P9-BJE-546

H77 $13.00

physiological chemistry

review of
physiological
chemistry

16th
EDITION

HAROLD A. HARPER, PhD

Professor of Biochemistry
University of California School of Medicine
San Francisco
Biochemist Consultant to the Clinical Investigation Center
Naval Regional Medical Center
Oakland, California

VICTOR W. RODWELL, PhD

Professor of Biochemistry
Purdue University
Lafayette, Indiana

PETER A. MAYES, PhD, DSc

Reader in Biochemistry
Royal Veterinary College
University of London

and Associate Authors

Los Altos, California 94022   LANGE Medical Publications

Copyright © 1977

All Rights Reserved By

Lange Medical Publications
Drawer L   Los Altos, California 94022

Copyright in Canada

Italian Edition: *Piccin Editore, Padua, Italy*
Spanish Edition: *El Manual Moderno, S.A., Mexico, D.F.*
French Edition: *Les Presses de l'Université Laval, Quebec, Canada*
Japanese Edition: *Maruzen Co., Ltd., Tokyo, Japan*
Portuguese Edition: *Atheneu Editora São Paulo, S.A., São Paulo, Brazil*
Polish Edition: *Panstwowy Zaklad Wydawnictw Lekarskich, Warsaw, Poland*
German Edition: *Springer-Verlag, Heidelberg, Germany*
Turkish Edition: *Ege Üniversitesi, Izmir, Turkey*

International Standard Book Number: *0–87041–034–2*
Library of Congress Catalogue Card Number: *77–70095*

A Concise Medical Library for Practitioner and Student

Review of Physiological Chemistry, 16th ed. $13.00

Current Medical Diagnosis & Treatment 1977 (annual revision). Edited by M.A. Krupp   1977
and M.J. Chatton. 1066 pp.

Current Pediatric Diagnosis & Treatment, 4th ed. Edited by C.H. Kempe, H.K. Silver,   1976
and D. O'Brien. 1053 pp, *illus.*

Current Surgical Diagnosis & Treatment, 3rd ed. Edited by J.E. Dunphy and L.W. Way.   1977
About 1130 pp, *illus.*

Current Obstetric & Gynecologic Diagnosis & Treatment. Edited by R.C. Benson.   1976
911 pp, *illus.*

Review of Medical Physiology, 8th ed. W.F. Ganong. 599 pp, *illus.*   1977

Review of Medical Microbiology, 12th ed. E. Jawetz, J.L. Melnick, and E.A. Adelberg.   1976
542 pp, *illus.*

Review of Medical Pharmacology, 5th ed. F.H. Meyers, E. Jawetz, and A. Goldfien.   1976
740 pp, *illus.*

Basic & Clinical Immunology. Edited by H.H. Fudenberg, D.P. Stites, J.L. Caldwell, and   1976
J.V. Wells. 653 pp, *illus.*

Basic Histology, 2nd ed. L.C. Junqueira, J. Carneiro, and A.N. Contopoulos. 453 pp, *illus.*   1977

General Urology, 8th ed. D.R. Smith. 492 pp, *illus.*   1975

General Ophthalmology, 8th ed. D. Vaughan and T. Asbury. 379 pp, *illus.*   1977

Correlative Neuroanatomy & Functional Neurology, 16th ed. J.G. Chusid. 448 pp, *illus.*   1976

Principles of Clinical Electrocardiography, 9th ed. M.J. Goldman. 412 pp, *illus.*   1976

Handbook of Psychiatry, 3rd ed. Edited by P. Solomon and V.D. Patch. 706 pp.   1974

Handbook of Obstetrics & Gynecology, 6th ed. R.C. Benson. 772 pp, *illus.*   1977

Physician's Handbook, 18th ed. M.A. Krupp, N.J. Sweet, E. Jawetz, E.G. Biglieri, and   1976
R.L. Roe. 754 pp, *illus.*

Handbook of Pediatrics, 12th ed. H.K. Silver, C.H. Kempe, and H.B. Bruyn.   1977
About 710 pp, *illus.*

Handbook of Poisoning: Diagnosis & Treatment, 9th ed. R.H. Dreisbach. About 520 pp.   1977

Copyright © 1939, 1944, 1951, 1953, 1955, 1957, 1959, 1961,
1963, 1965, 1967, 1969, 1971, 1973, 1975

Table of Contents

Harold A. Harper, PhD

Preface

This *Review,* which first appeared in 1939, has continued to be prepared through the years with the intention of supplying a reasonably concise presentation of those aspects of chemistry that are most relevant to the study of biology and medicine. Through the past 15 editions, as in this one, a "whole organ" or systemic concept of biochemical phenomena has been favored, while still giving due regard to the burgeoning information on the subcellular and molecular aspects of biologic material. It is hoped that such an approach will continue to maintain the book as a direct service to students and practitioners of the health sciences related to medicine without neglecting fundamental advances in modern molecular chemistry and biology.

In the 16th edition, it was decided to reorganize the textual material completely and to recognize as co-authors the 2 colleagues who have for many years served as major contributors to the work, Professors Victor Rodwell and Peter Mayes. In addition, we have enlisted the services of several contributors who have written chapters in their specialized areas as identified in the table of contents. Laurel V. Schaubert has continued to exert her considerable artistic talents in the preparation of illustrations, structural formulas, and metabolic schemes.

It cannot be a surprise to those who have used this book over the years that it now contains substantially more pages then we started with. It can only be hoped that we have reached a satisfactory compromise between an adequate presentation of an ever-growing body of knowledge and our desire to maintain a concise presentation.

Harold A. Harper
Victor Rodwell
Peter A. Mayes

San Francisco
June, 1977

Authors

Kent C. Cochrum, DVM
Associate Professor of Veterinary Medicine, Department of Surgery, University of California School of Medicine, San Francisco.

Gerold M. Grodsky, PhD
Professor of Biochemistry and Research Biochemist, University of California School of Medicine, San Francisco.

Harold A. Harper, PhD
Professor of Biochemistry, University of California School of Medicine, San Francisco; Biochemist Consultant to the Clinical Investigation Center, Naval Regional Medical Center, Oakland.

David W. Martin, Jr., MD
Associate Professor of Medicine and Biochemistry, University of California School of Medicine, San Francisco; Investigator, Howard Hughes Medical Institute, Miami.

Peter A. Mayes, PhD, DSc
Reader in Biochemistry, Royal Veterinary College, University of London.

Victor W. Rodwell, PhD
Professor of Biochemistry, Purdue University, Lafayette, Indiana.

David D. Tyler, PhD
Lecturer in Biochemistry, Royal Veterinary College, University of London.

John David Wallin, MD
Director Clinical Investigation Center, Naval Regional Medical Center, Oakland.

1...
Introduction

The purpose of this chapter is (1) to review certain aspects of organic chemistry relevant to the understanding of physiologic chemistry and (2) to provide certain guidelines designed to assist the learning and integration of the information presented in this book.

The early chapters of this book deal with the structures and properties of chemical compounds important in physiologic chemistry. Some of these structures will be familiar from the study of organic chemistry, but many are highly complex structures (eg, heterocyclic structures*) perhaps not previously encountered. The chemistry and the physiologic chemistry of unfamiliar molecules are largely predictable from those of structurally similar molecules as well as from the structure of molecules that possess identical functional groups.† In general, each functional group in a molecule will behave in a predictable way with respect to the reactions it will undergo. This will be a valuable guide also to the kinds of enzyme-catalyzed transformations that the group undergoes in living cells. The chemical elements which comprise functional groups will first be considered.

THE ELEMENTS OF THE SECOND & THIRD PERIODS OF THE PERIODIC TABLE

With the exception of certain metal ions, physiologic chemistry is, for the most part, related to the chemistry of the elements of the second and third periods of the periodic table.

In 1976, instruments designed to detect either new or the known forms of life were landed on the planet Mars. The experiments that were conducted assumed the existence of certain probable similarities

*Hetero atoms (Greek *heteros* = "other") such as O, N, and S also form covalent bonds with carbon, eg, in ethylamine, $C_2H_5NH_2$, ethyl alcohol, C_2H_5OH, and ethyl mercaptan, C_2H_5SH. Hetero atoms have one or more pairs of electrons not involved in covalent bonding. Since these unshared electrons have a negative field, **compounds with hetero atoms** attract protons, ie, they **act as bases** (see Chapter 2). Heterocyclic structures are cyclic structures that contain hetero atoms.
†A **functional group** (eg, $-NH_2$, $-COOH$, $-OH$) is a specific arrangement of linked chemical elements that has well-defined chemical and physical properties.

Table 1–1. The elemental composition of living cells.

Element	Composition by Weight (%)	Element	Composition by Weight (%)
O	65		
C	18	Cu, Zn	
H	10	Se, Mo	
N	3	F, Cl, I	0.70
Ca	1.5	Mn, Co, Fe	
P	1.0		
K	0.35	Li, Sr	
S	0.25	Al, Si, Pb	
Na	0.15	V, As	Traces†
Mg	0.05	Br	
Total	99.30		

†Variable occurrence in cells. No known function in most cases.

between terrestrial life and hypothetical life elsewhere in the universe. One central assumption was that extra-terrestrial life would use some or all of the same elements used by terrestrial life.

On earth, all cells, regardless of their origin (animal, plant, or microbial), contain the same elements in approximately the same proportions (Table 1–1). Thus, of the more than 100 known elements, only 19 are essential for terrestrial life. Perhaps there is some logical chemical explanation for their selection.

Six nonmetals (O, C, H, N, P, and S), which contribute almost 98% of the total mass of cells, provide the structural elements of protoplasm. From them the functional components of cells (walls, membranes, genes, enzymes, etc) are formed. These 6 elements all occur in the first 3 periods of the periodic table (Table 1–2).

The relative abundance of these 6 elements in the seas, crust, and atmosphere of earth does not by itself explain their utilization for life. Aluminum is more abundant than carbon but performs no known func-.

Table 1–2. The structural elements of protoplasm.

Period	Group							
	I	II	III	IV	V	VI	VII	VIII
1	H							He
2	Li	Be	B	C	N	O	F	Ne
3	Na	Mg	Al	Si	P	S	Cl	Ar

tion essential to life. By contrast, the intrinsic chemical properties of these 6 elements suggest their unique suitability as building blocks for life. Desirable features for structural elements apparently are as follows: (1) Small atomic radius. (2) The versatility conferred by the ability to form 1-, 2-, 3-, and 4-electron bonds. (3) The ability to form multiple bonds.

Small atoms form the tightest, most stable bonds—a distinct advantage for structural elements. H, O, N, and C are the **smallest atoms capable of forming 1-, 2-, 3-, and 4-electron bonds**, respectively. Utilization of all possible types of electron bonds permits maximum versatility in molecular design. So also does the ability to form multiple bonds, a property confined almost entirely to P, S, and the elements of period 2. Advantages of C- versus Si- based life include: (1) Greater chemical stability of C–C versus Si–Si bonds. (2) The ability of C, but not of Si, to form multiple bonds (eg, the oxides of C are diffusible, monatomic gases, whereas the oxide of Si is a viscous polymer). (3) The stability of C–C bonds, but not of Si–Si bonds, to rupture by nucleophilic reagents* such as O_2, H_2O, or NH_3.

Similar factors uniquely qualify P and S for utilization in energy transfer reactions. Energy transfer is facilitated by bonds susceptible to nucleophilic attack† (eg, nucleophilic attack of the 6-OH of glucose on the terminal P–P bond of ATP, forming ADP plus glucose-6-phosphate). P and S resemble Si in that P–P or S–S bonds, like Si–Si bonds, are susceptible to nucleophilic rupture by virtue of their unoccupied third orbitals. However, unlike Si, P and S form multiple bonds (more versatile), a consequence of their smaller atomic diameters. Most energy transfer reactions in biochemistry may be visualized as resulting from attack of a nucleophil (N) on the unoccupied third orbital of a phosphorus atom:

$$
\begin{array}{c}
\overset{\displaystyle O}{\underset{\displaystyle \overset{|}{\underset{-O}{O}}\cdots \overset{..}{N}}{{}^-O-P-O-R}}
\end{array}
$$

The characteristic chemical and physical properties of the chemical elements of life are the same throughout the known universe. It thus seems probable that if life exists elsewhere, the same elements are employed for the same or similar reasons. Taking this one step further, it seems likely that the kinds of biologic molecules formed from these elements and the kinds of reactions they might undergo would bear strong similarities to those on earth. For this reason, a biochemist is probably the scientist most likely to recognize and understand extraterrestrial life in whatever size or physical shape it might occur.

*Electron-rich elements or compounds.
†Attack of an electron-rich center upon an electron-deficient center.

REVIEW OF ORGANIC CHEMISTRY

It is believed that a sound understanding of organic chemistry is an essential prerequisite to the study of physiologic chemistry. Satisfactory knowledge of organic chemistry will enhance an understanding of the reactions of chemical compounds that are catalyzed in cells by the class of proteins known as enzymes.

This section is not intended as a complete review of organic chemistry but rather as a summary of the main points. The material should be quite familiar to those who have only recently completed the study of this branch of chemistry.

The Covalent Bond

The region in space where an electron is most likely to be found is termed an **orbital**. The sizes and shapes of different orbitals may be thought of as determining the spatial arrangements of atoms in molecules. The most fundamental of the "rules" that describe the electronic configurations of **atoms** is the **Pauli exclusion principle: only 2 electrons can occupy any given orbital, and these must have opposite spins**. Electrons of like spin tend to get as far away from each other as possible. Electrons in **molecules** occupy orbitals in accordance with similar rules.

To form a covalent bond, 2 atoms must be positioned so that an orbital of one overlaps an orbital of the other. Each orbital must contain a single electron, and these must have opposite spins. The 2 atomic orbitals merge, forming a single **bond orbital** containing both electrons. Since this new arrangement contains less energy (ie, is more stable) than that of the isolated atoms, **energy is evolved when bonds are formed**. The amount of energy (per mol) given off when a bond is formed is called the **bond dissociation energy**. For a given pair of atoms, the greater the overlapping of atomic orbitals, the stronger the bond.

The carbon atom (atomic number = nuclear charge = 6) has 6 electrons, 2 of which are unpaired and occupy separate $2p$ orbitals:

Although this suggests that C should form 2 bond orbitals with H, 4 bonds are formed, giving CH_4. Since bond formation is an exergonic (stabilizing) process, as many bonds as possible tend to be formed. This occurs even if the resulting bond orbitals bear little resemblance to the original atomic orbitals.

To produce a tetravalent C atom, mentally "promote" one of the $2s$ electrons to the empty p orbital:

While this representation suggests C should form 3 bonds of one type (using the *p* orbitals) and a fourth of another type (using the *s* orbital), the 4 bonds of methane are known to be equivalent. The **molecular orbitals** have a mixed or hybridized character and are termed *sp³* orbitals since they are considered to arise from mixing of one *s* and 3 *p* orbitals:

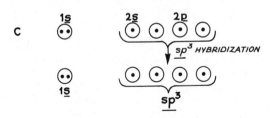

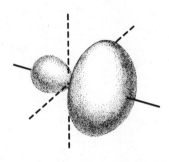

sp³ Orbitals have the following shape:

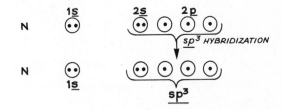

We shall neglect the back lobe and represent the front lobe as a sphere:

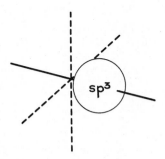

Concentrating atomic orbitals in the direction of a bond permits greater overlapping and strengthens the bond. The most favored hybrid orbital is therefore much more strongly directed than either *s* or *p* orbitals, and the 4 orbitals are exactly equivalent. Most important, these hybrid orbitals are directed toward the corners of a regular **tetrahedron**. This permits them to be as far away from each other as possible (recall Pauli exclusion principle).

Bond Angle

For maximum overlapping of the *sp³* orbitals of C with the *s* orbitals of hydrogen, the 4 H nuclei must be along the axes of the *sp³* orbitals and at the corners of a tetrahedron. The angle between any 2 C–H bonds must therefore be the **tetrahedral angle 109.5°**:

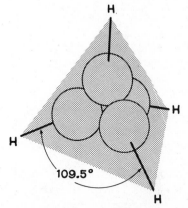

Methane has been shown experimentally to conform to this model. Each C–H bond has exactly the same length (0.109 nm) and dissociation energy (102 kcal/mol), and the angle between any pair of bonds is 109.5°. **Characteristic bond lengths, bond energies, and bond angles thus are associated with covalent bonds.** Unlike the ionic bond, which is equally strong in all directions, **the covalent bond has directional character.** Thus, the chemistry of the covalent bond is much concerned with molecular size and shape. Three kinds of C atom are encountered: **tetrahedral** (*sp³* hybridized), **trigonal** (*sp²* hybridized), and **digonal** (*sp* hybridized).

In ammonia (NH_3), nitrogen (atomic number = 7) has a valence state similar to that described for carbon: 4 *sp³* orbitals directed to the corners of a tetrahedron.

Each of the unpaired electrons of N occupying one of the *sp³* orbitals can pair with that of a H atom, giving NH_3. The fourth *sp³* orbital contains an unshared electron pair. The unshared electron pair appears to occupy more space and to compress the bond angles slightly to 107°. It is a region of high electron density and confers on NH_3 its basic properties (attracts protons).

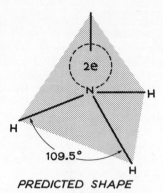

PREDICTED SHAPE

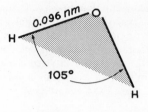

ACTUAL SHAPE

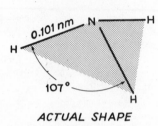

ACTUAL SHAPE

In H_2O, the O (atomic number = 8) has only 2 unpaired electrons and hence bonds to only 2 hydrogens.

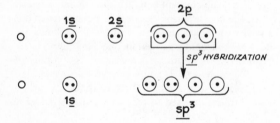

Water also is tetrahedral. The 2 hydrogens occupy 2 corners of the tetrahedron and the 2 unshared electron pairs the remaining corners. The bond angle (105°) is even smaller than that in NH_3.

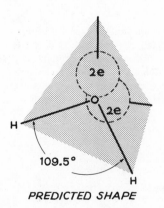

PREDICTED SHAPE

Isomers

Isomers (Greek *isos* = same; *meros* = part) are chemical compounds that have identical elemental compositions. For example, for the empirical formula C_3H_6O, three isomers are possible.

$CH_3CH_2CH_2OH$

1-Propanol

$$\begin{array}{c} CH_3 \\ \diagdown \\ CH_3 \diagup \end{array} CHOH$$

2-Propanol
(1-methylethanol)

$CH_3-O-CH_2CH_3$

Methylethyl ether

The chemical properties of compounds having the same empirical formula are frequently quite different (eg, 1-propanol and methylethyl ether). Occasionally, they are quite similar (eg, 1-propanol and 2-propanol), and in certain special cases discussed below they are identical.

Stereoisomers

Stereoisomers differ only in the way in which the constituent atoms are oriented in space; they are like one another with respect to which atoms are attached to which other atoms. In methane, CH_4, the 4 hydrogen atoms are at the vertices of an imaginary equilateral tetrahedron (4-sided pyramid) with the carbon atom at the center.

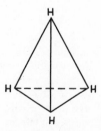

A carbon atom to which 4 different atoms or groups of atoms are attached is known as an asymmetric carbon

atom. For example, in the formula for alanine, the asymmetric (alpha) carbon atom is starred (*).

$$CH_3 - \overset{\overset{\displaystyle H}{|}}{\underset{\underset{\displaystyle NH_2}{|}}{C^*}} - COOH$$

Alanine

Many carbohydrates, peptides, steroids, nucleic acids, etc contain 2 or more asymmetric C atoms. A thorough understanding of the stereochemistry of systems with more than one asymmetric center is therefore essential.

Representations of Spatial Relationships Between Atoms

Certain spatial relationships are readily visualized using ball-and-stick atomic models. A compound having asymmetric carbon atoms exhibits **optical isomerism.** Thus, lactic acid has 2 nonequivalent optical isomers, one being the mirror image or **enantiomer** of the other (Fig 1−1).

The reader may convince himself that these structures are indeed different by changing the positions of either enantiomer by rotation about any axis and attempting to superimpose one structure on the other.

Although enantiomers of a given compound have the same chemical properties, certain of their physical and essentially all of their physiologic properties are different. Enantiomers rotate plane-polarized light to an equal extent but in opposite directions. Since enzymes act on only one of a pair of enantiomers, only half of a **racemic mixture** (a mixture of equal quantities of both enantiomers) generally is physiologically active.

The number of possible different isomers is 2^n, where n = the number of different asymmetric carbon atoms. An aldotetrose, for example, contains 2 asymmetric carbon atoms; hence, there are $2^2 = 4$ optical isomers (Fig 1−2).

To represent 3-dimensional molecules in 2 dimensions, **projection formulas,** introduced by Emil Fischer, are used. The molecule is placed with the asymmetric carbon in the plane of the projection. The groups at the top and bottom project **behind** the plane of projection. Those to the right and left project equally **above** the plane of projection. The molecule is then projected in the form of a cross (Fig 1−3).

Unfortunately, the orientation of the tetrahedron differs from that of Fig 1−1. **Fischer projection formulas may never be lifted from the plane of the paper and turned over.** Since the vertical bonds are really **below** the projection plane while the horizontal bonds are above it, **it also is not permissible to rotate the Fischer projection formula within the plane of the paper by either a 90-degree or a 270-degree angle, although it is permissible to rotate it 180 degrees.**

A special representation and nomenclature for molecules with 2 asymmetric carbon atoms derives from the names of the 4-carbon sugars erythrose and threose. If 2 like groups (eg, 2 −OH groups) are on the same side, the isomer is called the "erythro" form; if on the opposite side, the "threo" isomer. Fischer projection formulas inadequately represent one feature of these molecules. Look at the models from which these formulas are derived. The upper part of Fig 1−2 represents molecules in the "eclipsed" form in which the groups attached to C_2 and C_3 approach each other as

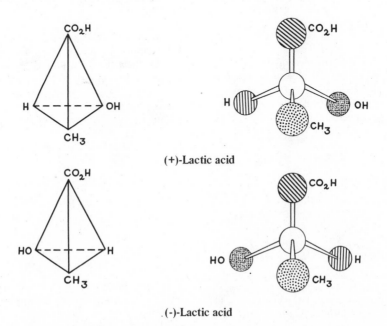

(+)-Lactic acid

(-)-Lactic acid

Figure 1−1. Tetrahedral and ball-and-stick model representation of lactic acid enantiomers.

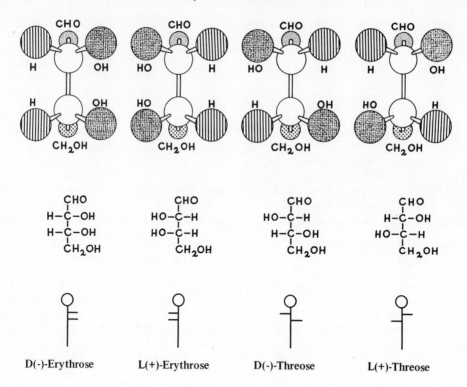

Figure 1—2. The aldotetroses. *Top:* Ball-and-stick models. *Middle:* Fischer projection formulas. *Bottom:* Abbreviated projection formulas.

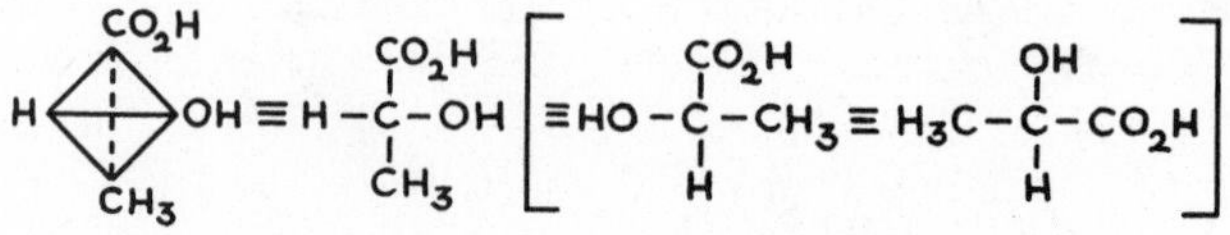

Figure 1—3. Fischer projection formula of (-)-lactic acid.

closely as possible. The real shape of the molecule more closely approximates an arrangement with C_2 and C_3 rotated with respect to each other by an angle of 60 degrees, so that their substituents are **staggered** with respect to each other and are as far apart as possible. One way to represent "staggered" formulas is to use **"sawhorse"** representations (Fig 1—4).

A second representation is the **Newman projection formula** (Fig 1—5). The molecule is viewed front-to-back along the bond joining the asymmetric carbon atoms. These 2 atoms, which thus exactly eclipse each other, are represented as 2 superimposed circles (only one is shown). The bonds and groups attached to the asymmetric C atoms are projected in a vertical plane

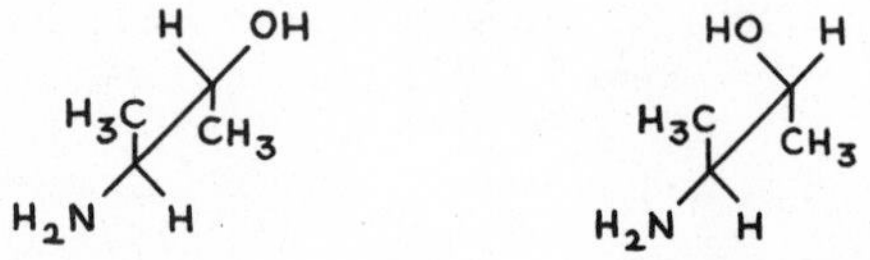

Figure 1—4. Sawhorse representations of the erythro and threo isomers of 3-amino-2-butanol. The **erythro** and **threo** refer to the relative positions of —OH and —NH_2 groups. Note that there are 3 ways to stagger C_2 with respect to C_3. That shown represents a structure with the bulky CH_3 groups oriented as far away from each other as possible.

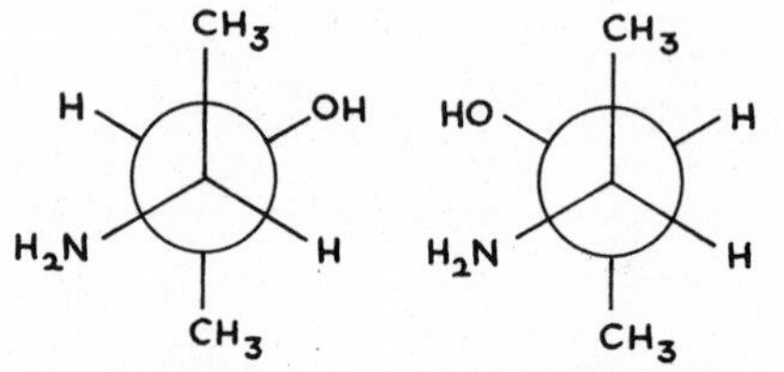

Figure 1—5. Newman projection formulas for the erythro and threo isomers of 3-amino-2-butanol.

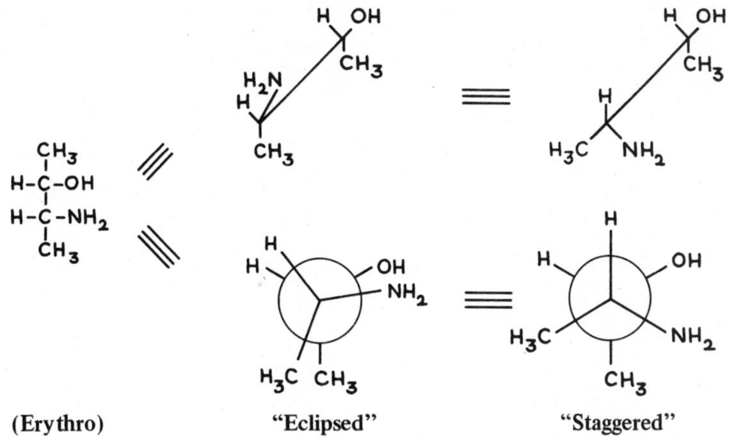

Figure 1–6. Transformation from Fischer to sawhorse or Newman formula.

and appear as "spokes" at angles of 120 degrees for each C atom. The spokes on the rear atom are offset 60 degrees with respect to those on the front C atom. To distinguish the 2 sets of bonds, those for the front carbon are drawn to the center of the circle and those for the rear carbon only to its periphery (Fig 1–5).

It is desirable to be able to shift between the Fischer projection formulas most often used in books and articles to either the sawhorse or Newman projection formulas, which most accurately illustrate the true shape of the molecule and hence are most useful in understanding its chemical and biologic properties. One way is to build a model* corresponding to the Fischer projection formula, stagger the atoms, and draw the sawhorse or Newman formulas. Fig 1–6 shows how to interconvert these formulas without models. The Fischer projection formula is converted to an "eclipsed sawhorse" or Newman projection which then is rotated 180 degrees about the C_2–C_3 bond, producing a staggered sawhorse or Newman projection.

Cis-Trans Isomerism

Cis-trans isomerism (Latin *cis* = this side, *trans* = across) occurs in compounds with double bonds. Since the double bond is rigid, the atoms attached to it are not free to rotate as about a single bond. Thus the structures

H—C—COOH	H—C—COOH
‖	‖
H—C—COOH	HOOC—C—H

Maleic acid (cis)   **Fumaric acid (trans)**

are not equivalent and have different chemical and physiologic properties. Fumaric acid, but not maleic

*The student is urged to purchase an inexpensive set of models. These will prove invaluable in studying the chemistry of sugars, amino acids, and steroids in particular.

acid, is physiologically active. The **cis** isomer has the 2 more "bulky" groups on the same side of the double bond. If they are on opposite sides of the double bond, the **trans** isomer is produced.

Introduction of **trans** double bonds in an otherwise saturated hydrocarbon chain deforms the shape of the molecule relatively little. A **cis** double bond, by contrast, entirely changes its shape. It can thus be appreciated why cis and trans isomers of a compound are not interchangeable in cells. Membranes composed of trans and cis isomers would have entirely different shapes. Enzymes acting on one isomer might be expected to be entirely inert with the other.

Again, the usual formulas fail to represent the actual shape of the molecules. Portions of the hydrocarbon backbone of a saturated fatty acid such as stearic acid ($CH_3[CH_2]_{16}COOH$) and of the cis and trans isomers of an 18-carbon unsaturated fatty acid ($CH_3[CH_2]_7CH=CH[CH_2]_7COOH$) are represented in Fig 1–7.

FUNCTIONAL GROUPS IMPORTANT IN PHYSIOLOGIC CHEMISTRY

A **functional group** is a specific arrangement of elements (generally C, H, O, N, P, or S) that has well-defined chemical and physical properties. As will shortly be seen, the properties of the small and large molecules that constitute the subject matter of physiologic chemistry are most readily understood in terms of the chemical and physical properties of the functional groups that these molecules contain.

Alcohols

Many of the compounds that will be encountered (eg, sugars, certain lipids, and amino acids) are **alcohols**. These have both polar (hydroxy, OH) and nonpolar (alkyl) character. They are thus best regarded

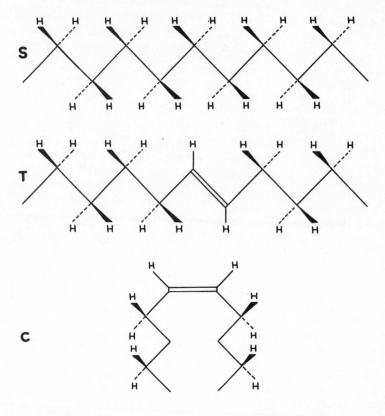

Figure 1—7. Representation of portions of the hydrocarbon backbones of a saturated fatty acid (**S**), an unsaturated fatty acid with a single trans double bond (**T**), and one with a single cis double bond (**C**). Bonds drawn as solid lines are in the plane of the paper. Bonds drawn as dotted lines project behind, and those drawn ◣ project in front of the plane of the paper.

both as **hydroxylated hydrocarbons** and as **alkyl derivatives of water**. Although alcohols with up to 3 carbon atoms are infinitely soluble in water, water solubility decreases with increasing length of the carbon chain, ie, with increasing nonpolar character. Primary, secondary, and tertiary alcohols have respectively one, 2, and 3 alkyl groups attached to the carbon atom bearing the –OH group.

$$CH_3CH_2CH_2CH_2 - OH$$

Primary butyl alcohol
(1-butanol)

$$CH_3 - CH_2 - \overset{\overset{\displaystyle H}{|}}{\underset{\underset{\displaystyle CH_3}{|}}{C}} - OH \qquad CH_3 - \overset{\overset{\displaystyle CH_3}{|}}{\underset{\underset{\displaystyle CH_3}{|}}{C}} - OH$$

Secondary butyl alcohol   **Tertiary butyl alcohol**
(1-methylpropanol)   **(1,1-dimethylethanol)**

Both monohydric (one –OH group) and polyhydric (more than one –OH group) alcohols are of physiologic significance. The sugars are derivatives of poly-

hydric alcohols. Cyclic or ring-containing alcohols such as the sterols or inositol are polyhydric alcohols. Their highly polar character makes polyhydric alcohols far more water-soluble than corresponding monohydric alcohols with equivalent numbers of carbon atoms. Thus, even polyhydric alcohols with 6 or more carbon atoms (eg, sugars) are highly water-soluble.

Some chemical reactions of alcohols with physiologic analogies include:

A. Oxidation: Primary and secondary (but not tertiary) alcohols are oxidized by strong oxidizing agents to aldehydes and carboxylic acids or ketones, respectively:

PRIMARY:
$$R-CH_2OH \xrightarrow{[O]} RCHO + COOH$$

SECONDARY:
$$\overset{R_1}{\underset{R_2}{>}}CHOH \xrightarrow{[O]} \overset{R_1}{\underset{R_2}{>}}C=O$$

Tertiary alcohols, which cannot be dehydrogenated without rupture of a C–C bond, are not readily oxidized.

B. Esterification: An ester is formed when water is split out between a primary, secondary, or tertiary alcohol and an acid.

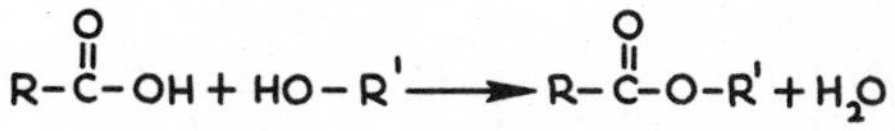

$$R-\overset{O}{\overset{\|}{C}}-OH + HO-R' \longrightarrow R-\overset{O}{\overset{\|}{C}}-O-R' + H_2O$$

Many lipids contain carboxylic ester linkages. The acid may be an organic acid, as shown above, or an inorganic acid. Thus, the esters of H_3PO_4 (see phosphorylated sugars and phospholipids) and H_2SO_4 are of great significance in biochemistry.

C. Ether Formation: Ethers are derivatives of primary, secondary, or tertiary alcohols in which the hydrogen of the —OH group is replaced by an alkyl group (R—O—R'). The ether linkage is comparatively uncommon in living tissues.

Sulfur, which is in the same group of the periodic table as oxygen, forms similar compounds. Thioalcohols (mercaptans), thioesters, and thioethers all occur in nature.

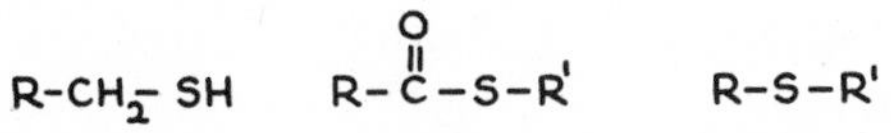

$$R-CH_2-SH \qquad R-\overset{O}{\overset{\|}{C}}-S-R' \qquad R-S-R'$$

Thioalcohol   **Thioester**   **Thioether**

In addition, the disulfides,

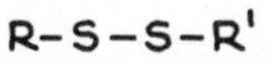

$$R-S-S-R'$$

which have no oxygen counterpart in biology, play an important role in protein structure.

Aldehydes & Ketones

Aldehydes and ketones possess the strongly reducing carbonyl group $>C=O$. Aldehydes have one and ketones 2 alkyl groups attached to the carbon bearing the carbonyl group:

$$R-\overset{H}{\overset{|}{C}}=O \qquad\qquad \overset{R}{\underset{R'}{}}C=O$$

Aldehyde   **Ketone**

The sugars, in addition to being polyhydric alcohols, are also either aldehydes or ketones.

Some chemical reactions of aldehydes and ketones of biochemical interest include the following:

A. Oxidation: Oxidation of an aldehyde to the corresponding carboxylic acid:

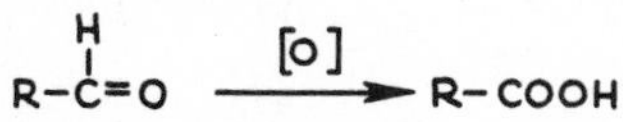

$$R-\overset{H}{\overset{|}{C}}=O \xrightarrow{[O]} R-COOH$$

Ketones are not readily oxidized since, like tertiary alcohols, they cannot lose hydrogen without rupture of a C—C bond.

B. Reduction: Reduction of an aldehyde yields the corresponding primary alcohol, and reduction of a ketone yields the corresponding secondary alcohol.

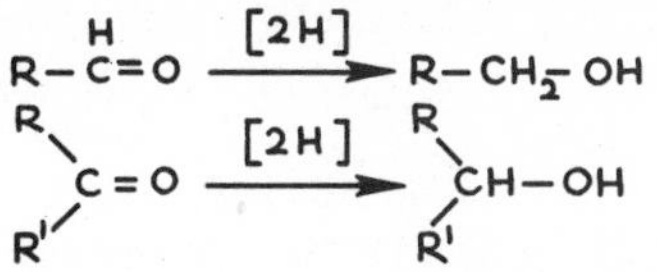

$$R-\overset{H}{\overset{|}{C}}=O \xrightarrow{[2H]} R-CH_2-OH$$
$$\overset{R}{\underset{R'}{}}C=O \xrightarrow{[2H]} \overset{R}{\underset{R'}{}}CH-OH$$

C. Hemiacetal and Acetal Formation: Under acidic conditions, aldehydes can combine with one or 2 of the hydroxyl groups of an alcohol, forming, respectively, a hemiacetal or an acetal:

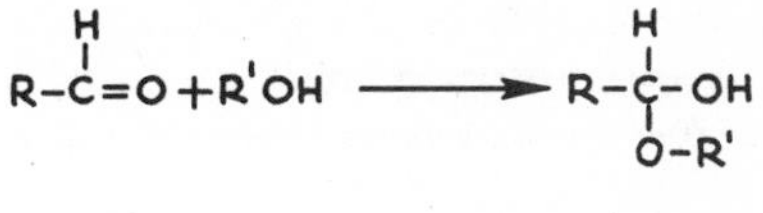

$$R-\overset{H}{\overset{|}{C}}=O + R'OH \longrightarrow R-\overset{H}{\underset{O-R'}{\overset{|}{C}}}-OH$$

Hemiacetal

$$R-\overset{H}{\overset{|}{C}}=O + 2R'OH \longrightarrow R-\overset{H}{\underset{OR'}{\overset{|}{C}}}-OR' + H_2O$$

An acetal

The carbonyl and alcohol functions may be part of the same molecule. For example, the aldose (aldehyde) sugars exist in solution primarily as internal hemiacetals. Analogous structures (hemiketals and ketals) are formed from alcohols and ketones.

Aldehydes may also form thiohemiacetals and thioacetals with thioalcohols:

$$R-\overset{H}{\overset{|}{C}}=O + R'-SH \longrightarrow R-\overset{H}{\underset{S-R'}{\overset{|}{C}}}-OH$$

A thiohemiacetal

Thiohemiacetals are involved as enzyme-bound intermediates in the enzymic oxidation of aldehydes to acids.

D. Aldol Condensation: Under alkaline conditions, aldehydes and, to a lesser extent, ketones undergo condensation between their carbonyl and their a-carbon atoms to form aldols or β-hydroxy aldehydes or ketones.

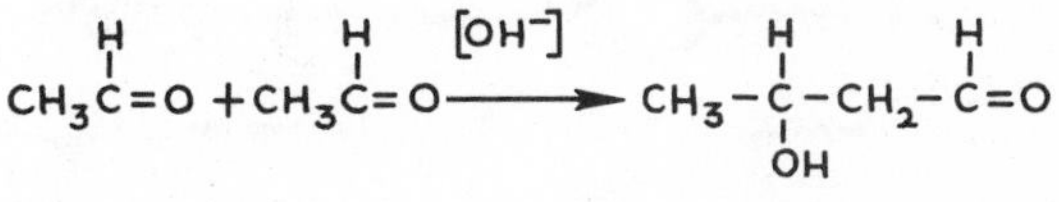

$$CH_3\overset{H}{\overset{|}{C}}=O + CH_3\overset{H}{\overset{|}{C}}=O \xrightarrow{[OH^-]} CH_3-\overset{H}{\underset{OH}{\overset{|}{C}}}-CH_2-\overset{H}{\overset{|}{C}}=O$$

The β-hydroxy acids derived from these are of great importance in fatty acid metabolism.

Carboxylic Acids

Carboxylic acids have both a carbonyl ($> C=O$) and a hydroxyl group on the same carbon atom. They are typical weak acids and only partially dissociate in water to form a hydrogen ion (H^+) and a **carboxylate anion** $R-COO^-$ with the negative charge shared equally by the 2 oxygen atoms.

Some reactions of carboxylic acids of physiologic interest include the following:

A. Reduction: Complete reduction yields the corresponding primary alcohol.

$$R-COOH \xrightarrow{[4H]} R-CH_2OH + H_2O$$

B. Ester and Thioester Formation: See alcohols.

C. Acid Anhydride Formation: A molecule of water is split out between the carboxyl groups of 2 acid molecules.

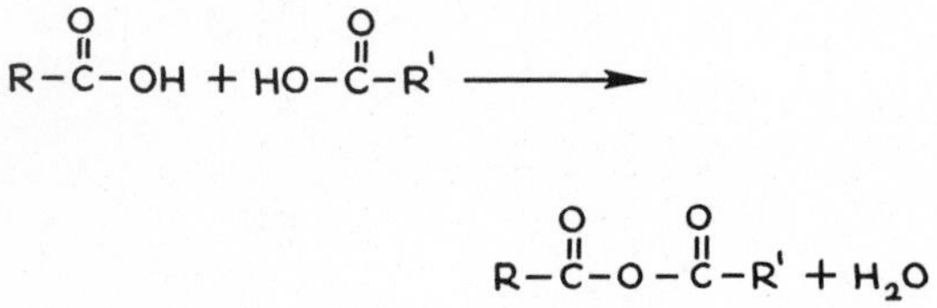

$$R-\overset{O}{\overset{\|}{C}}-OH + HO-\overset{O}{\overset{\|}{C}}-R' \longrightarrow$$

$$R-\overset{O}{\overset{\|}{C}}-O-\overset{O}{\overset{\|}{C}}-R' + H_2O$$

When both acid molecules are the same, a **symmetric anhydride** is produced. Different molecules yield **mixed anhydrides**. Anhydrides found in nature include those of phosphoric acid (in ATP) and the mixed anhydrides formed from phosphoric acid and a carboxylic acid, eg:

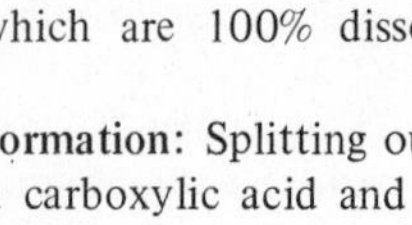

$$CH_3-\overset{O}{\overset{\|}{C}}-O-\overset{O}{\underset{\underset{OH}{|}}{\overset{\|}{P}}}-OH$$

Acetyl phosphate

D. Salt Formation: Carboxylic acids react stoichiometrically (equivalent for equivalent) with bases to form salts which are 100% dissociated in solution.

E. Amide Formation: Splitting out a molecule of water between a carboxylic acid and ammonia or an amine forms an amide:

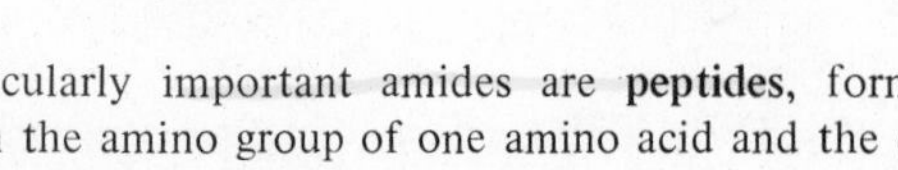

$$CH_3-\overset{O}{\overset{\|}{C}}-OH + H_3N \longrightarrow CH_3-\overset{O}{\overset{\|}{C}}-NH_2 + H_2O$$

Acetic acid   **Acetamide**

Particularly important amides are **peptides**, formed from the amino group of one amino acid and the carboxyl group of another.

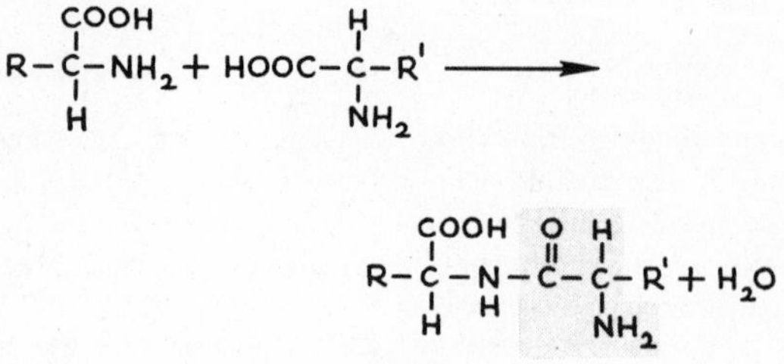

$$R-\overset{\overset{COOH}{|}}{\underset{\underset{H}{|}}{C}}-NH_2 + HOOC-\overset{\overset{H}{|}}{\underset{\underset{NH_2}{|}}{C}}-R' \longrightarrow$$

$$R-\overset{\overset{COOH}{|}}{\underset{\underset{H}{|}}{C}}-\overset{\overset{}{}}{\underset{\underset{H}{|}}{N}}-\overset{O}{\overset{\|}{C}}-\overset{\overset{H}{|}}{\underset{\underset{NH_2}{|}}{C}}-R' + H_2O$$

Peptide bond

Amines

Amines, which are alkyl derivatives of ammonia, are usually gases or fairly volatile liquids with odors similar to ammonia, but more "fish-like." Primary, secondary, and tertiary amines are formed by replacement of one, 2, or 3 of the hydrogens of ammonia, respectively.

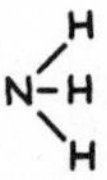

$$\underset{\underset{H}{|}}{\overset{\overset{H}{|}}{N}}-H \qquad\qquad R-NH_2$$

Ammonia   **Primary amine**

$$\underset{R'}{\overset{R}{\diagdown}}NH \qquad\qquad \underset{R''}{\overset{\overset{R}{|}}{R'-N}}$$

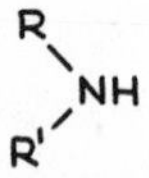

Secondary amine 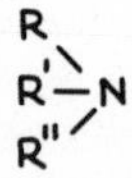   **Tertiary amine**

Ammonia in solution exists in both charged and uncharged forms:

$$NH_3 + H^+ \rightleftharpoons NH_4^+$$

Ammonia   **Ammonium ion**

The amines behave in an entirely analogous way:

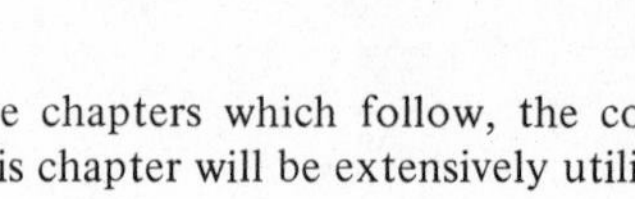

$$\underset{R'}{\overset{R}{\diagdown}}NH + H^+ \rightleftharpoons \underset{R' \quad H}{\overset{R \quad H}{N^\oplus}}$$

An amine   **An alkylammonium ion**

In the chapters which follow, the concepts outlined in this chapter will be extensively utilized.

2...
Water

INTRODUCTION

Physiologic chemistry is concerned, for the most part, with the chemical properties and chemical reactions of organic compounds. For this reason, it may be forgotten that in living cells most chemical reactions occur in an aqueous environment. There is, moreover, abundant evidence that water is an active participant in many biochemical reactions and that it is an important determinant of the properties of macromolecules such as proteins. Before beginning the study of bio-organic molecules and their reactions, it is therefore appropriate that brief consideration be given to those properties of water that enable it to play such a key role in the biochemical reactions of living cells.

MOLECULAR STRUCTURE OF WATER

The tetrahedral character of the carbon atom in a molecule such as methane (CH_4) (Fig 2–1) is familiar to all students of organic chemistry.

The 4 sp^3-hybridized orbitals of the carbon atom are symmetrically distributed about the center of a regular tetrahedron, and the bond angles between

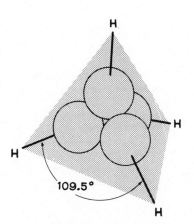

Figure 2–1. Methane.

hydrogen atoms are exactly 109.5 degrees (the so-called "tetrahedral angle"). In methane, the regions of high electron density (the sp^3 orbitals) and the regions of low electron density (the relatively unshielded nuclei of the hydrogen atoms) are symmetrically distributed about the molecule.

The water molecule also has tetrahedral character. It is best viewed as a nonregular tetrahedron with the oxygen atom at its center (Fig 2–2).

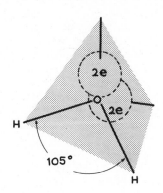

Figure 2–2. Water.

The 2 bonds with hydrogen are directed toward 2 corners of the tetrahedron, while the unshared electrons on the 2 sp^3-hybridized orbitals occupy the 2 remaining corners. The angle between the 2 hydrogen atoms (105 degrees) is slightly less than the tetrahedral angle (109.5 degrees), forming a slightly skewed tetrahedron. In contrast to methane, electrical charge is not uniformly distributed about the water molecule. The side of the oxygen opposite to the 2 hydrogens is relatively rich in electrons, while on the other side the relatively unshielded hydrogen nuclei form a region of local positive charge. Chemists use the term **dipole** to refer to molecules such as water that have electrical charge (electrons) unequally distributed about their structure. Ammonia also is a dipole and, like water, has a tetrahedral structure (Fig 2–3). In ammonia, the bond angles between the hydrogens (107 degrees) approach the tetrahedral angle even more closely than in water. Many organic compounds that occur in living cells are dipoles. Examples include alcohols, phospholipids, amino acids, and nucleic acids.

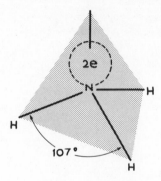

Figure 2—3. Ammonia.

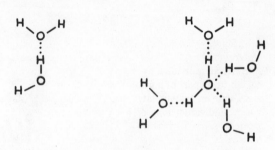

Figure 2—4. *Left:* Association of 2 dipolar water molecules. The dotted line represents a hydrogen bond. *Right:* Association of a central water molecule with 4 other water molecules by hydrogen bonding. This structure is typical of ice and, to a lesser extent, of liquid water.

MACROMOLECULAR STRUCTURE OF WATER

That water molecules can, on occasion, assume highly ordered arrangements should come as no surprise to anyone who has closely examined a snowflake. Molecular ordering of water molecules is not, however, restricted to ice. Even liquid water exhibits a substantial degree of macromolecular structure that closely parallels the geometric disposition of water molecules in ice. The ability of water molecules to associate with one another in both the solid and liquid states arises from the dipolar character of the water molecule. Water remains a liquid because of the transient nature of these macromolecular complexes (the half-life for the association-dissociation of water molecules is about 1 microsecond).

In the solid state, each water molecule is associated with 4 other water molecules. In the liquid state, the number is somewhat less (about 3.5). With the exception of the transient nature of intermolecular interactions in liquid water, it thus resembles ice in its macromolecular structure more closely than might at first be imagined.

HYDROGEN BONDS

The dipolar character of water molecules favors their mutual association in ordered arrays with a precise geometry dictated by the internal geometry of the water molecule (Fig 2—4).

The electrostatic interaction between the hydrogen nucleus of one water molecule and the unshared electron pair of another is termed a **hydrogen bond.** Compared to covalent bonds, hydrogen bonds are quite weak. To break a hydrogen bond in liquid water requires about 4.5 kcal of energy per mol—less than 3% of the energy required to rupture the O—H bond in water (110 kcal/mol). While individually weak, hydrogen bonds play a significant role in physiologic chemistry because they can be formed in large numbers. Taken together, many hydrogen bonds confer signif-

icant structure not only upon water but also upon other dipolar molecules as diverse as alcohols, DNA, and proteins. Fig 2—5 illustrates hydrogen bonds formed between representative molecules of physiologic significance.

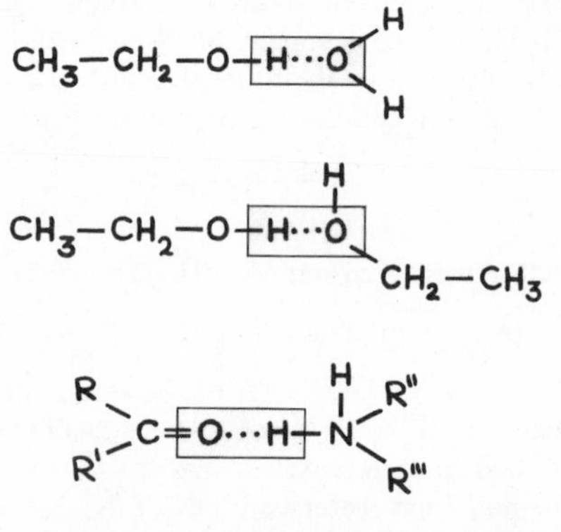

$$CH_3-CH_2-O \boxed{-H \cdots O} \begin{array}{c} H \\ \\ H \end{array}$$

$$CH_3-CH_2-O \boxed{-H \cdots O} \begin{array}{c} H \\ \\ CH_2-CH_3 \end{array}$$

$$\begin{array}{c} R \\ \diagdown \\ R' \end{array} C=O \cdots H \boxed{-N} \begin{array}{c} H \\ \diagup \\ \diagdown \\ R''' \end{array}$$

Figure 2—5. Formation of hydrogen bonds between an alcohol and water, between 2 molecules of ethanol, and between the peptide carbonyl oxygen and the hydrogen on the peptide nitrogen of an adjacent peptide.

Note that hydrogen bonds are not restricted to water molecules, and in particular that the hydrogens of nitrogen atoms can also participate in hydrogen bonding. This topic will again be considered in connection with the 3-dimensional structure of proteins and with base pairing within DNA in later chapters of this book.

DISSOCIATION OF WATER

Water molecules have a limited tendency to dissociate (ionize) into H^+ and OH^- ions:

$$H_2O \rightleftharpoons H^+ + OH^-$$

Since ions are continuously recombining to form water molecules and vice versa, it cannot be stated whether an individual hydrogen or oxygen is present as an ion or as part of a water molecule. At one instant it is an ion; an instant later, part of a molecule. Fortunately, individual ions or molecules need not be considered. Since 1 gram of water contains 3.76×10^{22} molecules, the ionization of water is described statistically. It is sufficient to know the **probability** that a hydrogen will be present as a hydrogen ion or as part of a water molecule.

If it is said that the probability that a hydrogen exists as an ion is 0.01, this means that a hydrogen atom has one chance in 100 of being an iron and 99 chances out of 100 of being in a water molecule. The actual probability of a hydrogen atom in pure water existing as a hydrogen ion is, however, approximately 0.0000000018, or 1.8×10^{-9}. Consequently, the probability of its being part of a molecule is almost unity. Stated another way, for every hydrogen ion and hydroxyl ion in pure water, there are 1.8 billion or 1.8×10^9 water molecules. Despite this disparity in numbers, hydrogen and hydroxyl ions contribute significantly to the properties of water.

The tendency of water to dissociate is expressed as follows:

$$K = \frac{[H^+] \, [OH^-]}{[H_2O]}$$

where the bracketed terms represent the molar concentrations* of hydrogen ions, hydroxyl ions, and undissociated water molecules, and K is termed the **dissociation constant**. To calculate the dissociation constant for water, recall that 1 mol of water weighs 18 g. One liter (1000 g) of water therefore contains $1000 \div 18 = 55.56$ mol. Pure water is thus 55.56 molar. Since the probability that a hydrogen in pure water will exist as an H^+ ion is 1.8×10^{-9}, the molar concentration of H^+ ions (or of OH^- ions) in pure water is calculated by multiplying the probability, 1.8×10^{-9}, by the molar concentration of water, 55.56 molar. This result is 1.0×10^{-7} molar.

We can now calculate K for water:

$$K = \frac{[H^+][OH^-]}{[H_2O]} = \frac{[10^{-7}] \, [10^{-7}]}{[55.56]}$$

$$= 0.018 \times 10^{-14} = 1.8 \times 10^{-16} \text{ molar}$$

The high concentration of molecular water (55.56 M) is not significantly affected by dissociation. It is therefore convenient to consider it as essentially constant. This constant may then be incorporated into the dissociation constant, K, to provide a new constant,

K_W, termed the **ion product** for water. The relationship between K_W and K is shown below:

$$K = \frac{[H^+] \, [OH^-]}{[H_2O]} = 1.8 \times 10^{-16} \text{ molar}$$

$$K_W = (K) \, [H_2O] = H^+] \, [OH^-]$$

$$= (1.8 \times 10^{-16} \text{ molar}) \, (55.56 \text{ molar})$$

$$= 1.00 \times 10^{-14} \text{ molar}^2$$

Note that the dimensions of K are moles per liter and of K_W moles^2 per liter^2. As its name suggests, the ion product, K_W, is numerically equal to the product of the molar concentrations of H^- and OH^-:

$$K_W = [H^+] \, [OH^-]$$

At 25° C, $K_W = (10^{-7})^2 = 10^{-14}$ molar^2. At temperatures below 25° C, K_W is greater than 10^{-14}, and, at the temperatures above 25° C, less than 10^{-14}. For example, at the temperature of the human body (37° C), the concentration of H^+ in pure water is slightly more than 10^{-7} molar. Within the stated limitations of the effect of temperature, $K_W = 10^{-14}$ **molar^2 for all aqueous solutions**—even those which contain acids or bases. In the following section, we shall make use of this constant in the calculation of pH values for acidic and basic solutions.

pH

The term **pH** was introduced in 1909 by Sørensen, who defined pH as **the negative log of the hydrogen ion concentration**:

$$pH = -\log [H^+]$$

This definition, while not rigorous,* is adequate for most purposes in physiologic chemistry. To calculate the pH of a solution:

(1) Calculate the hydrogen ion concentration, $[H^+]$.

(2) Calculate the base 10 logarithm of $[H^+]$.

(3) pH is the negative of the value found in step 2.

For example, for pure water at 25° C:

$$pH = -\log [H^+] = -\log 10^{-7} = -(-7) = 7.0$$

Low pH values (below 7.0) correspond to high concentrations of H^+ (acidic solutions), and high pH values (above 7.0) to low concentrations of H^+ (basic solutions).

Acids are defined as **proton donors** and bases as **proton acceptors**. A distinction is made, however, be-

---

*Strictly speaking, molar activity rather than molar concentration.

*pH = $-\log$ (H$^+$ activity).

tween strong acids (eg, HCl, H_2SO_4), which are completely dissociated even in strongly acidic solutions (ie, at low pH); and **weak acids,** which dissociate only partially in acidic solution. A similar distinction is made between **strong bases** (eg, KOH, NaOH) and **weak bases** (eg, $Ca[OH]_2$). Only strong bases are dissociated at very high pH. Most charged biochemical intermediates, including amino acids, are **weak acids.** Exceptions include phosphorylated intermediates (eg, sugar phosphates), which also possess the strongly acidic primary phosphoric acid group.

The following examples illustrate how to calculate the pH of acidic and basic solutions.

Example: What is the pH of a solution whose hydrogen ion concentration is 3.2×10^{-4} molar?

$$pH = -\log [H^+]$$
$$= -\log (3.2 \times 10^{-4})$$
$$= -\log (3.2) - \log (10^{-4})$$
$$= -0.5 + 4.0$$
$$= 3.5$$

Example: What is the pH of a solution whose hydroxide ion concentration is 4.0×10^{-4} molar?

To approach this problem, we define a quantity **pOH** that is equal to $-\log [OH^-]$ and that may be derived from the definition of K_w:

$$K_w = [H^+][OH^-] = 10^{-14}$$

therefore: $\log [H^+] + \log [OH^-] = \log 10^{-14}$

or: $$pH + pOH = 14$$

To solve the problem by this approach:

$$[OH^-] = 4.0 \times 10^{-4}$$
$$pOH = -\log [OH^-]$$
$$= -\log (4.0 \times 10^{-4})$$
$$= -\log (4.0) - \log (10^{-4})$$
$$= -0.60 + 4.0$$
$$= 3.4$$

Now: $pH = 14 - pOH = 14 - 3.40$
$$= 10.6$$

Example: What will be the pH of (a) 2.0×10^{-2} M KOH, (b) 2.0×10^{-6} M KOH? In these solutions, OH^- arises from 2 distinct sources: KOH and water. Since the pH is determined by the **total** $[H^+]$ (and the pOH by the **total** $[OH^-]$), both sources must be considered. In the first case, however, the contribution of water to the total $[OH^-]$ is negligible. The same cannot be said for the second case:

Molarity of KOH	2.0×10^{-2}	2.0×10^{-6}
$[OH^-]$ from KOH	2.0×10^{-2} M	2.0×10^{-6} M
$[OH^-]$ from water	1.0×10^{-7} M	1.0×10^{-7} M
Total $[OH^+]$	2.00001×10^{-2} M	2.1×10^{-6} M

Once a decision has been reached about the significance of the contribution by water, pH may be calculated as in the above example.

In the above examples, it was assumed that the strong base KOH was completely dissociated in solution and that the molar concentration of OH^- ions was thus equal to the molar concentration of KOH. This assumption is valid for relatively dilute solutions of **strong** bases or acids but **not for solutions of weak bases or acids.** Since these weak electrolytes dissociate only slightly in solution, we must calculate the concentration of H^+ (or $[OH^-]$) produced by a given molarity of the acid (or base) using the **dissociation constant** before calculating total $[H^+]$ (or total $[OH^-]$), and subsequently calculating the pH.

PROTONIC EQUILIBRIA OF FUNCTIONAL GROUPS THAT ARE WEAK ACIDS OR BASES

Dissociation Behavior & Acid Strength

A large fraction of the molecules present in living cells possess functional groups that are weak acids or bases. One or more of these functional groups—most frequently carboxyl groups, amino groups, or the secondary phosphate dissociation of phosphate esters—are present in all proteins and nucleic acids, most coenzymes, and most intermediary metabolites. The dissociation behavior (protonic equilibria) of weakly acidic and weakly basic functional groups is therefore fundamental to an understanding of the influence of intracellular pH on the structure and physiologic activity of these compounds. In addition, their separation and identification in research and clinical laboratories frequently is a result of knowledge of the dissociation behavior of their functional groups.

We refer to the protonated form of an acid (eg, HA or RNH_3^+) as the **acid** and the unprotonated form (eg, A^- or RNH_2) as its **conjugate base** (Table 2–1). Similarly, we may refer to a **base** (eg, A^- or RNH_2) and its **conjugate acid** (eg, HA or RNH_3^+) (Latin *coniungere* = to join together).

Table 2–1. Selected examples of weak acids and their conjugate bases.

Acid	Conjugate Base
CH_3COOH	CH_3COO^-
$CH_3NH_3^+$	CH_3NH_2

The relative strengths of weak acids and of weak bases is expressed quantitatively as their **dissociation constants**, which express their tendency to ionize. Shown below are the expressions for the dissociation constant (K) for a representative weak acid (R–COOH) and weak base (R–NH$_3^+$).

$$R–COOH \rightleftharpoons R–COO^- + H^+$$

$$K = \frac{[R–COO^-]\,[H^+]}{[R–COOH]}$$

$$R–NH_3^+ \rightleftharpoons R–NH_2 + H^+$$

$$K = \frac{[R–NH_2]\,[H^+]}{[R–NH_3^+]}$$

Since the numerical values of K for weak acids and bases are negative exponential numbers, it is convenient to express K as pK, where

$$pK = -\log K$$

Note that pK is related to K as pH is to H$^+$ concentration. Table 2–2 lists illustrative K and pK values for a monocarboxylic, a dicarboxylic, and a tricarboxylic acid. Observe that the **stronger acid groups have lower pK values.**

Table 2–2. Dissociation constants and pK values for representative carboxylic acids.

Acid		K	pK
Acetic		1.76×10^{-5}	4.75
Glutaric	(1st)	4.58×10^{-5}	4.34
	(2nd)	3.89×10^{-6}	5.41
Citric	(1st)	8.40×10^{-4}	3.08
	(2nd)	1.80×10^{-5}	4.74
	(3rd)	4.00×10^{-6}	5.40

From the above equations that relate K to [H$^+$] and to the concentrations of undissociated acid and its conjugate base, note that when

$$[R–COO^-] = [R–COOH]$$

or when

$$[R–NH_2] = [R–NH_3^+]$$

then

$$K = [H^+]$$

In words, **when the associated (protonated) and dissociated (conjugate base) species are present in equal concentration, the prevailing hydrogen ion concentration [H$^+$] is numerically equal to the dissociation constant, K.** If the logarithms of both sides of the

above equation are taken and both sides are multiplied by -1, the expressions would be as follows:

$$K = [H^+]$$

$$-\log K = -\log [H^+]$$

$-\log$ K is defined as pK, and $-\log$ [H$^+$] is the definition of pH. Consequently, the equation may be rewritten as

$$pK = pH$$

ie, **the pK of an acid group is that pH at which the protonated and unprotonated species are present at equal concentrations.** From this, many interesting facts may be inferred. For example, the pK for an acid may be determined experimentally by adding 0.5 equivalent of alkali per equivalent of acid. The resulting pH will be equal to the pK of the acid.

Inductive Effects of Neighboring Groups on Acid Strength

The electrons of a covalent bond between 2 dissimilar atoms tend to associate with the more electronegative (electron-attracting) atom. The result is a dipole:

$$\underset{-}{Cl} \xleftarrow{\quad} \underset{+}{CH_2–CH_3}$$

The arrow $\xleftarrow{}$ represents the direction of electron "drift." Factors which increase the electron density on the carboxyl group from which the positively charged proton must dissociate hinder its leaving and have an **acid weakening effect.** Conversely, anything which decreases the electron density on the carbonyl group will assist dissociation of the proton and have an **acid strengthening effect.** The closer an electronegative atom is to the carboxyl group, the more pronounced the acid strengthening effect. These effects are readily seen with the strongly electronegative atom chlorine:

	pK
CH_3CH_2COOH	4.9
$\underset{\underset{Cl}{\mid}}{CH_2}–CH_2–COOH$	4.1
$CH_3\underset{\underset{Cl}{\mid}}{CH}–COOH$	2.8

Alkyl groups supply electrons, but in a less dramatic manner:

	pK
CH_3COOH	4.7
$CH_3–CH_2COOH$	4.9
$(CH_3)_3\,C–COOH$	5.0

Charged groups may either supply or withdraw electrons:

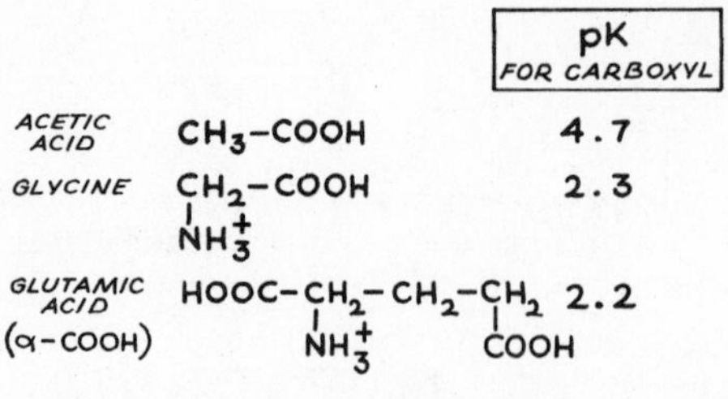

	pK FOR CARBOXYL
ACETIC ACID $CH_3–COOH$	4.7
GLYCINE $CH_2–COOH$ $\;\;\;\;|$ $\;\;\;\;NH_3^+$	2.3
GLUTAMIC ACID (α-COOH) $HOOC–CH_2–CH_2–CH_2$ $\;\;\;\;\;\;\;\;\;\;\;\;\;\;\;\;\;\;\;|\;\;\;\;\;\;\;\;\;|$ $\;\;\;\;\;\;\;\;\;\;\;\;\;\;\;\;\;\;\;NH_3^+\;\;\;\;\;COOH$	2.2

The second (γ) carboxyl dissociation of glutamic acid (pK = 4.2) is intermediate in acid strength between that of glycine and acetic acid since the molecule has both + and − charged groups.

The carbonyl group and hydroxyl groups also exert inductive effects and are acid strengthening:

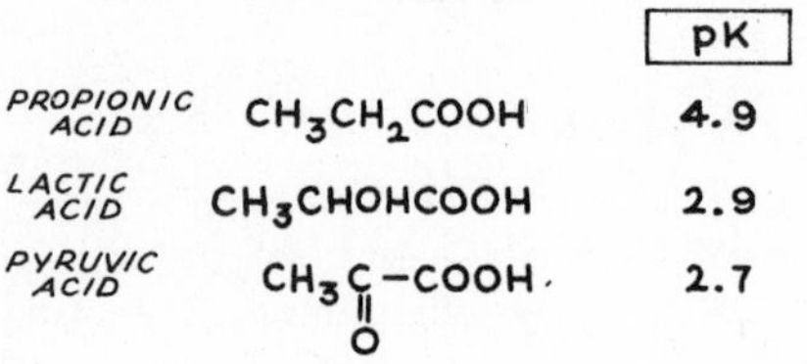

	pK
PROPIONIC ACID CH_3CH_2COOH	4.9
LACTIC ACID $CH_3CHOHCOOH$	2.9
PYRUVIC ACID $CH_3\underset{\underset{O}{\|}}{C}–COOH$	2.7

The aromatic amines such as aniline and nitrogen atoms of cyclic amines such as pyridine or purines and pyrimidines are, by contrast, moderately strong acids. Aromatic amines, therefore, exist for the most part in the dissociated or uncharged form at pH 7.4. Their acidity is attributable to their aromatic "electron sink" which reduces the negative charge on the nitrogen and facilitates dissociation of a proton.

The reaction of amines with acids to form amides is mentioned in Chapter 1. Amines and amine derivatives are involved in many important reactions of amino acids, lipids, and nucleic acids. Many drugs and other pharmacologically active compounds are amines. The uncharged forms are bases, ie, proton acceptors, whereas the charged forms are acids, ie, proton donors. The relative strengths of various amines may be expressed by the pK_a values for the dissociation:

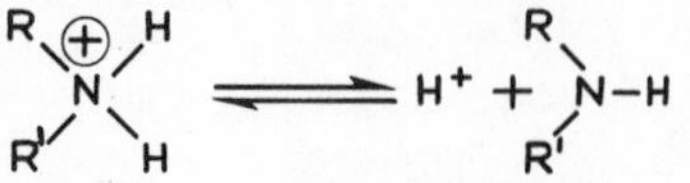

$$\underset{R'}{\overset{R}{\diagdown}}\underset{H}{\overset{\oplus}{N}}\underset{H}{\diagup} \;\;\rightleftharpoons\;\; H^+ + \underset{R'}{\overset{R}{\diagdown}}N–H$$

Some prefer to use pK_b values for amines. Conversion of pK_b to pK_a is accomplished from the relationship:

$$pK_a = 14 − pK_b$$

The pK_a values show that the aliphatic amines are weaker acids, or stronger bases, than ammonia. They also show that **at pH 7.4 essentially all of an aliphatic amine is in the charged form.** In body fluids, therefore, these amines are associated with an anion such as Cl^-.

Table 2–3. Acid dissociation constants of amines.*

	Acid Form	pK
Ammonia	NH_4^+	9.26
Methylamine	$CH_3NH_3^+$	10.64
Dimethylamine	$(CH_3)_2NH_2^+$	10.72
Trimethylamine	$(CH_3)_3NH^+$	9.74
Aniline	$C_6H_5NH_3^+$	4.58
Pyridine	$C_5H_5NH^+$	5.23

*From Weast RC (editor): *Handbook of Chemistry & Physics,* 46th ed. Chemical Rubber Publishing Co., 1965–1966.

THE HENDERSON-HASSELBALCH EQUATION

A weak acid, HA, ionizes as follows:

$$HA \rightleftharpoons H^+ + A^-$$

The equilibrium constant for this dissociation is written:

$$K = \frac{[H^+]\,[A^-]}{[HA]}$$

cross-multiply,

$$[H^+]\,[A^-] = K\,[HA]$$

divide both sides by $[A^-]$,

$$[H^+] = K\,\frac{[HA]}{[A^-]}$$

take the log of both sides,

$$\log[H^+] = \log\left(K\,\frac{[HA]}{[A^-]}\right) = \log K + \log\frac{[HA]}{[A^-]}$$

multiply through by −1,

$$-\log[H^+] = -\log K - \log\frac{[HA]}{[A^-]}$$

substitute pH and pK for $-\log[H^+]$ and $-\log K$, respectively; then

$$pH = pK - \log\frac{[HA]}{[A^-]}$$

Then, to remove the minus sign, invert the last term.

$$pH = pK + \log\frac{[A^-]}{[HA]}$$

In its final form as shown above, this is the **Henderson-Hasselbalch equation.** It is an expression of great predictive value in protonic equilibria, as illustrated below.

(1) When [A⁻] = [HA]: As mentioned above, this would occur when an acid is exactly half neutralized. Under these conditions:

$$pH = pK + \log \frac{[A^-]}{[HA]} = pK + \log \frac{1}{1} = pK + 0$$

Therefore, at half neutralization, pH = pK.

(2) When the ratio [A⁻]/[HA] = 100 to 1:

$$pH = pK + \log \frac{[A^-]}{[HA]}$$

$$pH = pK + \log 100/1 = pK + 2$$

(3) When the ratio [HA]/[A⁻] = 10 to 1:

$$pH = pK + \log 1/10 = pK - 1$$

If the equation is evaluated at several ratios of [A⁻]/[HA] between the limits 10^3 and 10^{-3}, and the calculated pH values plotted, the result obtained describes the titration curve for a weak acid (Fig 2–6).

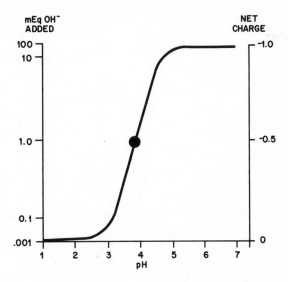

Figure 2–7. Titration curve for 100 mEq of an acid of the type HA having pK = 4.0 (●).

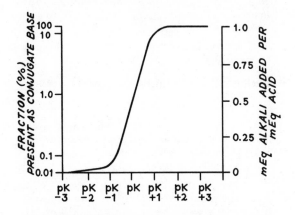

Figure 2–6. General form of a titration curve calculated from the Henderson-Hasselbalch equation.

BUFFERS & BUFFERING

Solutions of weak acids and their conjugate bases (or of weak bases and their conjugate acids) exhibit the phenomenon of **buffering**. Buffering is the tendency of a solution to resist a change in pH following addition of a strong acid or base more effectively than an equal volume of water. A redrawn version of Fig 2–6 in slightly different form illustrates this phenomenon (Fig 2–7).

Observe that the pH change per milliequivalent of OH⁻ added varies greatly depending on the pH. At pH values close to pK, the solution resists changes in pH most effectively, and it is said to exert a **buffering effect**. The 50:50 mixture of the acid (HA) and its conjugate base (A⁻) are therefore said to constitute a **buffer** or buffer system. For the example shown, this mixture is an effective buffer at or near pH 4.0 but not, for example, at pH 0.5 or at pH 7.0. **Solutions of weak acids and their conjugate bases buffer most effectively in the pH range pK ± 2.0 pH units.** This means that if it is desired to buffer a solution at pH X, a weak acid or base whose pK is no more than 2.0 pH units removed from pH X should be used.

Also shown in Fig 2–6 is the net charge on one molecule of the acid as a function of pH. A fractional charge of −0.5 does not mean that an individual molecule bears a fractional charge but that the statistical probability that a given molecule has a unit negative charge is 0.5. Consideration of the net charge on macromolecules as a function of pH provides the basis for many useful separatory technics, including the electrophoretic separation of amino acids, plasma proteins, and the abnormal hemoglobins (see Chapters 3 and 4).

3...
Amino Acids & Peptides

INTRODUCTION

Living cells produce an impressive variety of **macromolecules**, chiefly **proteins, nucleic acids,** and **polysaccharides**, that serve as structural components, as biocatalysts, as hormones, and as repositories for the genetic information characteristic of a species. These macromolecules are **biopolymers** constructed of distinct **monomer units** or **building blocks**. For nucleic acids, the monomer units are **nucleotides** (see Chapter 10); for complex polysaccharides, the monomer units are **sugar derivatives** (see Chapter 8); and for proteins, the monomer units are **amino acids**.

While many proteins contain substances in addition to amino acids, the 3-dimensional structure and many of the biologic properties of proteins are determined largely by the **kinds of amino acids present**, the **order in which they are linked together** in a polypeptide chain, and the **spatial relationship of one amino acid to another**. The unique biologic properties of proteins result primarily from specific interactions between the amino acids of which they are composed. To comprehend the chemistry of proteins, it is therefore necessary to have some knowledge of the chemistry of amino acids.

AMINO ACIDS

Alpha-amino acids have both an amino and a carboxylic acid function attached to the same (a) carbon atom.

$$R-\overset{\overset{\displaystyle H}{|}\overset{\displaystyle \alpha}{}}{\underset{\underset{\displaystyle COOH}{|}}{C}}-NH_2$$

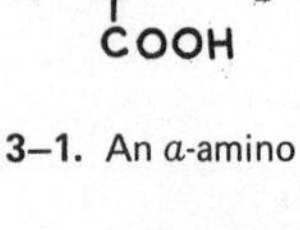

Figure 3–1. An a-amino acid.

Although over 200 different amino acids occur in nature, only about one-tenth of these occur in proteins. What is perhaps more remarkable is that proteins from all forms of life—plant, animal, or microbial—contain the same 20 amino acids. The reason for this becomes apparent when the universality of the genetic code is discussed (see Chapter 26).

Complete acid-, base-, or enzyme-catalyzed hydrolysis* of proteins produces the 20 L-a-amino acids listed in Table 3–2. Before we consider the properties of individual amino acids, properties common to all of them will first be discussed.

PROTONIC EQUILIBRIA OF AMINO ACIDS

Amino acids bear at least 2 ionizable weak acid groups, a $-COOH$ and an $-NH_3^+$. In solution, 2 forms of these groups, one charged and one neutral, exist in protonic equilibrium with each other:

$$R-COOH \rightleftharpoons R-COO^- + H^+$$

$$R-NH_3^+ \rightleftharpoons H^+ + R-NH_2$$

$R-COOH$ and $R-NH_3^+$ represent the **protonated** or **acid** partners in these equilibria. $R-COO^-$ and $R-NH_2$ are the **conjugate bases** (ie, proton acceptors) of the corresponding acids. Although both RCOOH and $R-NH_3^+$ are weak acids, RCOOH is a several thousand times stronger acid than is $R-NH_3^+$. At physiologic pH (7.4), carboxyl groups exist almost entirely as the conjugate base, ie, the **carboxylate ion,** $R-COO^-$. At the same pH, most amino groups are predominantly in the associated (protonated) form, $R-NH_3^+$. In terms of the prevalent ionic species present in blood and most tissues, amino acid structures should be drawn as shown in Fig 3–2(A).

Structure B (Fig 3–2) cannot exist at **any** pH. At any pH sufficiently low to repress ionization of the

---

*Hydrolysis = rupture of a covalent bond with addition of the elements of water.

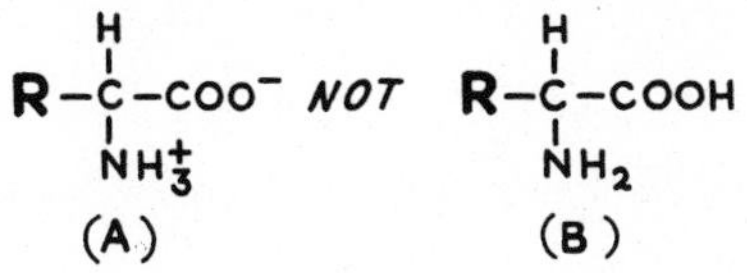

Figure 3–2. Ionically correct structure for an amino acid at or near physiologic pH *(A)*. The structure shown as *(B)* cannot exist at any pH but is frequently used as a convenience when discussing the chemistry of amino acids.

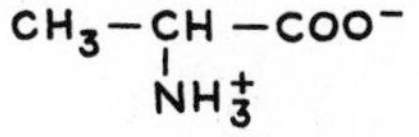

Figure 3–3. Isoionic or "zwitterionic" structure of alanine. Although charged, the zwitterion bears no *net* charge.

move in an electrical field. For an aliphatic amino acid such as alanine, the isoelectric species is the form shown in Fig 3–3.

Since pK_1 (RCOOH) = 2.35 and pK_2 (RNH$_3^+$) = 9.69, the isoelectric pH (pI) of alanine is:

$$pI = \frac{pK_1 + pK_2}{2} = \frac{2.35 + 9.69}{2} = 6.02$$

The situation is more complex for an amino acid that has ionizable groups in addition to those attached to the *a*-carbon atom. Fig 3–4 illustrates the different ionic forms of one such amino acid, aspartic acid.

From consideration of Fig 3–4, what would be the isoelectric pH (pI) for aspartic acid? An effective way to answer such a query is to write out all of the possible ionic structures for a compound in the order in which they occur as one proceeds from strongly acidic through neutral to basic solution (eg, as is done for aspartic acid in Fig 3–4). Next, identify the iso-ionic, zwitterionic, or neutral representation (as in Fig 3–4, structure [B]). pI is the pH exactly at the mid-point between the pK values on either side of the isoionic species. In this example,

$$pI = \frac{2.09 + 3.86}{2} = 2.98$$

comparatively strong carboxyl group, the more weakly acidic amino group would be protonated. If the pH is raised, the proton from the carboxyl will be lost long before that from the R–NH$_3^+$. At any pH sufficiently high to cause R–NH$_2$ to be the predominant species, the carboxylate ion (R–COO$^-$) must also be present. Convenience dictates, however, that the B representation be used for many equations involving reactions other than protonic equilibria.

As discussed in Chapter 2, the relative acid strengths of weak acids may be expressed in terms of their dissociation constants. More commonly, biochemists refer to the pK of an acid, which is simply the negative log of the dissociation constant, ie:

$$pK = -\log K$$

pK values for *a*-amino groups of free amino acids average about 9.8. They are thus much weaker acid functions than are carboxyl groups. The weak acid groups of amino acids are shown in Table 3–1.

The **isoelectric pH (pI)** of an amino acid is that pH at which it bears no net charge and hence does not

Table 3–1. Weak acid groups of amino acids.

	Conjugate Acid	Conjugate Base	Approximate pK$_a$
a-Carboxyl	R–COOH	R–COO$^-$	2.1 ± 0.5
Non-*a*-carboxyl	R–COOH ·	R–COO$^-$	4.0 ± 0.3
Imidazolinium (histidine)	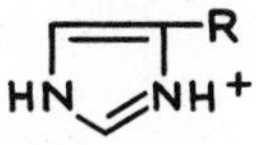	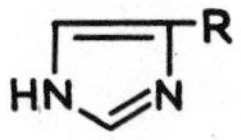	6.0
a-Amino	R–NH$_3^+$	R–NH$_2$	9.8 ± 1.0
ε-Amino (lysine)	R–NH$_3^+$	R–NH$_2$	10.5
Phenolic OH (tyrosine)	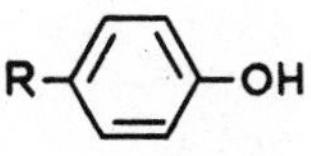	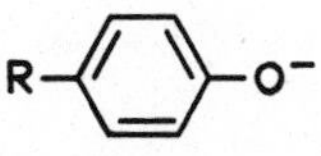	10.1
Guanidinium (arginine)			12.5
Sulfhydryl (cysteine)	R–SH	R–S$^-$	8.3

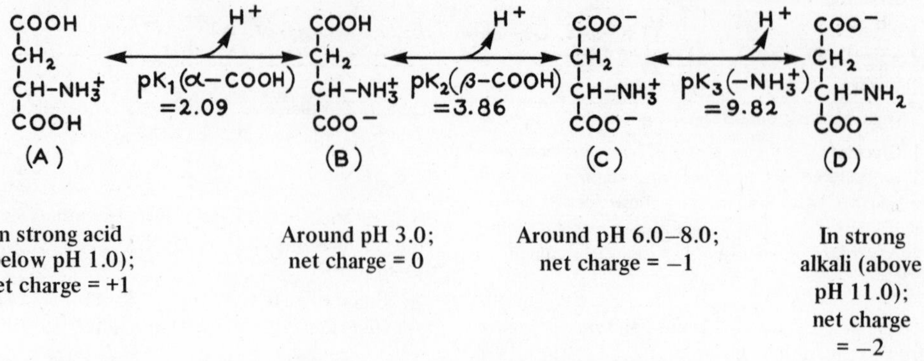

Figure 3—4. Protonic equilibria of aspartic acid.

The above method works equally well for amino acids with other dissociating groups, eg, lysine or histidine. It is also applicable to calculation of the charge on a molecule with any specified number of dissociating groups at any pH. The ability to perform calculations of this type is of value in the clinical laboratory to predict the mobility of known compounds in electrical fields and to select appropriate buffers for separation of one from another.

By writing the formulas for all possible charged species of the basic amino acids lysine and arginine, it will be observed that

$$pI = \frac{pK_2 + pK_3}{2}$$

For lysine, pI is 9.7, and for arginine 10.8.

STRUCTURES OF AMINO ACIDS

The amino acids present in proteins may be divided into 2 broad groups on the basis of the polarities of the R groups attached to the α-carbon atom (Fig 3—1). Table 3—2 illustrates such a classification.

For many purposes, it is convenient to subdivide the amino acids in proteins into 7 classes as in Table 3—3. In addition to their common names, this table also includes their systematic chemical names. At present, 2 systems of chemical nomenclature are used for amino acids. The older of these designates the carbon atom bearing the carboxyl and amino groups as the α-carbon. The adjacent carbon is termed β, the next γ, etc. While this system is slowly being supplanted by the familiar system of numbering the carbon atoms, it cannot be completely dispensed with at present. For example, reference is not made to a "2-amino acid" but to an "α-amino acid."

Table 3—3 gives, in addition, the 3-letter and single-letter abbreviations in common use among protein chemists. In this book, the 3-letter abbreviations will frequently be used. The shorter symbols are useful

Table 3—2. Classification of the L-α-amino acids present in proteins on the basis of the relative polarities of their R groups. A nonpolar group is one which has little or no charge difference from one region to another, whereas a polar group has a relatively large charge difference in different regions.

Nonpolar	Polar
Alanine	Arginine
Isoleucine	Aspartic acid
Leucine	Asparagine
Methionine	Cysteine
Phenylalanine	Glutamic acid
Proline	Glutamine
Tryptophan	Glycine*
Valine	Histidine
	Lysine
	Serine
	Threonine
	Tyrosine

*Glycine is a special case since the R is hydrogen, which ineffectively shields the polar groups on the α-carbon atom.

primarily when very long structures must be represented. They included here only as a guide to the terminology used by protein chemists.

Tables 3—4, 3—5, and 3—6 list selected examples of important amino acids that occur in various natural products but not in proteins.

OPTICAL ISOMERS OF AMINO ACIDS

With a single exception (glycine), each amino acid has at least one **asymmetric carbon atom** and hence is **optically active,** ie, it can rotate the plane of plane-polarized light. Although some of the amino acids found in proteins are dextrorotatory and some are levorotatory at pH 7.0, all have **absolute configurations** comparable to that of L-glyceraldehyde and hence are **L-α-amino acids.** Although D-amino acids do occur in cells and even in polypeptides (eg, in polypeptide antibiotics elaborated by certain microorganisms), they are not present in proteins.

Table 3–3. L-*a*-Amino acids found in proteins.*

Group	Trivial Name	Symbol	Systematic Name	Structural Formula
	With Aliphatic Side Chains			
	Glycinet	Gly [G]	Aminoacetic acid	$H-CH-COOH$ $\quad\ \ NH_2$
	Alanine	Ala [A]	2-Aminopropanoic acid	$CH_3-CH-COOH$ $\qquad\ NH_2$
	Valine	Val [V]	2-Amino-3-methylbutanoic acid	H_3C $\quad\ CH-CH-COOH$ $H_3C\qquad NH_2$
	Leucine	Leu [L]	2-Amino-4-methylpentanoic acid	H_3C $\quad\ CH-CH_2-CH-COOH$ $H_3C\qquad\qquad NH_2$
	Isoleucine	Ile [I]	2-Amino-3-methylpentanoic acid	CH_3 CH_2 $\quad\ CH-CH-COOH$ $CH_3\quad NH_2$
	With Side Chains Containing Hydroxylic (OH) Groups			
II	Serine	Ser [S]	2-Amino-3-hydroxypropanoic acid	$CH_2-CH-COOH$ $OH\quad NH_2$
	Threonine	Thr [T]	2-Amino-3-hydroxybutanoic acid	$CH_3-CH-CH-COOH$ $\qquad\ OH\quad NH_2$
	With Side Chains Containing Sulfur Atoms			
III	Cysteine‡	Cys [C]	2-Amino-3-mercaptopropanoic acid	$CH_2-CH-COOH$ $SH\quad NH_2$
	Methionine	Met [M]	2-Amino-4-(methylthio)butanoic acid	$CH_2-CH_2-CH-COOH$ $S-CH_3\qquad NH_2$
	With Side Chains Containing Acidic Groups or Their Amides			
IV	Aspartic acid	Asp [D]	Aminosuccinic acid	$HOOC-CH_2-CH-COOH$ $\qquad\qquad\ NH_2$
	Asparagine	Asn [N]	2-Aminosuccinamic acid	$H_2N-C-CH_2-CH-COOH$ $\quad\ \ \overset{\parallel}{O}\qquad NH_2$

*Except for hydroxylysine and hydroxyproline, which are incorporated into polypeptide linkages as lysine and proline and subsequently hydroxylated (see Chapter 23), specific transfer RNA molecules exist for all the amino acids listed in Table 3–3. Their incorporation into proteins is thus under direct genetic control.

tSince glycine has no asymmetric carbon atom, there can be no D or L form.

‡The amino acid cystine, 3,3-dithiobis-(2-aminopropionic acid), consists of 2 cysteine residues linked by a disulfide bond:

$$NH_2$$
$$HOOC-CH-CH_2-S-S-CH_2-CH-COOH$$
$$NH_2$$

Table 3–3 (cont'd). L-α-Amino acids found in proteins.

Group	Trivial Name	Symbol	Systematic Name	Structural Formula
IV	Glutamic acid	Glu [E]	2-Aminoglutaric acid	$HOOC-CH_2-CH_2-CH-COOH$ / NH_2
	Glutamine	Gln [Q]	2-Aminoglutaramic acid	*amide group* $H_2N-C-CH_2-CH_2-CH-COOH$ / O / NH_2
V	**With Side Chains Containing Basic Groups**			
	Arginine	Arg [R]	2-Amino-5-guanidovaleric acid	$H-N-CH_2-CH_2-CH_2-CH-COOH$ / $C=NH$ / NH_2 / NH_2
	Lysine	Lys [K]	2,6-Diaminohexanoic acid	$CH_2-CH_2-CH_2-CH_2-CH-COOH$ / NH_2 / NH_2
	Hydroxylysine*	Hyl	2,6-Diamino-5-hydroxyhexanoic acid	$CH_2-CH-CH_2-CH_2-CH-COOH$ / NH_2 OH / NH_2
	Histidine	His [H]	2-Amino-1H-imidazole-4-propanoic acid	$-CH_2-CH-COOH$ / NH_2 (imidazole ring, HN−N)
VI	**Containing Aromatic Rings**			
	Histidine (see above)			
	Phenylalanine	Phe [F]	2-Amino-3-phenylpropanoic acid	(phenyl)$-CH_2-CH-COOH$ / NH_2
	Tyrosine	Tyr [Y]	2-Amino-3-(4-hydroxyphenyl)propanoic acid	$HO-$(phenyl)$-CH_2-CH-COOH$ / NH_2
	Tryptophan	Trp [W]	2-Amino-3-(3-indolyl)propanoic acid	(indole ring)$-CH_2-CH-COOH$ / NH_2
VII	**Imino Acids**			
	Proline	Pro [P]	2-Pyrrolidinecarboxylic acid	(pyrrolidine ring) N H $COOH$
	4-Hydroxyproline	Hyp	4-Hydroxy-2-pyrrolidine-carboxylic acid	$HO-$(pyrrolidine ring) N H $COOH$

*Thus far, found only in collagen and in gelatin.

Table 3–4. Selected examples of α-amino acids that do not occur in proteins but perform essential functions in mammalian metabolism.

Common and Systematic Names	Formula	Significance
Homocysteine (2-amino-4-mercapto-butanoic acid)	$CH_2-CH_2-CH-COOH$ $\quad SH \qquad\quad NH_2$	An intermediate in methionine biosynthesis (see Chapter 23).
Cysteinesulfinic acid (1-amino-2-sulfinopro-panoic acid)	$CH_2-CH-COOH$ $\;SO_2H\;\;NH_2$	An intermediate in cysteine catabolism (see Chapter 22).
Homoserine (2-amino-3-hydroxy-butanoic acid)	$CH_2-CH_2-CH-COOH$ $\quad OH \qquad\quad NH_2$	An intermediate in threonine, aspartate, and methionine metabolism (see Chapter 22).
Ornithine (2,5-bisaminopentanoic acid)	$CH_2-CH_2-CH_2-CH-COOH$ $\;NH_2 \qquad\qquad\quad NH_2$	Intermediate in threonine, aspartate, and methionine metabolism (see Chapter 22).
Citrulline (2-amino-5-ureidopenta-noic acid)	$CH_2-CH_2-CH_2-CH-COOH$ $\;NH \qquad\qquad\quad NH_2$ $\;C=O$ $\;NH_2$	Intermediate in the biosynthesis of urea (see Chapter 22).
Argininosuccinic acid	$\qquad NH \qquad COOH$ $\qquad \| \qquad\quad \|$ $\qquad C-NH-CH$ $CH_2-NH \qquad CH_2$ $\;CH_2 \qquad\qquad COOH$ $\;CH_2$ $H-C-NH_2$ $\;COOH$	Intermediate in the biosynthesis of urea (see Chapter 22).
Dopa (3,4-dihydroxyphenyl-alanine)	HO-⬡-$CH_2-CH-COOH$ HO $\qquad\qquad NH_2$	Precursor of melanin.
3-Monoiodotyrosine	I HO-⬡-$CH_2-CH-COOH$ $\qquad\qquad NH_2$	Precursor of thyroid hormones.
3,5-Diiodotyrosine	I HO-⬡-$CH_2-CH-COOH$ I $\qquad\qquad NH_2$	Precursor of thyroid hormones.
3,5,3'-Triiodothyronine (T_3)	I $\qquad$ I HO-⬡-O-⬡-$CH_2-CH-COOH$ $\qquad\quad$ I $\qquad\qquad NH_2$	Precursor of thyroid hormones.
Thyroxine (3,5,3',5'-tetraiodo-thyronine) (T_4)	I $\qquad$ I HO-⬡-O-⬡-$CH_2-CH-COOH$ I $\qquad$ I $\qquad\qquad NH_2$	Precursor of thyroid hormones.

Table 3–5. Selected examples of α-amino acids that do not occur in proteins but perform essential functions in nonmammalian life forms.

Common and Systematic Names	Formula	Significance
α,γ-Diaminobutyric acid (2,4-bisaminobutanoic acid)	$CH_2(NH_2)-CH(NH_2)-COOH$	In polymyxin antibiotics.
2,3-Diaminosuccinic acid	$HOOC-CH(NH_2)-CH(NH_2)-COOH$	Excreted by *Streptomyces rimosus*, which produces oxytetracycline.
α-Aminoadipic acid (2-aminoadipic acid)	$HOOC-CH_2-CH_2-CH_2-CH(NH_2)-COOH$	Intermediate of lysine biosynthesis by yeast (see Chapter 23).
α,ε-Diaminopimelic acid (2,6-diaminopimelic acid)	$HOOC-CH(NH_2)-CH_2-CH_2-CH_2-CH(NH_2)-COOH$	Bacterial cell walls; intermediate of lysine biosynthesis by bacteria.
α,β-Diaminopropionic acid (2,3-diaminopropanoic acid)	$CH_2(NH_2)-CH_2-CH(NH_2)-COOH$	In the antibiotic viomycin.
Saccharopine	$HOOC-CH(NH_2)-CH_2-CH_2-CH_2-NH-CH(COOH)-CH_2-CH_2-COOH$	Intermediate of lysine biosynthesis by yeast and Neurospora (see Chapter 22).

Table 3–6. Selected examples of non-α-amino acids that perform important functions in mammalian metabolism.

Common and Systematic Names	Formula	Significance
β-Alanine (2-aminopropanoic acid)	$CH_2(NH_2)-CH_2-COOH$	Part of coenzyme A and of the vitamin pantetheine (see Chapter 12).
Taurine (2-aminoethylsulfonic acid)	$CH_2(NH_2)-CH_2-SO_3H$	Occurs in bile combined with bile acids (see Chapter 19).
γ-Aminobutyric acid (3-aminobutanoic acid)	$CH_2(NH_2)-CH_2-CH_2-COOH$	Formed from glutamate in brain tissue (see Chapter 22).
β-Aminoisobutyric acid (2-methyl-3-aminopropanoic acid)	$H_2N-CH_2-CH(CH_3)-COOH$	End product of pyrimidine catabolism (see Chapter 24); occurs in urine of patients with a heritable metabolic disorder (see Chapter 22).

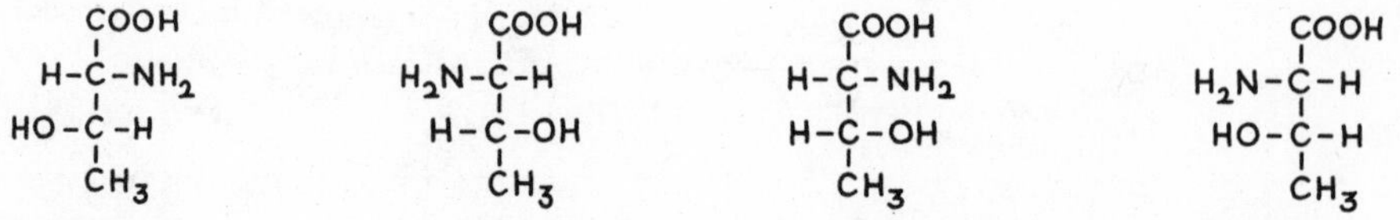

D-Threonine (I) — L-Threonine (II) — D-Allothreonine (III) — L-Allothreonine (IV)

Figure 3–5. Isomers of threonine.

Threonine, isoleucine, 4-hydroxyproline, and hydroxylysine each have 2 asymmetric carbon atoms and therefore exist in 4 isomeric forms. Of these, 2 are forms of allothreonine or of alloisoleucine, etc (Fig 3–5). Although a sheep liver enzyme (allothreonine aldolase) acts on allothreonine, neither allothreonine nor alloisoleucine appears to occur in nature.

Note (in Fig 3–5) that I–II and III–IV form **enantiomeric pairs** and hence have similar chemical properties. I–III and II–IV are **diastereoisomeric pairs** with different chemical properties.

The configurational structure for the 4-hydroxy-L-proline found in proteins is as shown in Fig 3–6.

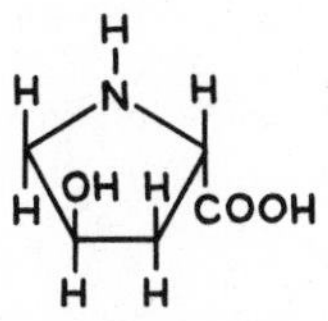

Figure 3–6. 4-Hydroxy-L-proline.

Various other amino acids (see Tables 3–4, 3–5, and 3–6) in free or combined states fulfill important roles in metabolic processes other than as constituents of proteins. Many additional amino acids occur in plants or in antibiotics. Over 20 D-amino acids occur naturally. These include the D-alanine and D-glutamic acid of certain bacterial cell walls and a variety of D-amino acids in antibiotics.

PHYSICAL PROPERTIES OF AMINO ACIDS

Solubility

The water solubility and high melting points of most amino acids reflect the presence of charged groups. They are readily solvated by and hence soluble in polar solvents such as water and ethanol, but they are insoluble in nonpolar solvents such as benzene, hexane, or ether. Their high melting points (above 200° C) reflect the energy needed to disrupt the ionic forces maintaining the crystal lattice.

Ultraviolet Absorption Spectrum of Aromatic Amino Acids

The aromatic amino acids tryptophan, tyrosine, histidine, and phenylalanine absorb ultraviolet light. As shown in Fig 3–7, most of the ultraviolet absorption of proteins is due to their tryptophan content.

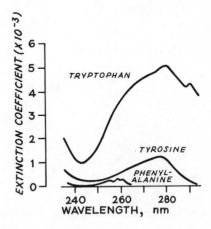

Figure 3–7. The ultraviolet absorption spectra of tryptophan, tyrosine, and phenylalanine.

CHEMICAL REACTIONS OF AMINO ACIDS

The carboxyl and amino groups of amino acids exhibit all the expected reactions of these functions, eg, salt formation, esterification, and acylation.

Color Reactions Useful for Identification of Amino Acids

Ninhydrin, a powerful oxidizing agent, causes oxidative decarboxylation of a-amino acids, producing CO_2, NH_3, and an aldehyde with one less carbon atom than the parent amino acid (Fig 3–8). The reduced

Table 3–7. Color reactions for specific amino acids.

Amino Acid Detected	Name	Reagents	Color
Arginine	Sakaguchi reaction	a-Naphthol and sodium hypochlorite	Red
Cysteine	Nitroprusside reaction	Sodium nitroprusside in dilute NH_4OH	Red
Cysteine	Sullivan reaction	Sodium 1,2-naphthoquinone-4-sulfonate and sodium hydrosulfite	Red
Histidine, tyrosine	Pauly reaction	Diazotized sulfanilic acid in alkaline solution	Red
Tryptophan	Glyoxylic acid reaction (Hopkins-Cole reaction)	Glyoxylic acid in 36 N H_2SO_4	Purple
Tryptophan	Ehrlich reaction	p-Dimethylaminobenzaldehyde in 12 N HCl	Blue
Tyrosine	Millon reaction	$HgNO_3$ in HNO_2; heat	Red
Tyrosine	Folin-Ciocalteu reaction	Phosphomolybdotungstic acid	Red
Tyrosine, tryptophan, phenylalanine	Xanthoproteic reaction	Boiling concentrated HNO_3	Yellow

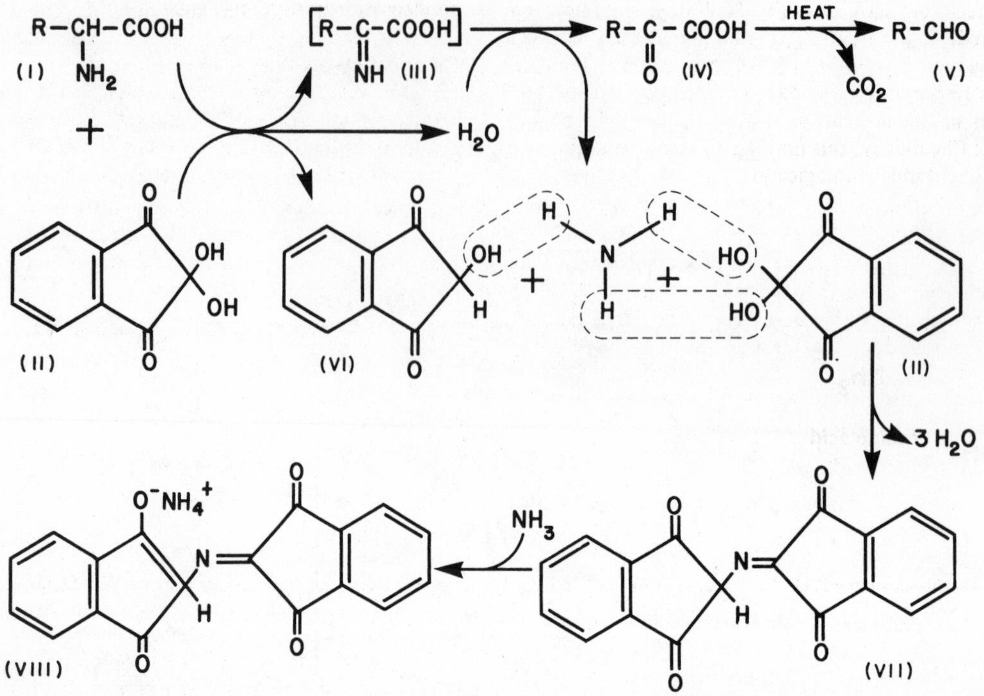

Figure 3—8. The reaction of an amino acid (I) with ninhydrin (II). The initial products formed are water, a partially reduced form of ninhydrin (VI), and an a-imino acid (III). This is shown in brackets because it is not actually isolated as an intermediate. (III) reacts rapidly with water, forming ammonia and an a-keto acid (IV). If the reaction is carried out at room temperature, (IV) may be isolated. In the presence of heat, however, (IV) is decarboxylated, forming CO_2 and an aldehyde (V) with one less carbon atom than the original amino acid. The formation of the typical blue-purple color of the ninhydrin reaction involves condensation of partially reduced ninhydrin (VI), ammonia, and ninhydrin (II) with the loss of 3 moles of water, forming the intermediate complex (VII). This then reacts with ammonia, forming the final color complex (VIII).

ninhydrin then reacts with the liberated ammonia, forming a blue complex which maximally absorbs light of wavelength 570 nm. The intensity of the blue color produced under standard conditions is the basis of an extremely useful quantitative test for a-amino acids. Amines other than a-amino acids also react with ninhydrin, forming a blue color but without evolving CO_2. The evolution of CO_2 is thus indicative of an a-amino acid. Even NH_3 and peptides react, although more slowly than do a-amino acids. Proline and 4-hydroxyproline produce a yellow rather than a purple color with ninhydrin.

A variety of color reactions specific for particular functional groups in amino acids are known. These are useful in both the qualitative and quantitative identification of particular amino acids. In many cases these color reactions may be used for amino acids combined in peptides or proteins. (See Table 3—7.)

Formation of Peptide Bonds

Without question, the most important reaction of amino acids is the formation of the peptide bond. In principle, peptide bond formation involves removal of 1 mole of water between the a-amino group of one amino acid and the a-carboxyl group of a second amino acid (Fig 3—9).

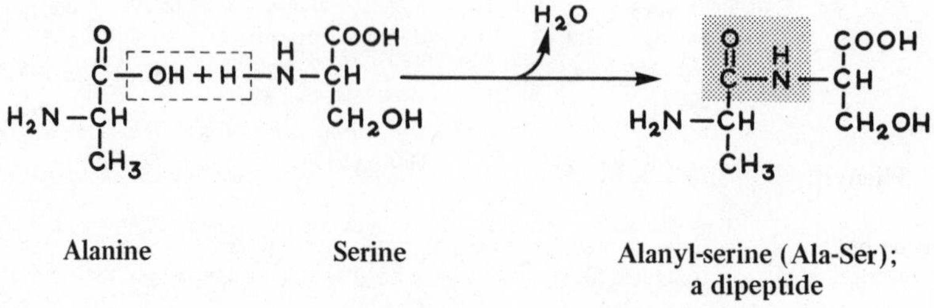

| Alanine | Serine | Alanyl-serine (Ala-Ser); a dipeptide |

Figure 3—9. Amino acids united by a peptide bond (shaded portion).

The reaction shown in Fig 3–9 does not, however, proceed as written since the equilibrium constant strongly favors hydrolysis of the peptide bond. In order to actually synthesize peptide bonds between 2 amino acids, the carboxyl group must first be activated. Chemically, this may involve prior conversion to an acid chloride. Biologically, activation involves initial condensation with ATP (Fig 3–10).

Other Reactions of Amino Acids

The reactions of the amino groups of amino acids shown in Figs 3–11 to 3–16 are used primarily in the synthesis of peptides and proteins or in the determination of peptide and protein structures.

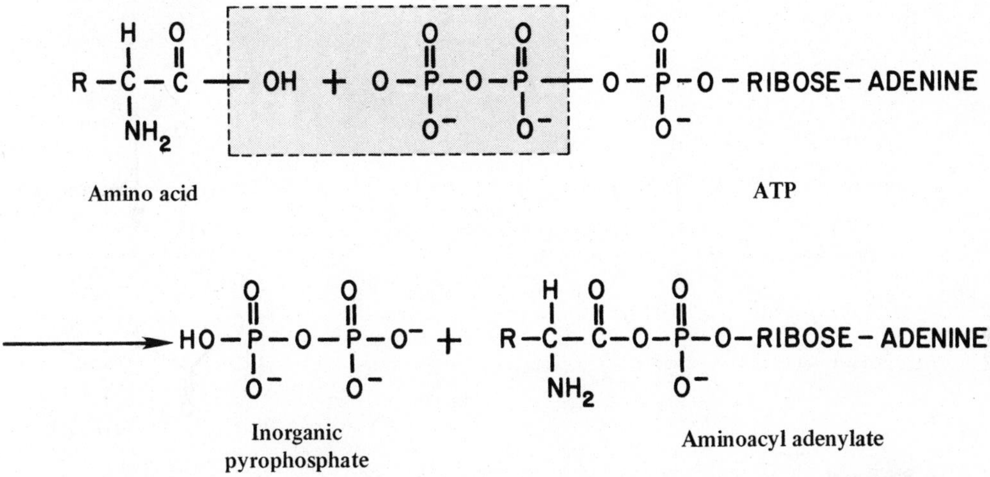

Figure 3–10. Condensation of the carboxyl group of an amino acid with ATP. The formation of the aminoacyl adenylate requires enzymic catalysis and is an important reaction in protein synthesis (see Chapter 26).

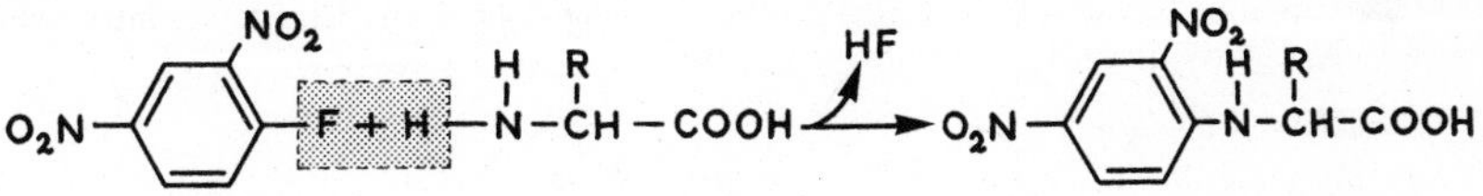

Figure 3–11. Reaction of an amino acid with 1-fluoro-2,4-dinitrobenzene (Sanger's reagent). The reagent is named for the Nobel laureate (1958) biochemist Frederick Sanger, who used it to determine the primary structure of insulin.

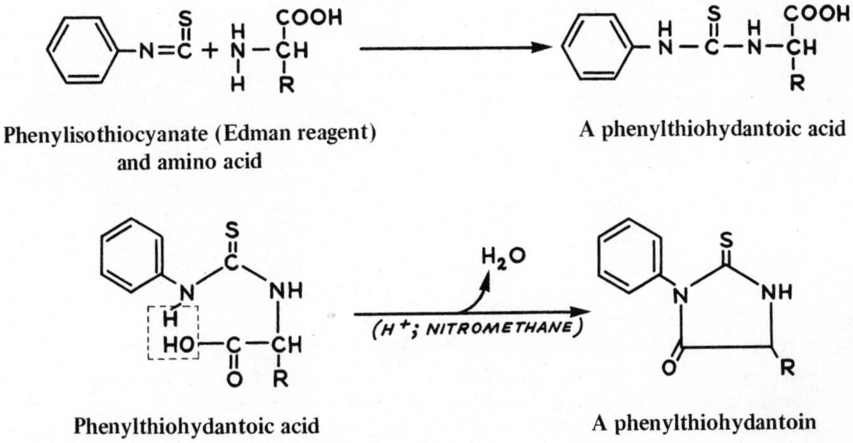

Figure 3–12. Conversion of an amino acid (or of the N-terminal residue of a polypeptide) to a phenylthiohydantoin derivative. The principal use of this reaction is to form a hydantoin derivative so that subsequently the N-terminal residues of a peptide can be identified.

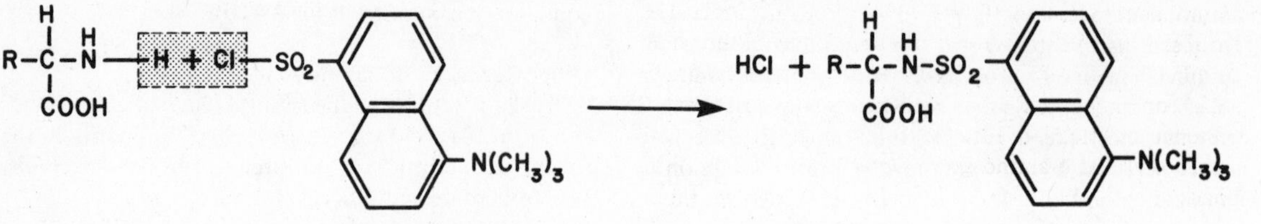

Dansyl chloride

Figure 3—13. Reaction of an amino acid with dansyl chloride. This reaction is used in the determination of the N-terminal residue of peptides.

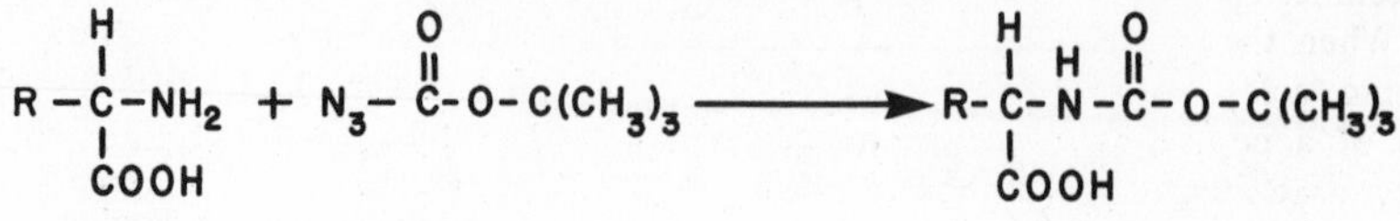

t-BOC-azide   t-BOC-amino acid

Figure 3—14. Reaction of an amino acid with t-butyloxycarbonyl azide (t-BOC-azide). Used to block the amino group of one amino acid while the other is reacted with an activated carboxyl group during the chemical synthesis of peptides.

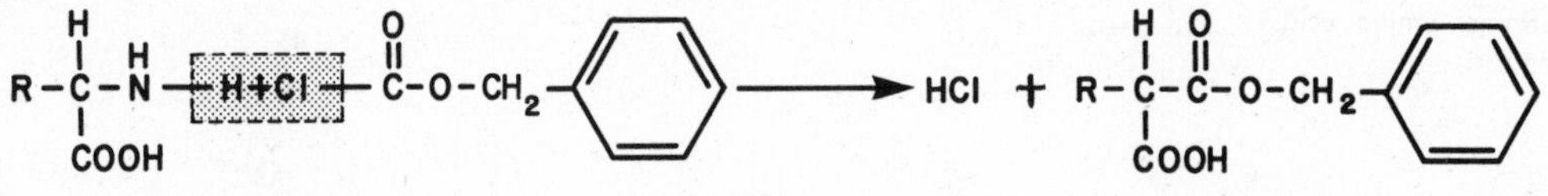

CBZ-chloride   CBZ-amino acid

Figure 3—15. Reaction of an amino acid with benzylchlorocarbonate. The carbobenzoxy (CBZ) derivative is used in the same way as the t-BOC derivative (Fig 3—14).

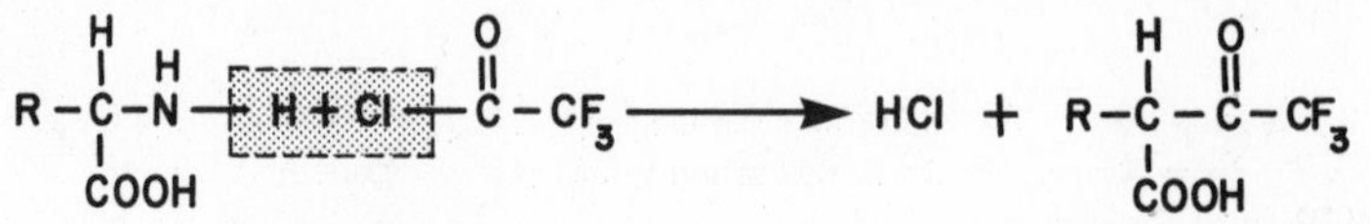

Trifluoroacetic   Trifluoracetyl
chloride   amino acid

Figure 3—16. Reaction of an amino acid with trifluoroacetic chloride. The resulting trifluoroacetyl derivative is relatively volatile and is prepared in order to separate amino acids by gas-liquid chromatography (GLC).

PEPTIDES

Definition

A peptide consists of 2 or more amino acids linked by a peptide bond. Polypeptides and simple proteins consist entirely of long chains of amino acids linked together by **peptide bonds** formed between the carboxyl group of one amino acid and the amino group of another. While a mole of water is removed during formation of a peptide bond (Fig 3—9), the synthesis of peptide bonds in cells involves a far more complex sequence of reactions (see Chapter 26).

Polypeptides are long peptide chains containing large numbers of peptide bonds. Although the term polypeptide thus should include proteins, polymers consisting of less than 100 amino acid residues are arbitrarily termed polypeptides and those with more than 100 are generally termed proteins.

Acid-Base Properties of Peptides

The peptide bond is an amide bond, and as such is neither basic nor acidic. In Fig 3—9, while the reactants on the left have 4 ionizable groups, the dipeptide on the right has but 2. Condensation of additional amino acids with a dipeptide produces tripeptides, tetrapeptides, etc. (*Note:* A pentapeptide is one formed from 5 amino acids, not one with 5 peptide bonds.) A pentapeptide formed solely from neutral amino acids (eg, pentaglycine) has only 2 ionizable groups: the C-terminal carboxyl and the N-terminal amino. Peptides formed from acidic or basic amino acids contain, in addition, ionizable groups due to the presence of ionizable functional groups other than the *a*-carboxyl and *a*-amino groups involved in the peptide bond.

Primary Structure of Peptides

The linear sequence of amino acid residues in a polypeptide is referred to as its **primary structure**. The determination of primary structure employs chemical methods whereas the higher orders of protein structure require physical technics such as x-ray crystallography (see Chapter 4). When the **number, kind,** and **linear order** of the amino acids are known, an accurate primary structure of a peptide or a protein may be obtained. In the conventional abbreviated form, a polypeptide might be shown (Fig 3–17). An even shorter representation is shown in Fig 3–18.

Glu-Lys-Ala-Gly-Tyr-His-Ala

Figure 3–17. Abbreviated representation of a heptapeptide. The N-terminal amino acid is glutamate and the C-terminal amino acid is alanine.

E K A G Y H A

Figure 3–18. Alternative representation of the peptide shown in Fig 3–17 using the single letter notation in wide use among protein chemists.

The **N-terminal** (amino terminal) amino acid is always shown at the left and the **C-terminal** (carboxyl terminal) amino acid at the right of the polypeptide chain. To assist in remembering this convention, visualize a snake moving across the page from left to right (Fig 3–19). The C-terminal residue forms the fangs and the N-terminal residue the tail.

Figure 3–19. Mnemonic device.

When the individual **amino acid residues** are linked by **straight lines**, as above, a definite and characteristic sequence is implied. The above structure (glutamyl-lysyl-alanyl-glycyl-tyrosyl-histidyl-alanine) is **named as a derivative of the C-terminal amino acid**, alanine. Uncertainty as to the exact order of specific residues is represented by enclosing that portion of the sequence, separated by **commas**, in **parentheses** (Fig 3–20).

Even small changes in the primary structure of proteins may produce profound physiologic effects.

Glu-Lys-(Ala,Gly,Tyr)-His-Ala

Figure 3–20. A heptapeptide with regions of uncertain primary structure.

Substitution of a single amino acid for another in a linear sequence of possibly 100 or more amino acids may reduce or abolish biologic activity with potentially serious consequences (eg, sickle cell disease; see Chapter 21). Indeed, many inherited metabolic errors may involve no more than a subtle change of this type. The introduction of new chemical and physical methods to determine protein structure has markedly increased knowledge of the biochemical bases for many inherited metabolic diseases.

DETERMINATION OF THE PRIMARY STRUCTURE OF PEPTIDES

Determination of primary structure may conveniently be considered in 2 aspects: (1) qualitative identification and estimation of the amino acid residues present; and (2) determination of sequence.

Determination of the Number & Kinds of Amino Acids Present

The peptide bonds linking the amino acids are first broken by hydrolysis. The free amino acids are then separated from one another and identified by chromatography and electrophoresis. The quantity of each amino acid present is then determined by quantitative chemical and physical technics (ninhydrin, specific color reactions, spectral properties of aromatic residues). Since peptide bonds are stable in water at pH 7.0, catalysis by acid, alkali, or enzymes must be employed to accomplish hydrolytic cleavage of these bonds. Each method has advantages and disadvantages.

A. Hydrolysis of Proteins by Acid: Most proteins are completely hydrolyzed to their constituent amino acids by heating at 110° C for 20–70 hours in 6 N HCl. Hydrolysis is carried out in a sealed, evacuated tube to exclude oxygen and prevent oxidative side reactions.

Undesirable side-effects of acid-catalyzed hydrolysis include the following:

(1) All the tryptophan and variable amounts of serine and threonine are destroyed. Formation of **humin,** a black polymer of breakdown products of tryptophan, accompanies acid hydrolysis.

(2) Glutamine and asparagine are deamidated to glutamate and aspartate.

(3) Glutamic acid undergoes intramolecular dehydration to pyrollidone 5-carboxylic acid (Fig 3–21).

(4) Other amino acids may undergo intermolecular dehydration forming cyclic anhydrides or **diketopiperazines** (Fig 3–22).

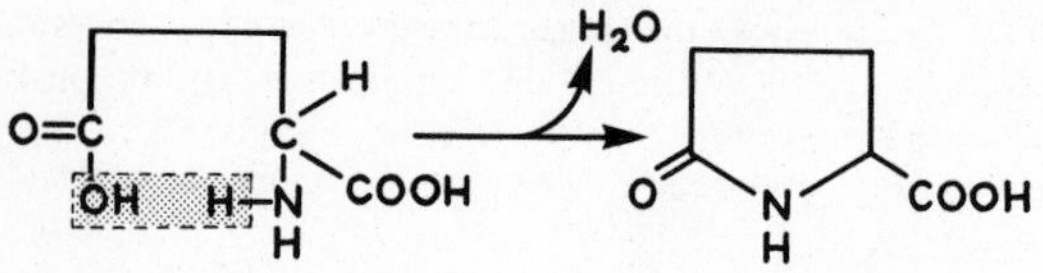

Glutamic acid   **Pyrollidone**
                                  5-carboxylic acid

Figure 3—21. Intramolecular dehydration of glutamic acid.

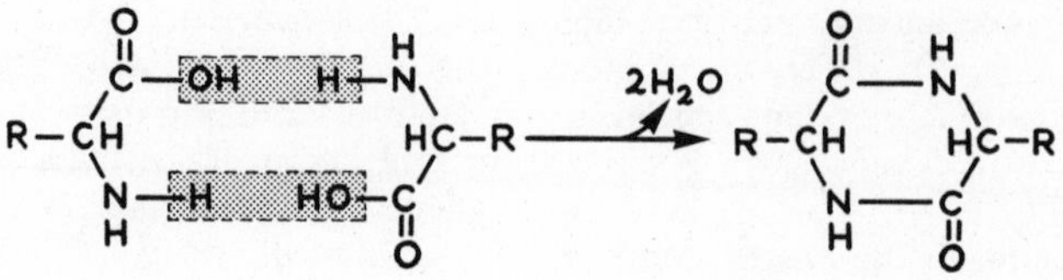

Paper Chromatography (Martin & Synge)

A small volume (about 0.005 ml) of an amino acid solution containing about 0.01 mg of amino acids is applied at a marked point 5 cm from the end of a filter paper strip. This is suspended in a sealed cylindrical jar or cabinet (Fig 3–24). One end of the paper dips into an aqueous solution of a solvent which typically consists of water, an acid or base, and an organic solvent such as n-butyl alcohol. The solvent may be placed in a trough from which the paper strip hangs ("descending paper chromatography"), or the strip

Two amino acids   **A diketopiperazine**

Figure 3—22. Intermolecular dehydration of amino acids.

B. Hydrolysis of Proteins by Alkali: This is used to recover tryptophan, which is not destroyed by alkaline hydrolysis. However, serine, threonine, arginine, and cysteine are lost, and all amino acids are racemized.

C. Enzyme-Catalyzed Hydrolysis: A variety of bacterial peptidases catalyze hydrolysis of all peptide bonds, but the reaction is slow compared to acid-catalyzed hydrolysis. Other proteolytic enzymes (trypsin, chymotrypsin) catalyze hydrolysis of certain peptide bonds quite rapidly. Other bonds are hydrolyzed slowly or not at all, and the polypeptide is incompletely hydrolyzed to free amino acids. This specificity is used to advantage in sequence studies (Fig 3–23).

may be suspended from the top of the jar and dip into a trough at the bottom of the jar ("ascending paper chromatography").

Strips are removed when the solvent has migrated over most of the available distance. When dry, the strips are sprayed with 0.5% ninhydrin in acetone and heated for a few minutes at 80–100° C. Purple spots appear where amino acids are present (Fig 3–25). In paper partition chromatography, the stationary phase, hydrated cellulose, is more polar than the mobile organic phase. Fig 3–25 shows that amino acids with large nonpolar side-chains (Leu, Ile, Phe, Trp, Val, Met, Tyr) migrate farther in n-butanol:acetic acid:water than those with shorter nonpolar side-chains (Pro, Ala,

$$\text{-Gly-Lys} \overset{C}{+} \text{Val-Phe} + \text{Arg} + \text{Leu-Cys-Tyr} \overset{C}{+} \text{Ile-Arg} + \overset{C}{\text{Trp}} + \text{Gln}$$
$$\text{T} \qquad\qquad \text{T} \qquad\qquad\qquad \text{T}$$

Figure 3—23. Hydrolysis of a polypeptide at the indicated peptide bonds catalyzed by trypsin (T) and chymotrypsin (C).

Separation & Identification of the Amino Acid Residues Present

The free amino acids of the protein hydrolysate are simultaneously separated one from another, identified, and prepared for quantitative analysis by partition chromatography or by electrophoresis. In paper, thin layer, column, or gas-liquid partition chromatography, amino acids are partitioned or divided between a stationary and a mobile phase. Separation depends on the relative tendencies of specific amino acids to reside in one or the other phase. Since the partitioning process is repeated hundreds or thousands of times, small differences in partition ratio permit excellent separations.

Gly) or with polar side-chains (Thr, Glu, Ser, Arg, Asp, His, Lys, Cys). This reflects the greater relative solubility of polar molecules in the hydrophilic stationary phase and of nonpolar molecules in organic solvents. Note further that, for a nonpolar series (Gly, Ala, Val, Leu), increasing length of the nonpolar side chain results in increased mobility.

The ratio of the distance traveled by an amino acid to that traveled by the solvent front, both measured from the marked point of application of the amino acid mixture, is called the R_f **value** for that amino acid. R_f values for a given amino acid vary with experimental conditions, eg, the solvent used. Although it is possible to tentatively identify an amino

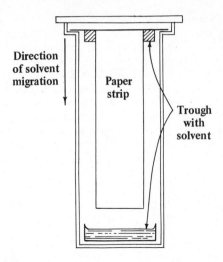

Figure 3—24. Cross-section of apparatus for descending paper chromatography.

acid by its R_f value alone, it is preferable to chromatograph known amino acid standards simultaneously with the unknown mixture. The spots on the test strip may then be readily identified by comparison with the standards.

Quantitation of the amino acids may be accomplished by cutting out each spot, removing (eluting) the compound with a suitable solvent, and performing a colorimetric (ninhydrin) or chemical (nitrogen) analysis. Alternatively, the paper may be sprayed with ninhydrin and the color densities of the spots measured with a recording transmittance or reflectance photometer device.

Modifications introduced to obtain better separation of components and to improve their quantitation include **2-dimensional paper chromatography**. In this technic, a square sheet rather than a strip of filter paper is used. The sample is applied to the upper left corner and chromatographed for several hours with one solvent mixture (eg, n-butanol:acetic acid:water). After drying to remove this solvent, the paper is turned through 90 degrees and chromatographed in a second solvent mixture (eg, collidine-water) (Fig 3—26).

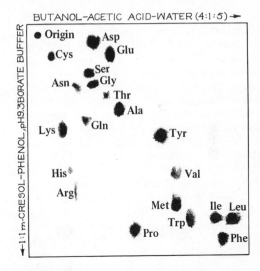

Figure 3—26. Two-dimensional chromatogram of natural amino acids. (Redrawn, slightly modified, from Levy & Chung: Two-dimensional chromatography of amino acids on buffered papers. Anal Chem 25:396, March 1953. Copyright © 1953 by American Chemical Society; reproduced with permission.)

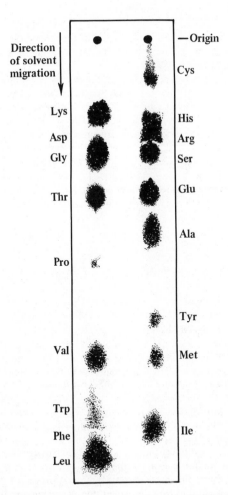

Figure 3—25. Identification of amino acids present in proteins. After descending paper chromatography in butanol-acetic acid, spots were visualized with ninhydrin.

Thin Layer Chromatography

One- or 2-dimensional thin layer chromatography (TLC) may be employed in place of paper chromatography. Thin layers of a chromatographic support or adsorbent (eg, cellulose powder, alumina, a cellulose ion exchange resin, Sephadex) are spread as a slurry on 8 X 8 inch glass plates. The plates are dried and used like paper sheets in paper chromatography. The advantage lies both in the choice of adsorbents, which permit separations not possible on paper, and in the

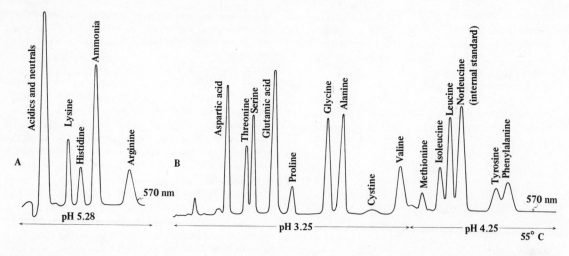

Figure 3—27. Automated analysis of an acid hydrolysate of corn endosperm on Moore-Stein Dowex 50 columns (at 55° C). *A:* A short (5.0 X 0.9 cm) column used to resolve basic amino acids by elution at pH 5.28. Time required = 60 minutes. *B:* A longer (55 X 0.9 cm) column used to resolve neutral and acidic amino acids by elution first with pH 3.25 and then with pH 4.25 buffer. An internal standard of norleucine is included for reference. Basic amino acids remain bound to the column. Time required = 180 minutes. Emerging samples are automatically reacted with ninhydrin and the optical density of samples recorded at 570 nm and 440 nm. The latter wavelength is used solely to detect proline and hydroxyproline (absent from corn endosperm). Ordinate = optical density plotted on a log scale. Abscissa = time in minutes. (Courtesy of Professor ET Mertz, Purdue University.)

rapidity of separation. Lipids, including sterols, may be rapidly and cleanly separated by adsorption chromatography on alumina. Amino acid mixtures which require 18 hours for separation on paper require as little as 3 hours using cellulose TLC.

Ion Exchange Column Chromatography

Moore and Stein utilized an ion exchange resin (Dowex) and various buffers as well as alterations in temperature to accomplish separation on a chromatographic column of all of the amino acids in a protein hydrolysate (Fig 3—27). Modifications in this procedure introduced by Moore, Spackman, and Stein permit a complete amino acid analysis of a peptide or of a protein hydrolysate in about 4 hours. The modified system can be used either with a fraction collector or with automatic recording equipment. In this method, columns of finely pulverized 8% cross-linked sulfonated polystyrene resin (Amberlite IR-120) are used. The method has been used for analysis of proteins such as histones, hemoglobin, and ribonuclease. With modifications it can be used for determination of amino acids and related compounds in plasma, urine, and plant and animal tissues.

High-Voltage Electrophoresis (HVE)

Separation of peptides and amino acids by placing them in an electrical field of 2000–5000 volts for 0.5–2 hours (high-voltage electrophoresis) is a valuable adjunct to chromatographic separation technics. As a support, paper or thin layers of powdered cellulose are most frequently used. Separations depend upon 2 factors: the net charge of a molecule at the pH selected and the molecular weight. For 2 molecules with iden-

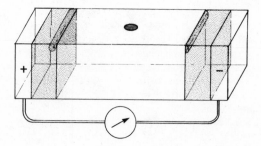

Figure 3—28. Apparatus for high-voltage electrophoresis.

tical charge, the lower molecular weight material will migrate farther in a given interval. Net charge is, however, the more important factor in determining the degree of separation achieved.

Fig 3—28 shows diagrammatically how high-voltage electrophoresis is conducted on cellulose thin layers. Samples are applied at the center of the supporting layer. This is then moistened with buffer of an appropriate pH, connected to buffer reservoirs by paper "wicks," and covered with a glass plate to reduce evaporative loss of buffer during passage of the current. When current is applied, molecules with a net positive charge at the selected pH move toward the cathode and those with a net negative charge toward the anode. For visualization of the separated materials, the dried **electropherogram** is treated with ninhydrin.

The choice of pH is dictated by the pK values of the dissociating groups on the molecules in the mixture. At pH 6.4, glutamate and aspartate bear a net charge of −1, move toward the anode, and are readily separated (30 minutes, 2000 volts) on the basis of their difference in molecular weight. Lysine, arginine, and histidine move in the opposite direction, whereas all of the other protein amino acids remain at or near the point of application.

For separation of the peptides resulting from enzymic digestion of a protein, a pH of 3.5 is better. The technic is also widely used for separation of oligonucleotides (pH 2.5) (see Chapter 11) or of nucleotides (pH 4.5).

TECHNICS USED IN DETERMINING PRIMARY PEPTIDE STRUCTURES

Determination by Manual Technics

Until 1967, the task of determining the primary structure of a large polypeptide or protein involved preparation of a large number of smaller peptides by specific enzymic hydrolysis (Fig 3–22). The peptides were then separated by a combination of electrophoretic and chromatographic technics, and the sequence of amino acids in many of these was determined by manual wet chemical technics such as those described below.

A. Hydrazinolysis: Peptides are treated with hydrazine, converting all peptide and amide bonds to acid hydrazides. The C-terminal carboxyl group does not react. The unchanged amino acid is thus that originally at the C-terminal end.

B. Treatment With 1-Fluoro-2,4-dinitrobenzene (Sanger's Reagent): This quantitatively arylates all free amino groups, producing intensely yellow 2,4-dinitrophenyl amino acids (Fig 3–11). These derivatives are readily quantitated by spectrophotometry. In a peptide, only the N-terminal residue can form a 1-fluoro-2,4-dinitrobenzene derivative. Following hydrolysis, this may be separated and identified.

Fluorodinitrobenzene also reacts with the ϵ-amino groups of lysine, the imidazole of histidine, the OH of tyrosine, and the SH of cysteine. Since the dinitrophenyl group is resistant to removal by acid hydrolysis, it is useful in structural analysis of the N-terminal amino acid of polypeptides and proteins.

C. Reactions With Phenylisothiocyanate (Edman Reagent): Phenylisothiocyanate reacts with the amino groups of amino acids, yielding phenylthiohydantoic acids. On treatment with acids in nonhydroxylic solvents, these cyclize to phenylthiohydantoins (Fig 3–12).

D. Digestion With Aminopeptidases or Carboxypeptidases: These enzymes catalyze successive removal of N- or C-terminal residues, respectively. The order in which residues appear in the nonprotein fraction as a function of time tells much of their order in a polypeptide.

The final task involved fitting together all the peptides which had overlapping regions in such a way as to give an unambiguous structure for the original polypeptide. Apart from the colossal effort involved, one serious shortcoming of this approach was that regions of minor or major uncertainty tended to remain unless exactly the right peptides were obtained.

Determination by Automated Technics

The determination of the primary structure of polypeptides—and thus also of proteins (see Chapter 4)—was revolutionized by Edman in 1967 by introduction of an automated system of analysis. Several companies now market fully automated apparatus for the determination of polypeptide sequences of up to 30–40 residues (or, in exceptional cases, up to 60 or even 80 residues) in one continuous operation. The apparatus is programmed to perform sequential Edman degradations on the N-terminal residue of a polypeptide. After the initial N-terminal amino acid has been removed, separated, and identified, an Edman derivative of the next one in the sequence is formed, etc. The apparatus lengthens the sequence that can be determined by manual technics 4- to 5-fold and is incomparably faster.

An early success using automated sequencing was the determination, in 1970, of the complete primary structure of bovine parathyroid hormone. Table 3–8 lists further examples.

Table 3–8. Examples of polypeptide structures determined by automated Edman technics.

Peptide	Number of Residues	Year
Ovine calcitonin	32	1970
Bovine neurophysin II	97	1971
Bovine neurophysin I	92	1972
Human amyloid protein A	76	1973

CONFORMATION OF PEPTIDES IN SOLUTION

From examination of molecular models, it is apparent that a large number of conformations (spatial arrangements) are possible for a polypeptide. The available evidence suggests, however, that peptides in solution may be more rigid than might be supposed and that one or a narrow range of conformations tends to predominate. These favored conformations result from the action of factors such as steric hindrance, coulombic interactions, H-bonding, and hydrophobic interactions (see Chapter 4). As is the case for proteins, there is evidence that specific conformations are required for physiologic activity of polypeptides such as angiotensin and vasopressin (see Chapter 29).

Association or aggregation of several identical polypeptide chains may also be a significant factor in their biologic activity. This appears to be the case for the tyrocidins.

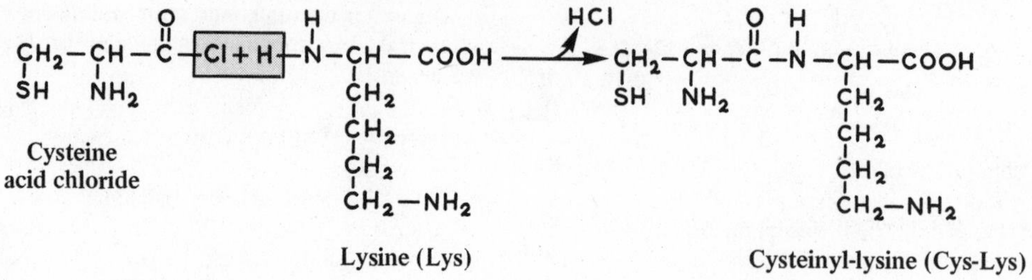

Figure 3–29. Reaction of an activated amino acid with the α-N of lysine.

SYNTHESIS OF PEPTIDES

Synthesis by Manual Technics

Peptides, like amides, may be synthesized by a reaction between an activated carboxyl group such as an acid chloride, an acid anhydride, or a thioester of one amino acid and the amino group of another, as for example between cysteine acid chloride and lysine (Fig 3–29). When this reaction is carried out, however, the activated carboxyl group also reacts with the ε-amino group of lysine, producing 2 isomeric Cys-Lys dipeptides. In addition, it may react with the amino group of another cysteinyl chloride producing Cys-Cys-Cl, and this process may continue, producing Cys-Cys-Cys-Cl, etc. To avoid these undesirable side products, all amino groups to be excluded from the reaction must be blocked. After the peptide bond is formed, the blocking group is removed, leaving the desired peptide.

Synthesis by Automated Technics

Synthesis of large polypeptides was difficult and extremely time-consuming. While classical chemical technics were adequate for synthesis of the octapeptides vasopressin and oxytocin, and later of bradykinin (see below), the yields of final product are too low to permit synthesis of long polypeptides or proteins. This has recently been achieved by the automated, solid-phase synthesis technic developed by RB Merrifield. In this process, an automated synthesis is carried out in a single vessel by a machine programmed to add reagents, remove products, etc at timed intervals. The steps involved are as follows:

(1) The amino acid that ultimately will form the C-terminal end of the polypeptide is attached to an insoluble resin particle.

(2) The second amino acid bearing an appropriately blocked amino group is introduced and the peptide bond formed in the presence of the strong dehydrating agent, dicyclohexylcarbodiimide.

(3) The blocking group is removed with acid, forming gaseous products which are removed.

(4) Steps 2 and 3 are repeated with the next amino acid in sequence, then the next, until the entire polypeptide attached to the resin particle has been synthesized.

(5) The polypeptide is cleaved from the resin particle.

The process proceeds rapidly and with excellent yields of final product. About 3 hours are required per peptide bond synthesized. Using the above-described technic, the A chain of insulin (21 residues) was synthesized in 8 days and the B chain (30 residues) in 11 days. The crowning achievement to date has been the total synthesis of pancreatic ribonuclease (124 residues; see Fig 4–6) in 18% overall yield. This constitutes the first total synthesis of an enzyme. It foreshadows a new era not only in confirmation of protein structures but in related areas such as immunology and perhaps in the treatment of inborn errors of metabolism.

A variety of physiologically important peptides, prepared synthetically from L-amino acids by routes which involve no racemization, have full physiologic activity. These include the octapeptides oxytocin and vasopressin, ACTH, and melanocyte-stimulating hormone (see Chapter 29).

PHYSIOLOGICALLY ACTIVE PEPTIDES

Although a large number of peptides exist in the free state in cells of animals, plants, and bacteria, the physiologic function of most of them is not clear. In some cases, they are thought to represent products of protein turnover; in others, they may be hormones, antibiotics, precursors of bacterial cell walls, or even potent poisons. Many bacterial and fungal peptides, including most antibiotics, are cyclic peptides containing both unusual amino acids and the D-isomers of the familiar protein amino acids. Frequently the peptide bonds involve the non-α carboxyl of glutamate or aspartate. D-Amino acids, despite their wide occurrence in microbial polypeptides, have not been found in plant or animal cells.

An example of one of the many known naturally occurring polypeptides is shown in Fig 3–30. This is the widely distributed tripeptide glutathione. Glutathione is required for the action of several enzymes, including insulin. Glutathione reductase is thought to function either in insulin degradation or possibly in the formation of the correct disulfide bonds.

Other important naturally occurring peptides include bradykinin and kallidin (lysyl-bradykinin), po-

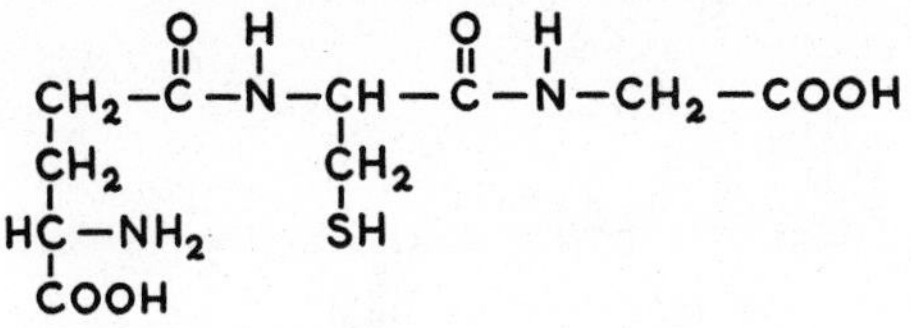

Figure 3–30. Glutathione (γ-glutamyl-cysteinyl-glycine).

tent smooth muscle hypotensive agents liberated from specific plasma proteins by treatment with snake venom or the proteolytic enzyme trypsin.

Arg-Pro-Pro-Gly-Phe-Ser-Pro-Phe-Arg

Bradykinin

Lys-Arg-Pro-Pro-Gly-Phe-Ser-Pro-Phe-Arg

Kallidin

The cyclic peptides tyrocidin and gramicidin are antibiotics, and they contain D-phenylalanine. (See structures below.)

```
Val-Orn-Leu-D-Phe-Pro
 |                    |   = (Val-Orn-Leu-D-Phe-Pro)₂
Pro-D-Phe-Leu-Orn-Val
```

Gramicidin S

```
Val-Orn-Leu-D-Phe-Pro
 |                   |
Tyr-Gln-Asn-D-Phe-Phe
```

Tyrocidin

•   •   •

References

Craig LC, Cowburn D, Bleich H: Methods for the study of small polypeptide hormones and antibiotics in solution. Annu Rev Biochem 44:509, 1975.

Greenstein JP, Winitz M: *Chemistry of the Amino Acids.* 3 vols. Wiley, 1961.

Heftman E: *Chromatography: A Laboratory Handbook of Chromatographic and Electrophoretic Methods,* 3rd ed. Van Nostrand, 1975.

Meister A: *Biochemistry of the Amino Acids,* 2nd ed. Academic Press, 1965.

Scott RM: *Clinical Analysis by Thin-Layer Chromatography Techniques.* Ann Arbor, 1969.

Stewart JM, Young JD: *Solid Phase Peptide Synthesis.* Freeman, 1969.

Touchstone JC: *Quantitative Thin Layer Chromatography.* Wiley-Interscience, 1973.

4 ...
Proteins

CLASSIFICATION OF PROTEINS

Knowledge of the molecular architecture of proteins has increased enormously in recent years. The total synthesis in 1969 of ribonuclease from its constituent amino acids ushered in a new era in protein chemistry wherein the effects of specific amino acid substitutions on structure and on biologic activity of proteins may be studied by the direct synthesis of such modified proteins. One consequence of the increase in knowledge has been the gradual disappearance of older terms and concepts.

When nothing was known concerning the primary structure of proteins, they were classified according to their solubilities. Vestiges of this approach persist at the present time, specifically in clinical laboratories, where the terms "albumin" and "globulin" remain in use.

While it might be possible to devise classification systems based on similarities in primary or higher orders of protein structure, no such system is currently in use. For the present, therefore, it will suffice to distinguish between simple proteins, which consist solely of amino acids (eg, insulin), and complex proteins, which additionally contain nonamino acids (eg, hemoglobin, glycoproteins, lipoproteins, nucleoproteins).

SIZE & SHAPE OF PROTEINS

Size

Molecular weights of proteins have been investigated by physical methods such as osmotic pressure measurements or by freezing point (cryoscopic) determinations. In general, the results lack precision because of variables due to pH, electrolytes, and the degree of hydration of the protein molecule. The method developed by Svedberg is the best yet advanced for determination of the molecular weight of proteins. This method depends upon measurement of sedimentation rates as determined in the ultracentrifuge. Molecular weights of representative proteins (ultracentrifuge measurements) are as follows: egg albumin, 44,000; bovine insulin, 12,000; serum albumin, 69,000; hemoglobin (horse), 68,000; serum globulin, 180,000; fibrinogen, 450,000; thyroglobulin, 630,000.

Overall Shape

One may distinguish 2 broad classes of proteins on the basis of their overall dimensions.

A. Globular Proteins: These have an axial ratio (length:width) of less than 10. They are characterized by the presence of peptide chains which are folded or coiled in a very compact manner. Axial ratios are usually not over 3:1 or 4:1. Examples of globular proteins are found among the fractions of the albumins and globulins in the plasma. **Insulin** is another globular protein.

B. Fibrous Proteins: These have an axial ratio greater than 10. **Keratin**, the protein of hair, wool, and skin, is a typical fibrous protein. It consists of a long peptide chain or groups of such chains. The peptide chains may be coiled in a spiral or helix formation and cross-linked by S–S bonds as well as by hydrogen bonds. The condensed form is referred to as alpha-keratin. This changes to beta-keratin by unfolding. **Myosin**, the major protein of muscle, is also a fibrous protein which undergoes a change in its structure during muscle contraction and relaxation.

Streaming Birefringence

This phenomenon is used to study the shape of protein molecules. A beam of light is passed through a polarizing lens. The polarized light is then passed through a solution of a protein and, finally, through a second polarizing lens which is oriented at right angles to the first lens. No light will emerge from the second lens if the protein solution does not affect the polarized light. This is the case with spherical protein molecules. It is also true of fibrous molecules when the solution is at rest because the protein molecules are then randomly oriented. However, when a solution of a fibrous protein is put in motion, the elongated molecules arrange themselves lengthwise in the axis of the stream and thus act as if another polarizer were added to the system. As a result the polarized light does pass through the second lens. This phenomenon is referred to as "streaming birefringence" or "double refraction of flow." It has been used to calculate the "axial ratio" of a fibrous protein, ie, the ratio of the length of the long axis to that of the short axis. An example is fibrinogen, which has a calculated axial ratio of 20:1.

BONDS RESPONSIBLE FOR PROTEIN STRUCTURE

Protein structures are stabilized by 2 classes of strong bonds (peptide and disulfide) and 2 classes of weak bonds (hydrogen and hydrophobic).

Peptide Bonds

The primary structure of proteins derives ultimately from linkage of L-a- amino acids by a-peptide bonds. The principal evidence for the peptide bond as the primary structural bond of proteins is summarized below.

(1) Proteases, enzymes which hydrolyze proteins, produce polypeptides as products. These enzymes also hydrolyze the peptide bonds of proteins.

(2) The infrared spectra of proteins suggest many peptide bonds.

(3) Two proteins, insulin and ribonuclease, have been synthesized solely by linking amino acids by peptide bonds.

(4) Proteins have few titratable carboxyl or amino groups.

(5) Proteins and synthetic polypeptides react with **biuret reagent** (an alkaline 0.02% cupric sulfate solution) to form a purple color. This reaction is specific for 2 or more peptide bonds.

(6) X-ray diffraction studies at the 0.2 nm level of resolution have conclusively identified the peptide bonds in the proteins, myoglobin and hemoglobin.

Disulfide Bond

The disulfide bond may interconnect 2 parallel chains through cysteine residues within each polypeptide (see structure of ribonuclease, Fig 4—6). This bond is relatively stable and thus is not readily broken under the usual conditions of denaturation. Performic acid treatment oxidizes the S—S bonds. This reagent is used, for example, to oxidize insulin in order to separate the protein molecule into its constituent polypeptide chains without affecting the other parts of the molecule (see Chapter 3). The union of 2 parallel peptide chains by an S—S linkage is illustrated in Fig 4—1.

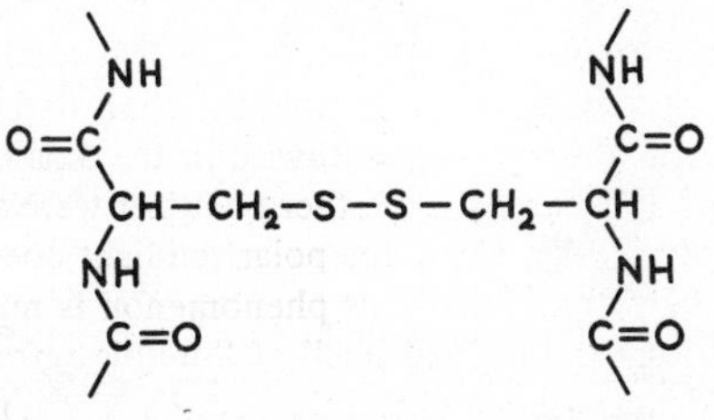

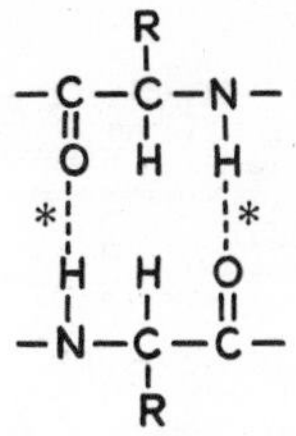

Figure 4—2. *Hydrogen bonds.

Hydrogen Bonds (Fig 4—2.)

The hydrogen bond results from the sharing of hydrogen atoms between the nitrogen and the carbonyl oxygen of different peptide bonds. These may be contributed by amino acid residues in the same or different polypeptide chains. Each hydrogen bond is by itself quite weak. Their importance in protein structure arises from the extremely large number of hydrogen bonds that may be formed. During denaturation of a protein, hydrogen and hyrophobic bonds (see below), but not peptide or disulfide bonds, are broken.

Hydrophobic Bonds

The nonpolar side chains of neutral amino acids tend to be closely associated with one another in proteins. The relationship is nonstoichiometric; hence no true bond may be said to exist. Nonetheless, these interactions play a significant role in maintaining protein structure.

Electrostatic Bonds

These are salt bonds formed between oppositely charged groups in the side chains of amino acids. The epsilon-amino group of lysine bears a net charge of +1 at physiologic pH and the gamma carboxyl of aspartate a net charge of −1. These may therefore interact electrostatically.

ORDERS OF PROTEIN STRUCTURE

Protein structure must be considered at several levels of organization. The first, or primary, level of organization is already familiar from the study of peptide sequences (see Chapter 3). The primary structure of a protein refers to the order of the individual amino acids in the polypeptide chain or chains that comprise the protein (Fig 4—3).

-Ala-Gly-Gly-His-Leu-
-Ala-Gly-His-Gly-Leu-

Figure 4—3. Portions of polypeptide chains of 2 proteins. While these contain the same amino acids, their order (sequence) differs. The proteins are therefore said to have different primary structures.

Figure 4—1. Two peptide chains united by a disulfide linkage.

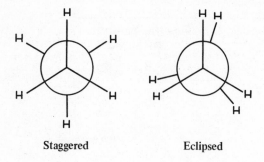

Staggered   **Eclipsed**

Figure 4–4. Staggered and eclipsed forms of ethane.

Secondary and tertiary structures of proteins refer to the conformation of polypeptide chains. The term **conformation** refers to the relative positions in space of each of the constituent atoms of a molecule. For a simple molecule like ethane (C_2H_6), 2 conformations are possible—"staggered" and "eclipsed" (Fig 4–4).

Since the carbon atoms can rotate freely about the single bond connecting them, the conformational forms of ethane are interconvertible. The staggered form is, however, favored thermodynamically over the sterically hindered eclipsed form. Free rotation about the bond connecting the carbon atom would not be possible if it were a double bond.

While the "backbone" of polypeptide chains consists of single bonds, free rotation does not occur about all these bonds. The peptide bond itself is planar and has some double bond character. Rotation about this bond does not occur. This semirigidity (Fig 4–5) has important consequences for orders of protein structure above the primary level.

The folding of the polypeptide chains into a specific coiled structure held together by disulfide bonds and by hydrogen bonds is referred to as the "**secondary structure**" of the protein (Fig 4–6).

The arrangement and interrelationship of the twisted chains of protein into specific layers or fibers is called the "**tertiary structure**" of the protein. This tertiary structure is maintained by weak interatomic forces such as hydrogen bonds or by what are termed Van der Waals' forces. For example, the protein of tobacco mosaic virus has a tertiary structure resembling a kernel of corn. These "kernels" line up along the "cob" of nucleic acid to produce the elongated nucleoprotein rods which have been seen under the electron microscope. Fig 4–7 illustrates the secondary and tertiary structure of a specific protein, the hemoprotein myoglobin.

In addition to primary, secondary, and tertiary structures, many proteins may display a fourth level of organization wherein several monomeric units, each with appropriate primary, secondary, and tertiary structures, may combine. The association of similar or dissimilar subunits confers on the protein a **quaternary structure** (Fig 4–8).

The secondary and tertiary structures of a protein are themselves determined by the amino acid structure of the primary polypeptide chain. Once the chain has been formed, the chemical groups which extend from the amino acids direct the specific coiling (secondary structure) and aggregation of the coiled chains (tertiary structure). Treatment of ribonuclease with a mild reducing agent inactivates it, but when it is gently reoxidized almost complete reactivation occurs. As illustrated in Fig 4–6, the disulfide bonds serve to maintain the specific coiled arrangement of the protein.

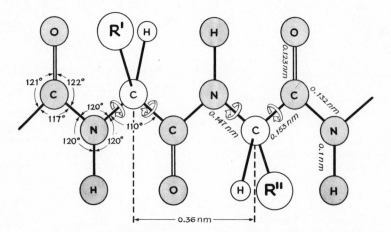

Figure 4–5. Dimensions of a fully extended polypeptide chain. The groups of 4 shaded atoms are **coplanar,** ie, they lie in the same plane. These same 4 atoms comprise the polypeptide bond. The unshaded atoms are the a-carbon atom, the a-hydrogen atom, and the a-R group of the particular amino acid. Free rotation can occur about the bonds connecting the a-carbon with the a-nitrogen and a-carbonyl functions (white arrows). The extended polypeptide chain is thus a semirigid structure with two-thirds of the atoms of the backbone held in a fixed planar relationship one to another. The distance between adjacent a-carbon atoms is 0.36 nm. The interatomic distances and bond angles, which are not equivalent, are also shown. (Redrawn and reproduced, with permission, from Corey LP, Branson HR: Proc Natl Acad Sci USA 37:205, 1951.)

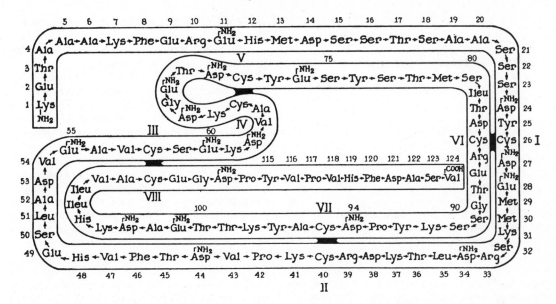

Figure 4–6. Structure of bovine ribonuclease. Two-dimensional schematic diagram showing the arrangement of the disulfide bonds and the sequence of the amino acid residues. Arrows indicate the direction of the peptide chain starting from the amino end. (Reproduced, with permission, from Smyth, Stein, & Moore: The sequence of amino acid residues in bovine pancreatic ribonuclease: Revisions and confirmations. J Biol Chem 238:227, 1963.)

Figure 4–7. Representation of primary, secondary, and tertiary structure of a protein. (In this instance, the whale muscle myoglobin molecule, drawn from x-ray analysis data of Kendrew.) The large dots represent α-carbon atoms of amino acids. The sequence of dots therefore denotes the primary structure of the molecule. This consists of a single polypeptide chain with a COOH end at the upper left and an α-amino end at the lower left. The spiral portions drawn in perspective represent regions where the polypeptide chain is coiled in an α-helix. The entire polypeptide chain is wound about itself, conferring tertiary structure. Since the myoglobin molecule contains but a single subunit, no quaternary structure is possible. Note also (in the upper right corner) the heme group attached by 2 histidine molecules to 2 different regions of the polypeptide chain. (Courtesy of RE Dickerson.)

Figure 4–8. Representation of quaternary structure of a protein. "Ping-pong ball" model of the apoferritin molecule. This consists of 20 subunits, each with a molecular weight of about 20,000. The subunits are arranged to form a hollow sphere which may become packed with iron salts forming the iron storage protein ferritin. (Courtesy of RA Fineberg.)

When these are broken by reduction (to SH groups), the characteristic coiling is lost; but gentle reoxidation (to S–S linkages) will reestablish it exactly as before.

Finally, aggregation of different proteins—each of which alone has all 4 orders of structure—into macromolecular complexes is encountered in electron transport (see Chapter 17) and in fatty acid biosynthesis (see Chapter 19).

PRIMARY STRUCTURE OF PROTEINS

Determination of Primary Structure

The methods used for the determination of primary structure of proteins are those discussed in Chapter 3.

Primary Structures of Specific Proteins

The technologic explosion that followed the introduction of automated Edman technics for sequencing polypeptides and proteins has resulted in literally hundreds of primary structures for proteins. Little purpose would be served by listing these here. Two famous examples will be discussed: insulin (the first protein sequence) and ribonuclease (the first protein chemically synthesized).

A. Insulin: This protein (or large polypeptide) consists of two polypeptide chains linked covalently by disulfide bonds (Fig 4–9). One (the A chain) has an N-terminal Gly and a C-terminal Asn; the other (the B chain) has Phe and Ala as the N- and C-terminal amino acid residues, respectively.

When insulin is oxidized with performic acid, the disulfide bonds linking the A and B chains are ruptured. By such a reaction, Sanger obtained 2 major polypeptide chains from the insulin molecule which he termed A and B. The A chain has a molecular weight of approximately 2750 and the terminal amino acid is glycine. The B chain, with a molecular weight of approximately 3700, has phenylalanine as the terminal amino acid. The complete sequence of all the amino

acids in both A and B chains of beef insulin is shown in Fig 4–10.

The A and B chains of insulin are synthesized as a single sequence of amino acids (proinsulin). One or more peptides are then cleaved between residues 30 and 1, forming active insulin (see Chapter 29).

The positions at which the chains are interconnected in an insulin residue of molecular weight 6000 (derived from beef pancreas) were also reported by Sanger. In the A chain, the cysteine residues at 6 and 11 (counting from the N-terminal acid, glycine) are connected by an S–S linkage. The A and B chains are interconnected by S–S linkages between 7A and 7B and between 20A and 19B, respectively (Fig 4–9).

The insulins of various mammalian species (pig, sheep, horse, whale) exhibit differences in the amino acid sequences at positions 8–10 of the A chain. The structure of human insulin in shown in Chapter 29.

B. Ribonuclease: The sequence of the amino acid residues in performic acid-oxidized ribonuclease was established by Hirs, Moore, & Stein (1960). This enzyme protein was found to be a single chain of 124 amino acid residues beginning with lysine as the N-terminal amino acid and ending with valine as the C-terminal amino acid. As described above for insulin, there are cysteine residues in the amino acid chain of ribonuclease that are joined to one another by disulfide bonds, thus accomplishing cross-linkages within the single polypeptide chain. The position of these disulfide bonds has been established as shown in the schematic diagram of the structure of bovine ribonuclease (Fig 4–6). It will be noted that there are 8 cysteine residues in the chain, thus providing 4 disulfide or S–S linkages.

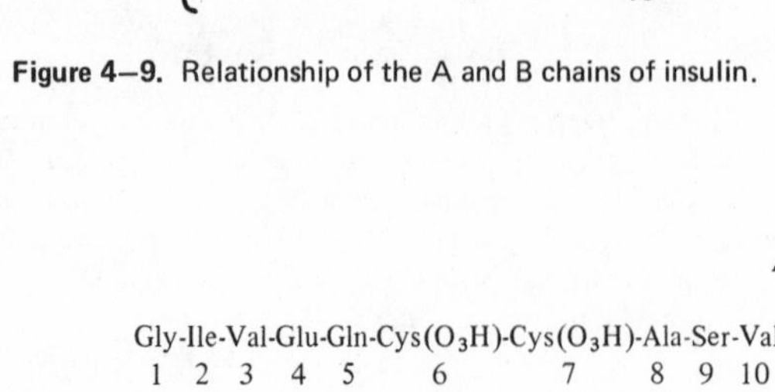

SECONDARY & TERTIARY STRUCTURE OF PROTEINS

Determination of Secondary & Tertiary Structure

A. X-Ray Diffraction: A single crystal of a protein or layers of protein or protein fibers will deflect x-rays, and the resultant image on a photographic plate

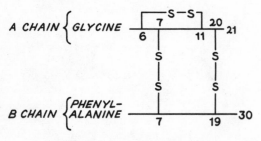

Figure 4–9. Relationship of the A and B chains of insulin.

A Chain

Gly-Ile-Val-Glu-Gln-Cys(O₃H)-Cys(O₃H)-Ala-Ser-Val-Cys(O₃H)-Ser-Leu-Tyr-Gln-Leu-Glu-Asn-Tyr-Cys(O₃H)-Asn
 1   2   3   4   5   6   7   8   9 10   11   12 13 14 15 16 17 18 19   20   21

B Chain

Phe-Val-Asn-Gln-His-Leu-Cys(O₃H)-Gly-Ser-His-Leu-Val-Glu-Ala-Leu-Tyr-Leu-Val-Cys(O₃H)-Gly-Glu-Arg-Gly-Phe-Phe-Tyr-Thr-Pro-Lys-Ala
 1   2   3   4   5   6   7   8   9 10 11 12 13 14 15 16 17 18   19   20 21 22 23 24 25 26 27 28 29 30

Figure 4–10. Amino acid sequence of the A and B chains of beef insulin. The acid at the left is the amino acid with a free amino group (the N-terminal amino acid). Cys(O₃H) is cysteic acid, the oxidized form of cysteine, which would be obtained after performic acid oxidation to break the S–S linkages that connect the chains in the intact molecule of insulin.

can be analyzed to yield information on the crystal or on the structure of the fiber. This technic has been the single most important factor in determination of complex, higher orders of protein structure. X-ray crystallographic analysis has provided detailed 3-dimensional structures, not only of myoglobin and hemoglobin, but of many enzymes, including ribonuclease, lysozyme, chymotrypsin, and lactate dehydrogenase. Progress has also been made in the elucidation of the structures of glyceraldehyde-3-phosphate dehydrogenase, carboxypeptidase A, carbonic anhydrase, papain, cytochome c, and phosphoglycerate mutase.

B. Optical Rotatory Dispersion: The ability of solutions of proteins to rotate the plane of plane-polarized light is examined at various wavelengths. Since proteins are composed of L-*a*- amino acids which are themselves optically active, proteins are highly optically active. In certain instances the optical rotation of a protein far exceeds that due solely to the sum of the individual rotations of its constituent amino acids. This suggests that the protein possesses asymmetry in addition to that of the *a*-carbon atoms. Helical structures (see below) can exist in right- or left-handed forms and hence are optically active. The presence of a high fraction of helical structure therefore contributes to the optical rotation. Other asymmetric structures can also contribute. The change in optical rotation accompanying the transition from helix to random coil or the reverse is used to assess the fraction of *a*-helix structure in proteins.

C. Electron Photomicrography: An actual picture of very small objects can be obtained with the electron microscope. Magnifications as high as 100,000 diameters can be obtained with this instrument. This permits the visualization of proteins of high molecular weight, such as virus particles.

The *a*-Helix

X-ray data obtained in the early 1930s indicated that hair and wool *a*-keratins possessed repeating units spaced 0.5–0.55 nm along their longitudinal axis. As shown in Fig 4–5, no dimension of the extended polypeptide chain appears to measure 0.5–0.55 nm. This apparent anomaly was resolved by Pauling and Corey, who proposed that the polypeptide chain of *a*-keratin is arranged as an *a*-helix (Fig 4–11).

In this structure, the R-groups on the *a*-carbon atoms protrude outward from the center of the helix. There are 3.6 amino acid residues per turn of the helix, and the distance traveled per turn is 0.54 nm—a reasonable approximation of the 0.5–0.55 nm spacing observed by x-ray diffraction. The spacing per amino acid residue is 0.15 nm, which also corresponds with x-ray data.

The main features of the *a*-helix are as follows:

(1) The *a*-helix is stabilized by inter-residue hydrogen bonds formed between the H atom attached to a peptide N and the carbonyl O of the residue fourth in line behind in the primary structure.

(2) Each peptide bond participates in the H-bonding. This confers maximum stability.

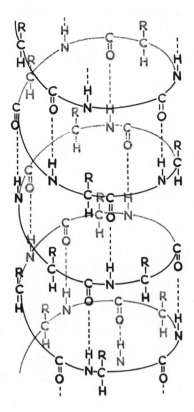

Figure 4–11. Alpha helix structure of a protein.

(3) An *a*-helix forms spontaneously as it is the lowest energy, most stable conformation for a polypeptide chain.

(4) The right-handed helix which occurs in proteins is significantly more stable than the left-handed helix when the residues are L-amino acids.

Certain amino acids tend to disrupt the *a*-helix. Among these are proline (the N-atom is part of a rigid ring and no rotation of the N–C bond can occur) and amino acids with charged or bulky R-groups which either electrostatically or physically interfere with helix formation (Table 4–1).

Table 4–1. Effect of various amino acid residues on helix formation.

Permit Stable *a*-Helix	Destabilize *a*-Helix	Break *a*-Helix
Ala	Arg	Pro
Asn	Asp	Hyp
Cys	Glu	
Gln	Gly	
His	Lys	
Leu	Ile	
Met	Ser	
Phe	Thr	
Trp		
Tyr		
Val		

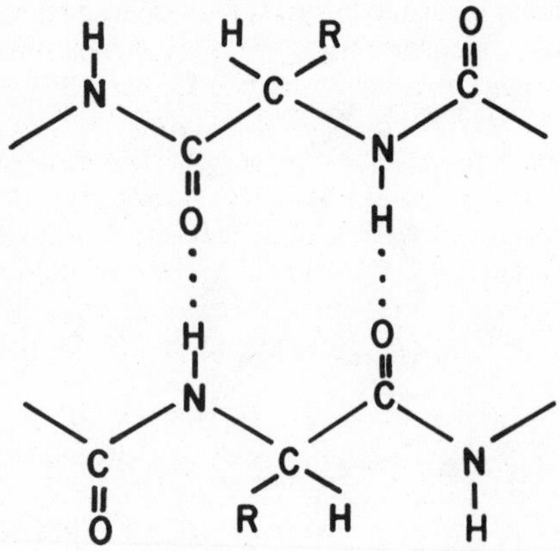

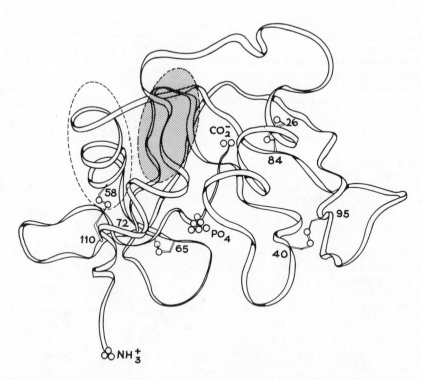

Figure 4–12. Diagrammatic representation of formation of a region of pleated sheet structure by formation of hydrogen bonds (. . .) between 2 regions of polypeptide chain. The bond angles are such that, when viewed on end, the polypeptide chains assume a conformation resembling a pleated sheet of paper.

Pleated Sheet

When sections of peptide chain are parallel to one another and close enough so that hydrogen bonds are formed between them, the protein is said to possess regions of pleated sheet structure (Fig 4–12).

If the 2 regions of polypeptide chain run in the same direction (ie, N-terminal to C-terminal), the sheet is said to be antiparallel. This form tends to be more common that the alternate antiparallel sheet arrangement. Regions of pleated sheet structure in a specific protein are shown shaded in Fig 4–13.

Random Coil

Regions of proteins that are not organized as a-helix or as pleated sheets are termed random coil. The word "random" is perhaps unfortunate, as it should not be taken to imply the absence either of structure or of biologic significance.

Figure 4–13. Schematic diagram of the main chain folding of bovine pancreatic ribonuclease. This protein is a single chain of 124 amino acid residues starting at the amino end (marked NH_3^+) and ending at the carboxy terminal (marked CO_2^-). The chain is cross-linked at 4 places by disulfide bridges from half cystine residues. The disulfide pairings for these bridges are 26–84, 40–95, 58–110, and 65–72 in the sequence. A region of a-helix is circled and a region of pleated sheet is shaded. Other portions of the molecule are predominantly random coil. The region of the active site (see Chapter 6) is indicated by the binding of the phosphate ion (PO_4^{3-}) in the cleft of the molecule. This model was obtained by x-ray diffraction studies of crystalline bovine pancreatic ribonuclease at 0.2 nm resolution. (Adapted from Kartha, Bello, & Harker: Nature 213:862, 1967.) The protein has recently been chemically synthesized in its entirety.

QUATERNARY STRUCTURE OF PROTEINS

Protomers and Oligomers

Proteins are said to possess **quaternary structure** if they consist of 2 or more polypeptide chains **united by forces other than covalent bonds** (ie, not peptide or disulfide bonds). The forces that stabilize these aggregates are hydrogen bonds and electrostatic or salt bonds formed between residues on the surfaces of the polypeptide chains. Such proteins are termed **oligomers,** and the individual polypeptide chains of which they are composed are variously termed **protomers, monomers,** or **subunits.**

The most commonly encountered oligomeric proteins contain 2 or 4 protomers and are termed dimers or tetramers, respectively. Oligomers containing more than 4 protomers are also common, however, particu-larly among regulated enzymes (eg, aspartate transcarbamoylase). Ferritin (Fig 4–8) is another example of an oligomeric protein with many oligomers. Oligomeric proteins play special roles in intracellular regulation because the protomers can assume different spatial orientations with resulting changes in the properties of the oligomer. The best-studied example is hemoglobin (see Chapter 34), in which a variety of conformations exist depending on the degree of oxygenation. Table 4–2 lists several oligomeric proteins which are enzymes.

Secondary, Tertiary, & Quaternary Structures of Specific Proteins

A. Ribonuclease: The results of x-ray diffraction studies of bovine ribonuclease indicate that the molecule of the enzyme has dimensions of about 3.2 $\times$ 2.8 $\times$ 2.2 nm. There is very little a-helix structure,

Table 4–2. Quaternary structure of enzymes.*

Enzyme (Oligomer)	Number of Protomers	Molecular Weight of Protomer
E coli galactoside acetyltransferase (acetyl-CoA:galactoside 6-O-acetyltransferase, E.C. 2.3.1.18)	2	29,700
Rat liver malate dehydrogenase (L-malate:NAD oxidoreductase, E.C. 1.1.1.37)	2	37,500
Rabbit muscle glycerol-3-phosphate dehydrogenase (L-glycerol-3-phosphate:NAD oxidoreductase, E.C. 1.1.1.8)	2	39,000
E coli UDP glucose epimerase (UDP glucose 4-epimerase, E.C. 5.1.3.2)	2	39,000
E coli alkaline phosphatase (orthophosphoric monoester phosphohydrolase, E.C. 3.1.3.1)	2	40,000
Chicken or rabbit muscle creatine kinase (ATP:creatine phosphotransferase, E.C. 2.7.3.2)	2	40,000
Horse liver alcohol dehydrogenase (alcohol:NAD oxidoreductase, E.C. 1.1.1.1)	2	40,000
Yeast aldolase (fructose-1,6-diphosphate D-glyceraldehyde-3-phosphate-lyase, E.C. 4.1.2.13)	2	40,000
Rabbit muscle enolase (2-phospho-D-glycerate hydro-lyase, E.C. 4.2.1.11)	2	41,000
E coli methionyl-t-RNA synthetase (L-methionine:t-RNA ligase [AMP], E.C. 6.1.1.10)	2	48,000
Chicken heart aspartate transaminase (L-aspartate:2-oxoglutarate aminotransferase, E.C. 2.6.1.1)	2	50,000
Yeast hexokinase (ATP:D-hexose 6-phosphotransferase, E.C. 2.7.1.1)	4	27,500
Rabbit liver fructose diphosphatase (D-fructose-1,6-diphosphate 1-phosphohydrolase, E.C. 3.1.3.11)	2†	29,000
	2†	37,000
Rat mammary gland glucose-6-phosphate dehydrogenase (D-glucose-6-phosphate:NADP oxido-reductase, E.C. 1.1.1.49)	2	63,000
Rat liver ornithine transaminase (L-ornithine:2-oxoacid aminotransferase, E.C. 2.6.1.13)	4	33,000
Aspartate transcarbamoylase (carbamoylphosphate:L-aspartate carbamoyltransferase, E.C. 2.1.3.2)	2†	17,000
	3†	33,000
Rattlesnake venom L-amino acid oxidase (L-amino acid:O_2 oxidoreductase [deaminating], E.C. 1.4.3.2)	2	70,000
Beef heart, liver, or muscle LDH (L-lactate:NAD oxidoreductase, E.C. 1.1.1.27)	4†	35,000
Rabbit muscle glyceraldehyde-3-phosphate dehydrogenase (D-glyceraldehyde-3-phosphate:NAD oxidoreductase [phosphorylating], E.C. 1.2.1.12)	4†	37,000
Yeast alcohol dehydrogenase (alcohol:NAD oxidoreductase, E.C. 1.1.1.1)	4	37,000
Rabbit muscle aldolase (ketose-1-phosphate aldehyde-lyase, E.C. 4.1.2.7)	4	40,000
Pig heart fumarase (L-malate hydro-lyase, E.C. 4.2.1.2)	4	48,500
Rabbit muscle pyruvate kinase (ATP:pyruvate phosphotransferase, E.C. 2.7.1.40)	4	57,200
Beef liver catalase (H_2O_2:H_2O_2 oxidoreductase, E.C. 1.11.1.6)	4	57,500
Beef heart mitochondrial ATPase (ATP phosphohydrolase, E.C. 3.6.1.3)	10	26,000
Pigeon liver fatty acid synthetase	2	230,000
Jack bean meal urease (urea amidohydrolase, E.C. 3.5.1.5)	6	83,000
E coli glutamine synthetase (L-glutamate:NH$_3$ ligase [ADP], E.C. 6.3.1.2)	12	48,500
Pig heart propionyl-CoA carboxylase (propionyl-CoA:CO_2 ligase [ADP], E.C. 6.4.1.3)	4	175,000
E coli RNA polymerase (nucleosidetriphosphate:RNA nucleotidyltransferase, E.C. 2.7.7.6)	2	440,000
Chicken liver acetyl-CoA carboxylase (acetyl-CoA:CO_2 ligase [ADP], E.C. 6.4.1.2)	2†	4,100,000
	10†	409,000

*Adapted from Klotz IM, Langerman NR, Darnall DW: Quaternary structure of enzymes. Annu Rev Biochem 39:25, 1970.
†Nonidentical subunits.

such structures being limited to 2 turns of the helix at the region of amino acid residues 5–12 and 2 more turns near the residues 28–35 (Fig 4–13). The 3-dimensional structure of myoglobin is shown in Fig 4–7. In contrast to myoglobin, ribonuclease has much of its structure exposed, no part being shielded by more than one layer of the main chain. A phosphate ion is associated directly with the active site of the enzyme. The amino acid residues nearest the phosphate are numbers 119 and 12. Both of these amino acid residues are histidine. Lysine residues at positions 7 and 41 and histidine at 48 have also been implicated as at the active sites, and all are also near the phosphate group. If ribonuclease is split by the enzyme subtilisin, 2 inactive peptides are produced. The shorter one (the so-called S-peptide) consists of the first 21 amino acids from the N-terminal. It can be reassociated with the longer peptide fragment (S-protein), and full activity of the enzyme returns.

B. Lactate Dehydrogenase: Although the primary structure has yet to be elucidated by chemical means, the complete tertiary structure of the LDH subunit has been described solely by interpretation of x-ray crystallographic data. This is the first and only example of the successful application of this technic to a subunit-containing enzyme; it is a noteworthy achievement. The subunit contains regions both of helix and of pleated sheet and is relatively compact save for the N-terminal end of the polypeptide chain, which projects out and is thought to interact with other subunits. The subunit contains a deep cleft which accommodates the coenzyme molecule (NAD). The nicotinamide portion of the NAD lies close to the essential thiol group in the region thought to contain the active site.

C. Carboxypeptidase A: X-ray crystallographic data indicate that substrates are bound in the region of the essential zinc atom and that the enzyme undergoes a conformational change when substrate is bound. Two groups, a tyrosyl and an aspartyl residue (which might well perform a role in catalysis), undergo a spatial shift of about 1.5 and 0.2 nm, respectively. Since removal of the zinc or its replacement by mercury destroys the activity without noticeable effect on the 3-dimensional structure, the zinc may be inferred to perform catalytic rather than structural functions.

D. Carbonic Anhydrase: X-ray data at the 0.55 nm level are available for human erythrocyte carbonic anhydrase C, a zinc metalloenzyme with a molecular weight of 30,000 which contains less than one-third α-helix. The zinc is located near the center of the molecule at the bottom of a large cavity. One sulfonamide inhibitor, acetoxymercurisulfanilamide, binds so that the sulfonamide group is adjacent to the zinc atom.

DENATURATION OF PROTEINS

The comparatively weak forces responsible for maintaining secondary, tertiary, and quaternary structure of proteins are readily disrupted by a variety of manipulations with a resulting loss of biologic activity. This loss of activity is termed **denaturation**. Physically, denaturation may be viewed as an altered conformation of polypeptide chains that does not affect their primary structure. For a protein consisting of a single polypeptide, the process may be represented diagrammatically as shown in Fig 4–14.

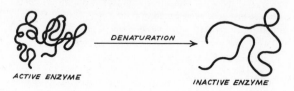

Figure 4—14. Representation of denaturation of a protein.

For an oligomeric protein, denaturation may involve dissociation of the protomers with or without subsequent unfolding or with or without accompanying changes in protomer conformation (Fig 4–15).

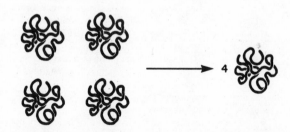

Figure 4—15. Representation of denaturation of an oligomeric protein under conditions not sufficiently severe to alter protomer conformation.

The biologic activity of most proteins is destroyed by treatment with strong mineral acids or bases, heat applied at or near 100° C, exposure to heavy metals (Ag, Pb, Hg), or treatment with organic solvents at or above room temperature. Denatured proteins generally are less soluble, and they often precipitate from solution. This property is used to advantage in the clinical laboratory. Blood or serum samples to be analyzed for small molecules (eg, glucose, uric acid, drugs) generally are first treated with acids such as trichloroacetic, phosphotungstic, or phosphomolybdic acid to precipitate most of the protein present. This is removed by centrifugation and the protein-free supernatant liquid is then analyzed.

The heat and acid lability of most enzymes pro-

vides a simple test to decide whether a reaction is enzyme-catalyzed. If a cell extract having catalytic activity loses this activity when boiled or when acidified and reneutralized, the catalyst probably was an enzyme.

Frequently, enzymes are either more or less readily denatured if their substrate is present. Either effect is attributed to a conformational change in the enzyme structure occurring when substrate is bound. The new conformation may be either more or less stable than before.

COLOR REACTIONS OF PROTEINS

Certain color reactions previously mentioned (Table 3–7) as specific for various amino acids are useful also to detect the presence of protein containing the amino acids for which the color test is indicative. These include the Millon, xanthoproteic, and ninhydrin reactions as well as the Hopkins-Cole (glyoxylic acid) test. The biuret reaction, specific to peptide linkages, is also used as a test for the presence of proteins.

•   •   •

References

Advances in Protein Chemistry. Academic Press, 1944–1977. [Annual publication.]

Blow DM, Steitz TA: X-ray diffraction studies of enzymes. Annu Rev Biochem 39:63, 1970.

Dayhoff MO (editor): *Atlas of Protein Structure.* Vol 5. National Biomedical Research Foundation, 1972.

Evergreen enzyme. (Editorial.) Nature 218:1202, 1968.

Ginsberg A, Stadtman ER: Multienzyme systems. Annu Rev Biochem 39:429, 1970.

Klotz IM, Langerman NR, Darnall DW: Quaternary structure of enzymes. Annu Rev Biochem 39:25, 1970.

Marglin A, Merrifield RB: Chemical synthesis of peptides and proteins. Annu Rev Biochem 39:841, 1970.

Neurath H, Hill RL (editors): *The Proteins,* 3rd ed. Academic Press, 1975.

5 . . .
General Properties of Enzymes

CATALYSIS

Catalysts accelerate chemical reactions. Although a catalyst is a participant in a reaction and undergoes physical change during the reaction, it reverts to its original state when the reaction is complete. **Enzymes are protein catalysts** for chemical reactions in biologic systems. Most chemical reactions of living cells would occur very slowly were it not for catalysis by enzymes.

By contrast to nonprotein catalysts (H^+, OH^-, or metal ions), each enzyme catalyzes a small number of reactions, frequently only one. Enzymes are thus **reaction-specific** catalysts. Since **essentially all biochemical reactions are enzyme-catalyzed**, many different enzymes must exist. Indeed, for almost every organic compound in nature, and for many inorganic compounds as well, there is an enzyme in some living organism capable of reacting with it and catalyzing some chemical change.

Although the catalytic activity of enzymes was formerly thought to be expressed only in intact cells (hence the term *en-zyme*, ie, "in yeast"), most enzymes may be extracted from cells without loss of their biologic (catalytic) activity. They can therefore be studied outside the living cell. Enzyme-containing extracts are used in studies of metabolic reactions and their regulation, of structure and mechanism of action of enzymes, and even as catalysts in the industrial synthesis of biologically active compounds such as hormones and drugs. Since the enzyme content of human serum may change significantly in certain pathologic conditions, studies of serum enzyme levels provide an important diagnostic tool for the physician (see Chapter 6).

COENZYMES

Many enzymes catalyze reactions of their substrates only in the presence of a specific nonprotein organic molecule called the coenzyme. Only when both enzyme and coenzyme are present will catalysis occur. Where coenzymes are required, the complete system or **holoenzyme** consists of the protein part or apoenzyme plus a heat-stable, dialyzable nonprotein **coenzyme*** that is bound to the apoenzyme protein. Types of reactions that frequently require the participation of coenzymes are oxidoreductions, group transfer and isomerization reactions, and reactions resulting in the formation of covalent bonds (classes 1, 2, 5, and 6; see below). By contrast, lytic reactions, including hydrolytic reactions such as those catalyzed by the enzymes of the digestive tract, are not known to require coenzymes (classes 3 and 4; see below).

Coenzymes frequently contain B vitamins as part of their structure (see Chapter 12). Thus, many enzymes concerned with the metabolism of amino acids require enzymes containing vitamin B_6. The B vitamins **nicotinamide, thiamin, riboflavin, pantothenic acid,** and **lipoic acid** are important constituents of coenzymes for biologic oxidations and reductions, and **folic acid** and **cobamide** coenzymes function in one-carbon metabolism.

It often is helpful to regard the coenzyme as a second substrate, ie, a **cosubstrate**. This is so for at least 2 reasons. In the first instance, **the chemical changes in the coenzyme exactly counterbalance those taking place in the substrate**; eg, in transphosphorylation reactions involved in the metabolism of sugars, for every molecule of sugar phosphorylated, one molecule of ATP is dephosphorylated and converted to ADP (Fig 5–1). Similarly, in oxidoreduction (dehydrogen-

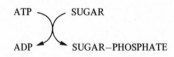

Figure 5–1. ATP acting as a cosubstrate.

ase) reactions (E.C. class 1.1), one molecule of substrate is oxidized (dehydrogenated) and one molecule of coenzyme is reduced (hydrogenated) (Fig 5–2).

*The term "prosthetic group" was formerly employed to denote coenzymes covalently bonded to the apoenzyme. The term is now largely obsolete.

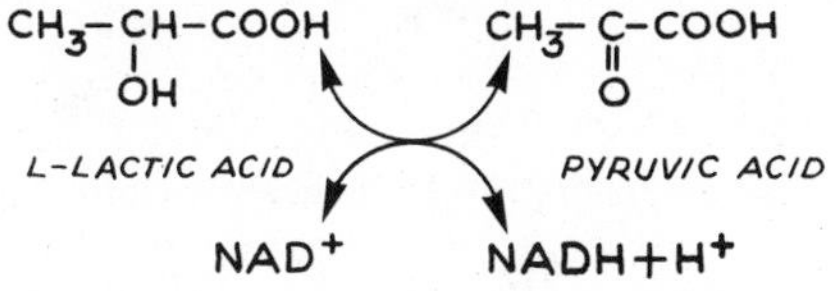

Figure 5–2. NAD$^+$ acting as a cosubstrate.

Table 5–1. Representative mechanisms for anaerobic regeneration of NAD$^+$.

Oxidant	Reduced Product	Life Form
Pyruvate	Lactate	Muscle, homolactic bacteria
Acetaldehyde	Ethanol	Yeast
Dihydroxyacetone phosphate	α-Glycerophosphate	*E coli*
Fructose	Mannitol	Heterolactic bacteria

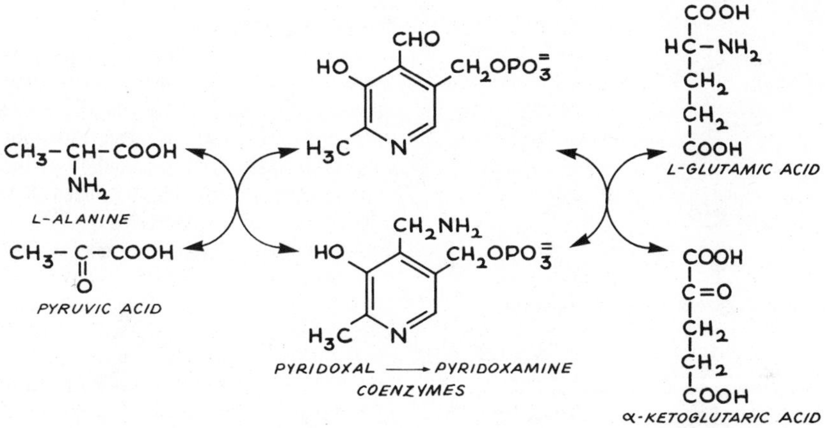

In transamination reactions (class 2.6), pyridoxal phosphate acts as a second substrate in 2 concerted reactions, and acts as carrier for transfer of an amino group between different α-keto acids (Fig 5–3).

Figure 5–3. Participation of pyridoxal phosphate in transamination reactions.

For every molecule of alanine converted to pyruvate, one molecule of the aldehyde form of pyridoxal phosphate is aminated. The amino form of the coenzyme does not appear as a reaction product since the aldehyde form is regenerated by transfer of the amino group to α-ketoglutarate, forming glutamate.

A second reason to give equal emphasis to the reactions of the coenzyme is that this aspect of the reaction may actually be of greater fundamental physiologic significance. For example, the importance of the ability of muscle working anaerobically to convert pyruvate to lactate resides not in pyruvate nor lactate themselves. The reaction serves merely to convert NADH to NAD$^+$. Without NAD$^+$, glycolysis cannot continue and anaerobic ATP synthesis (and hence muscular work) ceases. In summary, under anaerobic conditions, the conversion of pyruvate to lactate serves to reoxidize NADH and permit synthesis of ATP. Other reactions can serve the identical function equally well. In bacteria or yeast growing anaerobically a number of substances derived more or less directly from pyruvate are utilized as oxidants for NADH and are in the process themselves reduced (Table 5–1).

Classification of Coenzymes Based on Functional Characteristics

The classification of coenzymes might be done in many ways. Each of these would emphasize various features of significance. The feature emphasized here is the reaction type in which a given coenzyme is functional.

A. Coenzymes for group transfer of groups other than H.
  1. ATP and its relatives.
  2. Sugar phosphates.
  3. CoA.
  4. Thiamin pyrophosphate.
  5. B$_6$ phosphate.
  6. Folate coenzymes.
  7. Biotin.
  8. Cobamide (B$_{12}$) coenzymes.
  9. Lipoic acid.
B. Coenzymes for transfer of H.
  1. NAD$^+$, NADP$^+$
  2. FMN, FAD.
  3. Lipoic acid.
  4. Coenzyme Q.

Note that all coenzymes function in one or another type of group transfer reaction. Particularly striking is the frequent occurrence in the structure of coenzymes of the adenine ring joined to D-ribose and phosphate. Many coenzymes may therefore be regarded as derivatives of adenosine monophosphate which differ only in the substituents at positions R,R', and R'', and in the number of phosphate groups, n, attached to the 5' position of the ribose (Fig 5—4). This is illustrated in Table 5—2. Also included are 3 forms of activated amino acids.

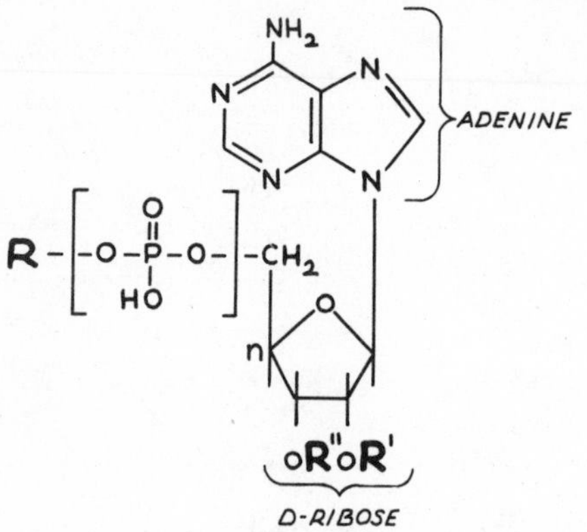

Figure 5—4. Adenosine monophosphate derivatives.

Table 5—2. Coenzymes and related compounds which are derivatives of adenosine monophosphate.

Coenzyme	R	R'	R''	n
AMP	H	H	H	1
ADP	H	H	H	2
ATP	H	H	H	3
Active methionine	Methio-nine*	H	H	0
Amino acid adenylates	Amino acid	H	H	1
Active sulfate	SO_3H_2	H	PO_3H	1
3',5'-Cyclic AMP	H	H	PO_3H	
NAD+	†	H	H	2
NADP+	†	PO_3H	H	2
FAD	†	H	H	2
CoA	†	H	PO_3H	2

*Replaces phosphate group.
†See Chapter 16.

ENZYME SPECIFICITY

Nonprotein catalysts typically accelerate a wide variety of chemical reactions. By contrast, a given enzyme catalyzes only a very few reactions (frequently only one). The ability of an enzyme to catalyze one specific reaction and essentially no others is perhaps its most significant property. The rates of a multitude of metabolic processes may thus be minutely regulated by suitable changes in the catalytic efficiency of particular enzymes (see Chapter 7). That such control be exerted via enzymes is essential if a cell, tissue, or whole organism is to function normally.

Close examination reveals that most enzymes can catalyze the same type of reaction (phosphate transfer, oxidation-reduction, etc) with several structurally related substrates. Frequently, reactions with alternate substrates take place if they are present in high concentration. Whether all of the possible reactions will occur in the living organism thus depends in part on the relative concentration of alternate substrates in the cell and their relative affinities for an enzyme. Some general aspects of enzyme specificity include those given below.

Optical Specificity

With the exception of epimerases (racemases), which interconvert optical isomers, **enzymes generally show absolute optical specificity for at least a portion of a substrate molecule.** Thus, maltase catalyzes the hydrolysis of *a*- but not *β*-glycosides, while enzymes of the Embden-Meyerhof and direct oxidative pathways catalyze the interconversion of D- but not L-phosphosugars. With a few exceptions, such as the D-amino acid oxidase of kidney, the vast majority of mammalian enzymes act on the L-isomers of amino acids. Other life forms may have enzymes with equal specificity for D-amino acids.

Optical specificity may extend to a portion of the substrate molecule or to its entirety. The glycosidases provide examples of both extremes. These enzymes, which catalyze hydrolysis of glycosidic bonds between sugars and alcohols, are highly specific for the sugar portion and for the linkage (*a* or *β*), but relatively nonspecific for the alcohol portion or aglycone.

Many substrates apparently form 3 bonds with enzymes. This "3-point attachment" can thus confer asymmetry on an otherwise symmetric molecule. A substrate molecule, represented as a carbon atom having 3 different groups (Fig 5—5), is shown about to attach at 3 points to a planar enzyme site. If the site can be approached only from one side and only com-

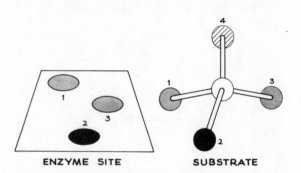

ENZYME SITE   SUBSTRATE

Figure 5—5. Representation of 3-point attachment of a substrate to a planar active site of an enzyme.

plementary atoms and sites can interact, the molecule can bind in only one way. The reaction itself—eg, dehydrogenation—may be confined to the atoms bound at sites 1 and 2 even though atoms 1 and 3 are identical. By mentally turning the substrate molecule in space, note that it can attach at 3 points to one side of the planar site with only one orientation. Consequently, atoms 1 and 3, although identical, become distinct when the substrate is attached to the enzyme. Extension of this line of reasoning can explain why the enzyme-catalyzed reduction of the optically inactive pyruvate molecule results in formation of L- and not D,L-lactate.

Representation of the substrate binding site (active site) of an enzyme as planar, while useful for illustrative purposes, is not strictly correct due to the 3-dimensional structure of the enzyme molecule. A somewhat more realistic representation might be to visualize the substrate bound to some organized portion of the enzyme molecule—perhaps a region of an a-helix, as shown in Fig 5—6.

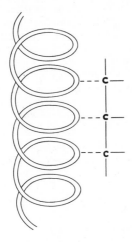

Figure 5—6. Representation of 3-point attachment of substrate to successive turns of a helical portion of an enzyme.

Group Specificity

A particular enzyme acts only on particular chemical groupings, eg, glycosidases on glycosides, alcohol dehydrogenase on alcohols, pepsin and trypsin on peptide bonds, and esterases on ester linkages. Within these restrictions, however, a large number of substrates may be attacked, thus, for example, lessening the number of digestive enzymes that might otherwise be required.

Certain enzymes exhibit a higher order of group specificity. Chymotrypsin preferentially hydrolyzes peptide bonds in which the carboxyl group is contributed by the aromatic amino acids phenylalanine, tyrosine, or tryptophan. Carboxypeptidases and aminopeptidases split off amino acids one at a time from the carboxyl- or amino-terminal end of polypeptide chains, respectively.

Although some oxidoreductases function equally well with either NAD or NADP as electron acceptor, most use one or the other preferentially. As a broad generalization, **oxidoreductases functional in biosynthetic processes in mammalian systems (eg, fatty acid synthesis) tend to use NADPH as reductant, while those functional in degradative processes tend to use NAD as oxidant.** Occasionally, a tissue may possess 2 oxidoreductases which differ only in their coenzyme specificity. One example is the NAD- and NADP-specific isocitrate dehydrogenases of rat mitochondria (Table 5—3).

Table 5—3. Distribution of NAD- and NADP-specific isocitrate dehydrogenases in mitochondria of rat tissue.*

Organ	Specific Activity (μmol/min/mg) of	
	NAD-Specific Enzyme	NADP-Specific Enzyme
Skeletal muscle	0.84	0.78
Heart	0.57	2.22
Kidney	0.28	1.20
Brain	0.25	0.054
Liver	0.16	0.33

*From Lowenstein JM: The tricarboxylic acid cycle. Page 168 in: *Metabolic Pathways.* Vol 1. Greenberg DM (editor). Academic Press, 1967.

In liver, about 90% of the NADP-specific enzyme occurs extramitochondrially. This may be concerned with biosynthetic processes, as the NAD-specific enzyme of mitochondria is specifically activated by ADP. Since ADP levels rise during depletion of ATP stores, this suggests a degradative role for the NAD-specific isocitrate dehydrogenase of mitochondria. High ADP (low ATP) levels would promote carbon flow through the citric acid cycle by activating the NAD-specific mitochondrial enzyme.

ENZYME CLASSIFICATION & NOMENCLATURE

The function of classification is to emphasize relationships and similarities in a precise and concise manner. Early attempts to devise a system of nomenclature for enzymes produced a confused series of ambiguous and generally uninformative names such as emulsin, ptyalin, and zymase. Enzymes were later named for the substrates on which they acted by adding the suffix **-ase.** Thus enzymes that split starch (amylon) were termed amylases; those that split fat (lipos), lipase; and those that acted on proteins, proteases. Groups of enzymes were designated as oxidases, glycosidases, dehydrogenases, decarboxylases, etc.

Recent studies of the mechanism of organic and

of enzyme-catalyzed reactions have led to a more rational classification of enzymes based on reaction types and reaction mechanisms. Although this International Union of Biochemistry (IUB) System is complex, it is precise, descriptive, and informative. No classification, of course, can be better than the information on which it is based, and periodic revisions are to be anticipated as more information becomes available.

The major features of the **IUB System for classification of enzymes** are as follows:

A. Reactions (and the enzymes catalyzing them) are divided into 6 major classes, each with 4–13 subclasses. The 6 major classes are listed below, together with examples of some important subclasses. The name appearing in brackets is the more familiar trivial name.

B. The enzyme name has 2 parts. The first is the name of the substrate or substrates. The second, ending in -ase, indicates the **type of reaction catalyzed.** The suffix -ase is no longer attached directly to the name of the substrate.

C. Additional information, if needed to clarify the nature of the reaction, may follow in parentheses. For example, the enzyme catalyzing the reaction L-malate + NAD^+ = pyruvate + CO_2 + NADH + H^+, known as the malic enzyme, is designated as 1.1.1.37 L-malate:NAD oxidoreductase (decarboxylating).

D. Each enzyme has a systematic code number (E.C.). This number characterizes the reaction type as to class (first digit), subclass (second digit), and sub-subclass (third digit). The fourth digit is for the particular enzyme named. Thus, E.C. 2.7.1.1 denotes class 2 (a transferase), subclass 7 (transfer of phosphate), sub-subclass 1 (an alcohol function as the phosphate acceptor). The final digit denotes the enzyme, hexokinase, or ATP:D-hexose-6-phosphotransferase, an enzyme catalyzing phosphate transfer from ATP to the hydroxyl group on carbon 6 of glucose.

The 6 major classes of enzymes with some illustrative examples are given below.

1. Oxidoreductases. Enzymes catalyzing oxidoreductions between 2 substrates, S and S'.

$$S_{reduced} + S'_{oxidized} = S_{oxidized} + S'_{reduced}$$

This large and important class includes the enzymes formerly known either as dehydrogenases or as oxidases. Included are enzymes catalyzing oxidoreductions of CH–OH, CH–CH, C=O, CH–NH_2, and CH=NH groups. Representative subclasses include:

1.1 Enzymes acting on the CH–OH group as electron donor. *For example:*
1.1.1.1 Alcohol:NAD oxidoreductase [alcohol dehydrogenase].

$$\text{Alcohol} + NAD^+ = \text{aldehyde or ketone} + NADH + H^+$$

1.4 Enzymes acting on the CH–NH_2 group as electron donor. *For example:*
1.4.1.3 L-Glutamate:NAD(P) oxidoreductase (deaminating) [glutamic dehydrogenase of animal

liver]. NAD(P) means that either NAD or NADP acts as the electron acceptor.

$$\text{L-Glutamate} + H_2O + NAD(P)^+ =$$
$$\text{a-ketoglutarate} + NH_4^+ + NAD(P)H + H^+$$

1.9 Enzymes acting on the heme groups of electron donors. *For example:*
1.9.3.1 Cytochrome c:O_2 oxidoreductase [cytochrome oxidase].

$$\text{4 Reduced cytochrome c} + O_2 + 4H^+ =$$
$$\text{4 Oxidized cytochrome c} + 2H_2O$$

1.11 Enzymes acting on H_2O_2 as electron acceptor. *For example:*
1.11.1.6 H_2O_2:H_2O_2 oxidoreductase [catalase].

$$H_2O_2 + H_2O_2 = O_2 + 2H_2O$$

2. Transferases. Enzymes catalyzing a transfer of a group, G (other than hydrogen), between a pair of substrates S and S'.

$$\text{S-G} + \text{S'} = \text{S'-G} + \text{S}$$

In this class are enzymes catalyzing the transfer of one-carbon groups, aldehyde or ketone residues, and acyl, alkyl, glycosyl, phosphorus or sulfur containing groups. Some important subclasses include:

2.3 Acyltransferases. *For example:*
2.3.1.6 Acetyl-CoA: choline O-acetyltransferase [choline acyltransferase].

$$\text{Acetyl-CoA} + \text{choline} = \text{CoA} + \text{O-acetylcholine}$$

2.4 Glycosyltransferases. *For example:*
2.4.1.1 a-1,4-Glucan:orthophosphate glycosyl transferase [phosphorylase].

$$(a\text{-}1,4\text{-Glucosyl})_n + \text{orthophosphate} =$$
$$(a\text{-}1,4\text{-Glucosyl})_{n-1} + a\text{-D-glucose-1-phosphate}$$

2.7 Enzymes catalyzing transfer of phosphorus containing groups. *For example:*
2.7.1.1 ATP:D-hexose-6-phosphotransferase [hexokinase].

$$\text{ATP} + \text{D-hexose} = \text{ADP} + \text{D-hexose-6-phosphate}$$

3. Hydrolases. Enzymes catalyzing hydrolysis of ester, ether, peptide, glycosyl, acid-anhydride, C–C, C-halide, or P–N bonds. *For example:*

$$\text{An acylcholine} + H_2O = \text{choline} + \text{an acid}$$

3.1 Enzymes acting on ester bonds. *For example:*
3.1.1.8 Acylcholine acyl-hydrolase [pseudo-cholinesterase].

3.2 Enzymes acting on glycosyl compounds. *For example:*
3.2.1.23 β-D-Galactoside galactohydrolase [β-galactosidase].

A β-D-galactoside + H_2O = an alcohol + D-galactose

3.4 Enzymes acting on peptide bonds. The classical names (pepsin, plasmin, rennin, chymotrypsin) have been largely retained due to overlapping and dubious specificities which make systematic nomenclature impractical at this time.

4. Lyases. Enzymes that catalyze removal of groups from substrates by mechanisms other than hydrolysis, leaving double bonds.

$$\begin{matrix} X & Y \\ | & | \\ C{-}C \end{matrix} = X{-}Y + C{=}C$$

Included are enzymes acting on C–C, C–O, C–N, C–S, and C-halide bonds. Representative subgroups include:

4.1.2 Aldehyde-lyases. *For example:*
4.1.2.7 Ketose-1-phosphate aldehyde-lyase [aldolase].

A ketose-1-phosphate = dihydroxyacetone phosphate
+ an aldehyde

4.2 Carbox-oxygen lyases. *For example:*
4.2.1.2 L-Malate hydro-lyase [fumarase].

L-Malate = fumarate + H_2O

5. Isomerases. This class includes all enzymes catalyzing interconversion of optical, geometric, or positional isomers. Some subclasses are:

5.1 Racemases and epimerases. *For example:*
5.1.1.1 Alanine racemase.

L-Alanine = D-alanine

5.2 Cis-trans isomerases. *For example:*
5.2.1.3 All trans-retinene 11-*cis-trans* isomerase [retinene isomerase].

All *trans*-retinene = 11-*cis*-retinene

5.3 Enzymes catalyzing interconversion of aldoses and ketoses. *For example:*
5.3.1.1 D-Glyceraldehyde-3-phosphate ketol-isomerase [triosephosphate isomerase].

D-Glyceraldehyde-3-phosphate =
dihydroxyacetone phosphate

6. Ligases. (Ligare = "to bind.") Enzymes catalyzing the linking together of 2 compounds coupled to the breaking of a pyrophosphate bond in ATP or a similar compound. Included are enzymes catalyzing reactions forming C–O, C–S, C–N, and C–C bonds. Representative subclasses are:

6.2 Enzymes catalyzing formation of C–S bonds. *For example:*
6.2.1.4 Succinate: CoA ligase (GDP) [succinic thiokinase].

GTP + succinate + CoA = GDP + P_i + succinyl-CoA

6.3 Enzymes catalyzing formation of C–N bonds. *For example:*
6.3.1.2 L-Glutamate:ammonia ligase (ADP) [glutamine synthetase].

ATP + L-glutamate + NH_4^+ =
ADP + orthophosphate + L-glutamine

6.4 Enzymes catalyzing formation of C–C bonds. *For example:*
6.4.1.2 Acetyl-CoA:CO_2 ligase (ADP) [acetyl-CoA carboxylase].

ATP + acetyl-CoA + CO_2 = ADP + P_i + malonyl-CoA

QUANTITATIVE MEASUREMENT OF ENZYME ACTIVITY

The extremely small quantities present introduce problems in determining the amount of an enzyme in tissue extracts or fluids quite different from those of determining the concentration of more usual organic or inorganic substances. Fortunately, **the catalytic activity of an enzyme provides a sensitive and specific device for its own measurement.** To measure the amount of an enzyme in a sample of tissue extract or other biologic fluid, the **rate of the reaction** catalyzed by the enzyme in the sample is measured. Under appropriate conditions, **the measured rate is proportionate to the quantity of enzyme present.** Where possible, this rate is compared with the rate catalyzed by a known quantity of the highly purified enzyme. Provided that both are assayed under exactly comparable conditions and under conditions where the enzyme concentration is the rate-limiting factor (high substrate and low product concentration, and favorable pH and temperature), the micrograms (μg) of enzyme in the extract may be calculated.

Many enzymes of clinical interest are not available in a purified state. It thus is not generally possible to determine the number of micrograms of enzyme present. Results therefore are expressed in terms of arbitrarily defined enzyme units. The relative amounts of enzyme in different extracts may then be compared. Enzyme units are expressed in micromols (μmols) of substrate reacting or product produced per minute or per hour under specified assay conditions. Frequently other units are used for convenience. For example, 1 Bodansky unit of phosphatase activity is that amount of the enzyme which will catalyze the formation of 1 mg of phosphorus (as inorganic phosphate) per 100 ml of serum in 1 hour under standardized conditions of pH and temperature. In reactions involving NAD^+ (dehydrogenases), advantage is taken of the property of NADH or NADPH (but not NAD^+ or $NADP^+$) to absorb light at a wavelength of 330 nm (Fig 5—7).

When NADH changes to NAD$^+$ (or vice versa), the absorbency (optical density) at 340 nm changes. Under specified conditions, the rate of change in absorbency depends directly on the enzyme activity. Hence, an enzyme unit of any dehydrogenase may be defined as a change in optical density at 340 nm of 0.001 per minute (Fig 5–7).

ISOLATION OF ENZYMES

Much knowledge about the pathways of metabolism and of regulatory mechanisms operating at the level of catalysis have come from studies of isolated, purified enzymes. Indeed, those areas of metabolism where the enzymes involved have not been purified are exactly those where information is fragmentary and controversial. In addition, reliable information concerning the kinetics, cofactors, active sites, structure, and mechanism of action also requires highly purified enzymes.

Enzyme purification involves the isolation of a specific enzyme protein from a crude extract of whole cells containing many other components. Small molecules may be removed by dialysis, nucleic acids by adsorption on charcoal, etc. The problem is to separate the desired enzyme from a mixture of hundreds of chemically and physically similar proteins. Useful methods include precipitation with varying salt concentrations (generally ammonium or sodium sulfate) or

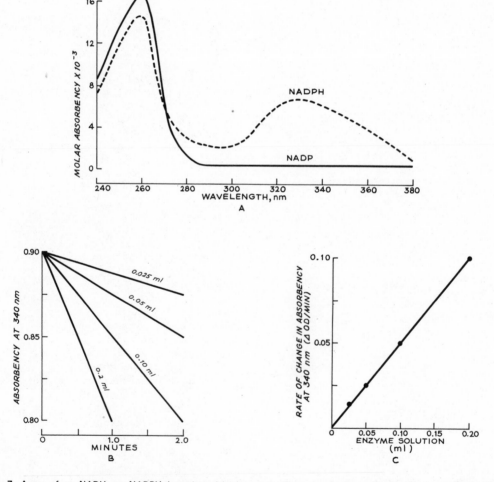

Figure 5–7. Assay of an NADH- or NADPH-dependent dehydrogenase. The rate of change in absorbency at 340 nm due to conversion of reduced to oxidized coenzyme is observed. For an enzyme-catalyzed reaction: S + NADH + H$^+$ = SH$_2$ + NAD$^+$, the oxidized form of the substrate (S) and the reduced form of the coenzyme (NADH) plus buffer is added to a cuvette and light of 340 nm wavelength is passed through it. Initially *(A)*, the absorbency or optical density (OD) is high since NADH (or NADPH) absorbs at this wavelength. On addition of 0.025–0.2 ml of a standard enzyme solution, the OD decreases *(B)*. Plotting the rate of change in OD per minute versus ml of enzyme used produces a more or less linear calibration curve *(C)*. Using this calibration curve, a given rate of change in absorbency at 340 nm may be related to the activity of the standard enzyme solution used to prepare (C). If the enzyme concentration of this is known, results may be expressed in terms of µg of enzyme present per ml of unknown tissue fluid. More frequently, results are expressed in enzyme units.

Table 5—4. Summary of a typical enzyme purification scheme.

Enzyme Fraction	Total Activity (enzyme units)	Total Protein (mg)	Specific Activity (enzyme units/mg)	Overall Recovery (%)
Crude liver homogenate	100,000	10,000	10	(100)
100,000 × *g* supernatant liquid	98,000	8,000	12.2	98
40–50% (NH$_4$)$_2$SO$_4$ precipitate	90,000	1,500	60	90
20–35% acetone precipitate	60,000	250	240	60
DEAE column fractions 80–110	58,000	29	2,000	58
43–48% (NH$_4$)$_2$SO$_4$ precipitate	52,000	20	2,600	52
First crystals	50,000	12	4,160	50
Recrystallization	49,000	10	4,900	49

solvents (acetone or ethanol), differential heat or pH denaturation, differential centrifugation, gel filtration, and electrophoresis. Selective adsorption and elution of proteins from the cellulose anion exchange diethylaminoethylcellulose and the cation exchanger carboxymethylcellulose have also been extremely successful for extensive and rapid purification. Recently, **affinity column chromatography** has been used with great success. A small molecule—eg, a substrate analogue—is bonded chemically to an inert support. Proteins which interact strongly with this material (eg, an enzyme whose active site "recognizes" the analogue) may then be separated from other proteins.

Ultimately, crystallization of the enzyme may be achieved, generally from an ammonium sulfate solution. Crystallinity does not, however, imply homogeneity. Exhaustive physical, chemical, and biologic tests must still be applied as criteria of purity.

The progress of a typical enzyme purification for a liver enzyme with good recovery and 490-fold overall purification is shown in Table 5—4. Note how specific activity and recovery of initial activity are calculated. The aim is to achieve the maximum specific activity (enzyme units per mg protein) with the best possible recovery of initial activity.

The sulfhydryl (SH) groups of many enzymes, notably the oxidoreductases (dehydrogenases), are essential for enzymatic activity. Oxidation (dehydrogenation) of these SH groups, forming disulfide linkages (S—S), brought about by many oxidizing agents including the O$_2$ of air, results in loss of activity. Frequently this also may cause a conformational change in the enzyme. Full activity may often be restored by reduced sulfhydryl compounds such as glutathione or cysteine (R—SH). These reduce the enzyme S—S to SH by disulfide exchange. (See Fig 5—8.)

The reverse is true for ribonuclease. Here reduction of certain disulfide bridges results in loss of secondary structure and of catalytic activity.

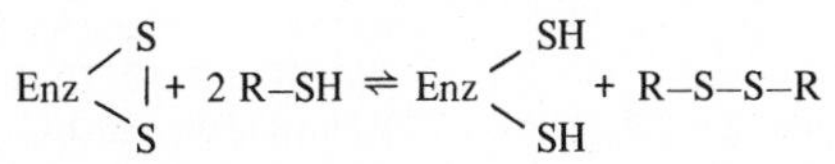

$$\text{Enz} \begin{matrix} \diagup S \\ \diagdown S \end{matrix} + 2\,R{-}SH \rightleftharpoons \text{Enz} \begin{matrix} \diagup SH \\ \diagdown SH \end{matrix} + R{-}S{-}S{-}R$$

Figure 5—8. Reversible reduction-oxidation of disulfide groups on an enzyme.

INTRACELLULAR DISTRIBUTION OF ENZYMES

Structure & Functions of Intracellular Components

In this and subsequent chapters reference will be made to various intracellular structures which are the sites of specific biochemical activities of the cell. The identity and the biochemical functions of many of these intracellular structures have been studied by electron microscopy, by histochemistry, and by technics involving separation by high-speed centrifugation.

Within multicellular organisms, diverse kinds of cells serve the specialized functions of the various tissues. Certain features are, however, common to all eukaryotic cells. All possess a cell membrane, a nucleus, and a cytoplasm containing cellular organelles and soluble proteins essential to the biochemical and physiologic functions of that cell. Although no "typical" cell exists, Fig 5—9 represents intracellular structures in general. In the electron micrograph of a section of an actual cell (rat pituitary gland), the cell membrane, mitochondria, and endoplasmic reticulum with associated ribosomes may be seen (Fig 5—10). In addition, the secretion granules, which in this instance are responsible for production of mammotropic (lactogenic) hormone, may also be noted.

Under a light microscope, the **cell membrane** appears only as a limiting boundary, since it is less than 10 nm thick. In electron micrographs, the membranes of many cells are seen to possess definite structures which often can be related to the specific functions of the tissue from which the cell is derived. That the membrane should possess such structures is not surprising, for it must maintain selective permeability in order to preserve within the cell the precise chemical environment necessary to the cell's function. Indeed, the mechanism of transport of metabolites in and out of cells is a highly significant aspect of cellular metabolic activity, and substances which affect transport across membranes thereby exert significant regulatory control of intracellular biochemical activities. Examples of substances which affect transport include hormones such as insulin and growth hormone.

If a solute of low molecular weight is present in extracellular fluid at a higher concentration than in the cell, it will tend to diffuse into the cell. The converse

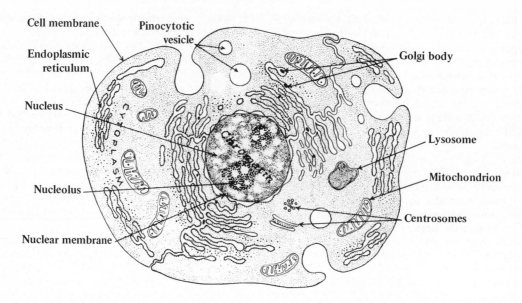

Cell membrane
Pinocytotic vesicle
Endoplasmic reticulum
Nucleus
Nucleolus
Nuclear membrane
Golgi body
Lysosome
Mitochondrion
Centrosomes

Figure 5—9. Structural components of an idealized "typical cell."

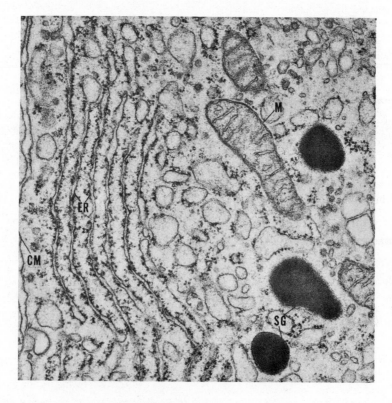

Figure 5—10. Portion of a mammotropic hormone-producing cell of rat anterior pituitary gland. (Reduced 30% from X 50,000.) Shown are several rows of endoplasmic reticulum with associated ribosomes (ER), mitochondria (M), secretion granules (SG), and a portion of cell membrane (CM). (Courtesy of RE Smith and MG Farquhar.)

also holds true, for solutes tend to diffuse from a region of high to a region of low concentration. **Passive transport** of solutes across cellular or intracellular membranes results from just such random molecular motion. It is believed that water, for example, is passively transported across membranes. Certain solutes, however, migrate across membranes in a direction opposite to that predicted from their concentrations on either side of the membrane (eg, K^+ in cells, Na^+ in extracellular fluid). This establishes a **solute gradient** which can only be maintained by expending energy. Maintaining these gradients by **active transport** thus requires ATP, which must be supplied by the cell. Many small molecules appear to be actively transported across membranes.

In many cells, large molecules and other macromaterials enter by **pinocytosis** ("cell drinking"). An inpocketing of the cell membrane forms a vesicle which surrounds and ultimately completely envelops the material to be ingested in a vacuole that enters the cytoplasm as a free-floating structure.

Among the largest cytoplasmic structures are the **mitochondria** (3–4 μm in length). These "power plants" of the cell extract energy from nutrients and trap the energy released by oxidative processes with simultaneous formation of the high-energy chemical bonds of adenosine triphosphate (ATP). The fine structure of the mitochondrion as visualized by electron microscopy is shown diagrammatically in Fig 5–11.

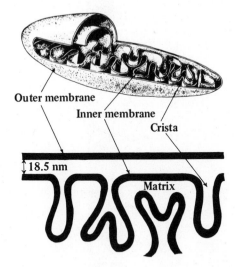

Figure 5–11. Representation of the structure of a mitochondrion.

Note that the mitochondrion has 2 membranes and that the inner one forms folded structures or **cristae** extending into the matrix of the structure. Each membrane is believed to consist of alternate layers of protein and lipid molecules. The components of the respiratory chain (see Chapter 16) associated with oxidative phosphorylation are present in the inner mitochondrial membrane. The enzymes of the citric acid cycle (see Chapter 17) are located in the fluid matrix, the soluble part of the mitochondrial interior.

Lysosomes, subcellular organelles approximately the same size as mitochondria, do not appear to possess internal structure. Lysosomes contain digestive enzymes which break down fats, proteins, nucleic acids, and other large molecules into smaller molecules capable of being metabolized by the enzyme systems of mitochondria. As long as the lipoprotein membrane of the lysosome remains intact, the enzymes within the lysosome are unable to act on substrates within the cytoplasm. Once the membrane is ruptured, release of lysosomal enzymes is quickly followed by dissolution (lysis) of the cell. This concept of lysosomal function as derived from studies of lysosomes from rat liver is illustrated in Fig 5–12.

In many cells a system of internal membranes termed the **endoplasmic reticulum** can be detected within the cytoplasm. This network of canaliculi may itself be continuous with the external membrane. The **Golgi bodies** may serve as a means of producing and maintaining this internal membrane. Closely associated with the inner surface of the endoplasmic reticulum are numerous granules rich in ribonucleic acid (RNA) termed **ribosomes**. The ribosomes are the sites of protein synthesis within the cell. As might be expected, the reticular system and the ribosomes are most highly developed in cells (such as those of the liver and pancreas) actively engaged in the production of proteins.

Other cytoplasmic structures include the **centrosomes** or centrioles which, although visible even under the ordinary light microscope, are apparent only when a cell is preparing to divide. At that time, the centrosomes form the poles of the spindle apparatus involved in chromosomal replication during mitosis.

The **nucleus** is characterized by its high content of chromatin, which contains most of the cellular deoxyribonucleic acid (DNA). When the cell is not in the process of dividing, the chromatin is distributed throughout the nucleus in a diffuse manner. Immediately before cell division, the chromatin assumes the organized structure of the chromosomes which will eventually be distributed equally to each daughter cell. The **nucleolus,** a discrete body within the nucleus, contains much ribonucleic acid (RNA), which under the electron microscope appears as extremely small granules resembling the ribosomes of the endoplasmic reticulum of the cytoplasm.

Intracellular Distribution of Enzymes

In addition to the morphologic details of the subcellular structures, there is great interest also in localization within the cell of various metabolic activities. The original concept of the cell as a "sack of enzymes" has given way to recognition of the cardinal significance of spatial arrangement and compartmentalization of enzymes, substrates, and cofactors within the cell. In rat liver cells, for example, the enzymes of the glycolytic pathway (see Chapter 18) are located in the nonparticulate portion of the cyto-

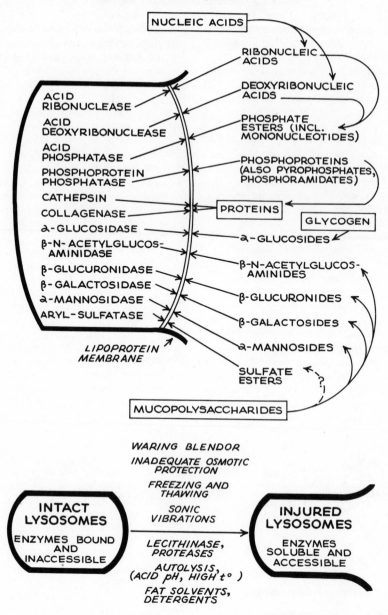

Figure 5–12. The lysosome. (Redrawn and reproduced, with permission, from De Duve C: The Lysosome Concept. Ciba Foundation Symposium: *Lysosomes.* Little, Brown, 1963.)

plasm, whereas enzymes of the citric acid cycle (see Chapter 17) are within the mitochondrion.

The metabolic functions of various cellular organelles may be studied following their separation by differential centrifugation. After rupture of the cell membrane, centrifugation of the cell contents in fields of 600–100,000 gravities ($\times$ g^*) separates the cell components into microscopically identifiable fractions: intact cells, cell debris and nuclei (600 $\times$ g for 5 minutes), mitochondria (10,000 $\times$ g for 30 minutes),

microsomes (100,000 $\times$ g for 60 minutes), and the remaining soluble or nonsedimentable fraction. The enzyme content of each fraction is then examined.

Localization of a particular enzyme activity in a tissue or cell in a relatively unaltered state may frequently be accomplished by histochemical procedures ("histoenzymology"). Thin (2–10 μm) frozen sections of tissue, prepared with a low-temperature microtome, are treated with a substrate for a particular enzyme. In regions where the enzyme is present, the product of the enzyme-catalyzed reaction is formed. If the product is colored and insoluble, it remains at the site of formation and serves as a marker for the localization

*$\times$ g refers to the amount by which the centrifugal field exceeds the force of gravity.

of the enzyme. Although quantitatively reliable technics have yet to be perfected, "histoenzymology" provides a graphic and relatively physiologic picture of patterns of enzyme distribution. Enzymes for which satisfactory histochemical technics are available include the acid and alkaline phosphatases, monoamine oxidase, and a variety of dehydrogenase activities.

• • •

References

General Enzymology

Boyer PD, Lardy H, Myrbäck K (editors): *The Enzymes,* 3rd ed. 7 vols. Academic Press, 1970–1973.

Dawes EA: *Quantitative Problems in Biochemistry.* Williams & Wilkins, 1962.

Dixon M, Webb EC: *Enzymes,* 2nd ed. Academic Press, 1964.

Nord FF (editor): *Advances in Enzymology.* Interscience. Issued annually.

Bioenergetics

Ingraham LL, Pardee AB: Free energy and entropy in metabolism. In: *Metabolic Pathways.* Vol 1. Greenberg DM (editor). Academic Press, 1967.

Klotz IM: *Energetics in Biochemical Reactions.* Academic Press, 1957.

Racker E: *Mechanisms in Bioenergetics.* Academic Press, 1965.

Coenzymes

Chaikin S: Nicotinamide coenzymes. Annu Rev Biochem 37:149, 1968.

Hogenkamp HPC: Enzymatic reactions involving corrinoids. Annu Rev Biochem 37:225, 1968.

Krampitz LO: Catalytic functions of thiamine diphosphate. Annu Rev Biochem 38:213, 1969.

Neims AH, Hellerman L: Flavoenzyme catalysis. Annu Rev Biochem 39:867, 1970.

Nomenclature

Enzyme Nomenclature. Recommendations of the International Union of Biochemistry on the Nomenclature and Classification of Enzymes, Together With Their Units and Symbols of Enzyme Kinetics. Elsevier, 1972.

Assay & Purification of Enzymes

Bergmeyer H-U (editor): *Methods of Enzymatic Analysis.* Academic Press, 1963.

Boyer PD, Lardy H, Myrbäck K (editors): *The Enzymes,* 3rd ed. 7 vols. Academic Press, 1970–1973.

Colowick SP, Kaplan NO (editors): *Methods in Enzymology.* 25 vols. Academic Press, 1955–1972.

Intracellular Distribution of Enzymes

Albers RW: Biochemical aspects of active transport. Annu Rev Biochem 36:727, 1967.

Greer DE, MacLennan DH: The mitochondrial system of enzymes. In: *Metabolic Pathways.* Vol 1. Greenberg DM (editor). Academic Press, 1967.

Korn ED: Cell membranes: Structure and synthesis. Annu Rev Biochem 38:263, 1969.

Lehninger AL: *The Mitochondrion: Molecular Basis of Structure and Function.* Benjamin, 1964.

Osawa S: Ribosome formation and structure. Annu Rev Biochem 37:109, 1968.

Reed LJ, Cox DJ: Macromolecular organization of enzyme systems. Annu Rev Biochem 35:57, 1966.

6 . . .
Kinetic Properties of Enzymes

To understand how enzymes control the rates of individual reactions and of overall metabolic processes, we must review briefly how certain factors affect the rates of chemical reactions in general.

KINETIC THEORY OF REACTION

The **kinetic** or **collision theory** states that for molecules to react they must collide and must also possess sufficient energy to overcome the **energy barrier for reaction.** If the molecules have sufficient kinetic energy to react, anything that increases the frequency of collision between molecules will increase their rate of reaction. Factors that decrease either the frequency of collision or the kinetic energy will decrease the rate of reaction.

If some molecules have insufficient energy to react, factors such as increased temperature, which increases their kinetic energy, will increase the rate of the reaction. These concepts are illustrated diagrammatically in Fig 6–1. In A none, in B a portion, and in C all of the molecules have sufficient kinetic energy to overcome the energy barrier for reaction.

Molecules are in motion at all temperatures above absolute zero (−273° C), the temperature at which all molecular motion ceases. Concrete evidence of molecular motion is provided by the phenomenon of diffu-

sion. This may be seen by use of a colored solute or gas which will in time become uniformly distributed throughout a solvent or container. With increasing temperature, the rate of diffusion (a result of increased molecular motion due to increased kinetic energy) increases. The pressure of a gas results from gas molecules colliding with the container walls. As the temperature of the gas increases, molecular motion, and hence the number of collisions with the vessel walls, increases. In a rigid container this causes increased pressure; in a flexible container it causes expansion. Lowering the temperature decreases the frequency of collisions with the container walls, causing a drop in pressure or a contraction in volume.

In the absence of enzymic catalysis, many chemical reactions proceed exceedingly slowly at the temperature of living cells. However, even at this temperature molecules are in active motion and are undergoing collision. **They fail to react rapidly because most possess insufficient kinetic energy to overcome the energy barrier for reaction.** At a considerably higher temperature (and higher kinetic energy), the reaction will occur more rapidly. That the reaction takes place at all shows that it is spontaneous (ΔG = negative). At the lower temperature it is spontaneous but slow; at the higher temperature, spontaneous and fast. What **enzymes** do is to **make spontaneous reactions proceed rapidly under the conditions prevailing in living cells.**

The mechanism by which enzymes accelerate reactions may be illustrated by a mechanical analogy.

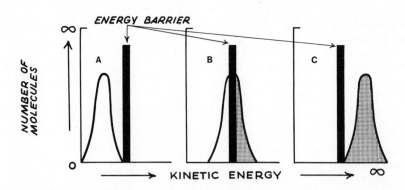

Figure 6–1. The energy barrier for chemical reactions.

Consider a boulder on the side of a hill (Fig 6–2).

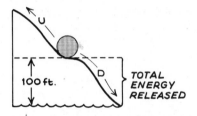

Figure 6–2.

Although the boulder might move up or down the hill, neither reaction is probable or likely to proceed rapidly. It is necessary to supply a small amount of energy to send the boulder rolling downhill. This energy represents the **energy barrier** for reaction D. Similarly, the energy required to move the boulder uphill corresponds to the energy barrier for reaction U.

Consider now the same boulder on a different hill, but the same height above ground level (Fig 6–3).

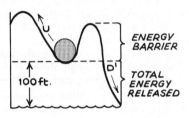

Figure 6–3.

The energy barrier for reaction D is now far greater. Note, however, that since the energy supplied in moving the boulder up from the initial position to the hump is released in its fall to ground level, the total energy released is the same as in Fig 6–2. This illustrates the concept that the **overall energy changes in chemical reactions are independent of the path or mechanism of the reaction.** The mechanism of the reaction determines the height of the hump or energy barrier only. In thermodynamic terms, the ΔG for the overall downhill reaction is exactly the same in both Figs 6–2 and 6–3. **Thermodynamics, which deals exclusively with overall energy changes, can therefore tell us nothing of the path a reaction follows (ie, its mechanism).** This, as will be shown below, is the task of kinetics.

If we now construct a tunnel through the energy barrier (Fig 6–4), reaction D would become more probable (proceed faster). Although ΔG remains the same, the activation energy requirement is reduced. The tunnel removes or lowers the energy barrier for the reaction. Enzymes may be considered to lower energy barriers for chemical reactions in roughly this

way—**by providing an alternate path with the same overall change in energy,** ie, by "tunneling through" the energy barrier.

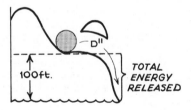

Figure 6–4.

Note also that since the initial and final states remain the same with or without enzymic catalysis, **the presence or absence of catalysts does not affect ΔG.** This is determined solely by the chemical potentials of the initial and final states.

EFFECT OF REACTANT CONCENTRATION

General Principles

At high reactant concentrations, both the number of molecules with sufficient energy to react and their frequency of collision is high. This is true whether all or only a fraction of the molecules have sufficient energy to react. For reactions involving 2 different molecules, A and B,

$$A + B \rightarrow AB$$

doubling the concentration either of A or of B will double the reaction rate. Doubling the concentration of both A and B will increase the probability of collision 4-fold. The reaction rate therefore increases 4-fold. **The reaction rate is proportionate to the concentrations of the reacting molecules.** Square brackets ([ ]) are used to denote molar concentrations;* ∝ means "proportionate to." The rate expression is:

$$Rate \propto [reacting\ molecules]$$

or

$$Rate \propto [A]\ [B]$$

For the situation represented by

$$A + 2B \rightarrow AB_2$$

the rate expression is given by

$$Rate \propto [A]\ [B]\ [B]$$

*Strictly speaking, molar activities rather than concentrations should be used.

or

$$\text{Rate} \propto [A][B]^2$$

For the general case where n molecules of A react with m molecules of B

$$nA + mB \rightarrow A_nB_m$$

the rate expression is

$$\text{Rate} \propto [A]^n[B]^m$$

Since all chemical reactions are reversible, for the reverse reaction:

$$A_nB_m \rightarrow nA + mB$$

the appropriate rate expression is

$$\text{Rate} \propto [A_nB_m]$$

We represent reversibility by double arrows:

$$nA + mB \rightleftharpoons A_nB_m$$

which reads: "n molecules of A and m molecules of B are in equilibrium with A_nB_m." We may replace the "proportionate to" symbol ($\propto$) with an equality sign by inserting a proportionality constant, k, characteristic of the reaction under study. For the general case

$$nA + mB \rightleftharpoons A_nB_m$$

expressions for the rates of the forward reaction (Rate_1) and back reaction (Rate_{-1}) are:

$$\text{Rate}_1 = k_1[A]^n[B]^m$$

and

$$\text{Rate}_{-1} = k_{-1}[A_nB_m]$$

When the rates of the forward and back reactions are equal, the system is said to be **at equilibrium**, ie,

$$\text{Rate}_1 = \text{Rate}_{-1}$$

Then $k_1[A]^n[B]^m = k_{-1}[A_nB_m]$

and $\dfrac{k_1}{k_{-1}} = \dfrac{[A_nB_m]}{[A]^n[B]^m} = K_{eq}$

The ratio of k_1 to k_{-1} is termed the **equilibrium constant, K_{eq}**. The following important properties of a system at equilibrium should be kept in mind.

1. **The equilibrium constant is the ratio of the reaction rate constants k_1/k_{-1}.**

2. **At equilibrium the reaction rates** (not the reaction rate constants) **of the forward and back reactions are equal.**

3. **Equilibrium is a dynamic state.** Although no **net** change in concentration of reactant or product molecules occurs at equilibrium, A and B are continu-

ally being converted to A_nB_m and vice versa.

4. **The equilibrium constant may be given a numerical value if we know the concentrations of A, B, and A_nB_m at equilibrium.** The equilibrium constant is related to ΔG^0 as follows:

$$\Delta G^0 = -RT \ln K_{eq}$$

R is the gas constant and T the absolute temperature. Since these are known, **knowledge of the numerical value of K_{eq} permits one to calculate a value for ΔG^0.** If the equilibrium constant is greater than 1, the reaction is spontaneous, ie, the reaction as written (from left to right) is favored. If it is less than 1, the opposite is true, ie, the reaction is more likely to proceed from right to left. In terms of the mechanical analogy, **if the equilibrium constant is greater than 1, the reaction from left to right is "downhill" and the reverse reaction "uphill."** Note, however, that although the equilibrium constant for a reaction indicates the **direction** in which a reaction is spontaneous, it does not indicate whether it will take place **rapidly**. That is, it does not tell us anything about the **magnitude of the energy barrier** for reaction. This follows from the fact that K_{eq} determines ΔG^0, which previously was shown to concern only initial and final states. **Reaction rates depend on the magnitude of the energy barrier, not that of ΔG^0.**

Most factors affecting the velocity of enzyme-catalyzed reactions do so by **changing reactant concentration.**

Enzyme Concentration

The **initial velocity, v,** of an enzyme-catalyzed reaction is **directly proportionate to the enzyme concentration [Enz].** (See Fig 5–7C). The initial velocity is that measured when almost no substrate has reacted. That the rate is not always proportionate to enzyme concentration may be seen by considering the situation at equilibrium. Although the reaction is proceeding, the rate of the reverse reaction equals it. In most practical situations it thus will appear that the reaction velocity is zero.

The enzyme is a reactant that combines with substrate forming an **enzyme-substrate complex, EnzS,** which decomposes to form a product, P, and free enzyme:

$$\text{Enz} + S \rightleftharpoons \text{EnzS} \rightleftharpoons \text{Enz} + P$$

Note that although the rate expressions for the forward, back, and overall reactions include the term [Enz],

$$\text{Enz} + S \rightleftharpoons \text{Enz} + P$$

$$\text{Rate}_1 = k_1[\text{Enz}][S]$$

$$\text{Rate}_{-1} = k_{-1}[\text{Enz}][P]$$

in the expression for the overall equilibrium constant, [Enz] cancels out.

$$K_{eq} = \frac{k_1}{k_{-1}} = \frac{[Enz][P]}{[Enz][S]} = \frac{[P]}{[S]}$$

The enzyme concentration thus has no effect on the equilibrium constant. Stated another way, since enzymes affect rates, not rate constants, they cannot affect K_{eq}, which is a ratio of rate constants. **The K_{eq} of a reaction is the same regardless of whether equilibrium is approached with or without enzymatic catalysis** (recall ΔG^0). In terms of the mechanical analogy, enzymes "dig tunnels" and change the path of the reaction but do not affect the initial and final positions of the boulder which determine K_{eq} and ΔG^0.

Substrate Concentration

If the concentration of the substrate [S] is increased while all other conditions are kept constant, the **measured initial velocity, v** (the velocity measured when very little substrate has reacted), increases to a maximum value, V, and no further (Fig 6–5).

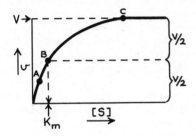

Figure 6–5. Effect of substrate concentration on the velocity of an enzyme-catalyzed reaction.

The velocity increases as the substrate concentration is increased up to a point where the enzyme is said to be "saturated" with substrate. The reason that the measured initial velocity reaches a maximal value and is unaffected by further increases in substrate concentration is that, even at very low substrate concentrations, the substrate is still present in excess of the

enzyme by a large molar ratio. For example, if an enzyme with a molecular weight of 100,000 acts on a substrate with a molecular weight of 100 and both are present at a concentration of 1 mg/ml, there are 1000 mols of substrate for every mole of enzyme. More realistic figures might be

$$[Enz] = 0.1\ \mu g/ml = 10^{-9}\ molar$$
$$[S] = 0.1\ mg/ml = 10^{-3}\ molar$$

giving a 10^6 molar excess of substrate over enzyme. Even if [S] is decreased 100-fold, substrate is present in 10,000-fold molar excess over enzyme.

The situation at points A, B, and C in Fig 6–5 is illustrated in Fig 6–6. At points A and B not all the enzyme present is combined with substrate, even though there are many more molecules of substrate than of enzyme. This is because the equilibrium constant for the reaction Enz + S ⇌ EnzS is not infinitely large. **At points A or B, increasing or decreasing [S] will therefore increase or decrease the amount of Enz associated with S as EnzS, and v will thus depend on [S].** At C, essentially all the enzyme is combined with substrate, so that a further increase in [S], although it increases the frequency of collision between Enz and S, cannot result in increased rates of reaction since no free enzyme is available to react.

Case B depicts a situation where exactly half the enzyme molecules "hold" or are "saturated with" substrate. The velocity is accordingly **half the maximal velocity** attainable at that particular enzyme concentration. **The substrate concentration that produces half-maximal velocity, termed the K_m value or Michaelis constant,** may be determined experimentally by graphing v as a function of [S] (Fig 6–5).

The Michaelis-Menten expression

$$v = \frac{V[S]}{K_m + [S]}$$

describes the behavior of many enzymes as substrate concentration is varied. The dependence of the initial velocity of an enzyme-catalyzed reaction on [S] and

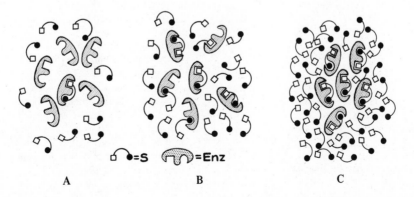

Figure 6–6. Representation of an enzyme at low *(A)*, at high *(C)*, and at the K_m concentration of substrate *(B)*. Points A, B, and C correspond to those of Fig 6–5.

on K_m may be illustrated by evaluating the Michaelis-Menten equation as follows:

1. **When [S] is very much less than K_m** (point A in Figs 6–5 and 6–6). Adding [S] to K_m now changes its value very little, so the [S] term is dropped from the denominator. Since V and K_m are both constants, we can replace their ratio by a new constant, K. [≈ means "approximately equal to."]

$$v = \frac{V[S]}{K_m + [S]} \ , \ v \approx \frac{V[S]}{K_m} \approx \frac{V}{K_m} [S] \ \approx K[S]$$

In other words, **when the substrate concentration is considerably below that required to produce half-maximal velocity (the K_m value), the initial velocity, v, depends upon the substrate concentration [S].**

2. **When [S] is very much greater than K_m** (point C, Figs 6–5 and 6–6). Now adding K_m to [S] changes the value of [S] very little, so the term K_m is dropped from the denominator.

$$v = \frac{V[S]}{K_m + [S]} \ , \ v \approx \frac{V[S]}{[S]} \approx \ V$$

This states that when the substrate concentration [S] far exceeds the K_m value, the initial velocity, v, is maximal, V.

3. **When [S] = K_m** (point B, Figs 6–5 and 6–6),

$$v = \frac{V[S]}{K_m + [S]} \ , \ v = \frac{V[S]}{[S] + [S]} = \frac{V[S]}{2[S]} = \frac{V}{2}$$

This states that **when the substrate concentration is equal to the K_m value, the initial velocity, v, is half-maximal.** It also tells how **to evaluate K_m,** namely, to **find the substrate concentration where the initial velocity is half-maximal.**

Since few enzymes give saturation curves which readily permit evaluation of V (and hence of K_m) when v is plotted versus S, it is convenient to rearrange the Michaelis-Menten expression to simplify evaluation of K_m and V. The Michaelis-Menten equation may be inverted and factored as follows:

$$v = \frac{V[S]}{K_m + [S]}$$

Invert:
$$\frac{1}{v} = \frac{K_m + [S]}{V[S]}$$

Factor:
$$\frac{1}{v} = \frac{K_m}{V} \times \frac{1}{[S]} + \frac{[S]}{V[S]}$$

$$\frac{1}{v} = \frac{K_m}{V} \times \frac{1}{[S]} + \frac{1}{V}$$

This is the equation for a **straight line**

$$y = ax + b$$

where if y, or 1/v, is plotted as a function of x, or

1/[S], the y intercept, b, is 1/V, and the slope, a, is K_m/V. The negative x intercept may be evaluated by setting y = 0. Then

$$x = -\frac{b}{a} = -\frac{1}{K_m}$$

From the **double-reciprocal or Lineweaver-Burk plot,** K_m may be estimated (Fig 6–7) either from the

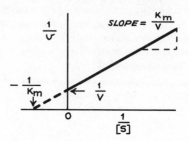

Figure 6–7. Double-reciprocal or Lineweaver-Burk plot of $\frac{1}{v}$ versus $\frac{1}{[S]}$ used for graphic evaluation of K_m and V.

slope and y intercept or from the negative x intercept. Since [S] is expressed in molarity, the dimension of K_m is molarity or moles per liter. Velocity, v, may be expressed in any units, since **K_m is independent of [Enz].** The double-reciprocal treatment requires relatively few points to define K_m and is therefore the method most often used to determine K_m. K_m values, apart from their usefulness in interpretation of the mechanisms of enzyme-catalyzed reactions, are of considerable practical value. At a substrate concentration of 100 times the K_m value, the enzyme will act at essentially maximum rate. This is generally desirable in the assay of enzymes. The **K_m value tells how much substrate to use.** The double-reciprocal treatment finds extensive use in the evaluation of inhibitors.

The Michaelis-Menten expression may be rearranged in other ways to give the equation of a straight line. If, for example, the substrate concentration [S] is plotted on the x axis and [S]/v on the y axis, the negative x intercept gives $-K_m$ directly. V may then be evaluated from the y intercept, which is K_m/V. Other forms are possible.

Coenzyme Concentration

As stated earlier (see Figs 5–1, 5–2, and 5–3), the coenzyme may frequently be regarded as a second substrate. In this instance, the comments of the previous section apply equally to substrates and to coenzymes. It also happens, however, that certain coenzymes (eg, pyridoxal phosphate) are covalently bonded to the enzyme or so tightly bound that their dissociation rarely occurs (eg, thiamin pyrophosphate). In these cases, it is preferable to regard the enzyme-coenzyme complex as the enzyme.

Temperature

Over a limited range of temperatures, the velocity

of enzyme-catalyzed reactions increases as temperature rises. The exact ratio by which the velocity changes for a 10° C temperature rise is the Q_{10}, or **temperature coefficient.** The velocity of many biologic reactions roughly doubles with a 10° C rise in temperature (Q_{10} = 2), and is halved if the temperature is decreased by 10° C. Many physiologic processes—eg, the rate of contraction of an excised heart—consequently exhibit a Q_{10} of about 2.

When the rate of enzyme-catalyzed reactions is measured at several temperatures, the result shown in Fig 6—8 is typical. There is an optimal temperature at which the reaction is most rapid. Above this, the reaction rate decreases sharply, mainly due to denaturation of the enzyme by heat.

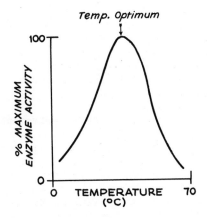

Figure 6—8. Effect of temperature on the velocity of a hypothetical enzyme-catalyzed reaction.

For most enzymes, optimal temperatures approximate those of the environment of the cell. For the homeothermic organism, man, this is 37° C. Enzymes from microorganisms adapted to growth in natural hot springs may exhibit optimal temperatures close to the boiling point of water.

The increase in rate below optimal temperature results from the increased kinetic energy of the reacting molecules. As the temperature is raised still further, however, the kinetic energy of the enzyme molecule becomes so great that it exceeds the energy barrier for breaking the secondary bonds that hold the enzyme in its native or catalytically active state. There is consequently a loss of secondary and tertiary structure and a parallel loss of biologic activity.

pH

Moderate pH changes affect the **ionic state of the enzyme** and frequently that of the substrate also. When enzyme activity is measured at several pH values, optimal activity is generally observed between pH values of 5.0 and 9.0. However, a few enzymes, eg, pepsin, are active at pH values well outside this range.

The shape of pH-activity curves is determined by the following factors:

1. Enzyme denaturation at extremely high or low pH values.

2. Effects on the charged state of the substrate or enzyme. For the enzyme, charge changes may affect activity either by changing structure or by changing the charge on an amino acid residue functional in substrate-binding or catalysis. If a negatively charged enzyme (Enz^-) reacts with a positively charged substrate (SH^+):

$$Enz^- + SH^+ \rightarrow EnzSH$$

then at low pH values Enz^- will be protonated and lose its negative charge.

$$Enz^- + H^+ \rightarrow Enz\text{-}H$$

Similarly, at very high pH values, SH^+ will ionize and lose its positive charge:

$$SH^+ \rightarrow S + H^+$$

Since the only forms that will interact are SH^+ and Enz^-, extreme pH values will lower the effective concentration of Enz^- and SH^+, thus lowering the reaction velocity shown in Fig 6—9. Only in the crosshatched area for both Enz and S in the appropriate ionic state, and the maximal concentrations of Enz and S are correctly charged at X. The result is a bell-shaped pH-activity curve.

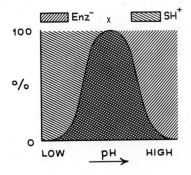

Figure 6—9. Effect of pH on enzyme activity.

Another important factor is a change in conformation of the enzyme when the pH is varied. A charged group far removed from the region where the substrate is bound may be necessary to maintain an active tertiary or quaternary structure. As the charge on this group is changed, the protein may unravel, or become more compact, or dissociate into subunits—all with a resulting loss of activity.

INHIBITION OF ENZYME ACTIVITY

It is customary to distinguish 2 broad classes of inhibitors–competitive and noncompetitive–depending on whether the inhibition is or is not relieved by increasing concentrations of substrate. In practice, many inhibitors do not exhibit the idealized properties of pure competitive or noncompetitive inhibition discussed below. An alternate way to classify inhibitors is by their site of action. Some bind to the enzyme at the same site as does the substrate (the catalytic or active site); others bind at some region (the allosteric site) other than the substrate site.

Competitive or Substrate Analog Inhibition

Classical competitive inhibition occurs at the substrate-binding or catalytic site. The chemical structure of a substrate analog inhibitor (I) closely resembles that of the substrate (S). It may therefore combine reversibly with the enzyme, forming an enzyme inhibitor (EnzI) complex rather than an EnzS complex. When both the substrate and this type of inhibitor are present, they compete for the same binding sites on the enzyme surface. A much studied case of competitive inhibition is that of malonate (I) with succinate (S) for succinate dehydrogenase.

Succinate dehydrogenase catalyzes formation of fumarate by removal of one hydrogen atom from each of the 2 a-carbon atoms of succinate (Fig 6–10).

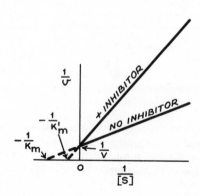

Succinic acid   **Fumaric acid**

Figure 6–10. Reaction catalyzed by succinate dehydrogenase.

Malonate (I) can combine with the dehydrogenase, forming an EnzI complex. This, however, cannot be dehydrogenated since there is no way to remove even one H atom from the single a-carbon atom of malonate without forming a pentavalent carbon atom. The only reaction the EnzI complex can undergo is decomposition back to free enzyme plus inhibitor. For the reversible reaction,

$$EnzI \underset{k_{-1}}{\overset{k_1}{\rightleftharpoons}} Enz + I$$

the equilibrium constant, K_i, is

$$K_i = \frac{[Enz]\,[I]}{[EnzI]} = \frac{k_1}{k_{-1}}$$

The action of competitive inhibitors may be understood in terms of the following reactions:

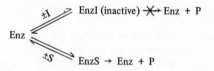

The rate of product formation, which is what is measured, depends solely on the concentration of EnzS. Suppose I binds very tightly to the enzyme (K_i = a small number). There now is little free enzyme (Enz) available to combine with S to form EnzS and to decompose to Enz + P. The measured reaction rate will thus be slow. For analogous reasons, an equal concentration of a less tightly bound inhibitor (K_i = a larger number) will not decrease the rate of the catalyzed reaction so markedly. Suppose that, at a fixed concentration of I, more S is added. This increases the probability that Enz will combine with S rather than with I. The ratio of EnzS/EnzI and the reaction rate also rise. At a sufficiently high concentration of S, the concentration of EnzI should be vanishingly small. If so, the rate of the catalyzed reaction will be the same as in the absence of I. This is shown in Fig 6–11.

Figure 6–11. Classical competitive inhibition.

The reaction velocity (v) at a fixed concentration of inhibitor was measured at various concentrations of S. The lines drawn through the experimental points coincide at the y-axis. Since the y-intercept is 1/V, this states that **at an infinitely high concentration of S** (1/S = O), **v is the same as in the absence of inhibitor.** However, the intercept on the x-axis (which is related to K_m) varies with inhibitor concentration and becomes a larger number ($-1/K'_m$ is smaller than $-1/K_m$) in the presence of I. Thus, **a competitive inhibitor raises the apparent K_m (K'_m) for the substrate.** Since K_m is the substrate concentration where the concentration of free enzyme is equal to the concentration of enzyme as EnzS, substantial free enzyme is available to combine with inhibitor. For simple competitive inhibition, the intercept on the x-axis is

$$y = \frac{1}{K_m \left(1 + \frac{[I]}{K_i}\right)}$$

K_m may be evaluated in the absence of I, and K_i evaluated using the above equation. If the number of moles of I added is very much greater than the number of moles of enzyme present, [I] may generally be taken as the added (known) concentration of inhibitor. The K_i values for a series of substrate analog (competitive) inhibitors indicate which are most effective. **At a low concentration, those with the lowest K_i values will cause the greatest degree of inhibition.**

Competitive inhibitors that block enzyme reactions in a parasite are potent **chemotherapeutic agents.** For example, many microorganisms require *p*-aminobenzoic acid to form the vitamin folic acid (Fig 6–12).

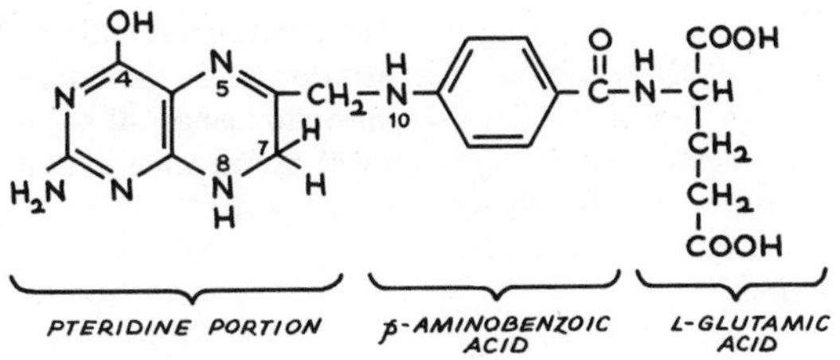

PTERIDINE PORTION   *p*-AMINOBENZOIC ACID   L-GLUTAMIC ACID

Figure 6–12. 7,8-Dihydrofolic acid.

Sulfanilamide, a structural analog of *p*-aminobenzoate, will block folic acid synthesis. The resulting deficiency of this essential vitamin is fatal to the microorganism. Since man lacks the enzymes necessary to synthesize folic acid, this compound is required as a vitamin in the diet. It follows that sulfonamides do not act as competitive inhibitors of folic acid synthesis in man.

Folic acid analogs used as chemotherapeutic agents against tumors include aminopterin (4-aminofolic acid) and amethopterin (Fig 6–13) which inhibit growth of Ehrlich ascites tumor cells. Amethopterin is a competitive inhibitor for dihydrofolate in the dihydrofolate reductase reaction. An aminopterin-resistant strain of Ehrlich cells has been shown to have as much as 14 times more dihydrofolate reductase than the

nonresistant strain, although levels of other folate-utilizing enzymes are unchanged. This illustrates one mechanism of drug resistance, ie, hyperproduction of the drug-sensitive enzyme.

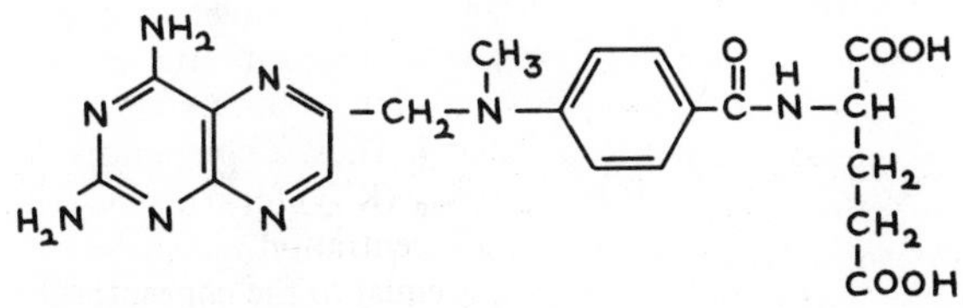

Other **antagonists to B vitamins** include pyrithiamine and oxythiamine (antagonists to thiamin), pyridine-3-sulfonic acid (to nicotinamide), pantoyl taurine and ω-methylpantothenic acid (to pantothenic acid), deoxypyridoxine (to pyridoxine), desthiobiotin (to biotin), and dicumarol to vitamin K. Purine and pyrimidine antimetabolites have also been prepared and studied as possible chemotherapeutic agents in the treatment of tumors. Examples are 6-mercaptopurine (Purinethiol, 6-MP), which may be a hypoxanthine antagonist, 5-fluorouracil, 5-fluorouridylic acid, and 5-iodouridine.

Many other drugs that inhibit enzyme action operate in a similar manner. D-Histidine competitively inhibits the action of histidase on L-histidine. **Physostigmine** competitively inhibits the hydrolysis of acetylcholine by cholinesterase, probably because it is structurally similar to acetylcholine. Even ATP and ADP are competitive inhibitors for many oxidoreductases where NAD and NADP are required as coenzymes. Recall that both the coenzymes and the inhibitors are derivatives of AMP (see Table 5–2).

The sulfonamide derivative **acetazolamide** (Diamox), although not bacteriostatic, is a potent inhibitor of carbonic anhydrase. Acetazolamide has been used to intensify renal excretion of water and electrolytes because of the importance of carbonic anhydrase in those functions of the renal tubule which affect reabsorption of electrolyte and thus of water (see Chapter 34).

Reversible Noncompetitive Inhibition

As the name implies, in this case no competition occurs between S and I. I usually bears little or no structural resemblance to S and may be assumed to bind to a different region on the enzyme. **Reversible noncompetitive inhibitors lower the maximum velocity attainable with a given amount of enzyme (lower V) but do not affect K_m.** Since I and S may combine at different sites, formation of both EnzI and EnzIS complexes is possible. Since EnzIS may break down to form product at a slower rate than does EnzS, the reaction is slowed but not halted. The following competing reactions may occur:

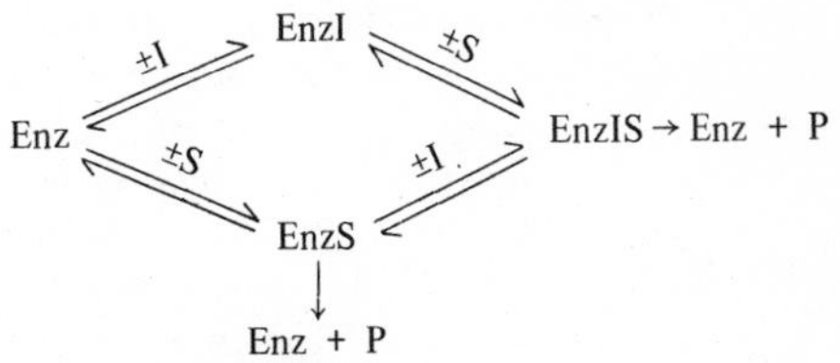

Figure 6–13. Amethopterin (methotrexate, 4-amino-N^{10}-methylfolic acid).

If S has equal affinity both for Enz and for EnzI (I does not affect the affinity of Enz for S), the results shown in Fig 6–14 are obtained when 1/v is plotted against 1/S in the presence of inhibitor. (It is assumed

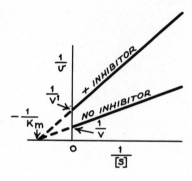

Figure 6–14. Reversible noncompetitive inhibition.

that there has been no significant alteration of the conformation of the active site when I is bound.)

Irreversible Noncompetitive Inhibition

A wide variety of enzyme "poisons" such as iodoacetamide, heavy metal ions (Ag^+, Hg^{2+}), oxidizing agents, etc reduce enzyme activity. Since these inhibitors bear no structural resemblance to the substrate, an increase in the substrate concentrations generally is ineffective in relieving this inhibition. Simple kinetic analysis of the type discussed above may not distinguish between enzyme poisons and true reversible noncompetitive inhibitors. Reversible noncompetitive inhibition is, in any case, rare. Unfortunately this is not always appreciated since both reversibly and irreversibly bound noncompetitive inhibition exhibit similar kinetics.

Extracts of the intestinal parasite Ascaris contain pepsin and trypsin inhibitors. The parasitic worm thus escapes digestion in the intestine. These protein inhibitors occur also in pancreas, soybeans, and raw egg white. Animals may also produce antibodies that irreversibly inactivate enzymes in response to the parenteral injection of the enzyme which functions as a foreign protein or antigen. This seriously limits the use of enzymes as chemotherapeutic agents.

THE CATALYTIC SITE

General Principles

The large size of proteins relative to their substrates led biochemists at the turn of the century to postulate that some restricted region of the enzyme was concerned with the process of catalysis. This region was termed the active site. Today, we refer to the **catalytic site,** since we now know that other sites are "active" (eg, allosteric sites). Initially, it was extremely puzzling to biochemists why enzymes were so large, when only a portion of their structure appeared to be required for substrate binding and catalysis. Today, it is recognized from 3-dimensional models of enzymes that a far greater portion of the protein inter-

acts with the substrate than was formerly supposed. When the need for allosteric sites of equal size also arises (see Chapter 7), the wonder is that proteins are as small as they are.

Rigid Model of the Catalytic Site

The original model of a catalytic site, proposed by Emil Fischer, visualized interaction between substrate and enzyme in terms of a "lock and key" analogy. This lock and key, or rigid template model (Fig 6–15), is still useful for understanding certain properties of enzymes—for example, the ordered binding of 2 or more substrates (Fig 6–16) or the kinetics of a simple substrate saturation curve.(Fig 6–6).

Flexible Model of the Catalytic Site

An unfortunate feature of the Fischer model is the implied rigidity of the catalytic site. A more refined and certainly a more useful model in terms of explaining properties of enzymes is the **"induced fit" model** of Koshland. Originally little more than an attractive hypothesis, this model now has received considerable experimental support.

An essential feature is the flexibility of the region of the catalytic site. In the Fischer model, the catalytic site is presumed to be pre-shaped to fit the substrate. In the induced fit model, the substrate induces a conformational change* in the enzyme. This aligns amino acid residues or other groups on the enzyme in the correct spatial orientation for substrate binding, catalysis, or both. At the same time, other amino acid residues may become buried in the interior of the molecule.

In the hypothetical example (Fig 6–17), hydrophobic groups (hatched portion) and charged groups (dots) both are involved in substrate binding. A phosphoserine (–P) and the –SH of a cysteine residue are involved in catalysis. Other residues involved in neither process are represented by the side chains of 2 amino acids, lysine and methionine. In the absence of substrate, the catalytic and the substrate-binding groups are several bond distances removed from one another. Approach of the substrate induces a conformational change in the enzyme protein, aligning the groups correctly for substrate binding and for catalysis. At the same time, the spatial orientations of other regions are also altered—the lysine and methionine are now closer together (Fig 6–17). An alternative representation is shown in Fig 6–18.

Substrate analogs may cause some, but not all, of the correct conformational changes. On attachment of the true substrate (A), all groups (shown as closed circles in the illustrations) are brought into correct

*Conformational change: A change in the average positions of atomic nuclei but not including bond changes. Unfolding or rotation about bonds of a protein is a conformational change, but the dissociation of a proton is not, even though it may accompany a conformational change. Polarizations of electrons without changes of the atomic nuclei are not conformational changes.

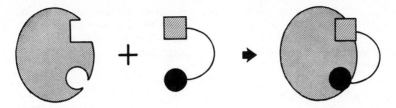

Figure 6—15. Representation of formation of an EnzS complex according to the Fischer template hypothesis.

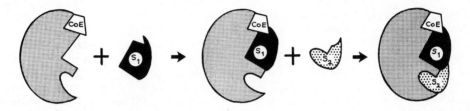

Figure 6—16. Representation of sequential adsorption of a coenzyme (CoE) and of 2 substrates (S_1 and S_2) to an enzyme in terms of the template hypothesis. The coenzyme is assumed to bear a group essential for binding the first substrate (S_1) which in turn facilitates binding of S_2.

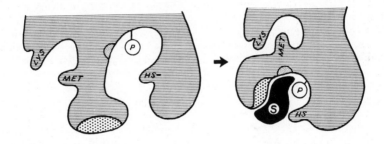

Figure 6—17. Representation of an induced fit by a conformational change in the protein structure. (After Koshland.)

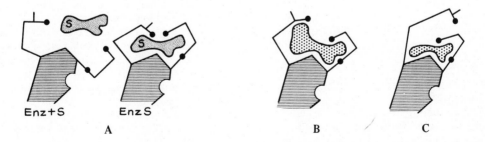

Figure 6—18. Representation of conformational changes in an enzyme protein when binding substrate *(A)* or inactive substrate analogs *(B,C)*. (After Koshland.)

alignment. Attachment of a substrate analog that is too "bulky" (Fig 6–18B) or too "slim" (Fig 6–18C) induces incorrect alignment. One final feature is the site shown as a small notch on the right of the enzyme. One may perhaps visualize a regulatory molecule attaching at this point and "holding down" one of the polypeptide arms bearing a catalytic group. Substrate binding, but not catalysis, might then occur.

Experimental evidence for the induced fit model includes demonstration of conformational changes during substrate binding and catalysis with creatine kinase, phosphoglucomutase, and several other enzymes. With phosphoglucomutase, compounds similar to the substrate (eg, inorganic phosphate or glycerol phosphate) produced noticeable but less extensive conformational changes. With carboxypeptidase, substrate binding induces an appreciable change in the location of 2 amino acid residues which may also be involved in catalysis.

The exact sequence of events in a substrate-induced conformational change remains to be established. Several possibilities exist (Fig 6–19).

Even when the complete primary structure of an enzyme is known, it may still be difficult to decide exactly which amino acid residues constitute the catalytic site. As so well illustrated by the induced fit model, these may be far distant one from another in terms of primary structure but spatially close in the sense of 3-dimensional or tertiary structure.

In the representation of a catalytic site shown in Fig 6–20, several regions of a polypeptide chain each contribute amino acid residues to the site. Furthermore, the residues contributed generally are not all sequential within a polypeptide chain. One may ask: "How far does the catalytic site extend?" To facilitate discussion, Koshland distinguishes 3 types of amino acid residues in enzymes.

(1) Contact residue. An amino acid residue within one bond distance (0.2 nm) of the substrate or other ligand* concerned. The term may include both specificity and catalytic residues.

(2) Specificity residue. An amino acid residue involved both in substrate binding and in subsequent catalytic process.

(3) Catalytic residue. An amino acid residue directly involved in covalent bond changes during enzyme action.

These are illustrated in Fig 6–20.

Modifiers of Enzyme Activity

The flow of carbon and of energy into various pathways of metabolism is profoundly influenced both by enzyme synthesis and by activation of proenzymes. However, these processes are irreversible. Like all mammalian proteins, enzymes eventually are degraded to amino acids (protein turnover). In bacteria, the activity is diluted out among daughter cells on successive divisions.† Although both mechanisms effectively reduce enzyme concentration and hence catalytic activity, they are slow, wasteful of carbon and energy, and rather like turning out a light by smashing the bulb,

---

*Ligand: Any small molecule bound to the enzyme by non-covalent forces. The term includes activators, substrates, and inhibitors.

†However, protein turnover does occur in bacteria at slow rates.

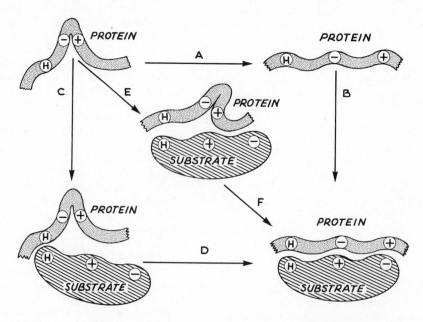

Figure 6–19. Representation of alternative reaction paths for a substrate-induced conformational change. The enzyme may first undergo a conformational change *(A)*, then bind substrate *(B)*. Alternatively, substrate may first be bound *(C)*, whereupon a conformational change occurs *(D)*. Finally, both processes may occur in a concerted manner *(E)* with further isomerization to the final conformation *(F)*. (Adapted from Koshland & Neet: Annu Rev Biochem 37:387, 1968.)

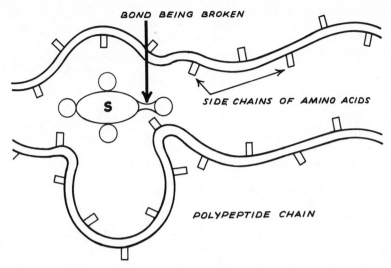

Figure 6–20. The catalytic site. This may be composed of amino acid residues far removed from one another in terms of primary structure. (After Koshland.)

then inserting a new one when light is needed. An "on-off" switch for enzymes clearly would be advantageous. It thus is not surprising that the **catalytic activity** of certain key enzymes can be reversibly decreased or increased by small molecules—in many cases themselves intermediary metabolites (Fig 6–21). Small molecule **modifiers** which decrease catalytic activity are termed **negative modifiers;** those which increase or stimulate activity are called **positive modifiers.**

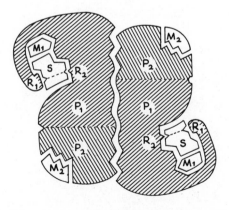

Figure 6–21. Schematic illustration of bond rupture by an enzyme consisting of 2 identical subunits. The substrates (S) are in contact with 2 catalytic residues (R_1 and R_2). Modifiers at the active site (M_1) and at an allosteric site (M_2) aid in maintaining the correct enzyme conformation. P_1 and P_2 may represent either 2 different polypeptide chains or parts of the same polypeptide chain. (Adapted from Koshland & Neet: Annu Rev Biochem 37:361, 1968.)

Examples of Catalytic Sites of Specific Enzymes

A. Lysozyme: Lysozyme is an enzyme, present in tears, nasal mucus, sputum, tissues, gastric secretions, milk, and egg white, which catalyzes the hydrolysis of β-1,4-linkages of N-acetylneuraminic acid (see Chapter 8) in mucopolysaccharides or mucopeptides. It performs the function, in tears and nasal mucus, of destroying the cell walls of many airborne gram-positive bacteria. Lysozyme (molecular weight about 15,000) consists of a single polypeptide chain of 129 amino acid residues having no coenzyme or metal ion cofactors. Since the lysozyme molecule may readily be unfolded and refolded, not only catalysis and specificity but also the 3-dimensional structure are determined solely by these residues. There are small regions of pleated sheet structure, little α-helix, and large regions without ordered secondary structure. A satisfactory representation of the structure of the enzyme consisting of a model of the molecule and its substrate, photographed in 3-dimensional color by the Parallax-Panoramagram technic, appears in J Biol Chem 243:1633, 1968. The molecule is seen to bear a deep central cleft which harbors a catalytic site with 6 subsites (Fig 6–22) which bind various substrates or inhibitors. The residues responsible for bond cleavage are thought to lie between sites D and E close to the carboxyl groups of asp 52 and glu 35. It is thought that glu 35 protonates the acetal bond of the substrate while the negatively charged asp 52 stabilizes the resulting carbonium ion from the back side.

B. Ribonuclease: Unlike lysozyme, considerable information about the catalytic site of ribonuclease was available prior to solution of the 3-dimensional structure by x-ray crystallography (Fig 4–13). The conclusions based on chemical investigations were largely confirmed by crystallography. The structure contains a cleft similar to that of lysozyme across

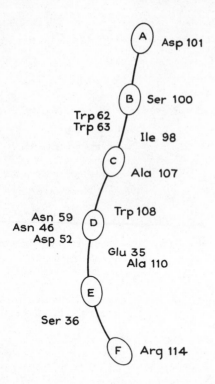

Figure 6–22. Schematic representation of the catalytic site in the cleft region of lysozyme. A to F represent the glycosyl moieties of a hexasaccharide. Some of the amino acids in the cleft region near these subsites of the catalytic site are shown together with their numbers in the lysozyme sequence. (Adapted from Koshland & Neet: Annu Rev Biochem 37:364, 1968.)

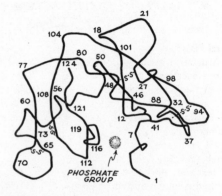

Figure 6–23. Structure of ribonuclease as determined from x-ray diffraction studies. (Numbers refer to specific amino acid residues.) (See also Fig 4–13.)

which lie 2 amino acid residues, his 12 and his 119. These previously were implicated by chemical evidence as being at the catalytic site. Both residues are near the binding site for uridylic acid (Fig 6–23).

Amino Acid Sequences at Catalytic Sites

Progress in partial decoding of the primary structures at some active sites has led to the discovery that there are many similarities between the sequences of several hydrolytic enzymes (see Table 6–1). This may mean that the number of bond-breaking mechanisms operating in biologic systems is relatively small. In view of the similarities, apparent in Table 6–1, it is perhaps not surprising that the amino acid sequences near the catalytic sites of the same enzyme from different species bear even greater similarity.

Table 6–1. Amino acid sequences in the neighborhood of the catalytic sites of several bovine proteases. Regions shown are those on either side of the catalytic site seryl (S) and histidyl (H) residues. For explanation of single letter abbreviations for amino acids, see Chapter 3. (Reproduced, with permission, from Dayhoff MO [editor] : *Atlas of Protein Sequence and Structure.* Vol 5. National Biomedical Research Foundation, 1972.)

Bovine Enzyme	Sequence Around Serine Ⓢ																
Trypsin	D	S	C	Q	D	G	Ⓢ	G	G	P	V	V	C	S	G	K	
Chymotrypsin A	S	S	C	M	G	D	Ⓢ	G	G	P	L	V	C	K	K	N	
Chymotrypsin B	S	S	C	M	G	D	Ⓢ	G	G	P	L	V	C	Q	K	N	
Thrombin	D	A	C	E	G	D	Ⓢ	G	G	P	F	V	M	K	S	P	

Bovine Enzyme	Sequence Around Histidine Ⓗ											
Trypsin	V	V	S	A	A	Ⓗ	C	Y	K	S	G	I	Q
Chymotrypsin A	V	V	T	A	A	Ⓗ	G	G	V	T	T	S	D
Chymotrypsin B	V	V	T	A	A	Ⓗ	C	G	V	T	T	S	D
Thrombin	V	L	T	A	A	Ⓗ	C	L	L	Y	P		

MECHANISM OF ENZYME ACTION

General Principles

A detailed discussion of the mechanisms whereby enzymes accelerate rates of reactions is beyond the scope of this book. Therefore, only 3 examples will be given: general acid and base catalysis, catalysis by metal ions, and catalysis by enzymes that contain pyridoxal phosphate.

General Acid-Base Catalysis

Reactions whose rates vary in response to changes in the hydrogen ion or hydronium ion concentration in solution, but are independent of the concentrations of other acids or bases present in the solution, are said to be subject to **specific acid** or **specific base catalysis.** Reactions whose rates are responsive to all the acids or bases present in solution are said to be subject to **general acid** or to **general base catalysis.** The mutarotation of glucose (see Chapter 8) is one reaction subject to general acid-base catalysis.

Role of Metal Ions

Metal ions perform essential catalytic and structural roles in proteins. Indeed, over one-fourth of all known enzymes contain tightly-bound metal ions or require them for activity. The functions of these metal ions are studied by physical methods, notably x-ray crystallography, nuclear magnetic resonance (NMR), and electron spin resonance (ESR). This information is coupled with knowledge of the formation and decay of metal complexes and of reactions within the coordination spheres of metal ions to provide insight into the roles metal ions play in enzyme-catalyzed reactions.

A. Metalloenzymes and Metal-Activated Enzymes: It is customary to distinguish between metalloenzymes and metal-activated enzymes. **Metalloenzymes** are those which contain a definite quantity of functional metal ion that is retained throughout purification. **Metal-activated enzymes** do not bind metals as tightly as do metalloenzymes but nonetheless require added metals for their activation. The distinction is, however, not particularly helpful, since many examples of borderline classification are known. Many enzymes retain metal ions throughout normal purification procedures but lose the metal when purified in the presence of chelating agents. Activity of the enzyme is then lost. It is restored only after addition of a metal ion. The distinction between metalloenzymes and metal-activated enzymes, if it is to be drawn, thus rests on the affinity of a particular enzyme for its metal ion. From the aspect of the mechanisms whereby metal ions perform their functions, it appears that these are similar both in metalloenzymes and in metal-activated enzymes.

B. Ternary Enzyme-Metal-Substrate Complexes: For the many ternary (3-component) complexes formed between the active site of an enzyme (Enz), a metal ion (M), and a substrate (S) which conform to a simple 1:1:1 stoichiometry, 4 schemes are possible:

Enz—S—M

Substrate-bridge complex

M—Enz—S

Enzyme-bridge complex

Enz—M—S

Simple metal-bridge complex

$$\text{Enz} \diagdown \overset{\displaystyle M}{\underset{\displaystyle S}{\big|}}$$

Cyclic metal-bridge complex

Although all 4 schemes are possible for metal-activated enzymes, metalloenzymes cannot form the substrate-bridge complex because they retain the metal throughout purification (ie, are already as Enz—M).

In addition to metal-binding data, the technics outlined in Table 6—2 assist in ascertaining which scheme is operable.

Table 6—3 lists some of the enzymes for which the coordination schemes have been established.

From these and other data, 2 generalizations emerge:

1. Most but not all kinases (ATP:phosphotransferases) form substrate-bridge complexes of the type Enz—nucleotide—M.

2. Phosphotransferases using pyruvate or phosphoenolpyruvate as substrate, enzymes catalyzing other reactions of phosphoenolpyruvate, and carboxylases form metal-bridge complexes.

C. Ternary Complexes: Table 6—3 lists 3 enzymes as forming both substrate-bridge and enzyme-bridge complexes. This is because they form one type of bridge complex with one substrate and a different type with the other. A useful technic for studying the metal complexes formed by 2 substrate enzymes has been to form "abortive" ternary (3-component) complexes

Table 6—2. Experimental technics for determining the coordination scheme existing between enzyme, metal ion, and substrate.* (NMR, nuclear magnetic resonance; ESR, electron spin resonance.)

Experimental Technic	Coordination Scheme		
	Enz—S—M	Enz—M—S or $\text{Enz}\diagdown\overset{M}{\underset{S}{\big|}}$	M—Enz—S
Effect of Ca^{2+}	Usually activates	Usually inhibits	Activates or inhibits
NMR of substrates with Enz—Mn	. . .	Enhanced relaxation of substrate nuclei	Deenhanced relaxation of substrate nuclei
ESR spectra of Mn in M—S and in the ternary complex	Spectra identical	Spectra different	. . .
ESR spectra of Fe or Cu in the ternary complex	. . .	Hyperfine splitting by magnetic nuclei of substrate	No hyperfine splitting

*Adapted from Mildvan AS: Metals in enzyme catalysis. Vol 2, p 465, in: *The Enzymes.* Boyer PD, Lardy H, Myrbäck K (editors). Academic Press, 1970.

Table 6–3. Coordination schemes of ternary enzyme-metal-substrate complexes of several enzymes.[*]

Enzymes marked with a dagger (†) form different coordination schemes with each of their substrates. In these cases, the substrate concerned is listed in parentheses.

Substrate Bridge (Enz–S–M)	Metal Bridge (Enz–M–S) or Enz⟨M/S	Enzyme Bridge (M–Enz–S)
Creatine kinase	Pyruvate kinase	Citrate lyase
Adenylate kinase	PEP carboxykinase	Dopamine hydroxylase
Arginine kinase	Pyruvate carboxylase	
3-Phosphoglycerate kinase	Ribose diphosphate carboxylase	Glutamine synthetase
Hexokinase	PEP carboxylase	†UDPG pyrophosphorylase
Tetrahydrofolate synthetase	PEP synthase	
†UDPG-pyrophosphorylase (S = UTP)	Enolase	†Tryptophan RNA synthetase (S = PP_i)
	Phosphoglucomutase	
†Tryptophan RNA synthetase (S = ATP)	Inorganic pyrophosphatase	†Valine RNA synthetase (S = PP_i)
†Valine RNA (S = ATP)	Histidine deaminase	
	D-Xylose isomerase	
	Aldolase	
	Carboxypeptidase	
	β-Methylaspartase	
	DNA-polymerase	
	Staphylococcal nuclease	

[*]Adapted from Mildvan AS: Metals in enzyme catalysis. Vol 2, p 472, in: *The Enzymes.* Boyer PD, Lardy H, Myrbäck K (editors). Academic Press, 1970.

between the enzyme, metal ion, one substrate, and one product. The complexes are termed abortive since they cannot give rise to a reaction (product is where substrate should be). Their stability facilitates their study. Proton relaxation data show that pyruvate kinase and creatine kinase form abortive ternary complexes of the types shown below.

$$\text{Pyruvate kinase} \underset{\text{Pyruvate}}{\overset{\overset{\displaystyle Mn}{|}}{-}} \text{ADP} \qquad \text{Creatine kinase} \overset{\text{ADP–Mn}}{\underset{\text{Creatine}}{\big\langle}}$$

Notice that Mn forms a cyclic metal-bridge complex with one kinase (pyruvate kinase) and a substrate-bridge complex with the other (creatine kinase). The products, pyruvate and creatine, form an enzyme-bridge complex with respect to the metal. Note also that, if the ADP of the abortive complex were replaced by ATP, a reaction would occur. Data of this type are used to infer the nature of active, catalytic complexes.

D. Enzyme-Bridge Complexes (M–Enz–S): Comparatively little is known concerning the role of metals in enzyme-bridge complexes. They are presumed to perform structural roles, possibly maintaining an active conformation (eg, glutamine synthetase). The role of a

metal ion need not be limited to conformational stabilization, for the metal may also form a metal bridge to a substrate. This occurs with pyruvate kinase:

$$\text{Pyruvate kinase} \underset{\text{Creatine}}{\overset{\overset{\displaystyle M}{|}}{-}} \text{ATP}$$

In addition to its structural role, the metal ion in pyruvate kinase appears to hold one substrate (ATP) in place and to activate it.

E. Substrate-Bridge Complexes (Enz–S–M): The formation of ternary substrate-bridge complexes of nucleoside triphosphates with enzyme, metal, and substrate appears to be attributable to displacement of water by ATP from the coordination sphere of the metal:

$$\text{ATP}^{4-} + \text{M(H}_2\text{O)}_6{}^{2+} \rightleftharpoons \text{ATP–M(H}_2\text{O)}_3{}^{2-} + 3\text{H}_2\text{O}$$

The substrate then binds to the enzyme forming the ternary complex:

$$\text{ATP–M(H}_2\text{O)}_3{}^{2-} + \text{Enz} \rightleftharpoons \text{Enz–ATP–M(H}_2\text{O)}_3{}^{2-}$$

While reaction of the enzyme first with ATP and subsequently with the metal may be faster, it is not thought to occur under physiologic conditions since intracellular concentrations of enzymes generally are far below those of ATP or of metal ions.

The function of metal ions in phosphotransferase reactions is thought to involve activation of the phosphorus atoms and formation of a rigid, polyphosphate-adenine complex of the appropriate conformation in the active, quaternary complex.

F. Metal-Bridge Complexes:

$$\text{Enz–M–S} \quad \text{or} \quad \text{Enz} \overset{\overset{\displaystyle M}{|}}{\underset{\displaystyle S}{\big\langle}}$$

X-ray crystallographic and peptide sequencing data have established that a histidyl residue is concerned with metal binding at the active site of many proteins (eg, carboxypeptidase A, cytochrome c, rubredoxin, metmyoglobin, and methemoglobin). Little, however, is known concerning the mechanism of formation of binary (2-component) Enz–M complexes except that the rate-limiting step is in many cases the departure of water from the coordination sphere of the metal ion. For many peptidases, activation by metal ions is a slow process requiring many hours for completion. Since Mn can move from one amino acid residue to another in microseconds, the rate of metal binding is thought to be rapid. The slow reaction probably is the subsequent conformational rearrangement of the binary Enz–M complex to an active conformation, eg:

Metal binding:

$$\text{Enz} + \text{M(H}_2\text{O)}_6 \xrightarrow{\text{Rapid}} \text{Enz–M(H}_2\text{O)}_{6\text{-n}} + \text{nH}_2\text{O}$$

Rearrangement to active conformation (Enz*):

$$\text{Enz–M(H}_2\text{O)}_{6\text{-n}} \xrightarrow{\text{Slow}} \text{Enz*–M(H}_2\text{O)}_{6\text{-n}}$$

For metalloenzymes, however, the ternary metal-bridge complex must be formed by combination of the substrate (S) with the binary M–Enz complex:

$$\text{Enz–M} + \text{S} \rightleftharpoons \text{Enz–M–S or Enz}\underset{\text{S}}{\overset{\text{M}}{<}}$$

G. Role of Metal Ions in Catalysis: Metal ions may participate in each of the 4 mechanisms by which enzymes are known to accelerate the rates of chemical reactions: (1) general acid-base catalysis, (2) covalent catalysis, (3) approximation of reactants, and (4) induction of strain in the enzyme or substrate.

Metal ions, like protons, are Lewis acids or electrophiles and can therefore accept a share in an electron pair forming a sigma bond. Metal ions may also be considered "super acids" since they exist in neutral solution, frequently have a positive charge of greater than one, and may form pi bonds. In addition (and unlike protons), metals can serve as a 3-dimensional template for the orientation and binding of basic groups present on the enzyme or substrate.

Metal ions can also accept electrons via sigma or pi bonds to activate electrophiles or nucleophiles (general acid-base catalysis). By donating electrons, metals can activate nucleophiles or act as nucleophiles themselves. The coordination sphere of a metal may bring together enzyme and substrate (approximation) or form chelate-producing distortion in either the enzyme or substrate (strain). A metal ion may also "mask" a nucleophile and thus prevent an otherwise likely side-reaction. Finally, stereochemical control of the course of an enzyme-catalyzed reaction may be achieved by the ability of the metal coordination sphere to act as a 3-dimensional template to hold reactive groups in a specific steric orientation. Table 6–4 lists a few examples where metal ions are known to perform some of these functions in enzymes.

Catalysis by Pyridoxal Phosphate Enzymes

A general view of the participation of pyridoxal phosphate bound to the surface of an enzyme in transamination is shown in Fig 5–3. In all pyridoxal phosphate-dependent reactions, a Schiff base intermediate is formed between the aldehyde group on pyridoxal phosphate and the a-amino group of an amino acid (Fig 6–24).

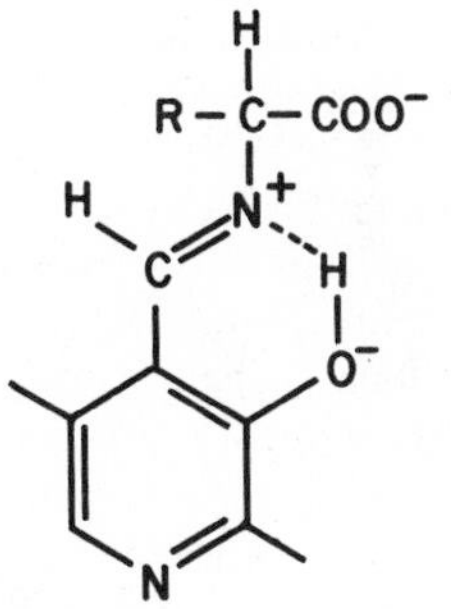

Figure 6–24. Major features of the Schiff base intermediate formed between enzyme-bound pyridoxal phosphate and an amino acid.

The protonated structure provides a conjugated system of double bonds extending from the pyridinium N to the a-carbon of the amino acid and the groups attached to this a-carbon. This system facilitates displacement of a pair of electrons from all 3 positions attached to the a-carbon atom (Fig 6–25).

Table 6–4. Selected examples of the roles of metal ions in the mechanism of action of enzymes.*

Enzyme	Role of Metal Ion
Histidine deaminase	Masking a nucleophile
Kinases, lyases, pyruvate decarboxylase	Activation of an electrophile
Carbonic anhydrase	Activation of a nucleophile
Cobamide enzymes	Metal acts as a nucleophile
Pyruvate carboxylase, carboxypeptidase, alcohol dehydrogenase	π-Electron withdrawal
Nonheme iron proteins	π-Electron donation
Pyruvate kinase, pyruvate carboxylase, adenylate kinase	Metal ion gathers and orients ligands
Phosphotransferase, D-xylose isomerase, hemoproteins	Strain effects

*Adapted from Mildvan AS: Metals in enzyme catalysis. Vol 2, p 456, in: *The Enzymes.* Boyer PD, Lardy H, Myrbäck K (editors). Academic Press, 1970.

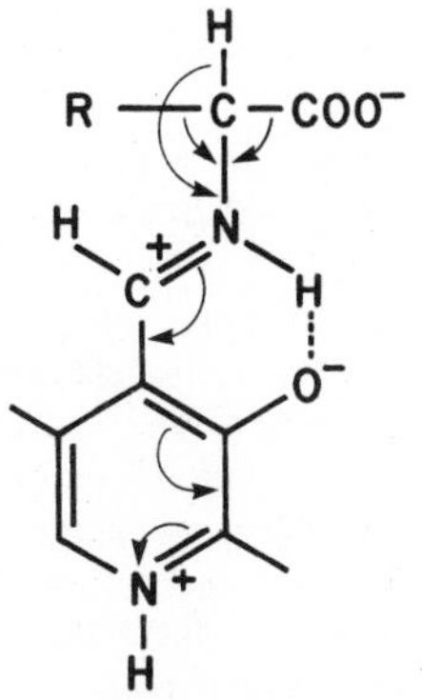

Figure 6–25. Representative electron shifts possible during pyridoxal phosphate catalyzed reactions.

ISOZYMES

Oligomeric enzymes that consist of 2 or more dissimilar protomers potentially can exist in several distinct forms. Frequently, one tissue produces one protomer predominantly and another tissue a different protomer. If these can combine in various ways to construct an active enzyme (eg, a tetramer), isozymes of that enzymic activity are said to be formed.

Isozymes are physically distinct forms of the same catalytic activity. They thus catalyze the same reaction. Isozymes of a particular enzyme are analogous to 10-cent coins minted at several different mints, eg, at Philadelphia, Denver, and San Francisco. The monetary value (reaction catalyzed = biologic value) is identical in each instance, and each coin (isozyme) is physically quite similar. But, just like "mint marks" on a coin, subtle physical, chemical, and immunologic differences between isozymes become apparent on careful examination.

Medical interest in isozymes was stimulated by the discovery in 1957 that **human sera contained several lactate dehydrogenase isozymes and that their relative proportions changed significantly in certain pathologic conditions.** Isozymes have also been reported in the sera and tissues not only of mammals but also of amphibians, birds, insects, plants, and unicellular organisms. Both the kind and the number of enzymes involved are equally diverse. Isozymes of numerous dehydrogenases and of several oxidases, transaminases, phosphatases, transphosphorylases, and proteolytic enzymes have been reported.

Serum lactate dehydrogenase isozymes may be visualized by subjecting a serum sample to electrophoresis, usually at pH 8.6, using a starch, agar, or polyacrylamide gel supporting medium. The isozymes have different charges at this pH and migrate to 5 regions of the electrophoretogram. Isozymes are then localized by means of their ability to catalyze reduction of a colorless dye to a colored form.

A typical dehydrogenase assay reagent contains the following:

(1) Reduced substrate (eg, lactate).

(2) Coenzyme (NAD).

(3) Oxidized dye (eg, nitroblue tetrazolium salt [NBT]).

(4) An intermediate electron carrier to transport electrons between NADH and the dye (eg, phenazine methosulfate [PMS]).

(5) Buffer; activating ions if required.

Lactate dehydrogenase catalyzes the transfer of 2 electrons and one hydrogen ion from lactate to NAD (Fig 6–26). The reaction proceeds at a measurable rate only in the presence of the enzyme catalyst, lactate dehydrogenase. When the assay mixture is spread on the electrophoretogram and incubated at 37° C, concerted electron transfer reactions take place only in those regions where lactate dehydrogenase is present (Fig 6–27). The bands are visible to the naked eye, and their relative intensities may be quantitated by a

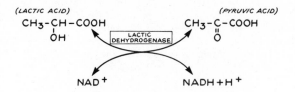

Figure 6–26. The L-lactate dehydrogenase reaction.

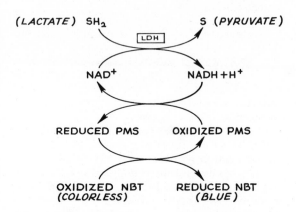

Figure 6–27. Coupled reactions in detection of lactate dehydrogenase activity on an electrophoretogram.

suitable scanning photometer (Fig 6–28). The most positive isoenzyme, as detected in an electrophoretogram, is I_1.

Lactate dehydrogenase isozymes differ from one another at the level of the quaternary structure. The active lactate dehydrogenase molecule (molecular weight 130,000) consists of 4 subunits of 2 types, H and M (molecular weight about 34,000). Only the tetrameric molecule possesses catalytic activity. If order is unimportant, these subunits might be combined in the following 5 ways:

HHHH
HHHM
HHMM
HMMM
MMMM

C. L. Markert used conditions known to disrupt and reform quaternary structure to clarify the relationships between the lactate dehydrogenase isozymes. Splitting and reconstitution of lactate dehydrogenase-I_1 or lactate dehydrogenase-I_5 produces no new isozymes. These therefore each consist of a single subunit type. When a mixture of purified lactate dehydrogenase-I_1 and lactate dehydrogenase-I_5 is subjected to the same treatment, lactate dehydrogenase-I_2, -I_3, and -I_4 are also produced. The approximate proportions of the isozymes found are those that would result if the relationship were:

Lactate Dehydrogenase Isozyme	Subunits
I$_1$	HHHH
I$_2$	HHHM
I$_3$	HHMM
I$_4$	HMMM
I$_5$	MMMM

Syntheses of H and M subunits have been shown to be controlled by distinct genetic loci.

ENZYMES IN CLINICAL DIAGNOSIS

Distinction Between Functional & Nonfunctional Plasma Enzymes

Certain enzymes and proenzymes are present at all times in the circulation of normal individuals. Their substrates also are present in the circulation either continuously or intermittently, and they perform a physiologic function in blood. Examples of these **functional plasma enzymes** include lipoprotein lipase, pseudocholinesterase, and the proenzymes of blood coagulation and of blood clot dissolution. They generally are synthesized in the liver, but they are also present in blood in equivalent or higher concentrations than in tissues.

As the name implies, **nonfunctional plasma enzymes** perform no known physiologic function in blood. Their substrates frequently are absent from plasma, and the enzymes themselves are present in the blood of normal individuals at levels up to a million-fold lower than in tissues. Their presence in plasma at levels elevated above normal values suggests an increased rate of tissue destruction. As such, the measurement of these nonfunctional plasma enzyme levels can provide the physician with valuable clinical evidence for diagnostic and prognostic purposes.

Among nonfunctional plasma enzymes are enzymes present in exocrine secretions and the true intracellular enzymes. The exocrine enzymes—pancreatic amylase, lipase, bile alkaline phosphatase, and prostatic acid phosphatase—diffuse passively into the plasma. The true intracellular enzymes which constitute the working machinery of the cell, and those which are tightly bound to particulate elements of the cell (see Chapter 5), are normally absent from the circulation.

Origin of Nonfunctional Plasma Enzymes

The low levels of nonfunctional enzymes found ordinarily in plasma arise apparently from the routine, normal destruction of erythrocytes, leukocytes, and other cells. With accelerated cell death, soluble enzymes enter the circulation. Although elevated plasma enzyme levels are generally interpreted as evidence of cellular necrosis, vigorous exercise also results in release of small quantities of muscle enzymes.

Concentration & Half-Life of Nonfunctional Plasma Enzymes in Pathologic States

While extensive tissue necrosis releases large quantities of intracellular enzymes into the circulation, the concentration and persistence in blood (half-life) of a given tissue enzyme depends on many factors. Among these are the following:

A. Intracellular Location: Depending on the nature and extent of necrosis, enzymes present in intracellular organelles (eg, mitochondria) may or may not be present in blood. Their presence generally suggests more extensive tissue damage than the presence of cytosol enzymes.

B. Biologic Half-Life in Blood: The rate of disappearance of an intracellular enzyme from blood depends on its size (may be filtered at the glomerulus), the presence in blood of factors that destabilize its activity (inhibitors, degradative enzymes), and other unknown factors.

C. Circulatory Factors: These involve the rate of circulation of extracellular fluid and vascularity of the injured area, and the presence or absence of an inflammatory barrier.

Diagnostic Value of Specific Enzymes

The determination by the clinical laboratory analyst of the activity of the following enzymes can provide the physician with valuable confirmatory or suggestive diagnostic evidence.

A. Lipase: The plasma lipase level may be low in liver disease, vitamin A deficiency, some malignancies, and in diabetes mellitus. It may be elevated in acute pancreatitis and pancreatic carcinoma.

B. Amylase: The plasma amylase level may be low in liver disease and increased in high intestinal obstruction, parotitis, acute pancreatitis, and diabetes.

C. Trypsin: Elevated levels of trypsin in the plasma occur during acute disease of the pancreas, with resultant changes in the coagulability of the blood reported as antithrombin titers. Direct measurement of the plasma trypsin in pancreatic disease may also be made. It is stated that elevation in concentration of plasma trypsin is a more sensitive and reliable indicator of pancreatic disease than plasma amylase or lipase.

D. Cholinesterase: This enzyme has been measured in plasma in a number of disease states. In general, low levels are found in patients ill with liver disease, malnutrition, chronic debilitating and acute infectious diseases, and anemias. High levels occur in the nephrotic syndrome. A large number of drugs produce a temporary decrease in cholinesterase activity, but the alkyl fluorophosphates cause irreversible inhibition of the enzyme. Some insecticides in common use depress cholinesterase activity, and tests for the activity of this enzyme in the plasma may be useful in detecting overexposure to these agents.

The content of cholinesterase in young red blood cells is considerably higher than in the adult red blood cells; consequently the cholinesterase titer of erythrocytes in the peripheral blood may be used as an indicator of hematopoietic activity.

E. Alkaline Phosphatase: The level of enzymes capable of catalyzing the hydrolysis of various phosphate esters at alkaline pH (alkaline phosphatase activity) may be increased in rickets, hyperparathyroidism, Paget's disease, osteoblastic sarcoma, obstructive jaundice, and metastatic carcinoma.

As is the case with several other enzymes, isozymes of alkaline phosphatase can be detected in body fluids. These include specific isozymes originating from bone, liver, placenta, and intestine. Measurement of specific alkaline phosphatase isozymes may therefore improve the diagnostic value of this test. Thus, serum alkaline phosphatase levels may increase in congestive heart failure as a result of injury to the liver. Of great value is the use of alkaline phosphatase isozyme measurements to distinguish liver lesions from bone lesions in cases of metastatic carcinoma.

F. Acid Phosphatase: The level of enzymes capable of catalyzing the hydrolysis of various phosphate esters at acidic pH (acid phosphatase activity) may be elevated in metastatic prostatic carcinoma.

G. Transaminases: Two transaminases are of clinical interest. **Glutamic oxaloacetic transaminase (GOT)** catalyzes the transfer of the amino group of aspartic acid to a-ketoglutaric acid, forming glutamic and oxaloacetic acids; **glutamic pyruvic transaminase (GPT)** transfers the amino group of alanine to a-ketoglutaric acid, forming glutamic and pyruvic acids. Serum transaminase levels in normal subjects are low, but after extensive tissue destruction these enzymes are liberated into the serum. An example is heart muscle, which is rich in transaminase; consequently, myocar-

dial infarcts are followed by rapid and striking increases in serum transaminase levels. Values decrease toward normal within a few days. The estimation of glutamic oxaloacetic transaminase is now widely used to confirm a diagnosis of myocardial infarction.

Liver tissue is rich in both transaminases, but it contains more GPT than GOT. Although both transaminases are elevated in sera of patients with acute hepatic disease, GPT, which is only slightly elevated by cardiac necrosis, is therefore a more specific indicator of liver damage.

Extensive skeletal muscle damage, as in severe trauma, also elevates serum transaminase levels.

H. Lactate Dehydrogenase: Lactate dehydrogenase (LD or LDH) can be detected by its ability to catalyze the reduction of pyruvate in the presence of NADH. In myocardial infarction, the concentration of serum LD rises within 24 hours of the occurrence of the infarct and returns to the normal range within 5–6 days. High levels of LD also occur in patients with acute and chronic leukemia in relapse, generalized carcinomatosis, and, occasionally, with acute hepatitis during its clinical peak, but not in patients with jaundice due to other causes. Serum LD is normal in patients with acute febrile and chronic infectious diseases as well as those with anemia, pulmonary infarction, localized neoplastic disease, and chronic disease processes.

I. LD Isozymes: Cardiac muscle contains a preponderance of one form of lactic dehydrogenase (designated LD-I_1). By measurement of the plasma isozyme pattern (Fig 6–28) it has been discovered that

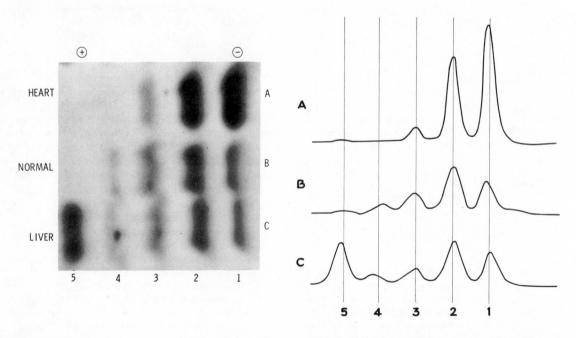

Figure 6–28. Normal and pathologic patterns of lactate dehydrogenase isozymes in human serum. LDH isozymes of serum were separated on cellulose acetate at pH 8.6 and stained for enzyme. The photometer scan shows the relative proportion of the isozymes. Pattern A is serum from a patient with a myocardial infarct, B is normal serum, and C is serum from a patient with liver disease. (Courtesy of Dr Melvin Black & Mr Hugh Miller, St Luke's Hospital, San Francisco.)

the pattern found in the course of myocardial infarction appears to be a more sensitive and lasting indication of myocardial necrosis than is simple measurement of the total serum or plasma lactate dehydrogenase activity.

J. Isocitrate Dehydrogenase: Measurement of serum **isocitric dehydrogenase** activity (ICD) has been found useful in the diagnosis of liver disease. The isocitric dehydrogenase levels of cerebrospinal fluid are also elevated in patients with cerebral tumors or meningitis of various types. With tumors, the values are about 10 times normal. With meningitis, the values may be as much as 50 times normal, but gradually decrease to normal as the patient recovers.

K. Creatine Phosphokinase: The measurement of serum creatine phosphokinase (CK or CPK) activity is of value in the diagnosis of disorders affecting skeletal and cardiac muscle as well as in studies of families affected with pseudohypertrophic muscular dystrophy. Nonmuscular tissues other than brain do not contain high levels of creatine phosphokinase, so that determinations of activity of this enzyme should be more specific to particular tissues than the transaminases or dehydrogenases which are more widely distributed. In human tissue, CK exists as 3 different dimeric isozymes composed of M (for muscle) and B (for brain) protomers. These are designated CK_1 (BB), CK_2 (MB), and CK_3 (MM). While measurement of CK levels is relatively routine in confirming a diagnosis of myocardial infarction, determination of differential levels of CK isozymes—as with LD—provides valuable additional information. In addition to electrophoretic separation (see Fig 6–28), CK isozymes may be separated by a variety of batch and column ion exchange chromatographic technics.

In normal individuals, the MB isozyme accounts for no more than about 2% of the total CK of plasma. By contrast, MB accounts for 4.5–20% of the total CK in plasma of patients with a recent myocardial infarct, and the total MB isozyme level is elevated up to 20-fold above normal.

L. Ceruloplasmin: This copper-containing serum globulin shows oxidase activity **in vitro** toward several amines, including epinephrine, 5-hydroxytryptamine, and dihydroxyphenylalanine. Plasma ceruloplasmin levels, determined as oxidase activity, are elevated in several circumstances, such as cirrhosis, hepatitis, bacterial infections, pregnancy, etc. Decreased levels, however, provide a useful confirmatory test for Wilson's disease (hepatolenticular degeneration).

● ● ●

References

Kinetics

Cleland WW: The statistical analysis of enzyme kinetic data. Adv Enzymol 29:1, 1967.

Cleland WW: Enzyme kinetics. Annu Rev Biochem 36:77, 1967.

Garfinkel D & others: Computer applications to biochemical kinetics. Annu Rev Biochem 39:473, 1970.

Piszkiwicz D: *Kinetics of Chemical and Enzyme-Catalyzed Reactions.* Oxford Univ Press, 1977.

Inhibitors

Webb JL: *Enzyme and Metabolic Inhibitors.* 2 vols. Academic Press, 1966.

The Active Site

Koshland DE Jr, Neet KE: The catalytic and regulatory properties of enzymes. Annu Rev Biochem 37:359, 1968.

Vallee BL, Riordan JF: Chemical approaches to the active sites of enzymes. Annu Rev Biochem 38:733, 1969.

Isozymes

Katunuma N & others: Regulation of glutaminase activity and differentiation of the isozyme during development. Adv Enzyme Regul 6:227, 1968.

Moog F, Vire HR, Grey RD: The multiple forms of alkaline phosphatase in the small intestine of the young mouse. Biochem Biophys Acta 113:336, 1966.

Multiple molecular forms of enzymes. Ann NY Acad Sci 94:art 3, 1961.

Stambaugh R, Post D: Substrate and product inhibition of rabbit muscle lactic dehydrogenase heart (H_4) and muscle (M_4) isozymes. J Biol Chem 241:1462, 1966.

Clinical Enzymology

Brewer GJ, Sing CF: *An Introduction to Isozyme Techniques.* Academic Press, 1970.

Crowley LV: Creatine phosphokinase activity in myocardial infarction, heart failure, and following various diagnostic and therapeutic procedures. Clin Chem 14:1185, 1968.

Esnouf MP, McFarlane RG: Enzymology and the blood clotting mechanism. Adv Enzymol 30:255, 1968.

Latner AL, Skiller AW: *Isozymes in Biology and Medicine.* Academic Press, 1968.

Wacker WEC, Coombs TL: Clinical biochemistry: Enzymatic methods: Automation and atomic adsorption spectroscopy. Annu Rev Biochem 38:539, 1969.

Weil-Malherbe H: The biochemistry of the functional psychoses. Adv Enzymol 29:479, 1967.

Wenner CE: Progress in tumor enzymology. Adv Enzymol 29:321, 1967.

Wilkinson JH: Clinical applications of isozymes. Clin Chem 16:733, 1970.

Wilkinson JH: Clinical significance of enzyme activity measurements. Clin Chem 16:882, 1970.

7 . . .
Regulation of Enzyme Activity

PHYSIOLOGIC ROLE
OF METABOLIC REGULATION

The Concept of Homeostasis

The concept of homeostatic regulation of the internal milieu advanced by Claude Bernard in the latter half of the 19th century stressed the ability of animals to maintain the constancy of their intracellular environments. This implies not only that all the necessary enzyme-catalyzed reactions proceed, but that they proceed at rates responsive to changes in both the internal and external environment. A cell or organism might be defined as diseased when it fails to respond or responds inadequately or incorrectly to an internal or external stress. Knowledge of factors affecting the rates of enzyme-catalyzed reactions is essential not only to understand homeostasis in normal cells but also to comprehend the molecular basis of disease.

All chemical reactions, including enzyme-catalyzed reactions, are to some extent reversible.* Within living cells, however, reversibility may not in fact occur because reaction products are promptly removed by further reactions catalyzed by other

enzymes. The flow of metabolites in a living cell is analogous to the flow of water in a water main. Although the main can transfer water in either direction, in practice the flow is unidirectional. Metabolite flow in the living cell also is largely unidirectional. True equilibrium, far from being characteristic of life, is approached only on the death of the cell.

The living cell is a steady-state system maintained by a unidirectional flow of metabolites (Fig 7–1). In the mature cell, the average concentration of a particular chemical compound remains relatively constant over considerable periods of time.* The flexibility of the steady-state system is well illustrated in the delicate shifts and balances by which an organism maintains the constancy of the internal environment in spite of wide variations in food, water, and mineral intake, work output, or external temperature.

Scope of Metabolic Regulation

For life to proceed in an orderly fashion, the flow of metabolites through anabolic and catabolic pathways must be regulated. Our concept of normal life incorporates the idea not only that all the requisite chemical events occur but also that they proceed at

*A readily reversible reaction has a small numerical value of ΔG. One with a large negative value for ΔG (> -5000 cal) might be termed "effectively irreversible" in most biochemical situations.

*Short-term oscillations of metabolite concentrations and of enzyme levels do occur, however, and are of profound physiologic importance.

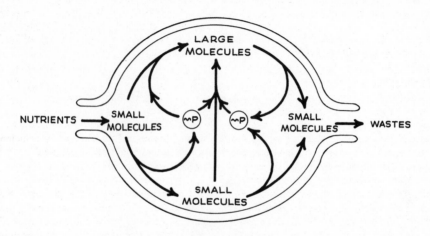

Figure 7–1. An idealized cell in steady state.

rates consistent with the activities and requirements of the intact organism in relation to its environment. Events such as ATP production, synthesis of macromolecular precursors, transport, secretion, and tubular reabsorption all must be responsive to subtle changes in the environment at the cellular, organ, and intact animal level. These processes must be coordinated and, in addition, must respond to short-term changes in the external environment (such as the addition or removal of an essential nutrient) as well as to periodic intracellular events (such as DNA production prior to cell division). The mechanisms by which cells and intact organisms regulate and coordinate overall metabolism are of concern to biochemists with as seemingly diverse research interests as cancer, heart disease, aging, microbial physiology, differentiation and metamorphosis, or the mechanism of hormone action. At present, the molecular details of regulation are best understood in microorganisms (particularly bacteria), which appear to lack the complexities of rapid protein turnover or of hormonal or nervous control that exist in higher animal systems.

While a knowledge of cellular regulatory processes in man is central to an understanding of metabolic diseases as well as to the therapeutic rationale, the molecular events that occur in the regulation of most metabolic processes in mammalian cells are little understood at present. It is clear, furthermore, that metabolic regulation in mammals differs significantly in detail even from superficially similar phenomena in bacteria. In the sections that follow, the regulation of metabolic processes in bacteria will be emphasized to a degree that may seem inappropriate to a book written with the interest of individuals concerned with human biology in mind. This emphasis is not intended to imply that metabolic regulation in man and other higher animals necessarily involves mechanisms identical to or even closely resembling those in bacteria. Although many analogies may be drawn, metabolic regulation in bacteria has relevance to mammals primarily because it has given rise to concepts which provide a conceptual framework for considering regulation in man. Throughout this section, the extent to which these concepts appear to be applicable—or nonapplicable—to man are noted.

In this chapter, the mechanisms are described by which metabolic processes are regulated via enzymes. These are illustrated by selected examples. The intention is to characterize the overall patterns of regulation that occur in cells and to convey some sense of the considerable progress achieved in this field in recent years. Throughout this book, reference is made to many other specific examples to illustrate these features of metabolic regulation in various areas of metabolism. Although it is hoped ultimately to explain physiologic processes in terms of simple chemical events, our present knowledge of the chemical and physical factors responsible for enzyme specificity, catalytic efficiency, and regulation of enzyme activity is incomplete, although in recent years substantial progress has been made.

AVAILABLE OPTIONS FOR REGULATION OF ENZYMES

Broadly speaking, the net flow of carbon through any enzyme-catalyzed reaction might be influenced (1) by changing the absolute quantity of enzyme present, (2) by altering the pool size of reactants other than enzyme, and (3) by altering the catalytic efficiency of the enzyme.

It will be shown that all 3 options are exploited in some form of life.

REGULATION OF ENZYME QUANTITY

General Principles

The absolute quantity of a given enzyme present in a cell at a particular time is determined by its rate of synthesis (k_s) and the rate of its degradation (k_d). (Fig 7—2.) The level of an enzyme in a cell may therefore

Figure 7—2. Regulation of enzyme quantity is determined by the net balance between enzyme synthesis and enzyme degradation.

be raised either by an increase in its rate of synthesis (increase in k_s), by a decrease in its rate of degradation (decrease in k_d), or by both effects together. Similarly, a lowered enzyme level can result from a decrease in k_s, an increase in k_d, or both. In all forms of life, enzyme (protein) synthesis from amino acids and enzyme (protein) degradation to amino acids are distinct processes catalyzed by entirely different sets of enzymes. Independent regulation of enzyme synthesis and enzyme degradation is thus readily achieved.

Outlined first are those factors that result in a net increase in the quantity of enzyme present, followed by those that result in a net decrease.

Control of Enzyme Synthesis: Genetic Basis

The primary structure of an enzyme, like that of other proteins, is dictated by the trinucleotide (triplet) code of messenger RNA attached to polyribosomes and by the matching bases of a transfer RNA-amino acid complex (see Chapter 25). The sequence of purine and pyrimidine bases of the messenger RNA is in turn dictated by a complementary base sequence that is part of a master DNA template or gene in the nucleus of the cell. Information for protein synthesis, stored in DNA, thus determines a cell's ability to synthesize a particular enzyme. One gene generally codes for one polypeptide, and 2 genes for a protein containing 2 dissimilar polypeptides. However, in 1977 Sanger announced the startling news that portions of the bacteriophage ϕX174 code not for one but for 2 **different polypeptides**. For example, the sequence **GAAUAGA** is read **both** as GAA-UAG and as AAU-AGA. While they may not prove true for life forms other than ϕX174, Sanger's observation destroys the generality of a widely held concept, ie, that one gene always codes for a single polypeptide.

The secondary, tertiary, and quaternary structure of enzymes may be dictated by the primary structure. It appears that, although many conformations are possible, the biologically active form is that with the lowest energy level and greatest stability. Supporting evidence that the **lowest energy conformation** (3-dimensional structure) may be the biologically active form includes the ability of several enzymes whose active conformations have been destroyed by mild denaturation (see Chapter 4) to regain activity on prolonged standing under conditions favoring breaking and reformation of secondary bonds. Assuming low energy conformations to be biologically active forms, computer programs have been designed which predict low-energy structures from the primary sequence and a limited amount of other data. These structures may then be projected on an oscilloscope screen and viewed from any angle. The ultimate aim of this approach is to predict correct, enzymically active conformations from primary structure data alone. At present, it is not necessary to postulate independent genetic control of orders of protein structure above the primary level.

A genetic **mutation** alters the DNA code and results in synthesis of a protein molecule with a modified primary structure. On occasion, this may result in altered structure at higher orders of organization also. Particularly if the new amino acid is significantly different from the old, changes in higher orders of structure may result. Depending on the nature of the structural change, a mutation may cause partial or complete loss of catalytic activity. Very rarely, a mutation may result in enhanced catalytic activity, as is sometimes seen in revertants of bacterial mutants to modified wild-types. Provided the mutation results in change which is not lethal, the modified genetic information is transmitted to the progeny of the cell. As a result, there frequently arises a **transmissible metabolic defect** which occurs at that step formerly catalyzed by the now defective enzyme. Examples of these inherited "molecular diseases" (Pauling) or "inborn errors of metabolism" (Garrod) include phenylketonuria, alkaptonuria, pentosuria, galactosemia, cystinuria, maple syrup urine disease, and the glycogen storage diseases. Many more heritable diseases are thought to be due to this phenomenon.

A much studied inherited defect is the formation in man of one or another of a variety of **abnormal hemoglobin molecules**. Some abnormal hemoglobins are of no clinical significance. With others, such as hemoglobin S, homozygous inheritance of the defect may result in early death, while the heterozygote (sickle cell trait) may experience only a mild anemia, although this is rare.

Since mutations at various genetic loci can produce an enzyme with impaired activity, in theory an almost infinitely large number of molecular diseases can result. However, not all genetic loci appear to be equally susceptible to mutagenic agents, and code changes tend to cluster about particular regions of a gene. Some portions of a polypeptide chain are therefore more susceptible to change than others.

Control of Enzyme Synthesis: Induction

For a molecule to be metabolized or for an inducer to act, it first must enter the cell. In some cases, a specific transport system or **permease** is needed. The permease itself may be inducible. Permeases share many properties in common with enzymes and appear to perform functions analogous to the cytochromes in electron transport insofar as they appear to transport substrates without causing a net change in substrate structure.

The phenomenon of enzyme induction is illustrated by the following experiment: *Escherichia coli* grown on glucose will not ferment lactose. Its inability to do so is due to the absence both of a specific permease for a β-galactoside (lactose) and of the enzyme β-galactosidase, which hydrolyzes lactose to glucose and galactose. If lactose or certain other β-galactosides are added to the medium during growth, both the permease and the β-galactosidase are induced and the culture can now ferment lactose.

In the example given, the inducer (lactose) is a substrate for the induced proteins, the permease, and the β-galactosidase. Although in general inducers serve as substrates for the enzymes or permeases they induce, compounds structurally similar to the substrate may be inducers but not substrates. These are termed **gratuitous inducers**. Conversely, a compound may be a substrate but not an inducer.

Frequently, a compound induces several enzymes which form part of a catabolic pathway. In the case cited above, β-galactoside permease and β-galactosidase were both induced by lactose.

Enzymes whose concentration in a cell is independent of an added inducer are termed **constitutive enzymes**. A particular enzyme may be constitutive in one strain of an organism, inducible in another, and neither constitutive nor inducible (ie, totally absent) in a third.

Cells capable of being induced for a particular enzyme always contain a small measurable **basal level** of the inducible enzyme even when grown in the absence of added inducer. The extent to which a particular organism responds to the presence of an inducer is also genetically determined and varies greatly from strain to strain. Increases in enzyme content ranging from 2- to 1000-fold may be observed on induction in different strains. The genetic heritage of the cell thus determines not only the nature but also the magnitude of the response to an inducer. The terms "constitutive" and "inducible" are therefore relative terms, like "hot" and "cold," which represent the extremes of a spectrum of responses to added inducers.

Bacteria exhibit complex patterns of enzyme induction of degradative enzymes. While the inducer frequently is either a substrate or the product of the inducible enzyme, this is not always the case. Examples of induction by the substrate, by the product, or by further products of catabolism all are well documented in bacteria. Where the inducer is something other than the substrate (eg, a product formed from the substrate), the formation of the inducer is thought to occur via the activity of low, basal levels of the inducible enzyme or enzymes required.

Variations in induction patterns in bacteria also occur at the genetic level. Where the structural genes which specify a group of catabolic enzymes comprise an operon, all of the enzymes of that operon are induced by a single inducer. This phenomenon is termed **coordinate induction.**

Examples of inducible enzymes in animals are tryptophan pyrrolase, threonine dehydrase, tyrosine-*a*-ketoglutaric transaminase, invertase, and enzymes of the urea cycle. An important example in bacteria is the inducible penicillinase that provides *Bacillus cereus* with a defense against penicillin.

Induction permits a microorganism to respond to the presence of a given nutrient in the surrounding medium by producing enzymes for its catabolism. In the absence of the inducer, little or no enzyme is produced. The ability to avoid synthesis of the enzyme in the absence of the nutrient permits the bacterium to use its available nutrients to maximum advantage, ie, it does not synthesize "unnecessary enzymes."

The genetic alternative to induction is **constitutivity,** the production of enzyme independent of the presence of small molecules acting as inducers.

Control of Enzyme Synthesis:
Repression & Derepression

In bacteria capable of synthesizing a particular amino acid, the presence of that amino acid in the culture medium curtails new synthesis of that amino acid via **repression.** The phenomenon is not restricted to amino acids and may operate in all biosynthetic pathways in microorganisms. A small molecule such as histidine or leucine, acting as a **corepressor,** can ultimately block the synthesis of the enzymes involved in its own biosynthesis.

In *Salmonella typhimurium,* addition of histidine represses the synthesis of all the enzymes of histidine biosynthesis, and addition of leucine represses synthesis of the first 3 enzymes unique to leucine biosynthesis. In both cases, these biosynthetic enzymes comprise **operons; coordinate repression** occurs following addition of the end products histidine or leucine. However, coordinate repression is not general for all biosynthetic pathways since the genetic information specifying the structure of biosynthetic enzymes may be organized into more than one operon. Following removal or exhaustion of an essential biosynthetic intermediate from the medium, the genetic information coding for the biosynthesis of enzymes is again expressed. This constitutes what is termed **derepression.** Depending on how many operons are involved, this derepression may be coordinate or noncoordinate.

In the above examples, histidine and leucine were used to illustrate the **product feedback repression** characteristic of biosynthetic pathways in bacteria. **Catabolite repression** is a related phenomenon that refers to the ability of a product or intermediate in a sequence of **catabolic** enzyme-catalyzed reactions to repress the synthesis of some or all of the catabolic enzymes concerned. This effect was first noted in cultures of *E coli* growing on a carbon source (X) other than glucose. It was observed that addition of glucose repressed the synthesis of the enzymes concerned with catabolism of X, and this phenomenon was initially termed the "glucose effect." With the recognition that many oxidizable nutrients other than glucose produced similar effects and that a catabolite of glucose (rather than glucose itself) was responsible for the repression observed, the term **catabolite repression** was adopted.

It is thought that the actual repressor substance is a macromolecule such as a protein, a nucleic acid, or a nucleoprotein which can bind the corepressor. In the absence of the corepressor, the macromolecule does not repress enzyme synthesis.

Examples are noted of the control the uptake of nutrients (mediated by permeases) may exert on the many reactions in intermediary metabolism and on the synthesis of large molecules. An organism capable of efficiently using substrates under a wide variety of conditions obviously has a biologic advantage. This may explain the widespread occurrence of these specific control mechanisms among living systems.

In branched or multiple-branched biosynthetic pathways such as those of the branched chain amino acids or the glutamate or aspartate families of amino acids, early enzymes of the biosynthetic pathways function in the biosynthesis of several amino acids. This is illustrated in Fig 7–3 for the aspartate family of amino acids.

Following addition of lysine to the medium of growing bacteria, synthesis of the enzymes unique to

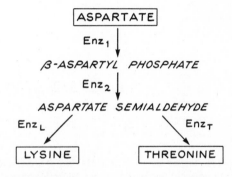

Figure 7–3. A portion of the aspartate family of amino acids. Enz_L and Enz_T denote groups of enzymes involved in lysine and threonine biosynthesis, respectively.

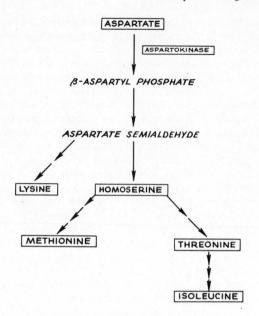

Figure 7—4. The aspartate family of amino acids.

lysine biosynthesis (Enz$_L$) are repressed. A similar repression of the enzymes unique to threonine biosynthesis (Enz$_T$) follows addition of threonine to the medium. These effects illustrate the simple product feedback repression just discussed. Enzymes Enz$_1$ and Enz$_2$, however, function both in lysine and in threonine biosynthesis. Product feedback repression of their synthesis by either lysine or threonine alone would therefore starve the bacterium of the other amino acid. If, however, both lysine and threonine are added to the medium, Enz$_1$ and Enz$_2$ become redundant, and repression of synthesis of Enz$_1$ and Enz$_2$ could be advantageous to survival of the organism, since it would permit more efficient use of available nutrients.

In the presence of all necessary end products of a branched or multiple-branched biosynthetic pathway, a phenomenon known as **multivalent repression** may occur. This occurs when, and only when, all end products of a particular set of biosynthetic enzymes are present in ample supply. How multivalent repression is

achieved, whether by binding of several end products to a single aporepressor or by other means, is not known. In Fig 7—3, a portion of the aspartate biosynthetic family was intentionally deleted to facilitate discussion. A more complete scheme is shown in Fig 7—4.

Complete repression of aspartokinase should therefore require methionine and isoleucine in addition to lysine and threonine. The concept of multivalent repression can, in principle, be extended to the hypothetical example shown in Fig 7—5.

As will be discussed below, multivalent feedback effects also occur with a second regulatory device, feedback inhibition.

Enzyme Turnover

In rapidly growing bacteria, the overall rate of protein degradation is relatively low (about 2% of the total cellular protein is degraded per hour), and control of enzyme levels appears to be achieved primarily by increases or decreases in rates of enzyme synthesis. This is not true for starving bacteria or for bacteria transferred to fresh medium providing a poorer source of carbon for growth (the so-called "stepdown culture"). Under these conditions, bacteria degrade protein at much faster rates (7—10% per hour).

The combined processes of enzyme synthesis and degradation constitute **enzyme turnover**. While turnover occurs both in bacteria and mammals, the importance of enzyme degradation as a device by which enzyme levels are regulated in bacteria has received little emphasis. This is not true for mammals, where turnover of protein was recognized as a characteristic property of all mammalian cells long before it was shown also to occur in bacteria. The existence of protein (enzyme) turnover in man was deduced from dietary experiments well over a century ago. It was, however, Schoenheimer's classical work, just prior to and during World War II, that conclusively established that turnover of cellular protein occurred throughout life. By measuring the rates of incorporation of ^{15}N-labeled amino acids into protein and the rates of loss of ^{15}N from protein, Schoenheimer deduced that body proteins are in a state of "dynamic equilibrium," a concept since extended to other body constituents, including lipids and nucleic acids.

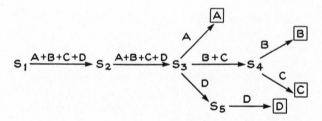

Figure 7—5. Representation of probable sites of repression in a hypothetical branched biosynthetic pathway in bacteria. $S_1 - S_5$ represent metabolic intermediates in the synthesis of the end products A–D, and the arrows represent the enzymes catalyzing the indicated reactions. Shown over the arrows are the end products whose presence in the medium should cause product feedback repression of synthesis of a particular enzyme. Where only a single product is required, simple repression is involved. Where 2 or more products are required, the repression is said to be multivalent.

In man and other animals, the regulation of intracellular levels of enzymes thus involves regulation both of enzyme synthesis and of enzyme degradation. The molecular details of these regulatory processes are, however, imperfectly understood at present. While the major events in protein synthesis are well understood, those involved in enzyme degradation are not. Enzyme degradation is known to involve hydrolysis by proteolytic enzymes, but little is known of the processes by which proteolytic activity is regulated. In some cases, the susceptibility of an enzyme to proteolytic degradation depends upon its conformation. The presence or absence of small molecules—such as substrates, coenzymes, or metal ions—which can alter protein conformation may thus alter proteolytic susceptibility. In certain cases, the presence of high levels of these small molecules renders mammalian enzymes insensitive to proteolytic attack. The concentrations of substrates, coenzymes, and possibly ions in cells may thus determine to a considerable extent the rates at which specific enzymes are degraded in mammalian cells. Two mammalian enzymes, arginase and tryptophan oxygenase (tryptophan pyrrolase), illustrate these concepts. The regulation of liver arginase levels can involve a change either in k_s or in k_d. Following ingestion of a diet rich in protein, liver arginase levels rise; this rise is known to result from an increased rate of arginase synthesis. Liver arginase levels also rise in starved animals. Here, however, it is arginase degradation that is decreased, while k_s remains unchanged. In a second example, injection of glucocorticoids and ingestion of tryptophan both result in elevated levels of tryptophan oxygenase in mammals. The effect of the hormones is to raise the rate of oxygenase synthesis (raise k_s). Tryptophan, however, has no effect on k_s but lowers k_d by stabilizing the oxygenase toward proteolytic digestion. These 2 examples should be contrasted with the previous section on enzyme induction in bacteria. In the case of arginase, the increased intake of nitrogen on a high-protein diet may elevate liver arginase levels (see Regulation of the Urea Cycle, Chapter 21). The increased rate of arginase synthesis thus superficially resembles that of substrate induction in bacteria. In the case of tryptophan pyrrolase, however, even though tryptophan may act as an inducer in bacteria (affects k_s), its effect in mammals is solely on the enzyme degradative process (affects k_d).

There is now a considerable body of evidence that enzyme levels in mammalian tissues may be altered by a wide range of physiologic, hormonal, or dietary manipulations. Examples are known for a variety of tissues and metabolic pathways (Table 7–1), but our

Table 7–1. Selected examples of rat liver enzymes which adapt to an environmental stimulus by changes in activity.*

Enzyme	E.C. Number	t½	Stimulus	Fold Change
Amino acid metabolism				
Arginase	3.5.3.1	4–5 days	Starvation or glucocorticoids.	+2
			Change from high- to low-protein diet.	−2
Alanine transaminase	2.6.1.2	3.5 days	Glucocorticoids.	+5
Serine dehydratase	4.2.1.13	20 hours	Glucagon or dietary amino acids.	+100
Tyrosine transaminase	2.6.1.5	1.5 hours	Glucocorticoids, glucagon, or insulin.	+4
Ornithine transaminase	2.6.1.13	20 hours	Glucocorticoids, dietary amino acids, or high-protein diet.	+20
Histidase	4.3.1.3	2.5 days	Change from low- to high-protein diet.	+20
Carbohydrate metabolism				
Glucokinase	2.7.1.2		Starvation or alloxan diabetes.	−5
			Re-fed glucose or insulin to diabetic.	+5
PEP-pyruvate carboxykinase	4.1.1.32		Insulin to diabetic rat.	+4
Glucose-6-P dehydrogenase	1.1.1.49	15 hours	Thyroid hormone or fasted rats re-fed a high-carbohydrate diet.	+10
α-Glycerophosphate dehydrogenase	1.1.2.1	4 days	Thyroid hormone.	+10
Malate:NADP dehydrogenase	1.1.1.40	4 days	Thyroid hormone.	+10
Fructose-1,6-phosphatase	3.1.3.11		Glucose.	+10
Lipid metabolism				
Citrate cleavage enzyme	4.1.3.8		Starved rats re-fed a high-carbohydrate, low-fat diet.	+30
Fatty acid synthetase			Starvation.	−10
			Starved animals re-fed a fat-free diet.	+30
HMG-CoA reductase	1.1.1.34	2–3 hours	Fasting or 5% cholesterol diet.	−10
			Twenty-four hour diurnal variation.	±10
			Insulin or thyroid hormone.	+2 to 10
Purine or pyrimidine metabolism				
Xanthine oxidase	1.2.3.2		Change to high-protein diet.	−10
Aspartate transcarbamoylase	2.1.3.2	2.5 days	One percent orotic acid diet.	+2
Dihydroorotase	3.5.2.3	12 hours	One percent orotic acid diet.	+3

*Data, with the exception of that for HMG-CoA reductase, from Schimke RT, Doyle D: Annu Rev Biochem 39:929, 1970.

knowledge of the molecular details which account for these changes is fragmentary.

Glucocorticoids increase the concentration of tyrosine transaminase by stimulating its rate of synthesis. This was the first clear case of a hormone regulating the synthesis of a mammalian enzyme. Insulin and glucagon—despite their mutually antagonistic physiologic effects—both independently increase the rate of synthesis 4- to 5-fold. The effect of glucagon probably is mediated via cyclic AMP since this can mimic the effect of the hormone in organ cultures of rat liver.

As discussed above, tryptophan does not affect the rate of tryptophan pyrrolase synthesis but retards its degradation. Hydrocortisone, however, increases the rate of enzyme synthesis 5-fold. Glucocorticoids appear to act in a similar manner with respect to hepatic glutamate-pyruvate transaminase. The rate of synthesis is increased without apparent effects on the rate of degradation.

The activity of δ-aminolevulinate synthetase, the first enzyme of heme biosynthesis, is increased as much as 50-fold by drugs which produce experimental porphyria, and this effect is blocked by glucose. Although the exact site of regulation is not known, the extremely short half-life (t½ = 1 hour) suggests control of enzyme degradation as a plausible site.

REGULATION OF THE CATALYTIC EFFICIENCY OF ENZYMES

Definition of Terms

In many texts, this section is referred to as "regulation of enzyme activity." The term "activity" is, however, somewhat ambiguous in certain instances. When we assay a tissue extract for an enzyme, we say that there is a certain activity present. If, as a result of physiologic manipulation, this measured activity changes, we have no way of knowing whether the quantity of enzyme has changed or whether the enzyme present is a more or less effective catalyst. **We shall refer to all changes in enzyme activity that occur without any change in the quantity of enzyme present as "effects on catalytic efficiency."**

Proenzymes

One method for the regulation of enzyme activity that has been known for a long time is the synthesis of the enzyme in a catalytically inactive or proenzyme form. To become catalytically active, the proenzyme must undergo limited proteolysis, a process attended by conformational changes that either reveal or, so to speak, "create" the catalytic site. The phenomenon of synthesis as a catalytically inactive proenzyme is best illustrated by certain digestive enzymes, as well as by enzymes of blood coagulation and of blood clot dissolution. This phenomenon is not restricted to proteolytic enzymes, as is suggested by the existence of pro-

insulin, a hormonally inactive insulin precursor that must undergo limited proteolysis before active insulin is produced (see Chapter 29).

Conversion of the proenzyme to the active enzyme is catalyzed either by proteolytic enzymes or by hydrogen ions (Fig 7–6).

Pepsinogen $\xrightarrow{\text{H}^+ \text{ or pepsin}}$ Pepsin

Trypsinogen $\xrightarrow{\text{Trypsin or enterokinase}}$ Trypsin

Chymotrypsinogen $\xrightarrow{\text{Trypsin}}$ Chymotrypsin

Procarboxypeptidase $\xrightarrow{\text{Trypsin}}$ Carboxypeptidase

Figure 7–6. Conversion of digestive proenzymes to the active proteases. Since activation of the enzyme precursor is catalyzed by the active form of the enzyme itself, the activation of pepsinogen and of trypsinogen proceeds with ever-increasing velocity and is said to be **autocatalytic.**

Conversion of fibrinogen to fibrin involves limited proteolysis catalyzed by thrombin. Under normal physiologic conditions, thrombin exists as the inactive precursor, prothrombin, and its activation requires a complex sequence of reactions. These involve a cascade of activation reactions, many of which involve proteolysis. Limited proteolysis is thus one key regulatory factor in the complex process of blood coagulation.

The activation process involves hydrolysis of peptide bonds, and it results in "unmasking" the active or catalytic center of the enzyme protein. Frequently, large portions of the proenzyme are removed on activation. The conversion of pepsinogen (molecular weight of 42,500) to pepsin (molecular weight of 34,500) involves the loss of almost one-fifth of the molecule. Similarly, the conversion of procarboxypeptidase to carboxypeptidase is accompanied by a drop in molecular weight from 96,000 to 34,300, a decrease of two-thirds. The conversion of trypsinogen to trypsin, however, involves the removal of only 6 amino acids. Certain nondigestive enzymes, eg, a bacterial histidase, may under certain conditions exist in an inactive proenzyme form.

Viewed as a physiologic control mechanism, synthesis of inactive enzyme precursors provides a mechanism for rapidly increasing the availability of an enzyme in response to physiologic demand. It would be serious, for example, if the enzymes of blood coagulation had first to be provided by the somewhat slower process of protein synthesis.

Treatment of several regulated enzymes by proteolytic enzymes can, in addition, mimic the effects of other forms of regulation. For example, the activation of phosphorylase b kinase or the conversion of the glucose 6-phosphate-dependent form of glycogen synthetase to the independent form may be achieved by limited proteolysis.

REGULATION OF CATALYTIC EFFICIENCY: AVAILABILITY OF REACTANTS

General Principles

The kinetic and regulatory properties of enzymes described in this and the 2 preceding chapters has value both in its own right and with respect to insights into physiologic processes in intact cells, tissues, and organisms. It is important to remember, however, that most available information was obtained by studying enzymes in free solution under conditions that differ substantially from those prevailing in living cells. The applicability of this knowledge to the in vivo situation must therefore be approached with considerable caution. One major reservation is that there generally is an enormous gap between the concentrations of substrates studied in vitro and those that actually prevail in vivo. Much of our knowledge is thus unfortunately restricted to conditions that cannot occur in living cells.

Role of Enzyme Compartmentation

The importance of compartmentation of metabolic processes in eukaryotic cells, including those of mammals, cannot be overemphasized. The localization of specific metabolic processes in the cytosol or within specific cellular organelles permits regulation of these processes independent of processes proceeding elsewhere. Product formed or utilized by a cytosolic metabolic process thus may be unavailable for mitochondrial processes and vice versa. The extensive compartmentalization of metabolic processes characteristic of higher forms of life carries with it the potential for a sophisticated and finely tuned regulation of metabolism. At the same time, it poses problems with respect to the translocation of essential metabolites across compartmental barriers. This is achieved via "shuttle mechanisms." In general, these shuttle mechanisms involve conversion of the material to be translocated to a form permeable to the compartmental barrier. This is followed by transport and conversion back to the original form on the other side of the barrier. Consequently, these interconversions require, for example, cytosolic and mitochondrial forms of the same catalytic activity. Since these 2 forms of the enzyme are physically separated from one another, their independent regulation is thereby facilitated. The role of "shuttle mechanisms" in achieving equilibration of metabolic pools of reducing equivalents, of citric acid cycle intermediates (see Chapter 18), and of other amphibolic intermediates is discussed in detail elsewhere in this book.

Regulatory Implications of Macromolecular Complexes

Organization of enzymes catalyzing a protracted sequence of metabolic reactions as a macromolecular complex serves to coordinate the activities of the enzymes concerned and to channel intermediates along a chosen metabolic path. Appropriate alignment of the enzymes can facilitate transfer of product from one enzyme to another without prior equilibration with metabolic pools of the intermediate concerned. This permits a finer level of metabolic control than is possible with the isolated components of the complex. In addition, conformational changes in one component of the complex may be transmitted by protein-protein interactions to other enzymes of the complex. Amplification of regulatory effects is thus readily achieved.

Effective Concentrations of Substrates & Coenzymes

From the preceding discussion of cellular compartmentation, it is clear that data for the **mean** cellular concentration of a substrate, coenzyme, or metal ion may have little or no meaning with respect to explaining the behavior of an enzyme in vivo. Information on the concentrations of essential metabolites **in the immediate neighborhood of the enzyme in question** is what is needed. As a first approximation, this implies measuring metabolite concentrations in different cellular compartments. However, even this does not account for local discontinuities in metabolite concentrations within compartments, brought about by factors such as proximity to the site of entry or of the production of a metabolite. Finally, little consideration is generally given to the often large discrepancy between total metabolite concentration and the concentration of the metabolite present in the free state (ie, available metabolite). To cite an example, the total concentration of 2,3-diphosphoglycerate in erythrocytes is extremely high, although the concentration of free diphosphoglycerate is probably comparable to that of other tissues. This arises from the presence in erythrocytes of approximately 5 mmol of hemoglobin, which binds 4 mol of diphosphoglycerate per mol of tetramer. For this concentration of hemoglobin, a **total** concentration of 20 mmol of diphosphoglycerate would result in a minuscule concentration of **free** diphosphoglycerate. While this is an extreme example, similar considerations apply to other metabolites in the presence of significant quantities of proteins that bind them effectively and reduce their concentration in the free state accordingly.

It will be recalled that one of the basic assumptions of the Michaelis kinetic approach was that the concentration of total substrate was essentially equal to the concentration of free substrate. As noted above, this assumption may well be invalid for in vivo situations. A second consequence is that the concentrations of free substrates in vivo often are of the same order of magnitude as those of the enzyme concentration in vivo. A more sophisticated kinetic approach for in vivo situations employs an equation of the Michaelis-Menten form, but assumes steady-state kinetics:

$$v = \frac{kE_t S_f}{K_m + S_f}$$

where S_f, the concentration of free substrate, is substituted for S. However, the application of this equation is hampered by the absence of exact values for S_f in the neighborhood of the enzyme in question. Also, it applies only to an unconstrained solution of enzyme, a situation that is not valid for macromolecular complexes.

Metal Ions

As is discussed in Chapter 6, metal ions perform key catalytic and structural roles in over one-fourth of all known enzymes. Particularly where a specific metal ion is required, ions may therefore be said to fulfill a regulatory role. This is particularly notable for reactions where ATP is a substrate. In many cases, the ATP-metal ion complex is the substrate for the reaction, and maximal activity is observed when the molar ratio of ATP to metal is about unity. Excess metal or excess ATP frequently is inhibitory. Since nucleoside diphosphates and triphosphates form stable complexes with divalent metal ions, the intracellular concentrations of the nucleotides represent one factor which can influence intracellular concentrations of free metal ions and hence regulate the activity of certain enzymes. Bacterial glutamine synthetase offers one well-documented example of metal ion regulation of enzyme activity. In the absence of metal ions, *E coli* glutamine synthetase assumes a "relaxed" configuration that is catalytically inactive. Addition of Mg^{2+} or Mn^{2+} converts the synthetase to the active, "tightened" form. In addition to metal ion regulation of these conformational changes, adenylation of the synthetase causes a complete change in divalent cation specificity. The unadenylated synthetase requires Mg^{2+}, whereas the adenylated form specifically requires Mn^{2+}. The activity of the adenylated enzyme is, furthermore, sensitive to the ATP to Mg^{2+} ratio, whereas that of the unadenylated form is not. The activity of the adenylated synthetase thus is susceptible to regulation by ATP to metal ion ratios, as discussed above. Despite these examples, the physiologic significance of regulation of enzyme activity by metal ions remains to be firmly established.

REGULATION OF CATALYTIC EFFICIENCY: FEEDBACK INHIBITION

General Principles

The catalytic efficiency of an enzyme is affected by changes in the concentration of substrates, coenzymes, activators, or inhibitors. Each can play a homeostatic role in regulation of catalytic efficiency. What follows relates solely to effects of activators or inhibitors on enzyme activity. The activity of certain key **regulatory enzymes** is modulated by low molecular weight **allosteric effectors** which generally have little or no structural similarity to the substrates or coenzymes for the regulatory enzyme.

Feedback inhibition refers to the phenomenon whereby a product of a protracted sequence of biosyn-

thetic reactions inhibits the activity of an enzyme early in the biosynthetic pathway. In the biosynthetic reaction sequence leading from A to D catalyzed by enzymes Enz_1 through Enz_3,

$$A \xrightarrow{Enz_1} B \xrightarrow{Enz_2} C \xrightarrow{Enz_3} D$$

a high concentration of D typically will inhibit conversion of A to B. This does not involve a simple "backing up" of intermediates but reflects the ability of D specifically to bind to and inhibit Enz_1. D thus acts as a **negative allosteric effector** or **feedback inhibitor** of Enz_1. This negative feedback, or **feedback inhibition** on an **early enzyme*** by an end product of its own biosynthesis, achieves regulation of synthesis of D. Typically, D binds to an **allosteric site** on the inhibited enzyme which is remote from the catalytic site. An electronic analogy would be to regard the reaction sequence $A \rightarrow \rightarrow D$ as an amplification circuit with an input signal A and an output signal D. In an amplifier with negative feedback, the output signal, D, decreases the magnitude of the input signal, A, by changing the grid bias of a triode or the base current of a transistor. The result is a decreased signal output.

The kinetics of feedback inhibition may be competitive, noncompetitive, partially competitive, uncoupled, or of mixed types. The same enzyme, Enz_1, may also be subject to activation by other small molecules acting either at the catalytic site (**autosteric effectors**) or at an allosteric site (**positive allosteric effectors**). Feedback inhibition is best illustrated within biosynthetic pathways. **Frequently the feedback inhibitor is the last small molecule before a macromolecule** as, eg, amino acids before proteins or nucleotides before nucleic acids. In general, **feedback regulation is exerted at the earliest functionally irreversible† step unique to a particular biosynthetic sequence.** Its relevance to metabolic regulation was emphasized by Umbarger, who in 1956 reported feedback inhibition by isoleucine of threonine dehydrase, an early enzyme of isoleucine biosynthesis.

Uncomplicated feedback inhibition of the type described above occurs in amino acid and in purine biosynthesis in microorganisms. Examples include inhibition by histidine of phosphoribosyl:ATP pyrophosphorylase, by tryptophan of anthranilate synthetase, and by CTP of aspartate transcarbamoylase. In each case the regulated enzyme is involved in biosynthesis of a single end product—histidine, tryptophan, or CTP. Frequently a biosynthetic pathway may be branched, with the initial portion serving for synthesis of 2 or more essential metabolites. Further branching may occur, as in the biosynthetic pathways for the essential amino acids (see Chapter 22).

---

*The term "early enzyme" means one catalyzing a remote or early step in a protracted reaction sequence.
†One strongly favored (in thermodynamic terms) in a single direction, ie, one with a large negative ΔG.

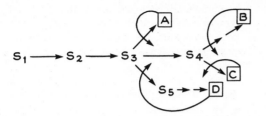

Figure 7–7. Sites of simple feedback inhibition in a hypothetical branched biosynthetic pathway. S_1–S_5 are intermediates in the biosynthesis of the end products A–D, and straight arrows represent the enzymes catalyzing the indicated conversions. The curved arrows represent feedback loops and indicate the probable sites of feedback inhibition by each of the indicated end products.

The hypothetical representation illustrated in Fig 7–7 shows the probable sites of simple feedback inhibition in a branched biosynthetic pathway such as those of amino acids or of purines or pyrimidines. S_1, S_2, and S_3 are precursors of all 4 end products (A, B, C, and D), S_4 is a precursor of B and C, and S_5 a precursor solely of D.

The sequences:

$$S_3 \longrightarrow A$$
$$S_4 \longrightarrow B$$
$$S_4 \longrightarrow C$$
$$S_3 \longrightarrow S_5 \longrightarrow D$$

constitute linear reaction sequences; they might be expected to be feedback-inhibited by their end products at an early stage. In general, this is what occurs. Frequently, however, more complex loops of feedback inhibition are observed (Fig 7–8).

These **multiple feedback loops** provide additional fine control of metabolism. For example, if B is present in excess, the requirement for S_2 decreases. The ability of B to decrease the rate of production of S_1 thus confers a distinct biologic advantage. However,

the very existence of multiple feedback loops poses difficulties. If excess B can inhibit not only the portion of the pathway unique to its own synthesis but also portions common to that for synthesis of A, C, or D, a large excess of B may cut off synthesis of all 4 end products. Clearly, this is undesirable. Several mechanisms have evolved which circumvent this difficulty but retain the additional fine control conferred by multiple feedback loops. These include: (1) **cumulative feedback inhibition**, (2) **concerted, or multivalent feedback inhibition**, (3) **cooperative feedback inhibition**, and (4) **enzyme multiplicity**, or the existence of 2 or more regulatory enzymes catalyzing the same biosynthetic reaction but having differing specificities with respect to their feedback inhibition by end products.

In **cumulative feedback inhibition** the inhibitory effect of 2 or more end products on a single regulatory enzyme is strictly additive. Cumulative feedback inhibition is encountered in regulation of glutamine utilization by *E coli* for synthesis of a spectrum of end products.

For **concerted** or **multivalent feedback inhibition**, no single end product alone greatly inhibits the regulatory enzyme. Marked inhibition occurs only when 2 or more end products are present in excess. Aspartokinase, which catalyzes conversion of aspartate to β-aspartyl phosphate (Fig 7–9), is a regulatory enzyme of the so-called "aspartate family" of amino acids—lysine, threonine, methionine, isoleucine, and homoserine. The aspartokinase of *Bacillus polymyxa* is only slightly inhibited by excess lysine, threonine, isoleucine, or methionine alone, but is essentially inactive

$$
\underset{\text{L-Aspartate}}{
\begin{array}{c}
COO^- \\
| \\
CH_2 \\
| \\
H{-}C{-}NH_3^+ \\
| \\
COO^-
\end{array}}
\;\xrightarrow[\boxed{\text{ASPARTOKINASE}}]{\text{ATP} \quad \text{ADP}}\;
\underset{\text{β-Aspartyl phosphate}}{
\begin{array}{c}
CO{-}O{-}\textcircled{P} \\
| \\
CH_2 \\
| \\
H{-}C{-}NH_3^+ \\
| \\
COO^-
\end{array}}
$$

Figure 7–9. The aspartokinase reaction.

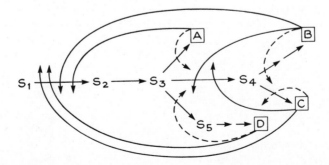

Figure 7–8. Sites of multiple feedback inhibition in a hypothetical branched biosynthetic pathway. The symbols are similar to those in the previous figures. Superimposed on the simple feedback loops of that figure (dashed, curved arrows) are multiple feedback loops (solid, curved arrows) which regulate the activity of enzymes common to the biosynthesis of more than one end product.

when both lysine and threonine are simultaneously present in excess. Since inhibition requires the concerted action of multiple inhibitors, it is therefore termed **concerted** or **multivalent feedback inhibition.**

Cooperative feedback inhibition embodies features both of cumulative and of multivalent inhibition. A single end product present in excess inhibits the regulatory enzyme, but **the inhibition observed when 2 or more inhibitors are present far exceeds the additive effects seen in cumulative feedback inhibition.** The regulatory enzyme phosphoribosylpyrophosphate amidotransferase, which catalyzes the first reaction unique to purine biosynthesis (see Chapter 23), is feedback-inhibited by several purine nucleotides. The mammalian amidotransferase is controlled by 6-aminopurine ribonucleotides (AMP, ADP) and the bacterial enzyme by 6-oxypurine ribonucleotides (GMP, IMP). Mixtures of both types of ribonucleotides (GMP + AMP or IMP + ADP etc) are more effective than the sum of the inhibitory activities of either tested alone. Cooperative effects are not observed with purines of the same class (ie, AMP + ADP or GMP + IMP). Since the purine end products are interconvertible, the ability of only 2 purines to curtail production of all purines does not pose special problems.

The aspartate family provides yet another variant of feedback inhibition: the existence within a single cell of **multiple enzymes** each with distinct regulatory characteristics. *E coli* produces 3 aspartokinases, each of which catalyzes formation of β-aspartyl phosphate from aspartate. Of these, one (AK_L) is specifically and completely inhibited by lysine, a second (AK_T) by threonine, and the third (AK_H) by homoserine, a precursor of methionine, threonine, and of isoleucine (Fig 7–10).

In the presence of excess lysine, AK_L is inhibited and β-aspartyl phosphate production decreases. This alone would not suffice to channel metabolites toward synthesis of homoserine and its products. Channeling is achieved by feedback inhibition at a secondary site or sites further along the pathway. Lysine thus also inhibits the first enzyme in the linear reaction sequence leading from β-aspartyl phosphate to lysine. This facilitates unrestricted synthesis of homoserine, and hence of threonine and isoleucine. Additional control points exist at the branch point where homoserine leads both to methionine and to threonine and isoleucine. Enzyme multiplicity in *E coli* occurs also in aromatic amino acid biosynthesis. Two distinct enzymes catalyze a reaction common both to tyrosine and phenylalanine synthesis. Each is separately and specifically inhibited either by tyrosine or by phenylalanine. As with the aspartate pathway, the individual aromatic amino acids also inhibit later steps in their own biosynthesis.

The above examples, chosen largely from microorganisms and from amino acid biosynthesis, illustrate the basic phenomenon of feedback inhibition and its major variants. Other examples are given throughout this book. That all the variations described are capable of exerting effective regulation of metabolism is suggested by the persistence in different strains of microorganisms of distinctive patterns of feedback inhibition of a single biosynthetic pathway (Table 7–2).

The most studied allosteric enzyme is **aspartate transcarbamoylase**, which catalyzes the first reaction (Fig 7–11) unique to pyrimidine biosynthesis (see Chapter 23), condensation of carbamoyl phosphate with aspartate forming carbamoyl aspartate.

Aspartate transcarbamoylase is **feedback-inhibited**

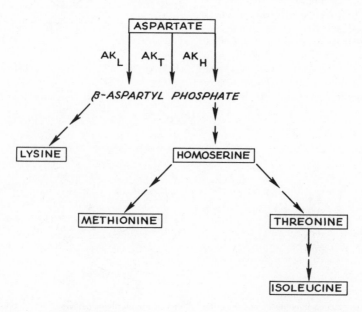

Figure 7–10. Regulation of aspartokinase (AK) activity in *E coli*. Multiple enzymes are subject to end product inhibition by lysine (AK_L), threonine (AK_T), or homoserine (AK_H).

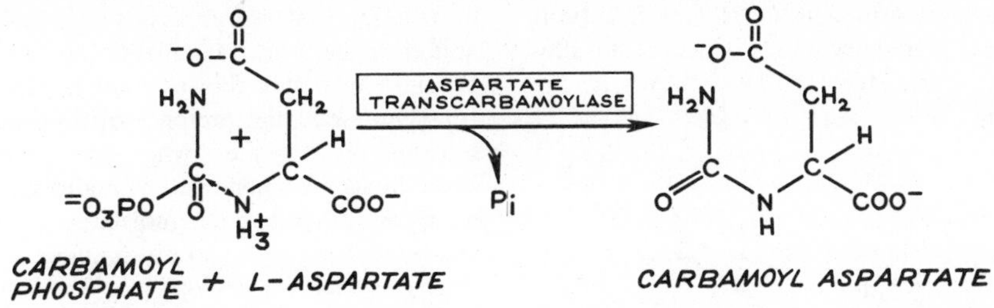

Figure 7—11. The aspartate transcarbamoylase (ATCase) reaction.

Table 7—2. Patterns of allosteric regulation of aspartokinase.

Organism	Feedback Inhibitor	Repressor
E coli (kinase I)	Homoser	. . .
E coli (kinase II)	Lys	Lys
E coli (kinase III)	Thr	. . .
R rubrium	Thr	. . .
B subtilis	Thr + Lys	. . .
S cerevisiae	Thr, Met, Homoser	Thr, Lys, Homoser

by cytidine triphosphate (CTP). Following treatment with mercurials, aspartate transcarbamoylase loses its sensitivity to inhibition by CTP but retains its full activity for carbamoyl aspartate synthesis. This strongly suggests that CTP is bound at a different (allosteric) site from either substrate. Aspartate transcarbamoylase apparently consists of 2 catalytic and 3 or 4 regulatory subunits. Each catalytic subunit contains 4 aspartate (substrate) sites and each regulatory subunit at least 2 CTP (regulatory) sites. Each type of subunit is subject to independent genetic control, as shown by the production of mutants lacking normal feedback control of CTP and, from these, of revertants with essentially normal regulatory properties.

Some general properties of some, but not all, allosteric enzymes include:

1. **Desensitization to allosteric control**—Treatment with mercurials, urea, proteolytic enzymes, high or low pH, etc may produce loss of feedback control with retention of catalytic activity.

2. **Heat stability**—Many allosteric effectors confer enhanced resistance to heat denaturation of the allosteric enzyme.

3. **Cold sensitivity**—Unlike most enzymes, many regulatory enzymes undergo reversible inactivation (loss of catalytic activity) at $0°$ C.

4. **Tertiary and quaternary structure**—All known allosteric enzymes possess tertiary, and in some cases also quaternary, structure. Aspartate transcarbamoylase, glycogen phosphorylase, pyruvate carboxylase, and acetyl-CoA carboxylase all undergo reversible association-dissociation reactions of subunits.

Evidence for Allosteric Sites on Regulated Enzymes

About 1963, Monod and his collaborators called attention to the lack of structural similarity between a feedback inhibitor and the substrate for the enzyme whose activity it regulated. Since the effectors are not isosteric with a substrate but **allosteric** ("occupy another space"), these workers proposed that enzymes whose activity is regulated by **allosteric effectors** (eg, feedback inhibitors) bind the effector at an **allosteric site** that is physically distinct from the catalytic site. **Allosteric enzymes** thus are enzymes whose activity at the active site may be modulated by the presence of allosteric effectors at an allosteric, effector-binding site. Several lines of evidence support the existence of physically distinct allosteric sites on regulated enzymes. These include the following:

(1) Isolated, regulated enzymes modified by appropriate chemical or physical technics frequently become insensitive to their allosteric effectors without alteration of their catalytic activity. Selective denaturation of allosteric sites has been achieved by treatment of regulated enzymes with mercurials, urea, x-rays, proteolytic enzymes, extremes of ionic strength or pH, aging at $0–5°$ C, or by freezing or heating. The nature and diversity of treatments giving rise to desensitization suggests specific denaturation of the presumed allosteric site.

(2) Allosteric effectors of enzyme activity frequently protect the **catalytic** site from denaturation under conditions where the substrates themselves do not protect. Since it seems unlikely that an effector bound at the catalytic site would protect when substrates do not, this is taken as evidence for a second, allosteric site elsewhere on the enzyme molecule.

(3) Bacterial mutants have been obtained in which the regulatory enzymes have altered regulatory properties. The catalytic properties are, however, identical to those of the wild-type from which the mutant was derived. This shows that the structure of the allosteric and catalytic sites are genetically distinct.

(4) Binding studies of substrates and of allosteric effectors to regulated enzymes show that, in many cases, each may be bound independently of the other.

(5) In certain cases (eg, aspartate transcarbamoylase), the allosteric effector binding site has been shown to be present on a different subunit from the catalytic site.

Kinetics of Inhibition of Allosteric Enzymes

When the rate of a reaction catalyzed by a typical

allosteric enzyme is measured at several concentrations of substrate in the presence and absence of an allosteric inhibitor, data similar to those shown in Fig 7–12 are obtained.

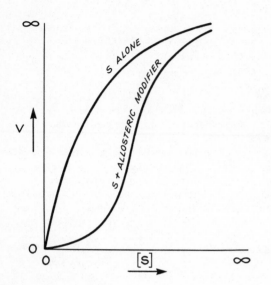

Figure 7–12. Sigmoid saturation curve for substrate in the presence of an allosteric inhibitor.

In the absence of the allosteric inhibitor, hyperbolic saturation kinetics are observed. However, in the presence of an allosteric inhibitor, the substrate saturation curve is distorted from a hyperbola into a sigmoid, which at high substrate concentrations may or may not merge with the hyperbola.

The kinetic analysis of feedback inhibition of regulated enzymes is complex and, as previously noted, may appear to be competitive, noncompetitive, partially competitive, or of other types. If, at high concentrations of S, comparable activity is observed in the presence or absence of the allosteric inhibitor, the kinetics superficially resemble those of competitive inhibition. However, since the substrate saturation curve is sigmoid rather than hyperbolic, it is therefore not possible to obtain meaningful results by graphing data for the allosteric inhibition of a regulated enzyme by the double-reciprocal technic. This method of kinetic analysis was developed for substrate competitive inhibition **at the active site**. Since allosteric inhibitors act at a different (allosteric) site, the kinetic model is no longer valid.

The detailed kinetic analysis of regulatory enzymes lies beyond the scope of this chapter. For our purposes, it will be sufficient to examine the consequences of the pronounced sigmoidicity of the substrate saturation curve (Fig 7–12). The sigmoid character of the V versus S curve in the presence of an allosteric inhibitor reflects the phenomenon known as **cooperativity**. At low concentrations of S, the activity in the presence of the inhibitor is low relative to that

in its absence. However, as S is increased, the extent of inhibition becomes relatively less severe (inhibitor becomes relatively less effective). These kinetics are consistent with the presence of 2 or more interacting substrate-binding sites, where the presence of a substrate molecule at one catalytic site facilitates binding of a second substrate molecule at a second site. Cooperativity of substrate binding has been most closely studied for hemoglobin, where the sigmoid O_2 saturation curve is known to result from cooperative interactions between 4 binding sites for O_2 located on different monomeric subunits.

Physiologic Consequences of Sigmoid Inhibition Kinetics

The consequences of cooperative substrate binding kinetics are analogous to those resulting from the sigmoid character of the hemoglobin O_2 saturation curve. At low substrate concentrations, the allosteric effector is an extremely effective inhibitor. It thus regulates most effectively at the time of greatest need, ie, when intracellular concentrations of substrate are low. As more substrate becomes available, stringent regulation is less necessary. As the substrate concentration rises, the degree of inhibition therefore lessens, and more product is formed. As with hemoglobin, the sigmoid character of the substrate saturation curve in the presence of the inhibitor also means that relatively small changes in substrate concentration result in large changes in activity. Sensitive control of activity thus is achieved by small changes in substrate concentration. Finally, by analogy with the differing O_2 saturation curves of hemoglobins from different species, regulatory enzymes from different sources may have sigmoid saturation curves shifted to the left or right to accommodate to the range of prevailing concentrations of substrate in a particular cell or organism.

Models of Allosteric Enzymes

Referring to the kinetics of allosteric inhibition as "competitive" or "noncompetitive" with substrate carries mechanistic implications which are misleading. As suggested by Monod, it is preferable to refer to 2 broad classes of regulated enzymes, K-series and V-series enzymes. K-series allosteric enzymes are those whose substrate saturation kinetics are generally competitive in the sense that K_m is raised (decreased affinity for substrate) without any effect on V_{max}. V-series allosteric enzymes are those wherein the presence of the allosteric inhibitor lowers V_{max} (lowered catalytic efficiency) without affecting the apparent K_m.

While various models have been proposed for the regulation of allosteric enzymes, it is unlikely that any single model can be expected to explain the behavior of all regulatory enzymes. Since sigmoidicity of the substrate-saturation curve confers a regulatory advantage, any mutation that gives rise to sigmoidicity should tend to be retained. To expect that these mutations would involve similar mechanisms is unrealistic.

Rather than discussing models, it will simply be

suggested that alterations in K_m or V_{max} probably result from conformational changes at the catalytic site induced by binding of the allosteric effector at the allosteric site. For a K-series allosteric enzyme, the primary effect of this conformational change may be to weaken the bonds between substrate and substrate-binding residues. Alternatively, for a V-series allosteric enzyme, the primary effect may be to alter the arrangement of catalytic residues so as to lower V_{max}. Even this simple model suggests, however, that intermediate effects (ie, both on K_m and on V_{max}) may be observed as a consequence of these conformational changes.

In conclusion, a variety of mechanisms adequately explain the sigmoid character of the substrate saturation curve in the presence of an allosteric inhibitor. The presence of sigmoid kinetics does not, therefore, imply a particular mechanism of inhibition.

REGULATION OF CATALYTIC EFFICIENCY: COVALENT MODIFICATION

In addition to allosteric effects, enzyme activity may also be regulated by **covalent modification** of specific amino acid residues on the enzyme surface. Covalent modification may either reinforce or counteract the effects of allosteric regulators and hence may either intensify or tend to nullify allosteric regulatory effects. Regulation by covalent modification is particularly well documented in animals (Table 7–3).

Covalent modification of a regulated enzyme typically requires ATP and involves either phospho-

Table 7–3. Regulated mammalian enzymes whose activity is determined by ATP-dependent, enzyme-catalyzed covalent modification.

Glycogen synthetase
Glycogen synthetase phosphatase
Glycogen phosphorylase
Phosphorylase a phosphatase
Phosphorylase b kinase
Fructose diphosphatase
Pyruvate dehydrogenase complex

rylation of the enzyme, catalyzed by a specific phosphotransferase, or adenylation, catalyzed by a specific adenyltransferase. Phosphorylase, glycogen synthetase, and pyruvate dehydrogenase all possess a seryl residue which may be phosphorylated by ATP in the presence of a specific phosphotransferase (kinase). This profoundly changes the catalytic properties of the enzyme concerned. Restoration of each enzyme to its original, unphosphorylated form is catalyzed by a specific phosphohydrolase (phosphatase) (Fig 7–13).

Notice that the reactions shown in Fig 7–13 closely resemble those involved in the interconversion of glucose and glucose 6-phosphate or of fructose 6-phosphate and fructose 1,6-bisphosphate (see Chapter 18). As is the case with the phosphosugars, the net result of phosphorylating and then dephosphorylating 1 mole of substrate (enzyme or sugar) is the hydrolysis of 1 mole of ATP.

1. $\text{Glucose} + \text{ATP} \longrightarrow \text{ADP} + \text{Glucose-6-}P$

2. $\text{H}_2\text{O} + \text{Glucose-6-}P \longrightarrow \text{P}_i + \text{Glucose}$

Net: $\text{H}_2\text{O} + \text{ATP} \longrightarrow \text{ADP} + \text{P}_i$

3. $\text{Enz–Ser–OH} + \text{ATP} \longrightarrow \text{ADP} + \text{Enz–Ser–O-}P$

4. $\text{H}_2\text{O} + \text{Enz–Ser–O-}P \longrightarrow \text{P}_i + \text{Enz–Ser–OH}$

Net: $\text{H}_2\text{O} + \text{ATP} \longrightarrow \text{ADP} + \text{P}_i$

It follows, therefore, that the activity of the kinases catalyzing reactions 1 and 3 and of the phosphatases catalyzing reactions 2 and 4 must themselves be subject to regulation. If they were not, they would act together to catalyze uncontrolled hydrolysis of ATP. For mammalian glycogen phosphorylase and glycogen synthetase, this is indeed the case (Table 7–3). The physiologic implications of regulation of the glycogen synthetase phosphatase enzymes are discussed in Chapter 18.

An alternative mechanism of covalent modification by ATP involves adenylation of the regulated enzyme (ie, transfer of AMP from ATP to the enzyme, with the accompanying formation of inorganic pyrophosphate). While this is not known to occur in mammalian systems, adenylation is responsible for regula-

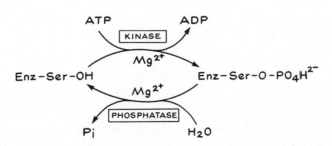

Figure 7–13. Representation of covalent modification of a regulated enzyme by phosphorylation-dephosphorylation of a seryl residue.

tion of the glutamine synthetase and RNA polymerase of *Escherichia coli.* For glutamine synthetase, covalent modification involves transfer of 12 mol of AMP to 1 mol of synthetase (see Chapter 22).

•   •   •

References

Gumaa KA, McLean P, Greenbaum AL: Compartmentation in relation to metabolic control in liver. Essays Biochem 7:39, 1971.

Kun E, Grisolia S: *Biochemical Regulatory Mechanisms in Eukaryotic Cells.* Wiley, 1972.

Newsholme EA, Stuart C: *Regulation in Metabolism.* Wiley, 1973.

Schimke RT, Doyle D: Control of enzyme levels in animal tissues. Annu Rev Biochem 39:929, 1970.

Sols A, Marco R: Concentrations of metabolites and binding sites: Implications in metabolic regulation. Curr Top Cell Regul 2:227, 1970.

Stanbury JB, Wyngaarden JB, Fredrickson DS (editors): *The Metabolic Basis of Inherited Disease,* 3rd ed. McGraw-Hill, 1972.

Umbarger HE: Regulation of amino acid metabolism. Annu Rev Biochem 38:323, 1969.

Weber G (editor): *Advances in Enzyme Regulation.* Vols 1–6. Pergamon Press, 1963–1977.

8...

Carbohydrates

The carbohydrates are widely distributed both in animal and in plant tissues. In plants, they are produced by photosynthesis and include the cellulose of the plant framework as well as the starch of the plant cells. In animal cells, carbohydrate in the form of glucose and glycogen serves as an important source of energy for vital activities. Some carbohydrates have highly specific functions (eg, ribose in the nucleoprotein of the cells, galactose in certain lipids, and the lactose of milk).

Carbohydrates may be defined chemically as aldehyde or ketone derivatives of the polyhydric (more than one OH group) alcohols or as compounds which yield these derivatives on hydrolysis.

Classification

Carbohydrates are divided into 4 major groups as follows:

(1) Monosaccharides (often called "simple sugars") are those which cannot be hydrolyzed into a simpler form. The general formula is $C_nH_{2n}O_n$. The simple sugars may be subdivided as trioses, tetroses, pentoses, hexoses, or heptoses, depending upon the number of carbon atoms they possess; and as aldoses or ketoses, depending upon whether the aldehyde or ketone groups are present. Examples are:

		Aldoses	Ketoses
Trioses	$(C_3H_6O_3)$	Glycerose	Dihydroxyacetone
Tetroses	$(C_4H_8O_4)$	Erythrose	Erythrulose
Pentoses	$(C_5H_{10}O_5)$	Ribose	Ribulose
Hexoses	$(C_6H_{12}O_6)$	Glucose	Fructose

(2) Disaccharides are carbohydrates which yield 2 molecules of the same or of different monosaccharides when hydrolyzed. The general formula is $C_n(H_2O)_{n-1}$. Examples are sucrose, lactose, and maltose.

(3) Oligosaccharides are those which yield $\frac{3}{2}$–6 monosaccharide units on hydrolysis.

(4) Polysaccharides yield more than 6 molecules of monosaccharides on hydrolysis. The general formula is $(C_6H_{10}O_5)_x$. Examples of polysaccharides, which may be linear or branched, are the starches and dextrins. These are sometimes designated as hexosans, pentosans, homopolysaccharides, or heteropolysaccharides depending upon the nature of the monosaccharides they yield on hydrolysis.

Structure of Glucose

Glucose is the principal sugar in blood, serving the tissues as a major metabolic fuel. Although the straight chain structural formula (aldohexose, Fig 8–1[A]) can account for some of its properties, a cyclic hemiacetal structure is favored on thermodynamic grounds and accounts completely for its chemical properties. For most purposes, the structural formula may be represented as a simple ring in perspective as proposed by Haworth (Fig 8–1[B]). X-ray diffraction analysis shows that the 6-membered ring containing one oxygen atom is actually in the form of a chair (Fig 8–1[C]).

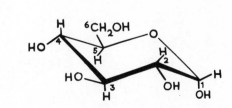

Figure 8–1. *a*-D-Glucose.

93

Isomerism

Compounds which have the same structural formula but differ in spatial configuration are known as **stereoisomers**. The presence of asymmetric carbon atoms (carbon atoms attached to 4 different atoms or groups) allows the formation of isomers. The number of possible isomers of a compound depends on the number of asymmetric carbon atoms (n) and is equal to 2^n. Glucose, with 4 asymmetric carbon atoms, therefore has 16 isomers. The more important types of isomerism found with glucose are as follows:

A. D and L: The designation of an isomer as D- or of its mirror image as the L- form is determined by its spatial relationship to the parent compound of the carbohydrate family, the 3-carbon sugar, glycerose. The L and D forms of this sugar are shown in Fig 8-2 together with the corresponding isomers of glucose. The orientation of the H and OH groups around the carbon atom adjacent to the terminal primary alcohol carbon (eg, carbon atom 5 in glucose) determines the family to which the sugar belongs. When the OH group on this carbon is on the right, the sugar is a member of the D series; when it is on the left, it is a member of the L series. The majority of the monosaccharides occurring in mammalian metabolism are of the D configuration.

The presence of asymmetric carbon atoms also confers **optical activity** on the compound. When a beam of polarized light is passed through a solution exhibiting optical activity, it will be rotated to the right or left in accordance with the type of compound, ie, the **optical isomer**, which is present. A compound which causes rotation of polarized light to the right is said to be dextrorotatory and a plus (+) sign is used to designate this fact. Rotation of the beam to the left (levorotatory action) is designated by a minus (−) sign.

When equal amounts of dextrorotatory and levorotatory isomers are present, the resulting mixture has no optical activity since the activities of each isomer cancel one another. Such a mixture is said to be a **racemic**, or a DL mixture. Synthetically produced compounds are necessarily racemic because the opportunities for the formation of each optical isomer are identical. The separation of optically active isomers from a racemic mixture is called resolution, ie, the racemic mixture is said to be "resolved" into its optically active components.

Stereoisomerism and optical isomerism are independent properties. Thus, a compound might be designated D (−) or L (+), indicating structural relationship to D or L glycerose but exhibiting the opposite rotatory power. The naturally occurring form of fructose, the D(−) isomer, is an example.

B. α and β Anomers: The cyclic structure of glucose is retained in solution, but isomerism takes place about position 1, the carbonyl or anomeric carbon atom, to give a mixture of α- and β-glucose. This equilibration is accompanied by optical rotation (**mutarotation**) as the hemiacetal ring opens and reforms with change of position of the −H and −OH groups on carbon 1. The change probably takes place via a hydrated straight-chain acyclic molecule, although polarography has indicated that glucose exists only to the extent of 0.0025% in the acyclic form (Fig 8-3).

C. Epimers: Isomers formed as a result of interchange of the −OH and −H on carbon atoms 2, 3, and 4 of glucose are known as epimers. Biologically, the most important epimers of glucose are mannose and galactose formed by epimerization at carbons 2 and 4, respectively (Fig 8-4).

D. Pyranose and Furanose Ring Structures: On the basis of the ring structures known to exist in glycosides (see below), Haworth in 1929 proposed similar structures for the sugars themselves. The terminology was based on the fact that the simplest organic compounds of similar structure exhibit similar ring structures to pyran and furan (Fig 8-5). Ketoses may also show ring formation (eg, D-fructofuranose or D-fructopyranose). Other ring forms may exist (eg, between C atoms 1 and 2 or 1 and 3), but they are unstable.

E. Aldose-Ketose Isomerism: Fructose has the same molecular formula as glucose but differs in its structural formula since carbon 2 is a part of a $>CO$ group, which makes fructose a ketose rather than an aldose. Generally, if there is a free −H on carbon 1, the sugar is an aldose, but if a $-CH_2OH$ group is substituted, the sugar is a ketose (Fig 8-6).

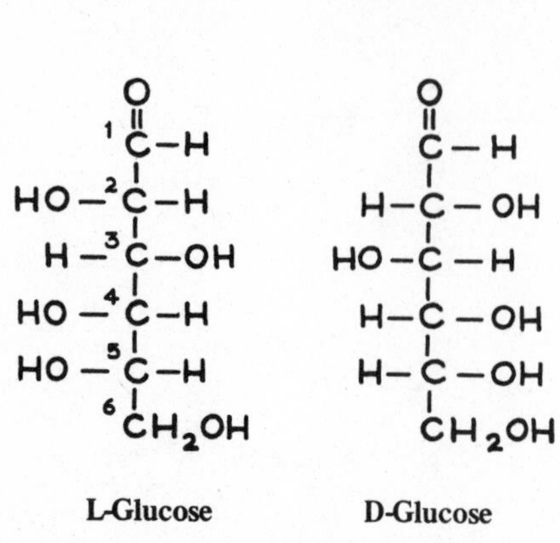

MONOSACCHARIDES

The monosaccharides include trioses, tetroses, pentoses, hexoses, and heptoses (3, 4, 5, 6, 7 carbon

Figure 8-2. D- and L-isomerism of glycerose and glucose.

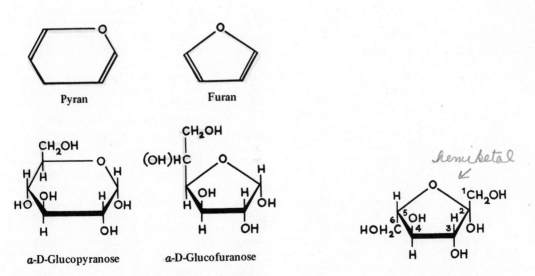

$+H_2O$ $-H_2O$

a-D-Glucose β-D-Glucose

$-H_2O$

CHO

Acyclic aldehyde form

Figure 8–3. Mutarotation of glucose.

a-D-Galactose a-D-Glucose a-D-Mannose

Figure 8–4. Epimerization of glucose.

Pyran   Furan

a-D-Glucopyranose a-D-Glucofuranose

hemiketal

Figure 8–5. Pyranose and furanose forms of glucose.

Figure 8–6. β-D-Fructose.

Table 8–1. Examples of pentoses.

Sugar	Source	Importance	Reactions
D-Ribose	Nucleic acids.	Structural elements of nucleic acids and co-enzymes, eg, ATP, NAD, NADP (DPN, TPN), flavoproteins.	Reduce Benedict's, Fehling's, Barfoed's, and Haynes' solutions. Forms distinctive osazones with phenylhydrazine.
D-Ribulose	Formed in metabolic processes.	Intermediates in hexose monophosphate shunt.	Those of keto sugars.
D-Arabinose	Gum arabic. Plum and cherry gums.	These sugars are used in studies of bacterial metabolism, as in fermentation tests for identification of bacteria. They have no known physiologic function in man.	With orcinol-HCl reagent gives colors: violet, blue, red, and green.
D-Xylose	Wood gums.		With phloroglucinol-HCl gives a red color.
D-Lyxose	Heart muscle.	A constituent of a lyxoflavin isolated from human heart muscle.	

atoms). The trioses are formed in the course of the metabolic breakdown of the hexoses; pentose sugars (Table 8–1) are important constituents of nucleic acids and many coenzymes; they are also formed in the breakdown of glucose by the hexose monophosphate shunt, and the hexoses glucose, galactose, and fructose are physiologically the most important of the monosaccharides (Table 8–2). A 7-carbon keto sugar, sedoheptulose, was first discovered in 1917 in the sedum plant. It also occurs in animal tissues, where it is formed as a phosphate ester in the metabolism of pentose phosphates by the hexose monophosphate shunt.

The structures of the aldo sugars are shown in Fig 8–7. Five keto sugars which are important in metabolism are shown in Fig 8–8.

HEXOSES

The hexoses are most important physiologically (Table 8–2). Examples are D-glucose, D-fructose, D-galactose, and D-mannose.

GLYCOSIDES

Glycosides are compounds formed as a result of a condensation reaction between a sugar and the hydroxyl group of a second compound which may or may not be another sugar. In these compounds, the carbohydrate residue is attached by an acetal linkage at the anomeric carbon atom 1 to the residue of the second compound or **aglycone**. If the carbohydrate portion is glucose, the resulting compound is a **glucoside**; if galactose, a **galactoside**, etc.

A simple example is the methyl glucoside formed when a solution of glucose in boiling methyl alcohol is treated with 0.5% hydrogen chloride as a catalyst. The reaction proceeds with the formation of anomeric *a*- and *β*-glucosides (Fig 8–9).

From *β*-D-glucose, *β*-methyl-D-glucoside would be formed.

Glycosides are found in many drugs, spices, and in the constituents of animal tissues. The aglycone may be methyl alcohol, glycerol, a sterol, a phenol, or another sugar (as in the disaccharides). The glycosides which are important in medicine because of their ac-

Table 8–2. Hexoses of physiologic importance.

Sugar	Source	Importance	Reactions
D-Glucose	Fruit juices. Hydrolysis of starch, cane sugar, maltose, and lactose.	The "sugar" of the body. The sugar carried by the blood, and the principal one used by the tissues. Glucose is usually the "sugar" of the urine when glycosuria occurs.	Reduces Benedict's, Haynes', Barfoed's reagents (a reducing sugar). Gives osazone with phenylhydrazine. Fermented by yeast. With HNO_3, forms soluble saccharic acid.
D-Fructose	Fruit juices. Honey. Hydrolysis of cane sugar and of inulin (from the Jerusalem artichoke).	Can be changed to glucose in the liver and intestine and so used in the body.	Reduces Benedict's, Haynes', Barfoed's reagents (a reducing sugar). Forms osazone identical with that of glucose. Fermented by yeast. Cherry-red color with Seliwanoff's resorcinol-HCl reagent.
D-Galactose	Hydrolysis of lactose.	Can be changed to glucose in the liver and metabolized. Synthesized in the mammary gland to make the lactose of milk. A constituent of glycolipids and glycoproteins.	Reduces Benedict's, Haynes', Barfoed's reagents (a reducing sugar). Forms osazone, distinct from above. Phloroglucinol-HCl reagent gives red color. With HNO_3, forms insoluble mucic acid. Not fermented by yeast.
D-Mannose	Hydrolysis of plant man-nosans and gums.	A constituent of prosthetic polysaccharide of albumins, globulins, mucoproteins. A sugar frequently occurring in glycoproteins.	Reduces Benedict's, Haynes', Barfoed's reagents (a reducing sugar). Forms same osazone as glucose.

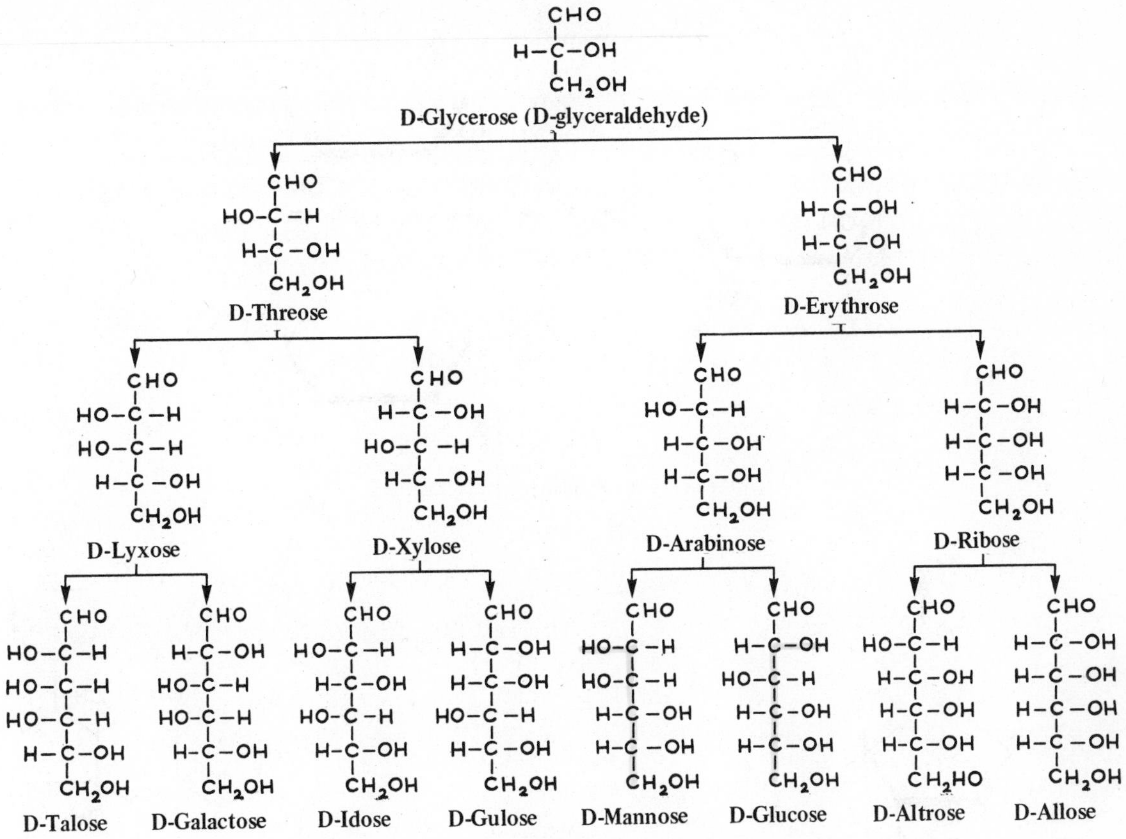

CHO
H—C—OH
CH₂OH

D-Glycerose (D-glyceraldehyde)

CHO
HO—C—H
H—C—OH
CH₂OH

D-Threose

CHO
H—C—OH
H—C—OH
CH₂OH

D-Erythrose

CHO
HO—C—H
HO—C—H
H—C—OH
CH₂OH

D-Lyxose

CHO
H—C—OH
HO—C—H
H—C—OH
CH₂OH

D-Xylose

CHO
HO—C—H
H—C—OH
H—C—OH
CH₂OH

D-Arabinose

CHO
H—C—OH
H—C—OH
H—C—OH
CH₂OH

D-Ribose

CHO
HO—C—H
HO—C—H
HO—C—H
H—C—OH
CH₂OH

D-Talose

CHO
H—C—OH
HO—C—H
HO—C—H
H—C—OH
CH₂OH

D-Galactose

CHO
HO—C—H
H—C—OH
HO—C—H
H—C—OH
CH₂OH

D-Idose

CHO
H—C—OH
H—C—OH
HO—C—H
H—C—OH
CH₂OH

D-Gulose

CHO
HO—C—H
HO—C—H
H—C—OH
H—C—OH
CH₂OH

D-Mannose

CHO
H—C—OH
HO—C—H
H—C—OH
H—C—OH
CH₂OH

D-Glucose

CHO
HO—C—H
H—C—OH
H—C—OH
H—C—OH
CH₂HO

D-Altrose

CHO
H—C—OH
H—C—OH
H—C—OH
H—C—OH
CH₂OH

D-Allose

Figure 8—7. The structural relations of the aldoses, D series.

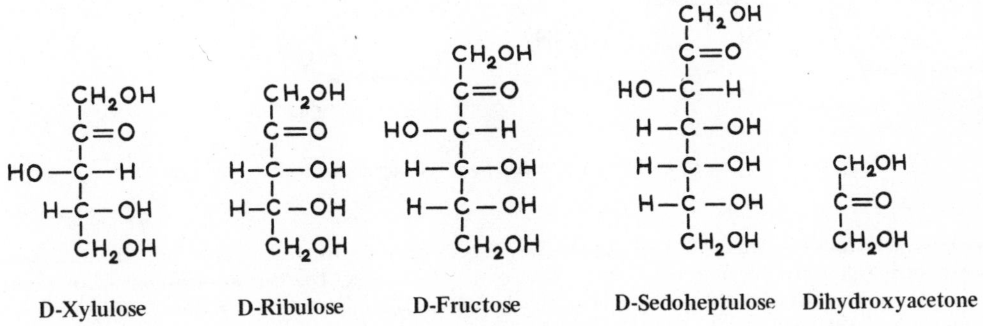

CH₂OH
C=O
HO—C—H
H—C—OH
CH₂OH

D-Xylulose

CH₂OH
C=O
H—C—OH
H—C—OH
CH₂OH

D-Ribulose

CH₂OH
C=O
HO—C—H
H—C—OH
H—C—OH
CH₂OH

D-Fructose

CH₂OH
C=O
HO—C—H
H—C—OH
H—C—OH
H—C—OH
CH₂OH

D-Sedoheptulose

CH₂OH
C=O
CH₂OH

Dihydroxyacetone

Figure 8—8. Examples of ketoses.

tion on the heart (**cardiac glycosides**) all contain steroids as the aglycone component. These include derivatives of digitalis and strophanthus such as ouabain, which is an inhibitor of the Na⁺-K⁺-ATPase of cell membranes. Other glycosides include antibiotics such as streptomycin (Fig 8—10).

IMPORTANT CHEMICAL REACTIONS OF MONOSACCHARIDES

Several reactions are of importance as proof of the structure of a typical monosaccharide such as glucose. These include the following:

Iodo Compounds

An aldose heated with concentrated hydriodic acid (HI) loses all of its oxygen and is converted into

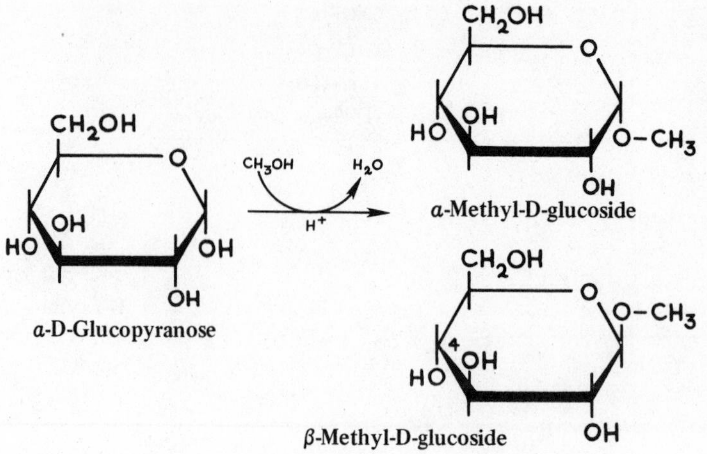

Figure 8—9. Formation of glucosides.

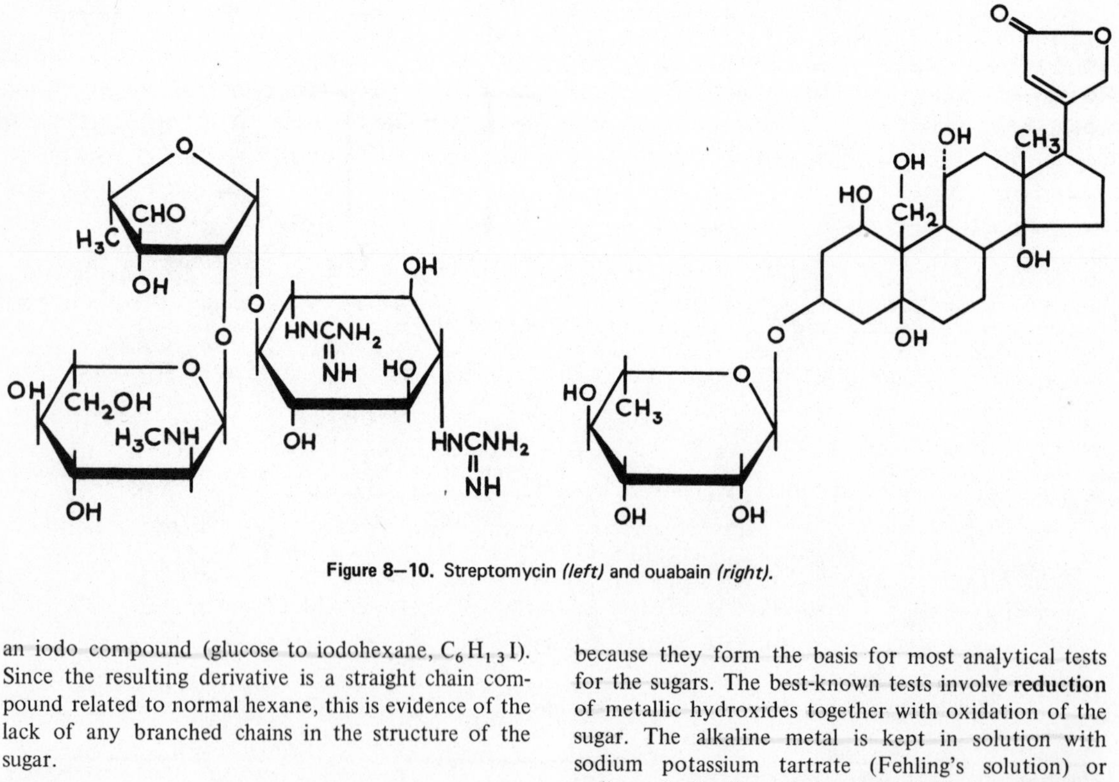

Figure 8—10. Streptomycin *(left)* and ouabain *(right).*

an iodo compound (glucose to iodohexane, $C_6H_{13}I$). Since the resulting derivative is a straight chain compound related to normal hexane, this is evidence of the lack of any branched chains in the structure of the sugar.

Acetylation

The ability to form sugar esters, eg, acetylation with acetylchloride ($CH_3CO.Cl$), indicates the presence of alcohol groups. The total number of acyl groups which can thus be taken up by a molecule of the sugar is a measure of the number of such alcohol groups. Because of its 5 OH groups, the acetylation of glucose, for example, results in a penta acetate.

Other Reactions

Various reactions dependent upon the presence of aldehyde or ketone groups are particularly important

because they form the basis for most analytical tests for the sugars. The best-known tests involve **reduction** of metallic hydroxides together with oxidation of the sugar. The alkaline metal is kept in solution with sodium potassium tartrate (Fehling's solution) or sodium citrate (Benedict's solution). Various modifications permit quantitative detection of the copper reduced as a measurement of the sugar content. Other metallic hydroxides may be used (bismuth, Nylander's test; ammoniacal silver, Tollens' test). Barfoed's test distinguishes between monosaccharides and disaccharides, since copper acetate in dilute acid is reduced by the former in 30 seconds but only after several minutes' boiling (to produce hydrolysis) of the disaccharides.

Osazone formation is a useful means of preparing crystalline derivatives of the sugars. These compounds have characteristic crystal structures, melting points,

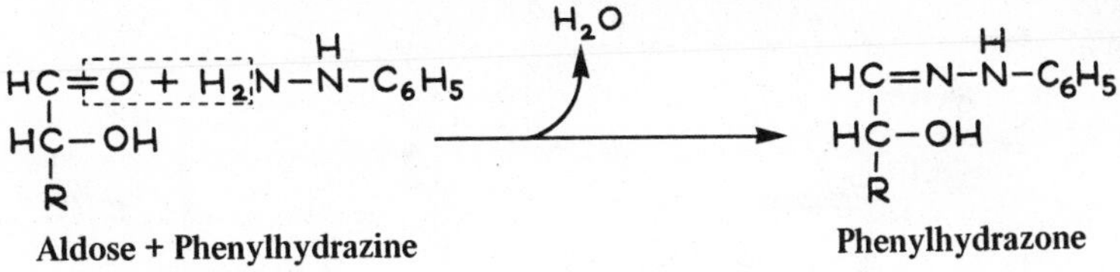

Figure 8—11. First stage of osazone formation.

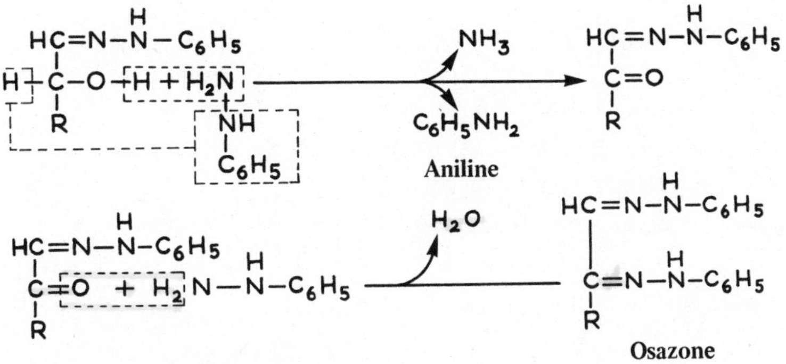

Figure 8—12. Second stage of osazone formation.

and precipitation times, and are valuable in the identification of sugars. They are obtained by adding a mixture of phenylhydrazine hydrochloride and sodium acetate to the sugar solution and heating in a boiling water bath. The reaction involves only the carbonyl carbon (ie, aldehyde or ketone group) and the next adjacent carbon. For example, with an aldose the reaction shown in Fig 8—11 occurs. The hydrazone then reacts with 2 additional molecules of phenylhydrazine to form the osazone (Fig 8—12). The reaction with a ketose is similar.

It will be noted from a comparison of their structures that glucose, fructose, and mannose would form the same osazones; but since the structure of galactose differs in that part of the molecule unaffected in osazone formation, it would form a different osazone.

Interconversion. Glucose, fructose, and mannose are interconvertible in solutions of weak alkalinity such as $Ba(OH)_2$ or $Ca(OH)_2$. These changes are easily visualized structurally through an enediol form common to all 3 sugars (Fig 8—13).

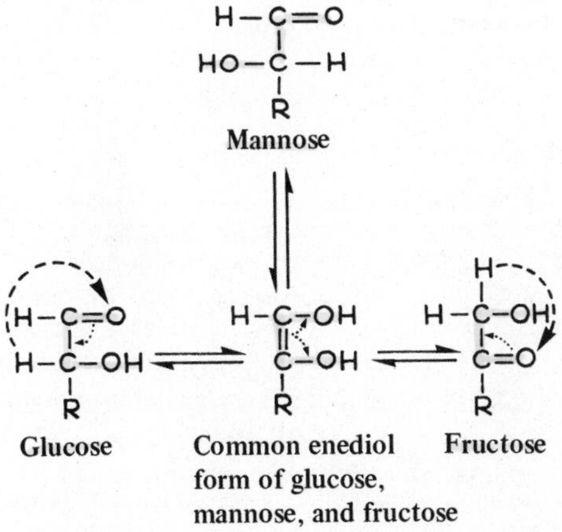

Oxidation of aldoses may form acids as end products (Fig 8—14). Oxidation of the aldehyde group forms "aldonic acids." However, if the aldehyde group remains intact and the primary alcohol group at the opposite end of the molecule is oxidized, "uronic acids" are formed instead (Fig 8—14).

Note that glucuronic acid exerts "reducing" activity because of the free aldehyde group. These so-called hexuronic acids are important in connection with conjugation reactions.

Oxidation of galactose with concentrated HNO_3 yields the dicarboxylic mucic acid. This compound crystallizes readily, and this is useful as an identifying test. Galacturonic acid is found in natural products (eg, pectins).

Reduction. The monosaccharides may be reduced to their corresponding alcohols by reducing agents such as sodium amalgam. (See Fig 8—15.)

Thus, glucose yields sorbitol; galactose yields dulcitol; mannose yields mannitol; and fructose yields mannitol and sorbitol.

With **strong mineral acids,** there is a shift of hydroxyl groups toward and of hydrogen away from the aldehyde end of the chain (Fig 8—16).

Reaction products with acid (furfural or one of its derivatives) will condense with certain organic phenols to form compounds of characteristic colors. Color

Figure 8—13. Interconversion.

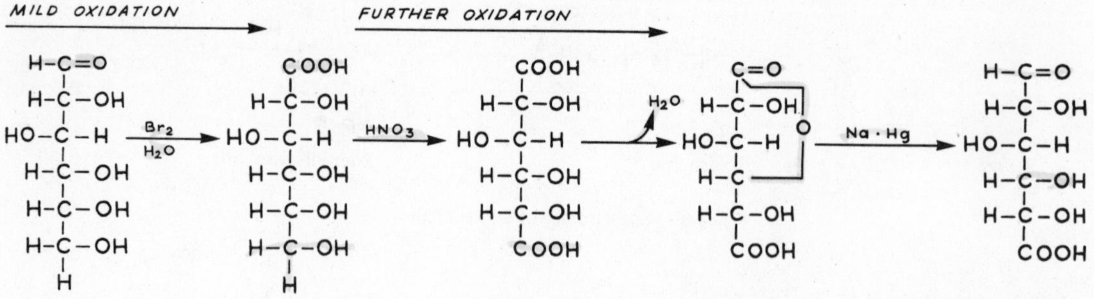

MILD OXIDATION ⟶   FURTHER OXIDATION ⟶

Glucose   Gluconic acid   Saccharic acid   Saccharolactone   Glucuronic acid

Figure 8–14. Oxidation of glucose.

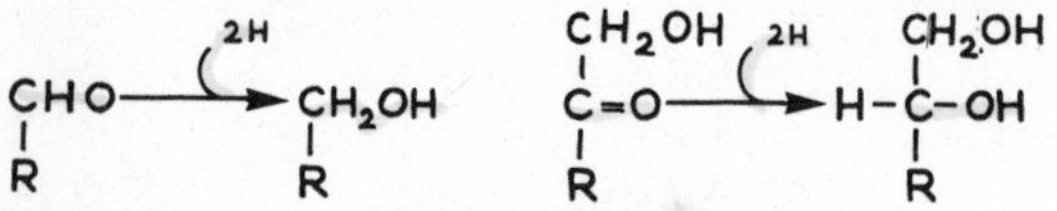

Aldo sugar   Keto sugar

Figure 8–15. Reduction of aldoses and ketoses.

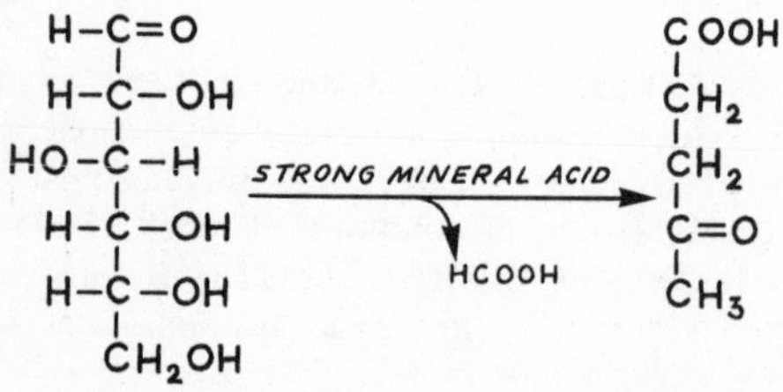

D-Glucose   Levulinic acid

Figure 8–16. Reaction with strong mineral acids.

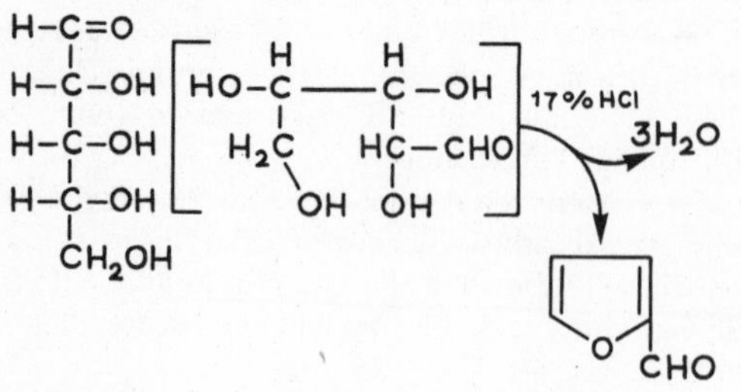

D-Ribose   Furfural

Figure 8–17. Reaction products with acid.

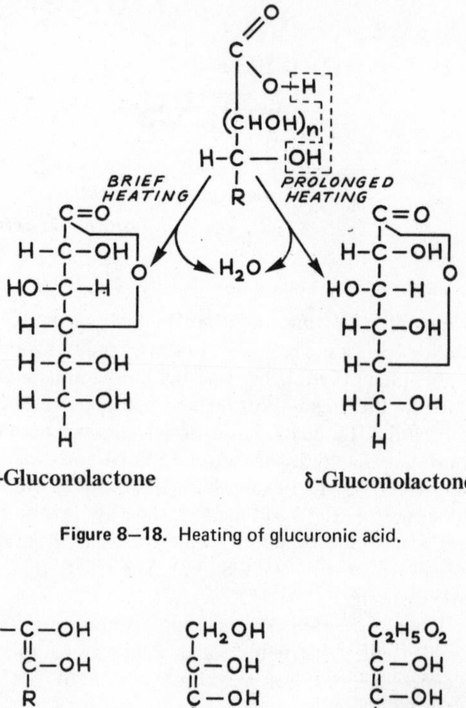

γ-Gluconolactone   δ-Gluconolactone

Figure 8–18. Heating of glucuronic acid.

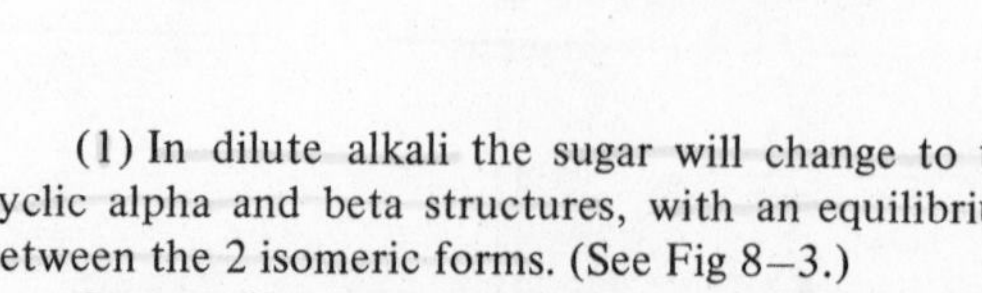

1,2-Enediol   2,3-Enediol   3,4-Enediol, etc

Figure 8–19. Formation of enols by heating.

tests for the various sugars are based on such reactions (Fig 8–17).

Heating of gluconic acid (Fig 8–18) produces lactones. These are cyclic structures resembling the pyranoses and furanoses described earlier.

With **alkali** monosaccharides react in various ways:

(1) In dilute alkali the sugar will change to the cyclic alpha and beta structures, with an equilibrium between the 2 isomeric forms. (See Fig 8–3.)

On standing, a rearrangement will occur which produces an equilibrated mixture of glucose, fructose, and mannose through the enediol form.

(2) If the mixture is heated to 37° C, the acidity increases and a series of enols are formed in which double bonds shift from the oxygen-carbon link to positions between various carbon atoms (Fig 8–19).

(3) In concentrated alkali, sugar caramelizes and produces a series of decomposition products. Yellow

and brown pigments develop, salts may form, many double bonds between carbon atoms are formed, and carbon-to-carbon bonds may rupture.

DEOXY SUGARS

Deoxy sugars are those in which a hydroxyl group attached to the ring structure has been replaced by a hydrogen atom. They are obtained on hydrolysis of certain substances which are important in biologic processes. An example is the deoxyribose occurring in nucleic acids (DNA).

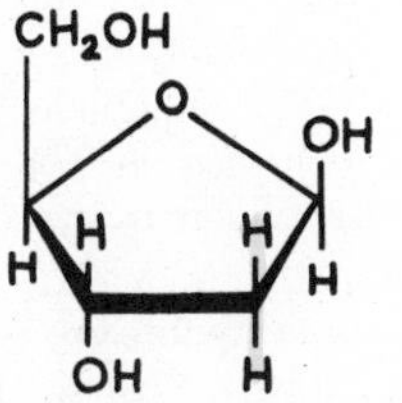

Figure 8—20. 2-Deoxy-D-ribofuranose (α form).

AMINO SUGARS (HEXOSAMINES)

Sugars containing an amino group are called **amino sugars.** Examples are D-glucosamine, D-galactosamine, and D-mannosamine, all of which have been identified in nature. Glucosamine is a constituent of hyaluronic acid. Galactosamine (chondrosamine) is a constituent of chondroitin. Mannosamine is an important constituent of mucoprotein.

Several antibiotics (erythromycin, carbomycin) contain amino sugars. Erythromycin contains a dimethylamino sugar. Carbomycin contains the first known 3-amino sugar, 3-amino-D-ribose. The amino sugars are believed to be related to the antibiotic activity of these drugs.

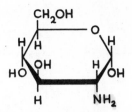

Figure 8—21. Glucosamine (2-amino-D-glucopyranose) (α form).

DISACCHARIDES

The disaccharides are sugars composed of 2 monosaccharide residues united by a glycosidic linkage (Fig 8—22). They are named chemically according to the structures of their component monosaccharides. The suffix **-furan** or **-pyran** refers to the structural resemblances to these compounds. The alpha and beta refer to the configuration at the starred (*) carbon atom, as indicated in examples shown in connection with the formulas in Fig 8—22. The physiologically important disaccharides are maltose, sucrose, lactose, and trehalose (Table 8—3).

Since sucrose has no free carbonyl group, it gives none of the reactions characteristic of "reducing" sugars. Thus it fails to reduce alkaline copper solutions, form an osazone, or exhibit mutarotation. Hydrolysis of sucrose yields a crude mixture which is often called "invert sugar" because the strongly levorotatory fructose thus produced changes (inverts) the previous dextrorotatory action of the sucrose.

POLYSACCHARIDES

Polysaccharides include the following physiologically important substances:

Starch $(C_6H_{10}O_5)_X$ is formed of an α-glucosidic chain. Such a compound, yielding only glucose on

Table 8—3. Disaccharides.

Sugar	Source	Reactions
Maltose	Digestion by amylase or hydrolysis of starch. Germinating cereals and malt.	Reducing sugar. Forms osazone with phenylhydrazine. Fermentable. Hydrolyzed to D-glucose.
Lactose	Milk. May occur in urine during pregnancy.	Reducing sugar. Forms osazone with phenylhydrazine. Not fermentable by yeasts. Hydrolyzed to glucose and galactose.
Sucrose	Cane and beet sugar. Sorghum. Pineapple. Carrot roots.	Nonreducing sugar. Does not form osazone. Fermentable. Hydrolyzed to fructose and glucose.
Trehalose	Fungi and yeasts. The major sugar of insect hemolymph.	Nonreducing sugar. Does not form an osazone. Hydrolyzed to glucose.

MALTOSE (a FORM)

O-a-D-Glucopyranosyl-(1→4)-a-D-glucopyranoside

SUCROSE

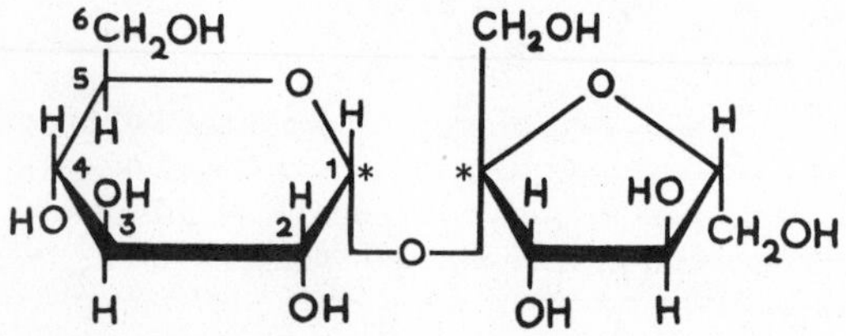

O-β-D-Fructofuranosyl-(2→1)-a-D-glucopyranoside

LACTOSE (β FORM)

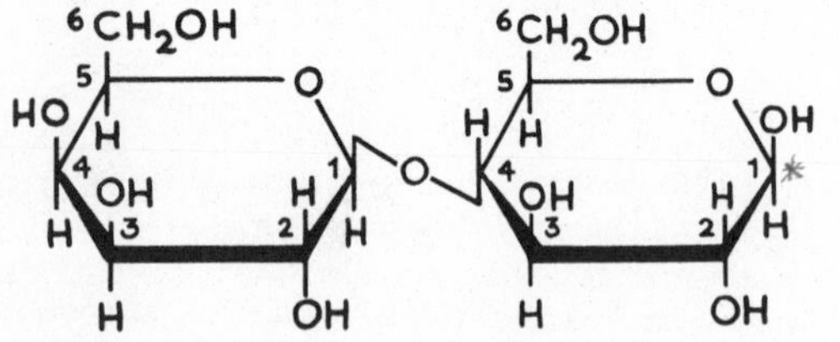

O-β-D-Galactopyranosyl-(1→4)-β-D-glucopyranoside

TREHALOSE (a FORM)

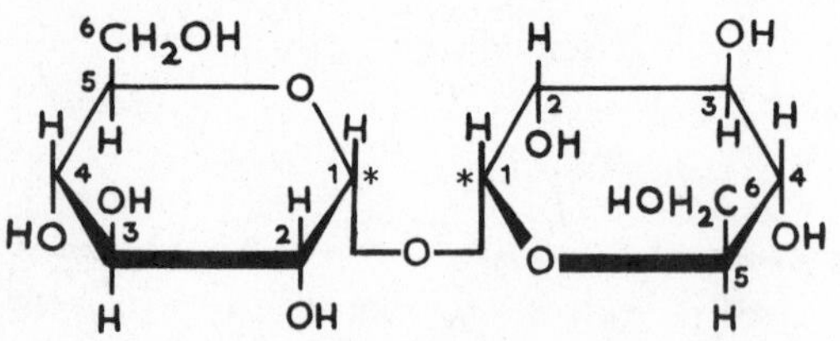

O-a-D-Glucopyranosyl-(1→1)-a-D-glucopyranoside

CELLOBIOSE

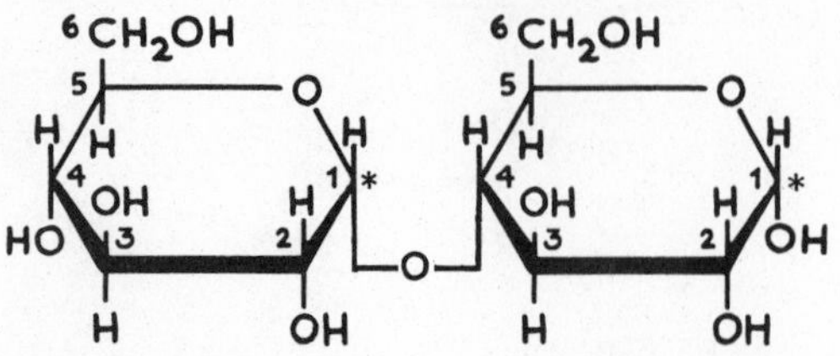

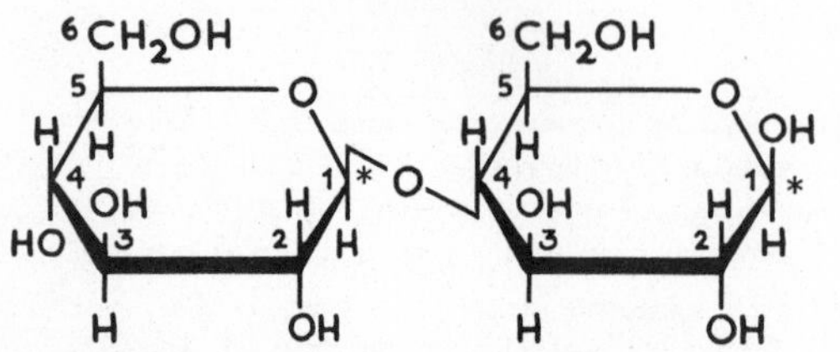

O-β-D-Glucopyranosyl-(1→4)-β-D-glucopyranoside

Figure 8–22. Structures of representative disaccharides.

hydrolysis, is called a **glucosan**. It is the most important food source of carbohydrate and is found in cereals, potatoes, legumes, and other vegetables. Natural starch is insoluble in water and gives a blue color with iodine solution. The microscopic form of the granules is characteristic of the source of the starch. The 2 chief constituents are amylose (15–20%), which is a nonbranching helical structure responsible for the color with iodine (Fig 8–23), and amylopectin (80–85%), which consists of highly branched chains which give only a red color with iodine because they do not coil effectively. Each is composed of a number of a-glucosidic chains having 24–30 glucose residues apiece. The glucose residues are united by 1:4 linkages in the chains and by 1:6 linkages at the branch points.

Glycogen is the polysaccharide of the animal body. It is often called animal starch. It is a branched structure with straight chain units of 11-18-a-D-glucopyranose (in a[1-4]-glucosidic linkage) with branching by means of a(1-6)-glucosidic bonds. Glycogen is nonreducing and gives a red color with iodine (Fig 8–24).

Inulin is a starch found in tubers and roots of dahlias, artichokes, and dandelions. It is hydrolyzable to fructose and hence it is a fructosan. No color is given when iodine is added to inulin solutions. This starch is easily soluble in warm water. It is used in physiologic investigation for determination of the rate of glomerular filtration.

Dextrins are substances which are formed in the course of the hydrolytic breakdown of starch. The partially digested starches are amorphous. Dextrins which give a red color when tested with iodine are first formed. These are called **erythrodextrins**. As hydrolysis proceeds the iodine color is no longer produced. These are the so-called **achroodextrins**. Finally, only reducing sugars will appear.

Cellulose is the chief constituent of the framework of plants. It gives no color with iodine and is not soluble in ordinary solvents. Since it is not subject to attack by the digestive enzymes of man, it is an important source of "bulk" in the diet. It consists of straight chains of β-D-glucopyranose.

Chitin is an important structural polysaccharide of invertebrates. It is found, for example, in the shells of crustaceans. Structurally, chitin apparently consists of N-acetyl-D-glucosamine units joined by β(1-4)-glucosidic linkages.

Polysaccharides which are associated with the structure of animal tissues are analogous to the cellulose of the plant cells. Examples are **hyaluronic acid** and the **chondroitin sulfates**. These substances are members of a group of carbohydrates, the **mucopolysaccharides**. They are characterized by their content of amino sugars and uronic acids and are now preferably referred to as **glucosaminoglycans**. Heparin, a powerful antithrombic agent produced and stored by mast cells, is also a mucopolysaccharide. On hydrolysis, heparin yields glucuronic acid and glucosamine as well as acetic and sulfuric acids probably derived from acetyl and

A

B

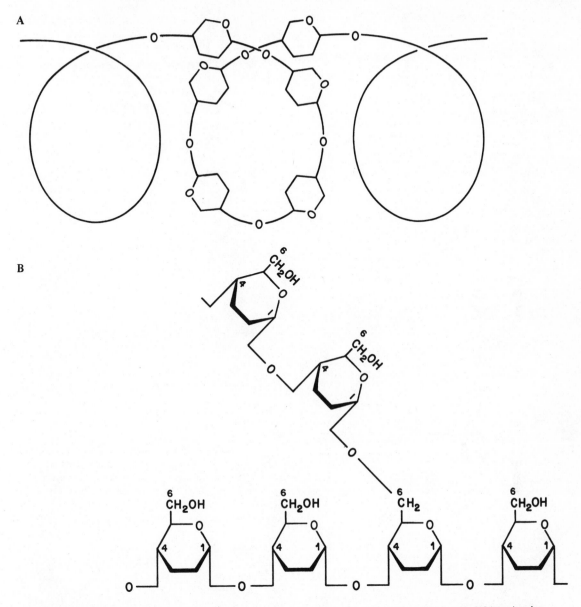

Figure 8–23. Structure of starch. *A:* Amylose, showing helical coil structure. *B:* Amylopectin, showing 1:6 branch point.

sulfate groups present in the intact molecule (Fig 8–26).

The **glycoproteins** (mucoproteins) are protein-polysaccharide compounds occurring in the tissues, particularly in mucous secretions. These compounds—in contrast to the glucosaminoglycans—do not contain uronic acids although they do contain acetyl hexosamines such as N-acetylglucosamine and N-acetylgalactosamine. Hexoses such as mannose or galactose are also found. In addition, a methyl pentose (L-fucose; see opposite) and the sialic acids commonly occur in these conjugated proteins. Examples of glycoproteins are also found among the alpha$_1$ and alpha$_2$ globulins of the plasma.

The sialic acids are actually a family of com-

L-Fucose (6-deoxy-L-galactose)

pounds derived from neuraminic acid. They are widely distributed in vertebrate tissues and have also been isolated from certain strains of bacteria. **N-Acetylneuraminic acid,** the structure of which is shown in Fig 8–25, is an example of a sialic acid. Enzymes have been identified in the liver of the rat and in bovine submaxillary glands which can accomplish the biosynthesis of N-acetylneuraminic acid.

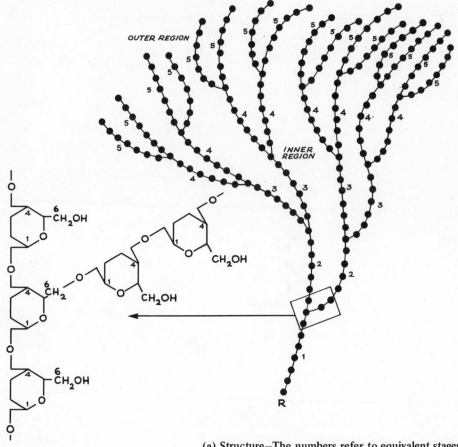

OUTER REGION

INNER REGION

R

(b) Enlargement of structure at a branch point.

(a) Structure—The numbers refer to equivalent stages in the growth of the macromolecule. R, primary glucose residue with free reducing-CHO group (carbon No. 1). The branching is more variable than shown, the ratio of 1,4 to 1,6 bonds being from 12 to 18.

Figure 8—24. The glycogen molecule.

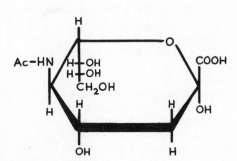

Figure 8—25. Structure of sialic acids. (Ac = CH_3-CO- in N-acetylneuraminic acid.)

The blood group substances of the erythrocytes (isoagglutinogens) which are responsible for the major immunologic reactions of blood (blood types) are glycoproteins. L-Fucose is an important constituent of human blood group substances (19% in blood group B substance).

Examples of mucopolysaccharides which produce specific immune reactions are found among the bacteria. The capsular polysaccharides (haptenes) of pneumococci have been the most extensively studied in this connection. Preparations of capsular polysaccharide from type I pneumococci yield, on hydrolysis, glucosamine and glucuronic acid.

Some of the pituitary hormones, although mainly proteins, also contain carbohydrate. Examples are human chorionic gonadotropin (HCG) and luteinizing hormone (LH). These hormones are therefore other examples of glycoproteins.

CHITIN

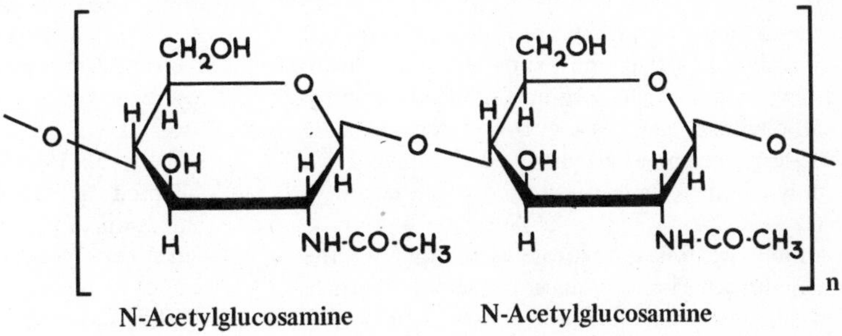

N-Acetylglucosamine   N-Acetylglucosamine

HYALURONIC ACID

ground substance of connective tissue

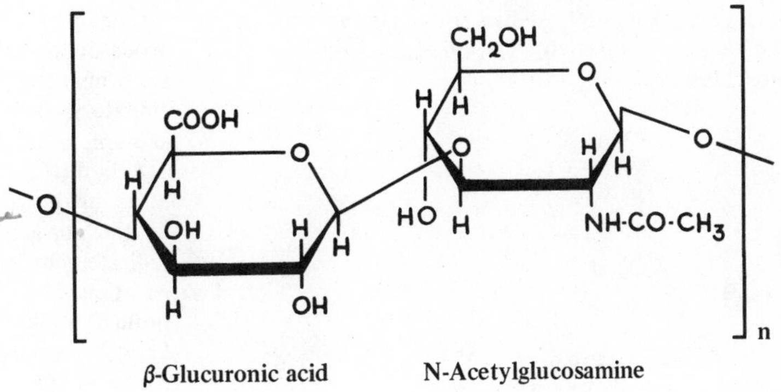

β-Glucuronic acid   N-Acetylglucosamine

CHONDROITIN-4-SULFATE

[Note: There is also a 6-sulfate.]

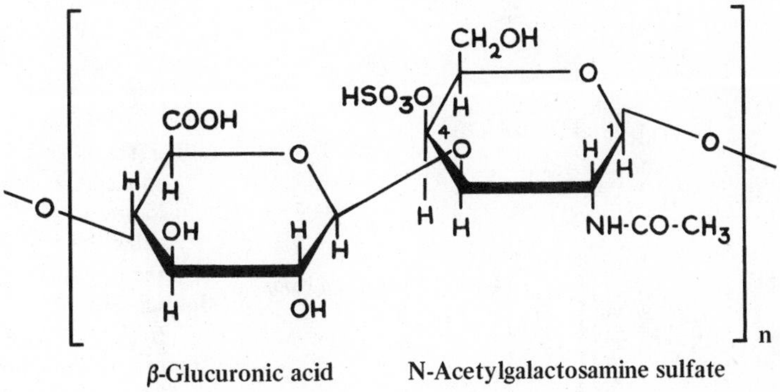

β-Glucuronic acid   N-Acetylgalactosamine sulfate

HEPARIN

anticoagulant

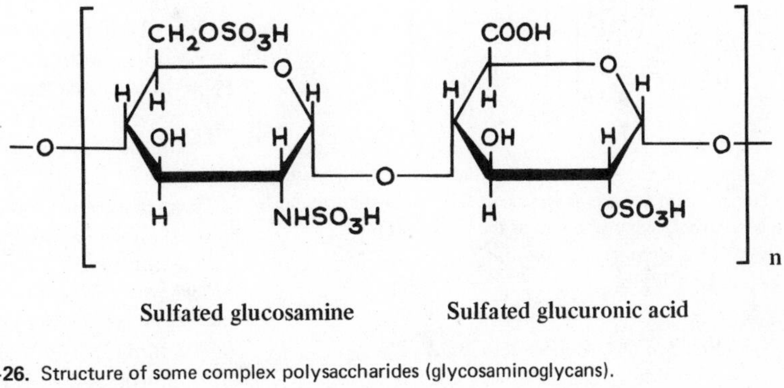

Sulfated glucosamine   Sulfated glucuronic acid

Figure 8—26. Structure of some complex polysaccharides (glycosaminoglycans).

CARBOHYDRATES OF CELL MEMBRANES

For a discussion of the structure of cell membranes, see Chapter 9. Analysis of mammalian cell membranes indicates that approximately 5% is carbohydrate, present as glycoproteins and glycolipids. These carbohydrate residues (eg, N-acetylglucosamine or N-acetylgalactosamine) are attached to amino acids in the polypeptide chains of proteins via the acetyl residue (see Fig 37–5). Fig 8–27 illustrates how these carbohydrates are linked to proteins or lipids in the plasma membrane. Their presence on the outer surface of the plasma membrane has been shown with the use of plant **lectins**, protein agglutinins which bind specifically with certain glycosyl residues. For example, **concanavalin A** has a specificity toward *a*-glucosyl and *a*-mannosyl residues.

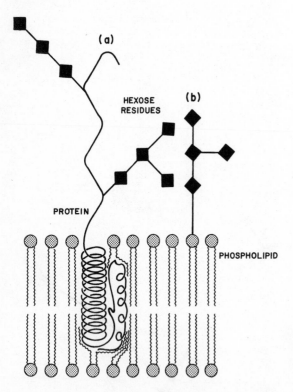

Figure 8–27. Glycoproteins and glycolipids of the cell membrane. The diagram illustrates hexose residues attached to an integral protein and a phospholipid of the cell membrane.

TESTS FOR CARBOHYDRATES

The separation and identification of carbohydrates can be accomplished by chromatographic technics (see p 30). There are, however, a number of time-honored qualitative tests that may be utilized in connection with chromatographic separations as well as independently. These are described briefly below.

Anthrone Test: To 2 ml of anthrone test solution (0.2% in concentrated H_2SO_4) add 0.2 ml of unknown. A green or blue-green color indicates the presence of carbohydrate. The test is very sensitive; it will give a positive reaction with filter paper (cellulose). The anthrone reaction has been adapted to the quantitative colorimetric determination of glycogen, inulin, and sugar of blood.

Barfoed's Test (copper acetate and acetic acid): To 5 ml of reagent add 1 ml of unknown. Place in boiling water bath.

Benedict's Test (copper sulfate, sodium citrate, sodium carbonate): To 5 ml of reagent in test tube add 8 drops of unknown. Place in a boiling water bath for 5 minutes. A green, yellow, or orange-red precipitate gives a semiquantitative estimate of the amounts of reducing sugar present.

Bial's Orcinol-HCl Test: To 5 ml of reagent add 2–3 ml of unknown and heat until bubbles of gas rise to the surface. Green solution and precipitate indicate pentose.

Fermentation Test: To 5 ml of a 20% suspension of ordinary baker's yeast add about 5 ml of unknown solution and 5 ml of phosphate buffer (pH 6.4–6.8). Place in a fermentation tube or test tube and let stand 1 hour. Bubbles of CO_2 indicate fermentation.

Haynes' Test (Rochelle salt, or potassium sodium tartrate, glycerol, copper sulfate): Performed similarly to Benedict's.

Iodine Test: Acidify the unknown solution with HCl and add 1 drop of the mixture to a solution of iodine in KI. The formation of a blue color indicates the presence of starch; a red color indicates the presence of glycogen or erythrodextrin.

Molisch Test: To 2 ml of unknown add 2 drops of fresh 10% *a*-naphthol reagent and mix. Pour 2 ml of concentrated H_2SO_4 so as to form a layer below the mixture. A red-violet ring indicates the presence of carbohydrate.

Pavy's Test (Rochelle salt, ammonium hydroxide, copper sulfate): Similar to Benedict's test.

Phenylhydrazine Reaction (osazone formation): Heat phenylhydrazine reagent with 2 ml of a solution of the sugar in a test tube in a boiling water bath for 30 minutes; cool, and examine crystals with a microscope. Compare with diagrams in laboratory manuals or with crystals prepared from known solutions.

Seliwanoff's Resorcinol Test: To 1 ml of unknown add 5 ml of freshly-prepared reagent. This is made by adding 3.5 ml of 0.5% resorcinol to 12 ml of concentrated HCl and diluting to 35 ml with distilled water. Place in boiling water bath for 10 minutes. Cherry-red color indicates fructose.

Tauber's Benzidine Test: To 1 ml of benzidine solution add 2 drops of unknown sugar; boil and cool quickly. A violet color indicates pentose.

Tollens' Naphthoresorcinol Reaction: To 5 ml of unknown in a test tube add 1 ml of 1% alcoholic solution of naphthoresorcinol. Heat gradually to boiling; boil for 1 minute with shaking; let stand for 4 minutes, then cool under tap. Then prepare ether extract. A violet-red color in the ether extract indicates presence of hexuronic acids and rules out pentoses.

Tollens' Phloroglucinol-HCl Test: To equal volumes of the unknown solution and HCl add phloroglucinol. Glucuronates may be distinguished from pentoses or galactose by the naphthoresorcinol test.

• • •

References

Advances in Carbohydrate Chemistry. Academic Press, 1945—current.

Conn EE, Stumpf PK: *Outlines of Biochemistry,* 3rd ed. Wiley, 1972.

Cook GMW, Stoddart RW: *Surface Carbohydrates of the Eukaryotic Cell.* Academic Press, 1973.

Davidson EA: *Carbohydrate Chemistry.* Holt, 1967.

Ferrier RJ, Collins PM: *Monosaccharide Chemistry.* Penguin Books, 1972.

Florkin M, Stotz E: *Comprehensive Biochemistry; Carbohydrates.* Section 2, vol 5. Elsevier, 1963.

McGilvery RW: *Biochemistry.* Saunders, 1970.

Percival EGV, Percival E: *Structural Carbohydrate Chemistry.* Prentice-Hall, 1962.

Pigman WW, Horton D (editors): *The Carbohydrates.* Vols 1A and 1B. Academic Press, 1972.

West ES & others: *Textbook of Biochemistry,* 4th ed. Macmillan, 1966.

9 . . .
Lipids

The lipids are a heterogeneous group of compounds related, either actually or potentially, to the fatty acids. They have the common property of being (1) relatively insoluble in water and (2) soluble in nonpolar solvents such as ether, chloroform, and benzene. Thus, the lipids include fats, oils, waxes, and related compounds.

A lipoid is a "fat-like" substance which may not actually be related to the fatty acids although occasionally the terms "lipid" and "lipoid" are used synonymously.

Lipids are important dietary constituents not only because of their high energy value but also because of the fat-soluble vitamins and the essential fatty acids which are found with the fat of natural foods. In the body, fat serves as an efficient source of energy—both directly and potentially, when stored in adipose tissue. It serves as an insulating material in the subcutaneous tissues and around certain organs. The fat content of nerve tissue is particularly high. Combinations of fat and protein (lipoproteins) are important cellular constituents, occurring both in the cell membrane and in the mitochondria within the cytoplasm, and serving also as the means of transporting lipids in the blood.

Classification

The following classification of lipids has been proposed by Bloor:

A. Simple Lipids: Esters of fatty acids with various alcohols.

1. **Fats**—Esters of fatty acids with glycerol. A fat which is in the liquid state is known as an oil.

2. **Waxes**—Esters of fatty acids with higher alcohols than glycerol.

B. Compound Lipids: Esters of fatty acids containing groups in addition to an alcohol and a fatty acid.

1. **Phospholipids**—Lipids containing, in addition to fatty acids and an alcohol, a phosphoric acid residue. They also have nitrogen-containing bases and other substituents. In many phospholipids—eg, the glycerophospholipids—the alcohol is glycerol, but in others—eg, the sphingophospholipids—it is sphingosine.

2. **Cerebrosides (glycolipids)**—Compounds of the fatty acids with carbohydrate, containing nitrogen but no phosphoric acid.

3. **Other compound lipids,** such as sulfolipids and aminolipids. Lipoproteins may also be placed in this category.

C. Derived Lipids: Substances derived from the above groups by hydrolysis. These include fatty acids (both saturated and unsaturated), glycerol, steroids, alcohols in addition to glycerol and sterols, fatty aldehydes, and ketone bodies (see Ketosis, Chapter 20).

Because they are uncharged, glycerides (acylglycerols), cholesterol, and cholesteryl esters are termed neutral lipids.

FATTY ACIDS

Fatty acids are obtained from the hydrolysis of fats. Fatty acids which occur in natural fats usually contain an even number of carbon atoms (because they are synthesized from 2-carbon units) and are straight-chain derivatives. The chain may be saturated (containing no double bonds) or unsaturated (containing one or more double bonds).

Nomenclature

The most frequently used systematic nomenclature is based on naming the fatty acid after the hydrocarbon with the same number of carbon atoms, -oic being substituted for the final e in the name of the hydrocarbon (Genevan system). Thus, saturated acids end in -anoic, eg, octanoic acid, and unsaturated acids with double bonds end in -enoic, eg, octadecenoic acid (oleic acid). Carbon atoms are numbered from the carboxyl carbon (carbon No. 1). The carbon atom adjacent to the carboxyl carbon (No. 2) is also known as the α-carbon. Carbon atom No. 3 is the β-carbon, and the end methyl carbon is known as the ω-carbon. Various conventions are in use for indicating the number and position of the double bonds, eg, Δ^9 indicates a double bond between carbon atoms 9 and 10 of the fatty acid. A widely used convention is to indicate the number of carbon atoms, number of double bonds, and the positions of the double bonds as shown in Figs 9–1 and 9–2.

A closer examination of the position of the

$$18:1;9$$

$$CH_3(CH_2)_7 \overset{10}{CH}=\overset{9}{CH}(CH_2)_7COOH$$

Figure 9–1. Oleic acid.

$$18:2;9,12$$

$$CH_3(CH_2)_4\overset{13}{CH}=\overset{12}{CH}CH_2\overset{10}{CH}=\overset{9}{CH}(CH_2)_7COOH$$

Figure 9–2. Linoleic acid.

double bonds in naturally occurring fatty acids reveals that they are related to the –CH$_3$ or ω-end of the fatty acid rather than the carboxyl group. Thus, a series of monounsaturated fatty acids of increasing chain length based on oleic acid may be described as ω-9 acids, and another series based on linoleic acid and which includes arachidonic acid constitutes the ω-6 series.

Saturated Fatty Acids

Saturated fatty acids may be envisaged as based on acetic acid as the first member of the series (general formula: $C_nH_{2n+1}COOH$). Examples of the acids in this series are shown in Table 9–1.

Other higher members of the series are known to occur, particularly in waxes. A few branched-chain fatty acids have also been isolated from both plant and animal sources.

Unsaturated Fatty Acids

These may be further subdivided according to degree of unsaturation.

Table 9–1. Saturated fatty acids.

Acetic	CH_3COOH	Major end product of carbohydrate fermentation by rumen organisms
Propionic	C_2H_5COOH	An end product of carbohydrate fermentation by rumen organisms
Butyric	C_3H_7COOH	In certain fats in small amounts (especially butter). An end product of carbohydrate fermentation by rumen organisms.
Caproic	$C_5H_{11}COOH$	
Caprylic (octanoic)	$C_7H_{15}COOH$	In small amounts in many fats (including butter), especially those of plant origin
Decanoic (capric)	$C_9H_{19}COOH$	
Lauric	$C_{11}H_{23}COOH$	Spermaceti, cinnamon, palm kernel, coconut oils, laurels
Myristic	$C_{13}H_{27}COOH$	Nutmeg, palm kernel, coconut oils, myrtles
Palmitic	$C_{15}H_{31}COOH$	Common in all animal and plant fats
Stearic	$C_{17}H_{35}COOH$	
Arachidic	$C_{19}H_{39}COOH$	Peanut (arachis) oil
Behenic	$C_{21}H_{43}COOH$	Seeds
Lignoceric	$C_{23}H_{47}COOH$	Cerebrosides, peanut oil

A. Monounsaturated (Monoethenoid) Acids: General formula: $C_nH_{2n-1}COOH$. *Examples:* Oleic acid, palmitoleic acid, found in nearly all fats.

B. Polyunsaturated (Polyethenoid) Acids:

1. Two double bonds. General formula: $C_nH_{2n-3}COOH$. *Example:* Linoleic acid* (18:2; 9, 12). Occurs in many seed oils, eg, corn, peanut, cottonseed, soybean oils.

2. Three double bonds. General formula: $C_nH_{2n-5}COOH$. *Example:* Linolenic acid* (18:3; 9, 12, 15). Found frequently with linoleic acid but particularly in linseed oil.

3. Four double bonds. General formula: $C_nH_{2n-7}COOH$. *Example:* Arachidonic acid* (20:4; 5, 8, 11, 14). Found in small quantities with linoleic and linolenic acids but particularly in peanut oil. (See p 294).

A group of compounds known as prostaglandins (see also p 297), found in seminal plasma and other tissues, is of interest because of its pharmacologic and biochemical activity on smooth muscle, blood vessels, and adipose tissue (see also p 298). In vivo, prostaglandins are synthesized from arachidonic acid. *Example:* Prostaglandin E_2 (PGE$_2$) (Fig 9–3).

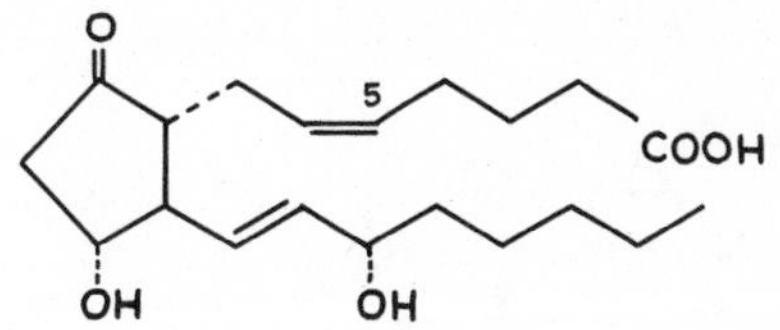

Figure 9–3. Prostaglandin E_2 (PGE$_2$).

C. Many other fatty acids have been detected in biologic material. For example, fish oil contains 22:5 and 22:6 unsaturated fatty acids. Various other structures, such as hydroxy groups (ricinoleic acid) or cyclic groups, have been found in nature. An example of the latter is chaulmoogric acid (Fig 9–4).

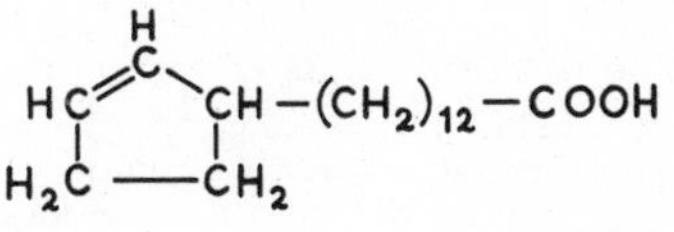

Figure 9–4. Chaulmoogric acid.

Isomerism in Unsaturated Fatty Acids

Variations in the location of the double bonds in unsaturated fatty acid chains produce isomers. Thus, oleic acid could have 15 different positional isomers.

Geometric isomerism depends on the orientation of radicals around the axis of double bonds. Some

*Linoleic, linolenic, and arachidonic are the so-called "essential" fatty acids (see p 294).

compounds differ only in the orientation of their parts around this axis. This is noteworthy in the chemistry of steroids. If the radicals which are being considered are on the same side of the bond, the compound is called "cis"; if on opposite sides, "trans." This can be illustrated with oleic and elaidic acids or with dicarboxylic acids such as fumaric and maleic acids (Fig 9–5).

In acids with a greater degree of unsaturation there are, of course, more geometric isomers. Naturally occurring unsaturated long chain fatty acids are nearly all of the "cis" configuration, the molecule being "bent" at the position of the double bond. Thus, arachidonic acid, having 4 double bonds, is U-shaped.

Alcohols

Alcohols found in lipid molecules include glycerol, cholesterol, and higher alcohols (eg, cetyl alcohol, $C_{16}H_{33}OH$), usually found in the waxes. The presence of glycerol is indicated by the acrolein test (Fig 9–6).

Among the unsaturated alcohols found in fats are a number of important pigments. These include phytol (phytyl alcohol), which is also a constituent of chlorophyll, and lycophyll ($C_{40}H_{56}O_2$), a polyunsaturated dihydroxy alcohol which occurs in tomatoes as a purple pigment.

$$H_2C-OH \quad\quad CH_2$$
$$HC-OH \xrightarrow[\text{HEAT PLUS } KHSO_4]{\text{DEHYDRATED WITH}} \ \overset{2H_2O}{\ } \quad CH$$
$$HC-H \quad\quad CHO$$
$$O-H$$

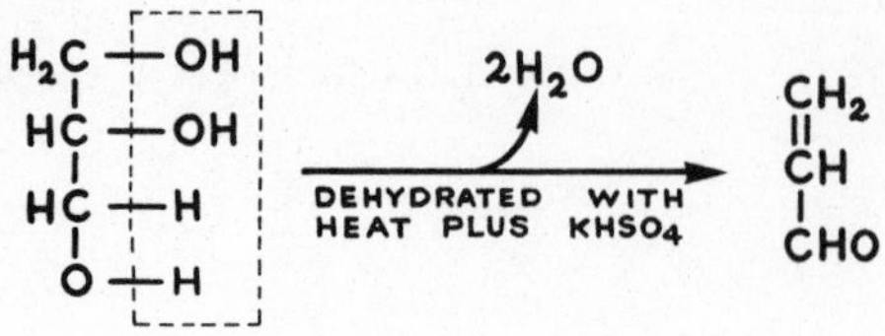

Figure 9–6. Conversion of glycerol to acrolein.

Fatty Aldehydes

The fatty acids may be reduced to fatty aldehydes. These compounds are found either combined or free in natural fats.

TRIACYLGLYCEROLS*
(Triglycerides)

The triacylglycerols (triglycerides), or so-called neutral fats, are esters of the alcohol glycerol and fatty acids. In naturally occurring fats, the proportion of triacylglycerol molecules containing the same fatty acid residue in all 3 ester positions is very small. They are nearly all mixed acylglycerols.

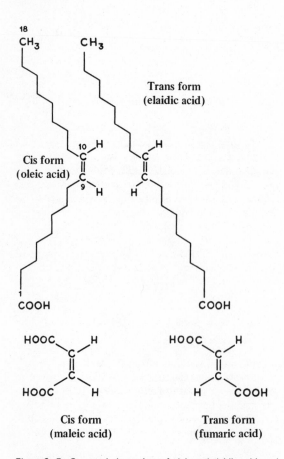

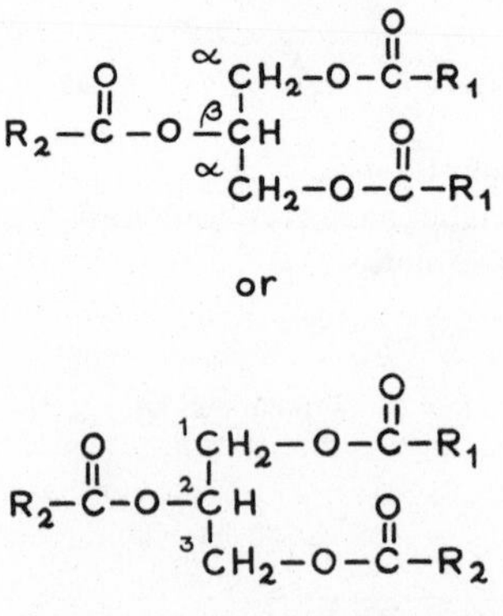

$$R_2-\overset{O}{\overset{\|}{C}}-O-\overset{\beta}{\underset{\alpha}{\overset{\alpha}{C}}}H \begin{array}{c} \overset{O}{\overset{\|}{CH_2-O-C-R_1}} \\ \overset{O}{\overset{\|}{CH_2-O-C-R_1}} \end{array}$$

or

$$R_2-\overset{O}{\overset{\|}{C}}-O-\overset{1}{\underset{3}{\overset{2}{C}}}H \begin{array}{c} \overset{O}{\overset{\|}{CH_2-O-C-R_1}} \\ \overset{O}{\overset{\|}{CH_2-O-C-R_2}} \end{array}$$

Figure 9–7. Triacylglycerols.

In Fig 9–7, if all 3 fatty acids were the same and if R were $C_{17}H_{35}$, the fat would be known as tristearin, since it consists of 3 stearic acid residues esterified with glycerol. In a mixed acylglycerol, more than one fatty acid is involved (Figs 9–8 and 9–9).

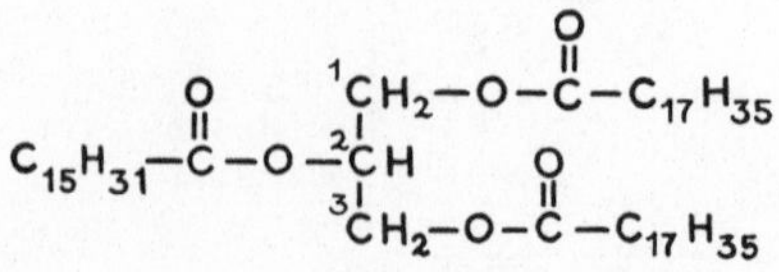

$$C_{15}H_{31}-\overset{O}{\overset{\|}{C}}-O-\overset{1}{\underset{3}{\overset{2}{C}}}H \begin{array}{c} \overset{O}{\overset{\|}{CH_2-O-C-C_{17}H_{35}}} \\ \overset{O}{\overset{\|}{CH_2-O-C-C_{17}H_{35}}} \end{array}$$

Figure 9–8. 1,3-Distearopalmitin (or a,a'-distearopalmitin).

Figure 9–5. Geometric isomerism of oleic and elaidic acids and of maleic and fumaric acids.

*See explanatory note on p 280.

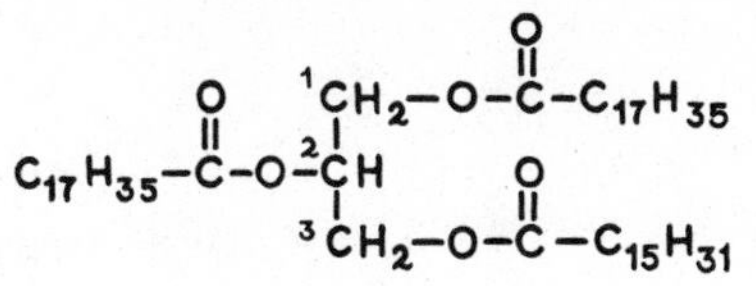

Figure 9–9. 1,2-Distearopalmitin (or α,β-distearopalmitin).

Nomenclature

The numbering system shown above has largely superseded the older α-, β- nomenclature. When it is required to number the carbon atoms of glycerol unambiguously, the -*sn*- (stereochemical numbering) system is used, eg, 1,2-distearyl-3-palmityl-*sn*-glycerol (as above).

Partial acylglycerols consisting of mono- and diacylglycerols wherein a single fatty acid or 2 fatty acids are esterified with glycerol are also found in the tissues. These are of particular significance in the synthesis and hydrolysis of triacylglycerols.

Waxes

If the fatty acid is esterified with an alcohol of high molecular weight instead of with glycerol, the resulting compound is called a wax.

PHOSPHOLIPIDS

The phospholipids include the following groups: (1) phosphatidic acid and phosphatidylglycerols, (2) phosphatidylcholine, (3) phosphatidylethanolamine, (4) phosphatidylinositol, (5) phosphatidylserine, (6) lysophospholipids, (7) plasmalogens, and (8) sphingomyelins.

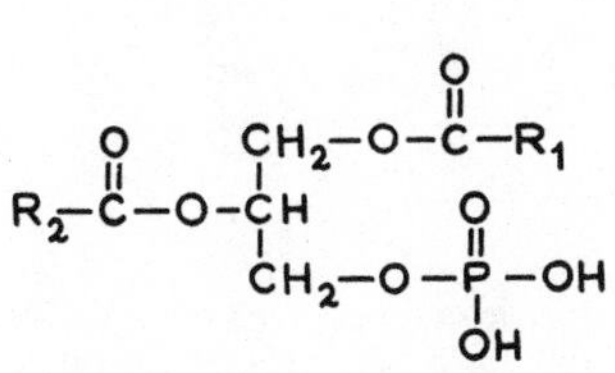

Figure 9–10. Phosphatidic acid.

Phosphatidic Acid & Phosphatidylglycerols

Phosphatidic acid is important as an intermediate in the synthesis of triacylglycerols and phospholipids but is not found in any great quantity in tissues (Fig 9–10).

Cardiolipin is a phospholipid which is found in mitochondria. It is formed from **phosphatidylglycerol** (Fig 9–11).

Phosphatidylcholine (Lecithin)

The lecithins contain glycerol and fatty acids, as do the simple fats, but they also contain phosphoric acid and choline. The lecithins are widely distributed in the cells of the body, having both metabolic and structural functions. Dipalmityl lecithin is a very effective surface active agent, preventing adherence, due to surface tension, of the inner surfaces of the lungs. However, most phospholipids have a saturated acyl radical in the C_1 position and unsaturated radical in the C_2 position. (Fig 9–12.)

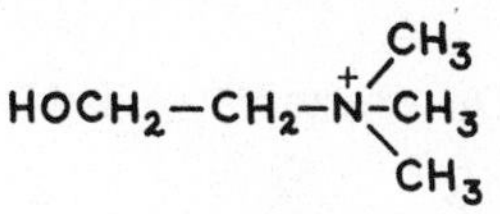

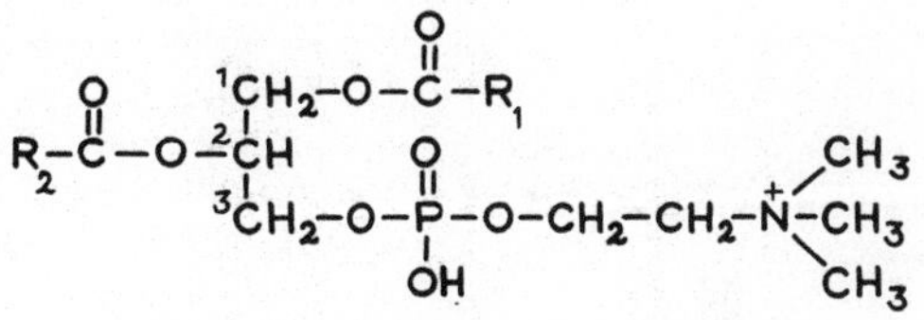

Figure 9–12. 3-Phosphatidylcholine.

Phosphatidylethanolamine (Cephalin)

The cephalins differ from lecithins only in that ethanolamine replaces choline (Fig 9–13).

Phosphatidylinositol (Lipositol)

Inositol (see p 173) as a constituent of lipids was first discovered in acid-fast bacteria. Later it was found to occur in phospholipids of brain tissue and of soybeans as well as in other plant phospholipids. The

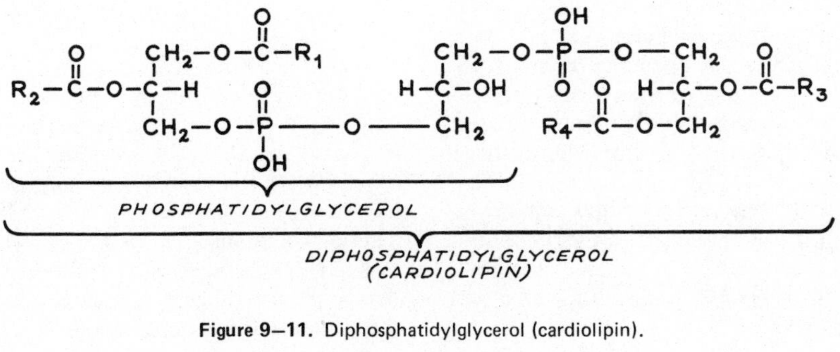

Figure 9–11. Diphosphatidylglycerol (cardiolipin).

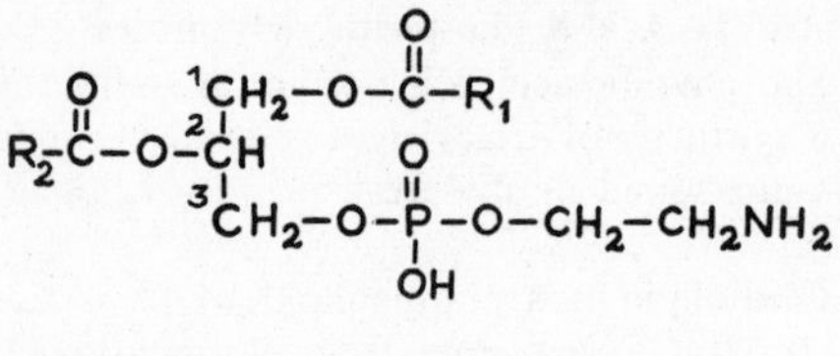

Figure 9–13. 3-Phosphatidylethanolamine.

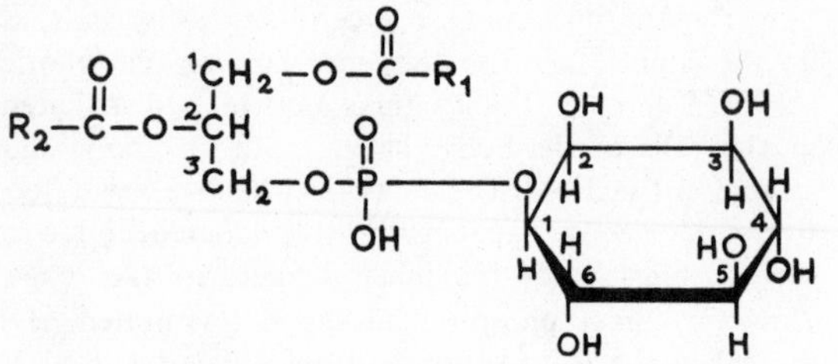

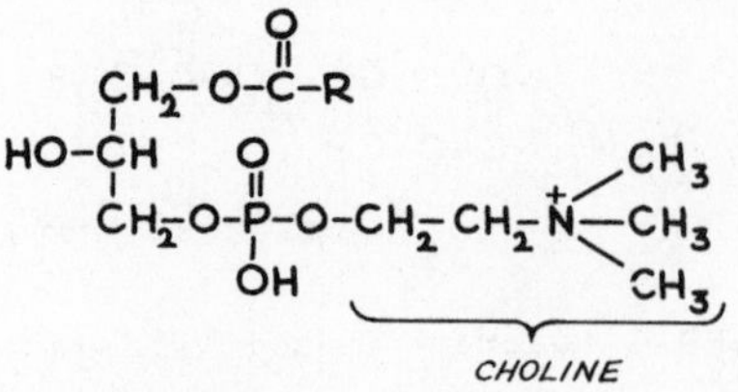

Figure 9–16. Lysolecithin.

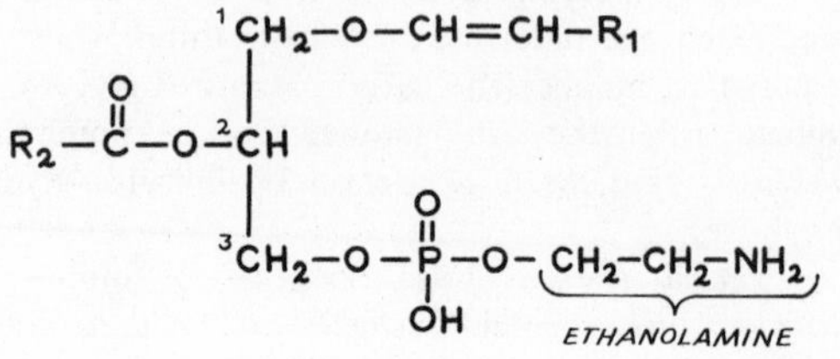

Figure 9–14. 3-Phosphatidylinositol.

Figure 9–17. Structure of plasmalogen (phosphatidal ethanolamine).

inositol is present as the stereoisomer, myo-inositol. (Fig 9–14.)

Phosphatidylserine

A cephalin-like phospholipid, phosphatidylserine, which contains the amino acid serine rather than ethanolamine, has been found in tissues. In addition, phospholipids containing threonine have been isolated from natural sources (Fig 9–15.)

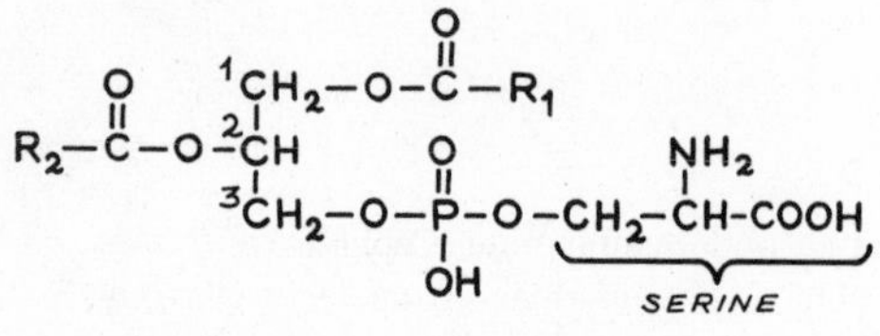

Figure 9–15. 3-Phosphatidylserine.

Lysophospholipids

These are phosphoacylglycerols containing only one acyl radical, eg, lysolecithin (Fig 9–16).

Plasmalogens (See Fig 9–17.)

These compounds constitute as much as 10% of the phospholipids of the brain and muscle. Structurally, the plasmalogens resemble lecithins and cephalins but give a positive reaction when tested for aldehydes with Schiff's reagent (fuchsin-sulfurous acid) after pretreatment of the phospholipid with mercuric chloride.

Plasmalogens possess an ether link on the C_1 carbon instead of the normal ester link found in most acylglycerols. Typically, the alkyl radical is an unsaturated alcohol; it is this group that gives rise to a positive aldehyde test after the above treatment.

In some instances, choline, serine, or inositol may be substituted for ethanolamine.

Sphingomyelins

Sphingomyelins are found in large quantities in brain and nerve tissue (see Chapter 37). No glycerol is present. On hydrolysis the sphingomyelins yield a fatty acid, phosphoric acid, choline, and a complex amino alcohol, sphingosine. (Fig 9–18.)

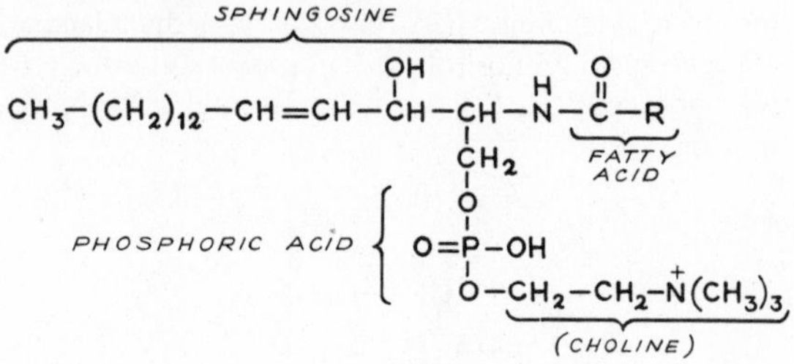

Figure 9–18. Structure of a sphingomyelin.

CEREBROSIDES
(Glycolipids)

Cerebrosides contain galactose, a high molecular weight fatty acid, and sphingosine. Therefore, they may also be classified with the sphingomyelins as sphingolipids. Individual cerebrosides are differentiated by the type of fatty acid in the molecule. These are **kerasin**, containing lignoceric acid; **cerebron**, with a hydroxy lignoceric acid (cerebronic acid); **nervon**, containing an unsaturated homologue of lignoceric acid called nervonic acid; and **oxynervon**, having apparently

$$CH_3-(CH_2)_{22}-COOH$$

LIGNOCERIC ACID

$$CH_3-(CH_2)_{21}-CH(OH)-COOH$$

CEREBRONIC ACID

$$CH_3-(CH_2)_7-CH=CH-(CH_2)_{13}-COOH$$

NERVONIC ACID

$$CH_3-(CH_2)_7-CH=CH-(CH_2)_{12}-CH(OH)-COOH$$

OXYNERVONIC ACID

Figure 9–19. Characteristic fatty acids of cerebrosides.

the hydroxy derivative of nervonic acid as its constituent fatty acid. Stearic acid is a major component of the fatty acids of rat brain cerebrosides. (Fig 9–19.)

The cerebrosides are found in many tissues besides brain. In Gaucher's disease, the cerebroside content of the reticuloendothelial cells (eg, the spleen) is very high and the kerasin is characterized by glucose replacing galactose in the cerebroside molecule. The cerebrosides are in much higher concentration in medullated than in nonmedullated nerve fibers.

Sulfatides are sulfate derivatives of the galactosyl residue in cerebrosides (Fig 9–20).

Gangliosides (Fig 9–21) are glycolipids occurring

in the brain. They contain N-acetylneuraminic acid (NANA; see p 12), fatty acids (of which 80–90% are of C-18 chain length), sphingosine, and 3 molecules of hexose (glucose and galactose). Hexosamine is a common constituent of virtually all naturally occurring gangliosides; the N-acetylneuraminic acid (NANA) content varies between 1 and 5 molecules per molecule of ganglioside.

STEROIDS

The steroids are often found in association with fat. They may be separated from the fat after saponification (see p 117), since they occur in the "unsaponifiable residue." All of the steroids have a similar cyclic nucleus resembling phenanthrene (rings A, B, and C) to which a cyclopentane ring (D) is attached. However, the rings are not uniformly unsaturated, so the parent (completely saturated) substance is better designated as cyclopentanoperhydrophenanthrene. The positions on the steroid nucleus are numbered as shown in Fig 9–22.

It is important to realize that in considering structural formulas of steroids a simple hexagonal ring denotes a completely saturated 6-carbon ring with all valences satisfied by hydrogen bonds unless shown

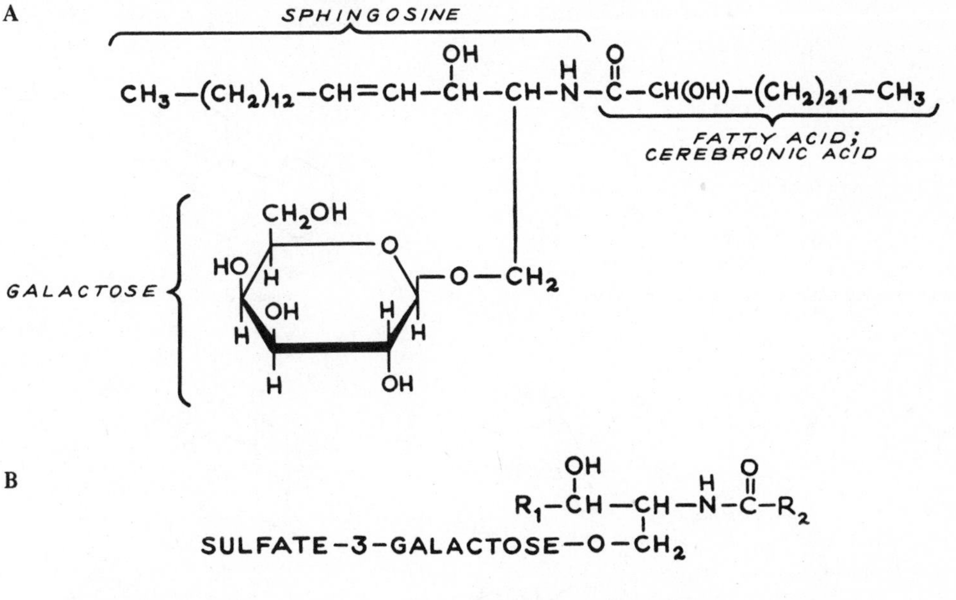

Figure 9–20. Structure of *(A)* a cerebroside and *(B)* a sulfatide (cerebroside sulfate).

CERAMIDE– GLUCOSE-GALACTOSE –N–ACETYLGALACTOSAMINE– GALACTOSE
(ACYLSPHINGOSINE)
|
NANA

Figure 9–21. A ganglioside.

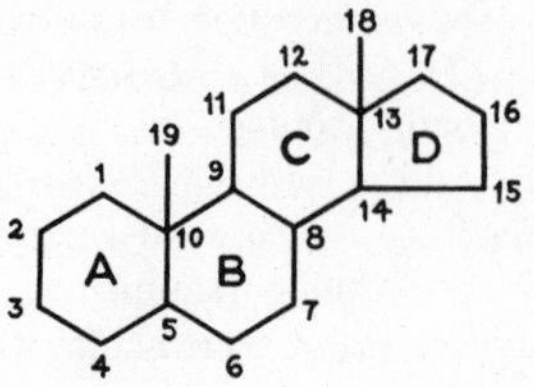

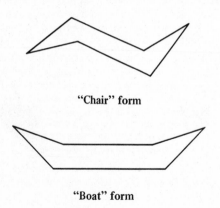

Figure 9—22. Cyclopentanoperhydrophenanthrene nucleus.

otherwise, ie, it is not a benzene ring. All double bonds are shown as such. Methyl side chains are shown as single bonds unattached at the farther (methyl) end. These occur typically at positions 10 and 13 (constituting C atoms 19 and 18). A side chain at position 17 is usual (as in cholesterol). If the compound has one or more hydroxyl groups and no carbonyl or carboxyl groups, it is a **sterol**, and the name terminates in -ol.

Stereochemical Aspects

Because of their complexity and the possibilities of asymmetry in the molecule, steroids have many potential stereoisomers. Each of the 6-carbon rings of the steroid nucleus is capable of existing in the 3-dimensional conformation either of a "chair" or of a "boat" (Fig 9—23).

In naturally occurring steroids, virtually all the rings are in the "chair" form, which is the more stable conformation. With respect to each other, the rings can be either -cis or -trans. (Fig 9—24.)

The junction between the A and B rings is -cis or -trans in naturally occurring steroids. That between B and C is -trans and the C/D junction is -trans except in cardiac glycosides and toad poisons (Klyne, 1965). Bonds attaching substituent groups above the plane of the rings are shown with bold solid lines (β), whereas those bonds attaching groups below are indicated with broken lines (a). The A ring of a 5a steroid is always -trans to the B ring, whereas it is -cis in a 5β steroid. The methyl groups attached to C_{10} and C_{13} are invariably in the β configuration.

Cholesterol (See Fig 9—25.)

Cholesterol is widely distributed in all cells of the body, but particularly in nervous tissue. It occurs in animal fats but not in plant fats. The metabolism of cholesterol is discussed on p 313. Cholesterol is designated as 3-hydroxy-5,6-cholestene.

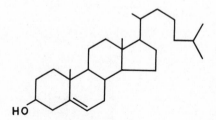

"Chair" form

"Boat" form

Figure 9—23. Conformations of stereoisomers.

Figure 9—25. Cholesterol.

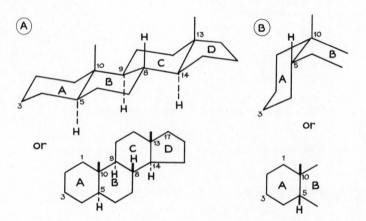

Figure 9—24. Generalized steroid nucleus, showing *(A)* an all-trans configuration between adjacent rings and *(B)* a cis configuration between rings A and B.

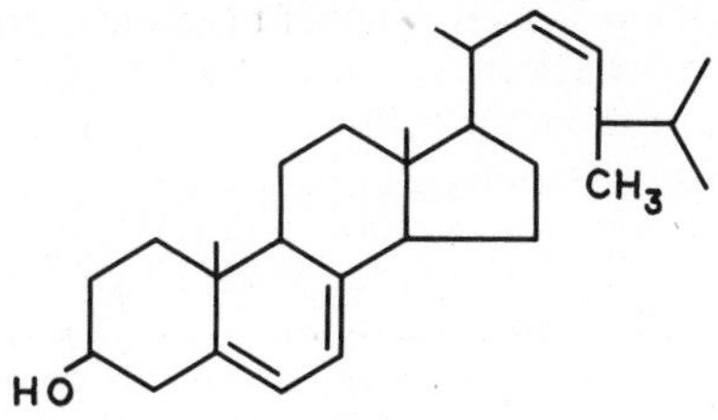

Figure 9—26. Ergosterol.

Ergosterol (See Fig 9—26.)

Ergosterol occurs in ergot and yeast. It is important as a precursor of vitamin D. When irradiated with ultraviolet light, it acquires antirachitic properties consequent to the opening of ring B.

Coprosterol

Coprosterol (coprostanol) occurs in feces as a result of the reduction by bacteria in the intestine of the double bond of cholesterol between C_5 and C_6. The orientation of rings A and B (between carbon atoms 5 and 10), which is **trans** in cholesterol, is **cis** in coprosterol.

Other Important Steroids

These include the bile acids, adrenocortical hormones, sex hormones, D vitamins, cardiac glycosides, the sitosterols of the plant kingdom, and some alkaloids.

Color Reactions to Detect Sterols

Saturated sterols (eg, coprosterol) do not give these color tests.

Liebermann-Burchard reaction. A chloroform solution of a sterol, when treated with acetic anhydride and sulfuric acid, gives a green color. The usefulness of this reaction is limited by the fact that various sterols give the same or a similar color. This reaction is the basis of a colorimetric estimation of blood cholesterol.

Salkowski test. A red to purple color appears when a chloroform solution of the sterol is treated with an equal volume of concentrated sulfuric acid.

Digitonin, $C_{56}H_{92}O_{29}$ (a glycoside occurring in digitalis leaves and seeds), precipitates cholesterol as the digitonide if the hydroxyl group in position 3 is free. This reaction serves as a method for the separation of free cholesterol and cholesteryl esters.

THE PLASMA LIPOPROTEINS

Extraction of the plasma lipids with a suitable lipid solvent and subsequent separation of the extract into various classes of lipids shows the presence of triacylglycerols, phospholipids, cholesterol and cholesteryl esters and, in addition, the existence of a much smaller fraction of unesterified long-chain fatty acids (free fatty acids, FFA) that accounts for less than 5% of the total fatty acid present in the plasma. This latter fraction, the free fatty acids, is now known to be metabolically the most active of the plasma lipids. An analysis of blood plasma showing the major lipid classes is given in Table 9—2.

Since lipids account for much of the energy expenditure of the body, the problem is presented of transporting a large quantity of hydrophobic material (lipid) in an aqueous environment. This is solved by associating the more insoluble lipids with more polar ones such as phospholipids and then combining them with cholesterol and protein to form a hydrophilic lipoprotein complex. It is in this way that triacylglycerols derived from intestinal absorption of fat or from the liver are transported in the blood as chylomicrons and very low density lipoproteins. Fat is released from adipose tissue in the form of free fatty acids and carried in the unesterified state in the plasma as an albumin-free fatty acid complex. Many classes of lipids are, therefore, transported in the blood as lipoproteins.

Pure fat is less dense than water; it follows that as the proportion of lipid to protein in lipoproteins increases, the density decreases. Use is made of this property in separating the various lipoproteins in plasma by ultracentrifugation. The rate at which each lipoprotein floats through a solution of NaCl (specific gravity 1.063) may be expressed in Svedberg (Sf) units of flotation. One Sf unit is equal to 10^{-13} cm/second/dyne/g at 26° C. The composition of the various lipoprotein fractions obtained by centrifugation is shown in Table 9—3; the density of lipoproteins increases as the protein content rises and the lipid content falls and as the size of the particle becomes smaller. The various chemical classes of lipids are seen to occur in varying amounts in most of the lipoprotein fractions. Since the fractions represent the physiologic entities present in the plasma, mere chemical analysis of the plasma lipids

Table 9—2. Lipids of the blood plasma in man.

Lipid	mg/dl	
	Mean	Range
Total lipid	570	360—820
Triacylglycerol	142	80—180*
Total phospholipid†	215	123—390
Lecithin		50—200
Cephalin		50—130
Sphingomyelins		15—35
Total cholesterol	200	107—320
Free cholesterol (nonesterified)	55	26—106
Free fatty acids (nonesterified)	12	6—16*

Total fatty acids (as stearic) range from 200—800 mg/dl; 45% are triacylglycerols, 35% phospholipids, 15% cholesteryl ester, and less than 5% free fatty acids.

*Varies with nutritional state.
†Analyzed as lipid phosphorus; mean lipid phosphorus = 9.2 mg/dl (range, 6.1—14.5). Lipid phosphorus X 25 = phospholipid as lecithin (4% phosphorus).

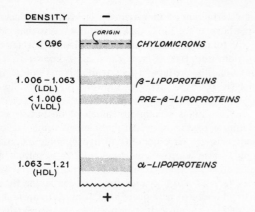

Figure 9–27. Separation of plasma lipoproteins by paper electrophoresis or by agarose gel electrophoresis.

(apart from free fatty acids) yields little information on their physiology.

In addition to the use of technics depending on their density, lipoproteins may be separated according to their electrophoretic properties (Fig 9–27) and may be identified more accurately by means of immunoelectrophoresis. Apart from FFA, 4 major groups of lipoproteins have been identified that are important physiologically and in clinical diagnosis. These are chylomicrons, very low density lipoproteins (VLDL or pre-β-lipoproteins), low density lipoproteins (LDL or β-lipoproteins), and high density lipoproteins (HDL or α-lipoproteins). Triacylglycerol is the predominant lipid in chylomicrons and VLDL, whereas cholesterol and phospholipid are the predominant lipids in LDL and HDL, respectively (Table 9–3).

The protein moiety of lipoproteins is known as an apolipoprotein or apoprotein, constituting nearly 60% of some HDL and as little as 1% of chylomicrons. Many lipoproteins contain more than one type of apoprotein polypeptide. They differ in their amino acid content and may be identified from their terminal amino acid residues by polyacrylamide gel electrophoresis and by immunochemical methods. Apoproteins are prepared by delipidation of isolated lipoproteins. The lipid-free apoproteins may be purified by gel filtration or by ion-exchange chromatography.

The larger lipoproteins—such as chylomicrons and VLDL—consist of a lipid core of nonpolar triacylglycerol and cholesteryl ester surrounded by more polar phospholipid, cholesterol, and apoproteins which can solubilize the particle in the surrounding aqueous plasma.

CHARACTERISTIC CHEMICAL REACTIONS & PROPERTIES OF THE LIPIDS

Hydrolysis

Hydrolysis of a lipid such as a triacylglycerol may be accomplished enzymatically through the action of lipases, yielding fatty acids and glycerol. Use may be made of the property of pancreatic lipase to attack the

Table 9–3. Composition of the lipoproteins in plasma of man. (Adapted from Olson & Vester, 1960.)

| | | | | | | | Composition | | | | |
| | | | | | | | Percentages of Total Lipid | | | | |
Fraction	Source	Diameter (nm)	Density	Sf	Protein (%)	Total Lipid (%)	Triacylglycerol	Phospholipid	Cholesteryl Ester	Cholesterol (Free)	Free Fatty Acids
Chylomicrons	Intestine	100–1000	< 0.96	> 400	1	99	88	8	3	1	. . .
Very low density lipoproteins (VLDL)	Liver and intestine	30–80	0.96–1.006	20–400	7	93	56	20	15	8	1
Low density lipoproteins LDL 1 or IDL	VLDL chylo-microns	25–30	1.006–1.019	12–20	11	89	29	26	34	9	1
LDL 2		20–25	1.019–1.063	2–12	21	79	13	28	48	10	1
High density lipoproteins HDL 1*	Liver; ? intestine	20	1.063	0–2							
HDL 2		10–20	1.063–1.125		33	67	16	43	31	10	. . .
HDL 3		7.5–10	1.125–1.210		57	43	13	46	29	6	6
Albumin-FFA	Adipose tissue		> 1.2810		99	1	0	0	0	0	100

IDL, intermediate density lipoprotein; FFA, free fatty acids.
*This fraction is quantitatively insignificant.

ester bonds in positions 1 and 3 preferentially to position 2 of triacylglycerols. **Phospholipases** attack the various ester linkages in phospholipids. Their specificity may be used to analyze the components of phospholipids. The sites of action of the various phospholipases are discussed on p 289.

Saponification

Hydrolysis of a fat by alkali is called **saponification**. The resultant products are glycerol and the alkali salts of the fatty acids, which are called **soaps**. Acid hydrolysis of a fat yields the free fatty acids and glycerol. Soaps are cleansing agents because of their emulsifying action. Some soaps of high molecular weight and a considerable degree of unsaturation are selective germicides. Others, such as sodium ricinoleate, have detoxifying activity against diphtheria and tetanus toxins.

Analytic Methods for the Characterization of Lipids

These include a determination of melting point, solidification temperature, and refractive index, as well as certain **chemical determinations**, as follows:

(1) **Saponification number:** The number of milligrams of KOH required to saponify 1 g of fat or oil. It varies inversely with the molecular weight of the fat or oil.

(2) **Acid number:** The number of milligrams of KOH required to neutralize the free fatty acid of 1 g of fat.

(3) **Polenske number:** The number of milliliters of 0.1 normal KOH required to neutralize the insoluble fatty acids (those not volatile with steam distillation) from 5 g of fat.

(4) **Reichert-Meissl number:** This is the same as the Polenske number except that, after a 5 g sample of the fat has been saponified, the **soluble** fatty acids are measured by titration of the distillate obtained by steam distillation of the saponification mixture.

(5) **Iodine number:** In the presence of iodine monobromide (Hanus method) or of iodine monochloride (Wijs method), unsaturated lipids will take up iodine. The iodine number is the amount (in grams) of iodine absorbed by 100 g of fat. This is a measure of the degree of unsaturation of a fat. Oils such as linseed oil or cottonseed oil have higher iodine numbers than solid fats such as tallow or beef fat because the former contain more unsaturated fatty acids in the fat molecule.

(6) **Acetyl number:** The number of milligrams of KOH required to neutralize the acetic acid obtained by saponification of 1 g of fat after it has been acetylated. This is a measure of the number of hydroxy-acid groups in the fat. Castor oil, because of its high content of ricinoleic acid, a fatty acid containing one OH group, has a high acetyl number (about 146).

The older methods of separation and identification of lipids, based on classical chemical procedures of crystallization, distillation, and solvent extraction, have now been largely supplanted by chromatographic procedures. Particularly useful for the separation of the various lipid classes is **thin layer chromatography** (TLC) and for the separation of the individual fatty acids, **gas-liquid chromatography** (GLC; Figs 9–28 and 9–29). Before these technics are applied to wet tissues, the lipids are extracted by a solvent system based usually on a mixture of chloroform-methanol (2:1).

Gas-liquid chromatography involves the physical separation of a moving gas phase by adsorption onto a stationary phase consisting of an inert solid such as silica gel or inert granules of ground firebrick coated with a nonvolatile liquid (eg, lubricating grease or silicone oils). In practice, a glass or metal column is packed with the inert solid and a mixture of the methyl esters of fatty acids is evaporated at one end of the column, the entire length of which is kept at temperatures of 170–225° C (Fig 9–28). A constantly flowing stream of an inert gas such as argon or helium

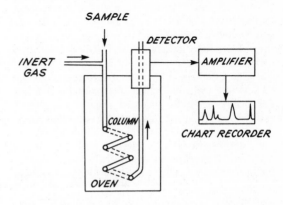

Figure 9–28. Diagrammatic representation of a gas-liquid chromatography apparatus.

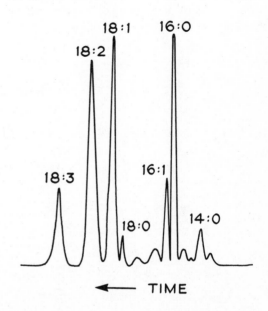

Figure 9–29. Separation of long chain fatty acids (as methyl esters) by gas-liquid chromatography. (A section of the record of a gas chromatogram.)

keeps the volatilized esters moving through the column. As with other types of chromatography, separation of the vaporized fatty acid esters is dependent upon the different affinities of the components of the gas mixture for the stationary phase. Gases which are strongly attracted to the stationary phase move through the column at a slower rate and therefore emerge at the end of the column later than those that are relatively less attracted. As the individual fatty acid esters emerge from the column, they are detected by physical or chemical means and recorded automatically as a series of peaks which appear at different times according to the tendency of each fatty acid ester to be retained by the stationary phase (Fig 9–29). The area under each peak is proportionate to the concentration of a particular component of the mixture. The identity of each component is established by comparison with the gas chromatographic pattern of a related standard mixture of known composition. A detector of radioactivity may also be incorporated into the gas stream, together with the mass detector. Thus, a measure of the specific radioactivity of each component separated is obtained.

The advantages of gas-liquid chromatography are its extreme sensitivity, which allows very small quantities of mixtures to be separated, and the fact that the columns may be used repeatedly. Application of the technic has shown that natural fats contain a wide variety of hitherto undetected fatty acids.

Thin layer chromatography (TLC) is carried out on glass plates which have been previously coated with a thin slurry of absorbent, usually silica gel. This is allowed to solidify and is then heated in an oven at a standard temperature and for a standard time. After cooling, the "activated" plate is "spotted" with the lipid mixture contained in a suitable solvent. The solvent is evaporated, the edge of the plate nearest the spots is dipped in an appropriate solvent mixture, and

the plate is run inside a closed tank until the solvent front arrives near the top edge of the plate. The plate is dried of solvent, and the position of the spots is determined by "charring" (spraying with sulfuric acid followed by heating) or fluorescence (with dichlorofluorescein) or by reacting with iodine vapor (Fig 9–30). Greater resolution of mixtures can be achieved by 2-dimensional development, using first one solvent in one direction and then, after drying, running the plate in a second solvent in a direction at right angles to the first. As well as being used for analytical purposes, thin layer chromatography may be used in purifying lipids when milligram quantities of lipid may be applied as a band to one plate. For recent reviews of general analytical methods applicable to lipids, see Lowenstein (1969) and Christie (1973).

Unsaponifiable Matter

Unsaponifiable matter includes substances in natural fats that cannot be saponified by alkali but are soluble in ether or petroleum ether. Since soaps are not ether-soluble, they may be separated from lipid mixtures by extraction with these solvents following saponification of the fat. Ketones, hydrocarbons, high molecular weight alcohols, and the steroids are examples of unsaponifiable residues of natural fats.

Hydrogenation

Hydrogenation of unsaturated fats in the presence of a catalyst (nickel) is known as "hardening." It is commercially valuable as a method of converting these fats, usually of plant origin, into solid fats as lard substitutes or margarines.

Rancidity

Rancidity is a chemical change that results in unpleasant odors and taste in a fat. The oxygen of the air is believed to attack the double bond in fatty acids to form a peroxide linkage. The iodine number is thus reduced, although little free fatty acid and glycerol are released. Lead or copper catalyzes rancidity; exclusion of oxygen or the addition of an antioxidant delays the process. Free radicals are produced during peroxide formation, and these can damage living tissues unless antioxidants, eg, tocopherols (vitamin E), are present which react with free radicals. Peroxidation is also catalyzed in vivo by heme compounds such as hemoglobin, myoglobin, and cytochromes.

Spontaneous Oxidation

Oils that contain highly unsaturated fatty acids (eg, linseed oil) are spontaneously oxidized by atmospheric oxygen at ordinary temperatures and form a hard, waterproof material. Such oils are added for this purpose to paints and shellacs. They are then known as "drying oils."

Membranes, Micelles, Liposomes, & Emulsions

In general, lipids are insoluble in water since they contain a predominance of nonpolar (hydrocarbon) groups. However, fatty acids, some phospholipids, and

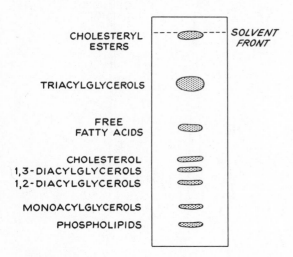

Figure 9–30. Separation of major lipid classes by thin layer chromatography. A suitable solvent system for the above would be hexane-diethyl ether-formic acid (80:20:2 v/v/v).

sphingolipids (the polar lipids) contain a great proportion of polar groups and are therefore partly soluble in water and partly soluble in nonpolar solvents. The molecules thus become oriented at oil-water interfaces with the polar group in the water phase and the nonpolar group in the oil phase. A bilayer of such polar lipids has been regarded as a basic structure in biologic membranes, being some 5 nm in thickness. When a critical concentration of polar lipids is present in an aqueous medium, they form micelles. Aggregations of bile salts into micelles and the formation of mixed micelles with the products of fat digestion may be important in facilitating absorption of lipids from the intestine. Liposomes are formed by sonicating a lipid in an aqueous medium. They consist of spheres of lipid bilayers which enclose part of the aqueous medium. Emulsions are much larger particles, formed usually by nonpolar lipids in an aqueous medium. These are stabilized by emulsifying agents such as polar lipids (eg, lecithin), which form a surface layer separating the main bulk of the nonpolar material from the aqueous phase (Fig 9–31).

THE CELL MEMBRANES

The plasma membrane of the living cell is a permeability barrier controlling the transfer of water and solutes between the external and internal environments. It was recognized (Overton) that the penetration of the cell by many classes of compounds was proportionate to their solubility in lipids rather than to molecular size. This led to the concept that the cell membrane is lipoid in nature. Gorter and Grendel observed in experiments using the Langmuir trough that the area occupied by lipids extracted from erythrocytes and spread as a monomolecular film on water was twice the surface area of the cells before extraction. This finding suggested that the membrane lipids were arranged in a bimolecular layer, with the nonpolar ends of the molecules toward each other within the membrane and the polar ends oriented toward the aqueous phase inside and outside the cell (Fig 9–31). In 1934, Danielli & Davson proposed that the lipid bilayer is sandwiched between protein (Fig 9–32[A]).

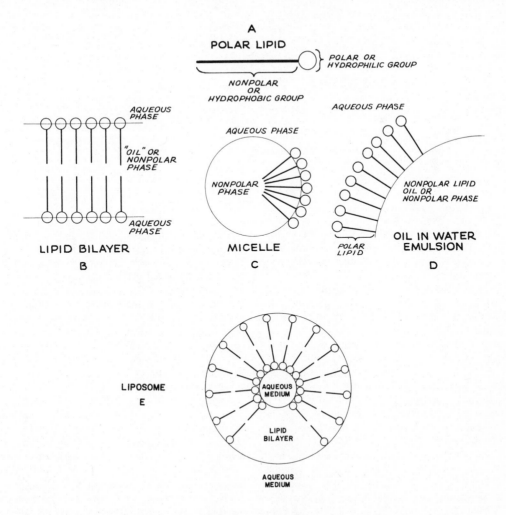

Figure 9–31. Formation of lipid membranes, micelles, emulsions, and liposomes.

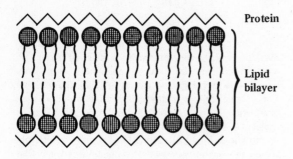

Protein

Lipid
bilayer

A. Danielli and Davson model.

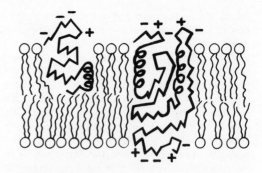

B. Fluid mosaic model: Section through membrane showing globular proteins embedded in a bilayer of phospholipids.

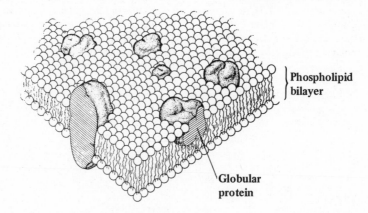

Phospholipid
bilayer

Globular
protein

C. Fluid mosaic model: Schematic 3-dimensional cross-section.

Figure 9–32. Cell membrane concepts.

However, this type of structure would not allow for the penetration of the membrane by lipophobic solutes, and it was suggested later that protein-lined pores traversed the lipid bilayer.

Analysis of rat liver plasma membranes reveals a composition of approximately 50–60% protein, 30% phospholipid, 5% cholesterol, and 5% carbohydrate. The spatial configuration of molecules of phospholipids such as phosphatidyl choline and sphingomyelins that make up the bulk of the membrane lipids is similar in that there are 2 hydrophobic fatty acid carbon chains lying parallel to each other with a hydrophilic group at the opposite end of the molecule (Fig 9–33[A]). The bulk of the membrane lipids can therefore be represented as polar end groups joined to 2 hydrophobic carbon chains (Fig 9–33[B]), and these readily arrange themselves into bilayers and micelles.

To overcome thermodynamic objections to the traditional concept of the simple lipid bilayer model of the plasma membrane, Singer & Nicolson (1972) proposed a **fluid mosaic model** (Fig 9–32[C]). This consists of a mosaic of globular proteins in a phospholipid bilayer, all of which are in a dynamic and fluid state. These investigators distinguish between 2 categories of proteins bound to membranes: "peripheral" proteins that can be removed without disrupting the membrane, and "integral" proteins that extend into and through the membrane. The hydrophilic portions of the polypeptides are located on both surfaces of the membranes and are considered to be in the irregular coil configuration, whereas the hydrophobic portions are in the helical form and within the membrane (Fig 9–32[B]). Groups of such structures might form a membrane pore and be important in transport. Thus, not only the lipids but also the proteins of the membrane are considered to be **amphipathic**, ie, they are structurally asymmetric, with a highly polar end and a nonpolar end. The polar end of the protein would be a region containing ionic amino acid residues and any covalently bound sugar residues which would be in contact with the aqueous phase (Fig 8–28). The results of electron micrography of freeze-etched preparations of membranes strongly suggest that a substantial amount of protein is deeply embedded in the membrane.

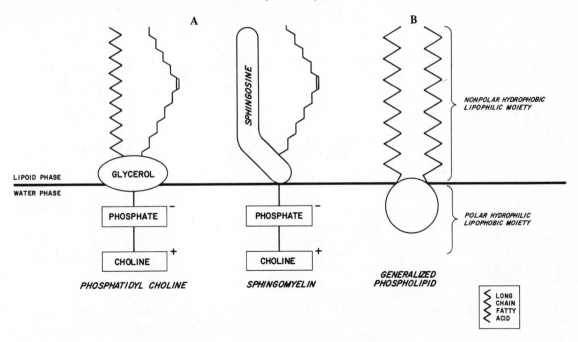

Figure 9–33. Orientation of phospholipid molecules at lipoid/water interfaces.

• • •

References

Ansell GB, Hawthorne JN, Dawson RMC (editors): *Form and Function of Phospholipids.* Elsevier, 1973.

Christie WW: *Lipid Analysis.* Pergamon Press, 1973.

Gunstone FD: *An Introduction to the Chemistry and Biochemistry of Fatty Acids and Their Glycerides,* 2nd ed. Chapman & Hall, 1967.

Gurr MI, James AT: *Lipid Biochemistry: An Introduction.* Chapman & Hall, 1975.

Hanahan DJ: *Lipide Chemistry.* Wiley, 1960.

Hilditch TP, Williams PN: *The Chemical Constitution of Natural Fats,* 4th ed. Chapman & Hall, 1964.

Johnson AR, Davenport JB: *Biochemistry and Methodology of Lipids.* Wiley, 1971.

Klyne W: *The Chemistry of the Steroids.* Methuen, 1965.

Lowenstein JM (editor): *Methods in Enzymology.* Vol 14. Academic Press, 1969.

Pecsok RL (editor): *Principles and Practice of Gas Chromatography.* Wiley, 1959.

Ralston AW: *Fatty Acids and Their Derivatives.* Wiley, 1948.

Rothfield LI (editor): *Structure and Function of Biological Membranes.* Academic Press, 1971.

Singer SJ, Nicolson GL: The fluid mosaic model of the structure of cell membranes. Science 175:720, 1972.

10 . . .
Nucleotides

The nucleotides are important intracellular molecules of low molecular weight which participate in a wide variety of biochemical processes. Perhaps the best known role of the purine and pyrimidine nucleotides is to serve as the monomeric precursors of RNA and DNA. However, the **purine** ribonucleotides serve also in biologic systems as the ubiquitous high-energy source, ATP, as regulatory signals (cyclic AMP [cAMP] and cyclic GMP) in a wide variety of tissues and organisms, and as components of the widely used coenzymes FAD, NAD, and NADP and of an important methyl donor, S-adenosylmethionine.

The **pyrimidine** nucleotides, in addition to providing monomeric precursors for nucleic acids, also serve as high-energy intermediates, such as UDP-glucose and UDP-galactose in carbohydrate metabolism and CDP-acylglycerol in lipid synthesis.

The various purine and pyrimidine bases which occur in the nucleotides are derived by appropriate substitution on the ring structures of the parent substances, purine or pyrimidine. Structures of these parent nitrogenous bases are shown in Fig 10–1. The positions on the rings are numbered according to the international system. Note that the direction of the numbering of the purine ring is different from that of the pyrimidine ring but that the number 5 carbon is the same in both heterocyclic compounds. Both the purine and the pyrimidine bases are planar molecules owing to their π electron clouds, the significance of which is discussed in Chapter 11.

The 3 major **pyrimidine bases** found in the nucleotides of both prokaryotes and eukaryotes are cyto-

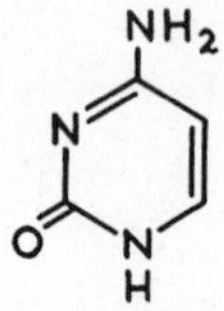

Cytosine
(2-oxy-4-aminopyrimidine)

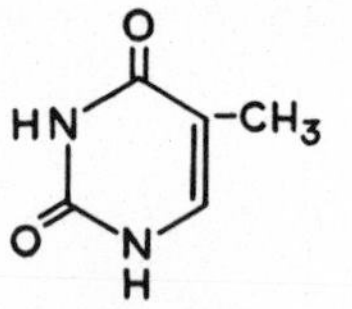

Thymine
(2,4 dioxy-5-
methylpyrimidine)

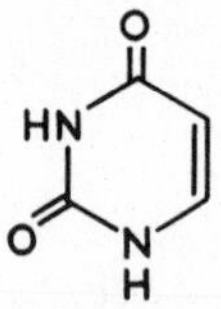

Uracil
(2,4-dioxypyrimidine)

Figure 10–2. The 3 major pyrimidine bases found in nucleotides.

sine, thymine, and **uracil** (Fig 10–2). The **purine bases**, **adenine** and **guanine**, are the 2 major purines found in living organisms. Two other purine bases, **hypoxanthine** and **xanthine**, also occur as intermediates in the metabolism of adenine and guanine. (Fig 10–3.) In humans, a completely oxidized purine base, **uric acid**, is formed as the end product of purine catabolism. This compound is discussed in greater detail in Chapter 24.

Because of their resonant structures, these aromatic molecules can exist in a lactim or lactam form (Fig 10–4); the latter is by far the predominant tautomer of uracil or thymine under physiologic conditions. (The importance of the lactim versus the lactam form becomes apparent in the discussions on base pairing and mutagenesis in Chapters 25 and 26.)

In plants, a series of purine bases containing methyl substituents occurs (Fig 10–5). Many have pharmacologic properties. Examples are coffee, which contains caffeine (1,3,7-trimethylxanthine); tea, which contains theophylline (1,3-dimethylxanthine); and cocoa, which contains theobromine (3,7-dimethylxan-

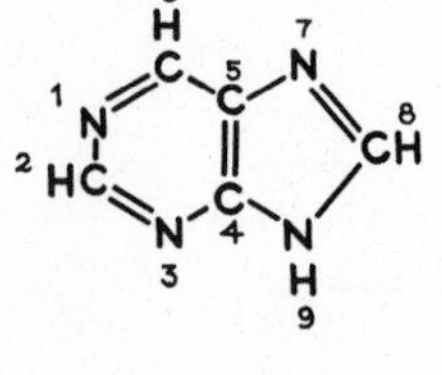

Purine

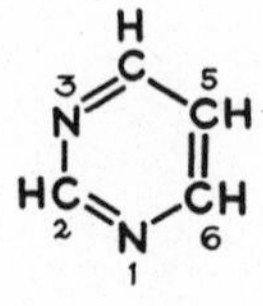

Pyrimidine

Figure 10–1. Structures of a purine and a pyrimidine with the positions of the elements numbered according to the international system.

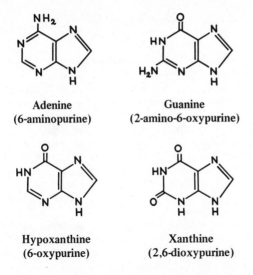

Adenine
(6-aminopurine)

Guanine
(2-amino-6-oxypurine)

Hypoxanthine
(6-oxypurine)

Xanthine
(2,6-dioxypurine)

Figure 10—3. The major purine bases present in nucleotides.

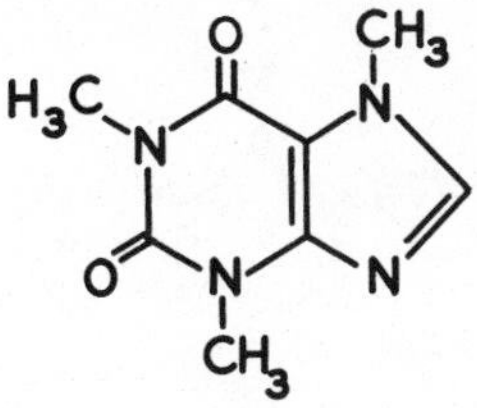

Caffeine
(1,3,7-trimethyl-
xanthine)

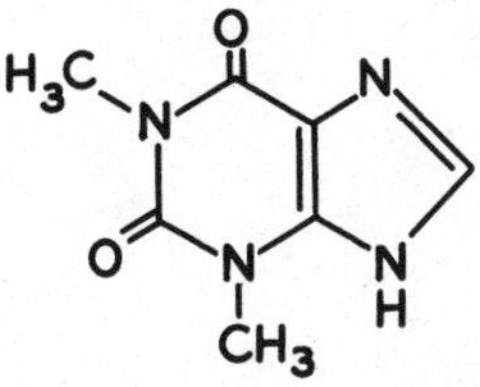

Theophylline
(1,3-dimethyl-
xanthine)

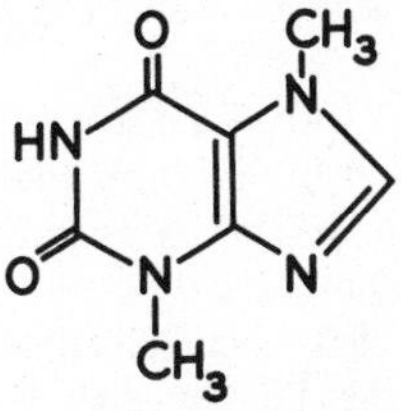

Theobromine
(3,7-dimethyl-
xanthine)

Figure 10—5. The structures of some methylxanthines commonly occurring in foodstuffs.

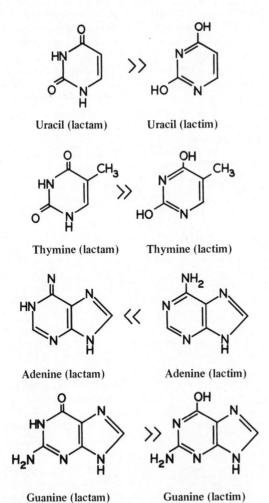

Uracil (lactam)

Uracil (lactim)

Thymine (lactam)

Thymine (lactim)

Adenine (lactam)

Adenine (lactim)

Guanine (lactam)

Guanine (lactim)

Figure 10—4. The structures of the tautomers of uracil, thymine, adenine, and guanine with the predominant forms indicated.

thine). The biologic properties of these compounds are described in Chapter 24 in the discussion of the metabolism of cyclic nucleotides.

In natural materials, numerous minor (ie, unusual) bases occur in addition to the 5 major bases—adenine, guanine, cytosine, thymine, and uracil—described above. Some of these unusual substituted bases are found only in the nucleic acids of bacteria and viruses, but many are also found in the transfer RNAs of both prokaryotes and eukaryotes. Both 5-methylcytosine and 5-hydroxymethylcytosine, for example, are significant components of bacteria and bacteriophage, respectively (Fig 10—6). More recently, several unusual bases have been discovered in the messenger RNA molecules of mammalian cells. N^6-methyladenine, N^6-dimethyladenine, and N^7-methylguanine are found in the nucleic acids of mammalian cells (Fig 10—7). A uracil modified at the N_3 position by the attachment

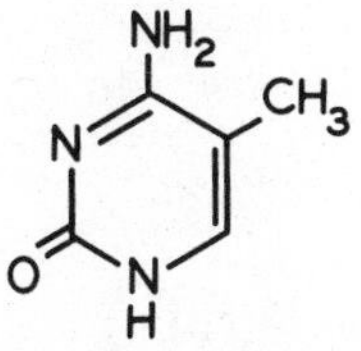

5-Methylcytosine

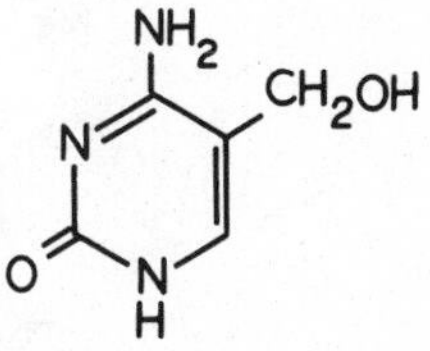

5-Hydroxymethylcytosine

Figure 10—6. The structures of 2 uncommon naturally occurring pyrimidine bases.

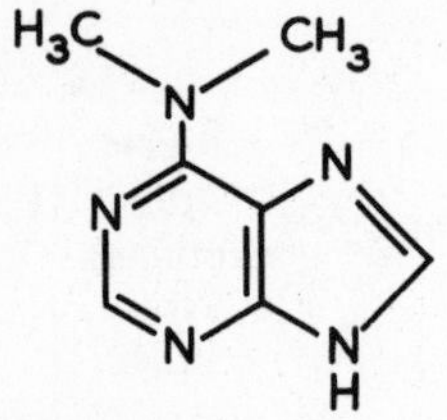

N^6,N^6-Dimethyladenine 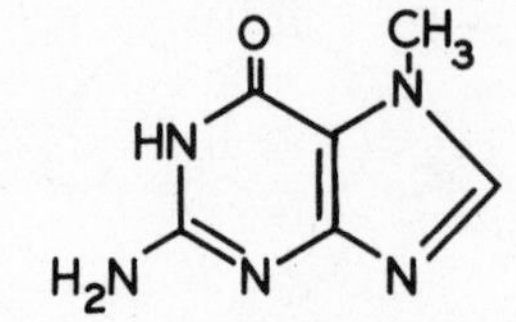   7-Methylguanine

Figure 10–7. The structures of 2 uncommon naturally occurring purine bases.

of an (*a*-amino, *a*-carboxyl)-propyl group has also been detected in bacteria. The functions of these substituted purine and pyrimidine nucleotide bases are not fully understood.

At neutral pH, guanine is the least soluble of the bases, followed in this respect by xanthine. Although uric acid as urate is relatively soluble at a neutral pH, its pK is 5.75, so that it becomes highly insoluble in a solution with a lower pH, such as urine. Guanine is not a normal constituent of normal human urine, but xanthine and uric acid do occur in human urine. In view of their low solubility, it is not surprising that these latter 2 purines are most likely to be found as constituents of stones formed within the urinary tract.

NUCLEOSIDES & NUCLEOTIDES

The **free** bases occurring in nature are much less abundant forms of purines and pyrimidines than are their nucleosides and nucleotides. A **nucleoside** (Fig 10–8) is composed of a purine or a pyrimidine base to which a sugar (usually either D-ribose or 2-deoxyribose) is attached at the N$_9$ or N$_1$, respectively. Thus, the adenine ribonucleoside **adenosine** consists of adenine with D-ribose attached at the 9 position. **Guanosine** consists of guanine with D-ribose attached at the 9 position. Cytidine is cytosine with ribose attached at its N$_1$ position. Uridine consists of ribose attached at the N$_1$ position of uracil.

The 2′-deoxyribonucleosides consist of 2-deoxyribose attached to the purine or pyrimidine bases at the same positions described above. The attachment of the ribose or 2-deoxyribose to the ring structures of the purine or pyrimidine bases is through an N-glycosidic bond, which is relatively acid labile. Although, theoretically, free rotation occurs about this N-glycosidic bond of the sugar moiety and the purine or pyrimidine ring structure, steric hindrance between these 2 moieties in fact prevents free rotation. In the naturally occurring nucleosides, the **anti** conformation is strongly favored over the **syn** form (Fig 10–9). As is discussed in Chapter 11, the anti form is necessary for the proper positioning of the complementary purine and pyrimidine bases in the double-stranded form of deoxyribonucleic acid.

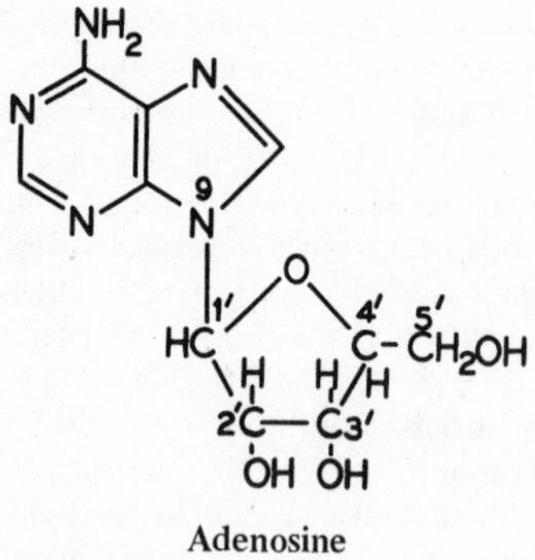

Adenosine

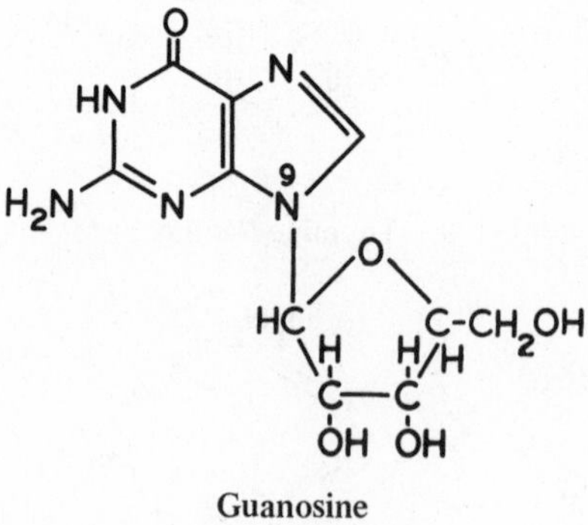

Guanosine

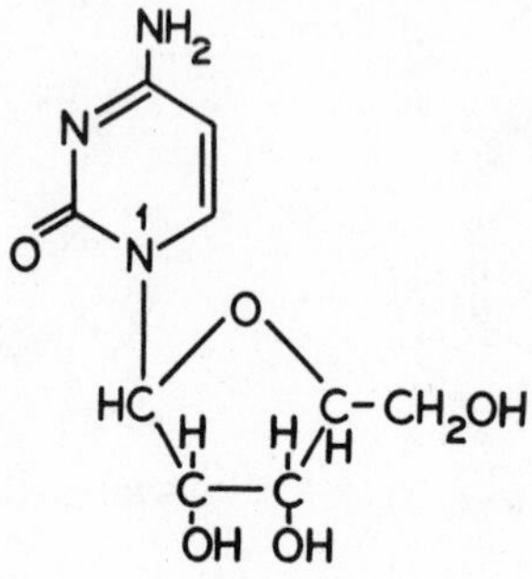

Cytidine

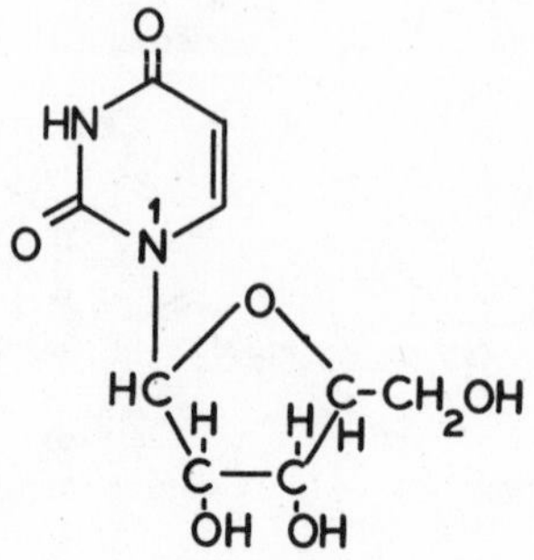

Uridine

Figure 10–8. Structures of ribonucleosides.

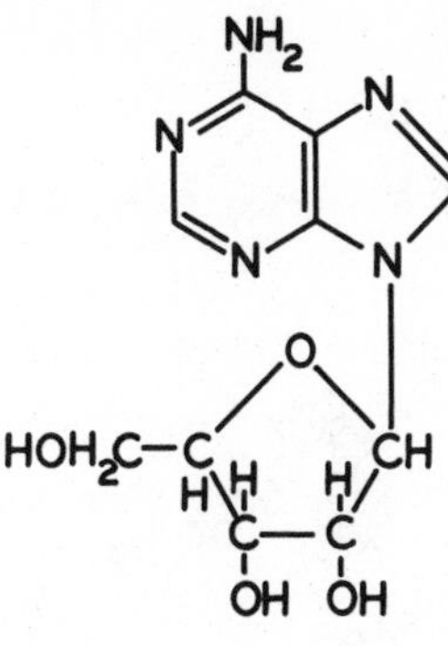

Syn

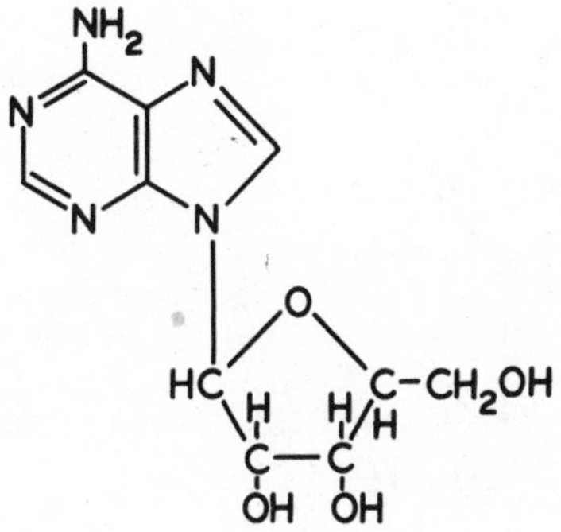

Anti

Figure 10–9. The structures of the **syn** and **anti** configurations of adenosine.

Nucleotides are nucleosides phosphorylated on one or more of the hydroxyl groups of the sugar (ribose or deoxyribose) (Fig 10–10). Thus, adenosine monophosphate (AMP or adenylate) is adenine + ribose + phosphate. 2'-Deoxyadenosine monophosphate (dAMP or deoxyadenylate) consists of adenine + 2-deoxyribose + phosphate. The only sugar commonly found attached to uracil is ribose, and that commonly found attached to thymine is 2-deoxyribose. Therefore, thymidylic acid (TMP) is thymine + 2-deoxyribose + phosphate and uridylic acid (UMP) is uracil + ribose + phosphate (Fig 10–11). DNA is a polymer of thymidylic acid, 2'-deoxycytidylic acid, 2'-deoxyadenylic acid, and 2'-deoxyguanylic acid. RNA is a polymer containing uridylate, cytidylate, adenylate, and guanylate.

There are exceptions to the above structures of nucleotides. For example, in tRNA the ribose moiety is occasionally attached to uracil at the 5 position, thus establishing a carbon-to-carbon linkage instead of the usual nitrogen-to-carbon linkage. This unusual compound is called pseudouridine (Ψ). The tRNA molecules contain another unusual nucleotide structure, ie, thymine attached to ribose monophosphate. This compound is formed subsequent to the synthesis of the tRNA by methylation of the UMP residue by S-adenosylmethionine (see below). Pseudouridylic acid (ΨMP) is similarly rearranged from uridylic acid after the tRNA molecule has been synthesized.

Nomenclature of Nucleosides & Nucleotides

The position of the phosphate in the nucleotide is indicated by a numeral. For example, adenosine with the phosphate attached to carbon 3 of the sugar ribose would be designated adenosine-3'-phosphate. The prime mark after the numeral is required to differentiate the numbered position on the sugar moiety from the numbered position on a purine or pyrimidine base, which would not be followed by the prime mark. A nucleotide of 2'-deoxyadenosine with the phosphate moiety attached to the carbon 5 position of the sugar would be designated 2'-deoxyadenosine-5'-phosphate. (Fig 10–12.)

The abbreviations A, G, C, T, and U may be used to designate a nucleoside in accordance with the purine or pyrimidine base it contains: adenine, guanine, cytosine, thymine, or uracil, respectively. The prefix d is added if the sugar of the nucleoside is 2'-deoxyribose. When the nucleoside occurs in the free form as a mononucleotide (ie, not a component of nucleic acid polynucleotide), the abbreviation MP (monophosphate) may be added to the abbreviation designating

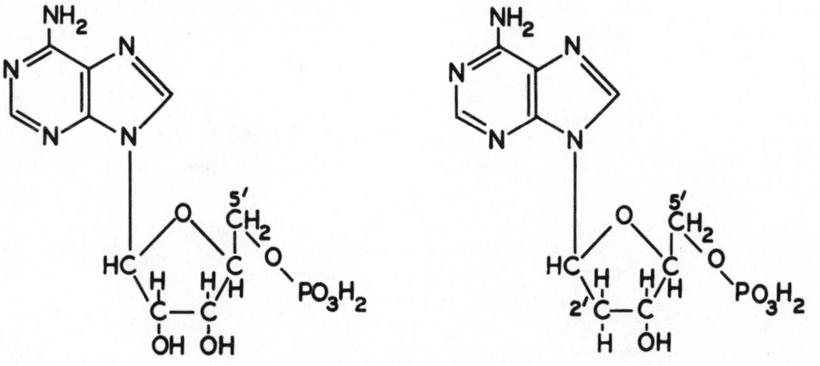

Figure 10–10. The structures of adenylic acid (AMP) *(left)* and 2'-deoxyadenylic acid (dAMP) *(right)*.

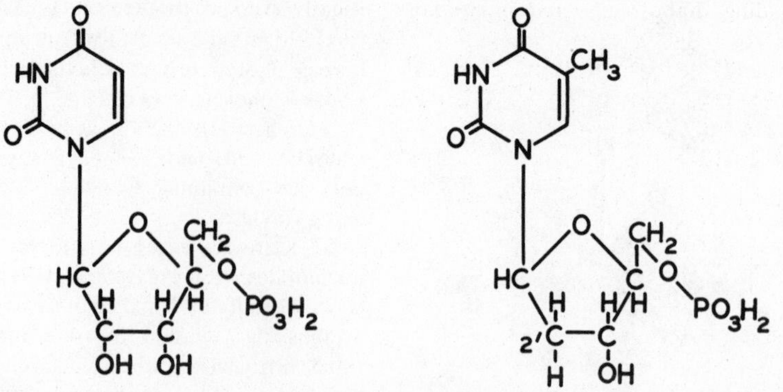

Figure 10–11. The structures of uridylic acid (UMP) *(left)* and thymidylic acid (TMP) *(right)*.

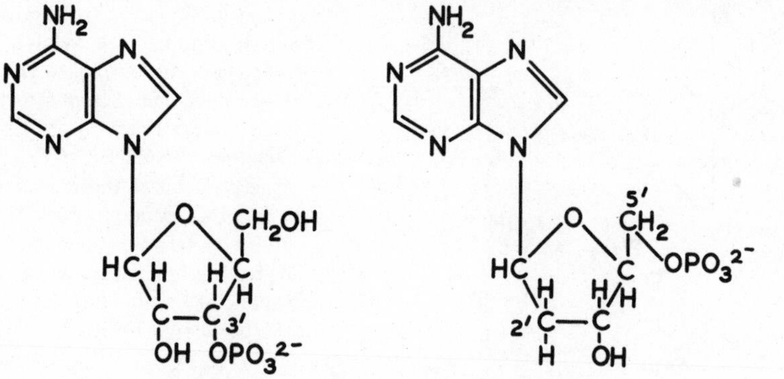

Figure 10–12. The structures of adenosine-3′-monophosphate *(left)* and 2′-deoxy-5′-monophosphate *(right)*.

the nucleoside. For example, guanosine containing 2′-deoxyribose would be designated dG (deoxyguanosine) and the corresponding monophosphate with the phosphate esterified to the carbon 3 of the deoxyribose moiety is designated dG-3′-MP. Generally, when the phosphate is esterified to the carbon 5 of the ribose or deoxyribose moiety, the prefixed primed number (5′) is deleted. For example, guanosine-5′-monophosphate would be abbreviated GMP, while the

5′-monophosphate of 2′-deoxyguanosine would be designated dGMP. When 2 or 3 phosphates are attached to the sugar moiety in the acid anhydride form, the abbreviations DP (diphosphate) and TP (triphosphate) are added to the abbreviations for the corresponding purine or pyrimidine nucleoside. Thus, adenosine triphosphate with the triphosphates attached to the 5′ carbon of the adenosine would be abbreviated ATP. The structure of ATP is shown in Fig 10–13 along

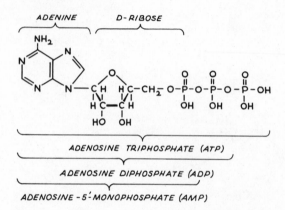

Figure 10–13. The structure of ATP and the structures of the corresponding diphosphate and monophosphate forms.

with its corresponding diphosphate and monophosphate forms. Because the phosphates are in the acid anhydride form—a low entropy situation—the phosphates are said to be high-energy, ie, high potential energy. The hydrolysis of 1 mol of ATP to ADP releases 7000 cal of potential energy.

NATURALLY OCCURRING NUCLEOTIDES

Free nucleotides which are not an integral part of nucleic acids are also found in tissues. Many have important functions. Some of these compounds are briefly described.

Adenosine Derivatives

Adenosine diphosphate and adenosine triphosphate are important compounds in view of their participation in oxidative phosphorylation and, in the case of ATP, as the source of high-energy phosphate for nearly every energy-requiring reaction in the cell. The ATP concentration in most living mammalian cells is nearly 1 mM. ATP is the most abundant intracellular free nucleotide.

Cyclic AMP ($3',5'$-adenosine monophosphate; cAMP) is an unusual but important adenosine derivative which is present in most animal cells. cAMP mediates a series of diverse extracellular signals of considerable importance to the function of the organism as a whole. cAMP is formed from ATP (Fig 10–14). The reaction is catalyzed by the enzyme **adenylate cyclase**, the activity of which is regulated by a series of complex interactions many of which involve hormone receptors. cAMP is destroyed in tissues by its conversion to AMP in a reaction catalyzed by **cAMP phosphodiesterase**. Intracellular cAMP concentrations are usually near 1 μM.

The incorporation of sulfate into ester linkages in compounds such as sulfated mucopolysaccharides requires the preliminary "activation" of the sulfate molecule. Sulfate is "activated" by reacting with ATP to form adenosine-$3'$-phosphate-$5'$-phosphosulfate (PAPS) in the reaction shown in Fig 10–15. The active

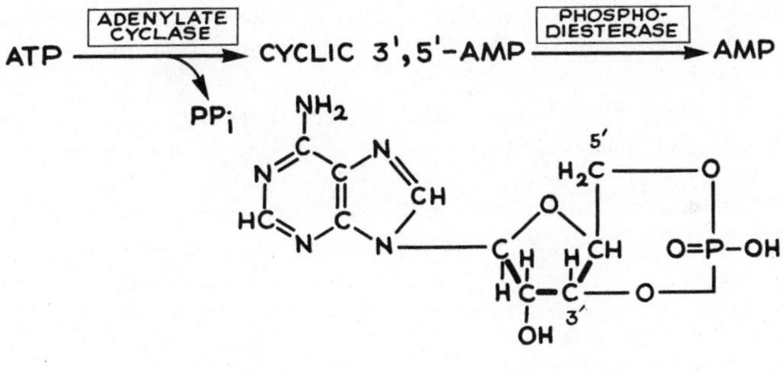

Figure 10–14. Formation of cAMP from ATP and destruction of cAMP by phosphodiesterase.

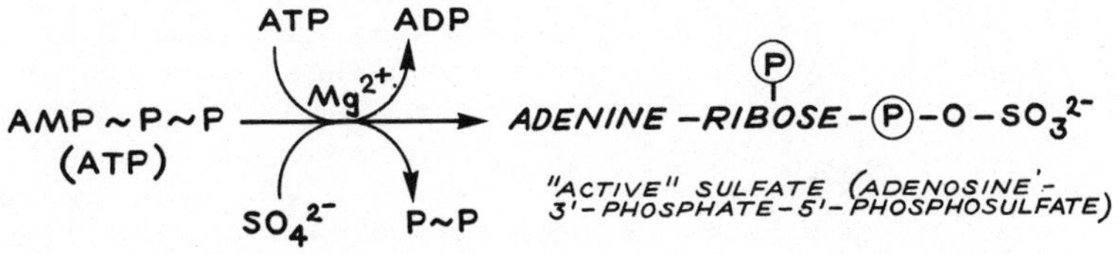

Figure 10–15. The formation and structure of adenosine $3'$-phosphate-$5'$-phosphosulfate.

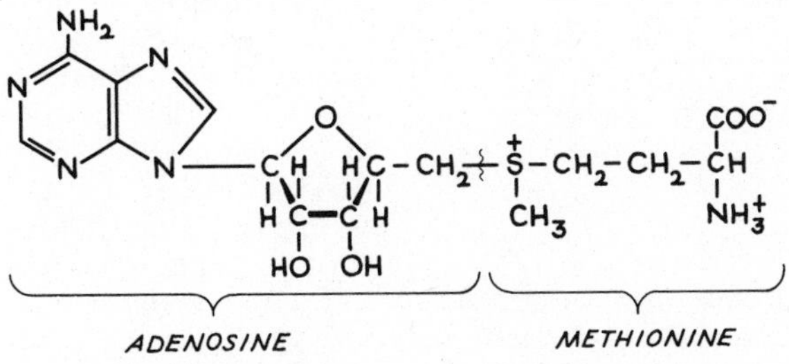

Figure 10–16. The structure of S-adenosylmethionine.

sulfate moiety is also required as the substrate for sulfate conjugation reactions.

Another important naturally occurring adenosine derivative, **S-adenosylmethionine** (Fig 10–16), serves as a form of "active" methionine. S-Adenosylmethionine serves widely as a methyl donor in many diverse methylation reactions and as a source of propylamine for the synthesis of polyamines.

Guanosine Derivatives

Guanosine nucleotides, particularly guanosine diphosphate and guanosine triphosphate, serve in several energy-requiring systems. These are analogs of ADP and ATP, respectively. For example, the oxidation of a-ketoglutaric acid to succinyl-CoA in the tricarboxylic acid cycle involves oxidative phosphorylation with transfer of phosphate to GDP to form GTP. This phosphorylation reaction is quite similar to those involving the phosphorylation of ADP to ATP. GTP also serves both as an allosteric regulator and as an energy source for protein synthesis on polyribosomes. It therefore has an important role in the maintenance of the internal milieu.

Cyclic GMP or 3'5'-guanosine monophosphate (Fig 10–17) appears also to be an important intracellular signal of extracellular events. In at least some cases, cyclic GMP acts antagonistically to cAMP. Cyclic GMP is formed from GTP by an enzyme called **guanylate cyclase** which is similar in many ways to adenylate cyclase. Guanylate cyclase, like adenylate cyclase, appears to be regulated by a variety of effectors, including hormones. Cyclic GMP is also catabolized by a phosphodiesterase to produce its respective 5'-monophosphate.

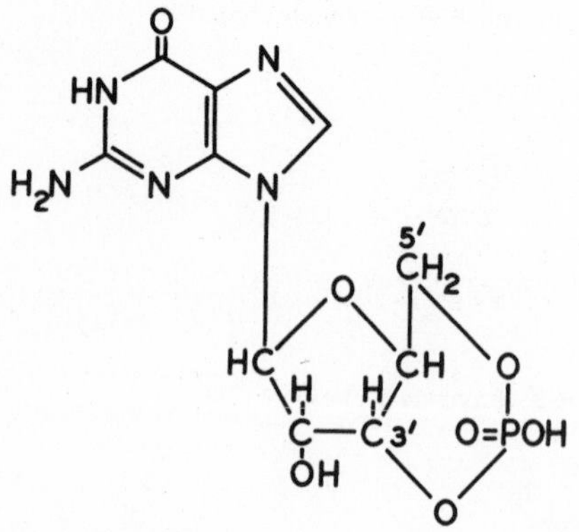

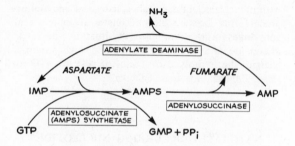

Figure 10–18. The purine nucleotide cycle.

AMP, a reaction which occurs particularly in muscle as part of the purine nucleotide cycle (Fig 10–18). Inosinate, derived from AMP, when reconverted to AMP results in the net production of ammonia from aspartate. Removal of the phosphate group from inosinate forms the nucleoside inosine (hypoxanthine riboside), an intermediate in another cycle referred to as the purine salvage cycle (see Chapter 24).

Analogs of ADP and ATP in which the purine nucleoside derivative is inosine rather than adenosine have been found occasionally to participate in phosphorylation reactions. These compounds are inosine diphosphate (IDP) and inosine triphosphate (ITP).

Uracil Derivatives

Uridine nucleotide derivatives are important coenzymes in reactions involving the metabolism of galactose and the polymerization of glucose. In these reactions the substrates are uridine diphosphoglucose (UDPGlu) and uridine diphosphogalactose (UDPGal). UDPGlu is the precursor of glycogen. Another uridine nucleotide coenzyme, uridine diphosphoglucuronic acid (UDPGlcUA), serves as the "active" glucuronide for conjugation reactions such as the formation of bilirubin glucuronide (see Chapter 14).

Uracil also participates in the formation of high-energy phosphate compounds analogous to ATP, GTP, or ITP. Uridine triphosphate (UTP) is utilized, for example, in the reactions involving conversion of galactose to glucose in which the UDPG and UDPGal also are formed. UTP is the precursor for the polymerization of uridine nucleotides into RNA.

Cytosine Derivatives

Cytidine (cytosine-ribose) may form the high-energy phosphate compounds cytidine diphosphate (CDP) and cytidine triphosphate (CTP); the latter serves also as the precursor for the polymerization of CMP into nucleic acids. CTP is a nucleotide required for the biosynthesis of phosphoglycerides in animal tissue. Reactions involving ceramide and CDP-choline are responsible for the formation of sphingomyelin and other substituted sphingosines.

Vitamin Nucleotides

The functional moieties of many vitamins are nucleotides with structures analogous to purine and

Figure 10–17. The structure of cyclic 3',5'-guanosine monophosphate (cyclic GMP).

Hypoxanthine Derivatives

Hypoxanthine ribonucleotide, usually called inosinic acid (or inosinate in the salt form), is a precursor of all purine ribonucleotides synthesized de novo. Inosinate can also be formed by the deamination of pyrimidine nucleotides. Riboflavin (vitamin B_2; see Chapter 12) functions as a ribose-5′-phosphate derivative linked to AMP by a pyrophosphate bridge (FAD). Niacin is a constituent of 2 coenzymes, nicotinamide adenine dinucleotide (NAD) and nicotinamide adenine dinucleotide phosphate (NADP). In both of these cases, nicotinamide ribose phosphate is joined to an adenosine monophosphate through a pyrophosphate linkage. Coenzyme A is pantetheine linked to adenosine-3′-phosphate through a pyrophosphate moiety. One of the biologically active derivatives of cobalamin (vitamin B_{12}) requires the attachment of a 5′-deoxyadenosyl moiety through the 5′ carbon to the cobalt.

It should thus be clear that the purine and pyrimidine nucleosides and nucleotides serve many diverse functions in living organisms beyond providing the monomers of the structures of nucleic acids in cells.

SYNTHETIC DERIVATIVES

Synthetic analogs of nucleobases, nucleosides, and nucleotides are widely used in the medical sciences and clinical medicine. In the past, most of these uses have depended upon the role of nucleotides as components of nucleic acids for cellular growth and division. For a cell to divide, its nucleic acids must be replicated, requiring that the precursors of nucleic acids—the normal purine and pyrimidine deoxyribonucleotides—be readily available. One of the most important components of the oncologist's pharmacopeia is the group of synthetic analogs of purine and pyrimidine nucleobases and nucleosides.

The pharmacologic approach has been to use an analog in which either the heterocyclic ring structure or the sugar moiety has been altered in such a way as to induce toxic effects when the analog becomes incorporated into various cellular constituents. Many of these effects result from inhibition by the drug of specific enzyme activities necessary for nucleic acid synthesis or from the incorporation of metabolites of the drug into the nucleic acids where they alter the required base pairing essential to accurate transmission of information.

The most commonly used analogs on the purine or pyrimidine rings have substituents which do not occur naturally and which alter the base pairing or the interaction of the nucleotides with specific enzymes (Fig 10–19). Examples of these would be the 5-fluoro or 5-iodo derivatives of uracil or deoxyuridine, all of which serve as thymine or thymidine analogs, respectively. Both 6-thioguanine and 6-mercaptopurine, in which naturally occurring hydroxyl groups are replaced with thiol groups at the 6 position, are widely used clinically. The analogs in which the purine or pyrimidine ring contains extra nitrogen atoms, such as 5- or 6-azauridine or azacytidine and 8-azaguanine (Fig 10–20), also have been tested clinically.

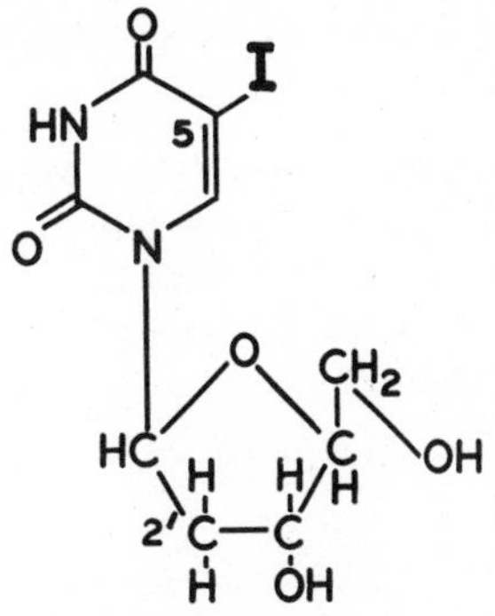

5′-Iodo-2′-deoxyuridine 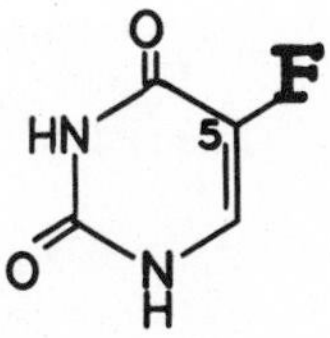   5-Fluorouracil

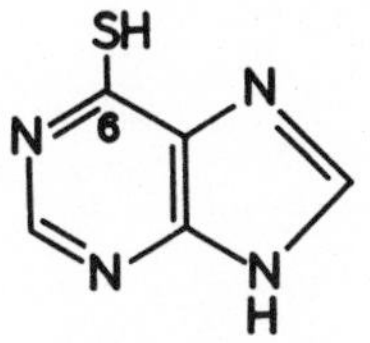

6-Mercaptopurine 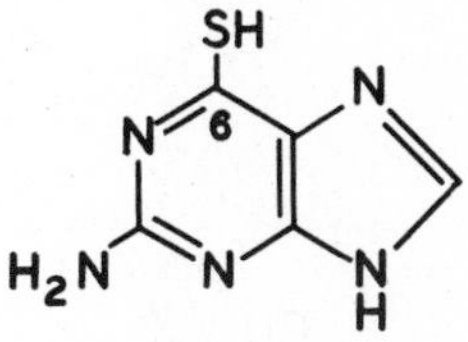   6-Thioguanine

Figure 10—19. The structures of 2 synthetic pyrimidine analogs *(above)* and 2 synthetic purine analogs *(below)*.

The purine analog 4-hydroxypyrazolo [3,4-d] pyrimidine (allopurinol) is widely marketed as an inhibitor of de novo purine biosynthesis and of xanthine oxidase. It is used for the treatment of hyperuricemia and gout. The 4-aminopyrazolopyrimidine is a potent hepatotoxin and is not clinically effective. Nucleosides containing arabinose rather than ribose as the sugar moieties, notably cytarabine (cytosine arabinoside, Ara(C) and vidarabine (adenine arabinoside, AraA), are used in the chemotherapy of cancer and viral infections. (See Fig 10—21 for structures of these substances.)

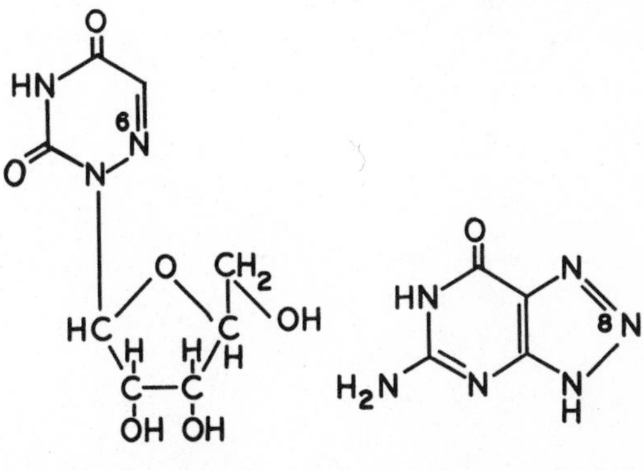

Figure 10—20. The structures of 6-azauridine *(left)* and 8-azaguanine *(right)*.

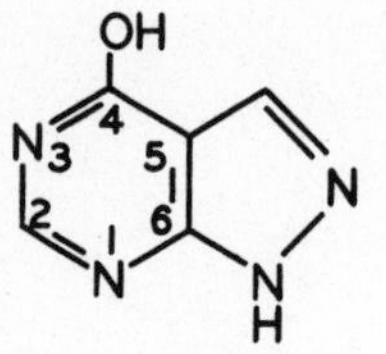

Allopurinol (lactim)

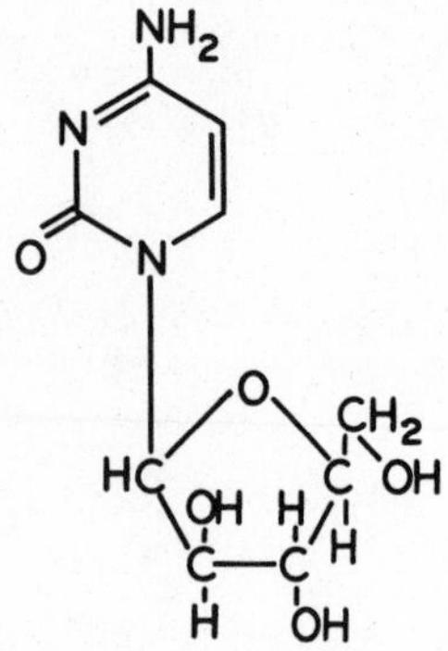

Cytosine arabinoside

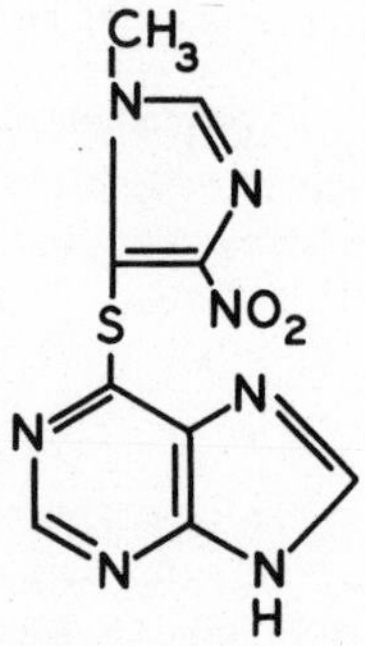

Azathioprine

Figure 10—21. The structures of 4-hydroxypyrazolopyrimidine (allopurinol), cytosine arabinoside (cytarabine), and azathioprine.

Azathioprine, which is catabolized to 6-mercaptopurine, is useful in organ transplantation as a suppressor of events involved in immunologic rejection. A series of nucleoside analogs with antiviral activities has been studied for several years; one, 5-iododeoxyuridine (see above), has been demonstrated to be highly effective in the local treatment of herpetic keratitis, an infection by herpesvirus of the cornea. Although many synthetic nucleoside analogs have been screened for antiviral efficacy both in clinical circumstances and experimentally in animals, none have been found to possess the characteristics of an ideal antiviral agent. However, many are still being synthesized and tested further.

More recently, with the advent of an understanding of the physiologic roles of cyclic nucleotides in both health and disease, there has occurred a rapid expansion of available analogs of cyclic nucleotides and of analogs of nucleosides which serve to alter their metabolism. Both aminophylline and theophylline are widely used clinically to inhibit the catabolism of intracellular cAMP.

• • •

References

Henderson JF, Paterson ARP: *Nucleotide Metabolism: An Introduction.* Academic Press, 1973.

Michelson AM: *The Chemistry of Nucleosides and Nucleotides.* Academic Press, 1963.

Prusoff WH, Ward DC: Nucleoside analogs with antiviral activity. Biochem Pharmacol 25:1233, 1976.

11...
Nucleic Acids & Chromatin

By any assessment of the major discoveries in science by the third quarter of the 20th century, it appears certain that the discovery that genetic information is coded along the length of a polymeric molecule composed of only 4 types of monomeric units will be regarded as a major scientific achievement of this century. This polymeric molecule, DNA, is the chemical basis of heredity. The demonstration that DNA contained the genetic information was first made in 1944 in a series of experiments by Avery, MacLeod, and McCarty, who showed that the genetic determination of the character (type) of the capsule of a specific pneumococcus could be transmitted to another of a distinctly different capsular type by introducing purified DNA from the former coccus into the latter. These authors referred to the agent (DNA) accomplishing the change as "transforming factor." (Fig 11–1.) Subsequently, this type of genetic manipulation has become commonplace in bacteriologic and genetic laboratories. For example, similar experiments have been performed utilizing cultured mammalian cells as recipients and isolated human chromosomes as the donors of genetic information.

Chemical Nature of DNA

The chemical nature of the monomeric units of DNA—**adenylate, guanylate, cytidylate,** and **thymidylate**—is described in Chapter 10. These monomeric units constituting a single strand of DNA are held in polymeric form by $3'5'$-phosphodiester bridges as depicted in Fig 11–2. The informational content of DNA resides in the sequence in which these monomers—purine and pyrimidine deoxyribonucleotides—are ordered. The polymer as depicted possesses a polarity; one end has a $5'$-hydroxyl or phosphate terminus while the other has a $3'$-phosphate or hydroxyl moiety. The importance of this polarity will become evident. Since the genetic information resides in the order of the monomeric units within the polymers, there must exist a mechanism of reproducing or replicating this specific information with a high degree of fidelity. That requirement, together with x-ray diffraction data from the DNA molecule and the observation of Chargaff that in DNA molecules the concentration of adenosine (A) nucleotides equals that of thymidine (T) nucleotides (A = T), while the concentration of guanosine (G) nucleotides equals that of cytidine (C) nucleotides (G = C), led Watson, Crick, and Wilkins to propose in the early 1950s a model of a double-stranded DNA molecule. The model of the currently accepted B form of

DNA is depicted in Fig 11–3. The 2 strands of this double-stranded molecule are held together by **hydrogen bonds** between the purine and pyrimidine bases of the respective linear molecules. The pairings between the purine and pyrimidine nucleotides on the opposite strands are very specific and are dependent upon hydrogen bonding of **A with T** and **G with C.** (Fig 11–4.)

Because of the restrictions imposed by the phosphodiester bond, the favored **anti** configuration of the glycosidic bond, and the predominant tautomers of the 4 bases (A, G, T, and C) in the polymer, A can pair only with T and G only with C as depicted in Fig 11–4. This base-pairing restriction explains the earlier observation that in a double-stranded DNA molecule the content of A equals that of T and the content of G equals that of C. The 2 strands of the double helical molecule, each of which possesses a polarity, are **antiparallel,** ie, one strand runs in the $5'$ to $3'$ direction and the other in the $3'$ to $5'$ direction. This is analogous to 2 parallel streets, each running one way but carrying traffic in opposite directions. In the double-stranded DNA molecules, since the information resides in the sequence of nucleotides on one strand, the opposite strand might be considered "antisense," ie, the complement of the "sense" strand.

As noted in the above base pairings, 3 hydrogen bonds hold the guanosine nucleotide to the cytosine nucleotide whereas the other pair, the A-T pair, is held together by 2 hydrogen bonds. Thus, the G-C bond is stronger by approximately 50%, and the higher the G-C content of a DNA molecule, the greater is its buoyant density. The B form has a pitch of 3.4 nm per turn. Within a single turn 10 base pairs exist, the plane of each base being stacked to resemble 2 winding stacks of coins side by side. The 2 stacks are held together by hydrogen bonding at each level between the 2 coins of opposite stacks and by 2 ribbons wound in a right-hand turn about the 2 stacks and representing the phosphodiester backbone.

This double-stranded structure in solution can be melted by increasing temperature or decreasing salt concentration. Not only do the 2 stacks of bases pull apart, but the bases themselves unstack while still connected in the polymer by the phosphodiester backbone. Concomitant with this **denaturation** of the DNA molecule is an increase in the optical absorbency of the purine and pyrimidine bases—a phenomenon referred to as **hyperchromicity** of denaturation. Because of the stacking of the bases and the hydrogen bonding be-

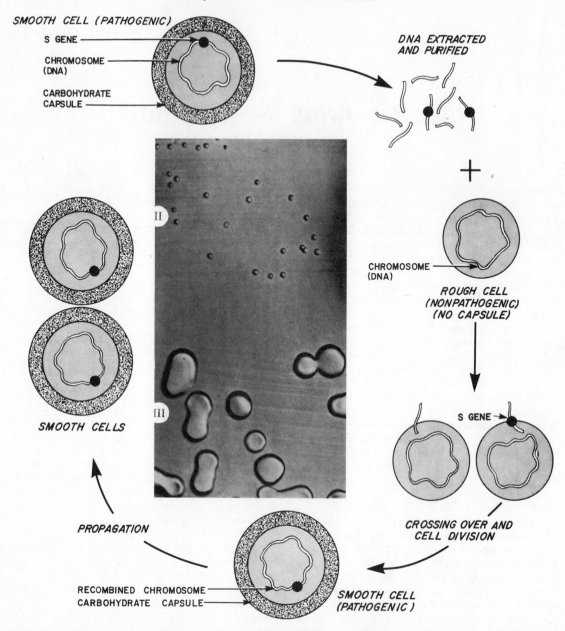

Figure 11–1. Diagrammatic representation of the Avery-MacLeod-McCarty experiment demonstrating that genetic information is contained in DNA. Pathogenic pneumococci with a capsule of carbohydrate resulting in the formation of smooth colonies were extracted, and the DNA containing the S gene was purified. The purified DNA was added to nonpathogenic, nonencapsulated pneumococci, which form rough colonies. The recipient nonencapsulated pneumococci were allowed to absorb and interact with the DNA and divide. Some of the resulting daughter pneumococci had acquired the ability (via the S gene) to form a carbohydrate capsule, smooth colonies, and thus pathogenicity. The photograph in the center (× 3.5) demonstrates smooth (pathogenic) type III and rough (nonpathogenic) type II colonies of these pneumococci. (Redrawn and reproduced, with permission, from Avery OT, MacLeod CM, McCarty M: J Exp Med 79:137, 1944.)

tween the stacks, the double-stranded DNA molecule exhibits properties of a fiber and in solution is a viscous material that loses its viscosity upon denaturation.

Careful examination of the model depicted in Fig 11–3 reveals a **major groove** and a **minor groove** winding along the molecule parallel to the phosphodiester backbones. In these grooves, specific proteins interact with DNA molecules.

In some organisms such as bacteria, bacteriophage, and many DNA-containing animal viruses, the 2 ends of the DNA molecules are joined to create a closed circle with no terminus. This of course does not destroy the polarity of the 2 molecules, but it elimi-

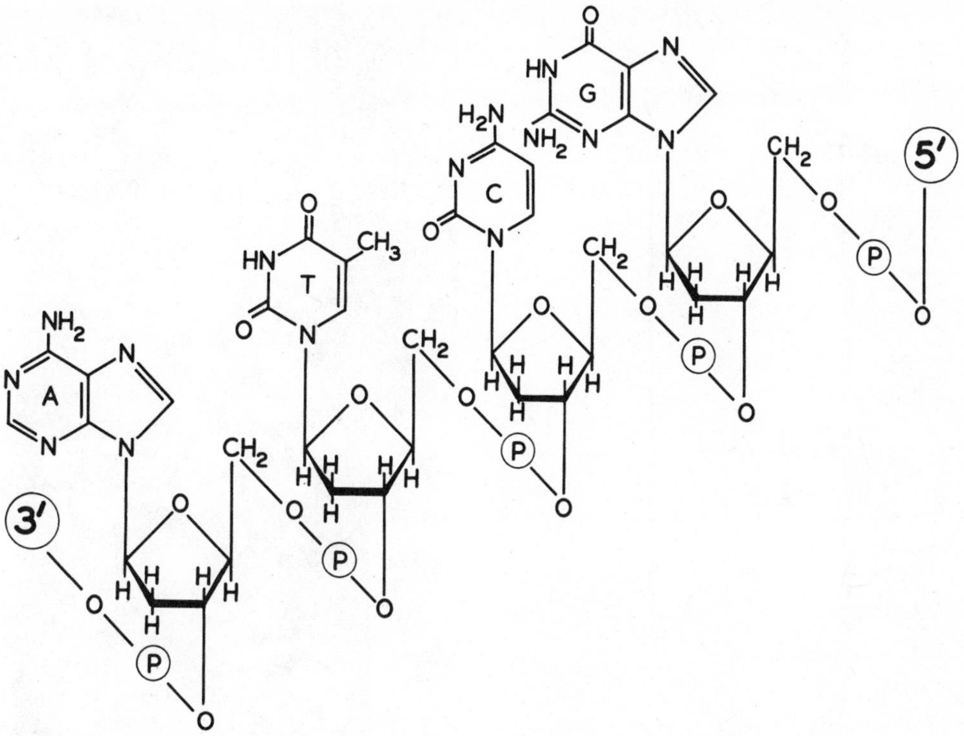

Figure 11–2. A segment of a structure of DNA molecule in which the purine and pyrimidine bases adenine (A), thymine (T), cytosine (C), and guanine (G) are held together by a phosphodiester backbone between 2′-deoxyribosyl moieties attached to the nucleobases by an N-glycosidic bond. Note that the backbone has a polarity (ie, a direction).

nates all 3′ and 5′ free hydroxyl and phosphoryl groups.

Chromatin

Chromatin is the chromosomal material extracted from nuclei of cells of eukaryotic organisms.*

Chromatin consists of very long double-stranded **DNA molecules** and a nearly equal mass of rather small basic proteins termed **histones** as well as a smaller amount of **nonhistone proteins** (most of which are acidic and larger than histones) and a small quantity of **RNA**. X-ray diffraction studies have suggested that chromatin contains a 10 nm repeating unit. More recent work using digestion with specific enzymes (nucleases) suggests that the repeating units occur every 200 base pairs. Note that these repeating units are in chromatin and not in the sequence of nucleotides of the double-stranded DNA molecule per se. Electron

microscopic studies have demonstrated spherical particles called **nucleosomes** which are approximately 12.5 nm in diameter and connected by DNA filaments (Fig 11–5). When one (H1) of the histone components is removed from chromatin, the nucleosomes are not so closely packed, suggesting that histone H1 is involved in the super-packing of nucleosomes in nuclei.

Histones & Nucleosomes

The H1 (lysine-rich) histones are somewhat heterogeneous, consisting of a series of closely related basic proteins. Among the histones, H1 histones are the least tightly bound to chromatin and are, therefore, easily removed with a salt solution, after which chromatin becomes soluble. The isolated nucleosomes contain 4 classes of histones: H2A, H2B, H3, and H4 (Table 11–1). The structures of slightly lysine-rich histones—

---

*So far as possible, the remaining discussion of this chapter and of Chapters 25, 26, and 27 will pertain to mammalian organisms, which are, of course, among the higher eukaryotes. At times it will be necessary to refer to observations made in prokaryotic organisms such as bacteria and viruses, but when such occurs it will be acknowledged as being information that must be extrapolated to mammalian organisms. The division of the material presented in this chapter and in Chapters 26 and 27 is somewhat arbitrary and should not be taken to mean that the processes described are not fully integrated and interdependent.

Table 11–1. Histone nomenclature.

	Original Schemes		New Scheme
Lysine-rich	fl	Ib	H1
	(f2c)	(V)	(H5)
Slightly lysine-rich	f2a2	IIb1	H2A
	f2b	IIb2	H2B
Arginine-rich	f3	III	H3
	f2al	IV	H4

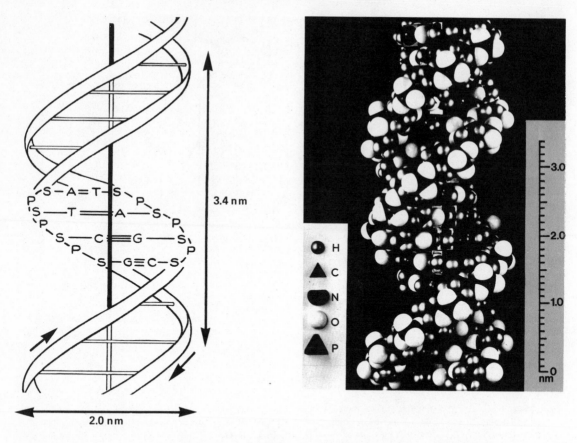

Figure 11–3. The Watson and Crick model of the double helical structure of DNA. *Left:* Diagrammatic representation of structure (modified). A = adenine, C = cytosine, G = guanine, T = thymine, P = phosphate, S = sugar (deoxyribose). *Right:* Space-filling model of DNA structure. (Photograph from James D. Watson, *Molecular Biology of the Gene,* 3rd ed. Copyright © 1976, 1970, 1965, by W.A. Benjamin, Inc, Menlo Park, California.)

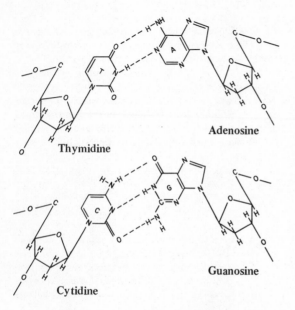

Thymidine

Adenosine

Cytidine

Guanosine

H2A and H2B—appear to have been significantly conserved between species, while the structures of arginine-rich histones—H3 and H4—have been highly conserved between species. This severe conservation implies that the function of histones is identical in all eukaryotes and that the entire molecule is involved quite specifically in carrying out this function. When removed from chromatin, the histones interact with each other in very specific ways. H3 and H4 aggregate to form a tetramer containing 2 molecules of each ($H3_2$-$H4_2$), while H2A and H2B form an oligomeric complex $(H2A\text{-}H2B)_n$. The tetrameric H3-H4 does not associate with the H2A-H2B oligomer, and H1 does not associate directly with any of the other histones.

Figure 11–4 (left). Base-pairing between the favored tautomers of adenosine and thymidine and between those of cytidine and guanosine, as proposed by Watson and Crick. The broken lines represent hydrogen bonds. (The phosphodiester bridges are not shown.)

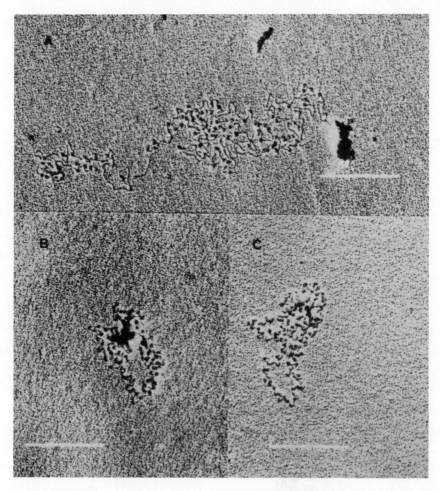

Figure 11–5. Electron micrograph of nucleosomes attached by strands of nucleic acid. (White bar represents 2.5 μm.) (Reproduced, with permission, from Chambon P: Cell 4:281, 1975.)

However, it was found by Roger Kornberg and Jean Thomas that when the tetramer and oligomer were mixed with purified, double-stranded DNA, the same x-ray diffraction pattern was formed as that observed in freshly isolated chromatin. Electron microscopic studies confirmed the existence of this self-assimilating structure. Furthermore, the reconstitution of chromatin from DNA and histones H2A, H2B, H3, and H4 was independent of the organismal or cellular origin of the various components. The histone H1 and the nonhistone proteins do not participate in the reconstitution of chromatin. On the basis of the relative masses of DNA and histone proteins, it has been proposed that the nucleosome, as the subunit of chromatin, consists of about 140 base pairs of DNA and 2 molecules of each of the histones H2A, H2B, H3, and H4.

The super-packing of nucleosomes in nuclei is seemingly dependent upon the interaction of the H1 histones with the double-stranded DNA connecting the nucleosomes. The topology of the interaction of the double-stranded DNA with the histones is not well delineated, but it is clear that the association of the histones with double-stranded DNA to form nucleosomes is not dependent upon the sequence of nucleotides in the DNA molecule. The associations occur at random sites, perhaps with some regular spacing.

Crick has proposed a model for the topology of chromatin (Fig 11–6).

When the DNA double-stranded molecule is associated with histones, it is folded to about one-seventh of its extended length, a packing ratio of 7. Crick's model proposes that folded DNA consists of relatively straight stretches of the B form terminated by large **kinks**, at which one base pair is completely unstacked from its adjacent one. At each kink the energy of stacking of a single base pair would be lost, whereas if the kinks are separated by sufficiently long straight portions of the DNA molecule the stability of the molecule would not be significantly reduced. The angle between the 2 axes of the straight parts of the DNA model can be 90 degrees but becomes sterically hindered as it approaches 100 degrees. If every kink has exactly the same angle, the structure formed will de-

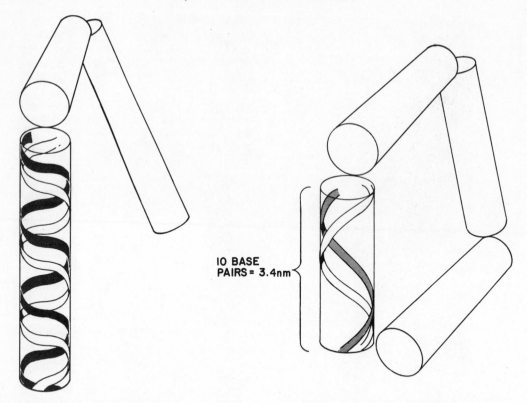

10 BASE
PAIRS = 3.4nm

Figure 11—6. Kinks in the B form of DNA as proposed by Crick. (Redrawn and reproduced, with permission, from Crick F, Klug A: Kinky helix. Nature 255:530, 1975.)

Figure 11—7. The formation of the left-handed kinky helix of DNA as proposed by Crick. (Redrawn and reproduced, with permission, from Crick F, Klug A: Kinky helix. Nature 255:530, 1975.)

pend upon the precise number of base pairs between the kinks. For example, remembering that the B form of DNA completes one exact turn for every 10 pairs of bases, if there are 10 base pairs between 2 kinks, the structure with 3 kinks bends into a square with the straight portions representing the sides of the square (Fig 11—7). If there are 5 base pairs between the kinks, or an odd multiple of 5, then the structure will approximate a zigzag. However, a kink imparts a small negative twist to the DNA, with the result that if successive kinks are made at intervals of 10 base pairs or multiples of 10, instead of the DNA folding back to form a closed square after 3 kinky turns, it will form a left-handed super helix, and the helix would be constructed of straight segments rather than of smooth turns. This model allows for the packing of DNA without defining the specific interrelationships between the histone complexes and the kinks.

Examination of human chromosomes by electron microscopy has revealed a fiber of a diameter of 25—30 nm in which a turn appears to be generated by the folding of a fiber with a diameter of 5—10 nm. This suggested model of a single continuous fiber folded upon itself many times with higher levels of organization is consistent with the nucleosome structure surrounded by kinky turns.

For years it has been suggested that histones act

as regulatory factors in the expression of genetic information; however, for numerous reasons that is not a likely assumption. It has also been proposed that the modification of histones by methylation, acetylation, or phosphorylation might allow histones to recognize specific DNA sequences and to play a regulatory role. From reconstruction experiments utilizing acidic chromatin proteins isolated from specific organs, it now appears that nonhistone proteins recognize specific sequences in the DNA molecule and that the specificity of gene expression resides actually in the acidic chromatin proteins.

Interestingly, some of the major nonhistone proteins in chromatin that have been identified include myosin, actin, tubulin, and tropomyosin. Their functions at this site are unknown, but they are involved in cytokinesis. From studies with viral DNA in animal cells, it appears that the histones cover about 20% of the DNA at random locations, leaving about 80% of the DNA molecule available for interaction with nonhistone proteins and other nucleic acids.

In sperm, many of the basic histone proteins are replaced with other basic proteins such as protamines, which serves to increase the density of nucleic acid packing.

At metaphase, mammalian chromosomes possess a 2-fold symmetry, with identical sister chromatids

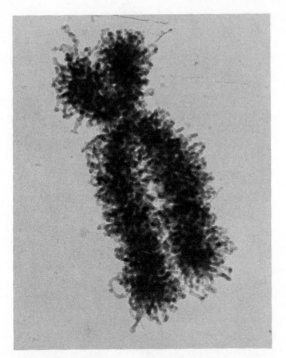

Figure 11—8. Human chromosome 12. (Reproduced, with permission, from DuPraw EJ: *DNA and Chromosomes.* Holt, Rinehart, & Winston, 1970.) (X 27,850)

connected at a centromere the relative position of which is characteristic for a given chromosome (Fig 11—8). Each sister chromatid probably contains one double-stranded DNA molecule. During interphase, the packing of the DNA molecule is less dense than it is in the condensed chromosome during the metaphase. The packaging of nucleoproteins within chromatids is not random, as evidenced by the characteristic patterns observed when chromatids are stained with specific dyes such as quinacrine or Giemsa's stain (Fig 11—9).

From individual to individual within a single species, the pattern of staining (banding) of the entire chromosome complement is highly reproducible; nonetheless, it differs significantly from other species, even those closely related. Thus, the packaging of the nucleoproteins in chromosomes of higher eukaryotes must in some way be dependent upon the nucleotide sequences in the DNA molecules.

Using fluorescent antibodies against specific nuclear proteins, Cohen has been able to provide some resolution to the association of these proteins with DNA in the giant chromosomes of Drosophila (Fig 11—10).

Chemical Nature of Ribonucleic Acid (RNA)

Ribonucleic acid is a polymer of purine and pyrimidine ribonucleotides linked together by 3′,5′-phosphodiester bridges analogous to those in DNA (Fig

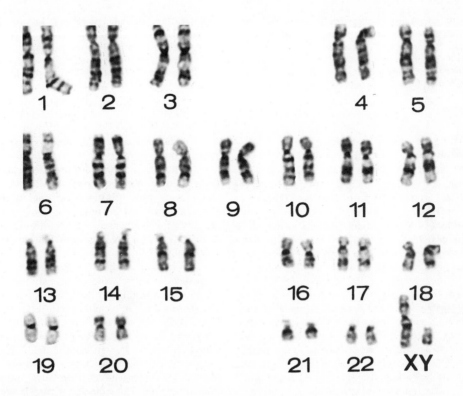

Figure 11—9. A human karyotype (of a man with a normal 46 XY constitution), in which the chromosomes have been stained by the Giemsa method and aligned according to the Paris Convention. (Courtesy of Helen Lawce and Dr. Felix Conte, Department of Pediatrics, University of California School of Medicine, San Francisco.)

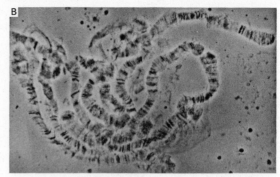

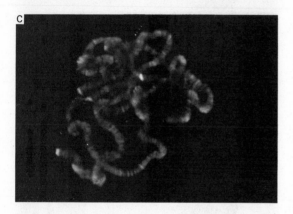

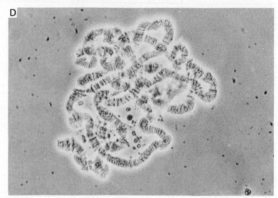

Figure 11—10. Localization of chromosomal proteins by immunofluorescence. Polytene chromosomes of *Drosophila melanogaster* salivary glands were treated with the serum of a rabbit immunized against a chromosomal protein. The locations of that protein were then visualized by means of a fluorescent antibody against rabbit antibodies. *(A)* Histone H1, shown to be generally distributed throughout the chromosomes in the same pattern as in *(B)* phase contrast density. *(C)* Nonhistone protein D1, widely distributed but highly concentrated in region 81F, also shown in *(D)* phase contrast. (Courtesy of CR Alfageme, GT Rudkin, & LH Cohen. The Institute for Cancer Research, Fox Chase, Philadelphia.)

11—11). Although sharing many features with DNA, RNA possesses several specific differences:

(1) As indicated by its name, the sugar moiety in RNA to which the phosphates and purine and pyrimidine bases are attached is **ribose** rather than the 2′-deoxyribose of DNA.

(2) Although RNA contains the ribonucleotides of adenine, guanine, and cytosine, it does not possess thymine except in the rare case mentioned below. Instead of thymine, RNA contains the ribonucleotide of **uracil.** Thus, the pyrimidine components of RNA differ from those of DNA.

(3) RNA exists natively as a **single-stranded** molecule rather than as a double-stranded helical molecule, as does DNA. However, given the proper complementary base sequence with opposite polarity, the single strand of RNA, as demonstrated in Fig 11–12, is capable of folding back on itself like a hairpin and thus acquiring double-stranded characteristics.

(4) Since the RNA molecule is single-stranded and complementary to only one of the 2 strands of a gene, its guanine content does *not* necessarily equal its cyto-

sine content, nor does its adenine content necessarily equal its uracil content.

(5) RNA can be **hydrolyzed by alkali** to 2′,3′ cyclic diesters of the mononucleotides. An intermediate in this hydrolysis is the 2′,3′,5′-triester, an intermediate which cannot be formed in alkali-treated DNA because of the absence of a 2′-hydroxyl group. The alkali lability of RNA is useful both diagnostically and analytically.

Information within the single strand of RNA is contained in its sequence ("primary structure") of purine and pyrimidine nucleotides within the polymer. The sequence is complementary to the "sense" strand of the gene from which it was transcribed. Because of this complementarity, an RNA molecule will hybridize with its template DNA strand, the strand which is thus necessarily referred to as being the "sense" strand; it will not hybridize with the "antisense" strand of the DNA of its gene. The sequence of the RNA molecule is (except for U replacing T) the same as that of the "antisense" strand of the gene (Fig 11–13).

Small quantities of double-stranded RNA other

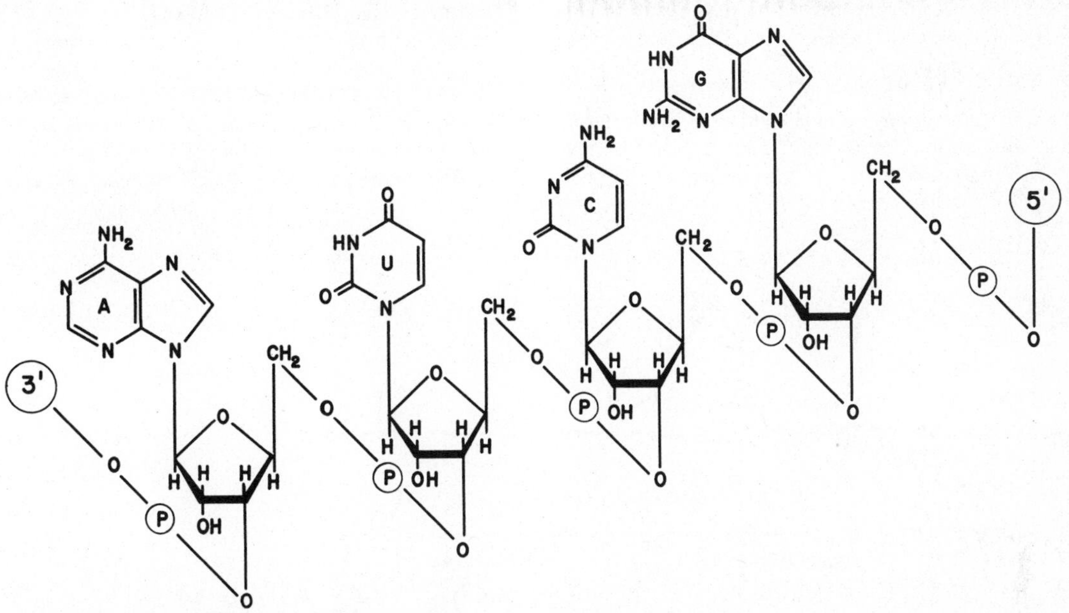

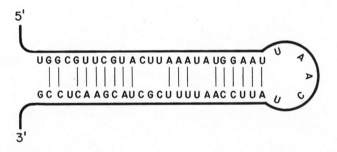

Figure 11—11. A segment of a ribonucleic acid (RNA) molecule in which the purine and pyrimidine bases—adenine (A), uracil (U), cytosine (C), and guanine (G)—are held together by phosphodiester bonds between ribosyl moieties attached to the nucleobases by N glycosidic bonds. Note that the polymer has a polarity.

5'

U G G C G U U C G U A C U U A A A U A UG G A A U U A A C

| | | | | | | | | | | | | | | | | | |

G C C U C A A G C A U C G C U U U U A A C C U U A U C

3'

Figure 11—12. Diagrammatic representation of the secondary structure of an RNA molecule in which a "hairpin" has been formed and is dependent upon the intramolecular base pairing.

DNA STRANDS:

ANTISENSE → 5'-T GG A A T T G T G A G C G G A T A A C A AT T T C A C A C A G G A A A C A G C T AT G A C C AT G – 3'
SENSE ─────→ 3'-A C C T T A A C A C T C G C C T A T T G T T A A A G T G T G T C C T T T G T C G A T A C T G G TA C – 5'

RNA TRANSCRIPT   5'   pA U U G U G A G C G G A U A A C A A U U U C A C A C A G G A A A C A G C U A U G A C C A U G   3'

Figure 11—13. The relationship between the sequences of an RNA transcript and its gene, in which the sense and antisense strands are shown with their polarities. The RNA transcript with a 5' to 3' polarity is complementary to the sense strand with its 3' to 5' polarity. Note that the sequence in the RNA transcript and its polarity is the same as that in the antisense strand, except that the U of the transcript replaces the T of the gene.

than transfer RNA have been detected in and isolated from mammalian organisms, including humans, but these are probably associated with RNA viruses. Double-stranded RNA may have some physiologic function such as serving as an inducer of **interferon**, an antiviral protein which most animal cells are capable of generating as a defense mechanism.

Structural Organization of RNA

In all prokaryotic and eukaryotic organisms, 3 main classes of RNA molecules exist: **messenger RNA (mRNA)**, **transfer RNA (tRNA)**, and **ribosomal RNA (rRNA)**. Each class differs from the others by size, function, and general stability.

The **messenger RNA (mRNA)** class is the most

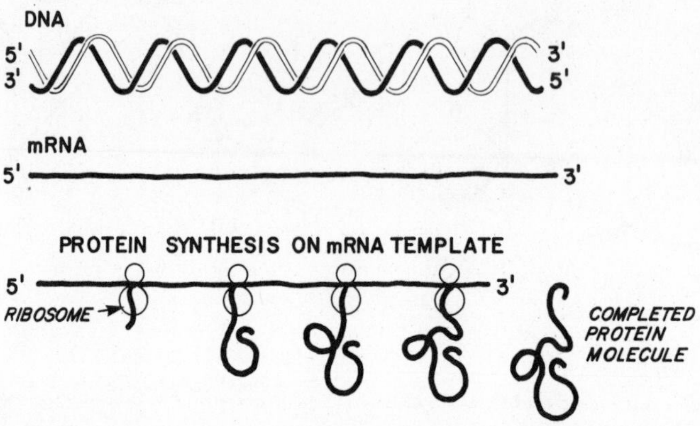

Figure 11—14. The expression of genetic information in DNA into the form of an mRNA transcript. This is subsequently translated by ribosomes into a specific protein molecule.

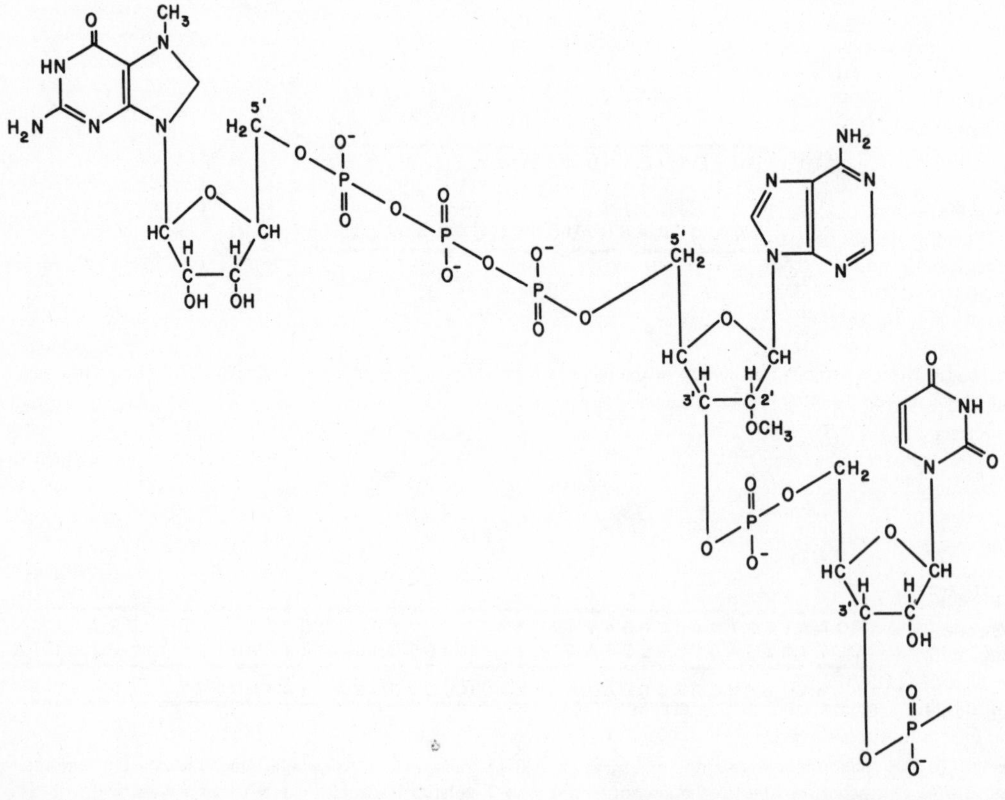

Figure 11—15. The cap structure attached to the 5′ terminus of most messenger RNA molecules. A 7-methylguanosine triphosphate is attached at the 5′ terminus of the mRNA, which usually contains a 2′-O-methylpurine nucleotide.

heterogeneous in size and stability, but all of the classes function as messengers conveying the information in a gene to the protein-synthesizing machinery, where each serves as a template on which a specific sequence of amino acids is polymerized to form a specific protein molecule, the ultimate gene product (Fig 11–14).

The messenger RNAs are single-stranded and complementary to the sense strand of their respective structural genes. The RNA molecules, particularly in mammals, have some unique chemical characteristics. The 5' terminus of mRNA is "capped" by a 7-methylguanosine triphosphate which is linked to an adjacent 2'-O-methyl ribonucleoside at its 5'-hydroxyl through the 3 phosphates (Fig 11–15). The mRNA molecules frequently contain internal 6-methyladenylates and other 2'-O-ribose methylated nucleotides. Although the function of this capping of mRNAs is not completely understood, the cap is probably involved in the recognition of mRNA. The protein-synthesizing machinery begins translating the mRNA into proteins at the 5' or capped terminus. The other end of most mRNA molecules, the 3'-hydroxyl terminus, has attached a polymer of adenylate residues 20–250 nucleotides in length. The specific function of the poly A "**tail**" at the 3'-hydroxyl terminus of mRNAs is not understood, but it has been suggested that it serves to maintain the intracellular stability of the specific mRNA. The mRNAs for the histones do not contain poly A.

In mammalian cells, including cells of humans, the mRNA molecules present in the cytoplasm do not appear to be the RNA products immediately synthesized from the DNA template but rather to have been processed from a precursor molecule before entering the cytoplasm. In mammalian nuclei, the immediate products of gene transcription constitute a fourth class of RNA molecules. These nuclear RNA molecules are very heterogeneous in size and are quite large. The **heterogeneous nuclear RNA (HnRNA)** molecules may exceed 10^7 daltons, whereas the mRNA molecules are generally smaller than 2×10^6 daltons. As is discussed in Chapter 25, the HnRNA molecules appear to be processed to generate the mRNA molecules which then enter the cytoplasm to serve as templates for protein synthesis.

The **transfer RNA (tRNA)** molecules consist of approximately 75 nucleotides and thus have a molecular weight of 25,000. The tRNA molecules serve as adaptors for the translation of the information in the sequence of nucleotides of the mRNA into specific amino acids. There are at least 20 tRNA molecules in every cell, at least one corresponding to each of the 20 amino acids required for protein synthesis. Although each specific tRNA differs from the others in its sequence of nucleotides, the tRNA molecules as a class have many features in common. The primary structure—ie, the nucleotide sequence—of all tRNA molecules allows extensive folding and intrastrand complementarity to generate a significant secondary structure which can appear like a cloverleaf (Fig 11–16).

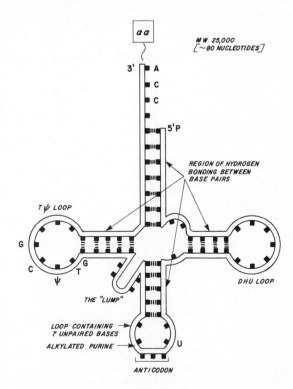

Figure 11–16. A typical aminoacyl tRNA in which the amino acid is attached to the 3' ACC terminus. The anticodon, TψC, and DHU loops are indicated, as are the positions of the intramolecular hydrogen bonding between these base pairs. (From James D. Watson, *Molecular Biology of the Gene*, 3rd ed. Copyright © 1976, 1970, 1965, by W.A. Benjamin, Inc, Menlo Park, California.)

X-ray diffraction studies have allowed the formulation of a schematic diagram illustrating the folding of the phenylalanine-accepting tRNA from yeast (Fig 11–17).

The features that all tRNA molecules have in common include a **CCA sequence** at the 3' termini. It is through an ester bond to the 3'-hydroxyl group of the adenosyl moiety that the carboxyl groups of amino acids are attached. The **anticodon loop** at the end of a base-paired stem recognizes the triplet nucleotide or codon (discussed in Chapter 26) of the template mRNA. In nearly all tRNA molecules there is a loop containing the nucleotides of ribothymine and pseudouridine and another loop containing the minor base dihydrouracil. (See also Chapter 26.)

Although tRNAs are quite stable in prokaryotes, they are somewhat less stable in eukaryotes. The opposite is true for mRNAs, which are quite unstable in prokaryotes but generally stable in eukaryotic organisms.

Ribosomal RNA

A ribosome is a cytoplasmic nucleoprotein structure which acts as the machinery for the synthesis of proteins from the mRNA templates. On the ribosomes, the mRNA and tRNA molecules interact to translate into a specific protein molecule the information trans-

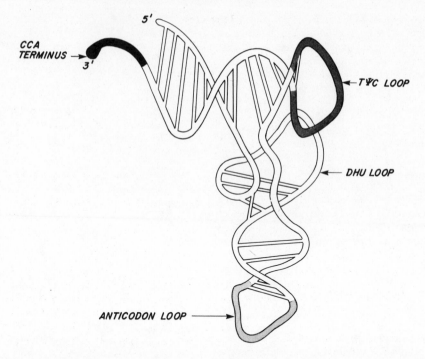

Figure 11–17. The 3-dimensional structure of a tRNA molecule as determined by x-ray crystallography. The specified amino acid is attached at the CCA 3′ terminus. The TψC loop, the dihydrouracil (DHU) loop, and the anticodon loop are indicated. (Redrawn and reproduced, with permission, from Stryer L: *Biochemistry.* Freeman, 1975. Copyright © 1975. [Based on a drawing by Dr. Sung-Han Kim.])

cribed from the gene. Ribosomal particles are very complex, having been self-assembled from at least 4 distinct RNA molecules and nearly 100 specific protein molecules (Table 11–2).

The mammalian ribosome contains 2 major nucleoprotein subunits, a larger one of 2.7 megadaltons

(60S) and a smaller subunit of 1.3 megadaltons (40S). The **60S subunit** contains a **5S ribosomal RNA** (rRNA), a **5.8S rRNA** (formerly 7S rRNA), and a **28S rRNA**; there are also probably more than 50 specific polypeptides. The smaller or **40S subunit** contains a single **18S rRNA** and approximately 30 polypeptide chains. All of these ribosomal RNA molecules except the 5S rRNA are processed from a single 45S precursor RNA molecule in the nucleolus (see Chapter 25). The 5S rRNA apparently has its own precursor which is independently transcribed. The highly methylated ribosomal RNA molecules are packaged in the nucleolus with the specific ribosomal proteins. In the cytoplasm, the ribosomes remain quite stable and capable of many translations. The functions of the ribosomal RNA molecules in the ribosomal particle are unknown, but they are necessary for ribosomal assembly and function.

Table 11–2. RNA components of mammalian ribosomes.

Subunit Size (Svedberg Units)	Subunit MW	RNA Size (Svedberg Units)	RNA MW
60S	2.7×10^6	5S	35,000
(> 50 polypeptides)		5.8S	45,000
		28S	1.5×10^6
40S	1.3×10^6	18S	750,000
(> 30 polypeptides)			

References

Brawerman G: Eukaryotic messenger RNA. Annu Rev Biochem 43:621, 1974.

Crick FHC, Klug A: Kinky helix. Nature 255:530, 1975.

Elgin SCR, Weintraub H: Chromosomal proteins and chromatin structure. Annu Rev Biochem 44:725, 1975.

Oudet P, Gross-Bellard M, Chambon P: Electron microscopic and biochemical evidence that chromatin structure is a repeating unit. Cell 4:281, 1975.

Rich A, Raj Bhandary UL: Transfer RNA: Molecular structure, sequence and properties. Annu Rev Biochem 45:805, 1976.

Thomas CA: The genetic organization of chromosomes. Annu Rev Genet 5:237, 1971.

Watson JD: *The Double Helix.* Atheneum, 1968.

Watson JD, Crick FHC: Molecular structure of nucleic acids. Nature 171:737, 1953.

12 . . .
The Fat-Soluble Vitamins

When animals are maintained on a chemically defined diet containing only purified proteins, carbohydrates, and fats, and the necessary minerals, it is not possible to sustain life. Additional factors present in natural foods are required, although often only minute amounts are necessary. These "accessory food factors" are called vitamins. The vitamins have no chemical resemblance to each other, but because of a similar general function in metabolism they are considered together.

Early studies of the vitamins emphasized the more obvious pathologic changes which occurred when animals were maintained on vitamin-deficient diets. Increased knowledge of the physiologic role of each vitamin has enabled attention to be concentrated on the metabolic defects which occur when these substances are lacking, and we may therefore refer to the biochemical changes as well as the anatomic lesions which are characteristic of the various vitamin deficiency states.

Before the chemical structures of the vitamins were known it was customary to identify these substances by letters of the alphabet. This system is gradually being replaced by a nomenclature based on the chemical nature of the compound or a description of its source or function.

The vitamins are generally divided into 2 major groups: fat-soluble and water-soluble. The fat-soluble vitamins, which are usually found associated with the lipids of natural foods, include vitamins A, D, E, and K. The vitamins of the B complex and vitamin C comprise the water-soluble group.

VITAMIN A

Chemistry

The structure of **vitamin A_1 aldehyde (retinal)** is shown in Fig 12–1. It may be derived from β-carotene by cleavage at the midpoint of the carotene in the polyene chain connecting the 2 β-ionone rings. The 2 hydrogen atoms attached to the 2 central carbon atoms of β-carotene are retained during the conversion of the carotene to vitamin A. The biosynthesis of vitamin A from β-carotene is most likely a dioxygenase reaction in which molecular oxygen reacts with the 2 central carbon atoms of β-carotene followed by cleavage of the central double bond of β-carotene to yield 2 moles of vitamin A aldehyde (retinal). These reactions are shown in Fig 12–1. **Vitamin A alcohol (retinol)** is then produced by reduction of the aldehyde in an NADH-dependent reaction catalyzed by retinene reductase.

Vitamin A_2 (3-dehydroretinol) has also been de-

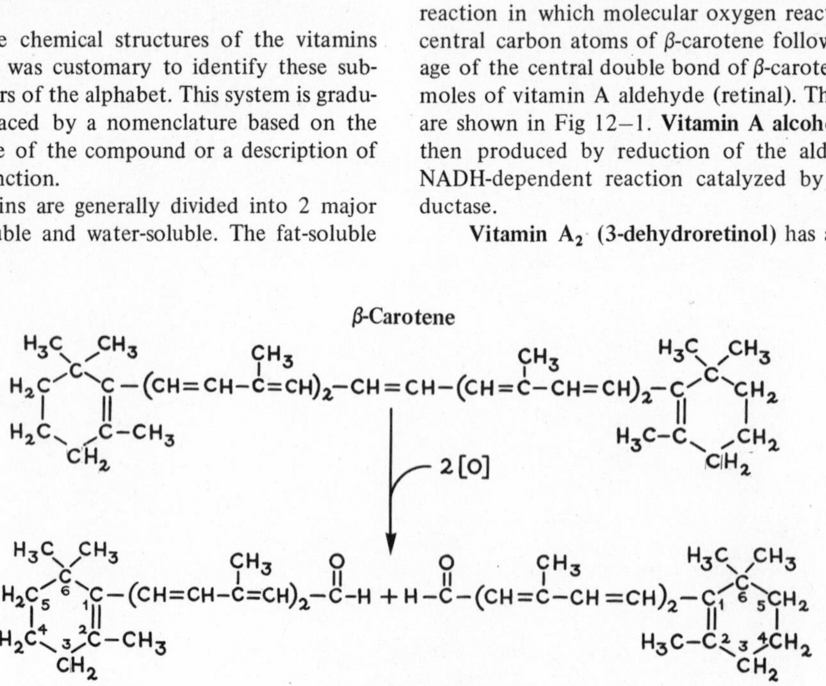

Figure 12–1. Conversion of β-carotene to retinal (vitamin A_1 aldehyde).

scribed. Its potency is 40% that of vitamin A_1; its structure differs from A_1 only by the presence of an additional double bond (between carbons 3 and 4 of the β-ionone ring).

Vitamin A alcohol occurs only in the animal kingdom, principally as an ester with higher fatty acids, in the liver, kidney, lung, and fat depots. The major dietary sources of all the vitamin A in animals are certain plant pigments known as **carotenes** (or carotenoids), the **provitamins A,** which are synthesized by all plants except parasites and saprophytes. In the human diet, vitamin A is derived both from the preformed vitamin (retinol) and from the provitamin carotenoids, of which β-**carotene** has the highest vitamin A activity and is the most plentiful in human diets.

Carotenes are active as a vitamin precursor only after conversion to retinol. Such conversion occurs in the intestinal wall in rats, pigs, goats, rabbits, sheep, and chickens, although in these animals the liver may also participate in the conversion. In man, the liver is believed to be the only organ capable of accomplishing the conversion of the carotenes to vitamin A. Retinol is transported in the blood in association with a specific **retinol binding protein**; the carotenoids are transported with the lipoproteins that transport the various lipid fractions.

The dietary provitamins are not absorbed from the intestine as well as vitamin A (retinol). Many factors affect the efficiency of absorption and utilization of preformed vitamin A and carotene. Small amounts of mineral oil added to the diet of experimental animals have been found to interfere with the utilization of both vitamin A and carotene, although the inhibition of carotene utilization was much greater than that of vitamin A.

The various provitamins A contribute differing amounts of the vitamin, in part because only the β-carotene isomer upon oxidative cleavage and subsequent reduction would yield 2 moles of vitamin A alcohol, but, also because of differing efficiency of absorption from the intestine and of conversion to vitamin A in the liver of man. For man, the average absorption of the provitamins A from different food sources is estimated to be about one-third of the amounts of the provitamins ingested. Because retinol (vitamin A alcohol) is assumed to be completely absorbed, it has now been decided to use **retinol equiv-**alents as the units for expressing vitamin A requirements in nutrition.

The overall utilization of β-carotene is taken as one-sixth that of retinol. Other carotenoids that have vitamin A activity (eg, α-carotene, cryptoxanthin) are only half as active as β-carotene; their efficiency as sources of vitamin A is therefore taken as one-twelfth that of retinol.

Physiologic Role

The maintenance of the integrity of epithelial tissue is an important function of vitamin A. In its absence, normal secretory epithelium is replaced by a dry, keratinized epithelium which is more susceptible to invasion by infectious organisms. **Xerophthalmia**, ie, keratinization of ocular tissue, which may progress to blindness, is a late result of vitamin A deficiency. Xerophthalmia is a major cause of blindness in childhood. It is still a major health problem in many parts of the world, especially in rapidly growing urban areas of the Far East such as Hong Kong, Djakarta, Manila, Saigon, and Dacca.

The specific role of vitamin A in the physiologic mechanisms of vision has been elucidated largely by Wald and by Morton. The retinal pigment **rhodopsin**, or visual purple, which has long been recognized in the rod cells of the retina, is a conjugated protein with a molecular weight of approximately 40,000. When light strikes the retina, rhodopsin is split into its protein component, **opsin**, and the associated nonprotein carotenoid, retinene. This latter compound has been identified as vitamin A_1 aldehyde and therefore is now termed **retinal**. In the light-bleached retina, vitamin A_1 itself, the alcohol **retinol** appears later, and it is therefore assumed that the aldehyde, retinal, is slowly converted by reduction to the alcohol, retinol. It follows that the regeneration of retinal from retinol requires oxidation of the terminal alcohol group to the aldehyde group. This is accomplished through the catalytic action of the enzyme **retinene reductase**, involving also NAD as coenzyme (Fig 12–2). These reactions are summarized below.

Retinene reductase appears to be very similar to alcohol dehydrogenase of liver; indeed, a crystalline preparation of alcohol dehydrogenase from horse liver was found to be able to catalyze the retinol-retinal reaction in vitro.

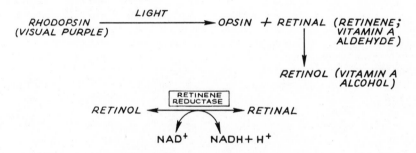

Figure 12–2. Role of vitamin A in chemistry of vision.

At least 2 colored intermediate compounds are formed in the course of the reactions whereby retinal is liberated from rhodopsin. One is a red or orange-red compound, **lumirhodopsin**, stable only at temperatures below −50° C. Beginning at a temperature of about −20° C, lumirhodopsin is converted to **metarhodopsin**, also orange-red in color. At temperatures above −15° C and in the presence of water, this compound hydrolyzes to retinal and opsin.

Regeneration of rhodopsin takes place in the dark. Under normal circumstances equilibrium is maintained in the retina of the eye such that the rate of breakdown of rhodopsin is equaled by the rate of regeneration. If, however, a deficiency of vitamin A exists, the rate of regeneration of rhodopsin is retarded, probably because of a shortage of precursor substances. This concept is supported by the observation that the retinas of rats maintained on a vitamin A-deficient diet contain less rhodopsin than do those of animals on an adequate diet.

The biochemical mechanism of cone vision is analogous to that of rod vision, described above. The photoreceptors of both rods and cones contain essentially the same chromophore (retinal), although the protein moiety (opsin) differs.

Night blindness (nyctalopia), which is a disturbance of rod vision, is one manifestation of vitamin A deficiency. Measurements of the rate of regeneration of a normal response to light have therefore been used to detect early vitamin A deficiency states because regeneration rates are considerably decreased by even moderate lack of the vitamin.

Although the role of vitamin A in the visual apparatus is now well established, the vitamin must also participate in the metabolism of the body in a much more generalized way. Animals on a diet free of vitamin A do not merely suffer visual impairment and ocular lesions but will eventually die unless the vitamin is supplied.

Reference has already been made to a function of vitamin A in connection with epithelial tissue. It has also been observed that in the absence of vitamin A the growth of experimental animals does not progress normally. The skeleton is affected first, and then the soft tissues. Mechanical damage to the brain and cord occurs when these structures attempt to grow within the arrested limits of the bony framework of the cranium and vertebral column. In the growing animal collagenous tissues are particularly affected by a deficiency of vitamin A. The mucopolysaccharides which form the ground substance are an important constituent of such tissues. Consequently it is of considerable interest that the rate of mucopolysaccharide formation was found to be inhibited in the tissues of vitamin A-deficient animals and restored to normal when the vitamin was provided.

Vitamin A may participate in reactions which affect the stability of cell membranes and of the membranes of subcellular particles. Vitamin A alcohol causes swelling of mitochondria in vitro. Vitamin A aldehyde or acid has considerably less effect. Mitochondria from the liver were the most readily swollen by vitamin A; those from spleen and brain were least affected. Heart mitochondria exhibited about one-fourth of the effect shown by liver mitochondria.

Vitamin A, when administered in excess to guinea pigs, causes a significant decrease in the activity of acid phosphatase, extractable from their peritoneal phagocytes. Large doses of vitamin A may reduce the stability or increase the permeability of the lysosomes within the peritoneal phagocytes. This would permit release of acid phosphatase (and presumably other enzymes) from the cells so that in subsequent measurements the acid phosphatase content would be lower than normal. A major function of vitamin A in normal metabolism may be the preservation of the structural integrity and the normal permeability of the cell membrane as well as that of the membranes of subcellular particles such as lysosomes and mitochondria.

Sources & Daily Allowance

All pigmented (particularly yellow) vegetables and fruits (eg, sweet potatoes, carrots, pumpkins, papayas, tomatoes, apricots, and peaches) and the leafy green vegetables supply provitamin A (carotene) in the diet. Yellow corn is the only cereal in common use that contains carotene. Preformed vitamin A is supplied by foods of animal origin, eg, liver, milk, butter, eggs, and, to a lesser extent, by kidney and the fat of muscle meats as well as by some fish.

Until recently, vitamin A activity in foods has been expressed in international units (IU), 1 IU being equivalent to 0.3 μg of retinol, 0.344 μg of retinyl acetate, or 0.6 μg of β-carotene. These relationships were derived from studies with the rat and were assumed to apply also to man. The recognition that the utilization of dietary provitamins is substantially less than that of retinol has meant that the total vitamin A activity of a diet must be more carefully calculated to indicate what percentage of vitamin A activity is derived from retinol and what amount from provitamins. It has now been decided to abandon the use of international units as a way to express the vitamin value of foods in favor of stating these values as an equivalent weight of retinol. In the most recent *Recommended Dietary Allowances,* these changes have been made (see Table 31–6). For a period of transition, it is desirable that the dietary allowances be stated both as retinol equivalents and as international units. It is further recommended that food analyses list separately retinol, carotene, and other provitamin A carotenoids so that total retinol equivalents (in micrograms) can be calculated.

One retinol equivalent is 1 μg of retinol, or 6 μg of β-carotene, or 12 μg of other provitamin A carotenoids, or 3.33 IU vitamin activity from retinol, or 10 IU vitamin A activity from β-carotene.

The results of several recent studies of human vitamin A requirements have indicated that 500–600 μg of retinol or twice as much β-carotene is the minimum amount necessary to permit adults to maintain an adequate concentration of vitamin A in the blood as well as to prevent all symptoms of deficiency. Since animal studies have indicated that at intakes of vitamin A just minimal for growth there is very little storage of the vitamin, the recommended allowance is in excess of this minimal quantity. Indeed, recent surveys of the amounts of vitamin A stored in the liver of humans revealed that significant numbers of the subjects studied had low reserves of this vitamin. In the USA, the usual foods available to the population are estimated to provide about half of the total vitamin A activity as retinol and the remaining half as provitamin A carotenoids. Because of a lack of better information, it is assumed that β-carotene comprises all of the provitamin A carotenoids in the food. The recommended daily dietary allowance for vitamin A in adults of 5000 IU would thus be made up of 2500 IU as retinol and 2500 IU as provitamin A; as retinol equivalents, this is 750 μg of retinol and 250 retinol equivalents as β-carotene, a total of 1000 retinol equivalents.

Toxicity of Vitamin A

A number of reports have emphasized the occurrence of **toxic effects** as a result of the ingestion of excess amounts of vitamin A. Hypervitaminosis A may occur as a consequence of the administration of large doses (in the form of vitamin A concentrates) to infants and small children. The principal symptoms are painful joints, periosteal thickening of long bones, and loss of hair. Preformed vitamin A in large amounts may be toxic to adults as well as children. Regular ingestion of more than 2000 retinol equivalents (6700 IU) of preformed vitamin A above that already in the diet may be hazardous and should be taken only under medical supervision. On the other hand, excess intake of carotenes is not harmful, although it may result in deposition of this yellow pigment in the skin. The pigment will disappear after reduction in excessive intake of the carotenoids.

Various congenital defects have been produced experimentally in the offspring of rats given a single large dose (75,000–150,000 IU) of vitamin A on the ninth, tenth, or eleventh day of pregnancy. No correlation has yet been established between the results of these experiments and a similar occurrence in humans, but it seems prudent to exercise caution in giving repeated large doses of vitamin A to pregnant women.

Deficiencies of Vitamin A

Vitamin A deficiency can occur not only from inadequate intake but also because of poor intestinal absorption or inadequate conversion of provitamin A, as occurs in diseases of the liver. In such cases, a high plasma carotene content may coincide with a low vitamin A level. It has recently been reported that zinc is necessary to maintain normal concentrations of vitamin A in the plasma. By using animals deficient in both zinc and vitamin A, it has been demonstrated that zinc is necessary for the normal mobilization of vitamin A from the liver. Patients suffering from cirrhosis of the liver have been shown to have lowered concentrations of zinc in the plasma, and cirrhotic patients

with impaired dark adaptation do not improve after therapy with vitamin A. Both of these facts point to the possibility that vitamin A metabolism may be adversely affected by zinc deficiency.

Carotene is poorly utilized in persons on a low-fat diet. Indeed, it is important to point out that the fat-soluble vitamins are all poorly absorbed from the intestine in the absence of bile, as in biliary obstruction. For this reason, any defect in fat absorption is likely to foster deficiencies of all fat-soluble vitamins. Intestinal diseases such as severe dysentery, celiac disease, and sprue all limit the absorption of vitamin A.

Determination of Vitamin A

Chemical and physical methods of determination of vitamin A are based on spectrophotometric measurements. Vitamin A_1 absorbs maximally at 610–620 nm and A_2 at 692–696 nm. A colorimetric determination of vitamin A utilizes the **Carr-Price reaction,** in which a blue color is obtained when a solution of antimony trichloride in chloroform is added to the vitamin-containing mixture. This reaction may be used to determine the vitamin A content of blood plasma. However, plasma vitamin A levels alone are not satisfactory as a means of detecting early deficiency of the vitamin because the levels are maintained at or near normal until there is advanced depletion of vitamin A. When lesions of the eyes are apparent, plasma levels of vitamin A are very low (5 μg/dl). Where it has been possible to measure the levels of vitamin A in the liver, it has been found that in malnourished children the normally large amounts of vitamin A stored in the liver are virtually exhausted, levels of less than 15 μg/g fresh liver tissue being reported.

THE VITAMINS D

The vitamins D are actually a group of compounds. All are sterols which occur in nature, chiefly in the animal organism. Certain of these sterols (known as provitamins D), when subjected to long-wave ultraviolet light (about 265 nm), acquire the physiologic property of curing or preventing rickets, a disease characterized by skeletal abnormalities, including failure of calcification.

Although all of the vitamins D possess antirachitic properties, there is a considerable difference in their potency when tested in various species. For example, irradiated ergosterol (vitamin D_2) is a powerful antirachitic vitamin for man and for the rat but not for the chicken. Vitamin D_3, on the other hand, is much more potent for the chicken than for the rat or the human organism.

Chemistry

For nutritional purposes the 2 most important D vitamins are D_2 (activated ergosterol; also known as ergocalciferol or viosterol) (Fig 12–4) and D_3 (acti-

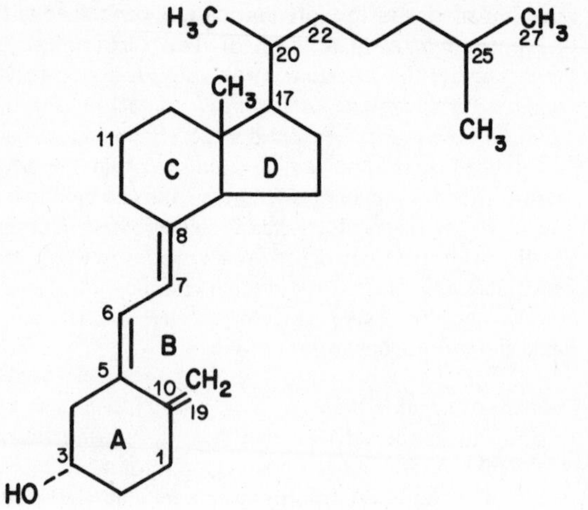

Figure 12—3. Cholecalciferol (vitamin D_3).

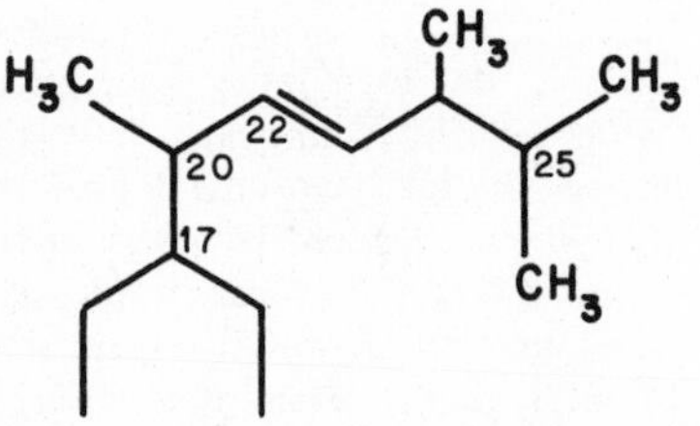

Figure 12—4. Ergocalciferol (vitamin D_2) (structure of side-chain).

vated 7-dehydrocholesterol, cholecalciferol), the form which occurs in nature in the fish liver oils (Fig 12—3). Provitamin D_2 (ergosterol) occurs in the plant kingdom (eg, in ergot and in yeast). The structure of vitamin D_3 is the same as that of D_2 except that the side-chain on position 17 is that of cholesterol. Man and other mammals can synthesize provitamin D_3 in the body. The vitamin is then activated in the skin by exposure to ultraviolet rays and carried to various organs in the body for utilization or storage (in liver).

Physiologic Role

The principal action of vitamin D is to increase the absorption of calcium and phosphorus from the intestine. The vitamin also has a direct effect on the calcification process. Evidence for this has been obtained by isotopic tracer studies, which indicate that the administration of vitamin D to animals deficient in this vitamin increases the rate of accretion and resorption of minerals in bone.

Vitamin D also influences the handling of phosphate by the kidney. In animals deficient in vitamin D, the excretion of phosphate and its renal clearance are decreased; in parathyroidectomized animals, vitamin D increases the clearance of phosphate and promotes lowering of the serum phosphate concentration,

7-Dehydrocholesterol is the form in which provitamin D_3 is found in natural foods. When it is irradiated with long-wave ultraviolet light, this compound acquires antirachitic properties to form the active vitamin D_3, now termed cholecalciferol. The provitamin D_3 can be synthesized within the body so that it may in fact not normally be required in the diet. In this sense, it is technically not a vitamin. When man lived mainly outdoors with minimal clothing and the atmosphere was clear so that there was no interference with the penetration of ultraviolet light from the sun, he was exposed to adequate radiation to convert the provitamin in his skin to active vitamin D_3. It is possible that in some regions, as in the far northern areas of the world, the amount of sunlight was not adequate to assure conversion of 7-dehydrocholesterol to vitamin D_3. In these circumstances, fish liver oils, which are virtually the only excellent source of vitamin D in nature, may have served to supply the vitamin. Otherwise, with adequate exposure to sunlight, it may be that vitamin D is not required in the diet, although the increased need for this substance in growth—and in pregnancy to provide for the needs of the fetus—undoubtedly makes it desirable to assure an adequate supply in the diets of infants, children, and pregnant and nursing women. Indeed, the long-described and well-known bone disease, rickets, which is the classic manifestation of severe deficiency of vitamin D, certainly points up the fact that under certain conditions the production of vitamin D within the body may not be adequate.

Cholecalciferol is not the *active* form of vitamin D in the tissues. Lund & DeLuca have shown that the metabolically active form of the vitamin which induces transport of calcium across the intestinal membrane is **1,25-dihydroxycholecalciferol** (1,25-[OH]$_2$-D$_3$) (Fig 12—5). This derivative is also responsible for the ability of vitamin D to promote mobilization of calcium from bone. Complete removal of the kidney in rats entirely

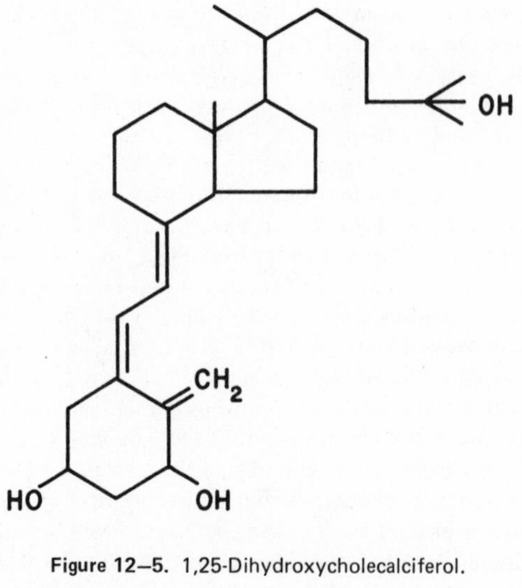

Figure 12—5. 1,25-Dihydroxycholecalciferol.

prevents the mobilization of calcium from bone in response to the administration of 25-hydroxycholecalciferol; however, $1,25\text{-}(OH)_2\text{-}D_3$ is still effective. This latter compound, as will be mentioned below, is produced by the kidney. The observation that in the anephric rat 25-hydroxycholecalciferol is ineffective in mobilizing calcium from bone provides further evidence that $1,25\text{-}(OH)_2\text{-}D_3$ is indeed the vitamin D_3 metabolite responsible for bone calcium mobilization.

The conversion of cholecalciferol to the metabolically active derivative begins with the formation of 25-hydroxycholecalciferol ($OH\text{-}D_3$) by a mitochondrial enzyme in liver. This compound is then further hydroxylated (at position 1) in the kidney to form 1,25-dihydroxycholecalciferol ($1,25\text{-}[OH]_2\text{-}D_3$). A more recently discovered additional active metabolite of D_3, also formed in the kidney, is 24,25-dihydroxycholecalciferol. This compound is believed to be active in kidney tissues where it exerts an effect on renal tubular mechanisms associated with the handling of calcium and phosphate.

The production of $1,25\text{-}(OH)_2\text{-}D_3$ in the kidney is strongly affected by the levels of calcium in the serum. When serum calcium is normal or elevated, synthesis of $1,25\text{-}(OH)_2\text{-}D_3$ is inhibited by feedback regulation; the reverse occurs in the presence of hypocalcemia. There appears also to be feedback control on the synthesis of 25-hydroxycholecalciferol in the liver.

It has been suggested that in chronic renal disease $1,25\text{-}(OH)_2\text{-}D_3$ may not be formed. This would account for signs of vitamin D resistance in such patients and a resultant lowering of serum calcium together with increased production of parathyroid hormone.

Administration of vitamin D to chicks with a vitamin D deficiency produces an increase in biosynthesis of proteins necessary for mobilization and transport of calcium ion at the brush border side of intestinal epithelium. It is hypothesized that the active form of vitamin D induces formation of the messenger RNA (mRNA) for the synthesis of calcium-binding proteins that comprise the calcium ion transport system in the intestinal mucosal cells. The effect of vitamin D on the intestine is blocked by the administration of dactinomycin, an observation which supports the concept that the vitamin is acting to stimulate mRNA synthesis. Vitamin D is thus pictured as functioning in the regulation of Ca^{2+} absorption from the intestine by controlling the expression of genetic information. In Chapter 29 is described the function of the steroid hormones in "unmasking" genetic information to bring about synthesis of enzyme proteins that catalyze the metabolic effects originally attributed to the hormone. It now appears that vitamin D, itself a steroid derivative, also functions similarly by effecting the synthesis of calcium transport proteins. Apparently, vitamin D functions more like a hormone than a vitamin.

It has been suggested that the action of vitamin D on calcium metabolism is not confined to certain organs but rather is generalized, and further that the vitamin controls translocation of divalent cations in a number of tissues that are particularly concerned with the turnover of these cations. The distribution of radioactively labeled vitamins D_2 and D_3 supports the concept of a generalized or systemic action for the vitamin. It is found in liver, small intestine mucosal cells, the membranes of the heart and of striated muscle, proliferating chondrocytes, and the epiphyseal plates of long bones. In homogenates of liver, kidney, and small intestine, the vitamin was found in the microsomal fraction.

Sources & Daily Allowance

In its active form, vitamin D is not well distributed in nature, the only rich sources being the liver and viscera of fish and the liver of animals which feed on fish. Eggs and butter also contain vitamin D. Milk is a poor source of the vitamin unless it is fortified by addition of the vitamin or has had its vitamin D content increased by irradiation with ultraviolet light. Much of the milk now available has vitamin D added to provide a concentration of 400 IU per quart (equivalent to 10 μg of vitamin D_3). Vitamin D is stable in foods; storage, processing, and cooking do not affect its activity.

For infants and children, a requirement of 400 IU/day has been suggested. Although the adult requirement is not known, 400 IU have been proposed for women during pregnancy and lactation as well as for other individuals of both sexes up to age 22 (see Table 31–6).

Excessive intakes of vitamin D are dangerous. Amounts of vitamin D above 2000 IU/day (5 times the maximum recommended daily allowance), when taken for prolonged periods, have produced hypercalcemia in infants and nephrocalcinosis in both infants and adults. The ingestion of vitamin D in excess of the recommended amounts is of no benefit and, furthermore, may produce serious and sometimes fatal results. The quantities of vitamin D necessary to produce toxic states of hypervitaminosis cannot be obtained from natural sources. The risk of overdosage is present only when there is improper use of pharmaceutical preparations of the vitamin.

One unit of vitamin D (1 USP unit or IU) is defined as the biologic activity of 0.025 μg of ergocalciferol. Substances intended for human nutrition are biologically assayed for vitamin D_2 by the "line test." Twenty-eight-day-old rats are put on a rachitogenic diet, characterized by a high cereal content and a high (4:1) ratio of calcium to phosphorus, until depleted of vitamin D (18–25 days). For the following 8 days one group, the **reference group**, is given daily test doses of cod liver oil of known potency (the USP Reference Oil) in a quantity sufficient to produce a narrow continuous line of calcification across the metaphysis of the tibia. This degree of healing is designated in the experimental protocol as "unit" or 2-plus healing. Other groups of rachitic test animals are given the test substance in varying amounts for a similar 8-day test period. All animals are sacrificed 10 days after the reference or test samples were first administered and the tibial bones examined for the degree of healing. The potency of the test material is calculated from the quantity required to produce healing equivalent to that of the reference sample. Substances intended for the chick, which responds better to vitamin D_3, are assayed by a method which determines the amount of ash in the bones of growing chicks which have been fed with the test materials.

Physical (spectrophotometric) methods are also used in assay of the vitamins D.

THE VITAMINS E

Chemistry

The vitamin E activity in foods is attributable to a series of compounds originating in plants: the tocopherols and the tocotrienols. Because of inadequate information on the content of some of these compounds having vitamin E activity, at present only a-tocopherol can be considered when calculating the vitamin E content of foods. The structure of a-tocopherol is shown in Fig 12–6.

The other compounds mentioned (a-, β-, and δ-tocopherols and tocotrienols) have lower biologic activities, estimated to be 1–50% that of a-tocopherol. One International Unit (IU) of vitamin E is defined as the activity of 1 mg of DL-a-tocopherol acetate. Synthetic free DL-a-tocopherol has a potency of 1.1 IU/mg and naturally occurring a-tocopherol (D-a-tocopherol) is considered to have an activity of 1.49 IU/mg; its acetate, 1.36 IU/mg.

All food analyses for vitamin E are now performed chemically rather than by biologic testing, as was formerly necessary. If suitable methods were available to distinguish the various tocopherols and trienols in foods, it would be appropriate to report the content of each in mg/100 g of foodstuff, but until such methods are developed allowances are based primarily on the D-a-tocopherol content of diets with an assumption that the non-a-tocopherol compounds contribute additional vitamin E activity equivalent to about 20% of the indicated a-tocopherol content of a mixed diet.

A deficiency of vitamin E in rats and some other animals causes resorption of the fetus in the female and, in the male, atrophy of spermatogenic tissue and permanent sterility. The susceptibility to hemolysis of erythrocytes treated in vitro with dilute solutions of hydrogen peroxide has been used as a test of vitamin E deficiency in humans. By this test it was shown that erythrocytes of full-term and, notably, of premature infants often had an increased susceptibility to hemolysis which could be reversed by administering vitamin E. It was later found that plasma levels of tocopherol may be low in newborn infants. In studies with adult male subjects on diets containing about 3 mg of a-tocopherol, deficiencies of vitamin E developed slowly as evidenced by the erythrocyte hemolysis test and direct measurements of plasma tocopherol levels. Depletion appeared to be hastened when the daily intake of polyunsaturated fatty acids, particularly linoleic acid, was increased. As a result of these and other studies, it has been concluded that a deficiency of vitamin E can occur in otherwise normal humans, and, further, that the intake of polyunsaturated fatty acids is the single most important factor in the determination of the requirement for vitamin E under normal circumstances.

In several studies of malnourished children in whom plasma tocopherol levels were low, it was found also that macrocytic anemia and a decreased erythrocyte survival time were associated abnormalities. After the administration of vitamin E, there were increases in plasma tocopherol, reticulocytosis, and disappearance of the anemia.

Infants, especially those of low birth weight, have on many occasions been reported to have low serum levels of tocopherol, particularly while subsisting on artificial formulas. Experimentally induced vitamin E deficiency produced in premature infants by feeding them a vitamin E-deficient formula has been shown to produce a syndrome characterized by anemia, reticulocytosis, thrombosis, and edema. The entire syndrome responded favorably to orally administered vitamin E.

Ritchie & others (1968) have reported on their observations and studies of 7 premature infants originally presenting with widespread edema as well as anemia found to be hemolytic in origin with an associated thrombocytosis. In all of these cases, serum tocopherol levels were low. The syndrome, which had developed spontaneously while the infants were being maintained on commercial formulas, was completely relieved by oral therapy with vitamin E, 75–100 IU daily. It was noted that the formula diet contained a low ratio of vitamin E to polyunsaturated fatty acids. Such formulas supply an amount of vitamin E that is not adequate to the needs of low birth weight premature infants. It seems apparent from these and simi-

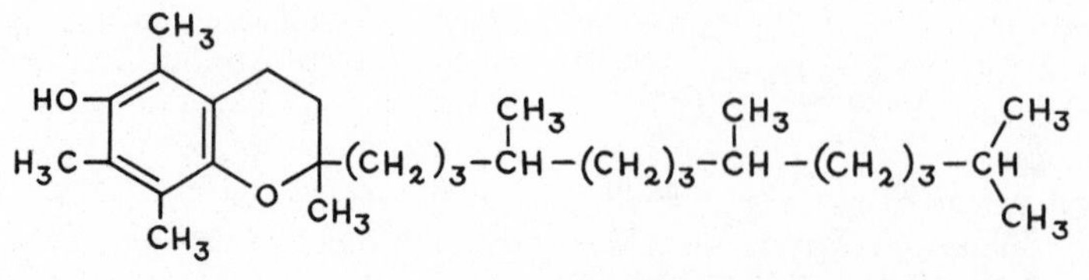

Figure 12–6. a-Tocopherol.

lar reports that vitamin E deficiency in newborn children may under some circumstances be an important cause of edema and hemolytic anemia.

Although vitamin E occurs in many foods, absorption of the vitamin from the intestine may be impaired in abnormal states characterized by malabsorption, particularly of lipids, as is the case with the other fat-soluble vitamins.

In a consideration of a recommendation for the dietary allowance of vitamin E in humans, Witting (1972) emphasized the relationship of vitamin E requirements to the dietary intake of polyunsaturated fatty acids. He states that the normal American starts with about 10% linoleic acid in his adipose tissues and a requirement for approximately 6 mg D-a-tocopherol (or about 9 IU) of vitamin E per day. After a few years of ingesting corn oil or safflower oil, linoleate may comprise 35–50% of the fatty acids of adipose tissue and the vitamin E requirement may be as much as 20–30 mg/day. A ratio of vitamin E intake to that of polyunsaturated acids of 0.6 has been recommended, although this may be higher than necessary since satisfactory diets in the USA have ratios that average only about 0.4 (milligrams tocopherol per gram of polyunsaturated acids), and normal levels of vitamin E in the plasma have been found in children fed a formula having a ratio of vitamin E to polyunsaturated fatty acids of 0.4.

Physiologic Role

The most striking chemical characteristic of the vitamins E is their antioxidant property. Polyunsaturated fatty acids are easily attacked by molecular oxygen, resulting in formation of peroxides. The tocopherols prevent this. Indeed, some believe that the deleterious effects of vitamin E deficiency are related to the accumulation of fatty acid peroxides in the tissues. The relationship of vitamin E requirements to the unsaturated fatty acid dietary intake is thus also explainable.

It has been suggested that vitamin E and other antioxidants obtained from the diet, such as vitamin C, may be important in inhibiting damage to lung tissue from oxidants in the air such as may be present in smog-contaminated atmospheres. In experimental studies, rats deficient in vitamin E were more damaged by ozone and nitrogen dioxide, which are among the oxidants in polluted air, than were those animals supplemented with vitamin E. Lipid peroxidation appears to be a damaging mechanism in ozone toxicity.

In some animal species, a lack of vitamin E produces muscular dystrophy. Such dystrophic muscles exhibit increased respiration (oxygen uptake). Treatment with tocopherol reduces the oxygen uptake of such tissue. However, vitamin E has not been shown to benefit any type of muscular dystrophy seen in man. In fact, despite the occurrence of a number of disorders in experimental animals maintained on vitamin E-deficient diets, no comparable clinical signs have been conclusively shown to result from a deficiency of vitamin E in man although there are some reports

which provide suggestive evidence that this may be the case.

The placental transfer of vitamin E is limited; mammary transfer is much more extensive. Thus the serum a-tocopherol level of breast-fed infants is increased more rapidly than that of bottle-fed infants. Furthermore, intake of vitamin E by the mother during her pregnancy is variable. As a result, the vitamin E nutriture of very young children could be inadequate. A relationship between vitamin E requirement and the quantity of unsaturated fats taken in the diet has been proposed. If such a relationship exists, it might be supposed that unsaturated fats in infant diets would further increase the need for vitamin E. Therefore, it is of interest that a group of infants fed a diet wherein the content of unsaturated fats was increased did develop anemia, edema, and certain changes in the skin. These changes, as well as a hemolytic anemia reported to have occurred in premature infants, responded to the administration of vitamin E.

Pathologic states characterized by malabsorption—eg, steatorrhea, cystic fibrosis, biliary atresia, nontropical sprue, and chronic pancreatitis—are reported to be associated with evidence of vitamin E deficiency as indicated by creatinuria, low levels of serum tocopherol, and increased hemolysis of erythrocytes. As a result of dietary surveys and studies of plasma tocopherol levels as well as resistance of erythrocytes to hemolysis, it is reported that there is widespread evidence for suboptimal vitamin E nutriture among the poorly nourished peoples of the world.

The level of tocopherol in the plasma after oral administration of DL-a-tocopheryl acetate has been measured. Single doses of 200, 400, 500, and occasionally of 100 mg were effective in increasing the free tocopherol levels of the plasma to a significant degree after 6 hours. Repeated daily oral doses produced somewhat greater maximum increases than did single doses. However, the parenteral administration of vitamin E failed to increase the free tocopherol level of the plasma regardless of the type of compound (free alcohol or monosodium phosphate) and the type of vehicle (oil or water) used.

Certain diets low in protein and especially in the sulfur-containing amino acids (particularly cystine) were found to produce an acute massive hepatic necrosis in experimental animals (Schwarz, 1954). A vitamin E deficiency enhances the effects of such diets, whereas added vitamin E exerts a preventive action upon the necrosis. Rats which have been kept on the deficient ration develop the fatal hepatic lesion suddenly (within a few hours or days) after a symptom-free latent period which averages 45 days. However, the occurrence of a metabolic defect in the livers of these animals can be demonstrated several weeks before the development of the necrotic lesion itself. Liver slices from these animals which are still histologically normal are able to respire in the Warburg apparatus for only 30–60 minutes; subsequently, oxygen consumption declines as incubation continues. The 3 major metabolic pathways for the utilization of acetate by the liver, viz, ketogenesis, lipogenesis, and oxidation to CO_2, are also deficient in the prenecrotic liver slice, probably as a result of the respiratory defect. If the diet is supplemented with cystine, vitamin E, or preparations of "factor 3," both the metabolic and the histologic lesions are prevented. A reversal of the respiratory decline in the necrotic liver can also be prevented by direct infusion of tocopherols into the portal vein.

Factor 3 has been identified as a selenium compound, and it is true that selenite gives complete protection against dietary liver necrosis in rats. However, the respiratory decline observed in the liver slices from rats kept on the deficient diet, as described above, is only partially prevented by supplementation with factor 3, whereas the liver slices from animals whose diets have been supplemented with vitamin E show no decline whatever. It now seems clear that the apparent potency of cystine in preventing dietary liver necrosis was in reality due to contamination with traces of factor 3-active selenium. It has therefore been concluded that dietary liver necrosis is the result of a simultaneous lack of factor 3-selenium and of vitamin E. A lack of one or the other alone produces relatively mild chronic diseases, but a simultaneous deficiency of both leads to severe tissue damage and death. A number of lesions hitherto attributed solely to vitamin E deficiency may actually be of dual origin, and the presence or absence of factor 3-active selenium may determine the fate of an animal on a vitamin E-deficient diet. However, some diseases are apparently caused entirely by a deficiency of vitamin E (eg, resorption sterility in rats and encephalomalacia in chicks), and there seem also to be other diseases which are little affected by administration of vitamin E but are cured by small supplements of factor 3-active selenium.

Sources & Requirements

The a-tocopherol content of foods has been measured, using modern analytical technics. Good sources of vitamin E include eggs, muscle meats, liver, fish, chicken, oatmeal, the oils of corn, soya, and cottonseed, and products made with such oils (eg, margarine, mayonnaise). It is of interest, however, that foods fried in vegetable oils and then frozen are low in tocopherol, indicating substantial losses of tocopherol during freezer storage. Concentrates of natural tocopherols are prepared by molecular distillation of wheat germ oil, which is particularly rich in vitamin E.

In the "average" American diet the daily intake of a-tocopherol ranges from 2.6–15.4 mg, with an average of 7.4 mg. This contrasts with a recommended daily allowance (Table 31–6) of 25–30 mg in adults.

Vitamin E was originally measured by a biologic assay based on the ability of the test material to support gestation when the pregnant rat is maintained on a vitamin E-deficient diet. A chemical method that permits the estimation of 2–5 μg of vitamin E has also been described. By this method, the vitamin E content of human blood was found to range from 361–412

μg/dl. At present, analyses for vitamin E may utilize paper, column, and gas-liquid chromatography. These technics permit more accurate and specific assays of a-tocopherol than were possible by the older methods. In particular, these more modern assay procedures differentiate between a-tocopherol and other less active or completely inactive forms of tocopherol.

Recommended daily allowances for vitamin E are listed in Table 31–6. These are lower than those suggested in former editions of the *Recommended Dietary Allowances* since the vitamin E content of diets in the USA, as consumed, is now known actually to be considerably less than that estimated—although higher than that reported from other Western countries. The wide distribution of vitamin E in vegetable oils, cereal grains, and animal fats makes it unlikely that a deficiency of this nutrient occurs in normal humans. Indeed, there is no clinical or biochemical evidence that vitamin E status is inadequate in normal individuals ingesting balanced diets. It has therefore been concluded that the vitamin E activity in average diets is satisfactory.

The minimum adult requirement for vitamin E when the diet contains the minimum of essential fatty acids is not known, but it is probably not more than 3–6 IU/day. The present state of our knowledge indicates that a dietary intake of vitamin E that maintains a blood concentration of total tocopherols above 0.5 mg/dl will also ensure an adequate concentration of the vitamin in all of the tissues.

THE VITAMINS K

Chemistry

A large number of chemical compounds which are related to 2-methyl-1,4-naphthoquinone possess some degree of vitamin K activity.

The naturally occurring vitamins K possess a phytyl radical on position 3 (vitamin K_1) (Fig 12–7) occurring in plants, or a difarnesyl radical (K_2; menaquinone; farnoquinone) (Fig 12–8) occurring in bacteria.

Several synthetic compounds containing the 2-methyl-1,4-naphthoquinone structure, such as menadione (Fig 12–9), exhibit vitamin K activity. This suggests that this portion of the molecule is essential for the formation of a second substance which actually exerts the biologic effects of the vitamin.

Physiologic Role

The best-known function of vitamin K is to catalyze the synthesis of prothrombin by the liver. In the absence of vitamin K a hypoprothrombinemia occurs in which blood clotting time may be greatly prolonged. It must be emphasized that the effect of vitamin K in alleviation of hypoprothrombinemia is dependent upon the ability of the hepatic parenchyma to produce prothrombin. Therefore advanced hepatic damage, as

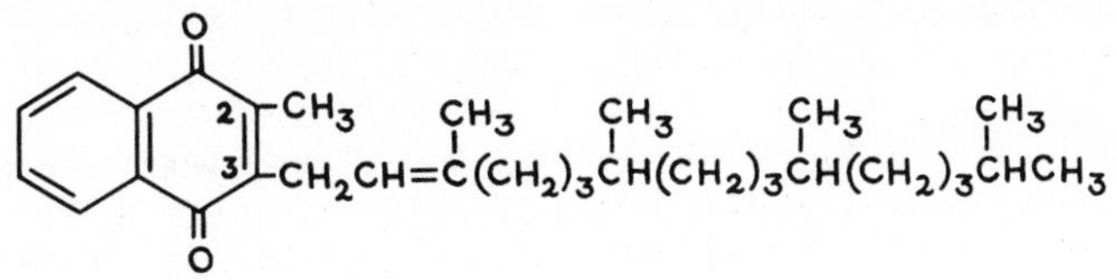

Figure 12–7. Vitamin K_1; phytonadione (phylloquinone; Mephyton [2-methyl-3-phytyl-1,4-naphthoquinone]).

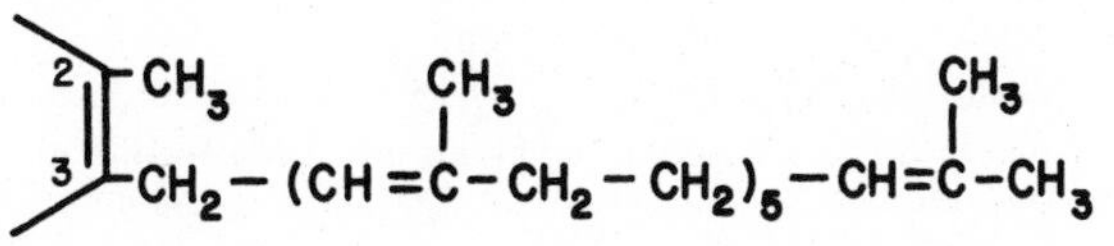

Figure 12–8. Vitamin K_2 (2-methyl-3-difarnesyl-1,4-naphthoquinone; farnoquinone) (side chain). It may also occur with 7 or 9 isoprene units ($-CH=C-CH_2-CH_2-$).

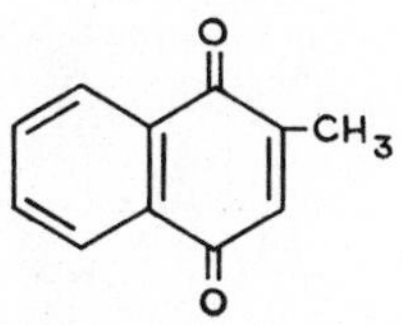

Figure 12–9. Menadione (2-methyl-1,4-naphthoquinone).

in carcinoma or cirrhosis, may be accompanied by a prothrombin deficiency which cannot be relieved by vitamin K.

The activities of several plasma thromboplastic factors are reduced in states of vitamin K deficiency or after administration of vitamin K antagonists such as dicumarol. The cause of delayed clotting in vitamin K deficiency states is therefore not confined to a prothrombin deficiency, although this is perhaps the most important factor.

The only generally accepted function of vitamin K in higher animals is that of regulating the synthesis of prothrombin and the other plasma clotting factors dependent on vitamin K (factors VII, IX, and X). It is known that the vitamin regulates the rate of synthesis of prothrombin after transcription from information carried on messenger RNA, but the nature of the control site is still not determined. Although it has been frequently suggested that vitamin K regulates the de novo synthesis of prothrombin, there is also evidence that protein synthesis is not required in connection with the step that is sensitive to vitamin K in the production of prothrombin. Suttie (1973) has demonstrated the presence of a precursor of prothrombin in the liver of rats. The experimental data derived from animal studies suggest that a prothrombin-precursor protein is produced in the liver which is converted to prothrombin in a step which requires vitamin K. In the rat, at least the absence of the vitamin, or the presence of vitamin K antagonists, causes an increase in the amount of this precursor. In the cow and in man, the precursor or, probably, some further modification of it is released into the plasma as an abnormal prothrombin which is detectable by the fact that normal and abnormal prothrombins differ in their electrophoretic mobility in the presence of calcium ions. It is proposed that the step sensitive to vitamin K involves the attachment of some as yet unrecognized prosthetic group or the modification of some amino acid residues to form metal (calcium) binding sites on the precursor. With respect to the latter function, vitamin K may be required to effect the carboxylation of the γ-carbon atom of glutamic acid residues in prothrombin protein. Such carboxyl groups would then serve as binding sites for calcium, as shown in Fig 12–10.

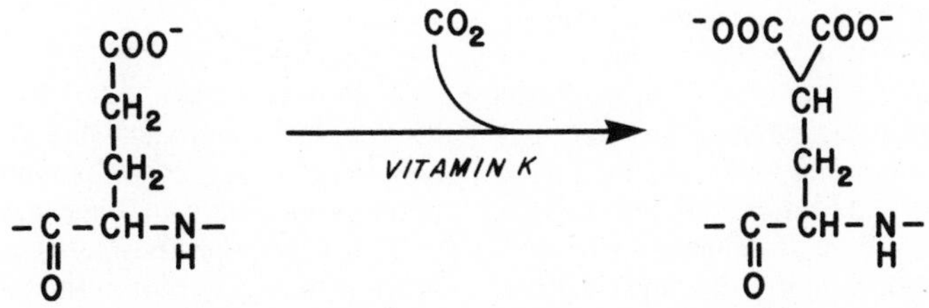

Figure 12–10. Carboxylation of a glutamic acid residue catalyzed by vitamin K.

It is known that vitamin K_1 is an essential component of the phosphorylation processes involved in photosynthesis in green plants, and it probably has a similar role in animal tissues, ie, that of cofactor necessary in oxidative phosphorylation. Vitamin K_1 is altered by the action of ultraviolet radiation. Rats fed beef sterilized by irradiation have developed vitamin K deficiency. It is reported that an impairment in the oxidative phosphorylative activity of mitochondria occurs when these cytoplasmic structures are irradiated with ultraviolet light at a wavelength of 236 nm. A similar effect on oxidative phosphorylation occurs when rat liver mitochondria are subjected to ultraviolet light. After addition of vitamin K_1 to the irradiated mitochondria, oxidative phosphorylation is restored almost to normal. The results of these experiments suggest that vitamin K, or a substance very closely related to it, does indeed play an important role in oxidative phosphorylation in the mitochondria.

The experiments with vitamin K_1 mentioned above are of considerable interest in the light of similar observations on the role of coenzyme Q. This biologically active quinone is so widely distributed in natural materials that it might be called "ubiquinone." The structure of coenzyme Q is shown in Fig 12–11. It is that of a 2,3-dimethoxy-5-methylbenzoquinone with a polyisoprenoid side chain at carbon 6. Thus far, 5 crystalline homologs that differ from one another in the number of isoprenoid units (formula: $-CH_2CH=C.CH_3-CH_2-$) in the side chain have been obtained from various sources. For example, coenzyme Q from beef heart has 10 isoprenoid units in the side-chain (Q_{10}). From a yeast, *Saccharomyces cerevisiae*, a Q_6 was isolated; from *Torula utilis*, Q_9, etc. The function of coenzyme Q as an electron carrier in terminal electron transport and in oxidative phosphorylation is described in Chapter 17.

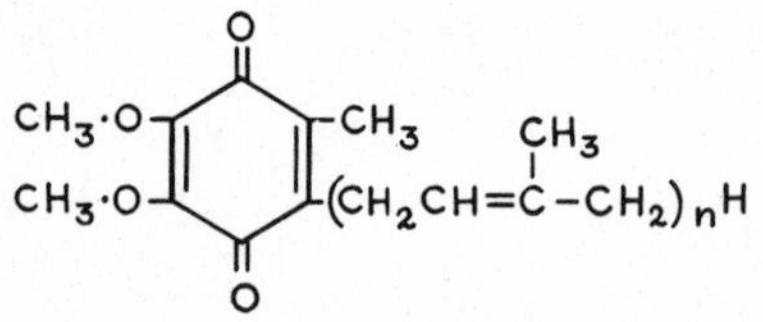

Figure 12–11. Coenzyme Q (ubiquinone).

A *dietary* deficiency of vitamin K is not likely to occur since the vitamin is fairly well distributed in foods and the intestinal microorganisms synthesize considerable vitamin K in the intestine. However, a deficiency may occur as a result of prolonged oral therapy with drugs (eg, sulfaguanidine or succinylsulfa-thiazole) capable of suppressing vitamin K-producing bacteria. Salicylates also are vitamin K antagonists. Furthermore, as has already been noted for the other fat-soluble vitamins, the absorption of vitamin K from the intestine depends on the presence of bile. A deficiency state will therefore result as a consequence of

biliary tract obstruction or if there is a defect in fat absorption, such as in sprue and celiac disease. Short-circuiting of the bowel as a result of surgery may also foster a deficiency which will not respond even to large oral doses of vitamin K. For such situations, water-soluble forms of vitamin K are available which may be absorbed even in the absence of bile. However, these derivatives are relatively ineffective in correcting the hypoprothrombinemia induced by oral anticoagulants, and they may produce some toxic manifestations in infants.

Synkayvite (sodium menadiol diphosphate) and Hykinone (menadione sodium bisulfite) are 2 water-soluble compounds with vitamin K activity. The chemical structures of these compounds are shown in Figs 12–12 and 12–13.

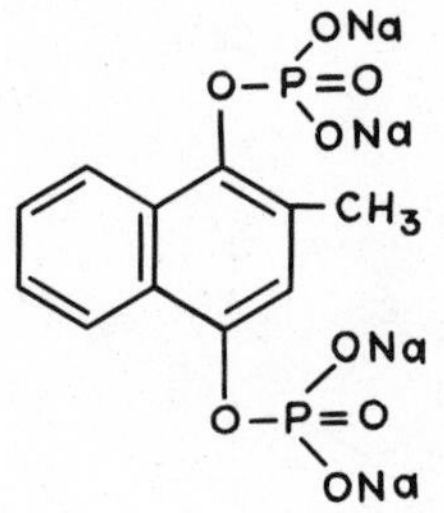

Figure 12–12. Sodium menadiol diphosphate (Synkayvite).

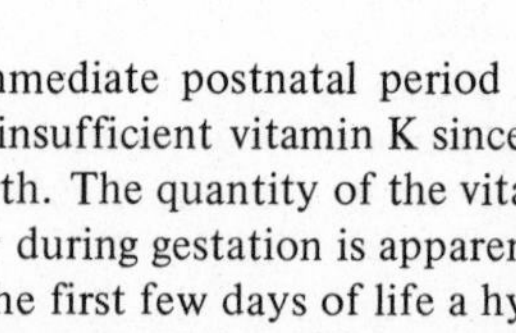

Figure 12–13. Menadione sodium bisulfite (Hykinone).

In the immediate postnatal period the intestinal flora produce insufficient vitamin K since the intestine is sterile at birth. The quantity of the vitamin supplied by the mother during gestation is apparently not large. Thus, during the first few days of life a hypoprothrombinemia may appear which will persist until the intestinal flora become active in the manufacture of the vitamin. This prothrombin deficiency can be prevented by administering vitamin K to the mother before parturition or by giving the infant a small dose of the vitamin.

The parenteral administration to infants of too large doses of vitamin K (eg, 30 mg/day for 3 days) has been shown to produce hyperbilirubinemia in some cases. Three mg of sodium menadiol diphosphate, which is equivalent to 1 mg of vitamin K_1, is adequate to prevent hypoprothrombinemia in the newborn, and there is no danger of provoking jaundice with this dosage. The oral administration of vitamin K has not been found to produce jaundice.

Uncontrollable hemorrhage is a symptom of vitamin K deficiency. The newborn child may bleed into the adrenal, brain, and gastrointestinal tract, and from the umbilical cord. In the adult, hemorrhage may also occur, most commonly after an operation on the biliary tract.

An important therapeutic use of vitamin K is as an antidote to the anticoagulant drugs such as dicumarol. For this purpose, large doses of vitamin K_1 may be used, either orally or, as an emulsion, intravenously. The prothrombin time, which is lengthened by the use of the anticoagulant drug, will usually return to normal in 12–36 hours after the administration of the vitamin provided liver function is adequate to manufacture prothrombin.

Sources

Vitamin K_1 is present in alfalfa and in such dark green vegetables as spinach, kale, and cabbage leaves as well as in cauliflower, peas, and cereals. Animal products in general contain little vitamin K, although cow's milk is a somewhat better source than human milk. Tomatoes, cheese, egg yolk, and liver are good sources. Fruits are poor sources, as are molds, yeasts, and fungi, which contain very little vitamin K; but, since it occurs in many bacteria, most putrefied animal and plant materials have considerable quantities of the vitamin.

• • •

References

See references for Chapter 13 on p 181.

13 . . .
The Water-Soluble Vitamins

VITAMIN C
(Ascorbic Acid)

Chemistry

The chemical structure of ascorbic acid (vitamin C) resembles that of a monosaccharide.

Vitamin C is readily oxidized to the dehydro form. Both forms are physiologically active, and both are found in the body fluids. The enediol group of ascorbic acid (from which removal of hydrogen occurs to produce the dehydro form, as shown in Fig 13—1) may be involved in the physiologic function of this vitamin. It is conceivable that this chemical grouping functions in a hydrogen transfer system; a role of the vitamin in such a system, ie, the oxidation of tyrosine, is described below.

The reducing action of ascorbic acid is the basis of the chemical determination of the compound. In most plant and animal tissues this is the only substance which exhibits this reducing action in acid solution. One of the most widely used analytic reactions for vitamin C is the quantitative reduction of the dye, 2,6-dichlorophenolindophenol, to the colorless leuco base by the reduced form of ascorbic acid. The method has been adapted to the microdetermination of blood ascorbic acid, so that only 0.01 ml of serum is needed for assay. Dehydroascorbic acid can be determined colorimetrically by the formation of a hydrazone with 2,4-dinitrophenylhydrazine. This method may also be used for the assay of total vitamin C after conversion of the reduced form.

Physiologic Role

Although ascorbic acid is undoubtedly widely required in metabolism, it can be synthesized in a variety of plants and in all animals studied except man and other primates and the guinea pig. The pathway of biosynthesis in animals—the uronic pathway (which is not the same as that of plants)—is shown in Chapter 19. Those animals which are unable to synthesize the vitamin presumably lack the enzyme system necessary to convert L-gulonic acid to ascorbic acid. In this sense scurvy may be considered to be the result of an inherited defect in carbohydrate metabolism.

Studies with L-ascorbic acid labeled in the various positions with isotopic carbon 14 have shown that the vitamin is extensively oxidized to respiratory CO_2 in rats and guinea pigs but that this is not the case in man. Correspondingly, ascorbic acid disappears slowly in man: it has a half-life of about 16 days in man compared to a half-life of about 4 days in the guinea pig. This correlates well with the fact that it takes 3—4 months for scurvy to develop in man on a diet containing no vitamin C, while the guinea pig becomes scorbutic in about 3 weeks.

L-Ascorbic acid-1-^{14}C is converted to labeled urinary oxalate in man, guinea pigs, and rats. In man, conversion of ascorbic acid to oxalate may account for the major part of the endogenous urinary oxalate.

Severe ascorbic acid deficiency produces scurvy. The pathologic signs of this deficiency are almost entirely confined to supporting tissues of mesenchymal origin (bone, dentine, cartilage, and connective tissue). Scurvy is characterized by failure in the formation and

Ascorbic acid
(reduced form)

Dehydroascorbic acid

Figure 13—1. Oxidation of vitamin C.

maintenance of intercellular materials, which in turn causes typical symptoms, such as hemorrhages, loosening of the teeth, poor healing of wounds, and the easy fracturability of the bones.

The biochemical function of ascorbic acid is still not known. Probably the most clearly established functional role of the vitamin is in maintaining the normal intercellular material of cartilage, dentine, and bone, as mentioned above. There is increasing experimental evidence for a specific role of ascorbic acid in collagen synthesis, with special reference to the synthesis of hydroxyproline from a proline precursor. There are also a number of reports of a possible function of ascorbic acid in oxidation-reduction systems, coupled with glutathione, cytochrome c, pyridine nucleotides, or flavin nucleotides. The vitamin has been reported to be involved in the oxidation of tyrosine and in the metabolism of adrenal steroids and of various drugs. However, its role in these reactions does not seem to be specific because it can usually be replaced by other compounds having similar redox properties.

The adrenal cortex contains a large quantity of vitamin C, and this is rapidly depleted when the gland is stimulated by adrenocorticotropic hormone. A similar depletion of adrenocortical vitamin C is noted when experimental animals (guinea pigs) are injected with large quantities of diphtheria toxin. Increased losses of the vitamin accompany infection and fever. These losses are particularly notable when bacterial toxins are present. All of these observations suggest that the vitamin may play an important role in the reaction of the body to stress.

Sources & Daily Allowances

The infant is usually well supplied with vitamin C at birth. However, infants 6–12 months of age who are fed processed milk formulas not supplemented with fruits and vegetables are very susceptible to the development of infantile scurvy. Adult cases appear from time to time, particularly in patients studied in municipal hospitals who may be living in depressed areas of cities. Elderly bachelors and widowers who may prepare their own foods are particularly prone to the development of vitamin C deficiency, a syndrome termed "bachelor scurvy." Food faddists may also develop vitamin C deficiencies if their diet avoids raw foods, particularly fruits and vegetables.

The best food sources of vitamin C are citrus fruits, berries, melons, tomatoes, green peppers, raw cabbage, and leafy green vegetables, particularly salad greens. Fresh (but not dehydrated) potatoes, while only a fair source of vitamin C on a per gram basis, are excellent sources in the average diet because of the quantities which are commonly consumed.

The vitamin is easily destroyed by cooking, since it is readily oxidized. There may also be a considerable loss in mincing of fresh vegetables such as cabbage, or in the mashing of potatoes. Losses of vitamin C during the storage and processing of foods are also extensive, particularly where heat is involved. Traces of copper and other metals accelerate this destruction.

Ascorbic acid is probably the most easily destroyed of all the vitamins. In consequence, it is very likely that persons consuming only small amounts of uncooked foods in their diets are not receiving adequate quantities of vitamin C.

The tissues and body fluids contain varying amounts of vitamin C. With the exception of muscle, the tissues of the highest metabolic activity have the highest concentration. Fasting individuals who are given liberal quantities of vitamin C (75–100 mg/day) have serum ascorbic acid levels of 1–1.4 mg/dl. Those on diets which provide only 15–25 mg/day will have serum levels correspondingly lower: 0.1–0.3 mg/dl. When the blood levels of ascorbic acid exceed 1–1.2 mg/dl, excretion of the vitamin occurs readily. For this reason the intravenous administration of vitamin C is usually attended by a considerable urinary loss. Large doses of the vitamin from pharmaceutical sources in amounts enitrely unobtainable from foods are also probably mainly excreted rapidly in the urine.

The recommended daily intakes of ascorbic acid for infants, children, and adults are listed in Table 31–6.

THE VITAMINS OF THE B COMPLEX

The recognized nutritionally important B vitamins are as follows:*

(1) Thiamin (vitamin B_1, antiberiberi substance, antineuritic vitamin, aneurine).

(2) Riboflavin (vitamin B_2, lactoflavin).

(3) Niacin (P-P factor of Goldberger, nicotinic acid).

(4) Pyridoxine (vitamin B_6, rat antidermatitis factor).

(5) Pantothenic acid (filtrate factor, chick antidermatitis factor).

(6) Lipoic acid (thioctic acid, protogen, acetate replacement factor).

(7) Biotin (vitamin H, anti-egg white injury factor).

(8) Folic acid group (liver *Lactobacillus casei* factor, vitamin M, *Streptococcus lactis* R (SLR) factor, vitamin B_c, fermentation residue factor, pteroylglutamic acid).

(9) Inositol (mouse anti-alopecia factor).

(10) *p*-Aminobenzoic acid.

(11) Vitamin B_{12} (cyanocobalamin, cobamide, antipernicious anemia factor, extrinsic factor of Castle).

---

*In parentheses are the various terms that may be regarded either as synonymous with the accepted current name for each B vitamin or as designations now regarded as historical and in use before the chemical identity of the vitamin was established.

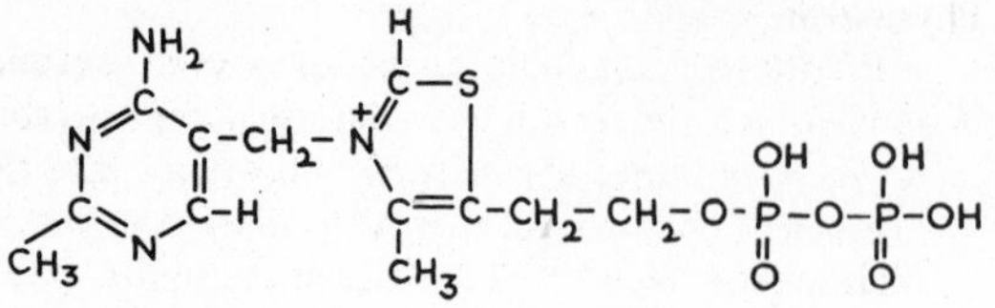

2,5,Dimethyl-   4-Methyl-5-hydroxy-
6-aminopyrimidine   ethylthiazole

Figure 13–2. Thiamin diphosphate.

THIAMIN

Chemistry

Thiamin ($C_{12}H_{17}N_4OS$) is 2,5-dimethyl-6-amino-pyrimidine bonded through a methylene linkage to 4-methyl-5-hydroxyethylthiazole (Fig 13–2).

Physiologic Role

Thiamin, in the form of thiamin diphosphate (thiamin pyrophosphate), acts as a coenzyme in the system for the oxidative decarboxylation of pyruvate or of a-ketoglutarate in the pyruvate or ketoglutarate dehydrogenase enzyme complex systems, respectively. These systems are discussed in detail in Chapter 19.

Thiamin diphosphate is also a coenzyme in the reactions of transketolation which occur in the direct oxidative pathway for glucose metabolism. The operation of this pathway in erythrocytes from thiamin-deficient rats is markedly retarded at the transketolase step so that pentose sugars accumulate to levels 3 times normal. The biochemical defect appears before growth ceases in the thiamin-deficient animal, and the defect can be significantly alleviated by addition of thiamin to the cells in vitro or by the intraperitoneal injection of thiamin in vivo.

Thiamin deficiency affects predominantly the peripheral nervous system, the gastrointestinal tract, and the cardiovascular system. Thiamin has been shown to be of value in the treatment of beriberi, alcoholic neuritis, and the neuritis of pregnancy or of pellagra. Beriberi occurs in endemic form where polished milled rice is a staple food. The disease is still an important public health problem in South and East Asia, especially in the Philippines, Vietnam, Thailand, and Burma.

In certain fish there is a heat-labile enzyme which destroys thiamin. Attention was drawn to this "thiaminase" by the appearance of "Chastek paralysis" in foxes fed a diet containing 10% or more of uncooked fish. The disease is characterized by anorexia, weakness, progressive ataxia, spastic paraplegia, and hyperesthesia. The similarity between the focal lesions of the nervous system in this paralysis in the fox and the lesions seen in Wernicke's syndrome in man have lent support to the concept that the latter is in part attributable to thiamin deficiency.

Chemical or microbiologic methods are used to determine thiamin in foods or in body fluids. The chemical procedures are based on conversion of thiamin to a compound which fluoresces under ultraviolet illumination. Quantitative measurement of the vitamin may then be accomplished with a photofluorometer.

For detection of thiamin deficiency in man, a determination of the amount of thiamin excreted in 4 hours may be used. This is sometimes modified to include the prior administration of a test dose of thiamin, and the percentage of the test dose which is excreted in the urine is observed (thiamin load test). Such studies may differentiate between persons with very high or moderate to low thiamin intakes, but their principal value in individual cases is to rule out thiamin deficiency. Another diagnostic test for thiamin deficiency is based on the measurement of the ratio of lactic to pyruvic acids in the blood after administration of glucose. Blood and urinary pyruvic acid levels are characteristically elevated in thiamin deficiency, as would be expected from the role of thiamin in pyruvic acid metabolism; but abnormal blood lactic acid-pyruvic acid ratios are said to be more specific indicators of vitamin B_1 deficiency than levels of pyruvic acid alone.

Sources & Daily Allowances

Thiamin is present in practically all of the plant and animal tissues commonly used as food, but the content is usually small. Among the more abundant sources are unrefined cereal grains, liver, heart, kidney, and lean cuts of pork. With improper cooking the thiamin contained in these foods may be destroyed. Since the vitamin is water-soluble and somewhat heat-labile, particularly in alkaline solutions, it may be lost in the cooking water. The enrichment of flour, bread, corn, and macaroni products with thiamin has increased considerably the availability of this vitamin in the diet. On the basis of the average per capita consumption of flour and bread in the USA, as much as 40% of the daily thiamin requirement is now supplied by these foods.

It is difficult to fix a single requirement for vitamin B_1. The requirement is increased when metabolism is heightened, as in fever, hyperthyroidism, increased muscular activity, pregnancy, and lactation. There is also a relationship to the composition of the diet. Fat and protein reduce—while carbohydrate increases—the quantity of the vitamin required in the daily diet. It is also possible that some of the thiamin synthesized by the bacteria in the intestine may be available to the organism. Deficiencies of thiamin are likely not only in persons with poor dietary habits, or in the indigent, but also in many patients suffering from organic disease.

Thiamin is readily absorbed from the intestine. However, it cannot be stored in the body to a significant degree. If the vitamin is taken in excessive amounts—as may occur by the use of thiamin-containing vitamin supplements—the excess vitamin is promptly excreted in the urine. As a result, there is no evidence of toxicity, but it is also apparent that proper amounts of the vitamin must be taken regularly in the diet because of the limited capacity of the tissues to accumulate significant stores of thiamin.

A detailed statement of thiamin requirements will be found in Table 31–6.

In a population subsisting on a high-carbohydrate (rice) diet low in fat and protein, an average daily intake of about 0.2 mg/1000 kcal is associated with widespread beriberi. Mild polyneuritis was produced in 2 human subjects maintained on a daily thiamin intake of 0.175 mg/1000 kcal for a period of about 4 months.

RIBOFLAVIN

The existence of a water-soluble, yellow-green, fluorescent pigment in milk whey was noted as early as 1879; but this substance, riboflavin, was not isolated in pure form until 1932. At that time it was shown to be a constituent of oxidative tissue-enzyme systems and an essential growth factor for laboratory animals.

Riboflavin (Fig 13–3) is relatively heat-stable but sensitive to light. On irradiation with ultraviolet rays or visible light it undergoes irreversible decomposition.

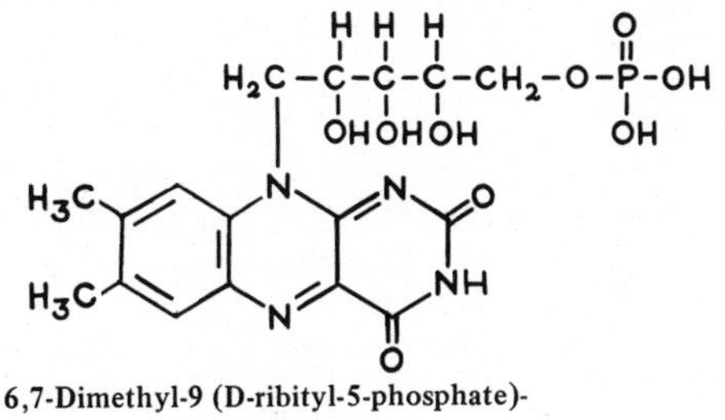

6,7-Dimethyl-9 (D-ribityl-5-phosphate)-isoalloxazine

Figure 13–3. Riboflavin phosphate (riboflavin mononucleotide).

Physiologic Role

Riboflavin is a constituent of several enzyme systems which are involved in intermediary metabolism. These enzymes are called flavoproteins. Riboflavin acts as a coenzyme for hydrogen transfer in the reactions catalyzed by these enzymes. In its active form riboflavin is combined with phosphate. This phosphorylation of riboflavin occurs in the intestinal mucosa as a condition for its absorption.

Two forms of riboflavin are known to exist in various enzyme systems. The first, riboflavin phosphate (riboflavin mononucleotide), is a constituent of the Warburg yellow enzyme, cytochrome c reductase, and the amino acid dehydrogenase for the naturally occurring L-amino acids. The other form is flavin adenine dinucleotide (FAD; see Fig 13–4), which contains 2 phosphate groups and adenine as well as ribose and ribitol. FAD is the prosthetic group of diaphorase, the D-amino acid dehydrogenase, glycine oxidase, and xanthine oxidase, which contains also iron and molybdenum. It is also an integral part of the prosthetic group of acyl-CoA dehydrogenase, the enzyme which mediates the first step in the oxidation of fatty acids.

Characteristic lesions of the lips, fissures at the angles of the mouth (cheilosis), localized seborrheic dermatitis of the face, a particular type of glossitis (magenta tongue), and certain functional and organic disorders of the eyes may result from riboflavin deficiency. However, these are not due to riboflavin deficiency alone and may result from various conditions.

It has been suggested that a determination of the riboflavin content of the serum is of value in the diagnosis of riboflavin deficiencies. The normal concentration of riboflavin in the serum is 3.16 µg/dl. Most of this is present as flavin adenine dinucleotide (FAD) (2.32 µg/dl); the remainder exists as free riboflavin (0.84 µg/dl). However, the relationship of blood levels of riboflavin to the amounts of the vitamin stored in the body remains to be elucidated. Urinary excretion of less than 50 µg riboflavin in 24 hours is usually associated with clinical signs of deficiency.

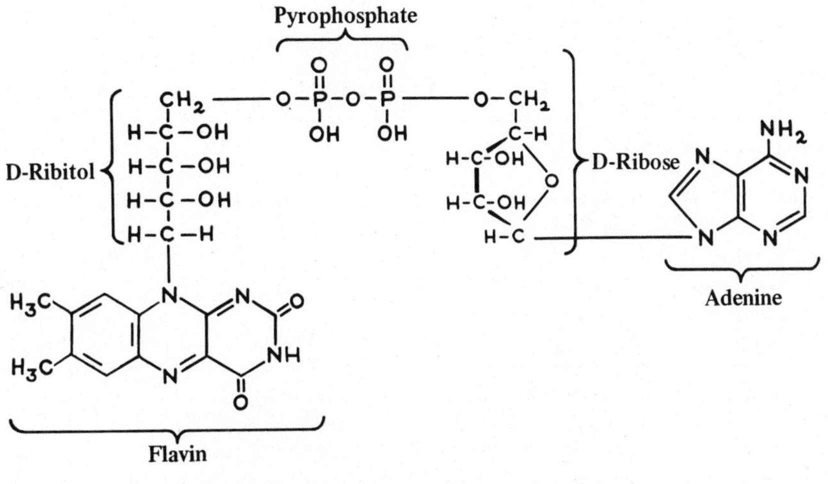

Figure 13–4. Flavin adenine dinucleotide (FAD).

From evidence gathered in dietary surveys, riboflavin deficiency should be among the most prevalent of the nutritional diseases attributable to lack of a vitamin. However, despite the fundamental role of riboflavin in metabolism, clinical signs of a riboflavin deficiency are relatively mild and rather nonspecific because of the frequent association of other nutritional deficiencies occurring simultaneously, such as pellagra and iron deficiency.

Sources & Daily Allowances

Riboflavin is widely distributed throughout the plant and animal kingdoms, with very rich sources in anaerobic fermenting bacteria. Milk, liver, kidney, and heart are excellent sources. Many vegetables are also good sources, but the cereals are rather low in riboflavin content. The riboflavin concentration in oats, wheat, barley, and corn is increased strikingly during germination.

Ordinary cooking procedures do not affect the riboflavin content of foods. Roasted, braised, or boiled meats retain 70–85% of the vitamin; an additional 15% is recovered in the drippings.

Unless proper precautions are taken, extensive losses of riboflavin in milk may occur during pasteurization, exposure to light in the course of bottling, or as a result of the irradiation of milk to increase its vitamin D content. Flour and bread, as a result of enrichment with crystalline riboflavin, may provide as much as 16% of the daily per capita requirement for this vitamin in the USA.

The riboflavin requirements are listed in Table 31–6.

NIACIN & NIACINAMIDE

Niacin and niacinamide are specific for the treatment of acute pellagra. It is important to remember that vitamin deficiencies seldom occur singly, as is well illustrated by patients with pellagra. Very often these patients exhibit symptoms caused by a lack of vitamins other than niacin, particularly a polyneuritis amenable to thiamin administration. Nevertheless, the dermatitis, diarrhea, dementia, stomatitis, and glossitis observed respond, often spectacularly, to niacin. Niacin is the P-P (pellagra-preventive) factor originally named by Goldberger.

Although the incidence of pellagra has declined as a result of greater diversification of the components of

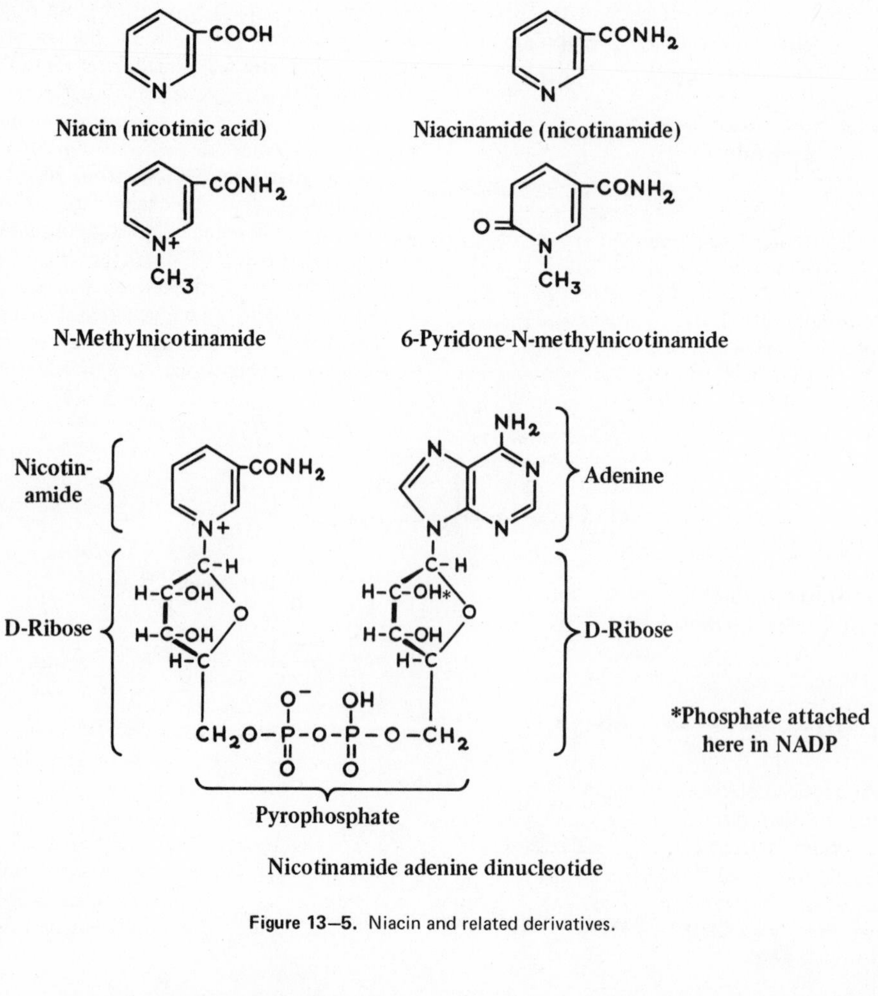

Niacin (nicotinic acid)

Niacinamide (nicotinamide)

N-Methylnicotinamide

6-Pyridone-N-methylnicotinamide

Nicotinamide adenine dinucleotide

*Phosphate attached here in NADP

Figure 13–5. Niacin and related derivatives.

the diet, it still occurs in parts of the Near East, Africa, southeastern Europe, and in the USA, usually in populations subsisting on diets high in corn. Alcoholism is an important precipitating factor in some areas.

The amino acid tryptophan normally contributes to the niacin supply of the body. For nutritional purposes, 60 mg of tryptophan is considered to produce 1 mg of niacin in man. Many of the diets causing pellagra are low in good quality protein as well as in vitamins. For this reason, pellagra is usually due to a combined deficiency of tryptophan and niacin.

Niacin is not excreted to any extent as the free nicotinic acid. A small amount may occur in the urine as niacinamide or as nicotinuric acid, the glycine conjugate. By far the largest portion is excreted as methyl derivatives, viz, N-methylnicotinamide and the 6-pyridone of N-methylnicotinamide, and N-methylnicotinic acid (Fig 13–5) and the glycine conjugates of these methyl derivatives. This methylation is accomplished in the liver at the expense of the labile methyl supply of the body. Methionine is the principal source of these methyl groups.

Physiologic Role

Niacinamide functions as a constituent of 2 coenzymes: nicotinamide adenine dinucleotide (NAD) and nicotinamide adenine dinucleotide phosphate (NADP). The reduced form of either coenzyme is designated by the prefix **dihydro-**, eg, dihydronicotinamide adenine dinucleotide **(NADH)** and dihydronicotinamide adenine dinucleotide phosphate **(NADPH).**

These coenzymes, which operate as hydrogen and electron transfer agents by virtue of reversible oxidation and reduction, play a vital role in metabolism. The function of niacin in metabolism explains its great importance in human nutrition and its requirement by many other organisms, including bacteria and yeasts.

The structure of NAD is known to be a combination of niacinamide with 2 molecules of the pentose sugar, D-ribose; 2 molecules of phosphoric acid; and a molecule of the purine base, adenine. It is shown in the oxidized form (see Fig 13–5). In changing to the reduced form it accepts hydrogen and electrons.

The mechanism of the transfer of hydrogen from a metabolite to oxidized NAD, thus completing the oxidation of the metabolite and the formation of reduced NAD, is shown in the abbreviated formula below. These reactions have been studied by observing the transfer of deuterium (heavy hydrogen) from labeled ethanol, CH_3CD_2OH, as catalyzed by alcohol dehydrogenase.

$$CH_3CD_2OH + NAD^+ \rightleftharpoons CH_3CDO + NADD + H^+$$

Both the reduced NAD and the aldehyde formed have one atom of deuterium per molecule. Hence one atom of deuterium is transferred to NAD; the other remains attached to the aldehyde carbon. The H atom, originally a part of the OH group of the alcohol, loses an electron and enters the medium as H^+.

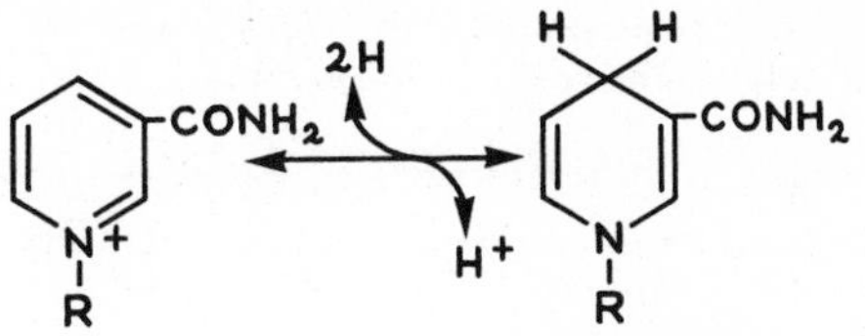

Figure 13–6. Reduction of NAD.

Reduction of NAD occurs in the **para-** position, as shown in Fig 13–6.

NADP differs only in the presence of one more phosphate moiety, esterified to the OH group on the second carbon of the ribose attached to the adenine (Fig 13–5). Its function is similar to that of NAD in hydrogen and electron transport. The 2 coenzymes are interconvertible.

Sources & Daily Allowances

Niacin is found most abundantly in yeast. Lean meats, liver, and poultry are good sources. Milk, tomatoes, canned salmon, and several leafy green vegetables contribute sufficient amounts of the vitamin to prevent disease, although they are not in themselves excellent sources. On the basis of the average per capita consumption, enriched bread and other enriched flour products may provide as much as 32% of the daily niacin requirement. Most fruits and vegetables are poor sources of niacin.

The recommended daily allowances for niacin are listed in Table 31–6.

The niacin requirements are influenced by the protein content of the diet because of the ability of the amino acid tryptophan to supply much of the niacin required by the body. There is also evidence that niacin may be synthesized by bacterial activity in the intestine and that some of this may be absorbed and utilized by the tissues. The niacin requirements specified in Table 31–6 are therefore to be considered "niacin equivalents," ie, to include both preformed niacin in the diet and that derived from tryptophan.

PYRIDOXINE

Pyridoxine was first discovered as essential for rats and named the rat antidermatitis factor or the rat antipellagra factor. Later work has shown that rats and man convert pyridoxine to other substances which far surpass pyridoxine in potency when tested with the lactobacilli or yeasts, which are used to assay foodstuffs for this vitamin. This suggested that pyridoxine is not the most active form of the vitamin in nature but that it is convertible to other derivatives which function as described below. These more active deriva-

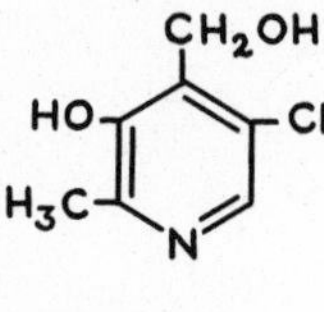

Pyridoxine 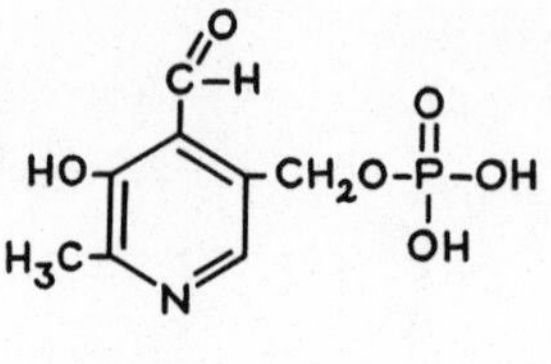   Pyridoxal phosphate

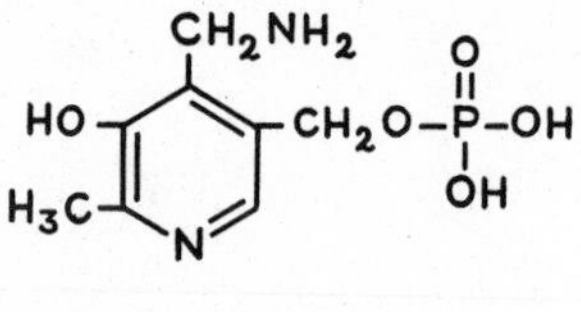

Pyridoxamine phosphate

Figure 13—7. Forms of pyridoxine.

tives are pyridoxal and pyridoxamine phosphates. Vitamin B_6 as it occurs in nature is probably a mixture of all 3 (Fig 13—7).

The predominant metabolite of vitamin B_6, which is excreted in the urine either from dietary B_6 or after ingestion of any of the 3 B_6 derivatives, is 4-pyridoxic acid (2-methyl-3-hydroxy-4-carboxy-5-hydroxymethyl pyridine) (Fig 13—8). This metabolite can be measured by a fluorometric method.

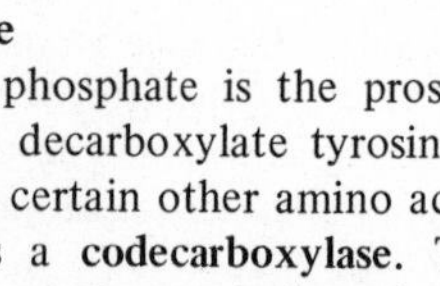

Figure 13—8. 4-Pyridoxic acid.

Physiologic Role

Pyridoxal phosphate is the prosthetic group of enzymes which decarboxylate tyrosine, arginine, glutamic acid, and certain other amino acids. In this way it functions as a **codecarboxylase**. The deaminases (dehydrases) for serine and threonine are also catalyzed by pyridoxal phosphate acting as coenzyme. A third and very important function of the vitamin is as a coenzyme for enzymes involved in transamination, ie, a **cotransaminase**. This function of pyridoxal phosphate probably is carried out by conversion to pyridoxamine phosphate. The reaction is reversible, so that the vitamin is actually functioning in an amino transfer system analogous to the hydrogen transfer systems described above in connection with niacinamide and riboflavin.

There is a specific relationship between vitamin B_6 and the metabolism of tryptophan because of the requirement for pyridoxal phosphate as a coenzyme for kynureninase. Failure to convert kynurenine to anthranilic acid results in the production of xanthurenic acid from kynurenine (see Chapter 22). In pyridoxine-deficient rats, dogs, swine, monkeys, and man, xanthurenic acid is found in the urine. When the vitamin is administered to the vitamin-deficient animals, xanthurenic acid disappears from the urine, and none can be found in the urine of normal animals. The examination of the urine for this metabolite after the feeding of a test dose of tryptophan has been used to diagnose vitamin B_6 deficiency.

The metabolism of cysteine is described in Chapter 22. In these reactions, vitamin B_6 is concerned with the transfer of sulfur from methionine to serine to form cysteine. This relates the vitamin to **transulfuration** as well as to transamination described above. The removal of sulfur from cysteine or homocysteine is catalyzed by desulfhydrases. These enzymes also require pyridoxal phosphate as coenzyme.

In studies on the factors which affect the transport of amino acids into the cells, it appears that pyridoxal participates in the mechanisms which influence intracellular accumulation of these metabolites. This may include a direct involvement of pyridoxal phosphate in the process of absorption of amino acids from the intestine.

It is thus apparent that vitamin B_6 is essential to amino acid metabolism in several roles: as a coenzyme for decarboxylation, deamination of serine and threonine, transamination, transulfuration, desulfuration of cysteine and homocysteine, the activity of kynureninase, and the transfer of amino acids into cells.

Vitamin B_6 is required by all animals investigated so far. Impaired growth results when immature animals are maintained on a vitamin B_6-free diet. Specific defects include acrodynia, edema of the connective tissue layer of the skin, convulsive seizures and muscular weakness in rats, and severe microcytic hypochromic anemia in dogs, swine, and monkeys accompanied by a 2- to 4-fold increase in the level of plasma iron and by hemosiderosis in the liver, spleen, and bone marrow. The anemia is not hemolytic in character, since there is no rise in icterus index or serum bilirubin. As is described in Chapter 14, pyridoxal is a coenzyme in the reaction by which α-amino-β-ketoadipic acid is decarboxylated to δ-aminolevulinic acid. The anemia of pyridoxine-deficient animals may be attributed to a defect at this point in the synthesis of heme.

Pyridoxine deficiency in humans may also be associated with a reversible hypochromic microcytic anemia with a high serum iron similar to that observed in pyridoxine-deficient animals.

Vitamin B_6 is unquestionably required in the diet of humans, although this vitamin is adequately supplied in the usual diets of adults, children, and all but very young infants. However, deficiency states in infants and in pregnant women have been described. In the first instance, epileptiform seizures were reported in a small percentage (3—5/1000) of very young infants maintained on an unsupplemented diet of a liquid infant food preparation which had been autoclaved at a very high temperature. The method of preparation presumably destroyed most of the vitamin B_6 content of the product. Supplementation of this material with pyridoxine promptly alleviated the symptoms. In the second instance, pregnant women given 10 g of DL-tryptophan excreted various intermediary metabolites of tryptophan breakdown, including xanthurenic acid. The administration of vitamin B_6 to these women suppressed to a large degree the excretion of these metabolites. This suggests that in pregnancy there may exist a B_6 deficiency which is brought about by the increased demand of the fetus for this vitamin.

There is increasing evidence that vitamin B_6 is intimately concerned with the metabolism of the central nervous system. Swine, after 9–10 weeks on a vitamin B_6-free diet, exhibit demyelinization of the peripheral nerves and degeneration of the axon. In humans, the effects of pyridoxine deficiency have been best demonstrated in infants and children. The epileptiform seizures in infants which were described above are examples. The abnormal central nervous system activity that accompanies low vitamin B_6 intake during infancy is characterized by a syndrome of increasing hyperirritability, gastrointestinal distress, and increased startle responses as well as convulsive seizures. During the actual periods of seizure, electroencephalographic changes may be noted. Clinical and electroencephalographic changes both respond quickly to pyridoxine therapy.

A syndrome resembling vitamin B_6 deficiency as observed in animals has also been noted in man during the treatment of tuberculosis with high doses of the tuberculostatic drug isoniazid (isonicotinic acid hydrazide, INH). Two to 3% of patients receiving conventional doses of isoniazid (2–3 mg/kg) developed neuritis; 40% of patients receiving 20 mg/kg developed neuropathy. Tryptophan metabolism (as indicated by xanthurenic acid excretion) was also altered. The signs and symptoms were alleviated by the administration of pyridoxine. Fifty mg of pyridoxine per day completely prevented the development of the neuritis. It is believed that isoniazid forms a hydrazone complex with pyridoxal that interferes with activation of the vitamin (Fig 13–9).

A role of pyridoxal in the metabolism of brain has been demonstrated. In connection with the function of this vitamin as a codecarboxylase for amino acids, there is one pyridoxal-dependent reaction which is specific to the central nervous system. This reaction

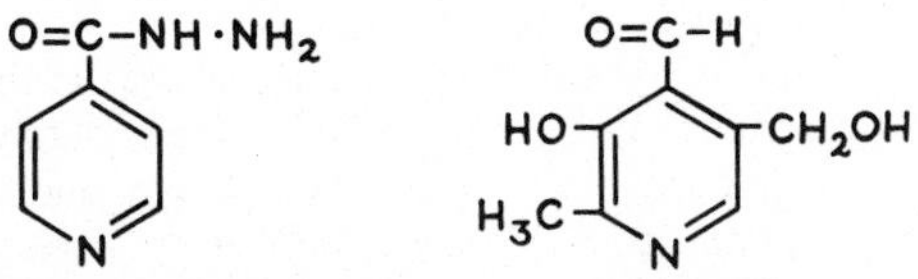

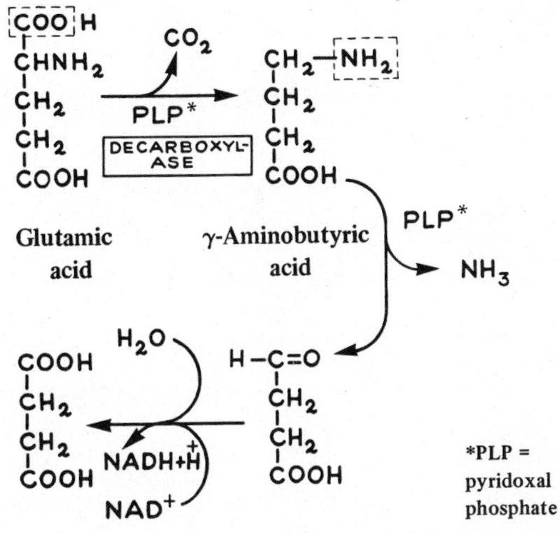

Figure 13–10. Metabolism of glutamic acid to succinic acid. Pyridoxal phosphate is a coenzyme for the decarboxylase.

is the decarboxylation of glutamic acid to γ-aminobutyric acid, which is further metabolized to succinic acid by way of an NAD-dependent soluble dehydrogenase in brain. The glutamic decarboxylase and the product of the decarboxylation, γ-aminobutyric acid, are found in the central nervous system, principally in the gray matter.

The effects of γ-aminobutyric acid on peripheral as well as central synaptic activity suggest that this compound may function as a regulator of neuronal activity. It is now believed that the epileptiform seizures in animals produced by a deficiency of B_6, the action of isoniazid, or the administration of pyridoxine antimetabolites, eg, deoxypyridoxine, may be related to a decrease in the activity of the glutamic acid decarboxylase with a resultant decrease in the amounts of γ-aminobutyric acid necessary to regulate neuronal activity in a normal manner. This idea is supported by the fact that the seizures can be controlled not only by the administration of vitamin B_6 but also by the administration of γ-aminobutyric acid.

Sources & Daily Allowances

It has been difficult to establish definitely the human requirement for vitamin B_6, probably because the quantity needed is not large and because bacterial synthesis in the intestine provides a portion of that requirement. There is some evidence that the requirement for vitamin B_6 is related to the dietary protein intake. For an adult, 2 mg/day has been recommended.

There are now a number of confirmed reports of disease states in which clinical or chemical abnormalities are not alleviated by a normal intake of vitamin B_6 but are ameliorated if the intake is increased very substantially—sometimes as much as 100 times the normal requirement. In one such series of cases of "vitamin B_6 dependency" in infants, it was observed that

Figure 13–9. Structure of isoniazid as compared to pyridoxal to show the possibility of formation of a hydrazone complex between the 2 compounds.

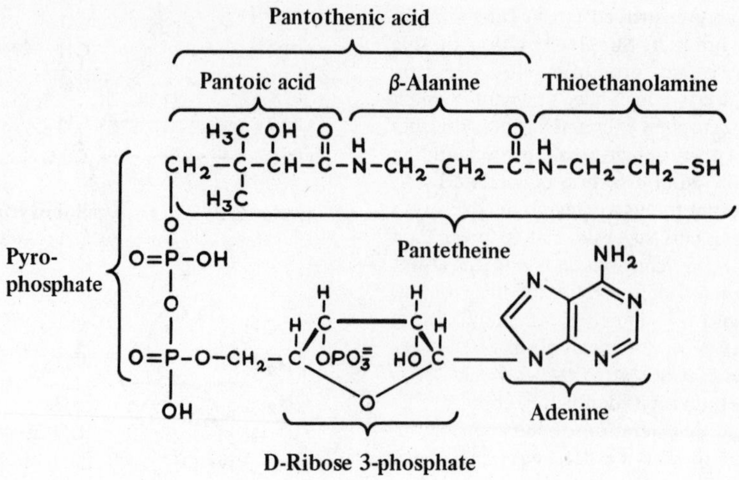

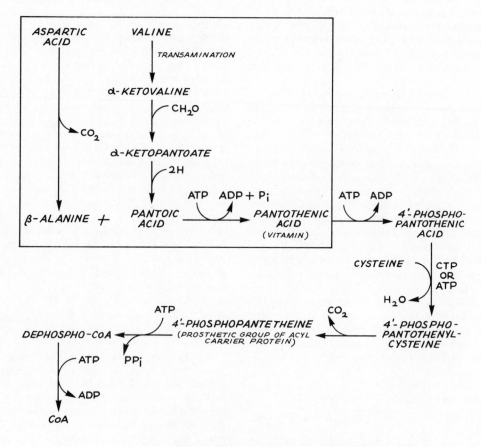

Pantothenic acid
Pantoic acid
β-Alanine
Thioethanolamine
Pyro-
phosphate
Pantetheine
Adenine
D-Ribose 3-phosphate

Figure 13–11. Structure of coenzyme A.

ASPARTIC ACID
VALINE
TRANSAMINATION
α-KETOVALINE
CH2O
CO2
α-KETOPANTOATE
2H
ATP
ADP + Pi
β-ALANINE +
PANTOIC ACID
PANTOTHENIC ACID
(VITAMIN)
ATP
ADP
4'-PHOSPHO-PANTOTHENIC ACID
CYSTEINE
CTP OR ATP
H2O
CO2
ATP
4'-PHOSPHOPANTETHEINE
(PROSTHETIC GROUP OF ACYL CARRIER PROTEIN)
4'-PHOSPHO-PANTOTHENYL-CYSTEINE
DEPHOSPHO-CoA
PPi
ATP
ADP
CoA

Figure 13–12. Biosynthesis of coenzyme A.

intakes in normals of less than 0.1 mg/day were associated with clinical manifestations of deficiency; however, no symptoms developed if the intake was 0.3 mg/day, and in most cases there was no increase in the excretion of xanthurenic acid after a tryptophan load. In the case of some infants studied, as much as 2—5 mg/day were required to prevent convulsions.

Mudd (1971) has reviewed the subject of what he terms "pyridoxine-responsive genetic disease." These diseases include vitamin B_6-responsive infantile convulsions, vitamin B_6-responsive anemia, vitamin B_6-responsive xanthurenic aciduria, primary cystathioninuria, and homocystinuria due to a primary deficiency of cystathionine synthase.

The currently recommended allowances for vitamin B_6 are listed in Table 31—6.

Good sources of the vitamin include yeast and certain seeds, such as wheat and corn, liver, and, to a limited extent, milk, eggs, and leafy green vegetables. There is little evidence that diets containing a reasonable balance of naturally occurring foodstuffs are ever seriously deficient in vitamin B_6. However, occasional cases of B_6 deficiency do arise as a result of malabsorption, alcoholism, antagonism to drugs, or the dependency mentioned above, which appears to be an inherited metabolic abnormality.

PANTOTHENIC ACID

Pantothenic acid is essential to the nutrition of many species of animals, plants, bacteria, and yeasts as well as for man. In experimental animals, symptoms due to pantothenic acid deficiency occur in such a wide variety of tissues that the basic function of this vitamin in cellular metabolism is amply confirmed. Gastrointestinal symptoms (gastritis and enteritis with diarrhea) are common to several species when a deficiency of this vitamin occurs. Skin symptoms, including cornification, depigmentation, desquamation, and alopecia also occur frequently. Lack of this vitamin also affects the adrenals. Animals deficient in pantothenic acid exhibit hemorrhage and necrosis of the adrenal cortex and an increased appetite for salt. If this condition persists the gland becomes exhausted, as shown by disappearance of lipoid material from the cortex and an acute state of adrenal cortical insufficiency, with sudden prostration and terminal dehydration. However, evidence of a dietary deficiency of pantothenic acid has not been clinically recognized in man.

Chemistry

In its active form, pantothenic acid is a constituent of **coenzyme A**, the coenzyme for acetylation reactions. The coenzyme has a nucleotide structure, as shown in Fig 13—11.

The biosynthesis of coenzyme A in many forms of life, including man, appears to proceed as shown in Fig 13—12. The reactions shown in the box are responsible for the biosynthesis of the vitamin pantothenic acid in plants and bacteria; these reactions do not occur in man.

In reactions involving coenzyme A, combination of the metabolite activated by the coenzyme occurs at the sulfhydryl (SH) group of the pantetheine moiety through a high-energy sulfur bond. It is therefore customary to abbreviate the structure of the free (reduced) coenzyme as CoA·SH, in which only the reactive SH group of the coenzyme is indicated.

Physiologic Role

As a constituent of coenzyme A, pantothenic acid is essential to several fundamental reactions in metabolism. An example is the combination of coenzyme A with acetate to form "active acetate." In the form of acetyl-coenzyme A (active acetate), acetic acid participates in a number of important metabolic processes. For example, it is utilized directly by combination with oxaloacetic acid to form citric acid, which initiates the citric acid cycle. Thus acetic acid derived from carbohydrates, fats, or many of the amino acids undergoes further metabolic breakdown via this "final common pathway" in metabolism. In the form of active acetate, acetic acid also combines with choline to form acetylcholine, or with the sulfonamide drugs which are acetylated prior to excretion.

The product of decarboxylation of a-ketoglutarate in the citric acid cycle is a coenzyme A derivative called "active" succinate (succinyl-CoA). Active succinate and glycine are involved in the first step leading to the biosynthesis of heme. Anemia frequently occurs in animals deficient in pantothenic acid. It may be assumed that this is referable to difficulty in formation of succinyl-CoA.

Coenzyme A has also an essential function in lipid metabolism. The first step in the oxidation of fatty acids catalyzed by thiokinases involves the "activation" of the acid by formation of the coenzyme A derivative, and the removal of a 2-carbon fragment in beta oxidation is accomplished by a "thiolytic" reaction, utilizing another mol of coenzyme A. The 2-carbon fragments thus produced are actually in the form of acetyl-CoA, which may directly enter the citric acid cycle for degradation to carbon dioxide and water or combine to form ketone bodies.

Although a major function of pantothenic acid is in conjunction with its role as a constituent of coenzyme A, the total pantothenic acid content of the cell cannot be accounted for as CoA. Furthermore, a significant amount of the cellular pantothenic acid is protein-bound. This latter form of pantothenic acid is that contained in a compound known as **acyl carrier protein**, a coenzyme required in the **biosynthesis** of fatty acids, whereas CoA is involved primarily in **catabolism** of fatty acids except for its function in connection with cholesterol biosynthesis.

Acyl carrier protein (MW 9100) possesses one SH group to which acetyl, malonyl, and intermediate chain-length acyl groups are attached in covalent linkages. The various changes that acyl groups undergo in fatty acid biosynthesis occur while they are in a thioester linkage with acyl carrier protein. This thiol-containing residue of acyl carrier protein is 2-mercaptoethanolamine (thioethanolamine), the same SH residue as on CoA. Indeed, the active SH-containing residue of acyl carrier protein is the phosphopantetheine portion of CoA (4'-phosphopantetheine); the remaining (adenine nucleotide) portion of the CoA molecule is not involved. The pantetheine residue of acyl carrier protein is linked covalently to a hydroxy group of a serine residue in the protein portion of the molecule. The amino acids which are immediately adjacent to this serine residue on the amino and carboxyl ends of the protein are aspartic acid (or asparagine) and leucine, respectively.

Acetyl-CoA is a precursor of cholesterol and thus of the steroid hormones. As was noted above, a pantothenic acid deficiency inevitably produces profound effects on the adrenal gland. The anatomic changes are accompanied by evidence of functional insufficiency as well. This is due to poor synthesis of cholesterol by the pantothenic acid-deficient gland.

Activation of some amino acids may also involve CoA. Examples occur among the branched-chain amino acids, valine and the leucines.

All of these facts point to an extremely important function for this vitamin in metabolism, involving as it does the utilization of carbohydrate, fat, and protein and the synthesis of cholesterol and steroid hormones as well as various acetylation reactions.

The combination of acetic acid or of fatty acids with CoA occurs at the terminal sulfhydryl group (SH) of the pantetheine residue. When an acyl group is transferred, the SH group is liberated to participate in the activation of another acyl radical. In bacteria, acetate may also be converted to acetyl phosphate, utilizing ATP as a phosphate donor. This high-energy compound can then be transferred directly to the SH site on CoA. The sulfur bond of acetyl-CoA (CoA·SH) is a high-energy bond equivalent to that of the high-energy phosphate bonds of ATP and other high-energy phosphorylated compounds. A similar high-energy sulfur bond is found in the derivatives of lipoic acid (thioctic acid). The formation of these high-energy bonds requires, therefore, a source of energy, either from a coupled exergonic reaction which yields the energy for incorporation into the bond, or from the transfer of energy from a high-energy phosphate bond or from another high-energy sulfur bond.

Although pantothenic acid contributes in a significant degree to many important biologic processes, there is no well-substantiated evidence for the existence of a deficiency in human subjects. Consequently, no quantitative data with respect to the daily requirements for this vitamin have yet been gathered.

Sources & Allowances

Pantothenic acid is widely distributed in food, particularly in that from animal sources, in whole grain cereals, and in legumes. Excellent food sources

(100–200 $\mu g/g$ of dry material) include egg yolk, kidney, liver, and yeast. Broccoli, lean beef, skimmed milk, sweet potatoes, and molasses are fair sources (35–100 $\mu g/g$). A 57% loss of pantothenic acid in wheat may occur during the manufacture of patent flour, and up to 33% is lost during the cooking of meat. Only a slight loss occurs in the preparation of vegetables.

Although the availability of pantothenic acid in foods is substantial and isolated dietary deficiencies are unlikely, subclinical deficiencies may well exist in individuals who are extensively malnourished. However, deficiencies of other B vitamins which are also likely to occur in such individuals mask any significant sign of a specific deficiency of pantothenic acid.

There is not yet adequate evidence on which to base recommended allowances for pantothenic acid. Dietary intakes in the adult population in the USA range between 5 and 20 mg/day. Diets that meet the other nutritional needs of children contain 4–5 mg/day of this vitamin. A daily intake of 5–10 mg is thought to be adequate for all adults; the upper level is suggested for pregnant and lactating women.

LIPOIC ACID

In connection with the oxidative decarboxylation of pyruvate to acetate, certain other coenzymes are required in addition to thiamin. Closely associated with thiamin in the initial decarboxylation of a-keto acids is **lipoic acid** (thioctic acid) (Fig 13–13). This factor was first detected in studies of the nutrition of lactic acid bacteria, where it was shown to replace the growth-stimulating effect of acetate. For this reason, the designation "acetate replacement factor" was assigned to it. A vitamin required for the nutrition of the protozoon *Tetrahymena geleii*, to which the term "protogen" was applied, and a factor from yeast (pyruvate oxidation factor) necessary for the oxidation of pyruvate to acetate by *Streptococcus faecalis*, which were studied at about the same time, were both later

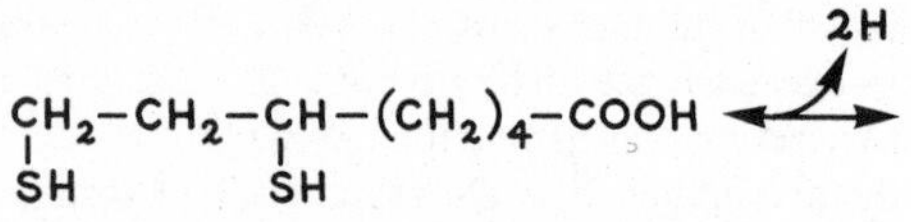

$$\underset{\overset{|}{SH}}{CH_2}-CH_2-\underset{\overset{|}{SH}}{CH}-(CH_2)_4-COOH \xrightleftharpoons{2H}$$

a-Lipoic acid (reduced form)
(6,8-dithio-octanoic acid)

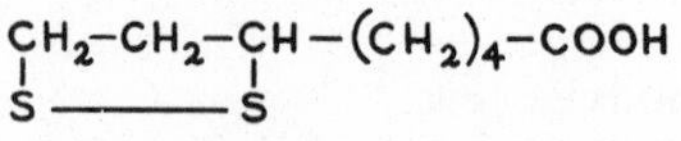

$$\underset{\overset{|}{S}\underline{}}{CH_2}-CH_2-\underset{\overset{|}{}S}{CH}-(CH_2)_4-COOH$$

a-Lipoic acid (oxidized form)

Figure 13–13. Forms of a-lipoic acid.

shown to be identical with the original acetate replacement factor of Guirard, Snell, and Williams. The active compound extracted from natural materials has been identified as a sulfur-containing fatty acid, **6,8-dithiooctanoic acid** (lipoic acid; thioctic acid).

Physiologic Role

Lipoic acid occurs in a wide variety of natural materials. It is recognized as an essential component in metabolism, although it is active in extremely minute amounts. It has not yet been demonstrated to be required in the diet of higher animals, and attempts to induce a lipoic acid deficiency in animals have so far been unsuccessful.

The complete systems for oxidative decarboxylation of pyruvic acid and of a-ketoglutaric acid involve both thiamin and lipoic acid as well as pantothenic acid, riboflavin, and nicotinamide derivatives (as CoA, FAD, and NAD, respectively). The reactions are shown in Figs 18–4 and 19–4.

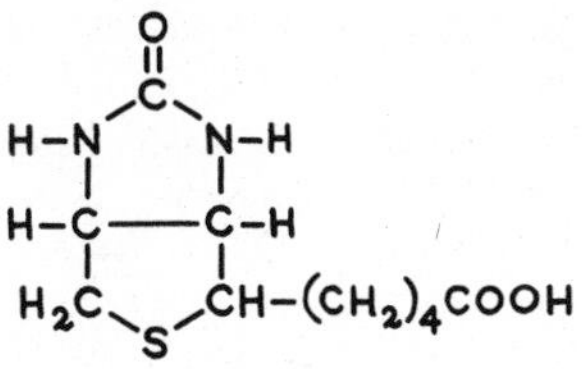

Figure 13–14. Biotin ($C_{10}H_{16}O_3N_2S$) (hexahydro-2-oxo-1-thieno-3,4-imidazole-4-valeric acid).

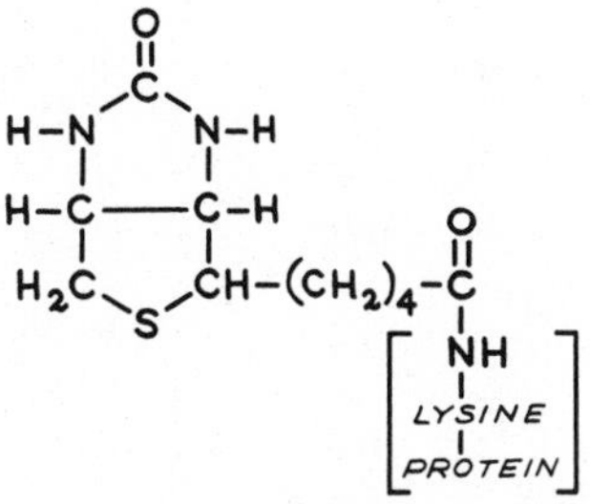

Figure 13–15. Attachment of biotin coenzyme to apoenzyme through epsilon nitrogen of lysine.

BIOTIN

Biotin was first shown to be an extremely potent growth factor for microorganisms. As little as 0.005 μg permits the growth of test bacteria. In experiments with rats, dermatitis, retarded growth, loss of hair, and loss of muscular control occurred when egg white was fed as the sole source of protein. Certain foods were then found to contain a protective factor against these injurious effects of egg white protein, and this protective factor was named biotin, or the anti-egg white injury factor. The antagonistic substance in raw egg white is a protein (**avidin**) which combines with biotin, even in vitro, to prevent its absorption from the intestine.

It is difficult to arrive at a quantitative requirement for biotin. A large proportion of the biotin requirement probably is supplied by the action of the intestinal bacteria, since a biotin deficiency can be induced more readily in animals which have been fed with those sulfonamide drugs which reduce intestinal bacteria to a minimum. Careful balance studies in man showed that in many instances urinary excretion of biotin exceeded the dietary intake, and that in all cases fecal excretion was as much as 3–6 times greater than the dietary intake. It is therefore difficult to conceive of a dietary biotin deficiency under the usual circumstances. Highly purified diets have produced the deficiency in chickens and monkeys, but it is possible that the observed symptoms were really due to the effect of the diets on the intestinal flora.

Chemistry

In the free state biotin has the structure shown in Fig 13–14.

In biologic systems, biotin functions as the coenzyme for **carboxylases**, enzymes which catalyze carbon dioxide "fixation," or carboxylation. The biotin coenzyme is tightly bound to the enzyme protein (the apoenzyme), probably by an amide linkage between the biotin carboxyl group and the terminal (epsilon) nitrogen of a lysine residue in the enzyme protein, as shown in Fig 13–15. This is suggested by the discovery in natural materials of a combined form of biotin, **biocytin**, identified as a lysine-biotin conjugate (ϵ-N-biotinyl lysine). Evidently, in the isolation of biotin from the naturally occurring biotin-enzyme complex, the vitamin may be split off from the enzyme protein together with the amino acid lysine, to which it is attached in the protein.

Physiologic Role

Human subjects placed on a refined diet containing a large amount of dehydrated egg white developed symptoms resembling those caused by biotin deficiency in animals. Urinary biotin decreased from a normal level of 30–60 μg/day to 4–7 μg/day. Prompt relief of symptoms occurred when a biotin concentrate was administered.

The best-demonstrated biochemical role of biotin is in connection with the reactions of carboxylation (CO_2 "fixation"). For this purpose, the biotin coenzyme-apoenzyme complex attaches CO_2, which can later be transferred to other substances as described below. The mechanism for formation of the CO_2-biotin enzyme complex may proceed as shown in Fig 13–16.

The CO_2 on the biotin enzyme complex may be transferred in a reaction catalyzed by **acetyl-CoA carboxylase** to acetyl-CoA to form **malonyl-CoA**, an important step in the extramitochondrial biosynthetic pathway for fatty acids.

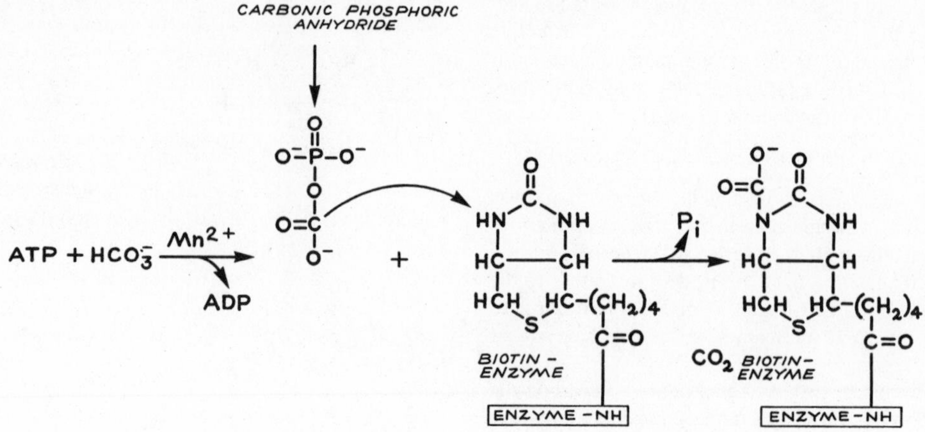

CARBONIC PHOSPHORIC
ANHYDRIDE

Figure 13—16. Formation of the CO_2-biotin enzyme complex.

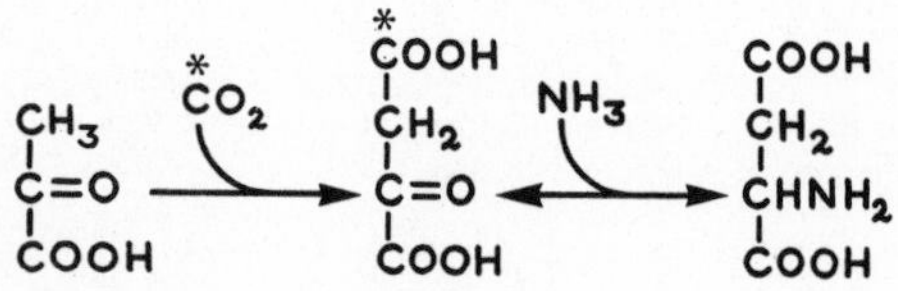

Pyruvic
acid

Oxaloacetic
acid

Aspartic
acid

Figure 13—17. Conversion of pyruvate to oxaloacetate.

Another example of a biotin-dependent reaction of carboxylation is the conversion of pyruvate to oxaloacetate (Fig 13—17). That the enzyme **pyruvate carboxylase**, catalyzing this reaction of CO_2 fixation, is biotin-dependent is confirmed by the observation that avidin, which specifically binds biotin, effectively inhibits pyruvate carboxylase. Furthermore, hydrolysates of purified preparations of pyruvate carboxylase have been shown by direct assay to contain biotin.

Fixation of CO_2 in formation of carbon 6 in purine synthesis is impaired in biotin-deficient yeast, which suggests that the vitamin plays a role in purine synthesis in connection with this step in formation of the purine structure.

A number of other enzyme systems are reportedly influenced by biotin. These include succinic acid dehydrogenase and decarboxylase, and the deaminases of the amino acids aspartic acid, serine, and threonine.

Sources & Requirements

The levels of biotin in human blood range between 14 and 55 $\mu g/dl$ in infants and 12 and 24 $\mu g/dl$ in adults, with slightly lower levels during pregnancy. Human milk contains an average of 0.16 $\mu g/dl$; the quantity seems little affected by variations in diet.

It seems doubtful whether any but the most severely deficient diet would result in a biotin deficiency in man. The daily intake is said to be between 100 and 300 μg. The vitamin is widely distributed in natural foods. Egg yolk, kidney, liver, tomatoes, and yeast are excellent sources.

THE FOLIC ACID GROUP

Folic acid (folacin, pteroylglutamic acid) is a compound made up of the pteridine nucleus, *p*-aminobenzoic acid, and glutamic acid.

There are at least 3 chemically related compounds of nutritional importance which occur in natural products. All may be termed pteroyl glutamates. These 3 compounds differ only in the number of glutamic acid residues attached to the pteridine-aminobenzoic acid complex. The formula for folic acid shown on p 170 is the monoglutamate. This is synonymous with vitamin B_C. The substance once designated as the fermentation factor is a triglutamate, and the vitamin B_C conjugate of yeast is a heptaglutamate. The deficiency syndrome which is now thought to be due to a lack of these substances has been recognized in the monkey since 1919. Since many investigators discovered the same deficiency state by varying technics, several names for these factors, in addition to those already mentioned, have appeared, including vitamin M, factors U and R, norit eluate factor, and *Streptococcus lactis* R factor.

Folic acid, when added to liver slices, is converted to a formyl derivative. Ascorbic acid enhances the activity of the liver in this reaction. This form of folic acid was first discovered in liver extracts when it was found to supply an essential growth factor for a lactobacillus, *Leuconostoc citrovorum*. It was thus termed the **citrovorum factor**. When its chemical structure was determined, the name **folinic acid** was applied.

The structure of folinic acid (leucovorin, folinic acid-SF [synthetic factor]) is shown on p 170. It is the reduced (tetrahydro) form of folic acid with a formyl group on position 5 (N^5-formyltetrahydrofolic acid).

A similar compound, but with the formyl group

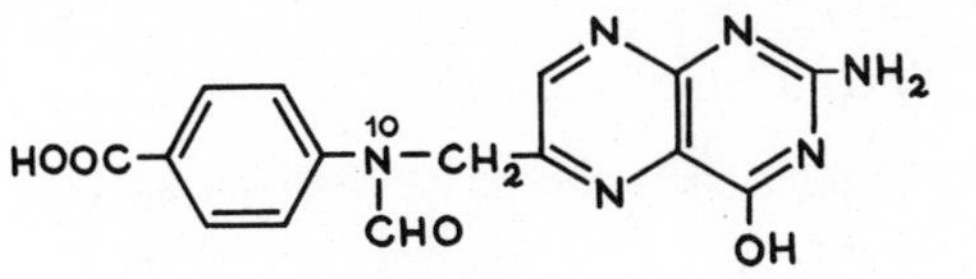

Figure 13-18. Rhizopterin (N^{10}-formylpteroic acid).

on position 10, has been recovered from liver (Fig 13-18). Rhizopterin, or the *Streptococcus lactis* R factor, is a naturally occurring compound which is a 10-formyl derivative of pteroic acid.

Physiologic Role

The folic acid coenzymes are specifically concerned with biochemical reactions involving the transfer and utilization of the single carbon (C-1) moiety (Fig 13-19). Before functioning as a C-1 carrier, folic acid must be reduced, first to 7,8-dihydrofolic acid

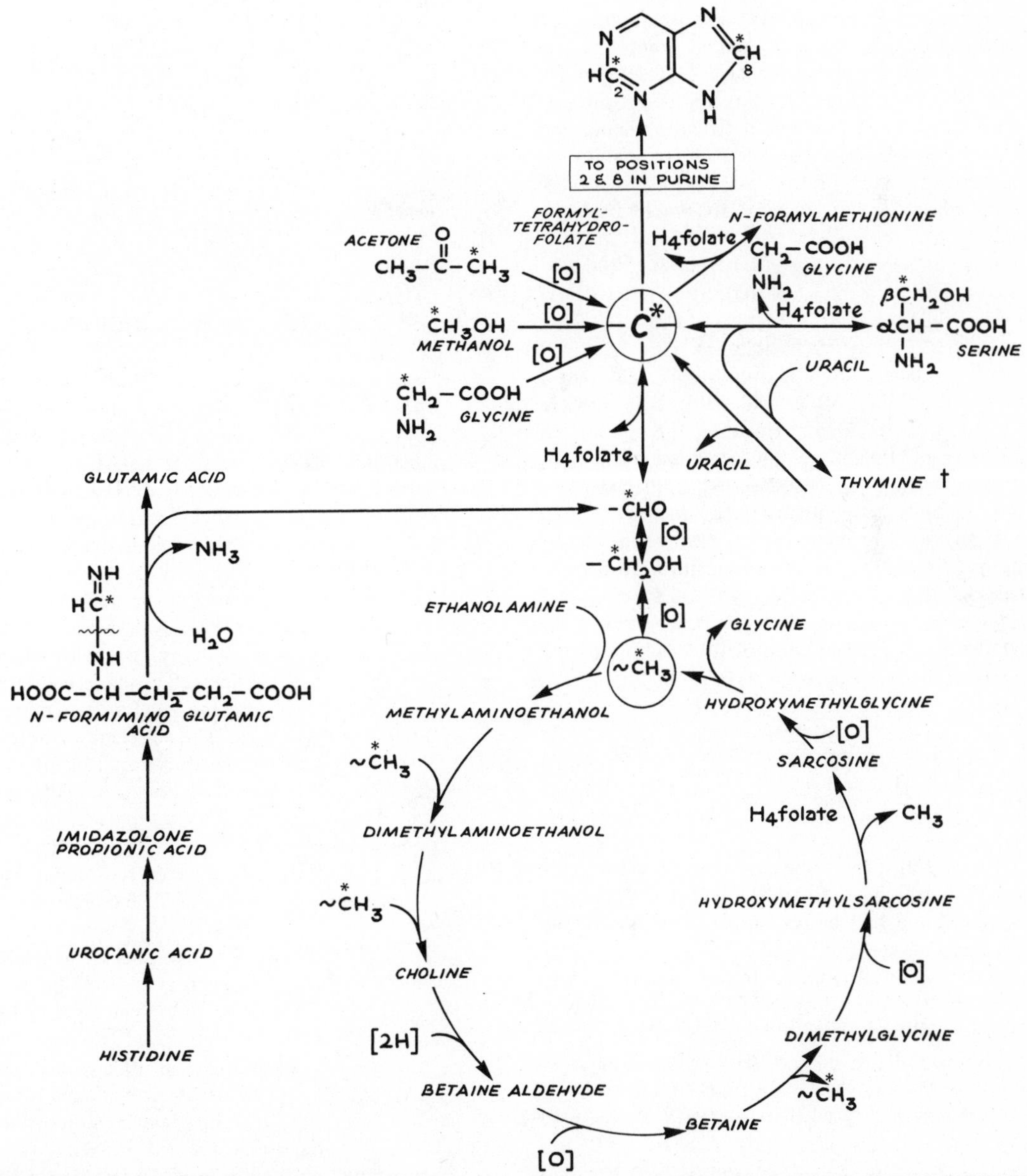

*Methyl groups from methionine (see Fig 13-29).
†C* for methylation of uracil to form thymine probably only from serine β-carbon via H_4folate.

Figure 13-19. Sources and utilization of the one-carbon moiety.

(H_2 folate) and then to the tetrahydro compound (H_4 folate), 5,6,7,8-tetrahydrofolic acid, catalyzed by **folic acid reductases** which use NADPH as hydrogen donor. The reactions are as follows:

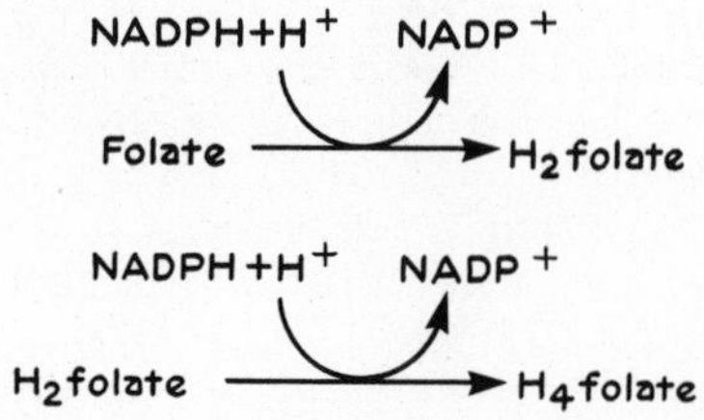

$$NADPH + H^+ \quad NADP^+$$
$$Folate \longrightarrow H_2\,folate$$

$$NADPH + H^+ \quad NADP^+$$
$$H_2\,folate \longrightarrow H_4\,folate$$

The folic acid antagonists such as methotrexate (amethopterin) are extremely potent competitive inhibitors of the reductase reaction H_2 folate → H_4-folate. In addition, there are clinically described cases of what appear to be folic acid deficiency anemias that have been proved to be due actually to inability to accomplish reduction of folic acid, presumably traceable to inherited deficiency of folic acid reductase activity.

The "one carbon" moiety carried on tetrahydrofolic acid may be formyl ($-CHO$), formate ($H \cdot COO^-$), methyl (CH_3-), or hydroxymethyl ($-CH_2OH$). These are metabolically interconvertible.

As has been noted above, folinic acid is a 5-formyl (f^5) tetrahydrofolic acid (H_4 folate); in abbreviated form, $f^5 \cdot H_4$ folate. However, except for the formylation of glutamic acid in the course of the metabolic degradation of histidine, the f^5 compound (folinic acid) is metabolically inert. Instead, the f^{10} ($f^{10} \cdot H_4$ folate), the tetrahydro derivative in which a single carbon group is bound on position 10 of tetrahydrofolic acid, is the active form of the folic acid coenzymes in metabolism. However, the f^5 can be converted to f^{5-10} by the action of the enzyme, formyltetrahydrofolic acid isomerase, as follows:

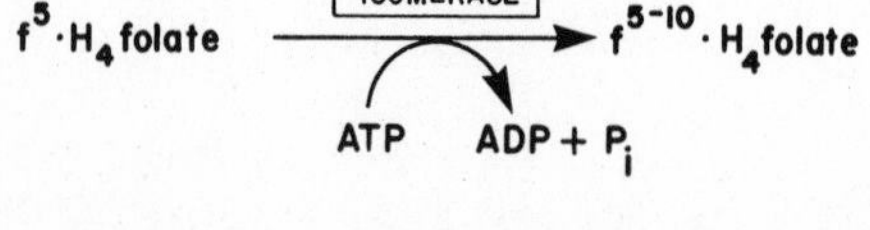

$$f^5 \cdot H_4\,folate \xrightarrow{\text{ISOMERASE}} f^{5-10} \cdot H_4\,folate$$
$$ATP \quad ADP + P_i$$

The structures of folic acid, the reduction compounds dihydro- and tetrahydrofolates (H_2 and H_4 folates), and important derivatives of the reduced compounds are shown in Fig 13—20.

N^5,N^{10}-methylenetetrahydrofolic acid ($f^{5-10} \cdot H_4$-folate) can be oxidized by $NADP^+$ to yield N^5,N^{10}-methylidyneltetrahydrofolic acid. Hydrolysis of this latter compound produces N^{10}-formyltetrahydrofolic acid ($f^{10} \cdot H_4$ folate), the form that is a major donor of the formyl (single carbon) in many synthetic pathways.

$f^{5-10} \cdot H_4$ folate can also be converted to N^5-methyltetrahydrofolic acid by an NAD-dependent reductase, and this methyl group is then transferable to deoxyadenosyl-B_{12} (cobamide coenzyme) to form methyl-B_{12}, an important donor of methyl groups as

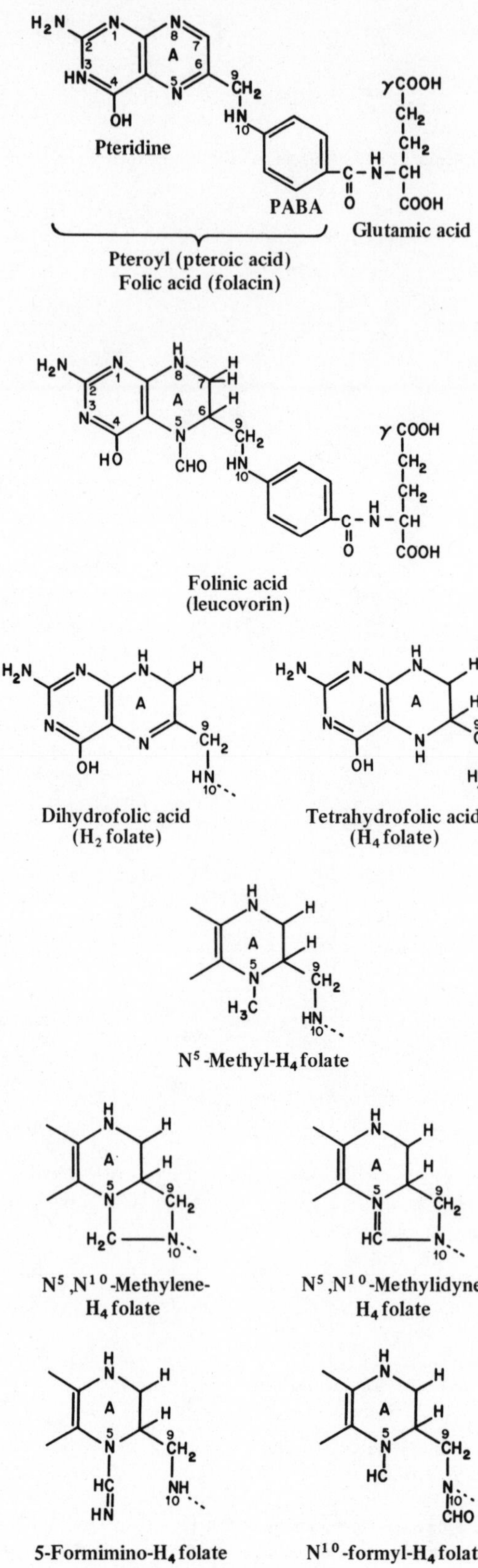

Figure 13—20. Forms of folic acid and its derivatives.

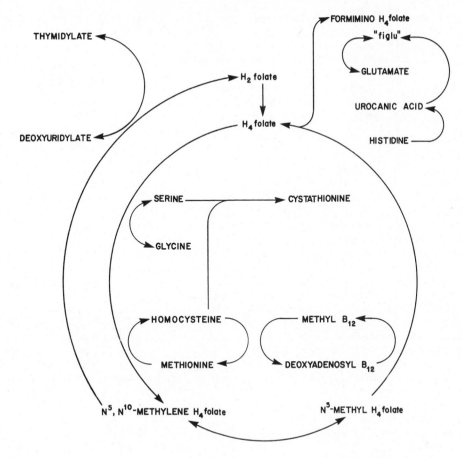

Figure 13—21. Interrelationships of folic acid derivatives and B_{12}.

illustrated by the methylation of homocysteine to form methionine.

Some of the interrelationships of the folic acid derivatives with B_{12} in a series of metabolic transformations are shown in Fig 13—21.

Sources & Utilization of the One-Carbon Moiety

The one-carbon moiety on tetrahydrofolic acid can be transferred to amino or to SH groups. An example of the first is the formimino (−HC=NH) group on glutamic acid, a product of histidine breakdown; the second is exemplified by the formation of thiazolidine carboxylic acid with cysteine.

The formimino group (fi) on glutamic acid can serve as a source of the one-carbon moiety as follows:

$$fi\text{-glutamate} + H_4\text{folate} \rightarrow fi^5 \cdot H_4\text{folate} + \text{glutamate}$$
$$fi^5 \cdot H_4\text{folate} \rightarrow f^{5-10} \cdot H_4\text{folate} + NH_3$$

Other sources of the one-carbon moiety are the methyl groups of (a) methionine, (b) choline, by way of betaine (Fig 13—29), and (c) of thymine—all of which are oxidized to hydroxy methyl (−CH$_2$OH) groups and carried as such on $f^{5-10} \cdot H_4$folate. The hydroxymethyl group (h) is then oxidized in an NADP-dependent reaction to a formyl (f) group:

$$\underset{h^{5-10} \cdot H_4\text{folate}}{} \xrightarrow{\quad NADP^+ \qquad NADPH+H^+ \quad} \underset{f^{5-10} \cdot H_4\text{folate}}{}$$

The beta carbon of serine as a hydroxy methyl group may also contribute to the formation of a single carbon moiety.

The single (formyl) carbon which is present on the tetrahydrofolic acids is utilized in several important reactions (Fig 13—19). The first is as a source of carbons 2 and 8 in the purine nucleus as described in Chapter 24. A second is the role of f^{10}-tetrahydrofolate ($f^{10} \cdot H_4$folate) as a source of the formyl group on N-formylmethionine-tRNA, which in microorganisms initiates synthesis of peptide chains on ribosomes (see Chapter 27). A third reaction involving the formyl carbon on $f^{10} \cdot H_4$folate is formation of the beta carbon of serine in conversion of glycine to serine. A fourth reaction is in the synthesis of methyl groups for (a) methylation of homocysteine to form methionine or (b) methylation of uracil to form thymine,* and (c) for the synthesis of choline by way of methyl groups from methionine.

*Probably from β-carbon of serine only.

The participation of the folic acid coenzymes in reactions leading to synthesis of purines and to thymine, the methylated pyrimidine of DNA, emphasizes the fundamental role of folic acid in growth and reproduction of cells. Because the blood cells are subject to a relatively rapid rate of synthesis and destruction, it is not surprising that interference with red blood cell formation would be an early sign of a deficiency of folic acid, or that the folic acid antagonists would readily inhibit the formation of leukocytes. But it must be remembered that the requirement for the folic acid coenzymes is undoubtedly generalized throughout the body and not confined to the hematopoietic system. This is supported by the observation that in folic acid-deficient monkeys there was a considerable decrease in the rate of synthesis of nucleoprotein, which rose to normal after administration of the vitamin. The function of the folic acid coenzymes in synthesis and utilization of methyl groups relates these vitamins also to phospholipid metabolism (choline synthesis; see Fig 13−29) and to amino acid metabolism.

A deficiency of folic acid has been produced experimentally in man by feeding a diet containing 5 μg of folate/day for a period of 4½ months (Herbert, 1962). During this period, hemoglobin fell from 15.5 g to 13.9 g/dl of blood. At the termination of the experiment, examination of bone marrow aspirates clearly revealed abnormalities in megaloblast cells.

When folic acid was first made available in crystalline form, it excited considerable interest because of its therapeutic effect in nutritional macrocytic anemia, pernicious anemia, and the related macrocytic anemias. At that time, vitamin B_{12} was not known. It was soon discovered that in those anemias which were due to other than simple folic acid deficiencies, or to deficiencies of other factors (as is the case in uncomplicated pernicious anemia), the hematologic response to folic acid was not permanent and the neurologic symptoms in pernicious anemia (combined system disease) remained unchanged. It is now apparent that while folic acid derivatives do have an effect on hematopoiesis, other factors are also necessary for the complete development of the blood cells. In pernicious anemia the most important factor is vitamin B_{12}; uncomplicated cases respond to this vitamin alone. Furthermore, vitamin B_{12} controls both the hematologic and the neurologic defect. It has therefore been concluded that folic acid has no place in the treatment of uncomplicated pernicious anemia. Although folic acid is harmless when administered to patients adequately treated with vitamin B_{12}, some have recommended that folic acid should not be included in multivitamin preparations because of the danger that it may mask pernicious anemia in susceptible patients and thus permit the disease to progress to the much more serious stage involving neurologic damage.

However, there are well-documented reports of megaloblastic anemias which were due apparently to simple nutritional deficiencies of folic acid. These reports, together with the results of the experimental production of folic acid deficiency mentioned above,

would seem to be ample proof that a megaloblastic anemia due entirely to dietary folic acid deficiency can occur.

In the metabolism of the amino acid histidine, there is a folic acid-dependent step at the point where formiminoglutamic acid is converted to glutamic acid. When folic acid-deficient patients are given a loading dose of histidine, the increased excretion of **formiminoglutamic acid ("figlu")** into the urine which occurs can be used as a chemical test of a lack of folic acid. Evidently the folic acid deficiency results in a metabolic block which is reflected in an accumulation and consequent excretion of formiminoglutamic acid. The use of this **"figlu" excretion test,** as well as direct assays (by microbiologic methods) of the serum content of folic acid and of vitamin B_{12}, should improve the accuracy of diagnosis of the causes of megaloblastic anemias.

In sprue, the administration of synthetic folic acid (5−15 mg/day) has been followed by rapid and impressive remissions, both clinically and hematologically. The glossitis and diarrhea subside in a few days, and a reticulocytosis occurs which is followed by regeneration of the erythrocytes and hemoglobin. Roentgenologic evidence of improved gastrointestinal function, improved fat absorption, and a return of the glucose tolerance curve to normal are also observed. The vitamin seems therefore to correct both the hematopoietic and gastrointestinal abnormalities in sprue.

Sources & Daily Allowances

According to some clinical nutritionists, folic acid deficiency is possibly the most common vitamin deficiency in North America and western Europe. This is especially true in pregnancy, wherein folic acid deficiency is said to be the most frequent cause of megaloblastic anemia. A suggested reason for this is that folic acid may not be contained in some vitamin preparations prescribed for pregnant women because, as noted above, folic acid can correct the anemia of vitamin B_{12} deficiency and thus mask the lack of B_{12}, thereby permitting neurologic damage to progress. It should be emphasized that combined deficiencies of folic acid, vitamin B_{12}, ascorbic acid, and iron—as well as other nutrients—are more common than isolated deficiencies of any one of these nutritional components. Folic acid deficiency should be considered in connection with alcoholism, hemolytic anemias, tropical and nontropical sprue, and the anemias occurring in infancy, pregnancy, or malignancies.

Folates are present in a wide variety of plant and animal tissues, mainly as polyglutamates in reduced methyl or formyl forms. The monoglutamate pteroylmonoglutamic acid, chemically designated folic acid (folacin), is actually a minor component of the folates contained in the diet.

The richest sources of the vitamin are yeast, liver, kidney, and green vegetables, with moderate amounts contained in dairy foods, meat, and fish. There is very little in fruits. The lability of the vitamin to cooking processes is said to be similar to that of thiamin, but some forms of the folates are unstable on exposure to air and are sensitive to ultraviolet light, and they steadily decline on storage. Cooking (particularly boiling) or heat preservation in canning destroys 50–90% of the folates present in the food.

The availability of folates for absorption is variable because of uncertainty as to bacterial enzymatic activity within the intestinal tract. The average daily diet contains 160 μg of folate before treatment with conjugase enzymes and 670 μg after treatment, indicating the greater availability of the vitamin as determined by the assay method after liberation from the conjugated forms. The dietary folate content will also vary greatly among various individuals in accordance with economic status and social habits.

Absorption probably occurs along the whole length of the mucosa of the small intestine. Within the intestinal mucosa, monoglutamates are produced from polyglutamates that may have been ingested, and dihydrofolates are further reduced to tetrahydro forms by the action of folic acid reductases. The tetrahydrofolates are then converted to methyltetrahydrofolate and in this form enter the portal blood to be transported to the liver. Subsequently, the vitamin appears in the systemic circulation to supply the tissues.

Transport in the plasma is as methyltetrahydrofolate bound to protein. In normal individuals, the plasma level of the vitamin varies from 3–21 ng/ml. When the dietary intake of folate is low, plasma levels fall within a few days. Although the folate level of plasma obtained from umbilical cord blood is about 3 times that of the maternal plasma, there is a rapid decline in the plasma during early neonatal life.

Excretion of folate in the feces represents the 20% of ingested folate that remains unabsorbed, as well as 60–90 μg in the bile that is not reabsorbed, and some synthesis of the vitamin by the flora of the colon. There is a small excretion in the urine (2–5 μg/day); this is much increased after an oral dose of folate if the tissues are saturated.

Tissue folate is about 70 mg in the whole body, of which about one third (5–15 μg/g) is in the liver. As might be expected, folate is incorporated into the erythrocytes during erythropoiesis and is retained there during their entire life span except for only a slight fall in concentration. In fact, red cell folate is a reliable indicator of the status of folate nutriture in the whole body. The average level is 300 ng/ml of whole blood based on a packed cell volume of 45%; the range is 160–640 ng/ml.

On a diet deficient in folate, the content of the vitamin in the liver is reported to fall to around 1.5 μg/g after about 130 days. The amounts of folate required per day to prevent this are a minimum of 200 μg or 300 μg in pregnancy. The recommended allowances as listed in Table 31–6 are considerably higher.

In a truly folic acid-deficient patient, the administration of 300–500 μg/day of folic acid will produce a hematologic response. However, this small dose will not effect a response in a patient with pernicious anemia. The use of this conservative but adequate dose

of folic acid will thus serve as a method of differentiating between vitamin B_{12} and folic acid deficiency.

Folic Acid Antagonists

The concept of competitive inhibition or metabolic antagonism is discussed in Chapter 6. Antagonists to folic acid have found clinical application in the treatment of malignant disease, and confirmation of the action of folic acid in cell growth has been obtained in studies of the effect of these antagonists on cells maintained in tissue culture.

Maximal inhibitory action is obtained when an amino group is substituted for the hydroxy group on position 4 of the pteridine nucleus. Thus **aminopterin** (4-amino folic acid) is the most potent folic acid inhibitor yet discovered. Another antagonist is **amethopterin**, (4-amino-10-methylfolic acid; **methotrexate**). In animals the inhibitory effect of aminopterin cannot be reversed by folic acid but only by folinic acid (leucovorin; 5-formyltetrahydrofolic acid). The interference of the antimetabolites occurs in the reduction of folic acid to the tetrahydro compound. It will be recalled that reduction is a necessary preliminary to the carriage of the one-carbon moiety.

In tissue cultures it has been found that aminopterin blocks the synthesis of nucleic acids, presumably by preventing the reduction of folic acid to the tetrahydro derivative and thus transport of the formyl carbon into the purine ring. Such inhibited cells fail to complete their mitoses; they do not progress from metaphase to anaphase because of a failure in the synthesis of nucleoprotein, a synthesis which is essential to chromosome reduplication.

Aminopterin has been used in the treatment of leukemia, particularly in children. A remission is induced temporarily in some patients, but after a time the leukemic cells apparently acquire the power to overcome the effects of the antagonist.

INOSITOL

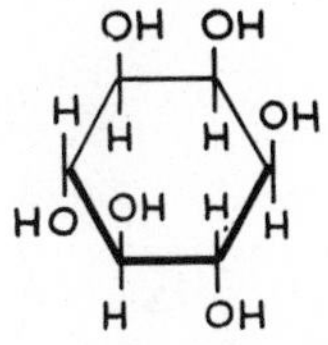

Figure 13—22. Meso-inositol ($C_6H_{12}O_6$, hexahydroxycyclohexane).

There are 9 isomers of inositol. Meso-inositol, also called myo-inositol (Fig 13–22), is the most important one in nature and the only isomer which is biologically effective.

The significance of this compound in human nutrition has not been established. However, in studies on the nutrient requirements of cells in tissue culture, it was found that 18 different human cell strains maintained on a semisynthetic medium failed to grow without the addition of meso-inositol. None of the other isomers were effective, a finding which is in agreement with the results of similar experiments in animals.

Together with choline, inositol has a lipotropic action in experimental animals. This lipotropic activity may be associated with the formation of inositol-containing lipids.

Deficiency symptoms in mice include so-called spectacled eye, alopecia, and failure of lactation and growth. In inositol-deficient chicks, an encephalomalacia and an exudative diathesis have been reported.

Sources

Inositol is found in fruits, meat, milk, nuts, vegetables, whole grains, and yeast.

PARA-AMINOBENZOIC ACID

Para-aminobenzoate is a growth factor for certain microorganisms and an antagonist to the bacteriostatic action of sulfonamide drugs. It forms a portion of the folic acid molecule, and it is suggested that its actual role is to provide this component for the synthesis of

folic acid by those organisms which do not require a preformed source of folic acid. However, it is not regarded as a vitamin for animals.

VITAMIN B_{12}

Vitamin B_{12}, the anti-pernicious anemia factor (extrinsic factor of Castle) was first isolated in 1948 from liver as a red crystalline compound containing cobalt and phosphorus. The vitamin can be obtained as a product of fermentation by *Streptomyces griseus*. Its concentration, either in liver or in the fermentation liquor, is only about one part per million.

Chemistry

The structure of vitamin B_{12} is shown in Fig 13–23. The central portion of the molecule (Fig 13–24) consists of 4 reduced and extensively substituted pyrrole rings surrounding a single cobalt atom. This central structure is referred to as a "corrin" ring system. It is very similar to that of the porphyrins but differs from the porphyrins in that 2 of the pyrrole rings (rings I and IV) are joined directly rather than through a single methylidyne carbon. It is of interest, however, that studies with an actinomyces organism that synthesizes vitamin B_{12} have revealed that the

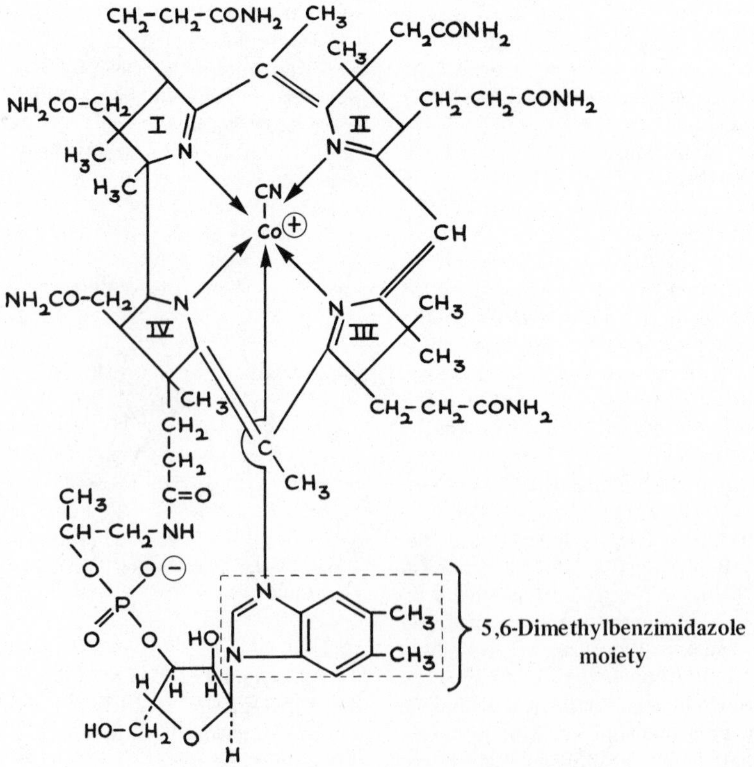

Figure 13–23. Cyanocobalamin; vitamin B_{12} ($C_{63}H_{88}O_{14}N_{14}PCo$).

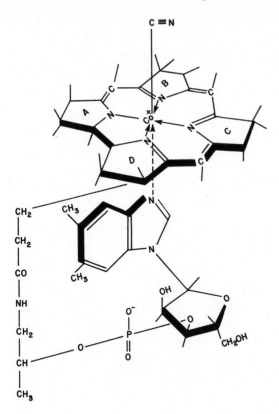

$C \equiv N$

CH_2
CH_2
CO
NH
CH_2
CH
CH_3

CH_3

CH_3

OH

O^-

O — P = O

CH_2OH

Figure 13—24. Molecular structure of cyanocobalamin (vitamin B_{12}).

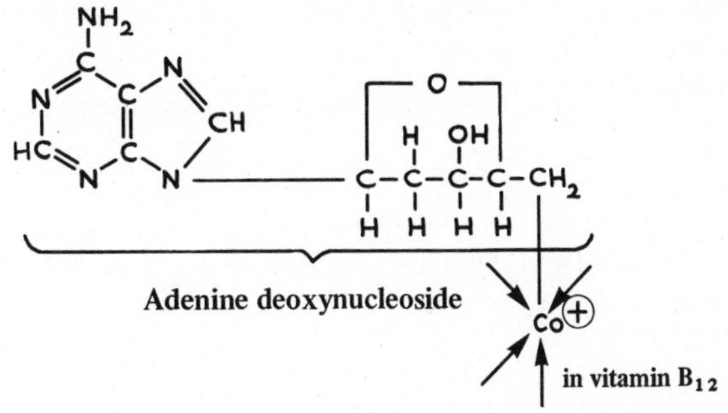

NH_2

Adenine deoxynucleoside

$C-C-C-C-CH_2$

Co ⊕

in vitamin B_{12}

Figure 13—25. Attachment of adenosyl moiety to vitamin B_{12} through C'-5 to cobalt in the B_{12} coenzymes.

Crystalline vitamin B_{12} is stable to heating at 100° C for long periods, and aqueous solutions at pH 4.0—7.0 can be autoclaved with very little loss. However, destruction is rapid when the vitamin is heated at pH 9.0 or above.

Although it had been suspected that vitamin B_{12} functions as a coenzyme in metabolism, such a function was not actually proved until Barker and others isolated 3 B_{12}-containing coenzymes from microbial sources. These coenzymes, the **cobamides**, do not contain the cyano group attached to cobalt as does cyanocobalamin. Instead there is an adenine nucleoside (5′-deoxyadenosine) which is linked to the cobalt by a carbon-to-cobalt bond, as shown in Fig 13—25.

The 5′-adenosyl moiety in coenzyme B_{12} is derived from adenosine triphosphate, which, after donating the adenosyl group, releases all 3 phosphate groups as inorganic tripolyphosphate. In the formation of the adenosyl coenzyme, cobalt undergoes successive reduction in a series of steps catalyzed by B_{12a} reductase and requiring NADH and FAD. Thus, in B_{12a}, which is red-colored, cobalt is present as Co^{3+}. This progresses to B_{12r} (orange) with cobalt as Co^{2+}, and to B_{12r} (gray-green) Co^+, the latter form reacting with ATP to form the adenosyl coenzyme as described above.

All 3 of the coenzymes possess the adenine deoxynucleoside described above, but they differ from one another in the benzimidazole portion of the B_{12} molecule. Here there may be found the 5,6-dimethyl-benzimidazole group, as occurs in vitamin B_{12}; an unsubstituted (methyl-free) benzimidazole; or an adenyl group. These 3 cobamide coenzymes are therefore designated 5,6-dimethylbenzimidazole cobamide, benzimidazole cobamide, or adenyl cobamide. The B_{12} coenzyme found in the largest quantities in natural materials is 5,6-dimethylbenzimidazole cobamide 5′-adenosine. Alternatively, it could also be called 5′-adenosyl cobalamin.

As already noted, there has also been detected another B_{12} coenzyme, a cobamide in which a methyl group is attached to the cobalt atom rather than the adenosyl moiety. All cobalamins are crystalline hygroscopic powders which are readily soluble in water and are heat stable. Molecular weights are around 1400.

The activity of the cobamide coenzymes has been

basic corrin structure is synthesized from the known precursors of porphyrins such as δ-aminolevulinic acid. The 6 "extra" methyl groups on B_{12} are derived from methionine (Bray & Shemin, 1963).

Below the corrin ring system there is a 5,6-dimethylbenzimidazole riboside that is connected at one end to the central cobalt atom and at the other end from the ribose moiety through phosphate and aminopropanol to a side chain on ring IV of the tetrapyrrole nucleus. A cyanide group which is coordinately bound to the cobalt atom may be removed; the resulting compound is called "cobalamin." Addition of cyanide forms "cyanocobalamin," identical with the originally isolated vitamin B_{12}. Substitution of the cyanide group with a hydroxy group forms "**hydroxocobalamin**"; with a nitro group, "**nitrocobalamin**"; and with a methyl group, "**methylcobalamin**." The biologic action of these derivatives appears to be similar to that of cobalamin, although hydroxocobalamin (B_{12a}) is more active in enzyme systems requiring B_{12} and therefore is used more often than B_{12} in experimental studies in vitro. Furthermore, although hydroxocobalamin given orally in large doses is absorbed as well as cyanocobalamin in similar doses, hydroxocobalamin is retained longer in the body; this suggests that hydroxocobalamin may be more useful for therapeutic administration of vitamin B_{12} by mouth.

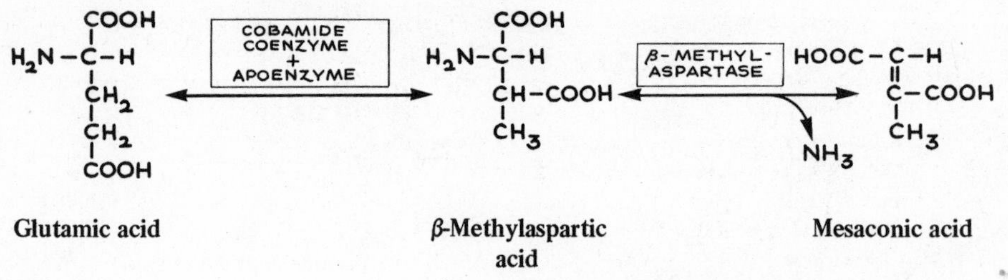

Figure 13-26. Conversion of glutamic acid to β-methylaspartic acid.

determined by means of their function in catalyzing the reaction shown in Fig 13-26, whereby glutamic acid is converted to β-methylaspartic acid (and thence to mesaconic acid in a reaction catalyzed by the enzyme β-methylaspartase, which is not cobamide-dependent). The apoenzyme system required in addition to the cobamide coenzyme is obtained from strain H1 cultures of *Clostridium tetanomorphum.*

In prokaryotic organisms (eg, bacteria), cobamide coenzyme plays an essential role in the cobamide-dependent ribonucleotide reductase reaction whereby the ribose moiety in a ribonucleotide is converted to deoxyribose when DNA is to be formed.

The B_{12} coenzymes have been isolated not only from several bacterial cultures but also from the liver of various animals (mainly dimethylbenzimidazole cobamide). The best source is a culture of *Propionibacterium shermanii* (ATCC 9614). The coenzymes are inactivated and converted to the vitamin form by visible light or by cyanide ion, the adenine nucleoside being removed or replaced by the cyano group. The methods originally used to extract the vitamin included heating in weak acid, addition of cyanide ion, and exposure to light. As a result it is likely that the coenzymes were converted to the vitamin and thus overlooked.

Absorption of Vitamin B_{12}

Vitamin B_{12} is absorbed from the ileum, but its absorption is dependent upon the presence of hydrochloric acid and a constituent of normal gastric juice designated **intrinsic factor (IF)** by Castle. Free vitamin B_{12} (cobalamin) is rapidly bound to intrinsic factor, a mucopolysaccharide secreted by the parietal cells of the gastric mucosa, in the proportion of 2 mol cobalamin to 1 mol IF dimer. Intrinsic factor is found in the cardia and fundus of the stomach but not in the pylorus. Atrophy of the fundus and a lack of free hydrochloric acid (achlorhydria) are usually associated with pernicious anemia. Patients who have sustained total removal of the stomach will also develop cobalamin deficiency and anemia because complete absence of intrinsic factor prevents absorption of the vitamin, although as long as 3 years may elapse after the operation before anemia will be apparent. This is because the vitamin B_{12} stores are depleted very slowly. In the liver, the biologic half-life for the vitamin is estimated to be about 400 days.

The combination of B_{12} with intrinsic factor results in the formation of a complex that is resistant to intestinal digestion. Vitamin B_{12} binds also to the proteins of gastric juice, bile, and saliva. This binding can be differentiated by immunologic means because an antibody to intrinsic factor has the same binding site on the molecule as vitamin B_{12}. Intrinsic factor concentration can be measured as the difference between the amount of radioactive (^{58}Co-labeled) B_{12} bound by gastric juice to which normal serum has been added and that bound by gastric juice to which serum containing intrinsic factor antibody has been added. One unit of intrinsic factor is that which binds 1 μg of ^{58}Co-B_{12}/ml of gastric juice. The assays are carried out one hour after stimulation of intrinsic factor secretion by an injection of pentagastrin. The range is 400-25,000 units/hour in subjects without evidence of gastric abnormality.

It is currently believed that intrinsic factor possesses 2 receptor sites, one for vitamin B_{12} and the other for ileal intestinal microvilli, which specifically requires a neutral pH and the presence of calcium ions. The latter receptor site is readily saturated, which results in limiting the absorption of vitamin B_{12} to 1.5 μg after any single dose. Intrinsic factor has not been detected in plasma, so it is assumed that it is released within the intestine, liberating B_{12} to pass into the intestinal mucosal cell. It has also been suggested that intrinsic factor protects vitamin B_{12}-peptide against bacterial attack and that it is in the peptide form that the vitamin is absorbed.

There is some passive absorption of B_{12}, thought to be about 1% of large concentrations of the vitamin. Indeed, it is known that if very large doses of vitamin B_{12} (3000 μg) are given orally to a patient with pernicious anemia, there occurs an increase in the plasma concentration of the vitamin. An intramuscular injection of 10-25 μg produces a similar rise in the serum concentration of the vitamin. Thus it can be seen that the vitamin can be effective without intrinsic factor. Apparently the only function of intrinsic factor is to provide for the absorption of the vitamin from the intestine, and then only when it is present in very small amounts (eg, in foods). Thus, vitamin B_{12} is both the **extrinsic factor** and the **anti-pernicious anemia factor** as originally described by Castle.

The normal partial intestinal mucosal block to absorption of B_{12} is complete or almost complete in sprue and in pernicious anemia when tested by the oral administration of radioactive cobalt-labeled B_{12} followed by measurements of hepatic uptake. The defect in sprue is not corrected by the administration of intrinsic factor because it is due to a generalized defect inherent in the absorptive mechanisms in the intestinal wall. In pernicious anemia caused by a lack of intrinsic factor, the administration of a test dose of labeled B_{12} together with 75–100 ml of normal human gastric juice, or with a potent source of intrinsic factor, results in a satisfactory hepatic uptake.

Another variety of pernicious anemia with vitamin B_{12} deficiency is that which occurs very early in the postnatal period—usually before age 2½. This appears to be due specifically to a lack of intrinsic factor, but it is not accompanied by absence of gastric acid secretion or by abnormalities in the histologic structure of the gastric mucosa. This syndrome does not appear to be related to adult pernicious anemia. It has been termed "congenital pernicious anemia." Later in childhood there may develop in other children a form of pernicious anemia which is characterized by a failure to secrete intrinsic factor and an associated achlorhydria and atrophic gastritis. Antibodies to intrinsic factor or to parietal cells have been detected in the serum of such patients. This latter form of pernicious anemia has been designated "juvenile pernicious anemia."

Transport of Vitamin B_{12}

Vitamin B_{12} is present in plasma as methylcobalamin, 5'-deoxyadenosylcobalamin, or hydroxocobalamin bound to proteins, of which there are at least 2: **transcorrin I** and **transcorrin II**. Transcorrin I is a strong binder of cobalamin; it migrates electrophoretically with proteins. Transcorrin II is a weak binder with β mobility. Probably the 1–10% of vitamin B_{12} carried on this latter protein is attached immediately after absorption and is readily released to be excreted in the urine. Hydroxocobalamin is more readily bound to the plasma-binding proteins that is cyanocobalamin. This may be the reason why hydroxocobalamin is retained longer in the body.

The plasma level of vitamin B_{12} in normal subjects ranges from 140–750 pg/ml. Daily variations may be as much as 80 pg/ml. Although there is no difference in the plasma levels between males and females, it tends to decline after the seventh decade of age. In any event, the plasma level represents only 0.1% of the total body content of the vitamin.

Cobalamin bound to plasma protein fractions is carried to the tissues where it is bound to a variety of protein receptors. Any excess is stored in the liver, probably as 5'-deoxyadenosylcobalamin. It is estimated that the total amount of cobalamin in the bodies of adults is 2.5 mg, of which about 1.5 mg is in the liver.

Excretion of Vitamin B_{12}

The main route of excretion of vitamin B_{12} is by way of the bile; by this pathway about 40 µg pass into the jejunum each day. By an enterohepatic circulation similar to that for the bile salts (see Chapter 14), most of this is reabsorbed in the ileum utilizing the intrinsic factor mechanism. Small amounts of the vitamin also enter the intestine from the gastric, pancreatic, and intestinal secretions. That which remains unabsorbed leaves the body in the feces; this amount, together with that produced in the colon by bacterial synthesis, is about 3–6 µg/day.

The urinary excretion of vitamin B_{12} is confined to that unbound to protein since the protein-bound fraction cannot be filtered by the renal glomerulus. This amounts to 0–0.25 µg/day. Because of its greater binding to protein, hydroxocobalamin is excreted in smaller amounts than cyanocobalamin after injection of the same amounts of each.

Functions in Metabolism

The vitamin B_{12} (cobamide) coenzyme has been shown to catalyze the enzymatic conversion in bacterial systems of glutamate to β-methylaspartate, as shown in Fig 13–26, and in animal tissue (eg, rat or ox liver) to catalyze the isomerase reaction whereby methylmalonyl-CoA is converted to succinyl-CoA (see below).

Methylmalonic acid can scarcely be detected in the urine of healthy humans (less than 2 mg/day), but it is excreted in significant amounts by patients with vitamin B_{12} deficiency such as occurs in untreated patients with pernicious anemia. Excretion of methylmalonic acid appears to be a sensitive index of the adequacy of body stores of vitamin B_{12}. The increased levels of methylmalonic acid in the urine begin to decrease as soon as treatment is started, but normal levels do not occur until hematologic abnormalities have been corrected and the content of vitamin B_{12} in the serum has reached normal. The abnormality in methylmalonic acid metabolism may be ascribed to a lack of adequate amounts of the vitamin B_{12} cobamide coenzyme, which, as indicated in the reaction shown below, is an essential cofactor with the enzyme methylmalonyl isomerase in catalyzing conversion of methylmalonyl-CoA to succinyl-CoA.

Methylmalonyl-CoA   Succinyl-CoA

The isomerization of methylmalonate to succinate catalyzed by 5'-deoxyadenosylcobalamin (the cobamide coenzyme) may be the essential reaction for the production of lipoprotein in myelin sheaths. If so, it would provide a biochemical explanation for the effects of B_{12} deficiency on the peripheral nervous system (the so-called combined system disease).

Methylmalonic aciduria has also been observed in infants and young children with severe metabolic acidosis who were not, however, deficient in vitamin B_{12}. The metabolic abnormality is ascribed to an inherited inability to convert methylmalonyl-CoA to succinyl-CoA because of a mutation which results in formation of an abnormal methylmalonyl isomerase enzyme protein. Rosenberg, Lilljequist, & Hsia (1968) have described the syndrome of methylmalonic aciduria in a 1-year-old male infant who during episodes of ketoacidosis excreted 800–1200 mg of methylmalonic acid per day as well as increased amounts of long-chain ketones. When the patient was given 1 mg of B_{12} IM each day, excretion of methylmalonic acid decreased to 220–280 mg/day. The authors suggest that this situation illustrates the existence in man of a vitamin B_{12} dependency state as distinguished from a B_{12} deficiency. The dependency is explained by the assumption that the mutant isomerase apoenzyme, in distinction to the normal apoenzyme, has a very low affinity for its coenzyme (cobamide). Thus it is only after relatively high concentrations of coenzyme (eg, following daily administration of 1 mg of B_{12}) that effective binding of coenzyme to apoenzyme occurs, with resultant partial restoration of catalytic activity.

The most characteristic sign of a deficiency of vitamin B_{12} in man is the development of a macrocytic anemia or characteristic lesions of the nervous system (or both—so-called "combined system disease"). Neurologic symptoms may supervene in B_{12} deficiency states without the prior development of anemia. In general it may be concluded that when the intake of B_{12} is low, the demand for this vitamin in hemopoiesis exceeds that for any other clinically recognizable physiologic function. Macrocytosis is therefore a sensitive indicator of a vitamin B_{12} deficiency.

As a component of the various coenzymes described above, vitamin B_{12} has its greatest effect on nucleic acid formation. This is by virtue of its action in cycling 5-methyltetrahydrofolate back into the folate pool (Silber & Moldow, 1970). It can be exemplified by the reaction whereby homocysteine is converted to methionine. For this purpose the single carbon unit on N^5-methyltetrahydrofolic acid is transferred to vitamin B_{12} coenzyme (deoxyadenosylcobalamin) to form methylcobalamin, which subsequently transfers the methyl group to homocysteine, thus forming methionine. The demethylated tetrahydrofolic acid can then return to the folate pool for use in the many other reactions of carriage of the one-carbon moiety involved in purine synthesis and the methylation of uracil, for example (Fig 13–21).

It is therefore not surprising that a deficiency of B_{12} would result in significant impairment of function of the hematopoietic system as demonstrated by megaloblastic erythropoiesis. However, in deficiency states, a fundamental role for this vitamin is also evident by the occurrence of other tissue and metabolic lesions. Thus, in B_{12} deficiency there are epithelial cell alterations in the gastrointestinal tract and impairment of the nervous system, including, perhaps, neuronal cell dysfunction.

Sources & Daily Allowances

The only source of cobalamins in nature is via synthesis by microorganisms in soil, water, and the animal intestine. In contrast to the other vitamins, plants contain no vitamin B_{12}; animal products are the primary dietary sources of the vitamin. Strict vegetarians may obtain enough cobalamin in the form of 5'-deoxyadenosylcobalamin, which is synthesized by microorganisms in legume nodules of root vegetables and is present in tap water. Bacterial synthesis of cobalamin occurs in the human colon but it is not absorbed. About 3–6 μg are excreted in the feces.

The average diet in the USA probably supplies 5–15 μg/day, but the range can be from as low as 1 μg to as high as 100 μg/day. Although the vitamin occurs in foods in a protein-bound form via peptide linkages, most of it is readily available for absorption during digestion. At intakes of less than 0.5 μg, at least 70% of the vitamin available is absorbed, a percentage value which decreases as the intestinal content of the vitamin increases. Pure dietary deficiencies of vitamin B_{12} are rare, being seen occasionally only in strict vegetarians.

As noted above, foods of animal origin are the only important dietary sources of B_{12}. The ingestion of 1 cup of milk, 4 ounces of meat, and 1 egg per day provides 2–4 μg of vitamin B_{12}. The use of beef liver or kidney would increase the intake to 15–20 μg/day.

The amounts of B_{12} in foods are very low. Of the dietary sources of the vitamin, the richest are liver and kidney, which may contain as much as 40–50 μg/100 g. Muscle meats, milk, cheese, and eggs contain 1–5 μg/100 g. The vitamin is almost if not entirely absent from the products of higher plants. Symptoms including sore tongue, paresthesia, amenorrhea, and nonspecific "nervous symptoms" have been reported from Great Britain and the Netherlands in groups living exclusively on vegetable foods. These are the only instances in which a dietary deficiency of the vitamin has been discovered. As already noted, a true dietary deficiency of vitamin B_{12} must be very rare. In most cases of B_{12} deficiency, an intestinal absorptive defect is responsible.

It is of great interest that probably the only original source of vitamin B_{12} is microbial synthesis. There is no evidence for its synthesis by the tissues of higher plants or animals. The activity of microorganisms in synthesizing B_{12} extends to the bacteria of the intestine. This is best illustrated by the microbial flora of the rumen in ruminant animals. A vitamin B_{12} concentration of 50 μg/100 g of dried rumen contents has been reported. Presumably this accounts for the superior B_{12} content of livers from ruminant animals as compared to other animals such as the pig or rat. It is probable that the synthetic activity of the intestinal bacteria also provides B_{12} for herbivorous animals other than ruminants.

The recommended daily requirements for vitamin B_{12} are listed in Table 31–6. It appears that 0.5–1 μg/day given parenterally will maintain patients with pernicious anemia in complete hematologic and neurologic remission. On the basis of this finding, and assuming that at least 50% of quantities up to 3 μg of the dietary vitamin B_{12} is absorbed, the recommended allowance for this vitamin is now set at 3 μg/day for adolescents and normal adults.

The vitamin B_{12} content of human milk closely parallels the serum level of the vitamin, so that the average daily output during lactation is about 0.3 μg. Because there is no apparent evidence of a B_{12} deficiency occurring in infants breast-fed by women with adequate levels of the vitamin in their serum, the allowance for infants artifically fed has been set at a level of 0.3 μg/day.

CHOLINE

Choline is an important metabolite, although probably it cannot be classified as a vitamin since it is synthesized by the body. Furthermore, the quantities of choline which are required by the organism are considerably larger than most substances considered as vitamins. However, in many animal species, a deficiency of choline, or of choline precursors, leads to certain well defined symptoms which are suggestive of vitamin deficiency diseases. Disturbances in fat metabolism are most prominently evidenced by the development of fatty livers. In the young growing rat there is also hemorrhagic degeneration of the kidneys and hemorrhage into the eyeballs and other organs. Older rats and the young animals which survive the acute stage develop cirrhosis. In chicks and young turkeys, choline deficiency causes perosis, or slipped tendon disease, a condition in which there is a defect at the tibiotarsal joint of the bird. Many other animals, such as rabbits and dogs, are also susceptible to choline deficiency.

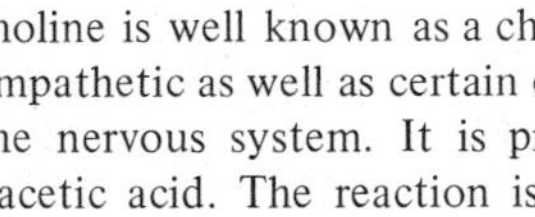

Figure 13—27. Choline.

Physiologic Role

Acetylcholine is well known as a chemical mediator of parasympathetic as well as certain other types of activity in the nervous system. It is produced from choline and acetic acid. The reaction is preceded by the synthesis of "active acetate," ie, acetyl-coenzyme A, which is formed from acetate and CoA. A source of high-energy phosphate, adenosine triphosphate, is also required. An enzyme (**acetyl thiokinase**) which catalyzes the formation of acetyl-CoA has been found in pigeon liver. After active acetate has been formed, acetylation of choline by acetyl-CoA occurs in the presence of a second enzyme, **choline acetylase** (Fig 13—28).

Acetylcholinesterase is an enzyme, present in many tissues, which hydrolyzes acetylcholine to choline and acetic acid. Its importance in nerve activity is discussed in Chapter 37. It has been found that red blood cells can synthesize acetylcholine and that both choline acetylase and acetylcholinesterase are present in red cells. Choline acetylase has also been detected not only in brain but in skeletal muscle, spleen, and placental tissue as well. The presence of this enzyme in tissues like placenta or erythrocytes which have no nerve supply suggests a more general function for acetylcholine than that in nerve alone. The formation and breakdown of acetylcholine may be related to cell permeability. With respect to red blood cells, it has been noted that when the enzyme choline acetylase is inactive either because of drug inhibition or because of lack of substrate, the cell loses its selective permeability and undergoes hemolysis.

The free choline level in the plasma of normal male adults averages about 4.4 μg/ml. Analyses made over a period of several months indicate that each individual maintains a relatively constant plasma level and that this level is not increased after meals or by the oral administration of large amounts of choline. This suggests that there is a mechanism in the body to maintain the plasma choline at a constant level. Excretion into the urine is a minor factor in this regulatory process, which must therefore be metabolic in origin.

Metabolism of Choline

The biosynthesis of choline has been established in the intact animal as well as with liver slices in vitro. In this process, the amino acid serine is decarboxylated in a pyridoxal-dependent reaction to ethanolamine. This latter compound is then progressively methylated to choline, as shown in Fig 13—29. Experiments with rat liver show that the methyl group of methionine (by way of S-adenosylmethionine) is apparently the sole precursor of the choline methyl groups. Although conversion of one-carbon fragments to the methyl groups of choline does occur (Fig 13—19), this is preceded by the incorporation of the one-carbon fragment into a methyl group of methionine. Because of the contributions of the amino acids to the biosynthesis of choline, the quantity of protein in the diet affects the choline requirement and a choline deficiency is usually coincident with some degree of protein deficiency.

The first reaction in the catabolism of choline is oxidation to betaine aldehyde, which is further oxidized to betaine. This latter compound is an excellent methyl donor and in fact, choline itself functions as a methyl donor only after oxidation to betaine. After loss of a methyl group by a direct methylation reaction in which a methyl group is transferred to homocysteine to form methionine, or to activated methyl donors, betaine is converted to dimethylglycine. Oxidation of one of the methyl groups on dimethylglycine produces N-hydroxymethylsarcosine. The hydroxymethyl group is then lost and sarcosine is formed by transfer of the hydroxymethyl to tetrahydrofolic acid. It is by this oxidative reaction and transfer to

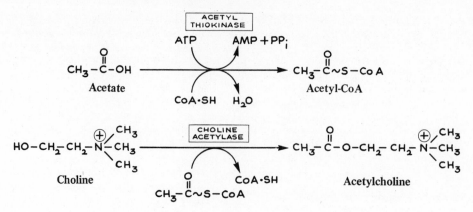

Figure 13—28. Formation of acetylcholine from "active acetate."

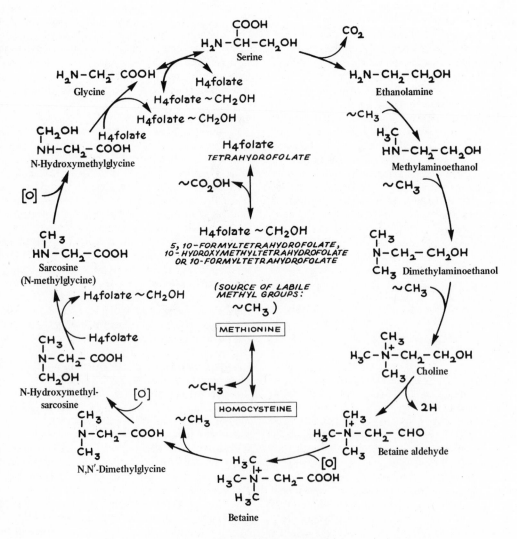

Figure 13—29. Metabolism of choline.

folic acid derivatives that methyl groups contribute to the one-carbon (formyl) pool (Fig 13–19). Sarcosine (N-methylglycine) is now converted to glycine by oxidation and transfer of its methyl group as described above. Glycine is readily converted to serine by addition of a hydroxymethyl group derived from the one-carbon pool of the formylated tetrahydrofolic acid derivatives; finally, the decarboxylation of serine to produce ethanolamine starts the cycle of choline synthesis once again. These reactions are diagrammed in Fig 13–29.

•　　•　　•

References

Annual Reviews of Biochemistry. Annual Reviews, Inc.

Bray RC, Shemin D: On the biosynthesis of vitamin B_{12}: The derivation of the corrin structure from δ-aminolevulinic acid and the methyl group of methionine. J Biol Chem 238:1501, 1963.

György P, Pearson WN (editors): *The Vitamins.* Vols 6 & 7. Academic Press, 1967.

Harris RS, Loraine TA, Wool IG (editors): *Vitamins and Hormones: Advances in Research and Applications.* (An annual publication.) Academic Press.

Herbert V: Experimental nutritional folate deficiency in man. Trans Assoc Am Physicians 75:307, 1962.

Mudd SH: Pyridoxine-responsive genetic disease. Fed Proc 30:970, 1971.

Recommended Dietary Allowances, 8th ed. National Academy of Sciences, 1974.

Ritchie JH & others: Edema and hemolytic anemia in premature infants. N Engl J Med 279:1185, 1968.

Rosenberg L, Lilljequist A-C, Hsia YE: Methylmalonic aciduria: An inborn error leading to metabolic acidosis, long-chain ketonuria, and intermittent hyperglycinemia. N Engl J Med 278:1319, 1968.

Schwarz K (editor): Nutritional factors and liver diseases. (2 parts.) Ann NY Acad Sci 57:378, 615, 1954.

Sebrell WH Jr, Harris RS (editors): *The Vitamins,* 2nd ed. Vols 1–5. Academic Press, 1972.

Silber R, Moldow CF: The biochemistry of B_{12}-mediated reactions in man. Am J Med 48:549, 1970.

Suttie JW: Mechanism of action of vitamin K: Demonstration of a liver precursor of prothrombin. Science 179:192, 1973.

Witting LA: Recommended dietary allowance for vitamin C. Am J Clin Nutr 25:257, 1972.

14 . . .
Porphyrins & Bile Pigments

Porphyrins are cyclic compounds formed by the linkage of 4 pyrrole rings through methylene bridges (Fig 6–1). A characteristic property of the porphyrins is the formation of complexes with metal ions bound to the nitrogen atom of the pyrrole rings. Examples are the iron porphyrins such as **heme** of hemoglobin and the magnesium-containing porphyrin **chlorophyll**, the photosynthetic pigment of plants.

In nature, the metalloporphyrins are conjugated to proteins to form a number of compounds of importance in biologic processes. These include the following:

A. Hemoglobins: Iron porphyrins attached to the protein, globin. These conjugated proteins possess the ability to combine reversibly with oxygen. They serve as the transport mechanism for oxygen within the blood. Hemoglobin has a molecular weight of 64,450.

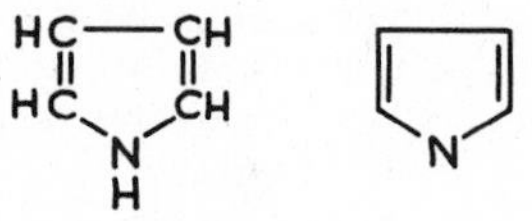

Pyrrole

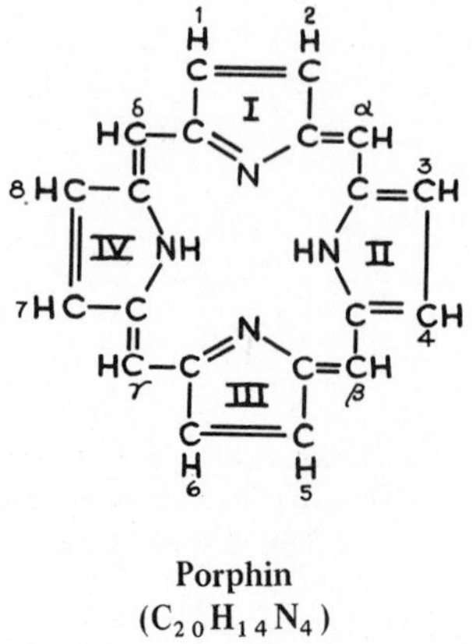

Porphin
$(C_{20}H_{14}N_4)$

Figure 14–1. The porphin molecule. Rings are labeled I, II, III, IV. Substituent positions on rings are labeled 1, 2, 3, 4, 5, 6, 7, 8. Methylene bridges are labeled $\alpha, \beta, \gamma, \delta$.

It contains 4 gram atoms of iron per mole in the ferrous (Fe^{2+}) state.

B. Erythrocruorins: Iron porphyrinoproteins which occur in the blood and tissue fluids of some invertebrates. They correspond in function to hemoglobin.

C. Myoglobins: Respiratory pigments which occur in the muscle cells of vertebrates and invertebrates. An example is the myoglobin obtained from the heart muscle of the horse and crystallized by Theorell in 1934. The purified prophyrinoprotein has a molecular weight of about 17,000. It contains only 1 gram atom of iron per mole.

D. Cytochromes: Compounds which act as electron transfer agents in oxidation-reduction reactions. An important example is **cytochrome c**, which has a molecular weight of about 13,000 and contains 1 gram atom of iron per mole.

E. Catalases: Iron porphyrin enzymes, several of which have been obtained in crystalline form. They are assumed to have a molecular weight of about 225,000 and to contain 4 gram atoms of iron per mol. In plants, catalase activity is minimal, but the iron porphyrin enzyme peroxidase performs similar functions. A peroxidase from horseradish has been crystallized; it has a molecular weight of 44,000 and contains 1 gram atom of iron per mole.

F. The Enzyme Tryptophan Pyrrolase: This enzyme catalyzes the oxidation of tryptophan to formyl kynurenine. It is an iron porphyrin protein.

Structure of Porphyrins

The porphyrins found in nature are compounds in which various side-chains are substituted for the 8 hydrogen atoms numbered in the porphin nucleus shown at left. As a simple means of showing these substitutions, Fischer proposed a shorthand formula in which the methylene bridges are omitted and each pyrrole ring is shown as a bracket with the 8 substituent positions numbered as shown below. Uroporphyrin, whose detailed structure is shown in Fig 14–11, would be represented as shown in Fig 14–2. (A = $-CH_2 \cdot COOH$; P = $-CH_2 \cdot CH_2 \cdot COOH$; M = $-CH_3 \cdot$)

The formation and occurrence of other porphyrin derivatives may be depicted as shown in Figs 14–3, 14–4, and 14–5.

It will be noted that the arrangement of the A and P substituents in the uroporphyrin shown in Fig

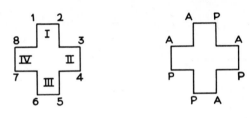

Figure 14—2. Uroporphyrin III.

14—2 is asymmetric (in ring IV, the expected order of the acetate and propionate substituents is reversed). This type of asymmetric substitution is classified as a type III porphyrin. A porphyrin with a completely symmetrical arrangement of the substituents is classified as a type I porphyrin. Only types I and III are found in nature, and the type III series is by far the more abundant.

The compounds shown in Figs 14—4 and 14—5 are all type III porphyrins (ie, the methyl groups are in the same substituent position as in type III coproporphyrin). However, they are sometimes identified as belonging to series 9 because they were designated ninth in a series of isomers postulated by Hans Fischer, the pioneer worker in the field of porphyrin chemistry.

These derivatives have one of 3 types of substituents: ethyl ($-CH_2CH_3$), E; hydroxyethyl ($-CH_2CH_2OH$), EOH; or vinyl ($-CH=CH_2$), V.

Deuteroporphyrins (Fig 14—6) and mesoporphyrins (Fig 14—7) may be formed in the feces by bacterial activity on protoporphyrin III.

Biosynthesis of Porphyrins

Both chlorophyll, the photosynthetic pigment of plants, and heme, the iron protoporphyrin of hemoglobin in animals, are synthesized in living cells by a common pathway. The 2 starting materials are "active succinate," the coenzyme A derivative of succinic acid, derived from the citric acid cycle, and the amino acid glycine. Pyridoxal phosphate is also necessary in this reaction to "activate" glycine. It is probable that pyridoxal reacts with glycine to form a Schiff base, whereby the alpha carbon of glycine can be combined with the carbonyl carbon of succinate. The product of the condensation reaction between succinate and glycine is α-amino-β-ketoadipic acid, which is rapidly decarboxylated to form δ-aminolevulinic acid (AmLev). This step is catalyzed by the enzyme **AmLev synthetase.** This appears to be the rate-controlling enzyme in porphyrin biosynthesis in mammalian liver. Synthesis of aminolevulinic acid occurs in the mitochondria, where succinyl-CoA is being produced in the reactions of the citric acid cycle.

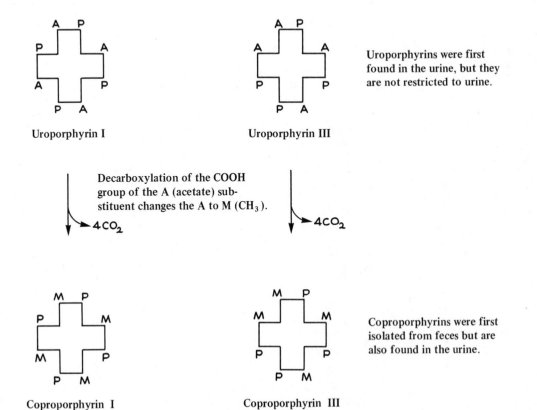

Uroporphyrin I   Uroporphyrin III

Uroporphyrins were first found in the urine, but they are not restricted to urine.

Decarboxylation of the COOH group of the A (acetate) substituent changes the A to M (CH$_3$).

Coproporphyrin I   Coproporphyrin III

Coproporphyrins were first isolated from feces but are also found in the urine.

Figure 14—3. Conversion of uroporphyrins to coproporphyrins.

Mesoporphyrin III (9) (from copro-porphyrin III by decarboxylation of propionates on positions 2 and 4)

Hematoporphyrin III (9) (may also be derived from coproporphyrin III by changing propionates on positions 2 and 4 to hydroxyethyl groups)

Figure 14—4. Conversion of mesoporphyrin to hematoporphyrin.

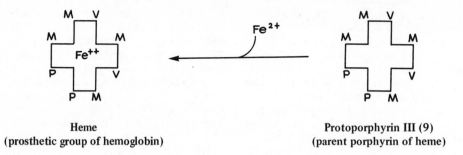

Heme
(prosthetic group of hemoglobin)

Protoporphyrin III (9)
(parent porphyrin of heme)

Figure 14—5. Addition of iron to protoporphyrin to form heme.

Schulman & Richert (1957) studied the incorporation of glycine and succinate into heme by avian red blood cells. It was found that blood samples from vitamin B_6- and from pantothenic acid-deficient ducklings utilized glycine and succinate for heme synthesis at a reduced rate, although δ-aminolevulinic acid incorporation into heme was essentially normal. The addition in vitro of pyridoxal-5-phosphate restored glycine and succinate incorporation without affecting aminolevulinic acid incorporation. Added coenzyme A was without effect in vitro, but the injection of calcium pantothenate 1 hour before the blood specimens were drawn restored to normal the rate of glycine incorporation into heme. These experiments suggest that the block in heme synthesis in pantothenic acid or in vitamin B_6 deficiency occurs at a very early step in heme synthesis, presumably in the formation of coenzyme A succinate and in the pyridoxal-dependent decarboxylation of a-amino-β-ketoadipic acid. The anemia which

has been found to accompany vitamin B_6 or pantothenic acid deficiency in several species of experimental animals may be explained on a biochemical basis by these observations.

The next step in porphyrin biosynthesis following formation of AmLev is characterized by the condensation of 2 mols of AmLev to form **porphobilinogen**, the monopyrrole precursor of the porphyrins. The reaction is catalyzed by **δ-aminolevulinase (AmLev dehydrase)**. All of these reactions are shown in Fig 14—8.

The pathway for the synthesis of porphobilinogen as described above has received support by the finding of both δ-aminolevulinic acid (1.3—7.0 mg/24 hours) and porphobilinogen (up to 2 mg/24 hours) in the urine of normal subjects as well as in the urine of patients with acute porphyria. In this group of patients, these compounds—which are involved in the synthesis of porphyrins—occur in greatly increased amounts.

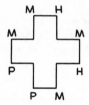

Figure 14—6. Deuteroporphyrin (type III).

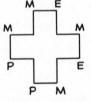

Figure 14—7. Mesoporphyrin (type III).

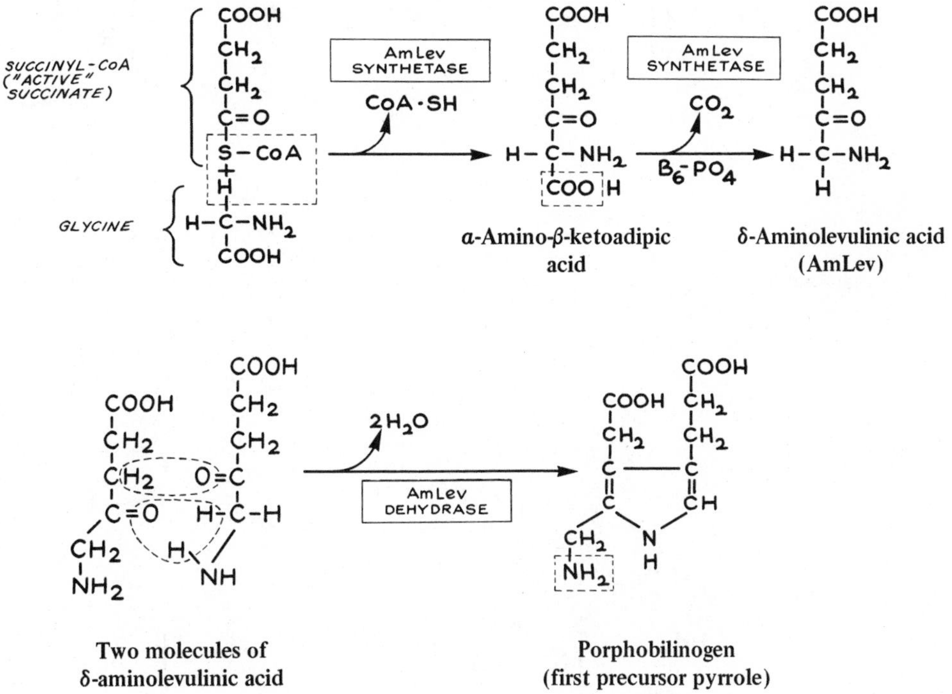

SUCCINYL-CoA
("ACTIVE"
SUCCINATE)

GLYCINE

COOH
CH₂
CH₂
C=O
S—CoA
+
H
H—C—NH₂
COOH

AmLev SYNTHETASE
CoA·SH

COOH
CH₂
CH₂
C=O
H—C—NH₂
COOH

a-Amino-β-ketoadipic acid

AmLev SYNTHETASE
CO₂
B₆⁻PO₄

COOH
CH₂
CH₂
C=O
H—C—NH₂
H

δ-Aminolevulinic acid (AmLev)

COOH
CH₂
CH₂
C=O
CH₂
NH₂

COOH
CH₂
CH₂
O=C
H—C—H
H
NH

2H₂O
AmLev DEHYDRASE

COOH
CH₂
CH₂
C
CH
N
H

COOH
CH₂
CH₂
C
CH₂
NH₂

Two molecules of δ-aminolevulinic acid

Porphobilinogen (first precursor pyrrole)

Figure 14—8. Biosynthesis of porphobilinogen.

The formation of a tetrapyrrole, ie, a porphyrin, occurs by condensation of 4 monopyrroles derived from porphobilinogen. In each instance, the amino carbon (originally derived from the alpha carbon of glycine) serves as the source of the methylene (alpha, beta, gamma, delta) carbons which connect each pyrrole in the tetrapyrrole structure. The enzymes involved in the conversion of AmLev to porphyrinogens occur in the soluble portion of the cell (the cytosol) in contrast to the mitochondrial location of the AmLev forming enzymes. Although the conversion of porphobilinogen to a porphyrin can be accomplished simply by heating under acid conditions, in the tissues this conversion is catalyzed by specific enzymes.

It has been pointed out that only types I and III porphyrins occur in nature, and it may be assumed that the type III isomers are the more abundant since the biologically important porphyrins such as heme and the cytochromes are type III isomers. Both type I and type III porphyrinogens may be formed as diagrammed in Fig 14—9. In this scheme, 3 moles of porphobilinogen condense first to form a tripyrrylmethane, which then breaks down into a dipyrrylmethane and a monopyrrole. The dipyrryl compounds are of 2 types depending upon where the split occurs on the tripyrryl precursor: at the point marked (A) or at (B). The formation of the tetrapyrrole occurs by condensation of 2 dipyrrylmethanes. If 2 of the (A) components condense, a type I porphyrin. results; if one (A) and one (B) condense, a type III results. Because of the structure of the side chains on porphobilinogen (acetate and propionate), it is clear that uroporphyrin-

ogens types I and III would result as the first tetrapyrroles to be formed.

At present, the detailed steps leading to the formation of the uroporphyrinogens from condensation of porphobilinogens remain obscure. Therefore, catalysis reactions by enzyme complexes designated uroporphyrinogen synthetase I or III are postulated to account for the formation of the 2 uroporphyrinogen isomers. The occurrence of partial blocks at the biosynthetic steps catalyzed by these synthetases will be described later. These blocks may represent additional factors in the etiology of some of the genetically determined porphyrias.

The uroporphyrinogens I and III are converted to coproporphyrinogens I and III by decarboxylation of all of the acetate (A) groups, which changes these to methyl (M) substituents. The reaction is catalyzed by **uroporphyrinogen decarboxylase**. The coproporphyrinogen III then enters the mitochondria, where it is converted to protoporphyrinogen and then to protoporphyrin. Several steps seem to be involved in this conversion. An enzyme, **coproporphyrinogen oxidase**, is believed to catalyze the decarboxylation and oxidation of 2 propionic side chains to form protoporphyrinogen. This enzyme is able to act only on type III coproporphyrinogen, which would explain why a type I protoporphyrin has not been identified in natural materials. The oxidation of protoporphyrinogen to protoporphyrin is believed to be catalyzed by an enzyme, **protoporphyrinogen oxidase**. In mammalian liver the reaction of conversion of coproporphyrinogen to protoporphyrin requires molecular oxygen.

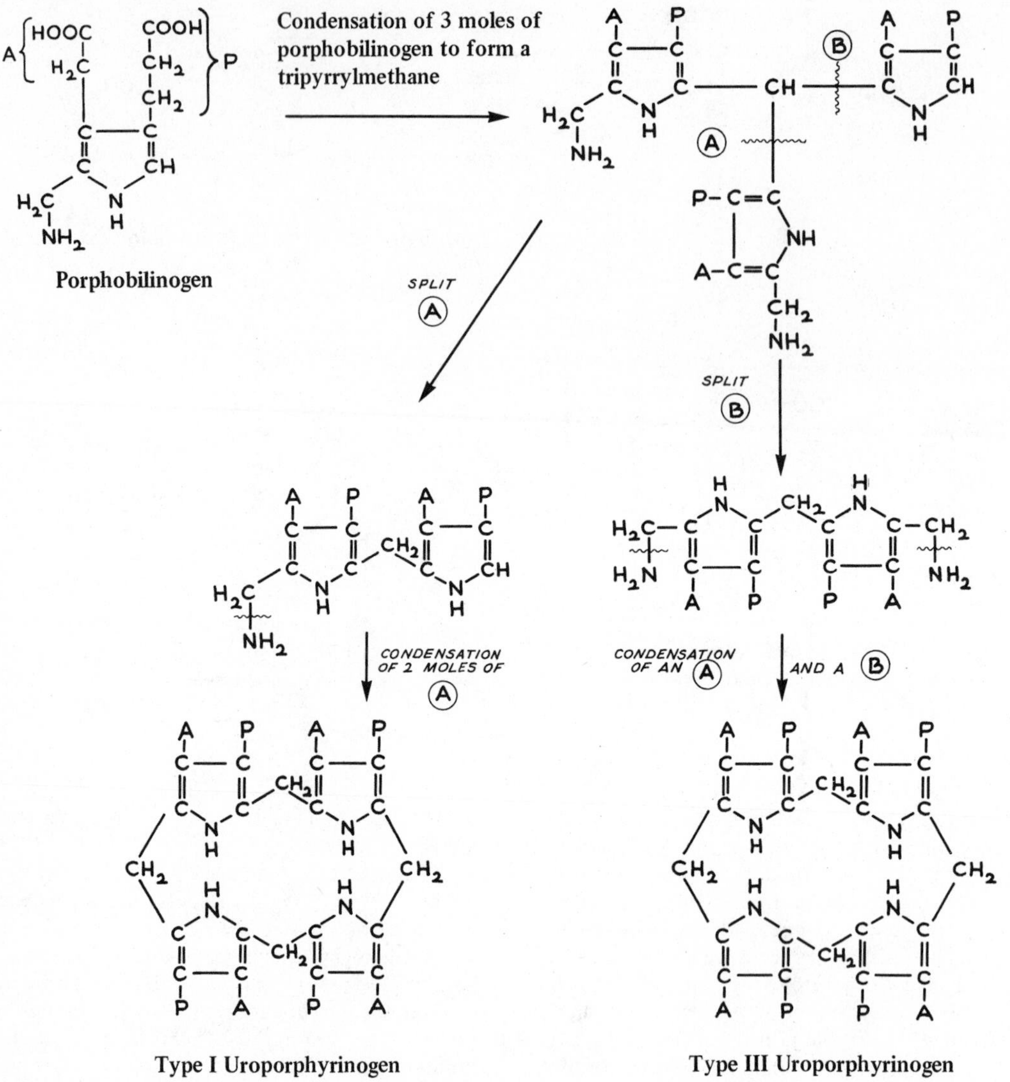

Figure 14—9. Conversion of porphobilinogen to uroporphyrinogens.

The final step in heme synthesis involves the incorporation of ferrous iron into protoporphyrin in a reaction catalyzed by **heme synthetase** or **ferrochelatase**. This reaction occurs readily in the absence of enzymes; but it is noted to be much more rapid in the presence of tissue preparations, presumably because of the tissue contribution of enzymes active in catalyzing iron incorporation.

A summary of the steps in the biosynthesis of the porphyrin derivatives from porphobilinogen is given in Fig 14—10.

The porphyrinogens which have been described above are colorless reduced porphyrins containing 6 extra hydrogen atoms as compared to the corresponding porphyrins. It is now apparent that these reduced porphyrins (the porphyrinogens) and not the corresponding porphyrins are the actual intermediates in the biosynthesis of protoporphyrin and of heme. This idea

is supported by the observation that the oxidized porphyrins cannot be used for heme or for chlorophyll synthesis either by intact or disrupted cells. Furthermore, the condensation of 4 moles of porphobilinogen (Fig 14—9) would directly give rise to uroporphyrinogens rather than to uroporphyrins.

The porphyrinogens are readily auto-oxidized to the respective porphyrins as shown in Fig 14—11 for uroporphyrinogen. These oxidations are catalyzed in the presence of light and by the porphyrins that are formed. The amounts of these porphyrin byproducts that are produced depend not only on the activities of the various enzymes involved but also on the presence of catalysts (light) or inhibitors (reduced glutathione) of their auto-oxidation.

Chemistry of Porphyrins

Because of the presence of tertiary nitrogens in

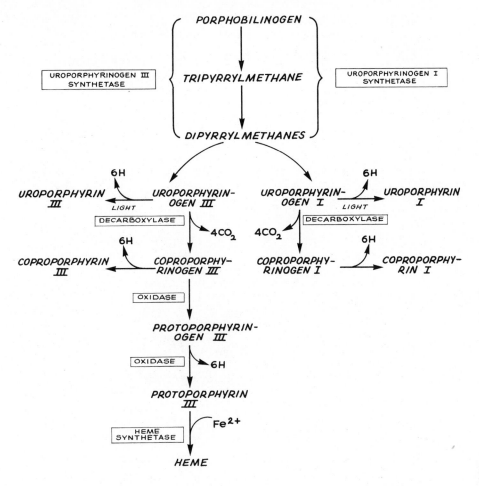

Figure 14—10. Steps in the biosynthesis of the porphyrin derivatives from porphobilinogen.

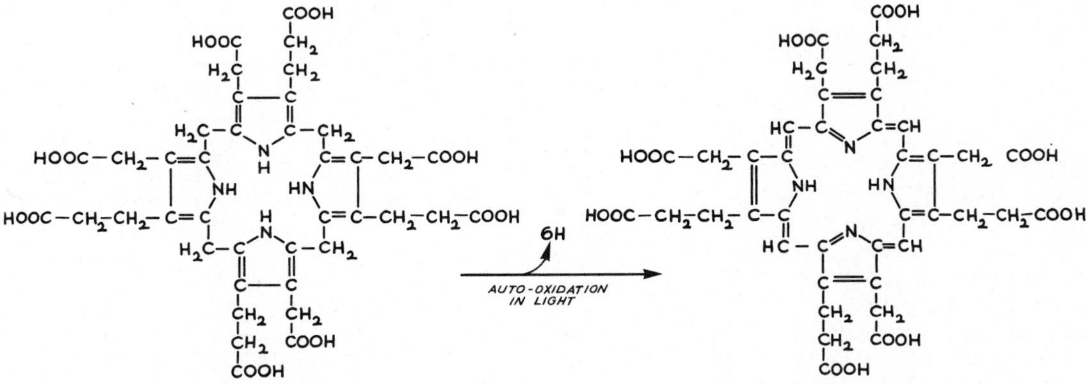

Uroporphyrinogen III

Uroporphyrin III

Figure 14—11. Oxidation of uroporphyrinogen to uroporphyrin.

the 2 pyrrolene rings contained in each porphyrin, these compounds act as weak bases. Those which possess a carboxyl group on one or more side-chains act also as acids. Their isoelectric points range from pH 3.0 to 4.5, and within this pH range the porphyrins may easily be precipitated from an aqueous solution.

The various porphyrinogens are colorless, whereas the various porphyrins are all colored. In the study of porphyrins or porphyrin derivatives, the characteristic absorption spectrum which each exhibits, both in the visible and the ultraviolet regions of the spectrum, is of great value. An example is the absorption curve for a solution of hematoporphyrin in 5% hydrochloric acid (Fig 14–12). Note the sharp absorption band near 400 nm. This is a distinguishing feature of the porphin ring and is characteristic of all porphyrins regardless of the side chains present. This band is termed the **Soret band,** after its discoverer. Hematoporphyrin in acid solution, in addition to the Soret band, has 2 weaker absorption bands with maxima at 550 and 592 nm.

In organic solvents, porphyrins have 4 main bands in the visible spectrum as well as the Soret band. For example, a solution of protoporphyrin in an ether-acetic acid mixture exhibits absorption bands at 632.5, 576, 537, 502, and 395 nm. When porphyrins dissolved in strong mineral acids or in organic solvents are illuminated by ultraviolet light, they emit a strong red fluorescence. This fluorescence is so characteristic that it is frequently used to detect small amounts of free porphyrins. The double bonds in the porphyrins are responsible for the characteristic absorption and fluorescence of these compounds, and, as previously noted, the reduction (by addition of hydrogen) of the methylene (C=H) bridges to CH_2 leads to the formation of colorless compounds termed **porphyrinogens.**

When a porphyrin combines with a metal, its absorption in the visible spectrum becomes changed. This is exemplified by protoporphyrin, the iron-free precursor of heme. In alkaline solution, protoporphyrin shows several sharp absorption bands (at 645, 591, and 540 nm), whereas heme has a broad band with a plateau extending from 540 to 580 nm.

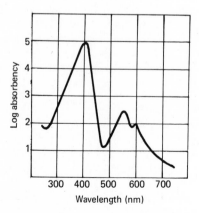

Figure 14–12. Absorption spectrum of hematoporphyrin (0.01% solution in 5% HCl).

Heme and other ferrous porphyrin complexes react readily with basic substances such as hydrazines, primary amines, pyridines, ammonia, or an imidazole such as the amino acid, histidine. The resulting compound is called a hemochromogen (hemochrome). The hemochromogens still show a Soret band but also exhibit 2 absorption bands in the visible spectrum. The band at the longer wavelength is called the alpha band; that at the shorter wavelength, the beta band. An example is the hemochromogen formed with pyridine. This has its alpha band at 559 nm and its beta band at 527.5 nm. In the formation of a hemochromogen, it is believed that 2 molecules of the basic substance replace 2 molecules of water which were loosely bound to iron in the ferrous porphyrin.

Hemoglobin & Cytochrome c

In hemoglobin, the iron in the protoporphyrin III (9) structure (heme) is thought to be coordinated to imidazole nitrogens contained in histidine residues within the protein globin. This coordination could occur to 2 imidazole nitrogens of histidine at positions 58 and 87 in the alpha chain and 63 and 92 in the beta chain. During oxygen transport, it has been suggested, one of the imidazole ligands (His α-58 and His β-63) becomes reversibly displaced by oxygen. This concept is diagrammatically indicated in Fig 14–13. In any event, the formation of oxyhemoglobin results in an increase in acidity of the compound precursor, ie, oxyhemoglobin is a stronger acid than is reduced (deoxygenated) hemoglobin.

Cytochrome c is also an iron porphyrin; it contains about 0.43% iron. The iron porphyrin is derived from protoporphyrin III (9), but the 2 vinyl side chains are reduced and linked by a thioether bond to 2 cysteine residues of the protein; in addition, the iron is linked to a histidine residue in the protein, as in the case of hemoglobin.

The amino acid sequence of that portion of the heme protein in horse heart cytochrome c which is responsible for the attachment of the heme prosthetic group has been described. To accomplish this attachment, 2 cysteine residues in the protein are utilized to form thioether bonds with 2 reduced vinyl side chains of hemin. Matsuhara & Smith (1963) reported the complete amino acid sequence of human heart cytochrome c. The peptide chain contains 104 amino acids. Acetylglycine is the N-terminal amino acid and glutamic acid the C-terminal amino acid. The 2 cysteine residues involved in linkage with the heme prosthetic group are located at positions 14 and 17 in the peptide chain. The linkage of iron in heme occurs through the imidazole nitrogen of a histidine residue at position 18 in the peptide chain. On the basis of these data, a partial structure of human heart cytochrome c can be depicted as shown in Fig 14–14.

Further studies have resulted in the determination of the amino acid sequence of the protein moieties in the cytochromes c of 13 different species. It is noteworthy that in all of them the primary structure is such that more than half of the amino acids are

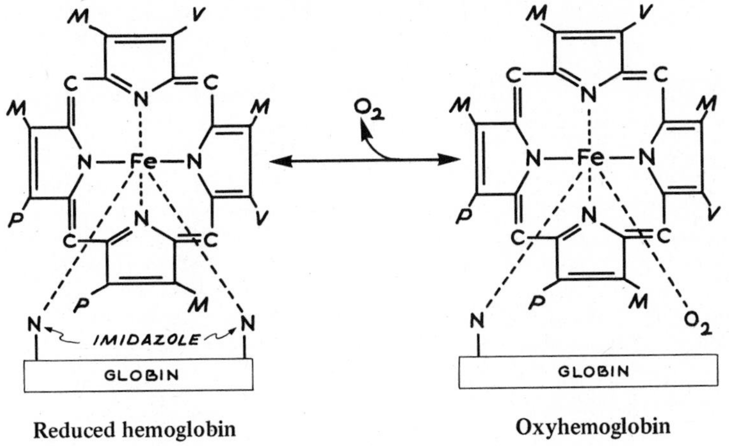

Reduced hemoglobin   Oxyhemoglobin

Figure 14—13. Imidazole conjugation in hemoglobin..

arranged in an identical sequence. It has been suggested that the degree of difference in primary structure among the 13 cytochromes c might be related to the degree of phylogenetic relationship between the species. For example, the cytochrome c of man as compared to that of a rhesus monkey differs by only one amino acid of the 104 amino acids comprising the whole chain. Human cytochrome c differs from that of the dog in 11 amino acid residues; from that of the horse, in 12. Between a species of fish (the tuna) and baker's yeast there are 48 differences in the amino acid sequences of the cytochromes c.

Tests for Porphyrins

The presence of coproporphyrins or of uroporphyrins is of clinical interest since these 2 types of compounds are excreted in increased amounts in the porphyrias. Coproporphyrins I and III are soluble in glacial acetic acid-ether mixtures, from which they may then be extracted by hydrochloric acid. Uroporphyrins, on the other hand, are not soluble in acetic acid-ether mixtures but are partially soluble in ethyl acetate, from which they may be extracted by hydrochloric acid. In the HCl solution, ultraviolet illumination gives a characteristic red fluorescence. A spectrophotometer may then be used to demonstrate the characteristic absorption bands. The melting point of the methyl esters of the various porphyrins may also be used to differentiate them (Dobriner, 1940; Watson, 1947). Paper chromatography (Petryka, 1968) has more recently been employed as a means of separating and identifying the porphyrins.

Porphyrinuria

The excretion of coproporphyrins may be increased under many circumstances, eg, acute febrile states; after the ingestion of certain poisons, particularly heavy metals such as lead or arsenic; blood

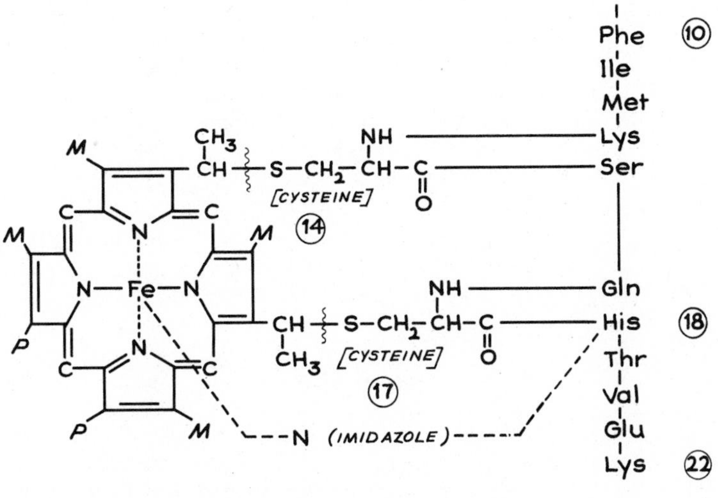

Figure 14—14. Partial structure of human heart cytochrome c.

dyscrasias, hemolytic anemia, or pernicious anemia; and sprue, cirrhosis, acute pancreatitis, and malignancies (eg, Hodgkin's disease). In these conditions, uroporphyrin is not present in the urine.

In healthy subjects, the total urinary coproporphyrin averages about 67 μg/24 hours; the type I isomer comprises on the average 14 μg/24 hours and type III 53 μg/24 hours. An alteration in the normal ratio of the excretion of types I and III coproporphyrins may be of value in detection of certain types of diseases of the liver. Thus, in the Dubin-Johnson syndrome it has been reported that patients may excrete more type I than type III coproporphyrin; this inverse ratio may occur also in carriers of the disease. The coproporphyrin excretion pattern is said to be normal in Gilbert's disease. The distribution of the 2 isomers in the urine of patients with obstructive jaundice or infectious hepatitis is not particularly significant for diagnostic purposes.

The Porphyrias

When the excretion of both coproporphyrin and uroporphyrin is increased because of their presence in the blood, the condition is referred to as **porphyria**.

Under this term are included a number of syndromes; some are hereditary and familial and some are acquired, but all are characterized by increased excretion of uroporphyrin and coproporphyrin in the urine or feces or both. Reduced catalase activity of the liver has also been reported in these cases.

A summary of these observation on the excretion of porphyrins is given in Table 14–1.

Several different classifications of the porphyrias have been proposed. Goldberg & Rimington summarized those extant in 1962. A more recent classification appears from the research group of Eales at Cape Town, South Africa (Eales, Grosser, & Sears, 1975).

It is convenient, however, to divide the porphyrias into 2 general groups based upon the porphyrin and porphyrin precursor content of the bone marrow or of the liver. Using this system, the porphyrias are classified as either **erythropoietic** or **hepatic**. Within each of these 2 general types, various subdivisions have been described as shown in Table 14–2.

Among the hepatic porphyrias there are 2 types (shown in the table as A and B) with focal centers in Sweden or in South Africa. In the Swedish type, early

Table 14–1. Excretion of porphyrins.

Type	Porphyrins Excreted		Remarks
Normal	Urine: Coproporphyrin I Coproporphyrin III	60–280 (avg 67) μg/day; mainly (78%) type III.	The excretion of uroporphyrins is negligible in normal individuals, averaging 15–30 μg/day, mostly type I.
	Feces: Coproporphyrin I Coproporphyrin III	300–500 μg/day; 70–90% is type I.	
Hereditary Acute (hepatogenic) porphyria (increased porphyrins in the liver)	Mainly type III porphyrins. Protoporphyrin: Up to 600 μg/day. Coproporphyrin III: 144–2582 μg/day. Coproporphyrin I: Small amounts. Uroporphyrin I and III[*]: 61,000–147,000 μg/day. Porphobilinogen δ-Aminolevulinic acid } in urine.		Hereditary as an autosomal dominant. Relatively common; metabolic defect is in the liver. Catalase activity of liver is markedly reduced. Patients are not light-sensitive.
Congenital (erythrogenic) porphyria (increased porphyrins in the marrow)	Mainly type I porphyrins. Type III coproporphyrin was reported in 2 cases. The fecal content of porphyrin is high.		Hereditary as an autosomal recessive. Rare. Patient shows sensitivity to light. Marrow is site of metabolic error.
Chronic porphyria (mixed)	Varies. There may be increased amounts of coproporphyrin I and III and no uroporphyrins; in other cases, uroporphyrin I and III are increased; still others have mixtures of copro- and uroporphyrins. Porphobilinogen may also be found in the urine.		Hereditary or acquired? Patient may be light-sensitive. Frequently associated with enlargement of the liver.
Acquired Toxic agents	Coproporphyrin III.		Eg, heavy metals, chemicals, acute alcoholism, and cirrhosis in alcoholics.
Liver disease	Coproporphyrin I.		Eg, infectious hepatitis, cirrhosis not accompanied by alcoholism, obstructive jaundice.
Blood dyscrasias	Coproporphyrin I.		Eg, leukemia, pernicious anemia, hemolytic anemias.
Miscellaneous	Coproporphyrin III.		Eg, poliomyelitis, aplastic anemias, Hodgkin's disease.

[*]According to Watson (1960), the uroporphyrins excreted in acute porphyria are a complex mixture of uroporphyrin I and a peculiar uroporphyrin III which has 7 rather than 8 carboxyl groups. The mixture is referred to as Waldenström porphyrin. It is extractable from urine by acetate but not by ether.

Table 14–2. Classification of porphyrias.*

I. Erythropoietic porphyrias
  A. Congenital erythropoietic porphyria (recessive)
  B. Erythropoietic protoporphyria (dominant?)
II. Hepatic porphyrias
  A. Acute intermittent porphyria, Swedish genetic porphyria, and pyrroloporphyria (dominant)
    1. Manifest
    2. Latent
  B. Porphyria variegata, mixed porphyria, South African genetic porphyria, porphyria cutanea tarda hereditaria, and protocoproporphyria (dominant)
    1. Cutaneous with little or no acute manifestations
    2. Acute intermittent without cutaneous symptoms
    3. Various combinations
    4. Latent
  C. Symptomatic porphyria, porphyria cutanea tarda symptomatica, urocoproporphyria, constitutional porphyria
    1. Idiosyncratic—Associated with alcoholism, liver disease, systemic disease, drugs, etc
    2. Acquired—Hexachlorobenzene-induced porphyria and hepatoma

*Reproduced, with permission, from Tschudy DP: Biochemical lesions in porphyria. JAMA 191:718, 1965.

intermediates of porphyrin biosynthesis such as aminolevulinic acid and porphobilinogen are excreted in the urine, whereas in the South African type coproporphyrin and protoporphyrin are excreted. It now seems established that the chemical manifestations of acute porphyria represent overproduction of porphyrin precursors as a result of increased activity of the hepatic enzyme **AmLev synthetase**. This enzyme, which catalyzes the production of aminolevulinic acid, is the rate-controlling enzyme in hepatic porphyrin synthesis (Granick, 1963). Normally it is under almost complete repression in the liver, whereas in patients with hepatic porphyria AmLev synthetase activity has been found to be more than 7 times that of nonporphyric controls (Tschudy, 1965). Granick (1966) has developed a hypothesis with respect to the etiology of hepatic porphyria which suggests that the increase in AmLev synthetase activity in this disease is due to a genetic mutation affecting the operator gene-repressor mechanism normally controlling AmLev synthetase production. This hypothesis extends also to an explanation of chemically induced porphyrias such as those following administration of certain drugs (eg, barbiturates) to sensitive individuals.

As has already been indicated above, there is now little doubt that the primary regulatory control of the biosynthesis of heme is exerted at the level of the action of AmLev synthetase. Furthermore, the end product, heme, is involved in a negative feedback type of regulation of AmLev synthetase activity both by direct inhibition of the activity of this enzyme and by contributing to suppression of its rate of synthesis. In this connection, it is pertinent to note that there is a close spatial relationship between the location of AmLev synthetase and its feedback inhibitor, heme, both being located in the mitochondrion. It follows

that local concentrations of heme would be sufficiently high to exert an inhibitory effect on AmLev synthetase activity when studied in organized cellular preparations, even though this cannot be demonstrated in liver homogenates.

Both experimentally and clinically, it has often been demonstrated that the administration of certain drugs as well as steroid hormones induces a significant overproduction of porphyrins as well as intermediates of their biosynthetic pathway. Some believe that this is brought about by increased synthesis of the enzyme, AmLev synthetase, induced by these drugs or the steroids. Furthermore, many of these same compounds, including phenobarbital, are known to induce formation of the microsomal hemoprotein, cytochrome P-450, as part of the adaptive response of the liver to the administration of drugs the metabolism of which requires cytochrome P-450. Consequently, the rise in hepatic AmLev synthetase activity following administration of these conpounds may be explained as necessary to provide the additional heme required for the synthesis of hemoproteins such as cytochrome P-450.

It now seems agreed that overproduction of aminolevulinic acid by increased activity of AmLev synthetase is the primary genetic defect in all of the inherited hepatic porphyrias, which are probably the most commonly encountered clinical entities involving disorders of porphyrin metabolism. The earliest observations on inherited metabolic diseases properly led to the conclusion that these were attributable to *diminished* activity of a critical enzyme in a metabolic pathway. In the inherited hepatic porphyrias, on the other hand, we have an example of a genetic defect produced by the opposite phenomenon, ie, *increased* activity of a specific enzyme.

In all types of inherited hepatic porphyria, increased activity of AmLev synthetase appears to be responsible for the overproduction of the porphyrin precursors, AmLev and porphobilinogen, as well as the porphyrins themselves. However, it has also been noted that there is a rather characteristic and distinct pattern in the excretion of the precursors, as contrasted with the tetrapyrroles (porphyrins), typical of each of the inherited hepatic porphyrias. For example, only AmLev and porphobilinogen are notably increased in acute intermittent porphyria; in hereditary coproporphyria, uroporphyrin and coproporhyrin are, in addition, also excreted in increased amount, whereas, in the so-called variegate porphyria, protoporphyrin in addition to the other metabolites mentioned is excreted in abnormal amounts. This suggests that, in addition to increased activity of AmLev synthetase, the defect common to all of the porphyrias, there must be other, secondary factors responsible for the characteristic excretory pattern of the 3 types of hepatic porphyria mentioned above.

Most explanations of the genetic abnormalities in these diseases focus on the role of heme in the feedback regulation of AmLev synthetase. Indeed, one aspect of this hypothesis was the basis of Granick's explanation of the cause of hepatic porphyria, wherein he suggests that there has occurred a mutation in the operator gene. Such operator mutants are known in microorganisms, and some of the biochemical manifestations of porphyria in humans are in fact similar to those noted in operator mutants in microorganisms, particularly the dominant mode of inheritance and the fluctuation of porphyrin precursor excretion (Meyer & Schmid, 1973).

Another possibility is that the catabolism of heme or of the hemoproteins of the liver might be increased. This would reduce the amount of heme available in the liver to act as a feedback repressor of the synthesis of AmLev synthetase, resulting in increased production of this key regulatory enzyme of porphyrin biosynthesis. The idea is supported by the observation that the well-known AmLev synthetase-inducing drug, allyisopropyl-acetylurea, which can produce experimental porphyria in rodents, has the unique ability to promote degradation of the microsomal hemoprotein cytochrome P-450, which constitutes the major fraction of the heme compounds in the liver. It has therefore been suggested that the increased turnover of cytochrome P-450 may explain the action of this drug to induce porphyria, by diverting heme from its role as a repressor of AmLev synthetase production. As yet, however, there is no evidence to support the idea that increased breakdown of hemoprotein in the liver is a factor in the production of the hepatic porphyrias in man.

A third suggestion with regard to the metabolic basis for the inherited hepatic porphyrias is the hypothesis that these inherited diseases are fundamentally the result of a partial block in heme biosynthesis. This effect, by limiting the amount of heme that can be formed, would then result in derepression of AmLev synthetase.

Acute intermittent porphyria is the most common form of the inherited hepatic porphyrias occurring in the USA. In this syndrome, urinary excretion of AmLev and porphobilinogen is markedly increased but there is no proportionate increase in the excretion of the tetrapyrroles formed beyond these earlier intermediates, beginning with the reactions catalyzed by uroporphyrinogen synthetase (Fig 14–10). If it is assumed that a partial block in biosynthesis of heme is also a factor in this disease, the site of this partial block would be at the steps involved in conversion of porphobilinogen to the uroporphyrinogens. This would explain how intermediates formed before this step could be increased (when AmLev synthetase formation is derepressed) but later intermediates would not. As has been noted (Fig 14–10), the condensation of porphobilinogen to the uroporphyrinogens is accomplished by a complex series of reactions that is as yet unknown; however, the rate-limiting enzyme appears to be uroporhyrinogen I synthetase. This is supported by the observation that, in patients with intermittent acute porphyria, uroporphyrinogen I synthetase activity in the liver is markedly decreased. A similar decline in activity of this enzyme was also detected in red cell hemolysates of the affected patients. As a result of all of these observations, a partial block in formation of uroporphyrinogens is assumed to explain the fact that, in intermittent acute porphyria, urinary excretion of AmLev and porphobilinogen is markedly increased whereas both urinary and fecal excretion of the porphyrins themselves is normal or only slightly elevated. It is also apparent that reduced formation of heme would occur as a result of the partial block in uroporphyrinogen synthetase activity, thus limiting negative feedback on AmLev synthetase activity.

If it is accepted that the liver of porphyric patients has a partial block in heme synthesis, it would be expected that any sudden demand for production of heme could not be met. An example of such a sudden demand would be that created by administration of barbiturates or any other drug that induces the formation of cytochrome P-450. Diversion of heme to the formation of this hemoprotein would reduce that available for feedback control of AmLev synthetase activity. This latter enzyme would be derepressed, and greatly increased quantities of AmLev and porphobilinogen would be excreted in the urine. If this is correct, it would explain why administration of certain drugs to patients with genetically transmitted hepatic porphyria may cause an acute clinical attack of porphyria.

Acute intermittent porphyria is inherited as an autosomal dominant genetic trait, although it may not manifest itself until the third decade of life. As indicated above, the biochemical defect in this disease is located in the liver—hence the term "hepatogenic porphyria" sometimes applied to this disease. The presenting symptoms occur most often in the gastrointestinal tract and nervous system. In the urine, which is characteristically pigmented and darkens on standing, there is an increased excretion of porphyrin precursors (aminolevulinic acid and porphobilinogen) as well as of type III coproporphyrin and uroporphyrin.

Congenital erythropoietic porphyria is a rare disease inherited as a recessive trait. It occurs more often in males than in females and usually manifests itself early in life. Chemically, the disease is characterized by the production of large quantities of uroporphyrin I, which is excreted in the urine together with increased amounts of coproporphyrin I. Increased amounts of uroporphyrin and coproporphyrin III may also be detected in the urine. That the bone marrow is the site of the increased production of porphyrin is supported by the finding of large concentrations of porphyrin in many of the normoblasts in the marrow, most of the porphyrin being located either in the nucleus of the cell or on its surface. In addition, the concentration of uro- and coproporphyrin in the marrow itself is greatly increased, whereas that of the liver is only slightly so— and that only secondarily as a result of uptake by the liver of the excess porphyrins originally produced in the marrow.

A significant clinical finding in erythropoietic porphyrias is marked sensitivity to light. Areas of the body exposed to light may become necrotic, scarred, and deformed. This photosensitivity is explained by the excessive porphyrin production followed by hemolysis which results in liberation of increased amounts of porphyrin and its accumulation under the skin. Porphyrins are photosensitizing agents because of their ability to concentrate radiant energy by absorption particularly at the wavelength of the Soret band (405 nm) as well as at infrared wavelengths (2600 nm). The presence of porphyrins near the surface of the body, as occurs in erythropoietic porphyria, permits light sensitization to occur; this is in contrast to the circumstances which prevail in hepatic porphyria, wherein accumulation of porphyrin takes place in areas of the body not exposed to light.

Erythropoietic protoporphyria is believed to be inherited by a dominant mode of transmission. The disease may occur in an active or in a latent form, depending perhaps on the plasma protoporphyrin level. In the so-called "complete syndrome" there is increased free erythrocyte and plasma protoporphyrin as well as increased fecal protoporphyrin. However, an increase in free erythrocyte protoporphyrin may occur without increase in plasma or fecal protoporphyrin, or there may occur only increased fecal protoporphyrin without other detectable abnormalities of porphyrin content in erythrocytes or plasma. When increased protoporphyrin is found, there is an increase in coproporphyrin as well.

Excessive amounts of protoporphyrin in erythrocytes characterizes this disorder and serves also to distinguish it from congenital erythropoietic porphyria, wherein the red cells contain predominantly uroporphyrin. (The normal range of protoporphyrin in the red cells of adults is 14–55 μg/dl red cells; in infants and children from ages 3 weeks to 15 years, 22–175 μg/dl red cells.) Plasma, fecal, and urine protoporphyrin levels are increased; fecal and urine uroporphyrin levels are normal. Coproporphyrin is usually normal in urine but may be increased in the feces. Type III porphyrins are the predominant types excreted in erythropoietic porphyria, in contrast to congenital erythropoietic porphyria, where type I isomers are the major forms excreted. The amounts of porphobilinogen and aminolevulinic acid excreted are normal.

The metabolic defect in erythropoietic protoporphyria is not yet known. It is apparently not due to inability to incorporate iron into protoporphyrin since studies of iron metabolism in vitro and in vivo have revealed no abnormalities. Photosensitivity in protoporphyria is related to the plasma content of protoporphyrin.

Porphyria variegata is transmitted genetically as a non-X-linked dominant characteristic. This disease is sometimes termed **South African genetic porphyria** because of its common occurrence among the white population of South Africa. The affected patients are said to be descendants of the original Boer stock that settled in the Cape area in 1688. However, the disease is not restricted to this particular group, having been described among all races in all parts of the world. In most cases (about 65%), the disease first manifests itself with neurologic disorders indistinguishable from those associated with attacks of acute intermittent porphyria. However, unlike this type of porphyria, the primary clinical manifestations are associated with cutaneous involvement.

Porphyria variegata usually does not manifest itself until after puberty; the peak period of onset is between 30 and 40 years of age. Cutaneous involvement is more common in males; acute episodes are more common in females. Skin photosensitivity and fragility extending to even the slightest trauma are cardinal signs.

Biochemically, variegate porphyria is characterized by persistent elevations of fecal uroporphyrin, coproporphyrin, and protoporphyrin, even during asymptomatic periods. In contrast to acute intermittent porphyria, urine aminolevulinic acid, porphobilinogen, uroporphyrin, and coproporphyrin levels do not remain persistently elevated during the latent period of the disease; furthermore, levels of porphyrins and of aminolevulinic acid and porphobilinogen return to normal within a few weeks after an acute attack of variegate prophyria subsides.

Porphyria cutanea tarda is a type of hepatic porphyria which occurs predominantly in older males. The patient characteristically develops blisters on the exposed surfaces of the skin following trauma or exposure to the sun. Other manifestations are hyperpigmentation, hypertrichosis, and abnormally high excretion of both uroporphyrin and coproporphyrin. In many of the reported cases there is an associated history of hepatic disease, so that porphyria cutanea tarda seems to develop secondary to a primary disease of the liver.

Schmid (1960) has described an outbreak of cutaneous porphyria which occurred in Turkey. All of the affected individuals excreted a dark or red urine which fluoresced readily under ultraviolet light and which contained large quantities of both ether-soluble and ether-insoluble porphyrins. Qualitative tests for urine porphobilinogen were negative. All of the patients were found to have consumed wheat intended for planting which had been treated with hexachlorobenzene to inhibit growth of a fungal parasite.

Porphyrin metabolism in lead poisoning. Because lead poisoning, among other toxic effects, often induces changes in porphyrin metabolism and clinical symptoms resembling acute intermittent porphyria, it must be included in any consideration of the clinical disorders of porphyrin metabolism. The erythrocyte is the primary site of the biochemical lesion in lead poisoning. Although the neurologic symptoms of lead intoxication are similar to those of acute intermittent porphyria, poisoning with lead is accompanied by anemia. Absence of any cutaneous manifestation in lead poisoning differentiates it clinically from other hepatic porphyrias.

Lead poisoning is usually associated with very high levels of aminolevulinic acid, coproporphyrin III, and, occasionally, porphobilinogen. Fecal porphyrin levels are usually normal. Mature red blood cells always contain high levels of protoporphyrin, which indicates that an effect of lead is to inhibit uptake of iron by protoporphyrin to form heme.

Effects of Chemical Substances on Induction of Porphyria

A characteristic feature of the porphyrias is the fact that a variety of drugs and other chemical substances may induce attacks of the disease. These include the following:

(1) Chemical agents that either bring about or enhance an attack of acute porphyria among patients with one of the inherited types of hepatic porphyria, ie, acute intermittent porphyria, porphyria variegata, or hereditary coproporphyria. Drugs included in this group are barbiturates, sulfonamides, griseofulvin, chloroquine, certain nonbarbiturate sedatives, and sex hormones.

(2) Chemicals found to cause an increase in excretion of porphyrins as well as clinical signs of photosensitivity. In this category, there is no evidence of a genetic predisposition to porphyria among these patients, so that the appearance of symptoms suggests that an induced metabolic defect has occurred; the clinical classification, therefore, is usually that of acquired or symptomatic cutaneous hepatic porphyria. Substances often implicated as causative agents include hexachlorobenzene, di- and trichlorophenols, phenobarbital, sulfonmethane, tolbutamide, chlorpropamide, estrogens, and alcohol.

(3) Chemicals which induce a moderate increase in porphyrins or their precursors but without clinical symptoms in normal individuals. Examples are griseofulvin and certain of the orally administered contraceptive agents.

CATABOLISM OF HEME; FORMATION OF BILE PIGMENTS

When hemoglobin is destroyed in the body, the protein portion, globin, may be reutilized, either as such or in the form of its constituent amino acids, and the iron enters the iron "pool"—also for reuse. However, the porphyrin portion, heme, is broken down in all likelihood mainly in the reticuloendothelial cells of the liver, spleen, and bone marrow (Fig 14–15). The initial step in the metabolic degradation of heme involves opening of the porphyrin ring between pyrrole residues I and II and elimination of the alpha methylene carbon as carbon monoxide (Fig 14–16). It is possible that the porphyrin ring may be opened and that the iron is still present before the protoporphyrin is released from the globin. Such a green, conjugated protein has been produced by oxidation of hemoglobin by oxygen in the presence of ascorbic acid. The prosthetic group of the protein is the iron complex of a

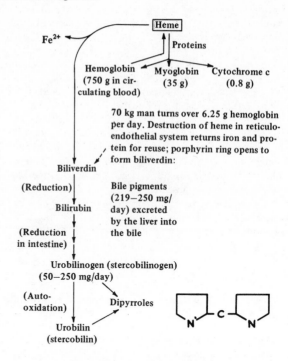

Figure 14–15. Catabolism of heme.

bile pigment resembling biliverdin. It has been called **choleglobin**.

After removal of iron and cleavage of the porphyrin ring of heme, as described above, **biliverdin**, the first of the bile pigments, is formed. Biliverdin is easily reduced to **bilirubin**, which is the major pigment in human bile. Biliverdin is the chief pigment of the bile in birds.

Normally, there are only slight traces of biliverdin in human bile, but the color of biliverdin is so much more intense than that of bilirubin that a relatively small amount, if present in the serum, is detectable even in the presence of a much larger amount of bilirubin. There is a report of a patient with so-called biliverdin jaundice in whom a definite green color was detected in the skin and in the serum when the serum biliverdin concentration was 3 mg/dl while that of bilirubin was 25 mg/dl. Watson (1969) states that biliverdin jaundice is largely limited to 2 conditions of which biliary obstruction as a result of carcinoma is the more common, the other being severe parenchymal liver disease, as in subacute atrophy or advanced cirrhosis of the liver. The amounts of biliverdin in the serum are very small in obstructive jaundice caused by the presence of a stone in the common bile duct; no biliverdin occurs in the serum in hemolytic jaundice.

Metabolism of Bile Pigments

The bile pigments originate in the reticuloendothelial cells of the liver, including the Kupffer cells, or in other reticuloendothelial cells wherein erythrocytes are destroyed. As indicated above, in the course of the destruction of erythrocytes, the protoporphyrin ring

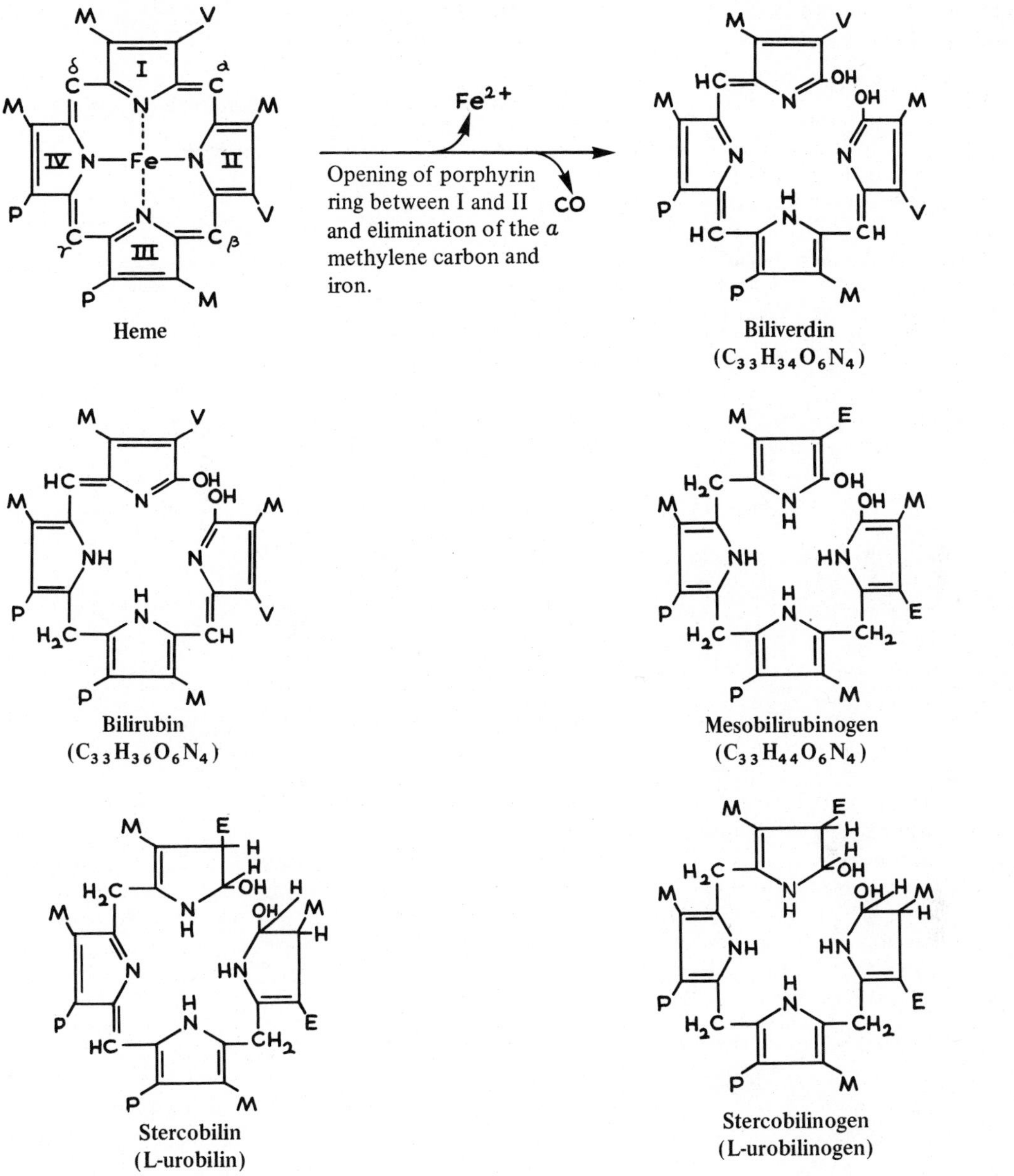

Heme

Opening of porphyrin ring between I and II and elimination of the a methylene carbon and iron.

Biliverdin
($C_{33}H_{34}O_6N_4$)

Bilirubin
($C_{33}H_{36}O_6N_4$)

Mesobilirubinogen
($C_{33}H_{44}O_6N_4$)

Stercobilin
(L-urobilin)

Stercobilinogen
(L-urobilinogen)

Figure 14—16. Structure of some bile pigments.

of heme derived from hemoglobin is opened to form the first bile pigment, biliverdin. This is reduced by the enzyme **bilirubin reductase** requiring also NADH or NADPH as cofactor.

Normally, 0.1–1.5 mg of bilirubin is present in 100 ml of human plasma. It is estimated that 1 g of hemoglobin yields 35 mg of bilirubin, which is carried in loose association with protein (mainly albumin) of the plasma. The protein-associated bilirubin is carried in the plasma to the liver, where it is conjugated with glucuronic acid (Fig 14–17). Bilirubin glucuronide is much more soluble in an aqueous medium than is the free (unconjugated) compound. For this reason, the bilirubin conjugate is readily excreted into the intes-

tine with the bile. The formation of conjugated bilirubin within the liver is apparently a necessary condition for its excretion in the bile. The bile pigments constitute 15–20% of the dry weight of human bile.

In the lower portions of the intestinal tract, especially the cecum and the colon, the bilirubin is released from the glucuronide conjugate and then subjected to the reductive action of enzyme systems present in the intestinal tract, mainly derived from anaerobic bacteria in the cecum. Fecal flora as well as a pure strain of a clostridium derived from the rat colon have been demonstrated (in vitro) to be able to complete the reduction of bilirubin to L-stercobilinogen, the normal end product of bilirubin metabolism in the colon. If

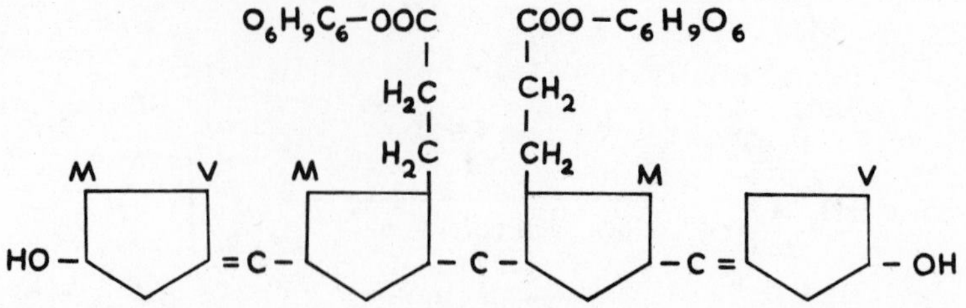

$$O_6H_9C_6-OOC \qquad COO-C_6H_9O_6$$

Figure 14—17. Structure of bilirubin diglucuronide (conjugated, "direct reacting" bilirubin). Glucuronic acid is attached to the 2 propionic acid groups to form an acylglucuronide.

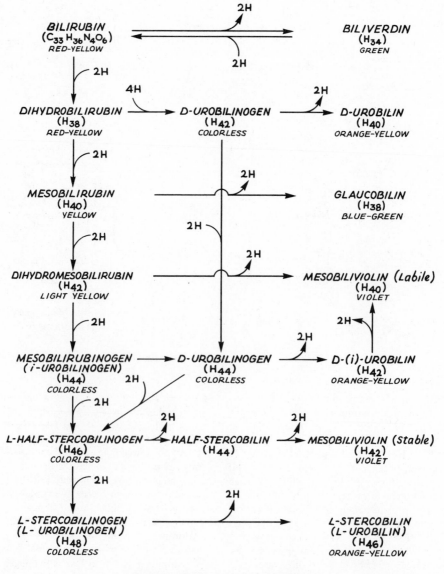

Figure 14—18. Formation of urobilinoids.

the intestinal flora is modified or diminished, as by the administration of orally effective antibiotic agents which are capable of producing partial sterilization of the intestinal tract, bilirubin may not be further reduced and may later be auto-oxidized, in contact with air, to biliverdin. Thus, the feces acquire a green tinge under these circumstances.

The metabolism of biliverdin and of bilirubin within the intestine is summarized in Fig 14–18 (Watson, 1969; Lightner & others, 1969). It will be noted that progressive hydrogenation occurs to produce a series of intermediary compounds which, beginning with mesobilirubinogen, comprise a number of colorless urobilinoids which may be oxidized, with loss of hydrogen, to colored compounds. The end product is colorless L-stercobilinogen (L-urobilinogen). Auto-oxidation in the presence of air produces stercobilin (L-urobilin), an orange-yellow pigment which contributes to the normal color of the feces. Stercobilin is strongly levorotatory ($[a_D]$ = 3600°).

Urobilin IX (D-[i]-urobilin, or inactive [i] urobilin), is an optically inactive urobilinoid that has been identified in the feces. It is less stable than stercobilin, becoming oxidized in air to form violet and blue-green pigments. In the feces of patients whose intestinal flora has been altered by oral administration of oxytetracycline or chlortetracycline, a dextrorotatory urobilinoid, D-urobilin ($[a_D]$ = +5000°), has been identified. It is believed to be derived from dihydrobilirubin by way of D-urobilinogen (Fig 14–18).

A portion of the urobilinogen produced in the colon is absorbed from the intestine into the blood. Some of this is excreted by the kidney and appears in the urine in amounts of 0–4 mg/day. The remainder of the absorbed urobilinogen is reexcreted in the bile.

The unabsorbed urobilinogen is excreted in the stool as fecal uroblinogen (40–280 mg/day). On exposure to oxygen, urobilinogen is oxidized to urobilin. This is the cause of the darkening of stools on exposure to air.

Summary of Porphyrin Metabolism

Types I and III uroporphyrinogens are synthesized from glycine and succinate precursors. By decarboxylation, these are converted to coproporphyrinogens. Both uroporphyrinogens and coproporphyrinogens are readily auto-oxidized to the corresponding uroporphyrins or coproporphyrins. The type I coproporphyrin is apparently a byproduct of the synthesis of heme protoporphyrin because the amount produced is proportionate to the production of hemoglobin. However, this pigment is useless and is excreted in the urine in amounts of 40–190 μg/day except under conditions of rapid hematopoiesis, as in hemolytic disease, where the daily urinary excretion of coproporphyrin I may exceed 200–400 μg/day. A somewhat larger amount of coproporphyrin is normally excreted in the feces: 300–1100 μg/day, 70–90% of which is coproporphyrin I.

Type III coproporphyrinogen is largely converted to protoporphyrin and then to heme, which conjugates with protein to form the hemoproteins: hemoglobin, myoglobin, cytochrome, etc. A small amount (20–90 μg/day) of type III coproporphyrin is normally excreted as such in the urine.

The excretion of uroporphyrins by normal subjects is negligible.

The breakdown of heme leads to the production of the bile pigments, so that the amount of bile pigment formed each day is closely related to the amount of hemoglobin created and destroyed. In hemoglobin, the porphyrin portion, exclusive of the iron, makes up 3.5% by weight of the hemoglobin molecule. Thus, 35 mg of bilirubin could be expected to appear for each gram of hemoglobin destroyed. It is estimated that in a 70 kg man about 6.25 g of hemoglobin are produced and destroyed each day (normal is 90 mg/kg/day). This means that about 219 mg of bilirubin (6.25 × 35) should be produced per day in this same individual. The bilirubin is excreted by the liver into the intestine by way of the bile and may be measured as fecal urobilinogen (stercobilinogen), to which it is converted by the action of the intestinal bacteria. However, 10–20% more than this estimated quantity actually appears each day as urobilinogen. This is most likely due to some porphyrin which is synthesized probably in the liver but never actually incorporated into red cells (early urobilinogen), as well as porphyrin derived from the catabolism of hemoproteins other than hemoglobin. Total daily bile pigment production is therefore close to 250 mg, but not all of this is recovered as urobilinogens because some of the urobilinogen is broken down by bacterial action to dipyrroles, which do not yield a color with the Ehrlich reagent used to measure urobilinogen. Fig 14–15 summarizes the catabolism of heme and the formation of bile pigments.

Jaundice

When bile pigment in the blood is excessive, it escapes into the tissues, which then become yellow. This condition is known as jaundice or icterus.

Jaundice may be due to the production of more bile pigment than the normal liver can excrete, or it may result from the failure of a damaged liver to excrete the bilirubin produced in normal amounts. In the absence of hepatic damage, obstruction of the excretory ducts of the liver by preventing the excretion of bilirubin will also cause jaundice. In all of these situations, bile pigment accumulates in the blood, and when it reaches a certain concentration, it diffuses into the tissues. Jaundice is frequently due to a combination of factors.

According to its mode of production, jaundice is sometimes subdivided into 3 main groups: hemolytic, hepatic, or obstructive.

A. Hemolytic Jaundice: Conditions which increase erythrocyte destruction also increase the formation of bile pigment. If erythrocytes are destroyed faster than their products, including bilirubin, can be excreted by the liver, the concentration of bilirubin in the serum rises above normal; hemolytic jaundice is the result.

B. Hepatic Jaundice: This type of jaundice is caused by liver dysfunction resulting from damage to the parenchymal cells. Examples are the jaundice caused by various liver poisons (chloroform, phosphorus, arsphenamine, carbon tetrachloride), toxins, hepatitis virus, engorgement of hepatic vessels in cardiac failure, and cirrhosis.

C. Obstructive (Regurgitation) Jaundice: This condition results from blockage of the hepatic or common bile ducts. The bile pigment is believed to pass from the blood into the liver cells as usual; however, failing to be excreted by the bile capillaries, it is absorbed into the hepatic veins and lymphatics.

The term "cholestatic" jaundice may be used to include all forms of extrahepatic obstructive jaundice in addition to some forms of parenchymal jaundice. The chemical findings in this type resemble those observed in the purely obstructive types of jaundice.

Constitutional Nonhemolytic Hyperbilirubinemia

In addition to the occurrence of elevated levels of bilirubin in the serum as a result of the various pathologic states described above, hyperbilirubinemia has been detected in individuals who are otherwise free of any aymptoms of hepatic disease or of hemolysis as a cause of hyperbilirubinemia. The abnormality is familial and is therefore believed to be genetically transmitted (Gilbert, 1902; Baroody, 1956). An impairment of excretion of bilirubin has been suggested as the cause of this syndrome, and the results of the bilirubin tolerance test (see below) in these subjects support this suggestion. The increased serum bilirubin is entirely of the indirect-reacting type (ie, unconjugated bilirubin; see below). This could be the result of excessive red blood cell destruction, ie, a hemolytic jaundice; but, as noted above, the metabolism of the red cells is not abnormal. An alternate explanation is that hyperbilirubinemic subjects have an impaired ability to conjugate bilirubin and thus to excrete it in the bile. This latter explanation has proved to be correct, the defect having been found to reside in an impairment in the mechanism for conjugation of bilirubin due to reduced activity of the hepatic enzyme, **glucuronyl transferase,** which catalyzes the transfer of the glucuronide moiety from uridine diphosphoglucuronic acid (UDPGlcUA) to bilirubin (Arias, 1957). Because the bile of an individual with constitutional nonhemolytic hyperbilirubinemia does contain some direct-reacting bilirubin, it must be assumed that the conjugative defect is not complete. However, there are also reports of rare instances of what appears to be a complete absence of conjugation of bilirubin. These individuals develop a very intense jaundice (serum bilirubin as high as 80 mg/dl). In one such case the bile contained no bilirubin ("white" bile), and there was also complete inability to form glucuronide conjugates with substances such as menthol and tetrahydrocortisone that are normally excreted in the urine as glucuronides. This defect resembles that which has also been found in a mutant strain of rats wherein there seems to be a complete absence of the mechanism for detoxification

by conjugation with glucuronic acid (Carbone, 1957). It is possible that the mild disease in humans (so-called Gilbert's disease) represents the "trait" or heterozygous form of inheritance of the genetic defect and that the severe form represents the homozygous inheritance of the defect.

The occurrence of some degree of jaundice in the newborn (icterus neonatorum) is not infrequent. Ordinarily, bilirubin levels in the serum rise of the first day of life to reach a maximum on the third or fourth day, after which a rapid decline to normal occurs. The maximum concentration of bilirubin in the serum rarely exceeds 10 mg/dl except in premature infants, in whom this so-called physiologic icterus may be more intense and more prolonged than in normal term infants. The phenomenon of icterus neonatorum is considered to be simply a reflection of immaturity ascribable to temporary inadequacy of the hepatic system for conjugating bilrubin. If, however, hemolysis (as in Rh incompatibility) occurs during this period of decreased ability to excrete bilirubin, it is likely that very high levels of bilirubin will be found in the serum. As a result bilirubin may accumulate in the tissues, producing a generalized jaundice. In the brain, the localized deep pigmentation of basal ganglia which occurs is termed "kernicterus." Such "brain jaundice" is associated with objective signs of disturbances in nervous system function, and permanent damage to the CNS will occur if death does not supervene.

Prolonged hyperbilirubinemia in the neonatal period has also been reported by Newman & Gross (1963) in a series of cases which appeared to be associated with breast feeding of the affected infants. Only the unconjugated ("indirect") bilirubin was elevated (as high as 8–19 mg/dl on the third to fifth days of life). All of the infants were in otherwise normal health, and there was no evidence of blood group incompatibility or a hemolytic process to account for the elevated indirect bilirubin. Although the bilirubin gradually declined during the first month of life, the rate of decline was much slower than normal unless breast feeding was discontinued in favor of feeding with cow's milk, when the elevated bilirubin levels promptly declined to normal. It was concluded that the hyperbilirubinemia in these infants was in some way related to breast feeding. Earlier it had been shown that serum from pregnant women and newborn infants exerted an inhibitory effect on bilirubin conjugation in rat liver slices and that the inhibitory substance in the serum was pregnanediol. This steroid hormone in quantities as high as 1 mg/day has been identified in the breast milk of mothers whose infants exhibited hyperbilirubinemia. In cow's milk the hormone cannot be detected. It should be emphasized that these effects of pregnanediol in breast milk were observed only in the very young infant at a time when the bilirubin conjugating system may not yet be fully developed.

Estimation of Bilirubin in Serum; the Van den Bergh Test

In clinical studies of liver dysfunction, measurement of bilirubin in the serum is of great value. A method for quantitatively assaying the bilirubin content of the serum was first devised by Van den Bergh by application of Ehrlich's test for bilirubin in urine. The Ehrlich reaction is based on the coupling of diazotized sulfanilic acid (Ehrlich's diazo reagent) and bilirubin to produce a reddish-purple azo compound. In the original procedure as described by Ehrlich, alcohol was used to provide a solution in which both bilirubin and the diazo reagent were soluble. Van den Bergh inadvertently ommitted the alcohol on an occasion when assay of bile pigment in human bile was being attempted. To his surprise, normal development of the color occurred "directly." This form of bilirubin which would react without the addition of alcohol was thus termed "direct-reacting." It was then found that this same direct reaction would also occur in serum for cases of jaundice due to obstruction. However, it was still necessary to add alcohol to detect bilirubin in normal serum or that which was present in excess in serum from cases of hemolytic jaundice where no evidence of obstruction was to be found. To that form of bilirubin which could be measured only after the addition of alcohol, the term "indirect-reacting" was applied.

In the years intervening since Van den Bergh first described the 2 types of bilirubin, a number of theories have been proposed in an attempt to explain the chemical and clinical significance of his observations. It has now been demonstrated that the indirect bilirubin is "free" (unconjugated) bilirubin en route to the liver from the reticuloendothelial tissues where the bilirubin was originally produced by the breakdown of heme porphyrins. Since this bilirubin is not water-soluble, it requires extraction into alcohol to initiate coupling with the diazo reagent. In the liver, the free bilirubin becomes conjugated with glucuronic acid, and the conjugate, bilirubin glucuronide, can then be excreted into the bile. Furthermore, conjugated bilirubin, being water-soluble, can react directly with the diazo reagent so that the "direct bilirubin" of Van den Bergh is actually a bilirubin conjugate (bilirubin glucuronide). In jaundice due to obstruction (regurgitation jaundice), the conjugated bilirubin may return to the blood, which accounts for the presence of direct as well as indirect bilirubin in such cases. In hemolytic jaundice there is no obstruction and the increase in bilirubin is confined to the indirect type, since the cause of the bilirubinemia is increased production and not an abnormality in hapatic conjugation or excretion.

When bilirubin appears in the urine, it is almost entirely of the direct type. It is thus probable that bilirubin is excreted into the urine only when conjugated and so made water-soluble. It also follows that bilirubinuria will be expected to occur only when there is an increase in the direct bilirubin content of the serum.

"Direct-reacting" bilirubin is a diglucuronide of bilirubin in which the 2 glucuronyl groups transferred from "active" glucuronide—ie, uridine diphosphoglucuronic acid (GlcUA)—by the catalytic action of glucu-

ronyl transferase are attached through ester linkages to the propionic acid carboxyl groups of bilirubin to form an acyl glucuronide. In the conjugation reaction, the monoglucuronide is formed first; this is followed by attachment of a second glucuronyl group to form the diglucuronide. Some monoglucuronide is normally found in the bile, but in hepatic disease, because of impairment of the conjugating mechanism, greater quantities of the monoglucuronide may be formed. Because the monoglucuronide does not react as rapidly with the Van den Bergh reagent as does the diglucuronide, it is possible that the so-called "delayed direct-reacting" bilirubin may reflect the presence of the monoglucuronide.

The determination of serum bilirubin is frequently carried out by the colorimetric method of Malloy and Evelyn as modified by Ducci and Watson. In this method, the color developed within 1 minute after addition of diluted serum (usually 1:10 with distilled water) to the diazo reagent is a measure of the "direct" bilirubin. This is therefore referred to as the "1-minute bilirubin." Another sample of diluted serum is then added to the mixture of the diazo reagent and methyl alcohol and the color developed after 30 minutes is measured. This "30-minute bilirubin" represents the total bilirubin content of the serum, ie, both conjugated (direct) and unconjugated (indirect). The indirect bilirubin concentration is then obtained simply as the difference between the 1-minute and the 30-minute readings. In summary:

> Total serum bilirubin = 30-minute bilirubin
> Direct (conjugated) bilirubin = 1-minute bilirubin
> Indirect (unconjugated) bilirubin =
>   30-minute minus 1-minute bilirubin

The normal concentrations of these various fractions of the serum bilirubin are given by Watson as follows:

	(mg/dl)		
	Total	**Direct**	**Indirect**
Mean	0.62 ± 0.25	0.11 ± 0.05	0.51 ± 0.20
Upper limit of normal	1.50	0.25	1.25

A quantitative measurement of the total serum bilirubin is of considerable value in the detection of latent jaundice, which is represented by concentrations between 1.5–2 mg/dl. Hyperbilirubinemia may be noted not only in diseases of the liver or biliary tract but also in disease states involving hemolysis such as occurs in infectious diseases, pernicious anemia, or hemorrhage.

The progress of a case of manifest jaundice may be followed by repeated serum bilirubin determinations. A rising concentration is an unfavorable sign; a progressive decline in serum bilirubin signifies improvement of liver disease or biliary obstructions.

Fecal Urobilinogen & Urobilin

Fecal urobilinogen usually varies directly with the rate of breakdown of red blood cells since it is derived from heme. It is therefore increased in hemolytic jaundice provided the quantity of hemoglobin available is normal. A decrease in fecal urobilinogen occurs in obstruction of the biliary tract or in extreme cases of diseases affecting the hepatic parenchyma. It is unusual to find a complete absence of fecal urobilinogen. When it does occur, a malignant obstructive disease is strongly suggested. The normal quantity of urobilinogen excreted in the feces per day is from 50–280 mg. Fecal urobilinogen is determined by conversion of urobilin into urobilinogen and determination of urobilinogen by methods similar to those used in the urine analyses (see below).

Test for Bilirubin in the Urine

The presence of bilirubin in the urine suggests that the direct bilirubin concentration of the blood is elevated due to hepatic parenchymatous or duct disease. Bilirubin in the urine may be detected even before clinical levels of jaundice are noted. Usually only direct-reacting bilirubin is found in the urine. The finding of bilirubin in the urine will therefore accompany a direct Van den Bergh reaction in blood (see above).

Urine Urobilinogen

Normally, there are mere traces of urobilinogen in the urine (average, 0.64 mg; maximum normal, 4 mg [in 24 hours]). In complete obstruction of the bile duct, no urobilinogen is found in the urine since biliru-

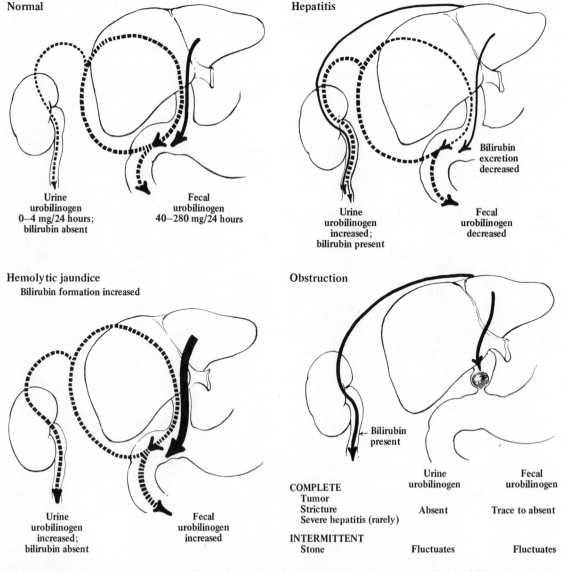

Figure 14–19. Bilirubin-urobilinogen cycle. (Solid arrows = bilirubin glucuronide; dotted arrows = urobilinogen.) (Reproduced, with permission, from Krupp MA & others: *Physician's Handbook*, 18th ed. Lange, 1976.)

bin is unable to get to the intestine to form it. In this case, the presence of bilirubin in the urine without urobilinogen suggests obstructive jaundice, either intrahepatic or posthepatic. In hemolytic jaundice, the increased production of bilirubin leads to increased production of urobilinogen, which appears in the urine in large amounts. Bilirubin is not usually found in the urine in hemolytic jaundice, so that the combination of increased urobilinogen and absence of bilirubin is suggestive of hemolytic jaundice. Increased blood destruction from any cause (eg, pernicious anemia) will, of course, also bring about an increase in urine urobilinogen. Furthermore, infection of the biliary passages may increase the urobilinogen in the absence of any reduction in liver function because of the reducing activity of the infecting bacteria.

Urine urobilinogen may also be increased in damage to the hepatic parenchyma because of inability of the liver to reexcrete into the stool by way of the bile the urobilinogen absorbed from the intestine.

The diagrams in Fig 14–19 summarize the events characterizing the handling of bilirubin and urobilinogen by the liver, intestine, and kidney under normal circumstances and in the presence of hemolytic jaundice, hepatitis, or jaundice associated with obstruction of the bile duct. A discussion of the types of jaundice occurs in the preceding text.

● ● ●

References

Arias IM, London IM: Science 126:563, 1957.

Baroody WG, Shugart RT: Am J Med 20:314, 1956.

Carbone JV, Grodsky GM: Proc Soc Exp Biol Med 94:461, 1957.

Dobriner K, Rhoads CP: Physiol Rev 20:416, 1940.

Gilbert A, Lereboullet P: Gas. hebd. d. sc. med. de Bordeaux 49:889, 1902.

Granick S: J Biol Chem 238:2247, 1963.

Granick S: J Biol Chem 241:1359, 1966.

Lightner DA, Moscowitz A, Petryka ZJ, Jones S, Weimer M, Davis E, Beach NA, Watson CJ: Arch Biochem 131:566, 1969.

Matsuhara H, Smith EL: J Biol Chem 238:2732, 1963.

Meyer UA, Schmid R: Fed Proc 32:1649, 1973.

Meyer UA, Strand LJ, Doss M, Rees AC, Marver HS: N Engl J Med 286:1277, 1972.

Newman AJ, Gross S: Pediatrics 32:995, 1963.

Petryka ZJ, Watson CJ: J Chromatogr 37:76, 1968.

Schmid R: N Engl J Med 263:397, 1960.

Schulman MP, Richert DA: J Biol Chem 226:181, 1957.

Tschudy DP, Perlroth MG, Marver HS, Collins A, Hunter G Jr: Proc Natl Acad Sci USA 53:841, 1965.

Watson CJ: Ann Intern Med 70:839, 1969.

Watson CJ, Berg MH, Hawkinson VE, Bossenmaier I: Clin Chem 6:71, 1960.

Watson CJ, Larson EA: Physiol Rev 27:478, 1947.

Bibliography

Eales L, Grosser Y, Sears WG: The clinical biochemistry of the human hepatocutaneous porphyrias in the light of recent studies of newly identified intermediates and porphyrin derivatives. Ann NY Acad Sci 244:441, 1975.

Goldberg A, Rimington C: *Diseases of Porphyrin Metabolism.* Thomas, 1962.

Lemberg R, Legge JW: *Hematin Compounds and Bile Pigments.* Interscience, 1949.

Rimington C: Haem pigments and porphyrins. Annu Rev Biochem 26:561, 1957.

Schmid R: The porphyrias. In: *The Metabolic Basis of Inherited Disease,* 3rd ed. Stanbury JB, Wyngaarden JB, Fredrickson DS (editors). McGraw-Hill, 1972.

Symposium: Porphyrin Biosynthesis and Metabolism. Ciba Foundation. Little, Brown, 1954.

15 . . .
Digestion & Absorption From the Gastrointestinal Tract

Most foodstuffs are ingested in forms which are unavailable to the organism, since they cannot be absorbed from the digestive tract until they have been broken down into smaller molecules. This disintegration of the naturally occurring foodstuffs into assimilable forms constitutes the process of digestion.

The chemical changes incident to digestion are accomplished with the aid of the enzymes of the digestive tract. These enzymes catalyze the hydrolysis of native proteins to amino acids, of starches to monosaccharides, and of fats to monoacylglycerols, glycerol, and fatty acids. It is probable that, in the course of these digestive reactions, the minerals and vitamins of the foodstuffs are also made more assimilable. This is certainly true of the lipid-soluble vitamins, which are not absorbed unless fat digestion is proceeding normally.

DIGESTION IN THE MOUTH

Constituents of the Saliva

The oral cavity contains saliva secreted by 3 pairs of salivary glands: parotid, submaxillary, and sublingual. The saliva consists of about 99.5% water, although the content varies with the nature of the factors exciting its secretion. The saliva acts as a lubricant for the oral cavity, and by moistening the food as it is chewed it reduces the dry food to a semisolid mass which is easily swallowed. The saliva is also a vehicle for the excretion of certain drugs (eg, alcohol and morphine) and of certain inorganic ions such as K^+, Ca^{2+}, HCO_3^-, iodine, and thiocyanate (SCN^-).

The pH of the saliva is usually slightly on the acid side, about 6.8, although it may vary on either side of neutrality.

Salivary Digestion

Saliva contains a starch-splitting enzyme, **salivary amylase (ptyalin)**. Although saliva is capable of bringing about the hydrolysis of starch and glycogen to maltose, this is of little significance in the body because of the short time it can act on the food. Salivary amylase is readily inactivated at pH 4.0 or less, so that digestive action on food in the mouth will soon cease in the acid environment of the stomach. Furthermore, other amylases, eg, pancreatic amylase, are capable of

accomplishing complete starch digestion. In many animals, a salivary amylase is entirely absent.

DIGESTION IN THE STOMACH

Stimulation of Gastric Secretion

Gastric secretion is initiated by nervous or reflex mechanisms. The effective stimuli for these reflexes are similar to those which operate in salivary secretion. The continued secretion of gastric juice is, however, due to a hormonal stimulus, **gastrin** (gastric secretin). This chemical stimulant is produced by the gastric glands and absorbed into the blood, which carries it back to the stomach where it excites gastric secretion. Histamine, produced by decarboxylation of the amino acid histidine, also acts as a potent gastric secretagogue.

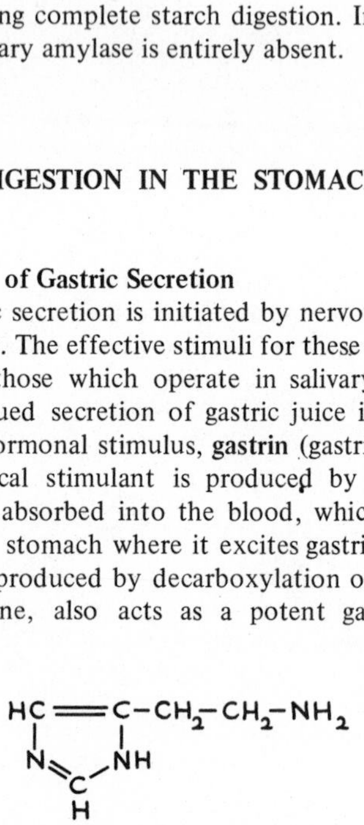

$$HC = C-CH_2-CH_2-NH_2$$

Figure 15—1. Histamine.

Gastric Constituents & Gastric Digestion

In the mucosa of the stomach wall, 2 types of secretory glands are found: those exhibiting a single layer of secreting cells (the chief cells), and those with cells arranged in layers (the parietal cells), which secrete directly into the gastric glands. The mixed secretion is known as gastric juice. It is normally a clear, pale yellow fluid of high acidity, 0.2—0.5% HCl, with a pH of about 1.0.

A. Hydrochloric Acid: The parietal cells are the sole source of gastric hydrochloric acid. HCl is said to originate according to the reactions shown in Fig 15—2.

The process is essentially similar to that of the "chloride shift" described for the red blood cell on p 591. There is also a resemblance to the renal tubular mechanisms for secretion of H^+, wherein the source of H^+ is also the carbonic anhydrase catalyzed formation

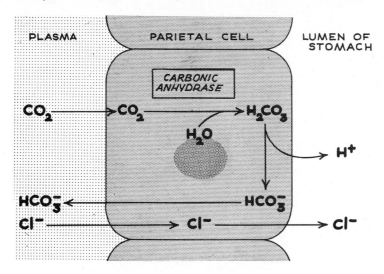

Figure 15—2. Production of gastric hydrochloric acid.

of H_2CO_3 from H_2O and CO_2.

An alkaline urine often follows the ingestion of a meal ("alkaline tide"), presumably as a result of the formation of extra bicarbonate in the process of hydrochloric acid secretion by the stomach in accordance with the reaction shown in Fig 15—2.

The gastric juice is 97—99% water. The remainder consists of mucin and inorganic salts, the digestive enzymes (pepsin and rennin), and a lipase.

B. Pepsin: The chief digestive function of the stomach is the partial digestion of protein. Gastric pepsin is produced in the chief cells as the inactive zymogen, **pepsinogen,** which is activated to pepsin by the action of HCl and, autocatalytically, by itself, ie, a small amount of pepsin can cause the activation of the remaining pepsinogen. The enzyme transforms native protein into proteoses and peptones which are still reasonably large protein derivatives.

C. Rennin (Chymosin, Rennet): The enzyme causes the coagulation of milk. This is important in the digestive processes of infants because it prevents the rapid passage of milk from the stomach. In the presence of calcium, rennin changes irreversibly the casein of milk to a paracasein which is then acted on by pepsin. This enzyme is said to be absent from the stomach of adults.

D. Lipase: The lipolytic action of gastric juice is not important, although a gastric lipase capable of mild fat-splitting action is found in gastric juice.

PANCREATIC & INTESTINAL DIGESTION

The stomach contents, or **chyme,** which are of a thick creamy consistency, are intermittently introduced during digestion into the duodenum through the pyloric valve. The pancreatic and bile ducts open into the duodenum at a point very close to the pylorus. The high alkaline content of pancreatic and biliary secretions neutralizes the acid of the chyme and changes the pH of this material to the alkaline side; this shift of pH is necessary for the activity of the enzymes contained in pancreatic and intestinal juice.

Stimulation of Pancreatic Secretion

Like the stomach, the pancreas secretes its digestive juice almost entirely by means of hormonal stimulation. The hormones are secreted into the blood by the duodenum and upper jejunum as a result of stimulation by hydrochloric acid, fats, proteins, carbohydrates, and partially digested foodstuffs. They are carried by the blood to the pancreas, liver, and gallbladder after absorption from the small intestine through the hepatic portal vein. The active hormonal components formed by the duodenum (originally termed "secretin" by Bayliss and Starling) have now been separated into several separate factors: (1) **secretin,** which stimulates the production by the pancreas of a thin, watery fluid, high in bicarbonate but low in enzyme content; (2) **pancreozymin,** stimulating the production by the pancreas of a viscous fluid low in bicarbonate but high in enzyme content; (3) **cholecystokinin,** which induces contraction and emptying of the gallbladder; and (4) **enterocrinin,** which induces the flow of intestinal juice.

Constituents of Pancreatic Secretion

Pancreatic juice is a nonviscid watery fluid which is similar to saliva in its content of water and contains some protein and other organic and inorganic compounds, mainly Na^+, K^+, HCO_3^-, and Cl^-. Ca^{2+}, Zn^{2+}, $HPO_4{}^{2-}$, and $SO_4{}^{2-}$ are present in small amounts. The pH of pancreatic juice is distinctly alkaline, 7.5—8.0 or higher.

The enzymes contained in pancreatic juice include trypsin, chymotrypsin, and carboxypeptidases,

Table 15–1. Summary of digestive process.

Source of Secretion and Stimulus for Secretion	Enzyme	Method of Activation and Optimal Conditions for Activity	Substrate	End Products or Action
Salivary glands of mouth: Secrete saliva in reflex response to presence of food in mouth.	Salivary amylase	Chloride ion necessary. pH 6.6–6.8.	Starch Glycogen	Maltose plus 1:6 glucosides (oligosaccharides) plus maltotriose.
Stomach glands: Chief cells and parietal cells secrete gastric juice in response to reflex stimulation and chemical action of gastrin.	Pepsin	Pepsinogen converted to active pepsin by HCl. pH 1.0–2.0.	Protein	Proteoses Peptones
	Renin	Calcium necessary for activity. pH 4.0.	Casein of milk	Coagulates milk
Pancreas: Presence of acid chyme from the stomach activates duodenum to produce (1) secretin, which hormonally stimulates flow of pancreatic juice; (2) pancreozymin, which stimulates the production of enzymes.	Trypsin	Trypsinogen converted to active trypsin by enterokinase of intestine at pH 5.2–6.0. Autocatalytic at pH 7.9.	Protein Proteoses Peptones	Polypeptides Dipeptides
	Chymotrypsin	Secreted as chymotrypsinogen and converted to active form by trypsin. pH 8.0.	Protein Proteoses Peptones	Same as trypsin. More coagulating power for milk.
	Carboxypeptidase	Secreted as procarboxypeptidase activated by trypsin.	Polypeptides at the free carboxyl end of the chain	Lower peptides. Free amino acids.
	Pancreatic amylase	pH 7.1	Starch Glycogen	Maltose plus 1:6 glucosides (oligosaccharides) plus maltotriose.
	Lipase	Activated by bile salts? pH 8.0.	Primary ester linkages of fats	Fatty acids, monoacylglycerols, diacylglycerols, glycerol
	Ribonuclease		Ribonucleic acid	Nucleotides
	Deoxyribonuclease		Deoxyribonucleic acids	Nucleotides
	Cholesteryl ester hydrolase	Activated by bile salts.	Cholesteryl esters	Free cholesterol plus fatty acids.
Liver and gallbladder	Bile salts and alkali	Cholecystokinin, a hormone from the intestinal mucosa—and possibly also gastrin and secretin—stimulate the gallbladder and secretion of bile by the liver.	Fats—also neutralize acid chyme	Fatty acid-bile salt conjugates and finely emulsified neutral fat—bile salt micelles
Small intestine: Secretions of Brunner's glands of the duodenum and glands of Lieberkühn.	Aminopeptidase		Polypeptides at the free amino end of the chain	Lower peptides. Free amino acids.
	Dipeptidases		Dipeptides	Amino acids
	Sucrase	pH 5.0–7.0	Sucrose	Fructose, glucose
	Maltase	pH 5.8–6.2	Maltose	Glucose
	Lactase	pH 5.4–6.0	Lactose	Glucose, galactose
	Phosphatase	pH 8.6	Organic phosphates	Free phosphate
	Isomaltase or 1:6 glucosidase		1:6 glucosides	Glucose
	Polynucleotidase		Nucleic acid	Nucleotides
	Nucleosidases		Purine or pyrimidine nucleosides	Purine or pyrimidine bases, pentose phosphate
	Phospholipase		Phospholipids	Glycerol, fatty acids, phosphoric acid, choline, or other bases

alpha-amylase, lipase, phospholipase A, cholesteryl ester hydrolase, ribonuclease, deoxyribonuclease, and collagenase. Some of these enzymes are secreted as inactive precursors (zymogens) such as trypsinogen or chymotrypsinogen, but are activated on contact with the intestinal mucosa. The activation of trypsinogen is attributed to **enterokinase,** which is produced by the intestinal glands. A small amount of active trypsin then autocatalytically activates additional trypsinogen and chymotrypsinogen.

A. Trypsin and Chymotrypsin: The protein-splitting action of pancreatic juice (proteolytic action) is due to trypsin and chymotrypsin, which attack native protein, proteoses, and peptones from the stomach to produce polypeptides. Chymotrypsin has more coagulative power for milk than trypsin, and, as previously noted, it is activated not by enterokinase but by active trypsin.

B. The "Peptidases": The further attack on protein breakdown products, ie, on the polypeptides, is accomplished by the following:

1. Carboxypeptidase—Carboxypeptidase is a zinc-containing enzyme of the pancreatic juice. It is an exopeptidase hydrolyzing the terminal peptide bond at the carboxyl end of the polypeptide chain.

2. Aminopeptidase and dipeptidase—The amino-peptidase attacks the terminal peptide bond at the free amino end of the chain. This system of intestinal proteases converts food proteins into their constituent amino acids for absorption by the intestinal mucosa and transfer to the circulation.

C. Amylase: The starch-splitting action of pancreatic juice is due to a pancreatic alpha-amylase. It is similar in action to salivary amylase, hydrolyzing starch and glycogen to maltose, maltotriose, and a mixture of branched (1:6) oligosaccharides and some glucose.

D. Lipase: Fats are hydrolyzed by a pancreatic lipase to fatty acids, glycerol, monoacylglycerols, and diacylglycerols. This is an important enzyme in digestion. Pancreatic lipase is specific for the hydrolysis of primary ester linkages such as occur in positions 1 and 3 of a triacylglycerol.

E. Cholesteryl Ester Hydrolase (Cholesterol Esterase): This enzyme may either catalyze the esterification of free cholesterol with fatty acids or, depending upon the conditions of equilibrium, it may catalyze the opposite reaction, ie, hydrolysis of cholesteryl esters. According to Goodman, under the conditions existing within the lumen of the intestine, the enzyme catalyzes the hydrolysis of cholesteryl esters, which are thus absorbed from the intestine in a nonesterified, free form.

F. Ribonuclease (RNase) and deoxyribonuclease (DNase) have been prepared from pancreatic tissue (see Chapter 25).

Constituents of Intestinal Secretions

The intestinal juice secreted by the glands of Brunner and of Lieberkühn under the influence of enterocrinin (see p 203) also contains digestive enzymes, including the following:

(1) Aminopeptidase and dipeptidase.

(2) The specific disaccharidases, ie, sucrase, maltase (including an isomaltase for splitting 1:6 glycosidic linkages), and lactase, which convert sucrose, maltose, or lactose, respectively, into their constituent monosaccharides for absorption.

(3) A phosphatase, which removes phosphate from certain organic phosphates such as hexosephosphates, glycerophosphate, and the nucleotides (a nucleotidase) derived from the diet.

(4) Polynucleotidases (nucleinases, phosphodiesterases), which split nucleic acids into nucleotides.

(5) Nucleosidases (nucleoside phosphorylases), one of which attacks only purine-containing nucleosides, liberating adenine or guanine and the pentose sugar which is simultaneously phosphorylated. The pyrimidine nucleosides (uridine, cytidine, and thymidine) are broken down by another enzyme which differs from the purine nucleosidase.

(6) The intestinal juice is also said to contain a phospholipase which attacks phospholipids to produce glycerol, fatty acids, phosphoric acid, and bases such as choline.

The Major Products of Digestion

The final result of the action of the digestive enzymes already described is to reduce the foodstuffs of the diet to forms which can be absorbed and assimilated. These end products of digestion are, for carbohydrates, the monosaccharides (principally glucose); for proteins, the amino acids; and for triacylglycerol, the fatty acids, glycerol, and monoacylglycerols.

Gastrointestinal Hormones

The gastrointestinal tract is not ordinarily considered as a source of hormones, although the total mass of endocrine cells in that organ exceeds that of all the other endocrine tissues. The gastrointestinal endocrine cells are distributed among the mucosal epithelial cells of the stomach and small intestine. For further discussion, see p 512.

THE BILE

In addition to many functions in intermediary metabolism, the liver, by producing bile, plays an important role in digestion. The gallbladder, a saccular organ attached to the hepatic duct, stores a certain amount of the bile produced by the liver between meals. During digestion, the gallbladder contracts and supplies bile rapidly to the small intestine by way of the common bile duct. The pancreatic secretions mix with the bile, since they empty into the common duct shortly before its entry into the duodenum.

Composition of Bile

The composition of hepatic bile differs from that

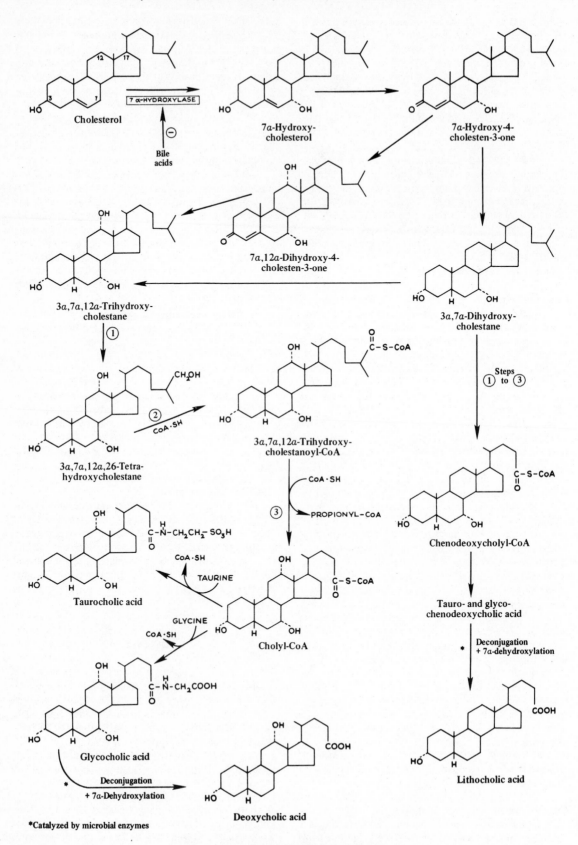

Figure 15—3. Biosynthesis and degradation of bile acids.

Table 15–2. The composition of hepatic and of gallbladder bile.

	Hepatic Bile (as secreted)		Bladder Bile
	Percent of Total Bile	Percent of Total Solids	Percent of Total Bile
Water	97.00	...	85.92
Solids	2.52	...	14.08
Bile acids	1.93	36.9	9.14
Mucin and pigments	0.53	21.3	2.98
Cholesterol	0.06	2.4	0.26
Fatty acids and fat	0.14	5.6	0.32
Inorganic salts	0.84	33.3	0.65
Specific gravity	1.01	...	1.04
pH	7.1–7.3	...	6.9–7.7

of gallbladder bile. As shown in Table 15–2, the latter is more concentrated.

Stimulation of Gallbladder & Bile Formation

Contraction of the gallbladder and relaxation of its sphincter are initiated by a hormonal mechanism. The hormone **cholecystokinin** (see Table 15–1) is secreted by the intestine in response to the presence of foods, mainly meats and fats. Bile salts act as stimulants to bile flow (**cholagogues**).

Bile Acids

The primary bile acids in human bile are cholic acid and chenodeoxycholic acid. These important compounds are synthesized in the liver from cholesterol by several intermediate steps (Danielsson & Sjövall, 1975). Cholic acid is the bile acid found in the largest amount in the bile itself. Both cholic acid and chenodeoxycholic acid are formed from a common precursor, itself derived from cholesterol (Fig 15–3).

The 7a-hydroxylation of cholesterol is the first committed step in the biosynthesis of bile acids, and it is probably this reaction that is rate-limiting in the pathway for synthesis of bile acids. The a-hydroxylation reaction is catalyzed by a microsomal system; it requires oxygen and NADPH, and it is partially inhibited by carbon monoxide. This system appears similar to that for the mono-oxygenases previously described in connection with hydroxylation of steroids and of certain drugs. It appears that cytochrome P-450 is a component of the system, as it is for the 12a- and 26-hydroxylation steps. Although pretreatment of experimental animals (rats) with phenobarbital sodium stimulates 7a-hydroxylation, this is not so with all strains of rats. This effect of phenobarbital on the oxygenase system has been observed in many other cytochrome P-450 catalyzed hydroxylation reactions using molecular oxygen, catalyzed by hydroxylases of the mixed function type.

Under normal circumstances in man, bile acids are synthesized by the liver at the relatively low rate of 200–500 mg/day. This rate is regulated to just replace the daily loss of bile acids in the feces. The bile acids may be thought of as the end products of cholesterol

catabolism in the body. These compounds, together with cholesterol itself, which is also present in the bile, represent the only significant route for elimination of cholesterol from the body. Because the tissues cannot break down the steroid nucleus, it must be converted to various steroid derivatives that can be eliminated as such. Measurement of the output of bile acids is therefore the most accurate way to estimate the amount of cholesterol lost from the body.

The bile acids normally enter the bile as glycine or taurine conjugates. The newly synthesized primary bile acids are considered to exist within the liver cell as esters of CoA, ie, cholyl- or chenodeoxycholyl-CoA (Fig 15–3). The CoA derivatives are formed with the aid of an activating enzyme occurring in the microsomes of the liver. A second enzyme catalyzes conjugation of the activated bile acids (the CoA derivatives) with glycine or taurine to form glycocholic or glycochenodeoxycholic and taurocholic or taurochenodeoxycholic acids. In man, the ratio of the glycine to the taurine conjugates is normally 3:1.

In the human, after storage and concentration in the gallbladder, the bile acids are transported to the small intestine in the bile when it is stimulated to flow by the ingestion of a meal, or by the hormone cholecystokinin. Since bile contains significant quantities of alkali cations (principally sodium and potassium) and the pH is alkaline, it is assumed that the bile acids and their conjugates are actually in a salt form—hence the term "bile salts," often used to describe these compounds in the bile. As will be discussed later, the bile acids play a very important role in fat digestion and absorption.

The Enterohepatic Circulation

A portion of the bile acids in the intestine may be subjected to some further changes by the activity of the intestinal bacteria. These include deconjugation and 7a-dehydroxylation, which produces the secondary bile acids, deoxycholic acid from cholic acid, and lithocholic acid from chenodeoxycholic acid. Although fat digestion products are normally absorbed in the first 100 cm of small intestine, the conjugated and deconjugated bile salts themselves are absorbed almost exclusively in the ileum, where a specific active transport system for both conjugated and unconjugated bile salts has been identified. Since fecal bile acids are present mainly as the products of bacterial metabolism, it is assumed that metabolism within the intestinal lumen with subsequent reabsorption by passive diffusion is a component of the **enterohepatic circulation** (Fig 15–4). This serves to return almost quantitatively to the liver by way of the portal circulation about 90% per day of the bile acids secreted into the intestine. However, lithocholic acid, because of its insolubility, is not reabsorbed to any significant extent.

A small fraction of the bile salts—perhaps only as little as 500 mg/day—escapes absorption and is therefore eliminated in the feces. Even though this is a very small amount, it nonetheless represents a major pathway for the elimination of cholesterol. The entero-

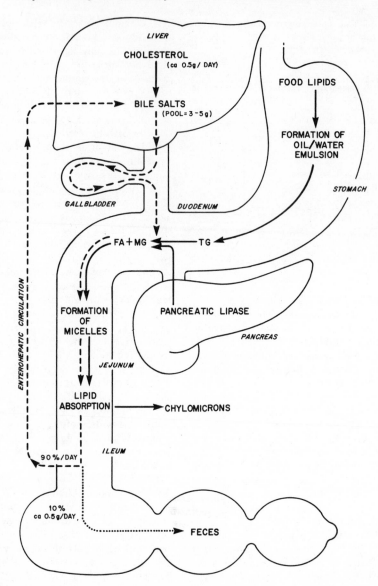

Figure 15–4. Enterohepatic circulation of bile salts and the digestion of lipids. Dashes (-----) indicate enterohepatic circulation of bile salts. TG, triacylglycerol; MG, monoacylglycerol; FA, long chain fatty acids.

hepatic circulation of bile salts is so efficient that each day the relatively small pool of bile acids (about 3–5 g) can be cycled through the intestine 6–10 times with only a small amount lost in the feces, ie, only approximately 1% per pass through the enterohepatic circulation. However, each day an amount of bile acid equivalent to that lost in the feces is produced from cholesterol by the liver so that a pool of bile acids of constant size is maintained. This is accomplished by a system of feedback control discussed below.

Bile acids have several useful important functions. As has been noted, the bile acids are the end products of cholesterol breakdown and are thus the major route of elimination of cholesterol from the body, via the feces. In fact, hepatic synthesis of cholesterol, in addi-

tion to being subject to feedback regulation by dietary intake of cholesterol, is also under profound regulatory control by the bile acids in the enterohepatic circulation. A number of observations support this fact. First, external diversion of bile flow leads to a striking increase in the rate of cholesterol synthesis both in the liver and in the intestine. Second, feeding of the bile acid binding resin **cholestyramine** also results in accelerated hepatic synthesis of cholesterol, which suggests that the bile acids are the bile components responsible for the feedback effect on cholesterol synthesis. Third, the oral administration of a variety of free and of conjugated bile acids in unphysiologically high amounts causes an inhibition of cholesterol synthesis. Finally, interference with the enterohepatic circulation of bile acids as a result of ileal bypass operations also results in a striking increase in cholesterol synthesis by the liver.

Changes in the rate of synthesis of bile acids are nearly always paralleled by corresponding changes in the rate of cholesterol synthesis in the liver. The principal rate-limiting step in the biosynthesis of bile acids is at the 7α-hydroxylase reaction, and in the biosynthesis of cholesterol it is at the HMG-CoA reductase step (Fig 20–31). The activities of these 2 enzymes change in parallel, and consequently it is difficult to ascertain whether inhibition of bile acid synthesis takes place primarily at the HMG-CoA reductase step or at the 7α-hydroxylase reaction. Bile acids do not seem to regulate these enzyme activities by a direct allosteric mechanism. A differential effect on the activities of the 2 enzymes has been reported upon feeding cholesterol to rats. HMG-CoA reductase is inhibited but 7α-hydroxylase activity increases with increase in bile acid formation. Man does not respond in a similar manner but rather may increase the excretion of neutral steroids in the feces and may suppress cholesterol synthesis. However, the ability to do this varies with different human subjects.

There is a lower excretion of bile acids in patients with type II hyperlipoproteinemia (see p 319) that is reflected by lower synthesis of cholic acid. A similar pattern is observed in hepatic cirrhosis and cholestasis where cholic and deoxycholic acid formation and presence in bile is reduced, whereas chenodeoxycholic acid production is normal.

Clinically, hypercholesterolemia may be treated by attempts to interrupt the enterohepatic circulation of bile acids. It is reported that significant reductions of plasma cholesterol can be effected by this procedure, which can be accomplished medically by the use of cholestyramine resin (Cuemid, Questran) or surgically by the ileal exclusion operations. Both procedures cause a block in the reabsorption of bile acids. Then, because of release from feedback regulation normally exerted by bile acids, the conversion of cholesterol to bile acids is greatly enhanced in an effort to maintain the pool of bile acids.

Functions of the Bile System

A. Emulsification: The bile salts have considerable ability to lower the surface tension of water. This enables them to emulsify fats in the intestine and to dissolve fatty acids and water-insoluble soaps. The presence of bile in the intestine is an important adjunct to accomplish the digestion and absorption of fats as well as the absorption of the fat-soluble vitamins A, D, E, and K. When fat digestion is impaired, other foodstuffs are also poorly digested, since the fat covers the food particles and prevents enzymes from attacking them. Under these conditions, the activity of the intestinal bacteria causes considerable putrefaction and production of gas.

B. Neutralization of Acid: In addition to its functions in digestion, the bile is a reservoir of alkali, which helps to neutralize the acid chyme from the stomach.

C. Excretion: Bile is also an important vehicle of excretion. It removes many drugs, toxins, bile pigments, and various inorganic substances such as copper, zinc, and mercury.

D. Cholesterol Solubility in Bile; Formation of Gallstones: Cholesterol—either derived from the diet, synthesized in the liver, or removed from the circulation by the liver—is eliminated almost entirely in the bile as cholesterol itself or as bile acids. Free cholesterol is totally insoluble in an aqueous vehicle such as bile; consequently, it must be incorporated into a lecithin-bile salt micelle. Indeed, lecithin, the predominant phospholipid in bile, is itself insoluble in aqueous systems but can be dissolved by bile salts in micelles. The large quantities of cholesterol present in the bile of humans are solubilized in these water-soluble mixed micelles, allowing cholesterol to be transported normally without precipitation in bile via the biliary tract to the intestine. Mixed micelles of bile salt, lecithin, and cholesterol, however, have a limited capacity to solubilize cholesterol. The actual solubility of cholesterol in bile depends on the relative proportions of bile salt, lecithin, and cholesterol. The solubility also depends on the water content of bile. This is especially important in dilute hepatic bile.

Using triangular coordinates (Fig 15–5), Redinger and Small were able to determine the maximum solubil-

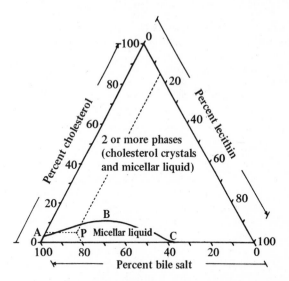

Figure 15–5. Method for presenting 3 major components of bile (bile salts, lecithin, and cholesterol) on triangular coordinates. Each component is expressed as a percentage mole of total salt, lecithin, and cholesterol. Line ABC represents maximum solubility of cholesterol in varying mixtures of bile salt and lecithin. Point P represents bile composition, containing 5% cholesterol, 15% lecithin, and 80% bile salt, and falls within the zone of a single phase of micellar liquid. Bile having a composition falling above the line would contain excess cholesterol in either supersaturated or precipitated form (crystals or liquid crystals). (Reproduced, with permission, from Redinger RN, Small DM: Bile composition, bile salt metabolism, and gallstones. Arch Intern Med 130:620, 1972. Copyright © 1972, American Medical Association.)

ity of cholesterol in human gallbladder bile. The diagram was constructed from in vitro studies of bile salt, lecithin, and cholesterol mixtures in water to illustrate the limits of cholesterol solubility in this quaternary system. The validity of representing the biologic system of bile in a similar way was confirmed by studies on the physical state and chemical composition of human gallbladder bile. For cholesterol solubility, reference to the figure indicates that any triangular point falling above the line ABC would represent a bile whose composition is such that cholesterol is either supersaturated or precipitated.

It is believed that at some time during the life of a patient with gallstones there is formed an abnormal bile that has become supersaturated with cholesterol. With time, various factors such as infection, for example, serve as seeding agents to cause the supersaturated bile to precipitate the excess cholesterol as crystals. Unless the newly formed crystals are promptly excreted into the intestine with the bile, the crystals will grow to form stones.

Utilizing the information concerning cholesterol solubility described above, attempts have been made to dissolve gallstones or to prevent their further formation. Eleven of 18 patients receiving chenodeoxycholic acid had a decrease in the size or the number of gallstones. No response was observed in 17 patients treated only with cholic acid or in the 18 patients receiving a placebo. However, of 13 patients with radiopaque gallstones, only 2 responded to therapy with chenodeoxycholic acid. It was concluded that chenodeoxycholic acid appears to offer specific medical treatment of asymptomatic radiolucent gallstones in functioning gallbladders.

E. Bile Pigment Metabolism: The origin of the bile pigments from hemoglobin is discussed on p 194.

INTESTINAL PUTREFACTION & FERMENTATION

Most ingested food is absorbed from the small intestine. The residue passes into the large intestine. Here considerable absorption of water takes place, and the semiliquid intestinal contents gradually become more solid. During this period, considerable bacterial activity occurs. By fermentation and putrefaction, the bacteria produce various gases, such as CO_2, methane, hydrogen, nitrogen, and hydrogen sulfide, as well as acetic, lactic, and butyric acids. The bacterial decomposition of lecithin may produce choline and related toxic amines such as neurine.

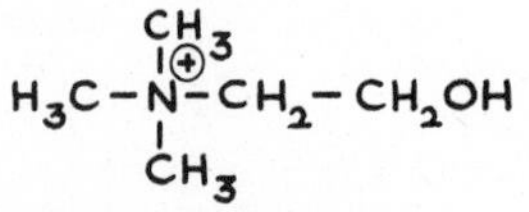

Choline

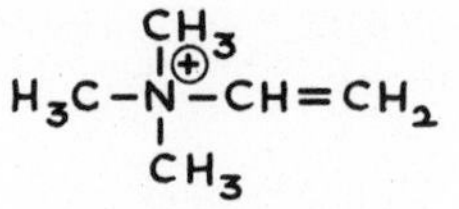

Neurine

Fate of Amino Acids

Many amino acids undergo decarboxylation as a result of the action of intestinal bacteria to produce toxic amines (ptomaines).

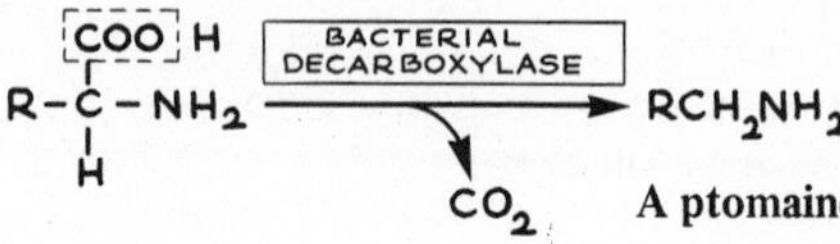

Such decarboxylation reactions produce cadaverine from lysine; agmatine from arginine; tyramine from tyrosine; putrescine from ornithine; and histamine from histidine. Many of these amines are powerful vasopressor substances.

The amino acid tryptophan undergoes a series of reactions to form indole and methylindole (skatole), the substances particularly responsible for the odor of the feces.

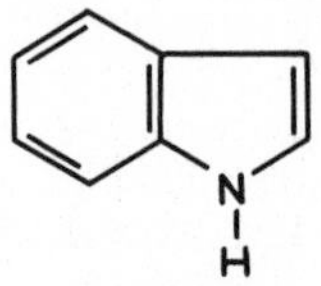

Indole 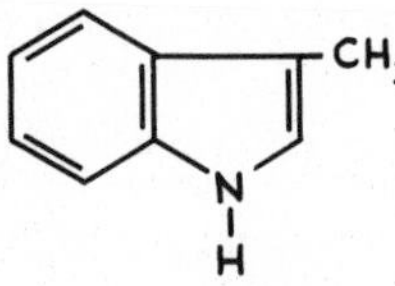   **Skatole**

The sulfur-containing amino acid cysteine undergoes a series of transformations to form mercaptans such as ethyl and methyl mercaptan as well as H_2S.

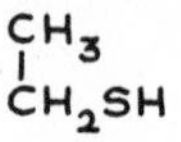

Ethyl mercaptan   **Methyl mercaptan**

**Methyl   Methane and hydrogen
mercaptan   sulfide**

The large intestine is a source of considerable quantities of ammonia, presumably as a product of the putrefactive activity on nitrogenous substrates by the intestinal bacteria. This ammonia is absorbed into the portal circulation, but under normal conditions it is rapidly removed from the blood by the liver. In liver disease this function of the liver may be impaired, in which case the concentration of ammonia in the peripheral blood will rise to toxic levels. It is believed that ammonia intoxication may play a role in the genesis of hepatic coma in some patients. In dogs on whom an Eck fistula has been performed (complete diversion of the portal blood to the vena cava), the feeding of large quantities of raw meat will induce symptoms of ammonia intoxication (meat intoxication) accompanied by elevated levels of ammonia in the blood. The oral administration of neomycin has been shown to reduce the quantity of ammonia delivered from the intestine to the blood. This is undoubtedly due to the antibacterial action of the drug. The feeding of high-protein diets to patients suffering from advanced liver disease, or the occurrence of gastrointestinal hemorrhage in such patients, may contribute to the development of ammonia intoxication. Neomycin is also beneficial under these circumstances.

Intestinal Bacteria

The intestinal flora may comprise as much as 25% of the dry weight of the feces. In herbivora, whose diet consists largely of cellulose, the intestinal or ruminal bacteria are essential to digestion, since they decompose this polysaccharide and make it available for absorption. In addition, these symbiotic bacteria may accomplish the synthesis of essential amino acids and vitamins. In man, although the intestinal flora is not as important as in the herbivora, nevertheless some nutritional benefit is derived from bacterial activity in the synthesis of certain vitamins, particularly vitamin K, and possibly certain members of the B complex, which are made available to the body. Information gained from experiments with animals raised under strictly aseptic conditions should help to define further the precise role of the intestinal bacteria.

ABSORPTION FROM
THE GASTROINTESTINAL TRACT

There is little absorption from the stomach, even of smaller molecules like glucose which can be absorbed directly from the intestine. Although water is not absorbed to any extent from the stomach, considerable gastric absorption of alcohol is possible.

The small intestine is the main digestive and absorptive organ. About 90% of the ingested foodstuffs is absorbed in the course of passage through the small intestine, and water is absorbed at the same time. Considerably more water is absorbed after the foodstuffs pass into the large intestine, so that the contents, which were fluid in the small intestine, gradually become more solid in the colon.

There are 2 general pathways for the transport of materials absorbed by the intestine: the veins of the hepatic portal system, which lead directly to the liver;

and the lymphatic vessels of the intestinal area, which eventually lead to the blood by way of the lymphatic system and the thoracic duct.

Absorption of Carbohydrates

The products of carbohydrate digestion are absorbed from the intestine into the blood of the portal venous system in the form of monosaccharides, chiefly the hexoses (glucose, fructose, mannose, and galactose), although the pentose sugars, if present in the food ingested, will also be absorbed. The oligosaccharides (compounds derived from starches which yield 2–10 monosaccharide units upon hydrolysis) and the disaccharides are hydrolyzed by appropriate enzymes derived from the mucosal surfaces of the small intestine, which may include pancreatic amylase adsorbed onto the mucosa. There is little free disaccharidase activity in the intestinal lumen. Most of the activity is associated with small "knobs" on the brush border of the intestinal epithelial cell (Shreeve, 1974). The monosaccharides derived from these hydrolytic reactions are then absorbed into the epithelial cells of the jejunum.

Two mechanisms are responsible for the absorption of monosaccharides: active transport against a concentration gradient and simple diffusion. However, the absorption of some sugars does not fit clearly into one or the other of these mechanisms. The chemical characteristics that seem necessary for active transport, both of which are present in glucose and galactose, are the following: the OH on carbon 2 should have the same configuration as in glucose, a pyranose ring should be present, and a methyl or substituted methyl group should be present on carbon 5. Fructose is absorbed more slowly than glucose and galactose. Its absorption appears to proceed by diffusion, which is different from the energy-dependent active transport mechanism for glucose and galactose.

To explain the active absorption of glucose, a mobile carrier has been postulated which binds both glucose and Na^+ at separate sites and which transports them both through the plasma membrane of the intestinal cell. It is envisaged that both the glucose and Na^+ are released into the cytosol, allowing the carrier to return for more "cargo." The Na^+ is transported down its concentration gradient and at the same time causes the carrier to transport glucose against its concentration gradient. The free energy required for this active transport is obtained from the hydrolysis of ATP linked to a sodium pump which expels Na^+ from the cell (Fig 15–6). The active transport of glucose is inhibited by ouabain (cardiac glycoside), an inhibitor of the sodium pump, and by phlorhizin, a known inhibitor of glucose reabsorption in the kidney tubule. Phlorhizin, a plant glycoside, probably displaces Na^+ from its binding site on the glucose carrier.

Hydrolysis of polysaccharides and oligosaccharides is a rapid process; therefore, the absorptive mechanisms for glucose-galactose and fructose are quickly saturated. A conspicuous exception is the hydrolysis of lactose, which proceeds at only half the rate for su-

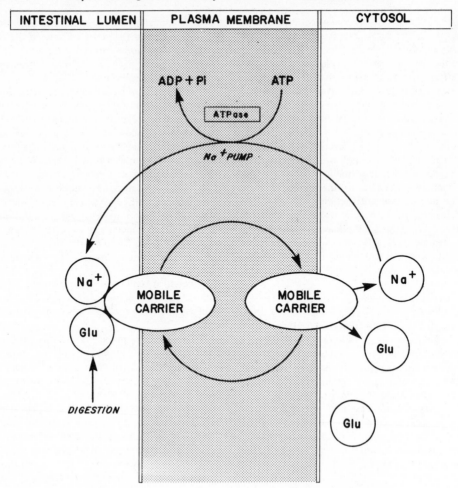

Figure 15—6. Active transport of glucose (Glu) across the intentinal mucosa.

crose. Thus it is the slower rate of hydrolysis of lactose that accounts for the fact that digestion of lactose does not lead to saturation of the transport mechanisms for glucose and galactose.

Defects in Digestion & Absorption of Carbohydrates

A. Lactase Deficiency: Intolerance to lactose, the sugar of milk, may be attributable to a deficiency of lactase. The syndrome should not be confused with intolerance to milk resulting from a sensitivity to milk proteins, usually to the β-lactoglobulin of milk.

There are 3 types of lactase deficiency:

1. Inherited lactase deficiency—In this syndrome, which is relatively rare, symptoms of intolerance to milk such as diarrhea and wasting, incident to fluid and electrolyte disturbances as well as inadequate nutrition, all develop very soon after birth. Withdrawal of milk and the feeding of a lactose-free diet results in disappearance of the symptoms, and the affected infant now begins to thrive. In an occasional case, it is reported that some infants who appeared to be able to digest and absorb lactose nonetheless developed very severe symptoms after ingestion of milk or lactose. The

appearance of lactose in the urine was a prominent feature of this strange syndrome, which appeared to be attributable to a direct toxic effect of lactose on the intestine. The immediate withdrawal of milk is essential.

2. Secondary low lactase activity—Because digestion of lactose is limited even in normal humans, intolerance to milk is not uncommon as a consequence of intestinal diseases. These include many gastrointestinal diseases prevalent in tropical as well as nontropical countries. Examples are tropical and nontropical (celiac) sprue, kwashiorkor, colitis, and gastroenteritis. The disorder may be noted also after surgery for peptic ulcer.

3. Primary low lactase activity—This is a relatively common syndrome, particularly among nonwhite populations in the USA as well as other parts of the world. Since intolerance to lactose was not a feature of the early life of adults with this disorder, it is presumed to represent a gradual decline in activity of lactase in susceptible individuals as they grow older.

The signs and symptoms of lactose intolerance are the same regardless of the cause. These include abdominal cramps, diarrhea, and flatulence or bloating. They are attributed to the results of accumulation of lactose within the intestinal lumen. The sugar is osmotically active, so that it holds water within the lumen, and the fermentative action on the sugar of the intestinal bacteria produces gases and other products which serve as intestinal irritants. Although avoidance of lactose-containing foods produces prompt relief as well as prevention of recurrence of symptoms, in most patients with primary low lactase activity it is not necessary to eliminate milk totally. It may be that over a period of time tolerance will develop. In view of the excellent qualities of milk as a nutrient, particularly among those populations where low levels of lactase may be prevalent, it seems desirable to attempt to establish what levels of milk ingestion may be tolerated by allowing milk in gradually increasing amounts. In only a minority of patients is lactose intolerance so severe that not even one 8-ounce glass of milk (12 g lactose) can be taken without symptoms.

B. Sucrase Deficiency: There are a number of reports of an inherited deficiency of the disaccharidases sucrase and isomaltase, occurring within the mucosa of the small intestine. Symptoms occur in early childhood following ingestion of the sugars in question. The symptoms are the same as those described in lactase deficiency except that they are evoked by ingestion of cane sugar rather than by milk. Patients eventually discover their inability to tolerate sucrose and modify their diet accordingly, although by the time of young adulthood a tolerance to the sugar seems to develop so that several grams of sucrose may be taken without incident.

C. Disacchariduria: An increase in the excretion of intact disaccharides may be observed in some patients with disaccharidase deficiencies. Although the intestine normally is virtually impermeable to disaccharides since, if it is absorbed, there is no metabolism of disaccharides, as much as 300 mg or more of disaccharide may be excreted in the urine of patients with intestinal damage (eg, sprue) or when there is accumulation of disaccharides within the intestine, as may occur in disaccharidase deficiencies.

D. Monosaccharide Malabsorption: There is a congenital condition in which glucose and galactose are absorbed only slowly due to a defect in the carrier mechanism. Because fructose is not absorbed via the carrier, its absorption is normal.

Absorption of Fats

The complete hydrolysis of triacylglycerols produces glycerol and fatty acids. However, the second and third fatty acids are hydrolyzed from the triacylglycerols with increasing difficulty, the removal of the last fatty acid requiring special conditions. Pancreatic lipase is virtually specific for the hydrolysis of primary ester linkages. If this lipase can hydrolyze the ester linkage at position 2 of the triacylglycerol at all, it does so at a very slow rate. An enzyme that can hydrolyze fatty acids esterified at the 2 position of a triacylglycerol was, however, found in rat pancreatic juice. This enzyme is not pancreatic lipase; it may be sterol ester hydrolase.

Because of the difficulty of hydrolysis of the secondary ester linkage in the triacylglycerol, it is suggested that the digestion of a triacylglycerol proceeds first by removal of a terminal fatty acid to produce a 1,2-diacylglycerol; the other terminal fatty acid is then removed to produce a 2-monoacylglycerol. Since this last fatty acid is linked by a secondary ester group, its removal requires isomerization to a primary ester linkage. This is a relatively slow process; as a result, monoacylglycerols are the major end products of fat digestion and less than one-fourth of the ingested fat is completely broken down to glycerol and fatty acids.

Within the intestinal wall, 1-monoacylglycerols are further hydrolyzed to produce free glycerol and fatty acids, whereas 2-monoacylglycerols may be reconverted to triacylglycerols. The utilization of fatty acids for resynthesis of triacylglycerols requires first their "activation." This is accomplished by formation of a coenzyme A (acyl) derivative of the fatty acid (see p 165). The reaction (which also requires ATP) is catalyzed by the enzyme **thiokinase.**

An ATP-dependent fatty acid thiokinase has been shown to be present in the mucosal cells of the intestine. It is likely, therefore, that the synthesis of triacylglycerols proceeds in the intestinal mucosa in a manner similar to that which takes place in other tissues, as described on p 287.

The free glycerol released in the intestinal lumen (from approximately 22% of the total amount of triacylglycerol originally present) is not reutilized but passes directly to the portal vein. However, the glycerol released within the intestinal wall cells can be reutilized for triacylglycerol synthesis by activation by ATP to glycerol 3-phosphate, followed by combination with acyl-CoA derived from fatty acids present in the intestinal wall as a result of absorption from the intestine or produced by hydrolysis of monoacylglycerols within the intestinal wall. Thus, normally, all long-chain fatty acids present in the intestinal wall are ultimately reincorporated into triacylglycerols which are transported to the lymphatic vessels of the abdominal region (the so-called lacteals) for distribution to the rest of the body.

All of the above factors relating to digestion and absorption of lipids are shown in Fig 15–7.

Triacylglycerols, having been synthesized in the intestinal mucosa after absorption as described above, are not transported to any extent in the portal venous blood. Instead, the great majority of absorbed fat appears in the form of **chylomicrons** which appear first in the lymphatic vessels of the abdominal region and later in the systemic blood. Chylomicrons are synthe-

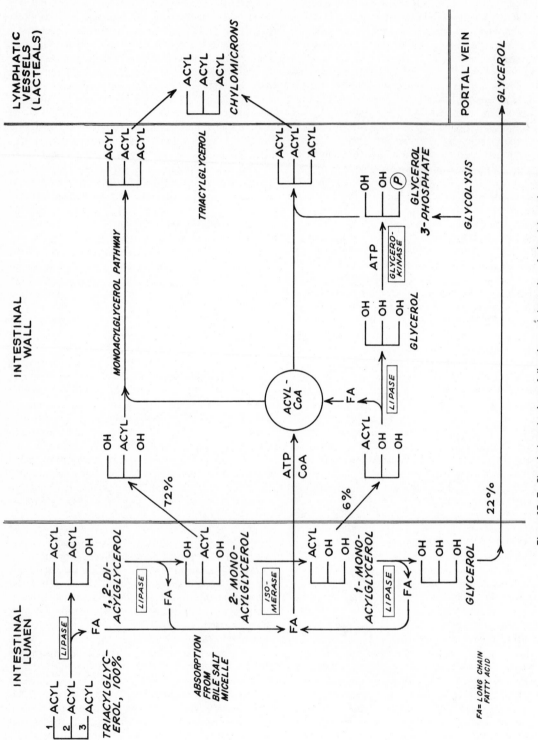

Figure 15–7. Chemical mechanisms of digestion and absorption of triacylglycerols. (Modified from Mattson & Volpenheim: J Biol Chem 239:2772, 1964.)

sized in the intestinal wall, and, although they contain largely triacylglycerol, cholesterol (both free and esterified), phospholipid, and a small (0.5%) but important amount of protein are also present. Indeed, administration of an inhibitor of protein synthesis (eg, puromycin) to rats prevents the formation of chylomicrons and results in accumulation of fat in the intestinal epithelial cells.

The majority of absorbed fatty acids of more than 10 carbon atoms in length, irrespective of the form in which they are absorbed, are found as esterified fatty acids in the lymph of the thoracic duct. Fatty acids with carbon chains shorter than 10–12 carbons are transported in the portal venous blood as unesterified (free) fatty acids. This was demonstrated in experiments in which labeled fatty acids were fed either as free acids or in neutral fat. About 90% of labeled palmitic (C_{16}) acid was found in the lymph after it was fed to experimental animals. Stearic (C_{18}) acid was poorly absorbed. Myristic (C_{14}) acid was well absorbed, mostly into the lymph; however, while almost all of the lauric (C_{12}) acid or decanoic (C_{10}) acid was absorbed, these were not found to any extent in the lymph. Presumably they passed into the portal blood. These lower fatty acids are, however, not important constituents of fats ordinarily taken in the diet except in the fats of milk.

Chyluria is an abnormality in which the patient excretes milky urine because of the presence of an abnormal connection between the urinary tract and the lymphatic drainage system of the intestine, a so-called "chylous fistula." In a similar abnormality, **chylothorax**, there is an abnormal connection between the pleural space and the lymphatic drainage of the small intestine which results in the accumulation of milky pleural fluid. As noted above, fatty acids of chain lengths less than 10–12 carbon atoms are transported almost entirely in the portal blood rather than in the lymph. With this fact in mind, a comparison was made of the effect on patients with chylous fistulas of feeding triacylglycerols in which the fatty acids were of medium-chain length (less than 12 carbons) with that of feeding dietary fat. Substitution of the medium-chain length fatty acids for other fat resulted in a disappearance of chyluria which reappeared when corn oil was given. In the patient with chylothorax, the use of triacylglycerol with short-chain fatty acids resulted in the appearance of clear pleural fluid as well as a reduction in its accumulation so that less frequent removal of the fluid by thoracentesis was required. There was also a reduction in protein losses to the body which would otherwise occur because of the presence of protein in the chylous fluid whether it accumulates in the pleural cavity or is lost into the urine.

A lipase distinct from that of the pancreas is present in the intestinal mucosa. It is probable that the principal action of the intestinal lipase is not within the lumen of the intestine, as is the case with pancreatic lipase, but within the cells of the intestinal wall. Here it may continue hydrolysis of monoacylglycerols that are not readily split by pancreatic lipase and thus

prepare fatty acids for resynthesis into neutral fat as described above. That resynthesis occurs from long-chain fatty acids (after formation of the "active" CoA derivatives) seems evident from the observation that ^{14}C-labeled palmitic acid given orally in olive oil to rats was later found to be randomly distributed in the 1, 2, and 3 positions of the acylglycerols recovered from the thoracic duct lymph.

There is evidence that unhydrolyzed fat can be absorbed if it is dispersed in very fine particles (not over 0.5 μm in diameter). A combination of bile salts, fatty acids, and a monoacylglycerol will bring about this fine degree of dispersion of neutral fats. Certain synthetic "wetting agents" such as Tween 80 (sorbitan monooleate) have a similar effect and are used therapeutically to promote fat absorption. Since bile salts play such an important role in the absorption of fats, it is obvious that fat absorption is seriously hampered by a lack of bile in the intestine such as results when the bile duct is completely obstructed.

Cholesterol appears to be absorbed from the intestine almost entirely in the free (unesterified) form. Nonetheless, 85–90% of the cholesterol in the lymph is in the esterified form, indicating that esterification of cholesterol, like that of fatty acids, must take place within the intestinal mucosal cells.

Summary of Fat Absorption

The dietary fat is digested, by the action of the pancreatic lipase present in the intestine, partially to glycerol and fatty acids and partially to split products such as monoacylglycerols. With the aid of the bile salts, these products of fat digestion enter the mucosal cells of the small intestine where digestion of fats may be completed through the action of the intestinal lipase, thus liberating long-chain fatty acids and glycerol. Resynthesis of triacylglycerols now occurs, utilizing the partial acylglycerols and the liberated fatty acids. Surplus fatty acids are converted to their acyl-CoA derivatives and esterified with glycerol 3-phosphate. The resynthesized fat then passes into the lymphatics (the lacteals) of the abdominal cavity and thence by way of the thoracic duct to the blood, where it may be detected as lipoprotein particles about 0.5 μm in diameter, the so-called chylomicrons. The bile salts are carried by the portal blood to the liver and excreted in the bile back to the intestine; this is the so-called enterohepatic circulation of the bile salts.

Phospholipid synthesis and turnover increase in the intestinal wall during the absorption of fat, although there is no evidence that they contribute substantially to lipid transport in the lymph or blood. Phospholipids are split by phospholipases, and their acyl chains are incorporated into chylomicrons. Their more hydrophilic components (such as choline) may be transported directly to the liver via the hepatic portal vein.

Cholesterol is absorbed into the lymphatics and recovered therein mainly as cholesteryl esters, although both free and esterified cholesterol are found in the blood plasma. Of the plant sterols (phytosterols), none is absorbed from the intestine except ergosterol, which is absorbed after it has been converted by irradiation to a vitamin D.

Absorption of Amino Acids & Protein

It is probable that under normal circumstances the dietary proteins are almost completely digested to their constituent amino acids and that these end products of protein digestion are then rapidly absorbed from the intestine into the portal blood. The amino acid content of the portal blood rises during the absorption of a protein meal, and the rise of individual amino acids in the blood a short time after their oral administration can be readily detected. It is possible that some hydrolysis, eg, of dipeptides, is completed in the intestinal wall. Animals may be successfully maintained with respect to protein nutrition when a complete amino acid mixture is fed to them. This indicates that intact protein is not necessary.

There is a difference in the rate of absorption from the intestine of the 2 isomers of an amino acid. The natural (L) isomer is actively transported across the intestine from the mucosa to the serosa; vitamin B_6 (pyridoxal phosphate) is involved in this transfer (see Chapter 13). The D-isomers, on the other hand, are transported only by free diffusion. This active transport of the L-amino acids is energy-dependent, as evidenced by the fact that, in studies of small pieces of segmented intestine, 2,4-dinitrophenol inhibits the concentration of L-amino acids. There is no such effect with the D-amino acids. It will be recalled that 2,4-dinitrophenol acts as an uncoupling agent in oxidative phosphorylation and thus interferes with production of ATP, which, in this case, is the energy source for active transport.

A valuable tool for the study of amino acid transport is the synthetic amino acid a-aminoisobutyric acid. This compound is transported across cell membranes as are the natural amino acids; but once within the cells it cannot be metabolized, so that it remains for identification and analysis. Another amino acid model has also been used to study transport of amino acids across the intestine. This compound, 1-aminocyclopentane-1-carboxylic acid, was found to behave somewhat differently from a-aminoisobutyric acid in intestinal transport. The latter resembled glycine, whereas the former behaved like valine and methionine in respect to transport across the intestinal wall.

When groups of amino acids are fed, there is some evidence that one amino acid fed in excess can retard the absorption of another. These observations are similar to those made with respect to reabsorption of amino acids by the renal tubules.

The absorption of small peptide fragments from the intestine is undoubtedly possible, and it is very likely that this normally occurs. During the digestion and absorption of protein, an increase in the peptide nitrogen of the portal blood has in fact been found.

A puzzling feature of protein absorption is that in some individuals sensitivity to protein (in the immunologic sense) results when they eat certain proteins. It is known that a protein is antigenic, ie, able to stimulate an immunologic response, only if it is in the form of a relatively large molecule; the digestion of a protein even to the polypeptide stage destroys its antigenicity. Those individuals in which an immunologic response to ingested protein occurs must therefore be able to absorb some unhydrolyzed protein. This is not entirely undocumented, since the antibodies of the colostrum are known to be available to the infant.

There is increasing support for the hypothesis that the basic defect in nontropical sprue is located within the mucosal cells of the intestine and that it consists of an enzymatic defect which permits the polypeptides resulting from the peptic and tryptic digestion of gluten, the principal protein of wheat, not only to exert a local harmful effect within the intestine but also to be absorbed into the circulation and thus to elicit the production of antibodies. It has been definitely established that circulating antibodies to wheat gluten or its fractions are frequently present in patients with nontropical sprue. Efforts to characterize chemically the peptic-tryptic digest of gluten which appears to be the harmful entity in the sprue patient have resulted in the finding that the digest is a mixture of peptides with a mean molecular weight between 820 and 928, suggesting that they are composed of 6 or 7 amino acids of which glutamine and proline must be present to ensure the harmful properties of the peptide. Mild acid hydrolysis which results in deamidation of glutamine renders the peptide harmless.

These observations on a disease entity that is undoubtedly the adult analog of celiac disease in children advance the possibility that protein fragments of larger molecular size than amino acids are absorbed from the intestine under certain conditions.

• • •

References

Digestion & Absorption

Johnston JM: Intestinal absorption of fats. In: *Comprehensive Biochemistry*. Vol 18. Florkin M, Stotz EH (editors). Elsevier, 1970.

Reiser R, Williams MC: J Biol Chem 202:815, 1953.

Senior JR: J Lipid Res 5:495, 1964.

Shreeve WW: *Physiological Chemistry of Carbohydrates in Mammals*. Saunders, 1974.

Smyth DH (editor): *Intestinal Absorption*. Plenum Press, 1974.

Bile Acids

Danielsson H, Sjövall J: Bile acid metabolism. Annu Rev Biochem 44:233, 1975.

Dietschy JM (editor): Symposium on bile acids. Arch Intern Med 130:473, 1972.

Nair PP, Kritchevsky D (editors): *The Bile Acids*. 2 vols. Plenum Press, 1971–1973.

16 . . .
Bioenergetics

INTRODUCTION

Bioenergetics or **biochemical thermodynamics** is the study of the energy changes accompanying biochemical reactions. These reactions are accompanied by liberation of energy as the reacting system moves from a higher to a lower energy level. Most frequently, the energy is liberated in the form of heat. In nonbiologic systems heat energy may be transformed into mechanical or electrical energy. Since biologic systems are essentially isothermic, no direct use can be made of heat liberated in biologic reactions to drive the vital processes that require energy. These processes—eg, synthetic reactions, muscular contraction, nerve conduction, and active transport—obtain energy by chemical linkage or **coupling** to oxidative reactions. In its simplest form this type of coupling may be represented as shown in Fig 16−1.

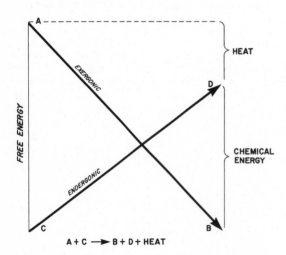

Figure 16−1. Coupling of an exergonic to an endergonic reaction.

The conversion of metabolite A to metabolite B occurs with release of energy. It is coupled to another reaction, in which energy is required to convert metabolite C to metabolite D. As some of the energy liberated in the degradative reaction is transferred to the synthetic reaction in a form other than heat, the normal chemical terms exothermic and endothermic cannot be applied to these reactions. Rather, the terms **exergonic** and **endergonic** are used to indicate that a process is accompanied by loss or gain, respectively, of free energy, regardless of the form of energy involved.

The Concept of Free Energy

Change in free energy (ΔG)* is that portion of the total energy change in a system which is available for doing work, ie, it is the useful energy.

If the reaction shown in Fig 16−1 is to go from left to right, then the overall process must be accompanied by loss of free energy as heat. One possible mechanism of coupling could be envisaged if a common obligatory intermediate (I) took part in both reactions, ie,

$$A + C \longrightarrow I \longrightarrow B + D$$

Some exergonic and endergonic reactions in biologic systems are coupled in this way. It should be appreciated that this type of system has a built-in mechanism for biologic control of the rate at which oxidative processes are allowed to occur since the existence of a common obligatory intermediate for both the exergonic and endergonic reactions allows the rate of utilization of the product of the synthetic path (D) to determine by mass action the rate at which A is oxidized. Indeed, these relationships supply a basis for the concept of **respiratory control**. An extension of this concept is provided by dehydrogenation reactions which are coupled to hydrogenations by an intermediate carrier (Fig 16−2).

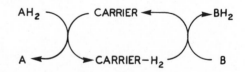

Figure 16−2. Coupling of dehydrogenation and hydrogenation reactions by an intermediate carrier.

*ΔG is the same as ΔF, which is used in some texts.

An alternative method of coupling an exergonic to an endergonic process is to synthesize a compound of high-energy potential in the exergonic reaction and to incorporate this new compound into the endergonic reaction, thus effecting a transference of free energy from the exergonic to the endergonic pathway (Fig 16–3).

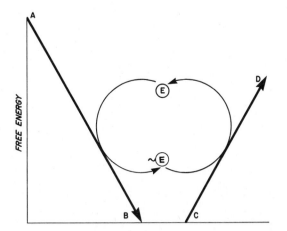

Figure 16–3. Transference of free energy from an exergonic to an endergonic reaction through the formation of a high-energy intermediate compound.

In Fig 16–3, ~ Ⓔ is a compound of high potential energy and Ⓔ is the corresponding compound of low potential energy. The biologic advantage of this mechanism is that Ⓔ , unlike I in the previous system, need not be structurally related to A, B, C, or D. This would allow Ⓔ to serve as a transducer of energy from a wide range of exergonic reactions to an equally wide range of endergonic reactions or processes, as shown in Fig 16–4.

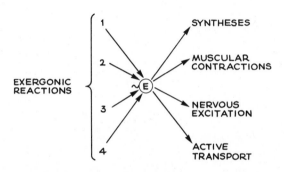

Figure 16–4. Transduction of energy through a common high-energy compound to energy-requiring (endergonic) biologic processes.

In the living cell, the principal high-energy intermediate or carrier compound (designated ~ Ⓔ) is **adenosine triphosphate** or **ATP**.

The Laws of Thermodynamics as Applied to Biochemical Systems

The first law of thermodynamics states that "the total energy of a system, plus its surroundings, remains constant." This is also the law of conservation of energy. It implies that within the total system, energy is neither lost nor gained during any change. However, within that total system, energy may be transferred from one part to another or may be transformed into another form of energy. For example, chemical energy may be transformed into heat, electrical, radiant, or mechanical energy.

The second law of thermodynamics states that "the total entropy of a system must increase if a process is to occur spontaneously." **Entropy** represents the extent of disorder or randomness of the system and becomes maximum in a system as it approaches equilibrium. Under conditions of constant temperature and pressure, the relationship between the free energy change (ΔG) of a reacting system and the change in entropy (ΔS) is given by the following equation which combines the 2 laws of thermodynamics:

$$\Delta G = \Delta H - T\Delta S$$

where ΔH is the change in enthalpy and T is the absolute temperature.

Under the conditions of biochemical reactions, because ΔH is approximately equal to ΔE, the total change in internal energy of the reaction, the above relationship may be expressed in the following way:

$$\Delta G = \Delta E - T\Delta S$$

If ΔG is negative in sign, the reaction proceeds spontaneously with loss of free energy, ie, it is **exergonic**. If, in addition, ΔG is of great magnitude, the reaction goes virtually to completion and is essentially irreversible. On the other hand, if ΔG is positive, the reaction proceeds only if free energy can be gained, ie, it is **endergonic**. If, in addition, the magnitude of ΔG is great, the system is stable with little or no tendency for a reaction to occur. If ΔG is zero, the system is at equilibrium and no net change takes place.

Relationship Between Equilibrium Constant & Standard Free Energy Change

In a model reaction

$$A + B \rightleftharpoons C + D$$

$$\Delta G = \Delta G^0 + RT\ln \frac{[C][D]}{[A][B]}$$

where R is the gas constant and T is the absolute temperature. When the reactants [A], [B], [C], and [D] are present in concentrations of 1.0 M, ΔG^0 is known as the **standard free energy change**.

At equilibrium, $\Delta G = 0$, ie,

$$0 = \Delta G^0 + RT\ln \frac{[C][D]}{[A][B]}$$

and therefore

$$\Delta G^0 = -RT\ln \frac{[C][D]}{[A][B]}$$

Since the equilibrium constant under standard conditions is

$$K'_{eq} = \frac{[C][D]}{[A][B]}$$

substitution gives

$$\Delta G^0 = -RT\ln K'_{eq}$$

or

$$\Delta G^0 = -2.303\,RT\log K'_{eq}$$

Thus, the standard free energy change can be calculated from the equilibrium constant K'_{eq}. It is important to note that ΔG may be larger or smaller than ΔG^0 depending on the concentrations of the various reactants.

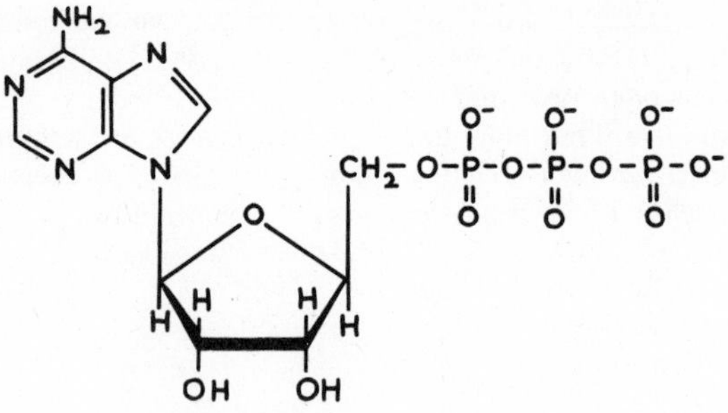

ROLE OF HIGH-ENERGY PHOSPHATES IN BIOENERGETICS & ENERGY CAPTURE

In order to maintain living processes, all organisms must obtain supplies of free energy from their environment. In the case of autotrophic organisms, this is achieved by coupling their metabolism to some simple exergonic process in their surroundings, eg, green plants utilize the energy of sunlight. On the other hand, heterotrophic organisms obtain free energy by coupling their metabolism to the breakdown of complex organic molecules in their environment. In all of these processes, ATP plays a central role in the transference of free energy from the exergonic to the endergonic processes (Figs 16–3 and 16–4). As can be seen from Fig 16–5, ATP is a specialized nucleotide containing adenine, ribose, and 3 phosphate groups. In its reactions in the cell it functions as the Mg^{2+} complex (Fig 16–6).

The importance of phosphates in intermediary metabolism became evident in the period between 1930 and 1940 with the discovery of the chemical details of glycolysis and of the role of ATP, ADP, and inorganic phosphate (P_i) in this process. ATP was considered to be a means of transferring phosphate radicals in the process of phosphorylation. The role of ATP in biochemical energetics was indicated in experiments demonstrating that ATP and creatine phosphate

Figure 16–5. Adenosine triphosphate (ATP).

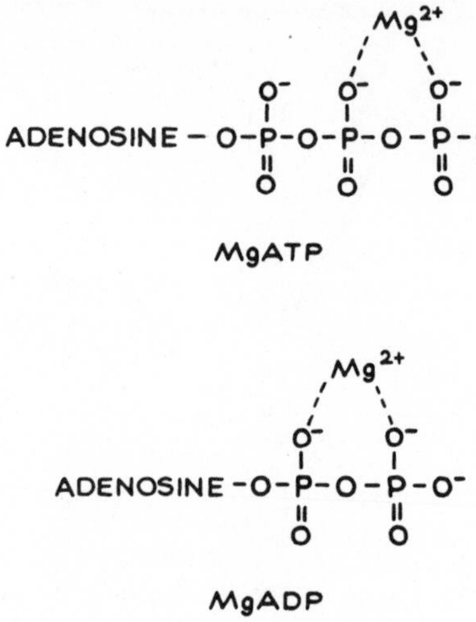

Figure 16–6. The magnesium complexes of ATP and ADP.

were broken down during muscular contraction and that their resynthesis depended on supplying energy from oxidative processes in the muscle. It was not until 1941, when Lipmann introduced the concept of "high-energy phosphates" and the "high-energy phosphate bond," that the role of these compounds in bioenergetics was clearly appreciated.

The Free Energy of Hydrolysis of ATP & Other Organophosphates

The standard free energy of hydrolysis of a number of biochemically important phosphates is shown in Table 16–1. An estimate of the comparative tendency of each of the phosphate groups to transfer to a suitable acceptor may be obtained from the $\Delta G^{0'}$ of hydrolysis. It may be seen from the table that the value for the hydrolysis of the terminal phosphate of ATP of -7.3 kcal/mol (as it is also for the terminal phosphate of ADP) divides the list into 2 groups. One group of "low-energy phosphates," exemplified by the ester phosphates found in the intermediates of glycolysis, have $\Delta G^{0'}$ values which are smaller than that of ATP, while in the other group, designated "high-energy phosphates," the value is higher than that of ATP. The components of this latter group are usually anhydrides (eg, ATP, ADP, the 1-phosphate of 1,3-bisphosphoglycerate), enolphosphates (eg, phosphoenolpyruvate), and phosphoguanidines (eg, creatine phosphate, arginine phosphate). Other biologically important compounds that are classed as "high-energy compounds" are thiol esters involving coenzyme A (eg, acetyl-CoA), acyl carrier protein, amino acid esters involved in protein synthesis, S-adenosylmethionine (active methionine), and UDPG (uridine diphosphate glucose).

High-Energy Phosphates

To indicate the presence of the high-energy phosphate group, Lipmann introduced the symbol $\sim P$, indicating **high-energy phosphate bond.** It is important to realize that the symbol denotes that it is the group attached to the bond which, on transfer to an appropriate acceptor, results in transfer of the larger quantity of free energy. For this reason, the term **group transfer potential** is preferred by some to "high-energy bond." Thus, ATP contains 2 high-energy phosphate groups and ADP contains one, whereas the phosphate bond in AMP (adenosine monophosphate) is of the low-energy type since it is a normal ester link (Fig 16–7).

Role of High-Energy Phosphates as the "Energy Currency" of the Cell

As a result of its position midway down the list of standard free energies of hydrolysis (Table 16–1), ATP is able to act as a donor of high-energy phosphate to those compounds below it in the table. Likewise, provided the necessary enzymic machinery is available, ADP can accept high-energy phosphate to form ATP from those compounds above ATP in the table. In ef-

Table 16–1. Standard free energy of hydrolysis of some organophosphates of biochemical importance.

Compound	$\Delta G^{0\prime}$	
	kJ/mol	kcal/mol
Phosphoenolpyruvate	−61.9	−14.8
Carbamoyl phosphate	−51.4	−12.3
1,3-Bisphosphoglycerate (to 3-phosphoglycerate)	−49.3	−11.8
Creatine phosphate	−43.1	−10.3
Acetyl phosphate	−42.3	−10.1
Arginine phosphate	−33.5	−8.0
ATP → ADP + P$_i$	−30.5	−7.3
Glucose 1-phosphate	−20.9	−5.0
Fructose 6-phosphate	−15.9	−3.8
Glucose 6-phosphate	−13.8	−3.3
Glycerol 3-phosphate	−9.2	−2.2

fect, an **ATP/ADP cycle** connects these processes which **generate** $\sim \text{P}$ to those processes which **utilize** $\sim \text{P}$ (Fig 16–8).

The processes which feed $\sim \text{P}$ into this cycle can be divided into 4 main groups. The greatest quantitative source of $\sim \text{P}$ in aerobic organisms is from reactions catalyzed by ATP synthetase, which, in effect, reverses the hydrolysis of ATP. The free energy to drive this process is derived from respiratory chain oxidation within the mitochondria (see p 231). This process **oxidative phosphorylation,** is part of the mechanisms within the cell that operate to achieve **energy conservation** or **energy capture.** Energy capture also results from the catabolism of glucose to lactic acid in the series of reactions known as the Embden-Meyerhof pathway of glycolysis (see p 253), wherein—per mole of

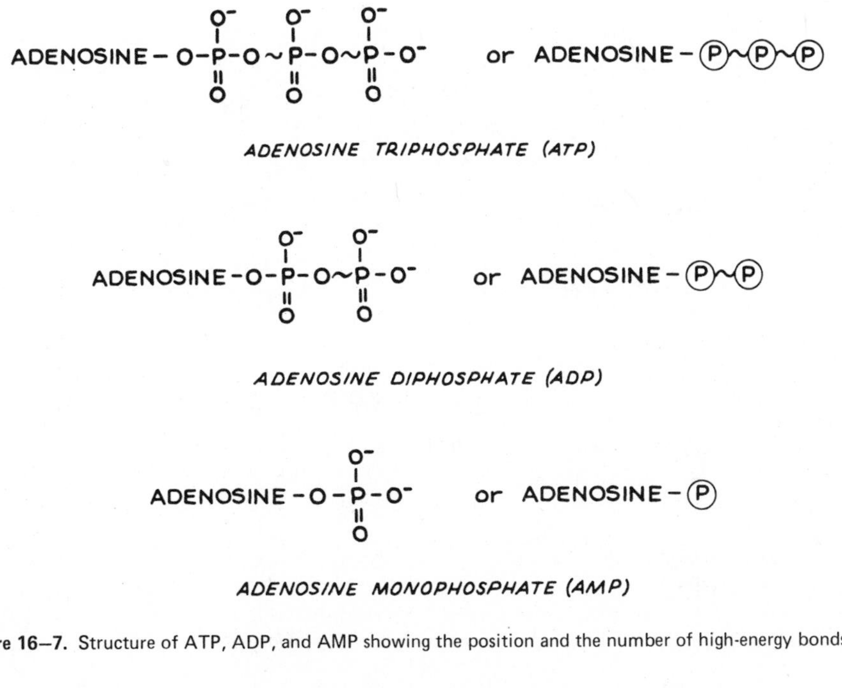

ADENOSINE TRIPHOSPHATE (ATP)

ADENOSINE DIPHOSPHATE (ADP)

ADENOSINE MONOPHOSPHATE (AMP)

Figure 16–7. Structure of ATP, ADP, and AMP showing the position and the number of high-energy bonds ($\sim$).

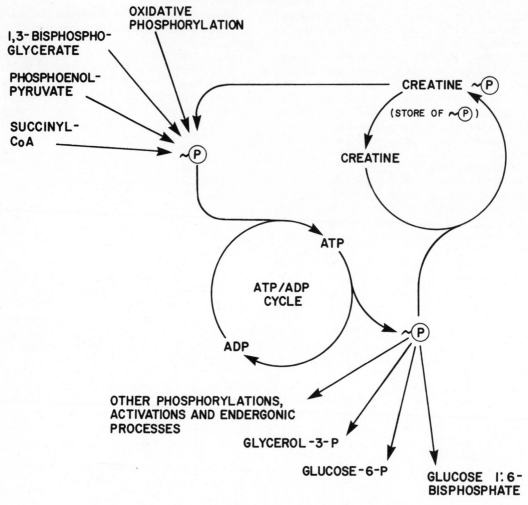

Figure 16—8. Role of ATP/ADP cycle in transfer of high-energy phosphate.

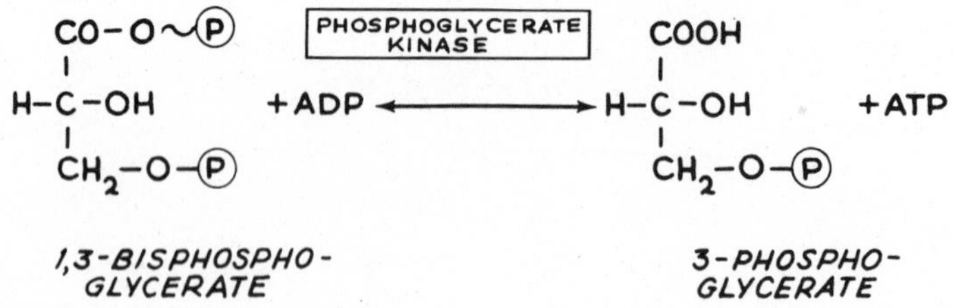

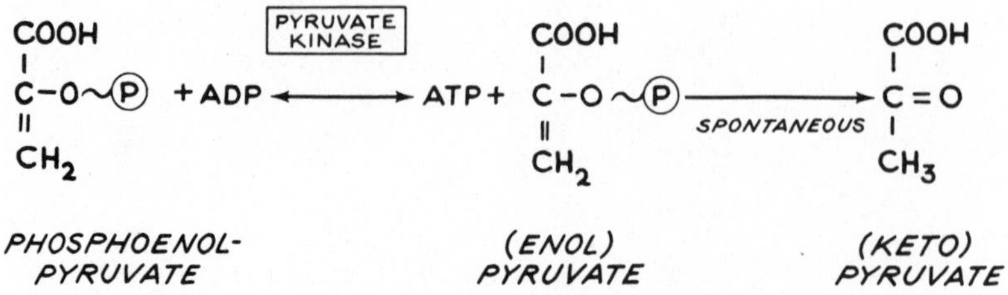

Figure 16—9. Transfer of high-energy phosphate from intermediates of glycolysis to ADP.

glucose catabolized—there is net formation of 2 high-energy phosphate groups, resulting in the formation from ADP of 2 moles of ATP. The chemical processes resulting in this net formation of ATP involve the incorporation of P_i into 3-phosphoglyceraldehyde, which, after dehydrogenation, forms 1,3-bisphosphoglycerate. This compound contains a high-energy phosphate that in turn reacts with ADP to form ATP. As a result of further molecular changes, another intermediate, phosphoenolpyruvate, is formed which contains a high-energy phosphate which is again transferred to ADP to form ATP (Fig 16–9). Further energy capture occurs at the succinyl thiokinase step of the citric acid cycle (see p 246), where additional high-energy phosphate is liberated.

Another group of compounds represented in Table 16–1 acts as storage forms of high-energy phosphate within muscle. These include creatine phosphate (phosphagen), occurring in vertebrate muscle, and arginine phosphate, within invertebrate muscle.

There is a substantial free energy loss in the reaction

$$\text{Creatine} \sim \textcircled{P} + \text{ADP} \xrightarrow{\boxed{\text{Creatine kinase}}} \text{Creatine} + \text{ATP} \ -3.0 \text{ kcal/mol}$$

Under physiologic conditions, the above reaction permits ATP concentrations to be maintained in muscle while ATP is rapidly being utilized as a source of energy for muscular contraction. On the other hand, when ATP is plentiful, its concentration can build up sufficiently to cause the reverse reaction to occur and allow the concentration of creatine phosphate to increase substantially so as to act as a store of high-energy phosphate. When ATP acts as a phosphate donor to form those compounds of lower free energy of hydrolysis (Table 16–1), the phosphate group is invariably converted to one of low energy, eg,

$$\text{Glucose} + \text{Adenosine} -\textcircled{P}\sim\textcircled{P}\sim\textcircled{P} \xrightarrow{\boxed{\text{Hexokinase}}} \text{Glucose} -\textcircled{P} + \text{Adenosine} -\textcircled{P}\sim\textcircled{P}$$

The reaction is accompanied by considerable loss of free energy which is used partly to raise the energy level of the substrate, but since some is also lost as heat, there is assurance that the reaction will go virtually to completion under physiologic conditions.

Interconversion of Adenine Nucleotides

The enzyme **adenylate kinase** (myokinase) is present in most cells. It catalyzes the interconversion of ATP and AMP to ADP:

This reaction has several functions. It allows the high-energy phosphate in ADP to be used in the formation of ATP, and it is also a means whereby AMP, formed as a consequence of several activating reactions involving ATP, can be rephosphorylated to form ATP. Finally, it allows AMP, which increases in concentration when ATP becomes depleted, to act as a metabolic (allosteric) signal to increase the rate of catabolic reactions, which in turn leads to the generation of more ATP.

When ATP reacts to form AMP, inorganic pyrophosphate (PP_i) is formed, as occurs, for example, in the activation of long-chain fatty acids:

$$\text{ATP} + \text{CoA.SH} + \text{R.COOH} \xrightarrow{\boxed{\text{Thiokinase}}} \text{AMP} + PP_i + \text{R.CO}\sim\text{SCoA}$$

This reaction is accompanied by loss of free energy as heat, which ensures that the activation reaction will go to the right; this is further aided by the hydrolytic splitting of PP_i, catalyzed by **inorganic pyrophosphatase**, a reaction which itself has a large $\Delta G^{0'}$ of −4.6 kcal/mol. Note that activations via the pyrophosphate pathway result in the loss of 2 $\sim\textcircled{P}$ rather than one $\sim\textcircled{P}$, as occurs when ADP and P_i are formed.

$$PP_i + H_2O \xrightarrow{\boxed{\begin{array}{c}\text{Inorganic}\\\text{pyrophosphatase}\end{array}}} 2 P_i$$

A combination of the above reactions catalyzed by these enzymes enables phosphate to be recycled and the adenine nucleotides to interchange (Fig 16–10).

Nucleoside Triphosphates Related to ATP

By means of the enzyme **nucleoside diphosphate kinase**, other nucleotides similar to ATP can be synthesized from their diphosphates, eg, **UTP** (uridine triphosphate), **GTP** (guanosine triphosphate), and **CTP** cytidine triphosphate), all of which take part in phosphorylations in the cell (Fig 16–11).

$$\underset{\text{(ATP)}}{\text{Adenosine} -\textcircled{P}\sim\textcircled{P}\sim\textcircled{P}} + \underset{\text{(AMP)}}{\text{Adenosine} -\textcircled{P}} \underset{\overrightarrow{}}{\overset{\boxed{\text{Adenylate kinase}}}{\rightleftarrows}} \underset{\text{(2 ADP)}}{2 \text{ Adenosine} -\textcircled{P}\sim\textcircled{P}}$$

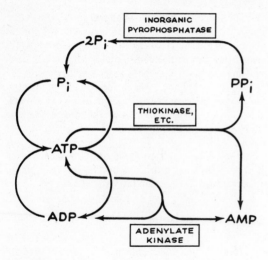

Figure 16–10. Phosphate cycles and interchange of adenine nucleotides.

Nucleoside diphosphate kinase

ATP + UDP ⟷ UTP + ADP
ATP + GDP ⟷ GTP + ADP
ATP + CDP ⟷ CTP + ADP

Figure 16–11. Reactions catalyzed by nucleoside diphosphate kinase.

• • •

References

Florkin M, Stotz EH (editors): *Bioenergetics.* In: *Comprehensive Biochemistry.* Vol 22. Elsevier, 1967.

Kaplan NO, Kennedy EP (editors): *Current Aspects of Biochemical Energetics.* Academic Press, 1966.

Klotz IM: *Energy Changes in Biochemical Reactions.* Academic Press, 1967.

Krebs HA, Kornberg HL: *Energy Transformations in Living Matter.* Springer, 1957.

Lehninger AL: *Biochemistry,* 2nd ed. Worth, 1975.

Lehninger AL: *Bioenergetics,* 2nd ed. Benjamin, 1972.

17...
Biologic Oxidation

Historical Review

    Chemically, oxidation is defined as the removal of electrons and reduction is the gain of electrons, as illustrated by the conversion of ferrous to ferric ion.

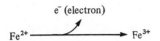

It follows that oxidation is always accompanied by reduction of an electron acceptor. The above definition covers a much wider range of reactions than did the older restricted definition which covered only the addition of oxygen or removal of hydrogen.

    Modern concepts of oxidation in biologic systems may be traced back to Lavoisier, who demonstrated that animals utilize oxygen from the air and replace this by carbon dioxide and water. He showed that respiration was similar in this respect to the burning of a candle. However, Pasteur, in his studies of the fermentation of glucose by yeast, firmly established that living organisms could respire in the absence of oxygen, ie, under anaerobic conditions. In the period around 1930, 2 diametrically opposed concepts of biologic oxidation prevailed. Warburg advocated the view that a widely distributed enzyme (**Atmungsferment**) catalyzed the activation of oxygen and its combination with substrate molecules. He believed that heavy metals, particularly iron, played a part in the catalysis, a conclusion that was supported by the fact that carbon monoxide and cyanide were potent inhibitors not only of respiration but also of heavy metal catalysis of the oxidation of organic molecules. Opposed to this concept was the thesis of Wieland that substrate molecules were activated and oxidized by removal of hydrogen in reactions catalyzed by specific enzymes called **dehydrogenases**. It was shown that the reduced dehydrogenases that resulted could in turn become reoxidized not only by oxygen but also by other acceptors such as methylene blue. With the discovery by Keilin of a group of respiratory catalysts designated the **cytochrome system**, the 2 concepts were reconciled, as it became clear that most substrates were in fact oxidized by a combination of both processes. Dehydrogenation initiated oxidation, and

the reducing equivalents were transported via the cytochrome system to react ultimately with molecular oxygen in the presence of Warburg's enzyme, the last member of the cytochrome system, now renamed **cytochrome oxidase**. The sequence of enzymes and carriers responsible for the transport of reducing equivalents from substrates to molecular oxygen is known as the **respiratory chain**. Further elucidation by Warburg and others of the role of **nicotinamide nucleotides** and **flavoproteins** made it possible by 1940 to construct the following sequence of components of the respiratory chain. The arrows indicate the direction of flow of reducing equivalents (H or electrons).

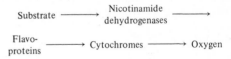

The respiratory chain is now known to be localized within mitochondria. By using mitochondria as a source, much purer preparations of the respiratory catalysts can now be studied than was possible with older methods of isolation from whole organs or tissue. At the present time the mechanism of coupling of oxidation in the respiratory chain to the production of the high-energy carrier, ATP, is a particularly active area of research.

Oxidation-Reduction Equilibria; Redox Potential

    In reactions involving oxidation and reduction, the free energy exchange is proportionate to the tendency of reactants to donate or accept electrons. This is expressed numerically as an **oxidation-reduction** or **redox potential**. It is usual to compare the redox potential of a system (E_o) against the potential of the hydrogen electrode, which at pH 0 is designated as 0.0 volts. However, for biologic systems it is normal to express the redox potential (E_o') at pH 7.0, at which pH the electrode potential of the hydrogen electrode is -0.42 volts. The redox potentials of some redox systems of special interest in mammalian physiology are shown in Table 17−1. The list of redox potentials shown in the table allows prediction of the direction of flow of electrons from one redox couple to another.

Table 17–1. Some redox potentials of special interest in mammalian oxidation systems.

System	E_0' volts
Oxygen/water	+0.82
Cytochrome a; Fe^{3+}/Fe^{2+}	+0.29
Cytochrome c; Fe^{3+}/Fe^{2+}	+0.22
Ubiquinone; ox/red	+0.10
Cytochrome b; Fe^{3+}/Fe^{2+}	+0.08
Fumarate/succinate	+0.03
Flavoprotein-old yellow enzyme; ox/red	−0.12
Oxaloacetate/malate	−0.17
Pyruvate/lactate	−0.19
Acetoacetate/β-hydroxybutyrate	−0.27
Lipoate; ox/red	−0.29
$NAD^+/NADH$	−0.32
H^+/H_2	−0.42
Succinate/α-ketoglutarate	−0.67

ENZYMES & COENZYMES INVOLVED IN OXIDATION & REDUCTION

In the Report of the International Union of Biochemistry, 1961, all enzymes concerned in oxidative processes are designated oxidoreductases. In the following account, oxidoreductases are classified into 5 groups.

(1) Oxidases: Enzymes that catalyze the removal of hydrogen from a substrate but use only oxygen as a hydrogen acceptor. They invariably contain copper and form water as a reaction product (with the exception of uricase and monoamine oxidase, which form H_2O_2) (Fig 17–1).

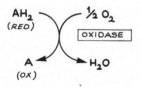

Figure 17–1. Oxidation of a metabolite catalyzed by an oxidase.

(2) Aerobic dehydrogenases: Enzymes catalyzing the removal of hydrogen from a substrate but which, as distinct from oxidases, can use either oxygen or artificial substances such as methylene blue as a hydrogen acceptor. Characteristically, these dehydrogenases are flavoproteins. Hydrogen peroxide rather than water is formed as a product. (Fig 17–2.)

(3) Anaerobic dehydrogenases: Enzymes catalyzing the removal of hydrogen from a substrate but not able to use oxygen as hydrogen acceptor. There are a large number of enzymes in this class. They perform 2 main functions:

(a) Transfer of hydrogen from one substrate to another in a coupled oxidation-reduction reaction not involving a respiratory chain (Fig 17–3).

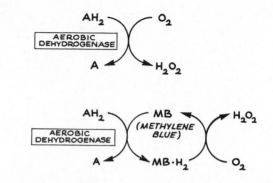

Figure 17–2. Oxidation of a metabolite catalyzed by an aerobic dehydrogenase.

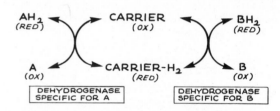

Figure 17–3. Oxidation of a metabolite catalyzed by anaerobic dehydrogenases, not involving a respiratory chain.

These dehydrogenases are specific for their substrates but often utilize the same coenzyme or hydrogen carrier as other dehydrogenases. As the reactions are reversible, these properties enable reducing equivalents to be freely transferred within the cell. This type of reaction, which enables a substrate to be oxidized at the expense of another, is particularly useful in enabling oxidative processes to occur in the absence of oxygen.

(b) As components in a respiratory chain of electron transport from substrate to oxygen (Fig 17–4).

(4) Hydroperoxidases: Enzymes utilizing hydrogen peroxide as a substrate. Two enzymes fall into this category: **peroxidase,** found in milk and in plants; and **catalase,** found in animals and plants.

(5) Oxygenases: Enzymes that catalyze the direct transfer and incorporation of oxygen into a substrate molecule.

Oxidases

Oxidases are conjugated proteins whose prosthetic groups contain copper.

Cytochrome oxidase is a hemoprotein widely distributed in many plant and animal tissues. It is the terminal component of the chain of respiratory carriers found in mitochondria and is therefore responsible for the reaction whereby electrons resulting from the oxidation of substrate molecules by dehydrogenases are transferred to their final acceptor, oxygen. The enzyme is poisoned by carbon monoxide (only in the dark), cyanide, and hydrogen sulfide. It is considered to be identical with Warburg's respiratory enzyme and

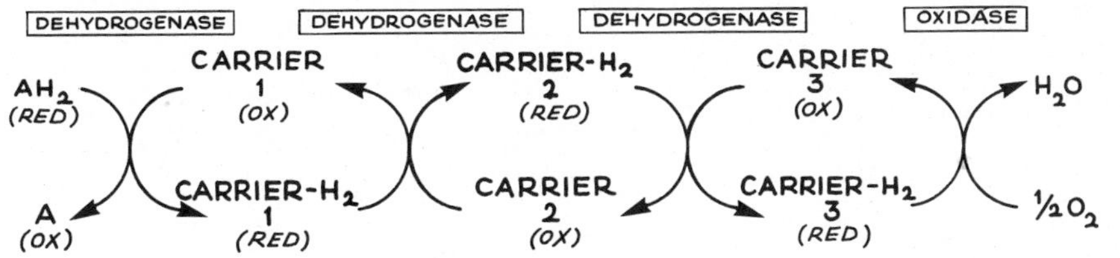

Figure 17—4. Oxidation of a metabolite by anaerobic dehydrogenases utilizing several components of a respiratory chain.

with what has also been termed cytochrome a_3. It was formerly assumed that cytochrome a and cytochrome oxidase were separate compounds since each has a distinct spectrum and different properties with respect to the effects of carbon monoxide and cyanide. More recent studies show that the 2 cytochromes are combined with the same protein, and the complex is known as **cytochrome aa$_3$**. It contains 2 molecules of heme A, each having one Fe atom, which oscillate between Fe^{3+} and Fe^{2+} during oxidation and reduction. Also, 2 atoms of Cu are present which are associated with the cytochrome oxidase activity and the reaction of electrons with molecular oxygen.

Phenolase (tyrosinase, polyphenol oxidase, catechol oxidase) is a copper-containing enzyme that is specific for more than one type of reaction. It is able to convert monophenols or o-diphenols to o-quinones. Other enzymes containing copper are **laccase**, which is widely distributed in plants and animals (converts p-hydroquinones to p-quinones), and **ascorbic oxidase**, found only in plants. Copper has been claimed to be present in a number of other enzymes such as **uricase**, which catalyzes the oxidation of uric acid to allantoin, and **monoamine oxidase**, found in the mitochondria of several tissues, an enzyme that oxidizes epinephrine and tyramine, for example.

Aerobic Dehydrogenases

Aerobic dehydrogenases are flavoprotein enzymes having **flavin mononucleotide (FMN)** or **flavin adenine dinucleotide (FAD)** as prosthetic groups (see Fig 13—4 for structure). The flavin groups vary in their affinity for their respective apoenzyme protein, some being detached easily and others not detached without destroying the enzyme. Many of these flavoprotein enzymes contain, in addition, a metal which is essential for the functioning of the enzyme; these are known as **metalloflavoproteins**.

Enzymes belonging to this group of aerobic dehydrogenases include **D-amino acid dehydrogenase** (D-amino acid oxidase), an FAD-linked enzyme, found particularly in liver and kidney, that catalyzes the oxidative deamination of the unnatural (D-) forms of amino acids. Other substrates include glycine, D-lactate, and L-proline, demonstrating that the enzyme is not completely specific for D-amino acids. **L-Amino acid dehydrogenase** (L-amino acid oxidase) is an FMN-linked enzyme found in kidney with general specificity for the oxidative deamination of the naturally occurring L-amino acids. **Xanthine dehydrogenase** (xanthine oxidase) has a wide distribution, occurring in milk and in liver. In the liver, it plays an important role in the conversion of purine bases to uric acid. It is of particular significance in the liver and kidneys of birds, which excrete uric acid as the main nitrogenous end product not only of purine metabolism but also of protein and amino acid catabolism. Xanthine dehydrogenase contains FAD as the prosthetic group. It is a metalloflavoprotein containing both nonheme iron and molybdenum, and it has a dual specificity in that it also oxidizes all aldehydes.

Aldehyde dehydrogenase (aldehyde oxidase) is an FAD-linked enzyme present in pig and other mammalian livers. It is similar to xanthine dehydrogenase in being a metalloflavoprotein containing molybdenum and nonheme iron and in acting upon aldehydes and N-heterocyclic substrates. However, it is distinguished from xanthine dehydrogenase by virtue of its inability to oxidize xanthine.

Of interest because of its use in estimating glucose is **glucose oxidase**, an FAD-specific enzyme prepared from fungi.

All of the above-mentioned aerobic dehydrogenases contain 2 molecules of the flavin nucleotide per mol. The metalloflavoproteins also have a fixed stoichiometry with regard to the number of atoms of metal per molecule, usually Mo:Fe as 2:8. The mechanisms of oxidation and reduction of these enzymes are complex. There seem to be different detailed mechanisms for each enzyme with the possible involvement of free radicals. However, evidence points to reduction of the isoalloxazine ring taking place in 2 steps via a semiquinone (free radical) intermediate (Fig 17—5).

Anaerobic Dehydrogenases

A. Dehydrogenases Dependent on Nicotinamide Coenzymes: A large number of dehydrogenase enzymes fall into this category. They are linked as coenzymes either to **nicotinamide adenine dinucleotide (NAD)** or to **nicotinamide adenine dinucleotide phosphate (NADP)**. The coenzymes are reduced by the specific substrate of the dehydrogenase and reoxidized by a suitable electron acceptor. They may freely and reversibly dissociate from their respective apoenzymes. The nicotinamide nucleotides are synthesized from the vitamin niacin (nicotinic acid and nicotinamide). The mechanism of oxidation of the coenzymes is as shown in Fig 17—6.

There is stereospecificity about position 4 of nicotinamide when it is reduced by a substrate AH_2.

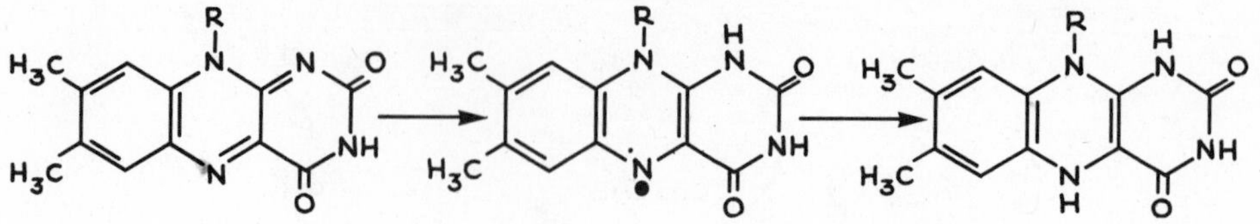

Figure 17—5. Reduction of isoalloxazine ring in flavin nucleotides.

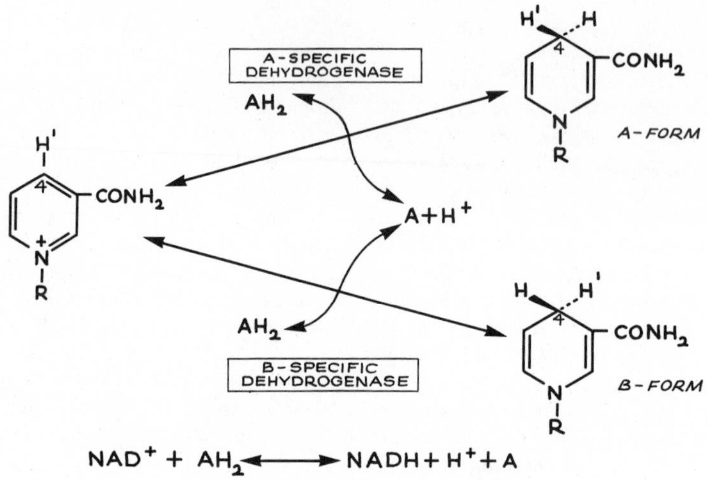

Figure 17—6. Mechanism of oxidation of nicotinamide coenzymes.

One of the hydrogen atoms is removed from the substrate as a hydrogen nucleus with 2 electrons (hydride ion) and is transferred to the 4 position where it may be attached in either the A- or B- position according to the specificity determined by the particular dehydrogenase catalyzing the reaction. The remaining hydrogen of the hydrogen pair removed from the substrate remains free as a hydrogen ion. Deuterium-labeled substrates have been used in elucidating these mechanisms.

Generally, NAD-linked dehydrogenases catalyze oxidoreduction reactions in the oxidative pathways of metabolism, particularly in glycolysis, the citric acid cycle, and in the respiratory chain of mitochondria. NADP-linked dehydrogenases are found characteristically in reductive syntheses, as in the extramitochondrial pathway of fatty acid synthesis and steroid synthesis. They are also to be found as coenzymes to the dehydrogenases of the hexose monophosphate shunt. Some nicotinamide coenzyme-dependent dehydrogenases have been found to contain zinc, notably alcohol dehydrogenase from liver and glyceraldehyde-3-phosphate dehydrogenase from skeletal muscle. The zinc ions are not considered to take part in the oxidation and reduction.

B. Dehydrogenases Dependent on Riboflavin Prosthetic Groups: The prosthetic groups associated with these flavoprotein dehydrogenases are similar to those of the aerobic dehydrogenase group, namely FMN and FAD. They are in the main more tightly bound to their apoenzymes than the nicotinamide coenzymes. Most of the riboflavin-linked anaerobic dehydrogenases are concerned with electron transport in (or to) the respiratory chain. NADH dehydrogenase is a member of the respiratory chain acting as a carrier of electrons between NADH and the more electropositive components. Other dehydrogenases such as succinate dehydrogenase, acyl-CoA dehydrogenase, and mitochondrial glycerol-3-phosphate dehydrogenase transfer electrons directly from the substrate to the respiratory chain. Another role of the flavin-dependent dehydrogenases is in the dehydrogenation (by dihydrolipoyl dehydrogenase) of reduced lipoate, an intermediate in the oxidative decarboxylation of pyruvate and a-ketoglutarate. In this particular instance, due to the low redox potential, the flavoprotein (FAD) acts as a carrier of electrons from reduced lipoate to NAD[+]. The electron-transferring flavoprotein is an intermediary carrier of electrons between acyl-CoA dehydrogenase and the respiratory chain.

C. The Cytochromes: Except for cytochrome oxidase (previously described), the cytochromes are classified as anaerobic dehydrogenases. Their identification and study are facilitated by the presence in the reduced state of characteristic absorption bands which disappear on oxidation. In the respiratory chain they are involved as carriers of electrons from flavoproteins on the one hand to cytochrome oxidase on the other. The cytochromes are iron-containing hemoproteins, in which the iron atom oscillates between Fe^{3+} and Fe^{2+}

during oxidation and reduction. Several identifiable cytochromes occur in the respiratory chain, viz, cytochromes b, c_1 c, a, and a_3 (cytochrome oxidase). Of these, only cytochrome c is soluble. Study of its structure has revealed that the iron porphyrin group is attached to the apoprotein by 2 thioether bridges derived from cystine residues of the protein. Besides the respiratory chain, cytochromes are found in other location, eg, the endoplasmic reticulum (cytochromes P-450 and b_5), plant cells, bacteria, and yeasts.

Hydroperoxidases

A. Peroxidase: Although typically a plant enzyme, peroxidase is found in milk and leukocytes. The prosthetic group is protoheme, which, unlike the situation in most hemoproteins, is loosely bound to the apoprotein. In the reaction catalyzed by peroxidase, hydrogen peroxide is reduced at the expense of several substances that will act as electron acceptors such as ascorbate, quinones, and cytochrome c. The reaction catalyzed by peroxidase is complex but the overall reaction is as follows:

$$H_2O_2 + AH_2 \xrightarrow{\boxed{\text{Peroxidase}}} 2H_2O + A$$

B. Catalase: Catalase is a hemoprotein containing 4 heme groups. In addition to possessing peroxidase activity, it is able to use one molecule of H_2O_2 as a substrate electron donor and another molecule of H_2O_2 as oxidant or electron acceptor. Under most conditions in vivo, the peroxidase activity of catalase seems to be favored.

$$2H_2O_2 \xrightarrow{\boxed{\text{Catalase}}} 2H_2O + O_2$$

Catalase is found in blood and liver. Its function is assumed to be the destruction of hydrogen peroxide formed by the action of aerobic dehydrogenases. Microbodies or **peroxisomes** are found in liver. These are rich in aerobic dehydrogenases and in catalase, which suggests that there may be a biologic advantage in grouping the enzymes which produce H_2O_2 with the enzyme which destroys it. In addition to the peroxisomal enzymes, mitochondrial and microsomal electron transport systems must be considered as sources of H_2O_2 (Fig 17–7).

Oxygenases

Enzymes in this group catalyze the incorporation of oxygen into a substrate molecule. They may be divided into 2 subgroups:

A. Dioxygenases (Oxygen Transferases, True Oxygenases): These enzymes catalyze the incorporation of both atoms of oxygen into the substrate:

$$A + O_2 \longrightarrow AO_2$$

Examples of this type include enzymes that contain iron as a prosthetic group such as **homogentisate dioxygenase** and **3-hydroxyanthranilate dioxygenase** from the supernatant fraction of the liver, and enzymes utilizing heme as a prosthetic group such as **L-tryptophan dioxygenase** (tryptophan pyrrolase) from the liver.

B. Mono-oxygenase (Mixed Function Oxidases, Hydroxylases): These enzymes catalyze the incorporation of only one atom of the oxygen molecule into a substrate. The other oxygen atom is reduced to water, an additional electron donor or cosubstrate being necessary for this purpose.

Example:

$$A-H + O_2 + ZH_2 \longrightarrow A-OH + H_2O + Z$$

Hayaishi has subdivided the mono-oxygenases into subgroups according to the nature of the cosubstrate electron donor involved. For example, many of the enzymes involved in steroid syntheses or transformations are mono-oxygenases utilizing NADPH as a cosubstrate. These are found mainly in the endoplasmic reticulum (microsomes) of the liver and in both the mitochondria and the endoplasmic reticulum of the adrenal glands.

The enzymes involved in the metabolism of many drugs by hydroxylation belong to this group. They are found in the microsomes of the liver together with cytochrome P-450 and cytochrome b_5. Both NADH and NADPH donate reducing equivalents for the reduction of these cytochromes (Fig 17–8), which in turn are oxidized by substrates in a series of enzymic reactions collectively known as hydroxylase (Fig 17–9).

Example: See below.

$$\text{DRUG} - H + O_2 + 2\,Fe^{2+} + 2\,H^+ \xrightarrow{\boxed{\text{Hydroxylase}}}$$
$$\text{(P-450)}$$
$$\text{DRUG} - OH + H_2O + 2\,Fe^{3+}$$
$$\text{(P-450)}$$

Among the drugs metabolized by this system are benzpyrene, aminopyrine, aniline, morphine, and benzphetamine. Many drugs such as phenobarbital have the ability to induce the formation of microsomal enzymes and of cytochrome P-450.

Oxygenases do not take part in reactions that have as their purpose the provision of energy to the cell; rather, they are concerned with the synthesis or degradation of many different types of metabolites.

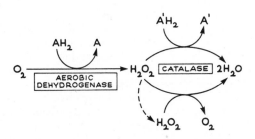

Figure 17–7. Role of catalase in oxidative reactions.

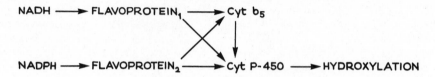

Figure 17–8. Electron transport chain in microsomes.

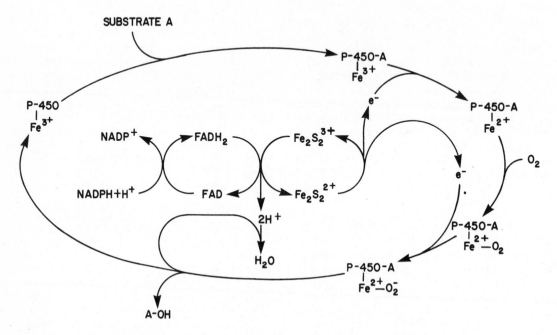

Figure 17–9. Cytochrome P-450 hydroxylase cycle in microsomes. The system shown is typical of steroid hydroxylases of the adrenal cortex. Liver microsomal cytochrome P-450 hydroxylase does not require the iron-sulfur protein Fe_2S_2.

Superoxide Metabolism

Oxygen is a potentially toxic substance, the toxicity of which has hitherto been attributed to the formation of H_2O_2. Recently, however, the ease with which oxygen can be reduced in tissues to the superoxide radical (O_2^-) and the occurrence of **superoxide dismutase** in aerobic organisms (although not in obligate anaerobes) has suggested that the toxicity of oxygen is due to its conversion to superoxide (Friedovich, 1975).

Superoxide is formed when reduced flavins, eg, xanthine dehydrogenase, are reoxidized univalently by molecular oxygen. It is also formed during univalent oxidations with molecular oxygen in the respiratory chain.

$$EnzH_2 + O_2 \longrightarrow EnzH + O_2^- + H^+$$

Superoxide can reduce oxidized cytochrome c

$$O_2^- + Fe^{3+} \longrightarrow O_2 + Fe^{2+}$$

or be removed by the presence of the specific enzyme superoxide dismutase.

$$O_2^- + O_2^- + 2\,H^+ \xrightarrow{\boxed{\text{Superoxide dismutase}}} H_2O_2 + O_2$$

It has been proposed that O_2^- bound to cytochrome P-450 is an intermediate in the activation of oxygen in hydroxylation reactions (Fig 17–9). However, the function of superoxide dismutase seems rather to be that of protecting aerobic organisms against the deleterious effects of superoxide. The cytosolic enzyme is composed of 2 similar subunits, each one containing one equivalent of Cu^{2+} and Zn^{2+}, whereas the mitochrondial enzyme contains Mn^{2+}, being similar to the enzyme found in bacteria. This finding supports the hypothesis that mitochondria have evolved from a prokaryote that entered into symbiosis with a protoeukaryote. The distribution of the dismutase is widespread, being present in all major aerobic tissues. Exposure of animals to an atmosphere of 100% O_2 causes an adaptive increase of the enzyme, particularly in the lungs.

THE RESPIRATORY CHAIN

The mitochondrion has appropriately been termed the "powerhouse" of the cell since it is within the mitochondria that most of the useful energy derived from oxidation within the tissues is captured in the form of the high-energy intermediate, ATP. All the useful energy formed during the oxidation of fatty acids and amino acids and virtually all of that from the oxidation of carbohydrate is made available within the mitochondria. To accomplish this, the mitochondria contain the series of catalysts known as the respiratory chain, which are concerned with the transport of reducing equivalents (hydrogen and electrons) and with their final reaction with oxygen to form water. Mitochondria also contain the enzyme systems responsible for producing the reducing equivalents in the first place, ie, the enzymes of β-oxidation and of the citric acid cycle. The latter is the final common metabolic pathway for the oxidation of all the major foodstuffs. These relationships are shown in Fig 17–10.

Organization of the Respiratory Chain in Mitochondria

The major components of the respiratory chain (Fig 17–11) are arranged sequentially in order of increasing redox potential (Table 17–1). Electrons flow through the chain in a stepwise manner from the more electronegative components to the more electropositive oxygen. Thus, the redox potential of a component of the respiratory chain contributes to the information necessary to assign it a tentative position in the chain. Several other approaches have been used to identify components and their relative positions. Chance and his associates have developed sophisticated technics for following the absorption spectra of the individual components in intact mitochondria. Other investigators, including Green, have broken the chain down into separate components or complexes and attempted to reconstruct it from the separate parts. Slater and others have used inhibitors which block specific reactions in the chain; these are frequently employed with artificial electron acceptors and donors. Chance and Williams introduced the concept of "crossover" to locate the site of action of inhibitors. The concept is based upon the assumption that when an inhibitor is introduced into an active series of redox components of the respiratory chain in the steady state, those components on the electronegative side of the block become more reduced while those on the electropositive side become more oxidized.

The main respiratory chain in mitochondria proceeds from the NAD-linked dehydrogenase systems on the one hand, through flavoproteins and cytochromes, to molecular oxygen on the other. The reducing equivalents are transported either as H^+ or as covalent hydrogen (Fig 17–11). Not all substrates are linked to the respiratory chain through NAD-specific dehydrogenases; some, because their redox potentials are more positive (eg, succinate), are linked directly to flavoprotein dehydrogenases, which in turn are linked to the cytochromes of the respiratory chain (Fig 17–12).

In recent years it has become clear that an addi-

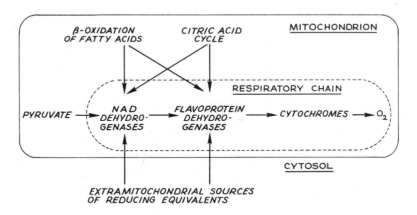

Figure 17–10. Relationship of electron transport in the respiratory chain to the β-oxidation of fatty acids, to the citric acid cycle, and to extramitochondrial sources of reducing equivalents.

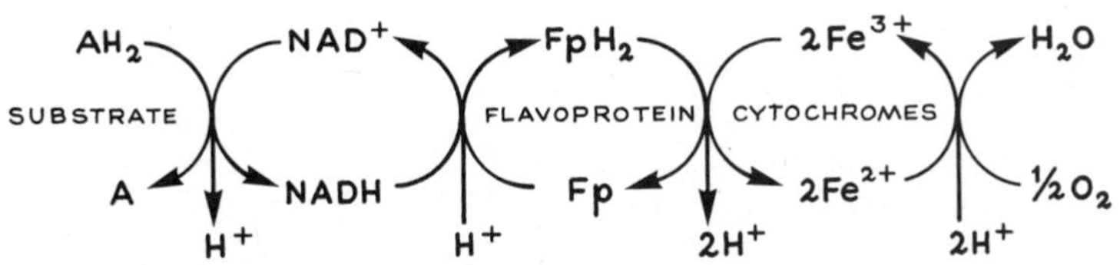

Figure 17–11. Transport of reducing equivalents through the respiratory chain.

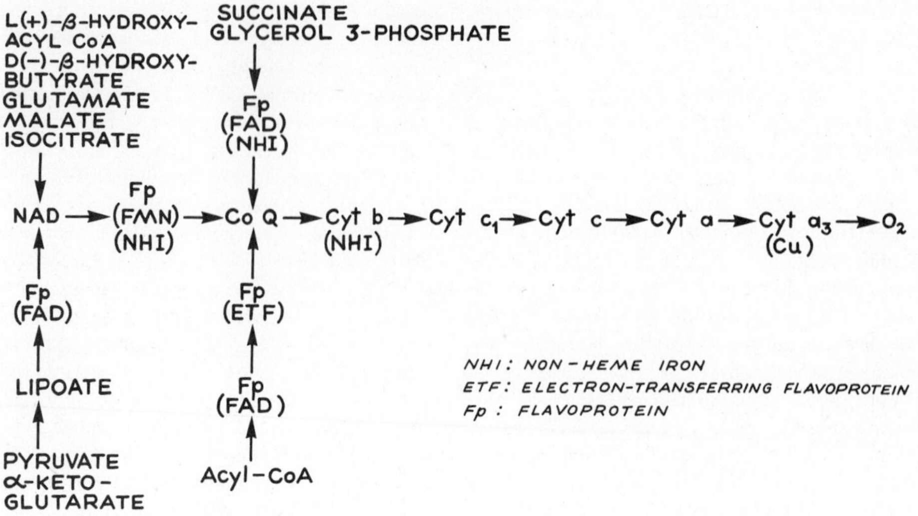

Figure 17—12. Components of the respiratory chain in mitochondria.

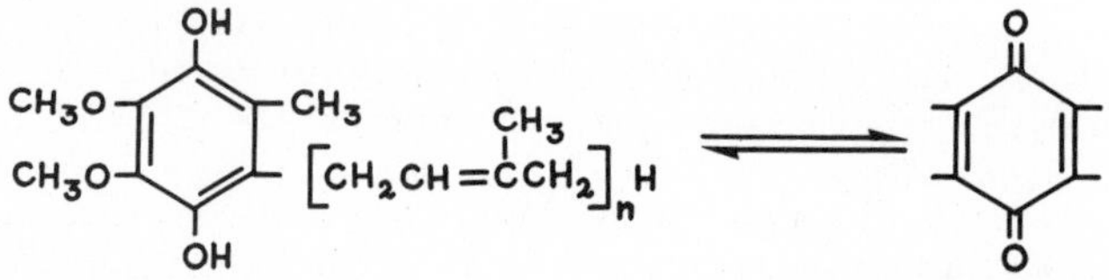

Reduced or quinol form   Oxidized or quinone form

n = number of isoprenoid units, which varies from 6 to 10, ie, coenzyme Q_{6-10}

Figure 17—13. Structure of coenzyme Q.

tional carrier is present in the respiratory chain linking the flavoproteins to cytochrome b, the member of the cytochrome chain of lowest redox potential. This substance, which has been named **ubiquinone** or **coenzyme Q** (CoQ; see Fig 17—13), exists in mitochondria in the oxidized quinone form under aerobic conditions and in the reduced quinol form under anaerobic conditions. CoQ is a constituent of the mitochondrial lipids, the other lipids being predominantly phospholipids that constitute part of the mitochondrial membrane. CoQ has a structure that is very similar to vitamin K and vitamin E. It is also similar to plastoquinone found in chloroplasts. All of these substances are characterized by the possession of a polyisoprenoid side chain. In mitochondria there is a large stoichiometric excess of CoQ compared to other members of the respiratory chain. It is possible that there is more than one pool of CoQ and that some of it is not in the direct pathway of oxidation.

An additional component found in respiratory chain preparations is **nonheme iron**. It is combined with protein and is associated with the flavoproteins (metalloflavoproteins) and with cytochrome b. The presence of a paramagnetic metal allows such prepara-

tions to be examined using the technic of electron paramagnetic resonance spectroscopy. The nonheme iron-protein complex is similar to the ferredoxins of bacteria and to iron proteins present in plants. On denaturation with acid or heat, H_2S is liberated in an amount which is stoichiometrically related to the iron present. The H_2S is derived from what is called "labile sulfur" attached to the iron. Both the sulfur and iron are thought to take part in the oxidoreduction mechanisms.

A current view of the principal components of the respiratory chain is shown in Fig 17—12. At the electronegative end of the chain, dehydrogenase enzymes catalyze the transfer of electrons from substrates to NAD of the chain. Several differences exist in the manner in which this is carried out. The a-keto acids pyruvate and a-ketoglutarate have complex dehydrogenase systems involving lipoate and FAD prior to the passage of electrons to NAD of the respiratory chain. Electron transfers from other dehydrogenases such as L(+)-β-hydroxyacyl-CoA, D(−)-β-hydroxybutyrate, glutamate, malate, and isocitrate dehydrogenases appear to couple directly with NAD of the respiratory chain, although it is possible that more than one pool of NAD may exist. Of these dehydrogenases, β-hydroxybutyrate dehydrogenase is much more firmly bound to the mitochondrion.

The reduced NAD of the respiratory chain is in turn oxidized by a metalloflavoprotein enzyme— **NADH dehydrogenase.** This enzyme contains nonheme iron and the prosthetic group FMN and is tightly bound to the respiratory chain. CoQ is the collecting point in the respiratory chain for reducing equivalents derived from other substrates that are linked directly to the respiratory chain through flavoprotein dehydrogenases. These substrates include succinate, glycerol 3-phosphate, and acyl-CoA. The flavin moiety of all these dehydrogenases appears to be FAD, and those catalyzing the dehydrogenation of succinate and glycerol 3-phosphate contain nonheme iron. In the dehydrogenation of acyl-CoA, an additional flavoprotein, the **electron-transporting flavoprotein,** is necessary to effect transference of electrons to the respiratory chain.

Electrons flow from CoQ, through the series of cytochromes shown in Fig 17–12, to molecular oxygen. The cytochromes are arranged in order of increasing redox potential. The terminal cytochrome a_3 (cytochrome oxidase) is responsible for the final combination of reducing equivalents with molecular oxygen. It has been noted that this enzyme system contains copper, an essential component of true oxidase enzymes. Cytochrome oxidase has a very high affinity for oxygen, which allows the respiratory chain to function at the maximum rate until the tissue has become virtually anoxic.

The structural organization of the respiratory chain has been the subject of considerable speculation. Of significance is the finding of nearly constant molar proportions between the components. The cytochromes are present in the approximate molar proportions, one with another, of 1:1. These findings, together with the fact that many of the components appear to be structurally integrated with the mitochondrial membranes, have suggested that these components have a definite spatial orientation in the membranes.

THE ROLE OF THE RESPIRATORY CHAIN IN ENERGY CAPTURE

ADP is envisaged as a molecule that captures, in the form of high-energy phosphate, some of the free energy resulting from catabolic processes and which as ATP passes on this free energy to drive those processes requiring energy. Thus, ATP has been called the energy "currency" of the cell.

As indicated in Chapter 16, under anaerobic conditions there is a net capture of 2 high-energy phosphate groups in the glycolytic reactions equivalent to approximately 15 kcal/mol of glucose. Since 1 mol of glucose yields approximately 686 kcal on complete combustion, the energy captured by phosphorylation in glycolysis is negligible. The reactions of the citric acid cycle, the final pathway for the complete oxidation of glucose, include only one phosphorylation step, the conversion of succinyl-CoA to succinate, which allows the capture of 2 more high-energy phosphates per mol of glucose. All of the phosphorylation described so far occur **at the substrate level.** Examination of intact respiring mitochondria reveals that when substrates are oxidized via an NAD-linked dehydrogenase, 3 mol of inorganic phosphate are incorporated into 3 mol of ADP to form 3 mol of ATP per half mol of O_2 consumed, ie, the P:O ratio = 3. On the other hand, when a substrate is oxidized via a flavoprotein-linked dehydrogenase, only 2 mol of ATP are formed, ie, P:O = 2. These reactions are known as **oxidative phosphorylation at the respiratory chain level.** Taking into account dehydrogenations in the pathway of catabolism of glucose in both glycolysis and the citric acid cycle, plus phosphorylations at the substrate level, it is now possible to account for at least 42% of the free energy resulting from the combustion of glucose, captured in the form of high-energy phosphate.

Assuming that phosphorylation is coupled directly to certain reactions in the respiratory chain in a manner analogous to phosphorylation in the glycolytic sequence of reactions, it is pertinent to inquire at what sites this could occur. There must be a redox potential of approximately 0.2 volts or a free energy change of approximately 9 kcal between components of the respiratory chain if that particular site is to support the coupled formation of 1 mol of ATP. Four sites in the respiratory chain fulfill these requirements, one between NAD and a flavoprotein, one between flavoprotein and cytochrome b, one between cytochrome b and cytochrome c, and one between cytochrome a and oxygen. Location of the phosphorylation sites has been elucidated by experiments in which the P:O ratio is measured in the presence of inhibitors of known reactions in the chain and in the presence of artificial electron acceptors.

The rate of respiration of mitochondria can be controlled by the concentration of ADP. This is because oxidation and phosphorylation are **tightly coupled** and ADP is an essential component of the phosphorylation process. When ADP is deficient in the presence of excess substrate, 3 crossover points can be identified since the component at the substrate side of the crossover point becomes more reduced and that on the oxygen side becomes more oxidized. These crossover points coincide with 3 of the possible sites previously identified on thermodynamic grounds. The 3 sites of phosphorylation have been designated as sites I, II, and III, respectively (Fig 17–14). The above findings explain why oxidation of succinate via the respiratory chain produces a P:O ratio of only 2, as site I would be bypassed by the flavoprotein-linked succinate dehydrogenase.

Respiratory Control

As stated above, oxidation and phosphorylation

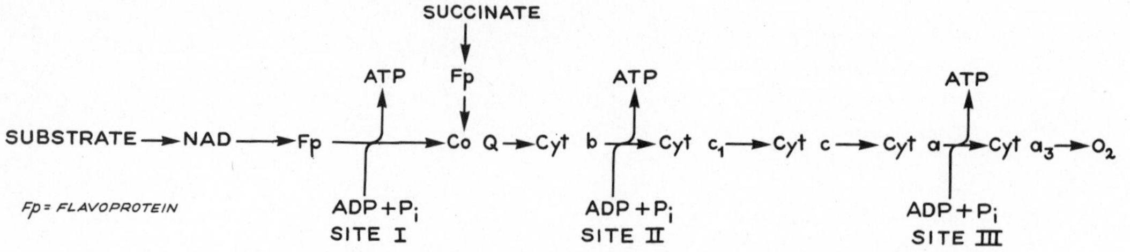

SUCCINATE

$$SUBSTRATE \longrightarrow NAD \longrightarrow Fp \underset{\substack{ADP+P_i \\ SITE\ I}}{\overset{ATP}{\longrightarrow}} Co\ Q \longrightarrow Cyt\ b \underset{\substack{ADP+P_i \\ SITE\ II}}{\overset{ATP}{\longrightarrow}} Cyt\ c_1 \longrightarrow Cyt\ c \longrightarrow Cyt\ a \underset{\substack{ADP+P_i \\ SITE\ III}}{\overset{ATP}{\longrightarrow}} Cyt\ a_3 \longrightarrow O_2$$

Fp = FLAVOPROTEIN

Figure 17—14. Probable sites of phosphorylation in the respiratory chain.

are tightly coupled in mitochondria. Thus, respiration cannot occur via the respiratory chain without concomitant phosphorylation of ADP. Chance and Williams have defined 5 conditions that can control the rate of respiration in mitochondria. These are listed in Table 17—2.

Generally most cells in the resting state seem to be in state 4, respiration being controlled by the availability of ADP. When work is performed, ATP is converted to ADP, allowing more respiration to occur, which in turn replenishes the store of ATP (Fig 17—15). It would appear that under certain conditions the concentration of inorganic phosphate and ATP could also affect the rate of functioning of the respiratory chain.

Thus, the manner in which biologic oxidative processes allow the free energy resulting from the oxidation of foodstuffs to become available and to be captured is stepwise, efficient (40–50%), and controlled rather than explosive, inefficient, and uncontrolled. The remaining free energy which is not captured is liberated as heat. This need not be considered as "wasted," since in the warm-blooded animal it contributes to maintenance of body temperature.

MECHANISMS OF OXIDATIVE PHOSPHORYLATION

Two principal hypotheses have been advanced to account for the coupling of oxidation and phosphorylation. The **chemical hypothesis** postulates direct chemical coupling at all stages of the process, as in the reactions that generate ATP in glycolysis. The **chemiosmotic hypothesis** postulates that oxidation of components in the respiratory chain generates hydrogen ions which are ejected to the outside of a coupling membrane in the mitochondrion. The electrochemical potential difference resulting from the asymmetric distribution of the hydrogen ions is used to drive the mechanism responsible for the formation of ATP.

Other hypotheses have been advanced in which it is envisaged that energy from oxidation is conserved in conformational changes of molecules which in turn lead to the generation of high-energy phosphate bonds.

Table 17—2. States of respiratory control.

	Conditions Limiting the Rate of Respiration
State 1	Availability of ADP and substrate only
State 2	Availability of substrate only
State 3	The capacity of the respiratory chain itself, when all substrates and components are present in adequate amounts
State 4	Availability of ADP only
State 5	Availability of oxygen only

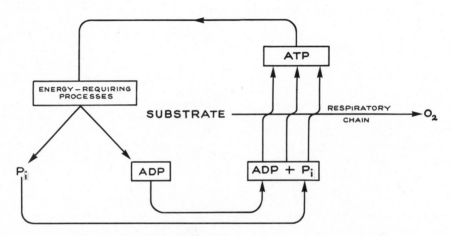

Figure 17—15. The role of ADP in respiratory control.

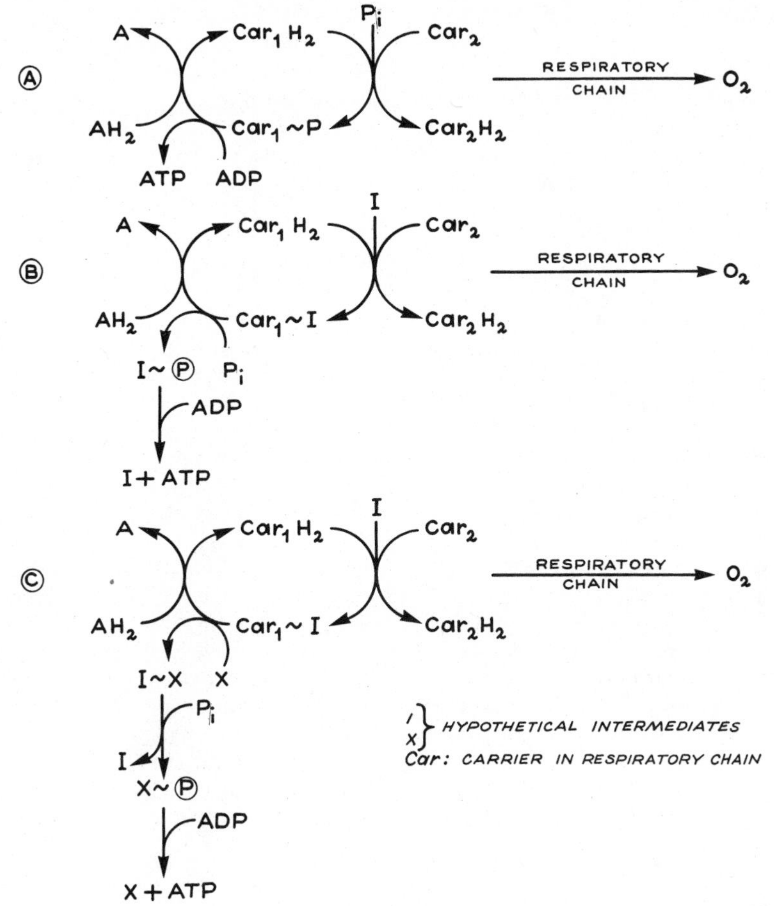

Figure 17—16. Possible mechanisms for the chemical coupling of oxidation and phosphorylation in the respiratory chain.

Table 17—3. Equations for oxidative phosphorylation occurring at the substrate level.

1.	3-Phosphoglyceraldehyde + NAD$^+$ + P$_i$ → 1~,3-Bisphosphoglycerate + NADH + H$^+$
	1~,3-Bisphosphoglycerate + ADP → 3-Phosphoglycerate + ATP
2.	2-Phosphoglycerate → 2~Phosphoenolpyruvate
	2~Phosphoenolpyruvate + ADP → Pyruvate + ATP
3.	a-Ketoglutarate + NAD$^+$ + CoA → Succinyl~CoA + NADH + H$^+$
	Succinyl~CoA + GDP* + P$_i$ → Succinate + GTP

*GDP is a compound analogous to ADP, adenine being replaced by guanine.

1. THE CHEMICAL HYPOTHESIS

Oxidative phosphorylation occurs in certain reactions of the Embden-Meyerhof system of glycolysis, in the citric acid cycle, and in the respiratory chain. However, it is only in those phosphorylations occurring at the substrate level in glycolysis and the citric acid cycle that the chemical mechanisms involved are known with any certainty. As these reactions have been used as models for investigating oxidative phosphorylation in the mitochondrial respiratory chain, their equations are shown in Table 17–3.

Several fundamental differences are evident in these equations. In equation 1, phosphate is incorporated into the product of the reaction **after** the redox reaction. In equation 2, phosphate is incorporated into the substrate **before** the internal rearrangement (redox change). In equation 3, the redox reaction leads to the generation of a high-energy compound other than a phosphate, which in a subsequent reaction leads to the formation of high-energy phosphate.

It is generally considered that oxidative phosphorylations in the respiratory chain follow the pattern shown in reactions 1 and 3, the latter being in effect an extension of 1 in which an extra nonphosphorylated high-energy intermediate stage is introduced. Of the possible mechanisms shown in Fig 17–16, mechanism C is favored since, in the presence of agents that uncouple phosphorylation from electron transport (eg, dinitrophenol), oxidation-reduction in the respiratory chain is independent of P_i. At present there is no definite knowledge of the identities of the hypothetical high-energy carrier (Car $\sim$ I) at any of the coupling sites of the respiratory chain. Likewise, the identities of the postulated intermediates I and X are not known. In recent years, several so-called "coupling factors" have been isolated that restore phosphorylation when added to disrupted mitochondria. These factors are mainly protein in nature and usually exhibit "ATPase" activity. In addition, attempts have been made to isolate high-energy intermediates of the respiratory chain and of its branches. A current view of the chemical coupling of phosphorylation to oxidation in the respiratory chain is shown in Fig 17–17.

Inhibitors of the Respiratory Chain & of Oxidative Phosphorylation

Much of the information shown in Fig 17–17 has been obtained by the use of inhibitors, and their proposed loci of action are shown. For descriptive purposes they may be divided into inhibitors of the respiratory chain, inhibitors of oxidative phosphorylation, and uncouplers of oxidative phosphorylation.

Inhibitors that arrest respiration by blocking the respiratory chain appear to act at 3 loci that may be identical to the energy transfer sites I, II, and III. Site I is inhibited by barbiturates such as amobarbital, by the antibiotic piericidin A, and by the fish poison rotenone. Some steroids and mercurials also affect this site.

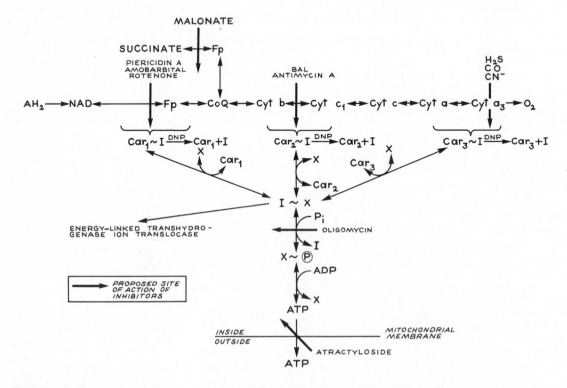

Figure 17–17. The coupling of phosphorylation to oxidation in the respiratory chain as interpreted by the chemical hypothesis. BAL = dimercaprol; DNP = dinitrophenol.

These inhibitors prevent the oxidation of substrates that communicate directly with the respiratory chain via an NAD-linked dehydrogenase, eg, β-hydroxybutyrate.

Dimercaprol and **antimycin A** inhibit the respiratory chain at or around site II, between cytochrome b and cytochrome c; and the inhibitors of cytochrome oxidase that have been known for many years are considered to act at or near site III.

The antibiotic **oligomycin** completely blocks oxidation and phosphorylation in intact mitochondria. However, in the presence of the uncoupler, dinitrophenol, oxidation proceeds without phosphorylation, indicating that oligomycin does not act directly on the respiratory chain but subsequently on a step in phosphorylation (Fig 17–17). As energy generated at one site of energy conservation may be used to reverse oxidation at another site, even in the presence of oligomycin and in the absence of Pᵢ, this inhibitor is considered to act after the stage represented by I ~ X.

Atractyloside inhibits oxidative phosphorylation which is dependent on the transport of adenine nucleotides across the inner mitochondrial membrane. It is considered to inhibit a "transporter" of ADP into the mitochondrion and of ATP out of the mitochondrion. Thus, it acts only on intact mitochondria but does not inhibit phosphorylation in particles which have no intact membrane.

The action of **uncouplers** is to dissociate oxidation in the respiratory chain from phosphorylation. This results in respiration becoming uncontrolled, the concentration of ADP or Pᵢ no longer limiting the rate of respiration. The uncoupler that has been used most frequently is 2,4-dinitrophenol, but other compounds act in a similar manner, including dinitrocresol, pentadichlorophenol, dicumarol, and CCCP (*m*-chlorocarbonyl cyanide phenylhydrazone). The latter, compared with dinitrophenol, is about 100 times as active. Dinitrophenol is considered to cause the hydrolysis of one of the high-energy intermediates (eg, Car ~ I), resulting in the release of the constituents Car + I and energy as heat. Because Car ~ I reacts to form, ultimately, ATP and because these reactions are reversible, dinitrophenol allows a reversal of the phosphorylation reactions, resulting in ATP hydrolysis, ie, release of latent ATP hydrolase activity. As mentioned earlier, oligomycin has no effect on respiration in the presence of dinitrophenol, but it does inhibit the latent ATP hydrolase resulting from the action of dinitrophenol because it inhibits the reactions involving phosphorylation (Fig 17–18).

Reversal of Electron Transport

Mitochondria catalyze the energy-dependent reversal of electron transport through the respiratory chain. The energy is provided either by ATP, where the effect is mediated by a complete reversal of oxidative phosphorylation; or the high-energy intermediate I ~ X can serve as a source of energy so that phosphorylation is not involved. A system demonstrating the latter effect may consist of mitochondria plus the addi-

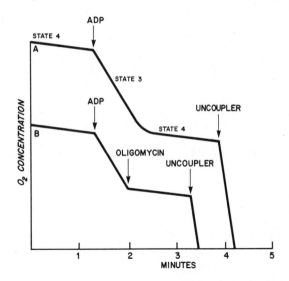

Figure 17–18. Respiratory control in mitochondria. Experiment A shows the basic state of respiration in state 4 which is accelerated upon addition of ADP. When the exogenous ADP has been phosphorylated to ATP, respiration reverts to state 4. The addition of uncoupler, eg, dinitrophenol, releases respiration from phosphorylation. In experiment B, addition of oligomycin blocks phosphorylation of added ADP and therefore of respiration as well. Addition of uncoupler again releases respiration from phosphorylation.

tion of succinate as electron donor and acetoacetate as electron acceptor. As succinate becomes oxidized, acetoacetate is reduced to β-hydroxybutyrate. It is considered that I ~ X is generated from sites II and III and used to drive reversed electron flow at site I, which enables NADH to be formed, which in turn reduces acetoacetate to β-hydroxybutyrate (Fig 17–17). Although these experiments demonstrate the reversibility of electron transport, the physiologic significance of the process is unknown.

Energy-Linked Transhydrogenase

There is evidence for an energy-linked transhydrogenase that can catalyze the transfer of hydrogen from NADH to NADP. It appears that the nonphosphorylated intermediate I ~ X supplies energy for the transfer as the process is inhibited by oligomycin only if ATP is used as energy source.

$$NADH + NADP^+ + I \sim X \longrightarrow NAD^+ + NADPH + I + X$$

Oxidation of Extramitochondrial NADH

Although NADH cannot penetrate the mitochondrial membrane, it is produced continuously in the cytosol by 3-phosphoglyceraldehyde dehydrogenase, an enzyme in the Embden-Meyerhof glycolysis sequence. However, under aerobic conditions, extramitochondrial NADH does not accumulate and is presumed to be oxidized by the respiratory chain in mitochondria. Several possible mechanisms have been

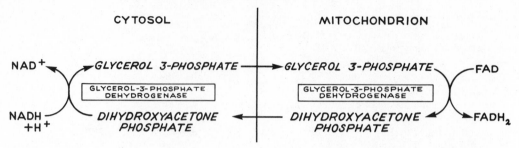

Figure 17—19. Glycerophosphate shuttle for transfer of reducing equivalents from the cytosol into the mitochondrion.

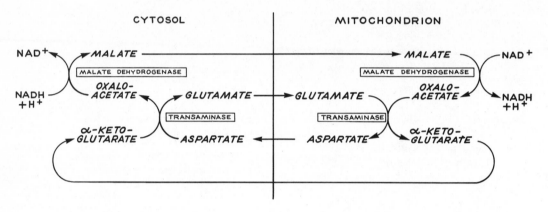

Figure 17—20. Malate shuttle for transfer of reducing equivalents from the cytosol into the mitochondria.

considered to permit this process. These involve transfer of reducing equivalents through the mitochondrial membrane via substrate pairs, linked by suitable dehydrogenases. Substrate pairs that have been considered include acetoacetate/β-hydroxybutyrate, lactate/pyruvate, dihydroxyacetone phosphate/glycerol 3-phosphate, and malate/oxaloacetate. It is necessary that the specific dehydrogenase be present on both sides of the mitochondrial membrane. However, β-hydroxybutyrate dehydrogenase is found only in mitochondria and lactate dehydrogenase only in the cytosol, ruling out these substrate pairs. Glycerol-3-phosphate dehydrogenase is NAD-linked in the cytosol, whereas the enzyme found in the mitochondria is a flavoprotein enzyme. The activity of the enzyme decreases after thyroidectomy and increases after administration of thyroxine. The mechanism of transfer using this system is shown in Fig 17—19. Although it is present in insect flight muscle and might be important in liver, in other tissues (eg, heart muscle) the mitochondrial glycerol-3-phosphate dehydrogenase is deficient. It is therefore believed that a transport system involving malate and malate dehydrogenase is of more universal occurrence. Rapid oxidation of NADH occurs only when aspartate-α-ketoglutarate transaminase and malate dehydrogenase, together with glutamate, aspartate, and malate, are added to mitochondria. The malate "shuttle" system is shown in Fig 17—20. The complexity of this system is due to the impermeability of the

mitochondrial membrane to oxaloacetate. However, the other anions are not freely permeable, requiring specific transport systems for passage across the membrane.

Energy-Linked Ion Transport in Mitochondria

Actively respiring mitochondria in which oxidative phosphorylation is taking place maintain or accumulate cations such as K^+, Na^+, Ca^{2+}, and Mg^{2+} and P_i from the mitochondria but the ion uptake is not inhibited by oligomycin, suggesting that the energy is supplied by a nonphosphorylated high-energy intermediate, eg, I $\sim$ X (Fig 17—17) in the case of the chemical hypothesis, or simply by cation exchange with protons in the case of the chemiosmotic hypothesis. Supporters of the chemiosmotic hypothesis envisage a primary proton pump, whereas in the chemical hypothesis an intermediate such as I $\sim$ X could drive either a proton or a cation pump.

2. THE CHEMIOSMOTIC HYPOTHESIS

Mitchell (1968) has provided a hypothesis that is able to explain the coupling of oxidation and phosphorylation without having to postulate an "energy-rich" intermediate common to both the respiratory

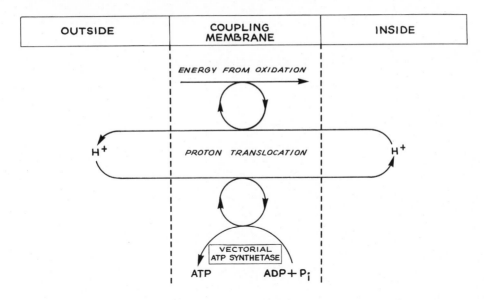

Figure 17—21. Principles of the chemiosmotic hypothesis of oxidative phosphorylation.

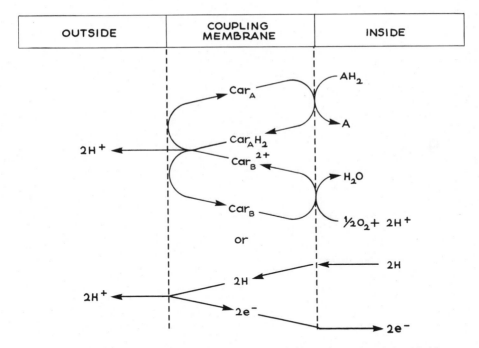

Figure 17—22. Proton-translocating oxidation/reduction (o/r) loop (chemiosmotic hypothesis).

chain and the phosphorylation pathway (ie, Car ~ I in Fig 17—17).

According to Mitchell, the primary event in oxidative phosphorylation is the translocation of protons (H^+) to the exterior of a coupling membrane (ie, the mitochondrial inner membrane) driven by oxidation in the respiratory chain. It is also postulated that the membrane is impermeable to ions in general but particularly to protons which accumulate outside the membrane, creating an electrochemical potential difference. This consists of a chemical potential (difference in pH) and a membrane potential. The electrochemical potential difference is used to drive a vectorial, membrane-located ATP synthetase (or the reversal of a membrane-located ATP hydrolase) which in the presence of P_i + ADP forms ATP. Thus, there is no high-energy intermediate which is common to both oxidation and phosphorylation (Fig 17—21).

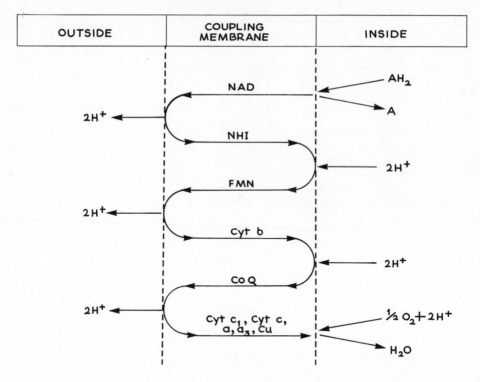

Figure 17—23. Possible configuration of o/r loops in the respiratory chain (chemiosmotic hypothesis). There is uncertainty with respect to the relative positions of cyt b and CoQ in the respiratory chain. In this scheme, cyt b is shown on the substrate side of CoQ as it fits the hypothesis and the redox potentials better in this position.

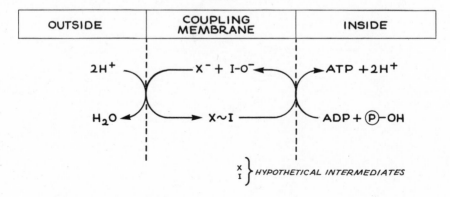

Figure 17—24. Proton-translocating reversible ATP synthetase of the chemiosmotic hypothesis.

It is proposed that the respiratory chain is folded into 3 oxidation/reduction (o/r) loops in the membrane, each loop corresponding functionally to coupling site I, site II, and site III of the chemical hypothesis, respectively. An idealized single loop consisting of a hydrogen carrier and an electron carrier is shown in Fig 17—22. A possible configuration of the respiratory chain folded into 3 o/r loops is shown in Fig 17—23.

The mechanism of coupling of proton translocation to the anisotropic (vectorial) ATP synthetase system is the most conjectural aspect of the hypothesis. Mitchell has postulated an anhydride intermediate X ~ I in a system depicted in Fig 17—24.

The existence of a membrane potential required to synthesize ATP would cause ions of a charge opposite to the internal phase to leak in through the coupling membrane. To prevent swelling and lysis, the ion leakage would have to be balanced by extrusion of ions against the electric gradient. It was therefore necessary to postulate that the coupling membrane contains exchange diffusion systems for exchange of anions against OH^- ions and of cations against H^+ ions. Such systems would be necessary for uptake of ionized metabolites through the membrane.

The chemiosmotic hypothesis can account for the phenomenon of respiratory control. The electrochemi-

•   •   •

cal potential difference across the membrane, once built up as a result of proton translocation, would inhibit further transport of reducing equivalents through the o/r loops unless it is discharged by back-translocation of protons across the membrane through the vectorial ATP synthetase system. This in turn depends on the availability of ADP and P_i as in the chemical hypothesis.

Several corollaries arise from the chemiosmotic hypothesis which have experimental support. These are as follows:

(1) Mitochondria are generally impermeable to protons and other ions. There is, however, evidence for the existence of specific transport systems which enable ions to penetrate the inner mitochondrial membrane.

(2) Uncouplers such as dinitrophenol increase the permeability of mitochondria to protons, thus reducing the electrochemical potential and short-circuiting the anisotropic ATP synthetase system for the generation of ATP.

(3) Addition of acid to the external medium, establishing a proton gradient, leads to the generation of ATP.

(4) The P/H^+ (transported out) quotient of the ATP synthetase is 1/2 and the H^+ (transported out)/O quotients for succinate and β-hydroxybutyrate oxidation are 4 and 6, respectively, conforming with the expected P/O ratios of 2 and 3, respectively. These ratios are compatible with the postulated existence of 3 o/r loops in the respiratory chain.

(5) Oxidative phosphorylation does not occur in soluble systems, where there is no possibility of a vectorial ATP synthetase. Some structural element involving a closed membrane must be present in the system to obtain oxidative phosphorylation.

The respiratory chain contains components organized in a sided manner as required by the chemiosmotic hypothesis.

Summary

The chemiosmotic hypothesis can explain oxidative phosphorylation, respiratory control, ion transport, the action of uncouplers, and the action of inhibitors as satisfactorily as the chemical hypothesis; but it has the virtue of being simpler, as it does not necessitate the postulation of a common high-energy intermediate of oxidation and phosphorylation. However, this subject is still surrounded by considerable controversy.

Anatomy & Function of the Mitochondrial Membranes

An account of the general structure of mitochondria is to be found in Chapter 5. Mitochondria have an outer membrane which is permeable to most metabolites, an inner membrane which is selectively permeable and which is thrown into folds or cristae, and a matrix within the inner membrane. The outer membrane may be removed by treatment with digitonin and is characterized by the presence of monoamine oxidase. Adenylate kinase is found in the space be-

tween the membranes. Cardiolipin is concentrated in the inner membrane where most of the lipid is phospholipid. The exact relationship of the lipid to the protein of the membranes is not understood. Delipidation of the inner membrane does not lead to its disruption.

The inner membrane consists of repeating units, each composed of a headpiece which projects into the matrix, joined by a stalk to a basepiece. Sonication leads to the formation of vesicles (submitochondrial particles) by the inner membrane with the headpieces facing the external medium (Fig 17–25). The whole of the electron transfer chain is found in the basepieces, and it is suggested that each basepiece is a complex containing a portion of the enzymes of the respiratory chain. Four of these complexes, together with mobile components (NADH, CoQ, and cytochrome c), constitute a complete respiratory chain. Cytochrome c is located in the outer side of the basepiece, and the ATP hydrolase (ATP synthetase) system resides in the headpiece. To be sensitive to oligomycin, the headpiece, stalk, and a juncture protein in the basepiece must be present. It has been postulated that each headpiece, stalk, and basepiece, together with one of the respiratory chain complexes, constitute a phosphorylating unit. Thus, energy released by electron transport in the basepiece could be conserved in the juncture protein of the basepiece and be transmitted through the stalk protein to the headpiece, where it is transduced into the phosphoryl bond of ATP. The soluble enzymes of the citric acid cycle and the enzymes of β-oxidation are found in the matrix, necessitating mechanisms for transporting ions, fatty and other organic acids, and nucleotides across the inner membrane.

Transport of Substances Into & Out of Mitochondria

The inner mitochondrial membrane is freely permeable to oxygen, water, CO_2, pyruvate, and other monocarboxylate ions such as β-hydroxybutyrate, acetoacetate, and acetate. Long chain fatty acids are transported into mitochondria via the carnitine system (Fig 20–2). However, dicarboxylate and tricarboxylate anions and amino acids require specific transporter or carrier systems to facilitate their transport across the membrane. It appears that monocarboxylate anions penetrate more readily because of the lesser degree of dissociation of these acids. It is the undissociated and more lipid-soluble acid that is thought to be the molecular species that penetrates the lipid membrane.

The transport of di- and tricarboxylate anions is closely linked to that of inorganic phosphate. Inorganic phosphate penetrates readily as the $H_2PO_4^-$ ion in exchange for OH^-. The net uptake of malate by the dicarboxylate transporter requires inorganic phosphate for exchange in the opposite direction. The net uptake of citrate, isocitrate, or cis-aconitate by the tricarboxylate transporter requires malate in exchange (Fig 17–26). α-Ketoglutarate transport also requires an exchange with malate. Thus, by the use of exchange mechanisms, osmotic balance is maintained. It will be

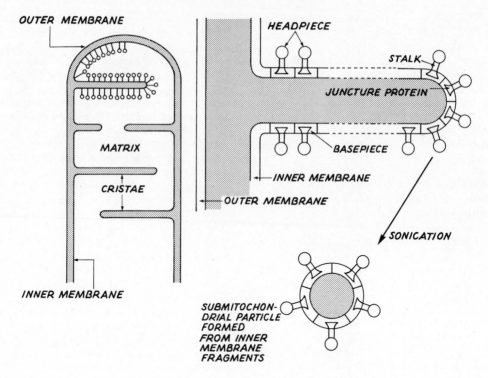

Figure 17—25. Structure of the mitochondrial membranes.

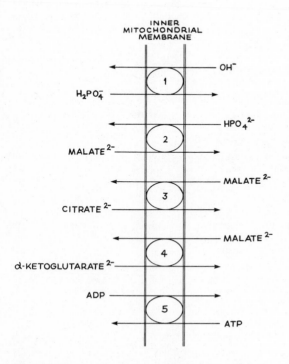

Figure 17—26. Transporter systems in the mitochondrial membrane. 1. Phosphate transporter. 2. Dicarboxylate transporter. 3. Tricarboxylate transporter. 4. α-Ketoglutarate transporter. 5. Adenine nucleotide transporter.

appreciated that citrate transport across the mitochondrial membrane depends not only on malate transport but on the transport of inorganic phosphate as well. The adenine nucleotide transporter allows the exchange of ATP and ADP but not AMP.

Action of Ionophores

These substances are so termed because of their ability to complex specific cations and thus to facilitate cation transport through biologic membranes. This property of ionophoresis is due to their lipophilic character, which allows penetration of lipoid membranes such as the mitochondrial membrane. An example is the antibiotic **valinomycin,** which allows penetration of K^+ through the mitochondrial membrane, which then discharges the electrochemical gradient between the inside and the outside of the mitochondrion and effectively uncouples respiration from phosphorylation.

References

Baltscheffsky H, Baltscheffsky M: Electron transport phosphorylation. Annu Rev Biochem 43:871, 1974.

Boyd GS, Smellie RMS (editors): *Biological Hydroxylation Mechanisms*. Academic Press, 1972.

Friedovich I: Superoxide dismutases. Annu Rev Biochem 44:147, 1975.

Gunsalus IC, Pederson TC, Sligar SG: Oxygenase-catalyzed biological hydroxylations. Annu Rev Biochem 44:377, 1975.

Hayaishi O (editor): *Oxygenases*. Academic Press, 1972.

Lehninger AL: *The Mitochondrion*. Benjamin, 1964.

Lemberg R, Barrett J: *Cytochromes*. Academic Press, 1973.

Lovenberg W (editor): *Iron-Sulfur Proteins*. 2 vols. Academic Press, 1973.

Mitchell P: *Chemiosmotic Coupling and Energy Transduction*. Glynn Research, Bodmin, United Kingdom, 1968.

Schenkman JB, Jansson I, Robie-Suh KM: The many roles of cytochrome b_5 in hepatic microsomes. Life Sci 19:611, 1976.

Singer TP (editor): *Biological Oxidations*. Interscience, 1968.

Sund H (editor): *Pyridine Nucleotide Dependent Dehydrogenases*. Springer, 1970.

Wainio WW: *The Mammalian Mitochondrial Respiratory Chain*. Academic Press, 1970.

18 . . .
The Citric Acid Cycle

The citric acid cycle (Krebs, or tricarboxylic acid cycle) is a series of reactions in mitochondria which catabolizes the oxidation of acetyl residues to CO_2 and water. The acetyl residues are in the form of **acetyl-CoA** (active acetate), an ester of coenzyme A. The latter is a complex nucleotide containing the vitamin pantothenic acid. Essentially, the cycle comprises the combination of a molecule of acetyl-CoA with the 4-carbon dicarboxylic acid oxaloacetate, resulting in the formation of a 6-carbon tricarboxylic acid, citrate. There follows a series of reactions in the course of which 2 molecules of CO_2 are lost and oxaloacetate is regenerated (Fig 18—1). Since only a small quantity of oxaloacetate is able to facilitate the conversion of a large quantity of acetyl units to CO_2, oxaloacetate may be considered to play a catalytic role.

Significance of the Citric Acid Cycle

The major contribution of the cycle is to act as the final common pathway for the oxidation of carbohydrate, lipids, and protein because glucose, fatty acids, and many amino acids are all metabolized to acetyl-CoA (Fig 18—2). Furthermore, the citric acid cycle is the mechanism by which much of the free energy liberated during respiration is made available. During the course of oxidation of acetyl-CoA in the cycle, reducing equivalents in the form of hydrogen or of electrons are formed as a result of the activity of specific dehydrogenases. These reducing equivalents then enter the respiratory chain, where large amounts of high-energy phosphate are generated in the process of oxidative phosphorylation (Fig 18—2; see also Chapter 17).

It is noteworthy that the enzymes of the citric acid cycle are located in the mitochondrial matrix, either free or attached to the inner surface of the inner mitochondrial membrane, which facilitates the transfer of reducing equivalents to the adjacent enzymes of the respiratory chain which is situated in the inner mitochondrial membrane.

It is of further significance that the citric acid cycle is dual or **amphibolic** in nature, which allows it to be a source of molecules for anabolic processes such as fatty acid and amino acid synthesis and gluconeogenesis.

Historical Aspects

By 1935 it was known that certain dicarboxylic and tricarboxylic acids were actively oxidized by respiring aerobic tissues. Szent-Györgyi had established that succinate was converted to oxaloacetate via fumarate and malate, and Martius and Knoop showed that succinate could be formed from citrate via a-ketoglutarate. In 1937, Krebs supplied a conceptual basis for these reactions by suggesting that they were arranged in a cyclic sequence termed the "citric acid cycle." Krebs came to this conclusion in the course of investigations on pigeon breast muscle, a very actively respiring tissue, in which he showed that oxidation of pyruvate or of endogenous carbohydrate was stimulated by only small amounts of citric acid cycle intermediates, ie, in a catalytic manner. In other experiments where malonate was added as an inhibitor of succinate dehydrogenase, it was noted that succinate accumulated after addition of pyruvate or any of the other intermediates of the citric acid cycle. The block in pyruvate utilization could be relieved by the addition of oxaloacetate on a mole-for-mole basis, thus establishing the existence of the initial condensation reaction which forms citrate.

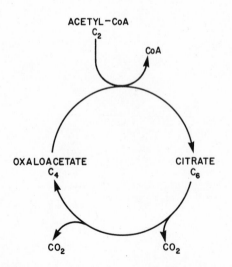

Figure 18—1. Citric acid cycle, illustrating the catalytic role of oxaloacetate.

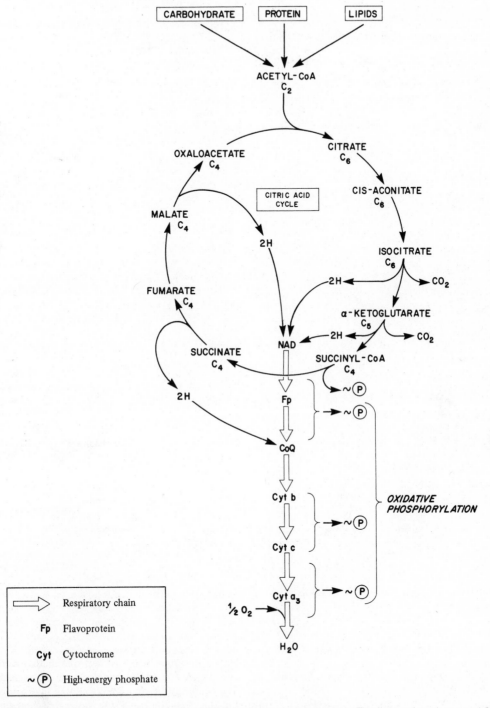

Figure 18–2. The citric acid cycle: the major pathway of respiration in aerobic organisms. The diagram shows how acetyl-CoA, the major product of carbohydrate, protein, and lipid catabolism, is oxidized by the cycle to CO_2 and water.

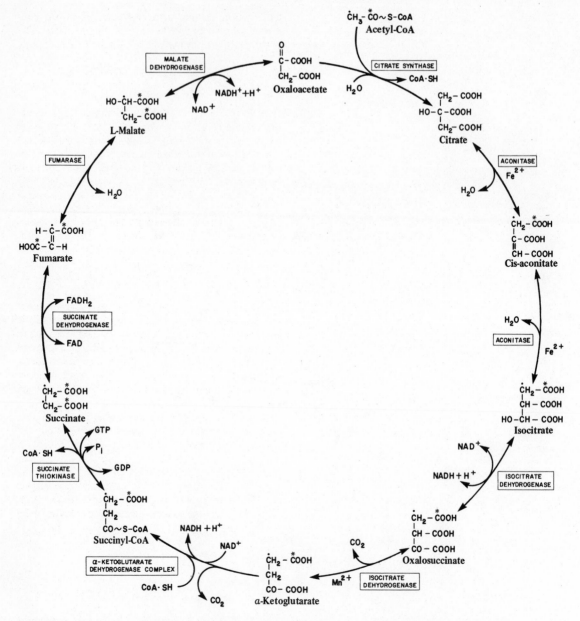

Figure 18—3. The citric acid (Krebs) cycle. Oxidation of NADH and FADH$_2$ in the respiratory chain leads to the generation of ATP via oxidative phosphorylation.

Reactions of the Citric Acid Cycle (See Fig 18—3.)*

$$\text{Acetyl-CoA + Oxaloacetate + H}_2\text{O} \rightarrow \text{Citrate + CoA·SH}$$

The initial condensation of acetyl-CoA with oxaloacetate to form citrate is catalyzed by a con-

densing enzyme, **citrate synthase**, which effects a carbon-to-carbon bond between the methyl carbon of acetyl-CoA and the carbonyl carbon of oxaloacetate. The condensation reaction is followed by hydrolysis of the thioester bond of CoA, which is accompanied by considerable loss of free energy as heat, ensuring that the reaction goes to completion.

Citrate is converted to isocitrate by the enzyme **aconitase** (aconitate hydratase), which contains iron in the Fe^{2+} state. This conversion takes place in 2 steps: dehydration to cis-aconitate, some of which remains bound to the enzyme, and rehydration to isocitrate. The reaction is inhibited by the presence of fluoroace-

*From Circular No. 200 of the Committee of Editors of Biochemical Journals Recommendations (1975): "According to standard biochemical convention, the ending -ate in, eg, palmitate, denotes any mixture of free acid and the ionized form(s) (according to pH) in which the cations are not specified." The same convention is adopted in this text for all carboxylic acids.

A

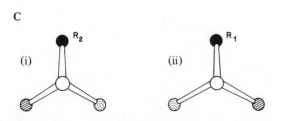

tate, which, in the form of fluoroacetyl-CoA, condenses with oxaloacetate to form fluorocitrate. The latter inhibits aconitase, causing citrate to accumulate.

$$\text{Citrate} \xrightleftharpoons[\text{H}_2\text{O}]{} \text{Cis-aconitate} \xrightleftharpoons[\text{H}_2\text{O}]{} \text{Isocitrate}$$

Experiments using ^{14}C-labeled intermediates indicate that citrate reacts in an asymmetric manner, with the result that aconitase always acts on that part of the citrate molecule which is derived from oxaloacetate. Ogston suggested that this was due to a 3-point attachment of the enzyme to the substrate (see Fig 18–4). The 3-point attachment would enable aconitase to differentiate the two $-\text{CH}_2\text{COOH}$ groups in citrate (Fig 18–4b), thus conferring asymmetry on an apparently symmetric molecule. However, the 3-point attachment hypothesis is not necessary to explain the asymmetric action of aconitase. It is now realized that the two $-\text{CH}_2\text{COOH}$ groups (R_1 and R_2 in Fig 18–4) are not identical in space with respect to the $-\text{OH}$ and $-\text{COOH}$ groups. This may be appreciated by reference to Fig 18–4c. The consequences of the asymmetric action of aconitase may be appreciated by reference to the fate of labeled acetyl-CoA in the citric acid cycle as shown in Fig 18–3. It is possible that cis-aconitate may not be an obligatory intermediate between citrate and isocitrate but may in fact be a side branch from the main pathway.

Isocitrate undergoes dehydrogenation in the presence of **isocitrate dehydrogenase** to form oxalosuccinate. Three different enzymes have been described. One, which is NAD-specific, is found only in mitochondria. The other 2 enzymes are NADP-specific and are found in the mitochondria and the cytosol, respectively. Respiratory chain-linked oxidation of isocitrate proceeds almost completely through the NAD-dependent enzyme.

$$\text{Isocitrate} + \text{NAD}^+ \longleftrightarrow \underset{\text{(enzyme bound)}}{\text{Oxalosuccinate}} \longleftrightarrow$$

$$a\text{-Ketoglutarate} + \text{CO}_2 + \text{NADH} + \text{H}^+$$

There follows a decarboxylation to a-ketoglutarate, also catalyzed by isocitrate dehydrogenase. Mn^{2+} is an important component of the decarboxylation reaction. It would appear that oxalosuccinate remains bound to the enzyme as an intermediate in the overall reaction.

Next, a-ketoglutarate undergoes oxidative decarboxylation in a manner which is analogous to the oxidative decarboxylation of pyruvate, both substrates being a-keto acids (Fig 18–5).

$$a\text{-Ketoglutarate} + \text{NAD}^+ + \text{CoA} \cdot \text{SH} \longleftrightarrow$$

$$\text{Succinyl-CoA} + \text{CO}_2 + \text{NADH} + \text{H}^+$$

The reaction catalyzed by an **a-ketoglutarate dehydrogenase** complex also requires identical cofactors—eg, thiamin diphosphate, lipoate, NAD^+, FAD, and CoA—

B

Enzyme surface with
points of attachment
to the substrate

C

(i)   (ii)

Figure 18–4. Asymmetry of citrate and the action of aconitase. *A:* Structure of citrate showing the 4 substituent groups attached to the central carbon atom at the apices of a regular tetrahedron. *B:* The Ogston hypothesis of a 3-point attachment of the substrate to the enzyme. Only bonds marked "X" are converted to the double bond in cis-aconitate. *C:* View of the molecule from (i) R_1 and (ii) R_2, showing the stereochemical difference of R_1 and R_2.

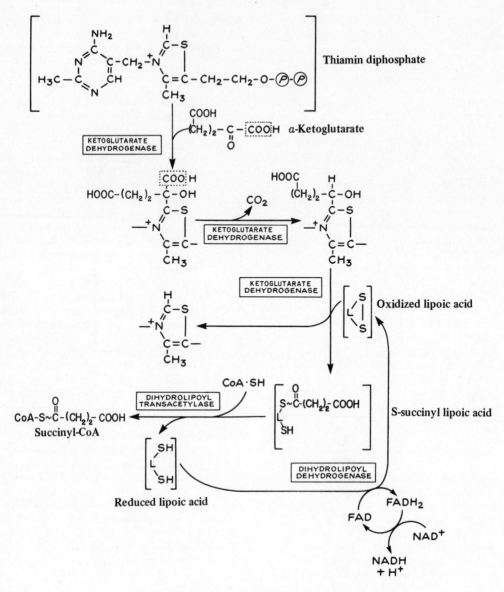

Figure 18—5. Oxidative decarboxylation of a-ketoglutarate.

and results in the formation of succinyl-CoA, a thio-ester containing a high-energy bond. The equilibrium of this reaction is so much in favor of succinyl-CoA formation that the reaction must be considered as physiologically unidirectional. Again, as in the case of pyruvate oxidation, arsenite inhibits the reaction, causing the substrate, **a-ketoglutarate**, to accumulate.

To continue the cycle, succinyl-CoA is converted to succinate by the enzyme **succinate thiokinase (succinyl-CoA synthetase).**

$$\text{Succinyl-CoA} + \text{P}_\text{i} + \text{GDP} \longleftrightarrow \text{Succinate} + \text{GTP} + \text{CoA} \cdot \text{SH}$$

This reaction requires GDP or IDP, which is converted in the presence of inorganic phosphate to either GTP

or ITP. This is the only example in the citric acid cycle of the generation of a high-energy phosphate at the substrate level. By means of a phosphokinase, ATP may be formed from either GTP or ITP,

$$\text{eg, GTP} + \text{ADP} \longleftrightarrow \text{GDP} + \text{ATP}$$

An alternative reaction in extrahepatic tissues, which is catalyzed by **succinyl-CoA-acetoacetate CoA transferase (thiophorase),** is the conversion of succinyl-CoA to succinate coupled with the conversion of acetoacetate to acetoacetyl-CoA. In liver there is also deacylase activity, causing some hydrolysis of succinyl-CoA to succinate plus CoA.

Succinate is metabolized further by undergoing a

dehydrogenation followed by the addition of water, and subsequently by a further dehydrogenation which regenerates oxaloacetate.

$$\text{Succinate} + \text{FAD} \longleftrightarrow \text{Fumarate} + \text{FADH}_2$$

The first dehydrogenation reaction is catalyzed by **succinate dehydrogenase**, which is bound to the inner surface of the inner mitochondrial membrane. It is the only dehydrogenation in the citric acid cycle which involves the direct transfer of hydrogen from the substrate to a flavoprotein without the participation of NAD. The enzyme contains FAD and nonheme iron. Fumarate is formed as a result of the dehydrogenation. Isotopic experiments have shown that the enzyme is sterospecific for the *trans* hydrogen atoms of the methylene carbons of succinate. Addition of malonate or oxaloacetate inhibits succinate dehydrogenase competitively, resulting in succinate accumulation.

Under the influence of **fumarase (fumarate hydratase)**, water is added to fumarate to give malate.

$$\text{Fumarate} + \text{H}_2\text{O} \longleftrightarrow \text{L-Malate}$$

In addition to being specific for the L-isomer of malate, fumarase catalyzes the addition of the elements of water to the double bond of fumarate in the *trans* configuration. Malate is converted to oxaloacetate by **malate dehydrogenase**, a reaction requiring NAD⁺.

$$\text{L-Malate} + \text{NAD}^+ \longleftrightarrow \text{Oxaloacetate} + \text{NADH} + \text{H}^+$$

Although the equilibrium of this reaction is much in favor of malate, the net flux is toward the direction of oxaloacetate because this compound together with the other product of the reaction (NADH) is removed continuously in further reactions.

The enzymes participating in the citric acid cycle are also found outside the mitochondria except for the a-ketoglutarate and succinate dehydrogenases. While they may catalyze similar reactions, some of the enzymes, eg, malate dehydrogenase, may not in fact be the same proteins as the mitochondrial enzymes of the same name.

In order to follow the passage of acetyl-CoA through the cycle (Fig 18–3), the 2 carbon atoms of the acetyl radical are shown labeled on the carboxyl carbon (using the designation [*]) and on the methyl carbon (using the designation [·]). Although 2 carbon atoms are lost as CO_2 in one revolution of the cycle, these particular atoms are not derived from the acetyl-CoA which has immediately entered the cycle but arise from that portion of the citrate molecule which was derived from oxaloacetate. However, on completion of a single turn of the cycle, the oxaloacetate which is regenerated is now labeled, which leads to labeled CO_2 being evolved during the second turn of the cycle. It is to be noted that because succinate is a symmetric compound and because succinate dehydrogenase does not differentiate between its 2 carboxyl groups, "random-

ization" of label occurs at this step such that all 4 carbon atoms of oxaloacetate appear to be labeled after one turn of the cycle. When gluconeogenesis takes place, some of the label in oxaloacetate makes its way into glucose and glycogen. In this process, oxaloacetate is decarboxylated in the carboxyl group adjacent to the CH_2 group. As a result of recombination of the resulting 3-carbon residues in a process which is essentially a reversal of glycolysis, the eventual location of label from acetate in glucose (or glycogen) is distributed in a characteristic manner. Thus, if oxaloacetate leaves the citric acid cycle after only one turn from the entry of labeled acetyl-CoA ("acetate"), label from the carboxyl carbon of acetate is found in carbon atoms 3 and 4 of glucose, whereas label from the methyl carbon of acetate is found in carbon atoms 1, 2, 5, and 6. For a discussion of the stereochemical aspects of the citric acid cycle, see Greville (1968).

Energetics of the Citric Acid Cycle

As a result of oxidations catalyzed by dehydrogenase enzymes of the citric acid cycle, 3 molecules of NADH and one of $FADH_2$ are produced for each molecule of acetyl-CoA catabolized in one revolution of the cycle. These reducing equivalents are transferred to the respiratory chain in the inner mitochondrial membrane (Fig 18–2). During passage along the chain, reducing equivalents from NADH will generate 3 high-energy phosphate bonds by the esterification of ADP to ATP in the process of oxidative phosphorylation (Chapter 17). However, $FADH_2$ produces only 2 high-energy phosphate bonds because it transfers its reducing power to CoQ, thus bypassing the first site for oxidative phosphorylation in the respiratory chain (see p 231). A further high-energy phosphate is generated at the level of the cycle itself (ie, at substrate level) during the conversion of succinyl-CoA to succinate. Thus, 12 new high-energy phosphate bonds are generated for each turn of the cycle (Table 18–1).

Amphibolic Role of the Citric Acid Cycle

In the introduction to this chapter, reference was made to the amphibolic role of the cycle. This involves

Table 18–1. Generation of high-energy bonds in the citric acid cycle.

Reaction Catalyzed By	Method of ~ P Production	Number of ~ P Formed
Isocitrate dehydrogenase	Respiratory chain oxidation of NADH	3
a-Ketoglutarate dehydrogenase	Respiratory chain oxidation of NADH	3
Succinate thiokinase	Oxidation at substrate level	1
Succinate dehydrogenase	Respiratory chain oxidation of $FADH_2$	2
Malate dehydrogenase	Respiratory chain oxidation of NADH	3
		Net 12

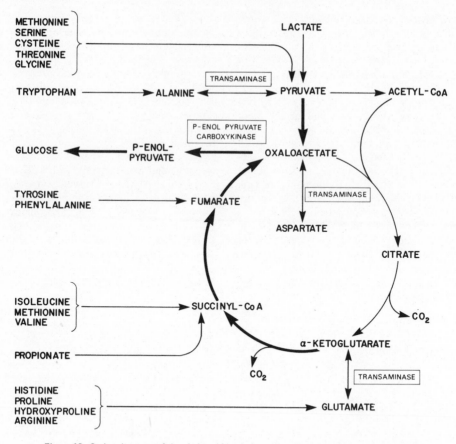

Figure 18—6. Involvement of the citric acid cycle in transamination and gluconeogenesis.

either metabolic pathways which end in a constituent of the cycle or pathways which originate from the cycle. These pathways concern the processes of gluconeogenesis, transamination, and deamination and fatty acid synthesis. Although these will be discussed in greater detail in subsequent chapters, they are summarized below.

Gluconeogenesis, Transamination, & Deamination

All chemical constituents of the cycle, from citrate to oxaloacetate, are potentially glucogenic since they can give rise to a net production of glucose in the liver or kidney, the organs which contain a complete set of enzymes necessary for gluconeogenesis (see p 267). The key enzyme that facilitates the net transfer out of the cycle into the main pathway of gluconeogenesis is **phosphoenolpyruvate carboxykinase**, which catalyzes the decarboxylation of oxaloacetate to phosphoenolpyruvate, GTP acting as the source of high-energy phosphate (Fig 18—6).

$$\text{Oxaloacetate} + \text{GTP} \rightarrow \text{Phosphoenolpyruvate} + CO_2 + \text{GDP}$$

Net transfer into the cycle (anaplerotic reactions) occurs as a result of several different reactions. Among the most significant is the formation of oxaloacetate

by the carboxylation of pyruvate, catalyzed by **pyruvate carboxylase**.

$$\text{ATP} + CO_2 + H_2O + \text{Pyruvate} \longleftrightarrow \text{Oxaloacetate} + \text{ADP} + P_i$$

This reaction is considered important in maintaining adequate concentrations of oxaloacetate for the condensation reaction with acetyl-CoA. If acetyl-CoA accumulates, it acts as an allosteric activator of pyruvate carboxylase, thereby ensuring a supply of oxaloacetate. Lactate, an important substrate for gluconeogenesis, enters the cycle via conversion to pyruvate and oxaloacetate.

Transaminase reactions produce pyruvate from alanine, oxaloacetate from aspartate, and α-ketoglutarate from glutamic acid. Because these reactions are reversible, the cycle also serves as a source of carbon skeletons for the synthesis of nonessential amino acids, eg,

$$\text{Aspartate} + \text{Pyruvate} \longleftrightarrow \text{Oxaloacetate} + \text{Alanine}$$

$$\text{Glutamate} + \text{Pyruvate} \longleftrightarrow \alpha\text{-Ketoglutarate} + \text{Alanine}$$

Other amino acids contribute to gluconeogenesis because all or part of their carbon skeletons is fed into

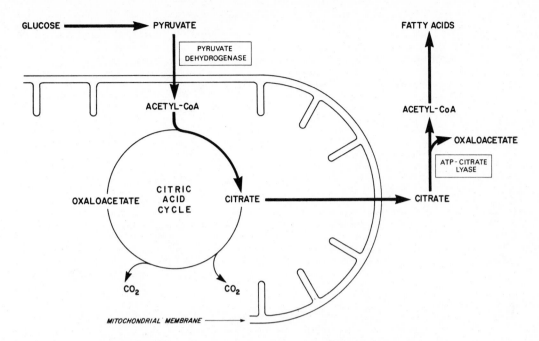

Figure 18—7. Participation of the citric acid cycle in fatty acid synthesis from glucose.

the citric acid cycle after deamination or transamination. Examples are alanine, cysteine, glycine, hydroxyproline, serine, threonine, and tryptophan, which form pyruvate, arginine, histidine, glutamate, and proline, which form α-ketoglutarate via glutamate, isoleucine, methionine, and valine, which form succinyl-CoA, and tyrosine and phenylalanine, which form fumarate. (See Fig 18–6.) It should be noted that substances forming pyruvate have the option of complete oxidation to CO_2 if they follow the **pyruvate** dehydrogenase pathway to acetyl-CoA, or they may follow the glucogenic pathway via carboxylation to oxaloacetate.

Of particular significance to ruminants is the conversion of propionate, the major glucogenic product of rumen fermentation, to succinyl-CoA via the methylmalonyl-CoA pathway.

Fatty Acid Synthesis (See Fig 18–7.)

Acetyl-CoA formed from pyruvate is the major building block for long-chain fatty acid synthesis in nonruminants. (In ruminants, acetyl-CoA is derived directly from acetate). As pyruvate dehydrogenase is a mitochondrial enzyme and the enzymes responsible for fatty acid synthesis are extramitochondrial, the cell has the problem of transporting impermeable acetyl-CoA through the mitochondrial membrane into the cytosol. This is achieved by allowing acetyl-CoA to form citrate in the citric acid cycle, transporting citrate out of the mitochondria, and finally making acetyl-CoA available in the cytosol by cleaving citrate in a reaction catalyzed by the enzyme **ATP-citrate lyase**, as shown below.

Citrate + ATP + CoA → Acetyl-CoA + Oxaloacetate + ADP + P_i

Another reaction whose function probably is to supply reducing equivalents in the form of NADPH for fatty acid synthesis is that catalyzed by the extramitochondrial **malic enzyme** (malate dehydrogenase [decarboxylating; NADP]).

$$\text{L-Malate} + \text{NADP}^+ \longleftrightarrow \text{Pyruvate} + CO_2 + \text{NADPH} + H^+$$

Regulation of the Citric Acid Cycle

The identification of regulatory enzymes of the citric acid cycle is difficult because of the many pathways with which the cycle interacts as well as its location within the mitochondrion wherein measurement of enzyme activity and substrate levels is relatively uncertain. In most tissues, where the primary function of the citric acid cycle is to provide energy, there is little doubt that respiratory control via the respiratory chain and oxidative phosphorylation is the overriding control on citric acid cycle activity. Thus, activity is immediately dependent on the supply of reduced dehydrogenase cofactors (eg, NADH), which in turn is dependent on the availability of ADP and ultimately, therefore, on the rate of utilization of ATP. In addition to this overall or coarse control, the properties of some of the enzymes of the cycle indicate that control might also be exerted at the level of the cycle itself. In a tissue such as brain, which is largely dependent on carbohydrate to supply acetyl-CoA, control of the citric acid cycle may occur at the pyruvate dehydrogenase step. In the cycle proper, control may be exercised by allosteric inhibition of citrate synthase by ATP or long chain fatty acyl-CoA. Allosteric activation of mitochondrial NAD-dependent isocitrate dehydrogenase by ADP is counteracted by

ATP and NADH. The a-ketoglutarate dehydrogenase complex appears to be under control analogous to that of pyruvate dehydrogenase. Succinate dehydrogenase is inhibited by oxaloacetate, and the availability of oxaloacetate, as controlled by malate dehydrogenase, depends on the NADH/NAD ratio. In the heart the cycle is controlled by the NADH/NAD ratio via the availability of oxaloacetate and by the ATP/ADP ratio via inhibition of citrate synthase by succinyl-CoA in competition with acetyl-CoA. An increased ATP/ADP ratio is considered to raise the GTP/GDP ratio at the succinate thiokinase step, thereby increasing the concentration of succinyl-CoA. Which (if any) of these mechanisms operates in vivo has still to be resolved.

•   •   •

References

Boyer PD (editor): *The Enzymes,* 3rd ed. Academic Press, 1971.

Goodwin TW (editor): *The Metabolic Roles of Citrate.* Academic Press, 1968.

Greville GD: Vol 1, p 297, in: *Carbohydrate Metabolism and Its Disorders.* Dickens F, Randle PJ, Whelan WJ (editors). Academic Press, 1968.

Lowenstein JM (editor): *Citric Acid Cycle: Control and Compartmentation.* Dekker, 1969.

Lowenstein JM (editor): *The Citric Acid Cycle.* Methods in Ezymology. Vol 13. Academic Press, 1969.

Lowenstein JM: Vol 1, p 146, in: *Metabolic Pathways,* 3rd ed. Greenberg DM (editor). Academic Press, 1967.

19...
Metabolism of Carbohydrate

Although the human diet is variable, in most instances carbohydrate accounts for a large proportion of the daily intake. However, much of the dietary carbohydrate is converted to fat and consequently is metabolized as fat. The extent of this process (lipogenesis) depends on whether or not the animal is a "meal eater" or a more continuous feeder. It is possible that in man the frequency of taking meals and the extent to which carbohydrates are converted to fat could have a bearing on disease states such as atherosclerosis, obesity, and diabetes mellitus. In herbivores, especially ruminants, much of the intake of carbohydrate is fermented by microorganisms to lower fatty acids prior to absorption from the alimentary tract.

The major function of carbohydrate in metabolism is as a fuel to be oxidized and provide energy for other metabolic processes. In this role, carbohydrate is utilized by cells mainly in the form of glucose. The 3 principal monosaccharides resulting from the digestive processes are glucose, fructose, and galactose. Fructose may assume considerable quantitative importance if there is a large intake of sucrose. Galactose is of major quantitative significance only when lactose is the principal carbohydrate of the diet. Both fructose and galactose are readily converted to glucose by the liver.

Pentose sugars such as xylose, arabinose, and ribose may be present in the diet, but their fate after absorption is obscure. D-Ribose and D-2-deoxyribose are synthesized in the body for incorporation into nucleotides.

INTERMEDIARY METABOLISM OF CARBOHYDRATE

The metabolism of carbohydrate in the mammalian organism may be subdivided as follows:

(1) Glycolysis: The oxidation of glucose or glycogen to pyruvate and lactate by the Embden-Meyerhof pathway.

(2) Glycogenesis: The synthesis of glycogen from glucose.

(3) Glycogenolysis: The breakdown of glycogen. Glucose is the main end product of glycogenolysis in the liver, and pyruvate and lactate are the main products in muscle.

(4) The oxidation of pyruvate to acetyl-CoA: This is a necessary step prior to the entrance of the products of glycolysis into the citric acid cycle, which is the final common pathway for the oxidation of carbohydrate, fat, and protein.

(5) The hexose monophosphate shunt (direct oxidative pathway, phosphogluconate oxidative pathway, pentose phosphate cycle): An alternative pathway to the Embden-Meyerhof pathway and the citric acid cycle for the oxidation of glucose.

(6) Gluconeogenesis: The formation of glucose or glycogen from noncarbohydrate sources. The pathways involved in gluconeogenesis are mainly the citric acid cycle and glycolysis. The principal substrates for gluconeogenesis are glucogenic amino acids, lactate, and glycerol, and, in the ruminant, propionate (Fig 19–1).

GLYCOLYSIS

At an early period in the course of investigations on carbohydrate metabolism it was realized that the process of fermentation in yeast was similar to the breakdown of glycogen in muscle. Although many of the early investigations of the glycolytic pathway were carried out on these 2 systems, the process is now known to occur in virtually all tissues.

In many of the first studies on the biochemical changes which occur during muscular contraction it was noted that when a muscle contracts in an anaerobic medium, ie, one from which oxygen is excluded, glycogen disappears and pyruvate and lactate appear as the principal end products. When oxygen is admitted, aerobic recovery takes place and glycogen reappears, while pyruvate and lactate disappear. However, if contraction takes place under aerobic conditions, lactate does not accumulate and pyruvate is oxidized further to CO_2 and water. As a result of these observations, it has been customary to separate carbohydrate metabolism into anaerobic and aerobic phases. However, this distinction is arbitrary since the reactions in glycolysis are the same in the presence of oxygen as in its absence except in extent and end products. When oxygen is in short supply, reoxidation of NADH formed during glycolysis is impaired. Under these circumstances

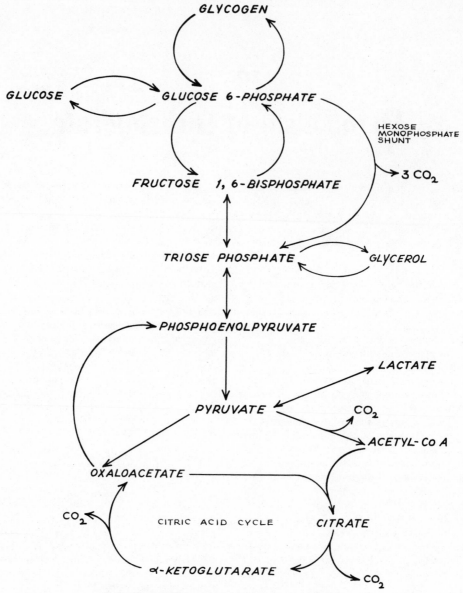

Figure 19–1. Major pathways of carbohydrate metabolism.

NADH is reoxidized by being coupled to the reduction of pyruvate to lactate, the NAD so formed being used to allow further glycolysis to proceed (Fig 19–2). Glycolysis can thus take place under anaerobic conditions, but this limits the amount of energy liberated per mol of glucose oxidized. Consequently, to provide a given amount of energy, more glucose must undergo glycolysis under anaerobic as compared with aerobic conditions.

The overall equation for glycolysis to lactate is

Glucose + 2 ADP + 2 P_i → 2 L(+)-Lactate + 2 ATP + 2 H_2O

Sequence of Reactions in Glycolysis

All of the enzymes of the Embden-Meyerhof

pathway (Fig 19–2) are found in the extramitochondrial soluble fraction of the cell, the cytosol. They catalyze the reactions involved in the glycolysis of glucose to lactate, which are as follows:

Glucose enters into the glycolytic pathway by phosphorylation to glucose 6-phosphate. This is accomplished by the enzyme **hexokinase** and by an additional enzyme in the liver, **glucokinase**, whose activity is inducible and affected by changes in the nutritional state. The reaction is accompanied by considerable loss of free energy as heat and must therefore be regarded as a "nonequilibrium" type reaction, ie, physiologically irreversible. ATP is required as phosphate donor, and, as in many reactions involving phosphorylation, it reacts as the Mg-ATP complex. One

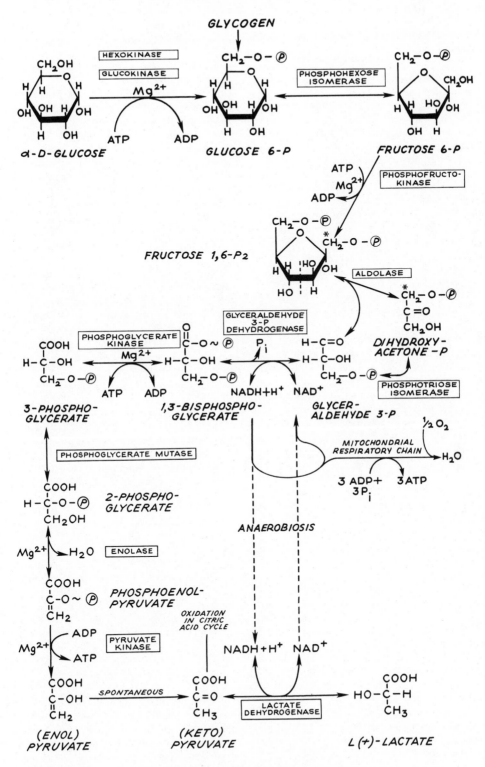

Figure 19—2. Embden-Meyerhof pathway of glycolysis.

high-energy phosphate bond of ATP is utilized and ADP is produced. Hexokinase activity is present in rat liver in as many as 3 different enzyme proteins (isozymes). It is inhibited in an allosteric manner by the product, glucose 6-phosphate.

$$a\text{-D-Glucose} + ATP \xrightarrow{Mg^{2+}} a\text{-D-Glucose 6-phosphate} + ATP$$

In contrast to glucokinase, hexokinase has a high affinity (low K_m) for its substrate, glucose. Its function is to ensure a supply of glucose for the tissues even in the presence of low blood glucose concentrations. It will also catalyze the phosphorylation of other hexoses but at a slower rate than glucose. The function of glucokinase is to remove glucose from the blood following a meal.

Glucose 6-phosphate is an important compound, being at the junction of several metabolic pathways (glycolysis, gluconeogenesis, the hexose monophosphate shunt, glycogenesis, and glycogenolysis) (Fig 19–1). In glycolysis it is converted to fructose 6-phosphate by **phosphohexose isomerase**.

$$a\text{-D-Glucose 6-phosphate} \longleftrightarrow a\text{-D-Fructose 6-phosphate}$$

This reaction is followed by another phosphorylation with ATP catalyzed by the enzyme **phosphofructokinase** to produce fructose 1,6-bisphosphate. Phosphofructokinase is another inducible enzyme whose activity is considered to play a major role in the regulation of the rate of glycolysis. The phosphofructokinase reaction is another that may be considered to be irreversible in the cell.

$$D\text{-Fructose 6-phosphate} + ATP \rightarrow D\text{-Fructose 1,6-bisphosphate}$$

The hexose phosphate, fructose 1,6-bisphosphate, is split by **aldolase** into 2 triose phosphates, glyceraldehyde 3-phosphate and dihydroxyacetone phosphate.

$$D\text{-Fructose 1,6-bisphosphate} \longleftrightarrow D\text{-Glyceraldehyde 3-phosphate} + \text{Dihydroxy-acetone phosphate}$$

Several different aldolases have been detected, all of which contain 4 subunits. Aldolase A occurs in most tissues, and, in addition, aldolase B occurs in liver and kidney.

Glyceraldehyde 3-phosphate and dihydroxyacetone phosphate are interconverted by the enzyme **phosphotriose isomerase**.

$$D\text{-Glyceraldehyde 3-phosphate} \longleftrightarrow \text{Dihydroxyacetone phosphate}$$

Glycolysis proceeds by the oxidation of glyceraldehyde 3-phosphate to 1,3-bisphosphoglycerate, and, because of the activity of phosphotriose isomerase, the dihydroxyacetone phosphate is also oxidized to 1,3-diphosphoglycerate via glyceraldehyde 3-phosphate.

$$D\text{-Glyceraldehyde 3-phosphate} + NAD^+ + P_i \longleftrightarrow 1,3\text{-Bisphosphoglycerate} + NADH + H^+$$

The enzyme responsible for the oxidation, **glyceraldehyde-3-phosphate dehydrogenase**, is NAD-dependent. Structurally, it consists of 4 identical polypeptides (monomers) forming a tetramer. Four SH groups are present on each polypeptide, probably derived from cysteine residues within the polypeptide chain. One of the SH groups is found at the active site of the enzyme. It is believed that the SH group participates in the reaction in which glyceraldehyde 3-phosphate is oxidized. The dehydrogenase enzyme may be inactivated by the SH poison iodoacetate, which is thus able to inhibit glycolysis at this point. The substrate initially combines with a cysteinyl moiety on the dehydrogenase forming a thiohemiacetal which is converted to a thiol ester by oxidation, the hydrogens removed in this oxidation being transferred to NAD bound to the enzyme. The NADH produced on the enzyme is not as firmly bound to the enzyme as is NAD. Consequently, NADH is easily displaced by a molecule of NAD. Finally, by phosphorolysis, inorganic phosphate (P_i) is added, forming 1,3-bisphosphoglycerate, and the free enzyme with a reconstituted SH group is liberated (Fig 19–3). Energy released during the oxidation is retained by the formation of a high-energy sulfur bond which becomes, after phosphorolysis, a high-energy phosphate bond in position 1 of 1,3-bisphosphoglycerate. This high-energy phosphate is captured as ATP in a further reaction with ADP catalyzed by **phosphoglycerate kinase**, leaving 3-phosphoglycerate.

$$1,3\text{-Bisphosphoglycerate} + ADP \longleftrightarrow 3\text{-Phosphoglycerate} + ATP$$

Since 2 molecules of triose phosphate are formed per molecule of glucose undergoing glycolysis, 2 molecules of ATP are generated at this stage per molecule of glucose, an example of phosphorylation "at the substrate level."

If arsenate is present, it will compete with inorganic phosphate (P_i) in the above reactions to give 1-arseno-3-phosphoglycerate, which hydrolyzes to give 3-phosphoglycerate without generating ATP. This is an important example of the ability of arsenate to accomplish uncoupling of oxidation and phosphorylation.

3-Phosphoglycerate arising from the above reactions is converted to 2-phosphoglycerate by the enzyme **phosphoglycerate mutase**. It is possible that 2,3-bisphosphoglycerate is an intermediate in this reaction.

$$3\text{-Phosphoglycerate} \longleftrightarrow 2\text{-Phosphoglycerate}$$

The subsequent step is catalyzed by **enolase** and involves a dehydration and redistribution of energy within the molecule, raising the phosphate on position 2 to the high-energy state, thus forming phosphoenolpyruvate. Enolase is inhibited by fluoride and is dependent on the presence of either Mg^{2+} or Mn^{2+}.

$$2\text{-Phosphoglycerate} \longleftrightarrow \text{Phosphoenolpyruvate} + H_2O$$

The high-energy phosphate of phosphoenolpyru-

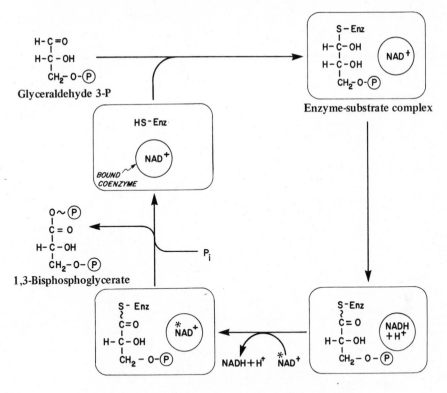

Figure 19–3. Oxidation of glyceraldehyde 3-phosphate.

vate is transferred to ADP by the enzyme **pyruvate kinase** to generate, at this stage, 2 mol of ATP per mol of glucose oxidized. Enolpyruvate formed in this reaction is converted spontaneously to the keto form of pyruvate. This is another physiologically irreversible step in glycolysis.

$$\text{Phosphoenolpyruvate} + \text{ADP} \rightarrow \text{Pyruvate} + \text{ATP}$$

The redox state of the tissue now determines which of 2 pathways is followed. If anaerobic conditions prevail, the reoxidation of NADH by H transfer through the respiratory chain to oxygen is prevented. Pyruvate, which is the normal end product of glycolysis under aerobic conditions, is reduced under anaerobic conditions by the NADH to lactate, the reaction being catalyzed by **lactate dehydrogenase**. Several isozymes of this enzyme have been described in Chapter 7. The reoxidation of NADH via lactate formation allows glycolysis to proceed in the absence of oxygen by regenerating sufficient NAD$^+$ for the reaction catalyzed by glyceraldehyde-3-phosphate dehydrogenase. Thus, tissues which may function under hypoxic circumstances tend to produce lactate. This is particularly true of skeletal muscle, where the rate at which the organ performs work is not limited by its capacity for oxygenation. The additional quantities of lactate produced may be detected in the tissues and in the blood and urine. Glycolysis in erythrocytes, even under aerobic conditions, always terminates in lactate,

because the enzymatic machinery for the aerobic oxidation of pyruvate is not present. The mammalian erythrocyte is unique in that about 90% of its total energy requirement is provided by glycolysis.

$$\text{Pyruvate} + \text{NADH} + \text{H}^+ \longleftrightarrow \text{L(+)-Lactate} + \text{NAD}^+$$

In the erythrocytes of many mammalian species, there is a bypass of the step catalyzed by phosphoglycerate kinase. Another enzyme, **bisphosphoglyceromutase**, catalyzes the conversion of 1,3-bisphosphoglycerate to 2,3-bisphosphoglycerate. The latter is converted to 3-phosphoglycerate by **2,3-bisphosphoglycerate phosphatase**, an activity which is also attributed to **phosphoglycerate mutase**. 2,3-Bisphosphoglycerate combines with hemoglobin, causing a decrease in affinity for oxygen and a displacement of the oxyhemoglobin dissociation curve to the right. Thus, its presence in the red cells aids oxyhemoglobin to unload oxygen.

Although most of the glycolytic reactions are reversible, 3 of them are markedly exergonic and must therefore be considered physiologically irreversible. These reactions are catalyzed by hexokinase (and glucokinase), phosphofructokinase, and pyruvate kinase. Cells which are capable of effecting a net movement of metabolites in the synthetic direction of the glycolytic pathway do so because of the presence of different enzyme systems which provide alternative routes to the irreversible reactions catalyzed by the above men-

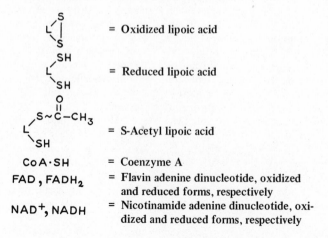

Legend and abbreviations

Square brackets mean that the intermediate is bound tightly to the enzyme interface.

$L\!\!\stackrel{S}{\underset{S}{|}}$ = Oxidized lipoic acid

$L\!\!\stackrel{SH}{\underset{SH}{}}$ = Reduced lipoic acid

$L\!\!\stackrel{S\sim\overset{O}{\overset{\|}{C}}-CH_3}{\underset{SH}{}}$ = S-Acetyl lipoic acid

CoA·SH   = Coenzyme A

FAD , FADH$_2$ = Flavin adenine dinucleotide, oxidized and reduced forms, respectively

NAD$^+$, NADH   = Nicotinamide adenine dinucleotide, oxidized and reduced forms, respectively

Figure 19—4. Oxidative decarboxylation of pyruvate.

tioned enzymes. These will be discussed under gluconeogenesis.

OXIDATION OF PYRUVATE TO ACETYL-CoA

Before pyruvate can enter the citric acid cycle, it must be oxidatively decarboxylated to acetyl-CoA ("active acetate"). This reaction is catalyzed by several different enzymes working sequentially in a multienzyme complex. They are collectively designated as the **pyruvate dehydrogenase** complex, shown in Fig 19–4. Pyruvate is decarboxylated in the presence of thiamin diphosphate to a hydroxyethyl derivative of the thiazole ring of enzyme-bound thiamin diphosphate, which in turn reacts with oxidized lipoate to form S-acetyl lipoate, all catalyzed by pyruvate dehydrogenase. In the presence of **dihydrolipoyl transacetylase**, S-acetyl lipoate reacts with coenzyme A to form acetyl-CoA and reduced lipoate. The cycle of reaction is completed when the latter is reoxidized by a flavoprotein in the presence of **dihydrolipoyl dehydrogenase**. Finally, the reduced flavoprotein is oxidized by NAD, which in turn transfers reducing equivalents to the respiratory chain. The pyruvate dehydrogenase complex consists of about 29 mol of pyruvate dehydrogenase and about 8 mol of flavoprotein (dihydrolipoyl dehydrogenase) distributed around 1 mol of transacetylase. Movement of the individual enzymes appears to be restricted, and the metabolic intermediates do not dissociate freely but remain bound to the enzymes.

It is to be noted that the pyruvate dehydrogenase system is sufficiently electronegative with respect to the respiratory chain that, in addition to generating a reduced coenzyme (NADH), it also generates a high-energy thio ester bond in acetyl-CoA. The presence of arsenite inhibits pyruvate dehydrogenase as does a

dietary deficiency of thiamine, allowing pyruvate to accumulate.

Energetics of Carbohydrate Oxidation

When 1 mol of glucose is combusted in a calorimeter to CO_2 and water, approximately 686 kcal are liberated as heat. When oxidation occurs in the tissues, some of this energy is not lost immediately as heat but is "captured" in high-energy phosphate bonds. At least 38 high-energy phosphate bonds are generated per molecule of glucose oxidized to CO_2 and water. Assuming each high-energy bond to be equivalent to 7.6 kcal, the total energy captured in ATP per mol of glucose oxidized is 288.8 kcal, or approximately 42% of the energy of combustion. Most of the ATP is formed as a consequence of oxidative phosphorylation resulting from the reoxidation of reduced coenzymes by the respiratory chain. The remainder is generated by phosphorylation at the "substrate level." Table 19–1 indicates the reactions responsible for the generation of the new high-energy bonds.

GLYCOGEN FORMATION & DEGRADATION

The formation of glycogen occurs in practically every tissue of the body, but chiefly in liver and muscle (Table 19–2). In man, the liver may contain as much as 5% glycogen when analyzed shortly after a meal high in carbohydrate. After 12–18 hours of fasting, the liver becomes almost totally depleted of glycogen. Muscle glycogen is only rarely elevated above 1% of the wet weight of the tissue.

The function of muscle glycogen is to act as a readily available source of hexose units for glycolysis within the muscle itself. In contrast, liver glycogen is largely concerned with maintenance of the blood glucose.

Table 19–1. Generation of high-energy bonds in the catabolism of glucose.

Pathway	Reaction Catalyzed By	Method of ~ P Production	Number of ~ P Formed per Mol Glucose
Glycolysis	Glyceraldehyde-3-phosphate dehydrogenase	Respiratory chain oxidation of 2 NADH	6
	Phosphoglycerate kinase	Oxidation at substrate level	2
	Pyruvate kinase	Oxidation at substrate level	2
			10
	Allow for consumption of ATP by reactions catalyzed by hexokinase and phosphofructokinase		−2
			Net 8
	Pyruvate dehydrogenase	Respiratory chain oxidation of 2 NADH	6
	Isocitrate dehydrogenase	Respiratory chain oxidation of 2 NADH	6
	a-Ketoglutarate dehydrogenase	Respiratory chain oxidation of 2 NADH	6
Citric acid cycle	Succinate thiokinase	Oxidation at substrate level	2
	Succinate dehydrogenase	Respiratory chain oxidation of 2 $FADH_2$	4
	Malate dehydrogenase	Respiratory chain oxidation of 2 NADH	6
			Net 30
	Total per mol of glucose under aerobic conditions		38
	Total per mol of glucose under anaerobic conditions		2

Table 19—2. Storage of carbohydrate in normal adult man (70 kg).

Liver	6.0% =	108 g*
Muscle glycogen	0.7% =	245 g†
Extracellular glucose	0.1% =	10 g‡
Total: 363 g × 4		= 1452 kcal

*Liver weight 1800 g.
†Muscle mass, 35 kg.
‡Total volume, 10 liters.

GLYCOGENESIS

Glucose is phosphorylated to glucose 6-phosphate, a reaction which is common to the first reaction in the pathway of glycolysis from glucose. Glucose 6-phosphate is then converted to glucose 1-phosphate in a reaction catalyzed by the enzyme **phosphoglucomutase.** This enzyme is phosphorylated and the phospho- group takes part in a reversible reaction in which glucose 1,6-bisphosphate is an intermediate.

Enz-P + Glucose 6-phosphate ⟷ Enz + Glucose 1,6-
bisphosphate ⟷ Enz-P + Glucose 1-phosphate

Next, glucose 1-phosphate reacts with uridine triphosphate (UTP) to form the active nucleotide **uridine diphosphate glucose (UDPG).***

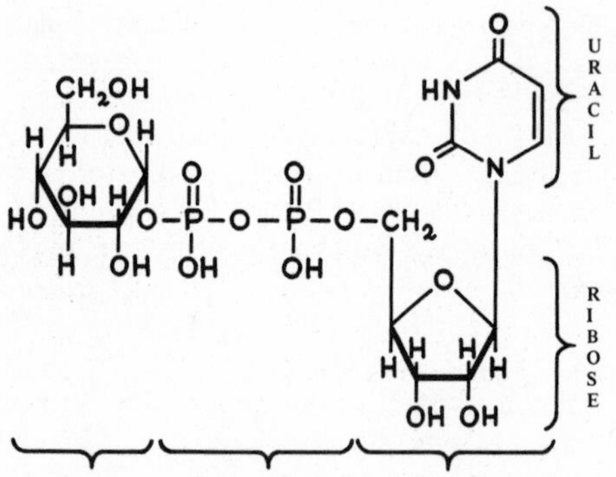

Glucose   Diphosphate   Uridine

Uridine diphosphate glucose (UDPG)

The reaction between glucose 1-phosphate and uridine triphosphate is catalyzed by the enzyme **UDPG pyrophosphorylase.**

UTP + Glucose 1-phosphate ⟷ UDPG + PP$_i$

The consequent hydrolysis of inorganic pyrophosphate

*Other nucleoside diphosphate sugar compounds are known, eg, UDPGal. In addition, the same sugar may be linked to different nucleotides. For example, glucose may be linked to uridine (as shown above) as well as to guanine, thymine, adenine, or cytosine nucleotides.

by inorganic pyrophosphatase pulls the reaction to the right of the equation.

By the action of the enzyme **glycogen synthetase** (or **glucosyl transferase**), the C_1 of the activated glucose of UDPG forms a glycosidic bond with the C_4 of a terminal glucose residue of glycogen, liberating uridine diphosphate (UDP) (Fig 19—5).

UDPG + $(C_6)_n$ → UDP + $(C_6)_n$ + 1
glycogen

The addition of a glucose residue to a preexisting glycogen chain occurs at the nonreducing, outer end of the molecule so that the "branches" of the glycogen "tree" become elongated as successive -1,4- linkages occur (Fig 19—6). When the chain has been lengthened to between 6 and 11 glucose residues, a second enzyme, the **branching enzyme (amylo-1,4→1,6-transglucosidase)** acts on the glycogen. This enzyme transfers a part of the -1,4- chain (minimum length 6 glucose residues) to a neighboring chain to form a -1,6- linkage, thus establishing a branch point in the molecule.

The action of the branching enzyme has been studied in the living animal by feeding ^{14}C-labeled glucose and examining the liver glycogen at intervals thereafter. At first only the outer branches of the chain are labeled, indicating that the new glucose residues are added at this point. Later, some of these outside chains are transferred to the inner portion of the molecule, appearing as labeled -1,6- linked branches (Fig 19—6). Thus, under the combined action of glycogen synthetase and branching enzyme, the glycogen molecule is assembled.

The structure of glycogen is shown in Fig 19—6. It will be seen to be a branched polysaccharide composed entirely of a-D-glucose units. These glucose units are connected to one another by glucosidic linkages between the first and fourth carbon atoms except at branch points, where the linkages are between carbon atoms 1 and 6. The molecular weight of glycogen may vary from 1 million to 4 million or more. If glycogen is a regularly branched structure as shown in Fig 19—6, a maximum molecular weight of $10-20 \times 10^6$ would be possible because of the fact that the molecule becomes more dense toward the periphery. However, if some of the glucose chains terminate in the interior, a larger molecule is theoretically possible.

In muscle (and possibly liver), **glycogen synthetase** is present in 2 interconvertible forms: **synthetase D** (dependent), which is totally dependent for its activity on the presence of glucose 6-phosphate; and **synthetase I** (independent), whose K_m for UDPG decreases in the presence of glucose 6-phosphate (Fig 19—7). However, only the latter effect occurs with physiologic concentrations of glucose 6-phosphate, implying that synthetase I is the active form of the enzyme. Synthetase D is converted to synthetase I by **synthetase phosphatase,** a reaction involving dephosphorylation of a serine residue within the enzyme protein. Synthetase I is phosphorylated to form synthetase D, with ATP acting as a phosphate donor, by an

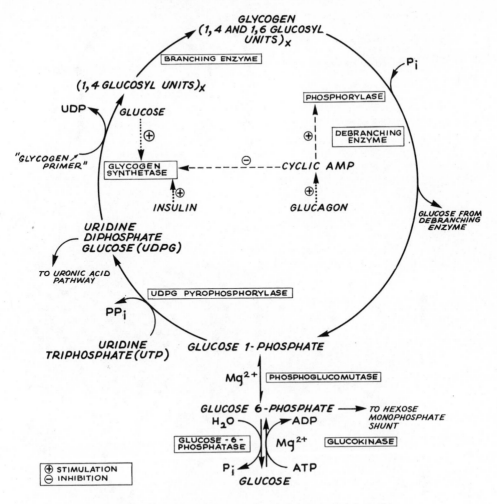

Figure 19—5. Pathway of glycogenesis and of glycogenolysis in the liver.

enzyme of rather wide specificity, **cAMP-dependent protein kinase** (synthetase kinase), which is active only in the presence of $3'5'$-cyclic adenylic acid (cAMP) (see Krebs, 1972).

3'5'-Adenylic acid (cyclic AMP; cAMP)

cAMP is the intracellular intermediate compound through which many hormones appear to act. It is formed from ATP by an enzyme, **adenylate cyclase,** occurring in cell membranes. Adenylate cyclase is activated by hormones such as epinephrine, norepinephrine, and glucagon, all of which lead to an increase in cAMP. cAMP is destroyed by a **phosphodiesterase** (Fig

19–7), and it is this activity that maintains the level of cAMP at its normally low level. Insulin has been reported to increase its activity in liver. Thyroid hormones may increase the synthesis of adenylate cyclase, thus potentiating the effects of epinephrine in stimulating the formation of cAMP.

In liver, glycogen synthetase also exists in an active **(a)** form as well as an inactive **(b)** form; (b) is formed from (a) by phosphorylation of the enzyme protein in a reaction catalyzed by a cAMP-dependent protein kinase, and (a) is formed from (b) by the action of **synthetase phosphatase.**

The reactions of glycogenesis in liver are summarized in Fig 19–5.

GLYCOGENOLYSIS

The breakdown of glycogen is initiated by the action of the enzyme **phosphorylase,** which is specific for the phosphorylytic breaking of the -1,4- linkages of glycogen to yield glucose 1-phosphate (Fig 19–5).

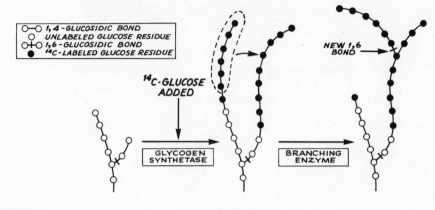

(a) Synthesis.

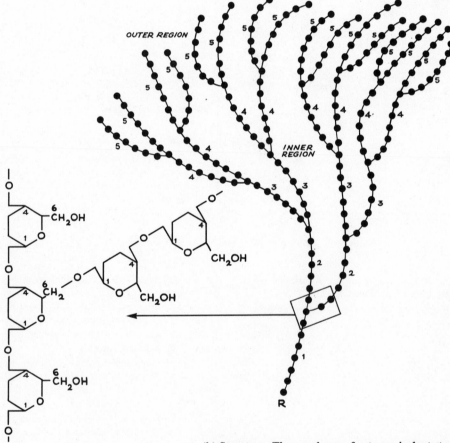

OUTER REGION

INNER REGION

(c) Enlargement of structure at a branch point.

(b) Structure—The numbers refer to equivalent stages in the growth of the macromolecule. R, primary glucose residue with free reducing-CHO group (carbon No. 1). The branching is more variable than shown, the ratio of 1,4 to 1,6 bonds being from 12 to 18.

Figure 19–6. The glycogen molecule.

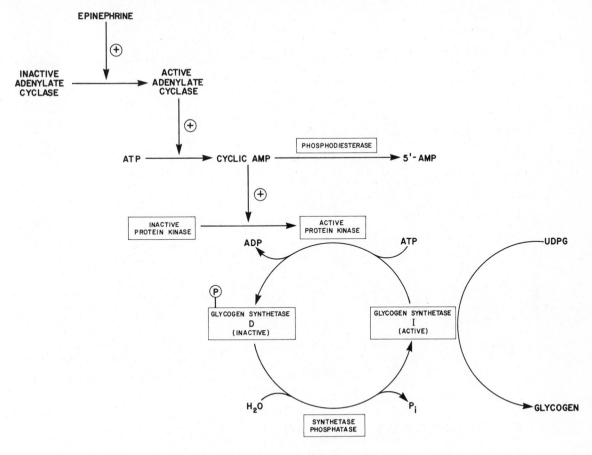

Figure 19—7. Control of glycogen synthetase in muscle.

Phosphorylase Activation & Inactivation (Fig 19—8.)

In liver, the enzyme protein (phosphorylase) was found to exist in both an active and an inactive form. The active phosphorylase (**phosphorylase a** or **phosphophosphorylase**) has one of its serine residues phosphorylated in an ester linkage with the hydroxyl group of the serine. By the action of a specific phosphatase (**phosphorylase phosphatase**), the enzyme can be inactivated to **dephosphophosphorylase** in a reaction which involves hydrolytic removal of the phosphate from the serine residue. Reactivation requires rephosphorylation

phosphorylase b, which is active only in the presence of 5′-AMP. Phosphorylase a is the physiologically active form of the enzyme. It is a tetramer containing 4 mol of pyridoxal phosphate. When it is hydrolytically converted to a dimer by **phosphorylase phosphatase**, which removes phosphate from phosphoserine residues, phosphorylase b is formed. This contains 2 mol of pyridoxal phosphate.

Conversion of phosphorylase b to phosphorylase a is considered to be the mechanism for increasing glycogenolysis.

$$\text{PHOSPHORYLASE } a + 4H_2O \xrightarrow{\text{PHOSPHORYLASE PHOSPHATASE}} 2 \text{ PHOSPHORYLASE } b + 4P_i$$
$$\text{(ACTIVE)} \qquad\qquad\qquad\qquad\qquad \text{(INACTIVE)}$$

with ATP and a specific enzyme, **phosphorylase b kinase** or **dephosphophosphorylase kinase.**

Muscle phosphorylase is immunologically distinct from that of liver. It is present in 2 forms: **phosphorylase a**, which is active in the absence of 5′-AMP, and

Two dimers of phosphorylase b may recondense to an active phosphorylase a tetramer in the presence of a specific enzyme, **phosphorylase b kinase**, which rephosphorylates the serine residues at the expense of ATP.

$$2 \text{ PHOSPHORYLASE } b + 4ATP \xrightarrow[\text{Mg}^{2+}]{\text{PHOSPHORYLASE b KINASE}} \text{PHOSPHORYLASE } a + 4 \text{ ADP}$$

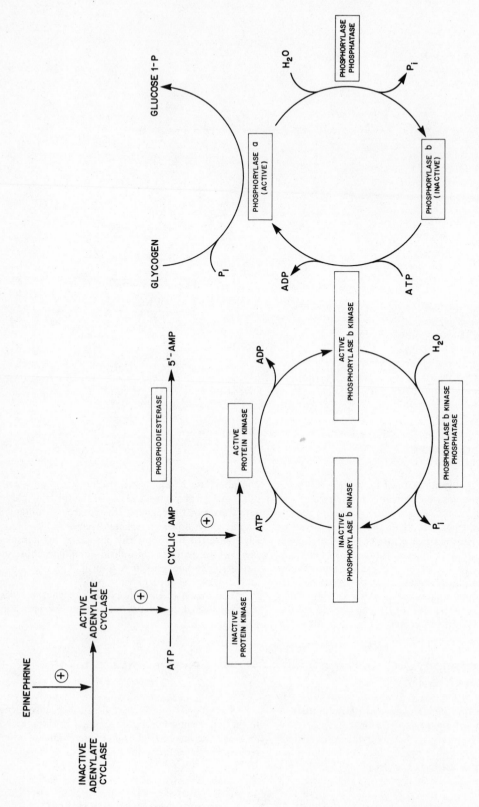

Figure 19–8. Control of phosphorylase in muscle.

Phosphorylase in muscle is activated by epinephrine (Fig 19–8). However, it is probable that this occurs not as a direct effect but rather by way of the effect of epinephrine on adenylate cyclase to form cAMP, which then serves to produce activation of phosphorylase b kinase by way of a second protein kinase system which is considered to be identical with the cAMP-dependent protein kinase responsible for inactivation of glycogen synthetase I (Fig 19–7). Liver phosphorylase kinase does not seem to be sensitive to a protein kinase. Activation of phosphorylase b kinase is also caused by muscular contraction, an effect which appears to be due to Ca^{2+} rather than cAMP. It is evident that glycogen metabolism is controlled by cAMP via a series of metabolic "cascades" (similar to the factors operating in the clotting of blood). This type of mechanism allows amplification of the original hormonal signal at each step of the cascade. Hence, a small change in [cAMP] can cause a large change in activity of glycogen synthetase and phosphorylase. The degradation of cAMP by phosphodiesterase allows the signal to be switched off rapidly.

The reactions for the inactivation of muscle phosphorylase are in some respects similar to those of the liver enzyme except that no cleavage of the protein molecular structure is involved in the case of liver phosphorylase. Furthermore, skeletal muscle phosphorylase is not affected by glucagon although heart muscle is. Another important difference is that liver synthetase phosphatase is inhibited by the active form of phosphorylase.

It is the step catalyzed by phosphorylase that is rate-limiting in glycogenolysis. This enzyme, phosphorylase, catalyzes the removal of 1,4-glucosyl residues from the outermost chains of the glycogen molecule until approximately 4 glucose residues remain on either side of a -1,6- branch (Fig 19–6). Another enzyme (**a-1,4→a-1,4 glucan transferase**) transfers a trisaccharide unit from one side to the other, thus exposing the -1,6- branch points (Illingworth and Brown, 1962). The hydrolytic splitting of the -1,6- linkages requires the action of a specific **debranching enzyme (amylo-1,6-glucosidase).*** The combined action of phosphorylase and these other enzymes converts glycogen to glucose 1-phosphate. The action of phosphoglucomutase is reversible, so that glucose 6-phosphate can be formed from glucose 1-phosphate. In liver and kidney (but not in muscle), there is a specific enzyme, **glucose-6-phosphatase**, that removes phosphate from glucose 6-phosphate, enabling the free glucose to diffuse from the cell into the extracellular spaces, including the blood. This is the final step in hepatic glycogenolysis which is reflected by a rise in the blood glucose.

*Because the -1,6- linkage is hydrolytically split, 1 mol of free glucose is produced rather than 1 mol of glucose 1-phosphate. In this way it is possible for some rise in the blood glucose to take place even in the absence of glucose-6-phosphatase, as occurs in type I glycogen storage disease (von Gierke's disease; see below) after glucagon or epinephrine is administered.

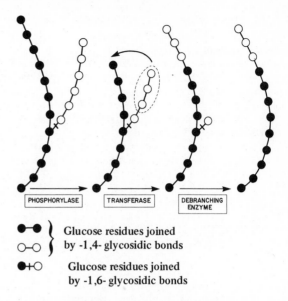

PHOSPHORYLASE   TRANSFERASE   DEBRANCHING ENZYME

●—● } Glucose residues joined
○—○ } by -1,4- glycosidic bonds

●+○ Glucose residues joined
     by -1,6- glycosidic bonds

Figure 19–9. Steps in glycogenolysis.

The control of glycogen metabolism in the liver has been reviewed by Hers (1976).

Diseases of Glycogen Storage

The term "glycogen storage disease" is a generic one intended to describe a group of inherited disorders characterized by deposition of an abnormal type or quantity of glycogen in the tissues. The subject has been reviewed by Brown & Brown (1968).

In **type I glycogenosis (von Gierke's disease)**, both the liver cells and the cells of the renal convoluted tubules are characteristically loaded with glycogen. However, these glycogen stores seem to be metabolically unavailable, as evidenced by the occurrence of hypoglycemia and a lack of glycogenolysis under stimulus by epinephrine or glucagon. Ketosis and hyperlipemia are also present in these patients, as would be characteristic of an organism deprived of carbohydrate. In liver, kidney, and intestinal tissue, the activity of glucose-6-phosphatase is either extremely low or entirely absent.

Other types of glycogen storage disease include the following: **type II (Pompe's disease)**, which is characterized by a deficiency of lysosomal a-1,4-glucosidase (acid maltase) whose function is to degrade glycogen, which otherwise accumulates in the lysosomes; **type III (limit dextrinosis)**, characterized by the absence of debranching enzyme, which causes the accumulation of a polysaccharide of the limit dextrin type; and **type IV (amylopectinosis)**, characterized by the absence of branching enzyme, with the result that a polysaccharide having few branch points accumulates.

An absence of muscle phosphorylase (myophosphorylase) is the cause of **type V glycogenosis (myophosphorylase deficiency glycogenosis; McArdle's syndrome)**. Patients with this disease exhibit a markedly diminished tolerance to exercise. Although their skeletal muscles have an abnormally high content of glycogen (2.5–4.1%), little or no lactate is detectable in their blood after exercise. A rise in blood sugar does occur, however, after administration of glucagon or epinephrine, which indicates that hepatic phosphorylase activity is normal. In some of the reported cases, myoglobinuria has been an associated finding.

Also described among the glycogen storage diseases are **type VI glycogenosis**, involving phosphoglucomutase deficiency in the liver, and **type VII glycogenosis**, characterized by a deficiency of phosphofructokinase in the muscles.

THE HEXOSE MONOPHOSPHATE SHUNT OR PENTOSE PHOSPHATE PATHWAY

This pathway for the oxidation of glucose occurs in certain tissues, notably liver, lactating mammary gland, and adipose tissue, in addition to the Embden-Meyerhof pathway of glycolysis. It is in effect a multicyclic process whereby 3 molecules of glucose 6-phosphate give rise to 3 molecules of CO_2 and 3 5-carbon residues. The latter are rearranged to regenerate 2 molecules of glucose 6-phosphate and one molecule of glyceraldehyde 3-phosphate. Since 2 molecules of glyceraldehyde 3-phosphate can regenerate a molecule of glucose 6-phosphate by reactions which are essentially a reversal of glycolysis, the pathway can account for the complete oxidation of glucose. As in the Embden-Meyerhof glycolysis pathway, oxidation is achieved by dehydrogenation; but in the case of the shunt pathway, NADP and not NAD is used as a hydrogen acceptor. The enzymes of the shunt pathway are found in the extramitochondrial soluble portion of the cell.

A summary of the reactions of the hexose monophosphate shunt is shown below.

step is catalyzed by **6-phosphogluconate dehydrogenase**, which also requires $NADP^+$ as hydrogen acceptor. Decarboxylation follows with the formation of the ketopentose ribulose 5-phosphate. The reaction probably takes place in 2 steps through the intermediate 3-keto-6-phosphogluconate.

Ribulose 5-phosphate now serves as substrate for 2 different enzymes. **Ribulose-5-phosphate epimerase** alters the configuration about carbon 3, forming the epimer, xylulose 5-phosphate, another ketopentose. **Ribose-5-phosphate ketoisomerase** converts ribulose 5-phosphate to the corresponding aldopentose, ribose 5-phosphate. This reaction is analogous to the interconversion of fructose 6-phosphate and glucose 6-phosphate in the Embden-Meyerhof pathway.

Transketolase transfers the 2-carbon unit comprising carbons 1 and 2 of a ketose to the aldehyde carbon of an aldose sugar. It therefore effects the conversion of a ketose sugar into an aldose with 2 carbons less, and simultaneously converts an aldose sugar into a ketose with 2 carbons more. In addition to the enzyme transketolase, the reaction requires thiamin diphosphate as coenzyme and Mg^{2+} ions. The 2-carbon moiety transferred is probably glycolaldehyde bound to thiamin diphosphate, ie, "active glycolaldehyde." In the hexose monophosphate shunt, transketolase catalyzes the transfer of the 2-carbon unit from xylulose 5-phosphate to ribose 5-phosphate, producing the 7-carbon ketose sedoheptulose 7-phosphate and the aldose glyceraldehyde 3-phosphate. These 2 products then enter another reaction known as transaldolation. Transaldolase allows the transfer of a 3-carbon moiety, "active dihydroxyacetone" (carbons 1–3), from the ketose sedoheptulose 7-phosphate to the aldose glyceraldehyde 3-phosphate to form the ketose fructose 6-phosphate and the 4-carbon aldose erythrose 4-phosphate.

A further reaction takes place, again involving transketolase, in which xylulose 5-phosphate serves as a donor of "active glycolaldehyde." In this case the

$$3 \; GLUCOSE \;\; 6-P \longrightarrow 3 \; CO_2 + 2 \; GLUCOSE \;\; 6-P$$
$$+ \qquad\qquad\qquad\qquad\qquad +$$
$$6 \; NADP^+ \qquad\qquad GLYCERALDEHYDE \;\; 3-P + 6\,NADPH + 6\,H^+$$

The sequence of reactions of the shunt pathway may be divided into 2 phases. In the first, glucose 6-phosphate undergoes dehydrogenation and decarboxylation to give the pentose ribulose 5-phosphate. In the second phase, ribulose 5-phosphate is converted back to glucose 6-phosphate by a series of reactions involving mainly 2 enzymes: **transketolase** and **transaldolase** (Fig 19–10).

Dehydrogenation of glucose 6-phosphate to 6-phosphogluconate occurs via the formation of 6-phosphogluconolactone catalyzed by **glucose-6-phosphate dehydrogenase**, an NADP-dependent enzyme. This reaction is inhibited by certain drugs, such as sulfonamides and quinacrine. The hydrolysis of 6-phosphogluconolactone is accomplished by the enzyme **gluconolactone hydrolase**. A second oxidative

erythrose 4-phosphate formed above acts as acceptor and the products of the reaction are fructose 6-phosphate and glyceraldehyde 3-phosphate.

In order to oxidize glucose completely to CO_2 via the shunt pathway, it is necessary that the enzymes are present in the tissue to convert glyceraldehyde 3-phosphate to glucose 6-phosphate. This involves the enzymes of the Embden-Meyerhof pathway working in a reverse direction and, in addition, the enzyme **fructose-1,6-diphosphatase**. A summary of the reactions of the direct oxidative pathway is shown in Fig 19–11. Most of the reactions are reversible, but the complete pathway is probably irreversible at the gluconolactone hydrolase step.

Metabolic Significance of the Hexose Monophosphate Shunt

It is clear that the direct oxidative pathway is markedly different from the Embden-Meyerhof pathway of glycolysis. Oxidation occurs in the first reactions, and CO_2, which is not produced at all in the Embden-Meyerhof pathway, is a characteristic product. This fact has been utilized in experiments designed to evaluate the relative proportions of glucose metabolized by the Embden-Meyerhof pathway compared with the shunt pathway. Most studies have been based on measurement of differences in the rate of liberation of $^{14}CO_2$ from [1-^{14}C] glucose and from [6-^{14}C] glucose. In the glycolytic pathway, carbons 1 and 6 of glucose are both converted to the methyl carbon of pyruvic acid and are therefore metabolized in the same manner. In the direct oxidative pathway, carbons 1 and 6 of glucose are treated differently, carbon 1 being removed early by decarboxylation with the formation of labeled CO_2. Interpretation of experimental results, however, is difficult because of the many assumptions which must be made, eg, whether or not fructose 6-phosphate formed by the direct oxidative pathway is recycled via glucose 6-phosphate.

Estimates of the activity of the shunt pathway in various tissues give an indication of its metabolic significance. It is active in liver, adipose tissue, adrenal cortex, thyroid, erythrocytes, testis, and lactating mammary gland. It is not active in nonlactating mammary gland, and its activity is low in skeletal muscle. Most of the tissues in which the pathway is active specialize in using NADPH in the synthesis of fatty acids or steroids and in the synthesis of amino acids via glutamate dehydrogenase. It is probable that the presence of active lipogenesis or of a system which utilizes NADPH stimulates an active degradation of glucose via the shunt pathway. The synthesis of glucose-6-phosphate dehydrogenase and 6-phosphogluconate dehydrogenase may also be induced during conditions associated with the "fed state." One of the major functions of the hexose monophosphate shunt would appear to be, therefore, the provision of reduced NADP required by anabolic processes outside the mitochondria.

Another important function of the hexose monophosphate shunt is to provide pentoses for nucleotide and nucleic acid synthesis. The source of the ribose is the ribose 5-phosphate intermediate. This compound may be isomerized to the 1-phosphate (cf glucose 6-phosphate ↔ glucose 1-phosphate interconversion, p 260), or it can react with ATP to give ribose 1,5-bisphosphate (cf fructose 6-phosphate → fructose 1,6-bisphosphate). Muscle tissue contains very small amounts of glucose-6-phosphate dehydrogenase and 6-phosphogluconate dehydrogenase. Nevertheless, skeletal muscle is capable of synthesizing ribose. This is probably accomplished by a reversal of the shunt pathway utilizing fructose 6-phosphate, glyceraldehyde 3-phosphate, and the enzymes transketolase and transaldolase. Thus, it is not necessary to have a completely functioning shunt pathway in order that a tissue may

synthesize ribose. In human tissues, ribose seems to be derived primarily by way of the oxidative reactions of the shunt pathway, whereas in the rat and mouse—except in muscle—the nonoxidative reactions appear to play a larger role than the oxidative.

In rabbit lens tissue, it was found that, while most of the glucose utilized was converted to lactate, at least 10% was metabolized via the shunt pathway. A relation between galactose accumulation and the experimental production of cataracts in rats has been recognized. Development of cataracts sometimes occurs as a complication of galactosemia, an inherited metabolic disease associated with the inability to convert galactose to glucose. In the light of the existence of a shunt pathway in the metabolism of the lens, it is of interest that galactose has been found to inhibit the activity of glucose-6-phosphate dehydrogenase of the lens in vivo when the sugar is fed to experimental animals and in vitro when galactose 1-phosphate is added to a homogenate of lens tissue.

Formation of NADPH seems to be an important function of the operation of the shunt pathway in red blood cells, and a direct correlation has been found between the activity of enzymes of the direct oxidative pathway, particularly of glucose-6-phosphate dehydrogenase, and the fragility of red cells (susceptibility to hemolysis), especially when the cells are subjected to the toxic effects of certain drugs (primaquine, acetylphenylhydrazine) or the susceptible individual has ingested fava beans (*Vicia fava*—favism). The majority of patients whose red cells are hemolyzed by these toxic agents have been found to possess a hereditary deficiency in the oxidative enzymes of the shunt pathway of the red blood cell.

L-Phenylalanine and phenylpyruvate, metabolites which accumulate in the blood in phenylketonuria, inhibit hexokinase, pyruvate kinase, and 6-phosphogluconate dehydrogenase of differentiating brain.

GLUCONEOGENESIS

Gluconeogenesis meets the needs of the body for glucose when carbohydrate is not available in sufficient amounts from the diet. A continual supply of glucose is necessary as a source of energy, especially for the nervous system and the erythrocytes. Glucose is also required in adipose tissue as a source of glyceride-glycerol, and it probably plays a role in maintaining the level of intermediates of the citric acid cycle in many tissues. It is clear that even under conditions where fat may be supplying most of the caloric requirement of the organism, there is always a certain basal requirement for glucose. In addition, glucose is the only fuel which will supply energy to skeletal muscle under anaerobic conditions. It is the precursor of milk sugar (lactose) in the mammary gland and it is taken up actively by the fetus. It is not surprising, therefore, to find that enzymatic pathways have been·

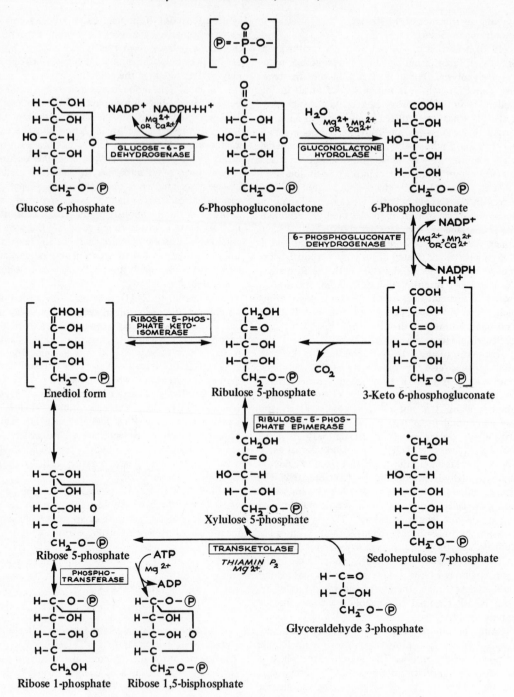

Figure 19—10. The hexose monophosphate shunt (pentose phosphate pathway).

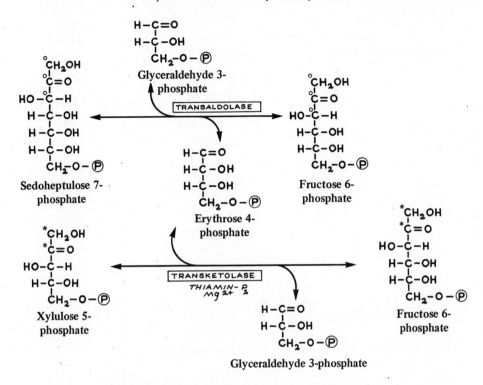

Figure 19—10 (cont'd). The hexose monophosphate shunt.

developed in certain specialized tissues for the conversion of noncarbohydrates to glucose. In addition, these gluconeogenic mechanisms are used to clear the products of the metabolism of other tissues from the blood, eg, lactate, produced by muscle and erythrocytes, and glycerol, which is continuously produced by adipose tissue.

In mammals, the liver and the kidney are the principal organs responsible for gluconeogenesis. As the main pathway of gluconeogenesis is essentially a reversal of glycolysis, this can explain why the glycolytic activity of liver and kidney is low when there is active gluconeogenesis.

Metabolic Pathways Involved in Gluconeogenesis
(Fig 19—12.)

These pathways are modifications and adaptations of the Embden-Meyerhof pathways and the citric acid cycle. They are concerned with the conversion of glucogenic amino acids, lactate, glycerol, and, in ruminants, propionate, to glucose or glycogen. It has been pointed out by Krebs that energy barriers obstruct a simple reversal of glycolysis (1) between pyruvate and phosphoenolpyruvate, (2) between fructose 1,6-bisphosphate and fructose 6-phosphate, (3) between glucose 6-phosphate and glucose, and (4) between glucose 1-phosphate and glycogen. These barriers are circumvented by special reactions described below:

(1) Present in mitochondria is an enzyme, **pyruvate carboxylase,** which in the presence of ATP, biotin, and CO_2 converts pyruvate to oxaloacetate. The func-

tion of the biotin is to bind CO_2 from bicarbonate onto the enzyme prior to the addition of the CO_2 to pyruvate. In the extramitochondrial part of the cell is found a second enzyme, **phosphoenolpyruvate carboxykinase,** which catalyzes the conversion of oxaloacetate to phosphoenolpyruvate. High-energy phosphate in the form of GTP or ITP is required in this reaction, and CO_2 is liberated. Thus, with the help of these 2 enzymes and lactate dehydrogenase, lactate can be converted to phosphoenolpyruvate. However, oxaloacetate does not diffuse readily from mitochondria. Alternative means are available to achieve the same end by converting oxaloacetate into compounds which can diffuse from the mitochondria, followed by their reconversion to oxaloacetate in the extramitochondrial portion of the cell. Such a compound is malate, but conversion via aspartate, a-ketoglutarate, glutamate, and citrate has also been proposed. Their formation from oxaloacetate within mitochondria and their conversion back to oxaloacetate in the extramitochondrial compartment involve citric acid cycle reactions and transaminations. There are species differences with regard to the distribution of phosphoenolpyruvate carboxykinase. The extramitochondrial location is true for the rat and mouse; but in the rabbit and chicken the enzyme is located in the mitochondria, and in the guinea pig it is found in both the mitochondria and cytosol.

(2) The conversion of fructose 1,6-bisphosphate to fructose 6-phosphate, necessary to achieve a reversal of glycolysis, is catalyzed by a specific enzyme, **fruc-**

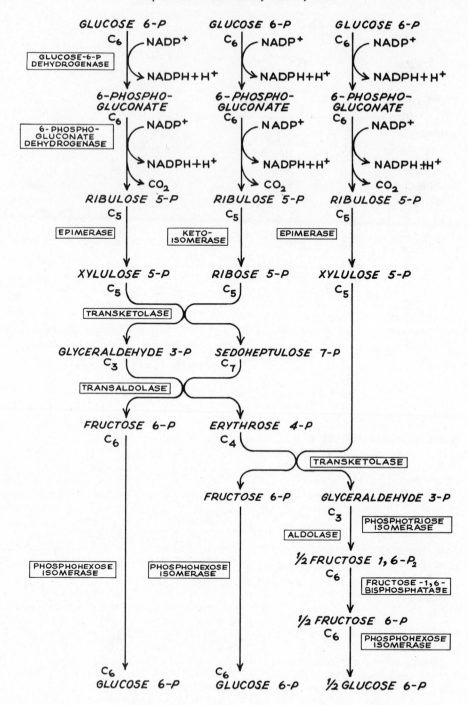

Figure 19—11. Flow chart of hexose monophosphate shunt and its connections with the Embden-Meyerhof pathway of glycolysis.

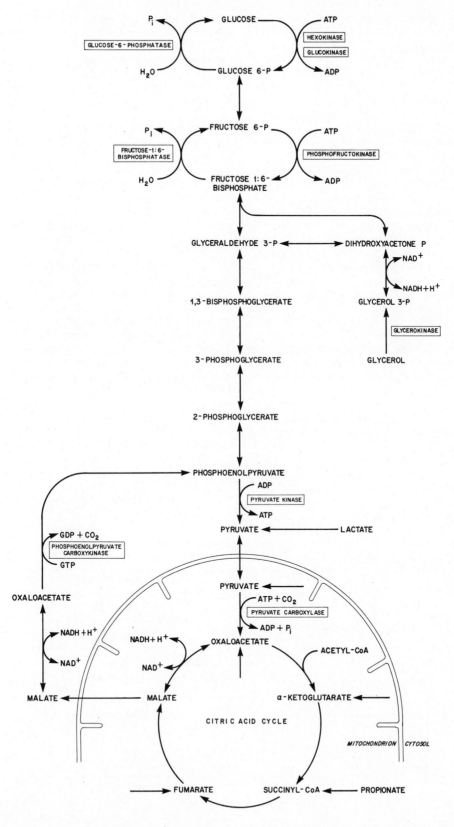

Figure 19–12. Major pathways in gluconeogenesis in the liver. Entry points of glucogenic amino acids after transamination are indicated by unlabeled arrows. (See also Fig 18–6.)

tose-1,6-bisphosphatase. This is a key enzyme in the sense that its presence determines whether or not a tissue is capable of resynthesizing glycogen from pyruvate and triosephosphates. It is present in liver and kidney and has been demonstrated in striated muscle. It is held to be absent from adipose tissue, heart muscle, and smooth muscle.

(3) The conversion of glucose 6-phosphate to glucose is catalyzed by another specific phosphatase, **glucose-6-phosphatase**. It is present in intestine, liver, and kidney, where it allows these particular tissues to add glucose to the blood. The enzyme, which is microsomal, also possesses pyrophosphatase activity. It is absent from muscle and adipose tissue.

(4) The breakdown of glycogen to glucose 1-phosphate is carried out by phosphorylase. The synthesis of glycogen involves an entirely different pathway through the formation of uridine diphosphate glucose and the activity of **glycogen synthetase** (Fig 19–5).

The relationships between these key enzymes of gluconeogenesis and the Embden-Meyerhof glycolytic pathway are shown in Fig 19–12. After transamination or deamination, glucogenic amino acids form either pyruvate or members of the citric acid cycle. Therefore, the reactions described above can account for the conversion of both glucogenic amino acids and lactate to glucose or glycogen. Thus, lactate forms pyruvate and enters the mitochondria before conversion to oxaloacetate and ultimate conversion to glucose. Propionate, which is a major source of glucose in ruminants, enters the main gluconeogenic pathway via the citric acid cycle after conversion to succinyl-CoA. Propionate, as with other fatty acids, is first activated with ATP and CoA by an appropriate **thiokinase**. Propionyl-CoA, the product of this reaction, undergoes a CO_2 fixation reaction to form D-methylmalonyl-CoA, catalyzed by **propionyl-CoA carboxylase** (Fig 19–13). This reaction is analogous to the fixation of CO_2 in acetyl-CoA by acetyl-CoA carboxylase (see Chapter 20) in that it forms a malonyl derivative and requires biotin as a coenzyme. D-Methylmalonyl-CoA

must be converted to its stereoisomer, L-methylmalonyl-CoA, by **methylmalonyl-CoA racemase** before its final isomerization to succinyl-CoA by the enzyme **methylmalonyl-CoA isomerase,** which requires vitamin B_{12} as a coenzyme. Vitamin B_{12} deficiency in man and animals results in the excretion of large amounts of methylmalonate (methylmalonic aciduria).

Although the pathway to succinate is its main route of metabolism, propionate may also be used as the priming molecule for the synthesis—in adipose tissue and mammary gland—of fatty acids which have an odd number of carbon atoms in the molecule. C 15 and C 17 fatty acids are found particularly in the lipids of ruminants.

Glycerol is a product of the metabolism of adipose tissue, and only tissues that possess the activating enzyme, **glycerokinase**, can utilize it. This enzyme, which requires ATP, is found in liver and kidney, among other tissues. Glycerokinase catalyzes the conversion of glycerol to glycerol 3-phosphate. This pathway connects with the triosephosphate stages of the Embden-Meyerhof pathway because glycerol 3-phosphate may be oxidized to dihydroxyacetone phosphate by NAD^+ in the presence of another enzyme, **glycerol-3-phosphate dehydrogenase,** although the equilibrium constant is very much in favor of glycerol 3-phosphate formation. Thus, liver and kidney are able to convert glycerol to blood glucose by making use of the above enzymes, some of the enzymes of the Embden-Meyerhof pathway, and the specific enzymes of the gluconeogenic pathway, fructose-1,6-bisphosphatase and glucose-6-phosphatase (Fig 19–12).

METABOLISM OF HEXOSES

Phosphorylation

The hexoses of metabolic importance—glucose, fructose, and galactose—enter most metabolic path-

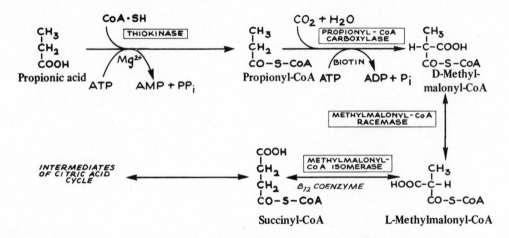

Figure 19–13. Metabolism of propionate.

ways, including glycolysis, after phosphorylation. As mentioned previously, glucose is phosphorylated by ATP in the presence of the enzyme **hexokinase**; but in liver there is in addition a more specific **glucokinase**. Hexokinase differs from glucokinase in that it is inhibited by glucose 6-phosphate (allosteric inhibition); it does not change in activity as a response to the nutritional or hormonal state of the animal; and it has a high affinity for glucose (low K_m). When glucose is the substrate, the product of the reaction with glucokinase or hexokinase is glucose 6-phosphate.

Fructose and galactose are not phosphorylated in the presence of glucokinase, but they have their own specific enzymes, **fructokinase** and **galactokinase**, which carry out phosphorylation in the liver. Unlike glucokinase or hexokinase, these enzymes always convert the hexose to the corresponding hexose 1-phosphate.

OTHER PATHWAYS OF GLUCOSE METABOLISM

THE URONIC ACID PATHWAY

Besides the major pathways of metabolism of glucose 6-phosphate that have been described, there exists a pathway for the conversion of glucose to glucuronic acid, ascorbic acid, and pentoses known as the **uronic acid pathway**. It is also an alternative oxidative pathway for glucose.

In the uronic acid pathway, glucuronic acid is formed from glucose by the reactions shown in Fig 19–14. Glucose 6-phosphate is converted to glucose 1-phosphate, which then reacts with uridine triphosphate

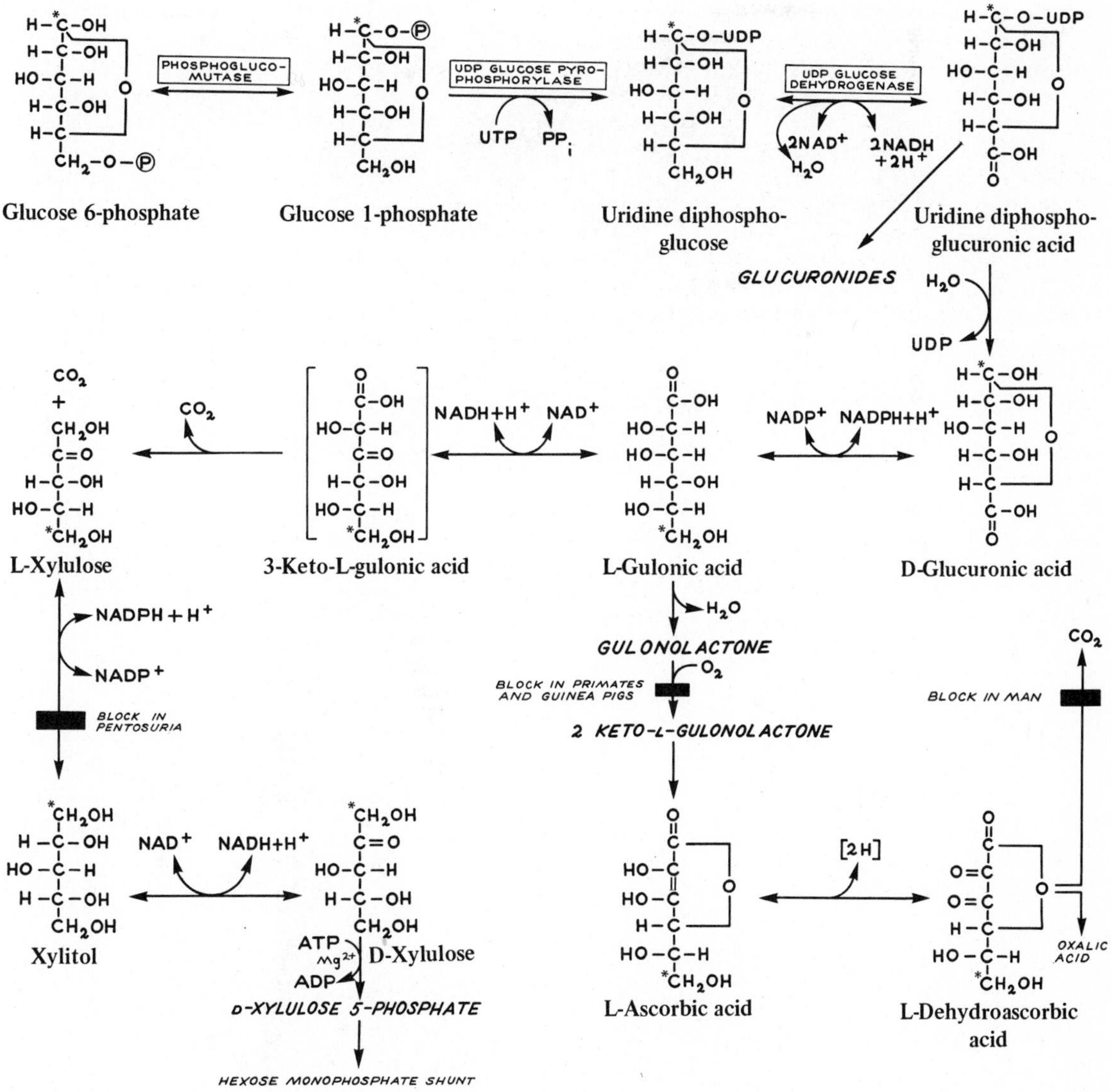

Figure 19—14. Uronic acid pathway.

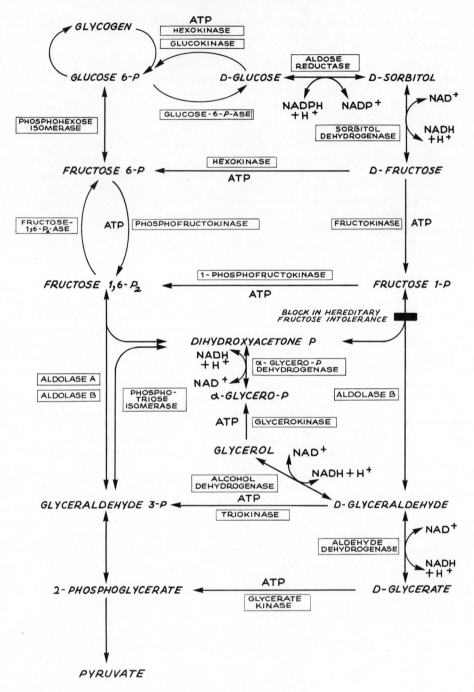

Figure 19–15. Metabolism of fructose.

(UTP) to form the active nucleotide, uridine diphosphate glucose (UDPG). This latter reaction is catalyzed by the enzyme **UDPG pyrophosphorylase**. All of the steps up to this point are those previously indicated as in the pathway of glycogenesis in the liver. Uridine diphosphate glucose is now oxidized at carbon 6 by a 2-step process to glucuronic acid. The product of the oxidation which is catalyzed by an NAD-dependent **UDPG dehydrogenase** is therefore, UDP-glucuronic acid.

Galacturonic acid is an important constituent of many natural products such as the pectins. It may be formed from UDP-glucuronic acid by inversion around carbon 4, as occurs when UDP-glucose is converted to UDP-galactose.

UDP-glucuronic acid is the "active" form of glucuronic acid for reactions involving incorporation of glucuronic acid into chondroitin sulfate or for reactions in which glucuronic acid is conjugated to such substrates as steroid hormones, certain drugs, or bilirubin (formation of "direct" bilirubin).

The further metabolism of glucuronic acid is shown in Fig 19–14. In an NADPH-dependent reaction, glucuronic acid is reduced to L-gulonic acid. This latter compound is the direct precursor of ascorbic acid in those animals which are capable of synthesizing this vitamin. In man and other primates as well as in guinea pigs, ascorbic acid cannot be synthesized and gulonic acid is oxidized to 3-keto-L-gulonic acid, which is then decarboxylated to the pentose L-xylulose.

Xylulose is a constituent of the hexose monophosphate shunt pathway; but in the reactions shown in Fig 19–14, the L-isomer of xylulose is formed from ketogulonic acid. If the 2 pathways are to connect, it is therefore necessary to convert L-xylulose to the D-isomer. This is accomplished by an NADPH-dependent reduction to xylitol, which is then oxidized in an NAD-dependent reaction to D-xylulose; this latter compound, after conversion to D-xylulose 5-phosphate with ATP as phosphate donor, is further metabolized in the hexose monophosphate shunt.

In the rare hereditary disease termed "**essential pentosuria**," considerable quantities of L-xylulose appear in the urine. It is now believed that this may be explained by the absence in pentosuric patients of the enzyme necessary to accomplish reduction of L-xylulose to xylitol, and hence inability to convert the L-form of the pentose to the D-form.

Various drugs markedly increase the rate at which glucose enters the uronic acid pathway. For example, administration of barbital or of chlorobutanol to rats results in a significant increase in the conversion of glucose to glucuronic acid, L-gulonic acid, and ascorbic acid. This effect on L-ascorbic acid biosynthesis is shown by many drugs, including various barbiturates, aminopyrine, and antipyrine. It is of interest that these last 2 drugs have also been reported to increase the excretion of L-xylulose in pentosuric subjects.

METABOLISM OF FRUCTOSE

Fructose may be phosphorylated to form fructose 6-phosphate, catalyzed by the same enzyme, hexokinase, that accomplishes the phosphorylation of glucose (or mannose). (See Fig 19–15.) However, the affinity of the enzyme for fructose is very small compared with its affinity for glucose. It is unlikely, therefore, that this is a major pathway for fructose utilization.

Another enzyme, **fructokinase**, is present in liver which effects the transfer of phosphate from ATP to fructose, forming fructose 1-phosphate. It has also been demonstrated in kidney and intestine. This enzyme will not phosphorylate glucose, and, unlike glucokinase, its activity is not affected by fasting or by insulin, which may explain why fructose disappears from the blood of diabetic patients at a normal rate. It is probable that this is the major route for the phosphorylation of fructose. The K_m for fructose of the enzyme in liver is very low, indicating a very high affinity of the enzyme for its substrate.

Fructose 1-phosphate is split into D-glyceraldehyde and dihydroxyacetone phosphate by **aldolase B**, an enzyme found in the liver. The enzyme also attacks fructose 1,6-bisphosphate. Absence of this enzyme leads to a **hereditary fructose intolerance**. D-Glyceraldehyde may gain entry to the glycolysis sequence of reactions via 3 possible routes. One is by the action of **alcohol dehydrogenase** to form glycerol, which, in the presence of **glycerokinase**, forms glycerol 3-phosphate. A second alternative involves **aldehyde dehydrogenase** which forms D-glycerate from D-glyceraldehyde. In rat liver, **D-glycerate kinase** catalyzes the formation of 2-phosphoglycerate, but this enzyme is not active in human liver. Another enzyme present in liver, **triokinase**, catalyzes the phosphorylation of D-glyceraldehyde to glyceraldehyde 3-phosphate. This appears to be the major pathway for the further metabolism of D-glyceraldehyde. The 2 triose phosphates, dihydroxyacetone phosphate and glyceraldehyde 3-phosphate, may be degraded via the Embden-Meyerhof pathway or they may combine under the influence of aldolase and be converted to glucose. The latter is the fate of much of the fructose metabolized in the liver.

Additionally, there is the possibility that fructose 1-phosphate may be phosphorylated directly in position 6 to form fructose 1,6-bisphosphate, an intermediate of glycolysis. The enzyme catalyzing this reaction, **1-phosphofructokinase**, has been found in muscle and liver. However, if this were a major pathway for fructose metabolism, hereditary fructose intolerance would probably not occur.

One consequence of hereditary fructose intolerance and of another condition due to **fructose-1,6-bisphosphatase deficiency** is a fructose-induced hypoglycemia despite the presence of high glycogen reserves. Apparently the accumulation of fructose 1-phosphate and fructose 1,6-bisphosphate inhibits the activity of liver phosphorylase.

If the liver and intestines of an experimental animal are removed, the conversion of injected fructose to glucose does not take place and the animal succumbs to hypoglycemia unless glucose is administered. It appears that brain and muscle can utilize significant quantities of fructose only after its conversion to glucose in the liver. In man but not in the rat, a significant amount of the fructose resulting from the digestion of sucrose is converted to glucose in the intestinal wall prior to passage into the portal circulation. Fructose is more rapidly glycolyzed by the liver than glucose. This is due most probably to the fact that it bypasses the steps in glucose metabolism catalyzed by glucokinase and phosphofructokinase, at which points metabolic control is exerted on the rate of catabolism of glucose.

Studies have indicated that fructose is metabolized actively by adipose tissue and that it is metabolized independently of glucose. At low concentrations, fructose is utilized by adipose tissue (epididymal adipose tissue of the rat) more slowly than glucose; at high concentrations, fructose is metabolized at a faster rate than glucose.

Free fructose is found in seminal plasma and is secreted in quantity by the placenta into the fetal circulation of ungulates and whales, where it accumulates in the amniotic and allantoic fluids. Experiments demonstrated that glucose was the precursor of fructose. One pathway proposed for this conversion is via sorbitol. Glucose undergoes reduction to sorbitol catalyzed by **aldose reductase** (polyol dehydrogenase) and NADPH. This is followed by oxidation of sorbitol to fructose in the presence of NAD and **ketose reductase** (sorbitol dehydrogenase).

METABOLISM OF GALACTOSE

Galactose is derived from the hydrolysis in the intestine of the disaccharide lactose, the sugar of milk. It is readily converted in the liver to glucose. The ability of the liver to accomplish this conversion may be used as a test of hepatic function in the galactose tolerance test. The pathway by which galactose is converted to glucose is shown in Fig 19–16.

In reaction 1, galactose is phosphorylated with the aid of **galactokinase**, using ATP as phosphate donor. The product, galactose 1-phosphate, reacts with **uridine diphosphate glucose (UDPG)** to form **uridine diphosphate galactose** and glucose 1-phosphate. In this

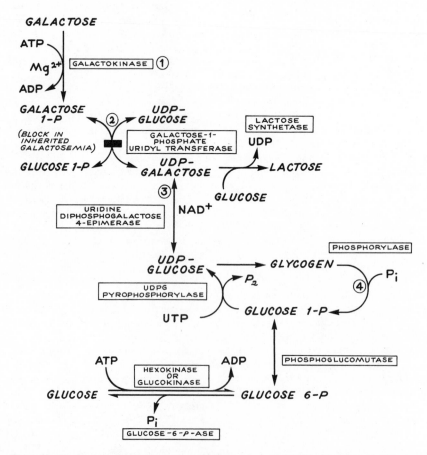

Figure 19—16. The pathway for conversion of galactose to glucose and for the synthesis of lactose.

step (reaction 2), which is catalyzed by an enzyme called **galactose-1-phosphate uridyl transferase**, galactose is transferred to a position on UDPG, replacing glucose. The conversion of galactose to glucose takes place (reaction 3) in a reaction of the galactose-containing nucleotide which is catalyzed by an **epimerase**. The product is uridine diphosphate glucose, UDPG. Epimerization probably involves an oxidation and reduction at carbon 4 with NAD as coenzyme. Finally (reaction 4), glucose is liberated from UDPG as glucose 1-phosphate, probably after incorporation into glycogen followed by phosphorolysis.

Reaction 3 is freely reversible. In this manner glucose can be converted to galactose, so that preformed galactose is not essential in the diet. It will be recalled that galactose is required in the body not only in the formation of milk but also as a constituent of glycolipids (cerebrosides), chondromucoids, and muco-proteins.

Galactokinase is an adaptive enzyme, responding with an increased activity upon the feeding of galactose. Young animals show higher activity than adults.

In the synthesis of lactose in the mammary gland, glucose is converted to UDP-galactose by the enzymes described above. UDP-galactose condenses with glucose to yield lactose, catalyzed by **lactose synthetase.**

Inability to metabolize dietary galactose occurs in **galactosemia**, an inherited metabolic disease in which galactose accumulates in the blood and spills over into the urine when this sugar or lactose is ingested. However, there is also marked accumulation of galactose 1-phosphate in the red blood cells of the galactosemic individual, which indicates that there is no deficit of galactokinase (reaction 1).

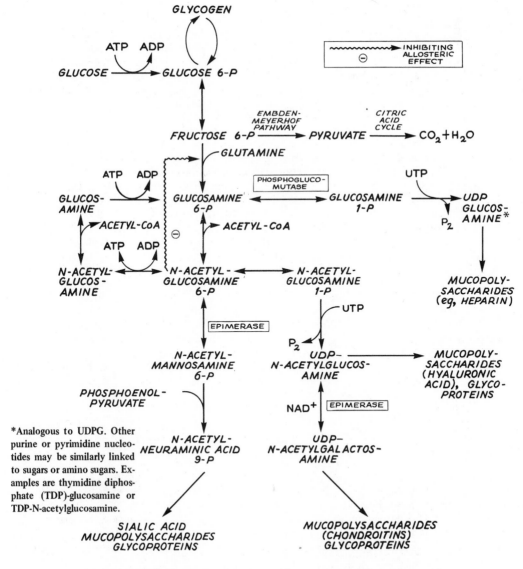

Figure 19—17. A summary of the interrelationships in metabolism of amino sugars.

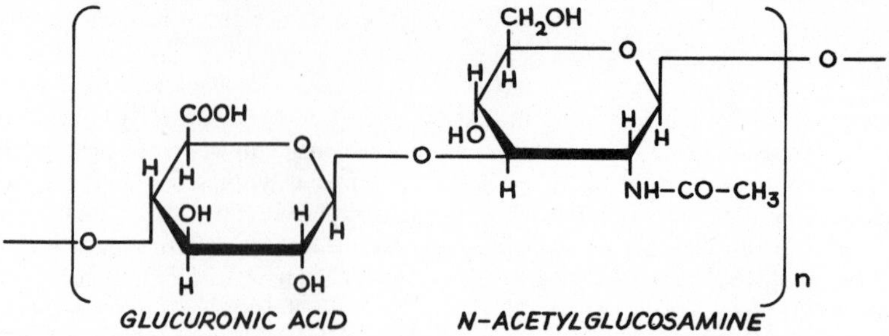

Figure 19—18. Disaccharide unit of hyaluronic acid.

Recent studies suggest that an inherited lack of galactose-1-phosphate uridyl transferase in the liver and red blood cells is responsible for galactosemia. As a result reaction 2 (see above) is blocked. The epimerase (reaction 3) is, however, present in adequate amounts, so that the galactosemic individual can still form UDP-galactose from glucose. This explains how it is possible for normal growth and development of affected children to occur regardless of the galactose-free diets which are used to control the symptoms of the disease.

Metabolism of Amino Sugars (Hexosamines)
(See Fig 19—17.)

Amino sugars are important components of the carbohydrate which is widely distributed throughout the body as a part of the structural elements of the tissues. The mucopolysaccharides (see p 639) are examples of these "structural" carbohydrates. In contrast to glycogen, in which each unit of the polysaccharide is identical (a glucosyl unit), the mucopolysaccharides appear to consist of 2 or more different units, one of which is an amino sugar. A familiar example of these mucopolysaccharides is hyaluronic acid (see p 641), which occurs in synovial fluid, vitreous humor, umbilical cord, skin, and bone. This compound contains, as a basic disaccharide unit, 1 mol of glucuronic acid linked to 1 mol of N-acetylglucosamine through a 1,3-glycosidic bond, as shown in Fig 19—18. UDP-glucuronic acid and UDP-N-acetylglucosamine are the precursors.

Another important group of mucopolysaccharides consists of the chondroitin sulfuric acids (see p 639), the prosthetic compounds of the polysaccharide-protein complexes known as chondromucoids. The chondromucoids are the chief components of cartilage, but they also occur in the walls of the large blood vessels and in tendons, in the valves of the heart, and in the skin. Chondroitin sulfuric acids A and C (see p 639) contain glucuronic acid, but the amino sugar is an acetylated galactosamine, N-acetyl-D-galactosamine. This is sulfated by "active sulfate" (3'-phosphoadenosine-5'-phosphosulfate). Glycoproteins (see p 642) are other examples of compounds containing amino sugars.

The enzymatic synthesis of glucosamine has been achieved (Fig 19—19). Using a purified enzyme obtained from typical bacterial, fungal, or mammalian (rat liver) cells, it was observed that the conversion of fructose 6-phosphate to glucosamine 6-phosphate was carried out by a transamidation reaction from glutamine. The catalyzing enzyme was termed **L-glutamine-D-fructose-6-phosphate transamidase (amino-transferase)**. The transamidase reaction may be unique in that the necessary energy is derived solely from the cleavage of the amide bond of glutamine in contrast to the usual reactions involving transfer of the amide nitrogen of glutamine to an acceptor other than water, all of which require an additional source of energy such as ATP.

The biosynthesis of N-acetylgalactosamine is accomplished through the catalytic action of an enzyme which has been identified in the liver. This enzyme acts on UDP-N-acetylglucosamine and epimerizes the glucosamine moiety to galactosamine, thus producing UDP-N-acetylgalactosamine. The enzyme is called **uridine diphosphate-N-acetylglucosamine epimerase** (cf uridine diphosphogalactose epimerase, Fig 19—16).

A summary of the interrelationships in the metabolism of the amino sugars is shown in Fig 19—17. Note the pathways for the synthesis from glucose of N-acetylglucosamine and N-acetylgalactosamine as their active uridine diphosphate derivatives. Also note the pathway of synthesis of N-acetylneuraminic acid, another important amino sugar in glycoproteins and mucopolysaccharides. For further details concerning glycoproteins consult Marshall (1972). For details concerning mucopolysaccharides, consult Dickens & others (1968).

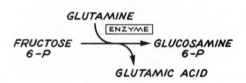

Figure 19—19. Synthesis of glucosamine from fructose.

●   ●   ●

References

Boyer PD (editor): *The Enzymes,* 3rd ed. Vols 5–9. Academic Press, 1972.

Brown BI, Brown DH in: *Carbohydrate Metabolism and Its Disorders.* Vol 2, p 123. Dickens F, Randle PJ, Whelan WJ (editors). Academic Press, 1968.

Cahill GF, Ashmore J, Renold AE, Hastings AB: Am J Med 26:264, 1959.

Cooper TG, Benedict CR: Biochem Biophys Res Commun 22:285, 1966.

Dickens F, Randle PJ, Whelan WJ (editors): *Carbohydrate Metabolism and Its Disorders.* 2 vols. Academic Press, 1968.

Exton JH, Jefferson LS, Butcher RW, Park CR: Am J Med 40:709, 1966.

Felig P, Wahren J: Fed Proc 33:1092, 1974.

Greenberg DM (editor): *Metabolic Pathways,* 3rd ed. Vol 1. Academic Press, 1967.

Hers HG: The control of glycogen metabolism in the liver. Annu Rev Biochem 45:167, 1976.

Hers HG: Rev internat d'hépatol 9:35, 1959.

Krebs EG in: *Current Topics in Cellular Regulation.* Vol 5, p 99. Academic Press, 1972.

Krebs HA: Gluconeogenesis. Proc R Soc Lond [Biol] 159:545, 1964.

Landau BR, Leanards JR, Barry FM: Am J Physiol 201:41, 1961.

Marshall RD: Glycoproteins. Annu Rev Biochem 41:673, 1972.

Miller LL: Fed Proc 24:737, 1965.

Miller ON, Olson RE: Arch Biochem 50:257, 1954.

Mortimore GE: Am J Physiol 204:699, 1963.

Newsholme EA, Start C: *Regulation in Metabolism.* Wiley, 1973.

Rapoport S in: *Essays in Biochemistry.* Vol 4, p 69. Campbell PN, Greville GD (editors). Academic Press, 1968.

Shull KH, Miller ON: J Biol Chem 235:551, 1960.

Stanbury JB, Wyngaarden JB, Fredrickson DS (editors): *The Metabolic Basis of Inherited Disease,* 3rd ed. McGraw-Hill, 1972.

Stetten D Jr: Am J Med 28:867, 1960.

Sutherland EW, Rall TW, Menon T: J Biol Chem 237:1220, 1962.

Sutherland EW, Wosilait WD: J Biol Chem 218:459, 1956.

Traut RR, Lipmann F: J Biol Chem 238:1213, 1963.

Weber G in: *The Biological Basis of Medicine.* Vol 2, p 263. Bittar EE, Bittar N (editors). Academic Press, 1968.

Whelan WJ (editor): *Control of Glycogen Metabolism.* Academic Press, 1968.

20 . . .
Metabolism of Lipids

The lipids of metabolic significance in the mammalian organism include triacylglycerols (triglycerides,* neutral fat), phospholipids, and steroids, together with products of their metabolism such as long chain fatty acids (free fatty acids), glycerol, and ketone bodies. For many years the tissue lipids were considered to be inactive storehouses of calorigenic material, called upon only in times of shortage of calories. However, Schoenheimer and Rittenberg showed by experiments in which deuterium-labeled fatty acids were fed to mice in caloric equilibrium that in only 4 days a considerable proportion of the depot lipid had been formed from the dietary lipid. Since the total mass of triacylglycerol in the depots remained constant, a corresponding quantity of triacylglycerol must have been mobilized during this period. These investigations demonstrated the dynamic state of body fat, a concept that forms the basis of present understanding of lipid metabolism.

Much of the carbohydrate of the diet is converted to triacylglycerol before it is utilized for the purpose of providing energy. As a result, triacylglycerol fatty acids may be the major source of energy for many tissues; indeed, there is evidence that in certain organs fatty acids may be used as fuel in preference to carbohydrate.

As the principal form in which energy is stored in the body, triacylglycerol has definite advantages over carbohydrate or protein. Its caloric value is over twice as great (9.3 kcal/g) and it is associated with less water in storage. Triacylglycerol is, therefore, the most concentrated form in which potential energy can be stored. In addition, fatty acids provide more metabolic water upon oxidation than other metabolic fuels, which is advantageous to mammals occupying dry environments.

A minimal amount of lipid is essential in the diet to provide an adequate supply of certain polyunsaturated fatty acids (the essential fatty acids) and of fat-

*According to the new standardized terminology of the International Union of Pure and Applied Chemistry (IUPAC) and the International Union of Biochemistry (IUB), the monoglycerides, diglycerides, and triglycerides are to be designated monoacylglycerols, diacylglycerols, and triacylglycerols, respectively. Both terms may be used occasionally in this book to remind the reader who is familiar with the older terminology of the change.

soluble vitamins which cannot be synthesized in adequate amounts for optimal body function. As well as acting as a carrier of these essential compounds, dietary lipid is necessary for their efficient absorption from the gastrointestinal tract. Apart from these functions, it is not certain how essential lipid is as a constituent of the diet. As a source of energy it can be replaced completely by either carbohydrate or protein, although the efficiency with which foodstuffs are utilized may suffer as a consequence.

OXIDATION OF TRIACYLGLYCEROL

Triacylglycerols must be hydrolyzed to their constituent fatty acids and glycerol before further catabolism can proceed. Much of this hydrolysis occurs in adipose tissue with release of free fatty acids into the plasma, where they are found combined with serum albumin. This is followed by free fatty acid uptake into tissues and subsequent oxidation. Many tissues (including liver, heart, kidney, muscle, lung, testis, brain, and adipose tissue) have the ability to oxidize long chain fatty acids although brain cannot extract them from the blood. The utilization of glycerol depends upon whether such tissues possess the necessary activating enzyme, **glycerokinase**. The enzyme has been found in significant amounts in liver, kidney, intestine, brown adipose tissue, and lactating mammary gland.

Oxidation of Fatty Acids

Knoop proposed that fatty acids are oxidized physiologically by β-oxidation. In experiments which were the forerunners of the modern technic of labeling, he tagged the methyl end of fatty acids by substitution of a phenyl radical. This prevented the complete oxidation of the fatty acids and resulted in urinary excretion of phenyl derivatives as end products of their metabolism. On feeding to dogs fatty acids with an even number of carbon atoms labeled in this manner, he noticed that phenylacetic acid was always excreted into the urine (as the glycine conjugate, phenylaceturic acid). However, on feeding labeled fatty acids with an odd number of carbon atoms, benzoic acid was always excreted (as the glycine conjugate, hippuric acid). These results could be explained only if the fatty acids were metabolized by a pathway involving the removal of 2 carbon atoms at a time from the carboxyl end of the molecule, ie, β-oxidation.

Several enzymes, known collectively as "fatty acid oxidase," are found in the mitochondrial matrix adjacent to the respiratory chain (which is found in the inner membrane). These catalyze the oxidation of fatty acids to acetyl-CoA, the system being coupled with the phosphorylation of ADP to ATP (Fig 20–1).

As in the metabolism of glucose, fatty acids must first be converted in a reaction with ATP to an active intermediate before they will react with the enzymes responsible for their further metabolism. This is the only step in the complete degradation of a fatty acid that requires energy from ATP. In the presence of ATP and coenzyme A, the enzyme **thiokinase** (acyl-CoA synthetase) catalyzes the conversion of a fatty acid (or free fatty acid) to an "active fatty acid" or acyl-CoA.

Thiokinases are found both inside and outside the mitochondria. Several thiokinases have been described,

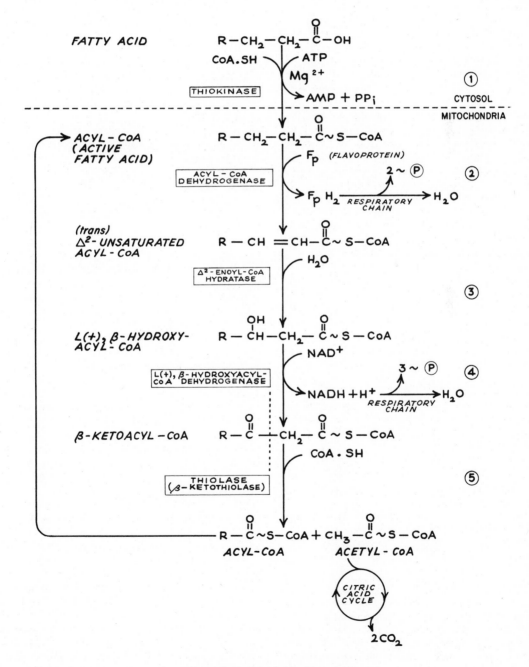

Figure 20–1. β-Oxidation of fatty acids.

each specific for fatty acids of different chain length. In addition, there is a GTP-specific mitochondrial thiokinase which, unlike the ATP-specific enzyme, forms GDP + P$_i$ as products and not pyrophosphate.

After the formation of acyl-CoA, there follows the removal of 2 hydrogen atoms from the a and β carbons, catalyzed by **acyl-CoA dehydrogenase**. This results in the formation of a,β-unsaturated or Δ^2-unsaturated acyl-CoA. The coenzyme for the dehydrogenase is a flavoprotein, containing flavin adenine dinucleotide (FAD) as prosthetic group, whose reoxidation by the respiratory chain requires the mediation of another flavoprotein, termed the electron-transferring flavoprotein (see p 228). Water is added to saturate the double bond and form β-hydroxyacyl-CoA, catalyzed by the enzyme Δ^2-**enoyl-CoA hydratase** (crotonase). The β-hydroxy derivative undergoes further dehydrogenation on the β carbon (**β-hydroxyacyl-CoA dehydrogenase**) to form the corresponding β-ketoacyl-CoA compound. In this case, nicotinamide adenine dinucleotide (NAD) is the coenzyme involved in the dehydrogenation. Finally, β-ketoacyl-CoA is split at the β position by **thiolase** (β-ketothiolase), which catalyzes a thiolytic cleavage involving another molecule of CoA. The products of this reaction are acetyl-CoA and an acyl-CoA derivative containing 2 carbons less than the original acyl-CoA molecule which underwent oxidation. The acyl-CoA formed in the cleavage reaction reenters the oxidative pathway at reaction (2) (Fig 20–1). In this way, a long chain fatty acid may be degraded completely to acetyl-CoA (C_2-units). As acetyl-CoA can be oxidized to CO_2 and water via the citric acid cycle (which is also found within the mitochondria), the complete oxidation of fatty acids is achieved.

Fatty acids with an odd number of carbon atoms are oxidized by the pathway of β-oxidation until a 3-carbon (propionyl-CoA) residue remains. This compound is converted to succinyl-CoA, a constituent

bonds/mol, or 129 × 7.6 = 980 kcal. As the caloric value of palmitic acid is 2340 kcal/mol, the process captures as high-energy phosphate at least 41% (980/2340 × 100) of the total energy of combustion of the fatty acid.

a- & ω-Oxidation of Fatty Acids

Quantitatively, β-oxidation is the most important pathway for fatty acid oxidation. However, a-oxidation, ie, the removal of one carbon at a time from the carboxyl end of the molecule, has been detected in brain tissue. It does not require CoA intermediates and does not lead to generation of high-energy phosphates. ω-Oxidation is brought about by hydroxylase enzymes involving cytochrome P-450 in microsomes (see p 191). The $-CH_3$ group is converted to a $-CH_2OH$ group which subsequently is oxidized to $-COOH$, thus forming a dicarboxylic acid. **Refsum's disease** is caused by an inherited inability to oxidize phytanic acid, formed from phytol present in plant foodstuffs. Phytanic acid contains a $-CH_3$ group on the β-carbon which blocks β-oxidation. Normal persons can overcome the block by employing an initial a-oxidation, but those with the disease apparently lack this ability.

Role of Carnitine in Fatty Acid Metabolism

Carnitine (β-hydroxy-γ-trimethylammonium butyrate), $(CH_3)_3 N^+-CH_2-CH(OH)-CH_2-COO^-$, stimulates the oxidation of long chain fatty acids by mitochondria. It is widely distributed, being particularly abundant in muscle. Activation of long chain fatty acids to acyl-CoA occurs in microsomes and on the outer membranes of mitochondria. Activation of lower fatty acids may occur within the mitochondria, independently of carnitine. Long chain acyl-CoA will not penetrate mitochondria and become oxidized unless carnitine is present, but carnitine itself will not penetrate mitochondria. An enzyme, **carnitine-palmityl acyltransferase**, is associated with the mitochondrial

$$ACYL-CoA + CARNITINE \underset{\text{CARNITINE - PALMITYL ACYL TRANSFERASE}}{\overset{}{\rightleftarrows}} ACYLCARNITINE + CoA$$

of the citric acid cycle (see also Chapter 18).

Energetics of Fatty Acid Oxidation

Transport in the respiratory chain of electrons from reduced flavoprotein and NAD will lead to the synthesis of at least 5 high-energy phosphate bonds (see Chapter 17) for each of the first 7 acetyl-CoA mol-

membranes and allows long chain acyl groups to penetrate the mitochondria and gain access to the β-oxidation system of enzymes. A possible mechanism to account for the action of carnitine in facilitating the oxidation of fatty acids by mitochondria is shown in Fig 20–2. In addition, another enzyme, **carnitine-acetyl acyltransferase**, is present in mitochondria

$$ACETYL-CoA + CARNITINE \underset{\text{CARNITINE -ACETYL ACYL TRANSFERASE}}{\overset{}{\rightleftarrows}} ACETYL-CARNITINE + CoA$$

ecules formed by β-oxidation of palmitate (7 × 5 = 35). Of the total of 8 mol of acetyl-CoA formed, each will give rise to at least 12 high-energy bonds on oxidation in the citric acid cycle, making 8 × 12 = 96 high-energy bonds derived from the acetyl-CoA formed from palmitate, minus 2 for the initial activation of the fatty acid, yielding a net gain of 129 high-energy

which catalyzes the transfer of short chain acyl groups between CoA and carnitine. The function of this enzyme is somewhat obscure. Two acetyl-CoA pools may be present in mitochondria—one derived from fatty acid oxidation, one from pyruvate oxidation; they may intercommunicate via the activity of carnitine-acetyl acyltransferase and reaction with carnitine.

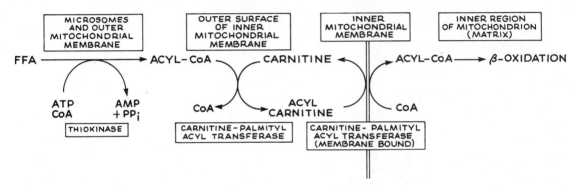

Figure 20—2. Proposed role of carnitine in the metabolism of long chain fatty acids.

BIOSYNTHESIS OF LIPIDS

Synthesis of Fatty Acids

Like many other degradative and synthetic processes (eg, glycogenolysis and glycogenesis), fatty acid synthesis was formerly considered to be merely the reversal of oxidation. However, it now seems clear that a **mitochondrial** system for fatty acid synthesis, involving some modification of the β-oxidation sequence, is responsible only for elongation of existing fatty acids of moderate chain length, whereas a radically different and highly active **extramitochondrial** system is responsible for the complete synthesis of palmitate from acetyl-CoA. There is also an active system for chain elongation present in rat liver microsomes.

A. Mitochondrial System: Under anaerobic conditions, mitochondria will catalyze the incorporation of acetyl-CoA into long chain fatty acids (mainly stearate [C_{18}] and palmitate [C_{16}], with some C_{20} and C_{14} fatty acids). The system requires the addition of ATP, NADH, and NADPH. The enzymes are probably the same as those involved in β-oxidation except for the conversion of the *a,β*-unsaturated acyl-CoA to the corresponding saturated compound which is catalyzed by **a,β-unsaturated acyl-CoA reductase** (enoyl-CoA reductase), requiring NADPH. It is likely that the incorporation of acetyl-CoA into the long chain fatty acids is due to its addition to existing fatty acids rather than to the synthesis de novo of the long chain fatty acids from acetyl-CoA. The ATP is probably required for the formation of acyl-CoA from endogenous fatty acids. A role for pyridoxal phosphate has been suggested as a coenzyme for the enzyme condensing acetyl-CoA with acyl-CoA; thus, thiolase may not be used in this synthetic pathway. The physiologic significance of this pathway is uncertain since it will operate only under anaerobic conditions.

B. Extramitochondrial System for De Novo Synthesis: (Fig 20—3.) This system has been found in the soluble fraction of many tissues, including liver, kidney, brain, lung, mammary gland, and adipose tissue. Its cofactor requirements include NADPH, ATP, Mn^{2+}, and HCO_3^- (as a source of CO_2). Free palmitate is the main end product. These characteristics contrast markedly with those of the mitochondrial system.

Bicarbonate as a source of CO_2 is required in the initial reaction for the carboxylation of acetyl-CoA to malonyl-CoA in the presence of ATP and **acetyl-CoA carboxylase.** Acetyl-CoA carboxylase has a requirement for the vitamin biotin. Activity is inhibited when biotin is bound by the protein avidin from egg white. As acyl-CoA derivatives are inactive in the system—unlike the situation in the mitochondria—it was concluded that acyl derivatives of CoA were not intermediates in the extramitochondrial pathway during the synthesis of palmitate and it was proposed that the acyl moiety remained attached to the enzyme as an acyl-S-enzyme complex.

There appear to be 2 types of fatty acid synthetase systems found in the soluble portion of the cell (cytosol). In bacteria, plants, and lower forms like Euglena, the individual enzymes of the system may be separate and the acyl radicals are found in combination with a protein called the **acyl carrier protein.** However, in yeast, mammals, and birds, the synthetase system is a multienzyme complex which may not be subdivided without loss of activity. The following account is based principally on the yeast system (Fig 20—3).

The multienzyme complex contains 2 types of —SH groups, "central" and "peripheral." In the "priming reaction," acetyl-CoA reacts with the "peripheral" —SH group and malonyl-CoA reacts with the "central" —SH group to transfer acetyl and malonyl residues to the enzyme (Fig 20—4). The acetyl group attacks the methylene group of the malonyl residue to liberate CO_2 and form acetoacetyl enzyme attached to the central —SH group. This decarboxylation allows the reaction to go to completion and acts as a driving force for the whole system. While attached to the central —SH group, acetoacetyl enzyme is reduced, dehydrated, and reduced again to form the corresponding saturated acyl-enzyme compound. The main stages of the reactions are analogous to those in β-oxidation except that the β-hydroxy acid is the D(−) isomer instead of the L(+) isomer. NADPH serves as the hydrogen donor in both reductions, with the mediation of flavin mononucleotide (FMN) in the reaction that saturates the

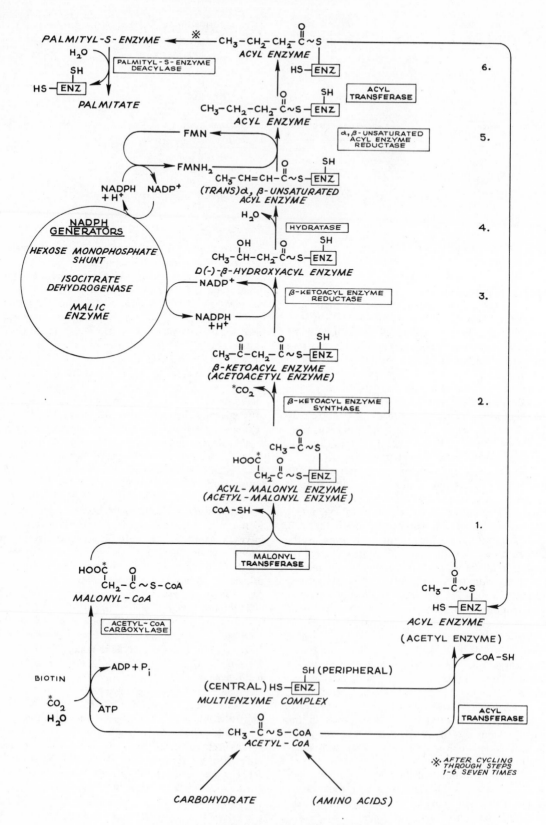

Figure 20—3. Extramitochondrial synthesis of palmitate.

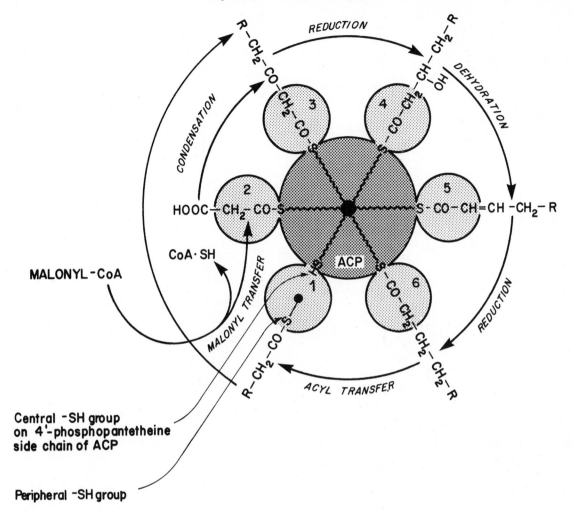

Figure 20-4. Operation of the multienzyme complex (fatty acid synthetase) as envisaged by Lynen. (**ACP:** Acyl carrier protein. **1:** Acyl transferase. **2:** Malonyl transferase. **3:** β-Ketoacyl enzyme synthase. **4:** β-Ketoacyl enzyme reductase. **5:** Hydratase. **6:** α,β-Unsaturated acyl enzyme reductase.)

double bond. FMN does not appear to play a part in the pigeon liver synthetase system. Finally, the saturated acyl radical is transferred to the "peripheral" –SH group, a new malonyl residue takes its place on the "central" –SH group, and the process is repeated until a saturated acyl radical of 16 carbon atoms is formed.

In mammalian systems, free palmitate is liberated from the enzyme complex by hydrolysis. The free palmitate must be activated to acyl-CoA before it can proceed via any other metabolic pathway. Its usual fate is esterification into acylglycerols. Both acyl carrier protein of bacteria and the multienzyme complex of yeast contain the vitamin pantothenic acid in the

form of 4'-phosphopantetheine. This is the carrier of the "central" –SH group and is responsible for the binding of acyl groups as in CoA. It is probable that the central –SH group is attached to a protein similar to the free acyl carrier protein of bacteria.

The aggregation of all the enzymes of a particular pathway into one multienzyme functional unit offers great efficiency and freedom from interference by competing processes, thus achieving the effect of compartmentalization of the process without the erection of permeability barriers.

The equation for the overall synthesis of palmitate from acetyl-CoA and malonyl-CoA is as follows:

$$CH_3CO \cdot S \cdot CoA + 7\,HOOC \cdot CH_2CO \cdot S \cdot CoA + 14\,NADPH + 14\,H^+ \longrightarrow$$
$$CH_3(CH_2)_{14}COOH + 7\,CO_2 + 6\,H_2O + 8\,CoA \cdot SH + 14\,NADP^+$$

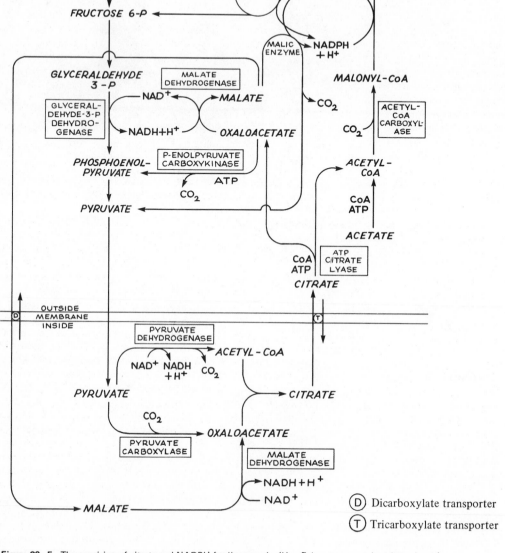

Figure 20–5. The provision of citrate and NADPH for lipogenesis. (Hex-P, hexose monophosphate shunt.)

The acetyl-CoA used as a primer forms carbon atoms 15 and 16 of palmitate. The addition of the subsequent C_2 units is via malonyl-CoA formation. Some recent evidence suggests that butyryl-CoA may be the primer molecule in mammalian liver and mammary gland. If propionyl-CoA acts as primer, long chain fatty acids having an odd number of carbon atoms result. These are found particularly in ruminants, where propionate is formed by microbial action in the rumen. NADPH is involved as coenzyme in both the reduction of the β-ketoacyl and of the α,β-unsaturated acyl derivatives. The oxidative reactions of the hexose monophosphate shunt are probably the chief source of the hydrogen required for the reductive synthesis of fatty acids. Tissues which possess an active hexose monophosphate shunt are also the tissues specializing in active lipogenesis, ie, liver, adipose tissue, and the lactating mammary gland. Moreover, both metabolic pathways are found in the extramitochondrial region of the cell, so that there are no membranes or permeability barriers for the transfer of NADPH/NADP from one pathway to the other. Other sources of NADPH include the extramitochondrial isocitrate dehydrogenase reaction (probably not a substantial source) and the reaction that converts malate to pyruvate catalyzed by the "malic enzyme" (see Fig 20–5).

Acetyl-CoA, the main building block for fatty acids, is formed from carbohydrate via the oxidation of pyruvate within the mitochondria, but acetyl-CoA does not diffuse readily into the extramitochondrial compartment, the principal site of fatty acid synthesis. The rate of incorporation of citrate into the fatty acids of a supernatant preparation of lactating mammary gland is greater than that of acetate. In addition, the activity of the extramitochondrial **ATP-citrate lyase (citrate cleavage enzyme)**, like the "malic enzyme," varies markedly with the nutritional state of the animal, closely paralleling the activity of the fatty acid synthesizing system. Utilization of pyruvate for lipogenesis by way of citrate involves the oxidative decarboxylation of pyruvate to acetyl-CoA and subsequent condensation with oxaloacetate to form citrate within the mitochondria, followed by the translocation of citrate into the extramitochondrial compartment, where in the presence of CoA and ATP it undergoes cleavage to acetyl-CoA and oxaloacetate catalyzed by ATP-citrate lyase. The acetyl-CoA is then available for malonyl-CoA formation and synthesis to palmitate (Fig 20–5). The oxaloacetate can form malate via NADH-linked malate dehydrogenase, followed by the generation of NADPH via the malic enzyme. In turn, the NADPH becomes available for lipogenesis. This pathway is a means of transferring reducing equivalents from extramitochondrial NADH to NADP. Alternatively, malate can be transported into the mitochondrion where it is able to reform oxaloacetate. It is to be noted that the citrate (tricarboxylate) transporter in the mitochondrial membrane requires citrate to exchange with malate (see p 241). Another alternative pathway open to oxaloacetate is that of decarboxylation to form phosphoenolpyruvate in a reaction catalyzed by phosphoenolpyruvate carboxykinase; after conversion to pyruvate, it can in this way reenter the mitochondria (Fig 20–5).

There is little ATP-citrate lyase in ruminants, probably because in these species acetate (derived from the rumen) is the main source of acetyl-CoA. Since the acetate is activated to acetyl-CoA extramitochondrially, there is no necessity for it to enter mitochondria and form citrate prior to incorporation into long chain fatty acids.

C. Microsomal System for Chain Elongation: This is probably the main site for the elongation of existing fatty acid molecules. The pathway converts acyl-CoA compounds of fatty acids to higher derivatives, using malonyl-CoA as acetyl donor and NADPH as reductant. Intermediates in the process are the CoA thioesters. The end product is the next higher homolog of the primer acyl-CoA molecule. The acyl groups that may act as a primer molecule include the saturated series from C_{10}–C_{16}, as well as some unsaturated C_{18} fatty acids. Fasting largely abolishes chain elongation.

BIOSYNTHESIS OF ACYLGLYCEROLS (GLYCERIDES) & METABOLISM OF PHOSPHOLIPIDS & SPHINGOLIPIDS

Although reactions involving the hydrolysis of triacylglycerols by lipase can be reversed, this does not seem to be the mechanism by which ester bonds of acylglycerols are synthesized in tissues. Tietz and Shapiro showed that ATP was required for the synthesis of neutral fat from fatty acids, and indeed both glycerol and fatty acids must be activated by ATP before they become incorporated into acylglycerols. If the tissue is liver, kidney, lactating mammary gland, or intestinal mucosa, the enzyme **glycerokinase** will catalyze the activation, by phosphorylation, of glycerol to sn-glycerol 3-phosphate.* If this enzyme is absent—or low in activity, as it is in muscle or adipose tissue—most of the glycerol 3-phosphate must be derived from an intermediate of the glycolytic system, dihydroxyacetone phosphate, which forms glycerol 3-phosphate by reduction with NADH catalyzed by **glycerol-3-phosphate dehydrogenase.**

Fatty acids are activated to acyl-CoA by the enzyme **thiokinase**, utilizing ATP and CoA. Two molecules of acyl-CoA combine with glycerol 3-phosphate to form 1,2-diacylglycerol phosphate (phosphatidic acid), catalyzed by **glycerol-3-phosphate acyl transferase.** This may take place in 2 stages via lysophosphatidic acid. Phosphatidic acid is converted by a phosphatase (**phosphatidate phosphohydrolase**) to a 1,2-diacylglycerol. In intestinal mucosa, a monoacylglycerol pathway exists whereby monoacylglycerol is converted to 1,2-diacylglycerol as a result of the presence of **monoacylglycerol acyl transferase**. A further molecule of acyl-CoA is esterified with the diacylglycerol to form a triacylglycerol, catalyzed by **diacylglycerol acyl transferase** (Fig 20–6). Most of the activity of these enzymes resides in the microsomal fraction of the cell, but some is found also in mitochondria; and phosphatidate phosphohydrolase activity is found mainly in the particle-free supernatant fraction. It has been reported that dihydroxyacetone phosphate may be acylated and converted to lysophosphatidic acid after reduction by NADPH. The quantitative significance of this pathway remains in dispute. The pathway appears to be more important in mitochondria than in microsomes.

Phospholipids

Phospholipids are synthesized either from phosphatidic acid, eg, phosphatidylinositol, or from 1,2-diacylglycerol, eg, phosphatidylcholine or phosphatidylethanolamine. In the synthesis of phosphatidylinositol, cytidine triphosphate (CTP) reacts with phosphatidic acid to form a cytidine-diphosphate-diacylglycerol (CDP-diacylglycerol). Finally, this compound reacts with inositol, catalyzed by the enzyme

---

*See p 111 for nomenclature of glycerol.

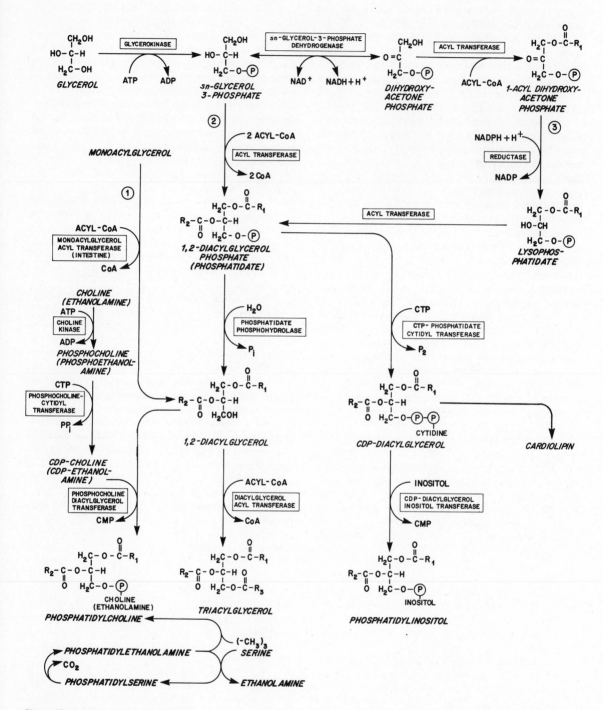

Figure 20–6. Biosynthesis of triacylglycerols and phospholipids. 1: Monoacylglycerol pathway; 2: Glycerol phosphate pathway; 3: Dihydroxyacetone phosphate pathway.

CDP-diacylglycerol inositol transferase, to form a phosphatidylinositol (Fig 20–6).

In the biosynthesis of phosphatidylcholine and phosphatidylethanolamine (lecithins and cephalins) (Fig 20–6), choline or ethanolamine must first be converted to "active choline" or "active ethanolamine," respectively. This is a 2-stage process involving, first, a reaction with ATP to form the corresponding monophosphate, followed by a further reaction with CTP to form either cytidine diphosphocholine (CDP-choline) or cytidine diphosphoethanolamine (CDP-ethanolamine). In this form, choline or ethanolamine reacts with 1,2-diacylglycerol so that a phosphorylated base (either phosphocholine or phosphoethanolamine) is transferred to the diacylglycerol to form either phosphatidylcholine or phosphatidylethanolamine, respectively. The enzyme responsible for the formation of phosphatidylethanolamine, **phosphoethanolamine-acylglycerol transferase,** is not present in liver. Phosphatidylserine is formed from phosphatidylethanolamine directly by reaction with serine. Phosphatidylserine may re-form phosphatidylethanolamine by decarboxylation. In the liver, but not in brain, an alternative pathway enables phosphatidylethanolamine to give rise directly to phosphatidylcholine by progressive methylation of the ethanolamine residue utilizing S-adenosylmethionine as the methyl donor.

A phospholipid present in mitochondria is **cardiolipin** (diphosphatidylglycerol; Fig 20–6). It is formed from phosphatidylglycerol, which in turn is synthesized from CDP-diacylglycerol and glycerol 3-phosphate according to the scheme shown in Fig 20–7.

Biosynthesis of Glycerol Ether Phospholipids & Plasmalogens

A plasmalogenic diacylglycerol is one in which the 1 (or 2) position has an alkenyl residue containing the vinyl ether aldehydogenic linkage ($-CH_2-O-CH=CH-R'$) as shown on p 112. It appears that dihydroxyacetone phosphate is the precursor of the glycerol moiety (Fig 20–8). This compound combines with acyl-CoA to give 1-acyl-dihydroxyacetone phosphate. An exchange reaction takes place between the acyl group and a long chain alcohol to give a 1-alkyl-dihydroxyacetone phosphate (containing the ether link) which in the presence of NADPH is converted to 1-alkyl-glycerol 3-phosphate. After further acylation in the 2 position, the resulting 1-alkyl, 2-acyl glycerol 3-phosphate (analogous to phosphatidic acid in Fig 20–6) is hydrolyzed to give the free glycerol derivative. Plasmalogens are formed by desaturation of the analogous glycerol ether lipid (Fig 20–8). Much of the phospholipids in mitochondria are plasmalogens.

Degradation & Turnover of Phospholipids

Degradation of many complex molecules in tissues is complete, eg, proteins. Thus, a turnover time can be determined for such a molecule. Although phospholipids are actively degraded, each portion of the molecule turns over at a different rate, eg, the turnover time of the phosphate group is different from that of the 1-acyl group. This is due to the presence of enzymes which allow partial degradation followed by resynthesis. **Phospholipase A_2** catalyzes the hydrolysis of the ester bond in position 2 of glycerophospholipids to form a lysophospholipid which, in turn, may be reacylated by acyl-CoA in the presence of an acyltransferase. Alternatively, lysophospholipid (eg, lysolecithin) is attacked by **lysophospholipase** (phospholipase B), removing the remaining 1-acyl group and forming the corresponding glyceryl phosphoryl base, which in turn may be split by a hydrolase liberating glycerol 3-phosphate plus base (Fig 20–9). **Phospholipase A_1** attacks the ester bond in position 1 of phospholipids. **Phospholipase C** attacks the ester bond in position 3, liberating 1,2-diacylglycerol plus a phosphoryl base. **Phospholipase D** is a plant enzyme which hydrolyzes the nitrogenous base from phospholipids (Fig 20–10).

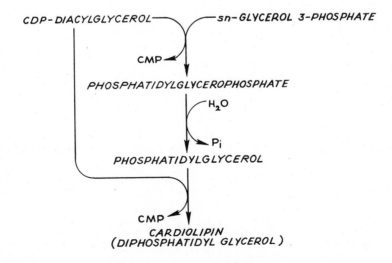

Figure 20–7. Biosynthesis of cardiolipin.

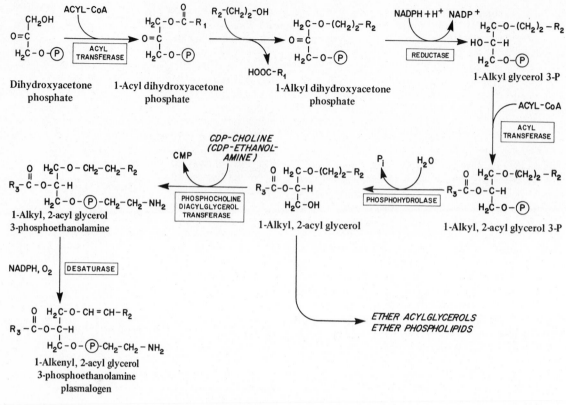

Figure 20—8. Biosynthesis of ether lipids and plasmalogens.

Lysolecithin may be formed by an alternative route involving **lecithin:cholesterol acyltransferase (LCAT).** This enzyme, found in plasma and possibly in liver, catalyzes the transfer of a fatty acid residue from the 2 position of lecithin to cholesterol to form cholesteryl ester and is considered to be responsible for much of the cholesteryl ester in plasma lipoproteins.

The synthesis of **sphingosine** (Fig 20—11) has been studied in microsomes. Following activation by combination with pyridoxal phosphate, the amino acid serine combines with palmityl-CoA to form 3-ketodihydrosphingosine after loss of CO_2. Sphingosine itself is formed after 2 reductive steps, one of which is known to utilize NADPH as H donor and the other to

$$\text{LECITHIN} + \text{CHOLESTEROL} \xrightarrow[\substack{\text{LECITHIN:} \\ \text{CHOLESTEROL} \\ \text{ACYLTRANSFERASE}}]{} \text{LYSOLECITHIN} + \text{CHOLESTERYL ESTER}$$

Long chain saturated fatty acids are found predominantly in the 1 position of phospholipids, whereas the polyunsaturated acids are incorporated more into the 2 position. The incorporation of fatty acids into lecithins occurs by complete synthesis of the phospholipid, by transacylation between cholesteryl ester and lysolecithin, and by direct acylation of lysolecithin by acyl-CoA. Thus, a continuous exchange of the fatty acids is possible, particularly with regard to introducing essential fatty acids into phospholipid molecules.

Sphingolipids

The **sphingomyelins** are phospholipids containing a fatty acid, phosphoric acid, choline, and a complex amino alcohol, sphingol (sphingosine). No glycerol is present.

involve a flavoprotein enzyme, analogous to the acyl-CoA dehydrogenase step in β-oxidation.

In vivo, sphingomyelin is synthesized from sphingosine phosphorylcholine. This is formed by the reaction of sphingosine with CDP-choline. Sphingosine phosphorylcholine is acylated at the amino group by an acyl-CoA of a long chain fatty acid to form sphingomyelin (Fig 20—12A). Alternatively, sphingomyelin may be synthesized from sphingosine via the formation of ceramide (N-acyl sphingosine), which in turn reacts with CDP-choline, giving CMP and sphingomyelin (Fig 20—12B).

Cerebrosides, Sulfatides, & Gangliosides

The cerebrosides are glycolipids which contain the sphingosine-fatty acid combination (ceramide) found in the sphingomyelins, but a galactose moiety is

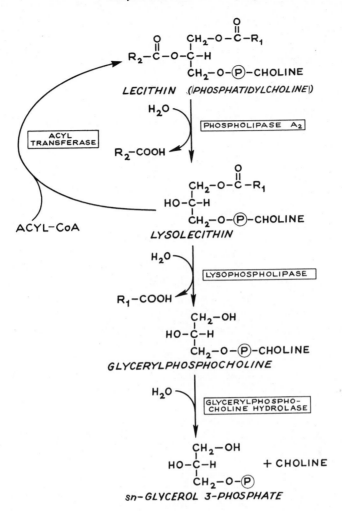

Figure 20—9. Metabolism of lecithin (phosphatidylcholine).

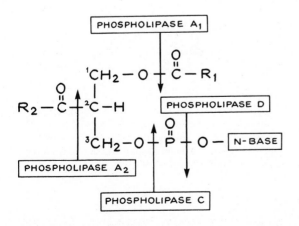

Figure 20—10. Sites of the hydrolytic activity of phospholipases on a phospholipid substrate.

attached to the ceramide in the place of the phosphorylcholine residue found in sphingomyelin. Characteristically, C_{24} fatty acids occur in cerebrosides (lignoceric, cerebronic, and nervonic acids). Lignoceric acid $(C_{23}H_{47}COOH)$ is completely synthesized from acetate. Cerebronic acid, the 2-hydroxy derivative of lignoceric acid, is formed from it. Nervonic acid $(C_{23}H_{45}COOH)$, a mono-unsaturated acid, is formed by elongation of oleic acid.

The requirement for galactose in the formation of cerebrosides, chondromucoids, and mucoproteins is the only known physiologic role of this sugar other than in the formation of lactose in milk.

The biosynthesis of the complete cerebroside molecule is catalyzed by an enzyme preparation obtained from young rat brain (Fig 20—13). **Uridine diphosphogalactose epimerase** utilizes uridine diphosphate glucose as substrate and accomplishes epimerization of the glucose moiety to galactose, thus forming uridine diphosphogalactose. The reaction in brain is similar to that described on p 276 for the liver and mammary gland. The reaction sequence suggested for

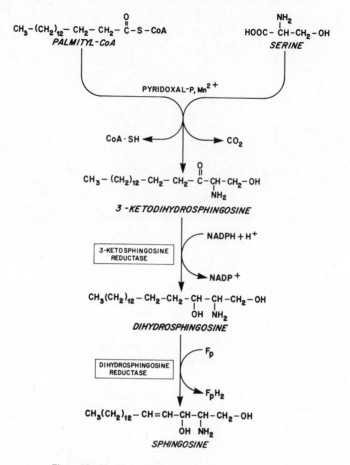

Figure 20—11. Biosynthesis of sphingosine. (Fp, flavoprotein.)

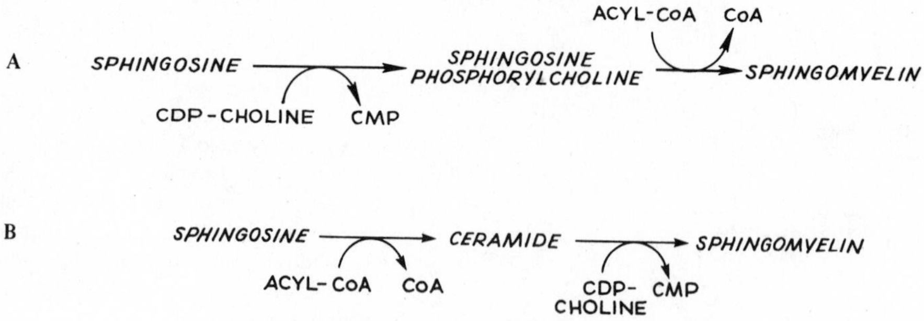

A   SPHINGOSINE ⟶ SPHINGOSINE PHOSPHORYLCHOLINE ⟶ SPHINGOMYELIN

B   SPHINGOSINE ⟶ CERAMIDE ⟶ SPHINGOMYELIN

Figure 20—12. Biosynthesis of sphingomyelin.

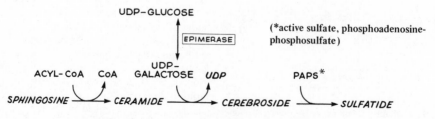

(*active sulfate, phosphoadenosine-phosphosulfate)

Figure 20—13. Biosynthesis of cerebrosides and sulfatides.

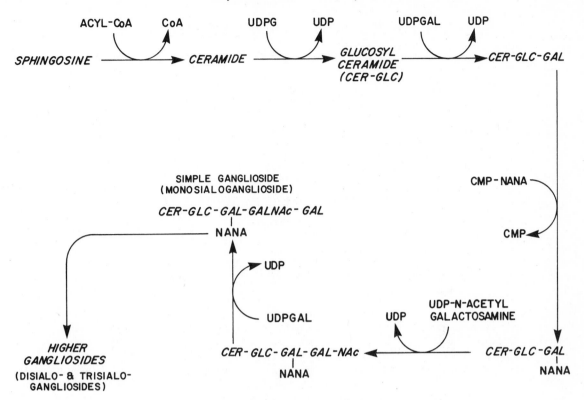

Figure 20–14. Biosynthesis of gangliosides. (NANA, N-acetylneuraminic acid.)

the biosynthesis of cerebrosides in brain tissue is shown in Fig 20–13.

In this reaction sequence, acyl-CoA represents the CoA derivative of a fatty acid which is to be incorporated into the cerebroside. Examples would be lignoceric, cerebronic, or nervonic acids, as noted above. Brady used labeled (1-^{14}C) stearic acid, a C_{18} saturated fatty acid which is a major component among the fatty acids of the cerebrosides in rat brain. The cerebrosides are found in high concentration in the myelin sheaths of nerves. **Sulfatides** are formed from cerebrosides after reaction with 3′-phosphoadenosine-5′-phosphosulfate ("active sulfate"). Gangliosides are synthesized from ceramide (acylsphingosine) by the stepwise addition of the activated sugars (eg, UDPG and UDPGal) and N-acetylneuraminic acid (Fig 20–14). A large number of gangliosides of increasing molecular weight may be formed.

Although glycosphingolipids are recognized as constituents of cell membranes, it is now realized that they are involved also as determinants in immunologic reactions such as in blood group substances.

Phospholipids & Sphingolipids in Disease (Lipidoses)

Certain diseases are characterized by abnormal quantities of these lipids in the tissues, often in the nervous system. They may be classified into 3 groups: (1) true demyelinating diseases, (2) sphingolipidoses, and (3) leukodystrophies.

In **multiple sclerosis**, which is a demyelinating dis-

ease, there is loss both of phospholipids, particularly ethanolamine plasmalogen, and of sphingolipids from white matter, such that an analysis of it resembles more the composition of gray matter. Cholesteryl esters are also found, though normally absent. The cerebrospinal fluid shows raised phospholipid levels.

The **sphingolipidoses** are a group of inherited diseases that often manifest themselves in childhood. They are part of a larger group of lysosomal disorders (Neufeld & others, 1975).

Lipid storage diseases exhibit several constant features: (1) The accumulation in various tissues of complex lipids which have a portion of their structure in common. This portion is **ceramide** (an N-fatty acyl derivative of sphingosine, Fig 20–12). (2) The rate of *synthesis* of the stored lipid is comparable to that of normal humans. (3) The enzymatic defect in each of these diseases is a *deficiency of a specific hydrolytic enzyme necessary to break down the lipid.* (4) The extent to which the activity of the affected enzyme is reduced is similar in all of the tissues of the individual afflicted with one of these inherited abnormalities of lipid metabolism. As a result of these unifying basic considerations, procedures for the diagnosis of patients with these disorders have been developed, and it has become possible to detect heterozygous carriers of the genetic abnormalities responsible for these diseases as well as to discover in the unborn fetus the fact that a sphingolipodystrophy is present. It is also expected that this new knowledge will supply approaches to the

Table 20–1. Summary of the more important lipidoses.

Disease	Enzyme Deficiency and Reaction Involved	Clinical Symptoms
Gaucher's disease	Glucocerebrosidase $Cer-Glc + H_2O \rightarrow Cer + Glc$	Enlarged liver and spleen, mental retardation
Fabry's disease	Ceramide trihexosidase $Cer-Glc-Gal-Gal + H_2O \rightarrow Cer-Glc-Gal + Gal$	Epidermal rash, progressive kidney failure; full symptoms only in males (X-linked recessive)
Metachromatic leukodystrophy	Sulfatidase $H_2O + Cer-Gal-3-SO_4 \rightarrow Cer-Gal + H_2SO_4$	Progressive nervous disorders due to demyelination; motor dysfunction
Krabbe's disease	Galactocerebrosidase $Cer-Gal + H_2O \rightarrow Cer + Gal$	Severe mental retardation in infants; myelin almost absent
Niemann-Pick disease	Sphingomyelinase Sphingomyelin + $H_2O \rightarrow$ Ceramide + Phosphocholine	Enlarged liver and spleen due to accumulation of sphingomyelin; fatal in early life
Tay-Sachs disease	G_{M2} Hexosaminidase $Cer-Glc-Gal\ (NANA)*-GalNAc + H_2O \rightarrow$ $Cer-Glc-Gal\ (NANA) + GalNAc$	Mental retardation, blindness, demyelination, accumulation of Tay-Sachs ganglioside (G_{M2})
Generalized (G_{M1}) gangliosidosis	G_{M1} Galactosidase $Cer-Glc-Gal\ (NANA)-GalNAc-Gal + H_2O \rightarrow$ $Cer-Glc-Gal\ (NANA)-GalNAc + Gal$	Mental retardation, liver enlargement, skeletal deformation, accumulation of G_{M1} gangliosides

*NANA = N-acetylneuraminic acid.

devising of methods for the treatment of patients afflicted with these diseases. A summary of the more important lipidoses is shown in Table 20–1. Individuals heterozygous for the Tay-Sachs mutant gene can be detected by an assay for the enzyme in serum; in fact, an automated assay has been developed for use in mass screening of population for the genetic defect. Using the technic of amniocentesis, prenatal diagnosis of many of the sphingolipidoses has been possible in cases where there is a risk that a pregnant woman may be carrying an affected child. Assessment of the risk is based on a history of having already had one or more affected children.

In **metachromatic leukodystrophy,** there is general demyelination characterized by the accumulation of sulfatides containing galactose rather than glucose.

METABOLISM OF THE UNSATURATED & ESSENTIAL FATTY ACIDS

The long chain unsaturated fatty acids of metabolic significance in mammals are as follows:

$$CH_3(CH_2)_5 CH=CH(CH_2)_7 COOH$$

Palmitoleic acid (16:1)

$$CH_3(CH_2)_7 CH=CH(CH_2)_7 COOH$$

Oleic acid (18:1)

$$CH_3(CH_2)_4 CH=CHCH_2 CH=CH(CH_2)_7 COOH$$

Linoleic acid (18:2)

$$CH_3 CH_2 CH=CHCH_2 CH=CHCH_2 CH=CH(CH_2)_7 COOH$$

Linolenic acid (18:3)

$$CH_3(CH_2)_4 (CH=CHCH_2)_4 (CH_2)_2 COOH$$

Arachidonic acid (20:4)

Other C_{20} and C_{22} polyenoic fatty acids may be detected by gas-liquid chromatography. These are derived from linoleic and linolenic acids by chain elongation. It is to be noted that all double bonds present in naturally occurring unsaturated fatty acids of mammals are of the cis configuration.

Palmitoleic and oleic acids are not essential in the diet because the tissues are capable of introducing one double bond into the corresponding saturated fatty acid. Experiments with labeled palmitate have demonstrated that the label enters freely into palmitoleic and oleic acids but is absent from linoleic, linolenic, and arachidonic acids. Linoleic, linolenic, and arachidonic acids are the only *fatty acids known to be essential* for the complete nutrition of many species of animals, and notably that of the human infant. As indicated above, linoleic acid cannot be synthesized by animals and therefore must be supplied preformed in the diet. However, arachidonic acid can be formed from linoleic acid in the animal body.

In 1928, Evans and Burr noticed that rats fed on a purified nonlipid diet to which vitamins A and D were added exhibited a reduced growth rate and a reproductive deficiency. Later work showed that the deficiency syndrome was cured by the addition of linoleic, linolenic, and arachidonic acids to the diet. Further diagnostic features of the syndrome include scaly skin, necrosis of the tail, and lesions in the urinary system, but the condition is not fatal.

Linoleic acid occurs in high concentrations in various edible vegetable oils, eg, corn, cottonseed, peanut, safflower, soybean (but not in olive or coconut oils). Arachidonic acid occurs in animal fats although only in rather small amounts.

$$STEARYL-CoA + ENZYME \longrightarrow STEARYL-Enz + CoA$$

$$STEARYL-Enz + O_2 + NADPH + H^+ \xrightarrow{\boxed{HYDROXYLASE}} HYDROXYSTERYL-Enz + NADP^+ + H_2O$$

$$HYDROXYSTEARYL-Enz \xrightarrow{\boxed{HYDRATASE}} OLEYL-Enz + H_2O$$

$$OLEYL-Enz + CoA \longrightarrow OLEYL-CoA + Enz$$

Microsomal desaturase system

Synthesis of Mono-unsaturated Fatty Acids

It is a common finding in the husbandry of animals that the degree of saturation of the fat laid down in the depots can be altered by dietary means. If, for example, an animal is fed a diet containing a large quantity of vegetable oil (ie, a high proportion of the unsaturated fatty acids), the animal lays down a soft type of depot fat. The converse situation is found in ruminants, where a characteristic hard, saturated fat is laid down as a result of the action of microorganisms in the rumen, which saturate the unsaturated fatty acids of the diet. As far as the nonessential mono-unsaturated fatty acids are concerned, the liver is considered to be the main organ responsible for their interconversion with the saturated fatty acids. An enzyme system in liver microsomes will catalyze the conversion of stearyl-CoA to oleoyl-CoA. Oxygen, NADPH, or NADH is necessary for the reaction. The enzymes appear to be those of a typical mono-oxygenase system involving cytochrome b_5 (hydroxylase). The sequence of reactions is shown above. It is specific for introducing a double bond in the Δ^9 position of saturated fatty acids, eg, palmitic and stearic acids.

Synthesis of Polyunsaturated Fatty Acids

Additional double bonds introduced into existing mono-unsaturated fatty acids are always separated from each other by a methylene group (methylene interrupted), except in bacteria. In animals, the additional double bonds are all introduced between the existing double bond and the carboxyl group but in plants they are introduced between the existing double bond and the ω-carbon. Thus, animals are able to completely synthesize the ω-9 (oleic acid) series of unsaturated fatty acids by a combination of chain elongation and desaturation but are unable to synthesize de novo the ω-6 series containing linoleic and arachidonic acids or the ω-3 series containing linolenic acid. It is for this reason that at least linoleic and linolenic acid must be supplied in the diet to accomplish the synthesis of the other members of the ω-6 and ω-3 series of polyunsaturated fatty acids. Linoleate may be converted to arachidonate. The pathway is first by dehydrogenation of the CoA ester through γ-linolenate followed by the addition of a 2-carbon unit (probably as acetyl-CoA in the mitochondrial system for chain elongation or as malonyl-CoA in the microsomal system, which appears

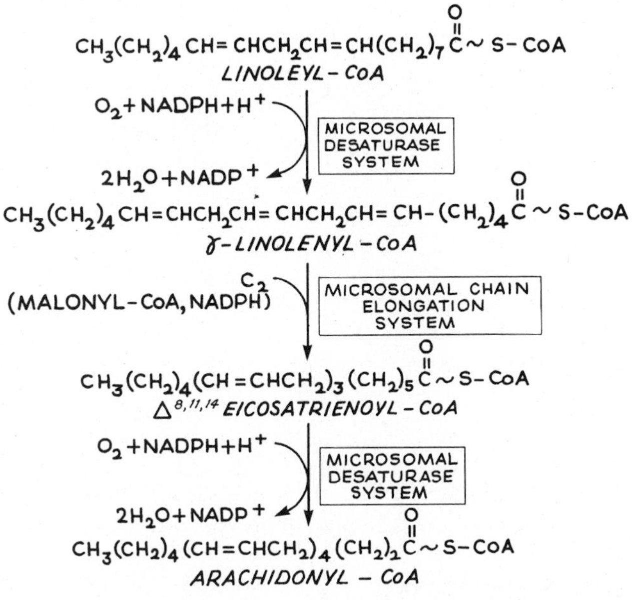

Figure 20-15. Conversion of linoleate to arachidonate.

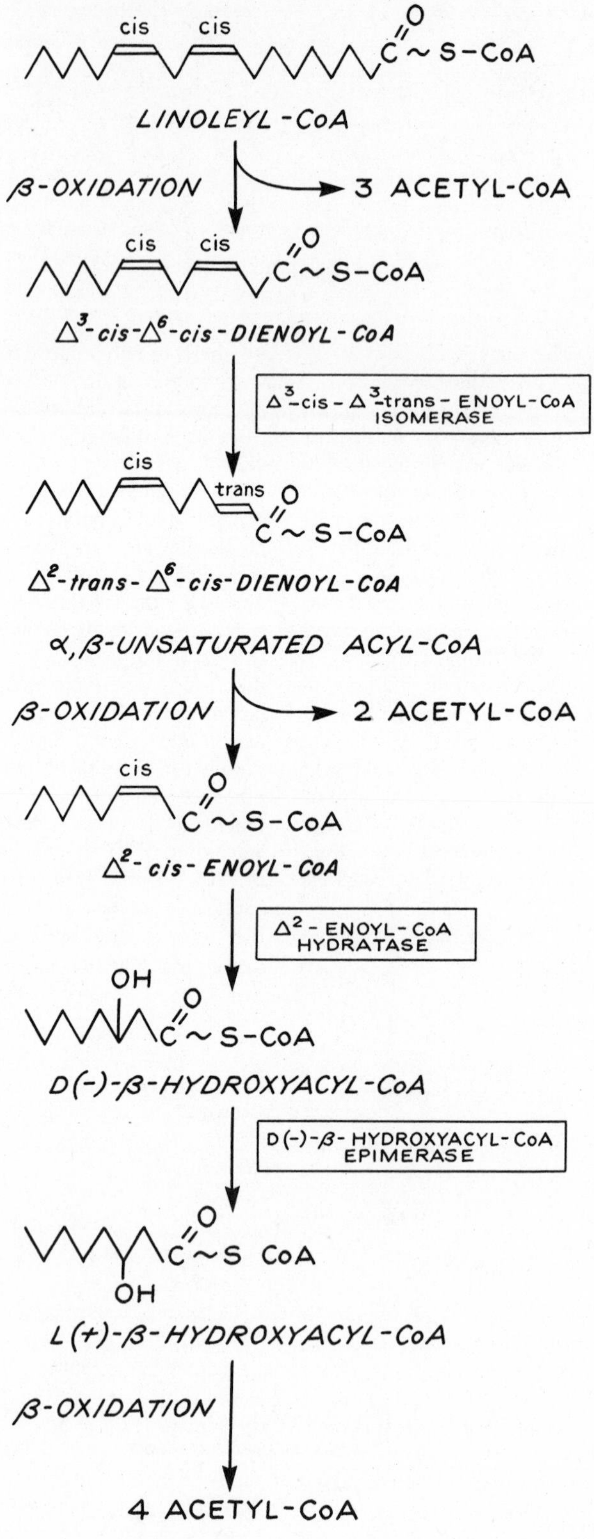

Figure 20—16. Sequence of reactions in the oxidation of unsaturated fatty acids, eg, linoleic acid.

to be the more active system) to give eicosatrienoate (homo γ-linolenate). The latter forms arachidonate by a further dehydrogenation (Fig 20–15). The dehydrogenating system is as described for saturated fatty acids above.

The nutritional requirement for arachidonate may thus be dispensed with if there is adequate linoleate in the diet.

The desaturation and chain elongation system is greatly diminished in the fasting state and in the absence of insulin.

The functions of the essential fatty acids appear to be various, though not well defined. Essential fatty acids are found in the structural lipids of the cell, are concerned with the structural integrity of the mitochondrial membrane, and occur in high concentration in the reproductive organs. In many of their structural functions, essential fatty acids are present in phospholipids, mainly in the 2 position. The roles of essential fatty acids in the genesis of fatty livers and in the metabolism of cholesterol are discussed later.

A deficiency of essential fatty acids has been produced in animals as well as in man using diets restricted in essential fatty acids. In experimental animals, signs of the deficiency include poor growth, dermatitis, decreased capacity to reproduce, lessened resistance to stress, and impaired transport of lipids. The skin symptoms and impairment of lipid transfer have also been noted in human subjects ingesting a diet lacking in essential fatty acids. In human adults subsisting on ordinary diets, no signs of essential fatty acid deficiencies have been reported. However, infants receiving formula diets low in fat developed skin symptoms that were cured by giving linoleate. Deficiencies attributable to a lack of essential fatty acids have also been reported to occur among patients being maintained for long periods exclusively by intravenous nutritional regimens.

The results of studies with animals or human subjects have indicated that a deficiency of essential fatty acids can be prevented by a very small intake—within a range of about 1–2% of the total caloric intake—of essential fatty acids. This quantity is easily obtained in the diet in all but the most extraordinary circumstances.

Oxidation of Unsaturated Fatty Acids

The CoA esters of these acids are degraded by the enzymes normally responsible for β-oxidation until either a Δ^3-cis-acyl-CoA compound or a Δ^2-cis-acyl-CoA compound is formed, depending upon the position of the double bonds. The former compound is isomerized (Δ^3-cis-Δ^2-trans-enoyl-CoA isomerase) to the corresponding Δ^2-trans-CoA stage, which in turn is hydrated by Δ^2-enoyl hydratase to L(+)-β-hydroxy-acyl-CoA. The Δ^2-cis-acyl-CoA compound is first hydrated by Δ^2-enoyl hydratase to the D(−)-β-hydroxy-acyl-CoA derivative. This undergoes epimerization (D[−]-β-hydroxy-acyl-CoA epimerase) to give the normal L(+)-β-hydroxy-acyl-CoA stage in β-oxidation (Fig 20–16).

Prostaglandins

Isotopic experiments have indicated that arachidonate and some related C_{20} fatty acids with methylene-interrupted bonds give rise to the group of pharmacologically active compounds known as **prostaglandins**. This series of compounds comprises fourteen 20-carbon (eicosanoic) acids, each with the same basic structure termed **prostanoic acid**. The carbon chains are bonded at the middle of the chain by a 5-membered ring. Variations in the double bonds and in the hydroxyl and ketone groups give rise to fatty acids that can be divided into 4 groups designated A, B, E, and F. There are 6 E and F compounds arising from eicosatri-, -tetra-, and -pentaenoic acids (ie, acids 20 carbon atoms in length and with 3, 4, or 5 double bonds). The "E" series of prostaglandins has a keto group, whereas the "F" series has a hydroxyl group in position 9 (Fig 20–17). These 6 **primary prostaglandins**, which occur in most cells, can be converted to the 8 **secondary prostaglandins** that have been identified to date in natural materials. Prostaglandin synthesis involves the consumption of 2 molecules of O_2 and 2 molecules of reduced glutathione. Synthesis is inhibited by aspirin.

The prostaglandins exhibit hormone-like activity. They are among the most potent biologically active substances yet discovered. As little as 1 ng/ml causes contraction of smooth muscle in animals. Potential therapeutic uses include prevention of conception, induction of labor at term, termination of pregnancy, the prevention or alleviation of gastric ulcers, control of inflammation and of blood pressure, and relief of asthma and nasal congestion.

Prostaglandins increase cAMP in platelets, thyroid, corpus luteum, fetal bone, adenohypophysis, and lung but lower cAMP in adipose tissue (see p 301).

Although the prostaglandins are synthesized from the "essential fatty acids," these compounds do not relieve symptoms of essential fatty acid deficiency, possibly because they are too rapidly metabolized. However, there is a marked correlation between essential fatty acid activity of various fatty acids and their ability to be converted to prostaglandins. It is therefore an open question whether essential fatty acids exert all of their physiologic effects via prostaglandin synthesis.

Even though the natural prostaglandins may be useful as drugs, several factors must be considered. One problem is the fact that these substances are metabolized very rapidly within the body. For example, prostaglandin E_2, when administered intravenously, is 96% inactivated in the first 90 seconds after it has been given. Furthermore, there is an unfortunate lack of tissue specificity for the effects of the prostaglandins. Prostaglandin E_2, in addition to causing uterine smooth muscle to contract when induction of labor is desired, causes gastrointestinal smooth muscle to contract as well, which leads to cramping and diarrhea. The same compound when inhaled into the nostrils immediately dilates the bronchi and alleviates an attack of asthma, but it simultaneously irritates the

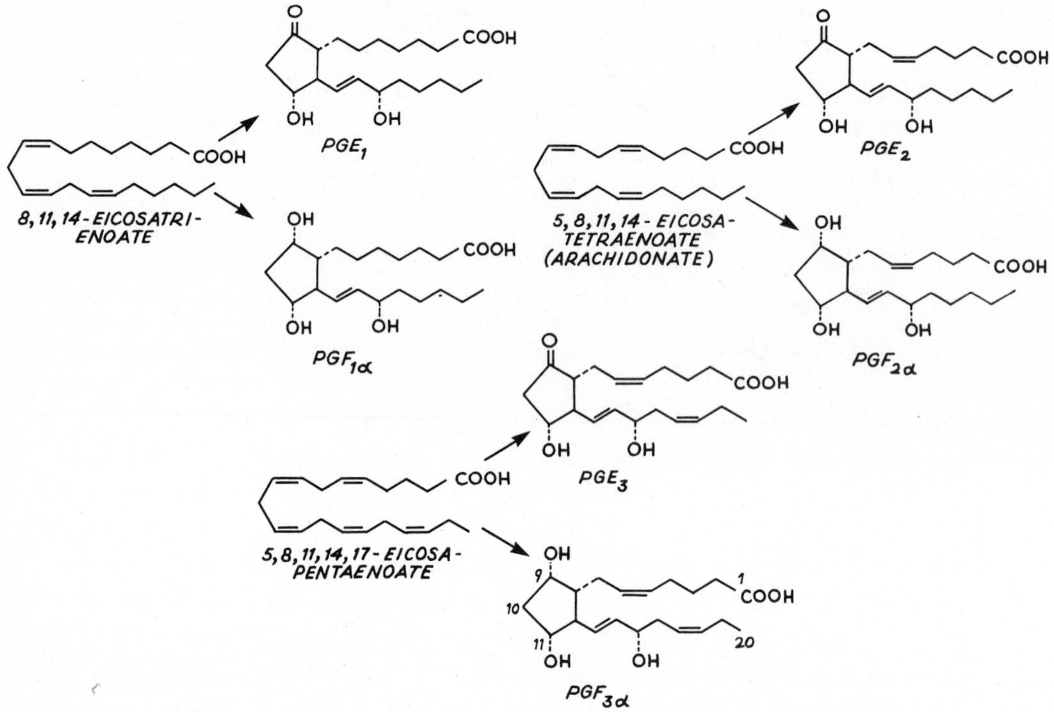

Figure 20–17. The 6 primary prostaglandins and their biosynthetic origins. (PG, prostaglandin.)

mucous lining of the throat, causing pain and coughing.

The presence of the enzyme **15-hydroxyprostaglandin dehydrogenase** in most mammalian tissues is probably the principal cause of the rapid metabolism of prostaglandins. It has been shown that blocking the action of this enzyme can prolong the half-life of prostaglandins in the body from 2- to 10-fold. Several analogs have been developed to bring about impairment of the action of the dehydrogenase. Furthermore, modifications to produce enzyme blocking also increase the tissue specificity of the action of the modified compound. Initial studies of prostaglandin analogs indicate that the introduction of a methyl group at the C_{15} position blocks the action of 15-hydroxyprostaglandin dehydrogenase while showing little effect on either contraction of smooth muscle or lowering of blood pressure. By using 15-methylated analogs of prostaglandins E_2 and F_{2a}, it may be possible to lower the dosage required for control of fertility to a level at which side-effects on smooth muscle and blood pressure are not significant. Another promising analog is the 16,16-dimethyl substituted prostaglandin E_2. This is more resistant to metabolic inactivation than the natural E_2 and shows a more specific ability to inhibit gastric acid secretion in dogs and man. The compound is therefore of interest for treatment of gastric ulcers.

The synthesis and metabolism of prostaglandins has been reviewed extensively by Samuelsson and others (1975).

Trans-fatty Acids

The presence of trans-unsaturated fatty acids in partially hydrogenated vegetable oils (eg, margarine) raises the question of their safety as food additives. Their long-term effects in man are not known, but up to 15% of tissue fatty acids have been found at autopsy to be in the trans configuration. They are metabolized more like saturated than like the cis-unsaturated fatty acids. This may be due to their similar straight chain conformation (see Chapter 9). Trans-polyunsaturated fatty acids do not possess essential fatty acid activity.

THE METABOLISM OF ADIPOSE TISSUE & THE MOBILIZATION OF FAT

The triacylglycerol stores in adipose tissue are continually undergoing lipolysis (hydrolysis) and re-esterification (Fig 20–18). These 2 processes are not the forward and reverse phases of the same reaction. Rather, they are entirely different pathways involving different reactants and enzymes. Many of the nutritional, metabolic, and hormonal factors that regulate the metabolism of adipose tissue act either upon the process of esterification or on lipolysis. The resultant of these 2 processes determines the magnitude of the free fatty acid pool in adipose tissue, which in turn is the source and determinant of the level of free fatty

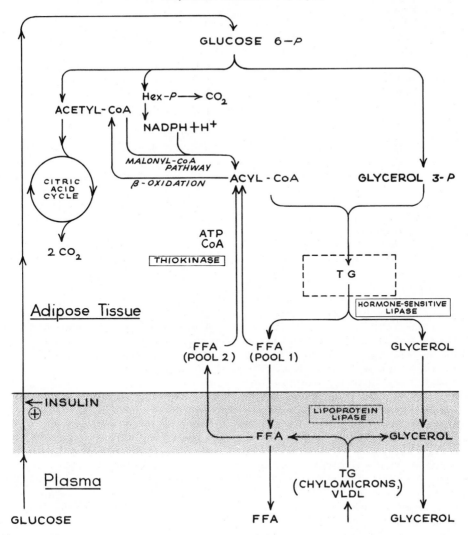

Figure 20–18. Metabolism of adipose tissue. Hormone-sensitive lipase is activated by ACTH, TSH, glucagon, epinephrine, norepinephrine, and vasopressin and inhibited by insulin, prostaglandin E_1, and nicotinic acid. Shaded area represents lipoprotein lipase region of the capillary wall. (Hex-*P*, hexose monophosphate shunt; TG, triacylglycerol; FFA, free fatty acids; VLDL, very low density lipoproteins.)

acids circulating in the plasma. Since the level of plasma free fatty acids has most profound effects upon the metabolism of other tissues, particularly liver and muscle, the factors operating in adipose tissue which regulate the outflow of free fatty acids exert an influence far beyond the tissue itself.

In adipose tissue, triacylglycerol is synthesized from acyl-CoA and glycerol 3-phosphate according to the mechanism shown in Fig 20–6. Because the enzyme **glycerokinase** is low in activity in adipose tissue, glycerol cannot be utilized to any great extent in the esterification of acyl-CoA. For the provision of glycerol 3-phosphate needed in this reaction the tissue is dependent on a supply of glucose. The triacylglycerol

undergoes hydrolysis by a **hormone-sensitive lipase*** to form free fatty acids and glycerol. Since glycerol cannot be utilized readily in this tissue, it diffuses out into the plasma, from where it is utilized by such tissues as liver and kidney, which possess an active glycerokinase. The free fatty acids formed by lipolysis can be resynthesized in the tissue to acyl-CoA by a **thiokinase** and reesterified with glycerol 3-phosphate to form triacylglycerol. Thus, there is a continual cycle within the tissue of lipolysis and reesterification. However, when

*This lipase is distinct from lipoprotein lipase that catalyzes lipoprotein triacylglycerol hydrolysis prior to its uptake into extrahepatic tissues (see p 305).

the rate of reesterification is not sufficient to match the rate of lipolysis, free fatty acid accumulates and diffuses into the plasma, where it raises the level of free fatty acids.

Under conditions of adequate nutritional intake or when the utilization of glucose by adipose tissue is increased, the free fatty acid outflow decreases and the level of plasma free fatty acid falls. However, the release of glycerol continues, demonstrating that the effect of glucose in reducing plasma free fatty acids is not mediated by reducing the rate of lipolysis. It is believed that the effect is due to the provision of glycerol 3-phosphate from glucose, which enhances esterification of free fatty acids via acyl-CoA. When the availability of glucose in adipose tissue is reduced, as in starvation or diabetes mellitus, less glycerol 3-phosphate is formed, allowing the rate of lipolysis to exceed the rate of esterification, with subsequent accumulation of free fatty acids and their release into the plasma.

Glucose can take several pathways in adipose tissue, including oxidation to CO_2 via the citric acid cycle, oxidation in the hexose monophosphate shunt, conversion to long chain fatty acids, and formation of acylglycerol via glycerol 3-phosphate (Fig 20–18). When glucose utilization is high, a larger proportion of the uptake is oxidized to CO_2 and converted to fatty acids. However, as total glucose utilization decreases, the greater proportion of the glucose is directed to the formation of glycerol 3-phosphate and acylglycerol, which helps to minimize the efflux of free fatty acids.

Free fatty acids liberated by adipose tissue may also be metabolized in that same tissue. In vitro studies have demonstrated uptake of ^{14}C-stearate (free fatty acids) into adipose tissue of both fed and fasting rats, but the uptake into the fed preparation was double that of the fasted one. However, in vivo the nutritional state has little effect on the deposition of 1-^{14}C-palmitate in adipose tissue, possibly because the free fatty acid uptake is limited by the blood flow. In the re-fed condition, most of the uptake was esterified and only a small percentage oxidized to CO_2, whereas in the fasting condition approximately equal amounts were oxidized and esterified.

From all of the foregoing observations, it would appear that, when carbohydrate is abundant, adipose tissue tends to emphasize the utilization of glucose for energy production and to esterify free fatty acids; when carbohydrate is in short supply, it conserves glucose for esterification via glycerol 3-phosphate formation and utilizes fatty acids for energy production.

Several laboratories have furnished evidence pointing to the existence of more than one free fatty acid pool within adipose tissue. Dole has shown that the free fatty acid pool (Fig 20–18, pool 1) formed by lipolysis of triacylglycerol is the same pool that supplies fatty acids for reesterification; also, it releases them into the external medium (plasma). This latter process is not reversible, since labeled fatty acids taken up from the external medium do not label pool 1 before they are incorporated into triacylglycerol. It is

necessary to postulate the existence of a second free fatty acid pool (pool 2) through which free fatty acids pass after uptake before they are incorporated into triacylglycerol or oxidized to CO_2. The work of Dole indicates that this second pool would be small and have a high turnover rate, since free fatty acids from the medium become esterified immediately upon entering the cell.

When unsaturated fatty acids are fed, they do not become incorporated very rapidly into all the depot fat but appear first of all to enter smaller and more active compartments, indicating that there are also several pools of triacylglycerol in adipose tissue.

Influence of Hormones on Adipose Tissue

The rate of release of free fatty acids from adipose tissue is affected by many hormones that influence either the rate of esterification or the rate of lipolysis. Insulin administration is followed by a fall in circulating plasma free fatty acids. In vitro, it inhibits the release of free fatty acids from adipose tissue, enhances lipogenesis and the synthesis of acylglycerol, and increases the oxidation of glucose to CO_2 via the hexose monophosphate shunt. All of these effects are dependent on the presence of glucose in the medium and can be explained, therefore, on the basis of the ability of insulin to enhance the uptake of glucose into adipose tissue cells. A second action of insulin in adipose tissue is to inhibit the activity of the hormone-sensitive lipase, reducing the release not only of free fatty acids but of glycerol as well. Adipose tissue is much more sensitive to insulin than is diaphragm muscle, which points to adipose tissue as a major site of insulin action in vivo. Both glucose oxidation and lipogenesis are reduced to the extent of 80–90% in adipose tissue from alloxan-diabetic rats. These metabolic effects are reversed by the addition of insulin in vitro. Prolactin has an effect upon adipose tissue similar to that of insulin, but only if given in large doses.

Other hormones accelerate the release of free fatty acids from adipose tissue and raise the plasma free fatty acid level by increasing the rate of lipolysis of the triacylglycerol stores. These include adrenocorticotropic hormone (ACTH), α- and β-melanocyte-stimulating hormones (MSH), thyroid-stimulating hormone (TSH), growth hormone (GH), vasopressin, epinephrine, norepinephrine, and glucagon. Many of these activate the hormone-sensitive lipase and increase glucose utilization as well. The latter process has been attributed to stimulation of esterification by the increased production of free fatty acids. For an optimum effect, most of these lipolytic processes require the presence of glucocorticoids and thyroid hormones. On their own, these particular hormones do not increase lipolysis markedly but act in a facilitatory or permissive capacity with respect to other lipolytic endocrine factors. These properties can be demonstrated in vivo using hypophysectomized or adrenalectomized animals. The need can be shown for a minimal level of circulating glucocorticoid in order to evoke the adipokinetic properties of growth hormone.

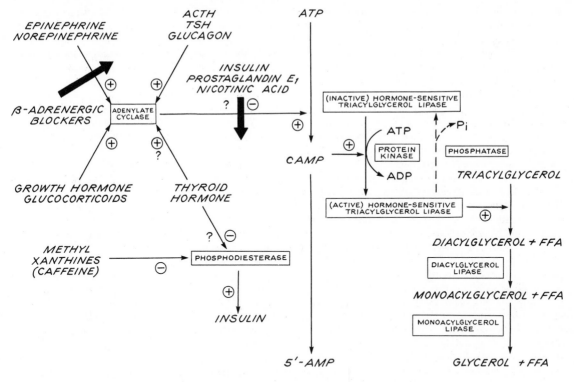

Figure 20—19. Control of adipose tissue lipolysis. (TSH, thyroid-stimulating hormone; FFA, free fatty acids.)

Adipose tissue contains a number of lipases, one of which is a hormone-sensitive triacylglycerol lipase. In addition, there is present a diacylglycerol lipase and monoacylglycerol lipase, which are not hormone-sensitive, but they are considerably more active than the hormone-sensitive triacylglycerol lipase; therefore, the latter is considered to catalyze the rate-limiting step in lipolysis (Fig 20–19). It appears that cAMP, by stimulating a **protein kinase**, converts inactive hormone-sensitive triacylglycerol lipase into active lipase. The hormones that act rapidly in promoting lipolysis do so by stimulating the activity of adenylate cyclase, the enzyme that converts ATP to cAMP. The mechanism is analogous to that responsible for hormonal stimulation of glycogenolysis. Lipolysis is controlled largely by the amount of cAMP present in the tissue. It follows that processes that destroy or preserve cAMP have an effect on lipolysis. cAMP is degraded to 5'-AMP by the enzyme **cyclic 3',5'-nucleotide phosphodiesterase**. This enzyme is inhibited by methyl xanthines such as caffeine and theophylline. Thus, at concentrations at which caffeine itself does not cause any increase in cAMP in isolated fat cells, and in the presence of a lipolytic hormone such as epinephrine, caffeine acts synergistically to cause a considerable increase in cAMP over that which would be caused by the epinephrine alone. It is significant that the drinking of coffee or the administration of caffeine causes marked and prolonged elevation of plasma free fatty acids in humans.

Insulin has a pronounced antilipolytic effect both in vivo and in vitro and antagonizes the effect of the lipolytic hormones. It is now considered that lipolysis may be more sensitive to changes in concentration of insulin than are glucose utilization and esterification. Nicotinic acid and prostaglandin E_1 also suppress free fatty acid mobilization. The antilipolytic effects of insulin, nicotinic acid, and prostaglandin E_1 may be accounted for by inhibition of the synthesis of cAMP, possibly at the adenylate cyclase site or by stimulating phosphodiesterase. Prostaglandins are synthesized in adipose tissue. Synthesis is increased by lipolytic hormones and is reduced by essential fatty acid deficiency. When infused in vivo at low concentration, prostaglandin E_1 causes the release of catecholamines with consequent increase in free fatty acid mobilization. However, when infused at high concentration, it inhibits mobilization, as it does in vitro. The site of action of thyroid hormones in facilitating lipolysis in adipose tissue is not clear. However, possible sites that have been reported include an augmentation of the level of cAMP and an inhibition of phosphodiesterase activity. The effect of growth hormone (in the presence of glucocorticoids) in promoting lipolysis is a slow process. It is dependent on new formation of proteins involved in the formation of cAMP. This finding also helps to explain the role of the pituitary gland and the adrenal cortex in enhancing fat mobilization.

Besides the recognized hormones, certain other adipokinetic principles have been isolated from pituitary glands. A "fat mobilizing substance" has been isolated from the urine of several fasting species, including man, provided the pituitary gland is intact. This substance is highly active both in vivo and in vitro.

The sympathetic nervous system, through liberation of norepinephrine in adipose tissue, plays a central role in the mobilization of free fatty acids by exerting a tonic influence even in the absence of augmented nervous activity. Thus, the increased lipolysis caused by many of the factors described previously can be reduced or abolished by denervation of adipose tissue, by ganglionic blockade with hexamethonium, or by depleting norepinephrine stores with reserpine.

Many of the facts reported above concern only the metabolism of adipose tissue in the young rat. However, data are now accumulating with respect to older rats, humans, and other species. In older rats (> 350 g), a much greater proportion of the glucose metabolized is converted to glycerol of acylglycerol and much less is synthesized into fatty acids, implying that in older rats there is a shift in lipogenesis from adipose to other tissues such as the liver. The tissue is also less sensitive to insulin. These changes in adipose tissue of the older rat are related to adiposity rather than age, since weight reduction is followed by a return in the metabolism of adipose tissue to a pattern similar to that of the young rat. Indeed, there are those who suggest that human adipose tissue is not an important site of lipogenesis. This is indicated by the observation that there is not significant incorporation of label into long chain fatty acids from labeled glucose or pyruvate and that ATP-citrate lyase, a key enzyme in lipogenesis, does not appear to be present. Other enzymes—eg, glucose-6-phosphate dehydrogenase, the malic enzyme—which in the rat undergo adaptive changes coincident with increased lipogenesis, do not undergo similar changes in human adipose tissue.

Human adipose tissue is unresponsive to most of the lipolytic hormones apart from the catecholamines. Of further interest is the lack of lipolytic response to epinephrine in the rabbit, guinea pig, pig, and chicken, the pronounced lipolytic effect of glucagon in birds, and the lack of acylglycerol glycerol synthesis from glucose in the pigeon. It would appear that, in the various species studied, a variety of mechanisms have been evolved for fine control of adipose tissue metabolism.

The fact that adipose tissue varies markedly between various species in its ability to react to lipolytic hormonal preparations, even to the extent of some preparations being inactive against tissue from the homologous species, poses a difficulty in interpreting experimental results. Nevertheless, on consideration of the profound derangement of metabolism in diabetes mellitus (which is due mainly to increased release of free fatty acids from the depots) and the fact that insulin to a large extent corrects the condition, it must be concluded that insulin plays a prominent role in the regulation of adipose tissue metabolism. To reach as firm a conclusion with respect to the role of the pituitary hormones is more difficult, since the rate of free fatty acid mobilization is only slightly depressed in fasting hypophysectomized animals. This depression could be accounted for by the reduced facilitatory or potentiating influence of the secretion of the thyroid and adrenal glands. Under physiologic conditions, it is likely that the main lipolytic stimulus in adipose tissue is due to liberation of norepinephrine through sympathetic activity.

Role of Brown Adipose Tissue in Thermogenesis

Brown adipose tissue is involved in metabolism particularly at times when heat generation is necessary. Thus, the tissue is extremely active in arousal from hibernation, in animals exposed to cold, and in heat production in the newborn animal. Brown adipose tissue is characterized by a high content of mitochondria, cytochromes, and a well developed blood supply. Metabolic emphasis is placed on oxidative processes, O_2 consumption being high with a large conversion of both glucose and fatty acids to CO_2. Lipolysis is active, but reesterification with glycerol could occur as glycerokinase is present in significant amounts in this tissue. Norepinephrine liberated from sympathetic nerve endings is important in increasing lipolysis in the tissue. Mitochondria from brown adipose tissue of cold-acclimatized rats oxidize a-ketoglutarate rapidly with a P:O $\leqslant 1$ and succinate and glycerol 3-phosphate with a P:O = 0. Addition of dinitrophenol has no effect, and there is no respiratory control by ADP. These experiments indicate that oxidation and phosphorylation are not coupled in mitochondria of this tissue. The phosphorylation that does occur appears to be at the substrate level. Thus, oxidation produces much heat, and little free energy is trapped in ATP. Under nonstimulated conditions, respiration in brown fat mitochondria is probably closely coupled, but the action of norepinephrine liberates free fatty acids within the tissue, which is presumably the cause of uncoupling. Glycerol 3-phosphate is oxidized readily via the mitochondrial flavoprotein-linked glycerol-3-phosphate dehydrogenase. If substrate level phosphorylation is important in brown adipose tissue, this pathway would be a means of maintaining glycolysis by transporting reducing equivalents generated in glycolysis into the mitochondria for oxidation in the respiratory chain. The presence of glycerokinase would enable free glycerol resulting from lipolysis to be converted to glycerol 3-phosphate and be oxidized directly in the tissue. It does not appear that much heat is generated by the energy-consuming futile cycle of lipolysis followed by resynthesis of triacylglycerol.

METABOLISM OF THE PLASMA LIPOPROTEINS

Five groups of lipoproteins having major roles in the transport and metabolism of lipids are present in plasma. These are **chylomicrons**, derived from intestinal absorption of triacylglycerol; and **very low density lipoproteins** (VLDL or pre-β-lipoproteins), also formed to a lesser extent from dietary lipids but mainly derived from the liver for the export of triacylglycerol. **Low density lipoproteins** (LDL or β-lipoproteins) represent a final stage in the catabolism of VLDL and possibly chylomicrons. **High density lipoproteins** (HDL or α-lipoproteins) are involved in VLDL and chylomicron metabolism and also in cholesterol metabolism. The fifth group, the **free fatty acids** (FFA), are not generally classified with the other plasma lipoproteins since their structure is different, consisting of long chain fatty acids attached to serum albumin. The physical characteristics of the lipoproteins and their separation and identification are discussed in Chapter 9.

Free Fatty Acids

The free fatty acids (nonesterified fatty acids, unesterified fatty acids) arise in the plasma from lipolysis of triacylglycerol in adipose tissue or as a result of the action of lipoprotein lipase during uptake of plasma triacylglycerols into tissues. They are found in combination with serum albumin in concentrations varying between 0.1 and 2 μEq/ml plasma and comprise the long chain fatty acids found in adipose tissue, ie, palmitic, stearic, oleic, palmitoleic, linoleic, and other polyunsaturated acids, and smaller quantities of other long chain fatty acids. Binding sites on albumin of varying affinity for the fatty acids have been described. Low levels of free fatty acids are recorded in the fully fed condition, rising to about 0.5 μEq/ml in the postabsorptive and between 0.7 and 0.8 μEq/ml in the fully fasting state. In uncontrolled diabetes mellitus, the level may rise to as much as 2 μEq/ml. In meal eaters, the level falls just after eating and rises again prior to the next meal, whereas in such continual feeders as ruminants—where there is a continual influx of nutrient from the intestine—the free fatty acids remain relatively constant and at a low level.

The rate of removal of free fatty acids from the blood is extremely rapid. Estimates suggest that the free fatty acids supply about 25–50% of the energy requirements in fasting. The remainder of the uptake is esterified and, according to evidence using radioactive free fatty acids, eventually recycled. In starvation, the respiratory quotient (RQ) (see Chapter 31) would indicate that considerably more fat is being oxidized than can be traced to the oxidation of free fatty acids. This difference may be accounted for by the oxidation of esterified lipids of the circulation or of those present in tissues. The latter is thought to occur particularly in heart and skeletal muscle, where considerable stores of lipid are to be found in the muscle cells. The free fatty acid turnover is related directly to free fatty acid concentration. Thus, the rate of free fatty acid production in adipose tissue controls the free fatty acid concentration in plasma, which in turn determines the free fatty acid uptake by other tissues. The nutritional condition does not appear to have a great effect on the fractional uptake of free fatty acids by tissues. It does, however, alter the proportion of the uptake which is oxidized to CO_2 compared to the fraction

which is esterified, more being oxidized in the fasting than in the fed state.

The Apolipoproteins (Apoproteins)

The lipoproteins are characterized by the presence of one or more proteins or polypeptides known as apoproteins. According to the ABC nomenclature, the 2 major apoproteins of HDL are designated A-I and A-II, respectively. The main apoprotein of LDL is apoprotein B, which is found also in VLDL and chylomicrons. Apoproteins C-I, C-II, and C-III are smaller polypeptides found in VLDL, HDL, and chylomicrons (Fig 20–20). Carbohydrates account for approximately 5% of apoprotein B and include mannose, galactose, fucose, glucose, glucosamine, and sialic acid. Thus, some lipoproteins are also glycoproteins (Table 20–2). The C apoproteins seem to be freely transferable between VLDL and chylomicrons on the one hand and HDL on the other. C-II is an important activator of extrahepatic lipoprotein lipase, involved in the clearance of triacylglycerol from the circulation.

Several apoproteins other than apo-A, B, or C have been found in plasma lipoproteins. One is the arginine-rich apoprotein isolated from VLDL; its name derives from the fact that it contains arginine to the extent of 10% of the total amino acids. It accounts for 5–10% of total VLDL apoproteins in normal subjects but is present in excess in the β-VLDL of patients with type III hyperlipoproteinemia. Animals made hypercholesterolemic by cholesterol feeding also have increased quantities of this apoprotein.

Formation of Chylomicrons & Very Low Density Lipoproteins (VLDL)

By definition, chylomicrons are found in chyle formed only by the lymphatic system draining the intestine. However, it is now realized that a smaller and denser particle having the characteristics of VLDL is also to be found in chyle. Chylomicron formation fluctuates with the load of triacylglycerol absorbed, whereas VLDL formation is quantitatively less but is more constant and occurs even in the fasting state. However, the bulk of the plasma VLDL is of hepatic origin, being the vehicle of transport of triacylglycerol from the liver to the extrahepatic tissues.

There are many similarities in the mechanism of formation of chylomicrons by intestinal cells and of VLDL by hepatic parenchymal cells (Fig 20–21). Apoprotein B is synthesized by ribosomes in the rough endoplasmic reticulum and is incorporated into lipoproteins in the smooth endoplasmic reticulum, which is the main site of synthesis of triacylglycerol, phospholipids, and cholesterol. Lipoproteins are also found in the Golgi apparatus, where, it is thought, carbohydrate residues are added to the lipoprotein. The chylomicrons and VLDL are released from either the intestinal or hepatic cell by fusion of the secretory vacuole with the cell membrane (reverse pinocytosis). Chylomicrons pass into the spaces between the intestinal cells, eventually making their way into the lymphatic system (lacteals) draining the intestine. VLDL are secreted by

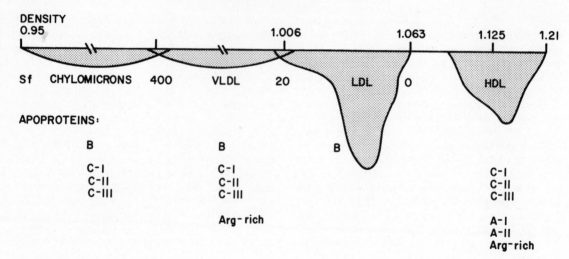

Figure 20–20. The 4 major plasma lipoprotein families depicted as Schlieren patterns obtained in the analytical ultracentrifuge. (Modified from Fredrickson, 1972–73.)

hepatic parenchymal cells into the space of Disse and then into the hepatic sinusoids. The similarities between the 2 processes and the anatomic mechanisms are striking, for—apart from the mammary gland—the intestine and liver are the only tissues from which particulate lipid is secreted. If particulate lipid was secreted by most tissues, the problem would exist of passing such a particle through the cell membrane of the endothelial cells of the capillaries. This is circumvented in the case of the intestine by secretion directly into the lymphatic system and in the liver by direct secretion into the space of Disse. Thus, the inability of particulate lipid to pass through cell membranes without prior

hydrolysis is probably the reason why dietary fat enters the circulation via the thoracic duct and not via the hepatic portal system.

Apoprotein B is essential for chylomicron and VLDL formation. In abetalipoproteinemia (a rare disease), apoprotein B is not synthesized, no lipoproteins are formed, and lipid droplets will accumulate in the intestine and liver. Although both chylomicrons and VLDL isolated from blood contain apoprotein C, the newly secreted or "nascent" lipoproteins contain little or none, and it would appear that the complement of apoprotein C polypeptides is taken up by transfer from HDL once the chylomicrons and VLDL

Table 20–2. Apoproteins of human plasma lipoproteins. (After Eisenberg & Levy, 1975.)

Apoprotein	Lipoprotein	C-Terminal Amino Acid	Number of Amino Acid Residues	Molecular Weight	Presence of Carbohydrate Residues	Additional Remarks
A-I	HDL	Glutamine	245	28,300	+	Activator of lecithin:cholesterol acyl transferase (LCAT).
A-II	HDL	Glutamine	77 × 2	17,000	–	Structure is 2 identical monomers joined by a disulfide bridge.
B	LDL, VLDL, chylomicrons	?	?	?	+	
C-I	VLDL, HDL, chylomicrons	Serine	57	6631	–	
C-II	VLDL, HDL, chylomicrons	Glutamic acid	?	10,000	–	Activator of extrahepatic lipoprotein lipase.
C-III	VLDL, HDL, chylomicrons	Alanine	79	8764	+	Several polymorphic forms depending on content of sialic acids.
Arginine-rich	VLDL, HDL	Alanine (?)	?	33,000 (?)	+	Present in excess in the β-VLDL of patients with type III hyperlipoproteinemia.

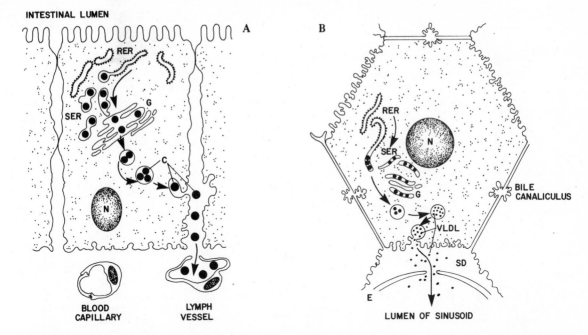

Figure 20—21. The formation and secretion of *(A)* chylomicrons by intestinal cells and *(B)* very low density lipoproteins by hepatic cells. (RER, rough endoplasmic reticulum; SER, smooth endoplasmic reticulum; G, Golgi complex; N, nucleus; C, chylomicrons; VLDL, very low density lipoproteins; E, endothelium; SD, space of Disse.)

have entered the circulation (Fig 20—22 and 20—23). A more detailed account of the factors controlling hepatic VLDL secretion is given on p 307.

Catabolism of Chylomicrons & Very Low Density Lipoproteins

The clearance of labeled chylomicrons from the blood is rapid, the half-time of disappearance being of the order of minutes in small animals like the rat but longer in larger animals like man, where it is still under 1 hour. Larger particles are catabolized more quickly than smaller ones. When chylomicrons labeled in the triacylglycerol fatty acids are administered intravenously, some 80% of the label is found in adipose tissue, heart, and muscle and approximately 20% in the liver. As experiments with the perfused organ have shown that the liver does not metabolize native chylomicrons or VLDL significantly, the label in the liver must result secondarily from their metabolism in extrahepatic tissues.

A. Role of Lipoprotein Lipase: Experiments using chylomicrons in which the triacylglycerol fatty acids were labeled with ^{14}C and the glycerol moiety with ^{3}H have shown that hydrolysis accompanies uptake by extrahepatic tissues. There is a significant correlation between the ability of a tissue to incorporate triacylglycerol fatty acids and the activity of the enzyme **lipoprotein lipase** (clearing factor lipase). It is located in the walls of blood capillaries and has been found in extracts of heart, adipose tissue, spleen, lung, renal medulla, aorta, diaphragm, and lactating mammary gland.

Normal blood does not contain appreciable quantities of the enzyme; however, following injection of heparin, lipoprotein lipase is released from the tissues into the circulation and is accompanied by the clearing of lipemia. A lipase is also released from the liver by large quantities of heparin, but this enzyme has properties different from those of lipoprotein lipase and does not react readily with chylomicrons.

Both phospholipids and apolipoprotein C-II are required as cofactors for lipoprotein lipase activity. It is noteworthy that both chylomicrons and VLDL provide the enzyme with both its substrate and cofactors. Hydrolysis takes place while the lipoproteins are attached to the enzyme on the endothelium. The triacylglycerol is hydrolyzed progressively through a diacylglycerol to a monoacylglycerol which is finally hydrolyzed by a separate monoacylglycerol hydrolase. Some of the released free fatty acids return to the circulation, but the bulk are transported into the tissue (Fig 20—22 and 20—23).

Reaction with lipoprotein lipase results in the loss of approximately 90% of the triacylglycerol of chylomicrons and with the loss of the apoprotein-C polypeptides which return to HDL. The resulting lipoprotein or **remnant** is about half the diameter of the parent chylomicron and in terms of the percentage composition becomes relatively enriched in cholesterol and cholesteryl esters because of the loss of triacylglycerol.

B. Role of the Liver: Chylomicron remnants are taken up by the liver in vivo (Redgrave, 1970) and by the perfused liver (Noel & others, 1975; Felts & others, 1975), in which system it has been shown that the

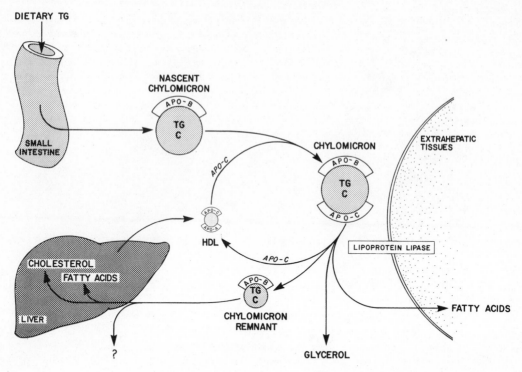

Figure 20—22. Metabolic fate of chylomicrons. (APO-B, apolipoprotein B; APO-C, apolipoprotein C; HDL, high density lipoprotein; TG, triacylglycerol; C, cholesterol and cholesteryl ester.)

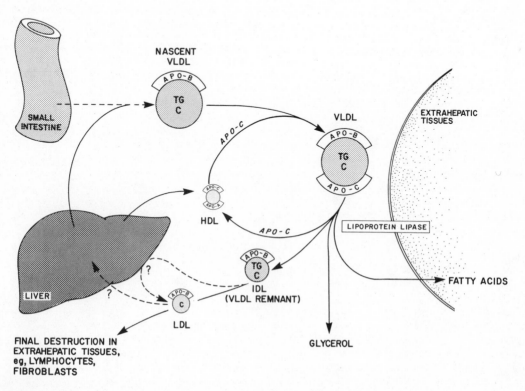

Figure 20—23. Metabolic fate of very low density lipoproteins (VLDL). (APO-B, apolipoprotein B; APO-C, apolipoprotein C; HDL, high density lipoprotein; TG, triacylglycerol; IDL, intermediate density lipoprotein; LDL, low density lipoprotein; C, cholesterol and cholesteryl ester.)

cholesteryl esters of remnants are hydrolyzed and the triacylglycerol fatty acids metabolized (Gardner & Mayes, 1976). Although lipoproteins in the LDL range of densities seem to be formed as a result of reaction between the liver and remnants, the nature and extent of this process remains to be evaluated.

When ^{125}I-VLDL were injected into humans, labeled apoprotein C was found in HDL as it became distributed between VLDL and HDL (Eisenberg & Levy, 1975). On the other hand, labeled apoprotein B disappeared from VLDL and appeared in a lipoprotein of intermediate density (1.006–1.019 IDL). Finally, the radioactivity was found in apoprotein B of LDL, showing that the B apoprotein of VLDL is the precursor of apoprotein B of LDL. The role of the liver in this process is speculative. However, the IDL may represent the end of the degradation of VLDL by lipoprotein lipase and may correspond to chylomicron remnants. Only one IDL particle is formed from each VLDL particle (Fig 20–23).

Metabolism of LDL

LDL does not appear to be secreted as such from either the liver or intestines. Rather, it seems to be formed from VLDL and possibly chylomicrons, as described above. The half-time of disappearance from the circulation of apoprotein B in LDL is approximately 2½ days. This time is increased in type III hyperlipoproteinemia. The liver was considered as the major site of LDL removal from the circulation. However, it has been shown that hepatectomy, in fact, shortens the T½ of LDL in the circulation. There is growing evidence that fibroblasts and lymphocytes may degrade LDL in extrahepatic tissues.

Metabolism of HDL

HDL is synthesized and secreted from both liver and intestine. However, nascent HDL from intestine does not contain apoprotein C but only apoprotein A. Thus, apoprotein C seems to be synthesized in the liver only and is transferred to intestinal HDL when the latter enters the plasma. Nascent HDL formed by the liver consists of discoid phospholipid bilayers containing apoprotein and free cholesterol (Hamilton & others, 1976). These lipoproteins are similar to the particles found in the plasma of patients with a deficiency of the plasma enzyme **lecithin:cholesterol acyl transferase (LCAT)** and in the plasma of patients with obstructive jaundice. Hamilton and others proposed that LCAT—and possibly the LCAT activator apoprotein A-I—bind to the disk. Catalysis by LCAT converts surface phospholipid and free cholesterol into cholesteryl esters and lysolecithin. The nonpolar cholesteryl esters move into the hydrophobic interior of the bilayer, whereas lysolecithin is transferred to plasma albumin. The reaction continues generating a nonpolar core that pushes the bilayer apart until a spherical, pseudomicellar HDL is formed, covered by a surface film of polar lipids and apoproteins. In LCAT deficiency, all lipoproteins contain abnormally low amounts of cholesteryl esters and high concentrations of free cholesterol and lecithin. In normal persons it is considered that the esterified cholesterol can be transferred nonenzymically from HDL to the lower density lipoproteins, eg, LDL. The LCAT system may be involved more with the removal of excess unesterified cholesterol from lipoproteins. In LCAT deficiency, a large LDL particle accumulates which is rich in unesterified cholesterol. The liver and possibly the intestines seem to be the final sites of degradation of HDL apoproteins.

THE ROLE OF THE LIVER IN LIPID METABOLISM

Much of the lipid metabolism of the body was formerly thought to be the prerogative of the liver. The discovery that most tissues have the ability to oxidize fatty acids completely and the knowledge that has accumulated showing that adipose tissue is extremely active metabolically have tended to modify the former emphasis on the role of the liver. Nonetheless, the concept of a central and unique role for the liver in lipid metabolism is still an important one. Apart from its role in facilitating the digestion and absorption of lipids by the production of bile, which contains cholesterol and bile salts synthesized within the liver, the liver has active enzyme systems for synthesizing and oxidizing fatty acids, for synthesizing triacylglycerols, phospholipids, cholesterol, and plasma lipoproteins, and for converting fatty acids to ketone bodies (ketogenesis). Some of these processes have already been described.

Triacylglycerol Synthesis & the Formation of VLDL

Experiments involving a comparison between hepatectomized and intact animals have shown that the liver is the main source of plasma lipoproteins derived from endogenous sources. Hepatic triacylglycerols are the immediate precursors of triacylglycerols contained in plasma VLDL. The fatty acids used in the synthesis of hepatic triacylglycerols are derived from 2 possible sources: (1) synthesis within the liver from acetyl-CoA derived in the main from carbohydrate and (2) uptake of free fatty acids from the circulation. The first source would appear to be predominant in the well fed condition, when fatty acid synthesis is high and the level of circulating free fatty acids is low. As triacylglycerol does not normally accumulate in the liver under this condition, it must be inferred that it is transported from the liver as rapidly as it is synthesized. On the other hand, during fasting, the feeding of high-fat diets, or in diabetes mellitus, the level of circulating free fatty acids is raised and more is abstracted into the liver. Under these conditions, free fatty acids are the main source of triacylglycerol fatty acids in the liver and in plasma lipoproteins because lipogenesis from acetyl-CoA is depressed. The enzyme mechanism responsible for the synthesis of triacylglycerols and phospholipids has been described on p 287. Factors which enhance both the synthesis of triacylglycerol and the secretion of VLDL by the liver include the feeding of diets high in carbohydrate (particularly if they contain sucrose or fructose), high levels of circulating free fatty acids, ingestion of ethanol, and the presence of high levels of insulin.

Fatty Livers & Lipotropic Factors

For a variety of reasons, lipid—mainly as triacylglycerol—can accumulate in the liver. Extensive accumulation is regarded as a pathologic condition. When accumulation of lipid in the liver becomes chronic, fibrotic changes occur in the cells which progress to cirrhosis and impaired liver function.

Fatty livers fall into 2 main categories. The first type is associated with raised levels of plasma free fatty acids resulting from mobilization of fat from adipose tissue or from the hydrolysis of lipoprotein or chylomicron triacylglycerol by lipoprotein lipase in extrahepatic tissues. Increasing amounts of free fatty acids are taken up by the liver and esterified. The production of plasma lipoprotein does not keep pace with the influx of free fatty acids, allowing triacylglycerol to accumulate, causing a fatty liver. The quantity of triacylglycerol present in the liver is significantly increased during starvation and the feeding of high-fat diets. In many instances (eg, in starvation), the ability to secrete VLDL is also impaired. In uncontrolled diabetes mellitus, pregnancy toxemia of ewes, or ketosis in cattle, fatty infiltration is sufficiently severe to cause visible pallor or fatty appearance and enlargement of the liver.

The second type of fatty liver is usually due to a metabolic block in the production of plasma lipoproteins. Theoretically, the lesion may be due to a block in lipoprotein apoprotein synthesis, a block in the synthesis of the lipoprotein from lipid and apoprotein, a failure in provision of phospholipids which are found in lipoproteins, or a failure in the secretory mechanism itself. It is often associated with deficiency of a substance known as a **lipotropic factor**. The deficiency causes triacylglycerol to accumulate even though only a normal rate of fatty acid synthesis and uptake of free fatty acids may be occurring. The exact mechanism by which many fatty livers in this category arise is still far from clear. One type of fatty liver which has been studied extensively is due to a deficiency of choline. As choline may be synthesized using labile methyl groups donated by methionine in the process of **transmethylation** (see Chapter 23), the deficiency is basically due to a shortage of the type of methyl group donated by methionine. Thus, choline, methionine, and betaine can all act as lipotropic agents in curing fatty livers due to choline deficiency, and, conversely, processes which utilize methyl groups excessively or diets poor in protein (containing methionine) or lecithin (containing choline) will all tend to favor the production of fatty livers.

Several mechanisms have been suggested to explain the role of choline as a lipotropic agent. The very low density lipoproteins are virtually absent from the blood of choline-deficient rats, indicating that the defect lies in the transport of triacylglycerol from the liver. In the perfused rat liver, the uptake of labeled free fatty acids and their oxidation is not reduced in choline-deficient livers; however, more of the label is incorporated into liver triacylglycerol and non-choline-containing phospholipids, and significantly less is incorporated into the choline-containing phospholipids. Mookerjea has suggested that, in addition to causing an impairment in synthesis of lipoprotein phospholipids containing choline, a choline deficiency may impair availability of phosphocholine, which stimulates incorporation of glucosamine into glycolipoproteins. Deficiency of phospholipids containing choline may impair synthesis of intracellular membranes concerned in lipoprotein synthesis. It has been suggested that depression of long chain fatty acid oxidation, which may occur in choline deficiency, may be due to depressed levels of carnitine (carnitine synthesis also being dependent on the provision of methyl groups). Reduced oxidation of fatty acids would be expected to enhance triacylglycerol formation. It is to be noted that the antibiotic puromycin, which inhibits protein synthesis, causes a fatty liver and a marked reduction in concentration of plasma esterified fatty acids in rats.

Other substances which cause fatty livers include ethionine (α-amino-γ-ethylmercaptobutyric acid), carbon tetrachloride, chloroform, phosphorus, lead, and arsenic. Choline will not protect the organism against these agents but appears to aid in recovery. The action of most of these substances is associated with inhibition of hepatic protein synthesis. However, while it appears that protein synthesis is impaired in most of these conditions, the rapidity of action of carbon tetrachloride (within minutes), compared with the several hours required to elicit an effect with ethionine, indicates some difference in mode of action. It is very likely that carbon tetrachloride also affects the secretory mechanism itself or the conjugation of the lipid with lipoprotein apoprotein. Its effect is not direct but depends rather on further transformation of the molecule. This probably involves formation of free radicals which may disrupt lipid membranes such as the endoplasmic reticulum, with formation of lipid peroxides. The action of ethionine is thought to be due to a decline in messenger RNA and protein synthesis caused by a reduction in availability of ATP. This results when ethionine, replacing methionine in S-adenosylmethionine, traps available adenine and prevents synthesis of ATP. This hypothesis is supported by the fact that the effect of ethionine may be reversed by administration of ATP or adenine. Administration of orotic acid also causes fatty livers due to a specific block in apo-B synthesis.

A deficiency of vitamin E enhances the hepatic necrosis of the choline deficiency type of fatty liver. Added vitamin E or a dietary factor termed "factor 3" (an organic compound containing selenium; see Chapter 30) has a protective effect. In addition to protein deficiency, essential fatty acid and vitamin deficiencies (eg, pyridoxine and pantothenic acid) can cause fatty infiltration of the liver. A deficiency of essential fatty acids is thought to depress the synthesis of phospholipids; therefore, other substances such as cholesterol which compete for available essential fatty acids for esterification can also cause fatty livers. Alcoholism also leads to fat accumulation in the liver, hyperlipidemia, and ultimately cirrhosis. The exact mechanism of action of alcohol in this respect is still uncertain. Whether or not extra free fatty acid mobilization plays some part in causing the accumulation of fat is not clear, but several studies have demonstrated elevated levels of free fatty acids in the rat after administration of a single intoxicating dose of ethanol. There is good evidence of increased hepatic triacylglycerol synthesis, decreased fatty acid oxidation, and decreased citric acid cycle activity, caused possibly by an increased NADH/NAD ratio generated by the oxidation of ethanol by alcohol dehydrogenase. This causes a shift to the left in the equilibrium malate ⇌ oxaloacetate, which may reduce activity of the citric acid cycle.

Other effects of alcohol may include increased lipogenesis and cholesterol synthesis from acetyl-CoA. Alcohol consumption over a long period leads to the accumulation of fatty acids in the liver which are derived from endogenous synthesis rather than from adipose tissue. There is no impairment of hepatic synthesis of protein after ethanol ingestion. Some of the constituents of lipoprotein secretion and factors concerned in the production of fatty livers are shown in Fig 20–24.

KETOSIS

Under certain metabolic conditions associated with a high rate of fatty acid oxidation, the liver produces considerable quantities of acetoacetate and

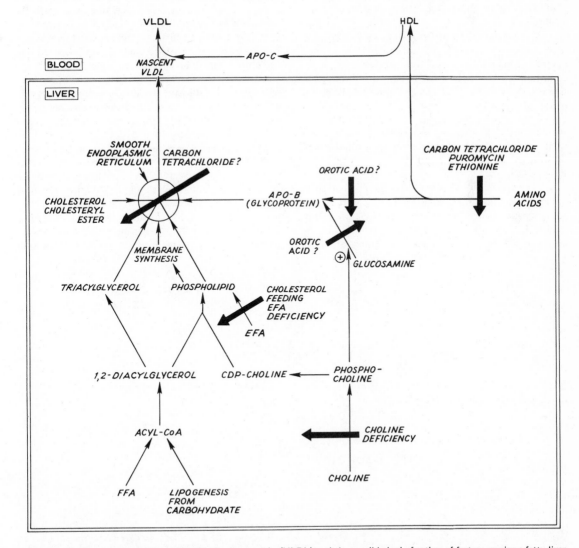

Figure 20—24. The secretion of very low density lipoprotein (VLDL) and the possible loci of action of factors causing a fatty liver. (EFA, essential fatty acids; LDL, low density lipoproteins; HDL, high density lipoproteins; APO-C, apolipoprotein C.)

D(–)-β-hydroxybutyrate which pass by diffusion into the blood. Acetoacetate continually undergoes spontaneous decarboxylation to yield acetone. These 3 substances are collectively known as the **ketone bodies** (also known as acetone bodies or "ketones") (Fig 20–25).

The concentration of total ketone bodies in the blood of well fed mammals does not normally exceed 1 mg/100 ml (as acetone equivalents). It is somewhat higher than this in ruminants. Loss via the urine is usually less than 1 mg/24 hours in man. Higher than normal quantities present in the blood or urine constitute **ketonemia** (hyperketonemia) or **ketonuria**, respectively. The overall condition is called **ketosis**. Acetoacetic and β-hydroxybutyric acids are both moderately strong acids and are buffered when present in blood or the tissues. However, their continual excretion in quantity entails some loss of buffer cation (in spite of ammonia production by the kidney) which progressively depletes the alkali reserve, causing **ketoacidosis**. This may be fatal in uncontrolled diabetes mellitus.

The simplest form of ketosis occurs in starvation and involves depletion of available carbohydrate coupled with mobilization of free fatty acids. No other condition in which ketosis occurs seems to differ qualitatively from this general pattern of metabolism, but quantitatively it may be exaggerated to produce the pathologic states found in diabetes mellitus, pregnancy toxemia in sheep, and ketosis in lactating cattle. Other nonpathologic forms of ketosis are found under conditions of high-fat feeding and after severe exercise in the postabsorptive state.

In vivo, the liver appears to be the only organ in nonruminants to add ketone bodies to the blood. Extrahepatic tissues utilize them as respiratory substrates. In ruminants, the rumen wall converts butyric acid, formed as a result of ruminal fermentation, to β-hydroxybutyrate, which enters the blood stream. The ruminant lactating mammary gland is also reported to produce ketone bodies. It is believed that these other sources of ketone bodies do not contribute significantly to the occurrence of ketosis in these species.

Enzymatic Mechanism for Ketogenesis in the Liver & for the Utilization of Ketone Bodies in Extrahepatic Tissues

The net flow of ketone bodies from the liver to the extrahepatic tissues results from an active enzymatic mechanism in the liver for the production of ketone bodies coupled with very low activity of enzymes responsible for their utilization. The reverse situation occurs in extrahepatic tissues (Fig 20–26).

Enzymes responsible for ketone body formation are associated mainly with the mitochondria. Originally it was thought that only 1 molecule of acetoacetate was formed from the terminal 4 carbons of a fatty acid upon oxidation. Later, to explain both the production of more than one equivalent of acetoacetate from a long chain fatty acid and the formation of ketone bodies from acetic acid, it was proposed that C_2 units formed in β-oxidation condensed with one another to form acetoacetate. This may occur by a reversal of the **thiolase** reaction whereby 2 molecules of acetyl-CoA condense to form acetoacetyl-CoA. Thus, acetoacetyl-CoA, which is the starting material for ketogenesis, arises either directly during the course of β-oxidation or as a result of the condensation of acetyl-CoA. Two pathways for the formation of acetoacetate from acetoacetyl-CoA have been proposed (Fig 20–28). The first is by simple deacylation catalyzed by the enzyme **acetoacetyl-CoA deacylase**. The second pathway (Fig 20–27) involves the condensation of acetoacetyl-CoA with another molecule of acetyl-CoA to form β-hydroxy-β-methylglutaryl-CoA (HMG-CoA),

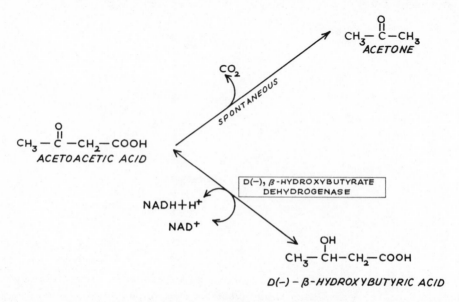

Figure 20–25. Interrelationships of the ketone bodies.

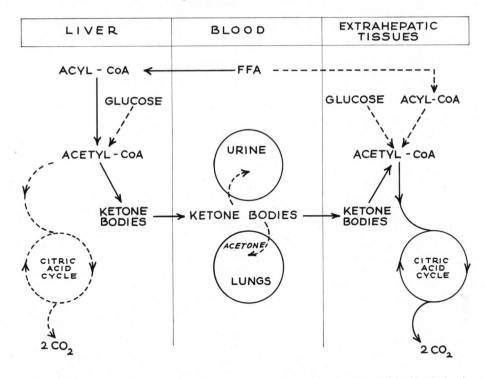

Figure 20—26. Formation, utilization, and excretion of ketone bodies. (The main pathway is indicated by the heavier arrows.)

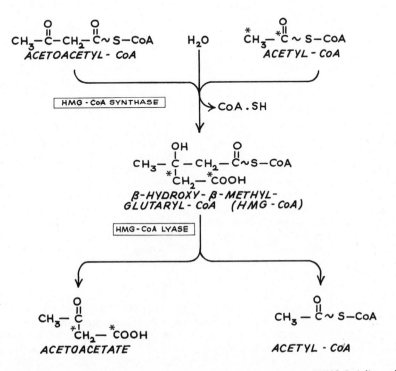

Figure 20—27. Formation of acetoacetate through intermediate production of HMG-CoA (Lynen).

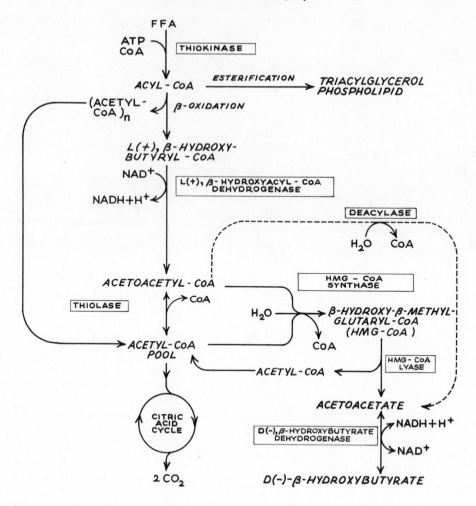

Figure 20—28. Pathways of ketogenesis in the liver. (FFA, free fatty acids; HMG, β-hydroxy-β-methylglutaryl.)

catalyzed by **β-hydroxy-β-methylglutaryl-CoA syn-thase.** The presence of another enzyme in the mito-chondria, **β-hydroxy-β-methylglutaryl-CoA lyase,** causes acetyl-CoA to split off from the β-hydroxy-β-methylglutaryl-CoA, leaving free acetoacetate. The carbon atoms split off in the acetyl-CoA molecule are derived from the original acetoacetyl-CoA molecule (Fig 20—27).

Present opinion favors the β-hydroxy-β-methyl-glutaryl-CoA pathway as the major route of ketone body formation. Although there is a marked increase in activity of HMG-CoA lyase in fasting, evidence does not suggest that this enzyme is rate-limiting in keto-genesis.

Acetoacetate may be converted to D(−)-β-hy-droxybutyrate by **D(−)-β-hydroxybutyrate dehydro-genase,** which is present in many tissues, including the liver. D(−)-β-hydroxybutyrate is quantitatively the pre-dominant ketone body present in the blood and urine in ketosis.

While the liver is equipped with an active enzy-matic mechanism for the production of acetoacetate from acetoacetyl-CoA, acetoacetate once formed can-not be reactivated directly in the liver. This accounts for the net production of ketone bodies by the liver. A thiokinase is present, however, which can convert D(−)-β-hydroxybutyrate to D(−)-β-hydroxybutyryl-CoA. This compound can reform acetoacetyl-CoA, but in view of the active degradation of acetoacetyl-CoA to acetoacetate in the ketotic liver it is doubtful whether this pathway of ketone body utilization is of great quantitative significance.

Two reactions take place in extrahepatic tissues which will activate acetoacetate to acetoacetyl-CoA. The enzymes responsible are absent from liver. One mechanism involves succinyl-CoA and the enzyme **succinyl-CoA-acetoacetate-CoA transferase** (thio-phorase). Acetoacetate reacts with succinyl-CoA, the CoA being transferred to form acetoacetyl-CoA and succinate.

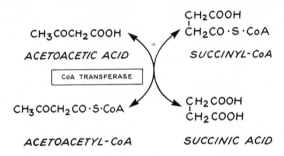

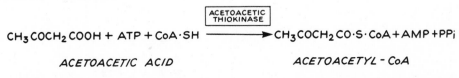

However, experiments with ^{14}C-labeled acetone have shown it to be converted, to a limited extent at least, to $^{14}CO_2$. Several pathways for the utilization of acetone have been proposed. One is that acetone is converted to acetoacetate by a reversal of decarboxylation. Another pathway involves the formation of propanediol, which may provide, if it is a significant process, a route for the net conversion of fatty acids to carbohydrate. Alternatively, propanediol may form a 1-carbon (formate) unit plus a 2-carbon unit (acetate).

The other reaction involves the activation of acetoacetate with ATP in the presence of CoA catalyzed by acetoacetic thiokinase.

D(−)-β-hydroxybutyrate may be activated directly in extrahepatic tissues by a thiokinase similar to the enzyme reported to be present in the liver. Conversion to acetoacetate with D(−)-β-hydroxybutyrate dehydrogenase and NAD⁺ followed by activation to acetoacetyl-CoA is an alternative route leading to its further metabolism. The acetoacetyl-CoA formed by these reactions is split to acetyl-CoA by thiolase and oxidized in the citric acid cycle (Fig 20−28).

Ketone bodies are oxidized in extrahepatic tissues proportionately to their concentration in the blood. They are also oxidized in preference to glucose and to FFA. If the blood level is raised, oxidation of ketone bodies increases until at a concentration of approximately 70 mg/100 ml, they saturate the oxidative machinery; any further increase in the rate of ketogenesis merely serves to raise the blood concentration and the rate of urinary excretion precipitously. At this point, a large proportion of the oxygen consumption of the animal may be accounted for by the oxidation of ketone bodies.

Most of the evidence suggests that ketonemia is due to increased production of ketone bodies by the liver rather than to a deficiency in their utilization by extrahepatic tissues. However, experiments on depancreatized rats support the possibility that ketosis in the severe diabetic may be aggravated by a reduced ability to catabolize ketone bodies.

In moderate ketonemia, the loss of ketone bodies via the urine is only a few percent of the total ketone body production and utilization. As there are renal threshold-like effects (there is not a true threshold) which vary between species and individuals, measurement of the ketonemia, not the ketonuria, is the preferred method of assessing the severity of ketosis.

While acetoacetate and D(−)-β-hydroxybutyrate are readily oxidized by extrahepatic tissues, acetone is difficult to oxidize in vivo. When acetone is injected into human subjects, its concentration in the blood rises sharply and is maintained at a high level for several hours, indicating a very slow rate of utilization.

CHOLESTEROL METABOLISM

The greater part of the cholesterol of the body arises by synthesis (about 1 g/day), whereas only about 0.3 g/day are provided by the average diet. Cholesterol is eliminated via 2 main pathways: conversion to bile acids and excretion of neutral sterols in the feces. The synthesis of steroid hormones from cholesterol and the elimination of their products of degradation in the urine are of minor quantitative significance. Cholesterol is typically a product of animal metabolism and occurs therefore in foods of animal origin such as meat, liver, brain, and egg yolk (a particularly rich source).

Synthesis of Cholesterol

Tissues known to be capable of synthesizing cholesterol include the liver, adrenal cortex, skin, intestines, testis, and aorta. The microsomal and cytosol fraction of the cell is responsible for cholesterol synthesis.

Acetyl-CoA is the source of all the carbon atoms in cholesterol. The manner of synthesis of this complex molecule has been the subject of investigation by many workers, with the result that it is possible at the present time to chart the origin of all parts of the cholesterol molecule (Figs 20−29, 20−30, and 20−31). Synthesis takes place in several stages. The first is the synthesis of mevalonate, a 6-carbon compound, from acetyl-CoA (Fig 20−29). The next major stage is the formation of isoprenoid units from mevalonate by loss of CO_2 (Fig 20−30). The isoprenoid units may be regarded as the building blocks of the steroid skeleton. Six of these units condense to form the intermediate, squalene, which in turn gives rise to the parent steroid lanosterol. Cholesterol is formed from lanosterol after several further steps, including the loss of 3 methyl groups (Fig 20−31).

Two separate pathways have been described for the formation of mevalonate. One involves the inter-

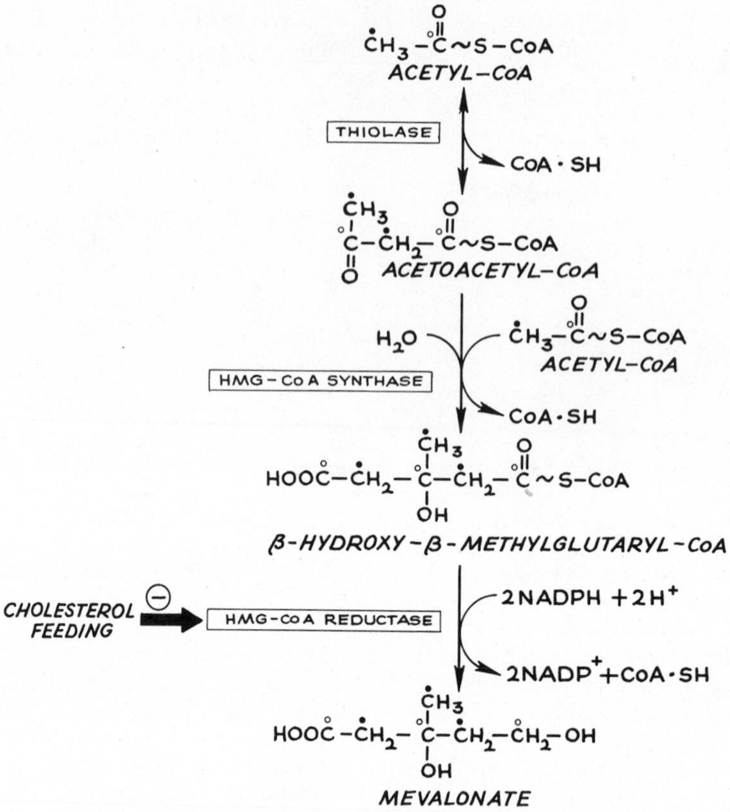

Figure 20–29. Biosynthesis of mevalonate. (HMG, β-hydroxy-β-methylglutaryl.)

mediate β-hydroxy-β-methylglutaryl-CoA and the other is through a β-hydroxy-β-methylglutaryl-S-enzyme complex. The pathway through β-hydroxy-β-methylglutaryl-CoA is considered to be quantitatively the more significant and follows the same sequence of reactions described previously for the synthesis of ketone bodies. However, since cholesterol synthesis is extramitochondrial, the 2 pathways are distinct. Thus, there are 2 β-hydroxy-β-methylglutaryl-CoA pools: The one in mitochondria is concerned with ketogenesis, and the other, extramitochondrial pool, is involved in the synthesis of isoprenoid units and cholesterol. It has also been proposed that the pathway may involve formation of malonyl-CoA, but this is unlikely because avidin, which inhibits biotin-linked enzymes such as acetyl-CoA carboxylase, does not inhibit the production of mevalonate from acetyl-CoA.

β-Hydroxy-β-methylglutaryl-CoA is converted to mevalonate in a 2-stage reduction by NADPH catalyzed by β-hydroxy-β-methylglutaryl-CoA reductase (Fig 20–29).

In the second stage, mevalonate is phosphorylated by ATP to form several active phosphorylated intermediates. By means of a decarboxylation, the active isoprenoid unit, isopentenylpyrophosphate, is formed. The next stage involves the condensation of molecules of isopentenylpyrophosphate to form farnesyl pyrophosphate. This occurs via an isomerization of isopen-

tenylpyrophosphate to form the 10-carbon intermediate, geranyl pyrophosphate. A further condensation with isopentenylpyrophosphate forms farnesyl pyrophosphate. Two molecules of farnesyl pyrophosphate condense at the pyrophosphate end in a reaction involving a reduction with NADPH with elimination of the pyrophosphate radicals. The resulting compound is squalene. Recently, evidence has been provided that an alternative pathway known as the "trans-methylglutaconate shunt" may be present. This pathway removes a significant proportion (20%) of the dimethylallyl pyrophosphate and returns it, via trans-3-methylglutaconate-CoA, to β-hydroxy-β-methylglutaryl-CoA. This pathway may have regulatory potential with respect to the overall rate of cholesterol synthesis.

Squalene has a structure which resembles the steroid nucleus very closely (Fig 20–31). It is converted to lanosterol by ring closures. Before closure occurs, the methyl group on C_{14} is transferred to C_{13} and that on C_8 to C_{14} and C_3 is hydroxylated. The latter reaction involves molecular oxygen, and the reaction is catalyzed by a microsomal hydroxylase system.

The last stage (Fig 20–31), the formation of cholesterol from lanosterol, involves changes to the steroid nucleus and side chain. The methyl group on C_{14} is oxidized to CO_2 to form 14-desmethyl lanosterol. Likewise, 2 more methyl groups on C_4 are removed to

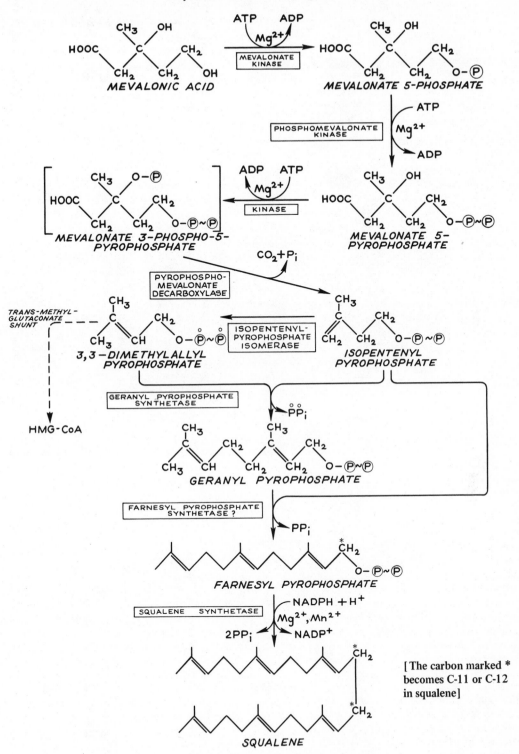

[The carbon marked * becomes C-11 or C-12 in squalene]

Figure 20—30. Biosynthesis of squalene. (HMG, β-hydroxy-β-methylglutaryl.)

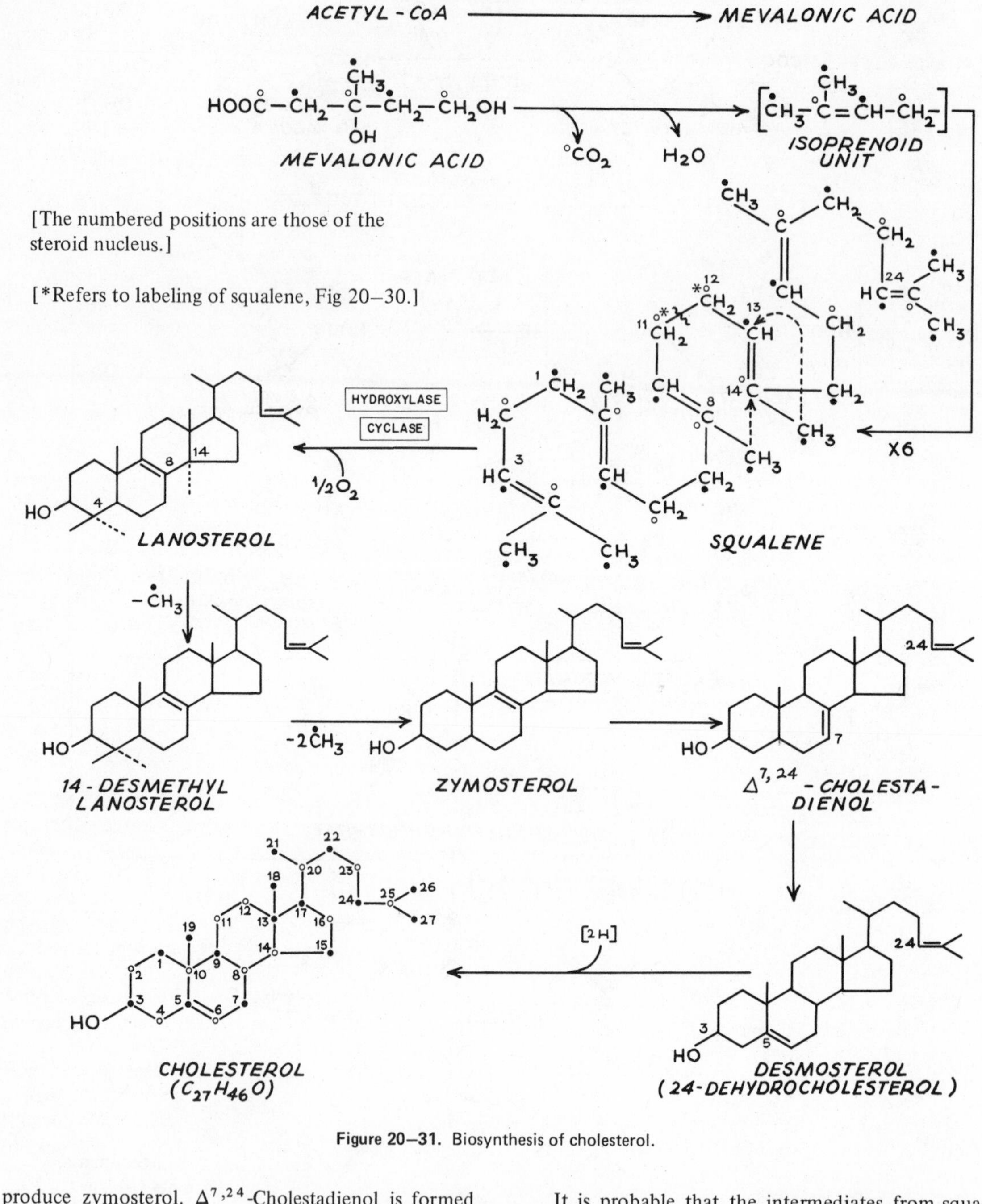

Figure 20—31. Biosynthesis of cholesterol.

produce zymosterol. $\Delta^{7,24}$-Cholestadienol is formed from zymosterol by the double bond between C_8 and C_9, moving to a position between C_8 and C_7. Desmosterol is formed at this point by a further shift in the double bond in ring II to take up a position between C_5 and C_6, as in cholesterol. Finally, cholesterol is produced when the double bond of the side chain is reduced. The exact order in which the steps described actually take place is not known with certainty. Some investigators favor the view that the double bond at C_{24} is reduced early and that desmosterol is not the immediate precursor of cholesterol. More than one pathway may operate simultaneously.

It is probable that the intermediates from squalene to cholesterol may be attached to a special carrier protein known as the **squalene and sterol carrier protein**. This protein binds sterols and other insoluble lipids, allowing them to react in the aqueous phase of the cell. In addition, it seems likely that it is in the form of cholesterol-sterol carrier protein that cholesterol is converted to steroid hormones and bile acids and participates in the formation of membranes and of lipoproteins. It is also as cholesterol-sterol carrier protein that cholesterol might affect the activity of β-hydroxy-β-methylglutaryl-CoA reductase (see below).

Control of cholesterol synthesis is exerted near

the beginning of the pathway. There is a marked decrease in the activity of β-hydroxy-β-methylglutaryl-CoA reductase in fasting rats, which might explain the reduced synthesis of cholesterol during fasting. On the other hand, the activity of this enzyme was not reduced in the livers of diabetic rats, which correlates well with the continued synthesis of cholesterol observed in the diabetic state. Siperstein has proposed a feedback mechanism whereby β-hydroxy-β-methylglutaryl-CoA reductase in liver is inhibited by cholesterol.. Since a direct inhibition of the enzyme by cholesterol cannot be demonstrated, cholesterol may act either by repression of the synthesis of new reductase or by inducing the synthesis of enzymes which degrade existing reductase. A diurnal variation occurs in both cholesterol synthesis and reductase activity. However, recent work indicates more rapid effects of cholesterol on reductase activity than can be explained solely by changes in the rate of protein synthesis. Administration of insulin or thyroid hormone increases β-hydroxy-β-methylglutaryl-CoA reductase activity, whereas glucagon or glucocorticoids reduce it.

After the administration of ^{14}C-labeled acetate, the label can be detected in plasma cholesterol. Synthesis takes place in the liver, and the cholesterol is incorporated into very low density lipoproteins and ultimately into low density lipoproteins. The effect of variations in the amount of cholesterol in the diet on the endogenous production of cholesterol in rats has been studied. When there was only 0.05% cholesterol in the diet, 70–80% of the cholesterol of the liver, small intestine, and adrenal gland was synthesized within the body, whereas on a diet containing 2% cholesterol the endogenous production fell to 10–30%. However, endogenous production could not be completely suppressed by raising the dietary intake. It appears that it is only hepatic synthesis which is inhibited. Experiments with the perfused liver have demonstrated that hypercholesterolemic serum inhibits sterol synthesis. There is a species variation in the relative importance of the liver as a source of endogenous cholesterol. In man, extrahepatic synthesis, mainly in the intestine, is more important, whereas in the dog and rat the liver is responsible for most cholesterol synthesis. Bile acids, rather than cholesterol, inhibit cholesterol synthesis in the intestine. A similar feedback control system at the β-hydroxy-β-methylglutaryl-CoA reductase step seems also to operate. More recent experiments in vitro have shown that cholesterol synthesis is inhibited by cAMP, indicating that one or more reactions in the synthetic pathway may be controlled by a cAMP-dependent protein kinase. Both mechanisms that are known to govern cholesterol synthesis in normal liver, feedback and caloric control, are lost when liver cells sustain malignant change.

Attempts to lower plasma cholesterol in humans by reducing the amount of cholesterol in the diet are effective. An increase of 100 mg in dietary cholesterol causes a rise of 5 mg cholesterol per dl serum.

Transport

Cholesterol in the diet is absorbed from the intestine and, in company with other lipids, incorporated into chylomicrons and VLDL. Of the cholesterol absorbed, 80–90% in the lymph is esterified with long chain fatty acids. Esterification may occur in the intestinal mucosa. The plant sterols (sitosterols) are poorly absorbed.

In man, the total plasma cholesterol is about 200 mg/dl, rising with age, although there are wide variations between individuals. The greater part is found in the esterified form. It is transported as lipoprotein in the plasma, the highest proportion of cholesterol being found in the LDL (β-lipoproteins), density 1.019–1.063. However, under conditions where the VLDL are quantitatively predominant, an increased proportion of the plasma cholesterol will reside in this fraction.

Dietary cholesterol takes several days to equilibrate with cholesterol in the plasma and several weeks to equilibrate with cholesterol of the tissues. The turnover of cholesterol in the liver is relatively fast compared with the half-life of the total body cholesterol, which is several weeks. Free cholesterol in plasma and liver equilibrates in a matter of hours.

Equilibration of cholesteryl ester with free cholesterol in plasma takes several days in man. In general, free cholesterol exchanges readily between tissues and lipoproteins, whereas cholesteryl ester does not exchange freely. Some plasma cholesteryl ester may be formed in HDL as a result of the transesterification reaction in plasma between cholesterol and the fatty acid in position 2 of phosphatidylcholine, catalyzed by lecithin:cholesterol acyltransferase (LCAT) (see p 290). A familial deficiency of this enzyme has been described. In affected subjects, the plasma concentration of cholesteryl esters and lysolecithin is low whereas the concentration of cholesterol and lecithin is raised. The plasma tends to be turbid. Abnormalities are also found in the lipoproteins. One HDL fraction contains disk-shaped structures in stacks or rouleaux, and LDL contains a larger particle having a lipid composition somewhat similar to VLDL. Also present as an abnormal LDL subfraction is lipoprotein-X, otherwise found only in patients with cholestasis. VLDL are also abnormal, migrating as β-lipoproteins upon electrophoresis. Patients with parenchymal liver disease also show a decrease of lecithin:cholesterol acyl transferase activity and abnormalities in the serum lipids and lipoproteins. It would appear that lecithin:cholesterol acyl transferase is necessary for the normal metabolism of the plasma lipoproteins.

Excretion of Cholesterol

Approximately half of the cholesterol eliminated from the body is excreted in the feces after conversion to bile salts. The remainder is excreted as neutral steroids. Much of the cholesterol secreted in the bile is reabsorbed, and it is believed that the cholesterol which serves as precursor for the fecal sterols is derived from the intestinal mucosa. Coprostanol is the principal sterol in the feces; it is formed from cholesterol in the lower intestine by the bacterial flora therein. A large proportion of the biliary excretion of bile salts is reabsorbed into the portal circulation, taken up by the liver, and reexcreted in the bile. This is known as the enterohepatic circulation. The bile salts not reabsorbed, or their derivatives, are excreted in the feces. Bile salts undergo changes brought about by intestinal bacteria. The rate of production of bile acids from cholesterol in the liver is reduced by infusion of bile salts, indicating the existence of another feedback control mechanism initiated by the product of the reaction.

Cholesterol, Coronary Heart Disease, & Atherosclerosis

Many investigators have demonstrated a correlation between raised serum lipid levels and the incidence of coronary heart disease and atherosclerosis. Of the serum lipids, cholesterol has been the one most often singled out as being chiefly concerned in the relationship. However, other parameters such as the cholesterol:phospholipid ratio, Sf 12–400 lipoprotein concentration, serum triacylglycerol concentration, etc show similar correlations. Patients with arterial disease can have any one of the following abnormalities: (1) elevated concentrations of VLDL (mainly triacylglycerols), with normal concentrations of LDL (D = 1.019–1.063) containing chiefly cholesterol; (2) elevated low density lipoproteins (cholesterol) with normal VLDL (triacylglycerols); (3) elevation of both lipoprotein fractions (cholesterol plus triacylglycerols).

Atherosclerosis is characterized by the deposition of cholesteryl ester and other lipids in the connective tissue of the arterial walls. Diseases in which prolonged elevated levels of low and very low density lipoproteins occur in the blood (eg, diabetes mellitus, lipid nephrosis, hypothyroidism, and other conditions of hyperlipidemia) are often accompanied by premature or more severe atherosclerosis.

Experiments on the induction of atherosclerosis in animals indicate a wide species variation in susceptibility. The rabbit, pig, monkey, and man are species in which atherosclerosis can be induced by feeding cholesterol. The rat, dog, and cat are resistant. Thyroidectomy or treatment with thiouracil drugs will allow induction of atherosclerosis in the dog and rat. Low blood cholesterol is a characteristic of hyperthyroidism. However, hyperthyroidism is associated with an increased rate of cholesterol synthesis. The fall in level of plasma cholesterol may be due to an increased rate of turnover and excretion.

Of the factors which lower blood cholesterol, the substitution in the diet of polyunsaturated fatty acids for some of the saturated fatty acids has been the most intensely studied. Naturally occurring oils which are beneficial in lowering plasma cholesterol include peanut, cottonseed, corn, and soybean oil, whereas butterfat and coconut oil raise the level. Reference to Table 20–3 indicates the high proportion of linoleic acid in the first group of oils and its relative deficiency or absence in butterfat or coconut oil, respectively. The effect of the low-fat (ie, high-carbohydrate) diet in raising total plasma lipids is presumably due to stimulation of the synthesis of VLDL in the liver and possibly also to a reduction in rate of removal. Sucrose and fructose have a greater effect in raising blood lipids than other carbohydrates. A correlation between the increased consumption of sucrose and atherosclerosis has been demonstrated by Yudkin and Roddy.

The reason for the cholesterol lowering effect of polyunsaturated fatty acids is still not clear. However, several hypotheses have been advanced to explain the effect, including the stimulation of cholesterol excretion into the intestine and the stimulation of the oxidation of cholesterol to bile acids. It is possible that cholesteryl esters of polyunsaturated fatty acids are more rapidly metabolized by the liver and other tissues, which might enhance their rate of turnover and excretion. There is other evidence that the effect is largely due to a shift in distribution of cholesterol

Table 20–3. Typical fatty acid analyses of some fats of animal and plant origin.[*]
(All values in weight percentages of component fatty acids.)

	Saturated			Unsaturated		
	Palmitic	Stearic	Other	Oleic	Linoleic	Other
Animal fats						
Lard	29.8	12.7	1.0	47.8	3.1	5.6
Chicken	25.6	7.0	0.3	39.4	21.8	5.9
Butterfat	25.2	9.2	25.6	29.5	3.6	7.2
Beef fat	29.2	21.0	3.4	41.1	1.8	3.5
Vegetable oils						
Corn	8.1	2.5	0.1	30.1	56.3	2.9
Peanut	6.3	4.9	5.9	61.1	21.8	...
Cottonseed	23.4	1.1	2.7	22.9	47.8	2.1
Soybean	9.8	2.4	1.2	28.9	50.7	7.0†
Olive	10.0	3.3	0.6	77.5	8.6	...
Coconut	10.5	2.3	78.4	7.5	trace	1.3

[*]Reproduced from NRC Publication No. 575: *The Role of Dietary Fat in Human Health: A Report.* Food and Nutrition Board, National Academy of Sciences.
†Mostly linolenic acid.

from the plasma into the tissues. Recently, it has been demonstrated that saturated free fatty acids cause higher rates of secretion of VLDL by the perfused liver than do unsaturated free fatty acids. Also, saturated fatty acids cause the formation of smaller VLDL particles which contain relatively more cholesterol, and they are utilized by extrahepatic tissues at a slower rate than are larger particles. All of these tendencies may be regarded as atherogenic.

Additional factors considered to play a part in atherosclerosis include high blood pressure, obesity, lack of exercise, and soft as opposed to hard drinking water. Elevation of plasma free fatty acids will also lead to increased VLDL secretion by the liver, involving extra triacylglycerol and cholesterol output into the circulation. Factors leading to higher or fluctuating levels of free fatty acids include emotional stress, nicotine from cigarette smoking, coffee drinking, and partaking of few large meals rather than more continuous feeding. Premenopausal women appear to be protected against many of these deleterious factors.

When dietary measures fail to achieve reduced serum lipid levels, the use of hypolipidemic drugs may be resorted to. Several drugs are known which block the formation of cholesterol at various stages in the biosynthetic pathway. Many of these drugs have harmful effects, and it is now considered that direct interference with cholesterol synthesis is to be avoided. Sitosterol is a hypercholesterolemic agent which acts by blocking the esterification of cholesterol in the gastrointestinal tract, thereby reducing cholesterol absorption. Drugs which are considered to increase the fecal excretion of cholesterol and bile acids include dextrothyroxine (Choloxin), neomycin, and possibly clofibrate (Atromid S). On the other hand, cholestyramine (Cuemid, Questran) prevents the reabsorption of bile salts by combining with them, thereby increasing their fecal loss. Clofibrate may also act by inhibiting the secretion of VLDL by the liver or by inhibiting hepatic cholesterol synthesis. Other hypocholesterolemic drugs include nicotinic acid and estrogens.

Disorders of the Plasma Lipoproteins

A few individuals in the population exhibit inherited defects in their lipoproteins leading to the primary condition of either hypo- or hyperlipoproteinemia. Many others having defects such as diabetes mellitus, hypothyroidism, and atherosclerosis show abnormal lipoprotein patterns which are very similar to one or the other of the primary inherited conditions. By making particular use of the technic of paper electrophoresis, Fredrickson has characterized the various types of lipoproteinemias.

A. Hypolipoproteinemia:

1. Abetalipoproteinemia—This is a rare inherited disease characterized by absence of β-lipoprotein (LDL) in plasma. Most of the blood lipids are present in low concentrations—especially acylglycerols, which are virtually absent since no chylomicrons or pre-β-lipoproteins (VLDL) are formed. Both the intestine

and the liver accumulate acylglycerols.

2. Hypobetalipoproteinemia—In hypobetalipoproteinemia, LDL or β-lipoprotein concentration is between 10–50% of normal, but chylomicron formation occurs. It must be concluded that β-lipoprotein is essential for triacylglycerol transport.

3. Familial alphalipoprotein deficiency (Tangier disease)—In the homozygous individual, there is near absence of plasma HDL or α-lipoproteins and accumulation of cholesteryl esters in the tissues. There is no impairment of chylomicron formation or secretion of endogenous triacylglycerol by the liver. However, on electrophoresis, there is no pre-β-lipoprotein, but a broad β-band is found containing the endogenous triacylglycerol. This finding provides evidence that the normal pre-β-band contains α-lipoprotein. Although α-lipoprotein does not appear to be essential for acylglycerol transport, clearance from the plasma is slow when it is absent, the patients tending to develop hypertriacylglycerolemia.

B. Hyperlipoproteinemia:

1. Type I—Characterized by very slow clearing of chylomicrons from the circulation, leading to abnormally raised levels of chylomicrons. The condition is due to a deficiency of lipoprotein lipase. Pre-β-lipoproteins may be raised, but there is a decrease in α- and β-lipoproteins. Thus, the condition is fat induced. It may be corrected by reducing the quantity of fat in the diet, but high-carbohydrate diets lead to raised levels of pre-β-lipoproteins due to synthesis in the liver.

2. Type II—Characterized by hyperbetalipoproteinemia, which is associated with increased plasma total cholesterol. There may also be a tendency for the pre-β-lipoproteins to be elevated. Therefore, the patient may have somewhat elevated triacylglycerol levels but the plasma—as is not true in the other types of hyperlipoproteinemia—remains clear. Lipid deposition in the tissue (eg, xanthomas, atheromas) is common. A type II pattern may also arise as a secondary result of hypothyroidism. The disease appears to be associated with reduced rates of clearance of β-lipoprotein (LDL) from the circulation. Reduction of dietary cholesterol and saturated fats may be of use in treatment.

3. Type III—Characterized by an increase in both β- and pre-β-lipoproteins, causing hypercholesterolemia and hypertriacylglycerolemia. Most of the β-lipoproteins tend to be in the D > 1.006 fraction after ultracentrifugation. Xanthomas and atherosclerosis are again present. Treatment by weight reduction and high fat diets containing unsaturated fats and little cholesterol is recommended.

4. Type IV—Characterized by hyperprebetalipoproteinemia with associated high levels of endogenously produced triacylglycerol. Cholesterol levels rise in proportion to the hypertriacylglycerolemia, and glucose intolerance is frequently present. Both α- and β-lipoproteins are subnormal in quantity. This lipoprotein pattern is also commonly associated with maturity onset diabetes, obesity, and many other conditions, including alcoholism and the taking of progestational hormones. Treatment of primary type IV hyperlipoproteinemia is by weight reduction, replacement of much of the carbohydrate in the diet with unsaturated fat, low cholesterol diets, and with hypolipidemic agents.

5. Type V—The lipoprotein pattern is complex since both chylomicrons and pre-β-lipoproteins are elevated, causing both triacylglycerolemia and cholesterolemia. Concentrations of α- and β-lipoproteins are low. Xanthomas are frequently present, but the incidence of atherosclerosis is apparently not striking. Glucose tolerance is abnormal and frequently associated with obesity and diabetes. The reason for the condition, which is familial, is not clear. Treatment has consisted of weight reduction followed by a diet not too high in either carbohydrate or fat.

● ● ●

References

Ansell GB, Hawthorne JN, Dawson RMC (editors): *Form and Function of Phospholipids.* Elsevier, 1973.

Eisenberg S, Levy RI: Lipoprotein metabolism. Adv Lipid Res 13:1, 1975.

Felts JM, Itakura H, Crane RT: Biochem Biophys Res Commun 66:1467, 1975.

Florkin M, Stotz EH (editors): *Comprehensive Biochemistry.* Vol 18. Elsevier, 1970.

Fredrickson DS: Plasma lipoproteins and apolipoproteins. Harvey Lecturers 68:185, 1972–73.

Gardner RS, Mayes PA: Biochem Soc Trans 4:715, 1976.

Hamilton RL & others: J Clin Invest 58:667, 1976.

Jeanrenaud B, Hepp D (editors): *Adipose Tissue Regulation and Metabolic Functions.* Academic Press, 1970.

Morrisett JD, Jackson RL, Gotto AM: Lipoproteins: Structure and function. Annu Rev Biochem 44:183, 1975.

Neufeld EF, Lim TW, Shapiro LJ: Inherited disorders of lysosomal metabolism. Annu Rev Biochem 44:357, 1975.

Noel SP, Dolphin PJ, Rubinstein D: Biochem Biophys Res Commun 63:764, 1975.

Ramwell PW (editor): *The Prostaglandins.* Vol 1. Plenum Press, 1973.

Redgrave TG: J Clin Invest 49:465, 1970.

Renold AE, Cahill GF (editors): *Handbook of Physiology.* Section 5. American Physiological Society, 1965.

Samuelsson G & others: Prostaglandins. Annu Rev Biochem 44:669, 1975.

Wakil S (editor): *Lipid Metabolism.* Academic Press, 1970.

Various authors: Disorders characterized by evidence of abnormal lipid metabolism: Pages 493–856 in: *The Metabolic Basis of Inherited Disease,* 3rd ed. Stanbury JB, Wyngaarden JB, Fredrickson DS (editors). McGraw-Hill, 1972.

21 . . .
Regulation of Carbohydrate
& Lipid Metabolism

The concept of respiratory control of the rate of oxidation of substrate provides a mechanism for the orderly burning of fuel molecules by each individual cell. It explains, in terms of availability of ADP, why the metabolic fuel is not burned in an uncontrolled or explosive fashion but rather at just that precise rate necessary to provide the immediate energy requirements of the cell in the form of high-energy phosphate. For such a mechanism to function efficiently, a continual supply of substrate or respiratory fuel molecules must always be available. Regulation of the metabolic pathways which provide these fuel molecules is essential if the supply is to be maintained under the variety of nutritional, metabolic, and pathologic conditions that are encountered in vivo. The term **caloric homeostasis** has been given to this type of metabolic regulation. It involves provision of the special fuel needs of each tissue, including the making available of alternative fuels. It also involves transport of various fuels about the body together with mechanisms to control their concentration in the blood.

GENERAL PRINCIPLES OF REGULATION OF METABOLIC PATHWAYS

Regulation of the overall flux along a metabolic pathway is often concerned with the control of only one or perhaps 2 key reactions in the pathway, catalyzed by "regulatory enzymes." The physicochemical factors which control the rate of an enzyme-catalyzed reaction, eg, substrate concentration (see Chapter 6), are of primary importance in the control of the overall rate of a metabolic pathway. However, temperature and pH, factors that can influence enzyme activity, are held constant in warm-blooded vertebrates and have little regulatory significance.

Equilibrium & Nonequilibrium Reactions

In a reaction at equilibrium, the forward and reverse reactions take place at equal rates and there is therefore no net flux in either direction. Many reactions in metabolic pathways are of this type, ie, "equilibrium reactions":

$$A \leftrightarrow B \leftrightarrow C \leftrightarrow D$$

In vivo, under "steady state" conditions, there would probably be a net flux from left to right owing to continual supply of A and continual removal of D. Such a pathway could function, but there would be little scope for control of the flux via regulation of enzyme activity since an increase in activity would only serve to speed up attainment of the equilibrium.

In practice, there are invariably one or more "nonequilibrium" type reactions in a metabolic pathway, where the reactants are present in concentrations that are far from equilibrium. In attempting to reach equilibrium, large losses of free energy occur as heat, making this type of reaction essentially nonreversible, eg,

$$A \leftrightarrow B \overset{\text{Heat}}{\nearrow} C \leftrightarrow D$$

Nonequilibrium reaction

Such a pathway has both flow and direction and would exhaust itself if control were not exerted. The enzymes catalyzing nonequilibrium reactions are usually low in concentration and are subject to other controlling mechanisms. This is similar to the opening and shutting of a "one-way" valve, making it possible to control the net flow.

IDENTIFICATION OF NONEQUILIBRIUM REACTIONS & REGULATORY ENZYMES

Comparison of the Mass Action Ratio With the Equilibrium Constant

$$A + B \rightleftharpoons C + D$$

In the above reaction, the apparent equilibrium constant is given by

$$K' = \frac{[C]\,[D]}{[A]\,[B]}$$

If a reaction is near equilibrium, the mass action ratio, which is the actual ratio

$$\frac{[C] \ [D]}{[A] \ [B]}$$

as determined in the tissue, should be similar to K'. On the other hand, if the mass action ratio is very different from K', then it can be assumed that the reaction is displaced from equilibrium in the cell, ie, it is a "nonequilibrium" reaction.

Measurement of Maximum Enzyme Activities

As the nonequilibrium reactions are displaced from equilibrium because the enzyme that catalyzes the reaction is not sufficiently active to bring the concentration of the reactants to equilibrium, assay of the maximum activity of each of the enzymes in the pathway enables those enzymes of low activity to be identified. These would be expected to catalyze the nonequilibrium reactions and to be of regulatory potential.

Study of the Properties of the Isolated Enzyme

If it is possible to purify or isolate an enzyme, its properties with respect to possible activators or modifiers can be studied in vitro. It is then necessary to ascertain whether such factors operate in vivo.

METABOLIC CONTROL OF AN ENZYME-CATALYZED REACTION

A hypothetical metabolic pathway, A,B,C,D, is shown in Fig 21−1, in which reactions A ⟷ B and C ⟷ D are equilibrium reactions and B → C is a nonequilibrium reaction. The flux through such a pathway can be regulated by the availability of substrate A. This might depend on its supply from the blood and on its ability to permeate the cell membrane. The flux will also be determined by the efficiency of removal of the end product D and on the availability of cosubstrate or cofactors represented by X and Y.

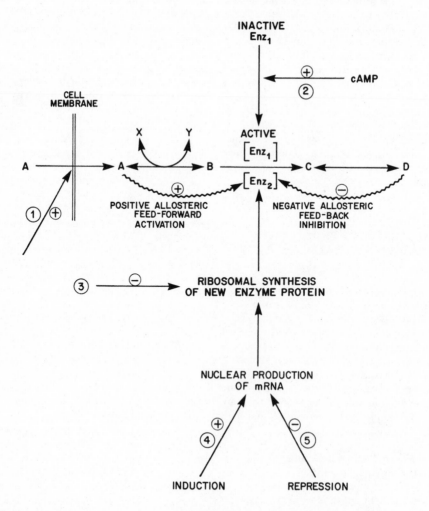

Figure 21−1. Possible mechanisms of control of an enzyme catalyzed reaction. Circled numbers indicate possible sites of action of hormones.

Enzymes catalyzing nonequilibrium reactions are often allosteric proteins subject to the action of "feedback" or "feed-forward" control by allosteric modifiers. Other control mechanisms depend on the action of hormones. These act by several different mechanisms. One, which is rapid, is mediated through the formation of cAMP, which in turn causes the conversion of an inactive enzyme into an active enzyme. This change is brought about via the activity of a protein kinase which phosphorylates the enzyme. The active form of the enzyme can be either the phosphorylated enzyme (eg, phosphorylase a) or the dephosphorylated enzyme (eg, glycogen synthetase I).

The synthesis of rate-controlling enzymes can be affected by hormones. Because this involves new protein synthesis, it is not a rapid change but is often a response to a change in nutritional state. Hormones can act as inducers or repressors of mRNA formation in the nucleus or as stimulators of the translation stage of protein synthesis at the ribosomal level.

THE REGULATION OF CARBOHYDRATE METABOLISM

It is convenient to divide the regulation of carbohydrate metabolism into 2 parts: (1) the regulation of carbohydrate metabolism at the cellular and enzymatic level, and (2) factors affecting the blood glucose. However, this is an arbitrary division as the 2 parts are functionally related.

REGULATION OF CARBOHYDRATE METABOLISM AT THE CELLULAR & ENZYMATIC LEVEL

Gross effects on metabolism of changes in nutritional state or in the endocrine balance of an animal may be studied by observing changes in the concentration of blood metabolites. By such technics as catheterization, it is also possible to study effects on individual organs by measuring arteriovenous differences, etc. However, the changes which occur in the metabolic balance of the intact animal are due to shifts in the pattern of metabolism in individual tissues which are usually associated with changes in availability of metabolites or changes in activity of key enzymes.

Changes in availability of substrates are either directly or indirectly responsible for most changes in metabolism. The concentration of glucose, fatty acids, and amino acids in blood influences their rate and pattern of metabolism in many tissues. Fluctuations in their blood concentrations due to changes in dietary availability may alter the rate of secretion of hormones which influence, in turn, the pattern of metabolism in metabolic pathways—often by affecting the activity of key enzymes which attempt to compensate for the original change in substrate availability. Three types of mechanisms can be identified as responsible for regulating the activity of enzymes concerned in carbohydrate metabolism: (1) changes in the rate of enzyme synthesis, (2) conversion of an inactive to an active enzyme, and (3) allosteric effects.

Some of the better-documented changes in enzyme activity that are considered to occur under various metabolic conditions are listed in Table 21–1. The information in this table applies mainly to the liver. The enzymes involved catalyze nonequilibrium reactions which may be regarded physiologically as "one way" rather than balanced reactions. Often the effect is reinforced because, invariably, the activity of the enzyme catalyzing the change in the opposite direction varies reciprocally. Thus, glucokinase catalyzes the conversion of glucose to glucose 6-phosphate. In the same compartment of the cell (the extramitochondrial region) is found glucose-6-phosphatase, the enzyme catalyzing the reaction in the reverse direction. Under conditions of a plentiful supply of carbohydrate, glucokinase activity is high whereas glucose-6-phosphatase activity is depressed. In starvation, glucokinase activity falls relative to glucose-6-phosphatase activity. In this way a so-called "futile cycle" whose net result would be hydrolysis of ATP is minimized. However, it appears that some recycling does occur at the glucokinase/glucose-6-phosphatase locus which may have the physiologic advantage of allowing large changes in net flux of metabolites in either direction, controlled by substrate concentration only. It is also of importance that the key enzymes involved in a metabolic pathway are all activated or depressed in a coordinated manner. Table 21–1 shows that this is clearly the case. The enzymes involved in the utilization of glucose are all activated under the circumstance of a superfluity of glucose, and under these conditions the enzymes responsible for producing glucose by the pathway of gluconeogenesis are all low in activity. It has been proposed by Weber that the coordination is achieved because the synthesis of a group of enzymes is controlled by the same functional genetic unit. Glucocorticoid hormones function as inducers, and insulin acts as a suppressor (repressor) of the biosynthesis of key hepatic gluconeogenic enzymes. Insulin is able to prevent induction of new enzymes by glucocorticoids; on the other hand, glucocorticoids have no effect on the activity of glycolytic enzymes which are sensitive to induction by insulin. Thus, according to this view, the secretion of insulin, which is responsive to the blood glucose concentration, controls the activity both of the enzymes responsible for glycolysis and those responsible for gluconeogenesis. All of these effects, which can be explained on the basis of new enzyme synthesis, can be prevented by agents which block the synthesis of new protein, such as actinomycin D, puromycin, and ethionine.

Both dehydrogenases of the hexose monophos-

Table 21–1. Regulatory and adaptive enzymes of the rat (mainly liver).

	Activity In		Inducer	Repressor	Activator	Inhibitor
	Carbo-hydrate Feeding	Starva-tion and Diabetes				[* = allosteric]
Enzymes of glycolysis and glycogenesis						
Glucokinase	↑	↓	Insulin			
Glycogen synthetase system	↑	↓	Insulin			cAMP, phosphorylase Glycogen
Phosphofructokinase	↑	↓	Insulin		*cAMP, *AMP, *fructose 6-P, *P_i, *fructose 1,6-bisphosphate	*Citrate (fatty acids, ketone bodies), *ATP
Pyruvate kinase	↑	↓	Insulin, fructose		*Fructose 1,6-bisphosphate	ATP, alanine
Pyruvate dehydrogenase	↑	↓			CoA, NAD, insulin, ADP, pyruvate	Acetyl-CoA, NADH ATP
Enzymes of gluconeogenesis						
Pyruvate carboxylase	↓	↑	Glucocorticoids, glucagon, epinephrine	Insulin	*Acetyl-CoA	*ADP
Phosphoenolpyruvate carboxykinase	↓	↑	Glucocorticoids	Insulin		
Fructose-1,6-bisphosphatase	↓	↑	Glucocorticoids, glucagon, epinephrine	Insulin		*Fructose 1,6-bisphosphate, *AMP
Glucose-6-phosphatase	↓	↑	Glucocorticoids, glucagon, epinephrine	Insulin		
Enzymes of the hexose monophosphate shunt and lipogenesis						
Glucose-6-phosphate dehydrogenase	↑	↓	Insulin			
6-Phosphogluconate dehydrogenase	↑	↓	Insulin			
"Malic enzyme"	↑	↓	Insulin			
ATP-citrate lyase	↑	↓	Insulin			ADP
Acetyl-CoA carboxylase	↑	↓	Insulin?		*Citrate	Long chain acyl-CoA
Fatty acid synthetase	↑	↓	Insulin?			

phate pathway can be classified as adaptive enzymes since they increase in activity in the well-fed animal and when insulin is given to a diabetic animal. Activity is low in diabetes or fasting. "Malic enzyme" and ATP-citrate lyase behave similarly, indicating that these 2 enzymes are probably involved in lipogenesis rather than gluconeogenesis (see Chapter 20).

In addition to phosphorylase and glycogen synthetase cited in Chapter 19 as examples of the second method of controlling enzyme activity (ie, conversion of an inactive to an active form of an enzyme), it has recently been shown that pyruvate dehydrogenase may exist in a phosphorylated as well as a dephosphorylated form. Thus, this enzyme may be regulated by phosphorylation involving an ATP-specific kinase which causes a decrease in activity, and by dephosphorylation by a phosphatase which causes an increase in activity of the dehydrogenase. The kinase is activated by increases in the [acetyl-CoA]/[CoA], [NADH]/[NAD], or [ATP]/[ADP] ratios. Thus pyruvate dehydrogenase and therefore glycolysis is inhibited under conditions of fatty acid oxidation or a surfeit of ATP (Fig 21–2). An increase in activity occurs after administration of fructose and insulin and a decrease occurs in starvation.

Several examples are available from carbohydrate

metabolism to illustrate the third method of control of the effective activity of an enzyme. The synthesis of oxaloacetate from bicarbonate and pyruvate, catalyzed by the enzyme **pyruvate carboxylase**, requires the presence of acetyl-CoA. The addition of acetyl-CoA results in a change in the tertiary structure of the protein, lowering the K_m value for bicarbonate. This effect has important implications for the self-regulation of intermediary metabolism, for, as acetyl-CoA is formed from pyruvate, it automatically ensures the provision of oxaloacetate and its further oxidation in the citric acid cycle by activating pyruvate carboxylase. The activation of pyruvate carboxylase by acetyl-CoA formed from the oxidation of fatty acids helps to explain the sparing action of fatty acid oxidation on the oxidation of pyruvate and the effect of free fatty acids in promoting gluconeogenesis in the liver (Fig 21–3). It is possible that the gluconeogenic effect of glucagon may be mediated via increased formation of cAMP, which in turn causes lipolysis and increased availability of fatty acids for oxidation of acetyl-CoA in the liver. The acetyl-CoA finally activates pyruvate carboxylase and gluconeogenesis. However, probably the main role of fatty acid oxidation in promoting gluconeogenesis is to supply energy in the form of ATP and reduced NAD (NADH). It is probable

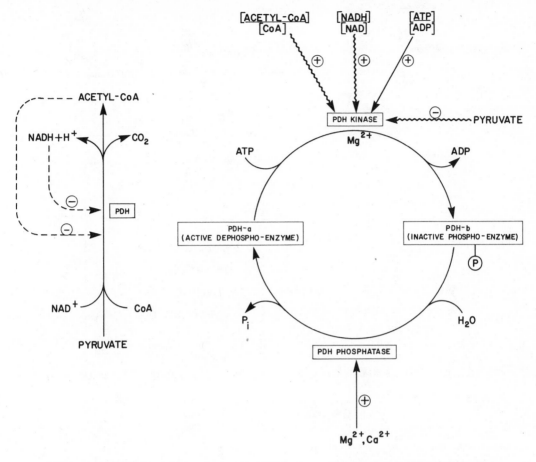

Figure 21—2. Regulation of pyruvate dehydrogenase (PDH). Arrows with wavy shafts indicate allosteric effects.

that the major effect of cAMP in promoting gluconeogenesis is by stimulating the flux of substrates between pyruvate and phosphoenolpyruvate.

Another enzyme which is subject to feedback control is **phosphofructokinase**. It occupies a key position in regulating glycolysis. Phosphofructokinase is inhibited by citrate and by ATP and is activated by AMP. The presence of **adenylate kinase** in liver allows rapid equilibration of the reaction: ATP + AMP ⇌ 2 ADP. Thus, when ATP is used in energy-requiring processes resulting in formation of ADP, the concentration of AMP rises. As the concentration of ATP may be 50 times that of AMP at equilibrium, a small fractional decrease in [ATP] will cause a several-fold increase in [AMP]. Thus, a large change in [AMP] acts as a metabolic amplifier of a small change in [ATP] This mechanism may allow the activity of phosphofructokinase to be highly sensitive to even small changes in energy status of the cell and may control the quantity of carbohydrate undergoing glycolysis prior to its entry into the citric acid cycle. The inhibition of phosphofructokinase by citrate and ATP could explain the sparing action of fatty acid oxidation on glucose oxidation and also the Pasteur effect whereby aerobic oxidation (via the citric acid cycle) inhibits the

anaerobic degradation of glucose. The inhibition by ATP and citrate and activation by AMP would also explain how the total quantity of carbohydrate undergoing oxidation is adjusted to fit the requirements of the tissue. A consequence of the inhibition of phosphofructokinase is an accumulation of glucose 6-phosphate which, in turn, inhibits further uptake of glucose by allosteric inhibition of hexokinase. In addition, the inhibition of pyruvate dehydrogenase by NADH and acetyl-CoA also reinforces the control of oxidation of carbohydrate at the phosphofructokinase step. There appears to be a reciprocal relationship between the regulation of pyruvate dehydrogenase and pyruvate carboxylase in both liver and kidney which alters the metabolic fate of pyruvate as the tissue changes from carbohydrate oxidation, via glycolysis, to gluconeogenesis. The reciprocal relationship in activities between phosphofructokinase and fructose-1,6-bisphosphatase in liver and the various factors affecting their activity (Table 21—1) with respect to the control of glycolysis and gluconeogenesis have been discussed by Newsholme & Start (1973).

Regulation of Glycogen Metabolism

Regulation of glycogen metabolism is effected by

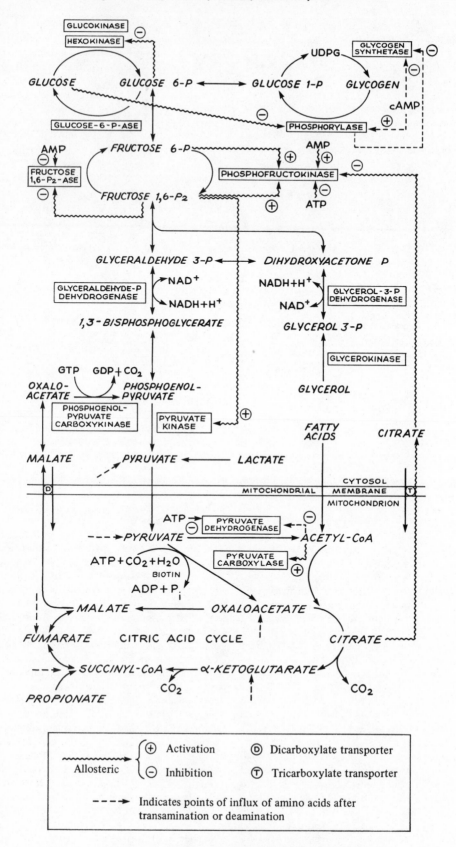

Figure 21–3. Key enzymes in the control of glycolysis and gluconeogenesis in liver.

a balance in activities between the enzymes of glycogen synthesis and of breakdown which are under substrate (through allosteric activity) as well as hormonal control. Not only is phosphorylase activated by a rise in concentration of cAMP, but glycogen synthetase is at the same time converted to the inactive form (see Chapter 19). Thus, breakdown and synthesis of glycogen do not occur simultaneously.

According to Hers (1976), the major factor that controls glycogen metabolism in the liver is the concentration of phosphorylase a. Not only does this enzyme control the rate-limiting step in glycogenolysis; it also controls the activity of synthetase phosphatase and thereby controls glycogen synthesis (Fig 21—3). The inactivation of phosphorylase is stimulated by glucose and inhibited by 5'-AMP and glycogen. Several observations have suggested that catecholamines, including epinephrine, stimulate glycogenolysis by an additional mechanism not involving cAMP. cAMP-independent glycogenolysis is also caused by vasopressin and angiotensin. Administration of insulin causes an immediate inactivation of phosphorylase followed by activation of glycogen synthetase.

Regulation of the citric acid cycle is discussed in Chapter 18.

THE BLOOD GLUCOSE

Sources of Blood Glucose

A. From Carbohydrates of the Diet: Most carbohydrates in the diet form glucose, galactose, or fructose upon digestion. These are absorbed into the portal vein. Galactose and fructose are readily converted to glucose in the liver.

B. From Various Glucogenic Compounds Which Undergo Gluconeogenesis: These compounds fall into 2 categories—those which involve a direct net conversion to glucose without significant recycling, such as some amino acids and propionate; and those which are the products of the partial metabolism of glucose in certain tissues and which are conveyed to the liver and kidney, where they are resynthesized to glucose. Thus, lactate, formed by the oxidation of glucose in skeletal muscle and by erythrocytes, is transported to the liver and kidney where it re-forms glucose, which again becomes available via the circulation for oxidation in the tissues. This process is known as the **Cori cycle** or lactic acid cycle (Fig 21—4). Glycerol for the triacylglycerols of adipose tissue is derived initially from the blood glucose since free glycerol cannot be utilized readily for the synthesis of triacylglycerols in this tissue. Acylglycerols of adipose tissue are continually undergoing hydrolysis to form free glycerol, which diffuses out of the tissue into the blood. It is converted back to glucose by gluconeogenic mechanisms in the liver and kidney. Thus, a continuous cycle exists in which glucose is transported from the liver and kidney to adipose tissue and whence glycerol is returned to be synthesized into glucose by the liver and kidney.

It has been noted that, of the amino acids transported from muscle to the liver during starvation, alanine predominates. This has led to the postulation of a glucose-alanine cycle, as shown in Fig 21—4, which has the effect of cycling glucose from liver to muscle and alanine from muscle to liver, effecting a net transfer of amino nitrogen from muscle to liver and of free energy from liver to muscle. The energy required for the hepatic synthesis of glucose from pyruvate is derived from the oxidation of fatty acids.

C. From liver glycogen by glycogenolysis.

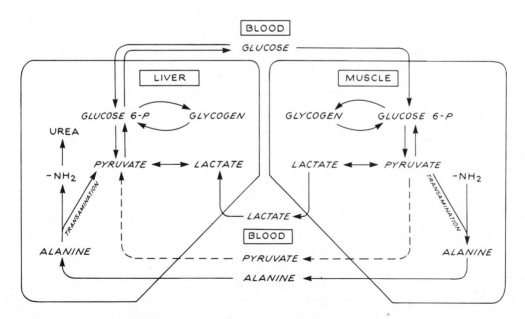

Figure 21—4. The lactic acid (Cori) cycle and glucose-alanine cycle.

The Concentration of the Blood Glucose

In the postabsorptive state the blood glucose concentration of man varies between 80 and 100 mg/100 ml. After the ingestion of a carbohydrate meal it may rise to 120–130 mg/100 ml. During fasting, the level falls to around 60–70 mg/100 ml. Under normal circumstances, the level is controlled within these limits. The normal blood glucose level of ruminants is considerably lower, being approximately 40 mg/100 ml in sheep and 60 mg/100 ml in cattle. These lower normal levels appear to be associated with the fact that ruminants ferment virtually all dietary carbohydrate to lower (volatile) fatty acids, and these largely replace glucose as the main metabolic fuel of the tissues in the fed condition.

Regulation of the Blood Glucose

The maintenance of stable levels of glucose in the blood is one of the most finely regulated of all homeostatic mechanisms and one in which the liver, the extrahepatic tissues, and several hormones play a part. Liver cells appear to be freely permeable to glucose whereas cells of extrahepatic tissues are relatively impermeable. This results in the passage through the cell membrane being the rate-limiting step in the uptake of glucose in extrahepatic tissues, whereas it is probable that the activity of certain enzymes and the concentration of key intermediates exert a much more direct effect on the uptake or output of glucose from liver. Nevertheless, the concentration of glucose in the blood is an important parameter in determining the rate of uptake of glucose in both liver and extrahepatic tissues. It is to be noted that hexokinase is inhibited by glucose 6-phosphate, so that some feedback control may be exerted on glucose uptake in extrahepatic tissues dependent on hexokinase for glucose phosphorylation. The liver is not subject to this constraint since glucokinase is not affected by glucose 6-phosphate. Glucokinase, which has a higher K_m for glucose than does hexokinase, seems to be specifically concerned with glucose uptake at the higher concentrations found in blood. Its absence in ruminants, which have low blood glucose concentrations, is compatible with this function.

At normal blood glucose concentrations (80–100 mg/100 ml), the liver appears to be a net producer of glucose. However, as the glucose level rises, the output of glucose ceases, and at high levels there is a net uptake. In the rat, it has been estimated that the rate of uptake of glucose and the rate of output are equal at a hepatic portal vein blood glucose concentration of 150 mg/100 ml. In dogs the blood glucose level at which there is net uptake by the liver varies with the type of diet. Thus, infusion of glucose into dogs maintained on a high-protein diet resulted in a rise in blood glucose, with a cessation of net hepatic glucose production only at hyperglycemic levels. In contrast, in carbohydrate-fed dogs, the blood glucose increased in concentration very little upon glucose infusion, and there was an immediate net uptake of glucose by the liver. An explanation of these differences due to changes in diet is probably to be found in changes in activity of enzymes in the liver concerned with glycolysis and gluconeogenesis.

In addition to the direct effects of hyperglycemia in enhancing the uptake of glucose into both the liver and peripheral tissues, the hormone **insulin** plays a central role in the regulation of the blood glucose concentration. It is produced by the beta cells of the islets of Langerhans in the pancreas and is secreted into the blood as a direct response to hyperglycemia. Its concentration in the blood parallels that of the blood glucose, and its administration results in prompt hypoglycemia. Substances causing release of insulin include amino acids, free fatty acids, ketone bodies, glucagon, secretin, and tolbutamide. Epinephrine and norepinephrine block the release of insulin. In vitro (and probably in vivo), insulin has an immediate effect on tissues such as adipose tissue and muscle in increasing the rate of glucose uptake. It is considered that this action is due to an enhancement of glucose transport through the cell membrane. In contrast, it is not easy to demonstrate an immediate effect of insulin on glucose uptake by liver tissue. This agrees with other findings which show that glucose penetration of hepatic cells is not rate-limited by their permeability. However, increased glucose uptake by liver slices can be demonstrated after administration of insulin in vivo, which indicates that other mechanisms are sensitive to the hormone. Perhaps the more unequivocal evidence that insulin does have a direct effect on glucose metabolism in the liver has been obtained in experiments with the isolated perfused liver where it has been demonstrated that insulin suppresses glucose production and diminishes oxidation of [U-^{14}C] glucose to $^{14}CO_2$.

The **anterior pituitary gland** secretes hormones that tend to elevate the blood sugar and therefore antagonize the action of insulin. These are growth hormone, ACTH (corticotropin), and possibly other "diabetogenic" principles. Growth hormone secretion is stimulated by hypoglycemia. Growth hormone decreases glucose uptake in certain tissues, eg, muscle. Some of this effect may not be direct since it mobilizes free fatty acids from adipose tissue which themselves inhibit glucose utilization. Chronic administration of growth hormone leads to diabetes. By producing hyperglycemia it stimulates secretion of insulin, eventually causing beta cell exhaustion. Although ACTH could have an indirect effect upon glucose utilization, since it enhances the release of free fatty acids from adipose tissue, its major effect on carbohydrate metabolism is due to its stimulation of the secretion of hormones of the adrenal cortex.

The **adrenal cortex** secretes a number of steroid hormones of which the glucocorticoids (11-oxysteroids) are important in carbohydrate metabolism. Upon administration, the glucocorticoids lead to gluconeogenesis. This is as a result of increased protein catabolism in the tissues, increased hepatic uptake of amino acids, and increased activity of transaminases and other enzymes concerned with gluconeogenesis in the liver. In addition, glucocorticoids inhibit the utilization of glucose in extrahepatic tissues. In all these actions, glucocorticoids act in an antagonistic manner to insulin.

Epinephrine, as secreted by the adrenal medulla, stimulates glycogen breakdown in muscle. However, administration of epinephrine leads to an outpouring of glucose from the liver provided glycogen is present. In muscle, as a result of the absence of glucose-6-phosphatase, glycolysis ensues with the formation of lactate. The lactate which diffuses into the blood is converted by the gluconeogenic mechanisms back to glycogen in the liver (Cori cycle). The stimulation of glycogenolysis by epinephrine is due to its ability to activate the enzyme phosphorylase. Hypoglycemia causes a sympathetic discharge. The increased epinephrine secretion stimulates glycogenolysis, which is followed by a rise in the level of blood glucose.

Glucagon is the hormone produced by the alpha cells of the islets of Langerhans of the pancreas. Its secretion is stimulated by hypoglycemia, and, when it reaches the liver (via the portal vein), it causes glycogenolysis by activating phosphorylase in a manner similar to epinephrine. Most of the endogenous glucagon is cleared from the circulation by the liver. Unlike epinephrine, glucagon does not have an action on muscle phosphorylase. Glucagon also enhances gluconeogenesis from amino acids and lactate.

Thyroid hormone should also be considered as affecting the blood sugar. There is experimental evidence that thyroxine has a diabetogenic action and that thyroidectomy inhibits the development of diabetes. It has also been noted that there is a complete absence of glycogen from the livers of thyrotoxic animals. In humans, the fasting blood sugar is elevated in hyperthyroid patients and decreased in hypothyroid patients. However, hyperthyroid patients apparently utilize glucose at a normal rate, whereas hypothyroid patients have a decreased ability to utilize glucose. In addition, hypothyroid patients are much less sensitive to insulin than normal or hyperthyroid individuals. All of these effects of thyroid hormone on carbohydrate metabolism may be related to differences in end organ response, rates of destruction of insulin, or both.

The Renal Threshold for Glucose

When the blood sugar rises to relatively high levels, the kidney also exerts a regulatory effect. Glucose is continually filtered by the glomeruli but is ordinarily returned completely to the blood by the reabsorptive system of the renal tubules. The reabsorption of glucose is effected by phosphorylation in the tubular cells, a process which is similar to that responsible for the absorption of this sugar from the intestine. The phosphorylation reaction is enzymatically catalyzed, and the capacity of the tubular system to reabsorb glucose is limited by the concentration of the enzymatic components of the tubule cell to a rate of about 350 mg/minute. When the blood levels of glucose are elevated, the glomerular filtrate may contain more glucose than can be reabsorbed; the excess passes

into the urine to produce **glycosuria**.

In normal individuals, glycosuria occurs when the venous blood sugar exceeds 170–180 mg/100 ml. This level of the venous blood sugar is termed the **renal threshold** for glucose. Since the maximal rate of reabsorption of glucose by the tubule (Tm_G—the tubular maximum for glucose) is a constant, it is a more accurate measurement than the renal threshold, which varies with changes in the glomerular filtration rate.

Glycosuria may be produced in experimental animals with phlorhizin, which inhibits the glucose reabsorptive system in the tubule. This is known as **renal glycosuria** since it is caused by a defect in the renal tubule and may occur even when blood glucose levels are normal. Glycosuria of renal origin is also found in human subjects. It may result from inherited defects in the kidney (see Chapter 35), or it may be acquired as a result of disease processes.

Carbohydrate Tolerance

The ability of the body to utilize carbohydrates may be ascertained by measuring its **carbohydrate tolerance**. It is indicated by the nature of the blood glucose curve following the administration of glucose. **Diabetes mellitus** ("sugar" diabetes) is characterized by decreased tolerance to carbohydrate due to decreased secretion of insulin. This is manifested by elevated blood glucose levels (hyperglycemia) and glycosuria and may be accompanied by changes in fat metabolism. Tolerance to carbohydrate is decreased not only in diabetes but also in conditions where the liver is damaged, in some infections, in obesity, and sometimes in atherosclerosis. It would also be expected to occur in the presence of hyperactivity of the pituitary or adrenal cortex because of the antagonism of the hormones of these endocrine glands to the action of insulin.

Insulin, the hormone of the islets of Langerhans of the pancreas, increases tolerance to carbohydrate. Injection of insulin lowers the content of the glucose in the blood and increases its utilization and its storage in the liver and muscle as glycogen. An excess of insulin may lower the blood glucose level to such an extent that severe hypoglycemia occurs which results in convulsions and even in death unless glucose is administered promptly. In man, hypoglycemic convulsions may occur when the blood glucose is lowered to about 20 mg/100 ml or less. Increased tolerance to carbohydrate is also observed in pituitary or adrenocortical insufficiency; presumably this is attributable to a decrease in the normal antagonism to insulin which results in a relative excess of that hormone.

Measurement of Glucose Tolerance

The glucose tolerance test is a valuable diagnostic aid. Glucose tolerance (ability to utilize carbohydrate) is decreased in diabetes and increased in hypopituitarism, hyperinsulinism, and adrenocortical hypofunction (such as in Addison's disease).

A. Standard Oral Glucose Tolerance Test: After

an overnight fast of 12 hours, the patient is given 0.75–1.5 g of glucose/kg (or a standard dose of between 50 and 100 g of glucose may be used). Specimens of blood and urine are taken before the administration of glucose and at intervals of one-half or 1 hour thereafter for 3–4 hours. The concentration of glucose in the blood is measured and plotted against time. As a result of the administration of glucose as described, the blood glucose in normal individuals increases in 1 hour from about 80 mg/100 ml to about 130 mg/100 ml; at the end of 2–2½ hours, a return to normal levels occurs. In a diabetic patient, the increase in the blood glucose level is greater than in normal subjects and a much slower return to the pre-test level is observed; ie, the glucose tolerance curve is typically higher and more prolonged than normal.

B. Intravenous Glucose Tolerance Test: An intravenous test is preferred if abnormalities in absorption of glucose from the intestine, as might occur in hypothyroidism or in sprue, are suspected. A 20% solution of glucose (0.5 g/kg) is given intravenously at a uniform rate over a period of one-half hour. A control (fasting) blood specimen is taken, and additional blood samples are obtained one-half, 1, 2, 3, and 4 hours after the glucose injection. In normal individuals, the control specimen of blood contains a normal amount

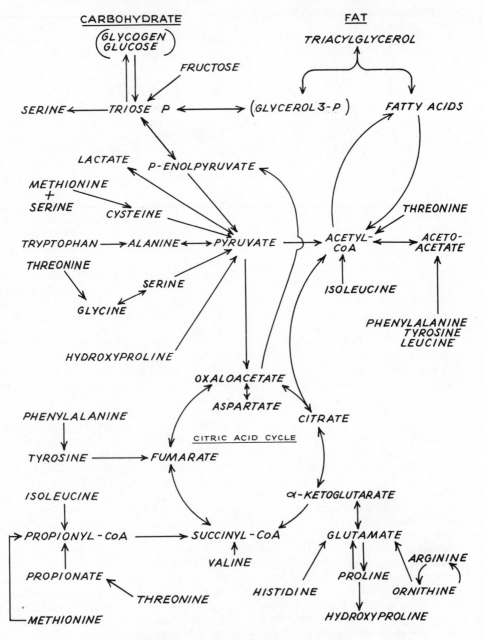

Figure 21–5. Interconversion of the major foodstuffs.

of glucose; the concentration does not exceed 250 mg/100 ml after the infusion has been completed; by 2 hours the concentration of glucose in the blood has fallen below the control level, and between the third and fourth hours it has returned to the normal fasting level.

C. Corticosteroid Tests: Administration of corticosteroids (eg, prednisone) causes glucose intolerance. This property has been utilized to detect latent diabetes.

Interconversion of Major Foodstuffs
(See Fig 21–5.)

That animals may be fattened on a predominantly carbohydrate diet demonstrates the ease of conversion of carbohydrate into fat. A most significant reaction in this respect is the conversion of pyruvate to acetyl-CoA, as acetyl-CoA is the starting material for the synthesis of long-chain fatty acids. However, the pyruvate dehydrogenase reaction is essentially non-reversible, which prevents the direct conversion of acetyl-CoA, formed from the oxidation of fatty acids, to pyruvate. There cannot be a net conversion of acetyl-CoA to oxaloacetate via the citric acid cycle since one molecule of oxaloacetate is required to condense with acetyl-CoA and only one molecule of oxaloacetate is regenerated. For similar reasons, there cannot be a net conversion of fatty acids having an even number of carbon atoms (which form acetyl-CoA) to glucose or glycogen.

Only the terminal 3-carbon portion of a fatty acid having an odd number of carbon atoms is glycogenic, as this portion of the molecule will form propionate upon oxidation. Nevertheless, it is possible for labeled carbon atoms of fatty acids to be found ultimately in glycogen after traversing the citric acid cycle; this is because oxaloacetate is an intermediate both in the citric acid cycle and in the pathway of gluconeogenesis. Many of the carbon skeletons of the nonessential amino acids can be produced from carbohydrate via the citric acid cycle and transamination. By reversal of these processes, glycogenic amino acids yield carbon skeletons which are either members or precursors of the members of the citric acid cycle. They are therefore readily converted by gluconeogenic pathways to glucose and glycogen. The ketogenic amino acids give rise to acetoacetate, which will in turn be metabolized as ketone bodies, forming acetyl-CoA in extrahepatic tissues (see Chapter 20).

For the same reasons that it is not possible for a net conversion of fatty acids to carbohydrate to occur, it is not possible for a net conversion of fatty acids to glucogenic amino acids to take place. Neither is it possible to reverse the pathways of breakdown of ketogenic amino acids, all of which fall into the category of "essential amino acids." Conversion of the carbon skeletons of glucogenic amino acids to fatty acids is possible, either by formation of pyruvate and acetyl-CoA or by reversal of nonmitochondrial reactions of the citric acid cycle from α-ketoglutarate to citrate followed by the action of ATP-citrate lyase to give

acetyl-CoA (see Chapter 20). However, under most natural conditions, eg, starvation, a net breakdown of protein and amino acids is usually accompanied by a net breakdown of fat. The net conversion of amino acids to fat is therefore not a significant process except possibly in animals receiving a high-protein diet.

REGULATION OF FATTY ACID SYNTHESIS
(Lipogenesis)

Many animals, including man, take their food as spaced meals and therefore need to store much of the energy in their diet for use between meals. The process of lipogenesis is concerned with the conversion of glucose and intermediates such as pyruvate and acetyl-CoA to fat, which constitutes the anabolic phase of this cycle. The nutritional state of the organism and tissues is the main factor controlling the rate of lipogenesis. Thus, the rate is high in the well-fed animal whose diet contains a high proportion of carbohydrate. It is depressed under conditions of restricted caloric intake, on a high-fat diet, or when there is a deficiency of insulin, as in diabetes mellitus. All of these conditions are associated with increased concentrations of plasma free fatty acids. Evidence has now been provided that there is an inverse logarithmic relationship between lipogenesis and the concentration of free fatty acids perfusing the rat liver (Fig 21–6). The greatest inhibition of lipogenesis occurs over the range of free fatty acids (0.3–0.8 μmol/ml of plasma) through which the plasma free fatty acids increase during transition from the fed to the starved state. As little as 2.5% of fat in the diet causes a measurable depression of lipogenesis in the liver as measured by the incorporation of acetate carbon into fatty acids. Lipogenesis from ^{14}C-acetate is higher in livers from rats consuming all their food in 2 hours. It is also higher when sucrose is fed instead of glucose. Masoro and others showed that almost no ^{14}C-glucose was incorporated into fatty acids of liver slices from fasting rats, whereas its conversion to ^{14}CO$_2$ was unaltered, demonstrating a metabolic block in the pathway of synthesis between acetyl-CoA and fatty acids. Because of the close association between the activities of the hexose monophosphate shunt on the one hand and of the lipogenic pathway on the other, it was considered that the block in lipogenesis was due to lack of NADPH generation from the shunt pathway. However, subsequent work in which an NADPH-generating system was added to a liver homogenate from fasting rats failed to promote fatty acid synthesis.

At present it is recognized that the rate-limiting reaction in the lipogenic pathway is at the acetyl-CoA carboxylase step (Fig 20–4), and more than one factor has been described which regulates the activity of this enzyme. Long chain acyl-CoA molecules inhibit acetyl-CoA carboxylase, an example of metabolic negative

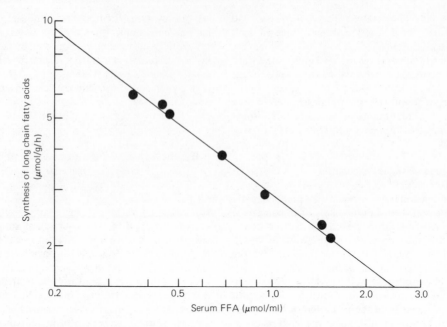

Figure 21–6. Direct inhibition of hepatic lipogenesis by free fatty acids. (Lipogenesis was determined from the incorporation of ^3H_2O into long chain fatty acids in the perfused rat liver. FFA = free fatty acids.)

feedback inhibition by a product of a reaction sequence inhibiting the initial reaction. Thus, if acyl-CoA accumulates because it is not esterified quickly enough, it will automatically damp down synthesis of new fatty acid. Likewise, if acyl-CoA accumulates as a result of increased lipolysis or an influx of free fatty acids into the tissue, this will also inhibit synthesis of new fatty acid.

Microsomes have a stimulatory effect on fatty acid synthesis when added to the extramitochondrial system present in the supernatant fraction of the cell. Since microsomes catalyze the esterification of acyl-CoA with glycerol 3-phosphate to form triacylglycerols and phospholipids, the mechanism of their stimulatory effect on fatty acid synthesis may be the removal of the feedback inhibition of acyl-CoA on acetyl-CoA carboxylase.

Acyl-CoA may also inhibit the mitochondrial tricarboxylate transporter, thus preventing egress of citrate from the mitochondria into the cytosol (Fig 20–4). There is also an inverse relationship between free fatty acids and the proportion of active to inactive pyruvate dehydrogenase. This would change the availability of citrate for lipogenesis.

Insulin stimulates lipogenesis by several possible mechanisms. It increases the transport of glucose into the cell (eg, in adipose tissue) and thereby increases the availability both of pyruvate and glycerol 3-phosphate. Several groups of investigators have shown that insulin may convert the inactive form of pyruvate dehydrogenase to the active form. There is also the possibility of a similar change occurring in acetyl-CoA carboxylase. Insulin, by its ability to depress the level of intracellular cAMP, inhibits lipolysis and thereby

reduces the concentration of long chain acyl-CoA, an inhibitor of lipogenesis.

Acetyl-CoA carboxylase is activated in an allosteric manner by citrate. However, whether citrate plays such a role in vivo is not clear. The inhibition to long chain acyl-CoA is competitive with citrate. Long chain acyl-CoA has also been reported to inhibit citrate formation at the citrate synthase step, essential in the pathway of fatty acid synthesis. It is also possible that oxidation of fatty acids—owing to increased levels of free fatty acids or to lack of insulin, allowing increased lipolysis of triacylglycerols—may increase the concentrations of acetyl-CoA/CoA and NADH/NAD$^+$ in mitochondria, inhibiting pyruvate dehydrogenase and thus blocking the supply of acetyl-CoA from carbohydrate via pyruvate.

Flatt has suggested that lipogenesis from glucose in adipose tissue is an energy-producing process and may be self-limiting because of respiratory control and availability of ADP. It is also clear that factors affecting the rate of glycolysis, which supplies acetyl-CoA for lipogenesis in nonruminants, must also exert an overall control on the process. In ruminants, acetate—not glucose—is the starting material for lipogenesis. It follows that, in these species, many of the control mechanisms discussed above are bypassed and thus do not apply.

Various reports indicate that both the fatty acid synthetase complex and acetyl-CoA carboxylase may be adaptive enzymes, increasing in total amount in the fed state and decreasing in fasting, feeding of fat, and diabetes. These effects on lipogenesis take several days to become fully manifested and augment the direct and immediate effect of free fatty acids (Fig 21–6).

REGULATION OF KETOGENESIS

In general, ketosis does not occur in vivo unless there is a concomitant rise in the level of circulating free fatty acids, severe ketosis being accompanied invariably by very high concentrations of plasma free fatty acids. In addition, numerous experiments in vitro have demonstrated that fatty acids are the precursors of ketone bodies. The liver, both in fed and in fasting conditions, has the ability to extract about 30% or more of the free fatty acids passing through it, so that at high concentrations of free fatty acids the flux passing into the liver is substantial. One of 2 fates awaits the free fatty acids upon uptake and after they are activated to acyl-CoA: (1) they are esterified to triacylglycerol, phospholipid, or cholesteryl ester; or (2) they are β-oxidized to acetyl-CoA (Fig 20–26). In turn, acetyl-CoA is oxidized in the citric acid cycle or used to form ketone bodies. Experiments with fasting rats have demonstrated that the magnitude of ketonemia is more directly related to the quantity of triacylglycerol present in the depots than to the quantity present in the liver, indicating that plasma free fatty acids (derived from the fat depots) are a more significant source of ketone bodies than fatty acids derived from lipolysis of liver triacylglycerol.

Among several possible factors, the capacity for esterification as an antiketogenic factor depends on the availability of precursors in the liver to supply sufficient glycerol 3-phosphate. The concentration of glycerol 3-phosphate in the livers of fasted rats is depressed when compared to that in fed animals. However, it was noted that the availability of glycerol 3-phosphate did not appear to limit esterification in fasting perfused livers, where, irrespective of the mass of free fatty acids taken up, a constant fraction was esterified. It has also been found in vivo that antiketogenic effects of glycerol and dihydroxyacetone are not correlated with the levels of glycerol 3-phosphate in the liver. Thus, whether the availability of glycerol 3-phosphate in the liver is ever rate-limiting on esterification is not clear; neither is there any information on whether the in vivo activities of the enzymes involved in esterification are rate-limiting.

Using the perfused liver, it has been shown that livers from fed rats esterify considerably more ^{14}C free fatty acids than livers from fasted rats, the balance not esterified in the livers from fasted rats being oxidized to either [14]CO_2 or ^{14}C ketone bodies. As the level of serum free fatty acids was raised, proportionately more of the free fatty acids were converted to ketone bodies and less were oxidized via the citric acid cycle to CO_2. The partition of acetyl-CoA between the ketogenic pathway and the pathway of oxidation of CO_2 was so regulated that the total energy production from free fatty acids (as ATP) remained constant. It will be appreciated that complete oxidation of 1 mol of palmitate involves a net production of 129 mol of ATP via CO_2 production in the citric acid cycle, whereas only 33 mol of ATP are produced when acetoacetate is the end product. Thus, ketogenesis may be regarded as a mechanism that allows the liver to oxidize large quantities of fatty acids within an apparently tightly coupled system of oxidative phosphorylation without increasing its total energy production.

Several hypotheses have been advanced to account for the diversion of fatty acid oxidation from CO_2 formation to ketogenesis. Theoretically, a fall in concentration of oxaloacetate, particularly within the mitochondria, could cause impairment of the citric acid cycle to metabolize acetyl-CoA. This has been considered to occur because of a decrease in ratio of $NAD^+/NADH$. Krebs has suggested that, since oxaloacetate is also on the main pathway of gluconeogenesis, enhanced gluconeogenesis leading to a fall in the level of oxaloacetate may be the cause of the severe forms of ketosis found in diabetes and the ketosis of cattle. Alternatively, it has been postulated that citrate synthase is inhibited, either by long chain acyl-CoA or by increased concentrations of ATP. Utter and Keech have shown that pyruvate carboxylase, which catalyzes the conversion of pyruvate to oxaloacetate, is activated by acetyl-CoA. Consequently, when there are significant amounts of acetyl-CoA, there should be sufficient oxaloacetate to initiate the condensing reaction of the citric acid cycle.

Evidence is accumulating which shows that lipolysis of liver triacylglycerols is under the control of a hormone-sensitive lipase, as in adipose tissue. This lipase is activated by increase in concentration of cAMP, which in turn is raised in concentration by the action of glucagon on adenylate cyclase and depressed by the presence of insulin. The combined action of these hormones may regulate lipolysis in the liver and, therefore, net esterification of free fatty acids. Thus, insulin and glucagon not only determine the rate of endogenous lipolysis but also affect the balance between esterification and oxidation of incoming plasma free fatty acids. Other recent evidence has indicated that when the redox state of the liver is more reduced (as it is in starvation), oxidation of fatty acids is enhanced and esterification is diminished. The increased [NADH]/[NAD] ratio present under these conditions may inhibit pyruvate dehydrogenase enabling more fatty acids to form acetyl-CoA.

In summary, ketosis arises as a result of a deficiency in available carbohydrate. This has 2 principal actions in fostering ketogenesis: (1) It causes an imbalance between esterification and lipolysis in adipose tissue, with consequent release of free fatty acids into the circulation. Free fatty acids are the principal substrates for ketone body formation in the liver, and therefore all factors, metabolic or endocrine, affecting the release of free fatty acids from adipose tissue influence ketogenesis. (2) Upon entry of free fatty acids into the liver, the balance between esterification and oxidation of free fatty acids is influenced by the hormonal state of the liver and possibly by the availability of glycerol 3-phosphate or by the redox state of the tissue. As the quantity of fatty acids presented for oxidation increases, more form ketone bodies and less form CO_2, regulated in such a manner that the total energy production remains constant. Ketone bodies are not oxidized significantly by the liver; they diffuse into the circulation whence they are extracted and oxidized by extrahepatic tissues preferentially to other fuels.

Ketosis in Vivo

The ketosis that occurs in starvation and fat feeding is relatively mild compared with the condition encountered in uncontrolled diabetes mellitus, pregnancy toxemia of ewes, ketosis of lactating cattle, or animals administered phlorhizin. The main reason appears to be that in the severe conditions carbohydrate is still less available to the tissues than in the mild conditions. Thus, in the milder forms of diabetes mellitus, in fat feeding, and in chronic starvation, glycogen is present in the liver in variable amounts, and free fatty acid levels are lower, which probably accounts for the less severe ketosis associated with these conditions. It is to be expected that the presence of glycogen in the liver is indicative of a greater capacity for esterification of fatty acids.

In ketosis of ruminants or in phlorhizin poisoning, there is a severe drain of glucose from the blood due to excessive fetal demands, the demands of heavy lactation, or impaired reabsorption by the kidney, respectively (Fig 21–7). Extreme hypoglycemia results, coupled with negligible amounts of glycogen in the liver. Ketosis in these conditions tends to be severe. As hypoglycemia develops, the secretion of insulin diminishes, allowing not only less glucose utilization in adipose tissue but also enhancement of lipolysis in adipose tissue and liver.

In diabetes mellitus, the lack (or relative lack) of insulin probably affects adipose tissue more than any other tissue because of its extreme sensitivity to this hormone. As a result, free fatty acids are released in quantities that give rise to plasma free fatty acid levels more than twice those in fasting normal subjects. Many changes also occur in the activity of enzymes within the liver which enhance the rate of gluconeogenesis and transfer of glucose to the blood despite high levels of circulating glucose.

THE ECONOMICS OF CARBOHYDRATE & LIPID METABOLISM IN THE WHOLE BODY

Many of the details of the interplay between carbohydrate and lipid metabolism in various tissues have been described. The conversion of glucose to fat is a process which occurs readily under conditions of optimal nutritional intake. With the exception of glycerol, fat (as fatty acids) cannot give rise to a net formation of glucose because of the irreversible nature of the oxidative decarboxylation of pyruvate to acetyl-CoA. Certain tissues, including the central nervous system

and the erythrocytes, are much more dependent upon a continual supply of glucose than others. A minimal supply of glucose is probably necessary in extrahepatic tissues to maintain the integrity of the citric acid cycle. In addition, glucose appears to be the main source of glycerol 3-phosphate in tissues devoid of glycerokinase. There is in all probability a minimal and obligatory rate of glucose oxidation. Large quantities of glucose are also required for the nutrition of the fetus and for the synthesis of milk, particularly in ruminants. Certain mechanisms operate which safeguard essential supplies of glucose in times of shortage, allowing other substrates to spare its general oxidation.

Randle and others have demonstrated that ketone bodies and free fatty acids spare the oxidation of glucose in muscle by impairing its entry into the cell, its phosphorylation to glucose 6-phosphate, the phosphofructokinase reaction, and the oxidative decarboxylation of pyruvate. Oxidation of free fatty acids and ketone bodies caused an increase in the concentration of intracellular citrate which in turn inhibited phosphofructokinase. These observations, taken with those of Olson, who demonstrated that acetoacetate was oxidized in the perfused heart preferentially to free fatty acids, justify the conclusion that under conditions of carbohydrate shortage available fuels are oxidized in the following order of preference: (1) ketone bodies (and probably other short chain fatty acids, eg, acetate), (2) free fatty acids, and (3) glucose. This does not imply that any particular fuel is oxidized to the total exclusion of any other.

These facts help to explain the experiments of several investigators who have shown in vivo that, under certain conditions, fat mobilization can be reduced after the administration of noncarbohydrate calorigenic substrates. For example, oral administration of fat reduces the level of circulating free fatty acids, and a similar result can be obtained in sheep after the administration of acetate. Fat mobilization and ketogenesis in rats on all-fat diets can be reduced substantially provided the quantity of fat ingested is increased to satisfy the caloric requirement of the animal. If substrates such as free fatty acids and ketone bodies spare the oxidation of glucose in muscle, more glucose will be available, causing a reduction in output of free fatty acids from adipose tissue (either directly or via stimulation of insulin secretion) and allowing the plasma level of free fatty acids to fall. As glucose is the fuel which is "burned last," it may be appreciated how adipose tissue is sensitive to a general deficiency in calorigenic substrates in the whole body through a mechanism based specifically on the availability of glucose. The combination of the effects of free fatty acids in sparing glucose utilization in muscle and heart and the effect of the spared glucose in inhibiting free fatty acid mobilization in adipose tissue has been called the "glucose-fatty acid cycle."

Starvation

On high-carbohydrate diets, free fatty acid oxidation is spared; it is generally considered that this is due

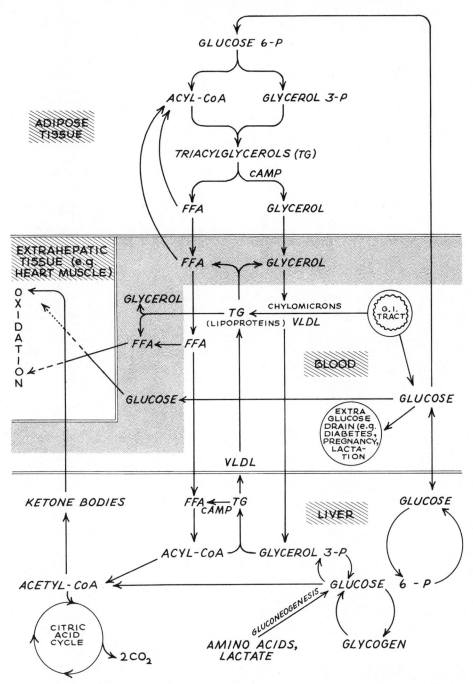

Figure 21—7. Metabolic interrelationships between adipose tissue, the liver, and extrahepatic tissues. (Stippled area, lipoprotein region of capillary wall; cAMP, cyclic AMP; FFA, free fatty acids; VLDL, very low density lipoproteins.)

to the high capacity in the tissues for esterification. As the animal passes from the fed to the fasting condition, glucose availability becomes less, liver glycogen being drawn upon in an attempt to maintain the blood glucose level. The level of insulin in the blood decreases, and glucagon rises. As glucose utilization diminishes in adipose tissue and the inhibitory effect of insulin on adipose tissue lipolysis becomes less, fat is mobilized as free fatty acids and glycerol. The free fatty acids are esterified in other tissues, particularly the liver, and the remainder are oxidized. Glycerol joins the carbohydrate pool after activation to glycerol 3-phosphate, mainly in the liver and kidney. During this transition phase from the fully fed to the fully fasting state, endogenous glucose production (from amino acids and glycerol) does not keep pace with its utilization and oxidation since the liver glycogen stores become depleted and blood glucose tends to fall. Thus, fat is mobilized at an ever increasing rate, but in several hours the free fatty acids and blood glucose stabilize at the fasting level. At this point it must be presumed that in the whole animal the supply of glucose balances the obligatory demands for glucose utilization and oxidation. This is achieved by the increased oxidation of free fatty acids and ketone bodies, sparing the non-obligatory oxidation of glucose. This fine balance is disturbed in conditions which demand more glucose or in which glucose utilization is impaired and which therefore lead to further mobilization of fat. The provision of carbohydrate by adipose tissue, in the form of glycerol, is probably as important a function as the provision of free fatty acids, for it is only this source of carbohydrate together with that provided by gluconeogenesis from protein which can supply the fasting organism with the glucose needed for those processes which must utilize glucose. In prolonged starvation in man, gluconeogenesis from protein is diminished due to reduced release of amino acids, particularly alanine, from muscle, the principal protein store. This coincides with adaptation of the brain to utilize ketone bodies in place of glucose.

A feedback mechanism for controlling free fatty acid output from adipose tissue in starvation may operate as a result of the action of ketone bodies and free fatty acids to directly stimulate the pancreas to produce insulin. Under most conditions, free fatty acids are mobilized in excess of oxidative requirements since a large proportion is esterified, even during fasting. As the liver takes up and esterifies a considerable proportion of the free fatty acid output, it plays a regulatory role in removing excess free fatty acids from the circulation. When carbohydrate supplies are adequate, most of the influx is esterified and ultimately retransported from the liver as VLDL to be utilized by other tissues. However, in the face of an increased influx of free fatty acids, an alternative route, ketogenesis, is available which enables the liver to continue to retransport much of the influx of free fatty acids in a form that is readily utilized by extrahepatic tissues under all nutritional conditions.

Most of these principles are depicted in Fig 21–7. It will be noted that there is a carbohydrate cycle involving release of glycerol from adipose tissue and its conversion in the liver to glucose, followed by its transport back to adipose tissue to complete the cycle. The other cycle, a lipid cycle, involves release of free fatty acids by adipose tissue, its transport to and esterification in the liver, and retransport as VLDL back to adipose tissue. Disturbances in carbohydrate or lipid metabolism often involve these 2 interrelated cycles where they interact in adipose tissue and in the liver. The role of cAMP and its hormonal control in these processes is particularly noteworthy.

● ● ●

References

Davies DD (editor): *Rate Control of Biological Processes.* Cambridge Univ Press, 1973.

Hers HG: The control of glycogen metabolism in the liver. Annu Rev Biochem 45:167, 1976.

Newsholme EA, Start C: *Regulation in Metabolism.* Wiley, 1973.

Söling HD, Willms B (editors): *Regulation of Gluconeogenesis.* Thieme, 1971.

22...
Catabolism of Amino Acids

AMINO ACID METABOLISM

The broad subject area of amino acid metabolism includes several major topics of both basic and medical interest. These include protein synthesis and degradation, conversion of the carbon skeletons of the amino acids to amphibolic intermediates, urea synthesis, and the formation of a wide variety of physiologically active compounds such as serotonin. This concept is diagrammed in Fig 22–1.

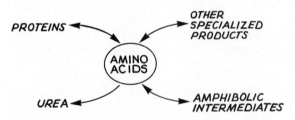

Figure 22–1. Outline of amino acid metabolism. All the indicated processes except urea formation proceed reversibly in intact cells. However, the catalysts and intermediates in biosynthetic and degradative processes frequently differ.

In this chapter, we shall consider how nitrogen is removed from amino acids and is converted to urea, by what reactions the carbon skeletons of the amino acids are converted to intermediates of amphibolic pathways, and the medical problems that arise when there are defects in these reactions.

NITROGEN CATABOLISM OF AMINO ACIDS

Overall View

In mammalian tissues the a-amino groups of amino acids, derived either from the diet or from breakdown of tissue proteins, ultimately are excreted in the urine as urea. The biosynthesis of urea involves the action of several enzymes. It may conveniently be divided for discussion into 4 processes: (1) transamination, (2) oxidative deamination, (3) ammonia transport, and (4) reactions of the urea cycle.

The relationship of these areas to the overall catabolism of amino acid nitrogen is shown in Fig 22–2. Vertebrates other than mammals share all features of this scheme except urea synthesis. Urea, the characteristic end product of amino acid nitrogen metabolism in man and other ureotelic organisms, is replaced by uric acid in uricotelic organisms (eg, reptiles and birds) or by ammonia in ammonotelic organisms (eg, bony fish).

Each of the above 4 processes will now be considered in detail. Although each also plays a role in amino acid biosynthesis (see Chapter 23), what follows is first discussed from the viewpoint of amino acid catabolism.

Transamination

Transamination, catalyzed by enzymes termed **transaminases** or **aminotransferases**, involves interconversion of a pair of amino acids and a pair of keto acids. These generally are a-amino and a-keto acids (Fig 22–3).

Pyridoxal phosphate, the coenzyme form of vitamin B_6, forms an essential part of the active site of

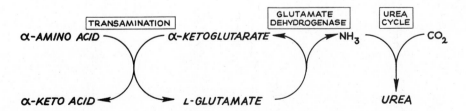

Figure 22–2. Overall flow of nitrogen in amino acid catabolism. Although the reactions shown are reversible, they are represented as being unidirectional to emphasize the direction of metabolic flow in mammalian amino acid catabolism.

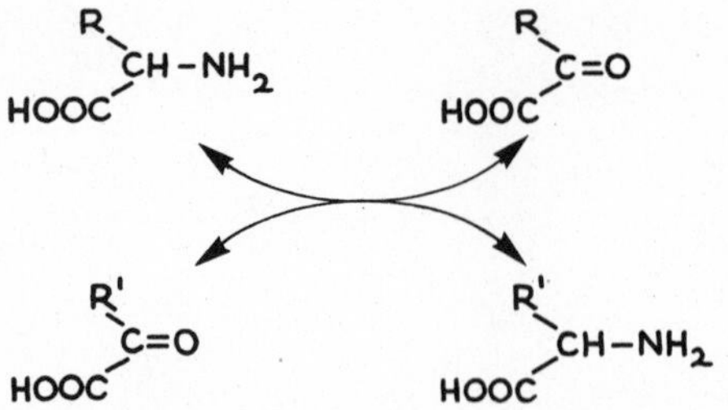

Figure 22–3. Transamination. The reaction is shown for 2 *α*-amino and 2 *α*-keto acids. Non-*α*-amino or carbonyl groups also participate in transamination, although this is relatively uncommon. The reaction is freely reversible with an equilibrium constant of about 1.

transaminases and of many other enzymes with amino acid substrates. In all pyridoxal phosphate-dependent reactions of amino acids, the initial step is formation of an enzyme-bound Schiff base intermediate (Fig 22–4).

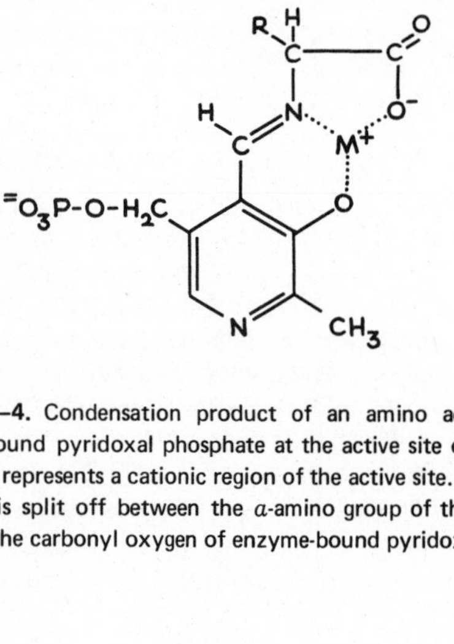

Figure 22–4. Condensation product of an amino acid with enzyme-bound pyridoxal phosphate at the active site of an enzyme. M+ represents a cationic region of the active site. One mol of water is split off between the *α*-amino group of the amino acid and the carbonyl oxygen of enzyme-bound pyridoxal phosphate.

This intermediate, stabilized by interaction with a cationic region of the active site, can be rearranged in ways that include release of a keto acid with formation of enzyme-bound pyridoxamine phosphate. The bound, amino form of the coenzyme can then form an analogous Schiff base intermediate with a keto acid. During transamination, the bound coenzyme thus serves as an intermediate carrier of amino groups (Fig 22–5).

Two transaminases, alanine-pyruvate transaminase (**alanine transaminase**) and glutamate-*α*-ketoglutarate transaminase (**glutamate transaminase**), present in most mammalian tissues, catalyze transfer of amino groups from most amino acids to form alanine (from pyruvate) or glutamate (from *α*-ketoglutarate) (Fig 22–6).

Since the equilibrium constant for most transaminase reactions is close to unity, transamination is a freely reversible process. This reversibility permits transaminases to function both in amino acid catabolism and biosynthesis.

Each transaminase is specific for the specified pair of amino and keto acids as one pair of substrates but nonspecific for the other pair, which may be any of a wide variety of amino acids and their corresponding keto acids. Since alanine is also a substrate for the glutamate transaminase reaction, all of the amino nitrogen from amino acids which can undergo transamination can be concentrated in glutamate. This is important because L-glutamate is the only amino acid in mammalian tissues which undergoes oxidative deamination at an appreciable rate. The formation of ammonia from *α*-amino groups thus occurs mainly via conversion to the *α*-amino nitrogen of L-glutamate.

Most (but not all) amino acids are substrates for transamination. Exceptions include lysine, threonine, and the cyclic imino acids, proline and hydroxyproline. Transamination is not restricted to *α*-amino groups. The δ-amino group of ornithine is, for example, readily transaminated, forming glutamate γ-semialdehyde (Fig 22–16). The serum levels of transaminases are markedly elevated in some disease states.

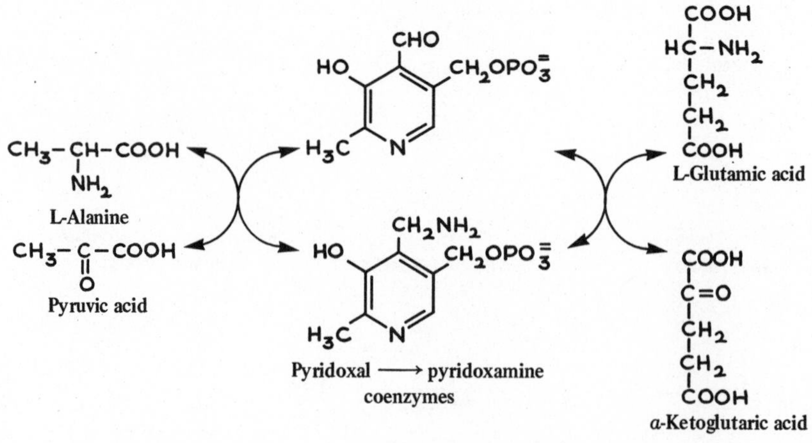

Figure 22–5. Participation of pyridoxal phosphate in transamination reactions.

ALANINE TRANSAMINASE

α-AMINO ACID + PYRUVATE ⇌ α-KETO ACID + ALANINE

GLUTAMATE TRANSAMINASE

α-AMINO ACID + α-KETOGLUTARATE ⇌ α-KETO ACID + GLUTAMATE

Figure 22–6. Alanine and glutamate transaminases.

Oxidative Deamination

Oxidative conversion of many amino acids to their corresponding a-keto acids occurs in homogenates of mammalian liver and kidney tissue. Although most of the activity of homogenates toward L-a-amino acids is due to the coupled action of transaminases plus L-glutamate dehydrogenase, both L- and D-amino acid oxidase activities do occur in mammalian liver and kidney tissue and are widely distributed in other animals and microorganisms. It must be noted, however, that the physiologic function of L- and D-amino acid oxidase of mammalian tissue is not known.

The amino acid oxidases are **auto-oxidizable flavoproteins**, ie, the reduced FMN or FAD is reoxidized directly by molecular oxygen forming hydrogen peroxide (H_2O_2) without participation of cytochromes or other electron carriers (Fig 22–7). The toxic product H_2O_2 is then split to O_2 and H_2O by **catalase**, which occurs widely in tissues, especially liver. Although the amino acid oxidase reactions are reversible, if catalase is absent the a-keto acid product is nonenzymically decarboxylated by H_2O_2, forming a carboxylic acid with one less carbon atom.

Both L- and D-amino acid oxidase activities are present in renal tissue, although the function of the D-amino acid oxidase is obscure.

In the amino acid oxidase reactions (Fig 22–7), the amino acid is first dehydrogenated by the flavoprotein of the oxidase, forming an a-imino acid. This spontaneously adds water, then decomposes to the corresponding a-keto acid with loss of the a-imino nitrogen as ammonia.

Mammalian L-amino acid oxidase, an FMN-flavoprotein, is restricted to kidney and liver tissue. Its activity is quite low, and it is essentially without effect on glycine or the L-isomers of the dicarboxylic or β-hydroxy a-amino acids. It thus is not likely that this enzyme fulfills a major role in mammalian amino acid catabolism.

Mammalian D-amino acid oxidase, an FAD-flavoprotein of broad substrate specificity, occurs in the liver and kidney tissue of most mammals. D-Asparagine and D-glutamine are not oxidized, and glycine and the D-isomers of the acidic and basic amino acids are poor substrates. The physiologic significance of this enzyme in mammals is not known.

L-Glutamate Dehydrogenase

The amino groups of most amino acids ultimately are transferred to a-ketoglutarate by transamination, forming L-glutamate (Fig 22–2). Release of this nitrogen as ammonia is catalyzed by **L-glutamate dehydrogenase**, an enzyme of high activity widely distributed in mammalian tissues (Fig 22–8). Liver glutamate dehydrogenase is a regulated enzyme whose activity is affected by allosteric modifiers such as ATP, GTP, and NADP, which inhibit the enzyme; and ADP, which activates the enzyme. Certain hormones appear also to influence glutamate dehydrogenase activity.

Glutamate dehydrogenase uses either NAD^+ or

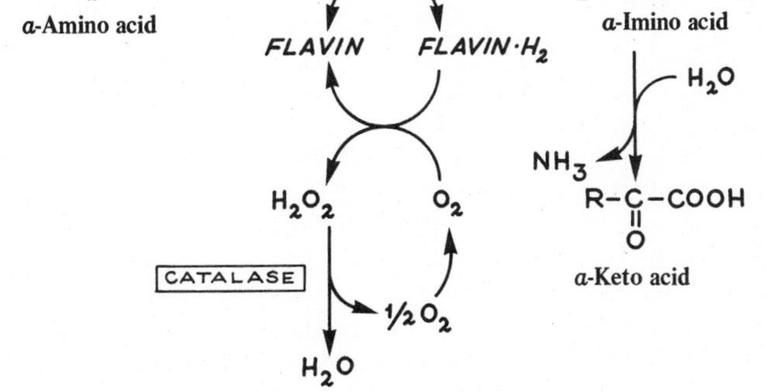

Figure 22–7. Oxidative deamination catalyzed by L-amino acid oxidase (L-*a*-amino acid:O_2 oxidoreductase). The *a*-imino acid, shown in brackets, is not a stable intermediate.

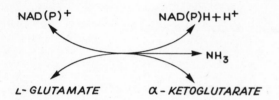

Figure 22–8. The L-glutamate dehydrogenase reaction. The designation NAD(P)$^+$ means that either NAD$^+$ or NADP$^+$ can serve as cosubstrate. The reaction is reversible, but the equilibrium constant favors glutamate formation.

NADP$^+$ as cosubstrate. The reaction is reversible and functions both in amino acid catabolism and biosynthesis. It therefore functions not only to funnel nitrogen from glutamate to urea (catabolism) but also to catalyze amination of a-ketoglutarate by free ammonia.

Formation of Ammonia

In addition to ammonia formed in the tissues, a considerable quantity is produced by intestinal bacteria both from dietary protein and from the urea present in fluids secreted into the gastrointestinal tract. This ammonia is absorbed from the intestine into the portal venous blood, which characteristically contains higher levels of ammonia than does systemic blood. Under normal circumstances the liver promptly removes the ammonia from the portal blood, so that blood leaving the liver (and indeed all of the peripheral blood) is virtually ammonia-free. This is essential since even minute quantities of ammonia are toxic to the central nervous system. The symptoms of **ammonia intoxication** include a peculiar flapping tremor, slurring of speech, blurring of vision, and, in severe cases, coma and death. These symptoms resemble those of the syndrome of hepatic coma which occurs when blood and, presumably, brain ammonia levels are elevated. Ammonia intoxication is assumed to be a factor in the etiology of hepatic coma. Therefore, treatment includes measures designed to reduce blood ammonia levels.

With severely impaired hepatic function or the development of collateral communications between the portal and systemic veins (as may occur in cirrhosis), the portal blood may bypass the liver. Ammonia from the intestines may thus rise to toxic levels in the systemic blood. Surgically produced shunting procedures (so-called Eck fistula, or other forms of portacaval shunts) are also conducive to ammonia intoxication, particularly after ingestion of large quantities of protein or after hemorrhage into the gastrointestinal tract.

The ammonia content of the blood leaving the kidneys via the renal veins always exceeds that of the renal arteries, indicating that the kidneys produce ammonia and add it to the blood. However, the excretion into the urine of the ammonia produced by renal tubular cells constitutes a far more significant aspect of renal ammonia metabolism. Ammonia production forms part of the renal tubular mechanisms for regulation of acid-base balance as well as conservation of cations (see Chapter 30). Ammonia production by the kidneys is markedly increased in metabolic acidosis and depressed in alkalosis. It is derived not from urea but from intracellular amino acids, particularly glutamine. Ammonia release is catalyzed by renal **glutaminase** (Fig 22–9).

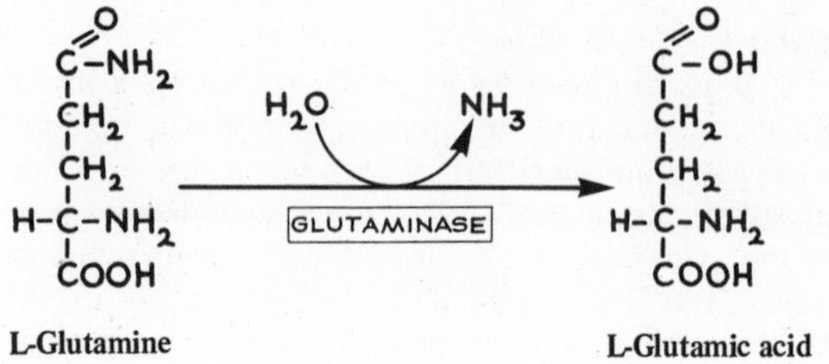

Figure 22–9. The glutaminase reaction. The reaction proceeds essentially irreversibly in the direction of glutamate formation.

Transport of Ammonia

Although ammonia may be excreted as ammonium salts—particularly in states of metabolic acidosis—the vast majority is excreted as urea, the principal nitrogenous component of urine. Ammonia, constantly produced in the tissues by the processes described above, is present only in traces in blood (10–20 $\mu g/dl$) since it is rapidly removed from the circulation by the liver and converted either to glutamate, to glutamine, or to urea. These trace levels of ammonia in blood contrast sharply with the more considerable quantities of free amino acids, particularly glutamine, in the blood (Table 22–1).

Removal of ammonia via the **glutamate dehydrogenase** reaction was mentioned above. Formation of glutamine is catalyzed by **glutamine synthetase** (Fig 22–10), a mitochondrial enzyme present in highest quantities in renal tissue. Synthesis of the amide bond of glutamine is accomplished at the expense of hydrolysis of one equivalent of ATP to ADP and P$_i$. The reaction is thus strongly favored in the direction of glutamine synthesis (see also Chapter 23).

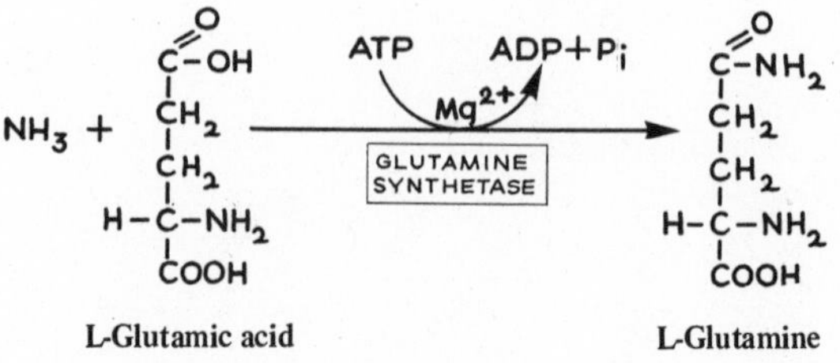

Figure 22–10. The glutamine synthetase reaction. The reaction strongly favors glutamine synthesis.

Table 22–1. Plasma amino acid concentrations (maximum normal levels).* (Expressed as mmol/dl.)

Amino Acid	Children	Adults
Alanine	41	66
a-Amino-n-butyric acid	3	4
Arginine	9	14
Asparagine	4	5
Aspartic acid	2	5
Citrulline	3	6
Cystine	8	14
Ethanolamine	9	11
Glutamic acid, glutamine	11	19
Glycine	52	56
Histidine	11	11
Hydroxyproline	3	
Isoleucine	5	10
Leucine	11	18
Lysine	27	24
Methionine	4	4
Ornithine	15	13
Phenylalanine	11	12
Proline	28	44
Serine	24	19
Taurine	22	17
Threonine	34	25
Tryptophan	7	7
Tyrosine	10	9
Valine	25	32

*From Dickinson JC & others: Pediatrics 36:2, 1965; Moore S, Stein W: J Biol Chem 211:908, 1954; and King JS: Clin Chim Acta 9:441, 1964. (Courtesy of Bio-Science Laboratories.)

Liberation of the amide nitrogen of glutamine as ammonia occurs not by reversal of the glutamine synthetase reaction but by hydrolytic removal of ammonia catalyzed by **glutaminase** (Fig 22–9). The glutaminase reaction, unlike the glutamine synthetase reaction, does not involve participation of adenine nucleotides, strongly favors glutamate formation, and does not function in glutamine synthesis. These 2 enzymes, glutamine synthetase and glutaminase (Fig 22–11), serve to catalyze interconversion of free ammonium ion and glutamine in a manner reminiscent of the interconversion of glucose and glucose 6-phosphate by glucokinase and glucose-6-phosphatase (see Chapter 18). An analogous reaction is catalyzed by **L-asparaginase** of animal, plant, and microbial tissue. Asparaginase and glutaminase have both been employed as antitumor agents since certain tumors exhibit abnormally high requirements for glutamine and asparagine.

Whereas in brain the major mechanism for removal of ammonia is glutamine formation, in the liver the most important pathway is urea formation. Brain tissue can form urea, although this does not play a significant role in ammonia removal. Formation of glutamine in the brain must be preceded by synthesis of glutamate in the brain itself because the supply of blood glutamate is inadequate to account for the increased amounts of glutamine formed in brain in the presence of high levels of blood ammonia. The immediate source of glutamate for this purpose is a-ketoglutarate. This would rapidly deplete the supply of citric acid cycle intermediates unless they could be replaced by CO_2 fixation with conversion of pyruvate to oxaloacetate (see Chapter 18). A significant fixation of CO_2 into amino acids does indeed occur in the brain, presumably by way of the citric acid cycle, and after infusion of ammonia more oxaloacetate is diverted to the synthesis of glutamine (rather than to aspartate) via a-ketoglutarate.

Circadian Changes in Plasma Amino Acid Levels

The plasma levels of most amino acids do not remain constant throughout a 24-hour day but rather change by varying in a circadian rhythm about a mean value. This was first noted for tyrosine by Wurtman. It has been confirmed for most other amino acids. In healthy young males fed equal meals spaced at approximately 4-hour intervals from 8 a.m. to 10 p.m. and confined to bed from 11 p.m. to 7 a.m., amino acid levels were lowest at 2 a.m. and highest at 10:30 a.m. Changes in physical activity had little effect on the levels or the times at which the highest or the lowest values occurred. However, the rhythm responds within 48 hours to an inversion of the sleeping-eating pattern. In general, plasma amino acid levels are lowest at 4 a.m. and rise 15–35% by noon to early afternoon. Amino acids present at the highest mean concentration (eg, glutamine, glycine, alanine, valine, or serine) change the least, whereas those present at a low mean concentration (tyrosine, tryptophan, phenylalanine, methionine, cysteine, or isoleucine) show the most striking changes in level as a function of time of day (eg, close to 2-fold for tyrosine). The exact physiologic significance of these circadian changes in plasma amino acid levels remains to be determined.

Urea Synthesis

A moderately active man consuming about 300 g of carbohydrate, 100 g of fat, and 100 g of protein daily must excrete about 16.5 g of nitrogen daily.

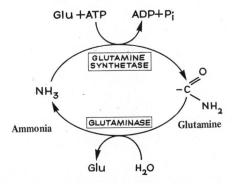

Figure 22–11. Interconversion of ammonia and of glutamine catalyzed by glutamine synthetase and glutaminase. Both reactions are strongly favored in the directions indicated by the arrows. Glutaminase thus serves solely for glutamine deamidation and glutamine synthetase solely for synthesis of glutamine from glutamate. (Glu = glutamate.)

Ninety-five percent is eliminated by the kidneys and the remaining 5%, for the most part as nitrogen, in the stool. The major pathway of nitrogen excretion in man is as urea synthesized in the liver, released into the blood, and cleared by the kidney (see Chapter 35). In man eating an occidental diet, urea constitutes 80–90% of the nitrogen excreted.

The reactions and intermediates in biosynthesis of 1 mol of urea from 1 mol each of ammonia, carbon dioxide (activated with Mg^{2+} and ATP), and of the a-amino nitrogen of aspartate are shown in Fig 22–12. The overall process requires 3 mols of ATP (2 of which are converted to ADP + P_i and 1 to AMP + PP_i), and the successive participation of 5 enzymes catalyzing the numbered reactions of Fig 22–12. Of the 6 amino acids involved in urea synthesis, one, N-acetylglutamate, functions as an enzyme activator rather

than as an intermediate. The remaining 5 amino acids—aspartate, arginine, ornithine, citrulline, and argininosuccinate—all function as carriers of atoms which ultimately become urea. Two (aspartate and arginine) occur in proteins, while the remaining 3 (ornithine, citrulline, and argininosuccinate) do not. The major metabolic role of these latter 3 amino acids in mammals is urea synthesis. Note that urea formation is in part a cyclical process. The ornithine used in reaction 2 is regenerated in reaction 5. There is thus no net loss or gain of ornithine, citrulline, argininosuccinate, or arginine during urea synthesis; however, ammonia, CO_2, ATP, and aspartate are consumed.

Reaction 1: Synthesis of carbamoyl phosphate. Condensation of 1 mol each of ammonia, carbon dioxide, and phosphate (derived from ATP) to form carbamoyl phosphate is catalyzed by **carbamoyl phos-**

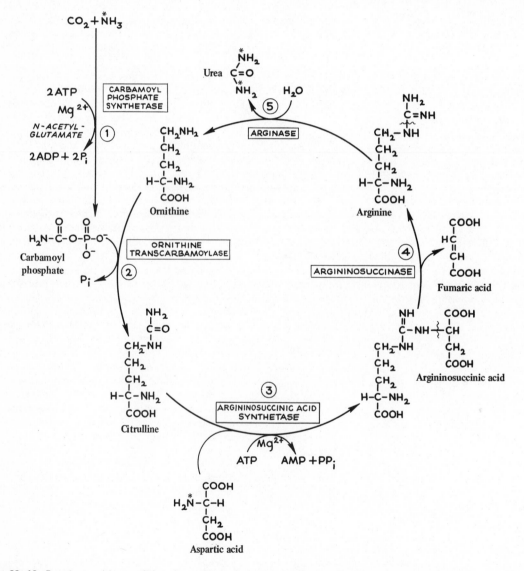

Figure 22–12. Reactions and intermediates of urea biosynthesis. The nitrogen atoms contributing to the formation of urea are starred.

phate synthetase, an enzyme present in liver mitochondria of all ureotelic organisms, including man. The 2 mol of ATP hydrolyzed during this reaction provide the driving force for synthesis of 2 covalent bonds—the amide bond and the mixed carboxylic acid-phosphoric acid anhydride bond of carbamoyl phosphate. In addition to Mg^{2+}, a dicarboxylic acid, preferably N-acetylglutamate, is required. The exact role of N-acetylglutamate is not known with certainty. Its presence brings about a profound conformational change in the structure of carbamoyl phosphate synthetase which exposes certain sulfhydryl groups, conceals others, and affects the affinity of the enzyme for ATP.

In bacteria, glutamine rather than ammonia serves as a substrate for carbamoyl phosphate synthesis. A similar reaction catalyzed by carbamate kinase is also important in citrulline utilization by bacteria.

Reaction 2: Synthesis of citrulline. Transfer of a carbamoyl moiety from carbamoyl phosphate to ornithine, forming citrulline + P_i, is catalyzed by **L-ornithine transcarbamoylase** of liver mitochondria. The reaction is highly specific for ornithine, and the equilibrium strongly favors citrulline synthesis.

Reaction 3: Synthesis of argininosuccinate. In the **argininosuccinate synthetase reaction**, aspartate and citrulline are linked together via the amino group of aspartate. The reaction requires ATP, and the equilibrium strongly favors argininosuccinate synthesis.

Reaction 4: Cleavage of argininosuccinate to arginine and fumarate. The reversible cleavage of argininosuccinate to arginine plus fumarate is catalyzed by **argininosuccinase**, a cold-labile enzyme of mammalian liver and kidney tissues. Loss of activity in the cold is associated with dissociation into 2 protein components. This dissociation is prevented by P_i, arginine, and argininosuccinate or by p-hydroxymercuribenzoate, which has no adverse effect on activity. The reaction proceeds via a **trans** elimination mechanism. The fumarate formed may be converted to oxaloacetate via the fumarase and malate dehydrogenase reactions and then transaminated to regenerate aspartate.

Reaction 5: Cleavage of arginine to ornithine and urea. This reaction completes the urea cycle and regenerates ornithine, a substrate for reaction 2. Hydrolytic cleavage of the guanidino group of arginine is catalyzed by **arginase**, which is present in the livers of all ureotelic organisms. Smaller quantities of arginase also occur in renal tissue, brain, mammary gland, testicular tissue, and skin. Highly purified arginase prepared from mammalian liver is activated by Co^{2+} or Mn^{2+}. Ornithine and lysine are potent inhibitors competitive with arginine.

Regulation of Urea Synthesis by Linkage of Glutamate Dehydrogenase With Carbamoyl Phosphate Synthetase

Carbamoyl phosphate synthetase is thought to act in conjunction with mitochondrial glutamate dehydrogenase to channel nitrogen from glutamate (and therefore from all amino acids; see Fig 22–2) into carbamoyl phosphate and thus into urea. While the equilibrium constant of the glutamate dehydrogenase reaction favors glutamate rather than ammonia formation, removal of ammonia by the carbamoyl phosphate synthetase reaction and oxidation of α-ketoglutarate by the citric acid cycle enzymes in the matrix of the mitochondrion serve to favor glutamate catabolism. This effect is enhanced by the presence of ATP, which, in addition to being substrate for carbamoyl phosphate synthesis, stimulates glutamate dehydrogenase activity unidirectionally in the direction of ammonia formation.

Metabolic Fates of Carbamoyl Phosphate

Carbamoyl phosphate has 2 major metabolic fates in mammals. The first is urea synthesis. The second is synthesis of pyrimidines destined primarily for incorporation into nucleic acids. Taking carbamoyl phosphate as a point of departure, the first enzyme of urea synthesis is **ornithine transcarbamoylase** and the first enzyme of pyrimidine synthesis is **aspartate transcarbamoylase**. Since carbamoyl phosphate is a **branch point compound**, we might anticipate independent regulation of its metabolism at the levels of aspartate transcarbamoylase and ornithine transcarbamoylase (Fig 22–13).

Aspartate transcarbamoylase is an allosteric, feedback-regulated enzyme in prokaryotic cells. Although similar evidence for regulation of ornithine transcarbamoylase in eukaryotic cells is lacking, independent regulation of these 2 enzymes is seen in regenerating mammalian liver tissue. Regeneration requires increased synthesis of nucleic acids, which would be facilitated by decreased use of carbamoyl phosphate for urea synthesis. During regeneration, ornithine transcarbamoylase levels decrease while aspartate transcarbamoylase levels increase. The process may be viewed as an example of **biochemical dedifferentiation.**

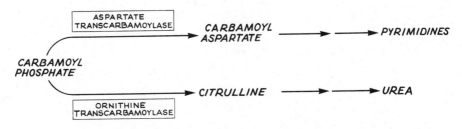

Figure 22–13. Metabolic fates of carbamoyl phosphate.

The urea cycle, a distinctive process of hepatic tissue, is an example of a biochemically differentiated system. Pyrimidine synthesis, which is necessary for all cell division, may be regarded as an undifferentiated process. When regeneration is complete, biochemical differentiation occurs, accompanied by a decrease in aspartate transcarbamoylase levels and an increase in those of ornithine transcarbamoylase. The physiologic factors regulating these processes are imperfectly understood.

CONVERSION OF THE CARBON SKELETONS OF THE COMMON L-α-AMINO ACIDS TO AMPHIBOLIC INTERMEDIATES

This section deals with the conversion of the carbon skeletons of the common L-amino acids to amphibolic intermediates. A subsequent section will consider the conversion of the carbon skeletons or of the intact L-amino acids themselves to certain specialized products.

The conclusion that the carbon skeletons of each of the common amino acids are converted to amphibolic intermediates arose from the results of nutritional studies performed in the period 1920–1940. These data, reinforced and confirmed by studies using isotopically labeled amino acids in the decade 1940–1950, supported the concept of the interconvertibility of fat, carbohydrate, and protein carbons and established that each amino acid is convertible either to carbohydrate (13 amino acids), fat (one amino acid), or both (5 amino acids) (Table 22–2). Although the knowledge of intermediary metabolism available at that time was incomplete and a detailed explanation of these interconversions was not possible, it was established that they indeed do occur.

How they occur is outlined in Fig 22–14. It will be noted that the carbon skeletons of all 13 "glycogenic" amino acids eventually form oxaloacetate, which is convertible to glycogen via phosphoenolpyruvate in the reactions of gluconeogenesis.

Individual amino acids are grouped for discussion on the basis of the principal amphibolic intermediates formed as end products of their catabolism.

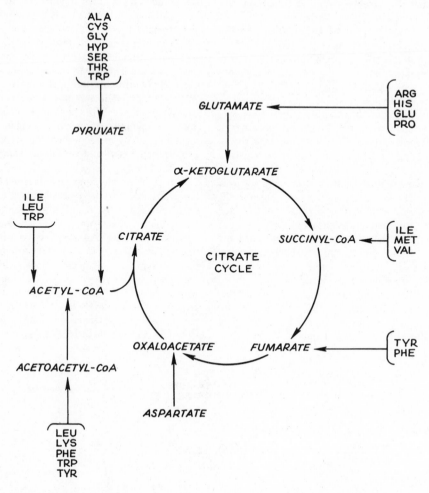

Figure 22–14. Amphibolic intermediates formed from the carbon skeleton of amino acids.

Table 22—2. Amphibolic fates of the carbon skeletons of the common amino acids.

Carbon skeleton ultimately converted to amphibolic intermediates forming:		
Glycogen ("Glycogenic" Amino Acids)	Fat ("Ketogenic" Amino Acids)	Both Glycogen and Fat ("Glycogenic" and "Ketogenic" Amino Acids)
L-Alanine L-Hydroxyproline L-Arginine L-Methionine L-Aspartate L-Proline L-Cystine L-Serine L-Glutamate L-Threonine L-Glycine L-Valine L-Histidine	L-Leucine	L-Isoleucine L-Lysine L-Phenylalanine L-Tyrosine L-Tryptophan

AMINO ACIDS FORMING OXALOACETATE

Aspartate & Asparagine

All 4 carbons of aspartate and of asparagine are converted to oxaloacetate as shown in Fig 22—15.

tarate. Deamination of histidine produces urocanate, so named because it was first detected as a histidine catabolite in the urine of dogs. The conversion of urocanate to 4-imidazolone-5-propionate, catalyzed by urocanase, involves both addition of H_2O and an internal oxidation-reduction. Although 4-imidazolone-5-

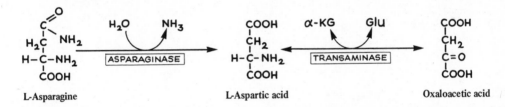

Figure 22—15. Catabolism of L-asparagine and of L-aspartate to oxaloacetate. (a-KG = a-ketoglutarate; Glu = glutamate.)

AMINO ACIDS FORMING a-KETOGLUTARATE

Glutamate, Glutamine, & Proline

All 5 carbon atoms of glutamate, glutamine, and proline are converted to a-ketoglutarate. Catabolism of glutamate and glutamine proceeds in a manner analogous to the conversion of aspartate and asparagine to oxaloacetate. Proline catabolism involves oxidation to a form of dehydroproline which on addition of water forms glutamate γ-semialdehyde. This is oxidized to glutamate and transaminated to a-ketoglutarate (Fig 22—16).

Arginine & Histidine

While arginine and histidine also form a-ketoglutarate, one carbon and 2 nitrogen atoms must first be removed from these 6-carbon amino acids. With arginine, this requires but a single step: the hydrolytic removal of the guanidino group catalyzed by arginase. The product, ornithine, then undergoes transamination of the δ-amino group, forming glutamate γ-semialdehyde, which is converted to a-ketoglutarate as described above for proline (Fig 22—16).

In the case of histidine, removal of the extra carbon and nitrogens requires 4 reactions. The product, glutamate, by transamination forms a-ketoglu-

propionate may undergo additional fates, conversion to a-ketoglutarate involves hydrolysis to N-formiminoglutamate followed by transfer of the forminino group on the a-carbon to tetrahydrofolate, forming N^5-formiminotetrahydrofolate. In patients suffering from folic acid deficiency, this last reaction is partially or totally blocked and N-formiminoglutamate is excreted in the urine. This forms the basis for a test for folic acid deficiency in which N-formiminoglutamate is detected in the urine following a large dose of histidine (see Chapter 23).

AMINO ACIDS FORMING PYRUVATE

Conversion of the carbon skeletons of alanine, cysteine, cystine, glycine, threonine, and serine to pyruvate is shown diagrammatically in Fig 22—17. Pyruvate may then be converted to acetyl-CoA. In this process, the 2 carbon atoms of glycine and all 3 carbon atoms of alanine, cysteine, and serine—but only 2 of the carbon atoms of threonine—form pyruvate.

Glycine

Amphibolic intermediates formed from glycine

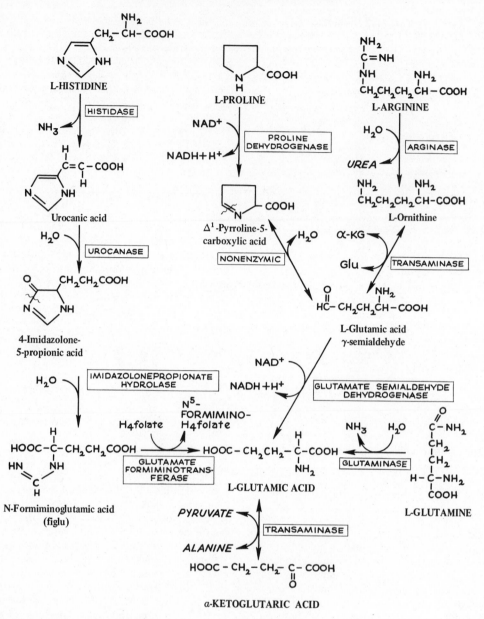

Figure 22—16. Catabolism of L-histidine, L-proline, and L-arginine to a-ketoglutarate. (a-KG = a-ketoglutarate; Glu = glutamate; H_4 folate = tetrahydrofolate.)

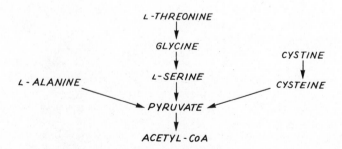

Figure 22—17. Diagrammatic representation of the conversion of the carbon skeletons of alanine, cystine, cysteine, threonine, glycine, and serine to pyruvate and to acetyl-CoA.

include pyruvate, CO_2, and 5,10-methylene tetrahydrofolate. Formation of pyruvate from glycine can occur by conversion to serine, a reaction catalyzed by serine hydroxymethyltransferase (Fig 22–18), followed by the reaction catalyzed by serine dehydratase (Fig 22–20) (see also Serine, below).

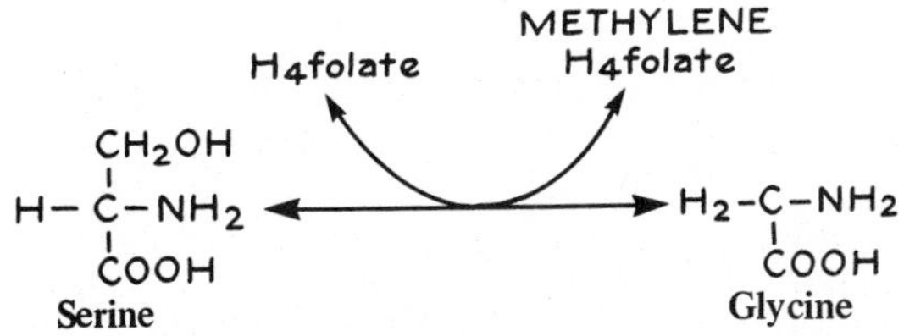

Figure 22–18. The serine hydroxymethyltransferase reaction. The reaction is freely reversible. (H_4folate = tetrahydrofolate.)

The major pathway for glycine catabolism in most vertebrates probably involves conversion to CO_2 and 5,10-methylene tetrahydrofolate. This reaction sequence (Fig 22–19), catalyzed by the enzymes of the glycine cleavage system, resembles the conversion of pyruvate to acetyl-CoA by the enzymes of the pyruvate dehydrogenase complex. Like the components of the pyruvate dehydrogenase complex, the enzymes of the glycine cleavage system (Fig 22–19) also comprise a macromolecular complex located within the liver mitochondria of most vertebrates.

The reactions of the glycine cleavage system occur readily in the liver tissue of most vertebrates, including man, other mammals, birds, and reptiles. In uricotelic organisms, the methylene tetrahydrofolate is converted primarily to purines, whereas in ureotelic and ammonotelic vertebrates the methylene tetrahydrofolate may either be converted to serine by the serine hydroxymethyltransferase reaction (Fig 22–18) or oxidized to CO_2.

The reactions of the glycine cleavage system (Fig 22–19) probably constitute the major route not only for glycine but also for serine catabolism in man and many other vertebrates (see also Serine, below). The most convincing evidence for its role in glycine catabolism derives from study of a patient with hyperglycinemia caused by defective hepatic catabolism of glycine. Liver tissue from normal human subjects readily catalyzes the conversion of glycine to CO_2 with the accompanying synthesis of serine. These reactions were found to occur at a far slower rate in tissues of a liver biopsy specimen obtained from the patient with hyperglycinemia. This disorder thus appears to have resulted solely from a defect in the glycine cleavage system and hence documents the physiologic importance of this system for glycine catabolism in man.

Alanine

Transamination of L-alanine (Figs 22–6 and 22–20) forms pyruvate, which may then be decarboxylated to acetyl-CoA (Fig 22–17).

Serine

Conversion of serine to pyruvate is catalyzed by

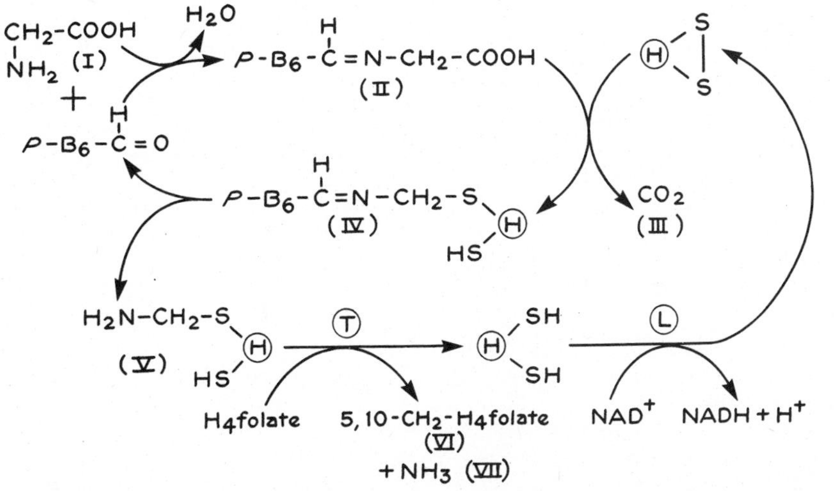

Figure 22–19. Catabolism of glycine to CO_2, NH_3, and methylene tetrahydrofolate by the components of the glycine cleavage system of vertebrate liver. Glycine (I) combines with the P-protein, a pyridoxal phosphoprotein, to form the Schiff base intermediate (II). The disulfide form of the H-protein then combines with (II), liberating the carboxyl carbon of glycine as CO_2 (III) and forming the Schiff base-H-protein complex (IV), which then decomposes to (V), reforming the P-protein. Decomposition of (V), which requires tetrahydrofolate (H_4folate) and is catalyzed by the T-protein, forms methylene tetrahydrofolate (5,10-CH_2-H_4folate) (VI), NH_3 (VII), and the reduced form of the H-protein. This is oxidized to the disulfide form by NAD^+ in a reaction catalyzed by the L-protein. Although the entire sequence of reactions is reversible, unidirectional arrows are used in order to illustrate the direction of flow of intermediates in the catabolism of glycine. (H_4folate = tetrahydrofolate.)

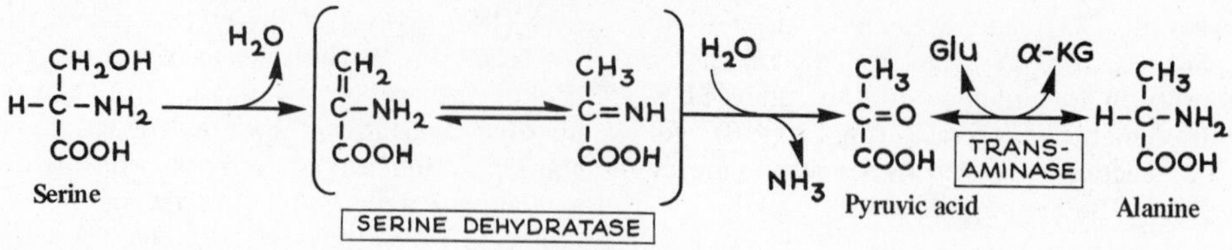

Figure 22-20. Conversion of alanine and serine to pyruvate. Both the alanine transaminase and serine dehydratase reactions require pyridoxal phosphate as a coenzyme. The bracketed intermediates in the serine dehydratase reaction are hypothetical. This reaction may be thought of as proceeding via elimination of H_2O from serine, forming an unsaturated amino acid. This rearranges to an α-imino acid which is spontaneously hydrolyzed to pyruvate plus ammonia. There is thus no net gain or loss of water during the serine dehydratase reaction. (Glu = glutamate; α-KG = α-ketoglutarate.)

serine dehydratase (Fig 22-20), a pyridoxal phosphate protein. The reaction involves both addition and loss of water and also loss of ammonia. This probably proceeds via formation of an imino acid intermediate, as shown in Fig 22-20.

The liver tissue of rats and of guinea pigs is rich in serine dehydratase, and in these species conversion of serine to pyruvate by the serine dehydratase reaction is no doubt of considerable physiologic significance. In many other vertebrates, including man, the evidence suggests that serine is degraded to glycine and to 5,10-methylene tetrahydrofolate. The initial reaction is catalyzed by serine hydroxymethyltransferase (Fig 22-18). The further catabolism of serine then becomes that of the catabolism of glycine, as was discussed above (Fig 22-19).

Cysteine & Cystine

Cystine is converted to cysteine by an NADH-dependent oxidoreductase (Fig 22-21). Conversion of

Serine is then converted to pyruvate by the serine dehydratase reaction (Fig 22-20). Both pyruvate and acetaldehyde then form acetyl-CoA (Fig 22-23). Alternatively, glycine is catabolized as shown in Fig 22-19.

Hydroxyproline

Three of the 5 carbons of 4-hydroxy-L-proline are converted to pyruvate by the reactions shown in Fig 22-24. The remaining 2 form glyoxylate. A mitochondrial dehydrogenase catalyzes conversion of hydroxyproline to L-Δ^1-pyrroline-3-hydroxy-5-carboxylate. This is in nonenzymic equilibrium with γ-hydroxy-L-glutamate-γ-semialdehyde, which is formed by addition of 1 mol of water. The semialdehyde is oxidized to the corresponding carboxylic acid, erythro-γ-hydroxyglutamate, and transaminated to α-keto-γ-hydroxyglutarate. An aldol type cleavage then forms glyoxylate plus pyruvate.

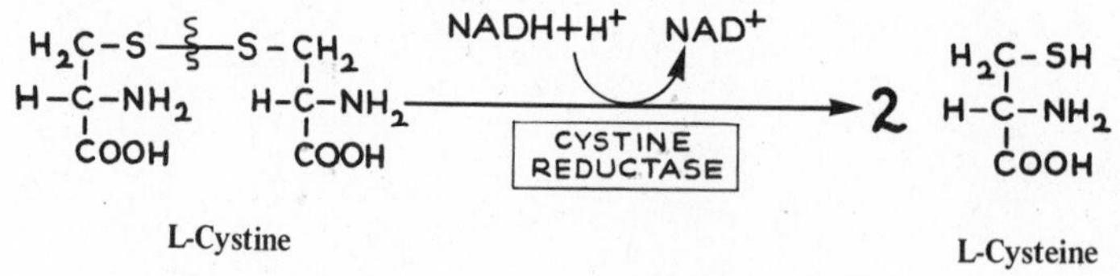

Figure 22-21. The cystine reductase reaction.

cysteine to pyruvate may then occur in any of 3 ways: (1) Via cysteine desulfhydrase, a pyridoxal phosphate-dependent reaction similar to that catalyzed by serine dehydratase (Fig 22-20). (2) By transamination and loss of H_2S. (3) By oxidation of the sulfhydryl group forming cysteine sulfinic acid, transamination, and loss of the terminal carbon's oxidized sulfur atom. These reactions are shown in Fig 22-22.

Threonine

Threonine is cleaved to acetaldehyde and glycine by **threonine aldolase.** Glycine then accepts a one-carbon moiety from $N^{5,10}$-methylene tetrahydrofolate in a reaction catalyzed by serine hydroxymethylase.

AMINO ACIDS FORMING ACETYL-COENZYME A

As shown above, all amino acids forming pyruvate are convertible to acetyl-CoA. In addition to alanine, cysteine, cystine, glycine, serine, and threonine, which form pyruvate prior to acetyl-CoA, 5 amino acids form acetyl-CoA directly without first forming pyruvate. These include the aromatic amino acids phenylalanine, tyrosine, and tryptophan; the basic amino acid lysine; and the neutral branched chain amino acid leucine.

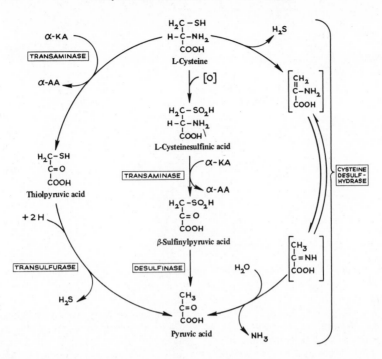

Figure 22–22. Conversion of cysteine to pyruvate. Bracketed intermediates in the cysteine desulfhydrase reaction are hypothetical. The reaction may be thought of as proceeding in a manner analogous to that catalyzed by serine dehydratase (Fig 22–20) except that the initial step involves loss of H_2S rather than H_2O. (a-AA = a-amino acid; a-KA = a-keto acid.)

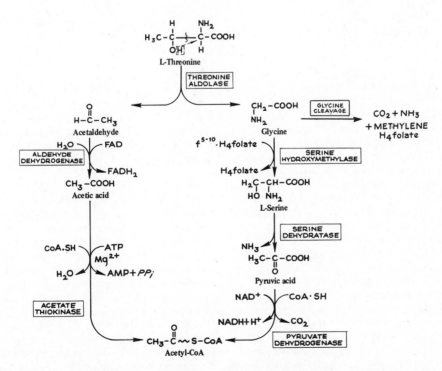

Figure 22–23. Conversion of threonine and glycine to serine, pyruvate, and acetyl-CoA. For details of the pyruvate dehydrogenase reaction, see Chapter 13. ($f^{5-10} \cdot H_4$ folate = formyl [5–10] tetrahydrofolic acid.) For details of glycine cleavage, see Fig 22–19.

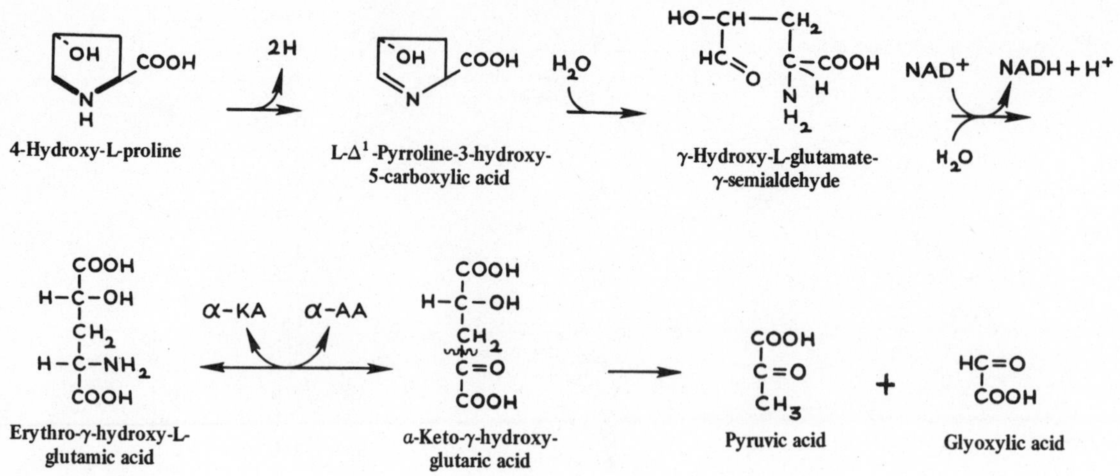

Figure 22—24. Intermediates in L-hydroxyproline catabolism in mammalian tissues. (a-KA = a-keto acid; a-AA = a-amino acid).

Tyrosine

A. Overall Reaction Sequence: Five enzymatically catalyzed reactions are involved in conversion of tyrosine to fumarate and to acetoacetate: (1) transamination to *p*-hydroxyphenylpyruvate; (2) simultaneous oxidation and migration of the 3-carbon side chain and decarboxylation, forming homogentisate; (3) oxidation of homogentisate to maleylacetoacetate; (4) isomerization of maleylacetoacetate to fumarylacetoacetate; and (5) hydrolysis of fumarylacetoacetate to fumarate and acetoacetate. Acetoacetate may then undergo thiolytic cleavage to acetate plus acetyl-CoA. These reactions are shown in Figs 22—25 and 22—26.

The intermediates in tyrosine metabolism were discovered in part as a result of studies of the human genetic disease alkaptonuria. Patients with alkaptonuria excrete substantial quantities of homogentisate in their urine, and much useful information was obtained by feeding suspected precursors of homogentisate to patients suffering from this disease. Early difficulties arising from the instability of several of the intermediates were resolved by the discovery that *a*-ketoglutarate and ascorbate were required for tyrosine oxidation by liver extracts. Subsequently, each of the individual enzymic steps was studied in detail.

B. Transamination of Tyrosine: Transamination of tyrosine to *p*-hydroxyphenylpyruvate is catalyzed by **tyrosine-*a*-ketoglutarate transaminase**, an inducible enzyme of mammalian liver tissue.

C. Oxidation of *p*-Hydroxyphenylpyruvate to Homogentisate: Although the reaction shown in Fig 22—25 appears to involve hydroxylation of *p*-hydroxyphenylpyruvate in the ortho position accompanied by oxidative loss of the carboxyl carbon, the reaction actually involves migration of the side chain. Ring hydroxylation and side chain migration appear to occur in a concerted manner. ***p*-Hydroxyphenylpyruvate hydroxylase** appears to be a copper metalloprotein with properties similar to those of **tyrosinase** (see Chapter 23). Although other reducing agents can re-

place ascorbate as a cofactor for this reaction, scorbutic patients excrete incompletely oxidized products of tyrosine metabolism. This suggests that one function of ascorbic acid is as a cofactor for *p*-hydroxyphenylpyruvate hydroxylase.

D. Conversion of Homogentisate to Fumarate and Acetoacetate: The benzene ring of homogentisate is ruptured, forming maleylacetoacetate in an oxidative reaction catalyzed by **homogentisate oxidase**, an iron metalloprotein of mammalian liver. The reaction is inhibited by *a,a'*-dipyridyl, a chelating agent that strongly binds iron. Treatment with *a,a'*-dipyridyl has been used to induce alkaptonuria in experimental animals.

Conversion of maleylacetoacetate to fumarylacetoacetate, which involves cis to trans isomerization about the double bond, is catalyzed by **maleylacetoacetate cis-trans isomerase**, a —SH enzyme present in mammalian liver. Hydrolysis of fumarylacetoacetate, catalyzed by **fumarylacetoacetate hydrolase**, forms fumarate and acetoacetate. As noted above, acetoacetate can then be converted to acetyl-CoA plus acetate by the β-ketothiolase reaction.

Lysine

Lysine provides an exception to the general observation that the first step in catabolism of an amino acid is removal of its *a*-amino group by transamination. Neither the *a*- nor ϵ-nitrogen atoms of L-lysine undergo transamination. It has long been known that mammals convert the intact carbon skeleton of L-lysine to *a*-aminoadipate and *a*-ketoadipate (Fig 22—27). Until quite recently, L-lysine was thought to be degraded via pipecolic acid, a cyclic imino acid resembling proline. It now appears that while liver degrades D-lysine via pipecolate, L-lysine is degraded via saccharopine as shown in Fig 22—28. Saccharopine is also an intermediate in lysine biosynthesis by yeast and other fungi (see Chapter 23).

L-Lysine first condenses with *a*-ketoglutarate,

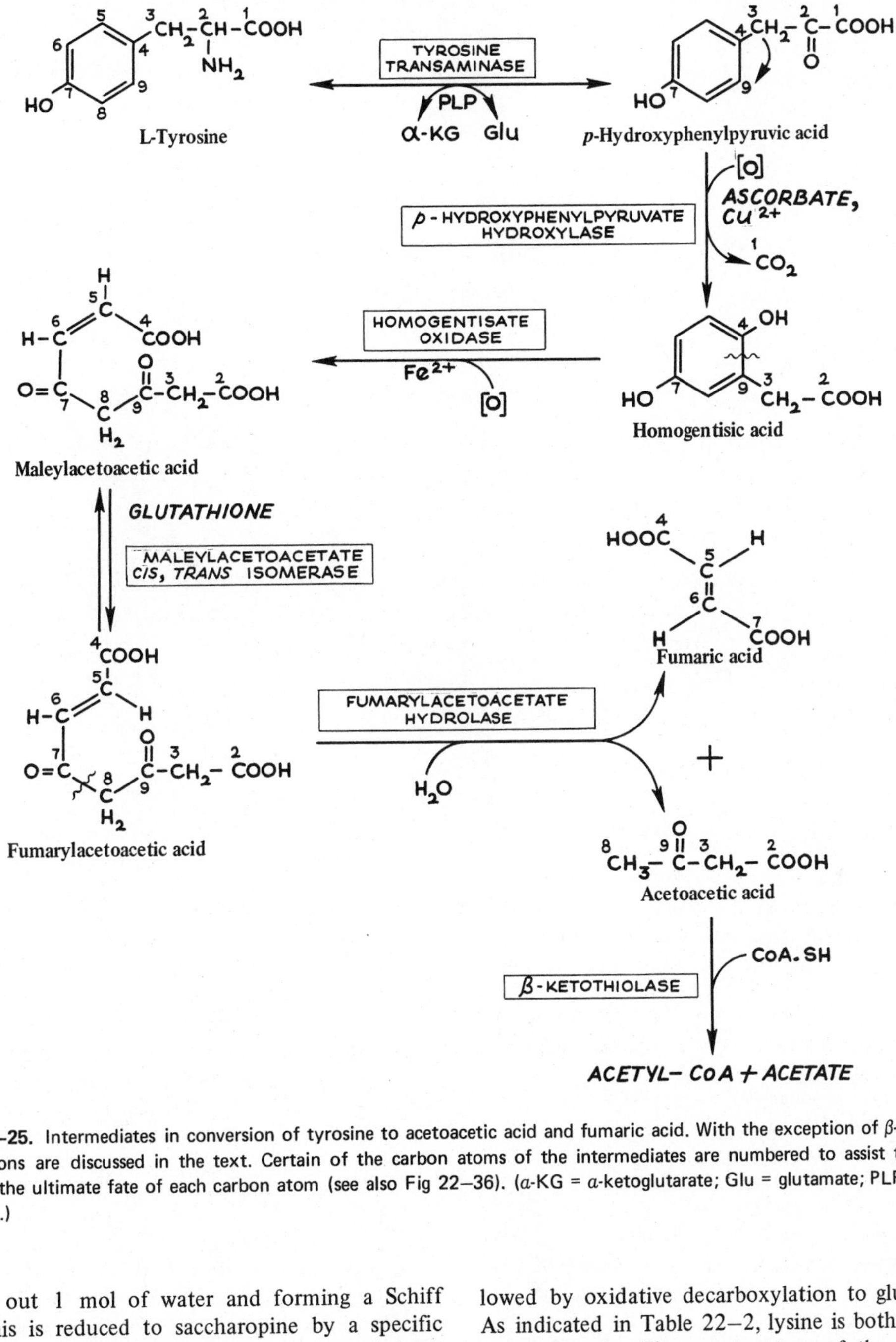

Figure 22–25. Intermediates in conversion of tyrosine to acetoacetic acid and fumaric acid. With the exception of β-ketothiolase, the reactions are discussed in the text. Certain of the carbon atoms of the intermediates are numbered to assist the reader in observing the ultimate fate of each carbon atom (see also Fig 22–36). (α-KG = α-ketoglutarate; Glu = glutamate; PLP = pyridoxal phosphate.)

splitting out 1 mol of water and forming a Schiff base. This is reduced to saccharopine by a specific dehydrogenase and then oxidized by a second dehydrogenase. Addition of water forms L-glutamate and L-α-aminoadipate-δ-semialdehyde. The net effect of this sequence of reactions is the same as that which would have resulted if the ε-nitrogen of lysine were removed by transamination. One mol each of L-lysine and of α-ketoglutarate are converted to α-aminoadipate-δ-semialdehyde and glutamate. NAD+ and NADH are specifically required as cofactors, however, even though no net oxidation or reduction has occurred.

The further catabolism of α-aminoadipate involves transamination to α-ketoadipate, probably fol-

lowed by oxidative decarboxylation to glutaryl-CoA. As indicated in Table 22–2, lysine is both glycogenic and ketogenic. The exact nature of the subsequent catabolites of glutaryl-CoA in mammalian systems are, however, not known with certainty.

Tryptophan

This amino acid is notable for its variety of important metabolic reactions and products. Originally isolated in 1901, it was among the first shown to be a nutritionally essential amino acid. Neurospora mutants and the bacterium Pseudomonas have proved invaluable aids in unraveling the details of tryptophan metabolism. Isolation of certain tryptophan metabolites

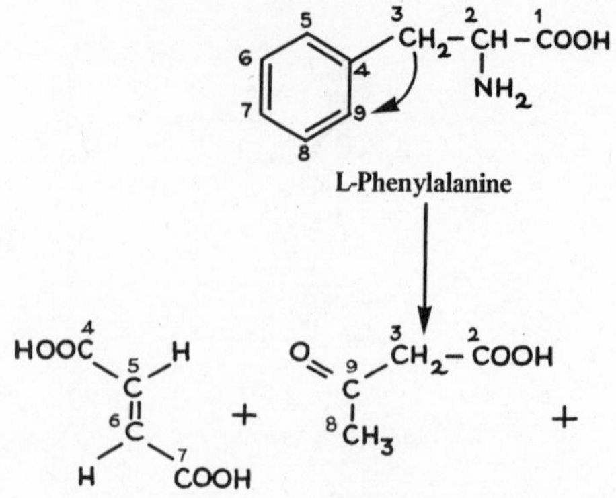

Figure 22—26. Ultimate catabolic fate of each carbon atom of phenylalanine. Pattern of isotopic labeling in the ultimate catabolites of phenylalanine (and tyrosine). The explanation of the observed labeling pattern is given in Fig 22—25 and in the accompanying text.

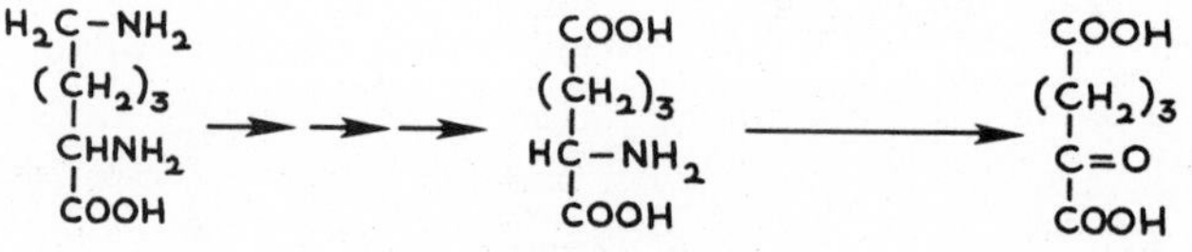

Figure 22—27. Conversion of L-lysine to α-aminoadipate and α-ketoadipate.

from urine has also contributed valuable information.

Although a large portion of the isotope of administered ^{14}C-L-tryptophan is retained by the tissue proteins, a considerable fraction appears in the urine in the form of various catabolites. The carbon atoms both of the side chain and of the aromatic ring may be completely degraded to amphibolic intermediates. This proceeds via what is known as the **kynurenine-anthranilate pathway** (Fig 22—29). The pathway is important not only for tryptophan degradation but also for conversion of tryptophan to niacin.

Tryptophan oxygenase (perhaps better known as **tryptophan pyrrolase**) catalyzes the cleavage of the indole ring with incorporation of 2 atoms of molecular oxygen, forming N-formylkynurenine. The oxygenase enzyme is an iron porphyrin metalloprotein which occurs in the liver of mammals, amphibians, birds, and insects and which has been obtained in highly purified form from liver and from Pseudomonas. Four forms of hepatic tryptophan pyrrolase have been described: the active holoenzyme, the apoenzyme, a third form that is combined with hematin, and a fourth that requires prolonged incubation or addition of small quantities of cell particles in order to be activated by hematin. Tryptophan pyrrolase is an inducible enzyme in liver. The chief inducing agents appear to be adrenal corticosteroids (eg, hydrocortisone) and tryptophan itself. De novo synthesis of tryptophan pyrrolase has been demonstrated by immunologic technics. Induction is blocked by administration of puromycin or dactino-

mycin. Tryptophan serves also to stabilize the enzyme toward proteolytic degradation. A considerable portion of newly synthesized enzyme is in a latent form that requires activation.

Hydrocortisone-induced activation of tryptophan pyrrolase consists of 2 steps: (1) conjugation of the apoenzyme with hematin, forming oxidized holoenzyme; and (2) reduction of the oxidized holoenzyme. The first step requires the presence of L-tryptophan or an analog (eg, ω-methyltryptophan). The second step is promoted by L-tryptophan and by ascorbate.

It has been observed that tryptophan analogs that promoted reaction 2 were inducers of the enzyme. Tryptophan analogs thus appear to induce higher levels of tryptophan pyrrolase in liver, both by promoting synthesis of new protein and by stabilizing existing enzyme against degradation. Tryptophan pyrrolase is subject to feedback inhibition by a variety of nicotinic acid derivatives, including NADPH.

Hydrolytic removal of the formyl group of N-formylkynurenine is catalyzed by **kynurenine formylase** of mammalian liver. When hydrolysis is performed in the presence of $H_2{}^{18}O_2$, one equivalent of [18]O is incorporated into the formate formed. The enzyme is not specific for N-formylkynurenine and will catalyze similar reactions with a variety of arylformylamines

The reaction catalyzed by kynurenine formylase produces **kynurenine** (Fig 22—29). This may be deaminated by transamination of the amino group of the side chain to ketoglutarate. The resulting keto deriva-

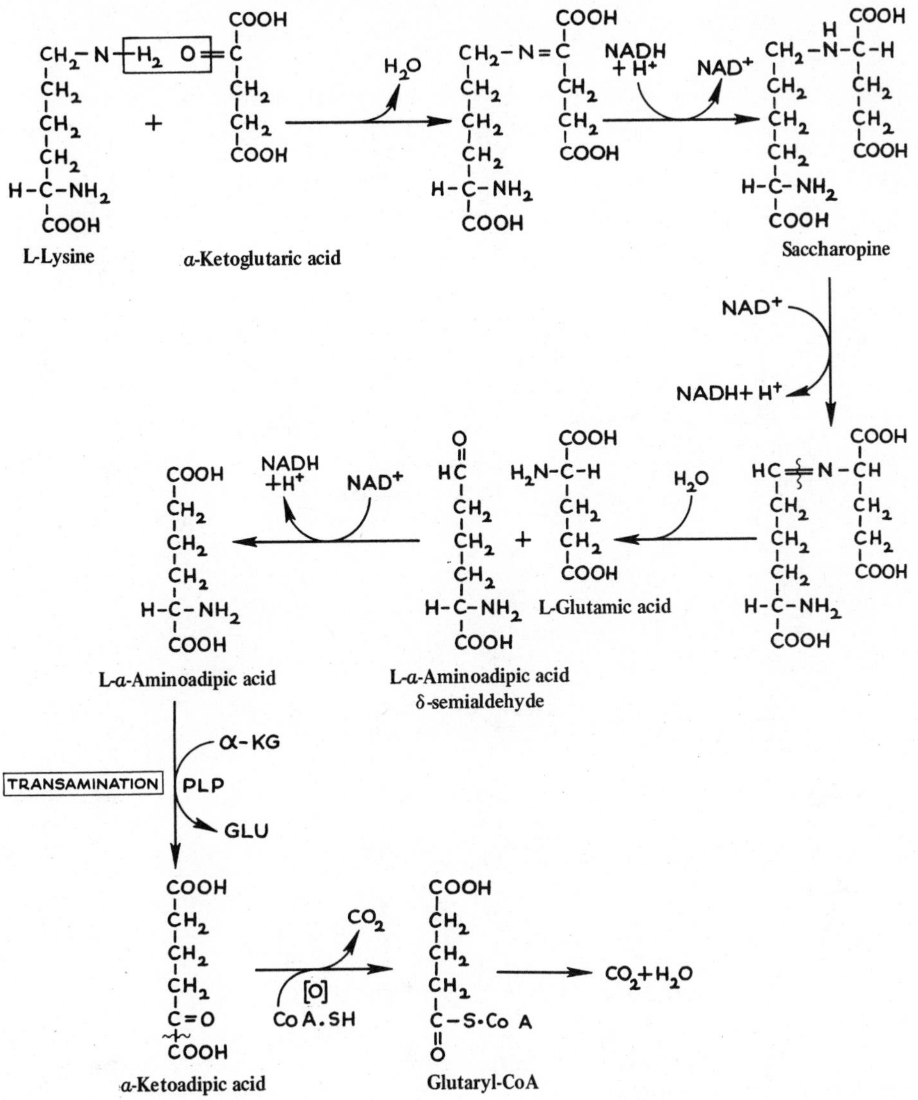

Figure 22–28. Catabolism of L-lysine. (a-KG = a-ketoglutarate; Glu = glutamate; PLP = pyridoxal phosphate.)

tive, 2-amino-3-hydroxybenzoyl pyruvate, loses water and then undergoes spontaneous ring closure, forming **kynurenic acid** (Fig 22–30). This compound is a byproduct of kynurenine; it is not formed in the main pathway of tryptophan breakdown shown in Fig 22–29.

The further metabolism of kynurenine involves its conversion to **hydroxykynurenine**, which in turn is converted to **3-hydroxyanthranilate**. The hydroxylation occurs with molecular oxygen in an NADPH-catalyzed reaction similar to that for the hydroxylation of phenylalanine to tyrosine (see Chapter 23).

The reaction by which kynurenine and hydroxykynurenine are converted to hydroxyanthranilate is catalyzed by the enzyme **kynureninase**, which requires vitamin B_6 (pyridoxal phosphate) as coenzyme. A deficiency of vitamin B_6 results in some degree of failure

to catabolize these kynurenine derivatives, which thus reach various extrahepatic tissues where they are converted to **xanthurenic acid** (Fig 22–30). This abnormal metabolite has been identified in the urine of humans, monkeys, and rats when dietary intakes of vitamin B_6 were inadequate. The feeding of excess tryptophan can be used to induce excretion of xanthurenic acid if vitamin B_6 deficiency exists. The kidney is one organ which has been shown to produce xanthurenic acid derivatives from kynurenine.

In many animals, the conversion of tryptophan to nicotinic acid makes a supply of the vitamin in the diet unnecessary. In the rat, rabbit, dog, and pig, tryptophan can completely replace the vitamin in the diet; in man and other animals, tryptophan increases the urinary excretion of nicotinic acid derivatives (eg, N-methylnicotinamide). In vitamin B_6 deficiency, it has

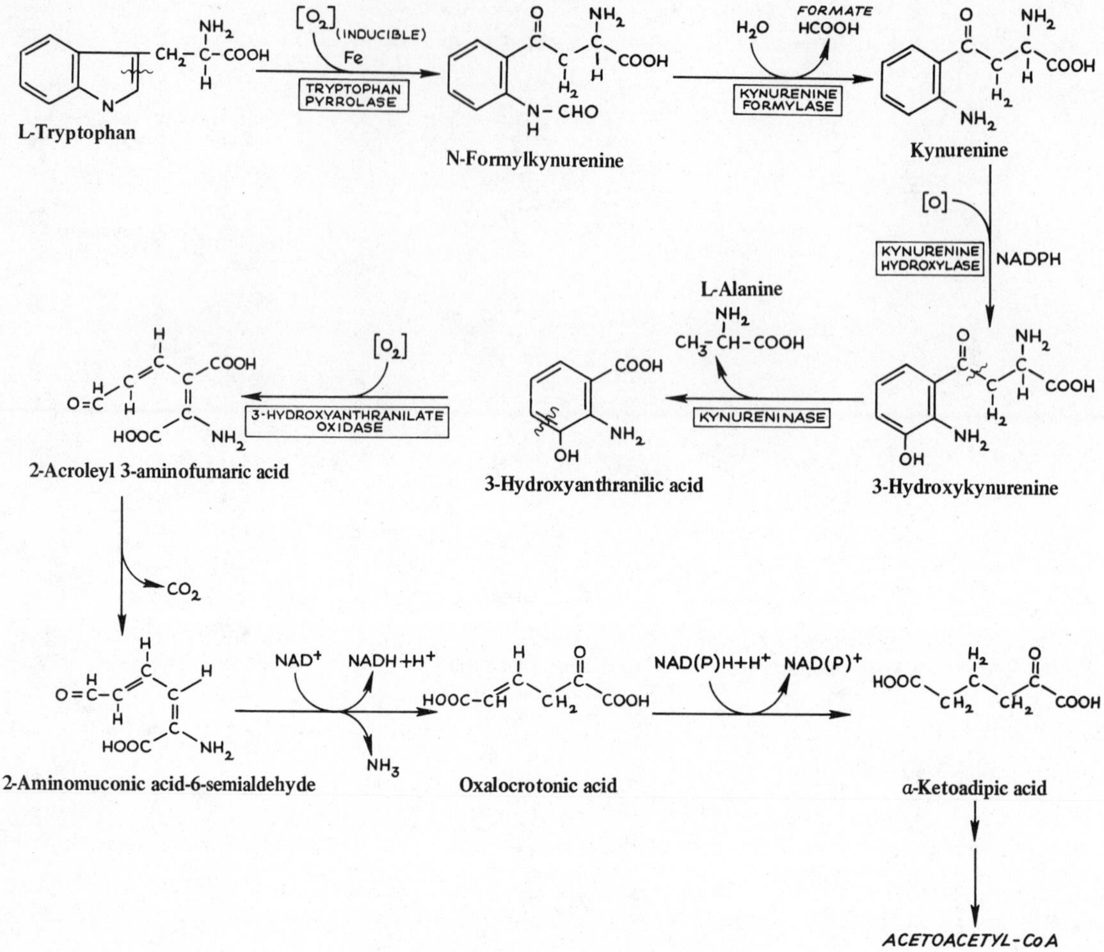

Figure 22–29. Catabolism of L-tryptophan.

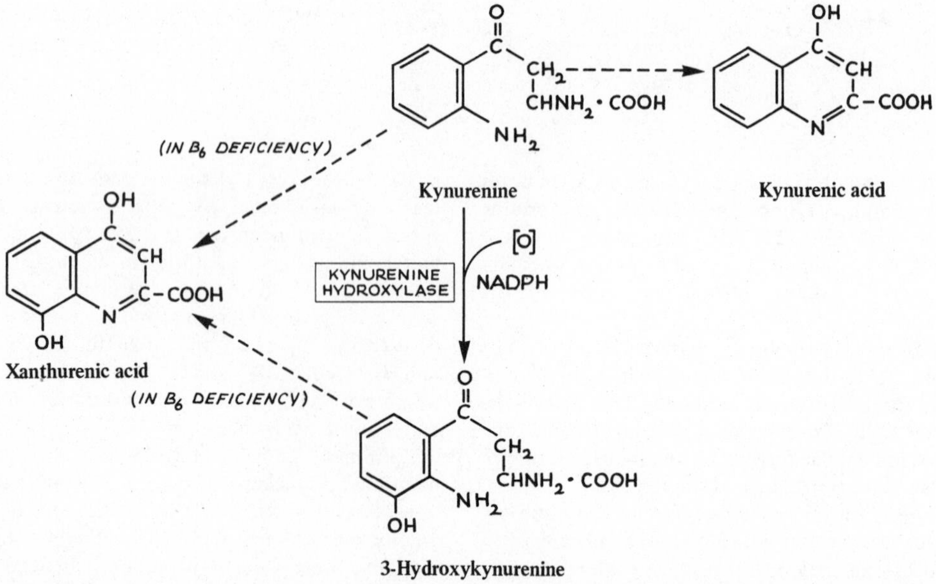

Figure 22–30. Conversion of kynurenine and hydroxykynurenine to xanthurenic acid in vitamin B_6 deficiency.

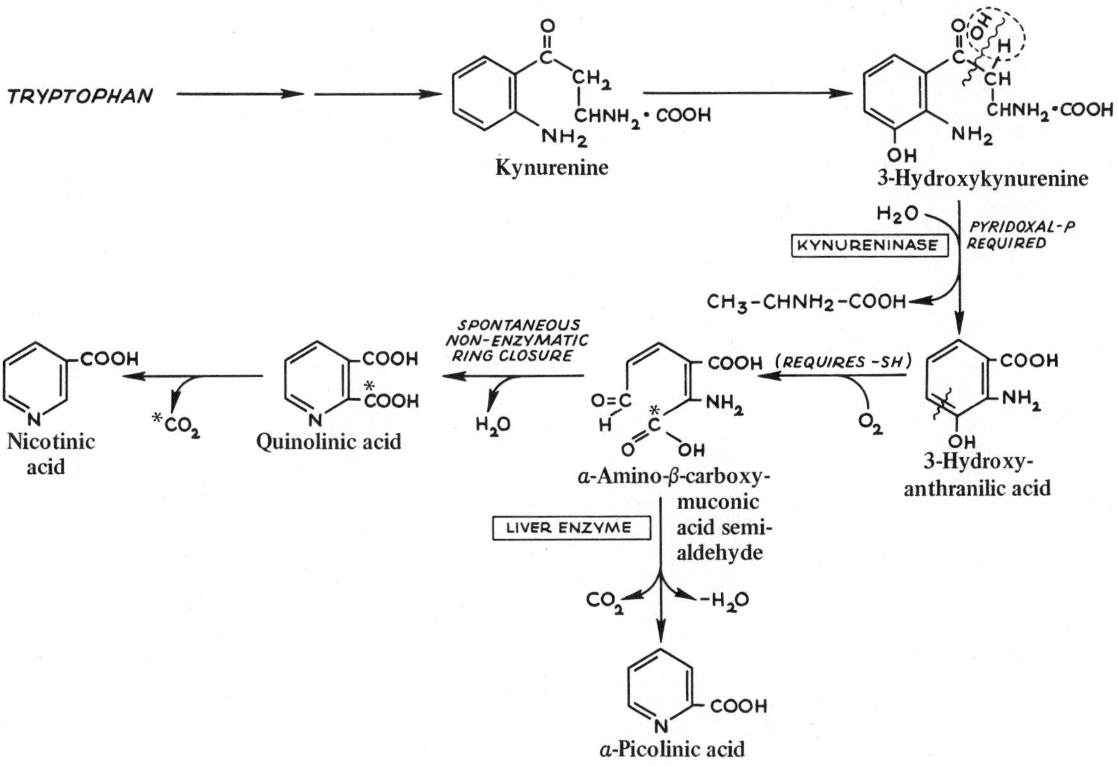

Figure 22–31. The catabolism of tryptophan to nicotinic acid via hydroxykynurenine.

been noted that the synthesis of pyridine nucleotides (NAD and NADP) in the tissues may be impaired. This is a result of the inadequate conversion of tryptophan to nicotinic acid for nucleotide synthesis; if an adequate supplement of nicotinic acid is supplied, nucleotide synthesis proceeds normally even in the absence of vitamin B_6.

It is likely that in many diets tryptophan normally provides a considerable amount of the nicotinic acid requirement. In man, approximately 60 mg of tryptophan produce 1 mg of nicotinic acid. Nutritional deficiency states such as pellagra must therefore be considered combined protein (tryptophan) as well as vitamin (nicotinic acid) deficiencies.

The pathway whereby tryptophan may produce nicotinic acid by way of kynurenine, an intermediate in the major pathway of tryptophan breakdown, is shown in Fig 22–31.

AMINO ACIDS FORMING SUCCINYL-COENZYME A

Overall Reactions

Whereas succinyl-CoA represents the amphibolic end product for the catabolism of methionine, isoleucine, and valine, only a portion of their carbon skeletons is in fact converted (Fig 22–32). Four-fifths of

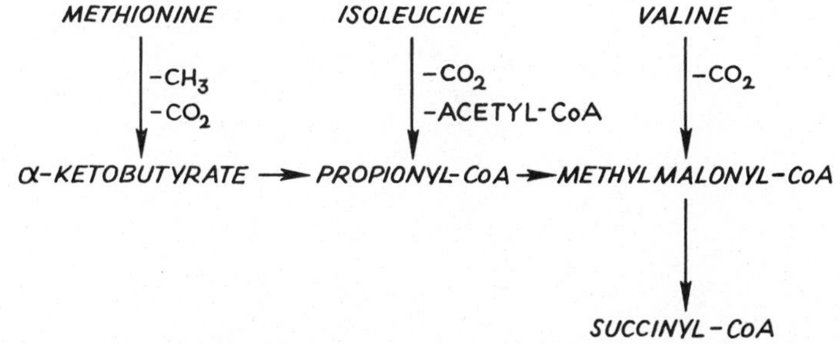

Figure 22–32. Overall catabolism of methionine, isoleucine, and valine. Conversion to succinyl-CoA.

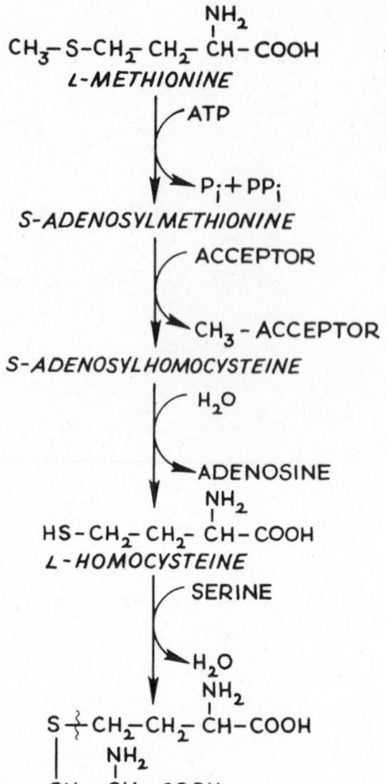

Figure 22–33. Intermediates in conversion of methionine to propionyl-CoA.

onate and of fatty acids containing an odd number of carbon atoms (see Chapter 18)—will not be further discussed here. What follows relates only to the conversion of methionine and isoleucine to propionyl-CoA and of valine to methylmalonyl-CoA.

Methionine

The intermediates formed during conversion of methionine to propionyl-CoA are shown in Fig 22–33. L-Methionine first condenses with ATP, forming S-adenosylmethionine ("active methionine"; Fig 22–34). The now activated S-methyl group is then transferred to any of a wide variety of acceptor compounds.* After removal of the methyl group, S-adenosylhomocysteine is formed. Hydrolysis of the S to C bond yields L-homocysteine plus adenosine. Homocysteine then condenses with a molecule of serine, forming the amino acid cystathionine. Hydrolytic cleavage of cystathionine forms L-homoserine plus cysteine, so that the net effect is the conversion of homocysteine to homoserine and of serine to cysteine. These 2 reactions are therefore also involved in biosynthesis of cysteine from serine (see Chapter 23). Homoserine is then converted to α-ketobutyrate in a reaction catalyzed by homoserine deaminase (Fig 22–35). Conversion of α-ketobutyrate to propionyl-CoA then occurs in the usual manner for oxidative decarboxylation of α-keto acids to form acyl-CoA derivatives (eg, pyruvate, α-ketoglutarate).

Leucine, Valine, & Isoleucine

As might be suspected from their structural similarities, the catabolism of L-leucine, L-valine, and L-isoleucine initially involves the same reactions. Ultimately, this common pathway diverges, and each amino acid follows its own unique pathway to amphibolic intermediates (Fig 22–36). The nature of these amphibolic end products (β-hydroxy-β-methyl-glutaryl-CoA, succinyl-CoA, and acetyl-CoA) determines whether each amino acid is glycogenic (valine), ketogenic (leucine), or both (isoleucine) (Table 22–2). Many of the reactions involved are closely analogous to reactions of straight and branched chain fatty acid catabolism. The structures of intermediates in leucine, valine, and isoleucine catabolism are given in Figs 22–37, 22–38, and 22–39. Because of the similarities noted in Fig 22–36, it is convenient to discuss the initial reactions in catabolism of all 3 amino acids together. In what follows, reaction numbers correspond to the numbered reactions of Figs 22–36, 22–37, 22–38, and 22–39.

A. Transamination: Reversible transamination (reaction 1) of all 3 branched L-α-amino acids in mammalian tissues probably is due to catalysis by a single transaminase. The reversibility of this reaction accounts for the ability of the corresponding α-keto acids

the carbons of valine—but only three-fifths of those of methionine and only half of those of isoleucine—contribute to the formation of succinyl-CoA. The carboxyl carbons of all 3 amino acids form CO_2 whereas the terminal 2 carbons of isoleucine form acetyl-CoA. In addition, the S-methyl group of methionine is removed as such.

The reactions leading from propionyl-CoA through methylmalonyl-CoA to succinyl-CoA—already discussed in connection with the catabolism of propi-

*Compounds whose methyl groups are derived from S-adenosylmethionine include betaines, choline, creatine, epinephrine, melatonin, sarcosine, various N-methylated amino acids, and various alkaloids of plant origin.

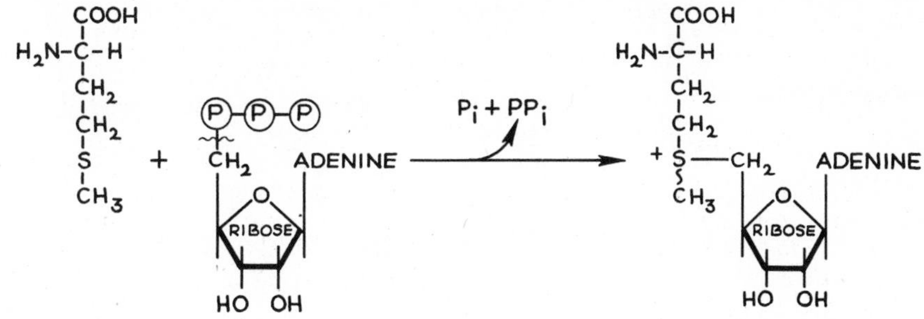

L-Methionine **ATP** **S-Adenosylmethionine ("active methionine")**

Figure 22–34. Formation of S-adenosylmethionine.

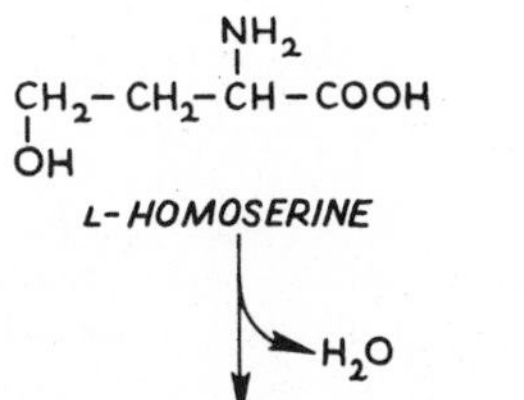

Figure 22–35. Conversion of L-homoserine to α-ketobutyrate, catalyzed by homoserine deaminase.

to replace a dietary requirement for the L-α-amino acids.

B. Oxidative Decarboxylation to Acyl-CoA Thioesters: These reactions (reaction 2) closely resemble the analogous oxidations of pyruvate to CO_2 and acetyl-CoA and of α-ketoglutarate to CO_2 and succinyl-CoA. Indirect evidence suggests the presence in mammals of at least 2 oxidative decarboxylases specific for only one or 2 α-keto acids. A partially purified mammalian decarboxylase is known which catalyzes oxidative decarboxylation of α-ketoisocaproate (from leucine) and of α-keto-β-methylvalerate (from isoleucine) but not of α-ketoisovalerate (from valine). In man, the available evidence suggests a single oxidative decarboxylase for all 3 α-keto acids. In **maple syrup urine disease,** a rare genetic defect in infants, a metabolic block due to a nonfunctional oxidative decarboxylase prevents further catabolism of all 3 α-keto acids (Fig 22–36). These acids accumulate in the blood and urine, imparting to urine the characteristic odor for which the defect is named. The accumulation of all 3 α-keto acids suggests a single oxidative decarboxylase. Menkes and others (1954) described 4 cases occurring in one family in which the disease was associated with severe functional impairment of the central nervous system. Death occurred in all cases at an early age. Another patient described by MacKenzie and Woolf (1959) first showed symptoms at 4 months of age consisting of jerking movements of the legs with occasional episodes of respiratory distress and cyanosis. During these episodes, the electrocardiogram indicated a severe generalized abnormality with multifocal discharges typical of metabolic disorders accompanied by seizures. During these acute episodes of the disease, the urinary excretion of the keto acids of the branched-chain amino acids was much increased and the urine emitted a characteristic odor similar to that of maple syrup.

C. Dehydrogenation to α,β-Unsaturated Acyl-CoA Thioesters: This reaction is analogous to dehydrogenation of straight chain acyl-CoA thioesters in fatty acid catabolism. It is not known whether a single enzyme catalyzes dehydrogenation of all 3 branched acyl-CoA thioesters; indirect evidence suggests that at least 2 enzymes are required. This evidence derives from chemical observations in **isovaleric acidemia,** wherein, following the ingestion of protein-rich foods, there occurs an increase of isovalerate in the blood. An increase in other branched α-keto acids does not occur. Isovalerate is formed by deacylation of isovaleryl-CoA, the substrate for the above dehydrogenase. Its formation suggests accumulation of isovaleryl-CoA, possibly due to a defective isovaleryl-CoA dehydrogenase. If a single

LEUCINE, VALINE, ISOLEUCINE
1
CORRESPONDING α-KETO ACIDS
2
CO2 + CORRESPONDING ACYL–CoA THIOESTERS
3
CORRESPONDING α,β–UNSATURATED ACYL–CoA THIOESTERS
LEU
VAL
ILE
β-HYDROXY-β-METHYL-GLUTARYL–CoA
SUCCINYL-CoA
PROPIONYL–CoA + ACETYL–CoA

Figure 22–36. Overall catabolism of the branched chain amino acids leucine, valine, and isoleucine in mammals. The first 3 reactions are common to all 3 amino acids; thereafter, the pathways diverge. Double lines intersecting arrows mark the sites of metabolic blocks in 2 rare human diseases: at 2, maple syrup urine disease, a defect in catabolism of all 3 amino acids; and at 3, isovaleric acidemia, a defect of leucine catabolism.

Leucine
α-KA
α-AA
α-Keto isocaproic acid
CoA·SH
CO2
Isovaleryl-CoA
[2H]
β-Methylcrotonyl-CoA
ADP
ATP
BIOTINYL-CO2
BIOTIN
4L
β-Methylcrotonyl-CoA
H2O
5L
β-Methylglutaconyl-CoA
β-Hydroxy-β-methyl-glutaryl-CoA
6L
Acetoacetic acid
Acetyl-CoA

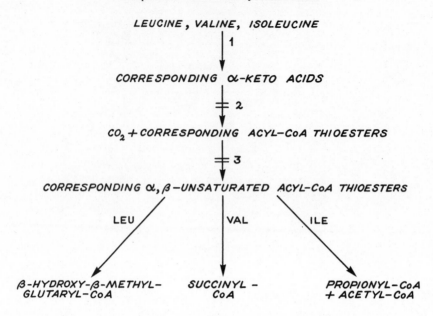

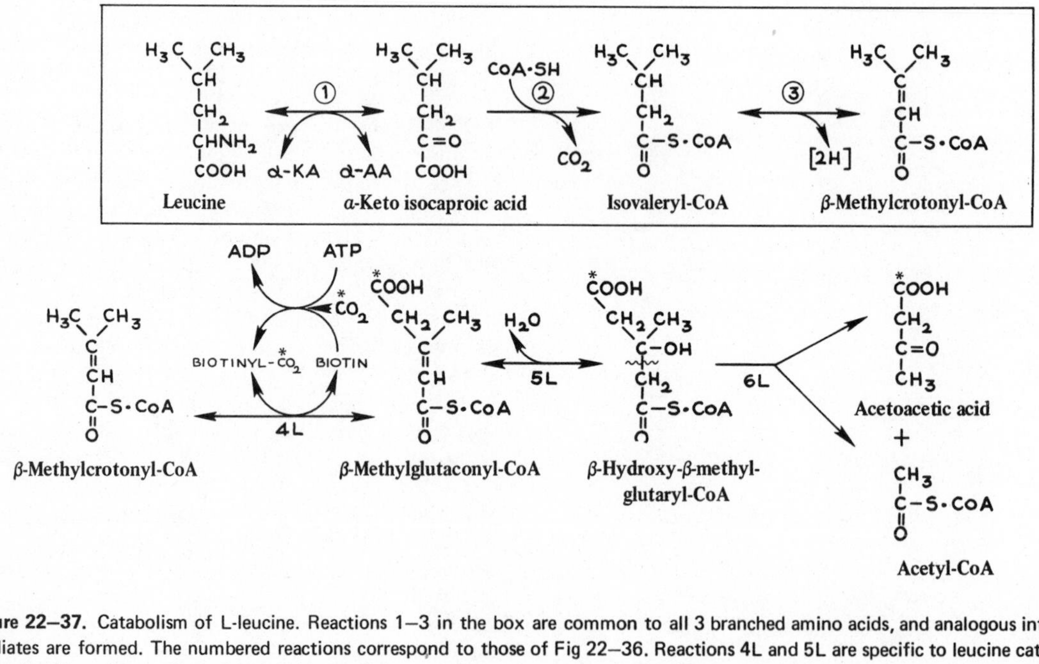

Figure 22–37. Catabolism of L-leucine. Reactions 1–3 in the box are common to all 3 branched amino acids, and analogous intermediates are formed. The numbered reactions correspond to those of Fig 22–36. Reactions 4L and 5L are specific to leucine catabolism. (α-KA = α-keto acids; α-AA = α-amino acids.)

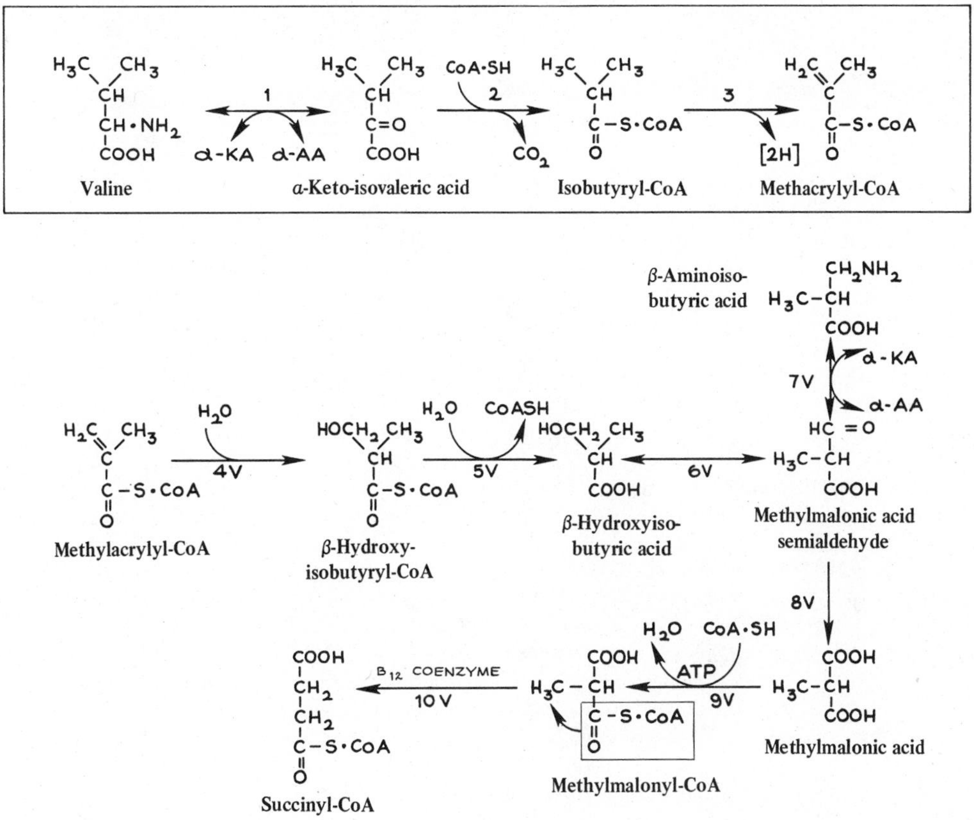

Figure 22—38. Catabolism of valine. Reactions 1—3 in the box are common to all 3 branched amino acids, and analogous intermediates are formed. The numbered reactions correspond to those of Fig 22—35. Reactions 4V through 10V are specific to valine catabolism. (a-KA = a-keto acid; a-AA = a-amino acid.)

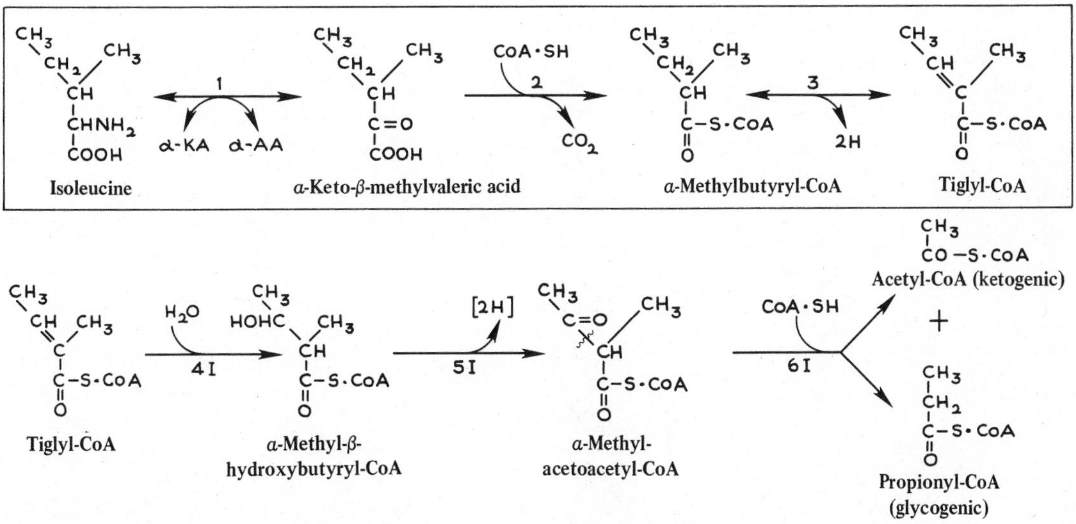

Figure 22—39. Catabolism of L-isoleucine. Reactions 1—3 in the box are common to all 3 branched amino acids, and analogous intermediates are formed. The numbered reactions correspond to those of Fig 22—35. Reactions 4I, 5I, and 6I are specific to isoleucine catabolism. (a-KA = a-keto acid; a-AA = a-amino acid.)

dehydrogenase served to dehydrogenate all 3 branched acyl-CoA thioesters, accumulation of isobutyrate (from valine) and α-methylbutyrate (from isoleucine) would be anticipated following a protein-rich meal.

Reactions Specific to Leucine Catabolism (Fig 22–37.)

Reaction 4L: Carboxylation of β-methylcrotonyl-CoA. A key observation leading to explanation of the ketogenic action of leucine (Table 22–2) was the discovery that 1 mol of CO_2 was "fixed" (ie, covalently bound) for every mol of isopropyl groups (from the terminal isopropyl group of leucine) converted to acetoacetate. This CO_2 fixation (reaction 4L, Fig 22–37) requires biotinyl-CO_2, formed from enzyme-bound biotin and CO_2 at the expense of ATP. Both in bacteria and in mammalian liver, this reaction forms β-methylglutaconyl-CoA as a free intermediate.

Reaction 5L: Hydration of β-methylglutaconyl-CoA. Very little is known about this reaction except that the product is β-hydroxy-β-methylglutaryl-CoA, a precursor not only of ketone bodies (reaction 6L, Fig 22–37) but also of mevalonate, and hence of cholesterol and other polyisoprenoids (see Chapter 19).

Reaction 6L: Cleavage of β-hydroxy-β-methylglutaryl-CoA. Cleavage of β-hydroxy-β-methylglutaryl-CoA to acetyl-CoA and acetoacetate occurs in mammalian liver, kidney, and heart mitochondria. It explains the strongly ketogenic effect of leucine, since not only is 1 mol of acetoacetate formed per mol of leucine catabolized but another ½ mol of ketone bodies may be formed indirectly from the remaining product, acetyl-CoA (see Chapter 19).

Reactions Specific to Valine Catabolism (Fig 22–38.)

Reaction 4: Hydration of methylacrylyl-CoA. Although this reaction occurs nonenzymatically at a relatively rapid rate, it is catalyzed by crystalline crotonase, a hydrolyase of broad specificity for L-β-hydroxyacyl-CoA thioesters possessing 4–9 carbon atoms.

Reaction 5V: Deacylation of β-hydroxyisobutyryl-CoA. Since the CoA thioester is not a substrate for the subsequent reaction (reaction 6V, Fig 22–38), it must first be deacylated to β-hydroxyisobutyrate (reaction 5V, Fig 22–38). This is catalyzed by a deacylase, present in many animal tissues, whose only other substrate is β-hydroxypropionyl-CoA.

Reaction 6V: Oxidation of β-hydroxyisobutyrate. Extracts of pig heart and other mammalian tissues catalyze the NAD-dependent oxidation of the primary alcohol group of β-hydroxyisobutyrate to an aldehyde (reaction 6V, Fig 22–38), forming methylmalonate semialdehyde. The reaction, which is readily reversible, is catalyzed by a purified, substrate-specific oxidoreductase from hog kidney.

Reaction 7V: Fate of methylmalonate semialdehyde. Two fates are possible for methylmalonate semialdehyde in mammalian tissues: transamination to β-aminoisobutyrate (reaction 7V, Fig 22–38) and conversion to succinyl-CoA (reactions 8V through 10V, Fig 22–38). Transamination to α-aminoisobutyrate, a

normal urinary amino acid, is catalyzed by various mammalian tissues including hog kidney. The second major fate involves oxidation to methylmalonate, acylation to methylmalonyl-CoA, and isomerization to succinyl-CoA (reactions 8V through 10V, Fig 22–38). This last reaction is of considerable interest and importance. The isomerization (reaction 10V, Fig 22–38) requires cobamide coenzyme and is catalyzed by methylmalonyl-CoA mutase. This reaction is important not only for valine catabolism but also for that of propionyl-CoA, a catabolite of isoleucine (Fig 22–39). In cobalt deficiency, the mutase activity is impaired. This produces a "dietary metabolic defect" in ruminants that utilize large quantities of propionate (from fermentation in the rumen) as an energy source. The purified mutase from sheep liver contains about 2 mols of deoxyadenosyl-B_{12} per mol. Rearrangement to succinyl-CoA, an intermediate of the citric acid cycle, occurs via an intramolecular shift of the CoA-carboxyl group. Although the reaction closely resembles the isomerization of threo-β-methylaspartate to glutamate, the reaction mechanisms appear to differ in significant details.

Reactions Specific to Isoleucine Catabolism (Fig 22–39.)

As with valine and leucine, the first data concerning isoleucine catabolism came from dietary studies using intact animals. These revealed that isoleucine was glycogenic and weakly ketogenic (Table 22–2). Glycogen synthesis from isoleucine was later confirmed using D_2O. Use of ^{14}C-labeled intermediates and liver slice preparations revealed that the isoleucine skeleton was cleaved, forming acetyl-CoA and propionyl-CoA (Fig 22–39).

Reaction 4I: Hydration of tiglyl-CoA. This reaction, like the analogous reaction in valine catabolism (reaction 4V, Fig 22–38), is catalyzed by crystalline mammalian crotonase.

Reaction 5I: Dehydrogenation of α-methyl-β-hydroxybutyryl-CoA. This reaction is analogous to that occurring in valine catabolism (reaction 5V, Fig 22–38). In valine catabolism, it will be recalled, the hydroxylated acyl-CoA thioester is first deacylated and then oxidized.

Reaction 6I: Thiolysis of α-methylacetoacetyl-CoA. Thiolytic cleavage of the covalent bond linking carbons 2 and 3 of α-methylacetoacetyl-CoA resembles the thiolysis of acetoacetyl-CoA to 2 mols of acetyl-CoA catalyzed by β-ketothiolase. The products, acetyl-CoA (ketogenic) and propionyl-CoA (glycogenic), account for the ketogenic and glycogenic properties of isoleucine.

METABOLIC DEFECTS IN AMINO ACID METABOLISM

This section discusses certain metabolic disorders of amino acid metabolism occurring in humans. Historically, these disorders played key roles in the elucidation of the pathways by which amino acids are metabolized in normal human subjects. Most of these diseases are rare, and in some cases have been reported in fewer than 6 individuals. As such, they are unlikely to be encountered by most practicing physicians. Their apparently low incidence in part reflects the absence, until quite recently, of automated technics for the identification and quantitation of individual amino acids in blood, urine, and spinal fluid. Recently developed technics for screening the blood and urine of large populations for abnormal amino acids or for abnormal levels of common amino acids may lead to more frequent recognition of these disorders. Technics have also been developed to assay enzymes present in the blood cells or in cultures of skin fibroblasts of patients. Technics yet to be developed will expand the horizons still further. It seems safe to predict an increase both in the number and in the apparent incidence of human metabolic disorders of amino acid metabolism.

Even though uncommon, these disorders present a formidable challenge to the psychiatrist, pediatrician, genetic counselor, or biochemist. They are detected most frequently at infancy, often are fatal at an early age, and often result in irreversible brain damage if left untreated. Their early detection and the rapid initiation of appropriate treatment, if available, are essential. Since several of the enzymes concerned are detectable in cultures of amniotic fluid cells, the prepartum diagnosis of these disorders by amniocentesis is now a distinct possibility. While current treatment consists primarily of feeding diets low in the amino acids whose catabolism is impaired, more effective treatment may some day be available. For example, circulating the patient's blood through a column containing the missing enzyme in an immobilized state may "replace" the deficient or defective enzyme in question.

These metabolic disorders result from alterations in the genetic code (see Chapter 26). Mutations which alter the triplet code of nucleotides present in the DNA of the genes cause production of proteins with modified primary structures (see Chapter 4). Depending on the nature of the primary change, other orders of protein structure may also be affected. While some changes in the primary structures of enzymes may have little or no effect, others may profoundly modify the 3-dimensional structure of catalytic or regulatory sites (see Chapter 6). The modified or mutant enzyme may possess altered catalytic efficiency (low V_{max} or high K_m) or altered ability to bind an allosteric regulator of its catalytic activity. Since most proteins contain over 100 amino acid residues, there are a great number of possible alterations in the primary structure of even a single enzyme. To this fact must be added a consideration of the large number of enzymes involved in amino acid catabolism. Predictably, the number of discrete disorders of amino acid catabolism is potentially extremely high. In principle, any of a wide variety of mutations may cause the same disease. For example, any mutation that causes a total or substantial loss of

the catalytic activity of argininosuccinase (Fig 22–12) will cause the metabolic disorder known as argininosuccinic acidemia. It is extremely unlikely, however, that all cases of argininosuccinic acidemia represent the same alteration in primary structure of argininosuccinase. In this sense they are, therefore, distinct molecular diseases.

Some of the known disorders of amino acid metabolism will be discussed in the text that follows.

Glycine

A. Glycinuria: Glycinuria is an extremely rare disorder of glycine metabolism which has so far been described in only one family. It is characterized by excess urinary excretion of glycine (glycinuria) in association with a tendency to formation of oxalate renal stones, although the amount of oxalate excreted in the urine is normal. Glycinuria appears to be inherited as a dominant, possibly X-linked, trait. The plasma content of glycine is normal in the glycinuric patients that have been studied while the urinary excretion of glycine ranges from 600–1000 mg/day. Consequently, it is assumed that glycinuria is attributable to a defect in renal tubular transport of glycine whereby decreased reabsorption of glycine by the renal tubule permits the amino acid to escape into the urine in greatly increased amounts.

B. Primary Hyperoxaluria: Primary hyperoxaluria is a metabolic disease characterized biochemically by a continuous high urinary excretion of oxalate which is unrelated to the dietary intake of oxalate. The history of the disease is that of progressive bilateral calcium oxalate urolithiasis, nephrocalcinosis, and recurrent infection of the urinary tract. Death occurs in childhood or early adult life from renal failure or hypertension. The excess oxalate is apparently of endogenous origin, possibly from glycine, which may be deaminated to form glyoxylate, itself a direct source of oxalate. The metabolic defect in this disease is considered to be a disorder of glyoxylate metabolism associated with failure to convert glyoxylate to formate or to convert it back to glycine by transamination. As a result, the excess glyoxylate is oxidized to oxalate. Glycine transaminase deficiency, together with some impairment of oxidation of glyoxylate to formate, may be the biochemical explanation for the inherited metabolic disease primary hyperoxaluria.

As might be expected, vitamin B_6-deficient animals (rats) excrete markedly increased quantities of oxalate because the glutamic or alanine-glyoxylic transaminase reactions are vitamin B_6-dependent. The excretion of oxalate in B_6-deficient rats can be enhanced by feeding glycine or by feeding vitamin B_6 antagonists. However, administration of vitamin B_6 has not been of benefit in clinical cases of endogenous hyperoxaluria.

Disorders Involving the Urea Cycle

Urea synthesis in the liver involves 5 enzymes (Fig 22–12); metabolic disorders associated with a deficiency of each of these 5 enzymes are known. The rate-limiting reactions of urea synthesis appear to be catalyzed by carbamoyl phosphate synthetase (reaction 1), ornithine transcarbamoylase (reaction 2), and arginase (reaction 5). Since the sole function of the urea cycle is to convert ammonia to the nontoxic compound urea, all disorders of urea synthesis cause ammonia intoxication. This intoxication is more severe when the metabolic block occurs at reactions 1 or 2, since some covalent linking of ammonia to carbon has already occurred if citrulline can be synthesized. Clinical symptoms common to all urea cycle disorders include vomiting in infancy, avoidance of high-protein foods, intermittent ataxia, irritability, lethargy, and mental retardation. The individual enzymic defects are discussed below.

The clinical features and the treatment of all 5 of the disorders discussed below are similar. Significant improvement is noted on a low-protein diet, and much of the brain damage may thus be prevented. The daily food intake should be given in frequent small feedings to avoid sudden increases in blood ammonia levels. Decreasing the absorption of ammonia formed by bacterial decomposition of amino acids in the intestines by attempts at intestinal sterilization using appropriate antibiotic drugs is not, apparently, of value.

A. Hyperammonemia Type I: One case of carbamoyl phosphate synthetase deficiency (reaction 1, Fig 22−12) has so far been reported. This probably is a familial disorder.

B. Hyperammonemia Type II: There are reports of at least 8 patients that have been shown to suffer from a deficiency of ornithine transcarbamoylase (reaction 2, Fig 22−12). All but one were females. The mothers also exhibited hyperammonemia and an aversion to high-protein foods. The only consistent clinical finding was an elevation of glutamine in the blood, cerebrospinal fluid, and urine. This probably reflects enhanced synthesis of glutamine by the glutamine synthetase reaction (Fig 22−10) consequent to elevated tissue levels of ammonia.

C. Citrullinemia: This extremely rare disorder (3 patients known) probably is recessively inherited. Large quantities (1−2 g/day) of citrulline are excreted in the urine, and both plasma and cerebrospinal fluid citrulline levels are markedly elevated. In one patient, complete absence of argininosuccinate synthetase activity (reaction 3, Fig 22−12) was noted. In another, a less profound modification of this enzyme appears to have occurred. The K_m value for citrulline for the synthetase from cultured fibroblasts from this patient was about 25 times normal. This strongly suggests a mutation causing a significant but not "lethal" modification of the catalytic site of the synthetase.

D. Argininosuccinic Aciduria: This rare recessive heritable disease (22 cases reported) is characterized by elevated levels of argininosuccinic acid in the blood, cerebrospinal fluid, and urine. It frequently is associated with the occurrence of friable, tufted hair **(trichorrhexis nodosa)**. While both early- and late-onset types are known, the disease is always manifest by age 2; it usually terminates fatally at an early age.

Argininosuccinic aciduria reflects the absence of **argininosuccinase** activity (reaction 4, Fig 22−12). Cultured skin fibroblasts from normal patients contain this enzyme, whereas those from patients with argininosuccinic acidemia do not. Argininosuccinase is also absent from brain, liver, kidney, and erythrocytes of patients with this disease. While the diagnosis is readily made by 2-dimensional paper chromatography of the urine, additional abnormal spots appear in urine on standing due to the tendency of argininosuccinate to form cyclic anhydrides. Confirmatory diagnosis is by measurement of erythrocyte levels of argininosuccinase. This test can be performed on cord blood for early detection. Since argininosuccinase is present in cultivated amniotic fluid cells, diagnosis by amniocentesis is also possible.

E. Hyperargininemia: This defect in urea synthesis (2 cases reported) is characterized by elevated blood and cerebrospinal fluid arginine levels, low erythrocyte levels of **arginase** (reaction 5, Fig 22−12), and a urinary amino acid pattern resembling that of lysine-cystinuria. Possibly this pattern reflects competition by arginine with lysine and cystine for reabsorption in the renal tubule. In the patients afflicted with this disease, a low-protein diet resulted in a lowering of plasma ammonia levels and the disappearance of the urinary lysine-cystinuria pattern.

Phenylalanine & Tyrosine

A. Phenylketonuria: Phenylketonuria is an inherited disorder of phenylalanine metabolism that occurs with a frequency of about one in 10,000 births. The disorder is biochemically attributable to absence of activity of a functional component I of phenylalanine hydroxylase (see Chapter 23). The patient is therefore unable to convert phenylalanine to tyrosine and, as a result, alternative catabolites of phenylalanine are produced (Fig 22−40); these include phenylpyruvic acid, the product of deamination of phenylalanine; phenyllactic acid, the reduction product of phenylpyruvic acid; and phenylacetic acid, produced by decarboxylation and oxidation of phenylpyruvic acid. Much of the phenylacetate is conjugated in the liver with glutamine and excreted in the urine as the conjugate, phenylacetylglutamine. Table 22−3 illustrates the chemical pattern in the blood and urine of a phenylketonuric patient. It is the presence in the urine of the keto acid phenylpyruvate that gives the disease its designation phenylketonuria.

Among infants and children exhibiting this metabolic defect, retarded mental development occurs for as yet unknown reasons. In the absence of a normal catabolic pathway for phenylalanine, several reactions of otherwise minor quantitative importance in normal liver assume a major catabolic role. In phenylketonurics, phenylpyruvate, phenyllactate, phenylacetate, and its glutamine conjugate phenacetylglutamine are formed and occur in the blood and urine (Fig 22−40). Although phenylpyruvate, which occurs in the urine of most phenylketonuric patients, can be detected by a simple biochemical spot test, a definitive diagnosis re-

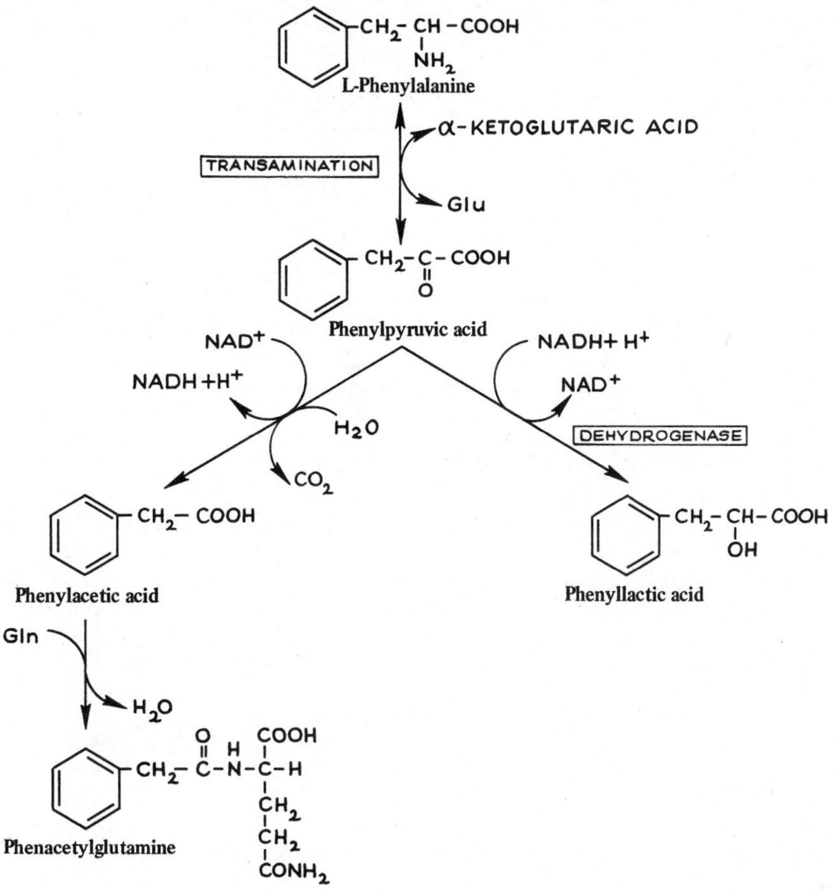

Figure 22—40. Alternative pathways of phenylalanine catabolism of particular importance in phenylketonuria. The reactions shown also occur in the liver tissue of normal individuals but are of minor significance if a functional phenylalanine hydroxylase is present. (Glu = glutamate; Gln = glutamine.)

quires determination of elevated plasma phenylalanine levels.

The mental performance of phenylketonuric children can be improved if they are maintained on a diet containing very low levels of phenylalanine. Clinical improvement is accompanied by a return to the normal range of blood phenylalanine levels and a reduced excretion of "alternative catabolites." Detection of the disease as early in infancy as possible is important if dietary treatment is to yield favorable results in mental development. The diet can be terminated at 6 years of age, when high concentrations of phenylalanine no longer are injurious to the brain.

Plasma phenylalanine may be measured by an automated micro method that requires as little as 20 μl of blood per determination. It is important to note, however, that abnormally high blood phenylalanine levels may not occur in phenylketonuric infants until the third or fourth day of life. Furthermore, false positive tests may occur in premature infants due to delayed maturation of the enzymes required for phenylalanine catabolism. A useful but somewhat less reliable

Table 22—3. Metabolites of phenylalanine accumulating in the plasma and urine of phenylketonuric patients.

Metabolite	Plasma (mg/dl)		Urine (mg/dl)	
	Normal	Phenylketonuric	Normal	Phenylketonuric
Phenylalanine	1–2	15–63	30	300–1000
Phenylpyruvate		0.3–1.8		300–2000
Phenyllactate				290–550
Phenylacetate				Increased
Phenylacetylglutamine			200–300	2400

screening test depends on detecting the elevated urinary levels of phenylpyruvate with ferric chloride.

It would be expected that the administration of phenylalanine to a phenylketonuric subject would result in prolonged elevation of the level of this amino acid in the blood, ie, diminished tolerance to phenylalanine. However, it has been found that an abnormally low tolerance to injected phenylalanine and a high fasting level of phenylalanine are also characteristic of the parents of the phenylketonuric individual. Evidently the recessive gene responsible for phenylketonuria can be detected biochemically in the phenotypically normal parents.

Several metabolic disorders of tyrosine catabolism are recognized, characterized by the excretion in urine of tyrosine itself and of tyrosine catabolites. Tyrosinosis has been reported thus far in only one patient; thus, it appears to be of very limited clinical interest. Its significance lies solely in the information it provides on the normal pathways of tyrosine catabolism in human liver. A range of familial disorders of tyrosine catabolism with associated liver cirrhosis and defective renal tubular reabsorption is reported under the descriptions of hereditary tryosinemia, atypical tyrosinosis, genuine tyrosyluria, or tyrosinemia. While these appear to be familial disorders, the relationship between them is not clear at present. There is doubt that, despite the clinical findings, all represent true metabolic defects of tyrosine catabolism.

B. Tyrosinosis: The enzymic defect in this syndrome is probably the absence either of hepatic **p-hydroxyphenylpyruvate hydroxylase** or of **tyrosine transaminase** activities (Fig 22–25). The patient described as afflicted with tyrosinosis excreted large quantities (1.5–3 g/day) of tyrosine in the urine. On a diet rich in tyrosine, other p-hydroxyphenyl acids, including 3,4-dihydroxyphenylalanine (dopa) (see Chapter 23) and p-hydroxyphenyllactic acid, were also excreted.

C. Tyrosinemia: Over 100 cases in which plasma tyrosine levels are elevated far above normal have been reported. While these may represent a spectrum of metabolic defects, the common clinical findings include hepatosplenomegaly, a nodular cirrhosis of the liver, abnormalities of tyrosine and methionine metabolism, p-hydroxyphenyllactic aciduria, multiple defects in renal tubular reabsorption, rickets, hyperphosphaturia and proteinuria, and aminoaciduria. While the enzyme defect appears to be hereditary, its exact nature is unknown. Treatment with a diet low in tyrosine and phenylalanine improves renal function and possibly also retards degenerative liver changes.

D. Alkaptonuria: This inherited metabolic disorder was noted in the medical literature as early as the 16th and 17th centuries, although it was not characterized in detail until 1859. The disease is of considerable historical interest because it formed the basis for Garrod's ideas concerning heritable metabolic disorders. Its most striking clinical manifestation is the occurrence of dark urine on standing in air. Late in the disease there occur generalized pigmentation of connective tissues (ochronosis) and a form of arthritis. The metabolic defect is attributable, therefore, to lack of activity of **homogentisate oxidase** (Fig 22–25). The substrate, homogentisate, is excreted in the urine, where it is oxidized in air to a brownish-black pigment. Over 600 cases have been reported; the estimated incidence of alkaptonuria is 2–5 per million live births.

Histidine

A. Histidinemia: Histidinemia is an inherited disorder of histidine metabolism. In addition to increased levels of histidine in the blood and urine, there is also increased excretion of imidazole pyruvic acid (which in a color test with ferric chloride may be mistaken for phenylpyruvic acid, so that a mistaken diagnosis of phenylketonuria could be made). Speech development may be retarded. The metabolic block in histidinemia is considered to be inadequate activity of liver histidase, which would impair conversion of histidine to urocanic acid. The alternative route of histidine metabolism, which involves transamination to form imidazole pyruvic acid, would then be favored and the excess imidazole pyruvic acid would be excreted in the urine. Imidazole acetic acid and imidazole lactic acid, the reduction product of imidazole pyruvic acid, have also been detected in the urine of histidinemic patients.

The quantity of histidine found in normal urine is relatively large. For this reason it may be more readily detected than most other amino acids. It has been reported that a conspicuous increase in histidine excretion is a characteristic finding in normal pregnancy but does not occur in toxemic states associated with pregnancy. The normally increased excretion of histidine during pregnancy apparently does not result from a metabolic defect in the metabolism of histidine. The phenomenon may be explained largely on the basis of the changes in renal function which are characteristic of normal pregnancy as well as the pregnancy toxemias. Furthermore, the alterations in amino acid excretion during pregnancy are not confined to histidine.

B. Imidazole Aminoaciduria: Three families in which there were 5 patients with cerebromacular degeneration have been found to have a generalized imidazole aminoaciduria. Some other members of the immediate family also exhibited a generalized imidazole aminoaciduria. The patients excreted large amounts of carnosine and anserine as well as histidine and 1-methylhistidine. In normal urine, the excretion of carnosine and of anserine is 2–3 mg/day and 5–7 mg/day, respectively; in these patients, 20–100 mg/day were excreted. The patients also had a greatly increased urinary content of histidine and of 1-methylhistidine. The parents and unaffected siblings had urinary biochemical abnormalities similar to those of the patients but without the symptoms of neurologic and retinal disease (cerebral degeneration and blindness). The imidazoluria appears to be genetically transmitted as a dominant trait and the cerebromacular degeneration as a recessive trait. The fact that the 2 traits have been found in 3 unrelated families suggests that both traits are manifestations of the same gene. The disease seems to resemble biochemically the findings in Hart-nup's disease, a disorder of tryptophan metabolism (to be described below), in that both diseases are characterized by defects in transport: one for the imidazoles and the other (Hartnup's disease) for the indoles.

Proline & Hydroxyproline

Defects in proline or hydroxyproline catabolism are extremely rare, having been reported in only 2 and 3 patients, respectively. Both were afflicted with severe mental retardation. Diets restricted in proline and hydroxyproline appear to be of dubious therapeutic benefit.

· **A. Prolinemia:** This heritable disorder is characterized by elevated plasma proline levels and by the urinary excretion of large quantities of proline, hydroxyproline, and serine. Two distinct types appear to exist. Type I appears to reflect a deficiency of **proline hydroxylase** activity; type II, a lack of activity of an enzyme concerned with the further catabolism of Δ^1-pyrroline-5-carboxylate (Fig 22–16).

B. Hydroxyprolinemia: This rare heritable disorder probably reflects the absence of activity of the enzyme catalyzing conversion of 4-hydroxy-L-proline to L-Δ^1-pyrroline-3-hydroxy-5-carboxylate (Fig 22–24). As such, it represents an enzyme deletion analogous to that of type I prolinemia. The clinical findings include severe mental retardation, elevated plasma hydroxyproline levels, and the urinary excretion of abnormal quantities of hydroxyproline and hydroxyprolyl peptides.

Lysine

Two rare metabolic abnormalities of lysine catabolism are known:

A. Hyperlysinemia With Associated Hyperammonemia: Only a single case has been reported. The exact metabolic defect is not known. The hyperammonemia does not reflect a defect in any of the enzymes of urea synthesis.

B. Persistent Hyperlysinemia: In this rare disorder (7 reported cases), plasma lysine levels are significantly (but not greatly) elevated. Hyperammonemia does not occur even after a test dose of lysine. In one case, plasma levels of saccharopine, a catabolite of L-lysine (Fig 22–28), was reported. No consistent mental retardation is associated with this disease.

Sulfur-Containing Amino Acids

A. Cystinuria (Cystine-Lysinuria): In this inherited metabolic disease, excretion of cystine in the urine is increased to 20–30 times normal. The excretion of lysine, arginine, and ornithine is also markedly increased. Cystinuria is considered to be due to a renal transport defect. The greatly increased excretion of lysine, arginine, and ornithine as well as cystine in the urine of cystinuric patients suggests that there exists in these individuals a defect in the renal reabsorptive mechanisms for these 4 amino acids. It is possible that a single reabsorptive site is involved. Thus, as far as renal mechanisms are concerned, cystinuria is not an uncomplicated defect which affects only cystine; the term "cystinuria" is therefore actually a misnomer, so that cystine-lysinuria may now be the preferred descriptive term for this disease.

Because cystine is a relatively insoluble amino acid, in cystinuric patients it may precipitate in the kidney tubules and form cystine calculi. This may be a major complication of the disease; were it not for this possibility, cystinuria would be an entirely benign anomaly and probably would escape recognition in many cases.

Although cystine is the principal sulfur-containing amino acid which occurs in the urine of the cystinuric patient, another sulfur-containing amino acid has also been detected in significant quantities in the urine of cystinurics. This amino acid has been identified as a mixed disulfide (Fig 22–41) composed of L-cysteine

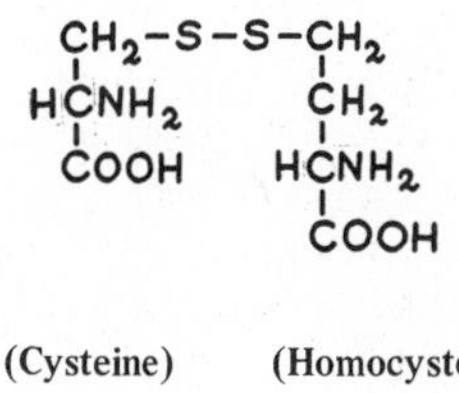

(Cysteine) (Homocysteine)

Figure 22–41. Structure of the "mixed" disulfide of cysteine and homocysteine.

and L-homocysteine. This compound is somewhat more soluble than cystine; to the extent that it may be formed at the expense of cystine, it would therefore reduce the tendency to formation of cystine crystals and calculi in the urine.

Evidence now indicates that there may be an intestinal transport defect for these amino acids as well. A failure in concentration of cystine and lysine in cells of the jejunal mucosa obtained by biopsy of the jejunal area of the intestine of cystinuric patients has been detected.

In an investigation of the transport of the affected amino acids in cystinuria into kidney slices obtained by biopsy from normal and cystinuric patients, it was found that lysine and arginine transport was defective in the cystinuric tissue but cystine transport was normal. All of the above experiments suggest that some revision of the present concepts of the etiology of cystinuria may be required.

B. Cystinosis (Cystine Storage Disease): Cystinuria should be differentiated from cystinosis. In the latter disease, which is also inherited, cystine crystals are deposited in many tissues and organs (particularly the reticuloendothelial system) throughout the body. It is usually accompanied by a generalized aminoaciduria in which all amino acids are considerably increased in the urine. Various other renal functions are also seriously impaired, and these patients usually die at an early age with all of the manifestations of acute renal failure. On the other hand, except for the likelihood of the formation of cystine calculi, cystinuria is compatible with a normal existence.

C. Homocystinuria: The incidence of this heritable defect of methionine catabolism is estimated at one in 160,000 births. Homocystine (up to 300 mg/day), together with S-adenosylmethionine in some cases, is excreted in the urine, and plasma methionine levels are elevated. Associated clinical findings include the occurrence of thromboses, osteoporosis, dislocated lenses in the eyes, and frequently also mental retardation. Two forms of the disease are known: a vitamin B_6-sensitive form and a B_6-insensitive form. Treatment, which involves feeding a diet low in methionine and high in cystine, effectively prevents pathologic changes if initiated early in life. The disease reflects impaired activity of **cystathionine synthetase** (Fig 22–33).

Branched Chain Amino Acids
(Leucine, Valine, Isoleucine)

Four defects in branched chain amino acid catabolism are known. Of these, maple syrup urine disease has been most extensively studied. Over 50 cases have been reported. The incidence of the disease has been estimated as 5–10 per million live births. Hypervalinemia, intermittent branched chain ketonuria, and isovaleric acidemia have been reported in only 1, 3, and 4 children, respectively.

A. Hypervalinemia: This metabolic disease, characterized by elevated plasma levels of valine (but not of leucine or isoleucine), reflects the inability to transaminate valine to α-ketoisovalerate (reaction 1, Fig 22–38). However, transamination of leucine and isoleucine (reaction 1, Figs 22–37 and 22–39) is unimpaired. (See Table 22–4.)

Table 22–4. Ability of leukocytes from a patient with hypervalinemia and of leukocytes from 2 normal individuals to catalyze transamination of branched chain amino acids.*

Amino Acid	Relative Rate of Transamination	
	Hypervalinemia	Control (Range)
Valine	0	70–135
Isoleucine	346	220–270
Leucine	387	140–185

*From Dancis & others: Pediatrics 39:813, 1967.

In the one known instance of hypervalinemia, feeding a diet low in valine prevented vomiting, improved weight gain, and reduced hyperkinesia.

B. Maple Syrup Urine Disease: As the name implies, the most striking feature of this hereditary disease is the characteristic odor of the urine, which resembles that of maple syrup or of burnt sugar. In afflicted individuals, both plasma and urinary levels of the branched chain amino acids leucine, isoleucine, and valine and their corresponding α-keto acids (Figs 22–37, 22–38, and 22–39) are greatly elevated (Table 22–5). For this reason, the disease has also been

Table 22–5. Plasma levels of branched chain amino acids in normal individuals and in 3 patients with maple syrup urine disease.

Amino Acid	Concentration (mg/dl)			
	Normal (Range)	Maple Syrup Urine Disease, Patient		
		A	B	C
Leucine	1.5–3.0	52	14	21
Valine	2.0–3.0	24	13	14
Isoleucine	0.8–1.5	18	2.2	8.5

termed branched chain ketonuria. Smaller quantities of branched chain α-hydroxy acids, formed by reduction of the α-keto acids, also are present in the urine.

Although the afflicted newborn infant initially appears to be normal, the characteristic signs of the disease are evident by the end of the first week of extrauterine life. In addition to the biochemical abnormalities described above, the infant is difficult to feed and may vomit. The patient may also exhibit a significant degree of lethargy. Diagnosis prior to 1 week of age is possible only by enzymic analysis. Extensive brain damage occurs in surviving children. Without treatment, death usually occurs by the end of the first year of life.

The biochemical defect is the absence or greatly reduced activity of the **α-keto acid decarboxylase** which catalyzes conversion of all 3 branched chain α-keto acids to CO_2 plus acyl-CoA thioesters (reaction 2, Figs 22–37, 22–38, and 22–39). This has been established by enzymic analysis of leukocytes and of cultured skin fibroblasts from children with this disease. The mechanism of toxicity, which is probably complex, is unknown. Possible factors in toxicity include the ability of large excesses of the branched chain amino acids to impair transport of other amino acids, alter amino acid pool sizes, and thus, possibly, to impair protein synthesis. All 3 branched chain α-keto acids also are competitive inhibitors of L-glutamate dehydrogenase activity (Fig 22–8).

Early diagnosis is very important, so that the patient can be placed on a diet in which protein is supplied only by a mixture of purified amino acids from which leucine, isoleucine, and valine are omitted. When the plasma levels of these amino acids fall within the normal range, they are restored to the diet in the form of milk and other foods in amounts adequate to supply—but not to exceed—the requirements for branched chain amino acids. There is no indication when, if ever, dietary restrictions may be eased. One fatality occurred as late as age 8. In those cases where treatment was initiated in the first week of life, considerable success was achieved in mitigating the dire consequences of the disease.

C. Intermittent Branched Chain Ketonuria: This disease, a variant of maple syrup urine disease, probably reflects a less severe structural modification of the **α-keto acid decarboxylase.** The decarboxylase activity of leukocytes and of fibroblasts, while distinctly lower than that of normal individuals, is well above those characteristic of classical maple syrup urine disease.

Since these individuals appear to possess an impaired but nevertheless distinct capability for catabolism of leucine, valine, and isoleucine, it is perhaps understandable that the typical symptoms of maple syrup urine disease occur later in life and only intermittently. The prognosis for successful use of dietary therapy would appear to be far more favorable in these individuals.

Taken together, maple syrup urine disease and intermittent branched chain ketonuria appear to illustrate the situation described in the introduction to this section—mutations causing different changes in the primary structure of the same enzyme. It is probable that a spectrum of activities ranging from frank disease through intermittent manifestations to normal values in fact occur in individual subjects.

D. Isovaleric Acidemia: The relevant findings include a persistent "cheesy" odor of the breath and body fluids, vomiting, acidosis, and coma precipitated by excessive ingestion of protein, or by an episode of infectious disease. Mild mental retardation was associated with the 3 known cases. The biochemical defect appears to be a deficiency of leucine catabolism. The impaired enzyme is **isovaleryl-CoA dehydrogenase** (reaction 3, Fig 22–37). Isovaleryl-CoA thus accumulates, is hydrolyzed to isovalerate, and is excreted in the urine and sweat.

Tryptophan

Hartnup's disease is a hereditary abnormality in the metabolism of tryptophan, characterized by a pellagra-like skin rash, intermittent cerebellar ataxia, and mental deterioration. The urine of patients with Hartnup's disease contains greatly increased amounts of indoleacetic acid (a-N[indole-3-acetyl]glutamine), as well as tryptophan.

The indole acids of human urine have been studied by paper chromatography. A total of 38 different indole acids were chromatographed. The most strikingly "abnormal" patterns of indole acid excretion were found in the urine of severely mentally retarded patients and in urine from the mentally ill. The significance of these findings has been questioned insofar as the causes of mental disease were concerned, particularly in view of the fact that the urinary excretion patterns tended to revert to normal after administration of broad-spectrum antibiotics.

Defects of Propionate, Methylmalonate, & Vitamin B_{12} Metabolism

Propionyl-CoA is formed from isoleucine (Fig 22–39) and methionine (Figs 22–32 and 22–33), as well as from the side chain of cholesterol and from fatty acids with odd numbers of carbon atoms. The conversion of propionyl-CoA to amphibolic intermediates involves biotin-dependent carboxylation to methylmalonyl-CoA. Methylmalonyl-CoA also is formed directly (ie, without prior formation of propionyl-CoA) from valine (Figs 22–32 and 22–38, reaction 9V). A vitamin B_{12} coenzyme-dependent isomerization converts malonyl-CoA to succinyl-CoA, a citric acid intermediate, which is oxidized to CO_2 and water.

Shortly after the discovery that 5′-deoxyadenosylcobalamin is a cofactor for the isomerization of methylmalonyl-CoA to succinyl-CoA, patients with acquired vitamin B_{12} deficiency were observed to excrete large quantities of methylmalonate in their urine. This methylmalonic aciduria disappeared when sufficient vitamin B_{12} was administered. Recently, a number of instances involving seriously ill children have been reported. In all of these cases, the patients appear to be afflicted with similar defects in propionate or methylmalonyl-CoA metabolism.

A. Propionic Acidemia: Propionyl-CoA carboxylase deficiency is characterized by high serum propionate levels and by defective catabolism of propionate by leukocytes. Treatment involves feeding a low-protein diet and measures to counteract metabolic acidosis.

B. Methylmalonic Aciduria: Two forms of methylmalonic aciduria are known. One responds to administration of vitamin B_{12}; the other does not. In the B_{12}-unresponsive disease, the enzyme **methylmalonyl-CoA isomerase** is defective. A patient with this latter condition responded favorably to massive doses (1 g/day) of vitamin B_{12}. Cultured fibroblasts from this patient grown in media containing 25 pg of vitamin B_{12} per ml oxidized ^{14}C-propionate poorly. The cultured cells contained only about 10% as much 5′-deoxyadenosylcobalamin as did control cells. When the concentration of vitamin B_{12} in the medium was increased 10,000-fold, the rate of propionate oxidation and the intracellular concentration of 5′-deoxyadenosylcobalamin both approached normal. No defect in binding the coenzyme to the mutase apoenzyme was observed. The defect in the B_{12}-responsive form of methylmalonic aciduria thus appears to be the inability to form 5′-deoxyadenosylcobalamin from normal levels of the vitamin.

The above selection of inherited diseases of amino acid catabolism is generally confined to the adequately studied diseases now known. Further details are available in Stanbury & others (1972).

References

Nitrogen Catabolism of the Amino Acids

Allison JB, Bird JWC: Elimination of nitrogen from the body. Page 483 in: *Mammalian Protein Metabolism.* Vol 1. Munro HN, Allison JB (editors). Academic Press, 1964.

Fasella P: Pyridoxal phosphate. Annu Rev Biochem 36:185, 1967.

Hardy RWF, Burns RC: Biological nitrogen fixation. Annu Rev Biochem 37:331, 1968.

Katanuma N, Okada M, Nishii Y: Regulation of the urea cycle and TCA cycle by ammonia. Adv Enzyme Regul 4:317, 1966.

Meister A: The specificity of glutamine synthetase and its relationship to substrate conformation at the active site. Adv Enzymol 31:183, 1968.

Ratner S: Enzymes of arginine and urea synthesis. Adv Enzymol 39:1, 1973.

Sallach HJ, Fahien LA: Nitrogen metabolism of amino acids. Page 1 in: *Metabolic Pathways.* Vol 3. Greenberg DM (editor). Academic Press, 1969.

Snell EE & others: *Pyridoxal Catalysis: Enzymes and Model Systems.* Interscience, 1968.

Wurtman RJ: Time-dependent variations in amino acid metabolism: Mechanism of the tyrosine transaminase rhythm in rat liver. Adv Enzyme Regul 7:57, 1968.

Conversion of the Carbon Skeletons of the Common Amino Acids to Amphibolic Intermediates

Greenberg DM, Rodwell VW: Carbon catabolism of amino acids. Pages 95 and 191 in: *Metabolic Pathways.* Vol 3. Greenberg DM (editor). Academic Press, 1969.

Hayaishi O: Enzymic hydroxylation. Annu Rev Biochem 38:21, 1969.

Krebs HA: The metabolic fate of the amino acids. Page 125 in: *Mammalian Protein Metabolism.* Vol. 1. Munro HN, Allison JB (editors). Academic Press, 1964.

Meister A: *Biochemistry of the Amino Acids,* 2nd ed. Vol 2. Academic Press, 1965.

Tabor H, Tabor CW: Biosynthesis and metabolism of 1,4-diaminobutane, spermidine, spermine and related amines. Adv Enzymol 36:203, 1972.

Metabolic Defects in Amino Acid Metabolism

Aebi HE: Inborn errors of metabolism. Annu Rev Biochem 36:271, 1967.

Frimter GW: Aminoacidurias due to disorders of metabolism. (2 parts.) N Engl J Med 289:835, 895, 1973.

Holt LE Jr, Snyderman SE: Anomalies of amino acid metabolism. Page 321 in: *Mammalian Protein Metabolism.* Vol 2. Munro HN, Allison JB (editors). Academic Press, 1964.

Hsia DY-Y: Inborn errors of metabolism. Page 301 in: *Diseases of Metabolism,* 5th ed. Duncan GG (editor). Saunders, 1964.

Larner J: Inborn errors of metabolism. Annu Rev Biochem 31:569, 1962.

Motulsky AG: Science 185:653, 1974.

Shih VE: *Laboratory Techniques for the Detection of Hereditary Metabolic Disorders,* CRC Press, 1973.

Stanbury JB, Wyngaarden JB, Fredrickson DS (editors): *The Metabolic Basis of Inherited Disease,* 3rd ed. McGraw-Hill, 1972.

23...
Biosynthesis of Amino Acids

NUTRITIONALLY ESSENTIAL & NUTRITIONALLY NONESSENTIAL AMINO ACIDS

Most prokaryotic cells (eg, bacteria) and many eukaryotic cells (eg, plants, yeasts) are capable of synthesizing from amphibolic intermediates all the amino acids present in proteins. Higher animals, including man, possess this ability for certain amino acids but not for others. Those amino acids that cannot be synthesized in adequate quantities by higher animals must therefore be taken in the diet. These are the **nutritionally essential amino acids.** Those that can be synthesized from amphibolic intermediates are designated **nutritionally nonessential amino acids** (Table 23–1).

It should be emphasized that some 22 amino acids are essential in the sense that all are constituents of the body proteins. The terms sometimes used by nutritionists in categorizing amino acids as "essential" or "nonessential" ("indispensable" or "dispensable") are less than accurate unless understood in the proper context as mentioned above. It might even be argued that the nutritionally nonessential amino acids are more important to the cell than the nutritionally essential amino acids, since organisms (eg, man) have evolved that lack the ability to manufacture the latter but not the former group.

The existence of nutritional requirements for amino acids in man can be interpreted as evidence that dependence on an external supply of a required intermediate can be of greater survival value than the ability to manufacture it. If a specific intermediate (eg, an amino acid) is present in the food supply, an organism that can synthesize it is reproducing and transferring to future generations genetic information of negative survival value. The reason that the survival value is negative rather than nil is that ATP and nutrients are being used to synthesize useless DNA. The number of enzymes required by prokaryotic cells to synthesize the nutritionally essential amino acids is large in relation to the number of enzymes required to synthesize the nutritionally nonessential amino acids (Table 23–2). This suggests that there is a positive survival advantage in retaining the ability to manufacture "easy" amino acids while losing the ability to make "difficult" amino acids.

Table 23–2. Enzymes required for the synthesis of amino acids from amphibolic intermediates. (Adapted from Davis BD: The teleonomic significance of biosynthetic control mechanisms. Cold Spring Harbor Symposia 26:1, 1961.)

Number of Enzymes Required to Synthesize:			
Nutritionally Essential		Nutritionally Nonessential	
Arg*	7	Ala	1
His	6	Asp	1
Thr	6	Asn†	1
Met	5 (4 shared)	Glu	1
Lys	8	Gln*	1
Ile	8 (6 shared)	Pro*	3
Val	1 (7 shared)	Ser	3
Leu	3 (7 shared)	Gly‡	1
Tyr	10	Cys§	2
Phe	1 (9 shared)		14
Trp	5 (8 shared)		
	60		

*From Glu.
†From Asp.
‡From Ser.
§From Ser plus S²⁻.

Table 23–1. Amino acid requirements of humans.

Essential; Must Be Supplied Preformed in Dietary Proteins	Essential but May Be Synthesized by the Tissues
Arginine*	Alanine
Histidine*	Asparagine
Isoleucine	Aspartic acid
Leucine	Cystine
Lysine	Glutamic acid
Methionine	Glutamine
Phenylalanine	Glycine
Threonine	Hydroxyproline
Tryptophan	Proline
Valine	Serine
	Tyrosine

*Arginine and histidine are sometimes classified as "semi-essential" because, as in the case of arginine, they may be synthesized in the tissues but not at adequate rates to support growth in younger individuals.

Biosynthesis of the nutritionally essential amino acids by bacteria from glutamate or aspartate or from nonnitrogenous amphibolic intermediates is discussed below. Since these reactions do not occur in mammalian tissues, the discussion is limited to general principles.

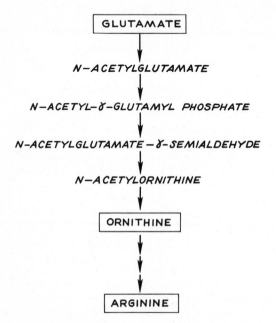

Figure 23—1. Biosynthesis of L-arginine from L-glutamate via acylated intermediates in bacteria. The reactions from glutamate to ornithine do not occur in mammalian tissues. The reactions leading from ornithine to arginine are those of the urea cycle (see Chapter 22) and are common to both bacteria and mammals. Some ornithine is formed in mammalian liver by reversal of the reactions of ornithine catabolism (see Chapter 22). This accounts for the status of arginine as only a partially essential amino acid in man and other animals.

BIOSYNTHESIS OF NUTRITIONALLY ESSENTIAL AMINO ACIDS FROM GLUTAMATE

Arginine (Bacteria)

Arginine is properly considered a nutritionally essential amino acid for man. It can be synthesized by rats, but not in quantities sufficient to permit normal growth. Microorganisms biosynthesize arginine from glutamate, utilizing N-acetylated intermediates (Fig 23—1). One intermediate in this pathway, N-acetyl-glutamate-γ-semialdehyde, is also a precursor of proline in bacteria. In man and other animals, however, proline is formed from glutamate.

BIOSYNTHESIS OF NUTRITIONALLY ESSENTIAL AMINO ACIDS FROM ASPARTATE

The Aspartate Family of Amino Acids (Bacteria)

As shown in Fig 23—2, aspartate is the precursor of a family of amino acids that includes lysine, methionine, threonine, and isoleucine. The regulatory implications of this relationship in bacteria are discussed in Chapter 7.

The initial reactions in synthesis of the aspartate family of amino acids are the conversion of aspartate to β-aspartyl phosphate, a reaction catalyzed by aspartate kinase (see Chapter 7), and the conversion of β-aspartyl phosphate to aspartate-β-semialdehyde (Fig 23—3).

Methionine & Threonine (Bacteria)

Following conversion of aspartate-β-semialdehyde to homoserine, the pathways for methionine and threonine biosynthesis diverge (Fig 23—3). The interconversion of homoserine and methionine is discussed in Chapter 22.

Lysine (Bacteria)

In bacteria, biosynthesis of lysine from aspartate-β-semialdehyde involves an initial condensation with pyruvate. The dihydropicolinate formed serves, in

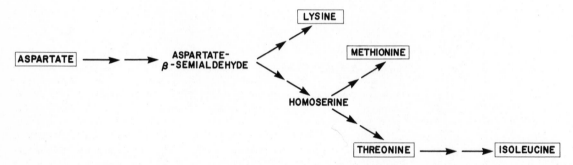

Figure 23—2. The aspartate family of amino acids. In bacteria, L-aspartate serves as a precursor of the indicated amino acids. Double arrows indicate that several reactions are required to achieve the indicated conversions.

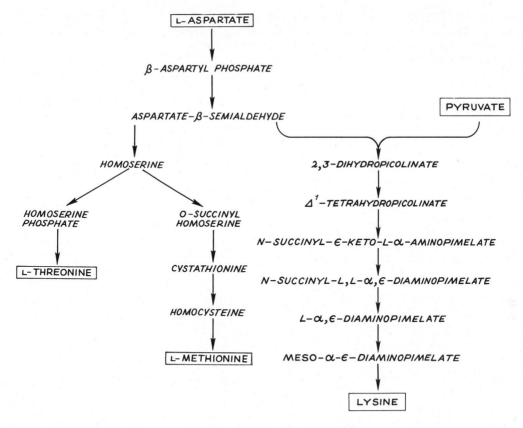

Figure 23–3. The aspartate family of amino acids: intermediates in threonine, methionine, and lysine biosynthesis in bacteria. All known intermediates are indicated. For lysine, additional carbon is provided by pyruvate.

addition, a role in spore formation in certain spore-forming bacteria (Fig 23–3), and the diaminopimelate performs a role in bacterial cell wall synthesis.

Isoleucine

The biosynthesis of isoleucine is considered below together with that of the other branched chain amino acids, valine and leucine.

BIOSYNTHESIS OF NUTRITIONALLY ESSENTIAL AMINO ACIDS FROM AMPHIBOLIC INTERMEDIATES

Lysine (Bacteria and Yeast)

Whereas in bacteria—as far as a biosynthetic precursor is concerned—lysine is a member of the aspartate family of amino acids, lysine biosynthesis in yeast involves an entirely different set of reactions, starting from α-ketoglutarate and acetyl-CoA as shown in Fig 23–4.

Reactions 1–5 are analogous to reactions of the citric acid cycle. They are not, however, catalyzed by the enzymes of this cycle but by a set of enzymes with slightly different substrate specificities. Reactions 7–9

are similar to those of L-lysine catabolism in man but proceed in the opposite direction (see Chapter 22).

Leucine, Valine, & Isoleucine

While leucine, valine, and isoleucine are all nutritionally essential amino acids for man and other higher animals, mammalian tissues do contain transaminases that reversibly catalyze interconversion of all 3 amino acids with their corresponding α-keto acids (see Chapter 22). This explains the ability of the appropriate keto acids to replace their amino acids in the diet. Although D-leucine is utilized to some extent by chicks and rats, the rate of deamination of the D-isomers to the α-keto acids is too slow to support growth.

The intermediates in the biosynthesis of the 3 branched chain amino acids are shown in Fig 23–5. The initial amphibolic starting materials are pyruvate (valine, leucine) or its next higher homologue α-ketobutyrate (isoleucine). These condense with active acetaldehyde derived from pyruvate. The details of the regulation of these pathways have been studied in considerable detail by Umbarger and others in a variety of organisms. While the exact mechanisms of organization and regulation differ from organism to organism, the biosynthesis of these amino acids is tightly controlled both at the level of the genome and at the level of

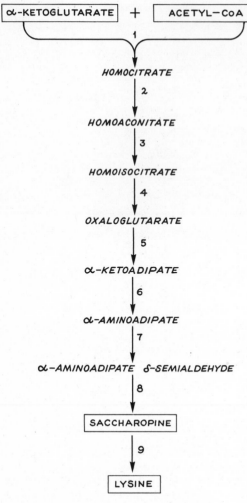

Figure 23—4. Lysine biosynthesis by yeast.

enzymic activity. Reaction 6, the first reaction unique to leucine biosynthesis, is catalyzed by an allosteric enzyme that is feedback-inhibited by the end product, leucine. Addition of leucine alters both the molecular architecture and the substrate affinities of the salmonella **a-isopropylmalate synthetase,** the catalyst for reaction 6. In neurospora, a eukaryotic organism, leucine represses the synthesis of a-isopropylmalate synthetase. Both feedback inhibition and repression thus are involved in regulation of leucine biosynthesis. When bacteria are grown on media containing all 3 amino acids in adequate quantities, synthesis of the enzymes catalyzing all 9 reactions of branched chain amino acid synthesis is repressed. Repression of enzymes 2—4 is "multivalent," ie, repression only occurs in the presence of **all 3** amino acids. In addition, *Escherichia coli* contains a pyruvate oxidase whose function is closely linked to production of active acetaldehyde destined for valine synthesis. Growth of *E coli* on media containing growth-limiting quantities of valine then derepresses the synthesis of this biosynthetic pyruvate oxidase.

Histidine

This amino acid, like arginine, is nutritionally semiessential. Adult human beings and adult rats have been maintained in nitrogen balance for short periods in the absence of histidine. The growing animal does, however, require histidine in the diet. If studies were to be carried on for longer periods, it is probable that a requirement for histidine in adult human subjects would also be elicited.

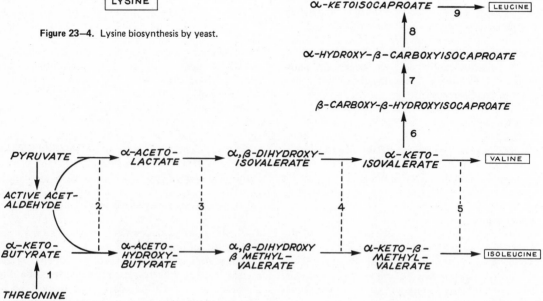

Figure 23—5. Intermediates in leucine, valine, and isoleucine biosynthesis in bacteria. Since these reactions do not occur in man or other animals, these 3 amino acids are nutritionally essential and must be supplied in the diet. Reactions 2—5 appear to be catalyzed by single enzymes functional for synthesis of all 3 amino acids. Considerable information is available about feedback regulation of the enzymes of this pathway. (Redrawn from Freundlich, Burns, & Umbarger: Proc Natl Acad Sci USA 48:1804, 1962.)

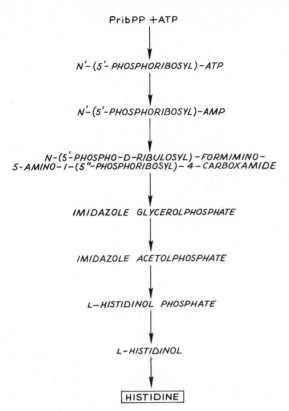

Figure 23–6. Intermediates in histidine biosynthesis in microorganisms. (PribPP = phosphoribosyl pyrophosphate.)

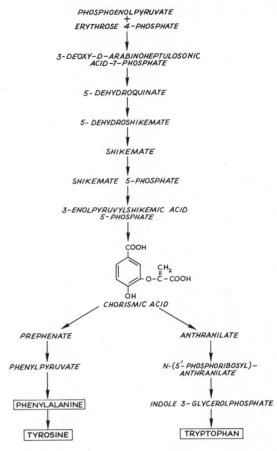

Figure 23–7. Intermediates in phenylalanine, tyrosine, and tryptophan biosynthesis in microorganisms.

An outline of the intermediates involved in histidine biosynthesis in microorganisms is shown in Fig 23–6. Biosynthesis starts with 5-phosphoribosyl-1-pyrophosphate (PribPP), which condenses with ATP, forming N′-(5-phosphoribosyl)-ATP. This reaction thus closely resembles the initial reaction of purine biosynthesis. The catalyst for this reaction, PribPP-ATP phosphorylase, is feedback-inhibited by histidine, the end product of the biosynthetic pathway.

Phenylalanine, Tryptophan, & Tyrosine (Bacteria)

The conversion of phosphoenolpyruvate, an intermediate in glycolysis, and of erythrose-4-phosphate, an intermediate in the pentose phosphate pathway, to phenylalanine and tryptophan is outlined in Fig 23–7. Chorismate, a key intermediate, is the precursor not only of the 3 aromatic amino acids but also of the quinone ring of coenzyme Q.

NUTRITIONALLY NONESSENTIAL AMINO ACIDS FORMED FROM AMPHIBOLIC INTERMEDIATES

Alanine (All Life Forms)

In all forms of life, alanine is formed from pyruvate by transamination (Fig 23–8).

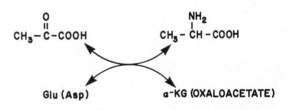

Figure 23–8. Formation of alanine by transamination of pyruvate. The amino donor may be glutamate or aspartate. The other product thus is α-ketoglutarate (α-KG) or oxaloacetate.

Glutamate (All Life Forms)

In all forms of life, glutamate is formed by the reaction catalyzed by L-glutamate dehydrogenase (Fig 23–9).

Yeast and fungi contain 2 separate glutamate dehydrogenases specific for NAD⁺ and for NADP⁺. Bacteria contain only an NAD⁺-dependent dehydrogenase and, as discussed below, can synthesize glutamate by a reaction distinct from that catalyzed by

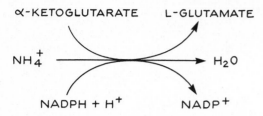

Figure 23-9. The glutamate dehydrogenase reaction. Reductive amination of a-ketoglutarate by NH_4^+ proceeds at the expense of NAD(P)H.

glutamate dehydrogenase. Since beef liver glutamate dehydrogenase has dual specificity for NAD^+ and for $NADP^+$, it is tempting to speculate that NAD^+ functions in glutamate catabolism and $NADP^+$ in glutamate biosynthesis by glutamate dehydrogenase in animals.

The biosynthetic function of glutamate dehydrogenase is of particular importance in plants and bacteria, which can synthesize large quantities of amino acids from glucose plus ammonia. When beef cattle are fed diets rich in carbohydrate plus nitrogen in the form of urea, the rumen bacteria first convert the urea to ammonia, then utilize the glutamate dehydrogenase reaction to provide the cattle with a diet rich in glutamate and other amino acids.

Glutamate (Bacteria)

In many bacteria, glutamate can also be formed by a reaction catalyzed by glutamate synthetase (Fig 23-10).

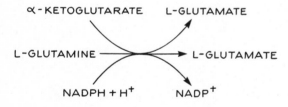

Figure 23-10. The glutamate synthetase reaction.

Despite its name, the glutamate synthetase reaction resembles the glutamate dehydrogenase reaction (Fig 23-9) more closely than that catalyzed by glutamine synthetase (Fig 23-11). Since glutamine (glutamate synthetase) rather than NH_4^+ (glutamate dehydrogenase) serves as the nitrogen donor, a second molecule of glutamate is formed from the remaining portion of the glutamine molecule. A mutant of *Bacillus megaterium* that lacks glutamate synthetase but not glutamate dehydrogenase requires large quantities of glutamate for growth. The principal mechanism for bacterial synthesis of glutamate may thus be via glutamate synthetase rather than glutamate dehydrogenase.

Glutamate formation via glutamate synthetase is more strongly favored thermodynamically than gluta-

mate formation via glutamate dehydrogenase. This is because the formation of the amino donor group (glutamine) requires 1 mol of ATP. This is shown below, where synthesis of glutamate by the combined action of glutamine synthetase and glutamate are compared.

Reaction 1:

$$\text{L-Glu} + NH_4^+ + \text{ATP} \xrightarrow{\text{Glutamine synthetase}} \text{L-Gln} + \text{ADP} + P_i$$

Reaction 2:

$$\text{L-Gln} + a\text{-KG} + NADPH_2 \xrightarrow{\text{Glutamate synthetase}} 2 \text{ L-Glu} + NADP^+.$$

Sum of reactions 1 and 2 = reaction 3:

$$a\text{-KG} + NH_4^+ + NADPH_2 + \text{ATP} \longrightarrow$$
$$\text{L-Gln} + NADP^+ + \text{ADP} + P_i$$

Reaction 4:

$$a\text{-KG} + NH_4^+ + NADPH_2 \xrightarrow{\text{Glutamate dehydrogenase}}$$
$$\text{L-Gln} + NADP^+ + H_2O$$

The difference (reaction 4 minus reaction 3) = reaction 5:

$$\text{ATP} + H_2O \longrightarrow \text{ADP} + P_i$$

Despite the requirement for ATP, this mechanism for glutamate synthesis has great utility in bacterial cells starved for nitrogen. The condition is known to favor glutamate formation via glutamine synthetase and glutamate synthetase. Glutamate dehydrogenase has a high K_m for ammonia and hence probably is essentially nonfunctional when intracellular levels of NH_4^+ are low. Glutamine synthetase, however, has a low K_m for NH_4^+, so glutamate formation via the 2 synthetases proceeds readily even at extremely low intracellular concentrations of NH_4^+. Under these conditions, loss of 1 mol of ATP may be a small price to pay to ensure survival.

Aspartate (All Life Forms)

Aspartic acid is formed by transamination of oxaloacetate (Fig 23-8).

Glutamine (All Life Forms)

L-Glutamine and L-glutamate are of fundamental importance for amino acid biosynthesis in all forms of life. In plants, animals, and bacteria, synthesis of glutamine is catalyzed by glutamine synthetase. In this reaction, NH_4^+ aminates glutamate in a reaction requiring ATP (Fig 23-11).

Glutamine (Bacteria)

A. Regulation of Glutamine Synthetase: The regulation of bacterial glutamine synthetase activity, which is exceedingly complex, has been intensively

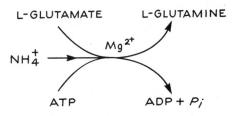

Figure 23–11. The glutamine synthetase reaction.

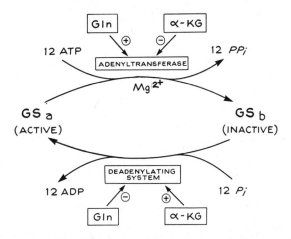

Figure 23–13. Representation of the regulation of *E coli* glutamine synthetase by covalent modification. Shown also are the effects of the 2 principal positive (+) and negative (−) effectors on the activity of the adenyltransferase and of the deadenylating system. (*a*-KG = *a*-ketoglutarate.)

studied in bacteria. Purified *E coli* glutamine synthetase (MW 600,000) consists of 12 apparently identical subunits. Its activity is regulated by (1) repression of enzyme synthesis, (2) cumulative feedback inhibition of enzyme activity, and (3) covalent modification. Of these, the third is perhaps the most important.

E coli glutamine synthetase (GS) exists both in active and inactive forms. The inactive form (GS_b) has only about 5% of the glutamine synthetase activity of the active form (GS_a). The relative proportions of GS_a and GS_b present in cells depend upon the nitrogen source used for growth. Following addition of NH_4^+ to the medium, glutamine synthetase is rapidly inactivated by conversion of GS_a to GS_b. This reaction involves adenylation of GS_a by up to 12 mols of AMP. GS_b therefore equals $GS_a(AMP)_{12}$. For the adenylation of GS_a, ATP, Mg^{2+}, and a GS_a-specific adenyltransferase are required. The AMP is linked by a phosphodiester bond to the OH of the tyrosyl residue on each of the 12 subunits of glutamine synthetase. The primary structure of a 21-amino-acid peptide surrounding the adenylation site is shown in Fig 23–12.

ferase and a protein that modifies the adenyltransferase so that it now catalyzes the transfer of AMP from GS_b to P_i. This regenerates GS_a. (See Fig 23–13.)

B. Regulation of Glutamine Synthetase by Glutamine: The most important low-molecular-weight effectors which influence the interconversion of GS_a and GS_b are glutamine and *a*-ketoglutarate. Glutamine acts as a positive effector for the adenyltransferase and stimulates its activity about 20-fold. Other positive effectors (glutamate, methionine, tryptophan, fructose

Ile-His-Pro-(Ala,Glu,Gly,Met)-Lys-Asp-Asp-Leu-Tyr-Asp-Leu-Pro-Pro-Glu-Gly-Glu-Ala-Lys

|
O
|
AMP

Figure 23–12. Primary structure of the region surrounding the adenylation site on *E coli* glutamine synthetase.

In addition to the catalytic site and the tyrosyl residue where adenylation occurs, each subunit also possesses separate binding sites for allosteric inhibitors. The affinity of glutamine synthetase for its substrates (L-glutamate, ATP, and a divalent metal ion) depends upon the degree of adenylation; the affinity of the inhibitors for their allosteric sites does not.

Following removal of NH_4^+ from the medium, reactivation of glutamine synthetase occurs by deadenylation of GS_b to GS_a. During deadenylation, AMP is transferred to P_i, forming ADP (Fig 23–13). The energy released during hydrolysis of the phosphodiester bond of the AMP-tyrosine residue of a GS_b subunit about equals the energy required for synthesis of ADP from AMP + P_i. Phosphorolytic cleavage of GS_b, forming ADP, thus is energetically feasible. Among the proteins involved in deadenylation are an adenyltrans-

1,6-bisphosphate, 3-phosphoglycerate, and phosphoenolpyruvate) exert similar but less pronounced effects. Glutamine also acts as a negative effector for deadenylation. *a*-Ketoglutarate has effects which are diametrically opposed to those of glutamine (Fig 23–13). Glutamine and *a*-ketoglutarate levels therefore regulate glutamine synthesis. High intracellular concentrations of glutamine decrease glutamine formation by favoring formation of the inactive form of glutamine synthetase (GS_b). When glutamine levels decrease, formation of the active form (GS_a) is favored and glutamine synthesis is enhanced.

C. Regulation of Adenyltransferase Activity: The adenyltransferase that catalyzes conversion of GS_a to GS_b also exists in 2 forms (P_I and P_{II}), each of which catalyzes adenylation of GS_a. P_I—but not P_{II}—also catalyzes deadenylation of GS_b to GS_a (Fig 23–13).

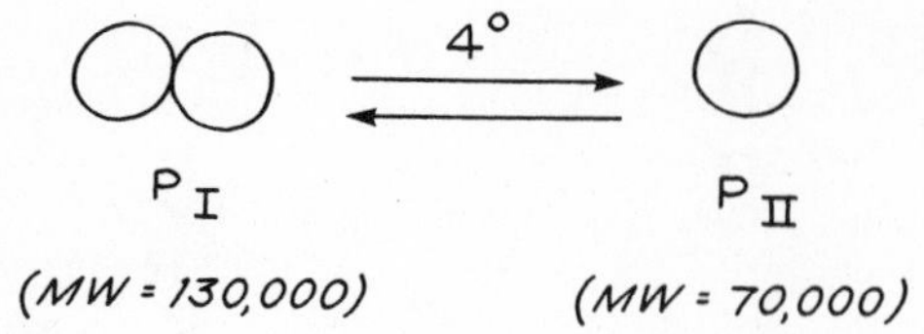

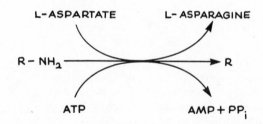

Figure 23–14. Structure of the *E coli* adenyltransferase that catalyzes conversion of GS_a to GS_b. P_I and P_{II} both catalyze the adenyltransferase reaction, but only P_I has deadenylating activity. The dimeric form (P_I) dissociates to the monomeric form (P_{II}) at low temperatures. P_I and P_{II} are separable by disk gel electrophoresis.

These relationships are summarized in Fig 23–14.

P_{II} also exists in 2 forms, P_{II}-AT and P_{II}-DA. Interconversion of P_{II}-AT and P_{II}-DA (Fig 23–15) involves a set of reactions analogous to those involved in interconversion of GS_a and GS_b (Fig 23–13).

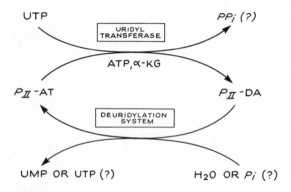

Figure 23–15. Representation of the interconversion of the 2 forms of the P_{II} component of the adenyltransferase for *E coli* glutamine synthetase. Both P_{II}-AT and P_{II}-DA stimulate the adenylation of GS_a, but only P_{II}-DA stimulates the deadenylating activity of P_I.

P_{II} is a regulatory protein that affects both the adenylation and deadenylation of GS (Fig 23–13). Whether the effects of P_{II} are primarily on adenylation or on deadenylation depends upon its state of uridylation. The fully uridylated form of P_{II} (Fig 23–15) is termed P_{II}-DA because it stimulates the deadenylation of GS_b by P_I. P_{II}-DA also stimulates the adenyltransferase activity of P_I, but only in the presence of glutamine. The other form of P_{II} is termed P_{II}-AT because it promotes the adenyltransferase reaction (adenylation of GS_a forming GS_b) by stimulating the adenyltransferase activity of P_I in the absence of glutamine. In addition, it makes the adenyltransferase reaction sensitive to stimulation by a-ketoglutarate. Unlike P_{II}-DA, P_{II}-AT has no effect on the deadenylating activity of P_I.

The complex cascade system of enzymes acting on enzymes that characterized the regulation of *E coli*

glutamine synthesis is reminiscent of the regulation of muscle phosphorylase activity (see Chapter 18).

Asparagine

The biosynthesis of asparagine is catalyzed by asparagine synthetase (Fig 23–16).

Figure 23–16. The asparagine synthetase reaction. Note similarities to and differences from the glutamine synthetase reaction (Fig 23–11). The nature of the amino donor (R–NH$_2$) differs depending on the life form considered (see accompanying text).

The reaction catalyzed by asparagine synthetase has many similarities to the glutamine synthetase reaction (Fig 23–11). In both cases, synthesis of the amide bond requires the free acid (aspartate or glutamate) and an amino donor, and the reaction is driven at the expense of ATP with Mg^{2+} as a catalyst. A major difference is that while ATP is converted to ADP + P_i in the glutamine synthetase reaction, AMP + PP_i are formed in the reaction catalyzed by asparagine synthetase. If, as is frequently the case, there are enzymes present that catalyze the hydrolysis of PP_i to 2 P_i (pyrophosphatases), the overall reaction

$$\text{Asp} + \text{R–NH}_2 + \text{ATP} \xrightarrow{Mg^{2+}} \text{Asn} + \text{R} + \text{AMP} + 2\,P_i$$

will be more favored than that of glutamine synthesis by about 8 kcal.

In mammalian systems, the amino donor probably is glutamine, whereas in bacteria it is ammonia. Plants use yet another amino donor, the cyano group of β-cyanoalanine.

Serine

Two pathways for serine biosynthesis exist in mammalian tissues. In both cases the carbon skeleton of serine is provided by D-3-phosphoglycerate, an intermediate in glycolysis (see Chapter 18). The 2 pathways differ with respect to the nature of the intermediates involved. One pathway uses nonphosphorylated intermediates and the other involves phosphorylated intermediates (Fig 23–17).

Synthesis via phosphorylated intermediates involves oxidation of 3-phosphoglycerate to phosphohydroxypyruvate, transamination to phosphoserine, and, finally, hydrolytic removal of the phosphate catalyzed by a phosphatase. For synthesis via nonphos-

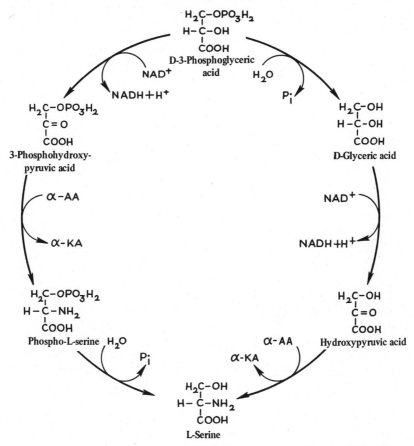

Figure 23—17. Serine biosynthesis via phosphorylated and nonphosphorylated intermediates. (a-AA = a-amino acids; a-KA = a-keto acids.)

phorylated intermediates, phosphoglycerate is dephosphorylated to glycerate by a phosphatase, oxidized to hydroxypyruvate, and, finally, transaminated to form L-serine. It is probable that the pathway involving phosphorylated intermediates accounts for the majority of the serine synthesized by mammalian tissues. This also appears to be true for plants and for a variety of microorganisms.

Glycine

Synthesis of glycine in mammalian tissues can occur in several ways. The cytosol of liver tissue contains active glycine transaminases that catalyze synthesis of glycine from glyoxylate and either glutamate or pyruvate. Unlike most transaminase reactions, these strongly favor glycine synthesis.

Two important routes for glycine formation are from choline (Fig 23—18) and from serine via the serine hydroxymethyltransferase reaction (Fig 23—19).

Glycine may be formed from CO_2, ammonia, and methylene tetrahydrofolate by reversal of the sequence of reactions that comprise the glycine cleavage system (see Chapter 22). Reversal of glycine cleavage is not, however, thought to account for a major fraction of glycine synthesis in mammals.

Finally, clostridia form glycine from L-threonine or L-allothreonine by an aldol-type cleavage that forms glycine plus acetaldehyde. The presence of this pathway may reflect the absence in clostridia of the enzymes of the phosphorylated pathway for serine biosynthesis.

NUTRITIONALLY NONESSENTIAL AMINO ACIDS FORMED FROM OTHER NUTRITIONALLY NONESSENTIAL AMINO ACIDS

Proline

In mammals and some other life forms, proline is biosynthesized from glutamate by reversal of the sequence of reactions for proline catabolism (Fig 23—20).

Hydroxyproline

Since proline serves as a precursor of hydroxyproline, both proline and hydroxyproline are members of the glutamate family of amino acids.

Both 3- and 4-hydroxyprolines occur in mammalian tissues. Little is known of the metabolic significance of 3-hydroxyproline other than that it is present in rat

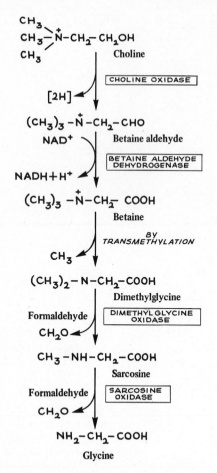

Figure 23–18. Formation of glycine from choline by way of betaine.

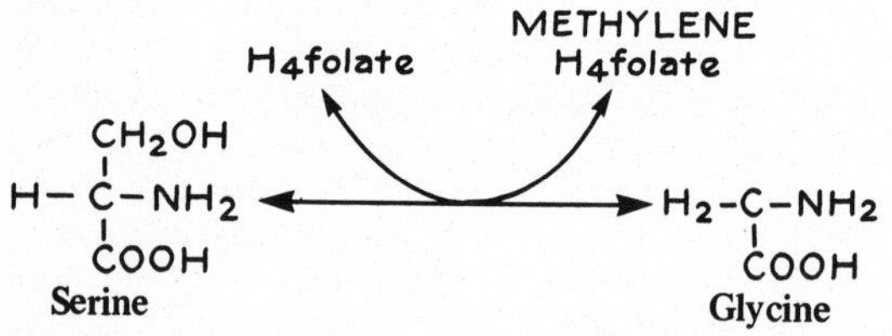

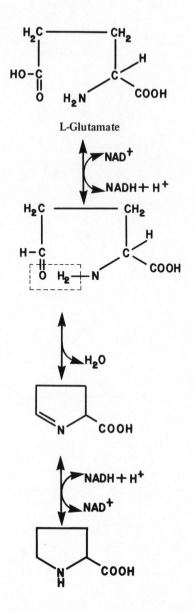

Figure 23–20. Biosynthesis of proline from glutamate by reversal of the reactions of proline catabolism.

Figure 23–19. The serine hydroxymethyltransferase reaction. The reaction is freely reversible. (H_4folate = tetrahydrofolate.)

tail tendon and, in addition, in the antibiotic telomycin. What follows refers solely to trans-4-hydroxyproline.

Hydroxyproline, like hydroxylysine, is almost exclusively associated with collagen, the most abundant protein of mammalian tissues. Collagen, an unusual protein in many respects, is composed of about one-third glycine and two-thirds proline and hydroxyproline. Hydroxyproline itself accounts for almost half of the total amino acid residues of collagen. Hydroxyproline appears to fulfill a structural role, stabilizing the collagen triple helix to digestion by proteolytic

enzymes. Unlike the hydroxyl groups of hydroxylysine, which serve as sites for the attachment of galactosyl and glucosyl residues, the hydroxyl groups of collagen hydroxyproline are unsubstituted.

A unique feature of the metabolism both of hydroxyproline and of hydroxylysine is that these preformed amino acids, as they may occur in ingested food protein, are not incorporated into collagen. There appears to be no tRNA species capable both of accepting hydroxyproline or hydroxylysine and inserting them into an elongating polypeptide chain. Dietary proline is, however, a precursor of collagen hydroxy-

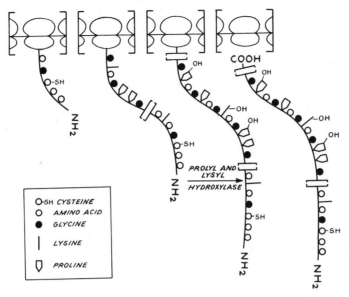

Figure 23–21. Representation of the hydroxylation of nascent chains of elongating collagen peptide by prolyl and lysyl hydroxylases. The best available evidence suggests that hydroxylation occurs prior to release from the ribosomes. (Redrawn and reproduced, with permission, from Cardinale CJ, Udenfriend S: Adv Enzymol 41:245, 1974.)

proline, and dietary lysine is a precursor of collagen hydroxylysine. Hydroxylation of proline or lysine is catalyzed by prolyl hydroxylase or by lysine hydroxylase, enzymes associated with the microsomal fraction of a wide variety of tissues including skin, liver, lung,

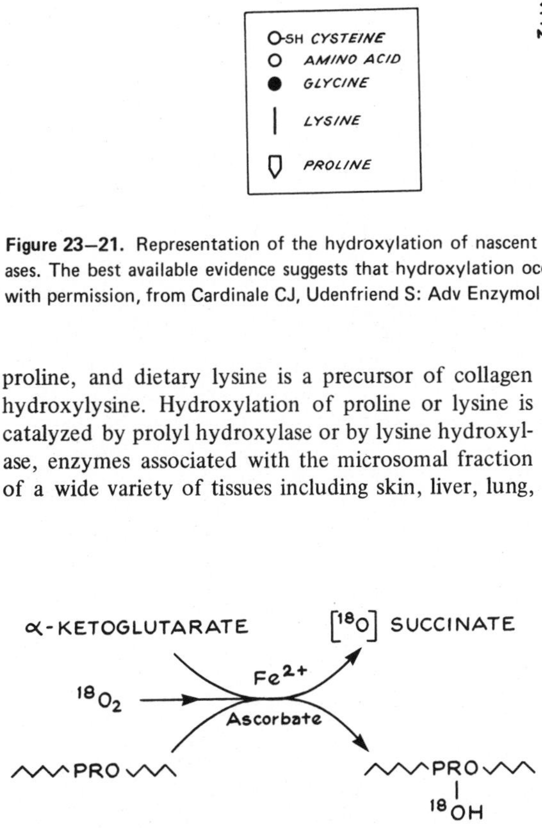

heart, skeletal muscle, and granulating wounds. These enzymes are peptidyl hydroxylases, since the hydroxylation occurs only subsequent to the incorporation of proline or lysine into polypeptide linkage (Fig 23–21).

Proline-rich peptides, including the vasoactive peptide bradykinin (see Chapter 3), can serve as substrates for proline hydroxylase. Copolymers of the type $(Pro-Gly-Pro)_n$ of MW 1200–8000 are satisfactory synthetic substrates. Both hydroxylases are mixed function oxygenases that require, in addition to substrate, molecular O_2, ascorbate, Fe^{2+}, and a-ketoglutarate. Prolyl hydroxylase has been more extensively studied, but lysyl hydroxylase appears to be an entirely analogous enzyme. For every mol of proline hydroxylated, 1 mol of a-ketoglutarate is decarboxylated to succinate. During this process, one atom of molecular O_2 is incorporated into proline and one into succinate (Fig 23–22).

Several aspects of this reaction remain unknown. It appears, however, that either enzyme-bound peroxysuccinate (Fig 23–23) or some form of superoxide

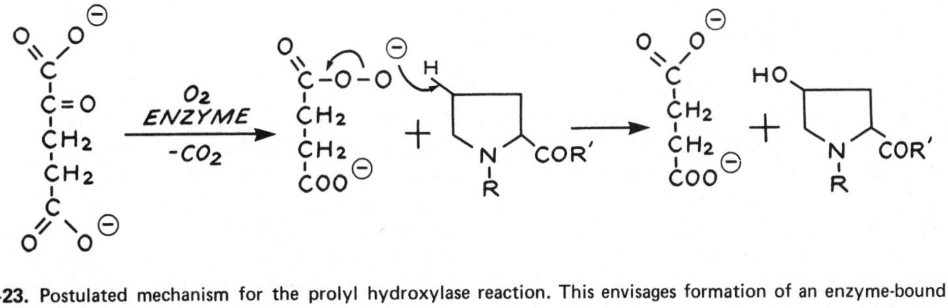

Figure 23–22. The proline hydroxylase reaction. The substrate is a proline-rich peptide. During the course of the reaction, molecular oxygen is incorporated into both succinate and proline (shown by the use of heavy oxygen, $^{18}O_2$).

Figure 23–23. Postulated mechanism for the prolyl hydroxylase reaction. This envisages formation of an enzyme-bound form of peroxysuccinate which subsequently attacks the peptidyl proline.

intermediate is involved. Much the same type of mechanism is thought to be responsible for the lysyl hydroxylase reaction.

Both 4-hydroxyproline and 4-ketoproline occur in the polypeptide actinomycin antibiotics. In contrast to mammalian systems, free hydroxyproline is incorporated directly into the actinomycin polypeptide elaborated by *Streptomyces antibioticus.*

NUTRITIONALLY NONESSENTIAL AMINO ACIDS FORMED FROM NUTRITIONALLY ESSENTIAL AMINO ACIDS

Cysteine

Cysteine, while not itself nutritionally essential, is formed from methionine (essential) and serine (nonessential). Methionine is first converted to homocysteine via S-adenosylmethionine and S-adenosylhomocysteine (see Chapter 22). The conversion of homocysteine and serine to cysteine and homoserine is shown in Fig 23–24.

Tyrosine

Tyrosine is formed from phenylalanine by the reaction catalyzed by phenylalanine hydroxylase (Fig 23–25). Thus, whereas phenylalanine is a nutritionally essential amino acid, tyrosine is not—provided the diet contains adequate quantities of phenylalanine.

Conversion of phenylalanine to tyrosine was inferred from nutritional experiments which showed that sufficiently high levels of dietary phenylalanine can replace the requirement for dietary tyrosine. The reaction is not reversible, so that tyrosine cannot replace the nutritional requirement for phenylalanine. Direct evidence was later provided when it was shown that intact rats converted ^{2}H-DL-phenylalanine to ^{2}H-L-tyrosine. Conversion of phenylalanine to tyrosine is catalyzed by the **phenylalanine hydroxylase** complex, a mixed function oxygenase present in mammalian liver but absent from other tissues. The overall reaction involves incorporation of one atom of molecular oxygen into the para position of phenylalanine while the other atom is reduced, forming water (Fig 23–25). The reducing power, supplied ultimately by NADPH, is immediately provided in the form of tetrahydrobiopterin, a pteridine resembling that in folic acid.

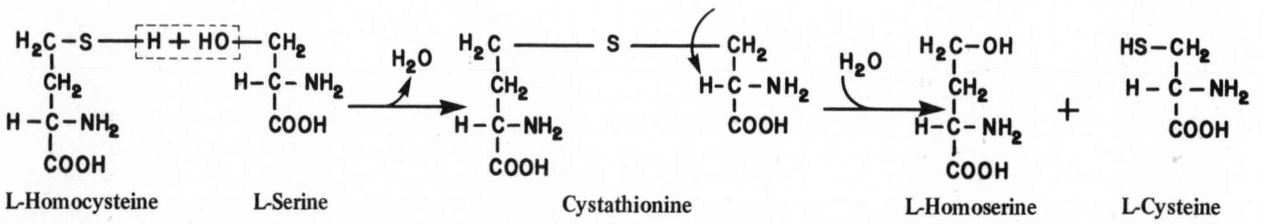

Figure 23–24. Conversion of homocysteine and serine to homoserine and cysteine. Note that while the sulfur of cysteine derives from methionine by transulfuration, the carbon skeleton is provided by serine.

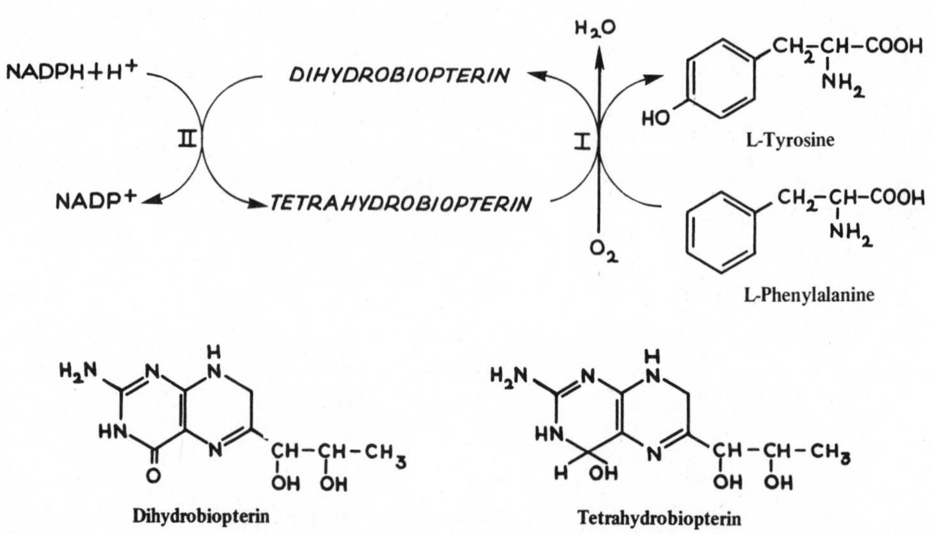

Figure 23–25. The phenylalanine hydroxylase reaction. Two distinct enzymic activities are involved. Activity II catalyzes reduction of dihydrobiopterin by NADPH, and activity I the reduction of oxygen to water and conversion of phenylalanine to tyrosine.

Hydroxylysine

5-Hydroxylysine (a,ϵ-diamino-δ-hydroxycaproate) is present in collagen and collagen products such as gelatin or isinglass but is probably absent from other mammalian proteins. Small quantities are reported to occur in wool, in trypsin, and as a phosphatide in *Mycobacterium phlei*. In rats, collagen hydroxylysine arises directly from dietary lysine, not dietary hydroxylysine. Before lysine is hydroxylated, it must first be incorporated into peptide linkage (Fig 23–21). Hydroxylation of the lysyl peptide is thencatalyzed by lysyl hydroxylase, a mixed function oxidase analogous to prolyl hydroxylase (Fig 23–22). As with proline hydroxylation, the oxygen of hydroxylysine is derived exclusively from molecular oxygen. The mechanism of the lysyl hydroxylase reaction probably closely resembles that of prolyl hydroxylase (Fig 23–23).

CONVERSION OF AMINO ACIDS TO SPECIALIZED PRODUCTS

This section considers the conversion of the carbon skeletons of the amino acids, the amino acids themselves, or portions of their structures to products of biochemical interest. Since most of these products are not themselves amino acids, the discussion merges at several points with metabolic pathways discussed elsewhere in this book.

Glycine

A. Synthesis of Heme: The a-carbon and nitrogen atoms of glycine are used in the synthesis of the porphyrin moiety of hemoglobin (see Chapter 14). The nitrogen in each pyrrole ring is derived from the glycine nitrogen and an adjoining carbon from the a-carbon of glycine. The a-carbon is also the source of the methylene bridge atoms linking the pyrrole rings together as a tetrapyrrole. For every 4 glycine nitrogen atoms utilized, 8 a-carbon atoms enter the porphyrin molecule. The relationship of glycine to heme synthesis and to the citric acid cycle is summarized in Fig 23–26 as the "succinate-glycine cycle."

Succinyl-CoA condenses on the a-carbon atom of glycine to form a-amino-β-ketoadipic acid. It is at this point that the metabolism of glycine is linked to the citric acid cycle, which provides succinyl-CoA.

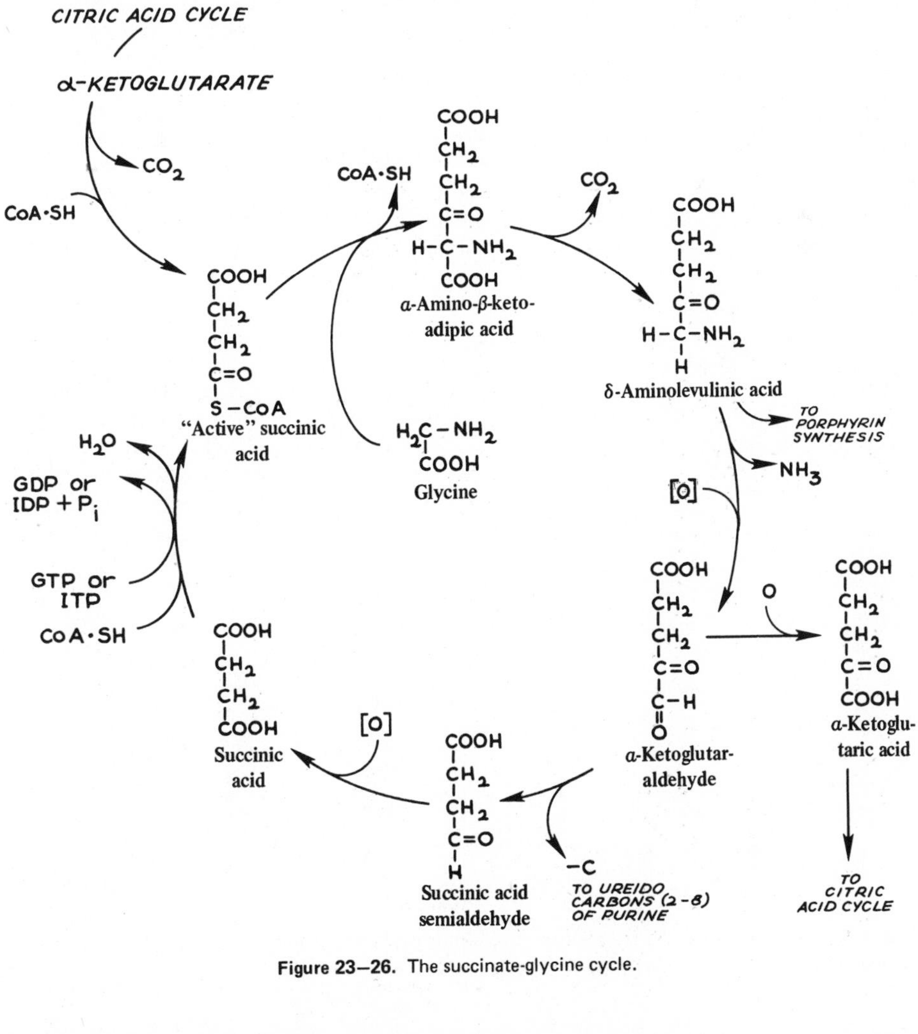

Figure 23–26. The succinate-glycine cycle.

a-Amino-*β*-ketoadipic acid is then converted by loss of CO_2 to δ-aminolevulinic acid. This compound serves as a common precursor for porphyrin synthesis as well as, after deamination, a carrier molecule for the introduction of the ureido carbons (2 and 8) into the purine ring (see Chapter 24). Succinate and ketoglutarate, which may return to the citric acid cycle, are also formed.

B. Synthesis of Purines: The entire glycine molecule is utilized to form positions 4, 5, and 7 of the purine skeleton.

The δ-carbon atom of δ-aminolevulinic acid is derived from the *a*-carbon of glycine. This δ-carbon is incorporated into positions 2 and 8 (the ureido carbons) of the purine nucleus to an even greater extent than *a*-carbons of glycine or *β*-carbons of serine. This suggests that δ-aminolevulinic acid is actually the carrier molecule for the transfer of the carbon atom to purines (Fig 23–26).

C. A Constituent of Glutathione: The tripeptide glutathione is a compound of glutamic acid, cysteine, and glycine. The nitrogen in glutathione is not available for transamination. Note that the peptide bond is with the γ-COOH of glutamate (Fig 23–27).

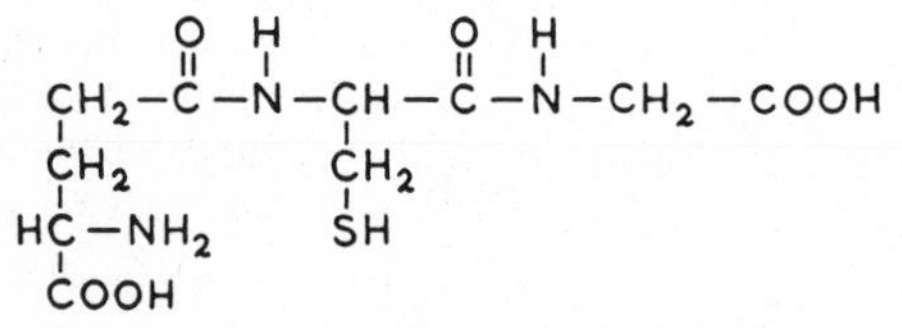

Figure 23–27. Glutathione (reduced form).

D. Conjugation With Glycine: Glycine conjugates with cholic acid, forming the bile acid glycocholic acid (see Chapter 14). With benzoic acid, it forms hippuric acid (Fig 23–28).

The quantitative ability of the liver to convert a measured dose of benzoic acid to hippuric acid was used as a test of liver function.

E. Synthesis of Creatine: The sarcosine (N-methylglycine) component of creatine (Fig 23–36) is derived from glycine.

Alanine

Except as a constituent of proteins, alanine is not known to have any other specific function, but together with glycine it makes up a considerable fraction of the amino nitrogen in human plasma. Both D- and L-alanine appear to be utilized by the tissues, but at differing rates.

Alanine is a major component of the cell walls of bacteria. In a number of species, part of the alanine is present as the D-isomer: 39–50% in *Streptococcus faecalis;* 67% in *Staphylococcus aureus.*

β-Alanine is a constituent of pantothenic acid and an end product in the catabolism of certain pyrimidines (cytosine and uracil). Studies on the catabolism of *β*-alanine in the rat indicate that this amino acid is degraded to acetate as shown in Fig 23–29.

Serine

Much of the serine in phosphoproteins appears to be present in the form of O-phosphoserine.

A cephalin fraction containing serine is present in the brain. The production of this compound, phosphatidylserine (see Chapter 9), may be another lipotropic function of serine.

Serine is involved directly in the synthesis of sphingol and therefore in the formation of sphingomyelins of brain. The details of this reaction are discussed in Chapter 19.

Serine participates in purine and pyrimidine synthesis. The *β*-carbon is a source of the methyl groups of thymine (and of choline) and of the carbon in positions 2 and 8 of the purine nucleus.

Threonine

This essential amino acid does not participate in transamination reactions. The D-isomer is not utilized by the body, probably because of the nonconvertibility of the keto acid to the amino acid. A specific function for threonine other than as a constituent of body

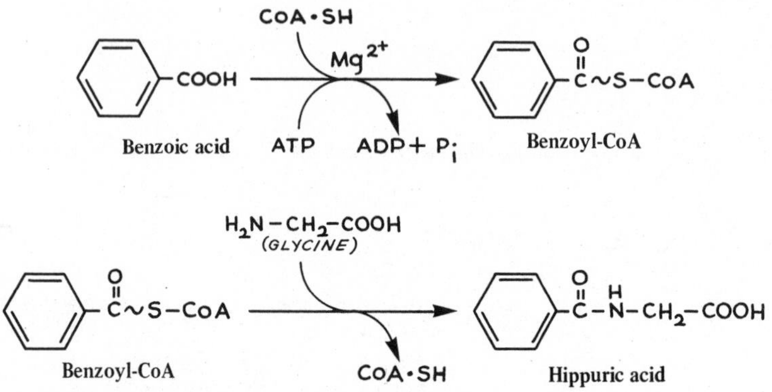

Figure 23–28. Formation of hippuric acid.

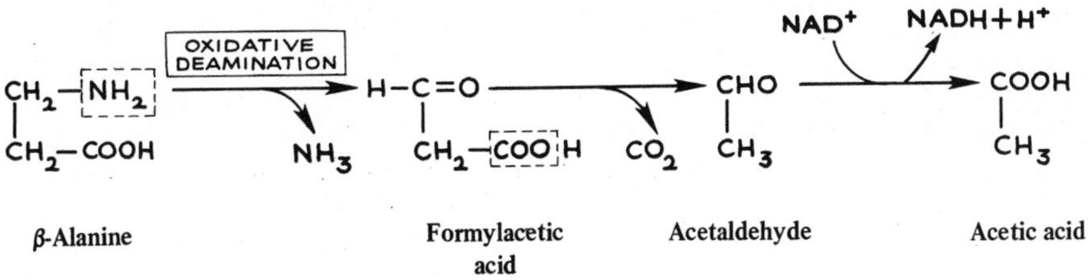

Figure 23—29. Catabolism of β-alanine in the rat. The conversion of acetaldehyde to acetic acid is catalyzed by aldehyde dehydrogenase.

proteins has not been discovered. It may be related to the utilization of fat in the liver (see Chapter 19). Threonine, like serine, may occur in proteins as O-phosphothreonine.

Methionine

The role of methionine as a methyl group donor is discussed in Chapter 22. This is one of its most important functions, for it is the principal source of methyl groups in the body. These can be transferred to pyridine derivatives, as occurs during the detoxification of drugs containing the pyridine ring.

In addition to utilization of the methyl group in the intact form, the methyl group is also oxidized. In the rat, one-fourth of the labeled methyl carbon appears in the expired CO_2 during the first day and about one-half is excreted in the urine, feces, or respiratory CO_2 in 2 days. The methyl carbon may also be used to produce the one-carbon moiety which conjugates with glycine in the synthesis of serine (Fig 23—30).

Homocysteine is involved in the utilization of the one-carbon (formate) moiety. This may occur through the formation of an intermediate compound of homocysteine with a one-carbon moiety derived from formate or formaldehyde. The single carbon could then be transferred to the synthesis of purines, the formation of the β-carbon of serine, or the methyl of

methionine. A scheme outlining this postulated role for homocysteine in utilization of formate is shown in Fig 23—30.

Methionine may undergo oxidative deamination to form the corresponding keto acid. This reaction is reversible, and conversion of the D- to the L-isomer is thus possible.

Cysteine

Cysteine is a major constituent of the proteins of hair and hooves and the keratin of skin. It is also present in smaller quantities in other proteins, where it may form disulfide bridges that stabilize protein structure (see Chapter 4).

Although D-cysteine is not utilized by animals for growth, it is oxidized in the body and contributes to the urinary sulfate. This sulfate arises almost entirely from oxidation of L-cysteine. The sulfur of methionine is transferred to serine (Fig 23—24) and thus contributes to the urinary sulfate indirectly (ie, by way of cysteine).

Cysteine is involved in the synthesis of coenzyme A (see Chapter 12), where it serves as a precursor of the thioethanolamine portion at the end of the CoA molecule that forms thioesters. Cysteine is also a precursor of the taurine that conjugates with cholic acid and other bile acids, forming taurocholic acid, etc (see Chapter 14).

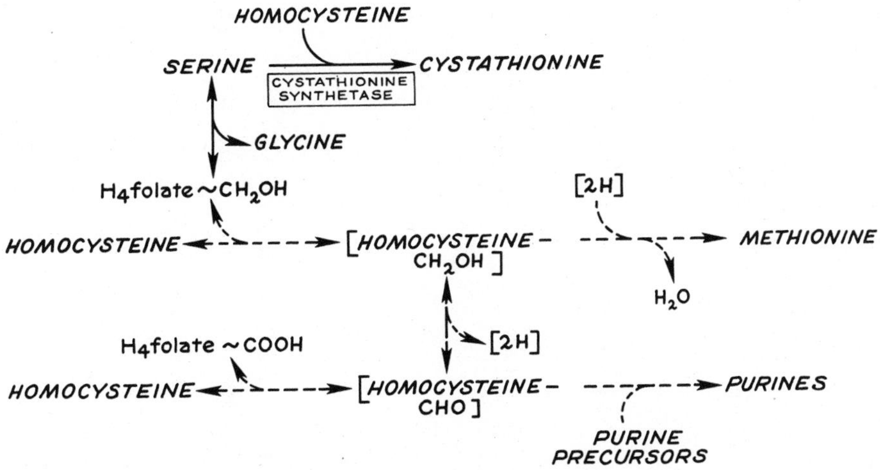

Figure 23—30. Role of homocysteine in utilization of formate.

Arginine

Arginine serves as a formamidine donor for creatine synthesis in primates (Fig 23–36) and for streptomycin synthesis in streptomyces (Fig 23–31).

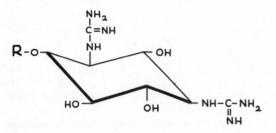

Figure 23–31. The streptidine portion of the streptomycins. In streptomyces, arginine serves as the donor of both guanido groups.

Other fates of interest include conversion to putrescine, agmatine, spermine, and spermidine by enteric bacteria (Fig 23–32) and synthesis of arginine phosphate (functionally analogous to creatine phosphate) in invertebrate muscle.

Although a functional role for arginine-derived polyamines in bacteria has not been discovered, bacteria typically convert large quantities of arginine to spermine and spermidine (Fig 23–32).

Histidine

Histamine is derived from histidine by decarboxylation. This reaction is catalyzed in mammalian tissues by an enzyme designated **aromatic L-amino acid decarboxylase**. The enzyme will also catalyze the decarboxylation of dopa (Fig 23–35), 5-hydroxytryptophan (Fig 23–34), phenylalanine, tyrosine, and tryptophan. The amino acid decarboxylase is present in kidney and in other tissues such as brain and liver. It is inhibited by *a*-methyl amino acids, which also inhibit amino acid decarboxylation in vivo and thus have clinical application as antihypertensive agents by preventing the formation of amines such as tyramine, norepinephrine, and serotonin derived from aromatic amino acids which act as pressor agents.

In addition to the aromatic amino acid decarboxylase, there is a completely different enzyme, a specific **histidine decarboxylase** present in most cells, which catalyzes the decarboxylation of histidine.

Three histidine compounds are found in the body: **ergothioneine**, in red blood cells and liver; **carnosine**, a dipeptide of histidine and *a*-alanine; and **anserine**, 1-methylcarnosine. The latter 2 compounds occur in muscle. The functions of these histidine compounds are not known (Fig 23–33).

Carnosine can replace histidine in the diet. When injected into animals, it has a circulatory depressant action similar to but not as potent as that of histamine, which in large doses may cause vascular collapse.

When rabbits were placed on vitamin E deficient diets, 1-methylhistidine appeared in the urine in easily detectable amounts about 1 week after the deficient

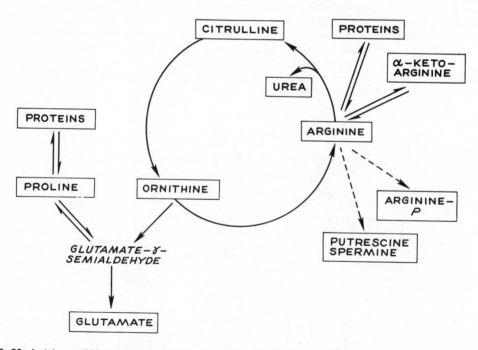

Figure 23–32. Arginine, ornithine, and proline metabolism. Reactions with solid arrows all occur in mammalian tissues. Putrescine and spermine synthesis occurs in *Escherichia coli,* a normal enteric bacterium. Arginine phosphate occurs in invertebrate muscle, where it functions as a phosphagen analogous to creatine phosphate in mammalian tissues (Fig 23–36).

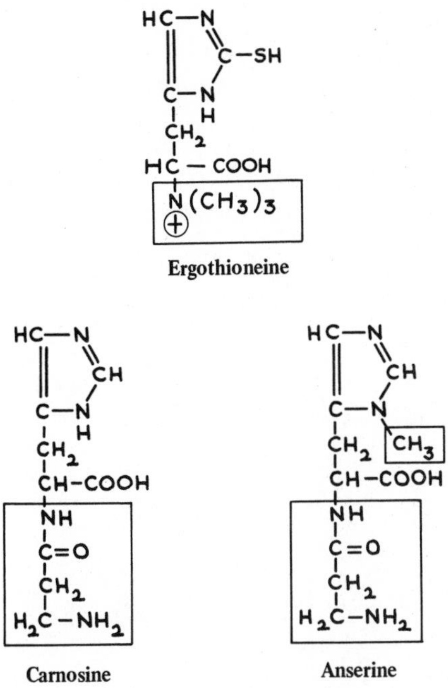

Ergothioneine

Carnosine

Anserine

Figure 23—33. Structures of compounds related to histidine.

diet had first been given; and the excretion of this compound increased progressively until it became the major amino acid in the urine. The methylhistidinuria could usually be detected a few days earlier than the creatinuria which is also characteristic of this deficiency state in rabbits, and it preceded by 1—2 weeks the appearance of the physical symptoms of muscular dystrophy.

The presence of 1-methylhistidine in human urine has been reported. This probably is derived from anserine. Larger amounts were found in the urine after the ingestion of rabbit muscle, which is particularly high in anserine content. 3-Methylhistidine has been identified in human urine in amounts of about 50 mg/day. The origin of this compound, an isomer of 1-methylhistidine (a component of anserine), is not known. There is no evidence that it occurs in muscle as a constituent of a peptide similar to anserine. It is of interest that 3-methylhistidine is unusually low in the urine of patients with Wilson's disease.

Tryptophan

A. Serotonin: A secondary pathway for the metabolism of tryptophan involves its hydroxylation to 5-hydroxytryptophan. The hydroxylation step is probably carried out by a system similar to that involved in the formation of hydroxykynurenine. The oxidation of tryptophan to the hydroxy derivative is analogous to the conversion of phenylalanine to tyrosine (Fig 23—25), and liver phenylalanine hydroxylase also catalyzes hydroxylation of tryptophan.

Decarboxylation of 5-hydroxytryptophan produces **5-hydroxytryptamine** (Fig 23—34). This compound, also known as **serotonin,** enteramine, or thrombocytin, is a potent vasoconstrictor as well as a stimulator of smooth muscle contraction. In these systemic effects it is probably equal in importance to epinephrine, norepinephrine, and histamine as one of the regulatory amines of the body.

It appears that serotonin is actually synthesized in the tissues where it is found rather than produced in one organ and carried by the blood to other organs. In mammals most of the serotonin is found in the gastrointestinal tract, so that it is not surprising that the amounts of serotonin in the blood and of its principal end product, 5-hydroxyindoleacetic acid, which is excreted in the urine, fall markedly after radical resection of the gastrointestinal tract.

Serotonin has a potent effect on the metabolism of the brain. As is the case with other tissues, the compound must be produced within the brain itself from precursors which gain access to the brain from the blood because serotonin itself does not pass the blood-brain barrier to any significant degree. While the functions of serotonin in the brain are not yet entirely clear, it seems reasonable to assume that an excess of serotonin brings about stimulation of cerebral activity and that a deficiency produces a depressant effect.

Most of the serotonin is metabolized by oxidative deamination to form 5-hydroxyindoleacetic acid. The enzyme which catalyzes this reaction is **monoamine oxidase.** A number of inhibitors of this enzyme have been found. Among them is iproniazid (Marsilid). It is hypothesized that the psychic stimulation which follows the administration of this drug is attributable to its ability to prolong the stimulating action of serotonin through inhibition of monoamine oxidase.

There is evidence that serotonin when first produced in the brain exists in a bound form which is not susceptible to the action of monoamine oxidase. The depressant drugs such as reserpine may effect a rapid release of the bound serotonin, thus subjecting it to rapid destruction by monoamine oxidase. The resultant depletion of serotonin would then bring about the calming effect which follows administration of reserpine.

The 5-hydroxytryptophan decarboxylase which forms serotonin from hydroxytryptophan is present in the kidney (hog and guinea pig) as well as in the liver and stomach. However, the widely distributed aromatic L-amino acid decarboxylase will also catalyze the decarboxylation of 5-hydroxytryptophan, so that a specific enzyme may not be required for this important reaction.

Although the blood platelets contain a considerable amount of serotonin, the lack of a decarboxylase in the platelets suggests that the serotonin is not manufactured but merely concentrated there.

The further metabolism of serotonin by deamination and oxidation results in the production of 5-hydroxyindoleacetic acid, and this end product is excreted in the urine. In normal human urine, 2—8 mg of 5-hydroxyindoleacetic acid are excreted per day, which indicates that the 5-hydroxyindole route is a significant pathway for the metabolism of tryptophan. Other metabolites of serotonin have been identified in the urine of patients with carcinoid. These include 5-hydroxyindoleaceturic acid (the glycine conjugate of 5-hydroxyindoleacetic acid), N-acetylserotonin, conjugated with glucuronic acid, some unchanged serotonin, and very small amounts of oxidation products of the nature of indican.

Greatly increased production of serotonin occurs in malignant **carcinoid** (argentaffinoma), a disease characterized by the widespread development of serotonin-producing tumor cells in the argentaffin tissue through-

out the abdominal cavity. Patients exhibit cutaneous vasomotor episodes (flushing) and occasionally a cyanotic appearance. There may also be a chronic diarrhea. These symptoms are attributed to the effects of serotonin on the smooth muscle of the blood vessels and digestive tract. In over half of the patients observed, there is also respiratory distress with bronchospasm. Cardiac involvement may occur late in the disease. The serotonin content in the blood of carcinoid patients—all of it in the platelets—is $0.5-2.7$ $\mu g/ml$ (normal is $0.1-0.3$ $\mu g/ml$). The most useful biochemical indication of increased production of sero-

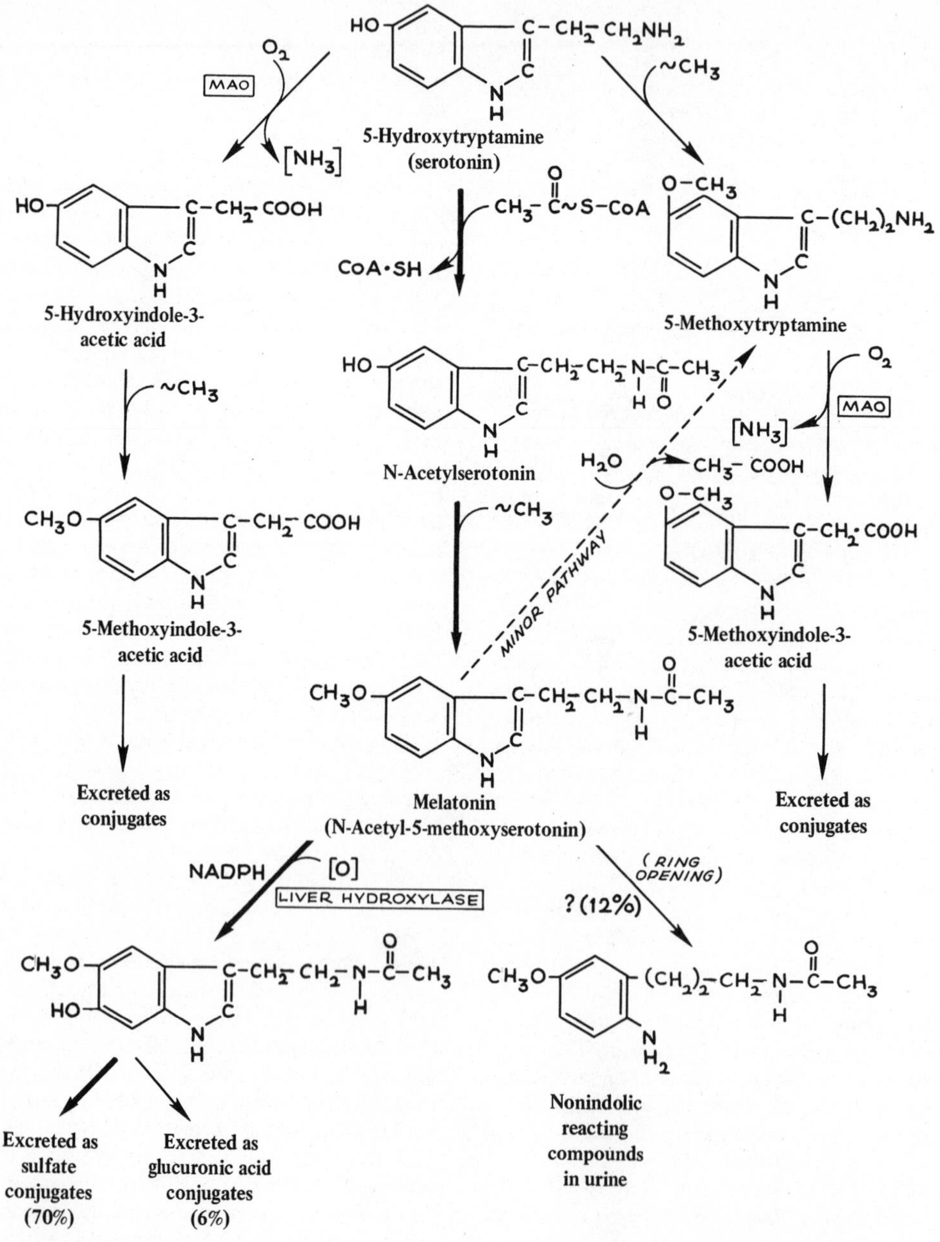

Figure 23–34. Biosynthesis and metabolism of melatonin. (Principal pathways indicated by heavy arrows. $[NH_3]$ = by transamination; MAO = monoamine oxidase.)

tonin, such as may occur in metastasizing carcinoid tumors, is the measurement of the urinary hydroxy-indoleacetic acid. In the carcinoid patient, excretion of 5-hydroxyindoleacetic acid has been reported as 76–580 mg in 24 hours (normal is 2–8 mg). Several assay methods for 5-hydroxyindoleacetic acid have been described. For diagnostic purposes, it is recommended that a quantitative measurement of 5-hydroxyindoleacetic acid excretion be made on a urine specimen collected over a 24-hour period. Random specimens of urine are useful for qualitative screening tests, but confirmation of the diagnosis should be made only on the 24-hour specimen.

From a biochemical point of view, carcinoid has been considered to be an abnormality in tryptophan metabolism in which a much greater proportion of tryptophan than normal is metabolized by way of the hydroxyindole pathway. One percent of tryptophan is normally converted to serotonin, but in the carcinoid patient as much as 60% may follow this pathway. This metabolic diversion markedly reduces the production of nicotinic acid from tryptophan; consequently, symptoms of pellagra as well as negative nitrogen balance may occur.

B. Melatonin: Melatonin (N-acetyl-5-methoxyserotonin) is a hormone derived from the pineal body and peripheral nerves of man, monkey, and bovine species. The hormone lightens the color of the melanocytes in the skin of the frog and blocks the action of the melanocyte-stimulating hormone. It also blocks the action of adrenocorticotropic hormone.

The pathway for the biosynthesis and metabolism of melatonin is shown in Fig 23–34. It will be noted that the compound is derived from serotonin by N-acetylation in which acetyl-CoA serves as acetate donor, followed by methylation of the 5-hydroxy group in which S-adenosylmethionine ("active" methionine) serves as methyl ($\sim CH_3$) donor. The reaction of methylation of the hydroxy group is localized in pineal body tissue. In addition to methylation of N-acetylserotonin, direct methylation of serotonin as well as of 5-hydroxyindoleacetic acid, the serotonin metabolite, also occurs.

The amines serotonin and 5-methoxytryptamine are metabolized to the corresponding acids through monoamine oxidase. Circulating melatonin itself is taken up by all tissues, including the brain. However, after administration of radioactively labeled melatonin to mice, it was noted that it was rapidly metabolized and only a small portion was bound and retained. The major catabolic pathway for degradation of melatonin is hydroxylation (in the liver) at position 6 followed by conjugation primarily with sulfate (70%) and with glucuronic acid (6%). A portion is also converted to nonindolic reacting compounds, which suggests that the indole ring has been opened.

C. Indole Derivatives in Urine: As shown in Fig 23–34, tryptophan may be converted to a number of indole derivatives. The end products of these conversions which appear in the urine are principally 5-hydroxyindoleacetic acid, the major end product of the

hydroxy tryptophan-to-serotonin pathway, and indole-3-acetic acid, produced by decarboxylation and oxidation of indolepyruvic acid, the keto acid of tryptophan. The daily excretion of indole-3-acetic acid in man is generally in the range of 5–18 mg, but it may rise to as high as 200 mg/day in certain pathologic states. As might be expected, the excretion of this compound is markedly increased by tryptophan loading.

Mammalian kidney and liver as well as bacteria obtained from human feces decarboxylate tryptophan to tryptamine, which can then be oxidized to indole-3-acetic acid. As noted in Fig 23–34, patients with phenylketonuria have been found to excrete increased quantities of indoleacetic acid (and indolelactic acid, probably derived by reduction of indolepyruvic acid). Traces of many other indole acids have been found as well.

Phenylalanine & Tyrosine

Melanin, the pigment of the skin and hair, is derived from tyrosine by way of dopa and its oxidation product, 3,4-dioxyphenylalanine (dopaquinone), which progresses to further melanin precursors (Fig 23–35).

The phenols which occur in the blood and urine are derived from tyrosine. In the urine, the phenols are largely conjugated with sulfate, and this comprises a portion of the so-called ethereal sulfate fraction of the total urinary sulfur. Tyrosine itself is also excreted in the urine, not only in the free state but also as a sulfate in which the sulfate moiety is conjugated through the para-hydroxy group. The excretion of tyrosine-O-sulfate averaged 28 mg/day in 5 adult males. This accounted for about half of the bound tyrosine and 3–8% of the ethereal sulfate sulfur in the urine. Sulfuration of tyrosine in vivo may actually occur on an N-terminal tyrosine within a peptide because free tyrosine does not act as a sulfate acceptor in a liver sulfate transfer system.

As shown in Fig 23–35, tyrosine is a direct precursor of epinephrine and norepinephrine. Tyrosine is also the direct precursor of the thyroid hormones which are iodinated tyrosine compounds (see Chapter 30).

Ascorbic acid and folic acid are both involved in tyrosine metabolism. Both vitamins prevent the defect in tyrosine oxidation observed in guinea pigs maintained on diets deficient in these substances. Alkaptonuria is observed not only in scorbutic guinea pigs but also in premature infants deprived of vitamin C. When the vitamin is supplied, the alkaptonuria promptly disappears. Vitamin C is not effective, however, in alkaptonuria of genetic origin. A direct association of ascorbic acid with tyrosine oxidation at the level of p-hydroxyphenylpyruvic acid as well as in the oxidation of homogentisic acid has been demonstrated. p-Hydroxyphenylpyruvic acid oxidase, the enzyme catalyzing conversion of p-hydroxyphenylpyruvic acid to homogentisic acid, is inhibited by its own substrate but ascorbic acid prevents this inhibition.

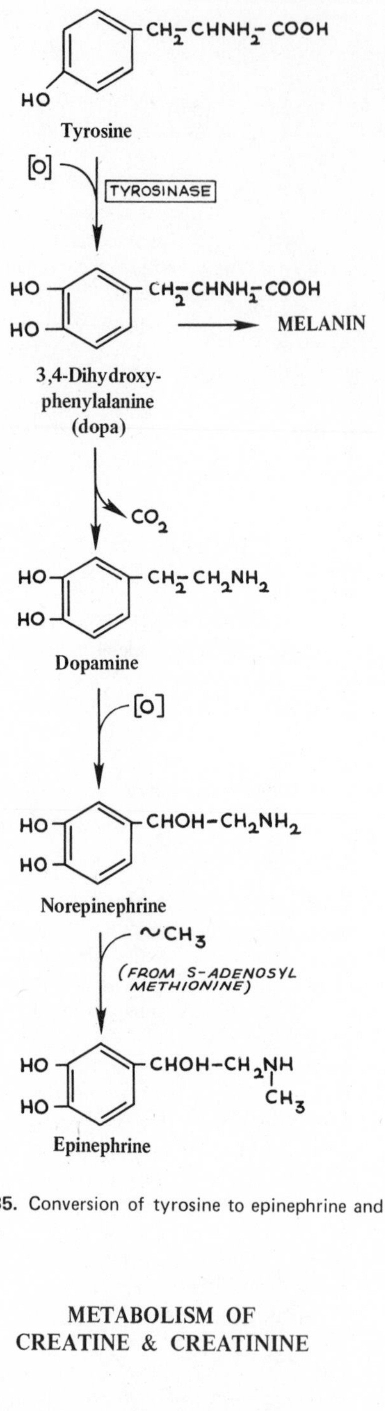

Figure 23–35. Conversion of tyrosine to epinephrine and norepinephrine.

METABOLISM OF
CREATINE & CREATININE

Creatine is present in muscle, brain, and blood, both phosphorylated as phosphocreatine and in the free state (Fig 23–36). Traces of creatine are also normally present in urine. Creatinine is the anhydride of creatine. It is formed largely in muscle by the irreversible and nonenzymatic removal of water from creatine phosphate. The free creatinine occurs in both blood and urine. Formation of creatinine is apparently a preliminary step required for the excretion of most of the creatine.

The 24-hour excretion of creatinine in the urine of a given subject is remarkably constant from day to day. The creatinine coefficient is the 24-hour urinary creatinine expressed in terms of body size. When expressed in this manner, the creatinine excretion of different individuals of the same age and sex is also quite constant.

The origin of creatine shown in the reactions below has been established by metabolic studies and confirmed by isotope technics. Three amino acids—glycine, arginine, and methionine—are directly involved. The first reaction is that of transamidination from arginine to glycine to form guanidoacetic acid (glycocyamine). This has been shown by in vitro experiments to occur in the kidney but not in the liver or in heart muscle. The synthesis of creatine is completed by the methylation of glycocyamine in the liver. In this reaction, "active" methionine is the methyl donor. Other methyl donors, such as betaine or choline after oxidation to betaine, may also serve indirectly by producing methionine through the methylation of homocysteine. The methylation of glycocyamine is not reversible. Neither creatine nor creatinine can methylate homocysteine to methionine. ATP and oxygen are required in the methylation of creatine.

The enzymatic mechanisms for the methylation of glycocyamine to form creatine are similar to those required for the formation of N-methylnicotinamide. The first step is the formation of active methionine (S-adenosylmethionine), which requires ATP, magnesium ions, and glutathione, and a methionine-activating enzyme. The second step involves the methylation of guanidoacetic acid by active methionine, a reaction which is catalyzed by a soluble enzyme, **guanidoacetate methylferase,** found in cell-free extracts of guinea pig, rabbit, beef, and pig liver. Glutathione or other reducing substances are required for the optimal activity of this enzyme; there is yet no evidence for the need of metal ions or other cofactors.

Until recently, the only site of the transamidinating enzyme in mammals was thought to be the kidney. Evidence has not been obtained to show that bilaterally nephrectomized rats can still synthesize creatine. This is interpreted as proof for the existence of an extrarenal site or sites of transamidination in this animal.

An enzyme preparation has been isolated from pancreatic tissue of beef as well as from the dog, which can catalyze the synthesis of creatine from glycocyamine and S-adenosylmethionine. It has also been found that the pancreas (in contrast to the liver) can synthesize glycocyamine. These observations suggest that the pancreas may play a unique role in the synthesis of creatine within the body of mammals.

The phenomenon of chemical feedback is discussed in Chapter 7. It is well illustrated by the effect of dietary creatine on creatine biosynthesis. In rats fed a complete diet containing 3% creatine, the transamidinase activity of the kidney was markedly lower than that of control animals. Gerber and others have studied the rate at which creatinine is synthesized from glyco-

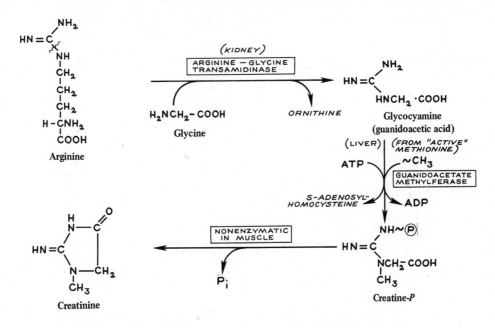

Figure 23-36. Biosynthesis of creatine and creatinine.

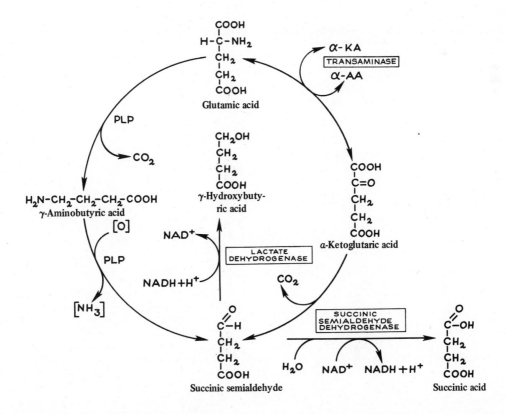

Figure 23-37. Metabolism of γ-aminobutyric acid. (α-KA = α-keto acids; α-AA = α-amino acids; PLP = pyridoxal phosphate.)

cyamine in the isolated perfused rat liver (1) in the presence of creatine precursors at levels normally present in the blood, and (2) in the presence of high concentrations of precursors (methionine and glycocyamine) added to the perfusion fluid. When the concentration of glycocyamine in the blood fell from 0.4 to 0.2 mg/dl, the rate of creatine synthesis decreased, whereas increasing glycocyamine to as high as 20 mg/dl together with additional methionine did not alter creatine synthesis significantly. Dietary creatine or a high blood creatine has no effect on the rate of synthesis of creatine in the liver. However, the fact that hepatic synthesis of creatine is related to the blood glycocyamine levels—and that this compound is produced in the kidney—suggests that the rate of creatine biosynthesis is actually dependent on kidney transamidinase activity, and, as noted above, the activity of this enzyme is in fact affected by creatine, apparently as a feedback mechanism.

Hyperthyroidism is one of the diseases which is characterized by disturbances in creatine metabolism. Consequently, it is of interest that hyperthyroidism is also associated with reduced kidney transamidinase activity. It may be that the effect of hyperthyroidism on kidney transamidinase is actually mediated by the elevated levels of blood creatine which occur in this disease, the creatine acting as described above to produce enzyme repression.

γ-Aminobutyrate

Decarboxylation of glutamate produces γ-aminobutyrate (Fig 23–37). An enzyme that catalyzes its formation from glutamate by alpha decarboxylation is found in the tissues of the central nervous system, principally in the gray matter. This enzyme requires pyridoxal phosphate as a coenzyme.

γ-Aminobutyrate is now known to serve as a normal regulator of neuronal activity, being active as an inhibitor when studied in various reflex preparations. It is further metabolized by deamination to succinic semialdehyde. The deamination is accomplished by a pyridoxal-dependent enzyme and the ammonia removed is transaminated to ketoglutarate, thus forming more glutamate.

Succinic semialdehyde may then be oxidized to succinate or reduced to γ-hydroxybutyrate, which has been found to exist in the brain in significant amounts. Reduction of succinic semialdehyde by homogenates of brain can be accomplished by an enzyme in the soluble protein fraction which was indistinguishable from lactic dehydrogenase.

When succinic semialdehyde is oxidized to succinic acid, there is completed what amounts to a "bypass" around the citric acid cycle in the brain in the sense that ketoglutarate, rather than going directly to succinate (as in the citric acid cycle), is transaminated to glutamate and thence by decarboxylation to γ-aminobutyrate, which is the source of succinic semialdehyde to form succinate.

γ-Aminobutyrate has also been detected in the kidneys of humans, indicating that this compound is not a unique constituent of the central nervous system in man.

•   •   •

References

Biosynthesis

Burnstein P: The biosynthesis of collagen. Annu Rev Biochem 43:567, 1974.

Cardinale GJ, Udenfriend S: Prolyl hydroxylase. Adv Enzymol 41:245, 1974.

Greenberg DM, Rodwell VW: Biosynthesis of amino acids and related compounds. Pages 237 and 317 in: *Metabolic Pathways.* Vol 3. Academic Press, 1969.

Holden JT (editor): *Amino Acid Pools.* Elsevier, 1962.

Meister A: *Biochemistry of the Amino Acids,* 2nd ed. Vol 2. Academic Press, 1965.

Truffa-Bachi P, Cohen GN: Some aspects of amino acid biosynthesis in microorganisms. Annu Rev Biochem 37:79, 1968.

Umbarger HE: Regulation of amino acid metabolism. Annu Rev Biochem 38:323, 1969.

Regulation

Calvo JM, Fink GR: Regulation of biosynthetic pathways in bacteria. Annu Rev Biochem 40:943, 1971.

Cohen GN: The aspartokinases and homoserine dehydrogenases of *Escherichia coli.* Curr Top Cell Regul 1:183, 1969.

Feigelson P: Studies on the allosteric regulation of tryptophan oxygenase: Structure and function. Adv Enzyme Regul 7:119, 1968.

Kenney FT: Mechanism of hormonal control of rat liver tyrosine transaminase. Adv Enzyme Regul 1:137, 1963.

Knox WE: The regulation of tryptophan pyrrolase activity by tryptophan. Adv Enzyme Regul 4:287, 1966.

Knox WE, Greengard O: The regulation of some enzymes of nitrogen metabolism: An introduction to enzyme physiology. Adv Enzyme Regul 3:247, 1965.

Schimke RT: On the roles of synthesis and degradation in regulation of enzyme levels in mammalian tissues. Curr Top Cell Regul 1:77, 1969.

Schimke RT, Doyle D: Control of enzyme levels in animal tissues. Annu Rev Biochem 39:929, 1970.

Umbarger HE: Regulation of the biosynthesis of the branched-chain amino acids. Curr Top Cell Regul 1:57, 1969.

Wood WA: Allosteric L-threonine dehydrases of microorganisms. Curr Top Cell Regul 1:161, 1969.

24 . . .
Metabolism of Purine
& Pyrimidine Nucleotides

The chemistry and, to some extent, the general roles of the purine and pyrimidine compounds have been discussed in Chapter 10. The chemistry of the nucleic acids has been described in Chapter 11. In this chapter, the metabolism of the purine and pyrimidine nucleotides will be discussed. A summary of these purine and pyrimidine derivatives is given in Table 24–1.

Digestion

Mammals and most lower vertebrates are said to be "prototrophic" for purines and pyrimidines, ie, capable of synthesizing purine and pyrimidine nucleotides de novo and thus not dependent upon exogenous sources of these important compounds. As a result, although mammals consume significant quantities of nucleic acids and nucleotides in their food, their survival is not dependent upon the absorption of these compounds or their breakdown products. Most dietary nucleic acids are ingested in the form of nucleoproteins from which the nucleic acids are liberated in the intestinal tract by the action of proteolytic enzymes. The pancreatic juice contains enzymes (nucleases) which degrade nucleic acids into nucleotides. These nucleases may be specific for the 2 major types of nucleic acids, RNA and DNA, and are appropriately termed ribonucleases and deoxyribonucleases. Intestinal enzymes—polynucleotidases or phosphoesterases—supplement the action of the pancreatic nucleases in producing mononucleotides from the nucleic acids. The mononucleotides are subsequently hydrolyzed to nucleosides by various nucleotidases and phosphatases, and the various nucleosides so produced can be either absorbed directly or further degraded by intestinal phosphorylase to the free purine or pyrimidine bases. The bases themselves may be oxidized, eg, guanine may be converted to xanthine and then to uric acid, or adenosine may be converted to inosine, to hypoxanthine, and then to uric acid (Fig 24–1). Uric acid can be absorbed across the intestinal mucosa and excreted in the urine as uric acid per se. In humans it appears that the majority of ingested nucleic acids is directly converted to uric acid without having previously been incorporated into the nucleic acids of the ingesting organism. However, there is evidence that some adenine is absorbed through the intestinal tract and incorporated into tissue nucleoproteins. Free pyrimidine orally administered to rats is mostly catabolized and excreted without having entered the nucleic acids of the ingesting organism. It would thus appear that, with the possible exception of adenine, none of the free purines or pyrimidines of the diet serve as a direct precursor of tissue nucleic acids.

Somewhat different results were obtained when

Table 24–1. The naturally occurring purine and pyrimidine bases and their related nucleosides and nucleotides.

Base	Nucleoside (Base + Sugar)	Nucleotide (Base + Sugar + Phosphoric Acid)
Purines		
Adenine (6-aminopurine)	Adenosine Deoxyadenosine	Adenylic acid Deoxyadenylic acid
Guanine (2-amino-6-oxypurine)	Guanosine Deoxyguanosine	Guanylic acid Deoxyguanylic acid
Hypoxanthine (6-oxypurine)	Inosine (hypoxanthine riboside) Deoxyinosine (hypoxanthine deoxyriboside)	Inosinic acid (hypoxanthine ribotide) Deoxyinosinic acid (hypoxanthine deoxyribotide)
Xanthine (2,6-dioxypurine)	Xanthosine	Xanthinylic acid
Pyrimidines		
Cytosine (2-oxy-4-aminopyrimidine)	Cytidine Deoxycytidine	Cytidylic acid Deoxycytidylic acid
Thymine (2,4-dioxy-5-methylpyrimidine)	Thymidine (thymine deoxyriboside)	Thymidylic acid (thymine deoxyribotide)
Uracil (2,4-dioxypyrimidine) Uracil	Uridine Pseudouridine (5-ribosyl linkage)	Uridylic acid Pseudouridylic acid

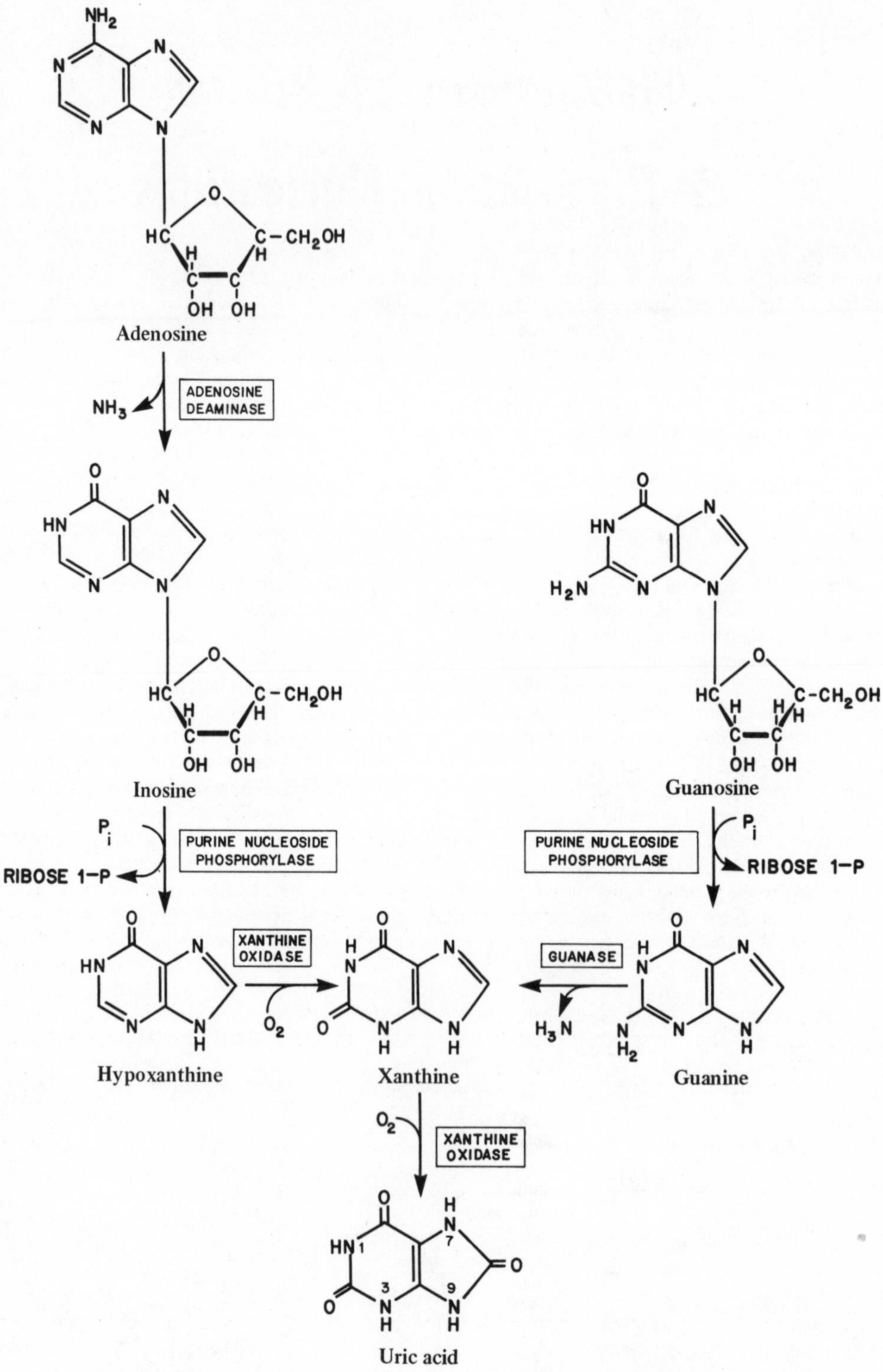

Figure 24—1. Generation of uric acid from purine nucleosides by way of the purine bases hypoxanthine, xanthine, and guanine.

purines or pyrimidines were administered parenterally as nucleosides or nucleotides. In rats, subcutaneous injection of labeled pyrimidine nucleosides—cytidine and uridine—resulted in the incorporation of these compounds into RNA and to a smaller extent into the cytosine and thymine of DNA. Injected thymidine was incorporated into DNA unaltered; demethylation of the thymidine apparently did not take place since no labeled uracil was detected in RNA. The fact that unchanged thymidine, when injected, can be incorporated into DNA has proved to be the basis of a valuable technic for labeling newly produced DNA in a great variety of biologic materials both in vivo and in vitro. For these purposes, ^{3}H-thymidine—ie, thymidine containing tritium (^{3}H), the radioactive isotope of hydrogen—is used.

Biosynthesis of Purine Nucleotides

In humans and other mammals, purine nucleotides are synthesized to meet the needs of the organism for the monomeric precursors of nucleic acids and for those other functions described in Chapter 10. In some organisms (birds, amphibians, and reptiles), the synthesis of purine nucleotides has an additional function, which is to serve as the chemical vehicle to excrete nitrogen waste products as uric acid. Such organisms are referred to as **uricotelic**, whereas those organisms that dispose of nitrogenous waste products in the form of urea, as humans do, are referred to as **ureotelic**. Because the uricotelic organisms must dispose of their nitrogenous wastes in the form of uric acid, they synthesize purine nucleotides at a relatively greater rate than do ureotelic organisms. Studies of the pigeon, particularly with pigeon liver, have provided much information about the process of de novo purine nucleotide synthesis. Subsequent studies in mammalian systems—especially mammalian cells in continuous culture—have demonstrated that the steps involved in de novo purine nucleotide synthesis in mammals are analogous to those in pigeon liver. These later studies provided information concerning the regulation of purine metabolism in mammals.

Information on the sources of the various atoms of the purine base has been obtained by tracer studies in birds, rats, and humans (Fig 24—2). The amino acid glycine is utilized intact to form the carbon positions 4 and 5, while its a nitrogen forms the nitrogen in position 7. The nitrogen for position 1 is derived from the amino nitrogen of aspartic acid; the N atoms at positions 3 and 9 are derived from the amide nitrogen of glutamine. The carbon atom at position 6 is derived from CO_2, while the carbons in position 2 and 8 come from a one-carbon (C-1) compound supplied by the tetrahydrofolate carrier.

The biosynthetic pathway for the synthesis of purine nucleotides is shown in Figure 24—3. In order to understand the regulation of de novo purine nucleotide synthesis, the first step (reaction 1, Fig 24—3) in the synthesis of purine nucleotides must be regarded as the formation of 1-pyrophosphorylribosyl-5-phosphate (PPriboseP). Although the conversion of ribose 5-phos-

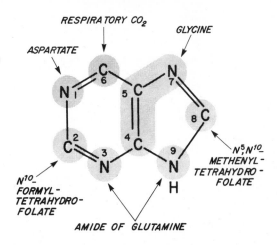

Figure 24—2. The sources of the nitrogen and carbon atoms of the purine ring.

phate of ATP to AMP + PPriboseP (Fig 24—4) is not uniquely committed to the synthesis of purine nucleotides, it appears from a regulatory aspect to be a most important process. As discussed in the latter part of this chapter, PPriboseP also serves as a precursor of the pyrimidine nucleotides and is required for the synthesis of NAD and NADP, 2 cofactors derived from niacin (See Chapter 12).

PPriboseP then reacts (reaction 2, Fig 24—3) with glutamine in a reaction catalyzed by the enzyme **phosphoribosylpyrophosphate amidotransferase** to form 5-phosphoribosylamine accompanied by the displacement of pyrophosphate and the formation of glutamic acid. Although other mechanisms have been proposed for the synthesis of 5-phosphoribosylamine in mammalian tissues, genetic experiments confirm that the physiologically important reaction is that catalyzed by the amidotransferase. The 5-phosphoribosylamine so formed then reacts (reaction 3, Fig 24—3) with glycine to produce glycinamide ribosylphosphate (glycinamide ribotide [GAR]). The amido group from glutamine contributes the 9 N of the eventual purine ring while the glycine contributes carbons 4 and 5 and the 7 N. The enzyme-catalyzing reaction 3 is designated **glycinamide kinosynthetase** since it requires ATP and generates ADP and phosphate in that reaction.

The N_7 of glycinamide ribosylphosphate is then formylated (reaction 4, Fig 24—3), which requires N^5,N^{10}-methenyltetrahydrofolate (See Chapter 12) and the enzyme **glycinamide ribosylphosphate formyltransferase** to transfer the C_1 moiety which becomes the C_8 of the purine base. In reaction 5, again with glutamine as the amide donor, amidation occurs at the C_4 of the formylglycinamide ribosylphosphate, catalyzed by **formylglycinamidine ribosylphosphate synthetase**, which requires ATP in addition to glutamine. The amide N becomes position 3 in the purine.

The closure of the imidazole ring is catalyzed by the enzyme **aminoimidazole ribosylphosphate synthetase**, which also requires ATP and which forms amino-

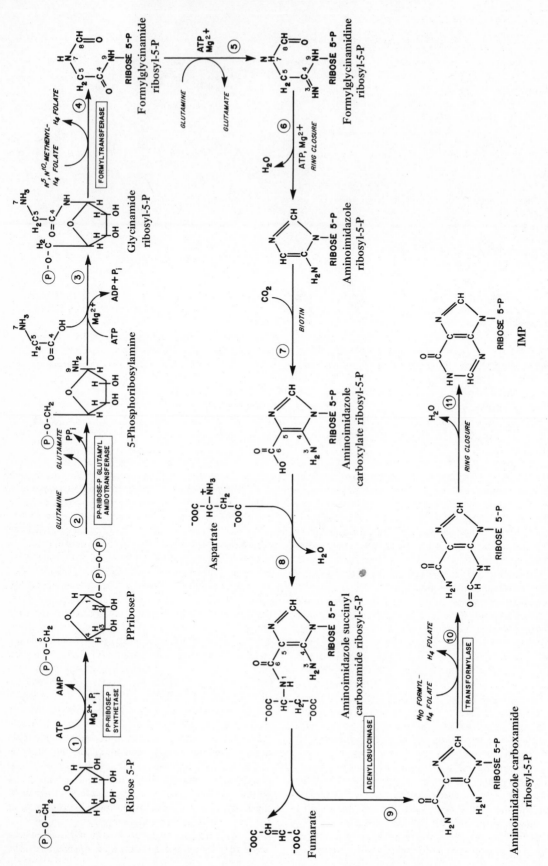

Figure 24–3. The pathway of de novo purine biosynthesis from ribose 5-phosphate and ATP. (See text for explanation.)

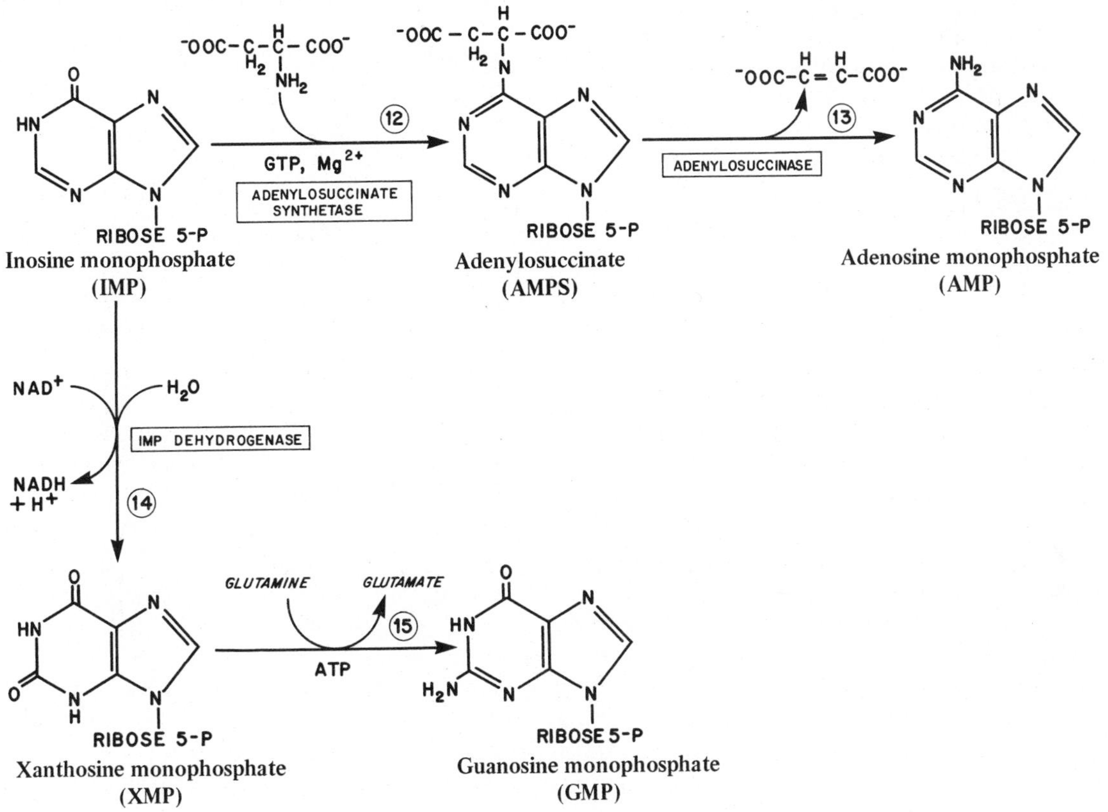

Figure 24—4. The conversions of IMP to AMP and GMP. (See text for explanation.)

imidazole ribosylphosphate. The synthesis progresses (reaction 7) to aminoimidazole carboxylate ribosyl phosphate by addition to the precursor compound of a carbonyl group, the source of which is respiratory CO_2. The utilization of CO_2, as in other CO_2 fixation reactions, apparently requires biotin; the precursor substance, aminoimidazole ribosylphosphate, has been found to accumulate in biotin-deficient animals. The source of the nitrogen in the 1 position is the a-amino group of aspartate (reaction 8), the remaining portion of which is indicated as the succinyl moiety of amino-imidazole succinylcarboxamide ribosylphosphate, abbreviated as SAICAR. In reaction 9, the succinyl group of SAICAR is split off as fumaric acid. Amino-imidazole carboxamide ribosylphosphate, which remains, is then formylated (reaction 10) by N^{10}-formyltetrahydrofolate ($f^{10} \cdot H_4$folate) to form amido-imidazole carboxamide ribosylphosphate in a reaction catalyzed by the appropriate **formyl transferase**. The newly added carbon, which, like the C_8 of the purine base, is derived from the C_1 pool via the tetrahydrofolate carrier, will be C_2 of the purine nucleus. Ring closure now occurs (reaction 11) via **IMP cyclohydrolase**, and the first purine nucleotide, **inosinic acid (inosine monophosphate, IMP)**, is thus formed.

The importance of folate metabolism (see Chapter 13) in the de novo synthesis of purine nucleotides

should be evident. Two one-carbon moieties are added to the purine ring at positions 8 and 2 by N^5,-N^{10}-methylidenyltetrahydrofolate and N^{10}-formyltetrahydrofolate, respectively. The latter is derived from the former. The N^5,N^{10}-methylidenyltetrahydrofolate is derived from the NADP-dependent dehydrogenation of N^5,N^{10}-methylenetetrahydrofolate. The N^5,N^{10}-methylenetetrahydrofolate can donate a one-carbon moiety to numerous acceptors, but once N^5,N^{10}-methylidenyltetrahydrofolate is formed the one-carbon group is committed to transfer only into purines, whence it is donated either directly or after conversion to N^{10}-formyltetrahydrofolate. Thus, any inhibition of the formation of these tetrahydrofolate compounds will have a detrimental effect upon the de novo synthesis of purines.

As is clear from the scheme in Fig 24—4, adenine nucleotides (reactions 12 and 13) and guanine nucleotides (reactions 14 and 15) are derived from inosine **monophosphate (IMP)** by amination and by oxidation and amination, respectively. The amination of IMP is accomplished through the formation of an intermediate compound in which aspartic acid is attached to inosinic acid to form adenylosuccinate. This reaction is similar to that of a preceding reaction (reaction 9) in which the nitrogen at position 1 of the purine nucleus was added by way of a nitrogen of aspartic acid. The formation of adenylosuccinate is catalyzed by **adenyl-succinate synthetase,** and it requires GTP, which provides a potential regulatory mechanism. The splitting off, as fumaric acid, of the remaining portion of aspartic acid from adenylosuccinate produces the final product, adenylic acid (adenosine monophosphate, AMP). Cleavage of fumaric acid from adenylosuccinate is catalyzed by the enzyme **adenylosuccinase,** which is responsible also for the cleavage of fumarate from the succinyl of aminoimidazole succinyl carboxamide ribosylphosphate (reaction 9). Also, in 2 steps, IMP is converted to guanosine monophosphate (GMP). The first reaction in this sequence (reaction 14) is an oxidation utilizing NAD as cofactor and water to form xanthosine monophosphate (XMP). XMP is aminated by the amido group of glutamine in a reaction which requires ATP, somewhat analogous to the requirement of GTP for the conversion of IMP to AMP.

Several antimetabolites which are glutamine analogs are effective inhibitors of various steps in purine biosynthesis. **Azaserine** (O-diazoacetyl-L-serine) is an antagonist to glutamine particularly at reaction 5. **Deoxynorleucine** ([6-diazo-5-oxo]-L-norleucine) blocks reaction 2 in purine synthesis, and **6-mercaptopurine,**

among its other actions, inhibits reactions 13 and 14 in the synthesis of AMP and GMP, respectively.

The conversions of AMP and GMP to their respective nucleoside diphosphates and nucleoside triphosphates occur in 2 successive steps (F ig 24—5). The successive transfers of the high-energy phosphate groups from ATP are catalyzed by **nucleoside monophosphate kinase** and **nucleoside diphosphate kinase,** respectively. The enzyme which phosphorylates adenylate is also referred to as **myokinase.**

The synthesis of the purine deoxyribonucleotides occurs by direct reduction of the 2′ carbon in the ribose moiety of the corresponding nucleotide rather than by the synthesis of the entire purine nucleotide utilizing a 2′-deoxy analog of PPriboseP. The reduction at the 2′ carbon occurs only after the purine and pyrimidine nucleotides have been converted to their respective nucleoside diphosphates. In prokaryotic organisms, cobalamin (vitamin B_{12}) is required for this reductive process, although it is not required for the same reaction in humans. The reduction of ribonucleoside diphosphates to deoxyribonucleoside diphosphates is a complex reaction in mammals. The reaction (Fig 24—6) requires **thioredoxin** (a protein cofactor), **thio-**

Figure 24—5. The reactions responsible for the conversion of nucleoside monophosphates to nucleoside diphosphates and nucleoside triphosphates.

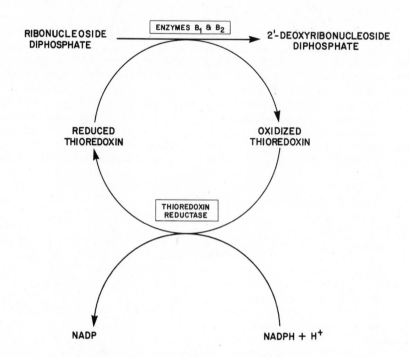

Figure 24—6. The reactions involved in the reduction of ribonucleoside diphosphates to 2′ deoxyribonucleoside diphosphates.

redoxin reductase (a flavoprotein), 2 other enzymes termed enzyme B_1 and enzyme B_2, and NADPH as a cofactor. The immediate electron donor to the nucleotide is the reduced form of thioredoxin which has accepted electrons from NADPH. The reversible oxidation-reduction of thioredoxin is catalyzed by **thioredoxin reductase**. The reduction of the ribonucleoside diphosphate by reduced thioredoxin is catalyzed by enzymes B_1 and B_2.

Not all tissues in the human body are capable of de novo synthesis of purine nucleotides. The erythrocyte is incapable of synthesizing 5-phosphoribosylamine and therefore is dependent upon exogenous purines for the formation of purine nucleotides. Polymorphonuclear leukocytes have little or no capacity for synthesizing phosphoribosylamine, but peripheral lymphocytes do possess some ability to synthesize purines de novo. Mammalian brain appears to have a reduced content of PPriboseP-glutamyl amidotransferase; indeed, it has been suggested that the human brain is dependent upon exogenous purines for the formation of purine nucleotides. It is evident that the mammalian liver is a major site of purine nucleotide synthesis so that this organ can provide purines to be salvaged and utilized by those tissues incapable of synthesizing purines de novo.

Purine Salvage Pathways

As described above, some tissues within mammalian organisms, including humans, are dependent upon exogenous purines or purine ribonucleosides for the formation of purine nucleotides. The salvage of these preformed purine compounds can occur by 2 general mechanisms. The quantitatively more important mechanism is the phosphoribosylation of the free purine bases by specific enzymes requiring PPriboseP as the ribose phosphate donor. The second general mechanism is the phosphorylation of purine nucleosides at their 5′-hydroxyl groups.

There are 2 enzymes in human tissues that can phosphoribosylate purine bases. One enzyme (Fig 24−7) is capable of phosphoribosylating adenine with PPriboseP to generate AMP: **adenine phosphoribosyl transferase**. The second (Fig 24−8) is capable of phosphoribosylating hypoxanthine and guanine with PPriboseP to yield IMP and GMP, respectively: **hypoxan-

thine-guanine phosphoribosyl transferase**. As will be discussed below, the latter pathway (the salvage of hypoxanthine and guanine to IMP and GMP) is more active than the formation of AMP from adenine.

The salvage of purine ribonucleosides to purine ribonucleotides is carried out in humans by an enzyme which utilizes only adenosine. This enzyme, **adenosine kinase** (Fig 24−9), can use inosine poorly if at all, and it demonstrates no ability to phosphorylate guanosine to its respective ribonucleotide.

However, there is more to the purine salvage pathways than simply the phosphorylation of adenosine and the phosphoribosylation of adenine, hypoxanthine, and guanine. In addition, in humans there is a cycle (Fig 24−10) in which IMP and GMP as well as their respective deoxyribonucleotides are converted to their respective nucleosides (inosine, deoxyinosine, guanosine, and deoxyguanosine) by a **purine 5′-nucleotidase**. These purine ribonucleosides and 2′-deoxynucleosides are converted to hypoxanthine or guanine by **purine nucleoside phosphorylase**, producing ribose 1-phosphate or 2′-deoxyribose 1-phosphate as phosphorolysis products. The hypoxanthine and guanine can then again be phosphoribosylated by PPriboseP to IMP and GMP to complete the cycle. The functions of this purine salvage cycle are unknown, but it is clear that, in the human organism as a whole, the consumption of PPriboseP by this salvage cycle is greater than the consumption of PPriboseP for the synthesis of purine nucleotides de novo.

There is a lateral pathway of this cycle which involves the conversion of IMP to AMP (reactions 12 and 13, Fig 24−4), with the subsequent conversion of AMP to adenosine. The latter is probably catalyzed by the same purine 5′-nucleotidase that hydrolyzes IMP to inosine. The adenosine so produced is then either salvaged directly back to AMP via **adenosine kinase** or is converted to inosine by the enzyme **adenosine deaminase**. Quantitatively, the function of this IMP→AMP→adenosine→inosine loop is less important than the previously described cycle. Qualitatively, the conversion of adenosine to inosine by adenosine deaminase is an important process, particularly for the immune system, as described in the discussion of inherited disorders of purine metabolism.

The salvage of the free purine adenine by adenine

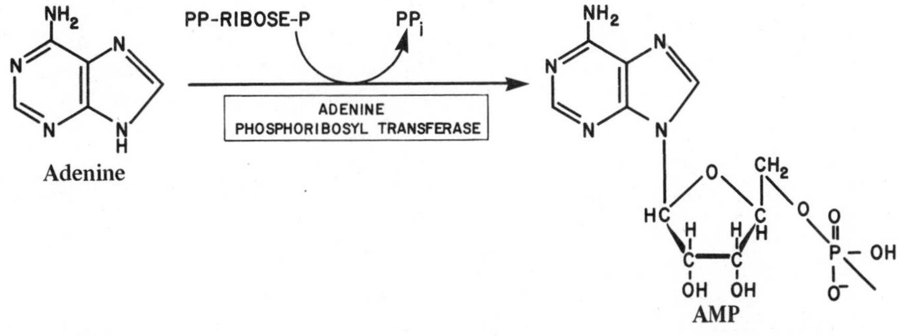

Figure 24−7. Phosphoribosylation of adenine catalyzed by adenine phosphoribosyl transferase.

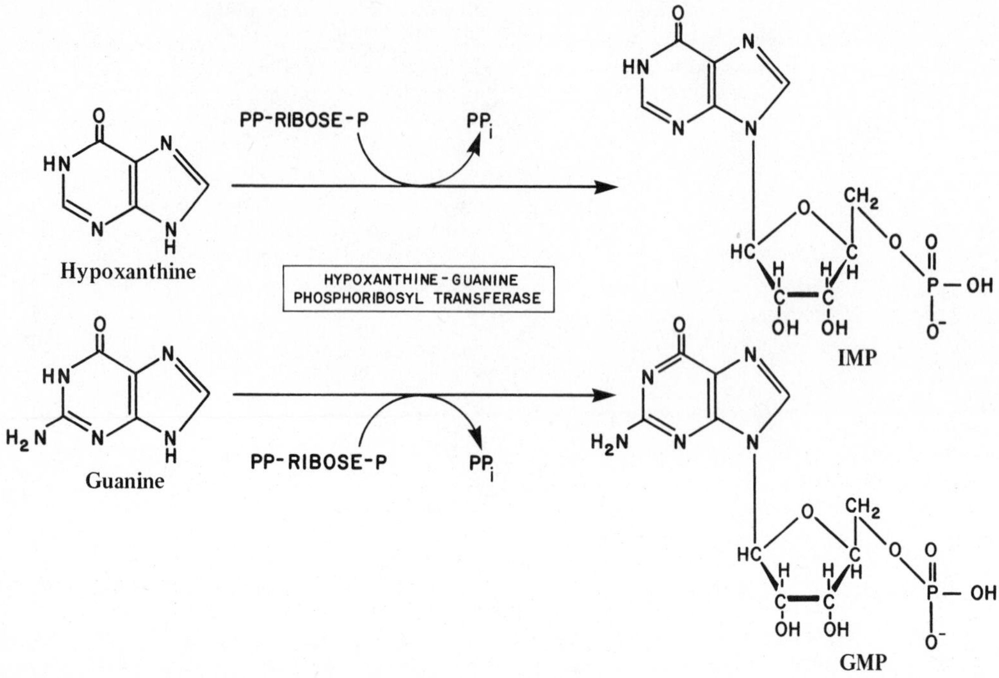

Figure 24—8. Phosphoribosylation of hypoxanthine and guanine to form IMP and GMP, respectively. The reactions are catalyzed by the enzyme hypoxanthine-guanine phosphoribosyl transferase.

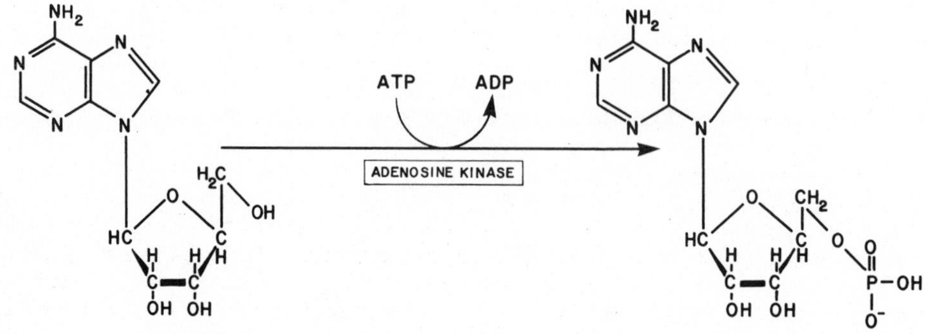

Figure 24—9. Phosphorylation of adenosine to AMP by adenosine kinase.

phosphoribosyl transferase seems to prevent the xanthine oxidase-mediated oxidation of adenine to 2,8-dihydroxyadenine (Fig 24—11). Dihydroxyadenine is a highly insoluble product which appears as kidney stones in patients devoid of adenine phosphoribosyl transferase activity. The source of free adenine for such a salvage process is not known with certainty, although it probably derives from the hydrolysis of 5'-methylthioadenosine, a by-product of the synthesis of polyamines from S-adenosylmethionine (Fig 24—12).

Regulation of Purine Biosynthesis

The de novo synthesis of IMP consumes the equivalent of 6 high-energy phosphodiester bonds (by ATP hydrolysis) along with the other required precursors, glycine, glutamine, methylenetetrahydrofolate,

and aspartate. Thus, it is important for the conservation of energy and nutrients that the cell economically regulate its rate of de novo purine biosynthesis. The single most important regulator of de novo purine biosynthesis is the intracellular concentration of PPriboseP. As with so many other intracellular compounds, the regulation of PPriboseP concentration is dependent upon the rate of synthesis versus the rate of utilization or degradation. The rate of synthesis of PPriboseP is dependent upon (1) the availability of its substrates, particularly ribose 5-phosphate, which is more likely to be limiting than is ATP; and (2) the catalytic activity of PPriboseP synthetase, which is dependent upon the intracellular phosphate concentration as well as the concentrations of the purine and pyrimidine ribonucleotides acting as allosteric regulators. In vitro, the

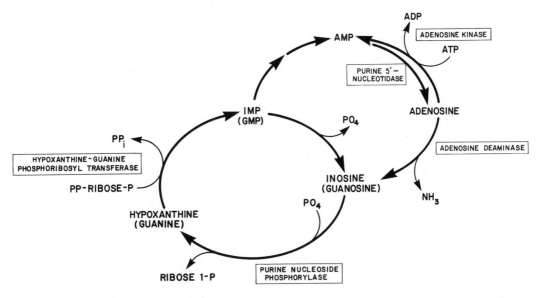

Figure 24–10. The purine salvage cycles involving the interconversion of AMP, IMP, and—to a lesser extent—GMP to their respective ribonucleosides and their eventual reconversion to purine ribonucleotides.

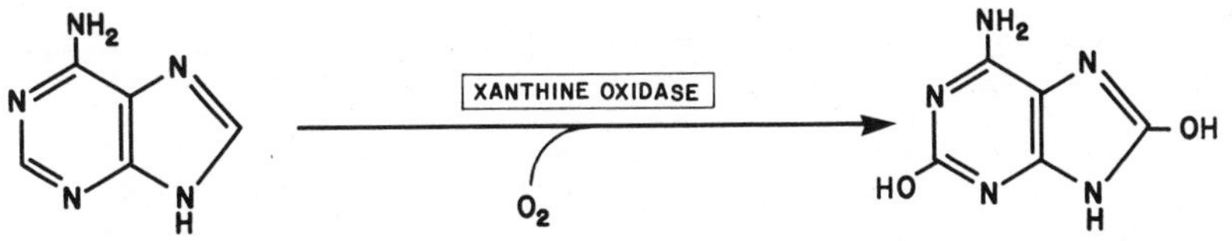

Adenine   2, 8-Dihydroxyadenine

Figure 24–11. The formation of 2,8-dihydroxyadenine from adenine by the catalytic action of xanthine oxidase.

PPriboseP synthetase from human erythrocytes and cultured fibroblasts is dependent upon inorganic phosphate and is most sensitive to inhibition by TDP, ADP, and AMP. The rate of utilization of PPriboseP is dependent to a large extent on its consumption by the salvage pathway which phosphoribosylates hypoxanthine and guanine to their respective ribonucleotides. To a lesser extent, utilization is dependent upon the rate of de novo purine synthesis. This conclusion stems from the observation that in males with inherited deficiencies of hypoxanthine-guanine phosphoribosyl transferase, the levels of PPriboseP in their erythrocytes and cultured fibroblasts are elevated severalfold.

The first enzyme uniquely committed to de novo purine synthesis, PPriboseP glutamyl amidotransferase, demonstrates in vitro a sensitivity to feedback inhibition by purine nucleotides, particularly adenosine monophosphate and guanosine monophosphate. These feedback inhibitors of the amidotransferase are competitive with the substrate PPriboseP, and thus, again, PPriboseP plays a major role in the regulation of de novo purine synthesis. Numerous indirect experiments suggest that the regulation of de novo purine synthesis by the amidotransferase is physiologically unimportant; in fact, as discussed later in this chapter, the search for feedback-resistant amidotransferase mutants among the population of gouty persons has not been successful despite a 15-year search. Thus, the regulation of the rate of synthesis of IMP occurs primarily at the level of PPriboseP synthetase and primarily by allosteric mechanisms responsible for feedback inhibition of that enzyme (Fig 24–13). There have been suggestions that repression or induction of enzymes in the de novo synthesis of purine occurs in cultured animal cells, but these have not been confirmed.

The conversion of IMP to GMP or to AMP is regulated by 2 mechanisms (Fig 24–14). AMP feedback regulates its own synthesis at the level of adenylosuccinate synthetase, GMP by feedback inhibition of IMP dehydrogenase. Furthermore, the conversion of IMP to adenylosuccinate en route to AMP requires the presence of GTP. The conversion of xanthinylate to GMP requires the presence of ATP. Thus, there is significant cross-regulation between the divergent pathways in the metabolism of IMP. This regulation prevents the synthesis of one purine nucleotide when there is a deficiency of the other. Hypoxanthine-guanine phosphoribosyl transferase, which converts hypoxanthine and guanine to IMP and GMP, respectively, is quite sensitive to product inhibition by these same nucleotides.

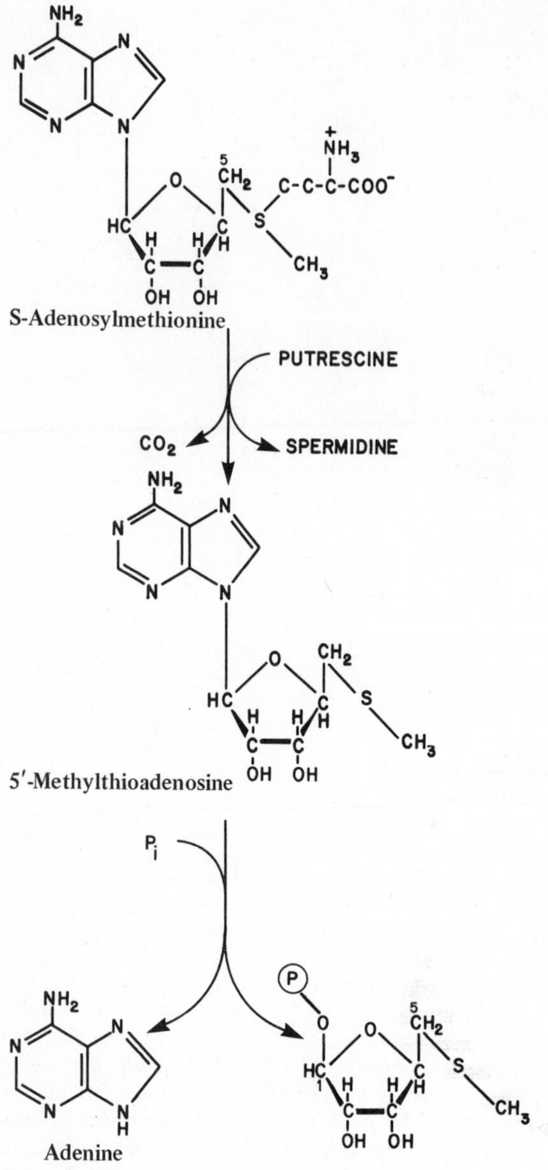

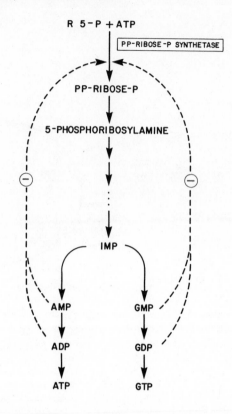

Figure 24–13. A regulatory scheme for the control of the rate of de novo purine synthesis. Solid lines represent chemical flow and dotted lines represent feedback inhibition by end products of the pathway.

S-Adenosylmethionine

PUTRESCINE

CO_2 SPERMIDINE

5′-Methylthioadenosine

P_i

Adenine

Figure 24–12. The formation of free adenine from S-adenosylmethionine during the formation of polyamines such as spermidine.

The reduction of ribonucleoside diphosphates to deoxyribonucleoside diphosphates is subject to complex regulation (Fig 24–15). The reduction of GDP to 2′-deoxy GDP is stimulated by deoxy TTP but inhibited by deoxy ATP; and the reduction of ADP to 2′-deoxy ADP is stimulated by deoxy GTP but inhibited by deoxy ATP. The reduction of the pyrimidine ribonucleoside diphosphates to their respective deoxyribonucleoside diphosphates is inhibited by deoxy TTP and deoxy ATP but stimulated by ATP. This process of regulation apparently provides for the proper balancing of deoxyribonucleotides for the synthesis of DNA.

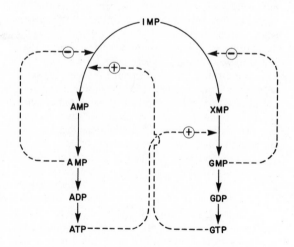

Figure 24–14. The regulation of the interconversion of IMP to adenosine nucleotides and guanosine nucleotides. Solid lines represent chemical flow and dotted lines represent both positive and negative feedback regulation.

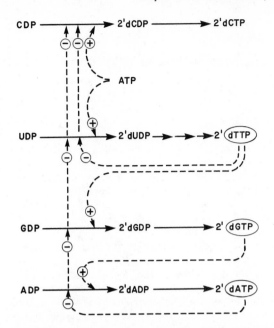

Figure 24–15. Regulation of the reduction of purine and pyrimidine ribonucleotides to their respective 2′ deoxyribonucleotides. Solid lines represent chemical flow and dotted lines represent negative or positive feedback regulation.

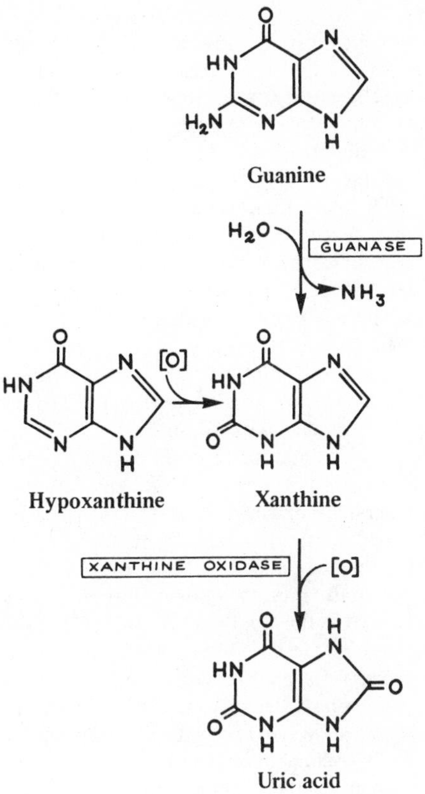

Catabolism of Purines

In humans, the ultimate catabolite (end product) of purines is uric acid. Reasoning from observations made in humans with inherited enzyme deficiencies, it appears that over 99% of the uric acid is derived from substrates of purine nucleoside phosphorylase, a component of the purine salvage pathway described above. The products of purine nucleoside phosphorylase, guanine and hypoxanthine, are converted to uric acid by way of xanthine in reactions catalyzed by the enzymes **guanase** and **xanthine oxidase**, respectively (Fig 24–16). Xanthine oxidase is very active in liver, small intestine, and kidney, and in its absence no uric acid is formed. As described above, some uric acid may be produced from nucleic acids by the bacterial flora of the intestinal tract, whence it is absorbed and directly excreted. This pathway seems to be a minor contributor to the urinary uric acid of persons on a normal diet.

As discussed below under the disorders of purine metabolism, the activity of xanthine oxidase is an important site for pharmacologic intervention in patients

Figure 24–16. The conversion of guanine and hypoxanthine to xanthine and uric acid.

with hyperuricemia and gout. In lower primates and other mammals, the enzyme **uricase** is responsible for the hydrolysis of uric acid to allantoin (Fig 24–17), a highly water-soluble end product of purine catabolism in those animals. Amphibians, birds, and reptiles do not possess uricase activity. These animals excrete uric acid and guanine as the end products of both purine metabolism and nitrogen (protein) metabolism. (In fact, the word guanine is derived from guano [huanu, dung], a white crystalline material deposited, for example, mainly by marine birds, on many coastal rocks.)

Organisms which form uric acid as the major nitrogenous waste product are said to be **uricotelic**. Aves, amphibia, and reptilia seem to have evolved a uricotelic system to regain water of hydration from uric acid

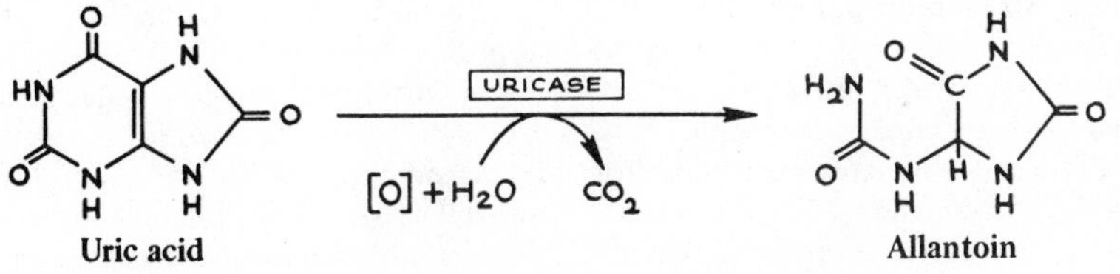

Figure 24–17. Conversion of uric acid to allantoin.

after it precipitates out, as it will at rather low concentrations. If they were to use urea as the end product of nitrogen metabolism, the water of hydration could not be regained since urea is water-soluble up to 10 M, a concentration far higher than any kidney can attain.

The metabolism of uric acid in humans has been studied by the use of isotopically labeled uric acid as well as its precursors, glycine and formate. Single doses of N^{15} uric acid were injected intravenously into normal human subjects and patients suffering from gout, a disease characterized by increased accumulation of uric acid and sodium urate. The dilution of the injected labeled isotope was used to calculate the quantity of total uric acid equilibrating with body water, a quantity referred to as the **miscible urate pool**. The mass of the rapidly miscible pool of uric acid in 25 normal male adult subjects averaged 1200 mg with a range of 866–1578 mg. In 3 normal female subjects the pool ranged from 541–687 mg. In gouty subjects the miscible urate pool was much larger, generally ranging from 2000–4000 mg in patients without tophi, ie, deposits of sodium urate in soft tissues. However, in severe tophaceous gout the pool was as high as 31,000 mg. The turnover of the miscible pool of total uric acid in normal persons is approximately 600 mg/24 hours. Isotope studies have demonstrated that 18–20% of the lost uric acid is not excreted in the urine but is degraded to CO_2 and ammonia and excreted in the feces, where it can be further metabolized by intestinal flora. It is known that some uric acid is excreted in the bile and thus is subject to degradation by intestinal flora. However, in humans, the breakdown of uric acid to CO_2 and NH_3 is independent of intestinal bacteria.

The handling of sodium urate, a salt of uric acid, by the mammalian kidney has been the subject of many studies. It appears from recent studies that sodium urate is freely filtered in the mammalian glomerulus, is partially reabsorbed and secreted in the proximal tubule, is further secreted in the loop of Henle, and perhaps is again partially reabsorbed in the distal convoluted tubule. The net excretion of total uric acid in normal men is 400–600 mg/24 hours. Many pharmacologic and naturally occurring compounds influence the renal absorption and secretion of sodium urate. Aspirin is a notable example of a commonly used drug which in high doses competitively inhibits urate excretion as well as reabsorption.

Biosynthesis of Pyrimidines

The pyrimidine nucleotides possess the heterocyclic ring structure which occurs also in the purine nucleus. These nucleotides have chemical and physiologic properties similar to those of purine nucleotides. Although the pyrimidine nucleus is simpler and its synthetic pathway briefer than that of the purine structure, the 2 share several common precursors. PPriboseP, glutamine, CO_2, and aspartate are required for the synthesis of all pyrimidine and purine nucleotides. For the thymidine nucleotides and for all purine nucleotides, tetrahydrofolate derivatives are also necessary. There is one striking difference between the

synthesis of pyrimidine nucleotides and that of purine nucleotides, namely, that the synthesis of the purine nucleotides commences with ribose phosphate as an integral part of the earliest precursor molecule, whereas the pyrimidine base is formed and attachment of the ribose phosphate moiety delayed until the later steps of the pathway.

The synthesis of the pyrimidine ring commences with the formation of carbamoyl phosphate from glutamine, ATP, and CO_2 in a reaction catalyzed by the carbamoyl phosphate synthetase located in the cytosol of the cell (Fig 24–18). In contrast, the carbamoyl phosphate synthetase molecule responsible for the early steps in urea synthesis resides in the mitochondria. The first step uniquely committed to the biosynthesis of pyrimidines is the formation of carbamoyl aspartate by the condensation of carbamoyl phosphate and aspartate, a reaction catalyzed by the enzyme **aspartate transcarbamoylase**. A ring structure can then be formed from carbamoyl aspartate by loss of H_2O catalyzed by the enzyme **dihydroorotase**. In a subsequent dehydrogenation step catalyzed by **dihydroorotate dehydrogenase** and utilizing NAD as a cofactor, **orotic acid** is formed. The next step is that in which a ribose phosphate moiety is added to orotic acid to form **orotidylate (orotidine monophosphate, OMP)**. This reaction is catalyzed by **orotate phosphoribosyl transferase**, an enzyme analogous to the hypoxanthine-guanine phosphoribosyl transferase and the adenine phosphoribosyl transferase involved in the phosphoribosylation of preformed purine rings. The first true pyrimidine ribonucleotide is formed by the decarboxylation of orotidylate to form **uridylate (uridine monophosphate, UMP)**. Thus, only at the penultimate step in the formation of UMP is the heterocyclic ring phosphoribosylated.

By mechanisms analogous to those described for the further phosphorylation of the purine nucleoside monophosphates, the pyrimidine nucleoside monophosphates are converted to their diphosphate and triphosphate derivatives. UTP is aminated to CTP, a reaction in which glutamine provides the amino group and which requires ATP. The reduction of the pyrimidine nucleoside diphosphates to the respective 2'-deoxynucleoside diphosphates occurs by a mechanism also analogous to that described for the purine nucleotides (Fig 24–6).

The formation of **thymidylate (thymidine monophosphate, TMP)** is the one reaction in pyrimidine nucleotide biosynthesis which requires a tetrahydrofolate donor of a single carbon compound. The 2'-deoxy UMP is methylated by **thymidylate synthetase**, which utilizes as a methyl donor N^5,N^{10}-methylenetetrahydrofolate. The methylene group of N^5,N^{10}-methylenetetrahydrofolate, which is added as a methyl group to the C_5 of deoxy-UMP, must be reduced in the process of its donation. While the methylene is reduced to a methyl group, the tetrahydrofolate carrier is oxidized to dihydrofolate, and the net redox state of the reaction is thus unchanged. The methylation of deoxy-UMP to TMP results in an overall reduction of the

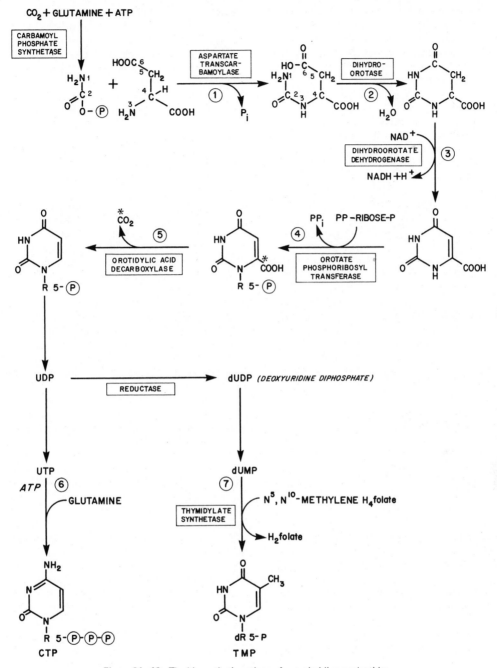

Figure 24—18. The biosynthetic pathway for pyrimidine nucleotides.

hydroxymethyl group from serine to a methyl group with the simultaneous oxidation of tetrahydrofolate to dihydrofolate. In order to continue to use the folate carrier, the cell must reduce dihydrofolate to tetrahydrofolate, a reaction carried out by the enzyme dihydrofolate reductase. The formation of TMP is therefore sensitive to inhibitors of dihydrofolate reductase. An example of such an inhibitor is methotrexate (amethopterin), a widely used anticancer drug.

Pyrimidine Salvage Pathways

Mammalian cells do not appear to possess efficient means of salvaging **free** pyrimidine bases to their respective pyrimidine nucleotides. However, they do have active salvage pathways for converting the pyrimidine **nucleosides** uridine, cytidine, and thymidine to their respective nucleotides (Fig 24—19). The enzyme required for de novo pyrimidine biosynthesis, **orotate phosphoribosyl transferase**, is capable of salvaging

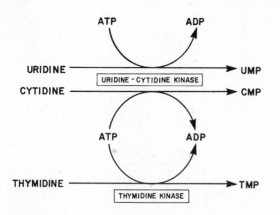

Figure 24—19. The pyrimidine nucleoside kinase reactions responsible for formation of the respective pyrimidine nucleoside monophosphates.

orotic acid to OMP, but in a strict sense orotic acid is not considered a complete pyrimidine base. The orotate phosphoribosyl transferase cannot use normal pyrimidine bases as substrates, although it is capable of converting allopurinol (4-hydroxypyrazolo[-2,4d-] pyrimidine) to a nucleotide in which the ribosyl phosphate is attached to the N_1 of the pyrimidine ring of that drug (Fig 24—20).

Catabolism of Pyrimidines

The catabolism of pyrimidines occurs mainly in the liver. It results in the production of a series of highly soluble end products. This contrasts with the production of the sparingly soluble uric acid and sodium urate by purine catabolism. The proposed pathways for the degradation of pyrimidines, based on fragmentary evidence, are shown in Fig 24—21. The release of respiratory CO_2 from the ureido carbon (C_2) of the pyrimidine nucleus represents a major pathway for the catabolism of uracil, cytosine, and thymine. β-Alanine and β-aminoisobutyric acid are the major end products of cytosine-uracil and thymine catabolism, respectively.

As indicated below, thymine is the precursor of β-aminoisobutyric acid, both in laboratory animals and in humans. The excretion of β-aminoisobutyric acid is increased in leukemia as well as after the body has been subjected to x-irradiation. This is undoubtedly a reflection of increased destruction of cells and their DNA. A familial occurrence of an abnormally high excretion of β-aminoisobutyric acid has also been observed in otherwise normal individuals. This genetic trait is traceable to a recessively expressed gene. High excreters result only when the trait is homozygous. It is of interest that approximately 25% of tested persons of Chinese or Japanese ancestry consistently excreted large amounts of β-aminoisobutyric acid. Although little is known about the mechanisms whereby β-aminoisobutyric acid is degraded in humans, an enzyme which catalyzes the reversible transamination reaction has been identified in pig kidney. The β-aminoisobutyric acid is converted to methylmalonic semialdehyde and thence to propionic acid, which in turn proceeds to succinate.

It should be noted that the initial steps in the degradation of pyrimidine nucleotides, including the removal of the sugar phosphate moiety by hydrolysis of the N-glycosidic bond, are similar to merely reversing the latter part of the synthetic pathway. For pseudouridine, which is formed in situ in tRNA by a rearrangement reaction, there is no mechanism to catalyze the hydrolysis or phosphorolysis of this unusual nucleoside to its respective pyrimidine base, uracil. Consequently, pseudouridine is excreted unchanged in the urine of normal persons.

Regulation of Pyrimidine Biosynthesis

The pathway of pyrimidine nucleotide biosynthesis is regulated by 2 general mechanisms. The first 2 enzymes in the pathway are sensitive to **allosteric regulation**, while the first 3 enzymes are regulated by an apparently coordinate **repression and derepression**. **Carbamoyl phosphate synthetase** is inhibited by UTP and purine nucleotides but activated by PPriboseP (Fig 24—22). **Aspartate transcarbamoylase** is particularly sensitive to inhibition by CTP. The allosteric properties

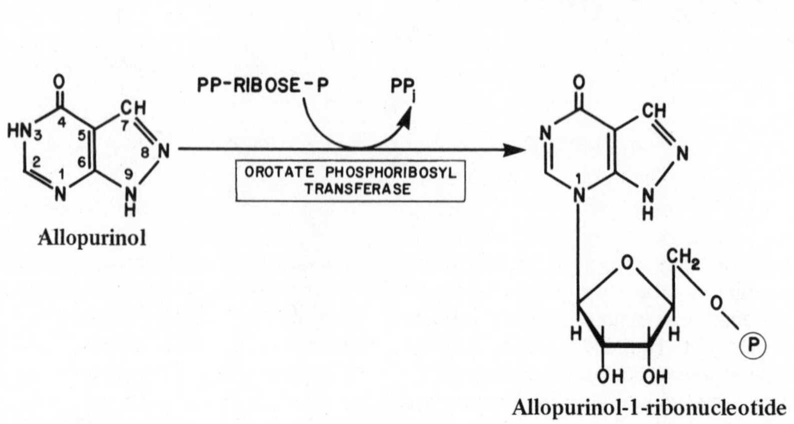

Figure 24—20. Formation of allopurinol-1-ribonucleotide by the phosphorylation of allopurinol in a reaction catalyzed by orotate phosphoribosyl transferase.

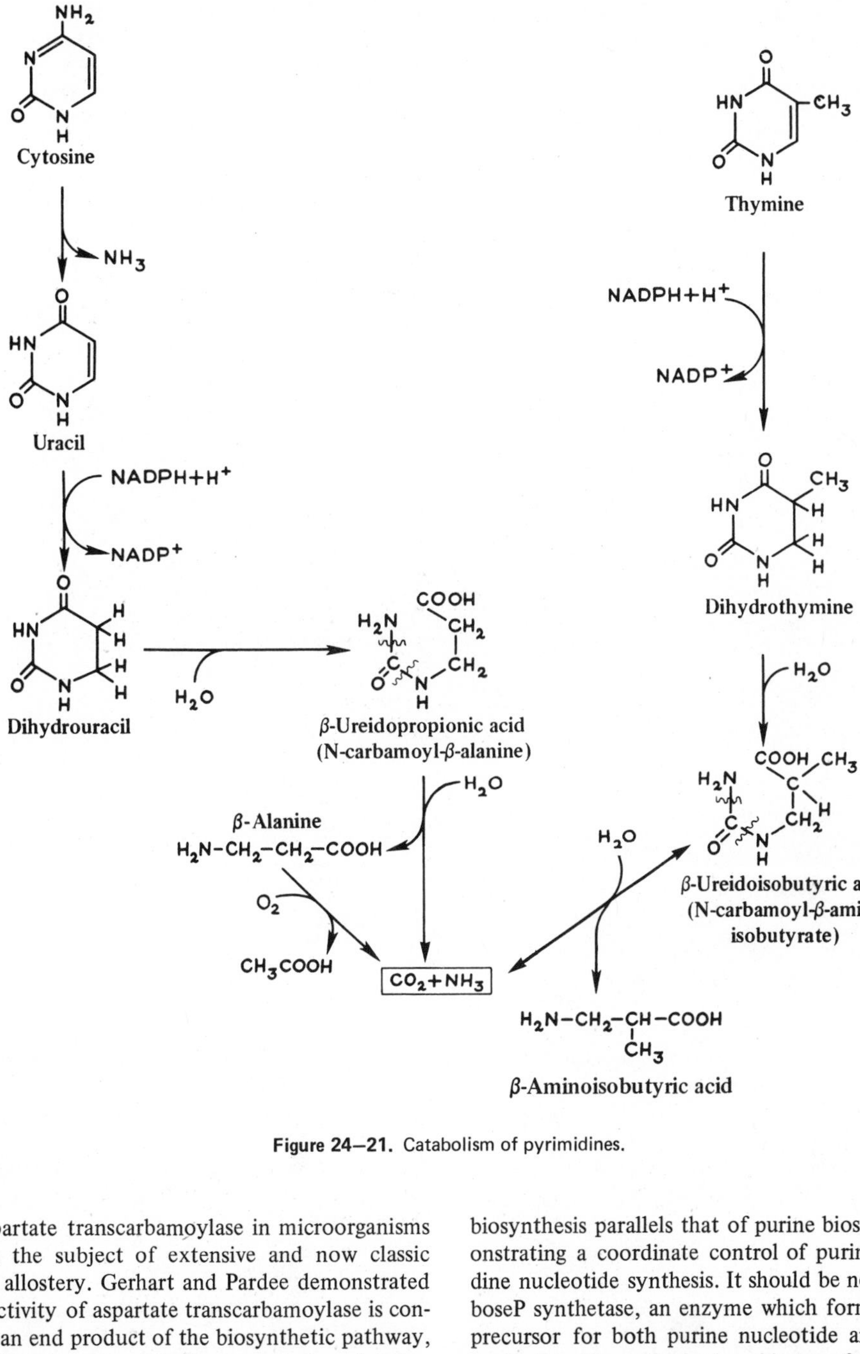

Figure 24–21. Catabolism of pyrimidines.

of the aspartate transcarbamoylase in microorganisms have been the subject of extensive and now classic studies in allostery. Gerhart and Pardee demonstrated that the activity of aspartate transcarbamoylase is controlled by an end product of the biosynthetic pathway, notably CTP. It was originally suggested, and it has been subsequently confirmed, that the enzyme **aspartate transcarbamoylase** possesses an allosteric site on a protein subunit. This allosteric site is distinct from that on the catalytic subunit. An end product of the pyrimidine biosynthetic pathway binds with a high affinity to the regulatory subunit. The binding of this end product (CTP), acting as a feedback inhibitor, reduces the affinity of the enzyme for its specific substrate and thereby creates a negative feedback loop.

It has been estimated from isotope incorporation studies that on a molar basis the rate of pyrimidine biosynthesis parallels that of purine biosynthesis, demonstrating a coordinate control of purine and pyrimidine nucleotide synthesis. It should be noted that PPriboseP synthetase, an enzyme which forms a necessary precursor for both purine nucleotide and pyrimidine nucleotide biosynthesis, is subject to feedback inhibition by both purine and pyrimidine nucleotides. Furthermore, carbamoyl phosphate synthetase is sensitive to feedback inhibition by both purine and pyrimidine nucleotides. Thus, there are several sites at which there is significant cross-regulation between purine and pyrimidine nucleotide synthesis.

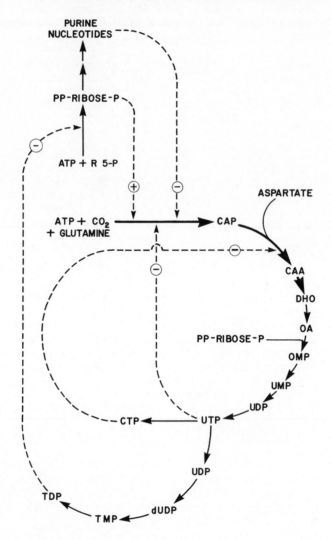

Figure 24–22. Regulatory scheme for the control of pyrimidine nucleotide synthesis. Solid lines represent chemical flow and broken lines represent positive and negative feedback regulation.

CLINICAL DISORDERS OF
PURINE METABOLISM
(See Table 24–2.)

Hyperuricemia & Gout

The predominant form of uric acid is determined by the pH of its milieu (eg, blood, urine, cerebrospinal fluid). The pK of the N^9 proton is 5.75, and the pK of the N^1 proton is 10.3. Thus, under physiologic conditions—ie, at the usual pH of physiologic fluids—only uric acid and its monosodium salt, sodium urate, are found. In a fluid where the pH is less than 5.75, the predominant molecular species will be uric acid. In a fluid at pH 5.75, the concentration of sodium urate will equal that of uric acid. At a pH greater than 5.75, sodium urate will predominate in the solution.

The miscible urate pool in the body is reflected by the sodium urate concentration in the serum. When this level exceeds the solubility of sodium urate in serum, a circumstance referred to as **hyperuricemia,** the serum becomes supersaturated and crystals of sodium urate may precipitate. The solubility of sodium urate in serum at 37° C is 7 mg/dl. There is currently no convincing evidence that under physiologic conditions sodium urate is bound by serum proteins. Crystals of sodium urate which precipitate out of solution can collect and deposit in soft tissues, particularly in or about joints. These urate deposits are referred to as **tophi.** Accumulation of sodium urate crystals in the tissues, including phagocytosis of the crystals by polymorphonuclear leukocytes in joint spaces, can lead to an acute inflammatory reaction called **acute gouty arthritis.** The chronic inflammatory changes induced by the deposition of sodium urate tophi can generate **chronic gouty arthritis,** resulting in joint destruction. Sodium urate can precipitate also in the renal interstices causing a **urate nephropathy.**

Table 24–2. Inherited disorders of purine metabolism and their associated enzyme abnormalities.

Clinical Disorder	Defective Enzyme	Nature of the Defect	Characteristics of Clinical Disorder	Inheritance Pattern
Gout	PPriboseP synthetase	Superactive (increased V_{max})	Purine overproduction and overexcretion	X-linked recessive
Gout	PPriboseP synthetase	Resistance to feedback inhibition	Purine overproduction and overexcretion	X-linked recessive
Gout	PPriboseP synthetase	Low K_m for ribose 5-phosphate	Purine overproduction and overexcretion	Probably X-linked recessive
Gout	HGPRTase*	Partial deficiency	Purine overproduction and overexcretion	X-linked recessive
Lesch-Nyhan syndrome	HGPRTase*	Complete deficiency	Purine overproduction and overexcretion; cerebral palsy and self-mutilation.	X-linked recessive
Immune deficiency	Adenosine deaminase	Severe deficiency	Combined (T cell and B cell) immunodeficiency	Autosomal recessive
Immune deficiency	Purine nucleoside phosphorylase	Severe deficiency	T cell deficiency, inosinuria, hypouricemia	Autosomal recessive
Renal lithiasis	Adenine phosphoribosyl transferase	Complete deficiency	2,8-Dihydroxyadenine renal lithiasis	Autosomal recessive
Xanthinuria	Xanthine oxidase	Complete deficiency	Xanthine renal lithiasis, hypouricemia	Autosomal recessive

*HGPRTase = hypoxanthine-guanine phosphoribosyl transferase.

In water, uric acid—the protonated form of urate—is only one-seventeenth as soluble as sodium urate. An aqueous solution becomes saturated with uric acid when its concentration is greater than 80 mg/dl. Because the pH of urine of normal persons generally is below the pK of uric acid (ie, 5.75), the predominant form of urate in urine is as uric acid, the highly insoluble form. Uric acid becomes the predominant form once the urine is acidified to a pH of less than 5.75, a process which occurs in the distal tubule and collecting ducts of the kidney. If crystals of this end product of purine catabolism are formed in the urinary system, they will be sodium urate at any site proximal to the site of acidification of urine; at any site distal to the acidification, uric acid crystals will be formed. Therefore, most stones of the urinary collecting system are uric acid. The precipitation of uric acid stones can be prevented to a considerable extent by alkalinization of the urine in an effort to ensure that sodium urate, the more soluble form, will predominate.

The needle-shaped sodium urate crystals are intensely negatively birefringent (optically anisotropic);

thus, when viewed through a polarizing microscope, they can be distinguished from other types of crystals. If the synovial or joint fluid of a patient shows polymorphonuclear leukocytes containing crystals whose color is yellow when viewed with their long axis parallel to the plane of polarized light and blue when perpendicular to the plane of light, then sodium urate crystals are present. The diagnosis is gout. It should be noted, however, that calcium pyrophosphate crystals, which are found in synovial fluid, are positively birefringent and can be responsible for a syndrome referred to as "pseudogout."

The classification of the disorders of purine metabolism includes those exhibiting **hyperuricemia**, those exhibiting **hypouricemia**, and the immunodeficiency diseases. As shown in Table 24–3, individuals with hyperuricemia can be divided into 2 groups: those with normal urate excretion rates and those excreting excessive quantities of total urates.

Among those individuals with hyperuricemia and no other associated disease, the majority excrete urates at a normal rate; a renal disorder is responsible for the hyperuricemia. This renal disorder is somewhat analogous to an elevated threshold wherein excretion of the normal amount of urate formed daily requires that the level of serum urate be elevated to "flow over the dam," so to speak.

Table 24–3. Classification of patients with hyperuricemia.

I. Normal excretion of urate; renal disorder responsible for elevated serum urate.
II. Excessive excretion of urate because of overproduction.
  A. Secondary to other diseases, eg, malignancy, psoriasis.
  B. Known enzyme defects responsible for overproduction.
    1. PPriboseP synthetase abnormalities.
    2. Hypoxanthine-guanine phosphoribosyl transferase deficiencies.
    3. Glucose-6-phosphatase deficiencies.
  C. Unrecognized defects.

Lesch-Nyhan Syndrome & Von Gierke's Disease

Some individuals with urate overexcretion (greater than 600 mg of uric acid per 24 hours) can be categorized as having secondary hyperuricemia. They have other disease processes such as malignancies or psoriasis that lead to enhanced tissue destruction.

Finally, there are persons with identifiable enzyme defects, including abnormalities of PPriboseP synthetase (feedback resistant and enhanced enzyme activities), the HGPRTase (hypoxanthine-guanine phosphoribosyl transferase) deficiencies (both the complete [Lesch-Nyhan syndrome] and incomplete deficiencies), and **glucose-6-phosphatase deficiency** (von Gierke's disease). There exists also a group of patients exhibiting idiopathic overproduction hyperuricemia, which will certainly be regarded as a heterogeneous group of diseases once the molecular bases for their metabolic defects are recognized.

The **Lesch-Nyhan syndrome** (complete HGPRTase deficiency) is an inherited X-linked recessive disorder characterized by cerebral palsy with choreoathetosis and spasticity, a bizarre syndrome of self-mutilation, and severe overproduction hyperuricemia. There is usually an associated urate nephropathy and uric acid lithiasis. The mothers of these children, who are heterozygous and mosaic for the HGPRTase deficiency, frequently exhibit overproduction hyperuricemia but without any neurologic manifestations. There also exist male patients with partial deficiencies of HGPRTase attributable to a different mutation of the same gene. These males have severe overproduction hyperuricemia but usually are without significant neurologic signs and symptoms.

Purine overproduction by patients deficient in hypoxanthine-guanine phosphoribosyl transferase is related to the increased intracellular concentrations of PPriboseP. Increased PPriboseP levels seem to result from the sparing of PPriboseP by the deficient salvage pathway. The biochemical basis for the neurologic disorder in Lesch-Nyhan syndrome is unknown.

The basis of purine overproduction and hyperuricemia in von Gierke's disease is purportedly secondary to the enhanced activity of the hexose monophosphate shunt and thus enhanced generation of ribose 5-phosphate, from which PPriboseP is synthesized. However, patients with glucose-6-phosphatase deficiency also have chronic lactic acidosis and thus have decreased secretion of urate contributing to the accumulation of total body urates.

All of the known enzyme defects (except the glucose-6-phosphatase deficiency, which has not been tested) are associated with increased intracellular concentrations of PPriboseP, and the theoretical basis for the purine overproduction in the glucose-6-phosphatase deficiency is probably similarly caused. Thus, it seems likely that many more disorders of overproduction hyperuricemia will eventually be discovered to be associated with increased accumulation of intracellular PPriboseP.

Other Purine Deficiency Disorders

Hypouricemia is due either to enhanced excretion or to decreased production of urate and uric acid. Dalmatian dogs, although possessing uricase activity, as do all dogs, are not capable of reabsorbing completely the filtered uric acid in their kidneys. They excrete urate and uric acid in amounts that are excessive in respect to their serum urate levels. A similar defect has been discovered in a human with hypouricemia.

Deficiency of the enzyme xanthine oxidase, either due to an inherited genetic defect or because of severe liver damage, results in hypouricemia and increased excretion of the oxypurines, hypoxanthine and xanthine. In severe xanthine oxidase deficiencies, patients frequently exhibit **xanthinuria** and xanthine lithiasis.

A deficiency of the enzyme purine nucleoside phosphorylase is associated with hypouricemia because individuals lacking this enzyme are not capable of producing hypoxanthine and guanine from inosine and guanosine, respectively. As a result, excessive quantities of purine nucleosides are excreted in their urine. One of the purine nucleosides excreted in significant quantities, guanosine, has limited solubility and can therefore result in renal lithiasis.

Two immunodeficiency diseases have been described in recent years as associated with deficiencies of purine metabolizing enzymes. **Adenosine deaminase deficiency** is associated with a severe combined immunodeficiency disease in which both thymus-derived lymphocytes (T cells) and bone marrow-derived lymphocytes (B cells) are sparse and dysfunctional. **Purine nucleoside phosphorylase deficiency** is associated with a severe thymus-derived lymphocyte deficiency with apparently normal B cell function, a much milder form of immunodeficiency. Both of these immunodeficiency diseases are inherited as autosomal recessive disorders. The molecular bases for the immune dysfunctions may be starvation of T lymphocytes for pyrimidine nucleotides with secondary effects on B cell function and survival.

Purine nucleoside phosphorylase deficiency results in the accumulation of intracellular inosine and guanosine, which are inhibitors of adenosine deaminase. These metabolites may induce a secondary, less severe adenosine deaminase deficiency. It has been proposed that both of these diseases might be responsive to exogenous uridine, but results from studies to confirm this suggestion are not yet definitive.

Purine deficiency states are rare in humans. These are limited to circumstances attributable primarily to deficiencies of folic acid and perhaps of vitamin B_{12} when the latter results in a secondary deficiency of folate derivatives.

CLINICAL DISORDERS OF PYRIMIDINE METABOLISM
(See Table 24–4.)

As described above, the end products of pyrimidine metabolism, unlike those of purine metabolism, are highly water-soluble compounds such as CO_2, ammonia, β-alanine, and propionate. Thus, in circumstances where pyrimidine overproduction occurs, clinically detectable abnormalities are rarely evident. In cases of hyperuricemia associated with severe PPriboseP overproduction, there is concomitant overpro-

Table 24—4. Inherited disorders of pyrimidine metabolism and their associated enzyme abnormalities.

Clinical Disorder	Defective Enzyme	Nature of the Defect	Characteristics of Clinical Disorder	Inheritance Pattern
β-Aminoisobutyric aciduria	Transaminase	Deficiency	No symptoms; frequent in Orientals.	Autosomal recessive
Orotic aciduria, type I	Orotate phosphoribosyl-transferase and oroti-dylate decarboxylase	Deficiencies	Orotic acid crystalluria, failure to thrive, and megaloblastic anemia. (?) Immune deficiency. Remission with oral uridine.	Autosomal recessive
Orotic aciduria, type II	Orotidylate decar-boxylase	Deficiency	Orotidinuria and orotic aciduria, megalo-blastic anemia. Remission with oral uridine.	Autosomal recessive
Orotic aciduria	Ornithine transcar-bamoylase	Deficiency	Protein intolerance, hepatic encephalop-athy, and mild orotic aciduria.	Autosomal recessive

duction of pyrimidine nucleotides with increased excretion of compounds such as β-alanine. Because of the requirement for N^5,N^{10}-methylenetetrahydrofolate for thymidylate synthesis, disorders of folate and vitamin B_{12} metabolism result in deficiencies of TMP (in the case of vitamin B_{12} deficiency, by an indirect mechanism).

β-Aminoisobutyric aciduria is an autosomal, recessively inherited disorder prevalent among the Oriental races. It is not associated with any pathologic state. It has been discussed above in connection with pyrimidine catabolism.

As described earlier, pseudouridine appears in normal urine. When increased nucleic acid turnover occurs in patients with leukemia or lymphoma, there is a markedly increased urinary excretion of pseudouridine. This compound is highly soluble and by itself produces no disease.

Two types of **hereditary orotic aciduria** have been reported. The more common type (type I), although still rare, is that in which both orotate phosphoribosyl transferase and orotidylate (OMP) decarboxylase are missing in all cell types tested (Fig 24—23). The patients are pyrimidine auxotrophs. They are readily treated with uridine. As infants, these patients fail to thrive and exhibit megaloblastic anemias and orange crystalluria (orotic acid). Unless treated with a source of pyrimidine nucleosides, they succumb to infections. The second type of hereditary orotic aciduria (type II) is due to a deficiency only of OMP decarboxylase (Fig 24—23). In patients with type I orotic aciduria, orotic acid is the major abnormal excretory product. In patients with type II, orotidine is the major excretory product, although some orotic acid is also excreted. In the erythrocytes of patients with type I orotic aciduria, the specific catalytic activities of aspartate transcarbamoylase and dihydroorotase were found to be greatly increased but returned to normal upon treatment of the patient with oral uridine. These observations suggest that one or more end products of the pathway are normally responsible for the maintenance of these enzyme activities at a regulated level. In a deficient state when the cells are deprived of the end products of this pathway, there is a derepression, perhaps a coordinate one, of at least those 2 enzymes.

The enzymology of this pathway has suggested that there is a common protein subunit shared between orotate phosphoribosyl transferase and OMP decarboxylase.

Increased excretion of orotic acid, uracil, and uridine has been described in patients deficient in ornithine transcarbamoylase, a liver mitochondrial enzyme responsible for an early step in urea and arginine biosynthesis. In these patients there is apparently mitochondrial carbamoyl phosphate accumulation in response to the enzyme block. The mitochondrial carbamoyl phosphate diffuses into the cytosol to be utilized as a substrate for de novo pyrimidine nucleotide synthesis. The excess production of orotic acid is then manifested as orotic aciduria, which usually occurs in a mild degree and appears without crystal formation.

At least 2 drugs, one of which is widely used clinically, can result in orotic aciduria. Allopurinol, 4-hydroxypyrazolo(-2,4d-)pyrimidine, a purine analog which directly inhibits xanthine oxidase, can be phosphoribosylated by orotate phosphoribosyl transferase, thereby competitively inhibiting the phosphoribosylation of orotic acid. Furthermore, the unusual nucleotide formed inhibits orotidylate decarboxylase, producing orotic aciduria and orotidinuria. In humans, at least, the pyrimidine pathway appears to readjust itself to this inhibition so that the organism is only transiently starved for pyrimidine nucleotides during the early stages of treatment.

6-Azauridine, after conversion to 6-azauridylate, is a competitive inhibitor of OMP decarboxylase, inducing high rates of excretion of orotic acid and orotidine as a result.

In specific liver mitochondrial failure, such as in Reye's syndrome, there is a secondary orotic aciduria. It is probably secondary to the inability of the mitochondria to utilize carbamoyl phosphate, which then, as in the inherited deficiency of ornithine transcarbamoylase, causes overproduction of orotic acid and a resultant orotic aciduria.

Perhaps in the future, the adenosine deaminase deficiencies and purine nucleoside phosphorylase deficiencies will rather be classified as secondary disorders of pyrimidine metabolism.

A

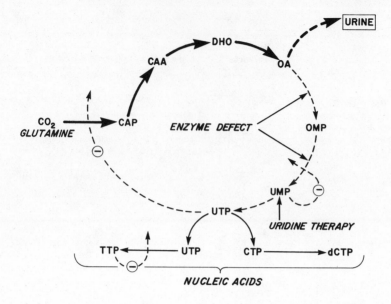

B

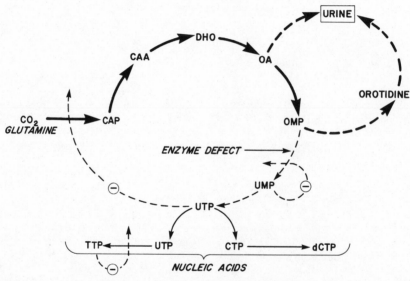

Figure 24–23. *Panel A:* The enzyme defect and consequences of orotic aciduria type I, in which both orotate phosphoribosyl transferase and orotidylic decarboxylase are deficient. *Panel B:* The defect and consequences of orotic aciduria type I, in which orotidylic decarboxylase is deficient. The dotted lines in which a negative sign is inserted represent feedback inhibition which exists under normal conditions. In type I orotic aciduria, orotic acid is spilled in the urine, whereas in type II both orotic acid and orotidine appear in the urine. (Redrawn and reproduced, with permission, from Smith LH Jr: Pyrimidine metabolism in man. N Engl J Med 288:764, 1973.)

• • •

References

Henderson JF: *Regulation of Purine Biosynthesis.* Monograph No. 170. American Chemical Society, 1972.

Henderson JF, Paterson ARP: *Nucleotide Metabolism: An Introduction.* Academic Press, 1973.

Kempe TD & others: Stable mutants of mammalian cells that overproduce the first three enzymes of pyrimidine nucleotide biosynthesis. Cell 9:541, 1976.

Smith LH Jr: Pyrimidine metabolism in man. N Engl J Med 288:764, 1973.

Stanbury JB, Wyngaarden JB, Fredrickson DS (editors): *The Metabolic Basis of Inherited Disease,* 3rd ed. McGraw-Hill, 1972.

Wyngaarden JB, Kelley WN: *Gout and Hyperuricemia.* Grune & Stratton, 1976.

25 . . .
Metabolism of Nucleic Acids

THE NATURE OF DNA

As described in Chapter 11, DNA is a very long polymer of purine and pyrimidine mononucleotide monomers bound one to another by phosphodiester bridges. DNA exists in nature as a double-stranded molecule, the strands being held together by the hydrophobic or Van der Waals forces between stacked planar purine and pyrimidine bases and by hydrogen bonding between the purine and pyrimidine bases of the 2 strands. The 2 strands have polarity and extend in opposite directions, ie, each is antiparallel as it runs in the double-stranded DNA molecule. For each purine or pyrimidine base in one strand there exists in the other strand a related pyrimidine or purine base whose specificity is determined by the base-pairing rules set forth in Chapter 11. The most favored tautomers and the anti configuration of the glycosidic bond of each nucleotide restrict the binding in the DNA double helix to adenine (A) paired with thymine (T) and guanine (G) paired with cytosine (C). Genetic information is contained in the primary structure, ie, the sequence of mononucleotides of the DNA molecule. For each gene in the DNA molecule there is a "sense" strand and its complementary "antisense" strand.

This complementarity of the Watson and Crick double-stranded model of DNA strongly suggests that replication of the DNA molecule occurs in a semiconservative manner. Thus, when each strand of the double-stranded DNA molecule separates from its complement during replication, each can then serve as a template on which a new complementary strand can be synthesized (Fig 25–1). The 2 newly formed double-stranded DNA molecules, each containing one strand (but complementary rather than identical) from the parent double-stranded DNA molecule during cell division, can then be sorted between the 2 daughter cells (Fig 25–2). Each daughter cell will contain DNA molecules with information identical to that which the parent possessed; yet in each daughter cell the DNA molecule of the parent cell has been only semiconserved.

The semiconservative nature of DNA replication in the bacterium *E coli* was unequivocally demonstrated by Meselson and Stahl in a now classical experiment using the heavy isotope of nitrogen and centrif-

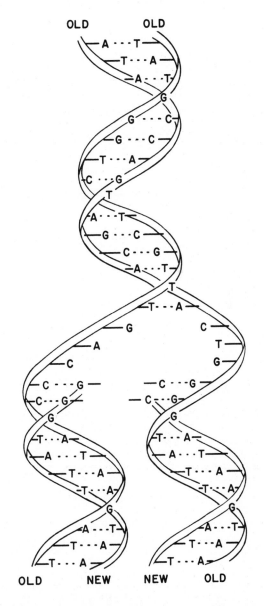

Figure 25–1. The double-stranded structure of DNA and the template function of each old strand on which a new complementary strand is synthesized. (From James D. Watson, *Molecular Biology of the Gene,* 3rd ed. Copyright © 1976, 1970, 1965, by W.A. Benjamin, Inc, Menlo Park, California.)

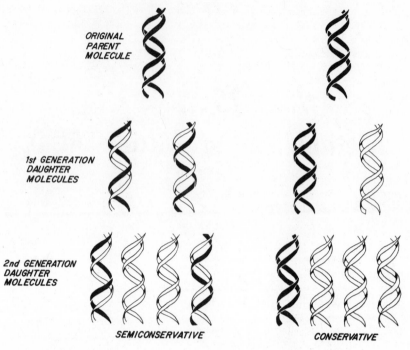

Figure 25—2. The expected distributions of parental DNA strands during semiconservative and conservative replication. The parental strands are solid and the newly synthesized strands are open. (Redrawn and reproduced, with permission, from Lehninger AL: *Biochemistry,* 2nd ed. Worth, 1975.)

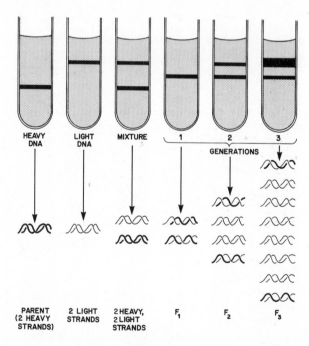

Figure 25—3. Schematic representation of the results of the Meselson-Stahl experiment demonstrating semiconservative replication of bacterial DNA. The tubes in which the equilibrium centrifugation conditions have been established are represented at the top and contain the bands of DNA with the indicated densities. In the lower part of the figure are represented the parent DNA strands containing the heavy isotope of nitrogen (^{15}N) and the strands isolated from daughter cells grown in the presence of the naturally occurring light isotope of nitrogen (^{14}N). The appearance of a band of DNA with an intermediate density and its persistence through 3 generations with the subsequent appearance of totally light DNA confirms the semiconservative nature of DNA replication in prokaryotes. (Redrawn and reproduced, with permission, from Lehninger AL: *Biochemistry,* 2nd ed. Worth, 1975.)

ugal equilibrium technics. This classical experiment is depicted in Fig 25–3. The DNA of *E coli* is chemically identical to that of humans, although the sequences of nucleotides are, of course, different, and the human cell contains about 1000 times more DNA per cell than does the bacterium. Furthermore, the chemistry of replication of DNA in prokaryotes such as *E coli* appears to be identical to that in eukaryotes, including humans, even though the enzymes carrying out the reactions of DNA synthesis and replication are different. Thus, any observations on the chemical nature or chemical reactions of nucleic acids of prokaryotes are very likely applicable to eukaryotic organisms. Indeed, the Meselson and Stahl type of experiment has now been performed in mammalian cells and has yielded results comparable to those obtained with *E coli*.

GENETIC ORGANIZATION OF THE MAMMALIAN GENOME

The diploid genome of human cells has a molecular weight of 3×10^{12}. It is subdivided into 23 pairs of chromosomes. The entire diploid genome contains sufficient DNA to code for nearly 1 million pairs of genes.

In Chapter 11, denaturation—ie, separation of the 2 strands—of a DNA molecule is described. The double-stranded structure of the DNA molecule is dependent upon proper base pairing to achieve proper complementary sequences of the 2 antiparallel strands. As a result, the process of renaturation, ie, reformation of the base complementarity and the double-stranded nature of the DNA molecule, requires that the sense strand of each gene find its proper antisense strand and vice versa (Fig 25–4). Only then, and after being

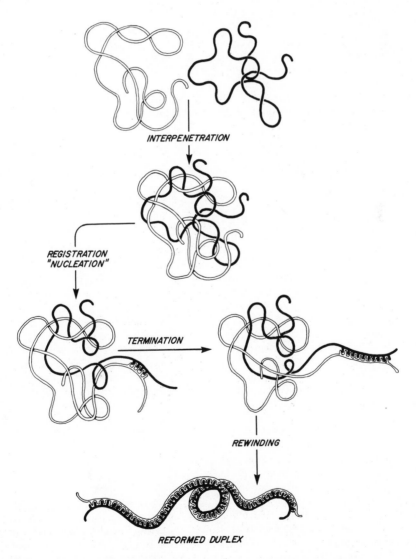

Figure 25–4. The steps in the process of renaturation of complementary single strands of DNA. The analogy to a zipper is emphasized.

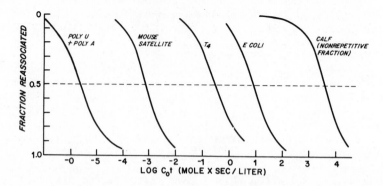

Figure 25—5. A series of C_0t curves for DNA molecules from different sources. The $C_0t_{1/2}$ values can be determined by extrapolating to the value of C_0t at the condition where half the material has reassociated. (Redrawn and reproduced, with permission, from Britten RJ, Kohne DE: Repeated sequences in DNA. Science 161:529, 1968. Copyright 1968 by the American Association for the Advancement of Science.)

properly aligned, can the strands by complementation reform the double-stranded molecule.

To illustrate the importance of DNA concentration in relation to renaturation, it might be noted that if, for example, the human genome contained a million different genes, the renaturation process, after denaturation of the human DNA, would require a very high concentration of DNA and frequent collisions of the different strands over a long period of time in order for complementation to be achieved. In this connection it can be noted that, in an organism such as a DNA virus or an *E coli* bacterium, the process of renaturation of denatured DNA requires a considerably lower concentration of DNA or less time (or both) because these organisms contain many fewer different genes. Thus, the concentration and time dependence of the renaturation of DNA from a specific organism can provide information about the genetic complexity of the genome of that organism. The product of the initial concentration (mass or moles of mononucleotide equivalents per unit volume) of DNA times the period required for the renaturation process to be half complete is proportionate to—and thus provides an index of—the degree of complexity of that DNA, ie, the number of different genetic sequences within its genome. This value, the product of the initial concentration of DNA (C_0) and the time (t) required for half renaturation is written as $C_0t_{1/2}$ and is referred to as the **half C_0t value**. The $C_0t_{1/2}$ value will be characteristic of the DNA being examined under standard conditions.

Fig 25—5 shows a series of C_0t curves for DNAs of different sources. In such a graph, the fraction reassociated is plotted against the arithmetical product (C_0t) of the initial concentration (C_0) of nucleotide pairs and the seconds (t) that the renaturation process was allowed to continue before the degree of renaturation was determined. The lower the value for $C_0t_{1/2}$, the fewer the different specific sequences or the less complex the genetic information in the DNA being examined. A line drawn parallel to the abscissa represents the half renaturation point; it intersects the rena-

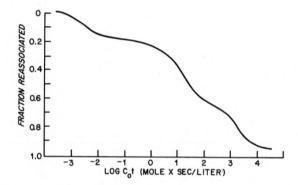

Figure 25—6. The complex C_0t curve for human DNA.

turation curve of each solution of DNA at its characteristic half C_0t value.

Surprisingly, mammalian DNA, including that from humans, reassociates more rapidly than one would predict based on the existence of one million pairs of different genes in the genome. Careful experiments have revealed that the reassociation or renaturation of mammalian denatured DNA has several components, as would be the case if different classes of genes are present in significantly different numbers of copies per genome (Fig 25—6). Approximately 10% of mammalian chromosomal DNA has very rapid reassociation kinetics (Table 25—1), suggesting that the sequences in this DNA (referred to as satellite DNA because it also separates by buoyant density from the main band of chromosomal DNA) occur in blocks of about 100 base residues and are repeated up to 10^7 times per cell. More will be said subsequently about this highly repetitive DNA. About half of the DNA of eukaryotic cells has an intermediate C_0t value, implying the existence of sequences several thousand residues in length each repeated $10^2 - 10^4$ times per genome. For another 10% of the total human DNA, approximately one copy is present for each haploid genome. Thus, this latter class among the human DNA comprises approximately

Table 25—1. Human DNA components by $C_o t$ analysis.

$C_o t_{1/2}$ (mol × sec/liter)	Approximate Size of Repeating Unit (Nucleotide Pairs)	Repeats per Haploid Genome	Percentage of Haploid Genome	Presumed Function
10^{-3}	100–500	10^7	10	Satellite DNA
10^0	500–5000	$10^2 - 10^4$	50	Nucleolar rRNA genes
3×10^3	2000	1	10	Unique sequence of structural genes

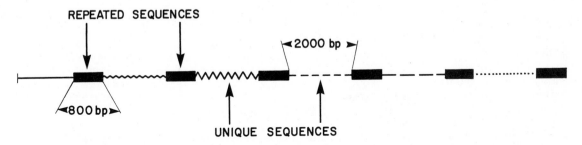

Figure 25—7. A distribution of repeated sequences among unique sequences of human DNA. (bp = base pairs.)

100,000 genes which, as already noted, occur once only in each haploid human genome (ie, there are 100,000 gene pairs among the diploid genomes).

Further studies have revealed that there is a pattern of sequence organization in mammals (Fig 25—7) in which the majority of the highly repetitive sequences are short, with an average length of 800 nucleotides, and that these alternate with those sequences which are present in only a single copy per haploid genome. The majority of the single copy sequences extend for less than about 2000 nucleotides before terminating in the repetitive sequence elements. There exists a small fraction of single copy sequences, up to several thousand nucleotides in length, which are also interspersed with repetitive sequences. The highly repetitive satellite DNA sequences, which in the mouse extend over approximately 400 nucleotide pairs and which comprise about 10^6 copies per genome, are primarily localized in the centromeric region of the chromosomes as seen at metaphase. The function of this satellite DNA is unclear.

The interspersed repetitive sequences between the single copy genes, which are distributed throughout the chromosomal structures of mammals, are thought to act as spacers with some regulatory function. As discussed below, the so-called spacers may be represented as integral parts of the transcription products of the structural genes of that organism. Although these interspersed repeats or spacers are very similar in sequence, a characteristic which is necessary in order that rapid renaturation kinetics (low half $C_o t$ values) will be exhibited, it is unlikely that they share absolutely identical sequences. However, their sequences appear to have been generally conserved throughout the genome of the organism.

The genes for ribosomal RNA are also present in a large number of copies per genome, and these multiple

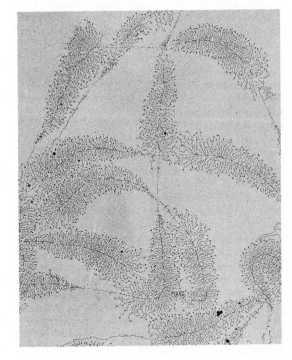

Figure 25—8. Electron photomicrograph of multiple copies of ribosomal RNA genes being transcribed in an amphibian cell. (X 6000) (Reproduced, with permission, from Miller OL Jr, Beatty BR: Portrait of a gene. J Cell Physiol 74[Suppl 1]:225, 1969.)

copies (perhaps a thousand per genome) are thought to represent gene amplification, the mechanism of which is currently unknown. Fig 25—8 is an electron micrograph of ribosomal RNA genes being transcribed.

Britten and Davidson have proposed a complex model of gene regulation based on their observations of the existence and interspersion of highly repetitive sequences of DNA among the structural genes of a genome.

DNA METABOLISM

DNA Synthesis & Replication

The primary function of DNA is understood to be the provision of progeny with the genetic information possessed by the parent. Thus, the replication of DNA must be complete and carried out with high fidelity to maintain genetic stability within the organism. The process of DNA replication is complex and involves many cellular functions and several verification procedures to ensure fidelity in replication. The first enzymologic observations on DNA replication were made in *E coli* by Arthur Kornberg, who described in that organism the existence of an enzyme now called DNA polymerase I. This enzyme has multiple catalytic activities, a complex structure, and a requirement for the triphosphates of the 4 deoxyribonucleosides of adenine, guanine, cytosine, and thymine. The polymerization reaction catalyzed by DNA polymerase I of *E coli* has served as a prototype for all DNA polymerases of both prokaryotes and eukaryotes, even though it is now recognized that the major role of this polymerase is to ensure fidelity and to repair rather than to replicate DNA.

The initiation of DNA synthesis (Fig 25–9) is surprisingly complex and occurs after the formation of a **short link of RNA**, about 10 nucleotides in length, to which, at its 3'-hydroxyl end, is attached the first deoxyribonucleotide. This process involves the nucleophilic attack by the 3'-hydroxyl group of the RNA initiator to the alpha phosphate of the deoxynucleoside triphosphate with the splitting off of pyrophosphate. The 3'-hydroxyl group of the recently attached deoxyribonucleoside monophosphate is then free to carry out a nucleophilic attack on the next entering deoxynucleoside triphosphate, again at its alpha phosphate moiety, with the splitting off of pyrophosphate. Of course, the selection of the proper deoxyribonucleoside whose terminal 3'-hydroxyl group is to be attacked is dependent upon proper pairing with the other (template) strand of the DNA molecule according to the rules proposed originally by Watson and Crick (Fig 25–10). When an adenine deoxyribonucleoside monophosphoryl moiety is in the template position, a thymidine triphosphate will enter and its alpha phosphate will be attacked by the 3'-hydroxyl group of the deoxyribonucleoside monophosphoryl most recently added to the polymer. By this stepwise process, the template dictates which deoxyribonucleoside triphosphate is complementary and by hydrogen bonding holds it in place while the 3'-hydroxyl group of the growing strand attacks and incorporates the new

nucleotide into the polymer. The polymerization of deoxyribonucleotides occurs by such a process in discontinuous pulses of about 100 nucleotides in length. These fragments of DNA attached to an RNA initiator component were discovered by Okazaki and are therefore referred to as **Okazaki pieces** (Fig 25–11). In mammals, after many Okazaki pieces are generated, the replication complex begins to remove the RNA primers, to fill in the gaps left by their removal with the proper base-paired nucleotide, and then to seal the fragments of newly synthesized DNA by enzymes referred to as **DNA ligases**.

As has already been noted, DNA molecules are double-stranded and the 2 strands are antiparallel, ie, running in opposite directions. The replication of DNA in prokaryotes and eukaryotes occurs on **both strands simultaneously**. However, an enzyme capable of polymerizing DNA in the 3' to 5' direction does not exist in any organism, so that both of the newly replicated DNA strands cannot grow in the same direction simultaneously. Instead, the same enzyme appears to replicate both strands at the same time. The single enzyme replicates one strand in short spurts in the **5' to 3' direction** with the same overall forward direction. It replicates the other strand by "turning its back," as it were, in the overall direction of replication, while polymerizing the nucleotides again in the 5' to 3' direction, but at the same time it faces toward the back end of the preceding RNA primer rather than toward the unreplicated portion. This process of discontinuous DNA synthesis on both strands is shown diagrammatically in Fig 25–12.

In the mammalian nuclear genome, all of the RNA primers are eventually removed as part of the replication process, whereas after replication of the mitochondrial genome the small piece of RNA remains as an integral part of the closed circular DNA structure.

In mammalian cells, on the different chromosomes there are **multiple origins** of DNA replication, and replication occurs in **both directions** up and down the chromosome and on both strands simultaneously. This replication process generates "replication bubbles" (Fig 25–13). During the replication of the double-stranded helix of DNA, there must be an **unwinding** of the molecule to allow the rewinding of the newly formed semiconserved DNA replicas. Given the time during which DNA replication must occur in prokaryotes, it can be calculated that the molecule must unwind at approximately 400,000 turns per second, which is clearly an impossible feat. Thus, there must be multiple "swivels" interspersed in the DNA molecules of all organisms. It is currently believed that the swivels are nothing more than nicks which allow unwinding and which are eventually resealed. In both prokaryotic and eukaryotic organisms, proteins have been detected which appear to have the specific function of promoting the unwinding of the DNA molecules during replication. These unwinding proteins act stoichiometrically by stabilizing the single-stranded structures of DNA while the replication fork advances.

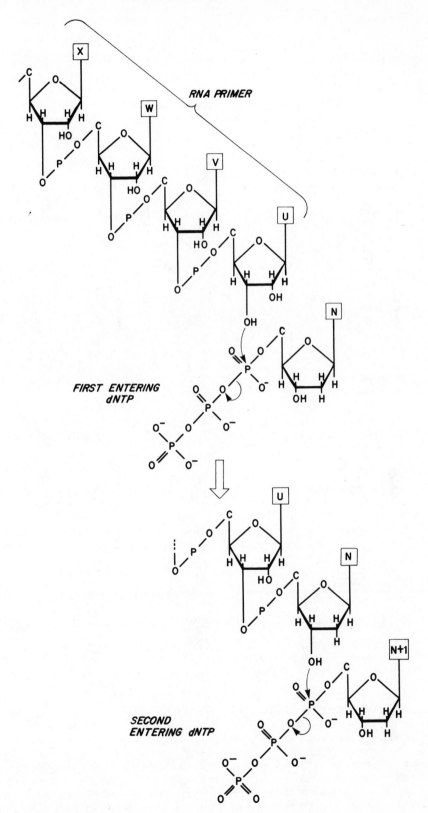

Figure 25–9. The initiation of DNA synthesis upon a primer of RNA and the subsequent attachment of the second deoxyribonucleoside triphosphate.

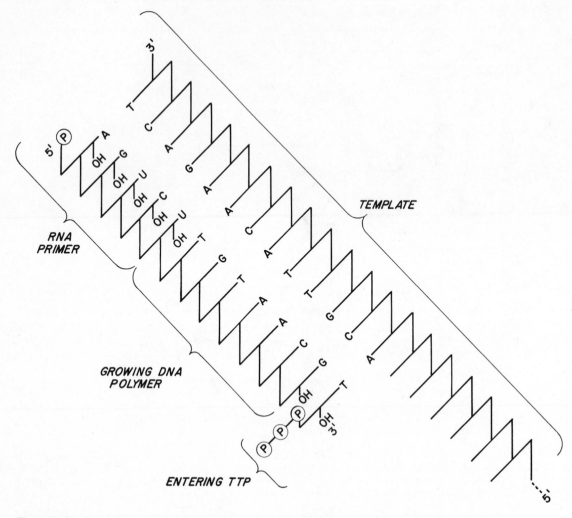

Figure 25–10. The synthesis of DNA on an RNA primer demonstrating the template function of the complementary strand of parental DNA.

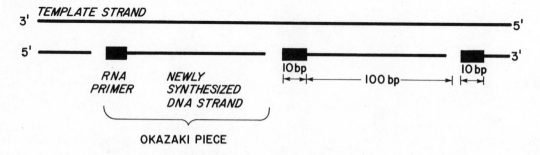

Figure 25–11. The discontinuous polymerization of deoxyribonucleotides in formation of Okazaki pieces.

In mammalian chromosomes, although little is known about the role of histones in DNA replication, there must be some shuffling of nuclear proteins during the process.

There is in mammalian cells one class of DNA polymerase enzymes, called maxi polymerase or polymerase alpha, responsible for chromosome replica-tion. A lower-molecular-weight polymerase is also present in mammalian nuclei, but it is probably not responsible for the usual DNA replication. These latter are referred to as mini polymerases or polymerase beta. Mitochondrial DNA polymerases have also been found, and many viruses carry their own DNA polymerase molecules.

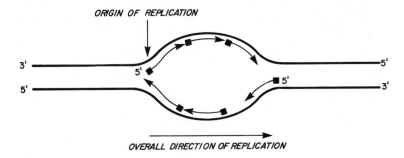

Figure 25—12. The process of discontinuous, simultaneous replication of both strands of double-stranded DNA.

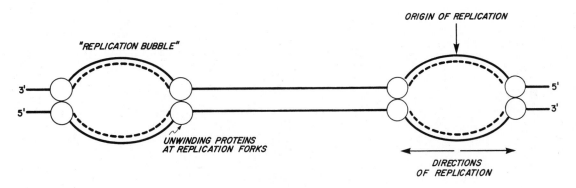

Figure 25—13. The generation of "replication bubbles" during the process of DNA synthesis. The bidirectional replication and the proposed positions of unwinding proteins at the replication forks are depicted.

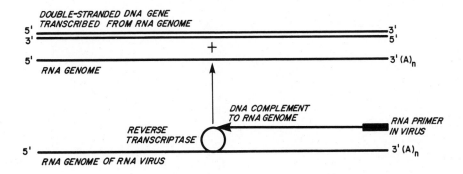

Figure 25—14. The generation of a double-stranded DNA molecule from an RNA template by the action of reverse transcriptase.

In recent years it has been discovered that there exists in many animal virus particles a class of enzymes capable of synthesizing a single-stranded and then a double-stranded DNA molecule from a single-stranded RNA template. This polymerase, RNA-dependent DNA polymerase or **"reverse transcriptase"** (Fig 25–14), synthesizes a double-stranded DNA molecule containing the information originally present in the RNA genome of the animal virus. Reverse transcriptases–ie, enzymes with the capacity to polymerize DNA on an RNA template–have been discovered in many different cells, including some which were not

known to be infected with viruses, as well as in numerous malignant cells, particularly leukemic cells. The functions of these enzymes in these latter groups of cells are not understood, but several different cellular roles have been proposed.

Regulation of DNA Synthesis

In animal cells, including human cells, the replication of the DNA genome occurs only at specified times during the life span of the cell. These periods are referred to as synthetic or S phases. They are usually temporally separated from the mitotic phase by non-

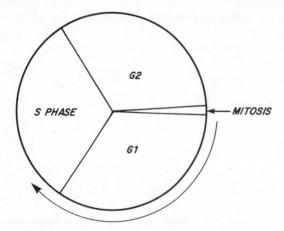

Figure 25—15. Mammalian cell cycle. The DNA synthetic phase (S phase) is separated from mitosis by gap 1 (G₁) and gap 2 (G₂). (Arrow indicates direction of cell progression.)

synthetic periods referred to as gap 1 (G₁) and gap 2 (G₂), occurring before and after the S phase, respectively (Fig 25–15). The cell regulates its DNA synthesis grossly by allowing it to occur only at specific times and mostly in cells preparing to divide by a mitotic process. The regulation of the entry of a cell into an S phase involves cyclic purine nucleotides, but the mechanisms are unknown.

During the S phase, mammalian cells contain greater quantities of polymerase alpha than during the nonsynthetic phases of the cell cycle. Furthermore, those enzymes responsible for the formation of the substrates for DNA synthesis, ie, deoxyribonucleoside triphosphates, are also increased in activity, and their activity will diminish following the synthetic phase until the reappearance of the signal for renewed DNA synthesis. Interestingly, the synthesis of the basic chromosomal proteins, the histones, occurs only during the S phase; furthermore, formation of the enzyme ornithine decarboxylase—which forms polyamines—is derepressed immediately prior to the S phase. The newly formed histones, however, do not attach specifically to the newly replicated DNA but seem to be randomly distributed on the expanding pool of DNA molecules.

Degradation & Repair of DNA

The maintenance of the integrity of the information in DNA molecules is of utmost importance to the survival of a particular organism as well as to survival of the species. Thus, it might be concluded that surviving species must have evolved mechanisms for repairing DNA damage incurred as a result of either replication errors or environmental insults. As described in Chapter 11, the major responsibility for the fidelity of replication resides in the specific pairing of nucleotide bases. Proper pairing is dependent upon the presence of the favored tautomers of the purine and pyrimidine nucleotides, but the equilibrium wherein one tautomer is more stable than another is only about 10^4 or 10^5 in

Table 25—2. Types of damage to DNA.

1. Single-base alteration
2. Two-base alteration
3. Chain breaks
4. Cross-linkage

favor of that with the greater stability. Although this is not sufficiently favorable to ensure the high fidelity that is necessary, the favoring of the preferred tautomers, and thus of the proper base pairing, could be assured by monitoring the base pairing twice. Such double monitoring does indeed appear to occur in mammalian systems: once at the time of insertion of the deoxyribonucleoside triphosphates, and later by a follow-up mechanism which removes all improper bases that now occur in the newly formed strand. This double monitoring does not permit errors of mispairing due to the presence of the unfavored tautomers to occur more frequently than once every 10^8-10^{10} base pairs. The enzymes responsible for this monitoring mechanism have not been identified.

Environmentally induced damage to DNA may be classified into 4 types (Table 25–2). The **one base damage** includes the hydration of the cytosine residue by ultraviolet irradiation and the alkylation of single bases with or without intercalation of the alkylating agent. The **2 base damage** includes thymine–thymine dimer formation via a cyclobutane moiety between juxtaposed thymine residues on the same strand or the cross-linking of nearby thymines on opposite strands (Fig 25–16). **Cross-linking** agents which link bases of opposite strands also induce 2 base alterations. Cross-links can also occur between the DNA molecule and nucleoproteins, particularly the histones, a phenomenon which clearly would alter the function of the DNA molecule if it were not repaired. **Chain breaks** may be created by irradiation such as x-ray exposure but also by radiochemical decay of incorporated atoms such as phosphorus.

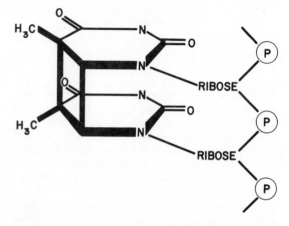

Figure 25—16. A thymine–thymine dimer formed via a cyclobutane moiety between juxtaposed thymine residues of DNA.

The repair of damaged DNA can occur in the following ways: (1) Direct cleavage of a thymine - thymine dimer can be accomplished by an enzyme present in mammalian cells which can be photoactivated by ultraviolet light. (2) Removal of the altered base or bases can occur by a process which involves incision, excision, repair replication, and ligation. (3) Damaged DNA can be replicated by an altered mechanism and then subjected to postreplication repair by a process which is not error-free and therefore is presumed to contribute significantly to the mutagenic effects of many agents. For example, caffeine, a methylxanthine present in coffee and many other food products, inhibits the gap sealing or ligation of postreplication repair immediately following the irradiation of cells in culture.

Xeroderma pigmentosum is an autosomal recessive genetic disease. The clinical syndrome includes marked sensitivity to sunlight with subsequent formation of multiple skin cancers and premature death. The inherited defect seems to involve the repair of damaged DNA. Cells cultured from patients with xeroderma pigmentosum exhibit low activity for the photoactivated thymine dimer cleavage process. However, the involved DNA repair processes in this disease are quite complex; there are at least 5 genetic complementation groups and a sixth variant of xeroderma pigmentosum. The major abnormality in xeroderma pigmentosum may be defective preparation of the chromatin for the various repair processes.

In patients with **ataxia-telangiectasia,** an autosomal recessive disease in humans resulting in the development of cerebellar ataxia and lymphoreticular neoplasms, there appears to exist an increased sensitivity to damage by x-ray. Patients with **Fanconi's anemia,** an autosomal recessive anemia characterized also by an increased frequency of cancer and by chromosomal instability, probably have defective repair of cross-linking damage. All 3 of these clinical syndromes are associated with increased frequency of cancer. It is likely that other human diseases resulting from disordered DNA repair capabilities will be found in the future.

ALTERATION & REARRANGEMENT OF GENETIC MATERIAL

An alteration in the sequence of purine and pyrimidine bases in a gene due to a change, a removal, or an insertion of one or more bases results in an altered gene product which in most instances ultimately is a protein. Such alteration in the genetic material results in a **mutation,** the consequences of which are discussed in detail in Chapter 26.

Prokaryotic and eukaryotic organisms are capable of exchanging genetic information between similar chromosomes. The exchange or **recombination** event occurs primarily during meiosis in mammalian cells and

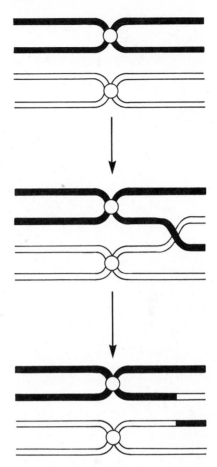

Figure 25–17. The process of crossing over between homologous chromosomes to generate recombinant chromosomes.

requires alignment of homologous chromosomes, an alignment which almost always occurs with great exactness. A process of crossing over occurs as shown in Fig 25–17. This results in a reciprocal exchange of genetic information between homologous chromosomes. If the homologous chromosomes possess different alleles of the same genes, the crossover will produce noticeable and heritable genetic linkage differences. In the rare case where the alignment of homologous chromosomes is not exact, the crossing over or recombination event may result in nonreciprocal exchange of information. One chromosome may receive less genetic material and thus a deletion, while the other partner of the chromosome pair receives more genetic material and thus an insertion (Fig 25–18). Unequal crossing over does occur (though rarely) in humans, as evidenced by the existence of hemoglobins designated Lepore and anti-Lepore.

Some bacterial viruses, ie, bacteriophage, are capable of recombining with the DNA of a bacterial host in such a way that the genetic information of the bacteriophage is incorporated in a linear fashion into the genetic information of the host. This integration, which is a form of recombination, occurs by the mech-

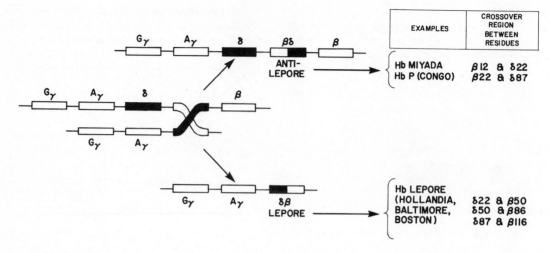

Figure 25–18. The process of unequal crossover in the region of the mammalian genome which harbors the structural genes for hemoglobin and the generation of the unequal recombinant products hemoglobin delta-beta Lepore and beta-delta anti-Lepore. The examples given show the locations of the crossover regions between amino acid residues. (Redrawn and reproduced, with permission, from Clegg JB, Weatherall DJ: β^0 Thalassemia: Time for a reappraisal? Lancet 2:133, 1975.)

anism shown in Fig 25–19. The backbone of the circular bacteriophage genome is broken, as is that of the DNA molecule of the host; the appropriate ends are resealed with the proper polarity. The bacteriophage DNA is figuratively straightened out as it is integrated into the bacterial DNA molecule—frequently a closed circle as well. The site at which the bacteriophage genome integrates or recombines with the bacterial genome is chosen by one of 2 mechanisms. If the bacteriophage contains a DNA sequence **homologous** to a sequence in the host DNA molecule, then a recombination event analogous to that occurring between homologous chromosomes can occur. However, many bacteriophages synthesize proteins which bind specific sites on bacterial chromosomes with a nonhomologous site specifically of the bacteriophage DNA molecule. Integration occurs at the site and is said to be **"site-specific."**

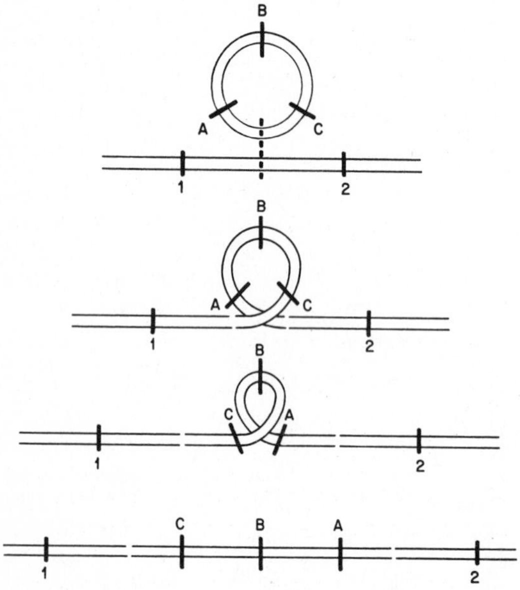

Many animal viruses, particularly the oncogenic viruses—either directly or, in the case of RNA viruses, their DNA transcripts—can be integrated into chromosomes of the mammalian cell. The integration of the animal virus into the animal genome is not "site-specific."

In diploid eukaryotic organisms such as humans, after cells progress through the S phase they contain a tetraploid content of DNA. This is in the form of sister chromatids of chromosome pairs. Each of these sister chromatids contains identical genetic information since each is a product of the semiconservative replication of the original parent DNA molecule of that chromosome. Crossing over occurs between these genetically identical sister chromatids. Of course, these **sister chromatid exchanges** (Fig 25–20) have no genetic consequence as long as the exchange is the result of an equal crossover. However, the frequency of sister chromatid exchanges appears to be an index of the frequency of genetic exchange events occurring generally within a mammalian cell.

It seems that cells which are incapable of minimizing the frequency of the sister chromatid exchanges (by unknown repair mechanisms) are susceptible to other events which are potentially mutagenic.

With the advancement of DNA chemistry and enzymology in recent years, it has been possible to synthesize specific genes in vitro. Some of these synthetic genes can express their genetic information in vivo in the form of an ultimate gene product—a

Figure 25–19. The integration of a circular genome (with genes A, B, and C) into the DNA molecule of a host (with genes 1 and 2) and the consequent ordering of the genes.

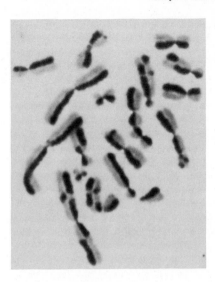

Figure 25–20. Sister chromatid exchanges between human chromosomes. These are detectable by Giemsa staining of the chromosomes of cells replicated for 2 cycles in the presence of bromodeoxyuridine. (Courtesy of Dr. Sheldon Wolff and Judy Bodycote, Laboratory of Radiobiology and Department of Anatomy, University of California School of Medicine, San Francisco.)

specific protein molecule which itself has normal function. Some of the genes have been synthesized, utilizing a purified naturally occurring specific mRNA and an RNA-dependent DNA polymerase (reverse transcriptase) which generates a double-stranded DNA (cDNA) gene complementary to the mRNA molecule. Other synthetic genes have been synthesized chemically using the information contained within the nucleotide sequence of the naturally occurring gene.

Recently, great interest has been shown in a series of enzymes (Table 25–3) capable of recognizing specific sequences of nucleotides in a DNA molecule and then subsequently catalyzing the cleavage of phosphodiester backbone at specific sites within the specific sequences. These enzymes, termed **restriction endonucleases,** are isolated from bacteria, in which they play a defensive role to destroy DNA from foreign organisms. The restriction endonucleases have provided scientists with the means of physically mapping DNA molecules and recombining DNA molecules from different sources to create new genetic sequences. These latter exercises are referred to as **recombinant DNA experiments.** Quite recently, they have received much attention both in the lay press and in the scientific literature.

Some bacteria harbor circular DNA molecules

Table 25–3. Substrate specificities of restriction endonucleases.*

Enzyme	Sequence	Number of Cleavage Sites			Microorganism
		λ	Ad2	SV40	
Hap II	CCGG	> 50	> 50	1	*Haemophilus aphrophilus*
Bsu I	GGCC	> 50	> 50	18	*Bacillus subtilis* strain X5
Alu I	AGCT	> 50	> 50	32	*Arthrobacter luteus*
Eco RII	CCTGG	> 35	> 35	16	*Escherichia coli* R245
Eco RII	CCAGG	> 35	> 35	16	*Escherichia coli* R245
Hind III	AAGCTT	6	11	6	*Haemophilus influenzae* R_d
Hinc II	GTPyPuAC	34	> 20	7	*Haemophilus influenzae* R_c
Hpa I	GTTAAC	11	6	5	*Haemophilus parainfluenzae*
Eco RI	GAATTC	5	5	1	*Escherichia coli* RY13
Bam HI	GGATTC	5	3	1	*Bacillus amyloliquefaciens* H
Bal I	CGGCCG	15	17	0	*Brevibacterium albidum*
Hae II	PuGCGCPy	> 30	> 30	1	*Haemophilus aegyptius*
Hha I	GCGC	> 50	> 50	2	*Haemophilus haemolyticus*
Mbo I	GATC	> 50	> 50	6	*Moraxella bovis*
Sma I	CCCGGG	3	12	0	*Serratia marcescens* Sb_b
Bgl II	AGATCT	5	10	0	*Bacillus globiggi*
Hinf I	GANTC	> 50	> 50	10	*Haemophilus influenzae* R_f
Taq I	TCGA	?	?	?	*Thermus aquaticus* YTI

*Arrows indicate the site of cleavage and sequence specificity of the endonucleases. The number of cleavage sites refers to the genomes of lambda bacteriophage (λ), adenovirus 2 (Ad2), and simian virus 40 (SV40).

which replicate autonomously in the bacterial proto-plasm. Such an autonomous DNA molecule is called a **plasmid**. Plasmids may carry genetic information to confer **resistance to antibiotics** on the host bacterium. Using **recombinant DNA technology**, a specific seg-ment of DNA can be integrated in vitro into a plasmid. In this manner, a bacterial culture can be utilized for the autonomous replication of the recombinant plas-mid and thus the new segment of DNA. Restriction endonucleases can then be used to clip out specifically the sequence originally inserted into the plasmid and thus to obtain milligram quantities of specific DNA sequences. Such technology would appear to provide great potential benefits for medical and agricultural purposes.

BIOLOGIC FUNCTION OF RIBONUCLEIC ACID (RNA)

As is the case with DNA, RNA contains informa-tion by way of its specific sequence of polymerized purine and pyrimidine ribonucleotides. However, the structure of RNA is somewhat different from that of DNA. RNA contains the same purine bases—adenine and guanine—present in DNA, but only one of the pyrimidine bases—cytosine—is the same as that in DNA. Thymine, present in DNA, has been replaced in RNA by uracil, whose structure, while similar to that of thymine, differs by lacking the 5-methyl substituent (see Chapter 10), As described in Chapter 11, RNA normally exists as a single-stranded molecule but is capable of folding back on itself to form hairpinlike loops with double-stranded portions of the single mole-cule. The information in RNA, contained within the specific sequence of nucleotides, is in nearly all circum-stances derived from a DNA molecule and dictated by base-pairing rules similar to those responsible for the double-stranded helix of DNA. The only difference in the base-pairing scheme dictating the sequence of the RNA nucleotides is that adenine of DNA pairs with a uracil while the complementary RNA molecule is being synthesized.

Although all naturally-occurring RNA molecules contain information in their sequences, only some of these molecules have their informational content trans-lated into the specific amino acid sequence of specific protein molecules. Those RNA molecules, which serve as templates for protein synthesis, are designated as mRNA. Many other RNA molecules have structural roles wherein they contribute to the formation of ribo-somes (the organellar machinery for protein synthesis) or serve as adapter molecules (tRNA) for the transla-tion of RNA information into specific sequences of polymerized amino acids. Much of the RNA synthe-sized from DNA templates in eukaryotic cells, includ-ing mammalian cells, is degraded within the nucleus, and it never serves as either a structural or an informa-tional entity within the cellular cytoplasm. As dis-cussed below under RNA processing, these portions of RNA molecules nonetheless are thought to play some regulatory roles.

Most RNA molecules transcribed in the cell nu-cleus appear to be involved in protein synthesis, but there are in cultured human cells small RNA species not directly involved in protein synthesis but which may have roles in the cellular architecture. These rela-tively small molecules vary in size from 90 to about 300 nucleotides and are apparently associated with specific cellular organelles.

The genetic material for some animal and plant viruses is RNA rather than DNA. Although some RNA viruses do not ever have their information transcribed into a DNA molecule, many animal RNA viruses—particularly the oncogenic viruses—are transcribed by an **RNA-dependent DNA polymerase** to produce a double-stranded DNA copy of their RNA genome. In most cases the resulting double-stranded DNA tran-script is integrated into the host genome and subse-quently serves as a template from which new viral RNA genomes can be transcribed. It is not clear whether animal cells that do not contain RNA viruses utilize an RNA molecule as a template for DNA synthesis and, if they do utilize it, what function that might serve.

RNA METABOLISM

RNA Synthesis

The process of synthesizing RNA from a DNA template has been characterized best in prokaryotes. Although in mammalian cells the regulation of RNA synthesis and the processing of the RNA transcripts is different from that in prokaryotes, the process of RNA synthesis per se is quite similar in these 2 classes of

DNA STRANDS:

ANTISENSE → 5'-T GG A ATT GTG AGC GGA TAACA AT T T CACACAG G AAAC AGC T ATG ACC ATG-3'
SENSE ──→ 3'-A CCT TA ACA CTC GCC TA TTGTTAA AGTGTGTC CTTTGTC GATACT GGTAC-5'

RNA   5'
TRANSCRIPT   pAU UGU G AGC G GAU AACA AUU UC AC ACAGG AAACA GCU AUG A CC AU G 3'

Figure 25–21. The relationship between the sense strand and antisense strand in the DNA molecule and the RNA molecule complementary to the sense strand.

organisms. Therefore, the description of RNA synthesis is prokaryotes will be applicable to eukaryotes even though the enzymes involved and the regulatory signals are different. The sequence of ribonucleotides in an RNA molecule is complementary to the sequence of deoxyribonucleotides in one strand of the DNA template molecule (Fig 25–21). The strand which is transcribed into an RNA molecule is referred to as the **sense strand** of the DNA. The other DNA strand is frequently referred to as the **antisense strand** of that gene. In the case of a double-stranded DNA molecule containing many genes, the sense strand for each gene will not necessarily be the same strand of the DNA double helix (Fig 25–22). Thus, a given strand of a double-stranded DNA molecule will serve as the sense strand for some genes and the antisense strand of other genes.

DNA-dependent RNA polymerase is responsible for the polymerization of ribonucleotides into a sequence complementary to the sense strand of the gene (Fig 25–23). The enzyme attaches at a specific site, the promoter, toward the 3' end of the sense strand of the gene to be transcribed. The DNA-dependent RNA polymerase of the bacterium *E coli* exists as a core molecule composed of 4 subunits; 2 of these are identical to each other (the a subunits), and 2 are similar to each other but not identical (the β subunit and the β' subunit). The core RNA polymerase utilizes a specific protein factor (the sigma [σ] factor) which assists the core enzyme to attach more tightly to the specific deoxynucleotide sequence of the promoter region (Fig 25–24). This holoenzyme (core polymerase + σ factor), in the presence of all 4 ribonucleoside triphosphates (ATP, GTP, CTP, UTP), commences movement along the sense strand toward its 5' terminus. The

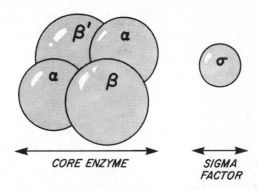

Figure 25–24. A diagrammatic representation of the subunit structure of DNA-dependent RNA polymerase and the sigma factor. (From James D. Watson, *Molecular Biology of the Gene*, 3rd ed. Copyright © 1976, 1970, 1965, by W.A. Benjamin, Inc, Menlo Park, California.)

enzyme polymerizes the ribonucleotides in a specific sequence which is dictated by the template (sense) strand and interpreted by the base-pairing rules. Pyrophosphate is released in the polymerization reaction. In both prokaryotes and eukaryotes, a purine ribonucleotide is the first to be polymerized into the RNA molecule.

The process of RNA synthesis, depicted in Fig 25–25, involves first the binding of the holo RNA polymerase molecule to the template at the promoter site. Initiation of formation of the RNA molecule at its 5' end then follows with the release of the σ factor, while the elongation of the RNA molecule from the 5' to its 3' end continues antiparallel to its template. Termination of the synthesis of the RNA molecule is signaled by a specific sequence in the sense strand of the DNA molecule, a signal which is recognized by a termination protein, the rho (ρ) factor. Following termination of synthesis of the RNA molecule, the core enzyme separates from the DNA template. With the assistance of another σ factor, the core enzyme then recognizes a promoter at which the synthesis of a new RNA molecule commences. More than one RNA polymerase molecule may transcribe the same sense strand of a gene simultaneously, but the process is phased and spaced in such a way that at any one moment each is transcribing a different portion of the DNA sequence. RNA synthesis is shown in an electron micrograph (Fig 25–8).

Mammalian cells possess several DNA-dependent RNA polymerases, the properties of which are described in Table 25–4. Each of these DNA-dependent RNA polymerases seems to be responsible for the transcription of different sets of genes. The subunit structures of mammalian polymerases have been described, but the functions of each of the subunits are not yet understood. Certainly, many must have regulatory functions, such as serving to assist the core polymerase in the recognition of specific sequences like promoters and termination signals. The antibiotic **rifampin** (rifam-

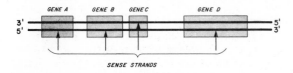

Figure 25–22. Sense strands of linked genes. These are not necessarily the same strand of the DNA double helix.

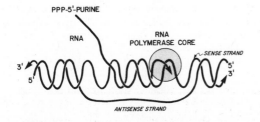

Figure 25–23. The RNA polymerase–catalyzed polymerization of ribonucleotides into an RNA sequence complementary to the sense strand of the gene. (From James D. Watson, *Molecular Biology of the Gene*, 3rd ed. Copyright © 1976, 1970, 1965, by W.A. Benjamin, Inc, Menlo Park, California.)

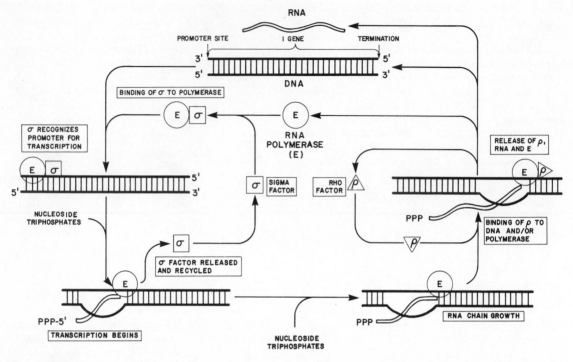

Figure 25—25. The process of RNA synthesis. It begins at the upper left-hand portion of the figure with the binding of sigma to polymerase to form a complex which recognizes the promoter for transcription. The process is completed as the RNA transcriptase is released from the gene, and all of the catalytic components are free to recycle. (From James D. Watson, *Molecular Biology of the Gene,* 3rd ed. Copyright © 1976, 1970, 1965, by W.A. Benjamin, Inc, Menlo Park, California.)

Table 25—4. Nomenclature and localization of animal DNA-dependent RNA polymerases.

Class of Enzyme	Sensitivity to α-Amanitin	Products	Principal Localization
I (A)	Insensitive	rRNA	Nucleolar
II (B)	Sensitive to low concentration (10^{-8} to 10^{-9} M)	hnRNA (mRNA)	Nucleoplasmic
III (C)	Sensitive to high concentration	tRNA and 5S RNA	Nucleoplasmic

picin) inhibits the binding of prokaryotic DNA-dependent RNA polymerase to promoter sites of genes.

One toxin from the mushroom *Amanita phalloides, α*-amanitin, is a specific inhibitor of the eukaryotic nucleoplasmic DNA-dependent RNA polymerase (RNA polymerase II).

The regulation of RNA synthesis in mammalian cells is poorly understood, but the nonhistone nucleoproteins probably have major responsibilities for indicating which genes are to be transcribed in a given cell, and when. The regulation of transcription in prokaryotes is described in more detail in Chapter 27.

Processing of RNA Molecules

In prokaryotic organisms, it appears that most RNA molecules transcribed from the sense strand of a gene are subjected to little modification and processing

prior to carrying out their intended function in protein synthesis. The exception is the tRNA molecules, which are transcribed in units considerably longer than the ultimate tRNA molecule. In fact, many of the transcription units contain more than one tRNA molecule. Thus, the processing of these tRNA precursor molecules is required for the generation of the ultimate functional molecules, the specific tRNAs.

The process is somewhat different in eukaryotic cells, particularly mammalian cells. Nearly all RNA molecules undergo extensive processing between the time they are synthesized and the time at which they serve their ultimate function, whether it be as mRNA or as a structural molecule. In many cases the processing occurs within the nucleus as well as after transportation from the nucleus to the cytoplasm. The processing includes **nucleolytic reactions, terminal additions** of nucleotides, and **nucleoside modifications.**

Heterogeneous Nuclear RNA (hnRNA)

The mRNA in mammalian cells is derived by post-transcriptional processing of large nuclear RNA precursor molecules 5000—50,000 nucleotides in length (hnRNA). Most mammalian mRNA molecules are 400—4000 nucleotides in length; the median is approximately 1200 nucleotides. Considerable uncertainty still exists concerning the precursor-product relationship between hnRNA and mRNA, the former being 10—100 times longer than the latter. The hnRNA population turns over in the nucleus quite rapidly, with a half-life of approximately 23 minutes. Only a small portion of these RNA molecules ever reaches the mammalian cytoplasm.

Three types of data suggest a precursor-product relationship between these RNA molecules: (1) In the nucleus, a sequence of polyadenylic acids (poly[A]) is added to the 3' terminus of many hnRNA molecules, and many, but not all, cytoplasmic mRNA molecules also contain a 3'-poly(A) tail comparable in size to that found in hnRNA. (2) The 5' terminus of mammalian mRNA contains a cap structure of a 7-methylguanine-5'-triphosphate linked to the 5'-terminal nucleotide (a purine nucleotide). The latter frequently contains a 2',O-methyl group. There is a remarkable compositional similarity between the 5'-terminal caps present on some hnRNA and the caps on mRNA. (3) The third piece of evidence is based on the demonstration by molecular hybridization that mRNA sequences are present in hnRNA fractions. However, to date the precursor-product relationship between hnRNA and mRNA has not been conclusively demonstrated. The precursors of some mRNAs such as those for ovalbumin and histones are considerably smaller than that class of nuclear RNA molecules considered to be hnRNA.

The processing of hnRNA (Fig 25—26) includes the **capping** of these heterogeneous molecules as well as the attachment of **poly(A) tails** to some. The 5'-terminal 7-methylguanosine trinucleotide caps and the methyl groups on the next few nucleotides of hnRNA

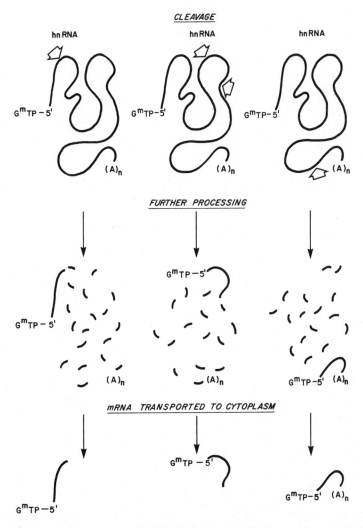

Figure 25—26. The processing of heterogeneous nuclear RNA (hnRNA) which has been previously capped at its 5' terminus by G^mTP and tailed with a polymer of adenylate. Three alternative processes are given. *Left:* The mRNA can be cleaved from the first part of the transcript with conservation of the original cap and degradation of all other portions of the hnRNA molecule. *Center:* The mRNA can be excised from a center portion of the hnRNA molecule with destruction of the original cap and the poly(A) tail and subsequent recapping. *Right:* The mRNA can be cleaved from the terminal portion of the transcript, ie, the 3' end of the hnRNA molecule. This allows for a conservation of the original poly(A) tail but destruction of the original cap and other portions of the molecule. The mRNA is eventually recapped. All 3 types of processing probably occur in mammalian cells.

can be added to the primary transcript or to 5′ termini arising by cleavages at internal sites. This implies that the 5′ terminus of mRNA molecules can be derived both from the 5′ terminus of the hnRNA molecule or from an internally cleaved 5′ terminus.

The observation that many hnRNA molecules contain poly(A) tails at their 3′ termini, as do many mRNA molecules, and that poly(A) tails can be attached in the nucleus, suggests that some mRNA molecules are derived from the 3′ portion of hnRNA molecules. However, a significant fraction of the poly(A) tails on hnRNA molecules is degraded within the nucleus, and poly(A) tails can also be attached to mRNA within the cytoplasm. Thus, different species of mRNA molecules might be located at different positions within their primary transcripts—probably hnRNA molecules.

The hnRNA contains both **unique sequences** and **repetitive sequences** within the same molecule, but mRNA molecules of the unique sequence class contain little if any repetitive sequences. This suggests that the repetitive sequences in hnRNA are not transported to the cytoplasm but might be regulatory elements removed from the precursor prior to the transport of the mRNA to cytoplasm.

The function of the **capped structure** on hnRNA molecules is presumed to be related to the function of the same on mRNA molecules, where it appears to be necessary for the initiation of **messenger translation**. The function of the poly(A) tail present on about 20% of the hnRNA molecules is also unknown, but clearly it does not serve as a qualitative signal responsible for the selection of those hnRNA molecules to be processed and transported to the cytoplasm. Many mRNA molecules do not contain poly(A). Many poly(A)-tailed RNA molecules receive their tails in the cytoplasm after transport from the nucleus.

A major unanswered question is whether each hnRNA molecule may contain more than a single messenger sequence. This is feasible even though each cytoplasmic mRNA molecule is probably monocistronic, ie, the genetic information it contains is confined to only a single gene.

The high rate of turnover and low rate of transmission of hnRNA information to cytoplasm appears to be a wasteful process. However, the expense must be worth the gain, which may be that of serving important regulatory roles for the degraded portions of the hnRNA molecules.

Messenger RNA (mRNA)

As mentioned above, most but not all mammalian mRNA molecules contain a capped structure at their 5′-phosphate terminus and a poly(A) tail at the 3′ terminus. The cap structures appear to be formed in the nucleus prior to transport of the mRNA molecule to the cytoplasm. The poly(A) tails (when present) appear to be added either in the nucleus or in the cytoplasm. The secondary methylations of mRNA molecules, those on the 2′-hydroxy groups, and the N_6 of adenylate residues occur after the mRNA molecule

has appeared in the cytoplasm. The function of the cap structures presumably is to assist in recognition of the proper site on the template mRNA at which to commence protein synthesis.

The function of the poly(A) tail is unknown. In any event, the presence or absence of the poly(A) tail does not determine whether a precursor molecule in the nucleus appears in the cytoplasm because all poly(A)-tailed hnRNA molecules do not contribute to cytoplasmic mRNA, nor do all cytoplasmic mRNA molecules contain poly(A) tails. Cytoplasmic processes in mammalian cells can both add and remove adenylate residues from the poly(A) tails, but this processing does not appear to influence the stability of the mRNA or its function in a homologous system. Ovalbumin mRNA, after the removal of its poly(A) tail, is translated less efficiently in both rabbit reticulocyte and wheat germ protein–synthesizing systems in vitro.

The turnover of poly(A)-containing mRNA in cultured mammalian cells is a first-order process with a half-time approximately equal to the doubling time of the cell culture. The kinetics of the degradation of histone mRNA which does not contain a poly(A) tail appears to be a zero-order process in which there is an age-dependent decay with a lifetime of approximately 6 hours. It is not clear whether this difference is related to the presence or absence of poly(A) or to some intrinsic property of these mRNA molecules.

The size of the cytoplasmic mRNA molecules after the poly(A) tail is removed is still considerably greater than the size required to code for the specific protein for which it is template. A summary of the required sizes and actual sizes of different mRNAs is given in Table 25–5. For several purified mammalian mRNA molecules there is a specific sequence (A·A·U·A·A·A) about 20 residues short of the 3′ terminal poly(A) sequence. This sequence seems to have been conserved in evolution since it is present in mRNA molecules from different species. Its function is unknown.

Nucleic acid hybridization analysis of mRNA from cultured human cells suggests the presence of 2 or 3 "abundance" classes. A HeLa cell contains about 1.25×10^9 nucleotides in mRNA. There appear to be 2 main abundance classes of the approximately 40,000 mRNA molecules per cell. Those mRNA molecules with the greatest complexity are present in very low abundance, whereas the majority of the mRNA molecules represent a smaller number of sequences, each of which is present in many copies.

Transfer RNA Molecules (tRNA)

The tRNA molecules, as described in Chapters 11 and 26, serve as adapter molecules for the translation of mRNA into protein sequences. The tRNAs contain many peculiar bases; some are simply methylated derivatives and some possess rearranged glycosidic bonds. The tRNA molecules are transcribed in both prokaryotes and eukaryotes as large precursors which are then subjected to **nucleolytic processing** and reduced in size by a specific class of ribonucleases, **ribo-**

Table 25–5. Lengths of isolated messenger RNAs.*†

Cell	Protein	Coding Length	mRNA Length	Poly(A) Length
Rabbit red blood cell	Globin	430	550 610 650	40
Mouse red blood cell	Globin			40, 60, 100
Duck red blood cell	Globin			100
Mouse myeloma	Light Ig	660	1200 1250 1300	200
Mouse myeloma	Heavy Ig	1350	1800	150–200
Chick oviduct	Ovalbumin	1164	1670 2640	Not known
Calf lens	α A2-Crystallin	520	1460	200
Calf lens	δ-Crystallin	1260	2000	Not known
Bombyx mori silk gland	Fibroin	14,000	16,000	100
Lytechinus pictus (sea urchin)	Histone f2al	310	370–400	None
HeLa	Molecules: 50% total 25% total 25% total	 < 1000 1000–2000 > 2000	 < 1400 1400–3000 > 3000	 150–200 150–200 150–200
	Mass: 50% total 50% total	 < 2100 > 2100	 < 2200 > 2200	 150–200 150–200

*Reproduced, with permission, from Lewin B: Units of transcription and translation: Sequence components of heterogeneous nuclear RNA and messenger RNA. Cell 4:480, 1975.

†Coding lengths are the number of nucleotides required to specify each protein, estimated from its number of amino acids or molecular weight. The lengths of the mRNAs are those determined experimentally; where more than one value is shown, each represents an independent determination. The length of poly(A) on a messenger is not constant but declines with age; thus, the apparent length depends on whether it is determined by steady state or by pulse labeling, which explains the variation in measured globin mRNA poly(A) lengths. "Not known" indicates that poly(A) is present but that its length has not been determined. ¶The distribution of HeLa protein and messenger sizes is only approximate; an estimate of the number of molecules in each size class suggests a median coding length in mRNA of about 1200 nucleotides (1400 less the poly[A] content), and an estimate of the mass of protein or mRNA in each size class suggests a number average molecular weight for the coding length of 2000 (ie, 2200 less the poly[A] content).

nuclease P. Some tRNA precursors in prokaryotes contain the sequence for 2 different tRNA molecules. The modification of the tRNA molecules includes the nucleoside **methylations** and rearrangements required for normal function, the proper **folding** to generate a partial double-stranded character, and the **attachment of the characteristic C·C·A terminus** at the 3' end of the molecule. This C·C·A terminus is the point of attachment for the specific amino acid that is to be for entrance into the polymerization reaction of protein synthesis. The methylation of mammalian tRNA precursors probably occurs in the nucleus, whereas the cleavage and C·C·A attachment are cytoplasmic functions. Enzymes within the cytoplasm of mammalian cells are required for the accomplishment of attachment of amino acids to the C·C·A residues, since the termini turn over more rapidly than do the tRNA molecules themselves. The tRNA molecules are more stable in growing eukaryotic cells than in resting cells. In the growing cells, the half-time is approximately 60 hours.

Ribosomal RNA (rRNA)

In mammalian cells, the 2 major rRNA molecules and one minor rRNA molecule are transcribed from a single large precursor molecule (Fig 25–27). The pre-

cursor is subsequently processed in the nucleolus to provide the ribosome subunits for the cytoplasm. The rRNA genes are located in the nucleoli of mammalian cells. Thousands of copies of these genes are present in every cell. The rRNA genes are transcribed as units, each of which contains, from 5' to 3', an 18S, a 5.8S (formerly 7S), and a 28S ribosomal RNA. The transcript is a 45S molecule which is highly methylated in the nucleolus. In the **45S precursor**, the eventual 28S segment contains 65 ribose-methyl groups and 5 base-methyl groups. Only those portions of the precursor which eventually become rRNA molecules are methylated. The 45S precursor is nucleolytically processed. Nearly half of the original transcript is discarded as "degradation products" by the mechanism shown in Fig 25–27. During the processing of rRNA, further methylation occurs, and eventually in the nucleoli the 28S chains self-assemble with ribosomal proteins newly synthesized in the cytoplasm to form the larger 60S subunit. The smaller (40S) ribosomal subunits may not be formed in the nucleoli from the 18S rRNA molecule. The 5.8S rRNA molecule also formed from the 45S precursor RNA in the nucleolus becomes an integral part of the smaller ribosomal subunit.

Both of the 2 major rRNA species present in the cytoplasm are stable in growing cells but unstable in

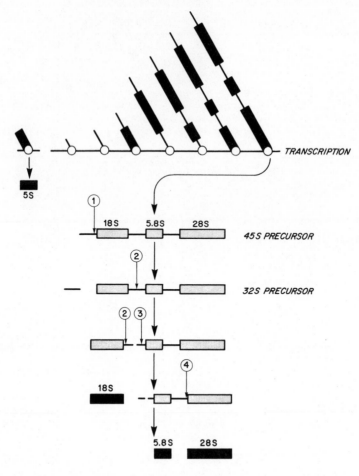

Figure 25—27. Diagrammatic representation of the processing of ribosomal RNA from precursor RNA molecules. (Reprinted, with permission, from Perry RP: Annu Rev Biochem 45:611, 1976.)

resting cells. In resting cells the 28S rRNA exhibits even greater instability than does the 18S rRNA.

INHIBITORS OF DNA & RNA SYNTHESIS

Many antibiotics and nucleotide analogs inhibit the synthesis of DNA and RNA. These are used both experimentally (in research) and clinically in the management of malignant diseases. A list of some of these inhibitors is shown in Table 25—6 with some indication of their mechanisms and effects.

NUCLEASES

Enzymes capable of degrading nucleic acids have been recognized for many years. These can be classified in several ways. Those which exhibit specificity for deoxyribonucleic acid are referred to as **deoxyribonucleases**. Those which specifically hydrolyze ribonucleic acids are **ribonucleases**. Within both of these classes are enzymes capable of cleaving internal phosphodiester bonds to produce a 3'-hydroxyl and a 5'-phosphoryl or a 5'-hydroxyl and a 3'-phosphoryl terminus. These are referred to as **endonucleases**. Some are capable of hydrolyzing both strands of a **double-stranded** molecule, whereas others can only cleave **single strands** of nucleic acids. Some nucleases can hydrolyze only unpaired single strands, while others are capable of hydrolyzing single strands participating in the formation of a double-stranded molecule. There exist classes of endonucleases which recognize specific base sequences in DNA; the majority of these are the **restriction endonucleases**, which have in recent years become an important and controversial tool in molecular genetics.

A list of the currently recognized restriction endonucleases is presented in Table 25—3.

Some nucleases are capable of hydrolyzing a nucleotide only when it is present at a terminus of a molecule; these are referred to as **exonucleases**.

Table 25—6. Inhibitors of DNA and RNA synthesis.[*]

Type of Inhibition	Inhibitor	Mechanism	Inhibition or Effect
Template binding Noncovalent	Actinomycin D	Binds to and intercalates between dG-dC pairs	RNA and DNA chain elongation
	Anthracyclines (eg, nogalamycin)	Binds and intercalates alternating A-T sequence	RNA and DNA chain elongation
	Acridine dyes (eg, acriflavine)	Intercalates	Frameshift mutation; RNA chain initiation
	Ethidium bromide	Intercalates	DNA replication and mutagenesis
	Kanchanomycin	Strong Mg^{2+} complex with template	*E coli* DNA polymerase I
	8-Aminoquinolines		*E coli* and *M luteus* DNA polymerase I; RNA polymerase only partially.
Covalent	Mitomycin (reduced) Bleomycin, phleomycin Anthramycin	Cross-links Chain breaks	DNA replication DNA replication DNA and RNA synthesis
Nucleotide analogs Chain terminator	Dideoxynucleoside triphosphates	Incorporated into DNA	DNA chain growth and $3' \rightarrow 5'$ degradation
	Arabinosyl nucleoside triphosphates	Incorporated into DNA	DNA chain growth and $3' \rightarrow 5'$ degradation; bacterial and animal cells.
	Cordycepin triphosphate ($3'$-deoxy ATP)	Incorporated into DNA and RNA	DNA and RNA chain growth
	$3'$-Amino ATP	Incorporated into DNA and RNA	DNA chain growth
Defective DNA	dUTP	Incorporated into DNA	Template degraded
	5-Hydroxyuridine or 5-aminouridine	Incorporated into RNA	RNA and DNA synthesis
	5-Bromouracil	Incorporated into DNA	Mutagenic, causes replication errors
	Tubericidin "ATP," formycin "ATP"	Incorporated into RNA and DNA	RNA and DNA synthesis and functions
Enzyme binding	Hydroxyphenylhydrazinouracil	Ternary complex with template and enzyme	*B subtilis* polymerase III; reversed by dGTP.
	Hydroxyphenylhydrazinoisocytosine	Ternary complex with template and enzyme	*B subtilis* polymerase III; reversed by dATP.
Enzyme binding	Rifampicin, streptovaricin	β-Subunit of bacterial RNA polymerase	RNA initiation
	Streptolydigin	β-Subunit of bacterial RNA polymerase	RNA chain growth
	α-Amanitin		Mammalian nuclear RNA polymerase
	Kanchanomycin		*E coli* RNA polymerase
Unknown mechanism	Edeine		DNA replication in bacteria
	Nalidixic acid		DNA replication in bacteria

[*]Reproduced, with permission, from Kornberg A: *DNA Synthesis.* Freeman, 1974.

• • •

References

Abelson HT & others: Changes in RNA in relation to growth of the fibroblast: The lifetime of mRNA, rRNA, and tRNA in resting and growing cells. Cell 1:161, 1974.

Bishop JO & others: Three abundance classes in HeLa cell messenger RNA. Nature 250:199, 1974.

Brawerman G: Eukaryotic messenger RNA. Annu Rev Biochem 43:621, 1974.

Chamberlin M: The selectivity of transcription. Annu Rev Biochem 43:721, 1974.

Chambon P: Eukaryotic nuclear RNA polymerases. Annu Rev Biochem 44:613, 1975.

Cleaver J, Bootsma D, Friedberg E: Human diseases with genetically altered DNA repair processes. Genetics 79:215, 1975.

Darnell JE, Jelinek WR, Molloy GR: Biogenesis of mRNA: Genetic regulation in mammalian cells. Science 181:1215, 1973.

Efstratiadis A & others: Enzymatic in vitro synthesis of globin genes. Cell 7:279, 1976.

Engelman DM, Moore PB: Neutron-scattering studies of the ribosome. Sci Am 235:44, 1976.

Glover D: Maintenance and evolution of repeated genes in eukaryotes. Nature 263:9, 1976.

Hamkalo B, Miller OL Jr: Electron microscopy of genetic activity. Annu Rev Biochem 42:379, 1973.

Kornberg A: *DNA Synthesis.* Freeman, 1974.

Lewin B: Units of transcription and translation: The relationship between heterogeneous nuclear RNA and messenger RNA. Cell 4:11, 1975.

Lewin B: Units of transcription and translation: Sequence of heterogeneous nuclear RNA and messenger RNA. Cell 4:77, 1975.

Nathans D, Smith HO: Restriction endonucleases in the analysis and restructuring of DNA molecules. Annu Rev Biochem 44:273, 1975.

Perry RP: Processing of RNA. Annu Rev Biochem 45:605, 1976.

Radding CM: Molecular mechanisms in genetic recombination. Annu Rev Genetics 7:87, 1973.

Rich A, RajBhandary UL: Transfer RNA: Molecular structure, sequence, and properties. Annu Rev Biochem 45:805, 1976.

Salim M, Maden BEH: Early and late methylations in HeLa cell ribosome maturation. Nature 244:334, 1973.

26...
Protein Synthesis & The Genetic Code

As previously described, the genetic information within the nucleotide sequence of DNA is transcribed in the nucleus into the specific nucleotide sequence of an RNA molecule. In higher eukaryotic cells, this transcript, heterogeneous nuclear RNA (hnRNA), is processed in the nucleus and seems to appear subsequently in the cytoplasm as messenger RNA (mRNA). The sequence of nucleotides in the mRNA is complementary to the nucleotide sequence of the "sense" strand of its gene in accordance with the base-pairing rules.

In a series of elegant experiments by Charles Yanofsky, it has been shown that there is a linear correspondence between the gene and its polypeptide product or protein. Using the technics of genetic mapping and protein sequencing, Yanofsky demonstrated that the order of mutants on the genetic map of tryptophan synthetase in *E coli* was the same as the order of the corresponding changes in the amino acid sequence of the tryptophan synthetase enzyme molecule (Fig 26–1).

The cell must possess the machinery necessary to translate information from the nucleotide sequence of an mRNA into the sequence of amino acids of the corresponding specific protein. This process, termed **translation**, was not understood for many years, until the recent clarification of our understanding of the process of translation and the deciphering of the genetic code, which is undoubtedly a major accomplishment of modern biology. It was realized early that mRNA molecules in themselves have no affinity for amino acids and, therefore, that the translation of the information in the mRNA nucleotide sequence into the amino acid sequence of a protein requires an intermediate, adapter molecule. This adapter molecule must recognize a specific nucleotide sequence on the one hand as well as a specific amino acid on the other. With such an adapter molecule, the cell can direct a specific amino acid into the proper sequential position of a protein as dictated by the nucleotide sequence of the specific mRNA. In fact, the functional groups of the amino acids do not themselves actually come into contact with the mRNA template.

In the nucleotide sequence of the mRNA molecule, code words exist for each amino acid. This is referred to as the **genetic code**. The adapter molecules which translate the code words into the amino acid sequence of a protein are the **transfer RNA (tRNA)** molecules. The **ribosome** is the cellular component on which these various functional entities interact to assemble the protein molecule. Many of these subcellular units (ribosomes) can aggregate to translate simultane-

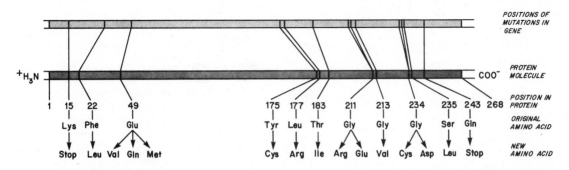

Figure 26–1. A diagram of the colinearity of the gene (Trp A) for the tryptophan synthetase A protein with the protein molecule itself. The positions of the mutations in the Trp A gene are indicated in the top bar, and the position of the corresponding altered amino acid determined by sequence analyses of the mutant protein molecule is shown in the lower bar. The numbers represent the number of the altered amino acid starting at the amino terminus of the protein molecule. Shown below the numbers of the altered amino acid residues are the original amino acids at those positions in the normal protein molecule. Below the normal amino acids are those occurring in the protein as the result of a mutation in the gene at the corresponding positions. (From *Biochemistry,* by Lubert Stryer. W.H. Freeman & Co. Copyright © 1975. Redrawn, with permission, from Yanofsky C: Gene structure and protein structure. Sci Am 216:89, May 1967.)

ously a single mRNA molecule and, in so doing, form what is called a **polyribosome.** In the cell, there are factories in which polyribosomes are gathered together for the formation of different classes of protein molecules. The **rough endoplasmic reticulum** is such a factory of polyribosomes attached to membrane structures which provides for the synthesis of proteins to be exported. Polyribosomal structures also exist free in the cytoplasm, where they synthesize proteins that remain within the cell.

Twenty different amino acids are required for the synthesis of proteins, and thus there must be at least 20 distinct code words which comprise the genetic code. Since there are only 4 different nucleotides in mRNA, each code word must consist of more than a single purine or pyrimidine nucleotide. Code words consisting of 2 nucleotides each could provide for only 16 (4 X 4) specific code words, whereas code words of 3 nucleotides could provide 64 (4 X 4 X 4) specific code words.

As a result of the initial observations of Matthaei and Nirenberg, it is now known that each code word, termed a **codon,** consists of a sequence of 3 nucleotides, ie, it is a triplet code. With 4 distinct bases in an mRNA molecule, in a triplet code there can be 64 triplets to provide for 20 amino acids. The deciphering of the genetic code (Table 26−1) was carried out largely in the laboratory of Marshall Nirenberg. It depended heavily on the chemical synthesis of nucleotide polymers, particularly triplets, by Khoṙana.

Three codons do not code for specific amino acids; these have been termed **nonsense codons.** At least 2 of these so-called nonsense codons are utilized

in the cell as signals to terminate the polymerization of amino acids where a protein molecule is to end. The remaining 61 codons code for 20 amino acids. Thus there must be "degeneracy" in the genetic code. An examination of the genetic code in Table 26−1 reveals that for many amino acids there exists more than one codon. Generally, the third nucleotide in a codon is less important than the other 2 in determining the specific amino acid to be incorporated, and this accounts for most of the **degeneracy** of the code. However, for any specific codon only a single amino acid is indicated; the genetic code is **unambiguous,** ie, given a specific codon, only a single amino acid is indicated. The distinction between ambiguity and degeneracy is an important concept to be emphasized.

The unambiguous but degenerate code can be described in molecular terms. The recognition of specific codons in the mRNA by the tRNA adapter molecules is dependent upon their **anticodon region** and the base-pairing rules. Each tRNA molecule contains a specific sequence, complementary to a codon, which is termed its anticodon. For a given codon in the mRNA, only a single species of tRNA molecule possesses the proper anticodon. Since each tRNA molecule can be charged with only one specific amino acid, each codon therefore specifies only one amino acid. However, some tRNA molecules can utilize the anticodon to recognize more than one codon. Nonetheless, all codons which the single species of tRNA molecules is capable of recognizing are able to code for the same amino acid. Given a specific codon, only a specific amino acid will be incorporated—although, given a specific amino acid, more than one codon may call for it.

As discussed below, the reading of the genetic code during the process of protein synthesis does not involve any overlap of codons. Furthermore, once the reading is commenced at a specific codon, there is **no punctuation** between codons, and the message is read in a continuing sequence of nucleotide triplets until a nonsense codon is reached.

The genetic code as given in Table 26−1 is universal; all known organisms utilize the same genetic code for the translation of their specific genes into specific proteins.

Transfer RNA Function

There exists at least one transfer RNA (tRNA) for each of the 20 amino acids. All of the tRNA molecules have extraordinarily similar functions and extraordinarily similar 3-dimensional structures. The adapter function of the tRNA molecules requires the charging of each specific tRNA with its specific amino acid. Since there is no affinity of nucleic acids for specific functional groups of amino acids, this recognition must be carried out by a protein molecule capable of recognizing both a specific tRNA molecule and a specific amino acid. At least 20 specific enzymes are required for these specific recognition functions and for the proper attachment of the 20 amino acids to specific tRNA molecules. The process of recognition and attachment (charging) is carried out in 2 steps by one

Table 26−1. The genetic code (codon assignments in messenger RNA).*

First Nucleotide	Second Nucleotide				Third Nucleotide
	U	C	A	G	
U	Phe	Ser	Tyr	Cys	U
	Phe	Ser	Tyr	Cys	C
	Leu	Ser	CT	CT	A
	Leu	Ser	CT	Trp	G
C	Leu	Pro	His	Arg	U
	Leu	Pro	His	Arg	C
	Leu	Pro	Gln	Arg	A
	Leu	Pro	Gln	Arg	G
A	Ile	Thr	Asn	Ser	U
	Ile	Thr	Asn	Ser	C
	Ile	Thr	Lys	Arg	A
	Met (CI)	Thr	Lys	Arg	G
G	Val	Ala	Asp	Gly	U
	Val	Ala	Asp	Gly	C
	Val	Ala	Glu	Gly	A
	Val	Ala	Glu	Gly	G

*The terms first, second, and third nucleotide refer to the individual nucleotides of a triplet codon. U = uridine nucleotide; C = cytosine nucleotide; A = adenine nucleotide; G = guanine nucleotide; CI = chain initiator codon; CT = chain terminator codon. (Abbreviations of amino acids are explained in Chapter 3.)

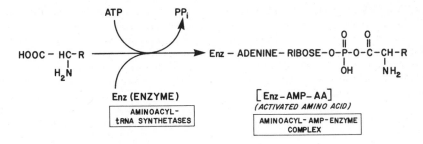

Figure 26–2. Activation of amino acids by the formation of an enzyme-AMP-amino acid complex. The formation of the complex is catalyzed by the specific aminoacyl-tRNA synthetase itself.

enzyme for each of the 20 amino acids. These enzymes are termed **aminoacyl-tRNA synthetases.** They form an activated intermediate of aminoacyl-AMP-enzyme complex as depicted in Fig 26–2. The specific amino-acyl-AMP-enzyme complex then recognizes a specific tRNA to which it attaches the aminoacyl moiety at the 3′-hydroxyl adenosine terminus (Fig 26–3). The amino acid remains attached to its specific tRNA in an ester linkage until it is polymerized at a specific position in the fabrication of a polypeptide precursor of a protein molecule.

The common features of tRNA molecules are diagrammatically represented in Fig 26–4. The 3′-hydroxyl terminus possesses an A·C·C sequence which, as described in Chapter 25, is continually turning over in the cell cytoplasm. At the 3′-hydroxyl adenosyl terminus, the specific amino acid is attached through an ester bond. The thymidine-pseudouridine-cytidine (T·Ψ·C) loop is involved in the binding of the aminoacyl-tRNA to the ribosomal surface at the site of protein synthesis. There exists an extra arm (the lump) which is variable among the different species of tRNA molecules. The loop containing dihydrouracil (DHU loop) is one of the sites important for the proper recognition of a given tRNA species by its proper charging enzyme or aminoacyl-tRNA synthetase.

The anticodon loop exists at a pole of the tRNA molecule quite distant from the pole to which the aminoacyl moiety is attached. The anticodon loop of tRNA molecules consists of 7 nucleotides. The sequence read from the 3′ to 5′ direction in that anti-

codon loop consists of a variable base·modified purine·X·Y·Z·pyrimidine·pyrimidine-5′. Note that this direction of reading the anticodon is 3′ to 5′, whereas the genetic code in Table 26–1 is read 5′ to 3′, since the codon and the anticodon loop of the mRNA and tRNA molecules, respectively, are antiparallel in their complementarity.

Fig 25–3 is a schematic diagram of the 3-dimensional structure of yeast phenylalanine tRNA as deduced from x-ray crystallographic studies.

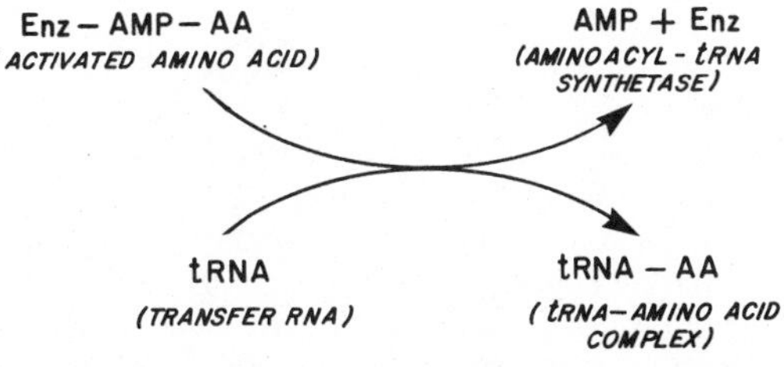

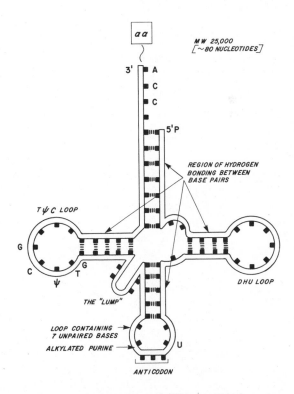

Figure 26–4. A typical aminoacyl-tRNA in which the amino acid is attached to the 3′ A·C·C terminus. The anticodon, TΨC, and DHU loops are indicated, as are the positions of the intramolecular hydrogen bonding between base pairs. (From James D. Watson, *Molecular Biology of the Gene,* 3rd ed. Copyright © 1976, 1970, 1965, by W.A. Benjamin, Inc, Menlo Park, California.)

Figure 26–3. Formation of the aminoacyl-tRNA from the activated amino acid and the appropriate tRNA. During the formation of the aminoacyl-tRNA complex, AMP and the aminoacyl-tRNA synthetase enzyme are released.

The degeneracy of the genetic code resides mostly in the last nucleotide of the codon triplet, suggesting that the base pairing between this last nucleotide and the corresponding nucleotide of the anticodon is not strict. This phenomenon is referred to as **wobble;** the pairing of the codon and anticodon can "wobble" at this specific nucleotide-to-nucleotide pairing site. This is depicted in Fig 26–5, in which the 2 anticodons for arginine, A·G·A and A·G·G, can bind to the same codon having a uracil at its 5′ end. Similarly, 3 codons for glycine, G·G·U, G·G·C, and G·G·A, are shown base-pairing with one anticodon, C·C·I. I is an inosine nucleotide, another of the peculiar bases appearing in tRNA molecules.

The codon recognition by a tRNA molecule does not depend upon the amino acid that is attached at its 3′-hydroxyl terminus. This has been ingeniously demonstrated by charging a tRNA specific for cysteine (tRNA$_{cys}$) with radioactively labeled cysteine. By chemical means, the cysteinyl residue was then altered to generate a tRNA molecule specific for cysteine but charged instead with alanine. The chemical transformation of the cysteinyl to the alanyl moiety did not alter the anticodon portion of the cysteine-specific tRNA molecule. When this alanyl-tRNA$_{cys}$ was used in the translation of a hemoglobin mRNA, a radioactive alanine was incorporated at what was normally a cysteine site in the hemoglobin protein molecule. The experi-

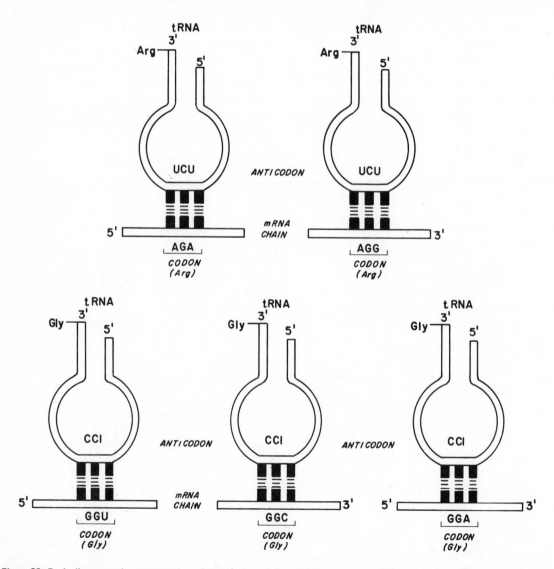

Figure 26–5. A diagrammatic representation of the binding of arginyl-tRNA and glycyl-tRNA to their respective codons of the mRNA chain. Note the antiparallel relationship of the tRNA and mRNAs and the "wobble" or lack of stringency of the base pairing between the nucleotide at the 5′ terminus of the anticodon loop and that at the 3′ terminus of the codon. I represents inosinate in phosphodiester linkage. (From James D. Watson, *Molecular Biology of the Gene,* 3rd ed. Copyright © 1976, 1970, 1965, by W.A. Benjamin, Inc, Menlo Park, California.)

ment demonstrated that the aminoacyl derivative of an aminoacyl-tRNA molecule does not play a role in the codon recognition. As already noted, the aminoacyl moiety never comes in contact with the template mRNA containing the codons.

Mutations

A mutation is a change in the nucleotide sequence of a gene. Although the initial change may not occur in the sense strand of the double-stranded DNA molecule for that gene, after replication, daughter DNA molecules with mutations in the sense strand will segregate and appear in the population of organisms. Single base changes may be **transitions** or **transversions**. In the former, a given pyrimidine is changed to the other pyrimidine or a given purine is changed to the other purine. Transversions are changes from a purine to either of the 2 pyrimidines or the change of a pyrimidine into either of the 2 purines, as shown in Fig 26−6.

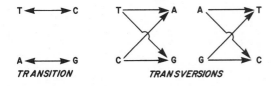

TRANSITION   **TRANSVERSIONS**

Figure 26−6. Diagrammatic representation of transition mutations and transversion mutations.

If the nucleotide sequence of the gene containing the mutation is transcribed into an mRNA molecule, then the mRNA molecule will possess a complementary base change at this corresponding locus.

Single base changes in the mRNA molecules may have one of several effects when translated into protein:

(1) There may be **no detectable effect** because of the degeneracy of the code. This would be more likely if the changed base in the mRNA molecule were to fall on the third nucleotide of a codon. The translation of a codon is least sensitive to a change at the third position.

(2) A **missense** effect will occur when a different amino acid is incorporated at the corresponding site in the protein molecule. This mistaken amino acid or missense, depending upon its location in the specific protein, might be **acceptable, partially acceptable,** or **unacceptable** to the function of that protein molecule. From a careful examination of the genetic code, one can conclude that most single-base changes would result in the replacement of one amino acid by another with rather similar functional groups. This is an effective mechanism to avoid drastic change in the physical properties of a protein molecule. If an acceptable missense effect occurs, the resulting protein molecule may not be distinguishable from the normal one. A partially acceptable missense will result in a protein molecule

with partial but abnormal function. If an unacceptable missense effect occurs, then the protein molecule will not be capable of functioning in its assigned role.

(3) A **nonsense** codon may appear which would then result in the **premature termination** of amino acid incorporation into a peptide chain and the production of only a fragment of the intended protein molecule. The probability is high that a prematurely terminated protein molecule would not function in its assigned role.

Much information is available on the amino acid sequences of the normal and abnormal human hemoglobins (see Chapter 32). The hemoglobin molecule can be used to demonstrate the effects of single-base changes in the hemoglobin structural gene. The **lack of effect** of a single-base change would be demonstrable only by sequencing the nucleotides in the messenger RNA molecules or structural genes for hemoglobin from a large number of humans with normal hemoglobin molecules. However, it can be deduced that the codon for valine at position 67 of the β chain of hemoglobin is not identical in all persons possessing the normal β chain of hemoglobin. Hemoglobin Milwaukee has at position 67 a glutamic acid; hemoglobin Bristol contains aspartic acid at position 67. In order to account for the amino acid change by the change of a single nucleotide residue in the codon for amino acid 67, one must infer that the precursor of hemoglobin Bristol possessed a G·U·U or G·U·C codon prior to a later change to G·A·U or G·A·C, both codons for aspartic acid (Fig 26−7). However the precursor of hemoglobin Milwaukee would have to possess at position 67 a codon G·U·A or G·U·G in order that a single nucleotide change could provide for the appearance of the glutamic acid codons G·A·A or G·A·G. Hemoglobin Sydney, which contains an alanine at position 67, could have arisen by the change of a single nucleotide in any of the 4 codons for valine (G·U·U, G·U·C, G·U·A, or G·U·G) to the alanine codons (G·C·U, G·C·C, G·C·A, or G·C·G, respectively).

An example of an **acceptable missense** mutation (Fig 26−8, top) in the structural gene for the β chain of hemoglobin could be detected by the presence of an electrophoretically altered hemoglobin in the red cells of an apparently healthy individual. Hemoglobin Hikari has been found in at least 2 families of Japanese people. This hemoglobin has asparagine substituted for lysine at the 61 position in the β chain. The corresponding transversion might be either A·A·A or A·A·G changed to either A·A·U or A·A·C. The replacement of the specific lysine with asparagine apparently does not alter the normal function of the β chain in these individuals.

A **partially acceptable missense** mutation (Fig 26−8, center) is best exemplified by hemoglobin S, sickle hemoglobin, in which the normal amino acid in position 6 of the β chain, glutamic acid, has been replaced by valine. The corresponding single nucleotide change within the codon would be G·A·A or G·A·G of glutamic acid to G·U·A or G·U·G of valine. Clear-

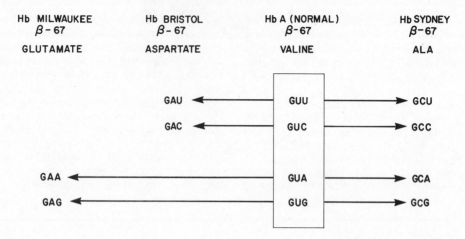

Figure 26–7. The normal valine at position 67 of the β chain of hemoglobin A can be coded for by one of the 4 codons shown in the box. In abnormal hemoglobin Milwaukee, the amino acid at position 67 of the β chain contains glutamate, coded for by G·A·A or G·A·G, either one of which could have resulted from a single-step transversion from the valine codons G·U·A or G·U·G. Similarly, the alanine present at position 67 of the β chain of hemoglobin Sydney could have resulted from a single-step transition from any one of the 4 valine codons. However, the aspartate residue at position 67 of hemoglobin Bristol could have resulted from a single-step transversion only from the G·U·U or G·U·C valine codons.

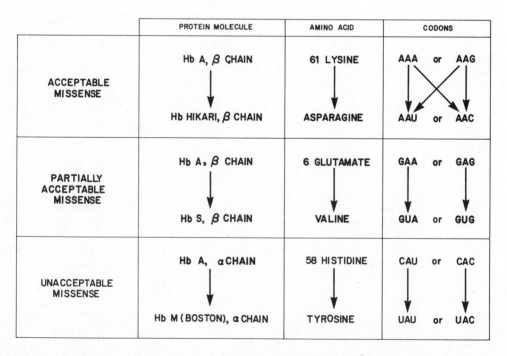

Figure 26–8. Examples of 3 types of missense mutations resulting in abnormal hemoglobin chains. The amino acid alterations and possible alterations in the respective codons are indicated. The hemoglobin Hakari β chain mutation has apparently normal physiologic properties but is electrophoretically altered. Hemoglobin S has a β chain mutation and partial function; hemoglobin S combines oxygen but precipitates when deoxygenated. Hemoglobin M Boston, an α chain mutation, permits the oxidation of the heme ferrous iron to the ferric state and thus will not bind oxygen at all.

ly, this missense mutation hinders normal function and results in sickle cell anemia when the mutant gene is present in the homozygous state. The glutamate-to-valine change may be considered to be partially acceptable because hemoglobin S does bind and release oxygen.

An **unacceptable missense** mutation (Fig 26–8, bottom) in a hemoglobin gene generates a nonfunctioning hemoglobin molecule. For example, the hemoglobin M mutations generate molecules which allow the Fe^{2+} of the heme moiety to be oxidized to Fe^{3+}, producing methemoglobin. Methemoglobin cannot transport oxygen.

Frame shift mutations as a result of the deletion or insertion of nucleotides in the gene generate altered nucleotide sequences of mRNA molecules. The deletion of a single nucleotide from the sense strand of a gene would result in an altered reading frame in the mRNA. The machinery translating the mRNA would not recognize that a base was missing since there is no punctuation in the reading of codons. A severe alteration in the sequence of polymerized amino acids, as depicted in Fig 26–9, would result. Altering the reading frame would result in a garbled translation of the mRNA distal to the single nucleotide deletion. Not only would the sequence of amino acids distal to this

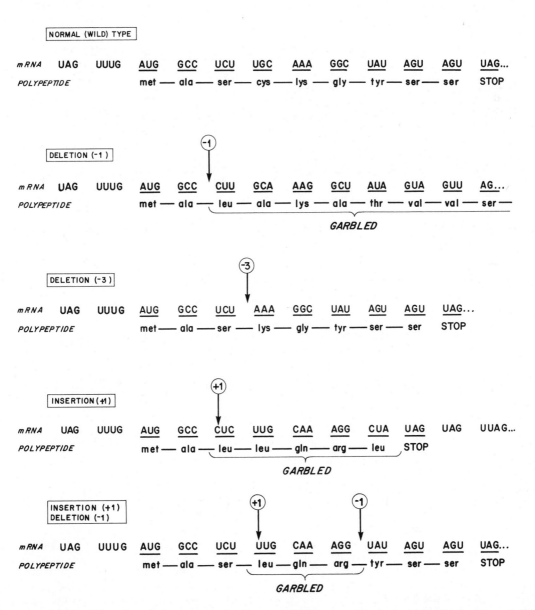

Figure 26–9. Demonstration of the effects of deletions and insertions in a gene on the sequence of the mRNA transcript and of the polypeptide chain translated therefrom. The arrows indicate the sites of deletions or insertions, and the numbers in the circles indicate the number of nucleotide residues deleted or inserted.

deletion be garbled, but the reading of the message might also result in the appearance of a nonsense codon and thus the production of a polypeptide prematurely terminated and garbled near its carboxyl terminus.

If 3 nucleotides or a multiple of 3 were deleted from a gene, the corresponding messenger when translated would provide a protein from which is missing the corresponding number of amino acids. Because the reading frame is a triplet, the reading phase would not be disturbed for those codons distal to the deletion. If, however, deletion of one or 2 nucleotides occurs just prior to or within the normal termination codon (nonsense codon), the reading of the normal termination signal would then be disturbed. Such a deletion might result in reading through a termination signal until another nonsense codon was encountered. Excellent examples of this phenomenon are described above in the discussion of hemoglobinopathies.

Insertions of one or 2 or nonmultiples of 3 nucleotides into a gene will result in an mRNA in which the reading frame will be distorted upon translation, and the same effects that occur with deletions would be reflected in the mRNA translation. This may be **garbled amino acid sequences** distal to the insertion, the generation of a **nonsense codon** at or distal to the insertion, or perhaps **reading through** the normal termination codon. Following a deletion in a gene, an insertion (or vice versa) can reestablish the proper reading frame. The corresponding mRNA, when translated, would contain a garbled amino acid sequence between the insertion and deletion. Beyond the reestablishment of the reading frame, the amino acid sequence would be correct. One can imagine that different combinations of deletions, of insertions, or of deletions and insertions would result in formation of a protein wherein a portion is abnormal, but this portion is surrounded by the normal amino acid sequences. Such phenomena have been demonstrated convincingly in the bacteriophage T4, a finding which contributed significantly to establishment of evidence that the reading frame is a triplet.

The hemoglobinopathies again provide examples of the effects of frame shift mutations. Generally, fragments of normal proteins resulting from premature termination or proteins containing significant portions which are garbled are rapidly degraded in the cell by normal protein monitoring processes. Examples are not currently available of hemoglobins demonstrating premature termination mutations or significant fractions which are garbled distal to deletions or insertions.

Hemoglobin Wayne results from a frame shift mutation at position 138 of the structural gene for the hemoglobin a chain. As shown in Fig 26—10, an adenosine nucleotide has been deleted so that the codon for amino acid 139 has been changed from A·A·A to A·A·U. The distal reading frame has been altered so that the normal termination signal, U·A·A, is read through but is out of phase. This results in the addition of 5 amino acids to the terminally garbled 3 amino acids of the protein. The reading is terminated when a new termination signal, U·A·G, appears in the out-of-phase reading.

Also shown in Fig 26—10 are 2 other mutants in the gene for the a chain of hemoglobin that result in an altered termination signal. In hemoglobin Icaria the normal termination signal U·A·A has been altered by a single base change to A·A·A in the mRNA, allowing the peptide-synthesizing machinery to read through this normal termination signal. Similarly, the first nucleotide of the normal termination signal U·A·A has been changed to a C in the message for hemoglobin Constant Spring. This mutation results in the addition of a similar abnormal peptide at the carboxy terminus of the a chain of the hemoglobin molecule.

Fig 26—11 summarizes the chain termination mutants which effect the codon U·A·A at position 142 of the a chain of the hemoglobin molecule. Note that all but 2 of the predicted mutations have been observed. Note also that, because of the degeneracy of the termination signal, 2 of the nucleotide changes (to U·G·A or to U·A·G) would not be detectable by examination of the hemoglobin molecule.

The above discussion of the altered protein products of gene mutations is based on the presence of normally functioning tRNA molecules. However, in prokaryotic and lower eukaryotic organisms, **abnormally functioning tRNA molecules** have been discovered which are themselves the results of mutations. Some of these abnormal tRNA molecules are capable of suppressing the effects of mutations in distant structural genes. These **suppressor tRNA molecules,** usually as the result of alterations in their anticodon regions, are capable of suppressing missense mutations, nonsense mutations, and frame shift mutations. However, since the suppressor tRNA molecules are not capable of distinguishing between a normal codon and one resulting from a gene mutation, their presence in a cell usually results in decreased viability. For instance, the nonsense suppressor tRNA molecules can suppress the normal termination signals to allow a read-through when this is not desirable. Frame shift suppressor tRNA molecules may read a normal codon plus a component of a juxtaposed codon to provide a frame shift, also when it is not desirable. Suppressor tRNA molecules have not been found in mammalian cells.

Protein Synthesis

The general structural characteristics of ribosomes and their self-assembly process have been discussed in Chapter 25. These particulate entities serve as the machinery on which the mRNA nucleotide sequence is translated into the sequence of amino acids of the specified protein. The translation of the mRNA commences near its 5′ terminus with the formation of the corresponding amino terminus of the protein molecule. The message is read toward its 3′ terminus, concluding with the formation of the carboxy terminus of the protein. As described in Chapter 25, the transcription of a gene into the corresponding mRNA or its precursor first forms the 5′ terminus of the RNA mole-

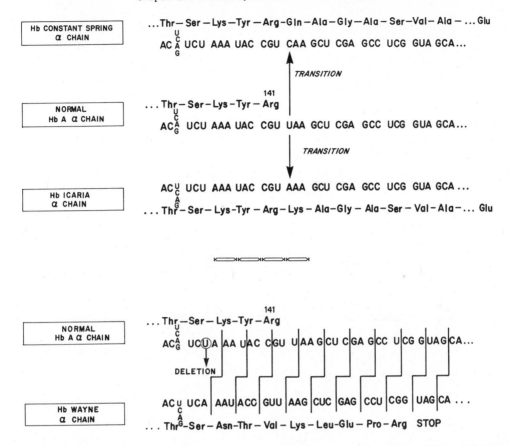

Figure 26—10. The demonstration of the effects of transitions or a deletion in the end of the hemoglobin α chain gene. Three abnormal hemoglobin molecules can result. The vertical lines in the lower portion represent the reading frame in the mRNA for hemoglobin Wayne and its origin.

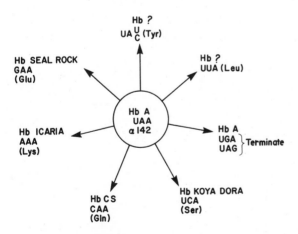

Figure 26—11. The results of all possible alterations of the normal termination signal (U·A·A) at position 142 of the mRNA for the α chain of hemoglobin A. Hemoglobin CS represents hemoglobin Constant Spring, and the hemoglobins with tyrosine or leucine at position 142 have yet to be discovered. (Redrawn and reproduced, with permission, from Weatherall DJ: Molecular pathology of the thalassemia disorders. West J Med 124:388, 1976.)

cule. In prokaryotes this allows for the beginning of mRNA translation before the transcription of the gene is completed. In eukaryotic organisms, the process of transcription is a nuclear one; mRNA translation occurs in the cytoplasm. This precludes simultaneous transcription and translation in eukaryotic organisms.

THE PROCESS OF PROTEIN SYNTHESIS

The process of protein synthesis, like that of gene transcription, can be described in 3 phases: initiation, elongation, and termination.

Initiation of Protein Synthesis (See Fig 26–12.)

The 5′ termini of most mRNA molecules in eukaryotes are "capped" as described in Chapter 25. This methyl-guanosyl triphosphate cap seems necessary for the binding of many mRNA molecules to the 40S ribosomal subunit. The first codon to be translated, usually A·U·G, is indented from the capped 5′ terminus. As the result of intramolecular base pairing, the 5′ por-

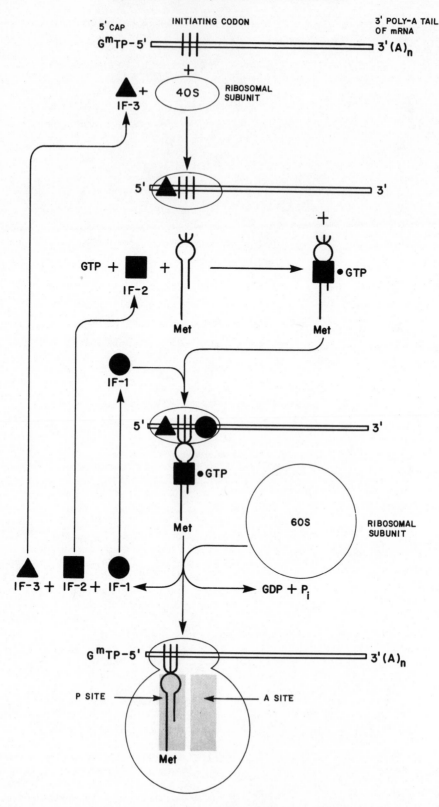

Figure 26–12. Diagrammatic representation of the initiation of protein synthesis on the mRNA template containing a 5' cap and 3' poly(A) terminus. IF-1, IF-2, and IF-3 represent initiation factor 1, initiation factor 2, and initiation factor 3, respectively; and the hairpinlike structure with Met at one end represents the methionyl tRNA. The P site and the A site represent the peptidyl tRNA and aminoacyl-tRNA binding sites of the ribosome, respectively.

tions of mRNA molecules have a secondary structure (folding) upon which the 40S ribosomal subunit depends for proper recognition of the first codon to be translated. The 18S ribosomal RNA (rRNA) of the 40S ribosomal subunit binds to a region of the mRNA that precedes the first translated codon. This binding of the mRNA to the 40S ribosomal subunit requires the presence of a protein factor, initiation factor 3 (IF-3).

The aminoacyl-tRNA called for by the first codon then interacts with GTP and initiation factor 2 (IF-2) to form a complex. This complex in the presence of initiation factor 1 (IF-1) attaches the anticodon of the tRNA to the first codon of the message to form an initiation complex with the 40S ribosomal subunit. Upon release of the initiation factors (IF-1, IF-2, and IF-3), the 60S ribosomal subunit attaches and the GTP is hydrolyzed. The formation of the 80S ribosome is thus complete.

The complete ribosome contains 2 sites for tRNA molecules. The peptidyl or **P site** contains the peptidyl-tRNA attached to its codon on the mRNA. The aminoacyl or **A site** contains the aminoacyl-tRNA attached to its respective codon on the mRNA. With the formation of the initiation complex for the first codon, the aminoacyl-tRNA molecule enters at what will become the P site, leaving the A site free. Thus, the reading frame is defined by attachment of the tRNA to the first codon to be translated in the mRNA. The recognition of this specific initiating codon is apparently dependent upon the secondary structure of the intramolecular base pairing of the mRNA molecule (Fig 26–13).

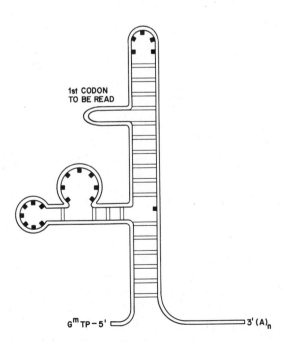

1st CODON TO BE READ

$G^m TP - 5'$ $3' (A)_n$

Figure 26–13. Diagrammatic representation of the suggested secondary structure of the mRNA of rabbit hemoglobin deduced from the known sequence of the corresponding gene.

In prokaryotes, a specific aminoacyl-tRNA is involved in the initiation of synthesis of most, if not all, protein molecules. N-Formylmethionyl-tRNA initiates most proteins in prokaryotes. Although methionine is the N-terminal amino acid in many eukaryotic proteins, the methionyl-tRNA is not formylated in eukaryotes. In prokaryotes, the N-formylation of the methionyl on the tRNA seems to deceive the P site of the ribosome by appearing to be a peptide bond. There exists also in prokaryotes an enzyme capable of removing the N-terminal formyl moiety or N-terminal methionly residue (or both) from proteins, in many cases even before the complete protein molecule has been formed.

Elongation

In the complete 80S ribosome formed during the process of initiation, the A site is free. The binding of the proper aminoacyl-tRNA in the A site requires proper codon recognition. Elongation factor 1 (EF-1) forms a complex with GTP and the entering aminoacyl-tRNA (Fig 26–14). This complex then allows the aminoacyl-tRNA to enter the A site with the release of EF-1·GDP and phosphate. As shown in Fig 26–12, EF-1·GDP then recycles to EF-1·GTP with the aid of other soluble protein factors and GTP.

The a amino group of the new aminoacyl-tRNA in the A site carries out a nucleophilic attack on the esterified carboxyl group of the peptidyl-tRNA occupying the P site. This reaction is catalyzed by a protein component, **peptidyl transferase**, of the 60S ribosomal subunit. Because the amino acid on the aminoacyl-tRNA is already "activated," no further energy source is required for this reaction. The reaction results in attachment of the growing peptide chain to the tRNA in the A site.

Upon removal of the peptidyl moiety from the tRNA in the P site, the discharged tRNA quickly vacates the P site. Elongation factor 2 (EF-2) and GTP are responsible for the **translocation** of the newly formed peptidyl-tRNA at the A site into the vacated P site. The GTP required for EF-2 is hydrolyzed to GDP and phosphate during the translocation process. The translocation of the newly formed peptidyl-tRNA and its corresponding codon into the P site then frees the A site for another cycle of aminoacyl-tRNA codon recognition and elongation.

The energy requirements for the formation of one peptide bond include the equivalent of the hydrolysis of 2 ATP molecules to ADP and 2 GTP molecules to GDP. The charging of the tRNA molecule with the aminoacyl moiety requires the hydrolysis of an ATP to an AMP, equivalent to the hydrolysis of 2 ATPs to 2 ADPs and phosphates. The entry of the aminoacyl-tRNA into the A site results in the hydrolysis of one GTP to GDP. The translocation of the newly formed peptidyl-tRNA in the A site into the P site by EF-2 similarly results in the hydrolysis of GTP to GDP and phosphate.

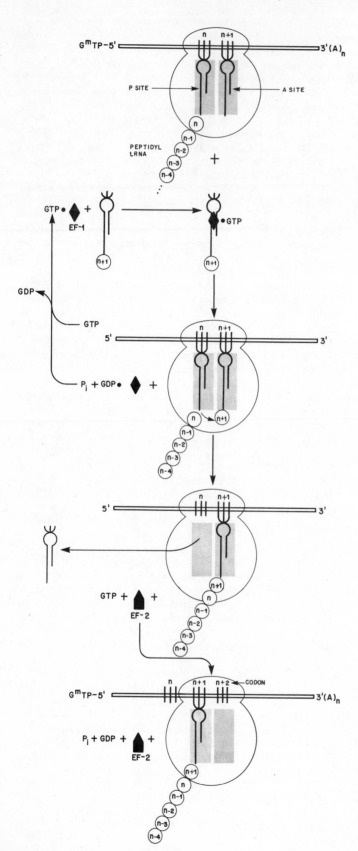

Figure 26–14. Diagrammatic representation of the peptide elongation process of protein synthesis. The small circles labeled n-1, n, n+1, etc represent the amino acid residues of the newly formed protein molecule. EF-1 and EF-2 represent elongation factors 1 and 2, respectively. The peptidyl-tRNA and aminoacyl-tRNA sites on the ribosome are represented by P site and A site, respectively.

Termination

After multiple cycles of elongation culminating in polymerization of the specific amino acids into a protein molecule, the nonsense or terminating codon of mRNA appears in the A site. There is no tRNA with an anticodon to recognize such a termination signal. **Releasing factors** are capable of recognizing that a termi- nation signal resides in the A site (Fig 26–15). The releasing factor hydrolyzes the bond between the pep- tide and the tRNA occupying the P site. This hydroly- sis releases the protein and the tRNA from the P site. Upon hydrolysis and release, the **80S ribosome dissoci- ates** into its 40S and 60S subunits, which are then recycled.

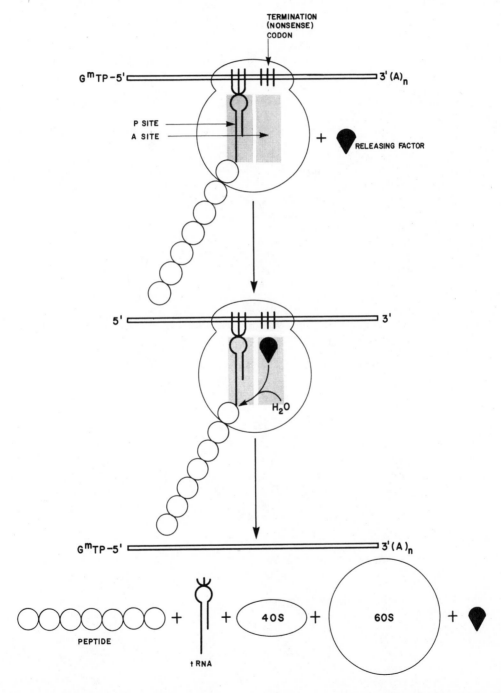

Figure 26–15. Diagrammatic representation of the termination process of protein synthesis. The peptidyl-tRNA and aminoacyl- tRNA sites are indicated as P site and A site, respectively. The hydrolysis of the peptidyl-tRNA complex is shown by the entry of H_2O.

The releasing factors are proteins—one of which (releasing factor 1) hydrolyzes the peptide bond when a U·A·A or U·A·G codon occupies the A site. The other, releasing factor 2, hydrolyzes the peptidyl-tRNA bond when either the U·A·A or the U·G·A codon occupies the A site.

Many ribosomes can translate the same mRNA molecule simultaneously. Because of their relatively large size, the ribosome particles cannot attach to an mRNA any closer than 80 nucleotides apart. Multiple ribosomes on the same mRNA molecule form a **polyribosome** or "polysome." In an unrestricted system, the number of ribosomes attached to an mRNA and thus the size of polyribosomes correlates positively with the length of the mRNA molecule. The mass of the mRNA molecule is, of course, quite small compared to the mass of even a single ribosome.

A single ribosome is capable of translating in 10 seconds about 400 codons into a protein with a molecular weight of approximately 40,000.

Polyribosomes actively synthesizing proteins can exist as free particles in the cellular cytoplasm or may be attached to sheets of membranous cytoplasmic material referred to as endoplasmic reticulum. The attachment of the particulate polyribosomes to the endoplasmic reticulum is responsible for their "rough" appearance as seen by electron microscopy. The proteins synthesized by the attached polyribosomes are extruded into the cisternal space between the sheets of rough endoplasmic reticulum and are exported from there. Some of the protein products of the rough endoplasmic reticulum are packaged by the Golgi apparatus into zymogen particles for eventual exportation. The polyribosomal particles free in the cytosol are responsible for the synthesis of proteins required for intracellular functions.

Protein Processing

Some animal viruses, notably poliovirus (an RNA virus), synthesize long polycistronic proteins from one long mRNA molecule. These protein molecules are subsequently cleaved at specific sites to provide the several specific proteins required for viral function. In animal cells, many proteins are modified following their synthesis from the mRNA template. Insulin, a low-molecular-weight protein of 2 polypeptide chains with interchain and intrachain disulfide bridges, is synthesized as a proinsulin molecule. The single polypeptide proinsulin folds to allow the disulfide bridges to form, and then a specific protease clips out a segment at the head of the hairpin (Fig 29–12). These posttranslational modifications are responsible for generation of the functional insulin molecule.

Many other peptide hormones are synthesized as **prohormones** which require modification before attaining biologic activity. Many of the posttranslational modifications involve the removal of N-terminal amino acid residues by specific aminopeptidases. Collagen, an abundant protein in the extracellular spaces of higher eukaryotes, is synthesized as procollagen. Three procollagen molecules, frequently not identical in sequence, align themselves in a way dependent upon the existence of specific amino terminal peptides. Specific enzymes then carry out hydroxylations and oxidations of specific amino acid residues within the procollagen molecules to provide cross-links for greater stability. Amino terminal peptides are cleaved off the molecule to form the final product, a strong insoluble collagen molecule.

Inhibitors of Protein Synthesis

Many clinically effective antibiotics act by specifically inhibiting protein synthesis in prokaryotic organisms. Most of these inhibitors interact specifically with the proteins of prokaryotic ribosomes. A number of the effective antibiotics do not interact with the specific proteins of eukaryotic ribosomal particles and are thus not toxic to eukaryotes.

Puromycin, the structure of which is shown in Fig 26–16, is a structural analog of tyrosinyl-tRNA. Puromycin is incorporated via the A site on the ribosome into the carboxyl terminal position of a peptide but

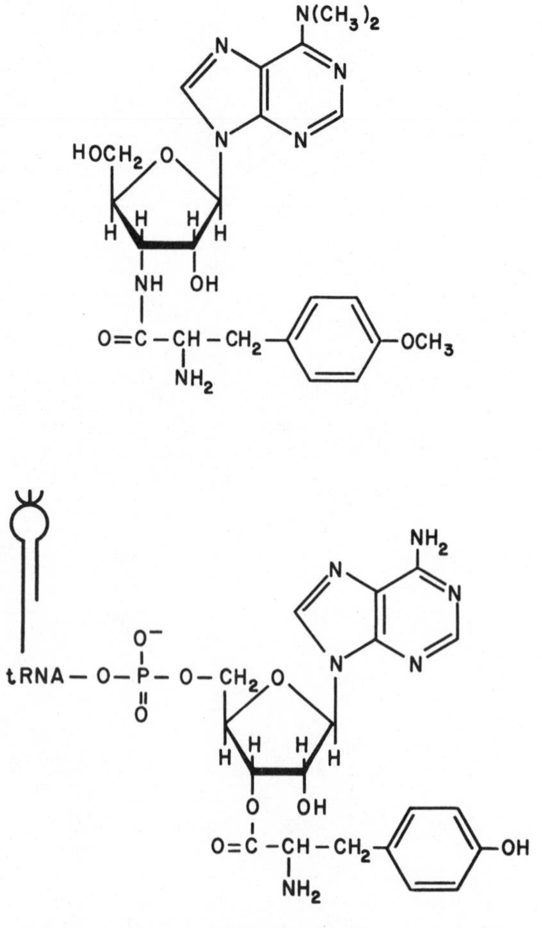

Figure 26–16. The comparative structures of the antibiotic puromycin and the 3′ terminal portion of tyrosyl-tRNA.

causes the premature release of the polypeptide. Puromycin, as a tyrosinyl-tRNA analog, effectively inhibits protein synthesis in both prokaryotes and eukaryotes.

Diphtheria toxin, an exotoxin of *Corynebacterium diphtheriae* infected with a specific lysogenic phage, catalyzes the ADP ribosylation of EF-2 in mammalian cells. This modification inactivates EF-2 and thereby specifically inhibits mammalian protein synthesis. Many organisms such as mice are resistant to diphtheria toxin. This resistance is due to inability of diphtheria toxin to cross the cell membrane rather than to insensitivity of mouse EF-2 to diphtheria toxin – catalyzed ADP ribosylation by NAD.

●　　●　　●

References

Drake JW, Baltz RH: The biochemistry of mutagenesis. Annu Rev Biochem 45:11, 1976.

Haselkorn R, Rothman-Denes LB: Protein synthesis. Annu Rev Biochem 42:397, 1973.

Roth JR: Frameshift mutations. Annu Rev Genet 8:319, 1974.

Schlessinger D: Genetic and antibiotic modification of protein synthesis. Annu Rev Genet 8:135, 1974.

Shafritz DA & others: Evidence for the role of $M^7G^{5'}$-phosphate group in recognition of eukaryotic mRNA by inhibition factor IF-M$_3$. Nature 261:291, 1976.

Weatherall D: Molecular pathology of the thalassemia disorders. West J Med 124:388, 1976.

Weissbach G, Ochoa S: Soluble factors required for eukaryotic protein synthesis. Annu Rev Biochem 45:191, 1976.

27...
Regulation of Gene Expression

The genetic information present in each somatic cell of a metazoan organism is practically identical. The exceptions are found in those few cells which have amplified genes in order to carry out specialized cellular functions. The expression of the genetic information must be regulated during ontogeny and differentiation of the organism and its cellular components. Furthermore, in order for the organism to adapt to its environment and to conserve energy and nutrients, the expression of genetic information must be responsive to extrinsic signals. As organisms have evolved, more sophisticated regulatory mechanisms have appeared to provide the organism and its cells with the responsiveness necessary for survival in its complex environment. Mammalian cells possess only about 1000 times more genetic information than does the bacterium *E coli;* however, much of this additional genetic information is involved in the regulation of gene expression.

In simple terms, there are only 2 types of gene regulation: **positive regulation** and **negative regulation** (Table 27–1). When the expression of genetic information is quantitatively **increased** by the presence of a specific regulatory molecule, regulation is said to be **positive;** whereas when the expression of genetic information is **diminished** by the presence of a specific regulatory molecule, regulation is said to be **negative.** The molecule mediating the negative regulation is said to be a negative regulator; that mediating positive regulation is a positive regulator. However, a **double negative** has the effect of acting as a **positive.** Thus, an effector which inhibits the function of a negative regulator will appear to bring about a positive regulation. In many regulated systems which appear to be induced, they are, in fact, derepressed at the molecular level. (See Chapter 7 for a description of these terms.)

In biologic organisms there are 3 types of temporal responses to a regulatory signal. These 3 responses are depicted diagrammatically in Fig 27–1 as rate of gene expression in temporal response to an inducing signal.

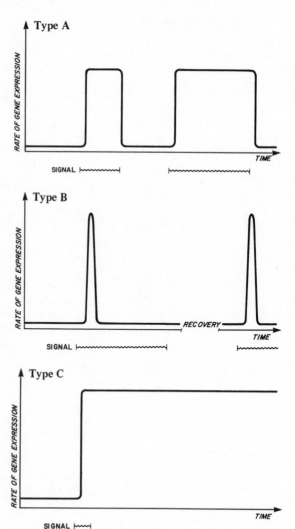

Figure 27–1. Diagrammatic representations of the responses of the rate of expression of a gene to specific regulatory signals such as a hormone.

Table 27–1. Effects of positive and negative regulation on gene expression.

	Rate of Gene Expression	
	Negative Regulation	**Positive Regulation**
Regulator present	Decreased	Increased
Regulator absent	Increased	Decreased

A **type A response** is characterized by an increased rate of gene expression which is **dependent** upon the continued presence of the inducing signal. When the inducing signal is removed, the rate of gene expression diminishes to its basal level, but the rate repeatedly increases in response to the reappearance of the specific signal. This type of response is commonly observed in many higher organisms after exposures to inducers such as steroid hormones.

A **type B response** exhibits an increased rate of gene expression which is **transient** even in the continued presence of the regulatory signal. After the regulatory signal has terminated and the cell has been allowed to recover, a second transient response to a subsequent regulatory signal may be observed. This type of response may commonly occur during development of an organism when only the transient appearance of a specific gene product is required although the signal persists.

The **type C response** pattern exhibits, in response to the regulatory signal, an increased rate of gene expression which persists **indefinitely** even after the termination of the signal. The signal acts as a trigger in this pattern. The response is typical of a differentiative process. Once the gene expression is initiated in the cell, it cannot be terminated even in the daughter cells; it is therefore an irreversible process.

Models for the Study of the Regulation of Gene Expression

In the last 20 years, with the understanding of how information flows from the gene through a messenger RNA to a specific protein molecule, there has developed sophisticated knowledge of the regulation of gene expression in prokaryotic cells. Most of the detailed knowledge about molecular mechanisms has been limited until recent years to prokaryotic and lower eukaryotic systems. This was due to the more advanced genetic analyses first available in the primitive organisms but yet to be obtained for mammalian cells or organisms. In this chapter, the discussion will center mostly on prokaryotic systems. The impressive genetic studies will not be described, but rather what may be termed the physiology of gene expression will be discussed. However, nearly all of the conclusions about this physiology have been derived from genetic studies.

Before the physiology can be explained, a few specialized genetic terms must be defined.

The **cistron** is the smallest unit of genetic expression. As described in Chapter 7, some enzymes and other protein molecules are composed of 2 or more nonidentical subunits. Thus, the so-called "one gene, one enzyme" concept is now known not to be necessarily valid. The cistron is the genetic unit coding for the structure of the subunit of a protein molecule, acting as it does as the smallest unit of genetic expression. Thus, the one gene – one enzyme idea might more accurately be regarded as a **one cistron – one subunit concept**.

An **inducible gene** is one the expression of which increases in response to an **inducer**, a specific regulatory signal.

The expression of some genes is constitutive, meaning that they are expressed at a reasonably high rate in the absence of any specific regulatory signal. As the result of mutation, some inducible gene products become constitutively expressed. A mutation resulting in constitutive expression of what was formerly an inducible gene is called a **constitutive mutation**.

The Lac Operon

François Jacob and Jacques Monod in 1961 described their **operon** model in what is now regarded as a classic paper. Their hypothesis was to a large extent based on observations on the regulation of lactose metabolism by the intestinal bacterium *E. coli*. The molecular mechanisms responsible for the regulation of the genes involved in the metabolism of lactose are among the best understood in any organism. β-Galactosidase hydrolyzes the β-galactoside lactose to galactose and glucose (Fig 27–2). The structural (Z) gene for β-galactosidase is clustered with the genes responsible for the permeation of galactose into the cell (Y) and for galactoside acetylase (A), whose function is not understood. The structural genes for these 3 enzymes are physically associated with regulatory genes

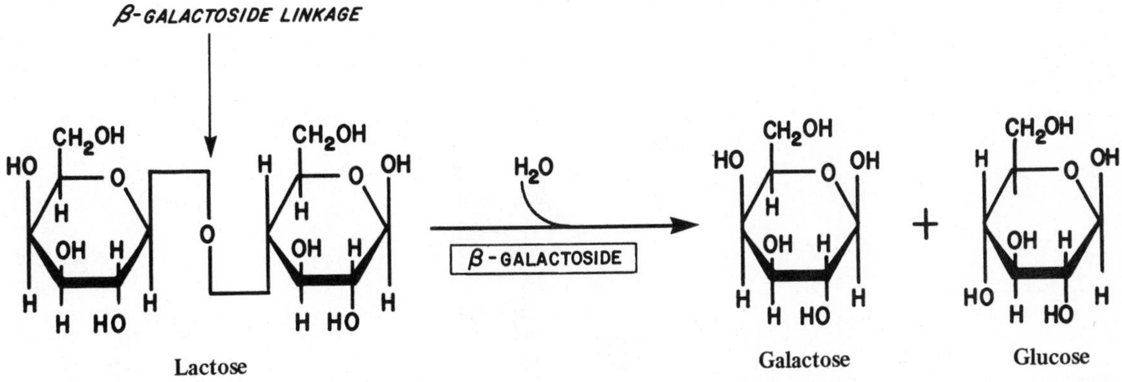

Figure 27–2. The hydrolysis by the enzyme β-galactosidase of lactose to galactose and glucose.

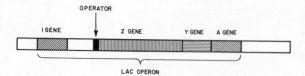

Figure 27—3. The positional relationships of the structural and regulatory genes of the lac operon.

to constitute the **lac operon** as depicted in Fig 27—3. This genetic arrangement of the structural genes and their regulatory genes allows for the **coordinate expression** of the 3 enzymes concerned with lactose metabolism.

When *E coli* is presented with lactose or some specific lactose analogs, the expression of the activities of β-galactosidase, galactoside permease, and galactoside acetylase is increased 10-fold to 100-fold. This is a type A response, as seen in Fig 27—1. Upon removal of the signal, ie, the inducer, the rate of synthesis of these 3 enzymes declines. Since there is no significant degradation of these enzymes in bacteria, the level of β-galactosidase as well as those of the other 2 enzymes will remain the same unless they are diluted out by cell division.

When *E coli* is exposed to both lactose and glucose as sources of carbon, the organisms first metabolize the glucose and then temporarily cease growing until the genes of the lac operon become induced to provide the ability to metabolize lactose. This type of growth in the presence of 2 carbon sources such as glucose and lactose is biphasic; it is termed **diauxie.** (Fig 27—4.)

Although lactose is present from the beginning of the bacterial growth phase, the cell does not commence to induce those enzymes necessary for catabolism of lactose until the glucose has been exhausted. This phenomenon was first thought to be

attributable to the repression of the lactose operon by some catabolite of glucose; hence it was termed **catabolite repression.** It is now known that "catabolite repression" is in fact mediated by a **catabolite gene activator protein (CAP)** and **cyclic AMP (cAMP).** The expression of many inducible enzyme systems or operons in *E coli* and other prokaryotes is sensitive to catabolite repression, as discussed below.

The physiology of the induction of the lac operon is well understood at the molecular level, and it will now be described (Fig 27—5).

The expression of the normal **i gene** of the lac operon is constitutive; it is expressed at a constant rate, resulting in the formation of the subunits of the **lac repressor.** Four subunits of MW 40,000 assemble into a lac repressor molecule. The repressor protein molecule, the product of the i gene, has a high affinity (formation constant of about 10^{11} molar) for the operator locus. The **operator locus** is between the **promoter site,** at which the DNA-dependent RNA polymerase attaches to commence transcription, and the beginning of the **Z gene,** the structural gene for β-galactosidase. When attached to the operator locus, the repressor molecule prevents the transcription of the operator locus as well as of the distal structural genes, Z, Y, and A. Thus, the repressor molecule is a **negative regulator;** in its presence the expression of the Z, Y, and A genes is prevented. There are normally present 20—40 repressor molecules and one or 2 operator loci per cell.

A lactose analog which is capable of inducing the lac operon while not itself serving as a substrate for β-galactosidase is called a **gratuitous inducer.** The addition of lactose or of a gratuitous inducer to bacteria growing on a limited carbon source (such as succinate) results in the prompt induction of β-galactosidase, permease, and acetylase. Small amounts of the gratuitous inducer or of lactose are able to enter the cell even in the absence of permease. The repressor molecules, both those attached to the operator loci and those free in the cytosol, have an affinity for the inducer. The binding of the inducer to a repressor molecule attached to the operator locus will cause the repressor to be detached. If DNA-dependent RNA polymerase has already attached to the sense strand at the promoter site, transcription will commence. The polymerase generates a polycistronic mRNA, the 5' terminus of which is complementary to the sense strand of the operator. In such a manner, an inducer derepresses the lac operon and allows the transcription of the structural genes for galactosidase, galactoside permease, and galactoside acetylase. The translation of the polycistronic mRNA can occur even before the transcription is completed. The derepression of the lac operon allows the cell to synthesize the enzymes necessary to catabolize lactose as an energy source. In order for the RNA polymerase to attach at the promoter site, there must also be present the catabolite gene activation protein (CAP) to which cAMP is attached. By an independent mechanism, the bacterium accumulates cAMP only when it is starved for a source of carbon. In the presence of glu-

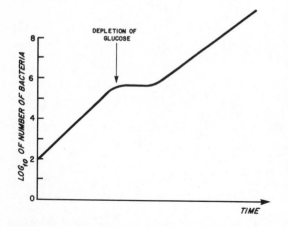

Figure 27—4. The rate of diauxic growth of *Escherichia coli* on a mixture of glucose and lactose.

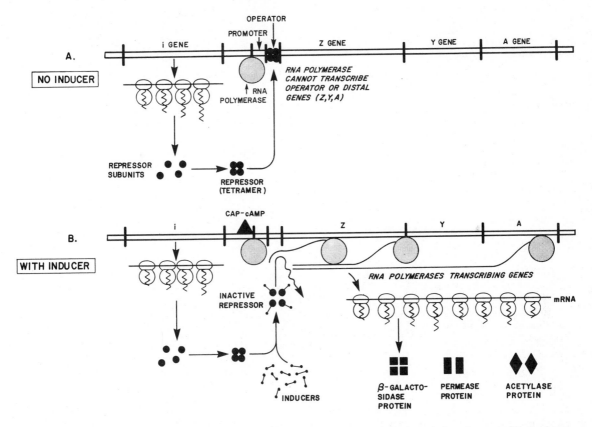

Figure 27—5. The mechanism of repression and of derepression of the lactose operon. When no inducer is present (A), the i gene products which are synthesized constitutively form a repressor molecule which binds at the operator locus to prevent the binding of RNA polymerase at the promoter locus and thus to prevent the subsequent transcription of the Z, Y, and A structural genes. When inducer is present, the constitutively expressed i gene forms repressor molecules which are inactivated by the inducer and cannot bind to the operator locus. In the presence of cAMP and its binding protein (CAP), the RNA polymerase can transcribe the structural genes Z, Y, and A, and the polycistronic mRNA molecule formed can be translated into the corresponding protein molecules β-galactosidase, permease, and acetylase, allowing for the catabolism of lactose.

cose or of glycerol in concentrations sufficient for growth, the bacteria will lack sufficient cAMP to bind to CAP. Thus, in the presence of glucose or glycerol, cAMP-saturated CAP is lacking, so that the DNA-dependent RNA polymerase cannot commence the transcription of the lac operon. In the presence of the CAP-cAMP complex on the promoter site, transcription then occurs. Thus, the CAP-cAMP regulator is acting as a **positive regulator** because its presence is required for gene expression. This phenomenon accounts for the diauxic growth of *E coli* on glucose and lactose.

With *E coli* wherein the i gene has been mutated so that its product, the lac repressor, is not capable of binding to DNA, the organism will exhibit **constitutive expression** of the lac operon. An organism with an i gene mutation that prevents the binding of an inducer to the repressor will remain repressed even in the presence of the inducer molecule because the inducer cannot bind to the repressor at the operator locus in order to derepress the operon.

Bacteria harboring mutations in their operator locus such that the operator sequence will not bind a normal repressor molecule are constitutive for the expression of the lac operon genes.

The Arabinose Operon

The structural genes of the arabinose operon in *E coli* are responsible for the formation of 3 enzymes required to metabolize arabinose. AraD, AraA, and AraB code for the enzymes L-ribulose-5-phosphate-4-epimerase, L-arabinose isomerase, and L-ribulokinase, respectively. (Fig 27—6.) The protein product of the AraC gene acts as a regulator and exists in 2 active conformational states. In the **P1** state the AraC gene product is the **repressor** and in the **P2** state it is the **activator**. P1, the repressor, binds to the AraO gene, the operator locus, to prevent the expression of the arabinose operon. The presence of L-arabinose, the first substrate for the pathway, changes the conformation of P1, the repressor, to P2, the activator. P2 binds to the i gene, also a regulatory site, and there promotes the expression of the arabinose gene. Thus, **P1 is a negative regulator and P2 a positive regulator,** and both

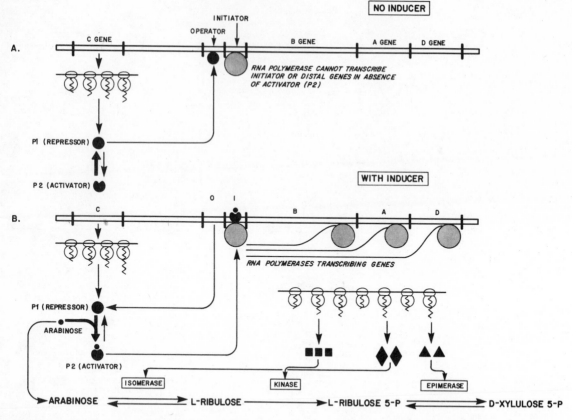

Figure 27—6. Diagrammatic representation of the repression *(A)* and induction *(B)* of the arabinose operon. When no inducer is present *(A)*, the C gene product—the repressor (P1)—binds at the operator locus, and the initiator locus lacks the activator (P2). Both conditions prevent the transcription of the distal B, A, and D genes by RNA polymerase. When inducer (arabinose) is present *(B)*, arabinose binds the C gene product—the P1 repressor—to form an activator (P2) molecule which can bind at the initiator site. The conversion of the P1 repressor to a P2 activator molecule not only shifts the equilibrium of the P1 repressor off the operator locus, but the presence of the P2 activator on the initiator locus allows the RNA polymerase to transcribe the distal structural genes B, A, and D. A messenger RNA transcribed from these genes can then be translated into the corresponding enzymes ribulokinase, isomerase, and polymerase, thus allowing the catabolism of arabinose.

are products of the **same gene,** AraC. The arabinose operon is also subject to catabolite repression. As expected, CAP-cAMP must bind at the controlling site in order for the structural genes of the arabinose operon to be expressed. Similarly, another regulatory nucleotide, guanosine tetraphosphate (ppGpp), stimulates the expression of the arabinose operon in a cell-free system. The mechanism of interaction of this latter regulatory nucleotide and the CAP-cAMP binding site is as yet unknown.

The Histidine Operon

Salmonella typhimurium is capable of synthesizing histidine from ATP and PPriboseP when this α-amino acid is not present in the environment. However, when the amino acid is present in the environment, histidine prevents the formation of those enzymes responsible for the de novo synthesis of histidine. Coding for the 10 enzymes required for the de novo synthesis of histidine is provided by 10 structural

Table 27—2. Relationship of His genes to histidine pathway enzymes.

His Gene	Enzyme
G	Phosphoribosyl-ATP synthetase
D	Dehydrogenase
C	Aminotransferase
B	Dehydratase
B	Phosphatase
H	Amidotransferase
A	Isomerase
F	Cyclase
I	Phosphoribosyl-AMP hydrolase
E	Phosphoribosyl-ATP pyrophosphohydrolase
S	Histidyl-tRNA synthetase

genes, all of which are genetically linked as the **histidine (His) operon.** The linkage map is shown in Fig 27—7.

In Table 27—2, the products of the 10 structural

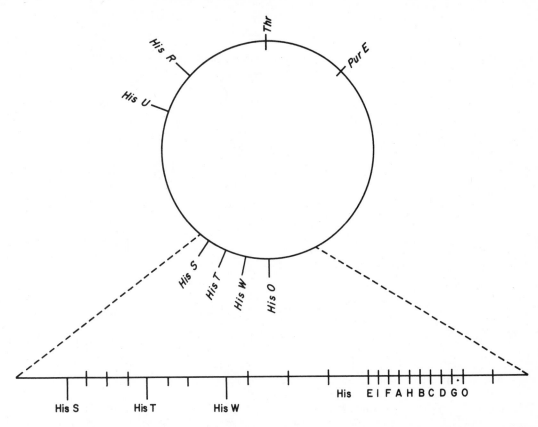

Figure 27—7. The genetic map of *Salmonella typhimurium* in which the His genes are represented and their relationship to threonine (Thr) and pure loci shown. (The portion of the salmonella genome which contains most of the His genes has been expanded in a linear form in the lower portion of the diagram.) (Redrawn and reproduced, with permission, from Brenner M, Ames BN: The histidine operon and its regulation. Chap 11 in: *Metabolic Regulation.* Vogel HJ [editor]. Vol 5 in: *Metabolic Pathways,* 3rd ed. Greenberg DM [editor]. Academic Press, 1971.)

genes are identified by the name of the enzyme. All 10 enzymes of the pathway are **coordinately expressed**.

There are in *S typhimurium* 6 gene mutations in 6 different genes which can cause constitutive expression of the His operon. The **His O** gene is the operator, and mutants in this region have an altered operator-promoter function. The **His S** gene codes for the histidinyl tRNA synthetase; **His R** gene is the structural gene for histidine tRNA. The **His W** gene codes for the tRNA maturation enzyme; and the **His T** gene codes for a protein which is responsible for the modification of 2 uridine residues to form pseudouridine in the His tRNA. The function of the **His U** gene is unknown. From the characterization of these genes, which, when altered, cause constitutive expression of the His operon, Ames and his colleagues have concluded that the histidinyl tRNA is involved directly or indirectly in the regulation of the expression of the His operon.

It has also been demonstrated that the first enzyme of the histidine de novo synthetic pathway (N-1,5'-phosphoribosyl-ATP:pyrophosphate phosphoribosyl transferase) (the product of the his G gene) specifically blocks the transcription of the histidine operon in vitro. It is not evident whether the histidinyl

tRNA interacts with the his G gene product to regulate in a negative manner the expression of the 10 structural genes of that operon.

The Regulation of Glutamine Synthetase Level in Cultured Mammalian Cells

Glutamine synthetase catalyzes the formation of glutamine from glutamate and ammonia. In mammalian cells, glutamine synthetase is not subject to the extensive allosteric regulation and adenylylation found in the corresponding enzyme in *E coli*. However, in cultured rat hepatoma cells, glucocorticoid hormones induce an increased rate of glutamine synthetase formation. (Fig 27—8.) Inhibitors of DNA-dependent RNA synthesis and inhibitors of protein synthesis prevent this 3- to 4-fold induction in the rate of synthesis of glutamine synthetase. The removal of the glucocorticoid effects a prompt decline in the rate of glutamine synthetase formation, a type A response. However, as with a number of other glucocorticoid-induced proteins, the "deinduction" upon the removal of the steroid hormone requires concomitant RNA synthesis. These observations imply the existence of an RNA molecule that rapidly turns over and is necessary for

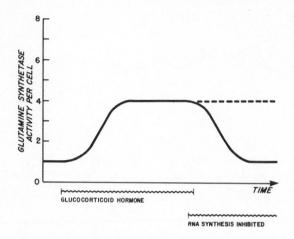

Figure 27–8. The induction of glutamine synthetase activity by the addition of glucocorticoid hormone to the culture medium of rat hepatoma cells. When the glucocorticoid hormone is removed, the activity of glutamine synthetase per cell declines back to the basal level (solid line). However, if RNA synthesis is inhibited prior to the removal of the glucocorticoid, the glutamine synthetase activity per cell does not decline (broken line).

deinduction (ie, repression). The molecule has not been identified. However, it is clear that the induction (or derepression) of glutamine synthetase and of another glucocorticoid-sensitive enzyme, tyrosine aminotransferase, is mediated by a steroid receptor protein with a high specific affinity for the glucocorticoid.

The removal of glutamine from the culture media in which cells of certain clones of rat hepatoma cells are growing effects a 15-fold increase in the level of glutamine synthetase activity (Fig 27–9). The increased accumulation of glutamine synthetase in response to deprivation of glutamine is secondary to a 15-fold decrease in the rate of glutamine synthetase

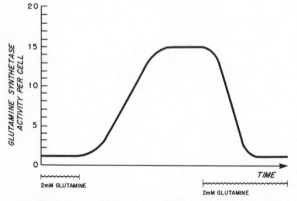

Figure 27–9. The effect of high (2 mmol) glutamine on glutamine synthetase activity per cell when added to the medium containing cultured rat hepatoma cells. When 2 mmol of glutamine are removed and replaced with a 10-fold lower concentration of glutamine, the activity of glutamine synthetase per cell increases 15-fold. The readdition of 2 mmol of glutamine results in a prompt decline in the glutamine synthetase activity per cell.

degradation. Degradation of glutamine synthetase is enhanced by the presence of a high concentration (2 mmol) of glutamine in the culture medium. From inhibitor studies it appears that glutamine or glutamine analogs such as diazonorleucine induce a specific function which is responsible for the enhanced specific degradation of glutamine synthetase. Other proteins, including other steroid hormone – induced proteins, are not degraded at an enhanced rate in the presence of excess exogenous glutamine.

Thus, the induction of glutamine synthetase by steroid hormones is mediated by an increased rate of synthesis of the glutamine synthetase protein. The increased accumulation of glutamine synthetase by deprivation of exogenous glutamine results from the decreased rate of degradation of the glutamine synthetase molecule. This is an example of a complex and sophisticated regulation of gene expression which has evolved in higher organisms.

Regulation of the Hemoglobin Genes in Cultured Mouse Cells

Mouse erythroleukemia cells as isolated by Charlotte Friend neither produce hemoglobin nor accumulate the mRNA for hemoglobin under the usual growth conditions, although these cells contain the genes for synthesis of the globin moiety of hemoglobin, as do all other somatic mouse cells. Under the usual growth conditions, this established line of erythroleukemia cells will grow in culture indefinitely. Exposure of the erythroleukemia cells to dimethyl sulfoxide (DMSO, a synthetic solvent) and a variety of other membrane-active agents induces a coordinate alteration of gene expression which appears to mimic at least a portion of normal erythroid differentiation. Over a 5-day period following an exposure to DMSO or other inducing agents, the rates of heme and globin synthesis increase 10- to 100-fold. The level of globin mRNA increases to a similar extent, and its accumulation is the first detectable biochemical event. Quantitation of specific globin mRNA was accomplished by utilizing molecular hybridization technics with a cDNA to globin mRNA (see Chapter 25). The response of erythroleukemia cells to inducer follows a type C pattern, as described in Fig 27–1. Following exposure to the inducing agent, the individual cells exhibit a latent period before becoming irreversibly committed to the expression of the differentiated function: hemoglobin synthesis. However, the continued presence of the inducer is not necessary to maintain the differentiated state.

Concomitant with the expression of the genes for hemoglobin, there is a programmed decline in the proliferative capacity of the cells wherein their proliferative capacity becomes limited to 4 divisions. The progeny have the potential to undergo 3, 2, 1, and eventually no divisions. Ultimately, a nondividing red differentiated clone of 16 cells is produced from the single newly "induced" parent cell.

It can be assumed that prokaryote models for regulation of gene expression will serve future investigations of this regulation in all mammals.

• • •

References

Arad G, Freikopf A, Kulka RG: Glutamine-stimulated modification and degradation of glutamine synthetase in hepatoma tissue culture cells. Cell 8:95, 1976.

Brenner M, Ames BN: The histidine operon and its regulation. Metabolic Pathways 5:350, 1971.

Englesberg E, Wilcox G: Regulation: Positive control. Annu Rev Genet 8:219, 1974.

Goldberg AL, St. John AC: Intracellular protein degradation in mammalian and bacterial cells. Annu Rev Biochem 45:747, 1976.

Gusella J & others: Commitment to erythroid differentiation by Friend erythroleukemia cells: A stochastic analysis. Cell 9:221, 1976.

Herskowitz I: Control of gene expression in bacteriophage lambda. Annu Rev Genet 7:289, 1973.

Jacob F, Monod J: Genetic regulatory mechanisms in protein synthesis. J Mol Biol 3:318, 1961.

Ross J, Ikawa Y, Leder P: Globin messenger-RNA induction during erythroid differentiation of cultured leukemia cells. Proc Natl Acad Sci USA 69:3620, 1972.

Zubay G, Chambers DA: Regulating the lac operon. Metabolic Pathways 5:297, 1971.

28 . . .
General Characteristics of Hormones

Most glands of the body deliver their secretions by means of ducts. These are the **exocrine glands.** Other glands manufacture chemical substances which they secrete into the blood stream for transmission to various "target" tissues. These are the **endocrine** or **ductless glands.** Their secretions, the hormones, catalyze and control diverse metabolic processes. Despite their varying actions and different specificities, depending on the target organ, the hormones have several characteristics in common. They act as body catalysts, resembling enzymes in some aspects since they are required only in very small amounts and are not used during their catalytic action. They differ from enzymes in the following ways:

(1) They are produced in an organ other than that in which they ultimately perform their action.

(2) They are secreted into the blood prior to use. Thus, circulating levels can give some indication of endocrine gland activity and target organ exposure. Because of the small amounts of hormones required,

blood levels can be extremely low. For example, circulating levels of protein hormones range from 10^{-10} to 10^{-12} M, and the circulating levels of thyroid and steroid hormones are from 10^{-6} to 10^{-9} M.

(3) Structurally, they are not always proteins; the known hormones include proteins with molecular weights of 30,000 or less, small polypeptides, single amino acids, and steroids.

The action of a hormone at a target organ is regulated by 5 factors: (1) rate of synthesis and secretion of the stored hormone from the endocrine gland of origin; (2) in some cases, specific transport systems in the plasma; (3) sometimes, conversion to a more active form; (4) hormone-specific receptors in target cell cytosol or membranes which differ from tissue to tissue; and (5) ultimate degradation of the hormone, usually by the liver or kidneys. Variation in any of these factors can result in a rapid change in the amount or activity of a hormone at a given tissue site.

It is characteristic of the endocrine system that a

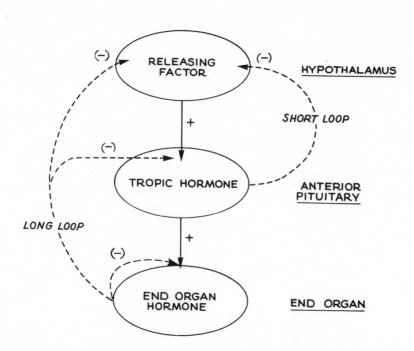

Figure 28–1. General feedback control of endocrine systems involving the hypothalamus, anterior pituitary, and end organ.

state of balance is normally maintained among the various glands. This is particularly notable with respect to releasing substances from the hypothalamus, which regulate synthesis and secretion of anterior pituitary hormones. The pituitary hormones in turn regulate activity of various target endocrine glands (Fig 28–1) (see pp 501–502). Characteristically, elevated hormone levels result in both direct and indirect feedback inhibition of their production by the originating gland.

General Mechanisms of Action of Hormones

Although the exact site of action of any hormone is still not established, 5 general sites have been proposed:

A. Induction of Enzyme Synthesis at the Nuclear Level: Many hormones, particularly the steroids, may act to stimulate RNA production in the target cell nucleus and thereby increase the synthesis of a specific enzyme or group of enzymes catalyzing a specific metabolic pathway. Steroid hormones initially act by binding to a specific high-affinity receptor protein in the cytosol (Fig 28–2). The complex that is formed (often involving structural transformation of the receptor protein) is then transported to the nucleus of the cell wherein it reacts with the nuclear chromatin. This combination in turn influences the synthesis of messenger RNA (mRNA) that will act as a template direct-

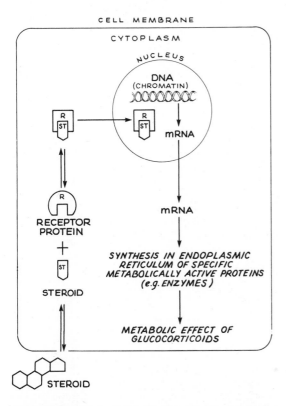

Figure 28–2. Steps in glucocorticoid action. St = steroid; R = specific glucocorticoid receptor; the dissimilar shapes of R are intended to represent different conformations of this protein. (Redrawn, with permission, from Baxter & Forsham [1972]).

ing the synthesis in the cytoplasmic endoplasmic reticulum of specific protein enzymes. Changes in metabolism are produced by this indirect route. It is to be noted that a direct chemical reaction of the hormone with DNA or RNA polynucleotide is not likely. Instead, it is postulated that the hormone must first combine with a specific receptor protein, and it is this combination that acts on DNA chromatin. It is probable that chromatin proteins may influence hormonal activity by modifying the ability of the receptor complex to bind to DNA. This action of certain chromatin proteins could account for the specific binding of preformed receptor complex to the DNA of the hormone's target cells, whereas DNA from other cells has less affinity.

Thyroid hormones act similarly to increase RNA and enzyme synthesis but may do so by directly binding to specific receptor proteins in the nuclear chromatin. Receptors in the cytosol are less effective in regulation.

Hormones acting as described above may be thought of as functioning to modify gene expression. Experimentally, such hormones, when isotopically labeled, are found to be localized in the nucleus. Other evidence of nuclear action is the frequent demonstration of an increase in RNA synthesis as measured by incorporation of labeled precursors, such as orotic acid or glycine, into the nuclear RNA fraction. The steroid hormones increase the synthesis of specific messenger, transfer, and ribosomal RNAs by the nucleus. In liver, a general increase in ribosomal RNA by glucocorticoids was found to result from induction of the RNA polymerase, which determines ribosomal RNA synthesis. A hormone which does not effect a net increase in RNA synthesis can still act by this mechanism by increasing the RNA for a specific enzyme while decreasing RNA synthesis for others. For example, the increase of ovalbumin in chick oviduct caused by estrogens has been associated with an increase of the specific mRNA for ovalbumin. Finally, the increase of activity of an enzyme after hormone administration can often be blocked by the administration of inhibitors of RNA synthesis such as dactinomycin, indicating that the hormonal action on enzyme activity was mediated by an effect on RNA synthesis. Hormone action leading to a change in the rate of RNA and enzyme synthesis with a consequent effect on cellular metabolism is comparatively slow. This type of action may therefore require hours or even days of exposure to the hormone before the effect may be detectable. Similarly, the effect of these hormones can persist long after their circulatory level has declined, since the induced enzymes may degrade slowly.

B. Stimulation of Enzyme Synthesis at the Ribosomal Level: Activity is at the level of translation of information carried by the messenger RNA on the ribosomes to the production of the enzyme protein. Ribosomes taken from a growth hormone-treated animal, for example, have a modified capacity to synthesize protein in the presence of normal messenger RNA.

C. Direct Activation at the Enzyme Level: Although the direct effect of a hormone on a pure enzyme is difficult to demonstrate, treatment of the intact animal or of isolated tissue with some hormones results in a change of enzyme activity not related to de novo synthesis; these hormonal effects are usually extremely rapid. Since cell membranes are usually required, it is probable that the initiating hormonal event is activation of a membrane receptor (see next paragraph).

D. Hormonal Action at the Membrane Level: Many hormones seem specifically involved in the transport of a variety of substances across cell membranes, including carbohydrates, amino acids, cations, and nucleotides. In general, these hormones specifically bind to cell membranes. They cause rapid secondary metabolic changes in the tissue but have little effect on metabolic activity of membrane-free preparations. Most protein hormones and catecholamines activate different membrane enzyme systems by direct binding to specific receptors on the cell membrane rather than in the cytosol.

Receptor levels themselves are highly sensitive to environmental and metabolic changes. Increased insulin and thyroid hormone **decrease** their respective receptors, suggesting that an inverse counterregulation between hormone and receptor may be a general endocrinologic phenomenon. Finally, the exact coupling between receptor binding and biologic action is unknown. In many cases, binding capacity exceeds the hormone levels required for maximum biologic response, suggesting that there is an excess of receptors or that nonfunctional receptors can exist.

E. Hormonal Action As It Relates to the Level of Cyclic Nucleotides: (Fig 28–3.) Cyclic AMP (cyclic 3′,5′-AMP) is a nucleotide which plays a unique role in the action of many hormones. Its level may be increased or decreased by hormonal action; the effect varies, depending on the tissue. Thus, glucagon may

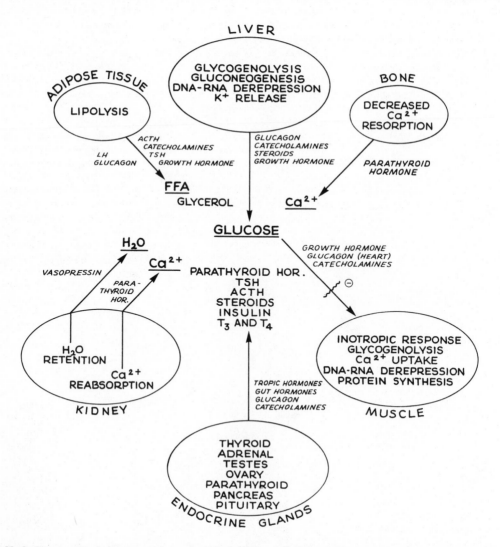

Figure 28–3. Tissue mechanisms increased by cyclic AMP (cAMP) and the hormones that generate it. Insulin and some prostaglandins often decrease cAMP and reverse the mechanisms in tissues. (LH = luteinizing hormone; TSH = thyrotropin.)

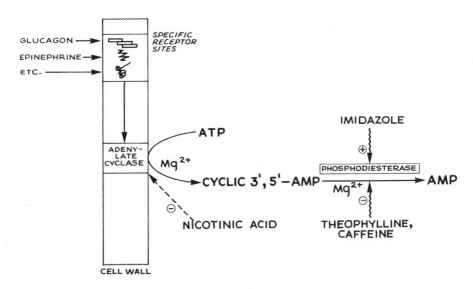

Figure 28—4. Factors involved in the production and degradation of cyclic 3′,5′-AMP (cAMP).

cause large increases of cyclic AMP (cAMP) in the liver but comparatively small increases in muscle. In contrast, epinephrine produces a greater increase of cAMP in muscle than in liver. Insulin can decrease hepatic cAMP in opposition to the increase caused by glucagon. Direct action of a hormone on purified adenylate cyclase (the enzyme responsible for the synthesis of cAMP from ATP) has been difficult to demonstrate. The hormones probably act at specific receptor sites in the different cell membranes which in turn activate the cyclase (Fig 28–4). It is probable that receptors for different hormones in a cell membrane activate a relatively common adenylate cyclase.

Most of the varied effects of cAMP appear to reflect its general ability to activate a large variety of phosphokinase enzymes. Thus, cAMP activation of phosphorylase is the result of a specific activation of the enzyme phosphorylase kinase, which results ultimately in the conversion of inactive dephosphophos-phorylase to active phosphorylase. In adipose tissue, cAMP may activate lipolysis by a similar stimulation of protein kinase which causes increased lipase activity. cAMP can increase also the activity of protein kinases which phosphorylate nuclear histones and possibly other nuclear proteins. Thus, changing levels of cAMP may influence the function of protein repressors in the nucleus and explain how some hormones regulate RNA and enzyme synthesis. The hydrolysis of cAMP results in the liberation of 1.6 kcal/mol more energy than the hydrolysis of a high-energy bond from ATP; this has led to the as yet unconfirmed suggestion that cAMP may activate kinase enzymes by adenylation. In the absence of cAMP, a kinase exists as a regulatory (inhibiting) subunit bound to the kinase catalytic subunit. cAMP binds to the regulatory subunit causing it to disassociate from, and thereby liberate, the active kinase (Fig 28–5). These kinases may not only phosphorylate enzymes, but they may also phosphorylate

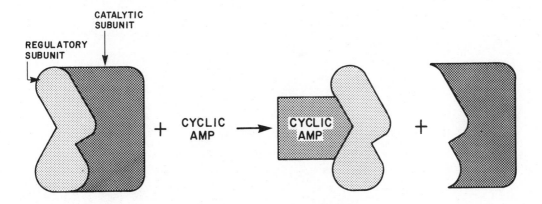

Figure 28—5. Activation of protein kinase by cyclic AMP (cAMP).

other proteins (eg, nucleoproteins). Thus, cAMP may affect regulatory systems at the chromatin level of transcription and possibly at the ribosomal protein level of translation.

Tissue levels of cAMP (approximately 10^{-7} M) can be influenced not only by hormones but also by nicotinic acid, imidazole, and methyl xanthines acting on its synthesis and degradation (Fig 28–4). However, the effects of these agents can vary with concentration or type of tissue and may not always relate to cAMP metabolism.

Adenylate cyclase is localized in the cell membrane; hormonal action on cAMP levels and membrane phenomena may therefore be related.

Though originally discovered as an endocrinologic phenomenon, cAMP is now recognized as a ubiquitous nucleotide which may be as important as ATP or AMP in controlling enzymatic reactions. A rise in cAMP is usually associated with beta-adrenergic reactions, and levels can be influenced by most metabolic changes caused by stress or diet.

Increased cAMP in cells can diffuse to extracellular fluid. Hormones which increase hepatic (glucagon) or renal (parathyroid hormone) cAMP bring about an increased level of the cyclic nucleotide in blood and urine, respectively. Although this may be useful for diagnostic purposes, extracellular cAMP has little or no biologic activity.

Cyclic GMP (guanosine monophosphate) is also found in most tissues. The exact role of this nucleotide is unknown, but tissue levels often rise and fall inversely to cAMP, suggesting its action also is inverse.

Role of Calcium in Hormone Action & Secretion

The action of most protein hormones is inhibited in the absence of calcium even though ability to increase or decrease cAMP is comparatively unimpaired. Thus, calcium may be a more terminal signal for hormonal action than cAMP (see section on parathyroid hormone in Chapter 29).

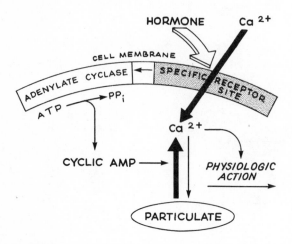

Figure 28–6. Interrelationships between hormone action, cyclic AMP, and calcium ion.

Rasmussen & Goodman (see reference on p 461) have suggested that ionized calcium of the cytosol is the important signal (Fig 28–6). The source of this calcium may be the extracellular fluid, or it may arise from mobilization of intracellular, tissue-bound calcium. Protein hormones increase the uptake of extracellular calcium, whereas cAMP primarily mobilizes tissue-bound calcium. Hormones which also activate adenylate cyclase have a dual action, increasing ionic cytosol calcium derived from both sources mentioned above. This observation would explain why cAMP can mimic the actions of many hormones but (usually) with different kinetic characteristics. It also casts cAMP in the role of a modulator of hormone action instead of as the final signal.

Similarly, the secretion of almost all hormones stored in granules requires calcium. Stimulators often increase uptake of calcium whether or not they increase cAMP. Furthermore, cAMP can partially initiate or modulate the action of primary stimulators by mobilizing intracellular bound calcium.

All of the mechanisms described above may be involved in the action of a given hormone and may vary in significance when the action of a hormone is studied in different tissues. For example, insulin has a major and rapid effect on membrane transport in adipose and muscle tissue, but its action is slower in liver, where secondary actions may be more demonstrable at the nuclear or translation level. Finally, all of the mechanisms are intimately related. An effect on transport would thus permit the entrance of substances which could act as enzyme activators or, at the nuclear level, as repressors or derepressors of RNA synthesis. Similarly, a direct effect on one enzyme system could modify the availability of substrates or products for other pathways or for activation or inactivation at the nuclear or membrane level. At present, therefore, because of the interdependency of these mechanisms, the primary action of a given hormone is not easily established.

Assay of Hormones

A. Biologic Assays: Biologic assays, in which an aspect of hormonal activity is measured in vitro or in vivo, remain important since they measure levels of functional activity. However, these assays often lack precision and sensitivity and are usually not specific.

B. Chemical Assays: These are often used in conjunction with isotope dilution and employ classical isolation and purification technics, including gas and column chromatography, electrophoresis, and differential solvent extraction. They provide a measure of the absolute quantity of a given hormone but can be burdensome and, in the case of protein hormones, are generally not applicable.

C. Radiodisplacement Chemical Assays: These have been widely adopted in recent years for both protein and nonprotein hormones. They are based on the competition for a specific binding protein of radiolabeled hormones with unlabeled hormone (Fig 28–7). The binding protein may be a specific antibody, mem-

Traces of radiolabeled hormone (●) incubated with excess antisera or specific binding protein (○). Little radioactivity remains in free fraction.

Addition of unlabeled hormone (sample or standard) (○) increased radioactivity in supernatant.

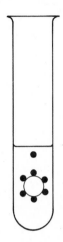

Figure 28–7. Principle of immunochemical assay for measuring hormone in biologic fluids. The amount of radioactivity in the supernatant is a direct function of the amount of hormone in the specimen.

brane receptor, or serum transport protein. Unlabeled hormone, present as either a standard or an unknown, competitively displaces the labeled hormone, resulting in an increase in radioactivity in the unbound fraction. Although many methods are available, they differ primarily in the technics used to separate the bound and free hormone fractions. These include hydrodynamic flow, electrophoresis, preferential salt precipitation, precipitation of the bound complex with antigamma globulin serum, and adsorption of the free hormone to charcoal or to cellulose. Radiodisplacement methods are more sensitive than most bioassays since they permit detection of hormones in concentrations less than 1 ng/ml. The radiodisplacement methods are highly specific and relatively convenient. One defect of these assays is that they can measure degradation fragments or precursors of the hormone which retain some binding activity but can vary in their biologic activity. When possible, both chemical and biologic assays should be performed on identical samples.

● ● ●

References

Baxter JD, Forsham PH: Tissue effects of glucocorticoids. Am J Med 53:573, 1972.

Catt KJ & others: Basic concepts of the mechanism of action of peptide hormones. Biol Reprod 14:1, 1976.

Cuatrecasas P, Hollenberg MD: Membrane receptors and hormone action. Adv Protein Chem 30:251, 1976.

Edelman IS: Mechanism of action of steroid hormones. J Steroid Biochem 6:147, 1975.

Hall R, Gomez-Pan A: Hypothalamic regulatory hormones and their clinical applications. Adv Clin Chem 18:173, 1976.

Posner BI: Polypeptide hormone receptors: Characteristics and applications. Can J Physiol Pharmacol 53:689, 1975.

Rasmussen H: Ions as second messengers. Hosp Practice 9:99, June 1974.

Rasmussen H, Goodman DBP: Calcium and cAMP as interrelated intracellular messengers. Ann NY Acad Sci 253:789, 1975.

Williams RH (editor): *Textbook of Endocrinology,* 5th ed. Saunders, 1974.

29 ...
The Chemistry & Functions of the Hormones*

THE THYROID

The thyroid gland consists of 2 lobes, one on each side of the trachea, with a connecting portion making the entire gland more or less H-shaped in appearance. In the adult, the gland weighs about 25–30 g and consists of closely packed sacs (follicles) filled with proteinaceous colloid. Although there is some evidence of extrathyroidal production of thyroid-like hormones, the thyroid gland is the primary source of their production.

Function

Thyroid hormone is particularly important as a regulator of development. A closely related function is that of a catalyst for the oxidative reactions and regulation of metabolic rates in the body. The tissues of hypothyroid animals exhibit a low rate of oxygen consumption, and the patient has a slow pulse, lowered systolic blood pressure, decreased mental and physical vigor, and often, although not always, obesity. Cholesterol levels in the blood are increased, but lipolysis and the liberation of fatty acids from the tissue decrease. In hyperthyroid states, the reverse occurs, including increased oxygen consumption and pulse rate, increased irritability, and loss of weight.

Although a number of effects of thyroid hormone on specific metabolic reactions have been demonstrated, a unifying concept of the mechanism by which it produces acceleration of metabolism is not yet apparent. This is in part due to the different effects noted when the hormone is studied at physiologic levels or at unphysiologically high doses.

The fact that thyroid hormones act relatively slowly, taken together with the observation that these hormones enter a target cell where they are bound to a specific carrier, suggests that thyroid hormone acts primarily via the protein synthesizing machinery of the target cell in accordance with the processes described in paragraph A (p 457). In contrast to the steroids, however, the thyroid hormones bind directly to receptor proteins associated with chromatin in the nucleus, possibly without prior binding to any cytosol receptor.

In moderate concentrations the thyroid hormone has an anabolic effect, causing an increase in RNA and protein synthesis, an action that precedes increased basal metabolic rate. Facilitation of protein synthesis occurs not only by increasing RNA synthesis at the nuclear level but also by increasing translation of the message contained in messenger RNA at the ribosome where protein synthesis occurs. It may also increase protein synthesis by stimulating growth hormone production. When injected into animals, thyroxine appears to stimulate most of the oxidative enzyme systems that have been investigated.

In high concentrations, negative nitrogen balance is observed and protein synthesis is depressed. Carbohydrate and lipid turnover is increased, and calcium is mobilized from bone. An effect of thyroid hormone to uncouple oxidative phosphorylation and increase swelling in the mitochondria has been described. Such an action results in the production of heat rather than the storage of energy as ATP. However, these effects are observed only with very high concentrations of the hormone and may not reflect its effect in the small physiologic doses characteristic of the intact organism. Other uncoupling agents such as antimycin A or dinitrophenol also increase body heat but fail to duplicate the other biologic actions of thyroid hormone. Thyroxine can increase the association of ATPase with ion pumps. Thus, a primary action of the hormone may be to increase ATP utilization, the resulting ATP depletion being responsible for the observed increase in oxygen uptake.

Intestinal absorption of glucose is increased by thyroid hormone. This rapid absorption may be a factor in the abnormal glucose tolerance often observed in hyperthyroidism.

Thyroid hormone normally has a long latent period, requiring many hours or days before an effect is noted. Consequently, effects may occur early in the period after administration of the hormone which, at present, are not detectable.

Chemistry & Normal Physiology

The inorganic iodine in the body is largely taken up by the thyroid in connection with the synthesis of thyroid hormone. Of a total of 50 mg of iodine in the body, about 10–15 mg are in thyroid.

The normal daily intake of iodide is 100–200 μg. This iodide, absorbed mainly from the small intestine, is transported in the plasma in loose attachment to proteins. Small amounts of iodide are secreted by the

*Note: Throughout this chapter the hypothalamic agents which regulate pituitary function (p 502) are referred to as hormones (eg, thyroxine-releasing hormone, TRH). Current usage also refers to them as factors (eg, thryoxine-releasing factor, TRF).

salivary glands, stomach, and small intestine, and traces occur in milk. About two-thirds of the ingested iodide are excreted by the kidney; the remaining one-third is taken up by the thyroid gland. Thyroid-stimulating hormone (TSH, thyrotropin) of the pituitary (see p 507) stimulates iodide uptake by the gland. Thyroid activity appears also to be related to the total amount of iodine in the gland. For example, in the normal gland, an iodine content of 2 mg/g of dried tissue is found, whereas in hyperthyroidism the content may fall to 0.25 mg/g. It may be that a fall in the iodine content of the gland stimulates the production of more thyrotropin, which therefore prolongs and exacerbates the hyperthyroid state.

Iodine uptake is energy-dependent and moves against a gradient, since ratios of thyroid gland to plasma iodide vary from 100:1–10:1. The energy-dependent uptake can be inhibited by cyanide or dinitrophenol. It also requires an active sodium pump, uptake being inhibited by ouabain. Despite this high concentration effect, free iodide represents only about 1% of the total iodide in the thyroid. As shown in Fig 29–1, intracellular iodide exists in 2 pools. One pool is freely exchangeable with blood iodide; the other represents iodide arising from deiodination of unused iodo-tyrosines. Thiocyanate, perchlorate, and pertechnetate compete with iodide for the uptake mechanism and cause rapid discharge of the exchangeable iodide from the thyroid gland.

Within the thyroid, iodide is oxidized and transferred to tyrosine by a heme-containing particulate-bound peroxidase (a tetramer with a molecular weight of 90,000) which requires hydrogen peroxide as a source of oxygen. The hydrogen peroxide is produced by an NADPH-dependent enzyme resembling cytochrome c reductase. Oxidation of iodide thus involves both the production of peroxide and oxidation of the iodide by the peroxidase enzyme. Free iodine is not the iodinating species in the peroxidase reaction; instead, free radicals of iodine and tyrosine are combined at the active site of the enzyme. Thyrotropin is active in stimulating this reaction.

The receptor tyrosine residues are in the glycoprotein thyroglobulin. This 19S protein has a molecular weight of 660,000, and each molecule contains 115 tyrosine residues. The molecule is composed of a polymer of dissimilar subunits. Iodination of the tyrosines in thyroglobulin occurs first in position 3 of the

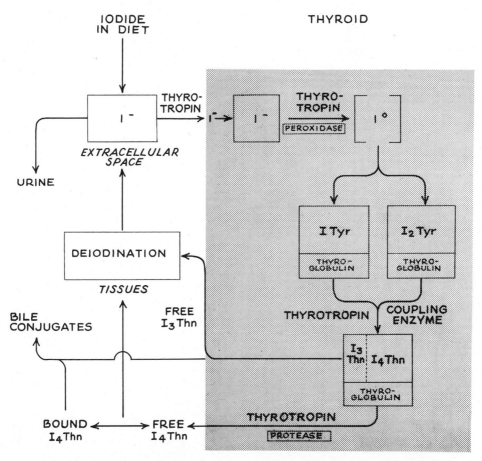

Figure 29–1. Metabolism of iodine and thyroid hormones. (ITyr = monoiodotyrosine; I_2Tyr = diiodotyrosine; I_3Thn = triiodothyronine; I_4Thn = thyroxine.)

aromatic nucleus and then at position 5, forming monoiodotyrosine and diiodotyrosine, respectively. Normally, the 2 are present in approximately equal concentrations, but with iodine deficiency more mono-iodotyrosine is formed. It is not likely that significant amounts of free tyrosine are iodinated and then incorporated into thyroglobulin, since thyroidal transfer RNA will not accept mono- or diiodotyrosine and since organification of iodine is not inhibited by concentrations of puromycin which block tyrosine incorporation into thyroglobulin.

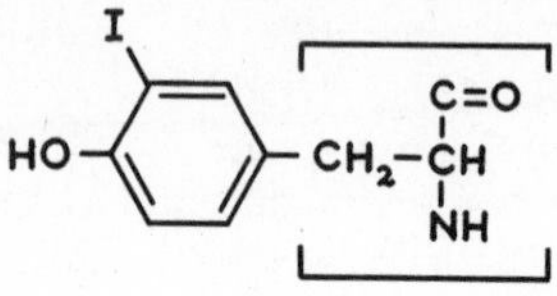

Figure 29–2. 3-Monoiodotyrosine (ITyr) (shown in peptide linkage in thyroglobulin).

It is assumed that coupling of 2 molecules of diiodotyrosine (I_2Tyr) then occurs within the thyroglobulin molecule to form tetraiodothyronine, or thyroxine (I_4Thn), in peptide linkage. Similarly, coupling of monoiodotyrosine (ITyr) with I_2Tyr also occurs to form triiodothyronine (I_3Thn). In these structures, the tyrosines are in perpendicular planes.

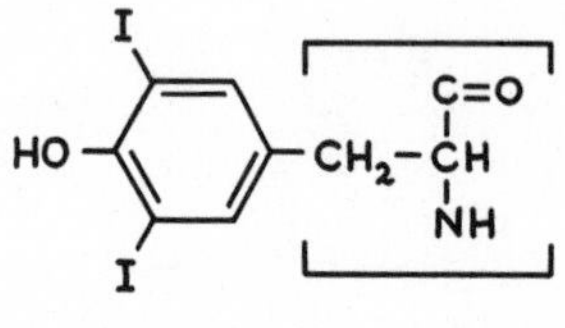

Figure 29–3. 3,5-Diiodotyrosine (I_2Tyr) (in peptide linkage).

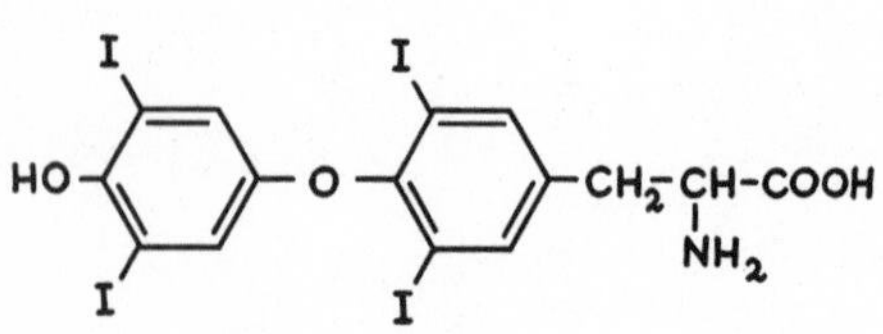

Figure 29–4. Thyroxine (I_4Thn).

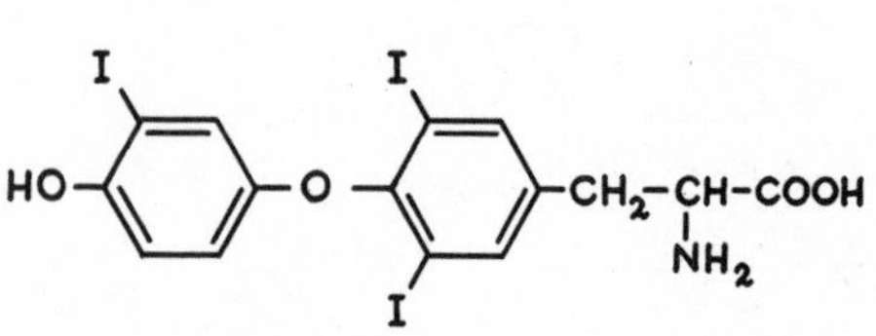

Figure 29–5. 3,5,3'-Triiodothyronine (I_3Thn).

The extensive structural changes in thyroglobulin to be expected following the combination of internal molecules of tyrosine do not occur. It is possible that the aromatic ring of a free iodotyrosine is transferred to the aromatic ring located in thyroglobulin. A possible active form of free iodotyrosine is 3,5-diiodo-4-hydroxyphenylpyruvic acid, whose iodinated ring was shown to be incorporated into thyroxine when it was incubated with thyroglobulin. The process is oxidative and dependent on a peroxidase system similar to or identical with that involved in the initial oxidation of iodide. This may explain why both steps of "organification" are often similarly affected by regulatory factors and drugs.

Distribution of organic iodine in the gland is as follows: I_2Tyr, 24–42%; ITyr, 17–28%; I_4Thn, 35%; I_3Thn, 5–8%. Approximately 20% of the thyroglobulin tyrosine residues are iodinated.

On stimulation (eg, by thyrotropin), thyroglobulin-containing colloid is taken up by the follicular cells via the process of endocytosis. The resulting secretory droplets combine transiently with lysosomes, the latter providing the proteolytic enzymes that break down thyroglobulin. Proteolysis of thyroglobulin may be facilitated by a disulfide cleavage step using a glutathione-catalyzed transhydrogenase similar to that which reduces insulin in the liver. Thyroxine and triiodothyronine are then released from the gland by a secretion process involving microtubules and microfilaments. The hydrolysis of thyroglobulin also liberates ITyr and I_2Tyr. If these iodinated amino acids were lost from the gland, considerable amounts of iodide would be biologically unavailable for the synthesis of active hormone. However, particulate thyroidal deiodinase (or dehalogenase) enzymes rapidly remove the iodide and permit its reutilization for the synthesis of new hormone (Fig 29–1). Approximately one-third of the total iodide in the thyroid is recycled in this manner. Both pituitary thyrotropin and exposure to a cold environment stimulate thyroglobulin breakdown and the release of active hormone. Thyroglobulin breakdown is directly inhibited by iodide, possibly by changing cellular reductive capacity. Intact thyroglobulin can enter the circulation during surgical manipulation or irradiation of the thyroid gland. Besides thyroglobulin, some albumin-like and hormonally inactive 4S iodoproteins can appear in the serum and contribute to the measured protein-bound iodine.

About 80% of the hormone iodine stored by the thyroid gland is thyroxine, and 20% is probably triiodothyronine. The accumulation of inorganic iodide and its conversion to diiodotyrosine and thyroxine in the thyroid are completed over about a 48-hour period, but the labeled protein-bound iodine does not appear in the plasma for several days after the original administration of the isotope.

Within the plasma, I_4Thn and I_3Thn are transported almost entirely in association with 2 proteins, the so-called thyroxine-binding proteins, which act as specific carrier agents for the hormones. A glycoprotein (MW 50,000) which migrates electrophoreti-

Table 29–1. Binding of thyroid hormones to serum proteins.

Protein	Relative Binding	Affinity	Capacity
Thyroxine-binding globulin	I_4 Thn > I_3 Thn; tetraiodothyroacetic acid = 0	High	Low
Thyroxine-binding prealbumin	Tetraiodothyroacetic acid > I_4 Thn; I_3 Thn = 0	Moderate	High
Serum albumin	Same for all	Low	Very high

cally in a region between the alpha$_1$ and alpha$_2$ globulins is designated **thyroxine-binding globulin.** Another protein, **thyroxine-binding prealbumin,** is detectable electrophoretically just ahead of the albumin fraction. When large amounts of I_4 Thn and I_3 Thn are present and the binding capacities of these specific carrier proteins are exceeded, the hormones bind to serum albumin. The comparative binding affinities for thyroxine and triiodothyronine are shown in Table 29–1. Approximately 0.05% of the circulating thyroxine is in the free, unbound state. "Free" I_3 Thn and I_4 Thn are the metabolically active hormones in the plasma.

I_4 Thn and I_3 Thn can be dissociated from their binding proteins by competing anions such as phenytoin, salicylates, or dinitrophenol.

In a normal subject, only about one-third of the maximum binding capacity is utilized; in a hyperthyroid patient, this may increase to one-half or more. In certain circumstances, thyroxine-binding globulin levels may become abnormal. An increase occurs in pregnancy as well as after the administration of estrogens. In nephrosis and after treatment with androgenic or anabolic steroids, decreased levels of thyroxine-binding globulin may occur. Generally, those circumstances which cause a decrease in thyroxine-binding globulin result in a reciprocal rise in thyroxine-binding prealbumin. However, I_4 Thn and I_3 Thn are less tightly bound to thyroxine-binding prealbumin and may quickly exchange to the "free" hormonal fraction. Thyroxine-binding globulin should therefore be considered the stable reservoir for both I_3 Thn and I_4 Thn.

Although the circulating levels of I_3 Thn are much lower than the corresponding I_4 Thn levels, I_3 Thn may be the major thyroid hormone. Because it is more loosely bound by the serum proteins, I_3 Thn disappears from the blood 20 times more rapidly than I_4 Thn (half-time of I_4 Thn is 6–7 days). I_3 Thn is 3–5 times more active than I_4 Thn and has a more rapid onset of action. It is also more rapidly degraded in the body. In rare subjects with chemical hyperthyroidism, in whom the circulating level of bound and free I_4 Thn is normal, the I_3 Thn concentration is elevated and accounts for the thyrotoxic state. Significant amounts of I_3 Thn may arise by conversion of I_4 Thn at the peripheral level. Total production of I_3 Thn from both thyroidal and peripheral tissue is about 50% of that for I_4 Thn. About half of the thyroidal I_4 Thn is rapidly converted in peripheral tissues to the more active

I_3 Thn. This represents the major source of body I_3 Thn and suggests that I_3 Thn may be the important active form of the hormone. Conversion rates are increased by phenytoin and phenobarbital and are decreased with age.

I_4 Thn can sometimes be converted in the tissues to reverse I_3 Thn (3,5',3'-triiodothyronine). Reverse I_3 Thn is less active than I_3 Thn; thus, its production can result in decreased thyroid hormone activity.

In contrast to the steroids, thyroid hormones may bind directly to specific receptor proteins in the acid nuclear chromatin; receptors in the cytosol are less effective as regulators. Although the exact chemical mechanism of action of I_3 Thn and I_4 Thn is not known, iodine is required at the 3,5 position, suggesting that binding of I_3 Thn and I_4 Thn to tissue receptors involves this portion of the molecule.

Both I_4 Thn and I_3 Thn are metabolized in the peripheral tissues by deamination and decarboxylation to **tetraiodothyroacetic acid** or **triiodothyroacetic acid.** These metabolites are about one-fourth as active on a weight basis as their hormonal precursors, although their onset of action, according to some observers, is much more rapid. Both substances have been used as agents to decrease serum cholesterol levels with a minimum of the less desired thyroxine actions.

Deiodination may also occur in the peripheral tissues, the liberated iodide being excreted in the urine. In the liver, thyroid hormone is rapidly conjugated with glucuronic acid and, to a lesser extent, with sulfate; and these inactive conjugates are excreted into the bile. Part of the conjugated thyroxine may be reabsorbed and transported to the kidney, where it may be deiodinated or excreted as intact conjugate.

Control of Thyroid Release

Thyroid-stimulating hormone of the pituitary gland has a general activating effect on uptake and oxidation of iodine as well as on synthesis and secretion of thyroxine by the thyroid gland. The broad effect of thyrotropin on these various metabolic steps

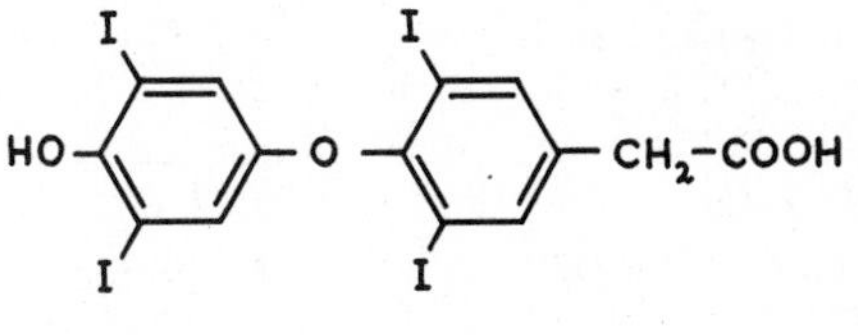

Figure 29–6. Tetraiodothyroacetic acid.

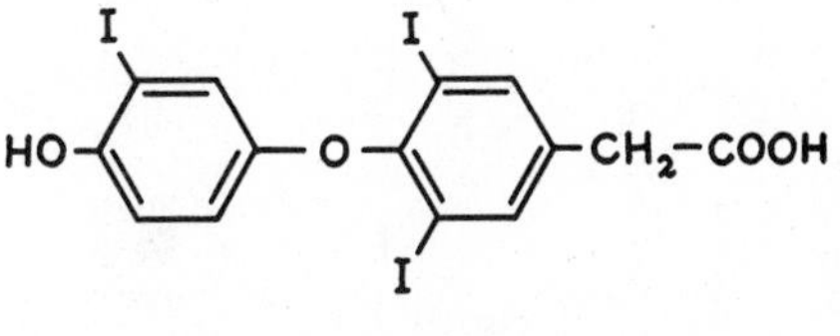

Figure 29–7. Triiodothyroacetic acid.

may be due to its ability to increase the vascularity of the gland. Exposure to cold causes a release of thyroid hormone, but this is probably mediated through thyrotropin release by the pituitary. Experimental lesions made in the hypothalamus can result in the inhibition of thyroid release, indicating the presence of a humoral factor in the hypothalamus which can activate the pituitary to secrete thyrotropin. This factor (**thyrotropin-releasing hormone**) has been identified in the sheep as a tripeptide (Fig 29–40).

Thyroxine is a feedback inhibitor of its own secretion. This inhibitory effect occurs at the pituitary by inhibition of thyrotropin secretion; it may be due to a direct action of thyroxine (or triiodothyronine) which decreases the pituitary sensitivity to thyroxine-releasing hormone. Except during cold exposure, thyroxine-releasing hormone secretion is fairly constant. Thus, most regulation occurs by interaction in the pituitary between thyroxine and thyroxine-releasing hormone-destroying enzymes. There is some evidence that thyroxine can, to a lesser extent, also inhibit thyroxine-releasing hormone secretion at the hypothalamic level.

The controlling effect of thyroxine on thyrotropin release in the pituitary is blocked by substances inhibiting protein synthesis, whereas the effect of thyroxine-releasing hormone is not. Thus, the 2 agents operate by different mechanisms. Iodine itself is an important autoregulator; decreased iodide (or, more likely, decreased organified iodine) rapidly increases subsequent iodide uptake as well as breakdown of thyroglobulin to I_4 Thn. Catecholamines can also directly stimulate thyroid hormone secretion.

Antithyroid drugs. Certain compounds act as antithyroid agents, inhibiting the production of thyroxine both at the organification and at the coupling steps. Examples of these antithyroid drugs are the goitrogens—thiouracil, propylthiouracil, methylthiouracil, carbimazole, thiourea, and methimazole (Tapazole, 1-methyl-2-mercaptoimidazole). Thiouracil is relatively toxic; the other compounds less so.

The Clinical Evaluation of Thyroid Abnormalities

Because of the differential activity of I_4 Thn and I_3 Thn and the major activity in the circulation, of these hormones as their free forms, an ideal evaluation should include measurement of the free and bound forms of each hormone. The older indirect methods for evaluation of thyroid gland activity such as the

basal metabolic rate, protein-bound iodine, butanol-extractable iodine, and the determination of I_4 Thn by column chromatography have been largely replaced by direct radioimmunoassays (RIA) for both I_4 Thn and I_3 Thn.

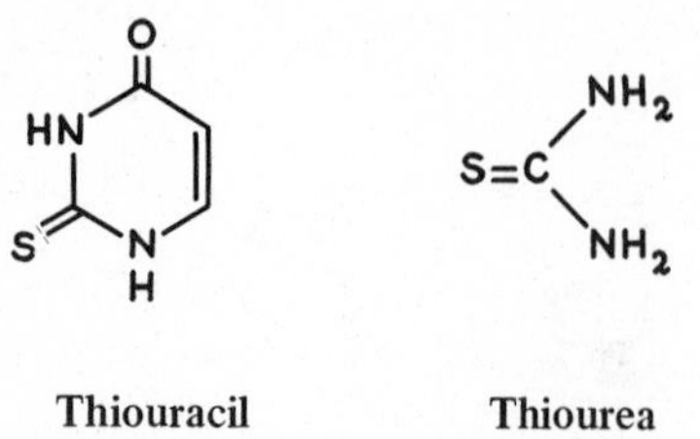

The proportion of free to bound hormones can be determined indirectly by the I_3 Thn binding test. This test is based on the in vitro uptake of radioiodine (^{131}I)-labeled I_3 Thn by adsorbents such as charcoal, resin, or the red blood cells. This I_3 Thn test is based upon the observation that, when labeled I_3 Thn is added to whole blood, the I_3 Thn is taken up and bound by the carrier proteins. The more I_3 Thn taken up by the serum carrier proteins, the less will be available for uptake by the adsorbent, and vice versa. Consequently, the amount of I_3 Thn bound by the adsorbent is an inverse measure of the degree of saturation of thyroxine-binding protein in the serum. As already noted above, thyroxine-binding capacity of hyperthyroid patients is more saturated than is normal. As a result, the residual serum-binding capacity for I_3 Thn is decreased so that adsorbent uptake is correspondingly increased. In some clinical states, such as pregnancy, where there is a compensatory increase in I_4 Thn binding protein, an individual may be euthyroid even though the total amount of thyroid hormones is elevated.

Thyroid uptake of ^{131}I is still a common procedure for evaluating thyroid function. Hyperfunction is indicated by the occurrence of more than 30% uptake when measured 24 hours after administration of the isotope.

Stimulation tests, evaluating the effect of administered thyrotropin on radiolabeled iodide uptake, are used to determine whether an abnormality is at the thyroid or the pituitary level. Direct immunoassay of circulating endogenous thyrotropin is used for the same purpose. The **thyroxine-releasing hormone stimulation test** in conjunction with I_4 Thn measurement is used to assess pituitary thyrotropin secretion and thyroid function.

Suppression tests involve administration of thyroid hormone to suppress thyrotropin secretion and thereby thyroid function. In thyrotoxicosis, thyroid hyperfunction is relatively insensitive to additional exogenous hormone.

Abnormalities of Thyroid Function

A. Hypothyroid States: A deficiency of thyroid hormone produces a number of clinical states depending upon the degree of the deficiency and the age at which it occurs.

It has recently become clear that hypothyroidism may result from an inherited inability to synthesize thyroid hormone. In such cases marked physical and mental retardation may result unless the condition is recognized and treated (with thyroid hormone) within the first years of life.

Though comparatively rare, congenital defects in iodine uptake, organification, coupling, deiodination, and hormone secretion have all been described.

Thiouracil   Thiourea

Figure 29–8. Antithyroid drugs.

1. **Cretinism** results from the incomplete development or congenital absence of the thyroid gland.

2. **Childhood hypothyroidism (juvenile myxedema)** appears later in life than cretinism and is less severe. The most important signs of juvenile myxedema are lack of bone growth, cessation of mental development, and, in some cases, changes in the skin as noted in cretinism.

3. **Myxedema** is caused by hypothyroidism in the adult. The basal metabolic rate and body temperature are lowered, and there is undue sensitivity to cold. Anemia and slowing of physical and mental reactions are also present.

4. **Hashimoto's disease** is a form of hypothyroidism in which all aspects of thyroid function may be impaired. This has now been established as an autoimmune disease in which the thyroid has been subjected to attack by cellular antibodies.

5. **Simple (endemic or colloid) goiter** is a deficiency disease caused by an inadequate supply of iodine in the diet. The decreased production of thyroid hormone causes overstimulation of the gland because of increased pituitary thyrotropin production incident to the lack of the "braking" effect of thyroid hormone.

Although treatment with iodine or with sodium iodide should be adequate for cases of simple goiter, thyroid hormone (L-thyroxine or desiccated thyroid) itself is more commonly used since there may be undetected defects in the pathway for synthesis of thyroxine, such as those, previously mentioned above, attributable to an inherited thyroid metabolic defect.

Simple goiter is common where the soil and water are low in iodine (eg, Great Lakes area). The use of iodized salt has done much to reduce its incidence.

B. Hyperthyroid States: Toxic goiter differs from simple goiter in that enlargement of the gland is accompanied by the secretion of excessive amounts of thyroid hormone, ie, hyperthyroidism together with enlargement (goiter). The term "toxic" does not refer to the secretion of the gland but to the toxic symptoms incident to the hyperthyroidism. Hyperthyroidism occasionally occurs without goiter.

The most common form of hyperthyroidism is **exophthalmic goiter**. The enlargement of the gland may be diffuse or nodular. In the latter case the terms **nodular toxic goiter** and **toxic adenoma** (Plummer's disease) are sometimes used, but the symptoms are the same. Symptoms include nervousness, fatigability, loss of weight, increased body temperature with excessive sweating, and an increase in the heart rate. A characteristic protrusion of the eyeballs (exophthalmos) usually accompanies hyperthyroidism.

The causes of nodular toxic goiter and of diffuse goiter (Graves' disease) are probably different. In the serum of patients with Graves' disease there occurs a thyroid-stimulating protein factor which is immunologically different from thyroid-stimulating hormone (thyrotropin) of the pituitary. The site of origin of this factor is not yet known, but it is apparently not the pituitary. When the factor is given intravenously, it disappears from the circulation more slowly than does thyrotropin. Qualitatively, it duplicates most actions of thyrotropin, but its maximal thyroid-stimulating effect occurs many hours after that of thyrotropin. For these reasons, it has been designated **long-acting thyroid stimulator**.

Long-acting thyroid stimulator is an antibody developed as an autoimmune phenomenon against thyroid protein. Hyperthyroidism can be produced by immunizing animals with thyroid microsomes. Long-acting thyroid stimulator activity is neutralized by anti-gamma globulin antibodies but not by antibody to thyrotropin. Many of the phenomena of Graves' disease, particularly the exophthalmos, may be related to this autoimmune reaction. In addition, transplacental transfer of long-acting thyroid stimulator antibody from mother to fetus may be responsible for neonatal thyrotoxicosis.

A substance called **LATS-protector** (long-acting thyroid stimulator protector), which in vitro can prevent inactivation of LATS by thyroid tissue fractions, has also been detected in the serum of hyperthyroid patients. It can directly stimulate the thyroid gland. LATS-protector, like LATS, is an antibody directed against some constituents of the tissues of the thyroid gland.

Hyperthyroidism can be treated by thyroid removal by surgery, or by radioactive iodine (^{131}I). It is also treated by antithyroid drugs (goitrogens) which prevent the gland from incorporating inorganic iodide into the organic forms, or by agents such as thiocyanate or perchlorate which compete with iodine for the uptake mechanism.

Calcitonin

Though now believed to be a hormone elucidated primarily by the C cells of the thyroid gland, calcitonin's metabolic actions and historical interest relate closely with parathyroid hormone. It is therefore discussed in the following section.

THE PARATHYROIDS

The parathyroid glands are 4 small glands so closely associated with the thyroid that they remained unrecognized for some time and were often removed during thyroidectomy. In man, the parathyroids are reddish or yellowish-brown egg-shaped bodies; the 4 glands together weigh about 0.05–0.3 g.

Function

The primary function of the parathyroid glands, mediated by their secretion of parathyroid hormone, is to maintain the concentration of ionized calcium in the plasma within the narrow range characteristic of this electrolyte despite wide variations in calcium intake, excretion, and deposition in bone. In addition to its effect on plasma ionized calcium via its action on

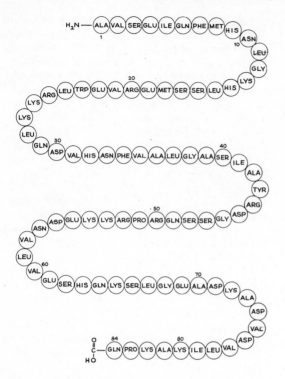

Figure 29–9. Structure of parathyroid hormone: a linear polypeptide of 84 amino acids. The physiologic activities of the peptide on both skeletal and renal tissues are contained within the 34 amino acids counting from the amino terminal end of the molecule.

Parathyroid extracts have been assayed biologically by their ability to increase the blood calcium in dogs or in rats after subcutaneous injection. In dogs, 1 unit of parathyroid activity is 0.01 of the amount necessary to raise the serum calcium by 1 mg/dl within 16–18 hours after injection. Other changes which may be observed in bioassays are rapidly induced rises in excretion of urinary phosphate and of 3'5'-cAMP. Bioassay in vitro is based on activation of renal adenylate cyclase and increase in cAMP in fetal rat skull or renal tissue. Radioimmunoassay for parathyroid hormone is used routinely for measuring levels of the hormone in the circulation. However, circulating precursor or breakdown products of variable biologic and immunologic activity can impair the accuracy of this assay.

Physiology

The administration of parathyroid hormone (1) raises the serum calcium and lowers the serum phosphorus; (2) increases urinary excretion of phosphate but decreases excretion of calcium; (3) removes calcium from bone, particularly if the dietary intake of calcium is inadequate; (4) increases serum alkaline phosphatase if changes in bone have been produced; and (5) activates vitamin D in renal tissue by increasing the rate of conversion of 25-hydroxycholecalciferol to 1,25-dihydroxycholecalciferol.

The action of parathyroid hormone to increase bone resorption results in the release not only of calcium but also of collagenase, lysosomal enzymes, and hydroxyproline. In the kidney, it affects renal tubular reabsorption of calcium and reabsorption or secretion of phosphate. There is also evidence that parathyroid hormone increases the rate of absorption of calcium from the intestine, an effect which is, however, comparatively minor and more likely a result of its renal action to increase production of 25-hydroxycholecalciferol.

The actions of the parathyroid hormone on bone and kidney are independent processes, as indicated by the fact that the hormone effectively mobilizes bone calcium in nephrectomized animals as well as from bone tissue incubated in vitro. The mechanism by which parathyroid hormone stimulates bone resorption is not known. The hormone increases the amounts of both lactic and citric acid in the tissues and both of these acids could act to make bone soluble. However, the amount of acid produced appears insufficient to explain the degree of bone resorption observed.

Parathyroid hormone may act to stimulate protein synthesis in the osteoclasts, which, in turn, effect resorption of bone. This idea is supported by the observation that inhibition of RNA synthesis (and thus, indirectly, protein synthesis) by dactinomycin blocks the activity of the hormone in vivo. However, the rapid acute effect of parathyroid hormone on bone resorption is not inhibited by dactinomycin, indicating that at least part of the activity is independent of RNA and possibly of protein synthesis as well.

A primary action of parathyroid hormone is to stimulate the uptake of extracellular calcium. In turn,

bone, parathyroid hormone controls renal excretion of calcium and of phosphate.

Chemistry

Parathyroid hormone is a linear polypeptide consisting of 84 amino acids. The amino acid sequence of the polypeptide is shown above (Fig 29–9). Parathyroid hormones from different species differ only slightly; bovine and porcine hormone are identical except for 7 amino acids. Studies of the synthetic parathyroid hormone polypeptide indicate that the essential requirements for the physiologic actions of this hormone on both skeletal and renal tissues are contained within the 1–29 or possibly the 1–34 N-terminal amino acids.

Parathyroid hormone is initially synthesized in the chief cells as a prohormone containing 15–20 extra amino acids.

The secreted hormone is degraded rapidly; it has a half-life of about 18 minutes. Circulating precursor or degradation products are found in the plasma (particularly ones of MW 7000) which have some biologic activity and may represent important active forms of the hormone. Parathyroid hormone from the salmon is the most active of several hormones derived from various animal species when tested in man, possibly because it is the most slowly degraded.

the increased calcium in the cytosol may trigger the metabolic events in bone and in kidney, including bone resorption and tubular reabsorption of calcium (Fig 28–6). cAMP also increases the bone resorption but does not increase calcium uptake. It may act by increasing cytosol calcium via mobilization of intracellular membrane-bound calcium. Parathyroid hormone increases cAMP by activating adenylate cyclase in both bone and kidney, the latter action being reflected by a rise in urinary cAMP. Therefore, the hormone has a dual action to increase cytosol calcium. In the absence of calcium, parathyroid hormone still increases cAMP but no longer stimulates bone resorption or osteoblastic activity. Thus, a major requirement for the parathyroid activation of calcium mobilization may be, paradoxically, to increase uptake of ionized calcium into the cells. Circulating phosphate ion can reverse the action of parathyroid hormone, presumably by influencing phosphate-calcium transport at the level of both mitochondria and cell membrane.

Parathyroid hormone requires vitamin D to bring about its effects on bone. It is therefore comparatively inactive in subjects with rickets. The effect of the hormone on renal excretion of phosphate, however, is not dependent on vitamin D.

Histologic evidence indicates that vitamin D and the hormone act by different mechanisms. The action of vitamin D is primarily on calcium ion transport systems both in the intestine and in bone.

Parathyroid hormone may affect organs other than bones and kidneys; indeed, patients with hyperparathyroidism may present without prominent renal or bone symptoms but with involvement of the central nervous system, the gastrointestinal tract, or the peripheral vascular system. Repeated doses of parathyroid extract may cause severe symptoms such as oliguria or anuria, anorexia, gastrointestinal hemorrhage, nausea and vomiting, and finally loss of consciousness and death. These symptoms are probably due to water and electrolyte depletion as well as to other body changes not clearly understood.

Control of Release of Parathyroid Hormone

In contrast to many protein hormones, parathyroid hormone is not stored in the gland; no storage granules are present. It is thus synthesized and secreted continuously.

Secretion of parathyroid hormone is subject to control by a negative feedback mechanism relating to the levels of ionized calcium in the plasma; parathyroid hormone concentrations are decreased abruptly by administration of calcium ion and rise when circulating ionized calcium is lowered by the administration of the chelating agent ethylenediaminetetraacetate. Calcium loss associated with uremia also results in an increase in circulating parathyroid hormone. Although calcium appears to be an important homeostatic regulator of parathyroid secretion, a change in the amount of phosphate has no effect on hormone release.

Administration of vitamin A decreases parathyroid hormone, possibly by increasing calcium uptake into the parathyroid gland.

Calcitonin (Thyrocalcitonin)

Calcitonin or thyrocalcitonin (Fig 29–10) is a calcium-lowering hormone originating from the thyroid gland. The release of calcitonin is stimulated by high levels of ionized calcium in the serum.

Calcitonin is directly effective on bone, where it results in metabolic effects opposite to those of parathyroid hormone though it does not act on the same mechanisms. It acts on circulating calcium levels faster than does parathyroid hormone, but the effects in general are quantitatively less as well as shorter in duration. Indeed, the half-time of calcitonin is 4–12 minutes, or about twice the rate for parathyroid hormone. Calcitonin may therefore be specifically involved in maintaining the constancy of calcium ion in the plasma only when minor changes are involved. In the kidney, calcitonin, in contrast to parathyroid hormone, increases calcium excretion and inhibits synthesis of 1,25-dihydroxycholecalciferol; however, it does not do so by affecting cAMP levels. Young animals are 50–100 times more sensitive to this hormone than adults.

In most species, including man, calcitonin is a peptide of MW 3600 (32 amino acids; see below). In contrast to parathyroid hormone, the complete structure of calcitonin is required for biologic activity, although large variations in the amino acid composition occur among different species. The hormone of salmon is particularly potent in man.

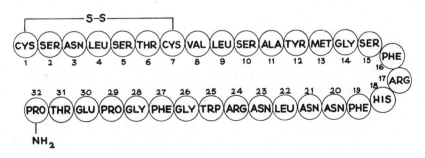

Figure 29-10. Structure of porcine calcitonin.

Abnormalities of Parathyroid Function

A. Hypoparathyroidism: This is usually the result of surgical removal of the parathyroids, as by accidental damage during thyroid surgery. It may also be caused by an autoimmune reaction. Idiopathic hypoparathyroidism, of unknown cause, has been reported. The symptoms of hypoparathyroidism include muscular weakness, tetany, and irritability. X-ray examination of the skull may reveal calcifications of the basal ganglia, and the bones may be more dense than normal. Early cataracts may be detected by slitlamp examination. If hypoparathyroidism begins early in childhood, there may be stunting of growth, defective tooth development, and mental retardation.

Serum calcium is low, serum phosphate is elevated, urinary calcium is low to absent, and urinary phosphate is low in the absence of renal failure. Serum magnesium and hydroxyproline levels are reduced. A decrease in the normally low levels of circulating hormone is difficult to detect.

Calcium, parathyroid hormone, and vitamin D precursors are used in treatment of hypoparathyroidism; the latter agent increases absorption of calcium from the intestine and phosphate excretion by the kidney.

In **pseudohypoparathyroidism**, there is a failure of the renal tubules to respond to the action of parathyroid hormone rather than a deficiency of the hormone itself.

B. Hyperparathyroidism: An increase in parathyroid hormone production is usually due to a tumor of the gland (parathyroid adenoma). Decalcification of the bones causes pain and deformities, including cystic lesions as well as spontaneous fractures. Deposits of calcium may form in the soft tissues, and renal stones may also occur. Deficiencies of magnesium may also result from long-continued hyperparathyroidism. Some extraparathyroid tumors associated with hyperparathyroidism contain active material immunologically indistinguishable from parathyroid hormone.

Enlargement of the parathyroid glands (**secondary hyperparathyroidism**), probably as a result of increased serum phosphate levels, is often a feature of chronic renal disease.

In primary hyperparathyroidism, serum calcium is high and serum phosphate low. Urine calcium is increased as well as urine phosphate (tubular reabsorption of phosphate decreased). In chronic renal disease, with secondary hyperactivity of the parathyroid, serum calcium is low. Urinary calcium and phosphate are both low, and there is apparent resistance to the action of vitamin D, in the presence of uremia and acidosis. As a result of associated bone abnormalities, serum alkaline phosphatase is often elevated. Radioimmunologically detectable parathyroid hormone is also elevated.

THE PANCREAS

The endocrine function of the pancreas is localized in the islets of Langerhans, epithelial cells that are dispersed throughout the entire organ. Two hormones which affect carbohydrate metabolism are produced by the islet tissue: insulin by the beta cells, and glucagon by the alpha cells. A delta cell has also been described, but its function is not known.

INSULIN

Insulin plays an important role in metabolism, causing increased carbohydrate metabolism, glycogen storage, fatty acid synthesis, amino acid uptake, and protein synthesis. It is thus an important anabolic hormone which acts on a variety of tissues including liver, fat, and muscle.

Chemistry

Insulin is a protein hormone produced from the islets of Langerhans which make up 1% of the pancreatic tissue. Crystallization of insulin requires traces of zinc, which may be a constituent of stored insulin since normal islets are relatively rich in this element.

The structure of human insulin is shown in Fig 29–11. In all species, the molecule consists of 2 chains connected by disulfide bridges. A third intradisulfide bridge also occurs on the A chain. Breaking the disulfide bonds with alkali or reducing agents inactivates insulin. Digestion of insulin protein with proteolytic enzymes inactivates the hormone, and for this reason it cannot be given orally.

The structures of a number of insulins obtained from various animal sources have been elucidated. That of pork pancreas is the most similar to human insulin. The 2 insulins differ only in the terminal amino acid (number 30) of the B chain, which is alanine in porcine insulin and threonine in human insulin. This terminal amino acid is easily removed with carboxypeptidase. The resulting altered molecule retains its biologic activity. Thus it is possible to convert porcine insulin into a compound with an active primary structure identical to human insulin save for the fact that the altered insulin is shorter by one amino acid in the B chain.

Insulins from the pig, whale, and dog are structurally identical. Those from the sheep, horse, and cow differ from porcine insulin only in 3 amino acids under the disulfide bridge in the A chain. Other species may differ in as much as 29 out of the 51 amino acids. Two structurally different insulins have been isolated from a single rat pancreas, differing by a single amino acid (lysine or methionine) in the A chain. The pancreas of certain fish contains more than one insulin, differences being found in both the A and B chains.

Despite the wide variation in primary (amino

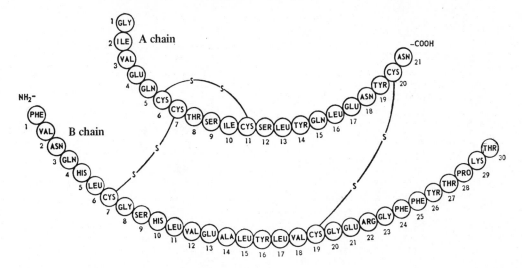

Figure 29—11. Structure of human insulin.

acid) structure, the biologic activity per unit weight is remarkably constant for all insulins.

Although the minimum calculated molecular weight of insulin is 5734, it can exist in different polymeric forms depending on the temperature, concentration, and pH. Most estimates of molecular weight by physical measurements range from 12,000–48,000. The molecular weight of insulin under normal physiologic conditions is not known—nor is it known whether insulin can exist under different physiologic conditions in more than one polymeric form.

The secondary and tertiary structures of bovine insulin have been determined by x-ray crystallography. These studies indicate that the A chain portion of the molecule is the more exposed, including the 6–11 disulfide bridge, possibly involved in hormonal activity (Fig 29–11). The B chain is in the internal portion of the molecule; noncovalent binding between B chains is responsible for the formation of the insulin dimer and probably higher polymers. The crystallized hexamer of insulin forms around zinc molecules which are held in place by imidazoles (on histidines) in the B chain.

Attempts have been made to determine the core of biologic activity in insulin by the controlled modification of side chains and by partial degradation of the molecule with proteolytic enzymes. Amino groups at the terminal amino acids or the epsilon amino groups of the lysine residues are not required since their acetylation causes no loss in biologic activity. Similarly, the removal of the amide from the terminal asparagine on the A chain (Fig 29–11) has no effect, though removal of the aspartic acid itself causes complete loss of activity. Removal of the terminal octapeptide on the B chain inactivates insulin, although removal of the terminal carboxyamino acid of the B chain and some amino acids in the amino terminal portion of the molecule does not affect activity. The hydroxyl groups of serine and threonine can be modified by sulfation with

little loss of potency, while destruction of the histidines by photo-oxidation results in inactivation. Although most side chains of insulin can be modified without interfering with activity, reaction at the same sites with molecules large enough to produce steric hindrance can cause inactivation.

Iodination of tyrosine residues (usually those of the exposed A chain) up to one atom per mol has little effect on the biologic activity of insulin, but increasing iodination causes progressive inactivation. Therefore, in the preparation of radioiodine-tagged insulin (used as a biologic and immunologic tracer), iodination must be restricted to less than one atom per mol.

Sulfated bovine insulin, porcine insulin, and fish insulins are sometimes used in resistant diabetics because of their reduced antigenicity and cross-reactivity with circulating antibody. A highly purified insulin (**monocomponent insulin**) with greatly reduced immunogenicity has been prepared. This insulin currently is proving preferable for routine clinical use.

Other modifications reduce the absorption of insulin from the injected sites, thus prolonging the action of the hormone. These preparations have the occasional disadvantage of being more immunogenic than crystalline insulin. **Protamine zinc insulin** is a combination of insulin with protamine which is absorbed more slowly than ordinary insulin; one injection of protamine zinc insulin may lower the blood glucose for more than 24 hours, whereas 2 or 3 injections of regular (crystalline) insulin might be required for the same effect.

Globin insulin, another combination of insulin with a protein (in this case globin) has an effect somewhere between those of regular and protamine insulin (a 12- to 15-hour duration of action).

Ultralente insulin is a slow-acting insulin prepared by controlled crystallization in the presence of high concentrations of zinc and acetate in order to produce large crystals which are therefore slowly absorbed. **Lente insulin** is a 7:3 mixture of ultralente and regular insulin which has a duration of effect between the two.

Assay of Insulin

Insulin preparations are standardized in units by measuring their effect on the blood glucose of rabbits. The international standard contains 24 units per mg recrystallized insulin.

In vitro bioassays can be used to measure circulating insulin. In these bioassays, the effects of plasma and insulin on glucose metabolism are measured in either incubating rat diaphragm or epididymal fat pad. Although adequately sensitive, the methods are nonspecific; results are therefore usually reported as insulin-like activity. Insulin-like activity in plasma is higher than the actual insulin content; this excess insulin-like activity has been called **bound, nonsuppressible,** or **atypical** insulin.

It is unlikely that "bound," "nonsuppressible," or "atypical" insulins actually represent protein-bound insulin or insulin in any form. However, they may be of physiologic significance as noninsulin humoral factors facilitating carbohydrate or lipid metabolism and they can compete with insulin for some membrane insulin receptors. Recent evidence suggests that much of the insulin-like activity in blood is the sulfation factor (**somatomedin**; see p 502) released from liver as a result of growth hormone activity. Whatever its role, insulin-like activity is not present in sufficient quantities to prevent ketosis in animals whose insulin supply is removed by pancreatectomy.

Radioimmunochemical assays are more specific than the bioassays and permit detection of insulin in concentrations less than 1 μU/ml. The insulin content of serum in the fasting state is reported to be about 25 μU/ml when measured immunochemically. In recent years, this method has gained ascendancy over the less specific and less reproducible bioassays. One defect of the radioimmunoassay is the fact that it may measure fragments or precursors of insulin in plasma. Those substances, while retaining some immunologic activity, have little or no biologic activity.

Biosynthesis of Insulin

In the beta cells of the pancreas, insulin is synthesized, as is any other protein, by the ribosomes of the endoplasmic reticulum. Studies in which mRNA from islets is translated in heterologous cell-free systems suggest that the initial, transient product is a peptide of 14–18,000 daltons. (See Yip & others reference, p 515.) However, the ultimate, stable product of ribosomal synthesis is the insulin precursor, **proinsulin**.

The structure of porcine proinsulin is shown in Fig 29–12. The molecule consists of a single polypeptide chain which begins with the normal B chain sequence at its amino terminus but contains a linking polypeptide of 33 amino acids which connects the carboxy terminus of the B chain to the amino terminus of the A chain amino acid sequence. The molecular weight of porcine proinsulin is 9082, about 50% great-

er than that of insulin. The connecting link is about the same size in proinsulins from other species, but it varies greatly in specific amino acid content. The molecule is comparatively inactive biologically, yet it can cross-react with antisera prepared against insulin. Proinsulin, after reduction to its open chain structure, is readily reconverted in high yield to the proper disulfide configuration with mild oxidation. Since the yields are higher than normally obtained with free A or B chains, the connecting link appears important in providing the proper alignment of the molecule for correct disulfide synthesis. Incubation of proinsulin with trypsin removes the linking peptide and liberates a completely biologically active product. Cleavage is not exact, however, and the final product, after trypsinization, is not insulin but **dalanated insulin**.* Therefore, the biologic mechanism by which the activation of proinsulin to insulin occurs requires proteolysis but may employ enzymes other than (or in conjunction with) trypsin itself. The conversion of proinsulin to insulin occurs in the granule package, not in the endoplasmic reticulum, where proinsulin is synthesized.

During biologic proteolysis, the 2 basic amino acids at either end of the connecting peptide (C-peptide) are removed (Arg 31, 21, and Lys 62, Arg 63). The free, biologically inactive C-peptide is retained in the granule and is ultimately secreted in equal molar ratio with the insulin.

Proinsulin can be measured by specific radioimmunoassay technics or, after separation from insulin, by "molecular sieving" chromatography. Normally, proinsulin represents only a small portion of the insulin stored in the pancreas or found in the plasma. Plasma proinsulin is not elevated in human diabetics or in normal individuals after glucose stimulation, but it may be the predominant circulating form in some subjects with islet cell tumors.

After conversion, the insulin inside the vesicle package condenses and forms the typical beta granules enclosed by membranous sacs. Current evidence suggests that stored insulin may exist in different "compartments" which differ in their sensitivity to stimulating agents.

Insulin Secretion

Approximately 50 units of insulin per day are required; this is about one-fifth of the amount stored in the human pancreas.

The secretion process for stored insulin after stimulation by glucose or tolbutamide has been visualized by electron microscopy. It is similar to the secretion of other proteins stored as granules, including those found in pituitary and pancreatic acinar cells. During secretion, the granules move to the plasma membrane of the cell, where the granule surface membrane fuses with the cell membrane. The fused membranes then rupture, and the granular contents are liberated into the pericapillary space. This process is called **emeiocy-**

---

*Dalanated insulin is the accepted term for insulin with alanine removed (dealaninated) at position 30 of the B chain.

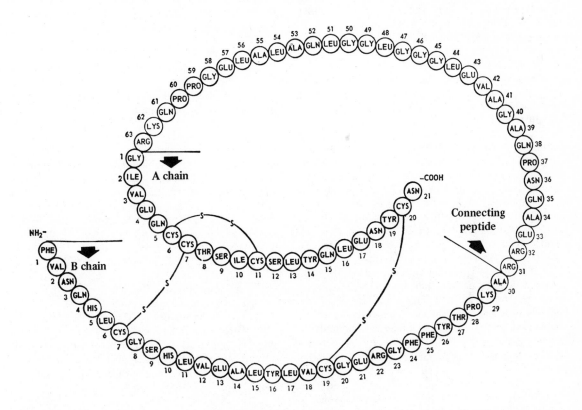

Figure 29–12. Structure of porcine proinsulin. (Reproduced, with permission, from Chance & others: Science 161:166, 1968.)

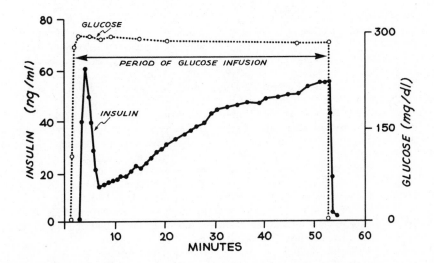

Figure 29–13. Multiphasic response of the in vitro perfused pancreas during constant stimulation with glucose. (Modified from Grodsky & others, 1969.)

tosis. Agents which destroy microtubules (vincristine, deuterium oxide) inhibit insulin secretion. Microfilamentous organelles have also been observed and implicated in the secretion process.

Since secretion of insulin is the resultant of a variety of phenomena, various agents may influence secretion at different levels. Those stimulating release of labile storage forms cause insulin secretion in seconds; those acting on provision of insulin to the secretion system may require 15–120 minutes. Agents acting on more than one phenomenon can produce multiphasic patterns of insulin release (Fig 29–13).

Glucose directly stimulates insulin release within 30–60 seconds. It acts directly on the mechanism controlling the release of stored insulin, and the effect is not inhibited by complete blocking of insulinogenesis with dinitrophenol or puromycin. In addition, glucose also stimulates insulin synthesis, an effect which requires a longer period and probably more chemical energy than that needed for insulin release.

It is not clear whether an intermediate produced in the course of glucose metabolism provides the secretory signal or whether the glucose molecule itself acts directly on a glucoreceptor in the beta cell membrane. In general, sugars which are readily metabolized—eg, mannose and, to a lesser extent, fructose—can stimulate insulin release; the nonmetabolizable sugars—galactose, L-arabinose, 2-deoxyglucose, and xylose—do not.

Stimulation of insulin secretion by glucose is blocked by inhibitors of glucose metabolism such as mannoheptulose, glucosamine, and 2-deoxyglucose.

Many agents (eg, amino acids, some gastrointestinal products, and fatty acids) can stimulate insulin release, but only if glucose is present. Possibly a dual action is required to bring about insulin release—activation of a receptor site and production of a metabolite. Glucose is capable of doing both, whereas other substances having only one of the 2 actions require a supplementary agent.

Nucleotide metabolism also plays a significant role since insulin secretion can be enhanced by cAMP and hormones (glucagon and, to a lesser extent, ACTH and thyrotropin) or agents such as theophylline which increase intracellular cAMP (Fig 28–4). cAMP is not the final signal for insulin release, however, since these agents alone are poor stimulators, acting primarily to potentiate the effect of glucose or amino acids. The in vitro effects of glucagon on insulin release usually require high concentrations. At physiologic levels in vivo, the major effect of glucagon is probably exerted on the liver.

Glucose stimulates both calcium uptake and beta cell cAMP. Thus, part of its action on insulin release is by increasing calcium localization in those compartments important for secretion (Fig 28–5). Translocation of calcium to insulin granules and plasma membrane occurs during glucose-stimulated secretion.

Amino acids, particularly leucine and arginine, can stimulate the pancreas to produce insulin both in vivo and in vitro. In children with spontaneous hypoglycemic episodes and in subjects with functioning islet cell tumors, leucine is particularly effective in causing a rise in circulating insulin. The metabolites of leucine, isovalerate and acetoacetate, have no effect, indicating that the amino acid itself is the primary stimulant.

Many hormones, such as growth hormone and glucocorticoids, can produce an increase in circulating insulin when administered to the intact animal. Since these agents also cause hyperglycemia, it is possible that they act on the pancreas primarily by way of increasing stimulation by glucose rather than by a direct effect.

Epinephrine, both in vivo and in vitro, is a potent and highly effective inhibitor of insulin secretion regardless of the blood glucose concentration. Thus, under extreme stress, epinephrine not only provides glucose to the circulation by glycogenolysis but preferentially preserves it for utilization by the brain since it simultaneously depresses insulin release. At the same time, it supplies fatty acids mobilized from adipose tissue to provide the major fuel for the exercising muscle.

Insulin secretion is enhanced by agents increasing beta-adrenergic action and is inhibited by agents stimulating the alpha-adrenergic systems. Epinephrine is both a beta- and alpha-adrenergic stimulator. Presumably, the alpha stimulation in the islet tissue is responsible for its inhibitory effect. When the alpha-adrenergic action is blocked with phentolamine, epinephrine actually increases insulin release.

Zinc is usually found associated with insulin in the beta cells, and the amount of zinc in those cells declines after administration of glucose. However, this element is not present in the beta cells of all species. Insulin secretion is intimately controlled by certain other cations. In vitro, calcium is an absolute requirement for insulin secretion regardless of glucose concentration. Magnesium is inhibitory. A decrease in the sodium pump or an increase of potassium ion causes an immediate secretion of insulin from the pancreas in vitro. In certain hypertensive diabetics with hypokalemia and impaired insulin secretion, replacement of potassium has improved the pancreatic sensitivity to normal stimulation.

Insulin release can also be indirectly influenced by the central nervous system. Lesions of the ventral medial nucleus or stimulation of the vagus increase insulin release. Finally, the sensitivity of pancreas to the above stimuli may vary with the developmental state. For example, the pancreases of fish, amphibians, ruminants, and the mammalian fetus are remarkably insensitive to glucose though they may respond normally to amino acids or other stimulants.

Hypoglycemic Agents

There are several hypoglycemic drugs, effective when taken by mouth, that are useful for the control of diabetes. One class of these drugs, the sulfonylureas, is not hypoglycemic in alloxanized diabetic animals, in animals or patients after pancreatectomy, or in juvenile diabetics whose pancreases contain little or no insulin. They are useful in the treatment of diabetics of the

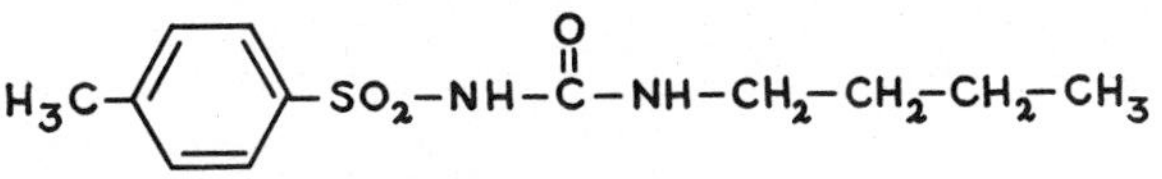

Figure 29–14. Orally effective hypoglycemic agents.

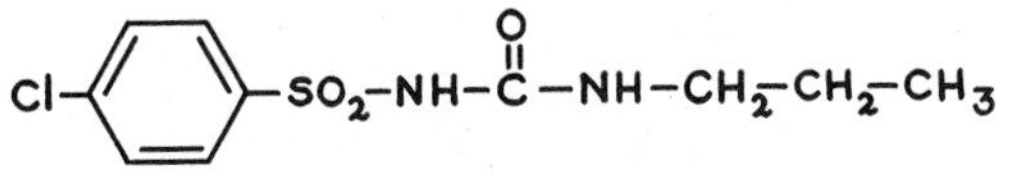

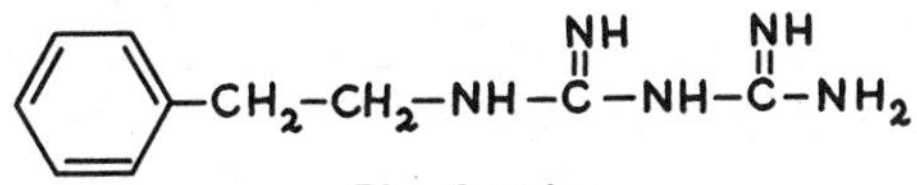

"adult-onset" type who have retained some pancreatic function. The orally effective sulfonamide agents most extensively used are tolbutamide (Orinase), chlorpropamide (Diabinese), and tolazamide (Tolinase), the last 2 being long-acting (Fig 29–14). Other sulfonylureas such as glyburide have actions similar to that of tolbutamide but are 50–100 times more potent.

Although sulfonylureas may have some peripheral effects on glucose metabolism, their primary action appears to be on the pancreas. Tolbutamide may act on insulin secretion by a different mechanism than that of glucose, which may explain its effectiveness in maturity-onset diabetes or in patients with islet cell tumors in whom the pancreas does not respond normally to glucose. In contrast to glucose, tolbutamide does not acutely stimulate insulin synthesis. The sulfonylureas also potentiate the action of glucose on the pancreas. Therefore, their total effect on the pancreas is dependent on the amount of metabolically available glucose in the circulation.

Phenethyl biguanide (phenformin, DBI) and chemically related drugs also produce hypoglycemia. The biguanides are active in severe diabetes as well as in alloxanized or pancreatectomized animals. In contrast to the sulfonylureas, the action of these hypoglycemic agents is exerted on the peripheral tissues. In muscle, glucose uptake is increased, partly as a result of an acceleration of glycolysis due to an uncoupling action on oxidative phosphorylation. In addition, the biguanides may produce hypoglycemia by decreasing gluconeogenesis in the liver and by decreasing intestinal glucose absorption.

An increase in serum lactate levels may often result from biguanide treatment, presumably as a result of its uncoupling action in muscle.

Intestinal Factors

Oral glucose tolerance tests cause greater insulin secretion than a comparable intravenous glucose tolerance test, even though blood glucose levels are usually higher in the latter case. Glucose administered orally stimulates the release of intestinal factors which in turn act on the pancreas. Gastrin, pancreozymin, secretin, and a glucagon-like substance are 4 such substances which are found in the intestine that can directly stimulate insulin secretion both in vivo and in vitro.

Metabolism of Insulin

Insulin is degraded primarily in liver and kidney by the enzyme **glutathione insulin transhydrogenase.** This enzyme brings about reductive cleavage of the S–S bonds which connect the A and B chains of the insulin molecule (Fig 29–11). Reduced glutathione, acting as a coenzyme for the transhydrogenase, donates the H atoms for the reduction and is itself thus converted to oxidized glutathione. After insulin has been reductively cleaved, the A and B chains are futher degraded by proteolysis. When insulin is bound to antibody, it is much less sensitive to enzymatic degradation.

Insulin-inactivating systems are rapid-acting; the half-life of circulating insulin is about 7–15 minutes.

Physiology: Mode of Action of Insulin

Despite the fact that insulin has for many years been available as a comparatively pure protein hormone, its primary site of action (if indeed there is a single primary site) is still virtually unknown. Insulin acts in such a variety of ways that it is difficult to establish whether a given effect is a primary or a secondary one. In addition, observations made in vivo can be misleading since a change in the metabolism of one tissue may occur as a result of the ability of insulin to influence the provision of metabolic substrates or inhibitors from a completely different tissue. In one or another tissue, insulin exhibits all of the activities ascribed to hormones, including transport at the membrane site, RNA synthesis at the nuclear site, translation at the ribosome for protein synthesis, and an influence on tissue levels of cAMP. Insulin is active in skeletal and heart muscle, adipose tissue, liver, the lens of the eye, and possibly leukocytes. It is comparatively inactive in renal tissue, red blood cells, and the gastrointestinal tract. The major metabolic actions of insulin are centered in the muscle, adipose tissue, and liver.

Insulin is firmly bound to the outer membrane fractions of those tissues on which it acts. This binding is to a highly specific receptor site, since other proteins and protein hormones of similar size do not compete. The amount of membrane-bound insulin parallels its biologic activity in the tissue, which suggests that binding is requisite to hormone activity. Additionally, the biologic activities of modified insulins are proportionate to their binding affinities. However, excess or nonfunctional binding sites can occur. Insulin is not changed in this process, as evidenced by the fact that, when reextracted from the membranes to which it is bound, it remains fully potent and immunologically fully reactive. The structure of the membrane receptor has not been elucidated but it is probably a glycoprotein. Thus, insulin may carry out most of its functions without actually entering the cell.

Muscle & Adipose Tissue

A primary effect of insulin in muscle and adipose tissue is to facilitate transport of a variety of substances. These include glucose and related monosaccharides, amino acids, potassium ion, nucleosides, inorganic phosphate, and calcium ion. These effects are not secondary to glucose metabolism since they can be demonstrated in in vitro systems when glucose is not present. Insulin need not enter the cell to activate transport since insulin bound covalently to large inert particles is fully active on the much smaller fat cells.

In muscle or adipose tissue, uptake of glucose by the cell is the rate-limiting step for all subsequent intracellular glucose metabolism. The ability of insulin to facilitate transport thus leads to an increase in all pathways of glucose metabolism, including glycogen deposition, stimulation of the hexose monophosphate shunt resulting in increased production of NADPH, increased glycolysis, increased oxidation (reflected by an increase in oxygen uptake and CO_2 production), and increased fatty acid synthesis. In adipose tissue, insulin increases lipid synthesis by providing acetyl-CoA and NADPH required for fatty acid synthesis, as well as the glycerol moiety (glycerophosphate) for triacylglycerol synthesis.

The action of insulin on carbohydrate transport does not require subsequent intracellular metabolism of the sugar. Insulin will increase transport and facilitate an increase in intracellular concentration of nonmetabolizable sugars such as L-arabinose and xylose, as well as galactose. The hormone promotes the entry into the cells of those sugars possessing the same configuration at carbons 1, 2, and 3 as D-glucose. Fructose does not require insulin for transport into the cells, possibly because of the ketone group at position 2. Intracellular transport of glucose is enhanced by anoxia or uncoupling agents such as dinitrophenol, indicating that exclusion of glucose from muscle or adipose tissue may require energy. Glucose uptake after

insulin administration can be demonstrated within a few minutes. Furthermore, it occurs in the presence of dactinomycin. Therefore, the insulin-mediated transport system does not require enzyme induction or the synthesis of RNA.

As previously stated, insulin increases the uptake of amino acids into muscle in the absence of glucose. This effect is not secondary to stimulation of protein synthesis since uptake is observed when all protein synthesis is blocked with puromycin. Insulin also increases the uptake of nonmetabolizable amino acids such as alpha-aminoisobutyrate. Insulin maintains muscle protein by decreasing protein degradation as well.

In adipose tissue, insulin sharply depresses the liberation of fatty acids induced by the action of epinephrine or glucagon. Part of this effect of insulin may be its role in glycolysis, which produces glycerophosphate from glucose and thus facilitates the deposition of the fatty acids as triacylglycerol. However, insulin will also depress fatty acid release in the absence of glucose, indicating that the hormone may act specifically on lipolysis. Since liberation of fatty acids from adipose tissue is stimulated by cAMP, insulin may decrease fatty acid liberation because it reduces tissue levels of cAMP. The effect may still be a membrane action of the hormone since adenylate cyclase, the enzyme responsible for the synthesis of cAMP, is membrane-bound. The reduction by insulin of fatty acid liberation from adipose tissue is extremely important as circulating fatty acid levels are responsible for many effects on intracellular metabolic events, both in muscle and liver. Release of fatty acids in various pathologic states may contribute to impairment of glucose metabolism by indirectly blocking glycolysis at several steps in the pathway. Indeed, many of the effects on liver noted after insulin administration in vivo may be the result of secondary changes induced by reduction in circulating free fatty acids.

Insulin may directly increase protein synthesis because the hormone facilitates incorporation of labeled intracellular amino acids into protein. Insulin can act at the ribosomal level to increase the capacity of this organelle to translate information from messenger RNA to the protein-synthesizing machinery. In the diabetic animal, the polysomes become disaggregated; insulin, in vivo, restores them to the normal aggregated form. This may not be a direct action of the hormone since it cannot be demonstrated in vitro.

Liver

Unlike muscle and adipose tissue, there is no barrier to glucose in liver cells. In this organ, extracellular and intracellular concentrations of glucose are approximately equal. However, an action of insulin on the hepatic cell membrane may still be the primary event since specific binding of insulin to hepatic membranes is demonstrable.

Whatever the site of action in liver, insulin does affect several aspects of hepatic metabolism. In vivo this can be explained, in part, as effects secondary to a decrease in the amounts of amino acids, potassium ion,

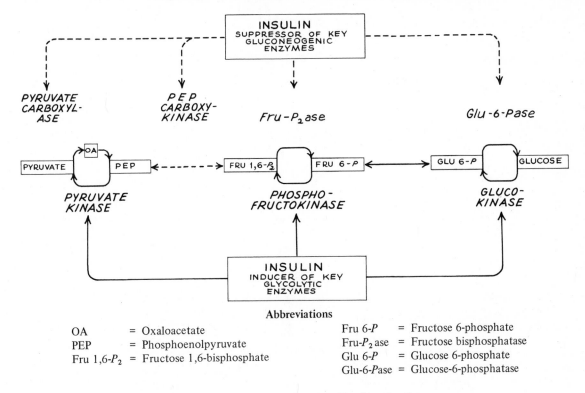

Abbreviations

OA	= Oxaloacetate		Fru 6-P	= Fructose 6-phosphate
PEP	= Phosphoenolpyruvate		Fru-P_2ase	= Fructose bisphosphatase
Fru 1,6-P_2	= Fructose 1,6-bisphosphate		Glu 6-P	= Glucose 6-phosphate
			Glu-6-Pase	= Glucose-6-phosphatase

Figure 29–15. Suppressor and inducer function of insulin on key liver enzymes.

glucose, and fatty acids presented to the liver. In addition, insulin acts directly; the following actions are demonstrable on the isolated perfused liver: decreased glucose output, urea production, protein catabolism, and cAMP; increased potassium and phosphate uptake.

There is a hepatic role for insulin on induction of specific enzymes involved in glycolysis and the simultaneous inhibition of specific gluconeogenic enzymes (Fig 29–15). It is suggested that insulin may act on a genetic locus in the nucleus which contains the functional genetic unit (genome) for a group of specific enzymes. Thus, insulin stimulates glycolysis by effecting a simultaneous increase in synthesis of the enzymes glucokinase, phosphofructokinase, and pyruvate kinase. Simultaneously, insulin represses the enzymes controlling gluconeogenesis: pyruvate carboxylase, phosphoenolpyruvate carboxykinase, fructose-1,6-bisphosphatase, and glucose-6-phosphatase. These changes in hepatic enzyme activity can be inhibited by blocking RNA and protein synthesis with dactinomycin and puromycin. Enzymes which are relatively unimportant in the control of either gluconeogenesis or glycolysis are not affected by insulin. In addition, insulin increases hepatic glycogen synthetase, thereby favoring glycogen synthesis.

The effects of insulin on specific enzyme synthesis in the liver are observed both in vivo and in intact cell preparations, but this may not imply direct action of the hormone at the nuclear level. The relative pattern of the enzyme induction is grossly influenced by

diet. Therefore, changes of intracellular metabolites or enzyme activities arising from the direct actions of the hormone on glucose output, potassium uptake, etc or from the effect of "signals" in the form of metabolites from the peripheral tissues could be responsible. Glucose itself may not be one of the signals, since glycolytic enzyme levels are not increased during the hyperglycemia of diabetes.

The Diabetic States (See Fig 29–16.)

Diabetes mellitus can be characterized as an insufficiency of insulin relative to the requirements of the tissues for this hormone. The juvenile diabetic has little detectable circulating insulin, and the pancreas fails to respond to a glucose load. On the other hand, the maturity-onset diabetic may show an impaired response to glucose, but because of the continued elevated glucose levels he may ultimately secrete more insulin for a given glucose load than a normal individual. Usually, however, continued impaired release is indicated since plasma glucose:insulin ratios are much higher than normal in these subjects. Excessive insulin release after a glucose load occurs in obese individuals who are not diabetic or who have only mild abnormalities in glucose tolerance. It has been suggested that this hyperinsulinism may be attributable both to a peripheral insensitivity to insulin and to a hypersensitivity of the pancreatic islet cells to glucose.

The increased peripheral resistance to insulin in obesity is at least partially the result of decreased in-

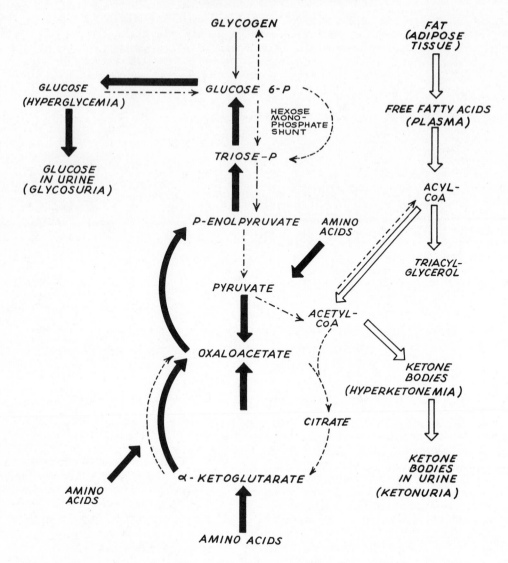

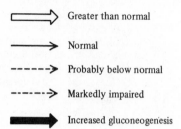

Activity of Pathway

Greater than normal

Normal

Probably below normal

Markedly impaired

Increased gluconeogenesis

Figure 29–16. Abnormal metabolism in the liver during uncontrolled diabetes.

sulin receptors on the target cell membranes. This is not a genetic characteristic, since receptors quickly increase after weight loss and concomitant increased insulin reduction. In animals, a close inverse correlation between the number of receptor sites and the degree of experimentally induced insulinization is found.

Most maturity-onset diabetics are also obese; it may be, therefore, that hyperinsulinism, when observed in the maturity-onset diabetic, is more closely related to obesity than to the diabetes. In nonobese prediabetic subjects (ie, persons with a strong family history of diabetes but no abnormalities in glucose tolerance), the insulin response to glucose is normal or slightly impaired. Subjects whose diabetes is secondary to acromegaly, Cushing's disease, or pheochromocytoma may suffer primarily from a peripheral defect in carbohydrate metabolism produced by growth hormone, corticosteroids, or catecholamines, and, in an effort to compensate, produce increased amounts of insulin for a given glucose load.

In diabetes, hyperglycemia occurs as a result of impaired transport and uptake of glucose into muscle and adipose tissue. Repression of the key glycolytic enzymes and derepression of gluconeogenic enzymes promotes gluconeogenesis in the liver, which further contributes to hyperglycemia. Transport and uptake of amino acids in peripheral tissues is also depressed, causing an elevated circulating level of amino acids, particularly alanine, which provide fuel for gluconeogenesis in the liver. The amino acid breakdown during gluconeogenesis in the liver results in increased production of urea nitrogen.

Because of the decreased production of ATP—and possibly because of a direct requirement for insulin—protein synthesis is decreased in all tissues. A decrease in acetyl-CoA, ATP, NADPH, and glycerophosphate in all tissues results in decreased fatty acid and lipid synthesis. Stored lipids are hydrolyzed by increased lipolysis, and the liberated fatty acids may then interfere at several steps of carbohydrate phosphorylation in muscle and liver, further contributing to hyperglycemia. Fatty acids reaching the liver in high concentration inhibit further fatty acid synthesis by a feedback inhibition at the acetyl-CoA carboxylase step. Increased acetyl-CoA from fatty acids activates pyruvate carboxylase, stimulating the gluconeogenic pathway required for the conversion of the amino acid carbon skeletons to glucose. Fatty acids also stimulate gluconeogenesis by entering the citric acid cycle and increasing production of citrate, an established inhibitor of glycolysis (at phosphofructokinase). Eventually, the fatty acids inhibit the citric acid cycle at the level of citrate synthetase and both pyruvate and isocitrate dehydrogenases. The acetyl-CoA which no longer can enter either the citric acid pathway or be used for fatty acid synthesis is shunted to the synthesis of cholesterol or ketones (or both). The rise in ketone concentration in the body fluids and tissues leads to acidosis. Glycogen synthesis is depressed as a result of decreased glycogen synthetase activity, by activation of phosphorylase through the action of epinephrine or glucagon,

and by the increased ADP:ATP ratio.

The insulin-deficient animal is in a state of hormonal imbalance favoring the action of corticosteroids, growth hormone, and glucagon, all of which add to the stimulation of gluconeogenesis, lipolysis, and decreased intracellular metabolism of glucose. Dehydration occurs because of the water required to excrete the excess glucose in the urine.

Liver and kidney are involved in the degradation of insulin. Thus, in renal or hepatic disease, there is an apparent increase in potency of administered insulin (hyperinsulinemia) and a decrease in insulin requirement. This has also been observed in some diabetics with associated kidney or liver disease.

Experimental Diabetes (See Fig 29–17.)

Experimental diabetes may be produced by total pancreatectomy or by a single injection of alloxan, a substance related to the pyrimidines; or with streptozotocin, an N-nitroso derivative of glucosamine. Such chemical ablation of insulin production is a simpler method of producing permanent diabetes than surgical removal of the pancreas, although it is not equally effective in all animals.

Diabetes may also be produced by injection of diazoxide, a sulfonamide derivative which inhibits insulin secretion.

Since a specific acute deficiency of insulin may be produced by the injection of large amounts of antibodies to insulin, this may also be considered another method for the experimental production of diabetes.

Phlorhizin diabetes, a syndrome produced by injection of the drug phlorhizin, is actually a renal diabetes in which glycosuria is produced by failure of reabsorption of glucose by the renal tubules rather than by virtue of any endocrine abnormality.

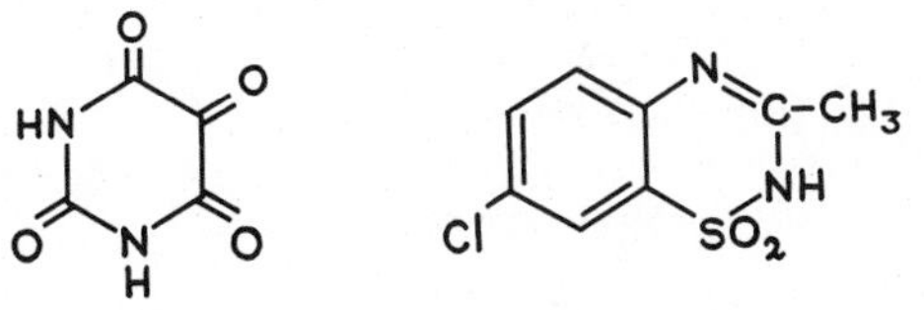

Alloxan   **Diazoxide**

Figure 29–17. Agents used in production of experimental diabetes.

Treatment of Hypoinsulinism & Hyperinsulinism

A. Hypoinsulinism (Juvenile Diabetes): Juvenile diabetes is usually treated with insulin and dietary regimens; a perfect maintenance treatment is not yet possible since subcutaneously administered crystalline insulin is slowly and continuously absorbed into the blood (half-time, 3–4 hours) so that the physiologic minute-to-minute regulation cannot be achieved. In the maturity-onset diabetic having only a mild degree of diabetes, the orally effective hypoglycemic agents (sulfonylureas and biguanides) may be used, but these may have significant cardiac side-effects.

B. Hyperinsulinism: Hyperinsulinism results from excessive production of insulin or overdosage with the hormone. A pancreatic tumor affecting islet tissue is a frequent cause of hyperinsulinism; however, other cases of hyperinsulinism are not associated with demonstrable tumor but are characterized by idiopathic hypoglycemia associated with a marked leucine sensitivity. Blood sugar levels are considerably reduced. The administration of glucose by any route will alleviate the condition. If the hyperinsulinism is due to hyperplasia or tumor of the islet tissue, surgical removal is necessary to correct the condition; however, cortisone, glucagon, and, recently, diazoxide or streptozotocin have all been used successfully to similar effect.

Antibodies

The repeated injection of insulin results in the production of low levels of an antibody to insulin in all subjects, whether diabetic or not, after 2 or 3 months of treatment. On occasion, high concentrations of the antibody are found in subjects who have clinically demonstrated resistance to insulin. Antibodies induced in animals by exogenous insulin can produce lesions in the islet cells and, occasionally, severe diabetes. Antibody-bound insulin is not available to the cells and is only slowly degraded; thus, much of the insulin, whether administered or secreted, is actually wasted. Occasionally, it is released, and after an acute episode of insulin resistance which has been treated with massive doses of insulin the released insulin may cause repeated bouts of hypoglycemia.

Much of the antigenic activity of commercial insulin resides in an impurity associated with a compound of high molecular weight. Highly purified "single component" or "monocomponent" insulin is now available.

Certain viruses can also produce immune islet cell lesions in experimental animals, similar to those seen in young juvenile diabetics. This and other data have led to a current interest in the possibility that some severe forms of this disease may be induced by viral infections.

GLUCAGON

Glucagon is now recognized as an important hormone involved in the rapid mobilization of hepatic glucose and, to a lesser extent, of fatty acids from adipose tissue. Thus, it acts as a hormone required to mobilize metabolic substrates from storage depots.

Glucagon is a polypeptide (Fig 29–18) with a molecular weight of 3485. It contains 15 different amino acids with a total of 29 amino acid residues, arranged in a straight chain. The sequence of the amino acids in the chain has also been determined, and the molecule has been completely synthesized. In contrast

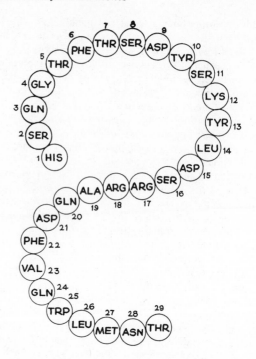

Figure 29–18. Glucagon polypeptide.

to insulin, glucagon contains no cystine, proline, or isoleucine but does contain considerable amounts of methionine and tryptophan. Further, it can be crystalized in the absence of zinc or other metals.

Glucagon originates primarily in the alpha (A) cells of the pancreas, although a significant amount comes from extrapancreatic alpha (A) cells in the stomach and other portions of the gastrointestinal tract. A glucagon-like immunoreactive factor (GLI) has also been identified in gastric and duodenal mucosa. It is immunologically similar though not identical to the alpha (A) cell hormone. Furthermore, it is less active than pancreatic glucagon in stimulating adenylate cyclase and therefore cannot duplicate many of the actions of the pancreatic hormone. Its physiologic role is unknown. Glucagon-like immunoreactive factor is stimulated by absorbed glucose, causing an apparent elevation of circulating pancreatic glucagon. The analytic error associated with this artifact is reduced by using pancreatic-specific antisera for the radioimmunoassay of glucagon.

In contrast to insulin, secretion of pancreatic glucagon increases with low blood glucose whether induced by starvation, insulin, or the sulfonylureas. Glucagon secretion is directly inhibited by glucose in vitro. The alpha cell may be an insulin-dependent tissue since inhibition of glucagon secretion by glucose in normal pancreas occurs only in the presence of insulin. Fatty acids also inhibit glucagon release, whereas exercise stimulates it.

Most amino acids, arginine in particular, cause a rapid secretion of glucagon from the pancreas. The overall effect of amino acids in vivo is not always predictable since they also stimulate hormones with antagonistic action such as insulin and growth hormone.

The alpha cells respond positively to beta-adrenergic stimulation but may be particularly insensitive to alpha-adrenergic signals. Thus, epinephrine, which has both alpha- and beta-adrenergic activity, causes beta stimulation of glucagon secretion. (In contrast, insulin secretion is most sensitive to the alpha-adrenergic activity of epinephrine and is inhibited.) In stress, therefore, insulin secretion is inhibited but glucagon secretion is stimulated.

The adenylate cyclase receptor sites in the liver are particularly sensitive to glucagon. Within minutes after the presentation of glucagon to the liver, cAMP levels increase. The cAMP in turn activates the enzyme dephosphophosphorylase kinase, and an increase of hepatic phosphorylase results. The activation of phosphorylase results in rapid glycogenolysis and hepatic output of glucose. In the dog, increased phosphorylase activity reaches its peak 10−15 minutes after administration of glucagon, further indicating that enzyme activation rather than the more delayed process of enzyme synthesis is involved. A stimulating effect of glucagon on gluconeogenesis has been observed in the isolated perfused liver. This enhanced gluconeogenesis may be mediated by cAMP activation of hepatic lipase which produces a fatty acid activation of the gluconeogenic process. The increased hepatic cAMP produced after glucagon has been shown to increase pyruvate carboxylase, thereby directly enhancing gluconeogenesis. It also activates protein kinases that catalyze phosphorylation of histones, ribosomal proteins, and membrane constituents. Thus, glucagon with time may effect the repression or derepression of hepatic enzyme synthesis.

Glucagon also increases potassium release from the liver, an action which may be related to its glycogenolytic activity.

In adipose tissue, and possibly liver, glucagon increases the breakdown of lipids to fatty acids and glycerol. This lipolytic activity may reside in a different portion of the molecule than does the glycogenolytic activity. In general, glucagon and epinephrine act similarly to increase cAMP synthesis and glycogen and lipid breakdown. However, glucagon is proportionately more active in liver, whereas epinephrine is more active in adipose tissue and skeletal muscle.

Since the target organ effects of insulin and glucagon are essentially opposite and since circulating levels of these hormones change reciprocally in response to glucose and stress, the alpha and beta cells may function as a bihormonal unit; thus, the ratio of insulin to glucagon can determine the quantitative relationship and direction of nutrient flow at the storage depot.

Glucagon may contribute to the etiology of the diabetic state in man. It is elevated in severe diabetes (with ketoacidosis) and rises to abnormally high levels when milder diabetics are stimulated with arginine. The defect in the diabetic alpha (A) cell may be an inability to "recognize" glucose in the absence of insulin.

Although acute replacement of insulin in the diabetic does not immediately restore alpha (A) cell sensitivity to glucose, chronic insulin administration or transplantation of normal islets into insulinopenic animals normalizes glucagon levels. Thus, although elevated glucagon may contribute to the diabetic state, the primary lesion in diabetes is probably at the level of the beta cell. Nevertheless, agents such as growth-hormone inhibiting hormone which inhibit glucagon release and other diabetogenic hormones may have application as an adjunct to insulin treatment for insulin-requiring diabetics.

Totally depancreatized patients do not require as much insulin as do some diabetics with an intact pancreas. This may be explained by the loss of the anti-insulin action of glucagon which would accompany pancreatectomy. Hyperglucagonemia has been reported in a patient with an alpha (A) cell tumor.

Little is known concerning the manner in which glucagon is metabolized. However, an enzyme capable of degrading glucagon has been identified in beef liver. The action of the enzyme is exerted at the N-terminal position of the glucagon polypeptide (Fig 29−18), where it removes the first 2 amino acids by hydrolysis of the peptide bond between serine and glutamine.

Crystalline glucagon polypeptide is now commercially available in the form of glucagon hydrochloride. It may be given by the intramuscular, subcutaneous, or intravenous route for treatment of hypoglycemic reactions, which may occur after overdosage with insulin used for the control of diabetes. Glucagon is also used as a diagnostic test for glycogen storage disease.

THE ADRENALS

THE ADRENAL MEDULLA

Function

The adrenal medulla is a derivative of the sympathetic portion of the autonomic nervous system. Despite its diverse physiologic functions, it is not essential to life.

The hormones synthesized by the adrenal medulla are **epinephrine (adrenaline)** and **norepinephrine (noradrenaline)**. Epinephrine is primarily synthesized and stored in the adrenal medulla and acts through the circulation on distant organs.

Epinephrine in general duplicates the effect of sympathetic stimulation of an organ. It is necessary to provide a rapid physiologic response to emergencies such as cold, fatigue, shock, etc. In this sense, it mobilizes what has been termed the "fight or flight" mechanism, a cooperative effort of the adrenal medulla and the sympathetic nervous system.

In addition to bringing about effects similar to

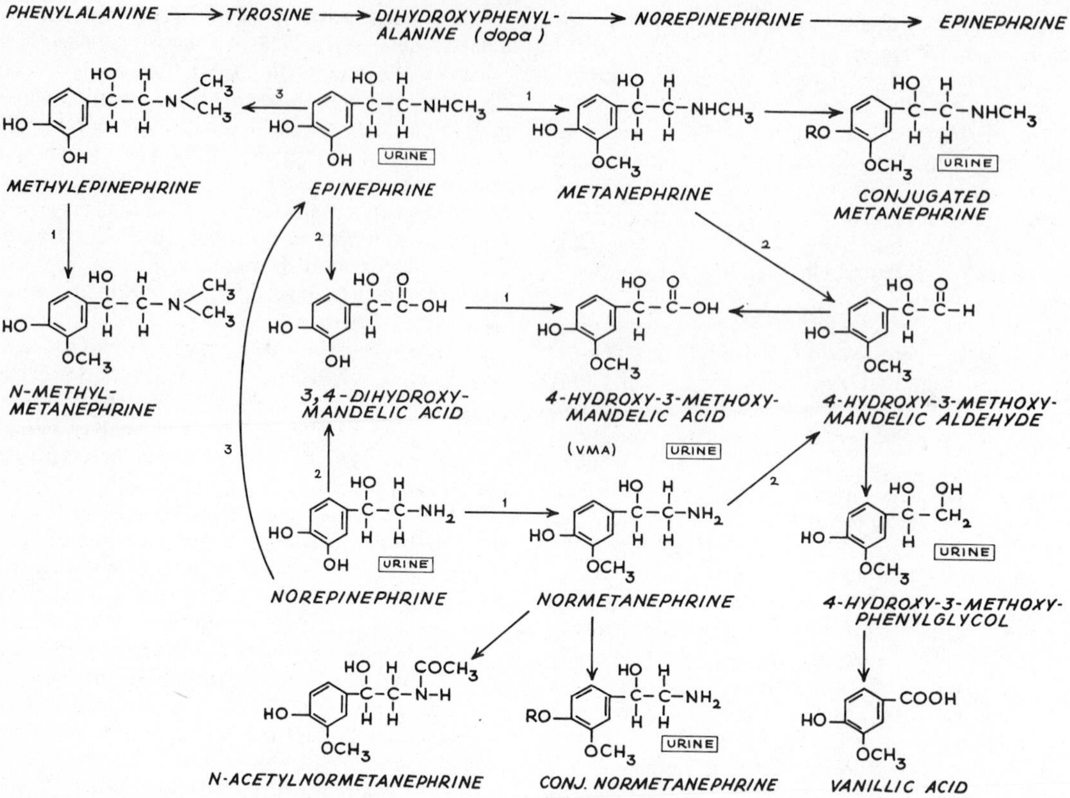

PHENYLALANINE ──────→ TYROSINE ──────→ DIHYDROXYPHENYL- ──────→ NOREPINEPHRINE ──────────→ EPINEPHRINE
                                       ALANINE (dopa)

Figure 29–19. Pathways for the metabolism of norepinephrine and epinephrine. 1, Catechol-O-methyltransferase; 2, monoamine oxidase; 3, phenylethanolamine N-methyltransferase. (Redrawn and reproduced, with permission, from Axelrod, 1965.)

those which follow stimulation of the sympathetic nervous system, both circulating epinephrine and norepinephrine induce metabolic effects, including glycogenolysis in the liver and skeletal muscle, and an increase in circulating free fatty acid levels as a result of stimulation of lipolysis in adipose tissue.

Chemistry

The hormones of the adrenal medulla are structurally related to a group of organic compounds designated as catechols. The group name is a contraction of the original term, which was pyrocatechol (1,2-dihydroxybenzene). The crystalline compound now designated as catechol was first prepared in 1839 by distilling catechin, a juice derived from an Asiatic plant, *Mimosa catechu*. Although the adrenal medullary hormones are spoken of as catecholamines, this term is not strictly accurate, as can be observed from their structural formulas shown in Fig 29–19. The aromatic nucleus of these hormones is indeed that of catechol (1,2-dihydroxybenzene), but the amino group is attached to an aliphatic side chain rather than directly on the aromatic ring as is implied by the term catecholamine. Nonetheless, the clinical literature today has elected to categorize the various dihydroxyphenylalkylamines under the generic term catecholamine, and this terminology will be used in subsequent sections of this book.

Eighty percent of the catecholamine hormone activity in the adrenal medulla is attributable to epinephrine, which occurs in the gland at a concentration of 1–3 mg/g of tissue. The chemical structure of epinephrine is shown in Fig 29–19. Naturally occurring epinephrine is the L-isomer. The unnatural D-form is only one-fifteenth as active. However, L-epinephrine produced synthetically is identical in activity with the natural product. Norepinephrine is found principally in the sympathetic nerves, where it acts as a neurotransmitter. This localization is a result of both synthesis in the nervous tissue and uptake by this tissue from the circulation.

As shown in Fig 29–19, epinephrine differs from norepinephrine only in that the former is methylated on the primary amino group of the aliphatic side chain.

Synthesis & Secretion

In either the adrenal medulla or the neurons, synthesis of the catecholamines is essentially the same (Figs 21–40, 29–19, and 29–20). The initial step in conversion of tyrosine to dihydroxyphenylalanine (dopa) occurs in the cytoplasm and requires the enzyme tyrosine hydroxylase. Inhibition of this enzyme (eg, with α-N-methyl-p-tyrosine) is used to block adrenergic activity in pheochromocytoma. Conversion of

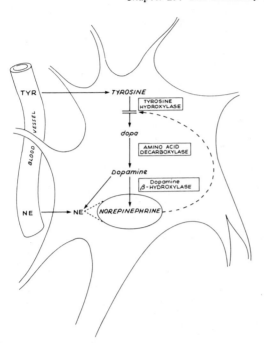

Figure 29—20. Biosynthesis of norepinephrine in the sympathetic neuron. NE = norepinephrine; dopa = dihydroxyphenylalanine. (Adapted from Axelrod & Weinshilbaum, 1972.)

dopa to dopamine also occurs in the cytoplasm and is catalyzed by an amino acid decarboxylase. This nonspecific enzyme is present in high concentration and is usually not a significant site of regulation. Dopamine enters vesicles in the adrenal medulla or neuronal cells where conversion to and storage of catecholamines occurs. These vesicles (chromaffin granules) contain dopamine β-hydroxylase for the synthesis of norepinephrine and, particularly in the medulla, phenylethanolamine N-methyltransferase, which specifically converts norepinephrine to epinephrine. S-Adenosylmethionine is the cofactor in this reaction. The hormones are stored in a complex containing ATP (about 4 mol hormone:1 mol ATP) and several incompletely characterized proteins. The contents of the vesicles, including calcium, are secreted by a calcium-dependent exocytosis in the same proportion as they are stored. The secreted catecholamines are then metabolized in the target tissue or the liver; or, particularly in the case of norepinephrine, they can be taken up again into the neuronal vesicles by an energy-dependent process. This reuptake into the neuron converts the catecholamines to the inactive storage form and is an important mechanism for quickly terminating hormonal or neurotransmitter activity.

Catecholamines do not penetrate the blood-brain barrier; thus, the norepinephrine in the brain must be synthesized within that tissue. L-Dopa, the precursor for catecholamines, does penetrate the barrier. It is therefore used to increase brain catecholamine synthesis in Parkinson's disease.

When radiotagged epinephrine is injected into animals, only about 5% is excreted in the urine unchanged, most of the hormone being metabolized in the tissues by a series of methylations of the phenolic groups or oxidations on the amine side chains (Fig 29–19). The main enzymes involved are monoamine oxidase for the oxidation reactions and catechol-O-methyltransferase for catalysis of the methylations. Monoamine oxidase is a mitochondrial enzyme (actually a series of isoenzymes) with a broad specificity capable of catalyzing the oxidation of side chains on a large variety of catechols. Catechol-O-methyltransferase rapidly catalyzes the inactivation of the catecholamines by methylation of the hydroxyl group at the 3 position. This Mg^{2+}-dependent enzyme is located in the cytosol. The enzyme is capable of methoxylating a variety of catecholamine intermediates with utilization of S-adenosylmethionine as the source of the methyl groups. Catechol-O-methyltransferase requires an active SH group and can therefore be inhibited by *p*-chloromercuric benzoate and iodoacetic acid. Catecholamines and pyrogallol can act as competitive inhibitors of epinephrine metabolism by serving as substrate for this enzyme. Although monoamine oxidase and catechol-O-methyltransferase are found in most tissues, their activity is particularly high in the liver where most of the degradation of the circulating catecholamines takes place.

The first step in the metabolism of the catecholamines can be either methoxylation or oxidation of the side chain, the preferred step varying with circumstances that have not yet been well established. The norepinephrine component which is tightly bound to tissue is initially metabolized by the mitochondrial monoamine oxidase, whereas the less tightly bound component is initially methoxylated by the methyltransferase (catechol-O-methyltransferase). In the neuron, metabolism of norepinephrine by monoamine oxidase is also favored since the levels of catechol-O-methyltransferase are low in this tissue. Since both enzymes usually react with the metabolic products in the liver, the final compounds appearing in the urine are often the same regardless of which of the 2 reactions occurred first.

One of the principal metabolites of epinephrine and of norepinephrine which occurs in the urine is **4-hydroxy-3-methoxy-mandelic acid**. This substance has also been called **vanilmandelic acid (VMA)**. Other metabolites occurring in the urine in significant quantities are 3-methoxyepinephrine (metanephrine) and 4-hydroxy-3-methoxy-phenylglycol. Minor excretion products are the catechols (dihydroxy compounds) which correspond to the methylated compounds mentioned above: 3,4-dihydroxymandelic acid and 3,4-dihydroxyphenylglycol, as well as vanillic acid.

Small quantities of acetylated derivatives are also found. The typical distribution of urinary products found after injection of radiotagged epinephrine is shown below:

Unchanged epinephrine	6%
Metanephrine	40%
Vanilmandelic acid	41%
4-Hydroxy-3-methoxy-phenylglycol	7%
3,4-Dihydroxymandelic acid	2%
Miscellaneous	4%

The urinary products are excreted mostly as conjugates with sulfate or glucuronide, sulfate being the preferred conjugation moiety in man.

Regulation

The amount of active catecholamines is controlled at the levels of synthesis, secretion, reuptake, and catabolism. Catecholamines are allosteric inhibitors of their synthesis at tyrosine hydroxylase. Thus, when the hormones are mobilized rapidly, synthesis is correspondingly reduced. During prolonged stress, β-adrenergic stimulation, pituitary hyperactivity, and ACTH or corticosteroid administration, all of the enzymes in the synthetic pathway are gradually increased. Glucocorticoids from the adjacent adrenal cortex particularly stimulate phenylethanolamine N-methyltransferase, the final enzyme required for epinephrine synthesis. Emeiocytotic secretion is highly sensitive to cholinergic control, and acetylcholine is a particularly positive modulator. This cholinergic stimulation, in turn, appears directly regulated by a stress-linked signal at the hypothalamus.

Disulfiram (Antabuse) inhibits dopamine β-hydroxylase, thereby decreasing catecholamine synthesis. This agent is therefore useful in regulating hypertension. Reserpine and guanethidine are antihypertensive and tranquilizing agents which decrease catecholamines by increasing their destruction, thereby depleting the amounts available in storage form. Cocaine and the antidepressive amphetamines inhibit the fixation and reuptake of the catecholamines by tissues, resulting in increased biologic availability. However, this is probably not the sole action and may not even be the major action of these drugs.

Many agents structurally similar to epinephrine and norepinephrine, though with less biologic activity, can be stored in the tissue sites normally reserved for the active hormones. The agents, known as "false neurotransmitters," prevent either the synthesis or storage of hormones and are released during normal sympathetic stimulation in their place. Thus, these agents or their precursors can be used clinically to reduce release of active hormone and therefore serve as hypotensive agents. "False transmitters" such as β-hydroxytyramine, α-methylnorepinephrine, and metaraminol (Aramine) are produced by administration of tyramine, methyldopa, α-methyltyrosine, or metaraminol itself. Initially, these agents often cause increased circulating hormones by preventing hormone binding in tissues.

Normal Physiology of Epinephrine & Norepinephrine

A. Action on Cardiovascular System: Epinephrine causes vasodilatation of the arterioles of the skeletal muscles and vasoconstriction of the arterioles of the skin, mucous membranes, and splanchnic viscera. It is also effective as a stimulant of heart action, increasing the irritability and the rate and strength of contraction of cardiac muscle and increasing cardiac output.

Norepinephrine has less effect on cardiac output than epinephrine, although it has an excitatory effect on most areas of the cardiovascular system. Norepinephrine exerts an overall vasoconstrictor effect, whereas epinephrine exerts, in general, an overall vasodilator effect, with exceptions as noted above. Both hormones lead to an elevation of blood pressure, more marked in the case of norepinephrine, as a result of their action on the heart and blood vessels.

B. Action on Smooth Muscle of the Viscera: Epinephrine causes relaxation of the smooth muscles of the stomach, intestine, bronchioles, and urinary bladder, together with contraction of the sphincters in the case of the stomach and bladder. Other smooth muscles may be contracted. The relaxing effect of epinephrine on bronchiolar smooth muscle makes this hormone particularly valuable in the treatment of asthmatic attacks.

C. Metabolic Effects: In the liver, epinephrine stimulates the breakdown of glycogen, an action that contributes to the ability of this hormone to elevate the blood glucose. The primary hepatic effect of epinephrine may be to increase cAMP by activating the enzyme adenylate cyclase. cAMP in turn ultimately activates a protein kinase, and this eventually results in conversion of the inactive form of phosphorylase to the phosphorylated active form (see p 261). This effect of epinephrine on increasing hepatic cAMP is similar to that of glucagon. However, measurements of the cAMP levels after epinephrine or glucagon indicate that glucagon is by far the more active hormone in liver tissue.

In muscle, epinephrine also causes the breakdown of glycogen by increasing cAMP, and in this tissue it is more active than glucagon. In exercising muscle, this can result in increased lactate secretion into the plasma. Increases in cAMP after administration of epinephrine can be determined in the isolated heart within 2–4 seconds; the effect of epinephrine on cardiac output (inotropic effect) is seen shortly afterward, whereas the activation of phosphorylase is not detectable for 45 seconds. Thus, the inotropic effect of epinephrine is not the result of an initial action on glycogenolysis, though both actions may result from the increased cAMP. In vivo, epinephrine action can result in an increase in heart glycogen. This is probably secondary to the action of the hormone on adipose tissue to increase circulating fatty acids which are rapidly utilized in the heart as fuel. Although total glucose uptake may be decreased, that glucose entering the heart is preferentially shunted to glycogen. In vivo, the lactic acid from muscle and the fatty acids released from adipose tissue are taken up by the liver and metabolized through the citric acid cycle. Eventually, the fatty acids activate the reversal of the glycolytic pathway, permitting lactate to be converted to glucose or glycogen. Therefore, despite the specific effect of epinephrine on glycogen breakdown in liver, liver glycogen can often be increased when the drug is administered in vivo.

In adipose tissue, epinephrine has a marked effect on lipolysis, resulting in the rapid release of both fatty acids and glycerol. These fatty acids serve as fuel in the muscle and can activate gluconeogenesis in the liver. The breakdown of fat in adipose tissue is usually accompanied by a compensating increase in glucose uptake and the synthesis of glycerophosphate. Epinephrine has a direct inhibitory action on insulin release in the pancreas. It therefore serves as an emergency hormone by (1) rapidly providing fatty acids, which are the primary fuel for muscle action; (2) mobilizing glucose, both by increasing glycogenolysis and gluconeogenesis in the liver and by decreasing glucose uptake in the muscle; and (3) decreasing insulin, thereby preventing the glucose from being taken up by peripheral tissues and preserving it for the central nervous system.

Epinephrine can stimulate both beta- and alpha-adrenergic receptors in tissue. Norepinephrine in small doses acts primarily, though not exclusively, on alpha receptors. Historically, adrenergic responses have been classified according to the comparative effectiveness of a series of related catechols on vascular, cardiac, and pulmonary physiologic responses. Thus, typical norepinephrine-stimulated responses such as vascular venous constriction were denoted as alpha-adrenergic. Typical epinephrine effects, such as increased heart rate and atrial contractibility, were beta phenomena. Fatty acid mobilization and glycogenolysis are beta-type metabolic reactions since they can be duplicated with beta-adrenergic stimulating drugs, eg, isoproterenol. It now appears that beta effects are those associated with an increase in cAMP, whereas alpha effects are associated with cAMP depression. Since epinephrine can stimulate both adrenergic responses, its effect in a tissue depends on the quantity or relative sensitivity of the alpha and beta receptors. Thus, in the pancreas, the alpha-adrenergic response to epinephrine predominates, cAMP decreases, and insulin release is inhibited. However, in the presence of an alpha-adrenergic blocker such as phentolamine (Regitine), the beta effect predominates and epinephrine causes increased cAMP and increased insulin release.

Abnormal Physiology

No clinical state directly attributable to a deficiency of the adrenal medulla is known. However, certain tumors of the medullary (chromaffin) cells result in **pheochromocytoma**, characterized by symptoms which simulate those of hyperactivity of the adrenal medulla. The symptoms of these tumors include intermittent hypertension which may progress to permanent hypertension and lead eventually to death from complications such as coronary insufficiency, ventricular fibrillation, and pulmonary edema.

Laboratory tests for adrenal medullary hyperactivity, as in the presence of pheochromocytoma, include chemical analyses for increased catecholamines in the blood and urine—in particular, vanilmandelic

acid (VMA) (see above), the principal urinary metabolite of epinephrine and norepinephrine. Excretion of vanilmandelic acid in the urine is normally 0.7–6.8 mg/24 hours. **Phentolamine (Regitine)** is a specific antagonist to norepinephrine. In the presence of sustained hypertension due to pheochromocytoma, the rapid intravenous injection of phentolamine should produce a sustained fall of blood pressure within 2–5 minutes. This test is another diagnostic aid in testing for pheochromocytoma.

The norepinephrine content of adrenal medullary tumors is much higher than that of epinephrine, suggesting that the hypertension produced by these tumors is attributable to norepinephrine.

As already noted, drugs increasing catecholamines are used as antidepressants; drugs decreasing catecholamines serve as antihypertensives and tranquilizers.

THE ADRENAL CORTEX*

The outer portion of the adrenal gland, the adrenal cortex, is essential to life. Its embryologic origin is quite different from that of the adrenal medulla.

The adrenal cortex produces a number of potent hormones all of which are steroid derivatives having the characteristic cyclopentanoperhydrophenanthrene nucleus. As will be noted later, the hormones of the gonads are also steroid hormones not remarkably different from those of the adrenal cortex. The similarity of embryologic origin of the adrenal cortex and of the gonads is of interest in connection with the close relationship of the chemistry of their respective hormones.

General Function

The steroid hormones of the adrenal cortex fall into 3 general classes, each with characteristic functions:

(1) The **glucocorticoids**, which primarily affect metabolism of protein, carbohydrate, and lipids.

(2) The **mineralocorticoids**, which primarily affect the transport of electrolytes and the distribution of water in tissues.

(3) The **androgens** or **estrogens**, which primarily affect secondary sex characteristics in their specific target organs.

Individual steroids usually have activities which are predominantly in one of the above categories but which may overlap into one or both of the others.

General Mechanism of Action

All of the steroids act primarily at the level of the cell nucleus to bring about RNA and protein synthesis.

*In cooperation with Tawfik ElAttar, PhD, Professor of Biochemistry, School of Dentistry, University of Missouri–Kansas City.

The first step (Fig 28–2) occurs within minutes. It involves the binding of the steroid to a receptor protein in the cytosol. These **receptor proteins** (MW approximately 100,000) are comparatively specific for a given steroid, although some competitive binding can occur. The levels of specific receptors vary in different cells and can decrease in clinical states causing decreased sensitivity to steroids (eg, steroid "resistance" in fibroblast and lymphoid cells). The steroid-receptor complex is able to enter the nucleus, where it binds reversibly to specific sites on the chromatin of the cell nucleus. The nuclear binding sites are possibly closely associated with the DNA itself, although chromatin proteins may play a role in the process. By this means, RNA synthesis and, ultimately, cellular protein and enzyme synthesis are modified. It is the enzyme changes that actually produce the effects attributable to the hormone. Since RNA and protein synthesis are initially required, the hormonal effects of steroids usually require 30 minutes to several hours to be apparent—indeed, these effects may be prevented by inhibitors of RNA and of protein synthesis.

At high concentrations, steroids may also act directly to alter membranes and enzymatic activity.

General Chemistry

All steroid hormones have a cyclopentanoperhydrophenanthrene ring system as their chemical nucleus. This 4-membered ring and its conventional numbering system is illustrated in the structure of cholesterol in Fig 29–21. Most naturally occurring steroids contain alcohol side chains and are therefore usually referred to as sterols.

A variety of stereoisomeric forms of the steroids are possible: (1) the A and B rings may be joined either in a trans or cis configuration. Estrogens are not capable of this form of isomerism since their A ring is aromatic; (2) hydrogens or other groups may be attached to the rings with an orientation either above (β-) or below (α-) the plane of the ring. The β-orientation is conventionally assigned to groups in the same plane as the C_{19} methyl group and is diagrammatically represented by solid lines. The opposite α-groups are normally represented by dashed lines. In natural steroids, both the chains attached at C_{17} and various substitutions at C_{11} are in the β-configuration. Some general terms of steroid nomenclature are given in Table 29–2.

About 50 steroids have been isolated from the adrenal gland, but only a few of them are known to possess physiologic activity. The most important ones are cortisone, hydrocortisone (cortisol, 17-hydroxycorticosterone), aldosterone, and the 2 androgens androstenedione (androst-4-ene-3,17-dione) and dehydroepiandrosterone (Figs 29–21 and 29–22). Cortisol is the major free circulating adrenocortical hormone in human plasma. The normal level of cortisol in plasma is about 12 μg/dl. The other steroid hormones are present in human plasma in relatively small concentrations.

Table 29–2. Nomenclature of steroids.

Prefix	Suffix	Chemical Significance
allo-		Trans (as opposed to cis) configuration of the A and B rings.
epi-		Configuration different from parent compound at a single carbon atom.
	-ane	Saturated carbon atom.
	-ene	A single double bond in ring structure.
hydroxy-, dihydroxy-, etc	-ol, -diol, etc	Alcohols.
oxo-	-one, -dione	Ketones.
dehydro-		Conversion of –C–OH to –C=O by loss of 2 hydrogen atoms.
dihydro-		Addition of 2 hydrogen atoms.
cis-		Arrangement of 2 groups in same plane.
trans-		Arrangement of 2 groups in opposing planes.
α-		A group trans to the 19-methyl.
β-		A group cis to the 19-methyl.
nor-		One less carbon in a side chain as compared to parent molecules. (*Example:* 19-Nor signifies that the methyl group constituting carbon 19 of a steroid is deleted.)

Biosynthesis of Adrenal Hormones (See Figs 29–21 and 29–22.)

Acetate is the primary precursor for the synthesis of all steroids. The pathway involves the initial synthesis of cholesterol, which, after a series of side chain cleavages and oxidations, is converted to Δ^5-pregnenolone. Pregnenolone is the "pivotal" steroid from which all the other steroid hormones are produced. There is evidence that pregnenolone (or progesterone) can be synthesized from acetate by a pathway other than through cholesterol, possibly from 24-dehydrocholesterol. However, in normal tissue this path is relatively minor. The adrenal cortex contains relatively large quantities of cholesterol, mostly as cholesterol esters which are derived both from synthesis and from extraadrenal sources.

Pregnenolone is converted to progesterone by a dehydrogenase or to 17-hydroxypregnenolone by a specific 17-hydroxylase. As shown in Figs 29–21 and 29–22, those 2 steroids are converted to a variety of active hormones by specific oxygenases and dehydrogenases which require molecular oxygen and NADPH. The result of these combined enzymatic reactions is the addition of hydroxyl or keto groups at the C_{11}, C_{17}, or C_{21} positions.

In general, C-21 hydroxylation is necessary for both glucocorticoid and mineralocorticoid activities. Those steroids with an additional –OH or C=O at the C_{11} position and an –OH at C_{17} have greater glucocorticoid and lesser mineralocorticoid action. Examples of the glucocorticosteroids are corticosterone,

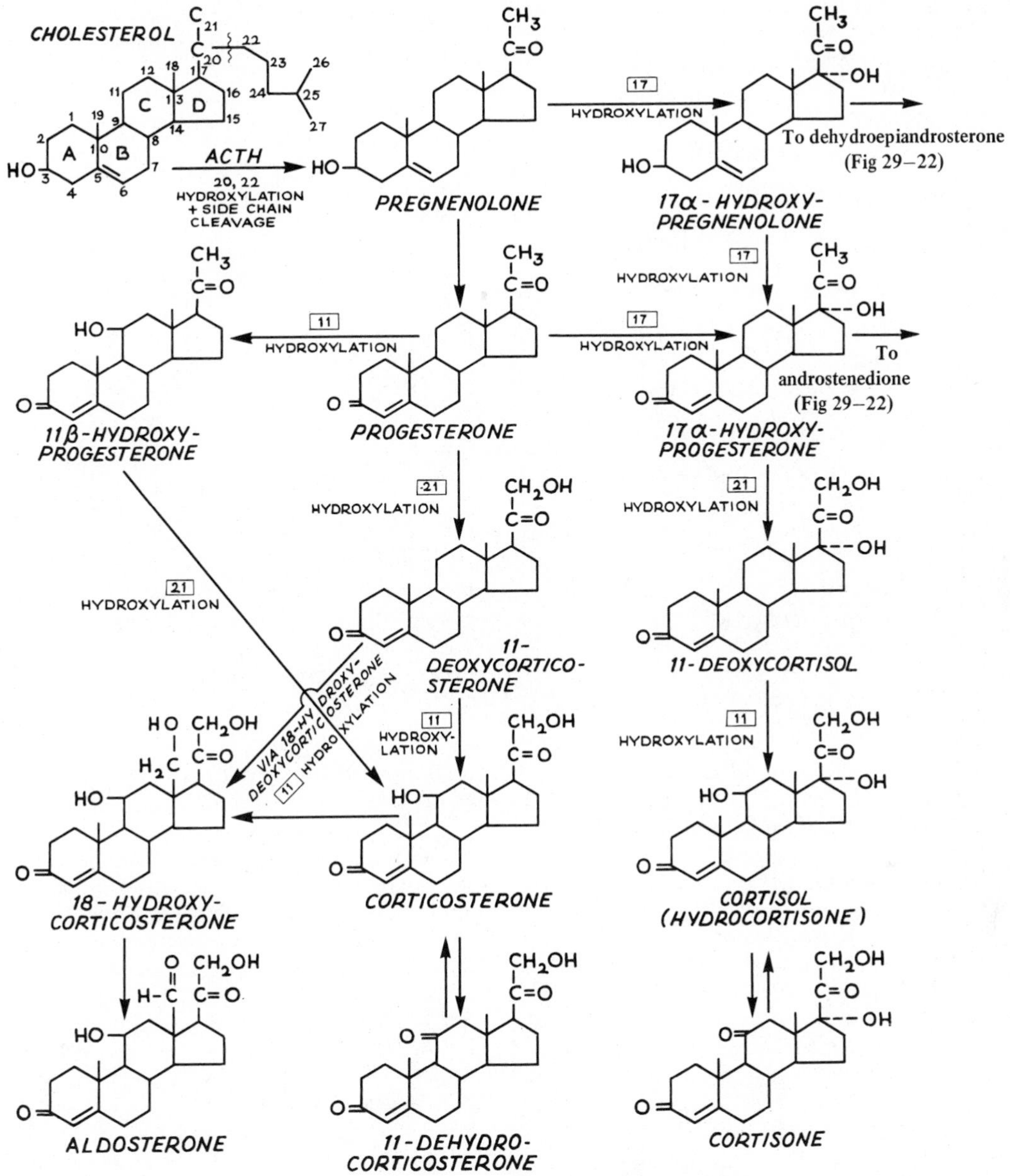

Figure 29—21. Biosynthesis of adrenal corticosteroids.

11-dehydrocorticosterone, cortisone, and hydrocortisone or cortisol. The 2 most important glucocorticoids are cortisol and corticosterone. Cortisol predominates in man and the fish, whereas corticosterone is the most important hormone in rodents.

The most potent mineralocorticoid is **aldosterone**. It has been detected in extracts of the adrenal cortex and in the blood of the adrenal vein. Its major pathway of synthesis requires a unique 18-hydroxylation (Fig 29—21). Although most hydroxylases involved in adrenal steroid synthesis are found throughout the gland, the 18-hydroxylase activity is restricted to the glomerular layer below the capsule. Thus, aldosterone synthesis is limited to this area.

The structure of aldosterone is shown in Fig 29—23 in the aldehyde form and in the hemiacetal form. It is believed that the hormone exists in solution in the hemiacetal form. It will be noted that aldosterone has the same structure as corticosterone except that the methyl group at position 18 is replaced by an aldehyde group. Deoxycorticosterone appears to be the precursor in the adrenal of both aldosterone and corticosterone.

11-Deoxycorticosterone is only 4% as potent as aldosterone. However, because it can be prepared synthetically (as the acetate, Doca) and because aldo-

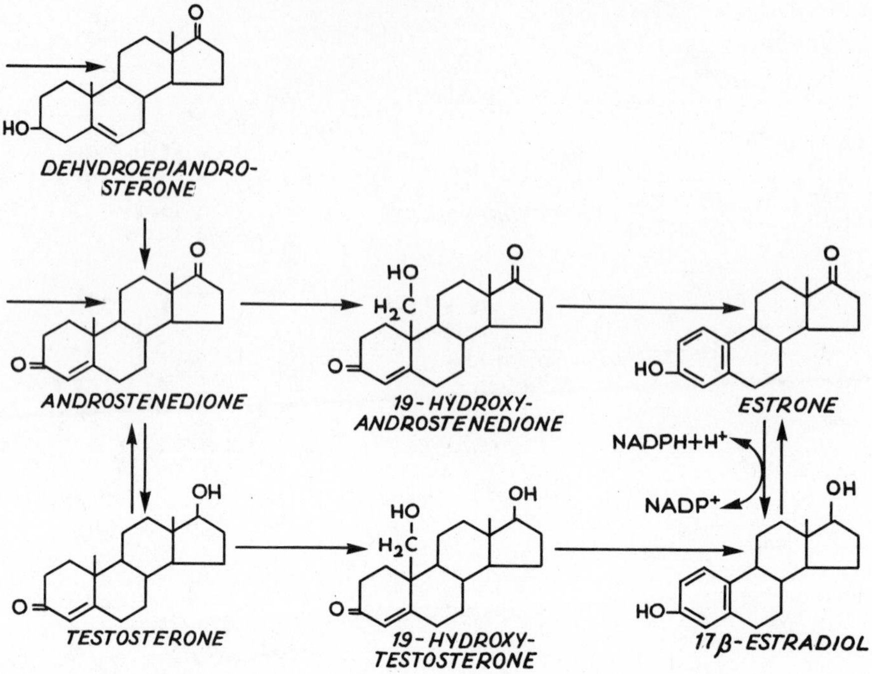

Figure 29—22. Biosynthesis of androgens and estrogens.

sterone is not yet available for therapeutic use, Doca is important in the treatment of Addison's disease. Doca may be administered sublingually, since absorption from the buccal mucosa occurs.

The major adrenal androgen, dehydroepiandrosterone, is produced by side chain cleavage of 17-hydroxypregnenolone. The smaller amounts of adrenal estrogens can arise from testosterone produced either from dehydroepiandrosterone or from 17-hydroxyprogesterone. Sulfate conjugates of some of the steroids, most notably of the androgen dehydroepiandrosterone, have been detected in the adrenal gland and in adrenal secretions. Conversion of pregnenolone sulfate to dehydroepiandrosterone sulfate has been reported to occur without the loss of the sulfate. Although sulfate conjugation is generally associated with inactivation mechanisms in the liver for drugs and other hormones, these results indicate that sulfate conjugates are involved in some pathways of biosynthesis of steroid hormones.

Metabolic Functions (See Fig 29—24.)

A. The Glucocorticoids: These steroid hormones (notably cortisol) act, as other steroids, to modify RNA and enzyme synthesis in their many target tissues. As noted previously (Fig 28—2), the first step is the binding to a specific receptor protein in the cytosol; this complex in turn is transported to the nucleus, binds to nuclear chromatin, and thereby alters the transcription of RNA. The resulting changes in metabolic processes are summarized in Fig 29—24. (Note that many of the glucocorticoid actions are metabolically antagonistic to insulin.) The glucocorticoids increase circulating glucose, fatty acids, and amino acids.

In the **peripheral tissues (muscle, adipose, and lymphoid tissue)**, the steroids are catabolic and tend to "spare" glucose. Glucose uptake and glycolysis are depressed. Protein synthesis is depressed, whereas protein degradation is increased. In **muscle**, there may be tissue wasting as protein stores are depleted. In **adipose tissue**, glucocorticoids increase lipolysis. The impairment of glucose metabolism in this tissue decreases the available glycerol phosphate, thereby impairing fat synthesis. In **Cushing's disease**, centripe-

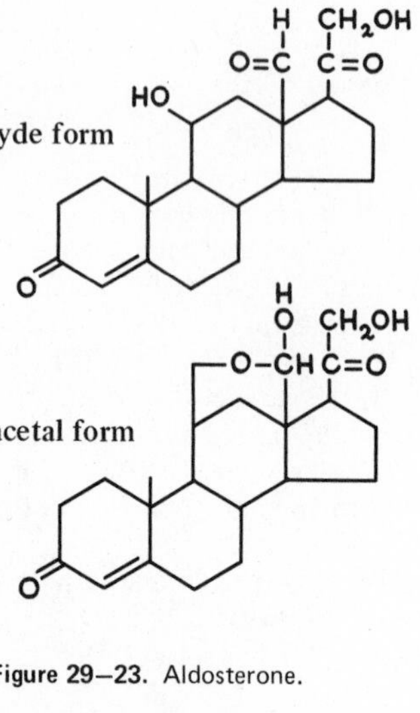

Figure 29—23. Aldosterone.

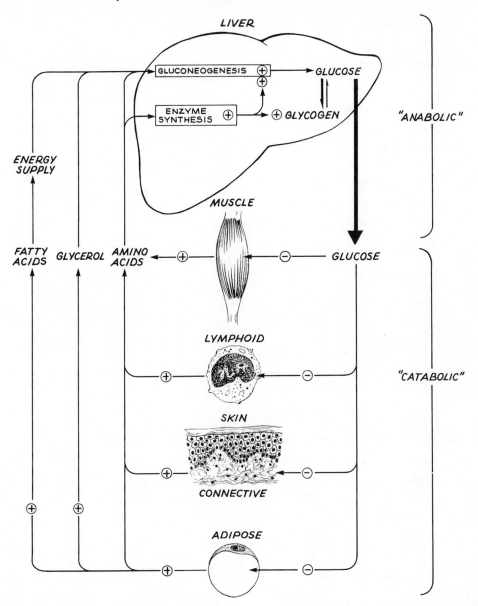

Figure 29—24. Glucocorticoid action on carbohydrate, lipid, and protein metabolism. The arrows indicate the general flow of substrate in response to the catabolic and anabolic actions of glucocorticoids when unopposed by secondary secretions of other hormones. Not shown is increased gluconeogenesis by kidney. The plus or minus signs indicate stimulation or inhibition, respectively. (Redrawn from Baxter & Forsham, 1972.)

tal redistribution of fat occurs without change in total body fat as lipid is mobilized from steroid-sensitive tissue and redeposited elsewhere.

In the livers of animals treated with adrenal steroids, all processes which help remove amino acids are increased. Thus, total protein synthesis, gluconeogenesis, glycogen deposition, amino acid conversion to CO_2, and urea are all enhanced. An increase in RNA synthesis occurs within 10 minutes after glucocorticoid administration, indicating that some of these effects may result from direct action of the glucocorticoids on

liver. Many of the gluconeogenic effects in the liver are caused by glycerol, fatty acids, and amino acids mobilized from peripheral tissues (Fig 29—24).

In particular, the adrenal steroids increase the amount of hepatic enzymes involved in amino acid metabolism such as alanine-α-ketoglutarate and tyrosine transaminases as well as tryptophan pyrrolase. The key enzymes in the regulation of gluconeogenesis (pyruvate carboxylase, phosphoenolpyruvate carboxykinase, fructose-1,6-bisphosphatase, and glucose-6-phosphatase) are also increased, possibly by the stimulation of a functional genetic unit in the nucleus which controls their synthesis. This seems to be a comparatively specialized action of the adrenal steroids since many other hepatic enzymes are not increased. In liver, adrenal steroids not only increase amino acid conversion to glucose but also conversion of CO_2 to glucose, suggesting that they may act on CO_2 fixation, particularly at the level of pyruvate carboxylase, a key enzyme involved in gluconeogenesis (see below). Conversion of fructose or glycerol to glucose is not specifically increased in vitro, thus supporting the concept of an action at some stage lower than the entry of these metabolites into the gluconeogenic pathway. The increase in glucose, glycogen, and protein synthesis observed in the liver indicates an important action of the adrenal steroids on increased metabolic availability of amino acids. However, the adrenal steroids have little effect on the concentration gradient of amino acids across cell membranes. In vivo, the hyperglycemia, particularly during later periods of treatment, is a result of increased gluconeogenesis in the liver and decreased glucose uptake in peripheral tissues. Though the primary source of the glucose moiety in the process of gluconeogenesis is usually considered to be amino acids, the amount of glucose produced cannot be entirely accounted for by amino acid breakdown. It is possible that lactate and glycerol derived from muscle and adipose tissue, respectively (the latter a product of the increased lipolysis), can also serve as sources of carbon for hepatic glucose synthesis.

The glucocorticoids are relatively inactive on heart, brain, and red cells. Other effects of the glucocorticoids can be extremely important:

1. Anti-inflammatory effects—At high concentrations, glucocorticoids decrease cellular protective reactions and in particular retard the migration of leukocytes into traumatized areas. Thus, cortisol is an anti-inflammatory agent and is used in this capacity in the so-called collagen diseases such as rheumatoid arthritis. The effectiveness of cortisol in rheumatoid arthritis may also be related to the immunosuppressive activity of this steroid.

2. Immunosuppressive effects—Cortisol decreases immune responses associated with infections, allergic states, and anaphylaxis. Indeed, glucocorticoids may be used for the purpose of repressing antibody formation when in organ transplantation procedures an effort to prevent rejection of the transplanted tissue or organ is essential.

Within 30 minutes after injection of cortisol, RNA synthesis in lymphocytes is modified. Thus, it appears that the primary effect of adrenal steroids that depress immune responses is at the nuclear site, leading to alterations in protein or enzyme synthesis of compounds that may inhibit normal cellular activity. In general, the glucocorticoids inhibit sensitization or primary response better than the anamnestic or later responses.

3. Exocrine secretory effects—Chronic treatment with glucocorticoids causes increased secretion of hydrochloric acid and pepsinogen by the stomach and trypsinogen by the pancreas; this can enhance the formation of gastrointestinal ulcers.

4. Effects on bone—Glucocorticoids reduce the osteoid matrix of bone, thus favoring osteoporosis and excessive loss of calcium from the body. Indeed, osteoporosis is a major complication of prolonged adrenal steroid therapy.

5. Cyclic AMP—In some tissues, the glucocorticoids decrease phosphodiesterase activity, thereby increasing cAMP. However, it is unlikely that steroids act primarily to increase cAMP since their action is at the nuclear site. Nevertheless, cAMP and the glucocorticoids have similar effects in almost all tissues (eg, increased protein metabolism, lipolysis, and gluconeogenesis), suggesting that they may have a mechanism of action in common.

6. Stress—The glucocorticoids reverse the decreased blood pressure resulting from emotional or surgical shock. In Addison's disease, external steroids are required to maintain blood pressure.

B. The Mineralocorticoids: With the exception of the androgens, all of the active corticosteroids increase the absorption of sodium and chloride by the renal tubules and decrease their excretion by the sweat glands, salivary glands, and the gastrointestinal tract. However, there is a considerable difference in the extent of these actions among various adrenal steroids. Cortisol has the least sodium-retaining action, whereas aldosterone is extremely potent, being at least 1000 times as effective as cortisol and about 35 times as effective as 11-deoxycorticosterone. Accompanying the retention of sodium by the kidney, there is increased excretion of potassium by an exchange of intracellular potassium with extracellular sodium.

Extracellular fluid volume is increased after the administration of mineralocorticoids. There is also an increase in the volume of the circulating blood and in the urinary output. After removal of the adrenal glands, these effects on water and salt metabolism are quickly reversed. The loss of water and of sodium can result in acute dehydration and death. Aldosterone also increases the renal clearance of magnesium to a degree which parallels its effect on potassium excretion.

Although the exact site of action of aldosterone is not known, it acts, like the other adrenal steroids, primarily at the nuclear site (Fig 28–2) via a specific cytosolic receptor to increase synthesis of RNA and thus indirectly to influence the synthesis of enzymes or other proteins. The comparatively long period of exposure of tissues, both in vitro and in vivo, that is required before physiologic effects are noted is consistent with this mechanism of action.

Spironolactone inhibits aldosterone action by competitively binding to the cytosol receptor protein and thereby forming an inactive complex (see below).

Although aldosterone resembles deoxycorticosterone in many of its metabolic effects, it also possesses other physiologic properties which distinguish it from deoxycorticosterone. These include increasing the deposition of glycogen in the liver, decreasing the

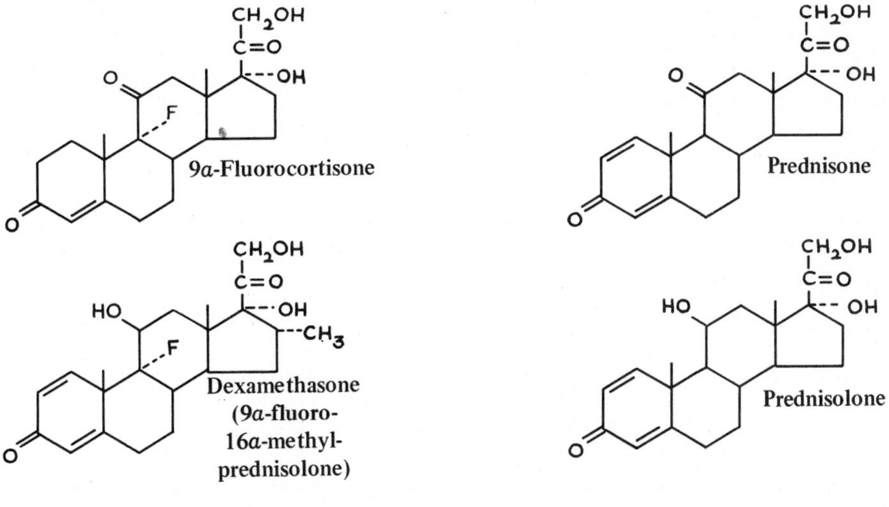

Figure 29—25. Synthetic adrenal steroids.

circulating eosinophils, and maintaining resistance to stress, such as exposure to low temperatures (so-called cold stress test). In maintaining the life of the adrenalectomized animal, aldosterone is more potent than any other known steroid.

C. Sex Hormones (C-19 Corticosteroids): The primary adrenal androgens are dehydroepiandrosterone and androstenedione (Fig 29—22). Testosterone can also be detected in certain adrenal tumors.

The adrenal origin of some sex hormones accounts for the fact that the urine of castrates still contains androgen derivatives. These adrenocorticosteroids of the androgenic type cause retention of nitrogen (a protein anabolic effect), phosphorus, potassium, sodium, and chloride. If present in excessive amounts, they also lead to masculinization in the female.

Analogs of Natural Steroids

Adrenal hormones have been synthesized which are in many instances more potent than the naturally occuring hormones and often more specific in their action (Fig 29—25).

This greater potency may arise from (1) a greater affinity of the steroid analog for the receptor protein in the cytosol; (2) an increased ability of this steroid-receptor complex to act at the nuclear level, or (3) less rapid degradation in the body.

The introduction of a halogen (eg, fluorine) at the 9a position of cortisone, cortisol, or corticosterone results in the production of compounds of high potency (Fig 29—25). However, their increased salt-retaining activity is relatively greater than their anti-inflammatory or metabolic activities. It is for this reason that these derivatives are of limited clinical usefulness. Introduction of a double bond between carbon atoms 1 and 2 results in the production of cortisone and cortisol analogs which in therapeutically useful doses are relatively inert as far as salt-retaining properties are concerned, although they retain the anti-in-

flammatory activity of the natural steroids. The cortisone analog is prednisone; the cortisol analog is prednisolone.

In steroids which have a hydroxy group on position 11 (eg, cortisol, 9a-fluorocortisol, or 11β-hydroxyprogesterone), the addition of the 2-methyl group markedly enhances the sodium-retaining and potassium-losing activity of the hormone.

A synthetic analog of prednisolone, having a similar but more potent anti-inflammatory action, is **dexamethasone** (9a-fluoro-16a-methylprednisolone). It is about 30 times more potent than cortisol.

Many steroids may act as an **antagonist** by competitively binding to the cytosol receptor normally used by another steroid. Although the antagonists may have a greater affinity for the receptor, the resulting receptor-steroid complex is comparatively inactive. Thus, **spironolactone (Aldactone)**, useful in hyperaldosteronism, acts by forming an inactive complex with the aldosterone receptor. Similarly, progesterone is an antagonist for glucocorticoids in some tissues; this may account for the reduced sensitivity to circulating free cortisol in the later stages of pregnancy.

Regulation of Steroid Secretion

The synthesis and secretion of adrenal steroids is controlled by adrenocorticotropin (ACTH) from the pituitary. The secretion of ACTH, in turn, is regulated by corticotropin-releasing factor which is released from the hypothalamus during stress (see p 509).

After stimulation of the gland, there is a rapid decline in the concentration of cholesterol within the adrenal. This and other evidence indicates that ACTH has its effect at some step involving conversion of cholesterol to pregnenolone.

It is still unclear whether the specific action of ACTH is to increase the initial 20-hydroxylation of cholesterol or to activate the "desmolase" step, a series of oxidative cleavages of the cholesterol side chain employing NADPH as cofactor. The ultimate products of these reactions are the C-21 steroids $20a,22\zeta$-dihydroxycholesterol and $17a,20a$-dihydroxycholesterol. These compounds are converted directly to pregnenolone or $17a$-pregnenolone by loss of an isocaproic aldehyde moiety from their side chains. Since ACTH stimulates synthesis of the substrate for all steroid hormone synthesis, it does not preferentially stimulate synthesis of a particular class of steroids.

The role of the large amounts of ascorbic acid found in the adrenal cortex is not known. It may act to provide reducing equivalents for the NADPH-dependent hydroxylations required for steroid synthesis mentioned below. Ascorbic acid is not synthesized in the adrenal but is concentrated there from extra-adrenal sources. ACTH reduces its uptake into the gland. The measurement of cholesterol or ascorbic acid depletion in the adrenal glands of hypophysectomized animals after the injection of ACTH was an early method of assay for the tropic hormone.

Stimulation of steroid synthesis and release by ACTH may be mediated through cAMP since the level of this substance is increased in adrenal slices within minutes by the tropic hormone. cAMP itself can directly simulate ACTH action.

Stimulation of steroid synthesis is usually associated with alterations in structure of the adrenal mitochondrial membrane and also is dependent on the presence of calcium ions. The ultimate effect of ACTH and cAMP, therefore, may involve changes in ionic flux across adrenal cell membranes. As in most reactions stimulated by cAMP, ATP is inhibitory.

The secretion of ACTH is under feedback control by circulating steroids; in man, cortisol is the most important regulator. Thus, when cortisol levels decrease, there is a concomitant rise in ACTH. For example, since ACTH nonspecifically stimulates all adrenal steroids, a defect in cortisol production will foster overproduction of androgens, resulting in various forms of adrenogenital syndrome. Pregnenolone is a feedback inhibitor of steroidogenesis, possibly by some unspecified "allosteric effect."

Unlike the other corticosteroids, the production of aldosterone by the adrenal is relatively uninfluenced by ACTH. Aldosterone production is increased mainly by deprivation of sodium, administration of potassium, and by any decline in the normal volume of the extracellular fluid; this latter circumstance is attributed to the presence of what are termed "volume receptors." It follows that activities resulting from an increase in aldosterone production—sodium retention, potassium excretion, and an expansion of extracellular fluid volume—would serve to reduce secretion of the hormone by a type of "feedback regulation." There is evidence that the regulatory effect of each of the above-mentioned factors is exerted independently of the others; however, the question of interdependence or the relative importance of each remains unsettled. Aldosterone production is also increased by beta-adrenergic stimuli- an observation that supports the idea that release of aldosterone is enhanced by cAMP.

Infusion of angiotensin II produces an increase in the rate of secretion of aldosterone. This fact suggests that the kidney, by means of the renin-angiotensin system (renal pressor system), is an important organ controlling aldosterone secretion.

Renin is secreted by the **juxtaglomerular cells** of the kidney. These cells are located in the walls of the renal afferent arterioles, and it may be that the "volume receptors" mentioned above are located here. Decreased arterial pressure and renal blood flow resulting from decreased extracellular fluid volume would increase renin secretion. Renin, in turn, converts hypertensinogen to angiotensin I; in plasma, angiotensin I is converted to angiotensin II, which acts directly on the aldosterone-producing cells of the zona glomerulosa of the adrenal cortex. At very high concentrations, renin may act in a similar way to increase nonspecifically the production of the other corticosteroids.

Secretion of aldosterone is increased in several diseases such as cirrhosis, nephrosis, and some types of cardiac failure. There is also an increase in malignant (accelerated) hypertension but not in the benign form of hypertension. The result is enhancement of retention of sodium and water, which further aggravates the edema characteristic of certain of these diseases. In nephritis, the renal loss of sodium and water may directly increase aldosterone production, which then leads to greater losses of potassium and hydrogen ion.

Compounds which block the action of aldosterone on sodium retention may be of value as diuretic agents in treatment of the edema which occurs in those disease states characterized by excess aldosterone production. Such an aldosterone blocking agent is **spironolactone (Aldactone)**, a compound belonging to a group of steroid spirolactones all of which are effective diuretics.

Transport & Metabolism of Adrenal Steroids

About 90% of serum cortisol circulates in the blood bound loosely to a specific alpha globulin (**corticosteroid-binding globulin, CBG, transcortin**). The bound hormone is essentially inactive. Corticosteroid-binding globulin can be increased by estrogens which thereby enhance the total amount of circulating cortisol though the actual amount of free steroid may be normal because of counter-regulation. Progesterone, on the other hand, is one of the few steroids with a high affinity for this binding protein and can cause displacement of cortisol to the free, active fraction. Some reversible binding to albumin may occur at high concentrations of circulating steroids.

In the resting state, the plasma contains $5-15$ $\mu g/dl$ of cortisol, the major corticosteroid of the blood. In the human subject, the level of cortisol in the plasma is highest in the early morning and lowest during the night hours. The content of aldosterone in plasma is very low (about 0.01 $\mu g/dl$). During a 24-hour period, the normal adult human secretes about $5-30$ mg of cortisol, $1-6$ mg of corticosterone, and $30-75$ μg of aldosterone.

The disappearance from the body of steroidal compounds such as cortisol is normally very rapid. ^{14}C-labeled cortisol injected intravenously has a half-life of about 4 hours. Within 48 hours, 93% of the injected dose disappears from the body: 70% by way of the urine, 20% by the stool, and the remainder presumably through the skin. The steroid nucleus is eliminated in the intact form; no significant breakdown to CO_2 and water occurs.

The corticosteroids are inactivated in the liver by ring reduction catalyzed by NADPH-requiring hydrogenases and by reduction of the 3-ketone group by NADH or NADPH, requiring reversible dehydrogenases (Fig 29–26). The resulting tetrahydro derivatives are in turn conjugated, mainly with glucuronic acid. Other tissues (eg, connective tissue) do not inactivate steroids since they lack the necessary hydrogenases and dehydrogenases.

Both free and conjugated corticosteroids are excreted into the intestine by way of the bile and, in part, reabsorbed from the intestine by the enterohepatic circulation. Excretion of free and, in particular, conjugated corticosteroids by the kidney takes place, although there is some tubular reabsorption.

Large amounts of aldosterone are produced from androstenedione in the liver. Aldosterone thus produced in the liver may, however, have little peripheral biologic activity since it could be inactivated by reduction and conjugation before leaving the liver. Aldosterone synthesized in the liver would, however, contribute to the conjugates of this hormone measured in the urine.

Hepatic inactivation of corticosteroids declines during prolonged malnutrition (protein and B vitamins) or in liver disease. Decreased excretion may also occur in renal insufficiency. Under any of these circumstances, the levels of corticosteroids in the blood are markedly raised. In chronic liver disease (cirrhosis) as well as in congestive heart failure, the liver does not completely inactivate salt-retaining steroids. This would lead to excessive salt retention, which may be an important cause of edema and ascites found in certain stages of these diseases.

Because of the effect of the liver on their metabolism, the dosage of many corticosteroids, when administered by mouth, must be increased, since the corticosteroids are initially carried by the portal circulation to the liver, where a portion of the dose may be inactivated.

Androgens are carried in the serum both in free and conjugated form in association with the serum proteins. These androgens consist mostly of dehydroepiandrosterone and androsterone, which is the male hormone found in both males and females. There is twice as much androsterone as dehydroepiandrosterone. The conversion of small amounts of cortisol and cortisone to 11-hydroxy androgens is believed to occur in the liver. In certain forms of liver disease, blood levels of 17-hydroxycorticoids are elevated whereas androgens are reduced. Most of the androgens are excreted into the urine as 17-ketosteroids (Fig 29–26).

Laboratory Studies of Adrenocortical Function

Adrenal activity is assessed by measuring the levels of circulating cortisol in the blood or, less specifically, by measuring broad chemical classes of corticosteroid or androgen metabolites in the urine. To differentiate the various forms of adrenal dysfunction, including those attributable to ACTH secretion of the pituitary, stimulation or suppression tests are employed. Some examples are as follows:

(1) **ACTH stimulation tests** evaluate the steroid response to injected ACTH. In this test, high levels of corticosteroids in blood or urine in response to ACTH indicate adrenal adenoma or hyperplasia, the latter condition often occurring as a result of pituitary hyperfunction. When the corticosteroid levels under basal conditions are high and stimulation fails to increase the levels, autonomous hypersecretion due to adrenal carcinoma should be suspected. If basal secretion of corticosteroids is low, a normal response to ACTH indicates adrenal insufficiency secondary to a lack of ACTH.

(2) **The dexamethasone suppression test** is performed using dexamethasone, a potent glucocorticoid, to suppress endogenous production of ACTH. The amount of dexamethasone used is too small to contribute significantly to a rise in normal amounts of corticosteroids in blood and urine; this makes it possible to evaluate response to the reduced ACTH output by observation of corticosteroid production under these circumstances.

(3) **The metyrapone (Metopirone) stimulation test** makes use of metyrapone, an inhibitor of adrenal 17β-hydroxylase, the enzyme which catalyzes the addition of the hydroxy group at position 11 of the steroid nucleus in the biosynthetic pathway for corticosteroid formation (Figs 29–21 and 29–22). Thus, a transient deficiency of cortisol is produced which normally results in stimulation of secretion of ACTH from the pituitary (see discussion of braking action of cortisol, p 510), followed in turn by a resultant increase in 11-deoxycortisol secretion. The test may also be used to assess adrenocortical as well as pituitary function.

(4) **The insulin hypoglycemia test** is based on the elevation of ACTH by the stress of insulin-induced hypoglycemia.

Plasma total cortisol can be measured, after a solvent extraction to eliminate various conjugated metabolites, by a comparatively specific fluorimetric technic. **Urinary 17-hydroxycorticoids** can be measured by a colorimetric test based on the Porter-Silber color reaction with phenylhydrazine and sulfuric acid. The reaction is positive for 17,21-dihydroxy-20-ketosteroids such as cortisone, cortisol, and 11-deoxycortisol, as well as for their reduced (tetrahydro) derivatives. After administration of ACTH, an increase in the amounts of Porter-Silber chromogens in the urine by as much as 300% is observed in normal subjects.

Urinary 17-ketosteroids are metabolites deriving from androgens produced both in the adrenals and the

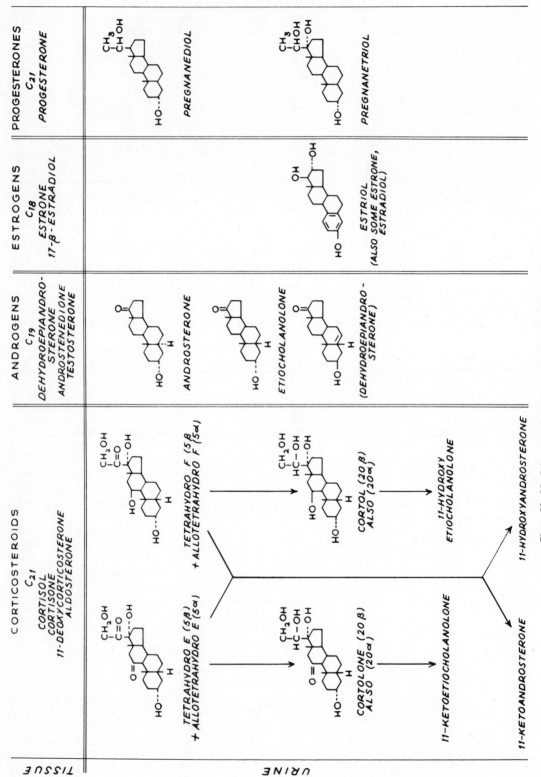

Figure 29—26. Primary excretion products of steroids. (As conjugates with glucuronic acid.)

gonads. The principal components of the "neutral" ketosteroid fraction of the urinary steroids are androsterone and its isomers, etiocholanolone and isoandrosterone, as well as dehydroepiandrosterone (Fig 29–26). The neutral 17-ketosteroids may be further subdivided into alpha and beta fractions, alpha and beta referring to the stereochemical configuration at carbon 3 of the steroid molecule. The beta fractions are those which are precipitated by digitonin; the alpha fractions are not.

Ketosteroids are estimated colorimetrically by means of the **Zimmermann reaction,** which involves coupling of the reactive 17-keto group of these compounds with **metadinitrobenzene.**

The **urinary neutral 17-ketosteroids** are a reflection of the androgenic function of the subject. In the female, 17-ketosteroids are produced entirely by the adrenal cortex; in the male, by the adrenal cortex and testes. The testes contribute one-third of the neutral urinary 17-ketosteroids. Dehydroepiandrosterone is probably derived mainly from the adrenal. It is found in the urine of both normal men and women, and it is greatly increased in some cases of hyperadrenocorticism, particularly those with excess production of androgens. While most androgens increase the excretion of neutral 17-ketosteroids, some injected forms (eg, methyltestosterone) do not.

17-Ketosteroid values are elevated in adrenocortical carcinoma, bilateral hyperplasia of the cortex, and testicular tumors (Leydig cell tumors). Cortisol may effect a fall in 17-ketosteroid excretion because of inhibition of ACTH production. Excretion of 17-ketosteroids is low in Addison's disease, pituitary dwarfism, Simmonds' disease, and occasionally in anorexia nervosa and myxedema.

Urinary aldosterone. Measurement of aldosterone in the urine is of value in the diagnosis of primary or secondary hyperaldosteronism. At present, measurement of this hormone requires chromatographic separation and quantitative determination by double isotope dilution (see below).

Specific methods for assay of steroids. Gas-liquid chromatography is used for separation and quantitation of steroids (including androgens and estrogens) after partial purification by column or paper chromatography.

The double isotope dilution technic uses 2 different isotopic forms (usually tritium and ^{14}C) of the steroid to be measured. One form is injected into the patient; the second is added in vitro to the sample taken for analysis. The steroid is rigorously purified by a series of chromatographic procedures, and the final chemical recovery is calculated from the recovery of the isotopic form added in vitro. The specific activity of the recovered injected steroid is used to calculate secretion rate.

Cortisol and other steroids can now be specifically measured by highly sensitive radiodisplacement technics using corticosteroid-binding globulin or antibody as the specific binding protein.

Abnormal Physiology

A. Hypoadrenocorticism: In humans, degeneration of the adrenal cortex, often due to a tuberculous process or in association with pernicious anemia as well as with multiple endocrine abnormalities such as diabetes and hypothyroidism, results in **Addison's disease.** The effects of this disease include decreased 17-hydroxycorticoid and aldosterone excretion, excessive loss of sodium chloride in the urine, elevated levels of potassium in the serum, low blood pressure, muscular weakness, gastrointestinal disturbances, low body temperature, hypoglycemia, and a progressive brownish pigmentation which increases over a period of months. The pigmentation is caused by the melanocyte-stimulating hormone (see p 509) activity inherent in the structure of ACTH which is present in increased amounts as a result of the deficiency of cortisol.

Adrenalectomy causes changes similar to those of Addison's disease, although they occur in a more severe form.

B. Hyperadrenocorticism: Adrenocortical hyperfunction may be caused by benign or malignant tumors of the cortex or by adrenocortical hyperplasia initiated by increased production of ACTH. To distinguish between the 2 etiologic forms of the disease (pituitary and adrenal), the term **Cushing's disease** has been restricted to those cases which are of pituitary origin, ie, pituitary basophilism. **Cushing's syndrome** denotes adrenocortical hyperfunction directly involving the adrenal gland.

The continuous administration of adrenal steroid hormones or ACTH may also induce signs of hyperadrenocorticism. These include (1) hyperglycemia and glycosuria (diabetogenic effect); (2) retention of sodium and water, followed by edema, increased blood volume, and hypertension; (3) negative nitrogen balance (protein anti-anabolic effect and gluconeogenesis); (4) potassium depletion and hypokalemic alkalosis; (5) hirsutism and acne; and (6) centripetal redistribution of fat.

Congenital hyperplasia as well as certain tumors of the adrenals cause the production of increased amounts of androgenic (C-19) steroids. The congenital form is almost always due to hyperplasia. The resulting disturbance is termed **congenital virilizing hyperplasia** when it is present at birth and **adrenogenital syndrome** when it occurs in the postnatal period. Under the influence of excess androgens, the female assumes male secondary sex characteristics. When it occurs in the male, there is excessive masculinization. Feminizing adrenal tumors may rarely occur in males. In the most common form, the metabolic defect is a virtual absence of C-21 hydroxylase. Consequently, cortisol and cortisone are not produced in normal amounts; aldosterone and other mineralocorticoid production is not impaired. Thus, there is little or no disturbance in salt and water metabolism. The urine of these patients contains large amounts of 17-ketosteroids and of pregnanetriol, but cortisol is very low in both blood and urine. The treatment of these patients with cortisol restores pituitary-adrenal balance, and ACTH production is therefore decreased. Androgenic steroid production by the adrenal is then reduced, as evidenced by a fall in the excretion of 17-ketosteroids to normal.

A variant of this adrenogenital syndrome is a more severe salt-losing form. Death may occur, as in addisonian crisis, shortly after birth, if the disease is not promptly recognized. In this case, both 17- and 21-hydroxylation are inhibited, resulting in decreased production of both glucocorticoids and the mineralocorticoids.

Other rare adrenogenital syndromes are known in which defects occur in the synthesis of C-11 hydroxylases and Δ^5-isomerase.

In some forms of testicular feminization, pituitary-adrenal balance may be normal; in these instances, the abnormality is attributable to an inability of the target organs to recognize androgens because of reduced specific receptors in the cytosol of target organ cells.

Aldosteronism

"Primary aldosteronism" results from tumors (aldosteronomas) of the adrenals in which the hyperactivity of the adrenal cortex is apparently confined to excess production of aldosterone. The primary metabolic defect may be an inability of the adrenals to perform 17-hydroxylations, thereby shunting progesterone to aldosterone (Fig 29–21). Aldosterone excretion in the urine, particularly after sodium loading, is helpful in establishing the diagnosis. A consistently low level of potassium in the serum is a characteristic finding in primary hyperaldosteronism. The administration of the aldosterone antagonist spironolactone (Aldactone) restores serum potassium to normal levels.

Conditions associated with excessive sodium and water loss such as congestive heart failure, cirrhosis, and nephrosis may produce **secondary aldosteronism** and a resultant edema.

THE ORGANS PRODUCING SEX HORMONES

The testes and ovaries, in addition to their function of providing spermatozoa or ova, manufacture steroid hormones which control secondary sex characteristics, the reproductive cycle, and the growth and development of the accessory reproductive organs, excluding the ovary and testis themselves. The sex hormones also exert potent protein anabolic effects.

Most of the regulation of hormone production in the testes and ovaries is controlled by tropic hormones from the pituitary which act, in part, by increasing intracellular cAMP.

MALE HORMONES

A number of androgenic hormones (C-19 steroids) have been isolated either from the testes or the urine. Their physiologic activity may be tested by the effects on the seminal vesicles and prostate or by their administration to castrated animals. In the capon, restoration of the growth of the comb and wattles, the secondary sex characteristics of the rooster, follows the administration of androgenic hormones.

Androsterone is used as the international standard of androgen activity; 1 IU = 0.1 mg of androsterone. Although this hormone does not occur in the testes, it is excreted in the urine of males (Fig 29–26) as a metabolite of testosterone.

The principal male hormone, **testosterone**, is synthesized by the interstitial (Leydig) cells of the testes from cholesterol through pregnenolone, progesterone, and hydroxyprogesterone, which is then converted to the C-19 ketosteroid, androstenedione, the immediate precursor of testosterone. Alternatively, the pathway through hydroxypregnenolone and dehydroepiandrosterone can be used to produce androstenedione. A direct conversion of dehydroepiandrosterone to testosterone has been established in which androstenedione is bypassed; dehydroepiandrosterone in this pathway is initially reduced to its 17-hydroxy derivatives, which are then converted to testosterone. These reactions are shown in Figs 29–21 and 29–22, since they are also a part of the biosynthetic pathway in the adrenal for the formation of the androgenic (C-19) steroids. It will also be noted that pregnenolone is a common precursor of the adrenocortical hormones and testosterone as well as of progesterone.

Circulating dehydroepiandrosterone sulfate from the adrenal can be converted in the testes to free dehydroepiandrosterone by a sulfatase and thus provide an additional source of testosterone precursor in this tissue.

In addition to testosterone, androstenedione and dehydroepiandrosterone (androgens also produced by the adrenal) are synthesized in the testes, although in amounts and with a total androgenic potency far less than that of testosterone.

The androgens as well as the estrogens are in part transported by binding to specific plasma proteins. These proteins increase in pregnancy or estrogen therapy, which results in a reduction of effective "free" androgenic action. About 99% of the testosterone circulating in the plasma is bound to protein (testosterone-binding globulin, TBG).

Testosterone is converted by the enzyme 5a-reductase in some but not all target tissues to the more potent dihydrotestosterone, which in adults is the active intracellular androgen.

As with other steroids, the androgens may initially bind to a specific cytosol receptor protein. The complex in turn is transported to the nucleus where it interacts with chromatin, triggering RNA and protein

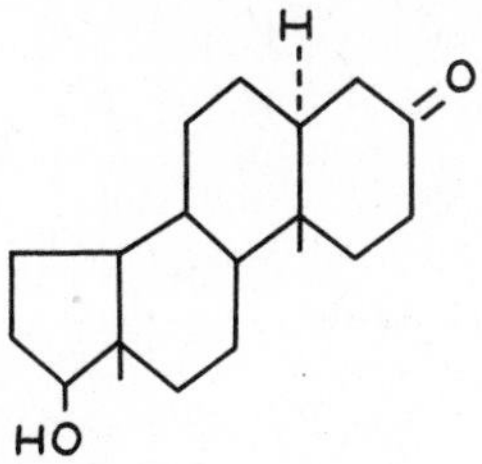

Figure 29–27. Dihydrotestosterone.

synthesis. Testicular feminization can result from defective testosterone or dihydrotestosterone binding to these cytosol receptors.

In general, the testes and the adrenals have similar qualitative capacities to synthesize androgens. Since the testis lacks 11-hydroxylase activity, however, only the adrenal can synthesize the glucocorticoids and mineralocorticoids (Figs 29–21 and 29–22).

In the normal male, 4–12 mg of testosterone are secreted per day. Direct measurement of testosterone in plasma by isotope dilution or radiodisplacement assay indicates that about 0.6 μg/dl is present in the normal male and about 0.03 μg/dl in the normal female. The small amount of testosterone in female plasma results mainly from peripheral conversion of androstenedione to testosterone by the ovary. Dehydroepiandrosterone is secreted in greater amounts than testosterone in normal men (15–50 mg/24 hours).

Testicular function is controlled by both pituitary FSH and LH, partially at least through activation of adenylate cyclase; increased testosterone levels cause feedback inhibition of LH secretion. Total blood testosterone is reduced during surgical or emotional stress.

The principal metabolites of testosterone are androsterone and etiocholanolone, the major 17-ketosteroids in the urine (Fig 29–26). In addition, small amounts of dehydroepiandrosterone are excreted as the sulfate. The principal pathway of degradation of testosterone involves oxidation in the liver to androstenedione and subsequent saturation of the double bond in ring A and reduction of the keto groups (Figs 29–22 and 29–26). Some 11-oxy or 11-hydroxy derivatives of androsterone and androstenedione are produced in the liver from adrenal cortisol and cortisone.

Testosterone promotes the growth and function of the epididymis, vas deferens, prostate, seminal vesicles, and penis. It is of value as replacement therapy in eunuchoidism. Its metabolic effect as a protein anabolic steroid exceeds that of any other naturally occurring steroid. It also contributes to the muscular and skeletal growth that accompanies puberty; this function is doubtless a necessary concomitant to its androgenic functions.

In vivo, androgens promote protein synthesis in male accessory glands by causing increased RNA and RNA polymerase in the nucleus and increased aminoacyl transferase at the ribosomal level. As a possible

result of these actions, androgens increase the activity of glycolytic enzymes, of hexokinase, and of phosphofructose kinase. The androgens also act at the mitochondrial level to increase the respiratory rate, the number of mitochondria, and the synthesis of mitochondrial membranes.

The protein anabolic effect of testosterone (nitrogen-retaining effect) is certainly as important as its androgenic effects. In many clinical situations where promotion of protein anabolism is required, testosterone has proved quite effective, but the accompanying androgenic effects are often undesirable. Consequently, efforts have been directed toward the production of synthetic steroids which, while retaining the protein anabolic action of testosterone, are relatively free of androgenicity. Some synthetic androgens include fluoxymesterone and 2a-methyldehydrotestosterone.

Excretion of 17-ketosteroids as their sulfates and glucuronides is in part a reflection of testicular hormone production. The testis contributes about one-third of the urinary neutral 17-ketosteroid, particularly androsterone, etiocholanolone, and epiandrosterone (see Fig 29–26). In normal children up to the eighth year of life, there is a gradual increase in 17-ketosteroid excretion up to 2.5 mg/day; an increase up to 9 mg occurs between the eighth year and puberty in both boys and girls; after puberty, the sex differences in ketosteroid excretion which were noted on p 493 occur. In eunuchs, ketosteroids may be normal or lowered, whereas in testicular tumors with associated hyperactivity of the Leydig cells ketosteroid excretion may be considerably increased.

FEMALE HORMONES

Two main types of female hormones are secreted by the ovary: the **follicular** or **estrogenic hormones** produced by the cells of the developing graafian follicle and the **progestational hormones** derived from the corpus luteum that is formed in the ovary from the ruptured follicle.

The Follicular Hormones

The estrogenic (follicular) hormones are C-18 steroids, differing from androgens in lacking the methyl group at C_{10}. In contrast to all other natural steroids, ring A is aromatic (Fig 29–22).

The principal estrogenic hormone in the circulation—and the most important active form of the estrogens—is estradiol, which is in metabolic equilibrium with estrone. It is bound to a specific plasma carrier protein (sex steroid-binding protein), which also transports the androgens.

The international standard for estrogen activity is estrone; 1 International Unit (IU) = 0.1 mg estrone. Comparable biologic activity of the estrogens to increase uterine weight in rodents varies with the mode of administration: estradiol > estrone > estriol when given subcutaneously: estriol > estradiol > estrone after oral administration.

Estriol (Fig 29–26) is the principal estrogen found in the urine of pregnant women and in the placenta. It is produced by hydroxylation of estrone at C_{16} and reduction of the ketone group at C_{17}.

The androgens, testosterone and androstenedione, are precursors for the synthesis of the estrogens in testes, ovaries, adrenals, and placenta (Fig 29–22). The conversion from testosterone involves 3 enzyme-catalyzed steps which require oxygen and NADPH: (1) 19-hydroxylation to 19-hydroxytestosterone or 19-hydroxyandrostenedione; (2) 19-oxidation to the keto derivatives; and (3) aldehyde lyolysis to remove the C_{19} keto group and cause aromatization of the A ring. **Metyrapone** inhibits estrogen synthesis by blocking 19-hydroxylation. As with the other steroids, estrogens (primarily estriol) can be found in urine either as a conjugate with sulfate or as a glucuronide (Fig 29–26).

Physiologic Effects of Estrogenic Hormones

In the lower animals, the estrogenic hormones induce estrus, a series of changes in the female reproductive system associated with ovulation. These changes may be detected by the histologic appearance of the vaginal smear.

In women, the follicular hormones prepare the uterine mucosa for the later action of the progestational hormones. The changes in the uterus include proliferative growth of the lining of the endometrium, deepening of uterine glands, and increased vascularity; changes in the epithelium of the fallopian tubes and of the vagina also occur. All of these changes begin immediately after menstrual bleeding has ceased.

The estrogens also suppress the production of the pituitary hormone (follicle-stimulating hormone, FSH) which initially started the development of the follicle. In contrast, they appear to stimulate pituitary LH; peak levels of estrogens precede peak level of LH by 1–2 days. Estrogens are effective in maintenance of female secondary sex characteristics, acting antagonistically to testosterone.

Mechanism of Action

A number of experiments have indicated that the activities of several enzyme systems in the uterus as well as the placenta are stimulated by the prior administration of estradiol to the intact rat. In contrast to testosterone, estradiol is the active form, metabolites playing only a minor role. Estradiol is bound to a specific cytosol receptor protein in the cells, the resulting complex then being translocated into the nucleus. During this process, the receptor protein is altered structurally ("receptor transformation"), thereby increasing the ability of the complex to bind chromatin proteins in the nucleus and to cause increased RNA synthesis. Binding to the cytosol receptor protein is relatively nonspecific, most of the tissue specificity for estradiol action occurring at the levels of subsequent

complex transformation and nuclear binding. It is possible that estrogens may act on target tissues at the level of RNA synthesizing enzymes; in ovariectomized rats, RNA polymerase activity in the nuclear fraction of uterine homogenates (but not liver homogenates) is increased by 2 hours after the administration of estrogen. As a result of the modified RNA synthesis and the entry of new messenger RNA into the cytoplasm, polyribosome metabolism is altered. Thus, as is the case with most other steroid hormones, estrogens indirectly affect protein synthesis at the translational level.

Estrogens may also act as cofactors in a transhydrogenation reaction in which H ions and electrons are transferred from reduced NADP to NAD.

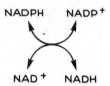

Figure 29–28. Transhydrogenation reaction involving estrogens.

The estrogen-dependent transhydrogenase which catalyzes the transfer of hydrogen from NADPH to NAD may bring about an increased rate of biologically useful energy in 2 ways: (1) Considering that the concentration of NADP in the cells is ordinarily very low, increased oxidation of NADPH would maintain availability of NADP for the activity of those dehydrogenases which require the oxidized form of this cofactor. (2) Because the direct oxidation of NADPH yields little if any high-energy phosphate, a method of deriving high-energy phosphate indirectly would be made available by transfer of hydrogen to NAD, thus forming NADH which could then be oxidized through the respiratory chain. This mechanism may in part explain the ability of estradiol to stimulate the rate of oxygen consumption, the conversion of acetate to CO_2, and the incorporation of acetate into protein, lipid, and the adenine and guanine of the total nucleic acid fraction of target tissues.

Synthetic Estrogens

A number of synthetic estrogens have been produced. The following are clinically valuable:

(1) Ethinyl estradiol is a synthetic estrogen which when given orally is 50 times as effective as water-soluble estrogenic preparations or 30 times as effective as estradiol benzoate injected intramuscularly.

(2) Diethylstilbestrol is an example of a group of para-hydroxyphenyl derivatives which, while not steroidal in structure, nonetheless exert potent estrogenic effects. However, as shown in the formula below, it is possible that ring closure may occur in the body to form a structure resembling the steroid nucleus.

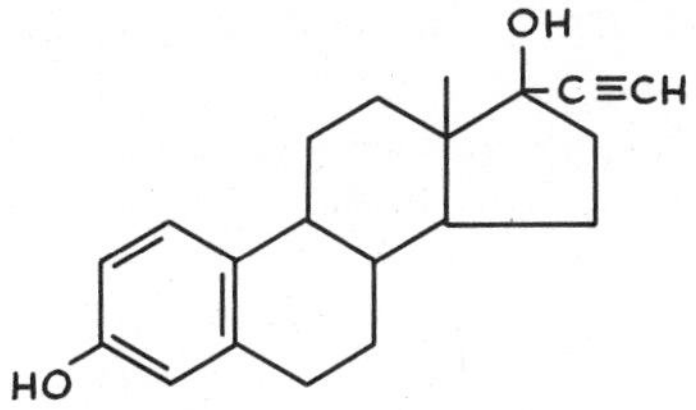

Figure 29–29. Ethinyl estradiol.

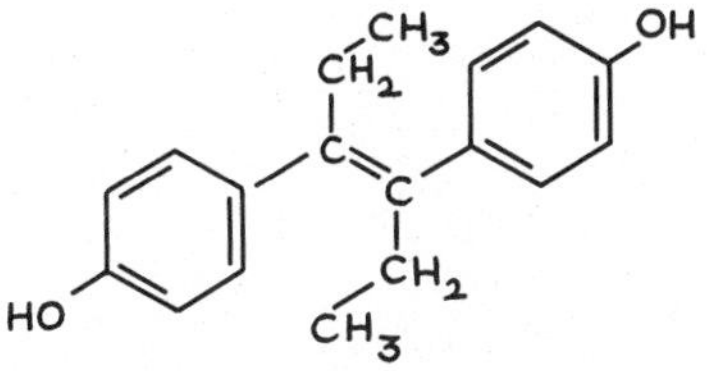

Figure 29–30. Diethylstilbestrol.

The Progestational Hormones (Luteal Hormones)

Progesterone (Fig 29–21) is the hormone of the corpus luteum, the structure which develops from the ruptured follicle. It is formed also by the placenta, which secretes progesterone, notably during the latter part of pregnancy. Progesterone is also formed in the adrenal cortex as a precursor of both C-19 and C-21 corticosteroids (Fig 29–21). In all of the above tissues, progesterone is synthesized from its immediate precursor, pregnenolone, by a combined dehydrogenase and isomerase reaction. The steroid analog cyanotrimethylandrostenolone can inhibit this conversion. In contrast to testosterone and estradiol, progesterone is bound in plasma to the corticosteroid-binding globulin. Intracellularly, it is bound to a specific binding protein in the cytosol which is chemically similar to corticosteroid-binding globulin but which has lost its ability to bind cortisol.

Functions of Progesterone

This hormone appears after ovulation and causes extensive development of the endometrium, preparing the uterus for the reception of the embryo and for its nutrition. The hormone also suppresses estrus, ovulation, and the production of pituitary luteinizing hormone, which originally stimulated corpus luteum formation. Progesterone antagonizes the action of estrogens in various tissues, including the cervical mucus, vaginal epithelium, and fallopian tubes. Progesterone also stimulates the mammary glands. When pregnancy occurs, the corpus luteum is maintained and menstruation and ovulation are suspended. The concentration of progesterone decreases near term. The Corner and Hisaw test for progesterone is based on the increase of secretory action caused by the hormone on the uterine endometrium.

If fertilization does not occur, the follicular and progestational hormones suddenly decrease on about the 26th day of the cycle; the new cycle then begins

with menstrual bleeding and sloughing of the uterine wall (Fig 29–33).

The metabolic fate of progesterone has been studied by the injection of ^{14}C-labeled hormone. About 75% of injected progesterone (or its metabolites) is transported to the intestine by way of the bile and eliminated in the feces. Large amounts occur in the urine only if the biliary route of excretion is blocked.

Other Progestational Hormones

In addition to progesterone, the corpus luteum may also produce a second hormone which has been termed **relaxin** because of its ability to bring about relaxation of the symphysis pubis of the guinea pig or of the mouse. Extracts of corpora lutea from the sow contain the active relaxing principle, and the blood of pregnant females of a number of species (including man) does also. Relaxin also occurs in the placenta. It is active only when injected into an animal in normal or artificially induced estrus. Relaxin appears chemically to be a polypeptide with a molecular weight of 9000. It is inactivated by treatment with proteolytic enzymes or by reagents which convert (by reduction) disulfide linkages to sulfhydryl groups.

The chief excretory product of progesterone is **pregnanediol** (Fig 29–26). It is present in quantities of 1–10 mg/day (as the glucuronide) during the latter half of the menstrual cycle. Its presence in the urine signifies that the endometrium is progestational rather than follicular.

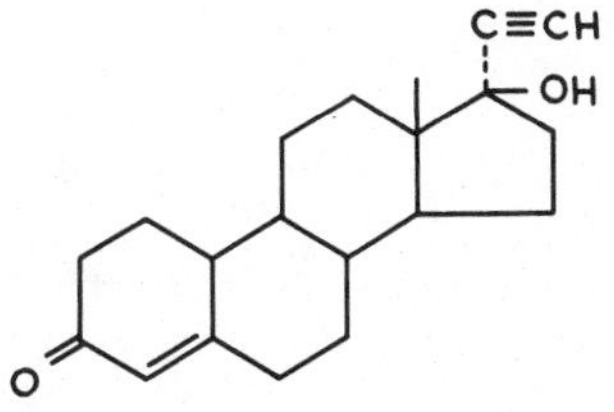

Figure 29–31. Norethindrone (Norlutin; 17α-ethinyl-19-nortestosterone).

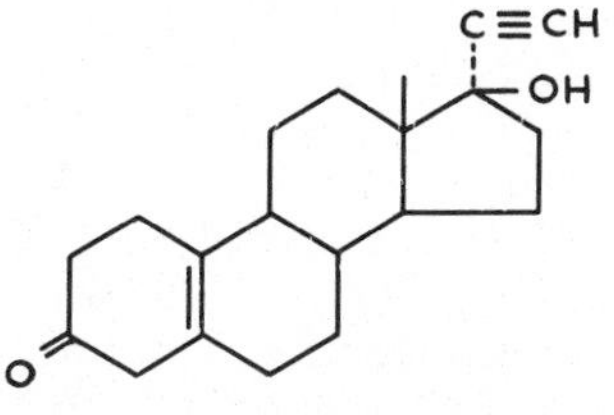

Figure 29–32. Norethynodrel (Enovid*; 17α-ethinyl-17-hydroxy-5[10]-estren-3-one).

*Enovid is a mixture containing, in addition to norethynodrel, a small portion of mestranol (ethinyl estradiol 3-methyl ether).

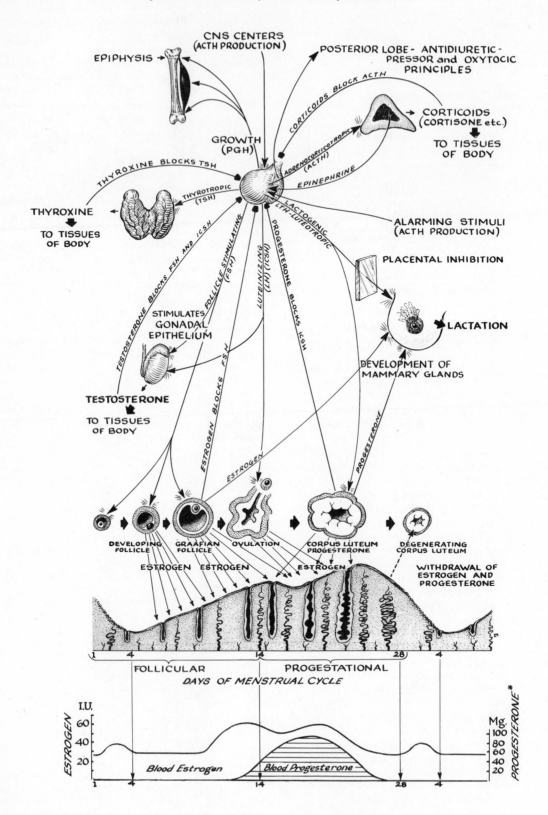

*Progesterone as determined from the urinary pregnanediol.

Figure 29–33. Relationships of the pituitary hormones to the target glands and tissues.

Pregnenolone also has some progestational activity. It may be used therapeutically to produce a secretory endometrium or to inhibit uterine motility in threatened abortion.

Orally Effective Progestational Agents

Progesterone is relatively ineffective when taken by mouth. In recent years, several synthetically produced progestational agents have been devised which are much more effective biologically than progesterone when taken orally. Two such compounds are shown above. Because, like progesterone, they have the ability to suppress ovulation, they have found application in association with estrogens as oral contraceptives.

Chorionic Gonadotropin (Anterior Pituitary-Like Hormones); Pregnancy Tests

The gonadotropic hormone found in urine during pregnancy is used as the basis for a test for pregnancy. For many years, the routine pregnancy test required maintenance of animal colonies. Injection of urine of a pregnant woman into immature female mice or rats caused rapid changes in the ovaries which could be easily seen as hemorrhagic spots and yellowish corpora lutea. This was the **Aschheim-Zondek test.** For the **Friedman test**, a virgin rabbit was used. The test urine was injected into an ear vein, and the ovaries were examined 24 hours later for ruptured or hemorrhagic follicles. The male frog *(Rana pipiens)*, the female toad *(Xenopus laevis)*, and the male toad *(Bufo arenarum)* were also used for pregnancy tests.

An immunoassay pregnancy test has since been developed which has superseded biologic testing. It is based upon precipitation of latex particles coated with antibodies to chorionic gonadotropin.

Chorionic gonadotropin is a product of the very early placenta. It is also produced when there is abnormal proliferation of chorionic epithelial tissue such as hydatidiform mole or chorioepithelioma; this would give rise to false results in pregnancy tests. Chorionic gonadotropin is used to induce ovulation in infertile women.

The effects of the female hormones on the menstrual cycle are illustrated in Fig 29–33.

For a summary of the interrelationships of FSH, LH, and female hormones during menstruation, see Catt reference on p 515.

Vitamin D₃ (cholecalciferol) is produced in the skin, activated by 25-hydroxylation in the liver, and metabolized to 1,25-hydroxycholecalciferol in the kidney. These active forms subsequently affect the bone, intestine, and kidney. Vitamin D is discussed in detail in Chapter 12. However, it could also be considered as among the steroid hormones.

THE PITUITARY GLAND (HYPOPHYSIS)

The human pituitary is a reddish-gray oval structure, about 10 mm in diameter, located in the brain just behind the optic chiasm as an extension from the floor of the hypothalamus. The average weight of the gland in the male is 0.5–0.6 g; in the female it is slightly larger, 0.6–0.7 g. The pituitary gland is composed of different types of tissue embryologically derived from 2 sources: a neural component and a buccal component. The terms **adenohypophysis** and **neurohypophysis** are used to differentiate the buccal and neural components, respectively.

The adenohypophysis includes the anterior lobe and the intermediate or middle lobe of the developed endocrine organ, both of which are glandular in structure. The neurohypophysis includes the posterior lobe of the gland and the infundibular or neural stalk which attaches the gland to the floor of the brain at the hypothalamus.

Complete removal of the pituitary (hypophysectomy) in young animals (eg, rats) causes a cessation of growth and a failure in maturation of the sex glands. Removal of the pituitary in the adult animal is followed by atrophy of the sex glands and organs, involution of the thyroid, parathyroids, and adrenal cortex, and a depression of their functions. In addition, there are alterations in protein, fat, and carbohydrate metab-

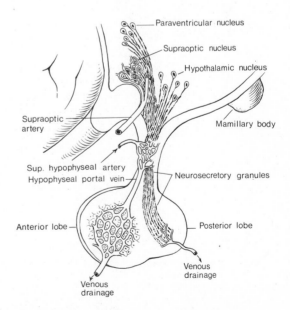

Figure 29–34. Simplified schematic reconstruction of the hypothalamus and the pituitary. (After Hansel; courtesy *International Journal of Fertility*. Redrawn and reproduced, with permission, from Schally & others: Science 179:341, 1973. Copyright © 1973 by The American Association for the Advancement of Science.)

olism. Also, there is abnormal sensitivity to insulin and resistance to the glycogenolytic effect of epinephrine.

Control of hormone secretion from the pituitary is in part modulated by regulating factors or hormones from the hypothalamus, that region of the brain immediately proximal to the pituitary (Fig 29–34). The median eminence of the hypothalamus is connected directly to the pituitary by the pituitary stalk. Within this stalk is a portal system of blood vessels required to maintain normal secretory activity of the pituitary gland. The regulating factors originating from endings of the hypothalamic nerve fibers are transported via the capillaries of the median eminence that empty with the portal vessels leading to the pituitary gland.

At present, 10 discrete regulating factors have been described that may affect the synthesis as well as the secretion of specific pituitary hormones (Table 29–3). In 3 instances (growth hormone, melanocyte-stimulating hormone, and prolactin), both stimulating and inhibiting regulators are known. This "on-off" regulation may be particularly useful for those pituitary hormones that are not under negative feedback control by the products of their target tissues. It should also be noted that the regulatory factors arising from hypothalamic centers provide an explanation for the ability of neurologic and psychic (eg, stress) stimulation to evoke endocrine and metabolic responses.

THE ANTERIOR PITUITARY GLAND

The anterior lobe is the largest and most essential portion of the pituitary. In man, this lobe comprises about 70% of the total weight of the gland. The ante-

Table 29–3. Hypothalamic hormones known to control the release of pituitary hormones.*

Hypothalamic Hormone (or Factor)	Abbreviation
Corticotropin (ACTH)-releasing hormone	CRH or CRF
Thyrotropin (TSH)-releasing† hormone	TRH or TRF
Luteinizing hormone (LH)-releasing† hormone	LH-RH or LH-RF
Follicle-stimulating hormone (FSH) releasing† hormone	FSH-RH or FSH-RF
Growth hormone (GH)-releasing† hormone	GH-RH or GH-RF
Growth hormone (GH) release-inhibiting hormone	GH-RIH or GIF
Prolactin release-inhibiting hormone	PRIH or PIF
Prolactin-releasing hormone	PRH or PRF
Melanocyte-stimulating hormone (MSH) release-inhibiting hormone	MRIH or MIF
Melanocyte-stimulating hormone (MSH) releasing hormone	MRH or MRF

*Reproduced, with permission, from Schally & others: Science 179:341, 1973. Copyright © 1973 by The American Association for the Advancement of Science.

†Or regulating hormone.

rior lobe of the hypophysis consists of epithelial glandular cells of varying sizes and shapes arranged in broad, circular columns separated by sinusoids containing blood. Three types of cells are differentiated by their staining qualities: (1) chromophobe cells (neutrophils), located in the center of the columns of epithelium, stain poorly; (2) and (3) chromaffin cells, located on the outside of the columns and therefore adjacent to the blood sinusoids, stain well. Those chromaffin cells which take the acid dyes are designated eosinophilic cells; those which stain with basic dyes, basophilic cells.

HORMONES OF THE ANTERIOR PITUITARY

Growth Hormone (Somatotropin)

A. Chemistry: Growth hormone, or somatotropin, was first isolated in sufficient quantity for study from the pituitary glands of cattle. The concentration of bovine growth hormone is 5–15 mg/gland, which is much higher than the μg/g quantities of other pituitary hormones.

Growth hormone from all mammalian species consists of a single polypeptide with a molecular weight of about 21,500. The proposed structure of human growth hormone consisting of 191 amino acids is shown in Fig 29–35. Although there is a high degree of similarity in the amino acid sequences of human, bovine, and porcine growth hormones, only human growth hormone or that of other primates is active in man.

Growth hormone can bring about some of the actions of lactogenic hormone (prolactin) and of human placental lactogen. Although all of these hormones are separate entities in the various species that have been studied, there is a considerable amount of similarity in their structures and, consequently, a significant degree of immunologic cross-reactivity.

Growth hormone from cattle is effective in stimulating growth in rats but not in man. The monkey and human preparations are active in both man and rat. It has been hypothesized that activity resides only in a portion of the molecule since partial hydrolysis of the hormone does not abolish its activity.

B. Function: Since actions of growth hormone can be demonstrated in vitro, it does act directly on target tissues. In addition, growth hormone stimulates production of **somatomedins (sulfation factors)**, from liver and possibly kidney, which can produce many of the anabolic effects of growth hormone. Somatomedin is similar to **serum insulin-like activity** described earlier (see p 472). Although both can bind to insulin receptors at high concentration, each has its own specific receptor and differs structurally from insulin.

Growth hormone has a variety of effects on different tissues, including muscle, adipose tissue, and liver. In general, it increases total growth and can cause

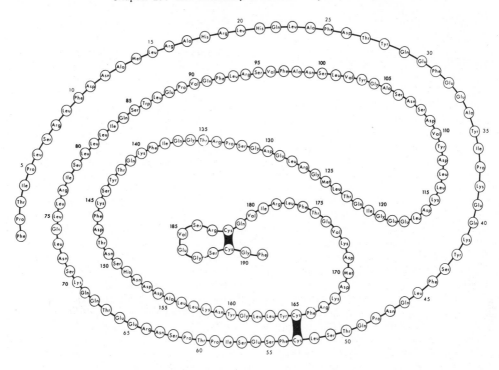

Figure 29–35. Proposed structure of human growth hormone. The numbers identify the amino acid residues, starting from the N-terminal. (Courtesy of CH Li.)

gigantism in children. Growth hormone deficiency in children results in dwarfism attended by low levels of the hormone in the serum. Dwarfism may also occur as a result of tissue insensitivity to normal amounts of growth hormone. As with steroids, part of the action of growth hormone is to spare circulating glucose. The hormone acts slowly, requiring from 1–2 hours to several days before its biologic effects are detectable.

1. Protein synthesis–Growth hormone stimulates over-all protein synthesis in the intact animal, resulting in a pronounced increase in nitrogen retention with an associated retention (actually increased renal tubular reabsorption) of phosphorus. Blood amino acids and urea are decreased. Thus, growth hormone in this regard acts synergistically with insulin. In muscle, growth hormone can stimulate protein synthesis by increasing the transport of amino acids into the cells, an action that can be demonstrated in vitro with rat diaphragm muscle. This effect is not inhibited by puromycin. Therefore, the facilitation of amino acid transport by the hormone is not mediated by a direct action on protein synthesis. In addition, growth hormone facilitates protein synthesis in muscle tissue by a mechanism independent of its ability to provide amino acids. Thus, increased protein synthesis can be demonstrated in vitro even when amino acid transport is blocked. In the intact animal, growth hormone administration results in an increase in DNA and RNA synthesis. It remains unclear whether increased RNA synthesis is a result of direct action of the hormone or a secondary result of an increase in metabolic signal

substance, possibly amino acids themselves. The hormone increases collagen synthesis. Since this protein is rich in hydroxyproline, an increase in turnover of collagen after growth hormone is reflected by an increase in urinary hydroxyproline and hydroxyproline peptides. The measurement of urinary hydroxyproline can therefore be used to assess growth hormone activity in the intact animal.

2. Lipid metabolism–Growth hormone is mildly lipolytic when incubated in vitro with adipose tissue, promoting release of free fatty acids and glycerol. In vivo, administration of growth hormone is followed 30–60 minutes later by an increase in circulating free fatty acids and increased oxidation of fatty acids in the liver. Under conditions of insulin deficiency (eg, diabetes), increased ketogenesis may occur.

3. Carbohydrate metabolism–In muscle, growth hormone antagonizes the effects of insulin. Impairment of glycolysis may occur at several steps, as well as inhibition of transport of glucose. Whether this latter effect is a direct effect on transport or a result of the inhibition of glycolysis has not yet been established. The mobilization of fatty acids from triacylglycerol stores may also contribute to the inhibition of glycolysis in the muscle. In liver there is an increase in liver glycogen, probably arising from activation of gluconeogenesis from amino acids. Hyperglycemia after growth hormone administration is a combined result of decreased peripheral utilization of glucose and increased hepatic production via gluconeogenesis. Prolonged administration of growth hormone results in an enhanced release of insulin from the pancreas during glucose stimulation. This effect may be secondary to the peripheral diabetogenic action of growth hormone to increase circulating pancreatic stimulants such as glucose, fatty acids, and ketones, or it may be caused by a direct but slow action on the pancreas.

4. Ion or mineral metabolism—Growth hormone increases intestinal absorption of calcium as well as its excretion. Since growth hormone stimulates the growth of the long bones at the epiphyses as well as the growth of soft tissue, increased calcium retention results for the most part from the increased metabolic activity of the bone. The hormone, by increasing somatomedin from the liver, thereby fosters sulfate incorporation into cartilage. In addition to calcium, sodium, potassium, magnesium, phosphate, and chloride are also retained. Serum phosphate levels are usually elevated in acromegaly and are often measured as an indication of the degree of excess growth hormone "activity" in the patient.

5. Prolactin properties—As already noted, growth hormone has many of the properties of prolactin such as stimulation of the mammary glands, lactogenesis, and stimulation of the pigeon crop sac.

C. Control of Secretion: The production of growth hormone in man is about 500 μg/day. In normal males, growth hormone (as measured by radioimmunoassay) ranges from 0–5 ng/ml of plasma; in females, values may occasionally be considerably higher, though most fall in the same range; the occasional high levels in females may be related to the fact that estrogens enhance the growth hormone released in response to various stimuli. Progesterones, in contrast, are inhibitory. In acromegalics, levels range from 15–80 or more ng/ml. Growth hormone is usually elevated in the newborn, decreasing to adult levels by 4 years of age.

Much of the control of growth hormone secretion occurs at the level of the hypothalamus. Positive control may be exerted by a specific **growth hormone releasing factor (GHRF)**, also termed growth hormone-releasing hormone (GRH). It has been extracted from the hypothalamus, where it is localized in the median eminence. The chemical nature of this substance as well as its physiologic role is not yet clear.

A negative modulator of growth hormone release, **growth hormone release-inhibiting hormone (GH-RIH or GIH) (somatostatin)** has been isolated and synthesized. This growth hormone-release inhibiting hormone is a peptide composed of 14 amino acids (Fig 29–36). It is active when injected either in its linear or in a cyclic form.

Injected growth hormone-release inhibiting hormone also inhibits release of insulin, glucagon, thyrotropin, and follicle-stimulating hormone (FSH). How-

ever, it does not appear to affect secretion of prolactin. Because of its ability to inhibit secretion of growth hormone and of glucagon, growth hormone-release inhibiting hormone (somatostatin) may have therapeutic application as an adjunct to insulin in the management of insulin-requiring diabetic patients. Somatostatin has now been found in the D cells of pancreatic islets and in the stomach, suggesting that the "hypothalamic" releasing hormones may actually be more widely distributed.

Control of these regulating factors is in turn regulated by signals from the ventromedial nucleus, which can be excited and bring about secretion of growth hormone by alpha-adrenergic stimulation or by glucagon or arginine. The inhibition by glucose of release of growth hormone may also occur at this level.

The plasma growth hormone level in the adult is not stable; depending on the nature of a stimulus, it may change as much as 10-fold within a few minutes. Plasma growth hormone concentration is increased following stress (pain, apprehension, cold, surgical stress, severe insulin hypoglycemia) and exercise, the response to exercise being greater in females than in males. The rapid rise after exercise necessitates careful control to ensure that the subject is resting before blood samples are taken for growth hormone measurements. The increased growth hormone after stress may be caused by increases in catecholamines acting at the hypothalamic level; infusion of either of these agents stimulates growth hormone secretion. Factors decreasing glucose availability to the hypothalamic regulating centers also stimulate release. This can be accomplished (1) by fasting, (2) by hypoglycemia associated with an insulin tolerance test, or (3) by administration of an agent such as 2-deoxyglucose, which inhibits the normal glycolysis of glucose, making it unavailable to the regulating centers even though circulating blood sugar becomes elevated. Since 2-deoxyglucose causes the prompt release of growth hormone while at the same time producing an elevated blood sugar, it is apparent that regulation in the hypothalamus is dependent on the normal metabolism of glucose, not on the circulating level of glucose as such.

Stimulation is also increased by protein meals and by amino acids, particularly arginine. This provides a regulatory system whereby increases in amino acids result in secretion of growth hormone which itself facilitates uptake of amino acids into protein. It will be recalled that arginine also facilitates the secretion of insulin, which, like growth hormone, is required for protein synthesis. Curiously, growth hormone is elevated in malnutrition with kwashiorkor. This may be due to abnormal glucose metabolism and decreased glucose availability at the control sites.

In the acromegalic patient, normal control mecha-

H–Ala–Gly–Cys–Lys–Asn–Phe–Phe–Trp–Lys–Thr–Phe–Thr–Ser–Cys–OH

Figure 29–36. Structure of growth hormone-release inhibiting hormone (GIH; somatostatin).

nisms for growth hormone release are lost. This is reflected in an inability to suppress plasma growth hormone values by administration of glucose or to respond to an arginine stimulation. In subjects with mild acromegaly or those who have been treated and in whom moderate hormonal overactivity persists, levels of growth hormone may overlap with those occasionally high normal values seen in normal females. In these cases, inability to suppress hormone production with glucose is used to evaluate residual acromegaly. Conversely, growth hormone deficiency may be documented by demonstration of inadequate responses to insulin-induced hypoglycemia or arginine infusion.

Peptides of variable metabolic activity which are not necessarily detectable by immunoassay have been prepared from growth hormone. Whether these peptides are released from the pituitary or indeed play any physiologic role is not yet established.

The Pituitary Tropins

The most characteristic function of the anterior pituitary is the elaboration of hormones which influence the activities of other endocrine glands, principally those involving reproduction or stress. Such hormones are called **tropic hormones.** They are carried by the blood to other target glands and aid in maintaining these glands and stimulating production of their respective hormones. For this reason, atrophy and decline in the function of many endocrine glands occur in pituitary hypofunction or after hypophysectomy.

With the possible exception of prolactin and melanocyte-stimulating hormone (MSH), the tropic hormones are under the positive and negative control of peptide factors from the hypothalamus (**releasing** and **inhibiting factors** or **hypothalamic neurohormones**). The production and release of the neurohormones, in turn, are sensitive to neural and metabolic stimuli and can be inhibited by their respective tropic hormones ("short loop feedback") (Fig 28–1).

In addition, the tropic hormones are usually subject to feedback inhibition at the pituitary or hypothalamic level by the hormone product of the final target gland. Thus, hydrocortisone, sex steroids, and thyroxine inhibit the release of their respective tropic hormones.

A. Lactogenic Hormone (Prolactin, PL, Mammotropin, Luteotropic Hormone, LTH): Pituitary luteotropic hormone is a protein with a molecular weight of approximately 23,000 which, like growth hormone, is produced by the pituitary acidophil cells. Its complete structure is shown in Fig 29–37. As has been noted, lactogenic hormone and growth hormone share some common structures and cross-react immunologically. Luteotropic hormone and growth hormone are distinct pituitary hormones in man and other species but probably evolved from a common ancestor.

In animals, luteotropic hormone activates the corpus luteum and stimulates continued progesterone production by the developed corpus luteum. It also stimulates enlargement of crop gland and formation of "crop milk" in pigeons. In man, the sheep hormone acts as an anabolic agent, mimicking the effects of growth hormone, but it is less active. It increases

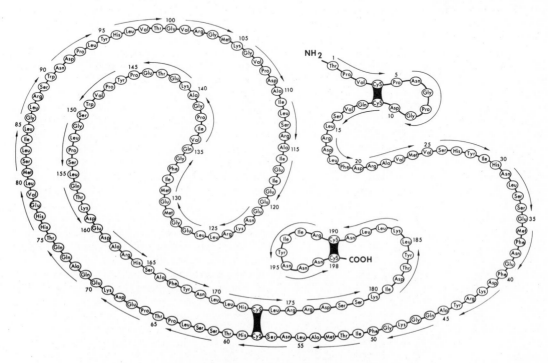

Figure 29–37. Ovine prolactin. (Courtesy of CH Li.)

during pregnancy and may stimulate mammary development and growth hormone-like metabolic changes. Its rapid decrease after parturition, however, suggests that it may have little to do with mammalian lactation. Luteotropic hormone can be inhibited by a hypothalamic factor, **prolactin inhibiting factor**, and may possibly be stimulated by a less well established releasing factor. Pharmacologic levels of thyrotropin-releasing hormone can also stimulate prolactin while L-dopa and certain ergot alkaloids are inhibitory.

B. The Gonadotropins: These tropic substances influence the function and maturation of the testis and ovary. They are glycoproteins with molecular weights of about 25,000 (FSH) and 40,000 (LH).

The gonadotropins follicle-stimulating hormone (FSH) and luteinizing hormone (LH) (as well as thyrotropin and human chorionic gonadotropin) consist of 2 nonidentical, noncovalently linked subunits, the a and β chains: The β chains vary in length from 110–120 amino acids, have partial homology only, and confer the specific biologic activity. The somewhat shorter a chains, if from the same species, are identical for all 3 hormones. The role of this common subunit is not established. However, it is necessary to maintain activity since the separated chains have little biologic action. The carbohydrate content of the gonadotropins consists of sialic acid, hexose, and hexosamine.

The secretion of luteinizing hormone and follicle-stimulating hormone is regulated by a single hypothalamic releasing factor, **luteinizing hormone/follicle-stimulating hormone-releasing hormone (LH/FSH-RH)** (Fig 29–38). Luteinizing hormone/follicle-stimulating hormone-releasing hormone is a decapeptide whose N-terminal amino acid is a derivative of glutamic acid, the cyclic compound (**pyroglutamic acid, pyroglu**) formed by removal of water to cause cyclization as

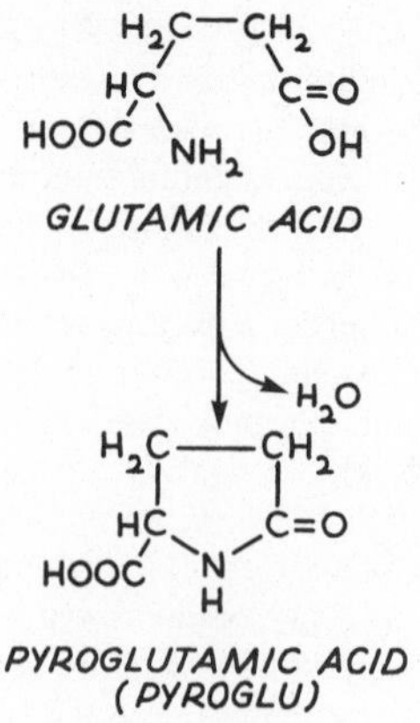

Figure 29–39. Structures of glutamic and pyroglutamic acids.

shown in Fig 29–39. LH/FSH-RH acts directly on the pituitary to increase cAMP elevation and gonadotropin release. It has been used to increase fertility in patients with hypothalamic amenorrhea. Although this single releasing factor probably mediates the hypothalamic control of gonadotropins, levels of follicle-stimulating hormone and luteinizing hormone do not always rise and fall together. Apparently much of the specific regulation of these gonadotropins, particularly by end-organ steroids, can occur at the pituitary level (Fig 28–1).

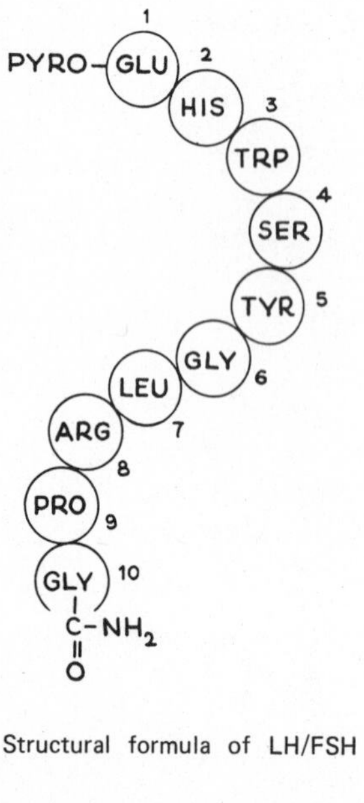

1. Follicle-stimulating hormone (FSH)—This hormone promotes follicular growth, prepares the follicle for the action of luteinizing hormone (LH), and enhances the release of estrogen induced by luteinizing hormone. In the male, it stimulates seminal tubule and testicular growth and plays an important role in the early stages of spermatogenesis. Plasma follicle-stimulating hormone concentrations increase through puberty from the low levels of infancy. In the female, there is marked cycling of levels, with peaks of the order of 10-fold or more over basal levels being reached at or slightly before the time of ovulation. Follicle-stimulating hormone secretion is inhibited at the pituitary and possibly the hypothalamic level by the administration of testosterone, progesterone, and possibly follicle-stimulating hormone itself. Estrogens may stimulate or inhibit depending on the circumstances.

Two **lipotropins** have been isolated from the pituitary. β-Lipotropin contains 91 amino acids, whereas a-lipotropin is a 58-amino-acid polypeptide consisting of a portion of β-lipotropin. Each possesses a heptapeptide also found in MSH. Though lipotropin when injected causes lipolysis and fatty acid mobilization, whether it exists as a true hormone in the circulation is unknown. β-Lipotropin may prove to be a precursor for β-**endomorphin** (identical to amino acids 61–91 of β-lipotropin, an interesting peptide with analgesic potency 18–33 times more active on a molar basis than morphine. (See Loh & others reference, p 515.)

2. Luteinizing hormone (LH) in the female stimu-

Figure 29–38. Structural formula of LH/FSH releasing hormone.

lates final maturation of the graafian follicle, ovulation, and the development of the corpora lutea. Both estrogen and progesterone secretion are stimulated.

In the ovary, luteinizing hormone can stimulate the nongerminal elements, which contain the interstitial cells, to produce the androgens androstenedione, dehydroepiandrosterone, and testosterone. In subjects with polycystic ovaries (Stein-Leventhal disease), part of the observed masculinization (hirsutism) may result from overactivity of the ovarian stroma to produce these androgens.

In the male, luteinizing hormone stimulates testosterone production by the testis, which in turn maintains spermatogenesis and provides for the development of accessory sex organs such as the vas deferens, prostate, and seminal vesicles.

Luteinizing hormone binds to relatively specific membrane plasma receptors in luteal and interstitial cells, which are not affected by FSH. This results ultimately in conversion of acetate to squalene (the precursor for cholesterol synthesis). Additionally, there is also acceleration of the conversion of cholesterol to 20α-hydroxycholesterol, a necessary intermediate in the synthesis of progesterone or testosterone (Fig 29–21).

The signal initiated by LH binding involves cAMP; this nucleotide is increased after addition of luteinizing hormone to incubating corpora lutea. Furthermore, added cAMP duplicates the stimulatory action of luteinizing hormone on progesterone synthesis both at the site of acetate incorporation into cholesterol and at the site of cholesterol incorporation into pregnenolone (Fig 29–21). The effects of cAMP and luteinizing hormone are blocked by puromycin, indicating that their action may be associated with protein synthesis, but the rapid rise in cAMP after hormone administration indicates that rapid effects also occur.

The plasma concentration and pituitary content of luteinizing hormone increase through puberty. In women, there is cycling of plasma luteinizing hormone levels, with midcycle (ovulatory) peaks many times the basal level. There is some evidence that the cycling observed in women may also occur to a lesser extent before adulthood, particularly in pubescence. The sequential relationship between blood levels of gonadotropins, estrogens, and progesterone to the events during cycling in females is still obscure.

Androgens inhibit LH secretion predominantly at the pituitary gland.

C. Thyrotropic Hormone; Thyroid-Stimulating Hormone (TSH): Thyrotropin is a glycoprotein of approximately 30,000 molecular weight. As is the case with the gonadotropins, this tropin consists of α and β subunits. (For review of structure, see Liu & Ward reference, p 515.) The α subunits of thyrotropin, luteinizing hormone, HCG, and follicle-stimulating hormone are nearly identical; the biologic specificity of thyrotropin must therefore reside in the β subunit.

Injection of thyrotropin will bring about all of the symptoms of hyperthyroidism. It increases thyroid growth and general metabolic activity, including glucose oxidation, oxygen consumption, and synthesis of phospholipids and RNA. Within minutes, thyrotropin rapidly increases each phase of thyroxine metabolism, including iodine uptake, organification, and, finally, the breakdown of thyroglobulin with the concomitant release of thyroid hormone. Thyrotropin binds to specific membrane receptors and activates thyroidal adenylate cyclase, resulting in increased cellular cAMP. It is not known if the major action of cAMP is to rapidly activate the enzymes involved in the above reactions or to increase their synthesis at the translation or transcription levels. It may be that it has both actions.

Thyrotropin is used clinically to differentiate primary hypothyroidism (myxedema) from secondary hypothyroidism (pituitary insufficiency).

Control of thyrotropin release. The reciprocal relationship between the target gland and pituitary thyrotropin is demonstrated by a reduction in thyrotropin after thyroxine or triiodothyronine administration. The thyroid hormone effect is primarily at the level of the pituitary.

As was described for other pituitary tropins, the release of thyrotropin is also controlled by a releasing factor originating in the hypothalamus. This factor has been designated **hypothalamic, hypophysiotropic thyrotropic releasing hormone (TRH).** This releasing hormone is a neutral tripeptide, ie, it has no terminal ionized groups. The tripeptide consists of pyroglutamic acid (Fig 29–39), histidine, and prolinamide as abbreviated below (Fig 29–40).

Thyrotropic releasing hormone obtained from the pig and that obtained from the sheep are identical. The synthetic tripeptide does not appear to be species-specific.

Inhibitors of protein synthesis have no effect on synthesis of thyrotropic releasing factor from the hypothalamus, indicating that the process is nonribosomal.

Thyrotropic releasing hormone causes an increase in thyrotropin within 1 minute; thus, it acts on thyrotropin secretion independently of an additional action on thyrotropin synthesis. As with most secretagogues, thyrotropic releasing hormone action is calcium-dependent (Fig 28–6). Thyrotropic releasing hormone is specific, acting primarily on the thyrotropin secreting cells. Thyrotropic releasing hormone, however, also stimulates prolactin secretion, and its possible use for stimulating milk production in cows is being investi-

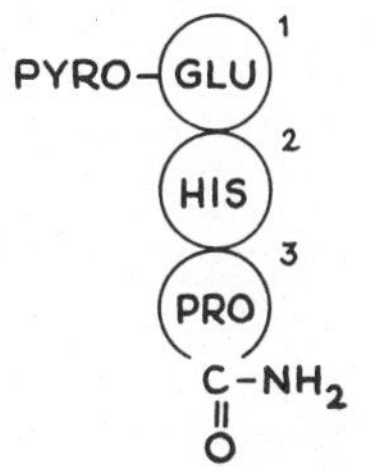

Figure 29–40. Amino acid sequence of hypothalamic thyrotropic releasing hormone.

gated. Administration of thyrotropic releasing hormone is now used to test the thyrotropin-secreting capacity of the pituitary as well as to distinguish between hypothalamic and pituitary lesions. Thyrotropic releasing hormone tripeptide retains much of its activity when given by mouth. This regulating hormone is rapidly destroyed in liver and kidney and has a half-time of disappearance from the blood of 4 minutes.

Plasma levels of thyrotropin. Blood levels determined by radioimmunoassay range from 0–3 ng/ml. Levels are low in subjects with hyperthyroidism and are increased in hypothyroidal myxedema. In simple goiter, thyrotropin levels are elevated only if hypothyroidism is still present.

D. Adrenocorticotropic Hormone (ACTH, Corticotropin): Adrenal function is regulated by the pituitary tropic hormone ACTH. ACTH is a straight chain polypeptide with a molecular weight of 4500 containing 39 amino acids (Fig 29–41). Only the first 23 amino acids (from the N-terminal end of the chain) are required for activity. The sequence of these 23 amino acids in the peptide chain is the same in all species examined including humans, whereas the remaining biologically inactive 16 amino acid chain varies according to the animal source.

1. Physiologic effects—ACTH not only increases the synthesis of corticosteroids by the adrenal but also

stimulates their release from the gland. It also increases total protein synthesis as indicated by increased incorporation of ^{14}C-labeled acetate into adrenal tissue proteins and increased adrenal RNA. Thus, ACTH produces both a tropic effect on steroid production and a trophic effect on adrenal tissue. In general, the tropic effects can be observed between 1–3 hours after administration of hormone, whereas the trophic actions, including stimulation of RNA synthesis, are much slower. Adrenal target organ specificity is apparent since other hormones such as thyrotropin, growth hormone, and gonadotropins are inactive.

ACTH affects steroid hormone synthesis in the adrenal at an early stage in the conversion of cholesterol to pregnenolone, the primary precursor for the synthesis of all adrenal steroids (Figs 29–21 and 29–22). Thus, ACTH stimulation results in an increase in mineralocorticoids, glucocorticoids, and androgens. As already noted, ACTH has only a mild effect on the output of aldosterone. The administration of ACTH to normal human beings, therefore, causes the following effects: (1) increased excretion of nitrogen, potassium, and phosphorus; (2) retention of sodium, chloride, and secondary retention of water; (3) elevation of fasting blood sugar and a diabetic glucose tolerance curve; (4) increase in circulating free fatty acids; (5) increased excretion of uric acid; (6) increased androgenicity (in extreme cases); and (7) decline in circulating eosinophils and lymphocytes and elevation of polymorphonuclear leukocytes.

The mechanism by which ACTH performs its tropic action remains unclear. However, its action appears to be primarily at the cell membrane level; ACTH diazotized to large cellulose fibers was still active in steroid biosynthesis when the large complex was suspended with adrenal cell cultures. Furthermore, the hormone is active only on preparations where the cell membrane is intact.

The primary action of ACTH may involve cAMP, since this compound is increased within seconds in the adrenal gland by ACTH and, if added directly, will in itself stimulate steroidogenesis. The effect of ACTH on the adrenal can be inhibited by blocking protein synthesis with puromycin, whereas the blocking of RNA synthesis by dactinomycin has little inhibitory effect. This action is consistent with a cAMP-mediated effect on protein kinases in the nucleus and indicates that ACTH may have a delayed effect on synthesis of adrenal enzymes. Perhaps because of its ability to activate adenylate cyclase and increase intracellular levels of cAMP, ACTH can increase lipolysis in adipose tissue and stimulate insulin secretion from the pancreas. However, the primary membrane receptor is the adrenal cell. Thus, these extra-adrenal effects are small, require large concentrations of the hormone, and are comparatively unimportant under normal physiologic conditions.

Prostaglandins (see p 297) may also play a role in ACTH action: ACTH mobilizes some prostaglandins in the adrenal, and prostaglandin E_2 can duplicate ACTH action to increase steroidogenesis.

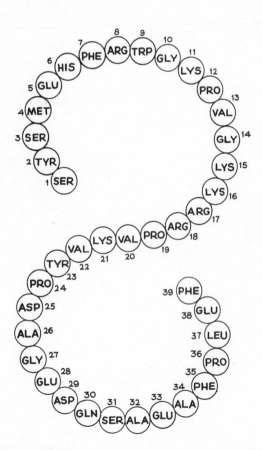

Figure 29–41. Structure of human ACTH.

2. Control of ACTH secretion—As with most of the other tropic hormones, ACTH is controlled by corticotropin-releasing hormones found in the hypothalamus. Three hormones have been designated as a_1-, a_2-, and β-corticotropin-releasing hormones, respectively. β-Corticotropin-releasing hormone may be vasopressin or a peptide similar in structure. (The similarity of vasopressin and one form of corticotropin-releasing hormone may explain why vasopressin is an effective stimulator of ACTH production.) The structures of a_1- and a_2-corticotropin-releasing hormone are similar to that of a-melanocyte-stimulating hormone (see p 510). Activation of the hypothalamic centers through the cerebral cortex by nonspecific stresses such as cold, pyrogens, insulin hypoglycemia, epinephrine, estrogens, or trauma or by psychic stimuli results in increased production of ACTH, leading to increased adrenal cortical activity and protective compensation against the stress. High levels of ACTH may inhibit its further synthesis by a "short loop" inhibition of corticotropin-releasing hormone production in the hypothalamus (Fig 28–1).

A reciprocal relationship between corticosteroid production and ACTH secretion is well established; exogenous cortisol causes feedback inhibition of ACTH release at the pituitary level. Androgens and progesterone may be less inhibitory at the same site.

Abnormalities of Pituitary Function

A. Hyperpituitarism:

1. Excess production of growth hormone (eosinophilic adenoma)—Gigantism results from hyperactivity of the gland during childhood or adolescence, ie, before closure of the epiphyses. The long bones increase in length so that the patient reaches an unusual height. There are also associated metabolic changes attributed to a generalized pituitary hyperfunction.

Acromegaly results from hyperactivity that begins after epiphysial closure has been completed and growth has ceased. The patient exhibits characteristic facial changes (growth and protrusion of the jaw, enlargement of the nose), growth and enlargement of the hands, feet, and viscera, and thickening of the skin.

2. Excess production of ACTH (basophilic adenoma) produces Cushing's disease.

B. Hypopituitarism: Hypopituitarism may occur as a result of certain types of pituitary tumors, or after hemorrhage (especially postpartum), infarct, or atrophy of the gland.

1. Dwarfism is a result of hypoactivity of the gland, sometimes caused by chromophobe tumors or craniopharyngioma. In either case, the underactivity is due to pressure of the tumor on the remainder of the gland. If the tumor begins early in life, dwarfism will result; if it occurs later, there will be cessation of growth and metabolic abnormalities similar to those observed after total hypophysectomy.

2. Pituitary myxedema, due to lack of thyrotropin, produces symptoms similar to those described for primary hypothyroidism.

3. Panhypopituitarism refers to deficiency of function of the hypophysis which involves all of the hormonal functions of the gland. This can result from destruction of the gland because of hemorrhage or infarct.

Milder forms of long-standing panhypopituitarism may result from the pressure of a tumor on the pituitary. In this condition, there is a tendency to hypoglycemia with sensitivity to insulin. The excretion of sex hormone products (17-ketosteroids) in the urine is much reduced in panhypopituitarism.

Pituitary-Like Hormones From the Placenta

Gonadotropic hormones not of pituitary origin are also found (eg, pregnancy hormone, chorionic gonadotropin).

A. Human Chorionic Gonadotropin (HCG) or Human Chorionic Somatomammotropin (HCS): This is a protein with immunologic and biologic properties similar to those of pituitary LH. As with the pituitary gonadotropins, the structure of human chorionic gonadotropin consists of a and β subunits. It has a high structural homology with LH, the a subunits in the 2 hormones being almost identical. Human chorionic gonadotropin is derived from the syncytiotrophoblast. It is elevated in the plasma of pregnant females. Because of its long half-life, human chorionic gonadotropin may remain in the circulation several days after parturition.

B. Human Placental Lactogen, Chorionic Growth Hormone Prolactin: This hormone has many physicochemical and immunologic similarities to human growth hormone. The complete structure has been determined, and a high degree of homology with growth hormone and to a lesser degree with pituitary prolactin was found. Human placental lactogen has lactogenic and luteotropic activity. It also has some metabolic effects which are qualitatively similar to those of growth hormone, including inhibition of glucose uptake, stimulation of free fatty acid and glycerol release, enhancement of nitrogen and calcium retention (despite increased urinary calcium excretion), reduction in the urinary excretion of phosphorus and potassium, and an increase in the turnover of hydroxyproline, as reflected by increased urinary excretion of that amino acid.

C. Thyrotropin: Recent evidence indicates that the placenta may also be the source of a thyrotropin-like substance.

THE MIDDLE LOBE OF THE PITUITARY

The middle lobe of the pituitary secretes a hormone, **intermedin,** which was first detected by its effect on the pigment cells in the skin of lower vertebrates. This hormone apparently also increases the deposition of melanin by the melanocytes of the human skin. In this role it is referred to as **melanocyte-stimulating hormone (MSH).** Both hydrocortisone and cortisone inhibit the secretion of melanocyte-stimulating hormone; this is similar to their action on ACTH. Epinephrine and, even more strongly, norepinephrine inhibit the action of melanocyte-stimulating hormone. When production of the corticosteroids is inadequate, as in Addison's disease, melanocyte-stimulating hormone is secreted, the synthesis of melanin is increased, and there is an accompanying brown pigmentation of the skin. In totally adrenalectomized patients, as much as 30–50 mg of orally administered cortisone must be supplied each day to prevent excess deposition of pigment in the skin. In patients suffering from panhypopituitarism (see above), in which case there is lack of melanocyte-stimulating hormone as well as corticosteroids, pigmentation does not occur.

Chemistry

Two peptides (a-MSH and β-MSH) have been isolated from the pituitaries of various species. In the human, there is about 50 times more β- than a-melanocyte-stimulating hormone. The structure of β-MSH is shown in Fig 29–42. a-MSH is smaller, containing only 13 amino acids. Both MSH peptides have considerable structural homology with ACTH. a-MSH is identical to the first 13 amino acids of ACTH (Fig 29–41), except that the N-terminal amino acid of a-MSH, serine, is acetylated and the C-terminal, valine, is in amide form. Amino acids 11–17 of β-MSH are common to both a-MSH and ACTH. This is of interest in view of the fact that ACTH has small but definite melanocyte-stimulating activity (about 1% that of MSH). This may be due to its content of the so-called intermedin sequence of amino acids, as described above. Although a-MSH has some corticotropic activity, this is not the

case with β-MSH.

Melatonin (N-acetyl-5-methoxy serotonin) is a hormone which lightens the color of the melanocytes of the skin of the frog and blocks the action of melanocyte-stimulating hormone as well as of ACTH. The chemistry and metabolism of melatonin are described in Chapter 23.

Regulation

The secretion of melanocyte-stimulating hormone is regulated at the hypothalamic level by **melanocyte-stimulating hormone release-inhibiting hormone**. A tripeptide and 2 pentapeptides have been isolated from the hypothalamus with melanocyte-inhibiting hormone activity, though the tripeptide appears to be the predominant and most important form. A **melanocyte-releasing hormone**, a pentapeptide, has also been described. All of these regulatory hormones have structures identical to fragments of oxytocin (Fig 29–43), suggesting that oxytocin may serve as their prohormone.

THE POSTERIOR LOBE OF THE PITUITARY

Extracts of the posterior pituitary contain at least 2 active substances: a pressor-antidiuretic principle, **vasopressin (Pitressin)**; and an oxytocic principle, **oxytocin (Pitocin)**. Both are produced primarily, however, in the neurosecretory neurons—specifically, the neurons of supraoptic and paraventricular nuclei of the hypothalamus. Thus, they may act as pituitary releasing hormones. The hormones are stored in the pituitary in association with 2 proteins, **neurophysin I and II**, with molecular weights of 19,000 and 21,000, respectively. Each neurophysin can bind either hormone. When secreted, the hormones circulate as free peptides preferentially to kidney, mammary gland, and liver. The half-life in plasma is extremely short, varying from 3–5 minutes depending on the chemical structure of the hormone and the particular species. Part of the vasopressin concentrated by the kidney is excreted in the urine, but most is degraded.

Function

A. Vasopressin: In high concentration, this substance raises blood pressure by its vasopressor effect on the peripheral blood vessels. Vasopressin has been used in surgical shock as an adjuvant in elevating blood pressure. It may also be used in the management of delayed postpartum hemorrhage and, at delivery, to overcome uterine inertia.

Vasopressin primarily acts on the kidney, where it exerts an antidiuretic effect as the so-called posterior pituitary **antidiuretic hormone**. The hormone affects the renal tubules and provides for the facultative reabsorption of water. The mechanism of action of vasopressin in the kidney is unknown. It binds firmly to

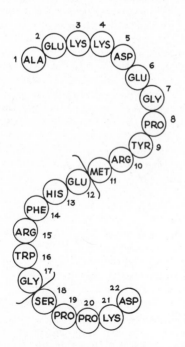

Figure 29—42. Amino acid sequence of human β-MSH.

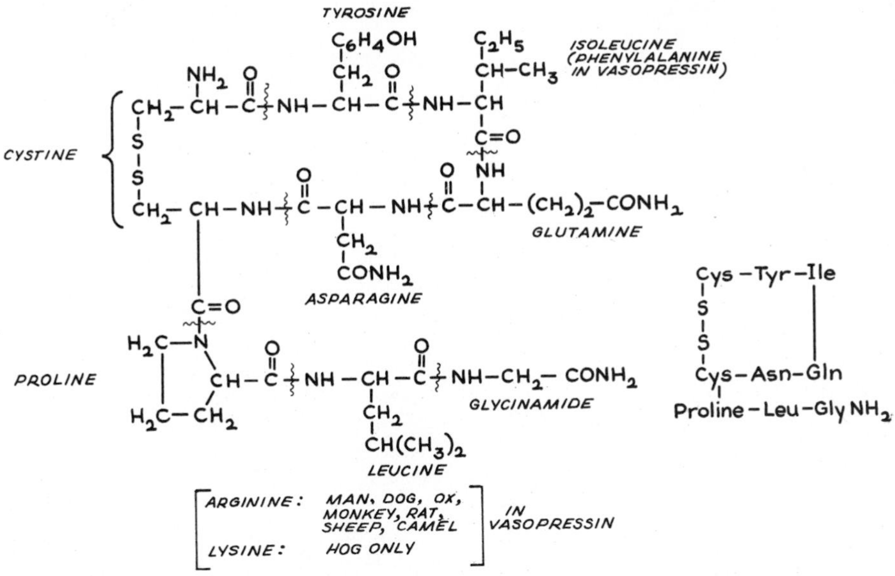

Figure 29—43. Structure of oxytocin.

renal tissue, an action that can be inhibited by sulfhydryl group (SH) blocking agents. Such observations have led to the suggestion that the action of vasopressin involves the opening of the disulfide (S—S) bridge (Fig 29—43), which is followed by a combination of the now available SH groups with other SH groups on membranes. Although such a binding can occur, there is as yet little support for the view that this is a required step in the action of the hormone. cAMP can duplicate many of the actions of vasopressin in kidney tissue, indicating that the hormone may act to increase levels of this substance.

Antidiuretic hormone may be increased by a variety of stimulators of neural activity. Emotional and physical stress, electrical stimulation, acetylcholine, nicotine, and morphine increase antidiuretic hormone secretion, as does dehydration or increased blood osmolality experimentally induced by injection of hypertonic saline. In general, these agents appear to increase synthesis of the hormones since their action does not cause a depletion of stored hormone. Furthermore, these stimulations are usually associated with an increase in RNA synthesis in the neuron, indicating an increased protein synthetic activity. Epinephrine and factors increasing blood volume are effective inhibitors of antidiuretic hormone secretion. Alcohol also inhibits antidiuretic hormone secretion.

In the absence of antidiuretic hormone, **diabetes insipidus** occurs. This is characterized by extreme diuresis—up to 30 liters of urine per day. The disease may be controlled by nasal administration of synthetic vasopressin or its derivatives. There is an additional form of diabetes insipidus (nephrogenic) where posterior pituitary production of antidiuretic hormone is normal but the target tissues are unresponsive to the hormone.

B. Oxytocin: (Fig 29—43.) This substance is increased during labor. It causes uterine contraction and is employed in obstetrics when induction of uterine contraction is desired. It also causes contraction of the smooth muscles in the mammary gland, resulting in milk excretion. Oxytocin levels are increased by suckling.

Chemistry

The structure of oxytocin is shown in Fig 29—43. It is a cyclic polypeptide containing 8 amino acids and has a molecular weight of about 1000.

The structure of vasopressin is quite similar to that of oxytocin. The differences are in 2 amino acids: (1) isoleucine of oxytocin is replaced in vasopressin by phenylalanine; and (2) leucine of oxytocin is replaced in vasopressin obtained from hog pituitary by lysine (**lysine vasopressin**) and in that from beef as well as many other animals by arginine (**arginine vasopressin**).

The functional chemical groups in oxytocin include the primary amino group of cystine; the phenolic hydroxyl group of tyrosine; the 3 carboxamide groups of asparagine, glutamine, and glycinamide; and the disulfide (S—S) linkage. By removal of certain of these groups, analogs of oxytocin have been produced. Examples are deoxy oxytocin, which lacks the phenolic group of tyrosine; and desamino oxytocin, which lacks the free primary amino group of the terminal cysteine residue. Desamino oxytocin has 5 times the antidiuretic activity of oxytocin itself.

For details of the comparative activities of a vast assortment of synthetic analogs and homologs, see Sawyer & Manning reference, p 515.

THE GASTROINTESTINAL HORMONES

The gastrointestinal hormones are polypeptides produced by mucosal endocrine cells of the stomach and small intestine. They are involved primarily in the regulation of motor and secretory functions of the stomach, small intestine, liver, biliary tract, and pancreas. The 3 major gastrointestinal hormones are **gastrin**, **secretin**, and **cholecystokinin-pancreozymin (CCK-PZ)**. A summary of the multiple and overlapping functions of these hormones is given in Table 29—4.

Demonstrable Actions of the Major Gastrointestinal Hormones

A. Gastrin: Two gastrins, I and II, each containing 17 amino acids, have been identified. They differ only in that gastrin II contains a sulfated tyrosine in position 12 whereas gastrin I contains an unmodified tyrosine (Fig 29—44). Most of the physiologic actions of gastrin reside in the carboxy terminal tetrapeptide, which is one-sixth as potent as the total molecule. Pentagastrin consisting of 4 of the 5 terminal amino acids has been synthesized and is used clinically.

Several larger gastrin polypeptides are found in the circulation and antral mucosa. "Big gastrin," a 34-amino-acid peptide containing a carboxy terminal heptadecapeptide similar to gastrin, is the major component in blood after feeding.

Gastrin is the most effective activator of gastric acid secretion known, though it can also stimulate pepsin and intrinsic factor release from gastric mucosa. To a lesser extent, it can duplicate many actions of the other gastrointestinal hormones (Table 29—4). It stimulates secretin release both directly and by stimulating acid secretion and can also delay delivery of gastric contents into the duodenum by reducing the rate of gastric emptying. Gastric acid secretion resulting from vagal stimulation is augmented by gastrin.

Gastrin release is increased by vagal stimulation (eg, caused by insulin-induced hypoglycemia), by acetylcholine, and by food intake, particularly protein or amino acids. Of the amino acids, glycine is the most potent. High levels of gastric acid can cause feedback inhibition of gastrin secretion. Cholecystokinin-pancreozymin has the same carboxy terminal peptide sequence as gastrin and, although less effective, can duplicate many of the actions of gastrin. Gastrin levels increase with age and other conditions where gastric acid secretion is low, including pernicious anemia. Zollinger-Ellison syndrome is characterized by gastrointestinal ulcers, high gastrin, and elevated gastric acid secretion caused by gastrin-producing pancreatic tumors (possibly from D [δ] cells in pancreatic islets).

Table 29—4. Gastrointestinal hormones.*

Activity	Gastrin	Hormone CCK-PZ	Secretin
Water and electrolyte secretion			
Stomach	↑	↑ (1)	↓
Pancreas	↑	↑	↑
Liver	↑	↑	↑
Brunner's glands	↑	↑	↑
Water and electrolyte absorption			
Ileum	↓	↓↑ (2)	↓↑ (2)
Gallbladder	0	0	↓
Enzyme secretion			
Stomach and pancreas	↑	↑	↑
Pancreatic islet secretion			
Insulin	↑	↑	↑
Glucagon	0	↑	↓
Smooth muscle			
Lower esophageal sphincter	↑	↓	↓
Stomach	↑	↑	↓
Pyloric sphincter	↓	↑	↑
Intestine	↑	↑	↓
Ileocecal sphincter	↓	NT	NT
Gallbladder	↑	↑	↑
Sphincter of Oddi	↓	↓	NT
Growth and amino acid uptake			
Gastric mucosa	↑	NT	↓
Pancreas	↑	↑	0
Metabolic			
Lipolysis	0	0	↑
Glycogenolysis	0	0	0
Glucose absorption			
Jejunum	↓	↑	NT

*Reproduced, with permission, from Williams RH (editor): *Textbook of Endocrinology,* 5th ed. Saunders, 1974.
(1) Inhibition of gastrin-mediated water and electrolyte secretion
(2) Conflicting results
NT = Not tested; ↑ = increase; ↓ = decrease; 0 = no effect.

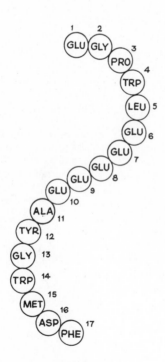

Figure 29—44. Human gastrin.

Table 29–5. Gastrointestinal polypeptide hormones.*

	Number of Amino Acid Residues	MW	Homologous Hormone	Cellular Location	Stimulus for Release	Actions
Established hormones						
Gastrin	17	2100	CCK-PZ	G cells of antrum and duodenum	Gastric distention and protein in the stomach	Stimulates acid and pepsin secretion; stimulates gastric mucosal growth; possibly stimulates lower esophageal sphincter.
Cholecystokinin-pancreozymin (CCK-PZ)	33	3883	Gastrin	Mucosa of entire small intestine	Fat, protein, and their digestion products in the intestine	Stimulates gallbladder contraction; stimulates pancreatic enzyme secretion; stimulates pancreatic growth; inhibits gastric emptying.
Secretin	27	3056	Glucagon	Mucosa of duodenum and jejunum	Low pH in the duodenum; threshold pH 4.5	Stimulates pancreatic and biliary HCO_3^- secretion; augments action of CCK-PZ on pancreatic enzyme secretion.
Candidate hormones†						
Gastric inhibitory polypeptide (GIP)	43	5105	Secretin	Mucosa of duodenum and jejunum	Glucose or fat in the duodenum	Stimulates release of insulin from pancreas; inhibits gastric H^+ secretion and gastric motility.
Vasoactive intestinal polypeptide (VIP)	28	3100	Secretin	Mucosa of entire small intestine and colon	?	Inhibits gastric H^+ and pepsin secretion; stimulates pancreatic HCO_3^- secretion and secretion from intestinal mucosa; inhibits gastric and gallbladder motility.
Motilin	22	2700	?	Mucosa of duodenum and jejunum	Alkaline pH (8.2) in the duodenum	Stimulates gastric motility.
Enterogastrone	?	?	?	Mucosa of small intestine	Fat in the intestine	Inhibits gastric H^+ secretion.
Entero-oxyntin (mediator of the "intestinal phase" of H^+ secretion)	?	?	?	Mucosa of small intestine	Protein in the intestine	Stimulates gastric H^+ secretion.
Enteroglucagon	?	3500–7000	Glucagon	Mucosa of small intestine	Glucose or fat in the intestine	Glycogenolysis.
Chymodenin	43	4900	?	Mucosa of small intestine	Fat in the intestine	Specific stimulation of chymotrypsin secretion by the pancreas.
Bulbogastrone	?	?	?	Duodenal bulb	Acid in the duodenal bulb	Inhibits gastric H^+ secretion.

*Slightly modified from Dunphy JE, Way LW (editors): *Current Surgical Diagnosis & Treatment,* 3rd ed. Lange, 1977.
†The candidate hormones are either peptides extracted from the gut which have not yet been proved to have a physiologic role or physiologic actions postulated as being due to as yet unidentified hormones.

B. Secretin: Historically, secretin (Fig 29–45) was the first substance to be identified as a hormone. It is the most powerful stimulant of water and bicarbonate secretion by the pancreas. Secretin is found in the duodenal and jejunal mucosa. It consists of a peptide with 27 amino acids, 14 of which are identical to those found in glucagon; the molecule has no structural homology with gastrin or cholecystokinin-pancreozymin. Though secretin stimulates pepsin secretion in the stomach, it inhibits gastric acid secretion as well as intestinal motor activity. The hormone also shares some of the actions of glucagon, eg, increasing cardiac output and lipolysis. However, its tissue binding sites are not the same as those for glucagon.

Ingestion of food and the resulting increase in acid stimulate secretin release. Secretin administration has been used to assess pancreatic exocrine function, responses being low in subjects with carcinoma of the pancreas.

C. Cholecystokinin-pancreozymin (CCK-PZ): Cholecystokinin-pancreozymin is an important stimulating agent for pancreatic enzyme secretion and gallbladder contraction. It has been isolated from duodenal-jejunal mucosa. The hormone is a polypeptide containing 33 amino acids, though a possible prohormone of 6 additional amino acids also occurs.

As noted earlier, the C-terminal pentapeptide is identical to that of gastrin. Most of the cholecystokinin-pancreozymin activity resides in the C-terminal octapeptide. Besides its activity on pancreatic enzyme synthesis and release, it shares many of the actions of gastrin and secretin on water, bicarbonate, and acid changes (Table 29–4). It is particularly effective in stimulating both insulin and glucagon release from pancreatic islets, which may explain why an oral glucose load is more effective in stimulating insulin release than is a comparable elevation of blood sugar produced by intravenous injection. Possibly, cholecystokinin-pancreozymin may represent one of the "gut factors" potentiating insulin release during oral administration of insulin secretagogues.

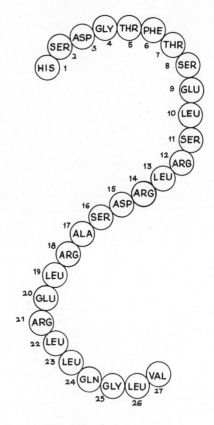

Figure 29–45. Porcine secretin.

Cholecystokinin-pancreozymin is secreted from the mucosa of the small intestine in response to acid, amino acids, fatty acids and a variety of cholinergic influences.

Table 29–5 contains summarizing information on the established gastrointestinal polypeptide hormones discussed above as well as a number of additional so-called "candidate" hormones.

•   •   •

References

Thyroid & Parathyroid

Field JB: Thyroid-stimulating hormone and cyclic adenosine 3'5'-monophosphate in the regulation of thyroid gland function. Metabolism 24:381, 1975.

Lissitzky S: Biosynthesis of thyroid hormones. Pharmacol Ther [B] 2:219, 1976.

Openheimer JH & others: Nuclear receptors and the initiation of thyroid hormone action. Recent Prog Horm Res 32:529, 1976.

Parfitt AM: The actions of parathyroid hormone on bone, etc. (3 parts.) Metabolism 25:809, 909, 1833, 1976.

Potts JT & others: The chemistry of parathyroid hormone and the calcitonins. Vitam Horm 29:41, 1971.

Rosenberg IN: Evaluation of thyroid function. N Engl J Med 286:924, 1972.

Pancreas (Insulin & Glucagon)

Chance RE, Ellis RM, Bromer WW: Porcine proinsulin: Characterization and amino acid sequence. Science 161:165, 1968.

Charles MA & others: Islet transplantation into rat liver: In vitro secretion of insulin from the isolated perfused liver and in vitro glucagon suppression. Endocrinology 98:738, 1976.

Cuatrecasas P, Hollenberg MD: Membrane receptors and hormone action. Adv Protein Chem 30:251, 1976.

Freychet P: Interactions of polypeptide hormones with cell membrane specific receptors: Studies with insulin and glucagon. Diabetologia 12:83, 1976.

Gerich JE & others: Normalization of fasting hyperglucagonemia and excessive responses to intravenous arginine in human diabetes mellitus by prolonged infusion of insulin. J Clin Endocrinol Metab 41:1178, 1975.

Gerich JE, Charles MA, Grodsky GM: Regulation of pancreatic insulin and glucagon secretion. Annu Rev Physiol 38:353, 1976.

Grodsky GM & others: Further studies on the dynamic aspects of insulin release in vitro with evidence for a 2-compartmental storage system. Acta Diabetol Lat 6 (Suppl 1):554, 1969.

Unger R: Diabetes and the alpha cell. Diabetes 25:136, 1975.

Yip CC, Hew C-L, Hsu H: Translation of messenger ribonucleic acid from isolated pancreatic islets and human insulinomas. Proc Natl Acad Sci USA 72:4777, 1975.

Adrenal Medulla

Axelrod J, Weinshilbaum R: Catecholamines. N Engl J Med 287:237, 1972.

Axelrod J: Relationship between catecholamines and other hormones. Recent Prog Horm Res 31:1, 1975.

Adrenal Cortex (Steroid Hormones)

Baxter JD, Forsham PH: Tissue effects of glucocorticoids. Am J Med 53:573, 1972.

Duax WL, Weeks CM, Rohrer DC: Crystal structure of steroids: Molecular conformation and biologic function. Recent Prog Horm Res 32:81, 1976.

Edelman IS: Mechanism of action of steroid hormones. J Steroid Biochem 6:147, 1975.

Means AR & others: Estrogen induction of ovalbumin in RNA: Evidence for transcription control. Mol Cell Biochem 7:33, 1975.

Minguell JJ, Sierralta WD: Molecular mechanism of action of the male sex hormones. J Endocrinol 65:287, 1976.

Anterior Pituitary (Hypothalamus)

Bewley TA, Li CH: The chemistry of human pituitary growth hormone. Adv Enzymol 42:73, 1975.

Catt KJ: Reproductive endocrinology. Lancet 1:1097, 1970.

Catt KJ & others: Basic concepts of the mechanism of action of peptide hormones. Biol Reprod 14:1, 1976.

Cowie AT, Forsyth IA: Biology of prolactin. Pharmacol Ther [B] 1:437, 1975.

Delofsen W: The chemistry of the adrenocorticotropins and of the melanotropins. Pharmacol Ther [B] 1:459, 1975.

Hall R, Gomez-Pan A: Hypothalamic regulatory hormones and their clinical applications. Adv Clin Chem 18:173, 1976.

Liu WK, Ward DN: Purification and chemistry of pituitary glycoprotein hormones. Adv Clin Chem 1:545, 1975.

Loh HH & others: β-Endorphin is a potent analgesic agent. Proc Natl Acad Sci USA 73:2895, 1976.

Posner BI: Polypeptide hormone receptors: Characteristics and applications. Can J Physiol Pharmacol 53:689, 1975.

Schally AV, Arimura A, Kastin AJ: Hypothalamic regulatory hormones. Science 179:341, 1973.

Vaitukayis JL & others: Gonadotropins and their subunits: Basic and clinical studies. Recent Prog Horm Res 32:289, 1976.

Vale W & others: Somatostatin. Recent Prog Horm Res 31:365, 1975.

Van Wyk JJ & others: Explorations of the insulin-like and growth-promoting properties of somatomedin by membrane receptor assays. Adv Metab Disord 8:127, 1975.

Middle and Posterior Pituitary

Chord IT: The posterior pituitary gland. Clin Endocrinol 4:89, 1975.

Kurtzman NA, Boonjarerns: Physiology of antidiuretic hormone and the interrelationship between the hormone and the kidney. Nephron 15:167, 1975.

Sawyer WH, Manning M: Synthetic analogs of oxytocin and the vasopressins. Annu Rev Pharmacol 13:1, 1973.

Gastrointestinal Hormones

Barrington EWJ, Dockray GT: Gastrointestinal hormones. J Endocrinol 69:299, 1976.

Williams RH (editor): *Textbook of Endocrinology,* 5th ed. Saunders, 1974.

30 . . .
Water & Mineral Metabolism

WATER METABOLISM

Properties of Water

Water is the most abundant compound in living cells, which usually contain 65–90% of water by weight. Because of the polarity and hydrogen-bonding properties of the molecule, water possesses several unique features which make it especially suited to perform its biologic functions. It is a powerful solvent for many ionic compounds and neutral molecules. Water or dilute salt solutions strongly influence the state of dissociation of the macromolecules of the cell (proteins and polynucleotides); thus, water not only serves as a dispersing medium but it also exerts a major influence on the structural and functional components of the cell. The high heat of vaporization of water is of vital importance in body cooling by evaporation of moisture in the lungs and from the skin.

Total Body Water

Total body water is distributed between 2 main compartments: intracellular and extracellular. The fluid within the body cells is designated the intracellular fluid. Since the fluid within each individual cell is fairly constant in composition, the concept of a single intracellular fluid compartment is a useful one, although it is in fact an aggregate of the fluid present in a huge number of minute separate compartments. All of the fluid outside the body cells is collectively termed the extracellular fluid. The extracellular fluid is heterogeneous. It can be subdivided into (1) plasma, (2) interstitial and lymph fluid, (3) dense connective tissue, cartilage, and bone, and (4) transcellular fluids.

The plasma is the extracellular fluid of the blood. The plasma and the cellular elements of the blood, principally red blood cells, fill the vascular system and together comprise the total blood volume. The interstitial fluid surrounds and bathes the cells of the tissues. The plasma and the interstitial fluid intermingle through pores in the blood capillaries, which allow water and most dissolved substances except protein to diffuse between the 2 fluids. This provides for continual mixing and exchange of nutrients and metabolic waste products. Interstitial and lymph fluid may be considered to represent an approximation of the actual fluid environment outside the cells. Dense connective tissue, cartilage, and bone, because of differences in structure and relative avascularity, do not exchange fluid or electrolyte readily with the remainder of the body water. For this reason, these tissues are classified as a distinct subdivision of the extracellular water. Finally, the extracellular water must include also a variety of extracellular fluid collections formed by the transport or secretory activity of the cells (transcellular fluids). Examples are the fluids found in the salivary glands, pancreas, liver and biliary tree, thyroid gland, gonads, skin, mucous membranes of the respiratory and gastrointestinal tracts, and the kidneys, as well as the fluids in spaces within the eye, the cerebrospinal fluid, and that within the lumen of the gastrointestinal tract.

Intake & Loss of Body Water

A. Water Intake: In the adult human, the normal intake of water, including that formed in the body, averages about 2500 ml/day. Most of this water enters orally, either as water or some other beverage (1200–1500 ml) and in foods (770–1000 ml). Water formed in the body ("metabolic water") is derived from the oxidation of foodstuffs. The quantity of metabolic water (200–300 ml/day) depends on the metabolic rate of the individual.

B. Water Losses: (See Table 30–1). Water is lost from the body by 4 routes: the skin, as sensible and insensible perspiration; the lungs, as water vapor in the expired air; the kidneys, as urine; and the intestines, in the feces. It is customary to refer to the sum of the dermal loss (exclusive of visible perspiration) and the pulmonary loss as the insensible losses. In very hot weather, or during periods of prolonged heavy exercise, water loss in sweat may increase to as much as 3000 ml/hour, which could obviously deplete the body fluids rapidly.

C. Additional Water Losses in Disease: In kidney disease in which concentrating ability is limited, renal water loss may be twice as high as that listed in Table 30–1. Insensible losses may rise much higher than normal as a consequence of operations, in fever, or in the physically debilitated. When subjected to high environmental temperatures, patients will also sustain extremely high extrarenal water losses, as much as 2000–5000 ml/day in some instances. Water losses from the intestine may be considerable, particularly in

Table 30—1. Daily water losses and water allowances for normal individuals who are not working or sweating.*

Size	Losses				Allowances	
	Urine (ml)	Stool (ml)	Insensible (ml)	Total (ml)	ml/person	ml/kg
Infant (2–10 kg)	200–500	25–40	75–300 (1.3 ml/kg/hr)	300–840	330–1000	165–100
Child (10–40 kg)	500–800	40–100	300–600	840–1500	1000–1800	100–45
Adolescent or adult (60 kg)	800–1000	100	600–1000 (0.5 ml/kg/hr)	1500–2100	1800–2500	45–30

*Butler & Talbot: New Engl J Med 231:585, 1944.

Table 30—2. Distribution of body water in "average" normal young adult male.*

Source	ml/kg of Body Weight	% of Total Body Water
Intracellular	330	55.0
Extracellular	270	45.0
Plasma	45	7.5
Interstitial-lymph	120	20.0
Dense connective tissue and cartilage	45	7.5
Inaccessible bone	45	7.5
Transcellular	15	2.5
Total body water	600	100.0

*Edelman & Leibman: Am J Med 27:256, 1959.

diarrhea and vomiting. These losses are debilitating and can be fatal, especially in infants.

Measurement of Distribution of Body Water
(Table 30–2.)

The volume of any body fluid compartment can be measured in principle by placing a substance in the compartment, allowing time for it to disperse evenly throughout the fluid, and then measuring the extent to which the substance has become diluted. The distribution of heavy water, deuterium oxide (D_2O), or tritium oxide has been used in the living animal and in human subjects as a method of measuring total body water. Antipyrine is also used. All of these substances diffuse almost uniformly in the cells of the body and can be measured by physical or chemical methods.

The value for body water given in Table 30–2 was obtained by measuring the volume of distribution of D_2O. However, in all studies of the proportion of the body which is water, considerable variation is to be expected when different subjects are compared even by the same analytic method. This is due mainly to variation in the amount of fat in the body. The higher the fat content of the subject, the smaller the percentage of water that subject will contain in his body. If a correction for the fat content of the subject is made, the total body water in various subjects is relatively constant (60–70% of body weight) when expressed as a percentage of the "lean body mass," ie, the sum of the fat-free tissue.

The composition of the adult human body has been determined by direct chemical analysis. The whole body contained 19.44% ether-extractable material (lipid), 55.13% moisture, 18.62% protein, and 5.43% ash, including 1.907% calcium and 0.925% phosphorus. When these data were recalculated on the fat-free basis, the moisture content was then 69.38%, which is in agreement with data obtained by indirect methods as described above.

Specific gravity of the body may also serve as a basis for calculations of total body water. The body is considered as a mixture of fat, which is of relatively low density, and fat-free tissue, which is of relatively high density. By measuring the specific gravity of the body (weighing the subject in air and under water), it is possible to calculate the proportion of the body which is fat tissue and that which is fat-free tissue. This technic has been used to arrive at an estimate of the lean body mass, described above.

Extracellular Fluid Volume

A. Total Volume: The volume of the extracellular fluid would be measured by the dilution of a substance which does not penetrate into the cells and which is distributed rapidly and evenly in all of the plasma as well as the remainder of the extracellular fluid. No such ideal substance has yet been found. However, the volume of distribution of certain saccharides such as mannitol or inulin has been found to give a reasonably accurate measurement of the **volume of the interstitial and lymph fluid.** It is believed that about 25% of the extracellular phase of dense connective tissue and cartilage also equilibrates rapidly with the saccharides, so that the measured volume must be corrected by this amount.

B. Plasma Volume: Plasma volume may be measured by the Evans blue dye (T-1824) technic. In this procedure, a carefully measured quantity of the dye is injected intravenously. After a lapse of time to allow for mixing, a blood sample is withdrawn and the concentration of the dye in the plasma is determined colorimetrically. The normal figures for plasma volume thus determined are 47–50 ml/kg body weight. Blood volume can be calculated from measurements of the plasma volume and the hematocrit (see Chapter 32). Other methods of plasma (or blood) volume measurement are based on the intravenous injection of radio-phosphorus-labeled red cells (^{32}P) or radioiodine-labeled human serum albumin (^{131}I). These substances distribute themselves in the blood stream and, after a mixing period of 10 or more minutes, their volume of distribution may be calculated from their concentration in an aliquot of blood or plasma.

C. Volume of Other Components: The volume of the remaining components of the extracellular fluid shown in Table 30–2 has been estimated by calculations from direct chemical analyses of representative samples of the individual tissues.

Intracellular Fluid Volume

This is calculated simply as the difference between the volume of total body water and that of the extracellular fluid.

Constituents of Extracellular and Intracellular Fluids

A. Measurements of Solutes: The solutes, the substances dissolved in the body water, are important not only in directing fluid distribution but also in maintaining acid-base balance (see Chapter 33). In describing chemical reactivity, particularly acid-base balance, all solutes must be expressed in identical units of concentration. Since one chemical equivalent of any substance is exactly equal in chemical reactivity to one equivalent of any other, this can be accomplished by converting the concentrations of each into equivalents/liter. Because of the small quantities involved in body fluids, the milliequivalent (mEq, 0.001 Eq) is preferred. Furthermore, when changes occur in the chemistry of the body fluid, there are usually compensatory shifts of one ion to make up for losses of another. For example, excessive losses of chloride over sodium in vomiting from the stomach result in a chloride deficit in the extracellular fluid. This is promptly compensated by an increase in bicarbonate to accompany the sodium left uncovered by the chloride loss. These changes can be readily understood and calculated when all reactants are expressed in the same units.

1. Conversion of electrolyte concentrations to mEq—For conversion of mg/dl to mEq/liter, (1) express the concentration on a per liter basis, ie, multiply the number of mg (per deciliter) by 10 to determine the number of mg/liter, and (2) divide the mg/liter by the appropriate mEq weight given in Table 30–3. The mEq weight of an element is the millimolecular weight divided by the valence.

Examples: Plasma sodium: 322 mg/dl. Multiply the mg by 10 (to express on a per liter basis). Then divide by mEq weight of sodium, 23.

$$322 \times 10 = 3220 \text{ mg/liter;}$$

$$\text{divided by } 23 = 140 \text{ mEq/liter}$$

Chloride (reported as NaCl): 603 mg/dl.

$$603 \times 10 = 6030 \text{ mg/liter;}$$

$$\text{divided by } 58.5 = 103 \text{ mEq/liter}$$

Table 30–3. Milliequivalent weights.

Na^+	23	Cl^-	35.5
K^+	39	Cl^- (as NcCl)	58.5
Ca^{2+}	20	$HPO_4{}^{2-}$ (as P)	17.2*
Mg^{2+}	12	$SO_4{}^{2-}$ (as S)	16

*The inorganic phosphorus in the serum exists as a buffer mixture in which approximately 80% is in the form of $HPO_4{}^{2-}$ and 20% as $H_2PO_4{}^-$. For this reason, the mEq weight is usually calculated by dividing the atomic weight of phosphorus by 1.8. Thus, the mEq weight for phosphorus in the serum is taken as 31/1.8, or 17.2. To avoid the problem presented by the 2 valences of the serum phosphorus, some laboratories prefer to express the phosphorus as millimols (mmol) rather than mEq. One mmol of phosphorus is 31 mg. To convert mg of phosphorus to mmol, divide mg/liter by 31, eg, serum phosphorus = 3.1 mg/100 ml = 31/31 = 1 mmol/liter.

Calcium: 10 mg/dl.

$$10 \times 10 = 100 \text{ mg/liter;}$$

$$\text{divided by } 20 = 5 \text{ mEq/liter.}$$

2. Conversion of bicarbonate to milliequivalents— The bicarbonate of the plasma is measured by conversion to CO_2 and reported in volumes percent (vol%); to convert to mEq of bicarbonate per liter, divide CO_2 combining power, expressed as vol%, by 2.3.*

3. Conversion of organic acids and proteins to mEq—The organic acids and the proteins in the anion column of plasma are calculated from their combining power with base. The base equivalence of protein, in mEq/liter, is obtained by multiplying the number of grams of total protein per deciliter by 2.43.

B. Electrolyte Composition of Body Fluids (Fig 30–1 and Table 30–4.)

1. Composition of interstitial fluid—The electrolyte composition of interstitial fluid is similar to that of plasma except that the plasma proteins do not pass to any significant extent into the interstitial fluid, and chloride largely replaces protein among the anions.

2. Composition of plasma and intracellular fluid— The electrolyte composition of intracellular fluid differs from that of plasma in that potassium rather than sodium is the principal cation and, largely as a result of the presence of phosphorylated organic compounds, phosphate rather than chloride is the principal anion. The intracellular chloride content is variable in accor-

*The conversion of the CO_2 combining power to mEq of bicarbonate is based on the following facts. One mol of a gas occupies 22.4 liters (at 0° C and 760 mm Hg), and therefore 1 mmol occupies 22.4 ml or, what is the same thing, each 22.4 ml of gas is equivalent to 1 mmol; 600 ml of CO_2/liter (a normal total blood CO_2) thus equals 600/22.4 = 26.8 mmol total CO_2/liter (1 mmol of CO_2 is the same as 1 mEq of CO_2).

The total CO_2 as determined in the blood includes carbonic acid, free CO_2, and bicarbonate. The bicarbonate fraction alone can be calculated by assuming that a 1:20 ratio exists between carbonic acid and bicarbonate. Under these conditions, the plasma bicarbonate fraction is derived by dividing the total CO_2 (as CO_2 combining power in vol%) by 2.3.

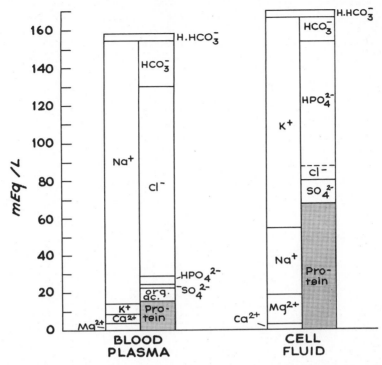

Figure 30—1. Electrolyte composition of blood plasma and intracellular fluid. (Modified from Gamble.)

Table 30—4. Plasma electrolyte concentrations (from Gamble).

Cations (+)	mEq/liter	Anions (−)	mEq/liter
Na^+	142	HCO_3^-	27
K^+	5	Cl^-	103
Ca^{2+}	5	HPO_4^{2-}	2
Mg^{2+}	3	SO_4^{2-}	1
		Organic acids	6
		Protein	16
Totals	155		155

dance with the metabolic circumstances. The amount of protein within the cell is also considerably larger than that in the extracellular environment.

The intracellular concentration of sodium is higher than had previously been assumed. Deane & Smith (1952) reported that the normal average intracellular sodium is 37 mEq/liter of intracellular water. Furthermore, it is now clear that sodium may replace potassium within the cell when sodium salts are administered to potassium-deficient subjects. The adrenocorticosteroids and ACTH also influence the concentration of sodium and potassium within the cell. Under the influence of these hormones, intracellular sodium may be increased.

Factors Which Influence the Distribution of Body Water

Water is retained in the body in a rather constant amount, but its distribution is continuously subject to change. Osmotic forces, directing the movement of water from one compartment to another in the body, are the principal factors which control the location and the amount of fluid in the various compartments. In a consideration of the various substances in solution in the fluids of the body and their effect on water retention and distribution, it is convenient to divide them into 3 categories, given below.

A. Electrolytes, Especially Sodium and Potassium: Because of the relatively large quantities of inorganic electrolytes in the body, especially sodium and potassium, these electrolytes are by far the most important substances influencing both the distribution and the retention of body water. As has been pointed out, in the normal individual sodium is largely confined to the extracellular space and potassium to the intracellular space. Since water is freely diffusible across the cell barrier, its movement is determined by changes in concentration of the osmotically effective electrolytes (principally sodium and potassium) on either side. Changes in extracellular electrolyte concentration are most commonly the basis for these shifts of water. As Gamble has so well expressed it, sodium is the "backbone" of the extracellular fluid in that it, more than any other element, determines the quantity of extracellular fluid to be retained. This is the reason that sodium intake is restricted in order to control overhydration in various pathologic states.

Under certain conditions, potassium leaves the cells. Important examples are found in prolonged gastrointestinal losses due to vomiting, diarrhea, or prolonged gastric suction. Replacement of the lost electrolytes with only sodium salts leads to migration of sodium into cells to replace the potassium deficit. This produces profound alterations in cellular metabolism such as persistent alkalosis even after apparently adequate salt and water therapy. It can be prevented by prompt and concomitant replacement of potassium deficits as well as sodium deficits.

B. Organic Substances of Large Molecular Size (Mainly the Proteins): The importance of the plasma proteins in the exchange of fluid between the circulating blood and the interstitial fluid is discussed in Chapter 32. The effect of the protein fraction of the plasma and tissues is mainly on the transfer of fluid from one compartment to another, not on the total body water.

C. Organic Compounds of Small Molecular Size (Glucose, Urea, Amino Acids, Etc): Since these substances diffuse relatively freely across cell membranes, they are not important in the distribution of water; if they are present in large quantities, however, they aid in retaining water, and thus they do influence total body water.

Dehydration

This term should not imply only changes in water balance. Almost always there must also be accompanying changes in electrolytes.

A. Water Loss or Restriction Causing Dehydration: When the supply of water is restricted for any reason, or when the losses are excessive, the rate of water loss exceeds the rate of electrolyte loss. The extracellular fluid becomes concentrated and hypertonic to the cells. Water then shifts from the cells to the extracellular space to compensate.

The symptoms of this intracellular dehydration are severe thirst, nausea and vomiting, a hot and dry body, a dry tongue, loss of coordination, and a concentrated urine of small volume. Intracellular dehydration is corrected by giving water by mouth, or dextrose and water parenterally, until symptoms are alleviated and the urine volume is restored.

B. Electrolyte Deficit: A relative deficit of electrolytes may occur when an excess of water is ingested. This condition of overhydration is commonly observed when large amounts of electrolyte-free solutions are administered to patients. More frequently, however, water and electrolytes are both lost, and replacement with only water leads to a deficiency of electrolytes in the presence of normal or excess total body water. The deficiency of sodium in the extracellular fluid is mainly responsible for the resulting hypotonicity of this fluid compartment. Some water passes into the cells, which are hypertonic to the extracellular fluid, causing the so-called intracellular edema. There follows a diminution in extracellular fluid volume which is very damaging. The resulting decrease in blood volume is conducive to a fall in blood pressure, slowing of circulation, and consequent impairment in renal function. Since the kidney is an essential aid in restoring the normal equilibrium, this latter complication is a serious one.

The patient becomes progressively weaker, but he does not complain of thirst and his urine volume is not notably changed. There is, however, reliable evidence of this type of dehydration in the elevated hematocrit or plasma total protein and the lowered sodium and chloride concentration in the plasma.

C. Correction of Dehydration: Because of the high content of electrolytes in the gastrointestinal secretions, loss of fluid from the gastrointestinal tract will readily produce serious fluid and electrolyte deficits if prompt and accurate replacement of the losses does not take place. In Table 30–5 the volume and composition of gastrointestinal fluids and of sweat are shown. Loss of chloride in excess of sodium will be expected when fluid is withdrawn from the upper gastrointestinal tract, as may occur in high intestinal obstruction, pyloric stenosis, gastric vomiting, or in continuous gastric suction. Ordinarily, sodium chloride solutions may be given parenterally to repair the losses since, in the presence of adequate kidney function, a proper adjustment of the electrolyte imbalance will occur. The importance of simultaneous replacement of potassium must also be kept in mind.

Fluid and electrolyte losses originating from the intestinal tract (as in prolonged diarrhea, pancreatic or biliary fistulas, etc) are characterized by the removal of

Table 30–5. Volume and composition of blood plasma, gastrointestinal secretions, and sweat.[*]

Fluid	Average Volume (ml/24 hours)	Electrolyte Concentrations (mEq/liter)			
		Na$^+$	K$^+$	Cl$^-$	HCO$_3^-$
Blood plasma		135–150	3.6–5.5	100–105	24.6–28.8
Gastric juice	2500	31–90	4.3–12	52–124	0
Bile	700–1000	134–156	3.9–6.3	83–110	38
Pancreatic juice	> 1000	113–153	2.6–7.4	54–95	110
Small bowel (Miller-Abbott suction)	3000	72–120	3.5–6.8	69–127	30
Ileostomy					
Recent	100–4000	112–142	4.5–14	93–122	30
Adapted	100–500	50	3	20	15–30
Cecostomy	100–3000	48–116	11.1–28.3	35–70	15
Feces	100	< 10	< 10	< 15	< 15
Sweat	500–4000	30–70	0–5	30–70	0

[*]Lockwood & Randall: Bull NY Acad Med 25:228, 1949; and Randall: Surg Clin North Am 32:3, 1952.

a fluid high in sodium and bicarbonate. This leads to a relative chloride excess and a bicarbonate deficit. This condition might best be repaired initially by the intravenous administration of a mixture of two-thirds isotonic saline solution and one-third sodium lactate solution (M/6).

Dehydration is frequently a complication of gastrointestinal tract disturbances, but it is not confined to these conditions. Other disorders in which dehydration is a problem include diabetes mellitus, Addison's disease, uremia, extensive burns, and shock.

Clinically, change in body weight during short periods is a reliable criterion of changes in hydration. When a patient is properly nourished and hydrated, his body weight remains relatively constant, with only a slight variation. Rapid daily gain in weight indicates overhydration. Loss of 8–12% in body weight represents a significant degree of dehydration if it is due to loss of fluids.

MINERAL METABOLISM

The mineral elements present in the animal body may be classified as **principal elements (macronutrients)** and **trace elements**.

Principal Mineral Elements (Macronutrients)

There are 7 essential elements: calcium, magnesium, sodium, potassium, phosphorus, sulfur, and chlorine. They constitute 60–80% of all the inorganic material in the body.

Trace Elements

These elements occur in living tissues in small amounts. They may be subdivided into 3 groups—essential, possibly essential, and nonessential—according to their dietary requirements in higher animals. The assignment of any particular element to a group depends on several factors, including the precise meaning attached to the word essential (Underwood, 1971).

The trace elements to be discussed are classified (roughly in order of importance) as follows: (1) Essential trace elements (micronutrients): iron, iodine, copper, zinc, manganese, cobalt, molybdenum, selenium, chromium, and fluorine. (2) Possibly essential trace elements: nickel, tin, vanadium, and silicon. (3) Nonessential trace elements: aluminum, boron, germanium, cadmium, arsenic, lead, and mercury.

Although in respect to their amounts the mineral elements are relatively minor components of the tissues, they are essential to many vital processes. The function of individual minerals is mentioned at various points in this book. A clear example is blood calcium and its role in neuromuscular irritability and in the clotting of blood. The metal requirements of a large number of enzymes (about one-third of the known enzymes), either as an integral part of the enzyme molecule or as enzyme "activators," are discussed in Chapter 6.

Certain mineral elements, principally sodium, potassium, and chlorine, are major factors in the maintenance of acid-base balance and the osmotic control of water metabolism. Other minerals are present in important physiologic compounds such as iodine in thyroxine, iron in hemoglobin, cobalt in vitamin B_{12}, and sulfur in the amino acids cysteine and methionine and in the enzyme cofactors thiamin, biotin, coenzyme A, and lipoic acid.

The balance (ie, ratio of one to another) of the ions in the tissues is often of physiologic importance. For example, normal ossification demands a proper ratio of calcium to phosphorus; the normal ratio between potassium and calcium in the extracellular fluid must be maintained to ensure the normal activity of muscle; and an excess of molybdenum in the diet can result in a deficiency of copper. Thus, both the principal mineral elements and the essential trace elements appear to operate in a delicate balance among themselves. All the essential trace elements are toxic when their intake is sufficiently in excess of dietary requirements.

CALCIUM

Functions

Calcium is present in the body in larger amounts than any other mineral element. The body of an adult male weighing 70 kg contains approximately 1200 g of calcium. About 99% of the body calcium is in the skeleton, where it is maintained as deposits of calcium phosphates in a soft, fibrous matrix. The very small quantity of calcium not present in skeletal structures is in the body fluids, where it is in part ionized. Indeed, this small amount of ionized calcium in the body fluids is of great importance in blood coagulation, in maintaining the normal excitability of the heart, muscles, and nerves, and in the differential aspects of membrane permeability.

The matrix of bone in which calcium is deposited has a unique structure essential to normal calcification. The major inorganic constituent of bone is comprised of a crystalline form of calcium phosphate closely resembling the mineral hydroxyapatite; in addition, however, the bone contains a substantial amount of noncrystalline, amorphous calcium phosphate. It appears that this amorphous material is predominant in early life but is superseded in later life by the crystalline apatite. Although it may appear that the mineral deposits in bone are more or less permanent, this material, like almost every other constituent of the tissues, is, in actual fact, in a dynamic state, constantly being formed and resorbed—more rapidly during early development and at a slower, declining rate during adult life. It is estimated that in adult males about 700 mg of calcium enter and leave the bones each day.

Sources

Of the common foods, milk and cheese are unquestionably the richest sources of calcium. Most other foods contribute smaller amounts: Examples are egg yolk, beans, lentils, nuts, figs, cabbage, turnip greens, cauliflower, and asparagus. In the USA, about 85% of the dietary intake of calcium is derived from milk and other dairy products.

Requirements (See also Table 31–6.)

Men and women after 18 years of age: 800 mg daily.

During second and third trimesters of pregnancy and during lactation: 1.2 g daily.

Infants under 1 year: 360–540 mg daily.

Children 1–18 years: 0.8–1.2 g daily.

To supply additional calcium, the carbonate, lactate, or gluconate salts as well as dicalcium phosphate may be administered.

The requirements for calcium listed above are thought to be excessive by some nutritional authorities. Excessively high levels of calcium in the serum and urine—or calcifications of soft tissues—are found in such conditions as idiopathic hypercalcemia of infancy, hypercalciuria, hyperparathyroidism, and in certain instances of renal stones. There are also reports of metastatic calcification associated with high intakes of calcium and of alkali in connection with dietary supplements prescribed for patients with peptic ulcer (so-called milk-alkali syndrome). Even though the high intakes of calcium may not be the primary cause of these complications, a substantial reduction in calcium intake is an important aspect of therapy.

Although it is still recommended that 800 mg of calcium should be consumed daily by adults, it is now evident that children develop healthy bones and adults remain in calcium balance despite lower intakes of calcium. Furthermore, in countries where the daily intake of calcium is 400–500 mg/day, there appears to be no evidence of calcium deficiency. It has been shown also that men may in time adapt to lower calcium intakes and become able to maintain calcium balance on intakes as low as 200–400 mg daily; what is more, a higher proportion of the ingested calcium is utilized when the intake is low than when it is more liberal. For the present, however, it is believed that the recommended intakes now suggested should be maintained to provide a suitable margin of safety as well as to take into account many variables among the populations of the world (such as climate and diet) that affect calcium needs.

Absorption

Ca^{2+} is absorbed by an active transport process occurring mainly in the upper small intestine. The process is regulated by 1,25-dihydroxycholecalciferol, a metabolite of vitamin D that is produced in the kidney in response to low plasma Ca^{2+} concentrations. Thus, Ca^{2+} absorption is adjusted to body needs. Absorption is facilitated by vitamin D, lactose, and pro-

Table 30—6. Distribution of calcium in body fluids or tissues.

Fluid or Tissue	mg/dl or dg	mEq/liter
Serum	9.0–11	5
CSF	4.5–5	2
Muscle	70	
Nerve	15	

tein. On a high-protein diet, about 15% of the dietary Ca^{2+} is absorbed, compared with 5% absorption on a low-protein diet. The more alkaline the intestinal contents, the less soluble the calcium salts. An increase in acidophilic flora (eg, the lactobacilli) is recommended to lower the pH, which favors calcium absorption.

Absorption of calcium is inhibited by a number of dietary factors which cause formation of insoluble calcium salts in the intestine, including phytate (eg, cereal grain), oxalates (eg, spinach), and phosphates. When fat absorption is impaired, much free fatty acid is present which reacts with Ca^{2+} to form insoluble calcium soaps.

Distribution

The calcium other than that in the bones and teeth is distributed as shown in Table 30–6.

Metabolism

The regulation of calcium metabolism by parathyroid hormone and calcitonin is discussed in Chapter 29.

The blood cells contain very little calcium. Most of the blood calcium is therefore in the plasma, where it exists in 3 fractions: ionized (so-called diffusible calcium), protein-bound (nondiffusible), and a small amount complexed probably as the citrate. All of these forms of calcium in the serum are in equilibrium with one another. In the usual determination of calcium, all 3 fractions are measured together.

An ultracentrifugal method for separation of protein-bound and free (ionized) calcium which requires only 5 ml of serum for a determination in duplicate has been devised. At a pH of 7.35 and a temperature of 37° C, the normal range of free calcium in the serum is 49.7–57.8% of the total calcium (mean, 53.1 ± 2.6%).

A decrease in the ionized fraction of serum calcium causes tetany. This may be due to an increase in the pH of the blood (alkalotic tetany; gastric tetany) or to lack of calcium because of poor absorption from the intestine, decreased dietary intake, increased renal excretion as in nephritis, or parathyroid deficiency. Increased retention of phosphorus, as in renal tubular disease, also predisposes to low serum calcium levels.

The Ca:P ratio is important in ossification. In the serum, the product of Ca X P (in mg/dl) is normally in children about 50. In rickets, this product may be below 30.

A relatively small quantity of the calcium lost from the body is excreted in the urine. In man, approximately 10 g of calcium are filtered in a 24-hour period by the renal glomeruli, but only about 200 mg appear in the urine. The maximal renal tubular re-absorptive capacity for calcium (Tm_{Ca}) is about 4.99 ± 0.21 mg/minute.

Most (70–90%) of the calcium eliminated from the body is excreted in the feces. The fecal calcium concentration is positively correlated with calcium intake. It is believed that most of the calcium in the feces is unabsorbed calcium and that only a very small amount is excreted into the intestine after absorption. The average daily loss of calcium in sweat is about 15 mg. Strenuous physical exercise increases the loss by way of the sweat even during periods of low intake of calcium.

Reference was made above to the influence of protein intake on calcium absorption. There is also a relationship between protein intake and urinary excretion of calcium. As an example, the amount of calcium in the urine of subjects taking a diet containing 600 g of protein was 8 times greater than it was when they consumed a protein-free diet.

Disease States

A. Relationship of Parathyroids: Calcium metabolism is profoundly influenced by the parathyroids.

1. In hyperparathyroidism caused by hyperactive, hyperplastic, or adenomatous parathyroid glands, the following signs are noted: hypercalcemia (serum calcium 12–22 mg/dl), decrease in serum phosphate, decreased renal tubular reabsorption of phosphate, increased phosphatase activity, rise in urinary calcium and phosphorus from bone decalcification, and dehydration and hemoconcentration. These signs are due to increased renal losses of phosphorus, causing a decrease in serum phosphate which elicits an increase in calcium to maintain the Ca:P ratio. The extra calcium and phosphorus is lost from soft tissues and from bone by increased osteoclastic (bone-destroying) activity.

In many cases of hyperparathyroidism, the total serum calcium may not be elevated sufficiently to permit diagnosis of this disease with certainty. In a group of patients with hyperparathyroidism due to parathyroid adenoma, ionized calcium ranged from 6.1–9.5 mg/dl (normal, 5.9–6.5 mg/dl), whereas the majority had levels of protein-bound calcium within normal limits or only slightly above normal. After surgical removal of the diseased parathyroid glands, there was a drop in total plasma calcium, again most marked in the ionized fraction. It has therefore been suggested that determination of the ionized fraction of the serum calcium may enhance the utility of the serum calcium for the diagnosis of hyperparathyroidism, particularly in patients who have normal total calcium levels.

2. In hypoparathyroidism, such as occurs after operative removal of the parathyroid glands, the concentration of the serum calcium may drop below 7 mg/dl. There is a concomitant increase in serum phosphate and a decrease in urinary phosphates. The urinary calcium is extremely low as well.

B. Osteoporosis: Osteoporosis is a disease of bone that has often been regarded as possibly related to inadequate intake of calcium. It has become increasingly evident, however, that such a simple etiologic relationship is not tenable. No relationship has been established between bone loss and intake of calcium; furthermore, intakes of calcium above 1500 mg/day do not seem to be "protective," nor are intakes below 300 mg/day unequivocally associated with bone tissue loss. There remains a possibility, however, that high protein intake associated with low calcium intake may play a role in the pathogenesis of osteoporosis since calcium losses can be significant when protein intake is high. Were this dietary situation to continue for prolonged periods, there would result a considerable loss in total body calcium.

C. Rickets: This disease is characterized by faulty calcification of bones due to a low vitamin D content of the body, a deficiency of calcium and phosphorus in the diet, or a combination of both. Usually the serum phosphate concentration is low or normal, except in renal disease (in which it may be elevated), and the serum calcium remains normal or may be lowered. There is an increase in fecal phosphate and calcium because of poor absorption of these elements, accompanied by a decrease in urine phosphate and calcium. An increase in alkaline phosphatase activity is also characteristic of rickets.

D. Renal Rickets: This condition should be distinguished from the common type of rickets mentioned above, which is a bone disease attributable to inadequate intestinal absorption of calcium, as well as faulty deposition of calcium in bones, as a result of a lack of vitamin D (see Chapter 12).

Renal rickets, now more accurately designated **familial hypophosphatemic rickets**, is inherited as an X-linked dominant trait. Affected males exhibit hypophosphatemia and severe rickets; heterozygous females—as compared to the males—tend to have higher serum phosphorus concentrations and less severe bone disease. Hypophosphatemic rickets is characterized biochemically not only by lowered serum phosphorus but also by hyperphosphaturia (increased loss of phosphorus in the urine) and a reduced intestinal absorption of calcium and phosphorus. The disease is thought to be caused by defective transport of phosphate by the intestine and by the renal tubules. Vitamin D in ordinary dosages does not relieve the symptoms in familial hypophosphatemic rickets; thus, it has sometimes been referred to as **vitamin D-resistant rickets**. It should be apparent that familial hypophosphatemic rickets is another example of a disease caused by a defective "end organ" response; in this instance, the renal tubule and the intestinal mucosa, the end organs, do not respond normally to the stimulus of regulators affecting phosphate transport.

E. Decrease of Serum Calcium: In severe renal disease, the serum calcium may decrease—in part because of increased losses into the urine. However, except for circumstances contributing to malabsorption of calcium from the intestine (as described previously), there is no clinical syndrome attributable exclusively to inadequate dietary intake of calcium. Certainly, inadequate dietary intake of calcium is not reflected by changes in serum calcium levels.

PHOSPHORUS

Functions

Phosphorus is found in every cell of the body, but most of it (about 80% of the total) is combined with calcium in the bones and teeth. About 10% is in combination with proteins, lipids, and carbohydrates, and in other compounds in blood and muscle. The remaining 10% is widely distributed in various chemical compounds. The great importance of the phosphate ester in energy transfer is discussed in Chapter 16.

Requirements & Sources (See also Table 31–6.)

Phosphorus is present in nearly all foods; consequently, a dietary deficiency is not known to occur in man. Since the distribution of calcium and of phosphorus in foods is very similar, an adequate intake of calcium generally ensures an adequate intake also of phosphorus. The average daily intake of phosphorus in adults in the USA is about 1.5 g.

The recommended allowance for phosphorus (except for the young infant) is the same as that for calcium. A rather wide variation in the calcium:phosphorus ratio can be tolerated if the amounts of vitamin D are adequate. With respect to young infants, it should be noted that the Ca:P ratio in cow's milk is about 1.2:1, whereas in human milk it is 2:1. Because an intake of phosphorus such as is provided in cow's milk may contribute to the occurrence of hypocalcemic tetany during the first week of life, it is now recommended that in early infancy the Ca:P ratio of the diet should be 1.5:1.

Distribution

The distribution of phosphorus in the body is shown in Table 30–7.

Metabolism

The metabolism of phosphorus is in large part related to that of calcium, as described heretofore. The Ca:P ratio in the diet affects the absorption and excre-

tion of these elements. If either element is given in excess, excretion of the other is increased. The optimal ratio is 1:1 when the intake of vitamin D is adequate.

An increase in carbohydrate metabolism, such as during absorption of carbohydrate, is accompanied by a temporary decrease in serum phosphate. A similar decrease may occur during absorption of some fats. In diabetes mellitus, there is a lower concentration of organic phosphorus but a higher concentration of inorganic phosphorus in the serum.

In rickets of the common low-phosphate variety, serum phosphate values may go as low as 1–2 mg/dl (0.64–1.3 mEq/liter).

Phosphate retention is a prominent cause of the acidosis in severe renal disease, and the resultant elevated serum phosphorus also contributes to the lowered serum calcium. Blood phosphorus levels are also high in hypoparathyroidism. A relationship of phosphorus metabolism to growth hormone is possibly indicated by the fact that growing children usually have high blood phosphorus levels and that in acromegaly an elevation of the blood phosphorus also occurs.

Blood phosphorus levels are low in hyperparathyroidism and in sprue and celiac disease. A low blood phosphorus together with an elevated alkaline phosphatase is also a characteristic finding in patients with an inherited or acquired renal tubular defect in the reabsorption of phosphate. Such cases include familial hypophosphatemic rickets (so-called renal rickets or vitamin D-resistant rickets), De Toni-Fanconi syndrome, and an inherited form of osteomalacia in adults called Milkman's syndrome. The greatly increased excretion of phosphate in the urine of these patients distinguishes them from those in whom a deficiency of vitamin D is the cause of the low serum phosphorus and the accompanying defects in the calcification of bone.

MAGNESIUM

Functions & Distribution

The body contains about 21 g of magnesium. Seventy percent is combined with calcium and phosphorus in the complex salts of bone; the remainder is in the soft tissues and body fluids. Magnesium is one of the principal cations of soft tissue. Whole blood contains 2–4 mg/dl (1.7–3.4 mEq/liter). The serum contains less than half that in the blood cells (1.94 mEq/liter). This is in contrast to calcium, almost all of which is in the serum. Cerebrospinal fluid is reported to contain about 3 mg/dl (2.40 mEq/liter). The magnesium content of muscle is about 21 mg/dg. In muscle and other tissues, intracellular magnesium ions probably function as activators for many of the phosphate group transfer enzymes.

A comprehensive listing of the magnesium content of foods is found in the reports of McCance &

Table 30–7. Distribution of phosphorus in body fluids or tissues.

Fluid or Tissue	mg/dl or dg	mEq/liter
Blood	40	
Serum (inorganic)		
Children	4–7	1.3–2.3
Adults	3–4.5	0.9–1.5
Muscle	170–250	
Nerve	360	
Bones and teeth	22,000	

Widdowson (1960). Derivatives of cocoa, various nuts, soybeans, and some seafoods are relatively rich in magnesium (100 to as high as 400 mg/dg). Whole grains and raw dried beans and peas may contain 100–200 mg magnesium per dg. Human milk contains approximately 4 mg magnesium per dl; cow's milk contains about 12 mg/dl.

Requirements (See also Table 31–6).

The current recommendation for magnesium in the diet is 350 mg/day for adult men and 300 mg/day for adult women.

In the diet of Oriental peoples there is a preponderance of foods high in magnesium, so that their intake of this mineral may approximate 6–10 mg/kg/day. The diet of Western peoples, however, provides less than 5 mg/kg/day for most adults (an average of 250–300 mg/day). It is claimed that several dietary constituents may interfere with retention or increase the requirement of magnesium. Examples are calcium, protein, and vitamin D. Alcohol is said to increase magnesium loss from the body. Since the Western diet may be high in calcium, protein, and vitamin D and because alcohol is also more commonly ingested by Western peoples, some authorities have suggested that the optimal daily intake of magnesium under these circumstances may be as high as 7–10 mg/kg/day.

Magnesium deficiency in man induces neuromuscular dysfunction as manifested by hyperexcitability with tremor and convulsions, and it is sometimes accompanied by behavioral disturbances. The wide occurrence of magnesium in foods makes a dietary deficiency under most circumstances extremely unlikely.

Estimates of the magnesium requirements for adult males range from 200 mg/day up to as high as 700 mg/day. Human milk contains approximately 4 mg magnesium per dl; cow's milk, about 12 mg/dl. The recommended allowances for infants have been estimated from this information; the allowances for children and adolescents given in Table 31–6 are only estimates but are intended to allow for increased needs during periods of rapid growth of bone.

Metabolism

The metabolism of magnesium is similar to that of calcium and phosphorus. Absorption and excretion of magnesium from the intestine has been measured in human subjects with the aid of isotopic ^{28}Mg. On an average diet (20 mEq Mg/day), 44.3% of the ingested radioisotope was absorbed. On a low Mg diet (1.9 mEq/day), 75.8% was absorbed; whereas on a high Mg intake (47 mEq/day), only 23.7% was absorbed. The rate and duration of absorption of the ingested magnesium indicated that most was absorbed from the small intestine and little or none from the colon. Absorption of magnesium from the intestine did not appear to be related to the status of magnesium stores in the body. In the first 48 hours after administration of radioactive magnesium, about 10% of the amount absorbed was excreted in the urine. Thus renal conservation of body magnesium appears to be excellent; in fact, the average urinary magnesium content is only about 6–20 mEq/liter. Aldosterone increases the renal clearance of magnesium as it does also the excretion of potassium.

An antagonism between magnesium and calcium has been noted in certain experiments. The intravenous injection of magnesium in a quantity sufficient to raise the magnesium ion concentration in the serum to about 20 mg/dl (normal, 2.4 mg/dl) results in immediate and profound anesthesia together with paralysis of voluntary muscles. The intravenous injection of a corresponding amount of calcium results in an instantaneous reversal of this effect. It is suggested that these 2 cations are exerting differing effects on cell permeability. In the case of magnesium, there is about 10 times as much of this element in the cells as in the extracellular fluid. For example, in plasma there is an average of 2.4 mg/dl; in muscle cells, 23 mg/dg. This differential distribution between plasma and muscle cells is not observed with calcium, but it is particularly prominent in the case of sodium and potassium as well as magnesium. Apparently magnesium and potassium are normally concentrated within the cell and sodium without. An alteration in this relationship is followed by profound physiologic changes. In this connection it is of interest, as already noted, that both magnesium and potassium excretion by the kidney are increased to the same extent by aldosterone.

In rats on a very low magnesium diet (0.18 mg/dg of food), vasodilation and hyperemia, hyperirritability, cardiac arrhythmia, and convulsions developed which were subsequently fatal. The tetany which developed when the diet was low in magnesium was probably due to the low magnesium content of the serum since the calcium levels remained normal.

It is difficult to produce a serious depletion of magnesium experimentally in man. A clinical syndrome characterized by muscle tremor, twitching, and more bizarre movements (occasionally with convulsions and often with delirium), was attributed to magnesium deficiency. The patients studied included a large group with chronic alcoholism and tremulousness and a few postoperative patients as well as those with pyloric obstruction and hypochloremic alkalosis. In all of these patients, however, the levels of magnesium in the serum were only moderately reduced. A decrease in the concentration of serum magnesium has also been noted in clinical hyperparathyroidism. It is possible that prolonged hyperparathyroidism could deplete the body stores of magnesium. After surgical correction of hyperparathyroidism, the development of tetany which is refractory to the administration of large amounts of calcium may indicate the need for magnesium.

As indicated above, serum magnesium levels may not correlate well with the intracellular concentration of this ion. Therefore, in an effort to assess the intracellular magnesium concentration, the content of this ion in the red blood cells has been measured. In healthy adults, the mean erythrocyte Mg was found to be 5.29 ∓ 0.34 mEq/liter when the mean plasma level was 1.80 ± 0.13 mEq/liter. In 12 patients with delirium tremens who were disoriented and confused, many with a pronounced tremor, some with hallucinations, the mean erythrocyte magnesium concentration was 3.9 ± 0.75 mEq/liter and the plasma concentration 1.5 ± 0.28 mEq/liter. After treatment with magnesium sulfate given intramuscularly, erythrocyte and plasma magnesium levels rose to normal.

In renal failure, magnesium tends to rise in the serum. Indeed, this might contribute to the somnolence and weakness characteristic of the uremic state. Thus it is of interest that 14 patients with uremia and associated depression of the central nervous system had mean erythrocyte magnesium levels of 8.84 ± 1.71 mEq/liter (upper limit of normal, 6.0 mEq/liter), and plasma levels of 3.17 ± 1.30 mEq/liter. It has been concluded that elevated serum or plasma levels are reliable evidence of a total body excess of magnesium. On the other hand, a deficit of magnesium may not be readily apparent from measurement of the serum level; in this instance, erythrocyte levels may be more informative.

SODIUM

Functions

This element is the major component of the cations of the extracellular fluid. It is largely associated with chloride and bicarbonate in regulation of acid-base equilibrium. The other important function of sodium is the maintenance of the osmotic pressure of body fluid and thus protection of the body against excessive fluid loss. It also functions in the preservation of normal irritability of muscle and the permeability of the cells.

Requirements & Sources

Daily requirements of 5 to as much as 15 g of sodium chloride have been recommended for adults by various authorities. These requirements were established from observations on urinary losses in subjects who were not on controlled low intakes of sodium chloride, and much of the salt in the urine therefore represented merely the excretion of the excess intake. Dahl (1958) has appraised the need for sodium chloride under conditions of controlled intakes. In his experiments, adults maintained on daily intakes of only 100–150 mg sodium lost a total of less than 25 mg sodium per day, which probably represents the minimum losses in the sweat. Dahl estimates the normal obligatory (irreducible) daily losses of sodium as follows: urine, 5–35 mg; stool, 10–125 mg; skin (not sweating), 25 mg; total, 40–185 mg.

The most variable loss of sodium occurs by way of the sweat. Ordinarily, sweat contains 20–50 mEq sodium per liter; excessive losses of sweat resulting from heavy exercise, environmental heat, or high fever can lead to sodium losses of as much as 350 mEq/day. However, the loss of sodium chloride in the sweat can be minimized during prolonged exposure to high temperatures if a period of a few days is allowed for adaptation.

It is suggested that whenever a water intake of more than 4 liters is required to replace sweat loss, extra sodium chloride should be provided. The need will vary from 2 g sodium chloride per liter of extra water loss up to an extra 7 g/day for persons doing heavy work under hot conditions.

A maximum sodium chloride intake of about 5 g/day may be recommended for adults without a history of hypertension. This is about half the daily amount which is ordinarily consumed. Furthermore, an intake of 5 g of sodium chloride per day is 10 times the amount at which adequate sodium chloride balance can apparently be maintained. For persons with a family history of hypertension, Dahl recommends a diet containing no more than 1 g of sodium chloride per day.

The main source of sodium is the sodium chloride used in cooking and seasoning; ingested foods contain additional sodium. It is estimated that about 10 g of sodium chloride (4 g of sodium) is thus ingested each day. In addition to salted foods, the content of sodium is high in bread, cheese, clams, oysters, crackers, wheat germ, and whole grains; relatively high in sodium are such foods as carrots, cauliflower, celery, eggs, legumes, milk, nuts, spinach, turnips, oatmeal, prunes, and radishes.

About 95% of the sodium which leaves the body is excreted in the urine. Sodium is readily absorbed mainly in the ileum, so that the feces contain very little except in diarrhea, when much of the sodium excreted into the intestine in the course of digestion escapes reabsorption.

Distribution

About one-third of the total sodium content of the body is present in the inorganic portion of the skeleton. However, most of the sodium is found in the extracellular fluids of the body (Table 30–8).

Metabolism

The metabolism of sodium is influenced by the adrenocortical steroids. In adrenocortical insufficiency, a decrease of serum sodium and an increase in sodium excretion occur.

Table 30–8. Distribution of sodium in body fluids or tissues.

Fluid or Tissue	mg/dl or dg	mEq/liter
Whole blood	160	70
Plasma	330	143
Cells	85	37
Muscle tissue	60–160	
Nerve tissue	312	

In chronic renal disease, particularly when acidosis coexists, sodium depletion may occur due to poor tubular reabsorption of sodium as well as to loss of sodium in the buffering of acids.

Unless the individual is well adapted to a high environmental temperature, extreme sweating may cause the loss of considerable sodium in the sweat; muscular cramps of the extremities and abdomen, headaches, nausea, and diarrhea may develop.

The levels of sodium as measured in the serum may not reflect accurately the total body sodium. Thus a low concentration of serum sodium (hyponatremia) may develop if patients are given large quantities of salt-free fluids. This obviously is not an indication of actual depletion of body sodium but rather the effect of overhydration. A similar situation prevails in edematous states such as cirrhosis or congestive heart failure, wherein low serum sodium is frequently observed although the total body sodium may actually be excessive.

However, in those clinical situations where depletion of sodium occurs (such as after excessive losses of gastrointestinal fluids or in renal disease accompanied by some degree of salt wasting), the low serum sodium which is found truly indicates depletion of total body sodium. In such hyponatremic states there will also be loss of water, which will be evident by rapid weight loss. Observations of changes in weight are of value in differentiating hyponatremic states due to dilution and overhydration, resulting in weight gain, from those in which true sodium depletion has occurred, resulting in weight loss due to dehydration.

Increased serum sodium (hypernatremia) is rare. It may occur as a result of rapid administration of sodium salts, or may be due to hyperactivity of the adrenal cortex, as in Cushing's disease. After the administration of corticotropin (ACTH), cortisone, or deoxycorticosterone, as well as some of the sex hormones, a rise in serum sodium concentration may also occur unless the concomitant retention of water acts to mask the sodium retention. The most common cause of hypernatremia, however, is rapid loss of water, such as in the dehydration associated with diabetes insipidus. Occasionally hypernatremia may also follow excessive sweating. This is so because sweat is a hypotonic salt solution; consequently, loss of this fluid engenders a loss of water at a rate exceeding loss of salt insofar as the ratio of water to salt in the body fluids is concerned.

Addison's disease, which is characterized by an increased sodium loss because of adrenocortical insufficiency, is ameliorated during pregnancy presumably because of the production of steroid hormones, which cause sodium retention. It has also been shown that the placenta elaborates hormones with sodium-retaining effects, and it is believed that these hormonal substances are responsible for the sodium and water retention, accompanied by rapid gains in weight, commonly observed in certain stages of pregnancy.

A study was made in rats of the effects of chronic ingestion of large amounts of sodium chloride on an otherwise standardized diet. Among the animals eating a diet with 7% sodium chloride or more there occurred a syndrome resembling nephrosis, characterized by the sudden onset of massive edema and by hypertension, anemia, pronounced lipemia, severe hypoproteinemia, and azotemia. All of the affected animals died, and at autopsy showed evidence of severe arteriolar disease. Significant hypertension was uniformly observed at all levels of sodium chloride (from 2.8–9.8%), and there was a tendency for the degree of elevation in blood pressure to parallel the amount of salt in the diet. At the higher levels of salt intake, there was also a significant decrease in the survival time of the experimental animals. However, the addition of potassium chloride to the high sodium chloride diets produced a striking increase in the survival times on the various diets, although a moderating effect of potassium on the blood pressure was observed only on the high levels of sodium chloride intake.

POTASSIUM

Functions

Potassium is the principal cation of the intracellular fluid; but it is also a very important constituent of the extracellular fluid because it influences muscle activity, notably cardiac muscle. Within the cells it functions, like sodium in the extracellular fluid, by influencing acid-base balance and osmotic pressure, including water retention. High intracellular potassium concentrations are essential for several important metabolic functions, including protein biosynthesis by ribosomes. A number of enzymes, including the glycolytic enzyme pyruvate kinase, require K^+ for maximal activity.

Requirements & Sources

The normal intake of potassium in food is about 4 g/day. This element is so widely distributed that a deficiency is unlikely except in the pathologic states discussed below.

A high content of potassium is found in the following foods (300–600 mg per serving): veal, chicken, beef liver, beef, pork; dried apricots, dried peaches, bananas, the juices of oranges, tangerines, and pineapples; yams, winter squash, broccoli, potatoes, and Brussels sprouts. There are other foods high in potassium but also high in sodium. Since in many situations the need for high potassium intake parallels that for a low sodium intake, these foods are of less value as sources of potassium.

Distribution

The predominantly intracellular distribution of potassium is illustrated in Table 30–9.

Metabolism

Variations in extracellular potassium influence

Table 30—9. Distribution of potassium
in body fluids or tissues.

Fluid or Tissue	mg/dl or dg	mEq/liter
Whole blood	200	50
Plasma	20	5
Cells	440	112
Muscle tissue	250–400	
Nerve tissue	530	

the activity of striated muscles so that paralysis of skeletal muscle and abnormalities in conduction and activity of cardiac muscle occur. Although potassium is excreted into the intestine in the digestive fluids (Table 30–5), much of this is later reabsorbed. The kidney is the principal organ of excretion for potassium. Not only is potassium filtered by the kidney in the glomeruli but it is also secreted by the tubules. The excretion of potassium is markedly influenced by changes in acid-base balance as well as by the activity of the adrenal cortex. (The renal mechanisms for potassium excretion are discussed in Chapter 35.) The capacity of the kidney to excrete potassium is so great that hyperkalemia will not occur, even after the ingestion or intravenous injection at a moderate rate of relatively large quantities of potassium, if kidney function is unimpaired. This is not so when urine production is inadequate. Potassium should **not** be given intravenously until circulatory collapse, dehydration, and renal insufficiency have been corrected.

A. Elevated Serum Potassium (Hyperkalemia):

1. Etiology—Toxic elevation of serum potassium is confined for the most part to patients with renal failure, advanced dehydration, or shock. A high serum potassium, accompanied by a high intracellular potassium, also occurs characteristically in adrenal insufficiency (Addison's disease). This elevated serum potassium is corrected by the administration of desoxycorticosterone acetate (Doca). Hyperkalemia may also occur if potassium is administered intravenously at an excessive rate.

2. Symptoms—The symptoms of hyperkalemia are chiefly cardiac and central nervous system depression; they are related to the elevated plasma potassium, not to increases in intracellular levels. The heart signs include bradycardia and poor heart sounds, followed by peripheral vascular collapse, and, ultimately, cardiac arrest. Characteristic electrocardiographic changes include elevated T waves, widening of the QRS complex, progressive lengthening of the P–R interval, and then disappearance of the P wave. Other symptoms commonly associated with elevated extracellular potassium include mental confusion; weakness, numbness, and tingling of the extremities; weakness of respiratory muscles; and a flaccid paralysis of the extremities.

B. Low Serum Potassium (Hypokalemia):

1. Etiology—Potassium deficiency is likely to develop in any illness, particularly in postoperative states when intravenous administration of solutions which do not contain potassium is prolonged. Potassium deficits are likewise to be expected in chronic wasting diseases with malnutrition, prolonged negative nitrogen balance, gastrointestinal losses (including those incurred in all types of diarrheas and gastrointestinal fistulas, and in continuous suction), and in metabolic alkalosis. In most of these cases intracellular potassium is transferred to the extracellular fluid, and this potassium is quickly removed by the kidney. Because adrenocortical hormones, particularly aldosterone, increase the excretion of potassium, overactivity of the adrenal cortex (Cushing's syndrome or primary aldosteronism) or injection of excessive quantities of corticosteroids or corticotropin (ACTH) may induce a deficit.

The excretion of potassium in the urine is increased by the activity of certain diuretic agents, particularly acetazolamide (Diamox) and chlorothiazide (Diuril). It is therefore recommended that potassium supplementation be provided when these drugs are used for more than a few days.

A prolonged deficiency of potassium may produce severe damage to the kidney. This may be associated secondarily with the development of chronic pyelonephritis. There is evidence that the initial damage to the kidney in potassium-depleted animals affects particularly the mitochondria in the collecting tubule.

During heart failure, the potassium content of the myocardium becomes depleted; with recovery, intracellular repletion of potassium occurs. However, intracellular deficits of potassium increase the sensitivity of the myocardium to digitalis intoxication and to arrhythmias. This fact is of importance in patients who have been fully digitalized and are then given diuretic agents which may produce potassium depletion. Administration of potassium may prevent or relieve such manifestations of digitalis toxicity.

Potassium deficits often become apparent only when water and sodium have been replenished in an attempt to correct dehydration and acidosis or alkalosis. Darrow states that changes in acid-base balance involve alterations in both intracellular and extracellular fluids and that the normal reaction of the blood cannot be maintained without a suitable relation between the body contents of sodium, potassium, chloride, and water.

When 1 g of glycogen is stored, 0.36 mmol of potassium are simultaneously retained. In treatment of diabetic coma with insulin and glucose, glycogenesis is rapid and potassium is quickly withdrawn from the extracellular fluid. The resultant hypokalemia may be fatal.

Familial periodic paralysis is a rare disease in which potassium is rapidly transferred into cells, lowering extracellular concentration.

2. Symptoms—The symptoms of low serum potassium concentrations include muscle weakness, irritability, and paralysis; tachycardia and dilatation of the heart with gallop rhythm are also noted. Changes in the electrocardiogram are also a prominent feature of hypokalemia, including first a flattened T wave; later, inverted T waves with sagging ST segment and atrioventricular block; and finally cardiac arrest.

It is important to point out that a potassium deficit may not be reflected in lowered (less than 3.5 mEq/liter) extracellular fluid concentrations until late in the process. This is confirmed by the finding of low intracellular potassium concentrations in muscle biopsy when serum potassium is normal. Thus the serum potassium is not an accurate indicator of the true status of potassium balance.

3. Treatment—In parenteral repair of a potassium deficit, a solution containing 25 mEq of potassium (KCl, 1.8 g) per liter may be safely given intravenously after adequate urine flow has been established. A daily maintenance dose of at least 50 mEq of potassium (KCl, 3.6 g) intravenously is probably necessary for most patients, with additional amounts to cover excessive losses, as from gastrointestinal drainage, up to 150 mEq of potassium per day. When these larger doses are required, as much as 50 mEq of potassium may be added to a liter of intravenous solution, although in this concentration a slower rate of injection is required (2½–3 hours). The potassium salts may be added to saline solutions or to dextrose solutions. Some prefer to add also magnesium and calcium in order to provide a better ionic balance, suggesting 10 mEq each of calcium and magnesium for each 25 mEq of potassium. The following formula contains these 3 cations in that proportion:

KCl	1.8 g (25 mEq K)
MgCl$_2$	0.5 g (10 mEq Mg)
CaCl$_2$	0.6 g (10 mEq Ca)

Whenever possible, the correction of a potassium deficit by the oral route is preferred. For adults, 4–12 g of KCl (as 1–2% solution) per day in divided doses is recommended.

In muscle, the proportion of potassium to nitrogen is 3 mmol to each g. Storage of nitrogen as muscle protein therefore demands additional potassium. It has been suggested that a loss of 5 kg of muscle protein requires 600 mEq of potassium together with the protein nitrogen necessary for its replacement. For this reason, the administration of potassium along with parenterally-administered amino acids has been recommended. Frost & Smith (1953) recommend that 5 mEq of potassium be given for each gram of amino acid nitrogen to provide for optimal nitrogen retention.

THE SODIUM-POTASSIUM PUMP

The high concentration gradients of Na$^+$ and K$^+$ that exist across the cell membrane are maintained by the activity of an energy-requiring pump that transports Na$^+$ out of the cell in exchange for K$^+$. The energy for pumping is provided by ATP generated during metabolic reactions in the cell. In the erythrocyte, where the most reliable data have been obtained, three Na$^+$ are pumped outward and two K$^+$ inward for each molecule of ATP hydrolyzed to ADP and inorganic phosphate.

An enzyme intimately related to the active transport of Na$^+$ and K$^+$ was discovered by Skou and has since been isolated from a variety of cell membrane preparations. The enzyme is an Mg^{2+}-activated adenosine triphosphatase (Na$^+$-K$^+$ ATPase) or "transport ATPase" (Skou, 1965; Dahl & Hokin, 1974). The requirement of the enzyme for Na$^+$ is absolute, but other ions, including Li$^+$, can substitute for K$^+$ to some extent. The enzyme has a molecular weight of 250,000–300,000 and appears to consist of 2 large subunits of MW 100,000–130,000 and one smaller subunit, possibly a glycoprotein, of MW 55,000.

Much recent evidence supports the conclusion that the Na$^+$-K$^+$ ATPase is involved in Na$^+$ and K$^+$ transport. For example, tissues with high transport activity, including nervous and secretory tissues, possess high Na$^+$-K$^+$ ATPase activity; most significantly, both transport Na$^+$ and K$^+$ and ATPase activity are inhibited specifically by cardiac glycosides, eg, ouabain; and the Na$^+$-K$^+$ ATPase in erythrocytes displays the same asymmetry as the Na$^+$ pump because Na$^+$ and ATP activate transport from the inside surface and K$^+$ and ouabain affect them from the outside.

Ouabain inhibits the respiration of many animal cell preparations, including brain and kidney, by 50% or more. Since cell respiration is regulated by the rate of intracellular ATP hydrolysis through the respiratory control mechanism of the mitochondria (see Chapter 5), the strong inhibition by ouabain indicates that much of the energy metabolism of a variety of cells is used to supply ATP for the Na$^+$-K$^+$ pump.

The activity of the Na$^+$-K$^+$ ATPase appears to be linked to the uptake of a variety of solutes by tissues, using carrier molecules that facilitate the specific and

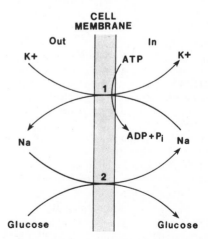

Figure 30–2. The sodium gradient hypothesis of glucose transport linked to Na$^+$-K$^+$ transport. **1** represents the Na$^+$-K$^+$ transport system and **2** represents a passive carrier for the cotransport of Na$^+$ and glucose (Crane, 1965).

compulsory cotransport of Na^+ and the solute molecule (Crane, 1965). When the external Na^+ concentration is maintained much higher than the internal Na^+ concentration by the Na^+-K^+ pump, Na^+ and solute bound to the carrier will move inward, down the Na^+ concentration gradient (see Fig 30—2). The Crane hypothesis was originally proposed to account for the Na^+- dependent transport of glucose during the process of glucose absorption from the intestine to the blood. Other solutes that appear to be transported in a similar manner in a variety of tissues include amino acids, iodide, thiamin, and uracil (Schultz & Curran, 1970). The energy stored in the Na^+ concentration gradient can thus be used to bring about the active transport of solutes without the requirement of separate and direct coupling of each of these systems to ATP.

LITHIUM

Lithium ion, in the form of lithium carbonate, is used in the treatment of manic-depressive illness. Li^+ is distributed more evenly between the extracellular and intracellular spaces than are Na^+ and K^+. As noted above, Li^+ can replace K^+ as an activator of Na^+-K^+ ATPase, although the ATPase activity is lower with Li^+ than with K^+. It is probable that Li^+ is transported across cell membranes by the Na^+-K^+ pump. Li^+ treatment modifies Na^+ and K^+ metabolism (Davis & Fann, 1971), but the possible relationship between these phenomena and the mode of action of Li^+ remains unknown.

CHLORINE

Function

As a component of sodium chloride, the element chlorine (as chloride ion) is essential in water balance and osmotic pressure regulation as well as in acid-base equilibrium. In this latter function, chloride plays a special role in the blood by the action of the chloride shift. In gastric juice, chloride is also of special importance in the production of hydrochloric acid.

Requirement & Metabolism

In the diet, the chloride occurs almost entirely as sodium chloride, and therefore the intake of chloride is satisfactory as long as sodium intake is adequate. In general, both the intake and output of this element are, in fact, inseparable from those of sodium. On low-salt diets, both the chloride and sodium in the urine drop to low levels.

Abnormalities of sodium metabolism are generally accompanied by abnormalities in chloride metabolism. When losses of sodium are excessive, as in diarrhea, profuse sweating, and certain endocrine dis-

Table 30—10. Distribution of chloride in body fluids or tissues.

Fluid or Tissue	mg/dl or dg	mEq/liter
Whole blood	250	70
Plasma or serum	365	103
Cells	190	53
Spinal fluid	440	124
Muscle tissue	40	
Nerve tissue	171	

turbances, chloride deficit is likewise observed.

In loss of gastric juice by vomiting or in pyloric or duodenal obstruction, there is a loss of chloride in excess of sodium. This leads to a decrease in plasma chloride, with a compensatory increase in bicarbonate and a resultant hypochloremic alkalosis (see Chapter 33). In Cushing's disease or after the administration of an excess of corticotropin (ACTH) or cortisone, hypokalemia with an accompanying hypochloremic alkalosis may also be observed. Some chloride is lost in diarrhea because the reabsorption of chloride in the intestinal secretions is impaired.

Distribution in the Body

The chloride concentration in cerebrospinal fluid is higher than that in other body fluids, including gastrointestinal secretions (Table 30—10).

SULFUR

Functions & Distribution

Sulfur is present in all cells of the body, primarily in the cell protein in the form of the 2 sulfur-containing amino acids, cysteine and methionine. The metabolism of sulfur and nitrogen thus tends to be associated. The cysteine residues of proteins have important functions, both in protein structure and in enzymic activity. Specific sulfhydryl groups of cysteine residues in some enzyme molecules are essential for catalytic activity, which is inhibited when these residues are modified by combination with alkylating reagents, heavy metal compounds, or oxidizing agents.

Methionine is the principal methyl group donor in the body. The "activated" form of methionine, S-adenosylmethionine, functions as a precursor in the synthesis of a large number of methylated compounds involved in intermediary metabolism and detoxification mechanisms (see Chapter 23).

Coenzyme A and lipoic acid are utilized for the synthesis of high-energy acyl-thioester intermediates (eg, acetyl-CoA, S-acetyl lipoate). Other organic compounds of sulfur are heparin, glutathione, thiamin, biotin, ergothioneine, taurocholic acid, the sulfocyanides, sulfur conjugates such as phenol esters and indoxyl sulfate, and the chondroitin sulfate in cartilage, tendon, and bone matrix. Small amounts of inorganic sulfates, with sodium and potassium, are present in blood and other tissues.

Sources & Metabolism

The main sources of sulfur for the body are the amino acids cysteine and methionine. Sulfate ions are only poorly absorbed from the intestine, and for this reason magnesium sulfate is useful as a saline cathartic. Elemental sulfur or sulfate sulfur is not known to be utilized for amino acid synthesis. Sulfate ions are incorporated into the mucopolysaccharides heparin and chondroitin sulfate after "activation" of sulfate as described on p 102.

Organic sulfur is mainly oxidized to sulfate and excreted as inorganic or ethereal sulfate. The various forms of urinary sulfur are described on p 627.

TRACE ELEMENTS

1. ESSENTIAL TRACE ELEMENTS

IRON

Function & Distribution

The role of iron in the body is almost exclusively confined to the processes of cellular respiration. Iron porphyrin (heme) groups are essential components of hemoglobin, myoglobin, the cytochromes, and the enzymes catalase and peroxidase. The remainder of the iron in the body (nonheme iron) is almost entirely protein-bound. These forms include the intracellular iron-containing flavoproteins (NADH dehydrogenase and succinate dehydrogenase) and iron-sulfur proteins as well as storage and transport forms of the mineral.

The approximate distribution of iron-containing compounds in normal adult humans is shown in Table 30–11.

Requirements & Sources

The need for iron in the human diet varies greatly at different ages and under different circumstances. It is determined by the requirements for tissue growth and hemoglobin synthesis and the replacement needs due to iron losses in urine, feces, and sweat, and, in the female, the additional losses in menstruation, gestation, and lactation. The need for iron is greatest during the first 2 years of life, during the period of rapid growth and hemoglobin increase in adolescence, and throughout the childbearing period in women.

Clinical studies have indicated that an additional 0.8–1 mg of iron per day is needed to maintain normal hemoglobin concentration in children and adolescents to provide for increased stores of iron in the growing body. The average loss of iron in the healthy adult male is estimated to be only about 1 mg/day, ranging from 0.4–2 mg depending upon the iron content of exfoliated cells. In adult women, the average loss of blood during a menstrual period is 35–70 ml, which represents a monthly loss of 16–32 mg of iron, or an additional average loss of 0.5–1 mg/day. This amount of iron is easily obtained from the diet. For women with excessive menstrual blood loss and a resultant chronic iron-deficiency anemia, a supplement of 100 mg of iron per day (as ferrous sulfate) is sufficient to produce a maximal response toward correction of anemia. Pregnancy increases the requirement to approximately 3.6 mg/day. In the latter part of pregnancy, iron requirements may reach 4 mg/day. It is clear that during growth, pregnancy, and lactation, when the demand for hemoglobin formation is increased, additional iron is needed in the diet. In the healthy adult male, or in healthy women after menopause, the dietary requirement for iron is almost negligible, and iron deficiency is very unlikely unless some loss of blood occurs. An exception is the possibility of iron deficiency as a result of malabsorption from the gastro-

Table 30–11. Distribution of iron-containing compounds in the normal human adult.

	Total in Body (g)	Iron Content (g)	Percent of Total Iron in Body
Iron porphyrins (heme compounds)			
Hemoglobin	900	3.0	60–70
Myoglobin	40	0.13	3–5
Heme enzymes			
Cytochrome c	0.8	0.004	0.1
Catalase	5.0	0.004	0.1
Other cytochromes	...	...	...
Peroxidase	...	...	...
Nonporphyrin iron compounds			
Siderophilin (transferrin)	10	0.004	0.1
Ferritin	2–4	0.4–0.8	15.0
Hemosiderin	...	...	...
Total available iron stores		1.2–1.5	
Total iron		4.0–5.0	

intestinal tract such as may occur after surgical resection of portions of the stomach and the small intestine, or in patients with disease characterized by malabsorption of iron.

A defect in hemoglobin synthesis, resulting in anemia, is commonly found during copper deficiency in most animals. Abnormalities in iron metabolism during copper deficiency appear to be due to defects in cellular and plasma transport of iron (see below).

The recommended daily amounts of iron currently suggested by nutritional authorities are as follows: (See also Table 31–6.)

A. Infants: 10–15 mg.

B. Children: 1–3 years of age, 15 mg; 4–10 years of age, 10 mg.

C. Older Children and Adults: *Males:* 11–18 years of age, 18 mg; after 19 years of age, 10 mg. *Females:* 11–50 years of age, and during pregnancy or lactation, 18 mg. After 51 years of age, 10 mg.

It should be noted that these requirements for iron take into account the low amount of iron actually absorbed from orally ingested iron.

The recommended allowance of 10 mg/day for adult males is readily obtained from the normal diet in the USA, which provides about 6 mg of iron per 1000 kcal. However, the recommended allowance for females (18 mg/day), based on 2000 kcal/day, is difficult to obtain from dietary sources without further iron fortification of foods.

The best dietary sources of iron are "organ meats": liver, heart, kidney, and spleen. Other good sources are egg yolk, whole wheat, fish, oysters, clams, nuts, dates, figs, beans, asparagus, spinach, molasses, and oatmeal.

Absorption From the Gastrointestinal Tract

A peculiar and possibly unique feature of the metabolism of iron is that it occurs in what is virtually a closed system. Under normal conditions very little dietary iron is absorbed, the amounts excreted in the urine are minimal, and a high proportion of the total body iron is continuously redistributed throughout the body in several metabolic circuits. Because there is no way to excrete excess iron, its absorption from the intestine must be controlled if it is not to accumulate in the tissues in toxic amounts. In the ordinary diet, 10–20 mg of iron are taken each day, but less than 10% of this is absorbed.

Infants and children absorb a higher percentage of iron from foods than do adults. Iron-deficient children absorb twice as much from foods as normal children. Iron deficiency in infants can usually be attributed to dietary inadequacy.

Factors Affecting Iron Absorption

Not all of the iron in foods is available to the body. An ordinary chemical determination for total iron of foodstuffs is thus not an accurate measure of nutritionally available iron. This can be determined by measuring the amount that will react with the a,a-dipyridyl reagent.

Most of the iron in foods occurs in the ferric (Fe^{3+}) state either as ferric hydroxide or as ferric organic compounds. In an acid medium, these compounds are broken down into free ferric ions or loosely bound organic iron. The gastric hydrochloric acid as well as the organic acids of the foods are both important for this purpose. Reducing substances in foods, SH groups (eg, cysteine), and ascorbic acid convert ferric iron to the reduced (ferrous) state. In this form, iron is more soluble and should therefore be more readily absorbed. Iron absorption is enhanced by protein, possibly as a result of the formation of low-molecular-weight digestive products (peptides, amino acids) which can form soluble iron chelates. Heme iron enters the mucosal cell without being released from the porphyrin ring. In humans, dogs, and rats, heme is broken down in the mucosa and the iron appears in plasma transferrin.

A diet high in phosphate causes a decrease in the absorption of iron since compounds of iron and phosphate are insoluble; conversely, a diet very low in phosphates markedly increases iron absorption. Phytic acid (found in cereals) and oxalates also interfere with the absorption of iron.

Absorption of iron occurs mainly in the stomach and duodenum. Impaired absorption of iron is therefore observed in patients who have had subtotal or total removal of the stomach or in patients who have sustained surgical removal of a considerable amount of the intestine. Iron absorption is also diminished in various malabsorption syndromes, such as steatorrhea.

In iron deficiency anemias, the absorption of iron may be increased to 2–10 times normal. It is also increased in pernicious anemia and in hypoplastic anemia.

Mechanism of Iron Absorption

The regulation of iron absorption is largely carried out by the intestinal epithelial cells, although the exact mechanism of this "control" is unknown. At one time, the so-called "mucosal block" theory was considered to account for the intestinal control of iron absorption. According to this theory, the amount of an iron-binding protein, **apoferritin**, in the mucosal cells was the controlling factor. Ferrous ion, once within the mucosal cells, is oxidized to the ferric state and then combined with apoferritin to form the iron-containing protein **ferritin**. It was believed that the binding capacity of apoferritin for iron limited the further absorption of iron; when saturated with iron, no further uptake of iron could occur.

More recent observations make it unlikely that ferritin is involved in the major regulation of iron absorption. Iron taken into the mucosal cell is bound to one or more specific carriers which appear to regulate its passage across the cell to the blood. It is probable that iron entering the cell in excess of that which can be bound by the carrier system becomes incorporated into ferritin. Intestinal ferritin appears therefore to act as a storage compound for iron rather than as a controller of absorption. Experimental support for the existence of nonferritin control of iron absorption has been provided by studies in mice with an X-linked inherited defect in iron absorption.

Transport in the Plasma

Nearly all the iron released from the mucosal cell enters the portal blood, mostly in the ferrous (Fe^{2+}) state. In the plasma, Fe^{2+} is oxidized rapidly to the ferric (Fe^{3+}) state and is then incorporated into a specific iron-binding protein, **transferrin**. This protein can bind 2 atoms of Fe^{3+} per molecule of protein to form a red ferric-protein complex. Transferrin (siderophilin) is a glycoprotein of MW 76,000 containing 5.3% carbohydrate. The carbohydrate consists of 2 identical branched side chains, each branch ending in a molecule of N-acetylneuraminic acid (sialic acid) (Jamieson & others, 1971).

Iron release from the mucosal cell is facilitated by a low degree of transferrin saturation by iron. Ceruloplasmin, a blue copper-binding plasma protein, exerts a catalytic activity (serum ferroxidase) in plasma to convert Fe^{2+} into Fe^{3+}, and it may thus promote the rate of iron incorporation into transferrin. Human serum also contains a yellow cuproprotein (ferroxidase II) which catalyzes the oxidation of ferrous ions (Topham & Frieden, 1970).

Under normal circumstances, almost all of the iron bound to transferrin is taken up rapidly by the bone marrow. It appears that only the reticulocytes are capable of utilizing the Fe^{3+} bound to transferrin, although both the reticulocytes and the mature erythrocytes can take up unbound ferric ion. Thus, transferrin in some manner diverts the plasma iron into those cells which are actively making hemoglobin.

The normal content of protein-bound iron (BI) in the plasma of males is 120–140 $\mu g/dl$; in females, 90–120 $\mu g/dl$. However, the total iron-binding capacity (TIBC) is about the same in both sexes: 300–360 $\mu g/dl$. This indicates that normally only about 30–40% of the iron-binding capacity of the serum is utilized for iron transport and that the iron-free siderophilin, ie, the unsaturated iron-binding capacity (UIBC), is therefore about 60–70% of the total.

In iron deficiency anemias the plasma protein-bound iron is low, whereas the total iron-binding capacity tends to rise, resulting in an unsaturated iron-binding capacity which is higher than normal. In hepatic disease, both the bound iron and the total iron-binding capacity of the plasma may be low, so that the percentage of the total iron-binding capacity which is unsaturated is not significantly altered from normal.

The amount of bound iron in the plasma is reported to exhibit a circadian variation which can be as much as 60 $\mu g/dl$ over a 24-hour period. The lowest values were found 2 hours following retirement for sleep; the highest values were found 5–7 hours later.

The failure of the kidney to excrete iron is probably due to the presence of iron in the plasma as a protein-bound compound which is not filtrable by the glomerulus. By the same token, losses of iron into the urine may occur in proteinuria. In nephrosis, for example, as much as 1.5 mg of iron per day may be excreted with protein in the urine.

Metabolism

The storage forms of iron, ferritin, and hemosiderin act as an internal iron reserve to protect against sudden losses of iron by bleeding. Ferritin is found not only in the intestine but also in liver (about 700 mg), spleen, and bone marrow. If iron is administered parenterally in amounts which exceed the capacity of the body to store it as ferritin, it accumulates in the liver as microscopically visible **hemosiderin**, a form of colloidal iron oxide in association with protein. The iron content of hemosiderin is 35% by weight. Ferritin stores iron in a soluble form; it consists of a spectrum of molecules with different affinities for iron. It therefore acts as both a short-term and a medium-term iron reserve. The mobilization of liver ferritin may require a ferric to ferrous transformation, involving the ferrireductase enzyme described by Osaki & Sirivech (1971).

The level of iron in the plasma is the result of a dynamic equilibrium in which iron from the plasma is redistributed in several metabolic circuits, each circuit terminating in the return of iron to the plasma iron pool. In the quantitatively most important circuit, iron is used for hemoglobin synthesis, involving the transfer of plasma iron to bone marrow, the red cell, the aging red cell, and back to the plasma (hemoglobin cycle). Studies of the turnover of iron, using isotopic ^{59}Fe, indicate that about 27 mg are utilized each day, 75% of this for the formation of hemoglobin. About 20 mg are obtained from the breakdown of red blood cells, a very small amount from newly absorbed iron, and the remainder from the iron stores. Normally there is a rather slow exchange of iron between the plasma and the storage iron; in fact, following an acute hemorrhage in a normal individual, the level of iron in the plasma may remain low for weeks, a further indication that mobilization of iron from the storage depots is a slow process.

Iron Deficiency

Iron deficiency anemias are of the hypochromic microcytic type. In experiments with rats made iron-deficient, it was found that cytochrome c levels were reduced even in the absence of anemia. This suggests that some of the symptoms in anemia may be due to decreased activity of intracellular enzymes rather than to low levels of hemoglobin.

A deficiency of iron may result from inadequate intake (eg, a high cereal diet, low in meat) or inadequate absorption (eg, gastrointestinal disturbances such as diarrhea, achlorhydria, steatorrhea, or intestinal disease, after surgical removal of the stomach, or after extensive intestinal resection) as well as from excessive loss of blood. If absorption is adequate, the daily addition of ferrous sulfate to the diet will successfully treat the iron deficiency type of anemia. A preparation of iron (iron dextran) for intramuscular injection in

patients who cannot tolerate or absorb orally administered iron has been used. Caution must be exercised
when iron is given parenterally because of the possibility of oversaturation of the tissues with resultant production of hemosiderosis.

Studies with isotopic iron have been used to
determine the rate of red blood cell production. [59]Fe
is given intravenously in tracer doses and the rate of
disappearance of the label is measured. Normally half
of the radioactivity disappears exponentially from the
circulating blood in 90 minutes. In hemolytic anemias,
where there is hyperplasia of the erythroid tissue, and
in polycythemia vera, half of the activity disappears in
11–30 minutes. In aplastic anemia the opposite situation prevails; the disappearance time is prolonged to as
long as 250 minutes. The reappearance of the label in
newly formed blood cells is then noted. In iron deficiency anemia, uptake of iron in the erythrocytes is
accelerated; in aplastic anemia, it is diminished.

Hemosiderosis

Because of the absence of an excretory pathway
for iron, excess amounts may accumulate in the
tissues. This is observed in patients with aplastic or
hemolytic anemia who have received many blood
transfusions over a period of years. The existence in
some individuals of an excessive capacity for the
absorption of iron from the intestine has been detected
by studies with radioactive iron. Such individuals
absorb 20–45% of an administered dose of the labeled
iron; a normal subject absorbs 1.5–6.5%. The anomaly
in iron absorption may be inherited. In such patients, a
very large excess (as much as 40–50 g) of iron accumulates in the tissues after many years. This hemosiderosis may be accompanied by a bronzed pigmentation of
the skin, **hemochromatosis**, and, presumably because
of the toxic effect of the unbound iron in the tissues,
there may be liver damage with signs of cirrhosis,
diabetes, and a pancreatic fibrosis. The condition is
sometimes referred to as bronze diabetes. As might be
expected, the unsaturated iron-binding capacity of the
serum of the patient with hemochromatosis is very
low. Thus, whereas the iron-binding proteins of the
serum in a normal individual are only about 30%
saturated, in patients with hemochromatosis they are
about 90% saturated, due to the excess absorption of
iron from the intestine.

An acquired siderosis of dietary origin is common
among the Bantu peoples of Africa. "Bantu siderosis"
is believed to be caused by the fact that the natives
consume a diet which is very high in corn and thus low
in phosphorus and that their foods are cooked in iron
pots. The combination of a low-phosphate diet and a
high intake of iron enhances absorption of iron sufficiently to produce siderosis with accompanying organ
damage as described above. Iron deficiency anemias,
common among pregnant women in other areas of the
world, are virtually unknown among the Bantu.

A recent survey of the study and uses of iron in
biochemistry and medicine has been prepared by
Jacobs & Worwood (1974).

COPPER

Functions & Distribution

Copper is an essential constituent of several proteins, metalloenzymes, and some naturally occurring
pigments. It is essential for hemoglobin synthesis, normal bone formation, and the maintenance of myelin
within the nervous system. Hemocyanin is a copper-
protein complex in the blood of certain invertebrates,
where it functions like hemoglobin as an oxygen
carrier.

Copper is present in 2 key enzymes of aerobic
metabolism: **cytochrome c oxidase**, which is responsible for the major part (probably more than 90%) of
the oxygen consumed by life on this planet; and cytosolic **superoxide dismutase**, which catalytically scav-
enges the toxic free radical superoxide ion (O_2^-) generated during aerobic metabolism. Cytosolic superoxide
dismutase has a molecular weight of 32,000, consists
of 2 identical subunits, and contains one Cu^{2+} and one
Zn^{2+} per subunit (Fridovich, 1975). Proteins identical
to superoxide dismutase were earlier isolated from several different sources and, in the absence of known
enzymic function, were given a variety of names, including erythrocuprein (from red blood cells), hepato-
cuprein (from liver), and cerebrocuprein (from brain).
A superoxide dismutase protein of markedly different
amino acid sequence and containing manganese instead
of copper and zinc is present in the matrix space of
mitochondria. Other cuproprotein enzymes present in
animal tissues include amine oxidase, tyrosinase, uricase, and dopamine hydroxylase.

Ceruloplasmin, a copper-binding plasma protein,
has a molecular weight of about 151,000 and contains
0.34% copper, or about 8 atoms of copper per mole.
Normal plasma contains about 30 mg of this protein
per dl. It is believed to function as a ferroxidase
enzyme during iron metabolism.

The adult human body contains 100–150 mg of
copper; about 64 mg are found in the muscles, 23 mg
in the bones, and 18 mg in the liver, which contains a
higher concentration of copper than that of any of the
other organs studied. It is of interest that the concentration of copper in the fetal liver is 5–10 times higher
than that in the liver of an adult. Both the blood cells
and serum contain copper; but the copper content of
the red blood cell is constant, while that of the serum
is highly variable, averaging about 90 µg/dl.

At least 80% of the red blood cell copper is present as superoxide dismutase (erythrocuprein). The copper in plasma occurs in 2 main forms, one firmly
bound and one loosely bound. The firmly bound
copper, comprising 80–95% of the total plasma copper, consists of ceruloplasmin. The loosely bound
copper is known as "direct-reacting" copper because it
reacts freely with copper complexing reagents (eg,
dithizon and diethyldithiocarbamate) and is loosely
bound to protein, probably serum albumin. The albu-
min-bound copper may represent copper in transport.
During copper estimations, since most of the plasma or

serum copper is tightly bound, it is necessary to first treat the serum with hydrochloric acid to free the copper so that it can react with the color reagent.

Requirements & Sources

The human requirement for copper has been studied by balance experiments. A daily allowance of 2.5 mg has been suggested for adults; infants and children require about 0.05 mg/kg body weight. This is easily supplied in average diets, which contain 2.5–5 mg of copper.

A nutritional deficiency of copper has never been positively demonstrated in man, although it has been suspected in cases of sprue or in nephrosis. However, there are reports of a syndrome in infants which is characterized by low levels of serum copper and iron and by edema and a hypochromic microcytic anemia. Therapy with iron easily cures the disease, and "spontaneous" cures are also reported.

Copper is widely distributed in foods; most diets provide the amount needed per day to maintain copper balance. The mixed diet of the later period of infancy meets or exceeds the value of 0.05 mg/kg/day suggested as needed by infants at this time. The richest sources of dietary copper are nuts, some shellfish, liver, kidney, raisins, and dried legumes. Cow's milk is a poor source of copper (concentrations of 0.015–0.18 mg/liter). Human milk ranges from 1.05 mg/liter at the beginning of lactation to 0.15 mg/liter at the end.

Metabolism

Experiments have been carried out with labeled copper (^{64}Cu). The copper was found to be largely associated with the albumin fraction of the plasma immediately after its ingestion. A decline in plasma radioactivity then occurs as copper attached to albumin is distributed to cuproproteins in the liver and elsewhere; a secondary rise in plasma radioactivity then takes place as copper incorporated into liver ceruloplasmin is released to the blood. In Wilson's disease (see below), this secondary rise does not occur.

Since copper in the plasma is largely bound to protein, it is not readily excreted in the urine. Most of it is excreted via the bile into the intestine and expelled with feces.

Copper Deficiency

Experimental animals on a copper-deficient diet lose weight and die; the severe hypochromic microcytic anemia which they exhibit is not the cause of death since an iron deficiency anemia of equal proportions is not fatal. This suggests that copper has a role in the body in addition to its function in the metabolism of red cells. This additional role of copper may be related to the activity of oxidation-reduction enzymes of the tissues, such as the cytochrome system. A relation between copper and iron metabolism has been detected. In the presence of a deficiency of copper, the movement of iron from the tissues to the plasma is decreased and hypoferremia results. Copper favors the absorption of iron from the gastrointestinal tract.

A bone disorder associated with a deficiency of copper in the diet of young dogs has been described. The bones of these animals were characterized by abnormally thin cortices, deficient trabeculae, and wide epiphyses. Fractures and deformities occurred in many of the animals. Anemia was present, and the hair turned gray. The disorder did not occur in any of the control animals, and was relieved by the administration of copper.

Wilson's disease (hepatolenticular degeneration) is associated with abnormalities in the metabolism of copper. In this disease the liver and the lenticular nucleus of the brain contain abnormally large amounts of copper, and there is excessive urinary excretion of copper and low levels of copper and of ceruloplasmin in the plasma. A generalized aminoaciduria also occurs in this disease.

Almost all patients with Wilson's disease have less than 23 mg of ceruloplasmin per dl of serum, which may be taken to represent the lower limit of normal. In some patients, ceruloplasmin cannot even be detected. Hence, in Wilson's disease, much of the plasma copper remains loosely bound to serum albumin, and the copper can therefore be more readily transferred to tissues such as the brain and liver or to the urine. The "direct-reacting" fraction of the serum copper (see above) is not decreased in these patients and may actually be increased. Thus, the total serum copper may appear to be normal or only slightly decreased.

If the deposition of copper in the liver becomes excessive, cirrhosis may develop. Accumulation of copper in the kidney may give rise to renal tubular damage, which leads to increased urinary excretion of amino acids and peptides and, occasionally, glucose as well.

It has been suggested that excessive copper absorption from the intestine and inadequate excretion of copper via the intestine may be factors in the genesis of Wilson's disease.

Hypercupremia occurs in a variety of circumstances. It does not seem to have any diagnostic significance.

IODINE

Function

Iodine is required exclusively for the biosynthesis of the iodinated thyroid hormones. Its metabolism is discussed in Chapter 29.

Requirements & Source (See also Table 31–6.)

The requirement for iodine is 5 µg/100 kcal or, for adults, about 100–150 µg/day. The use of iodized salt regularly will provide more than this.

The need for iodine is increased in adolescence and in pregnancy. Thyroid hypertrophy occurs if iodine deficiency is prolonged.

MANGANESE

Functions & Distribution

Manganese is essential for normal bone structure, reproduction, and the normal functioning of the central nervous system. The enzyme pyruvate carboxylase, involved in gluconeogenesis, and the superoxide dismutase present in the matrix space of mitochondria both contain tightly bound manganese. Arginase is specifically activated by manganese ions. In vitro, manganese or magnesium ions activate isocitrate dehydrogenase and several phosphotransferase enzymes, and manganese ions strongly inhibit lipid peroxidation reactions. In human serum, manganese is bound to a specific β-globulin.

The total body content of manganese is 12–20 mg. The kidney and liver are the chief storage organs for manganese. Mitochondria are the principal intracellular sites of manganese uptake. In blood, values of 4–20 μg/dl have been reported. Most of the manganese is excreted into the intestine by way of the bile. Very little manganese usually occurs in the urine.

Requirements & Sources

An evident deficiency of manganese is not known in man, suggesting that the average daily dietary intake of 2.5–7 mg is adequate, although a recommendation for the daily allowance cannot now be made. Nuts and whole grains are rich sources of manganese; vegetables and fruits are good sources. Meats, poultry, seafoods, and fish are poor sources.

COBALT

This element is a constituent of vitamin B_{12}, which is necessary for normal red blood cell formation. It is uncertain whether inorganic cobalt plays any separate essential biologic role. Enzymes requiring vitamin B_{12} for activity include methylmalonyl-CoA mutase, methyltetrahydrofolate oxidoreductase, homocysteine methyltransferase, and ribonucleotide reductase. Patients suffering from pernicious anemia due to vitamin B_{12} deficiency excrete large amounts of methylmalonic acid in the urine owing to a defective mutase reaction.

The total body content of cobalt averages about 1.1 mg. Cobalt is widely distributed throughout the body. The highest concentrations are usually found in the liver, kidneys, and bones. Cobalt administered orally as a soluble salt is poorly absorbed and is therefore largely eliminated in the feces. Injected isotopic cobalt is eliminated rapidly and almost completely by the kidneys into the urine.

Nutritional anemia in cattle and sheep living in cobalt-poor soil areas can be treated successfully with cobalt. Microorganisms in the rumens of these animals utilize cobalt to synthesize vitamin B_{12}.

Pharmacologic doses of inorganic cobalt salts induce an increase in red cell production (polycythemia) in many species including man. The toxic effects of the large amounts of cobalt required to induce this response limit the use of cobalt therapy in the management of human anemias.

ZINC

Functions & Distribution

Zinc is essential for the normal growth, reproduction, and life expectancy of animals and has a beneficial effect on the processes of tissue repair and wound healing. The element is an essential component of a number of enzymes present in animal tissues, including alcohol dehydrogenase, alkaline phosphatase, carbonic anhydrase, procarboxypeptidase, and cytosolic superoxide dismutase (which also contains copper). Acetazolamide (Diamox) inhibits carbonic anhydrase activity by binding to the zinc atom present in the enzyme molecule. The retina contains a zinc metalloenzyme, **retinene reductase**, which is required for the reconstitution of retinene (vitamin A aldehyde) during the rhodopsin cycle (see Chapter 12). Retinene reductase appears to be identical to liver alcohol dehydrogenase. Zinc is necessary to maintain normal concentrations of vitamin A in plasma. Zinc may be required for mobilization of vitamin A from the liver. When vitamin A concentrations in the plasma are lower than normal and are unresponsive to therapy with vitamin A, zinc supplementation may be effective.

Insulin forms complexes with zinc, which makes it possible for crystalline zinc insulin to be prepared during insulin purification. Zinc adhering to the insulin molecule increases the duration of insulin action when given by injection. Zinc-insulin complexes are also present in the B (β) cells of the pancreas, and there is evidence suggesting that zinc is used in these cells to store and release insulin as required (Davies, 1972).

The zinc content of leukocytes from the blood of normal human subjects is reported to be $3.2 \pm 3 \times 10^{-10}$ μg/million cells. The zinc content of white blood cells in human leukemia patients is decreased to about 10% of the normal amount. Temporary therapeutic amelioration of the leukemic process is accompanied by a rise in the zinc content of these cells to normal. Recent evidence suggests that superoxide ions produced by leukocytes have a bactericidal function (Babior & others, 1973) and the zinc-containing superoxide dismutase may therefore serve to regulate superoxide production in these cells.

Zinc is widely distributed in the tissues of the body. The human adult body is estimated to contain 1.4–2.3 g of zinc. About 20% of the total body zinc is present in the skin. A considerable proportion is also present in the bones and teeth. High concentrations of zinc are found in spermatozoa, prostate, and epididymis.

Metabolism

Zinc absorption occurs mainly in the small intestine, especially from the duodenum. Zinc given orally or by injection is mostly excreted in the feces. Endogenous zinc is secreted into the small intestine in the pancreatic juice, which contains carboxypeptidase.

The most rapid accumulation and turnover rate of zinc occurs in the soft tissues, especially the pancreas, liver, kidney, and spleen. Relatively large amounts of zinc are deposited in bones, but these stores do not move into rapid equilibrium with the rest of the organism. The body pool of biologically available zinc appears to be small and to have a rapid turnover.

Requirements & Sources

The average zinc content of a mixed diet in the USA is between 10 and 15 mg. The average intake of zinc in children has been estimated to range from 5 mg for 1–3 year olds to 13 mg for adolescents 10–13 years of age. The breast-fed newborn consumes from 0.7–5 mg of zinc per day. Metabolic studies have shown that in healthy adults an intake of 8–10 mg/day is sufficient to bring about equilibrium with respect to this element. The currently recommended allowance (Table 31–6) is 15 mg/day for adults, with an additional 15 mg during pregnancy and 10 mg during lactation. For preadolescent children, the recommended allowance for zinc is 6–10 mg/day; for infants during the first 6 months of life, the tentative recommendation is 3 mg/day.

A balanced diet containing sufficient animal protein should provide the recommended daily zinc allowance. Meat, liver, eggs, seafood (particularly oysters), milk, and whole grain products are good sources.

Zinc Deficiency

There are extensive areas within the USA in which the soil is deficient in available zinc. Pronounced zinc deficiency in man, resulting in hypogonadism and dwarfism, has been found in the Middle East; it probably does not exist in the USA except in a few cases of malabsorption syndrome. There are, however, reports that suggest the existence of marginal states of zinc nutrition in some segments of the United States population. Accelerated rates of wound healing and improved taste acuity observed as a result of increased zinc intake suggest that the requirement for zinc in these subjects was not being fully met by their diet.

The occurrence of a marginal deficiency of zinc was reported in a group of apparently healthy children who showed impaired taste acuity, poor appetite, and suboptimal growth as significant signs. Marked improvement was effected by increasing the daily intake of zinc in these children by 0.4–0.8 mg/kg.

Evidence for a conditioned deficiency of zinc in patients with so-called postalcoholic cirrhosis has been presented by Vallee & others (1959). Patients with Laennec's cirrhosis had a mean concentration of zinc of 66 ± 19 μg/dl serum (normal, 120 ± 19 μg/dl). There was also increased urinary excretion of zinc in the cirrhotic patients. When studied at autopsy, the livers of patients who had died of cirrhosis were found to have significantly less zinc than liver tissues from patients who had died of nonhepatic disease. It was suggested that the zinc deficiency in the cirrhotic patients was due to secondary factors related to the underlying disease which act to render a normal intake of zinc inadequate. Because of the importance of zinc in the activity of certain enzymes, as mentioned above, it may be supposed that a zinc deficiency would cause significant biochemical changes in the metabolism of those substrates affected by the enzymes concerned. One such substrate is alcohol, whose role in the etiology and exacerbation of cirrhosis has not been fully explained. Further studies of zinc metabolism in liver disease may therefore contribute to the understanding of this important clinical entity.

FLUORINE

Despite the toxic properties of fluoride at a high concentration, in trace quantities it is of unquestioned importance in the development of teeth and bones. The protective effect of fluoride against dental caries is well established, and fluoride is now accepted as a required mineral nutrient. The protective effect of fluoride in tooth development is most important during infancy and early childhood because these are the periods that coincide with tooth development, although the caries-preventive activity of fluoride continues into adulthood. In addition, appropriate levels of dietary fluoride decrease the incidence of osteoporosis, a defect in the maintenance of bone structure that occurs in older adults—notably in women after menopause. Fluoride has been shown to be a dietary essential for growth in rats and for fertility in mice.

In humans, fluoride is normally accumulated in small quantities only in the bones and teeth. The amount of fluoride present in these tissues depends on several factors, including the duration of fluoride intake and the age at which intake occurs. The amounts of fluoride in the soft tissues are generally very low and do not increase with age. Soluble fluorides in drinking water are rapidly absorbed. Fluoride is initially distributed in the same manner as chloride and remains mostly in the extracellular water. Most of the fluoride that escapes retention by the bones and teeth is excreted rapidly into the urine.

Requirements & Sources

Drinking water is the main source of fluoride for humans. At a concentration of 1 ppm, fluoride is supplied in nutritionally adequate amounts. When the drinking water in a given area contains less than that amount, it is regarded as an excellent public health practice to add fluoride to the water supply (fluoridation) in order to raise its concentration to an appropriate level. In long-term studies of the results of fluoridation, it has been shown that the incidence of dental caries in younger age groups (14—16 years) was reduced by 60—70%. When the water supply contains 1 ppm fluoride, 1—2 mg/day of fluoride will be ingested depending on the water intake in all forms, either as such or in beverages made with added water. This level of intake of fluoride is considered adequate.

Fluorosis

An excessively high intake of fluoride during childhood causes mottling and discoloration of the enamel of the teeth. Intake of fluoride in very large quantities also causes changes in bone, including increased bone density, calcification at the point of insertion of muscles, and bony exostoses. Fluorosis occurs only in geographic areas where the water naturally contains unusually high concentrations of fluoride (as much as 10—45 ppm); it does not occur in communities with a properly controlled system for fluoridation of the water supply.

Acute Toxicity of Fluoride

Fluoride is very toxic in large doses. A lethal dose may be as small as 0.5 g in a child, but doses many times as large are not always fatal. Fluoride is a powerful inhibitor of several magnesium-activated enzymes concerned in phosphate metabolism, including the glycolytic enzyme enolase. Fluoroacetate acts as a powerful inhibitor of the citric acid cycle after metabolic conversion ("lethal synthesis") to fluorocitrate, which blocks aconitase activity. The inhibitory properties of fluorinated pyrimidines are discussed elsewhere (see Chapter 24).

MOLYBDENUM

Functions & Distribution

Molybdenum is an essential component of the molybdoflavoproteins xanthine oxidase and aldehyde oxidase and the molybdohemoprotein sulfite oxidase of animal tissues. It is also present in the enzymes nitrate reductase in plants and nitrogenase, which function in nitrogen fixation by microorganisms (Johnson & others, 1974). Traces of molybdenum are required for the maintenance of normal levels of xanthine oxidase in animal tissues. In humans, a genetic deficiency of xanthine oxidase (xanthinuria) and of sulfite oxidase has been recognized. Xanthinuric individuals do not appear to suffer any ill effects, but the single reported case of human sulfite oxidase deficiency proved fatal. Sulfite oxidase catalyzes the detoxification of sulfur dioxide and sulfite to sulfate.

It has proved difficult to induce molybdenum deficiency diseases experimentally, which suggests that many animals have an extremely low requirement for molybdenum. Lambs fed a semipurified diet are reported to show a significant growth response when the diet is supplemented with 0.36 ppm of molybdenum, perhaps because molybdenum stimulates cellulose deg-

radation by rumen microorganisms. Excess dietary molybdenum may induce symptoms of copper deficiency. A complex relationship exists between the intake of molybdenum, copper, and sulfate and the copper status of the animal (Underwood, 1971).

Molybdenum concentrations in animal tissues are normally very low, comparable with those of manganese. The highest concentrations of molybdenum are usually found in liver and kidney.

SELENIUM

Functions & Distribution

Although not yet recognized as essential for man, selenium is clearly essential for many animal species. The element is required for normal growth and fertility and for the prevention of a wide variety of diseases that can be induced in experimental animals by dietary means. These diseases include dietary liver necrosis in rats, multiple necrosis in mice, muscular dystrophy and heart necrosis in minks, exudative diathesis in chicks and turkeys, stiff lamb disease and ill thrift in sheep, white muscle disease in calves, and liver dystrophy and muscle degeneration in pigs (Schwarz, 1974). The diseases can be prevented by supplementing the diet either with an organoselenium compound isolated by Schwarz and coworkers from bakers' yeast ("factor 3") or with certain other selenium compounds.

Selenium is an essential component of the enzyme glutathione peroxidase. Glutathione peroxidase isolated from sheep red blood cells has a molecular weight of approximately 84,000. The enzyme contains one atom of selenium per protein subunit of approximately 21,000 MW (0.34% of selenium). The enzyme catalyzes the oxidation of reduced glutathione to oxidized glutathione as shown below:

$$2\ GSH + H_2O_2 \longrightarrow GSSG + 2\ H_2O$$

Reduced glutathione protects membrane lipids and other cell constituents (eg, hemoglobin) against oxidative damage by destroying hydrogen peroxide and fatty acid hydroperoxides (of general structure ROOH) through reactions catalyzed by glutathione peroxidase, thus:

$$2\ GSH + ROOH \longrightarrow GSSG + ROH + H_2O$$

Oxidized glutathione is regenerated by the activity of the enzyme glutathione reductase.

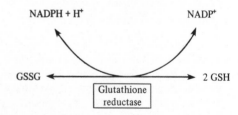

Recent studies suggest that selenium is involved in a variety of other important biologic processes including immune mechanisms, ubiquinone biosynthesis, and mitochondrial ATP biosynthesis (Frost & Lish, 1975).

Selenium is widely distributed in the animal body and is found in highest concentration in the kidney cortex, pancreas, pituitary, and liver. The amount of selenium in foodstuffs is highly variable, due largely to differences in soil selenium content in the areas where food is grown.

Relationship to Vitamin E

Some of the disorders of animals induced by dietary means are responsive either to selenium or to vitamin E, indicating that a close relationship exists between the 2 nutrients. However, certain diseases are apparently caused by a deficiency which responds specifically to one nutrient but not to the other. The role of selenium in hydroperoxide destruction through glutathione peroxidase activity, described above, serves to clarify the interrelationships between vitamin E and cysteine as a precursor of glutathione, as discussed in Chapter 12.

If vitamin E prevents fatty acid hydroperoxide formation, and the sulfur-containing amino acids (as precursors of glutathione) and selenium are involved in peroxide breakdown, all of these nutrients would obviously lead to a similar biochemical result, ie, lowering in the tissues of the concentrations of peroxides or products induced by them. Certain tissues or subcellular components that are inherently low in glutathione peroxidase would not be affected by selenium but would still be protected by vitamin E, which acts as an antioxidant by a mechanism not involving glutathione peroxidase.

Selenium Toxicity

Selenium is usually thought of as an element with pronounced toxic properties. When selenium is present in the diet in concentrations about 5–15 ppm, it is highly toxic to animals, as demonstrated in particular with ruminants maintained on pastures where the soil is rich in selenium. However, below about 3 ppm, selenium improves growth and is effective in combating several animal diseases. Selenium has long been known to inhibit alcoholic fermentation by yeast and the activity of certain respiratory enzymes, possibly by forming complexes with essential enzyme sulfhydryl groups.

A recent review of the biochemistry of selenium has been prepared by Stadtman (1974).

CHROMIUM

Chromium is widely distributed in the tissues, although in extremely small amounts. The total chromium content of the adult human body is estimated to be less than 6 mg. A severely restricted intake of chromium in the diets of rats and mice has been shown to impair growth and survival. These effects were ameliorated when the diet was supplemented with 5 ppm of chromium.

Some studies have suggested that trivalent chromium may act together with insulin in promoting utilization of glucose, a conclusion drawn from the observation that impairment of glucose tolerance occurs in animals maintained on low-chromium diets and that the diminished glucose tolerance can be reversed by supplementation of the diet with chromium. Recent evidence suggests that chromium is also involved in glucose tolerance in man (Davies, 1972).

2. POSSIBLY ESSENTIAL TRACE ELEMENTS

Nickel, silicon, tin, and vanadium have been suggested as essential trace elements in nutrition (Schwarz, 1974). Deficiencies of these elements have been produced in experimental animals that were raised under conditions allowing strict control of the metallic environment. These deficiencies resulted in suboptimal growth rates as well as other defects characteristically associated with the specific deficiency of each element. Nickel deficiency is characterized by suboptimal function and ultrastructural degeneration in the liver, suggesting a role for this element in the metabolism or structure of membranes. Silicon appears to be an integral component of acid mucopolysaccharides and may have a structural role in connective tissue, cartilage, skin, and bone. Tin and vanadium appear to influence lipid metabolism, possibly as oxidation-reduction catalysts.

3. NONESSENTIAL TRACE ELEMENTS

ALUMINUM

There is no conclusive evidence that aluminum performs any essential function in plants, animals, or microorganisms. This element is widely distributed in most plant and animal tissues in relatively low concentrations. Human blood has been found to contain approximately 0.15 µg of aluminum per milliliter.

Rats subsisting on a diet which supplied as little as 1 µg/day of aluminum showed no abnormalities. Large amounts fed to rats produced rickets by interfering with the absorption of phosphates.

The daily intake of aluminum in the human diet ranges from less than 10 mg to over 100 mg. In addition to the very small amounts naturally present in food and that derived from cooking utensils, aluminum may be added to the diet as sodium aluminum sulfate in baking powder and as alum, sometimes added to foods to preserve firmness. However, absorption of aluminum from the intestine is very poor. From measurements of urinary excretion it is estimated that only about 100 μg of aluminum are absorbed per day, most of the ingested aluminum being excreted in the feces even on a reasonably high intake. The total amount of aluminum in the body is about 50–150 mg.

BORON

Boron is essential for the growth of plants, and traces are found in animal tissues. Boron in food is almost completely absorbed and excreted, largely in the urine. Where high intake occurs, either by accident or during treatment of burns with boric acid, sufficient boron may be temporarily retained to cause serious toxic effects, especially in the brain.

The growth of rats maintained on diets very low in boron is not impaired.

CADMIUM

The total cadmium content of the adult human body is estimated to be about 30 mg, of which 10 mg is present in the kidney and 4 mg in the liver. Cadmium resembles zinc in its chemical characteristics.

Whole animal studies indicate that a mutual antagonism exists between cadmium and zinc, and important interactions also occur between cadmium and iron and copper. A protein, **metallothionein**, containing as much as 5.9% cadmium, 2.2% zinc, and 8.5% sulfur, has been isolated from equine renal cortex. About 25% of the amino acid residues are cysteine residues, which provide metal binding sites. This protein has a remarkably high metal content—about 10 times higher than any other known metalloprotein. A biologic function for metallothionein, in addition to its metal-sequestering role, has not yet been established.

OTHER NONESSENTIAL TRACE ELEMENTS

In addition to the elements discussed in the foregoing sections, a large number of other apparently nonessential trace elements are usually present in animal tissues in highly variable concentrations. These elements include antimony, arsenic, bismuth, germanium, gold, lead, mercury, rubidium, silver, and titanium. In the past century, the amounts of several of these elements contaminating food, water, and air have risen substantially as a consequence of man's industrial and agricultural activities. As a result, the intake of several toxic elements, including lead, mercury, and arsenic, has become important for human environmental health. A discussion of the clinical findings and treatment following intoxication by these elements and their compounds can be found in the book by Meyers & others (1976).

•   •   •

References

Babior B, Kipnes R, Curnutte J: The production by leukocytes of superoxide, a potential bactericidal agent. J Clin Invest 52:741, 1973.

Crane RK: Na$^+$-dependent transport in the intestine and other animal tissues. Fed Proc 24:1000, 1965.

Dahl JL, Hokin LE: Sodium-potassium adenosine triphosphatase. Annu Rev Biochem 43:327, 1974.

Dahl LK: Salt intake and salt need. (2 parts.) N Engl J Med 258:1152, 1205, 1958.

Davies IJT: *The Clinical Significance of the Essential Biological Metals.* Heinemann, 1972.

Davis JM, Fann WE: Lithium. Annu Rev Pharmacol 11:285, 1971.

Deane N, Smith HW: The distribution of sodium and potassium in man. J Clin Invest 31:197, 1952.

Fridovich I: Superoxide dismutases. Annu Rev Biochem 44:147, 1975.

Frost DV, Lish PM: Selenium in biology. Annu Rev Pharmacol 15:259, 1975.

Frost PM, Smith JL: Influence of potassium salts on efficiency of parenteral protein alimentation in the surgical patient. Metabolism 2:259, 1953.

Gamble JL: *Chemical Anatomy, Physiology, and Pathology of Extracellular Fluid,* 6th ed. Harvard Univ Press, 1954.

Goldberger E: *Water, Electrolyte, and Acid-Base Syndromes.* Lea & Febiger, 1975.

Jacobs A, Worwood M (editors): *Iron in Biochemistry and Medicine.* Academic Press, 1974.

Jamieson GA, Jett M, DeBernado SL: The carbohydrate sequence of the glycopeptide chains of human transferrin. J Biol Chem 246:3686, 1971.

Johnson JL, Rajagopalan KV, Cohen HJ: Molecular basis of the biological function of molybdenum: Effect of tungsten on xanthine oxidase and sulfite oxidase in the rat. J Biol Chem 249:859, 1974.

Mason EE: *Fluid, Electrolyte, and Nutrient Therapy in Surgery.* Lea & Febiger, 1974.

McCance RA, Widdowson EM: *The Composition of Food.* Her Majesty's Stationery Office, London, 1960.

Meyers FH, Jawetz E, Goldfien A: *Review of Medical Pharmacology,* 5th ed. Lange, 1976.

Osaki S, Sirivech S: Identification and partial purification of ferritin reducing enzyme in liver. Fed Proc 30:1292, 1971.

Schultz SG, Curran PF: Coupled transport of sodium and organic solutes. Physiol Rev 50:637, 1970.

Schwarz K: Recent dietary trace element research, exemplified by tin, fluorine, and silicon. Fed Proc 33:1748, 1974.

Skou JC: Enzymatic basis for active transport of Na^+ and K^+ across cell membrane. Physiol Rev 45:596, 1965.

Stadtman T: Selenium biochemistry. Science 183:915, 1974.

Thompson RHS, Wootton IDP: *Biochemical Disorders in Human Disease,* 3rd ed. Academic Press, 1970.

Topham RW, Frieden E: Identification and purification of a nonceruloplasmin ferroxidase of human serum. J Biol Chem 245:6698, 1970.

Underwood EJ: *Trace Elements in Human and Animal Nutrition,* 3rd ed. Academic Press, 1971.

Vallee BL & others: Zinc metabolism in hepatic dysfunction. Ann Intern Med 50: 1077, 1959.

31 . . .
Calorimetry:
Elements of Nutrition

Food is the source of the fuel which is converted by the metabolic processes of the body into the energy for vital activities. Calorimetry deals with the measurement of the energy requirements of the body under various physiologic conditions and of the fuel values of foods which supply this energy.

Energy Considerations in Nutrition

The unit of energy contained in foods as well as that involved in metabolic activities is most often expressed as a unit of heat, the calorie. A calorie is defined as the amount of heat required to raise the temperature of 1 g of water by 1° C (from 15° to 16° C). This amount of heat (a small calorie) is exceedingly small, so that in nutrition it is common to use instead the large calorie (written with a capital C and abbreviated Cal) or kilocalorie, which is 1000 times the energy of the small calorie.

The international unit of energy is the joule (10^7 ergs, or the energy expended when 1 kg is moved 1 meter by 1 newton). To convert energy allowances from kilocalories to joules, a factor of 4.2 may be used, ie, 1 kilocalorie = 4184 joules = 4.2 kilojoules (kJ).

All further references to calories in this chapter will be expressed as kilocalories (kcal).

Measurement of the Fuel Value of Foods

The combustion of a foodstuff in the presence of oxygen results in the production of heat. The amount of heat thus produced can be measured in a bomb calorimeter. By this technic, the caloric value of a foodstuff can be determined.

The caloric content of the 3 principal foodstuffs, determined originally by burning in a bomb calorimeter, is given in Table 31–1. Alcohol (ethyl alcohol) has

an energy value of 7 kcal/g. Energy values in kilojoules per gram are, for protein and carbohydrate, 17; for fat, 38; for ethanol, 30.

The full values given in Table 31–1 are average values, since variations occur within each class, eg, monosaccharides do not have exactly the same caloric content as polysaccharides.

When utilized in the body, carbohydrate and fat are completely oxidized to CO_2 and water, as they are in the bomb calorimeter also. Proteins, however, are not burned completely since the major end product of protein metabolism, urea, still contains some energy which is not available to the body. For this reason, the energy value of protein in the body (4.1 kcal/g) is less than that obtained in the bomb calorimeter.

It is customary to round off the energy value of foods as utilized in the body to the figures given in Table 31–1. These figures also correct for the efficiency of the digestion of foods.

Control of Body Heat

The heat generated by the body in the course of the metabolism of foodstuffs maintains the body temperature. Warm-blooded animals, such as birds and mammals, have heat-regulating mechanisms which either increase heat production or radiate or otherwise dissipate excess heat, depending on the temperature of their external environment. When the external temperature rises above the normal body temperature, 98.6° F (37° C), evaporation from the surface of the body becomes the only mechanism available for cooling the body.

Animal Calorimetry

Since all of the energy produced in the body is ultimately dissipated as heat, measurement of the vital heat production of an animal is a way to estimate its energy expenditure. There are 2 methods of accomplishing this.

A. Direct Calorimetry: In the direct calorimeter, the subject is placed in an insulated chamber; his heat production is measured directly by recording the total amount of heat transferred to a weighed quantity of water circulating through the calorimeter. The oxygen intake, the CO_2 output, and the nitrogen excretion in the urine and feces are also measured during the entire period of observation. These data are used as described below.

Table 31–1. Fuel values of foods.

| | Kilocalories per Gram | |
	In Bomb Calorimeter	In the Body*
Carbohydrate	4.1	4
Fat	9.4	9
Protein	5.6	4

*Figures are expressed in round numbers.

B. Indirect Calorimetry: Direct calorimetry is attended by considerable technical difficulties. By measuring gas exchange and determining the respiratory quotient, energy metabolism studies are considerably simplified and thus rendered applicable to field studies and to clinical analysis.

Respiratory Quotients (RQ) of Foodstuffs

The respiratory quotient is the ratio of the volume of carbon dioxide eliminated to the volume of oxygen utilized in oxidation.

A. Carbohydrates: The complete oxidation of glucose, for example, may be represented as follows:

$$C_6H_{12}O_6 + \boxed{6O_2} \longrightarrow \boxed{6CO_2} + 6H_2O$$

The RQ for carbohydrate is therefore:

$$\frac{CO_2}{O_2} = \frac{6}{6} \text{ or } 1$$

B. Fats have a lower RQ because the oxygen content of their molecule in relation to the carbon content is quite low. Consequently they require more oxygen from the outside. The oxidation of tristearin will be used to exemplify the RQ for fat.

$$2C_{57}H_{110}O_6 + \boxed{163O_2} \longrightarrow \boxed{114CO_2} + 110H_2O$$

$$\frac{CO_2}{O_2} = \frac{114}{163} = 0.70$$

C. Proteins: The oxidation of proteins cannot be so readily expressed because their chemical structure is variable. By indirect methods the RQ of proteins has been calculated to be about 0.8.

D. RQ of Mixed Diets Under Varying Conditions: In mixed diets containing varying proportions of protein, fat, and carbohydrate, the RQ is about 0.85. As the proportion of carbohydrate metabolized is increased, the RQ approaches closer to 1. When carbohydrate metabolism is impaired, as in diabetes, the RQ is lowered. Therapy with insulin is followed by an elevation in the RQ. A high carbohydrate intake, as used in fattening animals, will result in an RQ exceeding 1. This rise is caused by the conversion of much of the carbohydrate, an oxygen-rich substance, to fat, an oxygen-poor substance; a relatively small amount of oxygen is required from the outside, and the ratio of CO_2 eliminated to the oxygen taken in (the RQ) will be considerably elevated.

A reversal of the above process, ie, the conversion of fat to carbohydrate, would lower the RQ below 0.7. This has been reported but has not been generally confirmed.

Performance of Indirect Calorimetry

The use of the indirect method for calculating the total energy output and the proportions of various foodstuffs being burned may be illustrated by the following example:

The subject utilized oxygen at a rate of 414.6 liters/day and eliminated 353.3 liters of CO_2 in the same period. The urinary nitrogen for the day was 12.8 g.

Because of the incomplete metabolism of protein, the gas exchange is corrected for the amount of protein metabolized; a nonprotein RQ (nonprotein portion of the total RQ) is thus obtained.

One g of urinary nitrogen represents the combustion of an amount of protein which would require 5.92 liters of oxygen and would eliminate 4.75 liters of CO_2.

A. Calculate the Nonprotein RQ:

1. Multiply the amount of urinary nitrogen by the number of liters of oxygen required to oxidize that amount of protein represented by 1 g of urinary nitrogen.

$$12.8 \text{ g} \times 5.92 = 75.8 \text{ liters}$$

2. Multiply the amount of urinary nitrogen by the number of liters of CO_2 which result from this oxidation.

$$12.8 \text{ g} \times 4.75 = 60.8 \text{ liters of } CO_2$$

Thus, 75.8 liters of the total oxygen intake was used to oxidize protein, and 60.8 liters of the CO_2 eliminated was the product of this oxidation. The remainder was used for the oxidation of carbohydrates and fats. Therefore, to determine the nonprotein RQ, subtract these values for protein from the totals for the day.

$$\text{Oxygen: } 414.6 - 75.8 = 338.8 \text{ liters}$$
$$CO_2: 353.3 - 60.8 = 292.5 \text{ liters}$$

$$\frac{CO_2}{O_2} = \frac{292.5}{338.8} = 0.86 \text{ (nonprotein RQ)}$$

B. Convert the Nonprotein RQ to Grams of Carbohydrate and Fat Metabolized: Reliable tables have been worked out which give the proportions of carbohydrate and of fat metabolized at various RQs. According to the tables of Zuntz and Shunberg (as modified by Lusk and later by McLendon) (Table 31–2), when the nonprotein RQ is 0.86, 0.622 g of carbohydrate and 0.249 g of fat are metabolized per liter of oxygen used. Therefore, to determine the total quantities of carbohydrate and fat used, multiply these figures by the number of liters of oxygen (derived from the nonprotein RQ) consumed during the combustion of carbohydrate and fat.

$$338.8 \times 0.622 \text{ g} = 210.7 \text{ g carbohydrate}$$
$$338.8 \times 0.249 \text{ g} = 84.4 \text{ g fat}$$

C. Determine the Amount of Protein Metabolized: Each gram of urinary nitrogen represents the oxidation of 6.25 g of protein. Therefore, to determine

Table 31–2. The significance of the nonprotein respiratory quotient as regards the heat value of 1 liter of oxygen, and the relative quantity in calories of carbohydrate and fat consumed. (Zuntz & Schumberg, modified by Lusk, modified by McClendon.)*

| Nonprotein Respiratory Quotient | One Liter of Oxygen is Equivalent To | | |
| | Grams | | |
	Carbohydrate	Fat	Calories
0.707	0.000	0.502	4.686
0.71	0.016	0.497	4.690
0.72	0.055	0.482	4.702
0.73	0.094	0.465	4.714
0.74	0.134	0.450	4.727
0.75	0.173	0.433	4.739
0.76	0.213	0.417	4.751
0.77	0.254	0.400	4.764
0.78	0.294	0.384	4.776
0.79	0.334	0.368	4.788
0.80	0.375	0.350	4.801
0.81	0.415	0.334	4.813
0.82	0.456	0.317	4.825
0.83	0.498	0.301	4.838
0.84	0.539	0.284	4.850
0.85	0.580	0.267	4.862
0.86	0.622	0.249	4.875
0.87	0.666	0.232	4.887
0.88	0.708	0.215	4.899
0.89	0.741	0.197	4.911
0.90	0.793	0.180	4.924
0.91	0.836	0.162	4.936
0.92	0.878	0.145	4.948
0.93	0.922	0.127	4.961
0.94	0.966	0.109	4.973
0.95	1.010	0.091	4.985
0.96	1.053	0.073	4.998
0.97	1.098	0.055	5.010
0.98	1.142	0.036	5.022
0.99	1.185	0.018	5.035
1.00	1.232	0.000	5.047

*Reproduced, with permission, from Bodansky M: *Introduction to Physiological Chemistry*, 4th ed. Wiley, 1938.

the amount of protein metabolized, multiply the total urinary nitrogen by 6.25.

$$12.8 \text{ g} \times 6.25 = 80 \text{ g of protein}$$

D. Calculate the Total Heat Production: Multiply the quantity in grams of each foodstuff oxidized by the caloric value of that food to obtain the heat production due to its combustion. The sum of these caloric values equals the total heat production of the diet.

Carbohydrate: 210.7 g $\times$ 4 kcal = 842.8 kcal
Fat: 84.4 g $\times$ 9 kcal = 759.6 kcal
Protein: 80.0 g $\times$ 4 kcal = 320.0 kcal

Total heat production = 1922.4 kcal

BASAL METABOLISM

The total heat production or energy expenditure of the body is the sum of that required merely to maintain life (basal metabolism), together with such additional energy as may be expended for any additional activities. The lowest level of energy production consonant with life is the **basal metabolic rate.**

Conditions Necessary for Measurement of the Basal Metabolic Rate

1. A post-absorptive state; patient should have had nothing by mouth for the past 12 hours.

2. Mental and physical relaxation immediately preceding the test; usually one-half hour of bed rest is used, although ideally the patient should not arise from bed after a more prolonged rest.

3. Recumbent position during the test.

4. Patient awake.

5. Environmental temperature of 20–25° C.

Factors Influencing Basal Metabolism

A. Surface Area: The basal metabolic rates of different individuals, when expressed in terms of surface area (sq m), are remarkably constant. In general, however, smaller individuals have a higher rate of metabolism per unit of surface area than larger individuals.

B. Age: In the newborn the rate is low; it rises to maximum at age 5, after which the rate begins to decline, continuing into old age. There is, however, a relative rise just before puberty. Examples of influence of age on the basal metabolic rate: At age 6, the normal basal metabolic rate is between 50 and 53 kcal/sq m/hour; at age 21 it is between 36 and 41 kcal/sq m/hour.

C. Sex: Women normally have a lower basal metabolic rate than men. The basal metabolic rate of females declines between the ages of 5 and 17 more rapidly than that of males.

D. Climate: The basal metabolic rate is lower in warm climates.

E. Racial Variations: When the basal metabolic rate of different racial groups is compared, certain variations are noted. For example, the basal metabolic rates of Oriental female students living in the USA average 10% below the standard basal metabolic rate for American women of the same age; the basal metabolic rates of adult Chinese are equal to or below the lower limit of normal for Occidentals; high values (33% above normal) have been reported for Eskimos living in the region of Baffin Bay.

F. State of Nutrition: In starvation and undernourishment, the basal metabolic rate is lowered.

G. Disease: Infectious and febrile diseases raise the metabolic rate, usually in proportion to the elevation of the temperature. There is an increase of approximately 12% of the basal caloric requirement for each degree centigrade (8% per degree Fahrenheit) by which the body temperature is above normal. Diseases which are characterized by increased activity of cells also increase heat production because of this increased cellular activity. Thus, the metabolic rate may increase in such diseases as leukemia, polycythemia, some types of anemia, cardiac failure, hypertension, and dyspnea—all of which involve increased cellular activity. Perforation of an eardrum causes falsely high readings.

H. Effects of Hormones: The hormones also affect metabolism. Thyroxine is the most important of the hormones in this respect, and the principal use of calorimetry in clinical practice is in the diagnosis of thyroid disease. The rate is lowered in hypothyroidism and increased in hyperthyroidism. Changes in the basal metabolic rate are also noted in pituitary disease.

Other than thyroxine, the only hormone which has a direct effect on the rate of heat production is epinephrine, although the effect of epinephrine is rapid in onset and brief in duration. Tumors of the adrenal (pheochromocytoma) cause an elevation in the basal metabolic rate. In adrenal insufficiency (Addison's disease), the basal metabolism is subnormal, whereas adrenal tumors and Cushing's disease may produce a slight increase in the metabolic rate.

Measurement of Basal Metabolism

In clinical practice, the basal metabolic rate can be estimated with sufficient accuracy merely by measuring the oxygen consumption of the patient for 2 6-minute periods under basal conditions. This is corrected to standard conditions of temperature and barometric pressure. The average oxygen consumption for the 2 periods is multiplied by 10 to convert it to an hourly basis and then multiplied by 4.825 kcal, the heat production represented by each liter of oxygen consumed. This gives the heat production of the patient in kcal per hour. This is corrected to kcal per square meter body surface per hour by dividing the kcal per hour by the patient's surface area. A simple formula for calculating the surface area is as follows:

$$\frac{\text{Circumference of}}{\text{midthigh (in cm)} \times 2} \times \frac{\text{Height}}{\text{(in cm)}} = \frac{\text{Surface area}}{\text{(in sq cm)}}$$

The classical formula is that of Du Bois, as follows:

Du Bois' Surface Area Formula

$$A = H^{0.725} \times W^{0.425} \times 71.84$$

where A = surface area in sq cm,
H = height in cm,
and W = weight in kg

(Surface area in sq cm divided by 10,000 = surface area in sq m)

In practice, a nomogram which relates height and weight to surface area is used. It is based on the Du Bois formula.

Calculation of Basal Metabolic Rate

The normal basal metabolic rate for an individual of the patient's age and sex is obtained from standard tables. The patient's actual rate is expressed as a plus or minus percentage of the normal. *Example:* A male, age 35 years, 170 cm in height and 70 kg in weight, consumed an average of 1.2 liters of oxygen (corrected to normal temperature and pressure: 0° C, 760 mm Hg) in a 6-minute period.

1.2 × 10 = 12 liters of oxygen/hour
12 × 4.825 = 58 kcal/hour
Surface area = 1.8 sq m (from Du Bois' formula)
Basal metabolic rate = 58 kcal/1.8 = 32 kcal/sq m/hour

The normal basal metabolic rate for this patient, by reference to the Du Bois standards, is 39.5 kcal/sq m/hour. His basal metabolic rate, which is below normal, is then reported as:

$$\frac{39.5 - 32}{39.5} \times 100 = 18.98\% \text{ or } \textbf{minus 18.98}$$

A basal metabolic rate between −15 and +20% is considered normal. In hyperthyroidism, the basal metabolic rate may exceed +50 to +75%. The basal metabolic rate may be −30 to −60% in hypothyroidism.

MEASUREMENT OF ENERGY REQUIREMENTS

The metabolic rate increases with activity. Maximal increases occur during exercise—as much as 600–800% over basal. The energy requirement over a 24-hour period therefore will vary considerably in accordance with the amount of physical activity in which the subject is engaged. Examples of energy expenditures of mature men and women engaged in light occupations are given in Table 31–3.

It is suggested that the daily energy requirement of a moderately active person might be increased by about 300 kcal over the totals given in Table 31–3. For very active persons such as those engaged in heavy athletic pursuits, military personnel in training, or workers in heavy construction, the allowances might be increased by 600–900 kcal per day.

In attempts to regulate body weight, prime emphasis must be placed on restriction of excess caloric intake. Weight loss cannot be achieved under any circumstances as long as caloric intake exceeds expenditure, including provision for growth if applicable. However, exercise as a means to assist in weight loss or to control weight is useful in addition to caloric restriction. The limitations in weight reduction of exercise as compared to control of caloric intake may be appreciated by reference to Table 31–4, which shows how many minutes of various forms of exercise are required

Table 31–3. Examples of daily energy expenditures of mature men and women in light occupations.*

Activity Category	Time (hr)	Man, 70 kg		Woman, 58 kg	
		Rate (kcal/min)†	Total (kcal [kJ])†	Rate (kcal/min)	Total (kcal [kJ])
Sleeping, reclining	8	1.0–1.2	540 (2270)	0.9–1.1	440 (1850)
Very light Seated and standing activities, auto and truck driving, laboratory work, typing, playing musical instruments, sewing, ironing	12	Up to 2.5	1300 (5460)	Up to 2.0	900 (3780)
Light Walking on level, 2.5–3 mph, tailoring, pressing, garage work, electrical trades, carpentry, restaurant trades, cannery workers, washing clothes, shopping with light load, golf, sailing, table tennis, volleyball	3	2.5–4.9	600 (2520)	2.0–3.9	450 (1890)
Moderate Walking 3.5–4 mph, plastering, weeding and hoeing, loading and stacking bales, scrubbing floors, shopping with heavy load, cycling, skiing, tennis, dancing	1	5.0–7.4	300 (1260)	4.0–5.9	240 (1010)
Heavy Walking with load uphill, tree felling, work with pick and shovel, basketball, swimming, climbing, football	0	7.5–12.0		6.0–10.0	
Total	24		2740 (11,500)		2030 (8530)

*Reproduced from: *Recommended Dietary Allowances,* 8th ed. National Academy of Sciences, 1974. The data are from Durnin JVGA, Passmore R: *Energy, Work and Leisure.* Heineman, 1967.
†kcal = kilocalories (Cal); kJ = kilojoules = 4.2 kcal.

to dissipate the energy acquired by ingestion of various items of food or beverage.

SPECIFIC DYNAMIC ACTION (SDA)

The specific dynamic action of a foodstuff is the extra heat production, over and above the caloric value of a given amount of food, which is produced when this food is used by the body. For example, when an amount of protein which contains 100 kcal (25 g) is metabolized, the heat production in the body is not 100 kcal but 130 kcal. This extra 30 kcal is the product of the specific dynamic action of the protein. In the body, a 100 kcal portion of fat produces 113 kcal, and a 100 kcal portion of carbohydrate produces 105 kcal. The origin of this extra heat is not clear, but it is attributable to the activity of the tissues which are metabolizing these foodstuffs.

The specific dynamic action of each foodstuff, as given above, is obtained when each foodstuff is fed separately; but when these foods are taken in a mixed diet, the dynamic effect of the whole diet cannot be predicted by merely adding the individual effects of each foodstuff in accordance with its contribution to the diet, eg, 30% of the caloric value of protein, 13% of the caloric value of fat, and 5% of the caloric value of carbohydrate. According to Forbes, the dynamic effects of beef muscle protein, glucose, and lard, when each was fed separately, were 32, 20, and 16%, respectively, of their caloric content. But when the glucose and protein were combined, the dynamic effect was

12.5% less than predicted from the sum of their individual effects; combining lard, glucose, and protein produced 22% less dynamic effect than predicted; a glucose-lard combination was 35% less, and a protein-lard mixture 54% less than calculated from the individual percentages of each foodstuff.

These observations are of importance because they indicate that the high specific dynamic action of protein can be reduced depending on the quantities of other foodstuffs in the diet. Forbes's data show that fat (lard) has a greater influence on specific dynamic action than does any other nutrient, ie, fat decreases the specific dynamic action more than any other nutrient.

In calculating the total energy requirement for the day, it is customary to add 10% to the total caloric requirement to provide energy for the specific dynamic action, ie, expense of utilization of the foods consumed. This figure may be too large, particularly if the fat content of the diet is high.

THE ELEMENTS OF NUTRITION

The Components of an Adequate Diet

There are 6 major components of the diet. **Carbohydrate, fat,** and **protein** yield energy, provide for growth, and maintain tissue subjected to wear and tear. **Vitamins, minerals,** and **water,** although they do not yield energy, are essential parts of the chemical mechanisms for the utilization of energy and for the synthesis of various necessary metabolites such as hormones and enzymes. The minerals are also incorporated into the structure of the tissue and, in solution, play an important role in acid-base equilibrium.

The Energy Aspect of the Diet

Energy for physiologic processes is provided by the combustion of carbohydrate, fat, and protein. The daily energy requirement or the daily caloric need is the sum of the basal energy demands plus that required for the additional work of the day. During periods of growth, pregnancy, or convalescence, extra calories must be provided.

While all 3 major nutrients yield energy to the body, carbohydrate and, to a lesser extent, fat are physiologically the most economical sources. Protein serves primarily to provide for tissue growth and repair; but if the caloric intake from other foods is inadequate, it is burned for energy.

The caloric requirements of persons of varying sizes and under various physiologic conditions are tabulated in Table 31–6.

Obesity is almost always the result of excess consumption of calories. Treatment is therefore directed at reducing the caloric intake from fat and carbohydrate but maintaining the protein, vitamin, and mineral intake at normal levels. An adequate diet containing not more than 800–1000 kcal should be maintained and normal or increased amounts of energy expended until the proper weight is reached.

"Protein-Sparing Action" of Carbohydrates & Fats

Carbohydrate and fat "spare" protein and thus make it available for anabolic purposes. This is particularly important in the nutrition of patients, especially those being fed parenterally, when it is difficult or even impossible for them to take in enough calories. If the caloric intake is inadequate, giving proteins orally or amino acids intravenously is a relatively inefficient way of supplying energy because the primary function of proteins is tissue synthesis and repair and not energy production.

Distribution of Calories in the Diet

The amounts of each of the 3 energy-yielding components in the diet of persons in the USA have changed markedly during the present century. Most noteworthy is the decline in carbohydrate intake and a corresponding increase in the intake of fats. The total protein content of the diet has remained at an amount that supplies approximately 11–12% of the total caloric intake per day. Carbohydrate and fat now supply about the same amount of energy in the diet in the USA, ie, 46 and 42%, respectively.

Whereas starches supplied about 43% of dietary food energy during the first decade of this century, the amounts of starches have now declined so that they now comprise only about 29% of the total energy contained in the diet; furthermore, intake of simple sugars has increased to a point where they now supply 16–17% of the total energy supplied in the daily food consumed. The increase in fat intake is attributable mainly to the use of more separated fats and oils and, most significantly, to increased consumption of meat.

A. The Carbohydrate Intake: Carbohydrate is the first and most efficient source of energy for vital processes. The principal sources of carbohydrates in foods are the sugars, starches, and cellulose. Cereal grains, potatoes, and rice, the staple foods of most countries, are the main sources of dietary carbohydrate. Indeed, such carbohydrates may have to be depended on to furnish 60–80% of the total caloric intake when there is a scarcity of proteins and fats.

In the metabolic process of gluconeogenesis, carbohydrate can be supplied from most amino acids as well as from the glycerol moiety of fats. However, some preformed carbohydrate is necessary as well. It is considered that a minimum of 5 g of carbohydrate per 100 kcal of the total diet is necessary to prevent the development of ketosis, but prevention of the untoward effects of fasting or of high-fat diets will require 50–100 g of digestible carbohydrate per day.

B. The Fat Intake: Because of its high fuel value, fat is an important component of the diet. Furthermore, the palatability of foods is generally enhanced by their content of fat. As a form of energy storage in the body, fat has more than twice the value of protein or carbohydrate.

Fatty acids can be used directly as sources of energy by all of the cells of the body; indeed, skeletal muscle and the myocardium appear to utilize fatty acids preferentially as a source of fuel. Exceptions to the otherwise extensive use of fatty acids by the cells of most tissues are the erythrocytes and the cells of the central nervous system, although in total starvation, after a short period of adaptation, the brain can use ketones formed from fatty acids or certain amino acids.

The human requirement for fat is not precisely known. Important aspects of the contribution of fats to nutrition are their content of the essential fatty acids, linoleic and arachidonic acids, as well as the fact that dietary fats serve as the major carriers of the fat-soluble vitamins. With the exception of these specific contributions of fats to the diet, it appears that there is no absolute need for lipid in the diet. The specific contributions of fats can be supplied by the daily consumption of 15–25 g of appropriate lipids.

An important consideration in lipid nutrition relates to dietary factors influencing blood cholesterol levels. It is now well established that the level of serum cholesterol is decreased by the ingestion of polyunsaturated fatty acids and increased by saturated fatty acids as well as by dietary cholesterol itself. While there continues to be some disagreement about the relative importance of dietary cholesterol as compared to other factors known to influence the blood cholesterol levels, there is a growing body of evidence supporting the idea that over a certain range of dietary intake the amount of cholesterol ingested does exert a substantial influence on the levels of cholesterol in the serum. Mattson & others (1972) have concluded from studies of adult male subjects fed controlled diets containing 106–317 mg of cholesterol per 1000 kcal that

Table 31—4. Energy equivalents chart. Number of minutes required at the activities listed to expend the caloric energy of food items shown below.*

	Caloric Content	Reclining	Walking	Bicycle Riding	Swimming	Running
Beverages, alcoholic						
Beer, 8 oz glass	114	88	22	14	10	6
Gin, 1½ oz jigger	105	81	20	13	9	5
Manhattan, 3½ oz cocktail	164	126	32	20	15	8
Martini, 3½ oz cocktail	140	108	27	17	13	7
Old-fashioned, 4 oz glass	179	138	34	22	16	9
Rye whiskey, 1½ oz jigger	119	92	23	15	11	6
Scotch whiskey, 1½ oz jigger	105	81	20	13	9	5
Tom Collins, 10 oz glass	180	138	35	20	16	9
Wine, 3½ oz glass	84	65	16	10	8	4
Beverages, nonalcoholic						
Carbonated, 8 oz glass	106	82	20	13	9	5
Ice cream soda, chocolate	255	196	49	31	23	13
Malted milk shake, chocolate	502	386	97	61	45	26
Milk, 8 oz glass	166	128	32	20	15	9
Milk, skim, 8 oz glass	81	62	16	10	7	4
Milk shake, chocolate	421	324	81	51	38	22
Desserts						
Cake, 2-layer, 1/12	356	274	68	43	32	18
Cookie, chocolate chip	51	39	10	6	5	3
Doughnut	151	116	29	18	13	8
Ice cream, 1/6 qt	193	148	37	24	17	10
Gelatin, with cream	117	90	23	14	10	6
Pie, apple, 1/6	377	290	73	46	34	19
Sherbet, 1/6 qt	177	136	34	22	16	9
Strawberry shortcake	400	308	77	49	36	21
Fruits and fruit juices						
Apple, large	101	78	19	12	9	5
Banana, small	88	68	17	11	8	4
Orange, medium	68	52	13	8	6	4
Peach, medium	46	35	9	6	4	2
Apple juice, 8 oz glass	118	91	23	14	10	6
Orange juice, 8 oz glass	120	92	23	15	11	6
Tomato juice, 8 oz glass	48	37	9	6	4	2
Meats						
Bacon, 2 strips	96	74	18	12	9	5
Ham, 2 slices	167	128	32	20	15	9
Pork chop, loin	314	242	60	38	28	16
Steak, T-bone	235	181	45	29	21	12
Miscellaneous						
Bread and butter, 1 slice	78	60	15	10	7	4
Cereal, dry, 1/2 cup, with milk and sugar	200	154	38	24	18	10
French dressing, 1 tbsp	99	45	11	7	5	3
Mayonnaise, 1 tbsp	92	71	18	11	8	5
Pancake, with syrup	124	95	24	15	11	6
Spaghetti, 1 serving	396	305	76	48	35	20
Cottage cheese, 1 tbsp	27	21	5	3	2	1
Poultry and eggs						
Chicken, fried, 1/2 breast	232	178	45	28	21	12
Chicken, "TV dinner"	542	217	104	66	48	28
Turkey, 1 slice	130	100	25	16	12	7
Egg, fried	110	85	21	13	10	6
Egg, boiled	77	59	15	9	7	4
Sandwiches and snacks						
Club	590	454	113	72	53	30
Hamburger	300	269	67	43	31	18
Roast beef, with gravy	430	331	83	52	38	22
Tuna salad	278	214	53	34	25	14
Pizza, with cheese, 1/8	180	138	35	22	16	9
Potato chips, 1 serving	108	83	21	13	10	6
Cheddar cheese, 1 oz	111	85	21	14	10	6

*Adapted from Konishi FJ: J Am Diet Assoc 46:187, 1965.

Table 31–4 (cont'd). Energy equivalents chart. Number of minutes required at the activities
listed to expend the caloric energy of food items shown below.*

	Caloric Content	Reclining	Walking	Bicycle Riding	Swimming	Running
Seafood						
Clams, 6 medium	109	77	19	12	9	5
Cod, steamed, 1 piece	80	62	15	10	7	4
Crabmeat, 1/2 cup	68	52	13	8	6	4
Haddock, 1 piece	71	55	14	9	6	4
Halibut steak, 1/4 lb	205	158	39	25	18	11
Lobster, 1 medium	55	38	10	6	4	3
Shrimp, French fried, 1 serving	180	136	35	22	16	9
Vegetables						
Beans, green, 1 cup	27	21	5	3	2	1
Beets, canned, 1/2 cup	38	29	7	5	3	2
Carrot, raw	42	32	8	5	4	2
Lettuce, 3 large leaves	30	23	6	4	3	2
Peas, green, 1/2 cup	55	43	11	7	5	3
Potato, boiled, 1 medium	100	77	19	12	9	5
Spinach, fresh, 1/2 cup	20	15	4	2	2	1

dietary cholesterol can play a major role in determining blood cholesterol levels. The fatty acid composition of all of their experimental diets approximated that normally consumed in the USA, ie, 40% saturated and 12% polyunsaturated fatty acids. The intake of the experimental group that took a diet containing 317 mg cholesterol per 1000 kcal approximates the cholesterol intake of the typical American diet. In this group, the serum cholesterol level was increased by about 25% over that observed when the same subjects were subsisting on a cholesterol-free diet. Over the entire range of cholesterol feeding utilized in these experiments, the increase in serum cholesterol was linear; each 100 mg cholesterol per 1000 kcal resulted in approximately a 12 mg increase in serum cholesterol.

Up to a certain point, the isocaloric replacement of carbohydrate or protein by fat results in better growth in animals. This may be due to the effect of fat in reducing the specific dynamic action of the ration, thus improving the caloric efficiency of the diet.

At ordinary levels of intake, 20–25% of the calories of the diet might be derived from fats; for a 3000 kcal intake, this would represent 66–83 g of fat. When higher caloric levels are consumed, more fat is likely to be included. However, the American Heart Association recommends that the energy derived from fats should not exceed 35% of the total daily intake and that, of that amount, less than 10% of the total calories should be derived from saturated fatty acids and up to 10% from polyunsaturated fatty acids.

C. The Protein Requirement: A minimal amount of protein is indispensable in the diet to provide for the replacement of tissue protein, which constantly undergoes destruction and resynthesis. This is often spoken of as the **wear and tear quota.** The protein requirement is considerably increased, however, by the demands of growth, increased metabolism (as in infection with fever), in burns, and after trauma. The recommended intake of protein for individuals of vari-

ous age groups is shown in Table 31–6. As already noted, these presume that the caloric demand is adequately supplied by other foods so that the ingested protein is available for tissue growth and repair.

The requirement for protein in the diet is, however, not only quantitative; there is also an important qualitative aspect since the metabolism of protein is inextricably connected with that of its constituent amino acids. Certain amino acids are called indispensable in the diet in the sense that they must be obtained preformed and cannot be synthesized by the animal organism. The remainder, the so-called dispensable amino acids, are also required by the organism since they are found in the protein of the tissues, but they can apparently be synthesized, presumably from alpha-keto acids, by amination. The list of indispensable or "essential" amino acids varies with the animal species tested (eg, the chick requires glycine). It may also vary with the physiologic state of the animal. For some amino acids (eg, arginine) the rate of synthesis may be too slow to supply fully the needs of the animal. Histidine in the diet is also necessary to maintain growth during childhood. Such amino acids are said to be **relatively** indispensable. The nutritive value of a protein is now known to be dependent on its content of essential amino acids. Examples of incomplete proteins are gelatin, which lacks tryptophan; and zein of corn, which is low in both tryptophan and lysine. Such incomplete proteins are unable to support growth if given as the sole source of protein in the diet.

As was indicated above, 9 of the amino acids contained in natural proteins are indispensable nutrients for the human species. Cystine can spare as much as 80–90% of the methionine requirement by supplying some needs for organically bound sulfur, and tyrosine can spare 70–75% of the need for phenylalanine. This is so because normal metabolism of methionine and phenylalanine involves their conversion in whole or in part to cystine or tyrosine.

Table 31–5. Estimated amino acid requirements of man.*

Amino Acid	Requirement (per kg of body wt), mg/day			Amino acid Pattern for High Quality Proteins (mg/g of protein)
	Infant (3–6 mo)†	Child (10–12 yr)	Adult	
Histidine	33	?	?	17
Isoleucine	80	28	12	42
Leucine	128	42	16	70
Lysine	97	44	12	51
Total S-containing amino acids	45	22	10	26
Total aromatic amino acids	132	22	16	73
Threonine	63	28	8	35
Tryptophan	19	4	3	11
Valine	89	25	14	48

*Reproduced from page 44 in: *Recommended Dietary Allowances,* 8th ed. National Academy of Sciences, 1974.
†Two grams per kilogram of body weight per day of protein of the quality listed in the last column would meet the amino acid needs of the infant.

Some of the unnatural (D-) forms of the amino acids have been found to fulfill in whole or in part the requirement for a given amino acid. Thus, DL-methionine was as effective as L-methionine in supplying the requirement for this amino acid. Significant amounts of D-phenylalanine are utilized by the human organism, perhaps as much as 0.5 g/day. On the other hand, D-valine, D-isoleucine, and D-threonine individually do not exert a measurable effect upon nitrogen balance when the corresponding L-form is absent from the diet.

Amino acid requirements for infants (Holt & Snyderman, 1965), for children (Nakagawa & others, 1964), for men (Rose, 1957), and for women (Leverton, 1959) have been estimated. These are shown in Table 31–5. The values shown for adults are higher than those previously quoted because they have been adjusted upward by 30% to allow for individual variability. In summarizing his original observations on the amino acid requirements of men, Rose stated that when the diet furnished the 8 "essential" amino acids (histidine was not included) at their "recommended" levels of intake and extra nitrogen was provided as glycine to provide a total daily intake of only 3–5 g, nitrogen balance could be maintained in his subjects. Expressed as protein (N × 6.25), this quantity of nitrogen represents about 22 g of protein, an amount far below the recommended daily intake for adults. Subsequent studies have indicated that the maintenance of adult subjects in nitrogen equilibrium by the use of such limited amounts of amino acids is not uniformly successful. It is therefore probable that the requirements listed in Table 31–5 are to be regarded as minimal. Nonetheless, the amounts of the essential amino acids required for the maintenance of adult human need supply only about 20% of the total nitrogen requirement provided only that the pattern of

ingested essential amino acids is properly balanced. It should also be apparent that, in assessing protein requirements, consideration must be given to the intake of the essential amino acids rather than only to that of whole proteins of varying essential amino acid content.

Although it is not commonly appreciated, there is virtually no evidence that intakes of protein exceeding requirements in healthy adults have any nutritional benefit. On the other hand, low-protein diets tend to be limited in their content of foods of animal origin and thus low in important trace nutrients. They are also generally less palatable.

The caloric intake necessary for nitrogen balance in human subjects receiving amino acids (eg, casein hydrolysate) is higher than for subjects receiving whole protein (eg, whole casein, by mouth). For example, with whole protein, nitrogen balance could be attained with 35 kcal/kg, whereas as much as 53–60 kcal/kg were required when amino acids were used as the sole source of nitrogen.

Proteins differ in "biologic value" depending on their content of essential amino acids. The proteins of eggs, dairy products, kidney, and liver have high biologic values because they contain all of the essential amino acids. Good quality proteins, which are somewhat less efficient in supplying amino acids, include shellfish, soybeans, peanuts, potatoes, and the muscle tissue of meats, poultry, and fish. Fair proteins are those of cereals and most root vegetables. The proteins of most nuts and legumes are of poor biologic value. It is important to point out, however, that 2 or more proteins in themselves only "poor" or "fair" in quality may have a "good" biologic value when taken together because they may complement one another in supplying the necessary amino acids.

It is of interest to recall that proteins, in addition to their other important functions, also constitute the most important sources of nitrogen, sulfur, and phosphorus for the body.

Amino acid requirements for the human infant are, in general, higher than for the adult when expressed on the basis of body weight. It is also important to note that histidine is to be considered an essential amino acid for requirements of growth in the young infant.

Many amino acids have specific functions in metabolism in addition to their general role as constituents of the tissue proteins. Examples are cited in Chapter 23. They include the role of methionine as a methyl donor, cystine as a source of SH groups, the dicarboxylic acids in transamination, tryptophan as a precursor of niacin, arginine and the urea cycle, etc.

A deficiency of protein and calories among young children is the single most important nutritional problem in the world today. The clinical syndromes descriptive of these nutritional deficiency states are **kwashiorkor** and **marasmus**. In kwashiorkor, protein deficiency is the principal cause of the disease state, whereas in nutritional marasmus there is a generalized deficiency in food intake, most notably in respect to calories and protein. Although marasmus is commonly

Table 31–6. Recommended daily dietary allowances.[1] (Revised 1974.)

	Age (years)	Weight (kg)	Weight (lb)	Height (cm)	Height (in)	Energy (kcal)[2]	Protein (g)	Fat-Soluble Vitamins Vitamin A Activity (RE)[3]	Fat-Soluble Vitamins Vitamin A Activity (IU)	Vitamin D (IU)	Vitamin E Activity[4] (IU)	Water-Soluble Vitamins Ascorbic Acid (mg)	Folacin[5] (µg)	Niacin[6] (mg)	Riboflavin (mg)	Thiamin (mg)	Vitamin B6 (mg)	Vitamin B12 (µg)	Minerals Calcium (mg)	Phosphorus (mg)	Iodine (µg)	Iron (mg)	Magnesium (mg)	Zinc (mg)
Infants	0.0–0.5	6	14	60	24	kg × 117	kg × 2.2	420[7]	1400	400	4	35	50	5	0.4	0.3	0.3	0.3	360	240	35	10	60	3
	0.5–1.0	9	20	71	28	kg × 108	kg × 2.0	400	2000	400	5	35	50	8	0.6	0.5	0.4	0.3	540	400	45	15	70	5
Children	1–3	13	28	86	34	1300	23	400	2000	400	7	40	100	9	0.8	0.7	0.6	1.0	800	800	60	15	150	10
	4–6	20	44	110	44	1800	30	500	2500	400	9	40	200	12	1.1	0.9	0.9	1.5	800	800	80	10	200	10
	7–10	30	66	135	54	2400	36	700	3300	400	10	40	300	16	1.2	1.2	1.2	2.0	800	800	110	10	250	10
Males	11–14	44	97	158	63	2800	44	1000	5000	400	12	45	400	18	1.5	1.4	1.6	3.0	1200	1200	130	18	350	15
	15–18	61	134	172	69	3000	54	1000	5000	400	15	45	400	20	1.8	1.5	2.0	3.0	1200	1200	150	18	400	15
	19–22	67	147	172	69	3000	54	1000	5000	400	15	45	400	20	1.8	1.5	2.0	3.0	800	800	140	10	350	15
	23–50	70	154	172	69	2700	56	1000	5000		15	45	400	18	1.6	1.4	2.0	3.0	800	800	130	10	350	15
	51+	70	154	172	69	2400	56	1000	5000		15	45	400	16	1.5	1.2	2.0	3.0	800	800	110	10	350	15
Females	11–14	44	97	155	62	2400	44	800	4000	400	12	45	400	16	1.3	1.2	1.6	3.0	1200	1200	115	18	300	15
	15–18	54	119	162	65	2100	48	800	4000	400	12	45	400	14	1.4	1.1	2.0	3.0	1200	1200	115	18	300	15
	19–22	58	128	162	65	2100	46	800	4000	400	12	45	400	14	1.4	1.1	2.0	3.0	800	800	100	18	300	15
	23–50	58	128	162	65	2000	46	800	4000		12	45	400	13	1.2	1.0	2.0	3.0	800	800	100	18	300	15
	51+	58	128	162	65	1800	46	800	4000		12	45	400	12	1.1	1.0	2.0	3.0	800	800	80	10	300	15
Pregnant						+300	+30	1000	5000	400	15	60	800	+2	+0.3	+0.3	2.5	4.0	1200	1200	125	18+[8]	450	20
Lactating						+500	+20	1200	6000	400	15	80	600	+4	+0.5	+0.3	2.5	4.0	1200	1200	150	18	450	25

Reference: *Recommended Dietary Allowances*, 8th rev ed. Food and Nutrition Board, National Research Council – National Academy of Sciences, 1974.

[1] The allowances are intended to provide for individual variations among most normal persons as they live in the USA under usual environmental stresses. Diets should be based on a variety of common foods in order to provide other nutrients for which human requirements have been less well defined. See text for more detailed discussion of allowances and of nutrients not tabulated.

[2] Kilojoules (kJ) = 4.2 × kcal.

[3] RE = Retinol equivalents.

[4] Total vitamin E activity, estimated to be 80% as α-tocopherol and 20% other tocopherols. See text for variation in allowances.

[5] The folacin allowances refer to dietary sources as determined by *Lactobacillus casei* assay. Pure forms of folacin may be effective in doses less than one-fourth of the recommended dietary allowance.

[6] Although allowances are expressed as niacin, it is recognized that on the average 1 mg of niacin is derived from each 60 mg of dietary tryptophan.

[7] Vitamin A activity is assumed to be all as retinol in milk during the first 6 months of life. All subsequent intakes are assumed to be half as retinol and half as β-carotene when calculated from international units. As retinol equivalents, three-fourths are as retinol and one-fourth as β-carotene.

[8] This increased requirement cannot be met by ordinary diets; therefore, the use of supplemental iron is recommended.

Table 31–7. The vitamins in nutrition.

I. Fat-Soluble Vitamins

Nomenclature	Functions	Metabolism	Important Sources	Stability
Vitamin A (Retinol)	Maintenance of the integrity of epithelial tissue. Constituent of visual purple (rhodopsin) of retinal cells. Essential to growth, particularly of skeleton and other connective tissues.	*Absorption:* From gastrointestinal tract, vitamin A follows pathway of fats; consequently, any impairment in fat absorption impairs absorption of vitamin A. *Storage:* In liver (95%). *Deficiency:* Dry, keratinized epithelium; night blindness; xerophthalmia; arrested growth.	Fish liver oils, liver, butter, cream, whole milk, whole-milk cheese, egg yolk. Dark green leafy vegetables, yellow vegetables and fruits, fortified margarine. Principal source in foods is as the provitamin beta-carotene. The vitamin itself (Retinol) occurs relatively rarely in foods and is confined to lipids of animal tissues.	Insoluble in water; fat soluble. Associated with lipid in foods. Stable to heat by usual cooking methods. Destroyed by oxidation, drying, and very high temperatures.
Vitamin D Vitamin D_2: activated ergosterol (ergocalciferol). Vitamin D_3: activated 7-dehydrocholesterol (cholecalciferol).	Increases absorption of calcium and phosphorus from the intestine. Essential to ossification. Influences handling of phosphate by kidneys. Active form in tissues: 1,25-Dihydroxycholecalciferol.	*Absorption:* From intestine with fats, bile salts essential; can be synthesized in skin by activity of ultraviolet light on provitamin (D_3). *Storage:* Chiefly in liver. *Deficiency:* Rickets in children; tetanic convulsions in infants with severe deficiency.	Fish-liver oils, fortified milk, activated sterols, exposure to sunlight. Very small amounts in butter, liver, egg yolks.	Fat soluble. Relatively stable to heat and oxidation.
Vitamin E Mainly alpha-tocopherol; also beta-, gamma-, delta-tocopherol.	Exerts anti-oxidant effect to protect other vitamins in foods. May have auxiliary function in tissue respiration. In experimental animals, in association with other factors, prevents certain types of liver necrosis. No demonstrated function in human nutrition except in some infants immediately postpartum, particularly prematures. Need may be related to unsaturated fatty acid intake.	*Absorption:* Similar to other fat-soluble vitamins. Transfer via placenta is limited; mammary gland transfer better; hence, breast milk is effective source for infants. *Deficiency:* May occur in malabsorptive states associated with lipid malabsorption.	Plant tissues; oils of wheat germ, rice germ, cottonseed; green leafy vegetables, nuts, legumes, milk, eggs; muscle meats, fish.	Fat soluble. Not affected by heat or acid. Oxidized in rancid fats and in the presence of lead and iron salts, alkali, ultraviolet light.
Vitamin K Antihemorrhagic vitamin; coagulation vitamin. (Many compounds related to 2-methyl-1,4-naphthoquinone have some K activity.)	Catalyzes synthesis of prothrombin by the liver. Required for activity of some blood clotting (thromboplastic) factors. May also participate in tissue respiration.	*Absorption:* Similar to other fat-soluble vitamins. *Utilization:* Presence of bile needed; impairment in fat absorption seriously affects vitamin K absorption. Produced by intestinal microorganisms; therefore, antibiotic suppressive therapy may induce vitamin K deficiency. *Storage:* Limited amount in liver. *Deficiency:* Hypoprothrombinemia with resultant prolonged blood clotting; uncontrollable hemorrhage in newborn.	Green leaves, such as alfalfa, spinach, cabbage; liver. Synthesis in intestine by activity of microorganisms is probably most important source. Dietary deficiency unlikely.	Fat soluble. Unstable to alkali and light. Fairly stable to heat.

II. Water-Soluble Vitamins

Vitamin	Function	Absorption, Storage, Excretion, Deficiency	Sources	Stability
Ascorbic acid Vitamin C Antiscorbutic vitamin	Maintains normal intercellular material of cartilage, dentine, and bone. Probably has specific role in collagen synthesis by activity on proline hydroxylation. Association with oxidation-reduction systems in tissues. Metabolism of some amino acids, eg, tyrosine, proline.	*Storage:* Large quantity in adrenal cortex. With exception of muscle, tissues with high metabolic activity have increased concentrations. *Excretion:* Urine. *Deficiency:* Mild—petechial hemorrhages. Severe—loosening of teeth, lesions of gums, poor wound healing, easily fractured bones, scurvy.	Citrus fruits, tomatoes, strawberries, cantaloupe, cabbage, broccoli, kale, potatoes, green peppers, salad greens.	Soluble in water. Most easily destroyed of all vitamins—by heat, air, alkali, enzymes. Acid inhibits destruction. Copper accelerates destruction. Cooking generally reduces vitamin C content of food. Consumption of some uncooked foods essential to ensure adequate intake.
Thiamin Vitamin B$_1$ Antiberiberi vitamin	Constituent of enzyme systems of tissues, particularly in connection with decarboxylation (eg, pyruvic and ketoglutaric acids). Deficiency affects mainly peripheral nervous system, gastrointestinal tract, and cardiovascular system.	*Absorption:* Readily absorbed in aqueous solutions from both small and large intestines. *Storage:* Limited; hence, day-to-day supply needed. *Excretion:* Excess excreted in urine; also to some extent in perspiration; also in urine. *Deficiency:* Anorexia, gastrointestinal atony and constipation, beriberi (including polyneuritis, cardiac failure, and edema). Requirement increased by high carbohydrate intake; also in fever, hyperthyroidism, pregnancy, lactation.	Lean pork; liver, heart, kidney; brewer's yeast, wheat germ, whole-grain or enriched cereals and breads; soybeans, legumes, peanuts, milk.	Soluble in water. Stable in slightly acid solution. Quickly destroyed by heat in neutral or alkaline solution. Sulfite quickly destroys thiamin.
Riboflavin Vitamin B$_2$ (formerly lactoflavin [vitamin G])	Constituent of tissue respiratory enzyme systems, as well as some enzymes (flavoproteins) involved in amino acid and lipid metabolism.	*Absorption:* May require phosphorylation in intestinal mucosa. *Storage:* Limited in the body. *Excretion:* Excess excreted in urine. *Deficiency:* Cheilosis, seborrheic dermatitis of face, magenta tongue, certain functional and organic eye disorders.	Milk, powdered whey; liver, kidney, heart, meats; eggs; green leafy vegetables; dried yeast, enriched foods (flour, bread). Cereals low; germination of oats, wheat, barley, and corn increases content.	Sparingly soluble in water. Quickly decomposed by ultraviolet or visible light; very sensitive to alkali. Relatively resistant to heat in acid media.
Niacin Nicotinic acid Niacinamide Anti-pellagra vitamin (pellagra-preventive [P-P] factor)	Constituent of 2 coenzymes (NAD, NADH) which operate as hydrogen and electron transfer agents in respiration. Tryptophan normally contributes to niacin supply (60 mg tryptophan equivalent to 1 mg niacin).	*Storage:* Limited in the body. *Excretion:* Urine, mainly as methylated derivatives. *Deficiency:* Pellagra with gastrointestinal, skin, and neurologic changes.	Liver, kidney, lean meat, fish (salmon), poultry; whole-grain or enriched cereals, and breads; some leafy green vegetables, tomatoes; peanuts, brewer's yeast, tryptophan in proteins. Most fruits and vegetables are poor sources of niacin.	Soluble in water. Relatively stable to heat, oxidation, and light. Relatively stable to acid and alkali.
Vitamin B$_6$ Pyridoxine Pyridoxal Pyridoxamine	Pyridoxal phosphate is a prosthetic group of enzymes which decarboxylates tyrosine, arginine, glutamic acid, and certain other amino acids. Essential to transulfuration and in conversion of tryptophan to niacin; also as a coenzyme in transamination. Participates in metabolism of essential fatty acids. Essential in synthesis of porphyrins (eg, heme for hemoglobin and cytochromes).	*Absorption:* Intestinal bacteria synthesize some pyridoxine, and it is absorbed from the intestine. *Storage:* Limited in the body. *Excretion:* Urine. *Deficiency:* Hypochromic macrocytic anemia, lesions of central nervous system evidenced by epileptiform seizures and encephalographic changes, particularly in infants.	Wheat germ; meat, liver, kidney; whole-grain cereals, soybeans, peanuts, corn, yams; brewer's yeast. Synthesis by activity of microorganisms.	Fairly stable to heat, but sensitive to ultraviolet light and oxidation.

Table 31–7 (cont'd). The vitamins in nutrition.

Nomenclature	Functions	Metabolism	Important Sources	Stability
Pantothenic acid	Constituent of coenzyme A which participates in synthesis and breakdown of fatty acids, synthesis of cholesterol and steroid hormones, utilization of pyruvate and acetate, reactions of acetylation, metabolism of some amino acids, synthesis of heme for hemoglobin and cytochromes.	*Storage:* Limited in the body. *Excretion:* Urine. *Deficiency:* Gastrointestinal symptoms, skin symptoms, anemia, and impairment in functions of adrenal cortex in experimental animals.	Organ meats (liver, kidney), lean beef; egg yolk; peanuts; broccoli, cauliflower, cabbage; whole-grains, cereal bran; skim milk; fruits, sweet potatoes.	Easily destroyed by heat and alkali. Stable in neutral solution.
Folic acid Folacin Pteroylglutamic acid	Involved in transfer and utilization of the single-carbon moiety; participates in synthesis of purines, thymine, and methyl groups; has specific role in metabolism of histidine and well-demonstrated role in hematopoiesis.	*Excretion:* Excess in both urine and feces. *Deficiency:* May produce macrocytic anemia with concurrent glossitis, gastrointestinal lesions, diarrhea, and intestinal malabsorption (sprue). Deficiency in pregnancy not uncommon.	Liver, kidney; yeast; fresh green leafy vegetables, cauliflower. Synthesis by activity of intestinal microorganisms	Easily oxidized in acid medium and sunlight. Labile to heat. (Similar to thiamin.)
Vitamin B₁₂ Antipernicious anemia factor Cobalamin	Involved in purine and pyrimidine metabolism, synthesis of nucleic acid (DNA), maturation of red blood cells, methionine metabolism, and transmethylation. Contains cobalt, which is the only known function for this element.	*Absorption:* From ileum, but requiring intrinsic factor and hydrochloric acid contributed by stomach. *Storage:* Principally in liver, for long periods. *Excretion:* In feces (represents unabsorbed vitamin). *Deficiency:* Macrocytic anemia or pernicious anemia with degenerative changes in gastric mucosa, characteristic lesions in nervous system (combined system disease).	Foods of animal origin: liver, kidney, muscle meat, eggs, milk, cheese. No significant amounts in higher plants. Synthesis within intestine by activity of microorganisms.	Labile to heat, acids, alkali, and light.
Biotin Inositol Choline	Required by various animal species but of questionable need for humans. If they are in fact needed, the amounts required are very small and are probably synthesizable in tissues or provided by intestinal flora.			

associated with inadequate food intake for a variety of reasons, it may also represent a form of starvation secondary to such diseases as cystic fibrosis, celiac disease, or overwhelming infections. Other causes of marasmus are prematurity, mental deficiency, and gastrointestinal diseases involving severe diarrhea and malabsorption.

Vitamins

The chemistry and physiologic functions of the vitamins are discussed in Chapters 12 and 13. Normal individuals on an adequate diet can secure all of the required vitamins from natural foods; no supplementation with vitamin concentrates is necessary. In disease states in which digestion and assimilation are impaired or the normal requirement for the vitamins is increased, they must of course be supplied in appropriate quantities from other sources.

Many of the vitamins are destroyed by improper cooking. Some of the water-soluble vitamins, for example, are partially lost in the cooking water. Overcooking of meats also contributes to vitamin loss. Vitamin C is particularly labile both in cooking and storage. In fact, one can hardly depend on an adequate vitamin C intake unless a certain quantity of fresh fruits and vegetables is taken each day.

The refinement of cereal grains is attended by a loss of B vitamins. Enrichment of these products with thiamin, riboflavin, niacin, and iron is now used to restore these nutrients. Other foods are often improved by the addition of vitamins, eg, the addition of vitamin D to milk and of vitamin A to oleomargarine.

Because of the increasing tendency to fortify foods with additional vitamins and minerals, the Food & Drug Administration of the United States Public Health Service has found it necessary to issue additional regulations on vitamin and mineral preparations. For this purpose, all products containing vitamins and minerals have been divided into 3 categories:

(1) Products supplemented so that they contain up to 50% of the Recommended Daily Allowance (RDA) of vitamins and minerals are regarded as **ordinary foods.** Any natural food which already contains more than 50% of the RDA is, of course, classified as an ordinary food.

(2) With 3 exceptions, all products supplemented so that they contain 50–150% of the RDA are classified as **dietary supplements.** The 3 exceptions are vitamin A, vitamin D, and folic acid. The upper limits for these are set at 100% of the RDA.

(3) Vitamin and mineral preparations with potencies above 150% of the RDA exceed food requirements and therefore are regarded as appropriate only for the treatment of vitamin-mineral deficiencies or some other medical purpose. These products are classified as **drugs.**

Because of their toxicity, the FDA has directed particular attention to vitamins A and D. It is recommended that any preparation of vitamin A with more than 10,000 International Units (IU) per dosage unit or any preparation of vitamin D with more than 400 IU per dosage unit be supplied only on prescription.

A summary of the essential nutritional facts concerning the fat- and water-soluble vitamins is shown in Table 31–7.

Minerals

The minerals, while forming only a small portion of the total body weight, are nonetheless of great importance in the vital economy. Their functions and the requirements for each as far as now known are discussed in Chapter 30. Fruits, vegetables, and cereals are the principal sources of the mineral elements in the diet. Certain foods are particularly outstanding for their contribution of particular minerals, eg, milk products, which are depended on to supply the majority of the calcium and phosphorus in the diet.

A summary of the essential nutritional facts concerning the minerals required in the diet is shown in Table 31–8.

Water

Water is not a food, but since it is ordinarily consumed in the diet it is included as one of its components. The water requirements and the functions of water in the body are discussed in Chapter 30.

RECOMMENDED DIETARY ALLOWANCES

The Food and Nutrition Board of the National Academy of Sciences, National Research Council, has collected the best available data on the quantities of various nutrients required by normal persons of varying body sizes and ages and in different physiologic states. The first recommendations derived from such data were published in 1943. At intervals of approximately 5 years since that time, revisions of the recommendations have been issued. In the 1974 edition, the eighth revision (Table 31–6), recommendations for vitamins B_6, B_{12}, folacin, and vitamin E as well as for phosphorus, iodine, magnesium, and zinc have been added to the recommendations previously made for calories, protein, calcium, iron, thiamin, riboflavin, niacin, ascorbic acid, vitamin A, and vitamin D.

Unless the purposes of the Recommended Dietary Allowances are kept in mind, it might be concluded that the allowances are too high. The recommendations are designed to set levels suitable for maintenance of good nutrition in the majority of healthy individuals in the USA. Thus, they are proposed as a means of fixing goals in planning food supplies and interpreting food intakes of groups of people. It follows that the allowances may be higher than required for some individuals. Indeed, the allowances should not be interpreted as specific requirements for individuals unless it is understood that the stated amounts of each nutrient may in fact be too high for a given person. Therefore, the diet of an individual may not necessarily be regarded as deficient if it does not equal in every respect

Table 31–8. The mineral elements in nutrition.

Nomenclature	Functions	Metabolism	Important Sources
Calcium	Major constituent of bones and teeth. Essential to muscle contraction, normal heart rhythm, and nerve irritability. Activation of some enzymes. Most abundant mineral element in the body.	*Absorption:* According to tissue need; aided by vitamin D, ascorbic acid, lactose; oxalates and phytate interfere. *Utilization:* Regulated by parathyroid hormone and vitamin D. Storage in bone trabeculae. Excretion in urine and feces, the latter chiefly representing unabsorbed calcium. *Deficiency:* Retarded bone and tooth mineralization, fragile bones, stunted growth, rickets in children; may contribute to the occurrence of osteoporosis in adults.	*Best:* Milk, hard cheese; turnip, collard, kale, and mustard greens. *Good:* Ice cream, cottage cheese, broccoli, oysters, shrimp, salmon, clams.
Iron	Constituent of hemoglobin, myoglobin, and some oxidative enzymes. Present in all body cells, but stored as ferritin in liver, spleen, and bone marrow and principally in reticuloendothelial tissues. Transported in serum by the protein siderophilin (transferrin).	*Absorption:* According to body need (aided by gastric acidity and ascorbic acid); decreased by phosphatase, oxalate, and phytate. *Utilization:* Copper essential, iron from catabolized red blood cells used over again. *Excretion:* Minute amounts in urine and sweat; most of fecal iron represents unabsorbed iron from the diet. *Deficiency:* Reduced hemoglobin level; anemia.	*Best:* Liver. *Good:* Meat, egg yolk, enriched bread and cereals, peaches, apricots, prunes, raisins, dark green vegetables, molasses, legumes.
Chlorine	Constituent of gastric juice. Acid-base balance. In association with sodium and potassium, chlorine contributes to maintenance of normal body water content.	*Absorption:* Readily absorbed. *Excretion:* Excretion in urine parallels intake. Prolonged vomiting may lead to deficiency and resultant alkalosis.	Table salt, meat, milk, eggs.
Sulfur	Constituent of many proteins in the amino acids cysteine and methionine. High in proteins (keratin) of hair and also in insulin and glutathione.	Excess eliminated in urine largely as sulfates.	Eggs, cheese, milk, meat, nuts, legumes.
Magnesium	Constituent of bones, teeth, and many other tissues. Affects muscle and nerve irritability. Acts on some enzymes, particularly those of glycolysis.	*Deficiency:* Observed in alcoholism with cirrhosis and in severe renal disease. Dietary deficiency not known in man. *Excretion:* Mainly in bile; relatively little in urine.	Whole-grain cereals, nuts, cocoa, legumes, meat, sea foods, milk.
Manganese	Activates several enzymes such as blood and bone phosphatases, arginase, carboxylase, and cholinesterase.	Liver most active organ of metabolism. *Storage:* In liver and kidney. *Absorption:* Limited; elimination chiefly by intestine.	Whole-grain cereals, legumes, meat, fish, fowl, green leafy vegetables. Well distributed in human diets.
Copper	Essential to hemoglobin synthesis and to action of certain enzymes (eg, cytochrome oxidase, tyrosinase, catalase, uricase, ascorbic acid, oxidase, monoamine oxidase). Possibly plays a role in bone formation and maintenance of myelin.	*Storage:* In liver and central nervous system. Mainly protein-bound to ceruloplasmin in serum. *Excretion:* By bile into intestine. Erythrocuprein in erythrocytes. *Deficiency:* Leads to retarded hemoglobin production; occurs rarely, but occasionally in anemia of infants.	Liver, oysters, meat, fish, nuts, legumes, whole-grain cereals.
Zinc	Constituent of carbonic anhydrase, carboxypeptidase, and alcohol dehydrogenase as well as of insulin.	In liver, pancreas, muscles, bones and other organs (eg, prostate, testes, hair, red blood cells). *Excretion:* Chiefly by intestine.	Widely distributed in foods (eg, oysters, sea food, liver, wheat germ, yeast).
Iodine	Constituent of thyroxine.	*Storage:* Thyroid gland. *Excretion:* In urine. *Deficiency:* Nutritional deficiency may produce simple goiter, with enlarged thyroid. Cretinism due to incomplete development of the gland. Dietary deficiency very rare in USA.	Iodized salt is best protection. Sea foods; foods grown in nongoitrous regions.

Element	Function		Sources
Phosphorus	Major constituent of bones and teeth. Buffer salts. Metabolism of fat and carbohydrate and energy exchange via oxidative reactions associated with phosphorylation.	*Absorption:* Aided by vitamin D; about 1/3 lost in feces, related to Ca:P ratio of diet. *Storage:* About 80% in bones and teeth. *Excretion:* In urine. *Deficiency:* Poor mineralization of bones, poor growth, rickets, osteomalacia.	Milk, cheese, egg yolk, meat, fish, fowl, legumes, nuts, whole-grain cereals.
Potassium	Principal factor in maintenance of intracellular fluid balance. Affects rhythm of heart. Participates in the regulation of nervous and muscular irritability.	*Excretion:* In urine and sweat. *Deficiency:* Not usually as a result of dietary lack except following starvation; also during acidosis (such as diabetic acidosis) and with certain adrenal tumors, nausea, vomiting, diarrhea, and prolonged use of many oral diuretic agents.	Widely distributed in nature. Meat, fish, fowl, cereals, vegetables, fruits (notably dried apricots and peaches, bananas, juice of oranges and pineapples).
Sodium	Principal factor in maintenance of extracellular fluid balance. Buffer salts. Participates in the regulation of muscle and nerve irritability.	*Absorption:* Readily absorbed. *Excretion:* Parallels intake and is controlled by adrenocortical salt-regulating hormones, chiefly by kidneys. Sweat losses may be high in unadapted individuals. *Deficiency:* Nausea, diarrhea, muscular cramps, dehydration.	Table salt, meat, fish, fowl, milk, eggs, sodium compounds (eg, baking soda, baking powder).
Selenium	In very small amounts ($<$ 3 ppm), selenium improves growth and prevents certain diseases in some animals (eg, sheep). May be an essential factor in tissue respiration.	An essential component of the enzyme glutathione peroxidase. May act synergistically with vitamin E and/or cystine; exerts antagonistic effect to mercury; may be protective against naturally-occurring high levels of mercury in marine foods.	If required for man, amounts would be extremely small. Easily available in plants as obtained from soil. Marine fish and shellfish have higher selenium content than tissues of terrestrial animals.
Fluoride	Mainly in bones and teeth.	In trace amounts, essential to development of bones and teeth. Protects against dental caries. May be of benefit in osteoporosis.	Main source is drinking water; amounts highly variable—as high as 10–45 ppm in some areas. This amount is excessive and may lead to mottling and discoloration of tooth enamel. If water contains $<$ 1 ppm addition to bring to 1–2 ppm (a nutritionally adequate amount), fluoride improves tooth development in children and exerts preventive effect on development of caries.
Other elements	Present in trace amounts in animal tissues (eg, cobalt in vitamin B_{12}); those whose functions in humans, if any, are not yet defined include aluminum, boron, cadmium, chromium, molybdenum, nickel, silicon, tin, and vanadium.		

the recommendations specified.

Sebrell (1968), in commenting on the allowances, points out that they are intended for use in the USA under current conditions of living. Therefore, they take into account climate, economic status, distribution of population, and various other factors that make them particularly suitable for the USA. While they may serve as a reference for use in other countries, many variables such as population, food supply, climate, body size, and energy expenditure make it desirable that each country develop recommendations specific to the needs of its own people.

In order to simplify the concept of an adequate diet for normal individuals, foodstuffs have been arranged into 4 groups, each of which makes a major contribution to the diet. It is recommended that some food from each group be taken daily, as specified below.

(1) Milk group: For children, 3 or more 8 oz glasses (smaller servings for some children under 9 years of age); for teenagers, 4 or more glasses; for adults, 2 or more glasses. Cheese, ice cream, and other milk products can supply part of the milk recommended. 1 oz American cheese = 3/4 glass milk; 1/2 cup creamed cottage cheese = 1/3 glass milk; 1/2 cup ice cream = 1/4 glass milk.

(2) Meat group: Two or more servings of meat, fish, poultry, eggs, or cheese. Dry beans, peas, and nuts are alternates, although they cannot substitute entirely for meat, fish, poultry, or eggs.

(3) Vegetables and fruits: Four or more servings, including some dark green or yellow vegetables, citrus fruits, or tomatoes. Some uncooked vegetables should be included.

(4) Breads and cereals: Four or more servings of enriched or whole grain breads and cereals.

●　●　●

References

Bogert LJ, Briggs GM, Calloway DH: *Nutrition and Physical Fitness,* 9th ed. Saunders, 1973.

Holt LE Jr, Snyderman SE: Nutr Abstr Rev 35:1, 1965.

Leverton RM: P 477 in: *Protein & Amino Acid Nutrition.* Albanese AA (editor). Academic Press, 1959.

Mattson FH, Erickson BA, Kligman AM: Am J Clin Nutr 25:589, 1972.

Nakagawa I, Takahashi T, Suzuki T, Kobayashi K: J Nutr 83:115, 1964.

National Academy of Sciences–National Research Council: *Recommended Dietary Allowances,* 8th ed. National Academy of Sciences, 1974.

Rose WC: Nutr Abstr Rev 27:631, 1957.

Sebrell WH Jr: Nutr Rev 26:355, 1968.

General Bibliography

Albritton EC (editor): *Standard Values in Nutrition and Metabolism.* Saunders, 1954.

Block RJ, Weiss KW: *Amino Acid Handbook.* Thomas, 1956.

Brock JF: *Recent Advances in Human Nutrition.* Little, Brown, 1961.

Church CF, Church HN: *Food Values of Portions Commonly Used,* 11th ed. Lippincott, 1970.

Consolazio CF, Johnson RE, Marek E: *Metabolic Methods.* Mosby, 1951.

Cooper LF, Barber EM, Mitchell HS: *Nutrition in Health and Disease.* Lippincott, 1960.

Crampton EW, Lloyd LE: *Fundamentals of Nutrition.* Freeman, 1960.

Davidson S, Passmore R: *Human Nutrition and Dietetics,* 4th ed. Williams & Wilkins, 1969.

Goldsmith G: *Nutritional Diagnosis.* Thomas, 1959.

Institute of Home Economics, Agricultural Research Service: *Nutritive Value of Foods.* US Government Printing Office, 1970.

Pollack H, Halpern SL: *Therapeutic Nutrition.* Publication 234. National Research Council, 1952.

Sebrell WH Jr, Harris RS: *The Vitamins.* 3 vols. Academic Press, 1954.

Williams SR: *Nutrition & Diet Therapy,* 2nd ed. Mosby, 1973.

Wohl MG, Goodhart RS (editors): *Modern Nutrition in Health and Disease,* 5th ed. Lea & Febiger, 1973.

32 ...
The Blood, Lymph, & Cerebrospinal Fluid

BLOOD

Blood is a tissue which circulates in what is virtually a closed system of blood vessels. It consists of solid elements—the red and white blood cells and the platelets—suspended in a liquid medium, the plasma.

The Functions of the Blood

(1) Respiration: Transport of oxygen from the lungs to the tissues and of CO_2 from the tissues to the lungs.

(2) Nutrition: Transport of absorbed food materials.

(3) Excretion: Transport of metabolic wastes to the kidneys, lungs, skin, and intestines for removal.

(4) Maintenance of normal acid-base balance in the body.

(5) Regulation of water balance through the effects of blood on the exchange of water between the circulating fluid and the tissue fluid.

(6) Regulation of body temperature by the distribution of body heat.

(7) Defense against infection in the white cells and the circulating antibodies.

(8) Transport of hormones; regulation of metabolism.

(9) Transport of metabolites.

Volume of Packed Red Cells (VPRC)

When blood which has been prevented from clotting by the use of a suitable anticoagulant is centrifuged, the cells will settle to the bottom of the tube while the plasma, a straw-colored liquid, will rise to the top. Normally the cells comprise about 45% of the total volume. This has been termed the hematocrit or, in more modern terminology, the volume of packed red cells (VPRC). Expressed in International Units, the normal VPRC for males is 0.45 liters per liter (l/l); for females, it is about 0.41 l/l.

The specific gravity of whole blood varies between 1.054 and 1.060; the specific gravity of plasma is about 1.024–1.028.

The viscosity of blood is about 4.5 times that of water. Viscosity of blood varies in accordance with the number of cells present and with the temperature and degree of hydration of the body. Because these 3 factors are relatively constant under normal conditions, the viscosity of the blood does not ordinarily influence the physiology of the circulation.

Erythrocyte Sedimentation Rate

The erythrocyte sedimentation rate (ESR) is used clinically as a nonspecific screening test to detect the presence of infection. It has found wide use as a means of monitoring the status of chronic inflammatory diseases such as rheumatoid arthritis.

The erythrocyte sedimentation rate is dependent on the plasma concentration of asymmetric macromolecules (primarily fibrinogen and gamma globulin) and on the concentration of the red cells. The surface of the red cell normally has a negative electrical charge which is known as the "zeta potential." The repelling forces of these negative charges on the red cells normally assist in maintaining the red cells separated and suspended in plasma. Asymmetric macromolecules in plasma have the effect of decreasing the repellent forces of the red cell zeta potential. When there is an increase in the plasma concentration of macromolecules, such as in various inflammatory conditions, the red blood cells aggregate and settle more completely, thus increasing the erythrocyte sedimentation rate.

The 2 most common methods for measuring the erythrocyte sedimentation rate are the Wintrobe technic, introduced in 1924, and the Westergren technic, 1935. The former method employs a 100 mm tube in which the blood is suspended; the latter method uses a longer (180 mm) tube of smaller bore in which the blood is diluted 1:3 with saline. The blood (or diluted blood) is added to the measuring tube and the extent of settling (sedimentation) is recorded after 1 hour.

The Wintrobe method is thought to be a more accurate reflection of the status of the macromolecules in the blood when there is either a normal or only a slightly increased concentration of macromolecules, whereas the Westergren method is considered to reflect changes in the hematocrit, as would occur, for example, in anemia. In recent years, to improve correlation with disease states, it has become customary to apply a correction for anemia to the Wintrobe method to obtain what is called the "corrected" sedimentation rate.

In the Westergren method, saline dilution may

obscure the effects of a reduced red cell mass. Although certain advantages of both methods may still be recognized, a new method known as the "zeta sedimentation ratio" is more rapid and avoids errors resulting from the presence of anemia since results are expressed as a percentage, representing a comparison between a low-speed centrifugal erythrocyte sedimentation rate and the true hematocrit.

Blood Volume

The volume of the blood can be measured by several procedures, although the results obtained will vary somewhat with the method used. The method of Gregersen, which is employed frequently in clinical practice, utilizes T-1824, a blue dye (Evans blue). The dye is injected intravenously, and its concentration in the plasma is determined after sufficient time has elapsed to allow for adequate mixing (usually 10 minutes). The plasma volume thus obtained is then converted to total blood volume by the following formula:

$$\text{Total blood volume (dl)} = \frac{\text{Plasma volume (dl)}}{1 - \text{VPRC}}$$

Presumably the dye is bound to the plasma protein; for this reason it remains in the circulation for some time. Actually some of the dye does escape into the extracellular fluid; therefore the results obtained by this method are somewhat high. Normal volumes in males as found by the T-1824 method are given as follows: plasma volume, 45 ml/kg body weight; blood volume, 85 ml/kg. The corresponding values in the female are somewhat lower.

[131]I-labeled human serum albumin is also used to determine plasma volume. A carefully measured dose is injected, and the dilution of the label is then obtained.

There are objections to measurements of plasma volume as a means of determining whole blood volume. The blood volume is calculated from the plasma volume by the use of the hematocrit, which, since peripheral blood is used, may not represent the ratio of cells to plasma throughout the circulation. Consequently, a direct measurement of the whole blood volume by the use of labeled red cells is preferred when greater accuracy is required, particularly in states where there is an impairment of circulatory efficiency (eg, shock or cardiac failure). [32]P and radiochromium have both been used to label the red cells for the purpose of measuring whole blood volume.

Blood Osmotic Pressure

The osmotic pressure of the blood is kept relatively constant mainly by the kidney. Osmotic pressure can be determined by measurement of the freezing point depression. The average freezing point for whole blood has been established as $-0.537°$ C. This corresponds to an osmotic pressure of 7–8 atmospheres at body temperature. A solution of sodium chloride containing 0.9 g/dl has an osmotic pressure equal to that of whole blood. Such a saline solution is termed

Table 32–1. Composition of some saline solutions isotonic with blood.

	Saline (%)	Mammalian Ringer (%)	Ringer-Locke (%)	Tyrode (%)
NaCl	0.9	0.86	0.9	0.8
CaCl$_2$	...	0.033	0.024	0.02
KCl	...	0.03	0.042	0.02
NaHCO$_3$	...	...	0.01–0.03	0.1
Glucose	...	...	0.10–0.2	0.01
MgCl$_2$	...	...	...	0.01
NaH$_2$PO$_4$	...	...	...	0.005

"isotonic" or "physiologic" saline. Actually these sodium chloride solutions are not physiologic, since additional ions are lacking which are necessary for the function of the tissues. Other solutions, which are not only isotonic but which contain these ions in proper proportions, are more appropriate from a physiologic standpoint. Examples of these balanced ionic solutions are Ringer's, Ringer-Locke, and Tyrode's solutions. The formulas are given in Table 32–1.

THE CLOTTING OF BLOOD

When blood is drawn and allowed to clot, a clear liquid (serum) exudes from the clotted blood. Plasma, on the other hand, separates from the cells only when blood is prevented from clotting.

The blood clot is formed by a protein (**fibrinogen**) which is present in soluble form in the plasma and which is transformed to an insoluble network of fibrous material (**fibrin**, the substance of the blood clot) by the clotting mechanism.

According to the original **Howell theory** of blood coagulation, the change of fibrinogen into fibrin is caused by **thrombin**, which in fluid blood exists as **prothrombin**. The conversion of prothrombin to thrombin depends on the action of **thromboplastin** and calcium. These stages in the clotting process may be diagrammed as follows:

Stage I   Thromboplastin

                              ↓ + Ca^{2+}

Stage II Prothrombin ⟶ Thrombin

                                    ↓

Stage III   Fibrinogen ⟶ Fibrin (clot)

The many continuing studies on the details of the coagulation process have served to indicate how complex the system actually is. Lack of knowledge of the chemical nature of many of the factors involved has also resulted in much confusion in terminology. In an effort to introduce uniformity in nomenclature, the International Committee for the Standardization of the Nomenclature of Blood Clotting Factors has recommended a numerical system to designate the various factors presently accepted as involved in the clot-

Table 32–2. Numerical system for nomenclature of blood clotting factors.

Factor	Name
I	Fibrinogen
II	Prothrombin
III	Thromboplastin
IV	Calcium
V	Labile factor, proaccelerin, accelerator (Ac-) globulin
VII	Proconvertin, serum prothrombin conversion accelerator (SPCA), cothromboplastin, autoprothrombin I
VIII	Antihemophilic factor, antihemophilic globulin (AHG)
IX	Plasma thromboplastin component (PTC) (Christmas factor)
X	Stuart-Prower factor
XI	Plasma thromboplastin antecedent (PTA)
XII	Hageman factor
XIII	Laki-Lorand factor (LLF)

ting process. This system is given in Table 32–2, and each of the 12 factors will be described, together with some comments on function, in the text which follows.

Although a factor VI has been described, it is currently believed that no such separate factor exists; consequently it has been deleted.

Stage I: Origin of Thromboplastin

The term "thromboplastin" should not be interpreted as referring to a single substance. Instead it is meant to describe a function—namely, that of activating or catalyzing the conversion of prothrombin to thrombin.

Substances with thromboplastic activity are contributed by the plasma, the platelets, and the tissues.

A. From the *Plasma*:

1. Antihemophilic globulin (AHG)—This factor is relatively heat-stable but labile on storage. The antihemophilic globulins are principally β-2 globulins which occur in Cohn fraction I (see Fig 32–7). A deficiency of AHG is the cause of the classical type of hemophilia, sometimes designated **hemophilia A.**

2. Plasma thromboplastin component (PTC) (Christmas factor)—This factor is found in both serum and plasma. It occurs in the β-2 globulins in a concentration of less than 1 mg/dl of plasma. A deficiency of PTC is the cause of a hemophilioid disease sometimes referred to as Christmas disease after the surname of the first patient diagnosed as having this inherited coagulation defect.

3. Plasma thromboplastin antecedent (PTA)—A factor described by Rosenthal and others in 1953. Patients with PTA deficiency are usually rather mild bleeders.

4. Hageman factor—The absence of this factor is evident only from appropriate laboratory studies of the clotting system. If whole normal blood is collected in glass and in silicone-treated tubes, the blood in the silicone tube takes longer to clot than that in the glass tube. It is hypothesized that some reaction occurs on

exposure of the blood to glass, although many other substances such as kaolin, barium carbonate, Super-Cel Celite, bentonite, asbestos, and silicic acid will act like glass in this respect. This involves the Hageman factor and also PTA. The Hageman factor is thought to be activated by contact. The activated factor then reacts with a PTA factor to produce another activated product which is thought to be concerned with activation of PTA.

As noted above, Hageman factor deficiency is assumed to exist in patients with no clinically obvious clotting defect who manifest abnormalities in the clotting system when tested in vitro. In a laboratory test, blood from either PTA-deficient or Hageman factor-deficient patients exhibits a prolonged clotting time and an abnormal consumption of prothrombin (ie, excess prothrombin remains in the serum after clotting has taken place). Consequently, from laboratory tests alone the results of either defect are similar. However, the in vivo conditions are readily differentiated because of the bleeding tendency of the PTA-deficient patient which is not evident in the Hageman factor-deficient person.

5. Stuart-Prower factor (Stuart factor)—This plasma factor is required not only for the formation of thromboplastin but also for the conversion of prothrombin to thrombin. There appear to be no specific distinguishing clinical features corresponding to this defect, but it is detectable in a laboratory test by the presence of a prolonged clotting time or a long one-stage prothrombin time.

6. Factor V (labile factor, proaccelerin, accelerator [Ac] globulin)—A plasma (or serum) factor which disappears on heating or storing of oxalated plasma. The factor occurs in a more active form in serum than in plasma.

B. From the *Platelets*: The platelet thromboplastic factor (thromboplastinogenase) is obtained upon disintegration of the platelets, as by contact with a rough surface. Thrombin catalyzes the formation of the platelet factor.

C. From the *Tissues*: Thromboplastic precursors are also supplied by the tissues. These may be very important in initiating coagulation reactions because they are supplied from outside the circulation itself.

Stage II: Conversion of Prothrombin to Thrombin

Prothrombin is a globulin circulating in plasma. In the second stage of the clotting process it is activated by conversion to thrombin. The conversion requires a number of reactions involving the interaction of thromboplastic factors and including Stuart-Prower factor, factor V, and calcium. **Factor VII** (called "stable factor" because of its stability on storage) is also required. Factor VII is not consumed in coagulation. Synonyms applied to factor VII include the terms proconvertin, serum prothrombin conversion accelerator (SPCA), cothromboplastin, and autoprothrombin I.

Although factor VII is found among the coagulation factors circulating in plasma, it is believed to be required as an accessory only for the activity of tissue thromboplastin and not for plasma thromboplastin.

A prolonged one-stage plasma prothrombin time is characteristic of defects in any of the components of the second stage of clotting because each factor mentioned above is necessary for the conversion of prothrombin to thrombin. A lack of any one factor results in incomplete conversion of prothrombin to thrombin. Consequently, an excess of prothrombin remains in the serum after the clot has formed (abnormal prothrombin consumption).

Stage III: Formation of Fibrin From Fibrinogen

In the third stage of clotting, the protein fibrinogen loses one or more peptides under the influence of thrombin, which is actually a proteolytic enzyme. A factor from the platelets (platelet accelerator factor II) also catalyzes the conversion of fibrinogen to fibrin. The result of these reactions is the formation, first, of activated fibrinogen (F'), which then undergoes a spontaneous but reversible polymerization to produce fibrin, a protein of much larger molecular weight than the original fibrinogen.

Reversible polymerization is indeed the case in vitro, wherein a system composed of purified fibrinogen and thrombin and added calcium produces a clot which is soluble in 0.03% HCl, so-called **fibrin S** (soluble fibrin). However, in vivo an acid-insoluble clot of **fibrin** I (insoluble fibrin) is formed, but, if small amounts of serum are added to the in vitro system, fibrin I is then also formed. The serum evidently contains a factor responsible for inhibition of reversible polymerization of fibrin. This stabilizing factor in serum which enters the clotting sequence after fibrin has formed is called the **Laki-Lorand factor (LLF)** or **fibrin stabilizing factor (FSF)**. Using the numerical system for nomenclature of blood clotting factors shown in Table 32–2, LLF would be designated **factor XIII**.

To understand the role of the many factors involved in the clotting process, it is helpful to note that the protein clotting factors generally interact in pairs. As a result of this interaction, each clotting factor is in turn converted from an inactive to an active form. The process thus resembles conversion of enzymes from an inactive to an active form by specific activators, although the resemblance is not entirely accurate since some of the clotting factors are probably not enzymes.

In Fig 32–1, the sequence of action of factors necessary for initiation of clotting is outlined. The intrinsic system is that which is entirely present in the plasma and thus permits formation of fibrin without the need for contribution of clotting factors from the tissues. The extrinsic system differs from the intrinsic system by the presence of factors derived from outside the plasma. These extrinsic factors interact to produce active factor X (Stuart-Prower factor), and at that point the extrinsic and the intrinsic systems follow the same pathway to fibrin. The presence of both systems results in the formation of a greater amount of fibrin than is the case if the intrinsic system is operating alone.

Other Aspects of the Clotting Mechanism

A. Autocatalysis: In the first few seconds following an injury, little or nothing observable happens with respect to the clotting of shed blood. Clotting then begins suddenly, and the reactions become accelerated with the passage of time. This acceleration phenomenon is caused by **autocatalysis**, whereby certain products formed in the coagulation process actually catalyze the reactions by which they themselves were formed. The principal autocatalyst is thrombin.

B. Vasoconstrictor Action: In addition to the coagulation reactions at the site of the injury other factors may aid in securing hemostasis. These include:

1. A prompt reflex vasoconstriction in the region of the injury.

2. Compression of the vessels in the area of injury by the mass of clotted blood in the tissues (capillary adhesion). The capillary blood vessels become so compressed that their endothelial linings may actually adhere to one another.

3. Liberation of a vasoconstrictor principle upon lysis of the platelets. This may be **serotonin** (hydroxytryptamine), which is known to be adsorbed and concentrated in the platelets although it is not manufactured there.

C. Inhibitors of Prothrombin Activation and Conversion: The clotting of blood may be prevented by the action of substances which interfere with the conversion of prothrombin to thrombin. The best-known inhibitor of this reaction is **heparin**, a water-soluble, thermostable compound. It is extremely potent; as little as 1 mg will prevent the clotting of 1 dl or more of blood. Heparin is formed and stored in the metachromatic granules of the mast cells. These cells are located in the connective tissue surrounding capillaries and the walls of blood vessels. Liver and lung tissue are notably rich in heparin.

Heparin can act both in vivo and in vitro to prevent clotting of blood. In part, its anticoagulant effect is due to the direct and immediate combination of the highly sulfated heparin molecule with various coagulation factors.

Another inhibitor of clotting is referred to as "antithromboplastin," although it has not been proved that this substance acts specifically against thromboplastin. All that is known is that it inhibits the first phase of the process by which prothrombin is activated.

Plasma contains **antithrombic activity**, since it will cause the destruction of large quantities of thrombin by irreversible conversion to **metathrombin**. The antithrombin activity of the plasma is not influenced by heparin.

Calcium is also necessary for the conversion of prothrombin to thrombin. Citrates and oxalates which are commonly used as anticoagulants are effective because they remove calcium from the blood by the formation of insoluble citrate or oxalate salts of calcium. If calcium is added in excess, the clotting power of the blood is restored.

Blood may also be prevented from clotting by

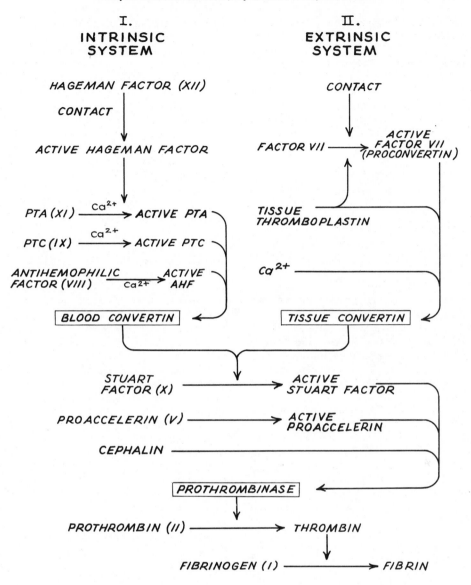

Figure 32—1. Intrinsic and extrinsic systems for initiation of clotting.

defibrination, ie, removal of fibrin by allowing it to form around a glass rod with which the blood has been stirred or on glass beads shaken in the flask with the blood.

The Fibrinolytic System

In addition to the mechanisms for the formation of a clot in the blood, there is also a mechanism which is concerned with the lysis of the clot. In plasma and serum there is a substance called **profibrinolysin (plasminogen)** which becomes activated to **fibrinolysin (plasmin),** the enzyme which lyses the clot. As was the case with prothrombin, profibrinolysin must be activated before it is converted to fibrinolysin. Plasminogen can be activated in various ways to yield the proteolytic enzyme, plasmin. One activator which

has been found in many tissues and in the plasma is called **fibrinolysokinase** (fibrinokinase). An activator is also present in the urine; it is termed **urokinase.** Simply shaking a concentrate of plasminogen with chloroform will also activate plasminogen.

Enzymes found in certain bacteria are effective as plasminogen activators. The ability of some bacteria to lyse fibrin clots is undoubtedly due to the presence of such activating enzymes. Examples of bacterial activating enzymes for plasminogen are **staphylokinase** and **streptokinase.** Activation by streptokinase appears to proceed in 2 stages. First, there is an interaction of streptokinase with a substance called "proactivator I." This reaction then yields "activator I" which in turn catalytically converts plasminogen to plasmin. The conversion of plasminogen to plasmin by streptokinase

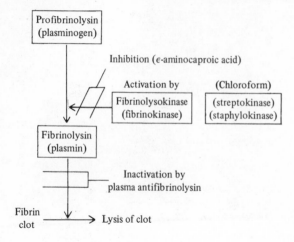

Figure 32–2. Fibrinolytic system.

results in a decrease in molecular weight from 143,000 to 120,000. It is this lower molecular weight product that exerts fibrinolytic activity.

There are also **inhibitors of plasminogen activation.** One such inhibitor is ϵ-aminocaproic acid, which competitively inhibits the activation of human or bovine plasminogen by streptokinase, urokinase, and probably fibrinokinase.

The fibrinolytic system is influenced by the neuroendocrine (pituitary) system. Thyroid stimulating hormone and growth hormone promote fibrinolysis, whereas adrenocorticotropic hormone inhibits it.

The essentials of the fibrinolytic system are diagrammed in Fig 32–2. Note the analogies to the clotting system as it pertains to prothrombin activation and conversion, and to the action of thrombin and antithrombin.

Prothrombin Production

Prothrombin, factor V, and factor VII are manufactured in the liver and vitamin K is necessary for their production and activity. Deficiencies of any of these substances or of Stuart-Prower factor are all characterized by a single laboratory finding—that of a prolonged one-stage prothrombin time. Most abnormalities associated with thrombin formation, the second stage of clotting, and formerly attributed to a deficiency of prothrombin itself, are now known to be related to deficiencies of factors V and VII. Stuart-Prower factor deficiency produces a hemorrhagic disease clinically indistinguishable from factor VII deficiency.

Although deficiencies of factor V (parahemophilia), factor VII, or of Stuart-Prower factor are among the inherited second-stage clotting diseases, these deficiencies may also occur in severe hepatic disease or as a result of long-term anticoagulant therapy.

A lack of prothrombin (hypoprothrombinemia) may be acquired or inherited. The latter is rare. Acquired hypoprothrombinemia results when liver damage is so extensive as to interfere with prothrombin synthesis or when the absorption of vitamin K

from the intestine is impaired—particularly when the flow of bile to the intestine is prevented, as in obstructive jaundice.

Dicumarol (Fig 32–3), acting as an antagonist to vitamin K, produces hypoprothrombinemia. This was the first drug to be used clinically to prolong the clotting time of blood, but a number of other antagonists (anticoagulant drugs) are also available to produce hypoprothrombinemia.

Prothrombin Time

Dicumarol may be used clinically to treat thrombosis or intravascular clotting. When this drug is used it is necessary to control the dosage carefully to avoid excessive prolongation of clotting time and the consequent hazard of hemorrhage. For this purpose, frequent determinations of the prothrombin level of the blood are required. This is accomplished by measuring **prothrombin time.** A technic for making these measurements is that of A.J. Quick, wherein an excess of thromboplastic substance (obtained from rabbit brain) and calcium are added to diluted plasma and the clotting time of the plasma is noted. A comparison of the clotting time of the patient with that of a normal control is always required for a valid test.

Prothrombin time is an indirect and inverse measure of the amount of prothrombin in the plasma, ie, an increased prothrombin time signifies a lower level of prothrombin. The prothrombin time is generally normal in hemophilia, in the purpuras, and in many types of jaundice. However, in obstructive jaundice as well as in conditions where there is significant involvement of the liver in the pathologic process, there will be a low level of prothrombin. Hemorrhage occurring in the newborn infant as well as any circumstance conducive to diminished absorption of vitamin K will also produce a lengthened prothrombin time.

When the prothrombin concentration declines below 30% of normal, prothrombin time rises above 30 seconds; however, coagulation time (see below) will probably remain normal until prothrombin time falls below 20% of normal.

Serum Prothrombin Consumption Test

In the normal process of clotting, no prothrombin remains in the serum. However, in certain abnormal conditions, such as in hemophilia, prothrombin is not all consumed and therefore determination of **serum prothrombin time** after clotting of blood measures the original amount of thromboplastin. For example, in normal individuals the **serum** prothrombin time (ie, the

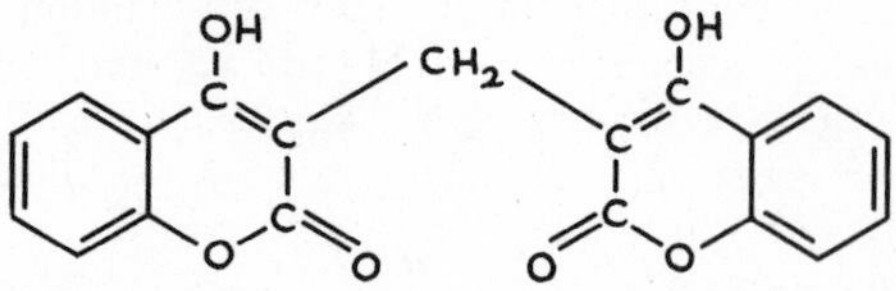

Figure 32–3. Dicumarol (bishydroxycoumarin; 3,3'-methylene-bishydroxycoumarin).

result of the serum prothrombin consumption test) exceeds 30 seconds, whereas in these abnormal cases it is less than 20 seconds (ie, the more rapid the clotting of the serum, the more prothrombin has remained after clotting). Hemophiliacs may have serum prothrombin times (ie, the result of a serum prothrombin consumption test) of 4–15 seconds.

Bleeding Time; Coagulation Time

Bleeding time is determined by noting the time at which blood exuding from a small cut no longer forms a spot on a piece of filter paper placed in contact with the cut surface.

To determine **coagulation time**, a commonly used method employs fine capillary glass tubes that are filled with blood obtained freely flowing from a rather deep cut in the skin. At short intervals, pieces of the blood-filled tube are broken off, and the exact time when coagulation occurs is noted as the point at which a thread of fibrin appears when the fragments of the broken capillary tube are separated.

THE PLASMA PROTEINS

The total protein of the plasma is about 7–7.5 g/dl. Thus, the plasma proteins comprise the major part of the solids of the plasma. The proteins of the plasma are actually a very complex mixture which includes not only simple proteins but also mixed or conjugated proteins such as glycoproteins and various types of lipoproteins.

The separation of individual proteins from a complex mixture is frequently accomplished by the use of various solvents or electrolytes (or both) to remove different protein fractions in accordance with their solubility characteristics. This is the basis of the so-called "salting-out" methods commonly utilized in the determination of protein fractions in the clinical laboratory. Thus it is customary to separate the proteins of the plasma into 3 major groups (fibrinogen, albumin, and globulin) by the use of varying concentrations of sodium or ammonium sulfate. Since it is likely that the subsequent analysis of the protein fractions will require a nitrogen analysis, sodium sulfate is preferred to ammonium sulfate.

Fibrinogen is the precursor of fibrin, the substance of the blood clot. It resembles the globulins in being precipitated by half-saturation with ammonium sulfate; it differs from them in being precipitated in a 0.75 molar solution of Na_2SO_4 or by half-saturation with NaCl. In a quantitative determination of fibrinogen, these reactions are used to separate this protein from other closely related globulins.

Fibrinogen is a large asymmetric molecule (see diagrams in Fig 32–4) which is highly elongated, having an axial ratio of about 20:1. The molecular weight is between 350,000 and 450,000. It normally constitutes 4–6% of the total proteins of the plasma.

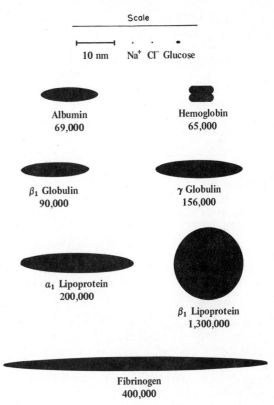

Figure 32–4. Relative dimensions and molecular weights of protein molecules in the blood (Oncley).

This protein is manufactured in the liver; in any situation where excessive destruction of liver tissue has occurred, a sharp fall in blood fibrinogen results.

The **serum proteins** include mainly the **albumin and globulin** fractions of the plasma since most of the fibrinogen is removed in the clotting process, which is incident to the preparation of the serum. These 2 fractions may be separated by the use of a 27% solution of sodium sulfate, which precipitates the globulins and leaves the albumins in solution. By analysis of the nitrogen* in the filtrate following such a separation, a measure of the serum albumin concentration is obtained.

Direct colorimetric methods for determination of albumin in the serum have also been proposed. These methods depend upon the ability of albumin to bind various ions, including certain dyes such as methyl orange or phenol red. Bromcresol green is a dye which appears to be more specific for albumin than the other dyes which have been employed for the colorimetric measurement of albumin. Analytical methods using bromcresol green for analysis of serum albumin are now in use in some clinical laboratories.

---

*It is customary to convert the nitrogen into protein by the use of the factor 6.25 (N × 6.25 = protein). However, the average nitrogen factor found by analyses of dried proteins from pooled human plasma was reported as 6.73 by Armstrong and others in 1947.

Analysis of the total protein of the serum, when corrected for the nonprotein nitrogen, may be used to estimate the total of the albumin and globulin. The globulin concentration is obtained by subtracting the albumin concentration (determined by direct analysis) from the total. The concentration of these 2 major protein fractions is often expressed as the ratio of albumin to globulin (A/G ratio). If proper separation of albumin and globulin fractions is accomplished, the normal value for this ratio is about 1.2:1. In many clinical situations, this ratio is reversed or "inverted."

Electrophoretic Determination of Serum Proteins

Electrophoresis is the migration of charged particles in an electrolyte solution which occurs when an electric current is passed through the solution. Various protein components of a mixture, such as plasma, at pH values above and below their isoelectric points will migrate at varying rates in such a solution because they possess different surface charges. The proteins will thus tend to separate into distinct layers. Tiselius has applied this principle to the analysis of plasma proteins. The sample for analysis is dissolved in a suitable buffer (for plasma, usually 0.1 N sodium diethylbarbiturate at pH 8.6). This mixture is then placed in the U-shaped glass cell of the Tiselius electrophoresis apparatus, and positive and negative electrodes are connected to each limb of the cell. When the current is applied, migration of the protein components begins. The albumin molecules, which are smaller and more highly charged, exhibit the most rapid rate of migration, followed by various globulins. After a time, boundaries between the separate fractions can be detected because of differences in the index of refraction due to variations in concentrations of protein. A photographic record of these variations constitutes what is termed an electrophoretic pattern. Fig 32–5 illustrates typical patterns as seen in each limb of the cell; these are called descending or ascending patterns in accordance with the direction of protein migration.

In normal human plasma, 6 distinct moving boundaries have been identified. These are designated in order of decreasing mobility as albumin, alpha₁ and alpha₂ globulins, beta globulin, fibrinogen, and gamma globulin. The distribution of electrophoretic components of normal human serum is as follows:

Albumin   52–65%   Of total plasma protein
Globulin   29.5–54%   (3.2–5.6 g/dl)
   α_1 2.5–5%   (0.1–0.4 g/dl)
   α_2 7–13%   (0.4–1.2 g/dl)
   β 8–14%   (0.5–1.1 g/dl)
   γ 12–22%   (0.5–1.6 g/dl)

Fibrinogen 6.5%

A/G ratio   1.2:1

Free or moving boundary electrophoresis as developed by Tiselius has not proved as readily applicable to the needs of clinical diagnosis as have the newly developed methods for determination of plasma pro-

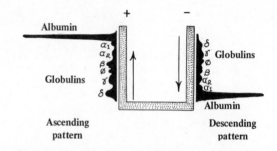

Figure 32–5. Diagrammatic representation of electrophoresis cell and electrophoretic patterns obtained from normal human plasma.

tein fractions based upon what is termed **zone electrophoresis** in a stabilizing medium such as paper or cellulose acetate. These latter methods have replaced the more complex free electrophoretic methods for clinical purposes.

An example of the patterns obtained with normal serum as well as the sera from patients afflicted with various abnormalities affecting plasma proteins is shown in Fig 34–4. These patterns were obtained by the technic of paper electrophoresis.

When cellulose acetate is used as the supporting medium in zone electrophoresis, separation of protein fractions can be accomplished much more rapidly than is the case with paper. For this and other reasons, cellulose acetate strips have almost completely replaced paper as the supporting medium for use in clinical zone electrophoretic determinations. The technic consists of placing micro quantities of serum (or other biologic fluids) at the point of origin and applying an electrical current for about 90 minutes to elicit migration of the proteins in the electrical field within an alkaline buffer solution. At the end of the period allowed for protein separation, the strips are stained and scanned with a densitometer. This instrument converts the band patterns into vertical peaks which can be quantitated. Fig 34–3 illustrates the technic of cellulose acetate zone electrophoresis.

Immunoelectrophoresis (see also Chapter 34) is a method that combines both electrophoretic separation and immune precipitation of proteins utilizing antigen- and antibody-specific precipitin reactions. This procedure is of particular value when zone electrophoresis determinations are also used for the diagnosis of the so-called paraproteinemias. Migration of the protein fractions is generally done in an agar gel medium. Immunologic identification of the electrically separated proteins is accomplished by the addition of immune serum to a trough in the agar block adjacent to the separated protein fractions, the specific precipitin antibodies in the immune serum reacting with the protein fractions acting as antigens to form visible lines of precipitation within a few hours. This is illustrated in Fig 32–6, which is a drawing of an immunoelectrophoretic pattern of normal human serum reacting with horse antiserum prepared against normal human serum

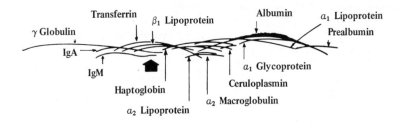

Figure 32–6. Immunoelectrophoresis of normal serum developed with a horse antiserum to whole normal serum. The broad vertical arrow indicates the starting point. (Reproduced, with permission, from White A, Handler F, Smith EL: *Principles of Biochemistry,* 5th ed. Blakiston, 1973.)

as antigen. The broad arrow marks the point at which electrophoretic migration was started.

Other Methods of Separation of Proteins in Plasma

The separation of proteins by electrophoretic analysis depends on a single property, the mobility of the proteins in an electric field. It is known that some plasma proteins which differ in size, shape, composition, and physiologic functions may nonetheless have identical or nearly identical mobilities under the usual conditions of electrophoretic analysis. Thus the conventional electrophoretic fractions are by no means single protein components. Other methods of analysis, such as ultracentrifugation, alcohol precipitation, or immunologic analysis, reveal a considerable number of individual entities within each electrophoretic component.

E.J. Cohn and his collaborators developed methods for the fractionation of plasma proteins which are particularly useful for the isolation in quantity of individual components. Their method is carried out at low temperatures and with low salt concentrations. Differential precipitation of the proteins is accomplished by variation of the pH of the solution and the use of different concentrations of ethyl alcohol.

The results of fractionation of pooled normal human plasma by the method of Cohn are shown in Fig 32–7. Five major fractions are obtained. These account for the vast majority of the total proteins of the plasma. The supernatant, after removal of fractions I–V (ie, fraction VI), contains less than 2% of the total protein. Fractions II and V are relatively homogeneous; the other fractions are very complex mixtures; subfractionation has revealed more than 30 protein components. By reprecipitation, albumin which is electrophoretically 97–99% homogeneous can be prepared from fraction V. This is the salt-poor human serum albumin which is used clinically. Fraction II is almost pure gamma globulin. It is rich in antibodies and has thus found application in prophylaxis and modification of measles and infectious (viral) hepatitis (epidemic jaundice).

A. Albumin: This fraction of the serum proteins, the most abundant of the proteins in the serum, is synthesized in the liver. It has a molecular weight of approximately 69,000. The primary structure of serum albumin consists of 610 amino acids arranged in a single peptide chain. The secondary structure of albumin appears to be one in which the chain is folded back upon itself to form layers which can be unfolded by lowering the pH and refolded by raising the pH again.

B. Globulins: The globulin fraction of the serum proteins is a very complex mixture. Certain components of particular interest will be described:

1. Mucoproteins and glycoproteins—These are combinations of carbohydrate (hexosamine) moieties with globulin, found principally in the alpha$_1$ and alpha$_2$ globulin fractions. Meyer defines mucoproteins (mucoids) as those containing more than 4% hexosamine and glycoproteins as those containing less.

2. The lipoproteins—About 3% of the plasma protein consists of combinations of lipid and protein migrating with the alpha globulins and about 5% of similar mixtures migrating with the beta globulins. By means of the ultracentrifuge, human serum was separated into various fractions to account for the total serum lipoproteins. Each fraction was analyzed for protein, phospholipid, free and esterified cholesterol, and triacylglycerols. The results of these analyses are shown in Table 32–3. Fraction A contains the beta lipoproteins, with densities less than 1.063; fraction B the alpha$_2$ lipoproteins, with densities of 1.063–1.107; and fraction C the alpha$_1$ lipoproteins, with densities of 1.107–1.220.

It will be noted that the beta lipoproteins (fraction A, above) are rich in fat and, consequently, low in protein. They are very large molecules, having molecu-

Table 32–3. Percentage composition of lipoproteins in man.

	Fraction		
	A	B	C
Density	< 1.063	1.063–1.107	1.107–1.220
Lipids			
Phospholipid	21%	29%	20%
Cholesterol			
Free	8%	7%	2%
Esterified	29%	23%	13%
Triacylglycerols	25%	8%	6%
	83%	67%	41%
Protein	17%	33%	59%

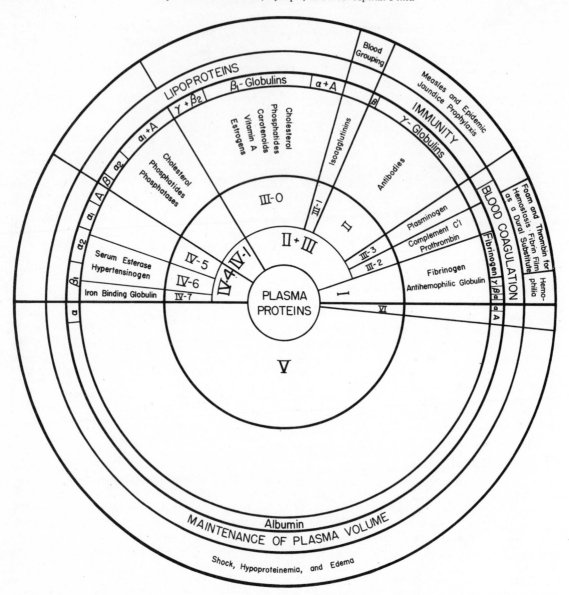

Figure 32–7. Plasma proteins: Their natural functions and clinical uses and separation into fractions. (Revised by LE Strong from Figure 1 in: Cohn EJ: Blood proteins and their therapeutic value. Science 101:54, 1945.)

lar weights in the range of 1,300,000. In contrast, the lipoproteins migrating with the alpha globulins have smaller amounts of fat and more protein, and their molecular weights tend to be much lower (in the range of 200,000). It is also apparent that the higher the fat and the lower the protein content of a lipoprotein, the lower is its specific gravity. As the fat content declines and the protein rises, there is a concomitant rise in the specific gravity of the lipoprotein so that the so-called high-density lipoproteins (sp gr > 1.220) contain relatively small amounts of lipid.

The lipoproteins probably function as major carriers of the lipids of the plasma since most of the plasma fat is associated with them. Such combinations

of lipid with protein provide a vehicle for the transport of fat in a predominantly aqueous medium such as plasma.

3. Metal-binding proteins—Globulins which combine stoichiometrically with iron and copper comprise about 3% of the plasma protein. **Siderophilin (transferrin)**, found in Cohn fraction IV-7, is an example of a protein in the plasma which binds iron. The main function of this protein is to transport iron in the plasma. In states of iron deficiency or in pregnancy, there is a significant increase in the concentration of this metal-binding protein in the plasma. In disease, such as in pernicious anemia, chronic infections, or liver disease, there is a reduction in the amount of this protein.

A blue-green copper-binding protein has been isolated from normal plasma. This protein, ceruloplasmin (MW 150,000), contains about 0.34% copper.

4. Gamma globulins—The gamma globulin fraction of the serum proteins is the principal site of the circulating antibodies, the so-called **immunoglobulins,** which constitute a family of closely related proteins possessing all of the known antibody activity of the serum.

On the basis of electrophoretic, immunologic, and ultracentrifugal studies, the immunoglobulins (Ig) have been divided into 5 groups. Of these, **IgG** (also known as γ-globulin or γG) is the major antibody-containing fraction, comprising approximately 80% of the gamma globulins. By ultracentrifugal analysis it would be designated a 7S gamma globulin in accordance with its sedimentation constant. Molecular weights are between 150,000 and 160,000.

The most extensive studies of antibody structures have been carried out with IgG. This topic and a more extensive discussion of the other immunoglobulins will be found in Chapter 34.

The normal (ie, adult) blood levels of IgG are not attained until 2 years of age. This emphasizes the importance of the immune substances contained in breast milk. Although immunoglobulins pass the placental barrier to some extent, the infant is much more dependent on immune bodies contained in breast milk to supply antibodies until his own immune system becomes operative.

The very early—ie, immediate postpartum—secretion of the mammary gland differs substantially from true breast milk. This first secretion, the **colostrum,** appears as a yellowish, alkaline, and slightly viscid fluid. It possesses a higher content of solids than breast milk, and the solid components are not exactly the same as those of breast milk. Colostrum coagulates on heating, whereas breast milk does not. The lipid components of colostrum contain more cholesterol and lecithins, and the fats have a higher iodine content than milk. The amount of colostrum secreted in humans is 150–300 ml/24 hours, but, on about the third or fourth postpartum day, true milk production begins and colostrum diminishes.

It is of considerable interest that colostrum is absorbed from the gastrointestinal tract of the infant without the necessity of any digestive change despite the great size of the globulin molecules contained therein.

Origin of the Plasma Proteins

The liver is the sole source of fibrinogen, prothrombin, and albumin. Most of the alpha and beta globulins are also of hepatic origin, but the gamma globulins originate from plasma cells and lymphoid tissue (see Chapter 34). Indeed, gamma globulins are the only proteins secreted by isolated lymph node cells. In plasmapheretic studies,* dogs on which an Eck

*Plasmapheresis is a technic for depleting the plasma proteins by withdrawal of blood and reinjection of washed cells suspended in Ringer's solution.

fistula has been performed (portal blood diverted to the vena cava) are able to regenerate plasma proteins at a rate only 10% of that of control dogs. The Eck operation results in progressive impairment of liver function. A similar decline in liver function occurs in chronic liver disease (cirrhosis), and here also low plasma protein levels (particularly albumin levels) are very characteristic.

A direct nutritional connection with plasma protein synthesis has long been known. Dietary protein serves as the source of the amino acids utilized for the synthesis of these proteins. Many studies have demonstrated a direct relationship between the quantity and especially the quality of ingested protein as it relates to the formation of plasma proteins, including antibody formation. In rats, antibody response to antigenic stimulus is decreased as a result of a dietary lack of the amino acids tryptophan and phenylalanine. As might be expected, all dietary proteins are not equally effective in supplying material for regeneration of plasma protein. For example, in the pioneer studies of this question, dogs were rendered hypoproteinemic by plasmapheresis and the efficacy was observed of various diet-supplied proteins to regenerate plasma protein. Fresh and dried beef serum and lactalbumin, a protein of milk, were most effective. Egg white, beef muscle, liver, casein, and gelatin (an incomplete protein which lacks tryptophan) followed in that order.

Functions of the Serum Proteins

A. Fluid Exchange: An important function of the serum proteins is the maintenance of osmotic balance between the circulating blood and the tissue spaces. The concentration of the electrolytes and of the organic solutes in plasma and tissue fluids is substantially the same; therefore, the osmotic pressures due to these substances are practically identical. However, the total osmotic pressure of the plasma, which exceeds 6.5 atmospheres (4940 mm Hg), is due not only to inorganic electrolytes and organic solutes but also to the plasma protein. These blood proteins are responsible for about 25 mm of the total osmotic pressure of the plasma. Because there is also a small amount of protein in the tissue fluids which exerts an osmotic pressure of about 10 mm Hg, the effective osmotic pressure of the blood over that of the tissue fluid is 15 (25 − 10) mm Hg. This has the effect of attracting fluid and dissolved substances into the circulation from the tissue spaces. Opposing this force is the hydrostatic pressure of the blood, which tends to force fluids out of the circulation and into the tissue spaces. On the arterial side of the capillary loop, the hydrostatic pressure may be considered to be about 30 mm Hg, and as the blood flows farther from the heart this pressure gradually decreases until it has fallen as low as 15 mm Hg in the venous capillaries and even lower in the lymphatics. The hydrostatic pressures of the capillary are opposed by approximately 8 mm Hg hydrostatic pressure in the tissue spaces. The effective hydrostatic pressure in the arterial capillary is therefore 22 mm Hg

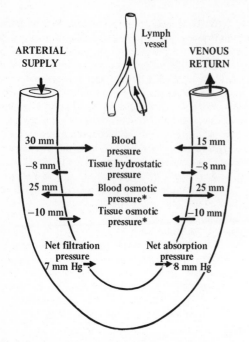

Figure 32–8. Capillary filtration and reabsorption ("Starling hypothesis"). The starred osmotic pressures are actually due only to the protein content of the respective fluids. They do not represent the total osmotic pressure.

osmotic effect to 500 ml of citrated plasma. This effect may be beneficial in treatment of shock or in any situation where it is desired to remove fluid from the tissues or to increase the blood volume.

B. Blood Buffers: The serum proteins, like other proteins, are amphoteric and can thus combine with acids or bases. At the normal pH of the blood, the proteins act as an acid and combine with cations (mainly sodium). The buffer pair which is formed constitutes a relatively small fraction of the total blood buffers, since only about 16 mEq/liter of sodium are combined with protein anions.

C. A Reserve of Body Protein: Serum albumin, when administered parenterally, is effective as a source of protein in hypoproteinemic patients. It is well assimilated and is not excreted unless a proteinuria already exists. Plasma is also effective as a source of nutrient protein.

The circulating plasma protein is not static; it constantly interchanges with a labile tissue reserve equal in quantity to the circulating protein. The term "dynamic equilibrium" has been applied to this interchange. In protein starvation, the body draws upon this tissue reserve as well as upon plasma protein for its metabolic needs.

D. Other Functions of Serum Proteins: These include transport of substances otherwise insoluble in plasma. Examples are the transport of bilirubin, steroid hormones, and the so-called free fatty acids by albumin. Many drugs are also transported in the plasma bound to albumin, such as certain antibiotics, coumarins, salicylates, and barbiturates. Lipids, including fat-soluble vitamins, are also transported by various fractions of the serum proteins, particularly the globulins, as illustrated by the lipoproteins which are lipid-globulin complexes. The gamma globulins are the sites of the circulating antibodies.

Plasma Protein Changes in Disease

The albumin component of the serum is either unchanged or, more usually, lowered in pathologic states. Albumin levels do not rise above normal except in the presence of hemoconcentration or dehydration. A decline in serum albumin levels (hypoalbuminemia) may follow prolonged malnutrition due to inadequate dietary intake of protein, impaired digestion of protein (as in pancreatic insufficiency), or inadequate absorption from the intestine. Hypoalbuminemia may also follow the chronic loss of protein, either in the urine (as in the nephrotic syndrome) or by extravasation (as in burns). Inability to synthesize albumin is a prominent feature of chronic liver disease (cirrhosis); indeed, hypoalbuminemia is a characteristic diagnostic and prognostic sign in this type of liver disease. Some types of hypoproteinemia are apparently due to an inherited inability to synthesize plasma protein fractions (so-called familial dysproteinemia), including albumin or the globulins. However, there are also patients with reduced levels of protein in the serum for which none of the above explanations suffice. Because these cases of "idiopathic hypoproteinemia" are

(30 − 8); in the venous capillary, 7 mm Hg (15 − 8). On the arterial side, the net result of these opposing pressures is a 7 mm Hg (22 − 15) excess of hydrostatic pressure over osmotic pressure; this favors filtration of materials outward from the capillary to the tissue spaces. On the venous side, the 8 mm Hg difference (15 − 7) is in favor of reabsorption of materials, because the intravascular osmotic pressure now predominates. Reabsorption is also aided by the lymphatics. This explanation of the mechanism of exchange of fluids and dissolved materials between the blood and tissue spaces is called the "Starling hypothesis." It is diagrammed in Fig 32–8.

The accumulation of excess fluid in the tissue spaces is termed "edema." Any alteration of the balance described above may result in edema. Decreases in serum protein concentration or increases in venous pressure, as in heart disease, are examples of pathologic processes which by altering the balance between osmotic and hydrostatic pressure would foster edema.

Each gram per dl of serum albumin exerts an osmotic pressure of 5.54 mm Hg, whereas the same quantity of serum globulin exerts a pressure of only 1.43 mm Hg. This is due to the fact that the albumin fractions consist of proteins of considerably lower molecular weight than those of the globulin fractions. Albumin is of major importance in maintaining serum osmotic pressure. One gram of albumin will hold 18 ml of fluid in the blood stream. Concentrated albumin infusions (25 g in 1 dl of diluent) are equivalent in characterized by excessively rapid disappearance of administered proteins from the plasma, the term "hypercatabolic hypoproteinemia" has been used to describe them. The rapid disappearance of protein from the plasma is now believed to be due to an excessive loss of protein into the gastrointestinal tract. Thus, the term "exudative enteropathy" has been suggested as more descriptive of the etiology of this syndrome.

The alterations which occur in the alpha and beta globulins are of considerable interest in disease. An increase in alpha globulins, particularly in the glycoproteins and mucoproteins, is a noteworthy feature of acute febrile disease. This seems to be related to inflammation or tissue destruction. It is also noted in moderate to advanced tuberculosis and in advanced carcinoma where tissue wasting is also occurring. In many diseases there is a constant association between decreased albumin and increased alpha globulin, eg, nephrosis, cirrhosis, and acute infections such as pneumonia, acute rheumatic fever, and typhus fever.

An abnormal constituent in the alpha globulin fraction of human serum is the so-called **C-reactive protein**. This protein is formed by the body in response to an inflammatory reaction. It is called C-reactive protein because it forms a precipitate with the somatic C-polysaccharide of the pneumococcus. Small amounts of this protein may be detected in human serum by a precipitin test using a specific antiserum from rabbits hyperimmunized with purified C-reactive protein.

Increases in beta globulins are often associated with accumulations of lipids.

Elevated levels of serum gamma globulin are characteristic of several diseases (see also Chapter 34). In the monoclonal gammopathies, one immunoglobulin predominates; it is detected as a single peak on the electrophoretic pattern. Upon analysis, the predominant globulin will be found to be a single protein species whose composition may be unique to a single patient. Examples of diseases in which hypergammaglobulinemias occur are multiple myeloma, Waldenström's macroglobulinemia, carcinoma, and lymphoma. In macroglobulinemia, large quantities of a protein of the IgM class are synthesized. In myeloma, the electrophoretic pattern is normal except for a superimposed protein boundary which generally possesses the mobility of a gamma or a beta globulin, although there have been a few reports of excessive alpha globulins.

The proteins described above as occurring in large amounts in the serum of myeloma patients have molecular weights in excess of 160,000. However, in about 30% of cases of this disease, an additional group of peculiar proteins of lower molecular weight may be detected in the serum and, because of their low molecular weights, may be excreted into the urine. These globulins, first described by Bence Jones in 1848, occur only in multiple myeloma and in a few cases of myeloid leukemia or other diseases which extensively involve the bone marrow. **Bence Jones proteins** have very unusual properties of solubility, precipitating at 45–60° C but redissolving on boiling. Recent chemical studies of the structure of Bence Jones proteins have revealed that these proteins are identical in composition to the light chains of normal immunoglobulins either of the κ or λ type. They appear as a result of synthesis by plasma cells of light chains in excess of heavy chains. The excess light chains, identical in composition to those of the myeloma proteins in the serum, are then excreted into the urine.

The Bence Jones proteins formed in any given interval are almost entirely excreted within 12 hours. As a result, a patient exhibiting Bence Jones proteinuria may excrete as much as half his daily nitrogen intake as Bence Jones protein.

Inherited Deficiencies of Plasma Protein Fractions

A. Thromboplastic Factors: The best example of a disease entity which is caused by an inherited lack of an essential factor in the clotting process is classical hemophilia. This hemorrhagic disease is due to a deficiency in the plasma content of antihemophilic globulin, a component of Cohn fraction I (see Fig 32–7). The defect is believed to be inherited as an X-linked recessive trait, transmitted exclusively through the females of an affected family although the females do not exhibit the bleeding tendency. The males, on the other hand, exhibit the disease but do not transmit the defect. The abnormality is characterized by a marked prolongation of the coagulation time of the blood with no abnormality in the prothrombin time. When antihemophilic globulin is added to hemophilic blood, clotting of such blood becomes normal. In the presence of hemorrhage, the hemophilic patient may be treated by injections of Cohn fraction I or by transfusions of fresh blood or plasma from normal donors.

Hemophilioid states have also been discovered, although these are less common than classical hemophilia. Each is due to a specific deficiency of a plasma thromboplastic factor.

Inherited as well as acquired deficiencies of the accelerator factors involved in conversion of prothrombin to thrombin have also been described.

B. Afibrinogenemia and Fibrinogenopenia: Afibrinogenemia is another inherited hemorrhagic disease which in its clinical manifestations superficially resembles hemophilia. It is characterized by the absence or near absence of fibrinogen, and transmitted as a non-X-linked recessive trait although it occurs slightly more frequently in males. In a typical case the clotting time and the prothrombin time are prolonged indefinitely. All of the clotting factors of the blood other than fibrinogen are present in normal amounts. In case of injury, death will occur from uncontrollable hemorrhage unless fibrinogen is supplied. Administered fibrinogen is lost from the body by normal decay in 12–21 days; therefore, the protein must be replaced every 10–14 days in quantities sufficient to maintain the fibrinogen level above 50 mg/dl of plasma.

Fibrinogenopenia and afibrinogenemia may also be acquired, most commonly as a complication of pregnancy where a long-standing intrauterine death of the fetus has occurred or where there has been premature separation of the placenta or the occurrence of amniotic fluid embolism following administration of oxytocin. It is thought that acute depletion of fibrinogen is brought about by release of thromboplastin-like substances from placenta and amniotic fluid, which results in extensive intravascular clotting and defibrination of the blood.

Acquired fibrinogen deficits may also occur as a consequence of surgical trauma, notably after thoracic or prostatic surgery. The cause may be an increase in fibrinolytic activity.

Totally incoagulable blood occurs only as a result of afibrinogenemia or in the presence of an excess of heparin. In the latter instance, correction of the clotting defect can be accomplished with either thrombin or thromboplastin; in the former situation, only fibrinogen will suffice to restore clotting.

C. Agammaglobulinemia and Hypogammaglobulinemia: Another apparently X-linked recessive factor is involved in the transmission of a defect in plasma protein production which is characterized by the complete or near-complete absence of gamma globulin from the serum. The cases reported so far have all been among males. Acquired forms of this disease have also been found; these occur in both sexes.

Patients afflicted with this inherited disorder of protein formation exhibit a greatly increased susceptibility to bacterial infection and an absence of gamma globulin from the serum and of circulating antibodies in the blood and tissues. Furthermore, there is a complete failure to produce antibodies in response to antigenic stimulation. Injections of gamma globulin may be used to aid in controlling bacterial infections in these patients. Peculiarly, their resistance to viral diseases seems normal.

In a study of several patients with agammaglobulinemia, some acquired and others congenital in origin, no abnormalities in the plasma clotting factors were found. This indicates that none of the factors involved in clotting mechanisms are gamma globulins. It is probable that congenital agammaglobulinemia is the result of an isolated deficiency of protein synthesis resulting from a lack of a single enzyme system. Furthermore, the deficiency of gamma globulin synthesis in these patients does not involve the liver but depends rather upon an anomaly of protein metabolism existing elsewhere in the reticuloendothelial system.

It is reported that in hypogammaglobulinemia there is a disturbance in the architecture of the lymphoid follicles, a lack of plasma cells, and a failure to form plasma cells after antigenic stimulation. There may also be a deficiency of at least 2 beta globulins which are immunochemically unrelated to gamma globulin.

HEMOGLOBIN

The red pigment of the erythrocyte is the conjugated protein hemoglobin. The normal concentration of hemoglobin in an adult is 14–16 g/dl of blood, all confined to the erythrocyte. It is estimated that there are about 750 g of hemoglobin in the total circulating blood of a 70 kg man and that about 6.25 g (90 mg/kg) are produced and destroyed each day.

Dilute acid will readily split hemoglobin into the protein globin and its prosthetic group **heme** (hematin). The hydrochloride of heme, called **hemin**, can easily be prepared in crystalline form. Heme is an iron porphyrin. The formation of porphyrins such as heme is described in Chapter 14.

Globin, the protein moiety of hemoglobin, consists of 4 subunits, ie, it has the structure of a tetramer. Each subunit consists of polypeptide chains. Two of the chains having identical amino acid composition are designated as a; the other 2, also identical with one another, are β chains. Adult human hemoglobin therefore possesses two a and two β chains. Each of the 4 chains has an associated heme group.

During fetal life, a hemoglobin is produced that differs from the hemoglobin A produced during adult life. This fetal hemoglobin (hemoglobin F) has two a chains, as in hemoglobin A, but there are two γ chains instead of the β chains.

The amino acid sequences of a, β, and γ chains derived from human hemoglobins are shown in Fig 32–9. It will be noted that an a chain has 141 amino acids. Valine is the N-terminal and arginine the C-terminal amino acid. The β chain has 146 amino acids, with valine as the N-terminal and histidine as the C-terminal amino acid. The γ chain also has 146 amino acids, but glycine is the N-terminal acid and histidine is the C-terminal amino acid.

The a chain has a molecular weight of 15,126; the β chain has a molecular weight of 15,866. Considering the fact that there are two a chains and two β chains in the entire globin molecule, it may be concluded that it contains a total of 574 amino acids, which, with 4 heme prosthetic groups (one for each chain), gives the hemoglobin molecule a molecular weight of 64,450. (Ultracentrifugal determinations of the molecular weight of hemoglobin had suggested a weight of 64,500.)

The iron contained in each heme group is coordinately bound to 2 histidine residues, probably at positions 58 and 87 in the a chains and at positions 63 and 92 in the β chains. It has been suggested that one of the imidazole bonds (possibly histidine 58 in the a chain and histidine 63 in the β chain) is reversibly displaced by oxygen when hemoglobin is oxygenated. This idea is shown diagrammatically in Fig 14–5. The relationship of heme iron to the porphyrin structures in heme as well as to histidine residues in globin when hemoglobin carries oxygen is also depicted in Fig 32–10.

The conformation of the tetrameric structure of

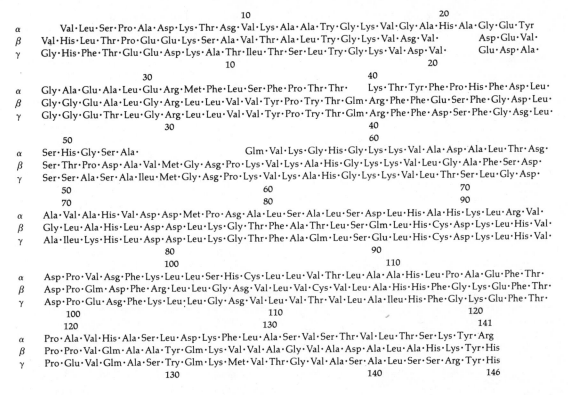

              10   20

α   Val·Leu·Ser·Pro·Ala·Asp·Lys·Thr·Asg·Val·Lys·Ala·Ala·Try·Gly·Lys·Val·Gly·Ala·His·Ala·Gly·Glu·Tyr

β   Val·His·Leu·Thr·Pro·Glu·Glu·Lys·Ser·Ala·Val·Thr·Ala·Leu·Try·Gly·Lys·Val·Asg·Val·   Asp·Glu·Val·

γ   Gly·His·Phe·Thr·Glu·Glu·Asp·Lys·Ala·Thr·Ileu·Thr·Ser·Leu·Try·Gly·Lys·Val·Asp·Val·   Glu·Asp·Ala·

              10   20

              30   40

α   Gly·Ala·Glu·Ala·Leu·Glu·Arg·Met·Phe·Leu·Ser·Phe·Pro·Thr·Thr·   Lys·Thr·Tyr·Phe·Pro·His·Phe·Asp·Leu·

β   Gly·Gly·Glu·Ala·Leu·Gly·Arg·Leu·Leu·Val·Val·Tyr·Pro·Try·Thr·Glm·Arg·Phe·Phe·Glu·Ser·Phe·Gly·Asp·Leu·

γ   Gly·Gly·Glu·Thr·Leu·Gly·Arg·Leu·Leu·Val·Val·Tyr·Pro·Try·Thr·Glm·Arg·Phe·Phe·Asp·Ser·Phe·Gly·Asg·Leu·

              30   40

   50   60

α   Ser·His·Gly·Ser·Ala·   Glm·Val·Lys·Gly·His·Gly·Lys·Lys·Val·Ala·Asp·Ala·Leu·Thr·Asg·

β   Ser·Thr·Pro·Asp·Ala·Val·Met·Gly·Asg·Pro·Lys·Val·Lys·Ala·His·Gly·Lys·Lys·Val·Leu·Gly·Ala·Phe·Ser·Asp·

γ   Ser·Ser·Ala·Ser·Ala·Ileu·Met·Gly·Asg·Pro·Lys·Val·Lys·Ala·His·Gly·Lys·Lys·Val·Leu·Thr·Ser·Leu·Gly·Asp·

   50   60   70

   70   80   90

α   Ala·Val·Ala·His·Val·Asp·Asp·Met·Pro·Asg·Ala·Leu·Ser·Ala·Leu·Ser·Asp·Leu·His·Ala·His·Lys·Leu·Arg·Val·

β   Gly·Leu·Ala·His·Leu·Asp·Asp·Leu·Lys·Gly·Thr·Phe·Ala·Thr·Leu·Ser·Glm·Leu·His·Cys·Asp·Lys·Leu·His·Val·

γ   Ala·Ileu·Lys·His·Leu·Asp·Asp·Leu·Lys·Gly·Thr·Phe·Ala·Glm·Leu·Ser·Glu·Leu·His·Cys·Asp·Lys·Leu·His·Val·

              80   90

             100   110

α   Asp·Pro·Val·Asg·Phe·Lys·Leu·Leu·Ser·His·Cys·Leu·Leu·Val·Thr·Leu·Ala·Ala·His·Leu·Pro·Ala·Glu·Phe·Thr·

β   Asp·Pro·Glm·Asp·Phe·Arg·Leu·Leu·Gly·Asg·Val·Leu·Val·Cys·Val·Leu·Ala·His·His·Phe·Gly·Lys·Glu·Phe·Thr·

γ   Asp·Pro·Glu·Asg·Phe·Lys·Leu·Leu·Gly·Asg·Val·Leu·Val·Thr·Val·Leu·Ala·Ileu·His·Phe·Gly·Lys·Glu·Phe·Thr·

   100   110   120

   120   130   141

α   Pro·Ala·Val·His·Ala·Ser·Leu·Asp·Lys·Phe·Leu·Ala·Ser·Val·Ser·Thr·Val·Leu·Thr·Ser·Lys·Tyr·Arg

β   Pro·Pro·Val·Glm·Ala·Ala·Tyr·Glm·Lys·Val·Val·Ala·Gly·Val·Ala·Asp·Ala·Leu·Ala·His·Lys·Tyr·His

γ   Pro·Glu·Val·Glm·Ala·Ser·Try·Glm·Lys·Met·Val·Thr·Gly·Val·Ala·Ser·Ala·Leu·Ser·Ser·Arg·Tyr·His

             130   140   146

Figure 32–9. Amino acid sequences in α, β, and γ chains derived from human hemoglobins; α and β from adult hemoglobin, and α and γ from fetal hemoglobin. Gaps are left in depicting the sequences only in order to emphasize sequence similarities in homologous portions of the 3 chains. In these sequences, Ileu = isoleucine; Try = tryptophan; Asg = asparagine; and Glm = glutamine. The numbers at the top indicate every tenth residue position in the α chain; at the bottom, the numbers refer to residues in the β and γ chains. (Reproduced, with permission, from White A, Handler P, Smith EL: *Principles of Biochemistry,* 5th ed. McGraw-Hill, 1973.)

hemoglobin is shown in Fig 32–11. This depicts the α and β chains with their N and C terminals indicated as well as the approximate positions of the heme porphyrin residues (shown as dark disks). It will be noted that the positively charged (cationic) N-terminal ammonium group of one α chain is close to the negatively charged (anionic) C-terminal group of the second α chain. A similar relationship exists between the β chains. The resultant electrostatic attraction is of considerable importance in the maintenance of the quaternary structure of the protein.

The most characteristic property of hemoglobin is its ability to carry oxygen to form oxyhemoglobin. The combination takes place with increasing tensions of oxygen as shown in Fig 33–1, where the sigmoidal curves of oxyhemoglobin formation are drawn at varying tensions of oxygen (P_{O_2}) and of CO_2. The effect of CO_2 on oxygen combination with hemoglobin, the so-called **Bohr effect,** is due to changes in pH in the medium surrounding the red cell. This is further discussed in Chapter 33. The combination of oxygen with hemoglobin is reversed merely by exposing oxyhemoglobin to lowered oxygen tensions. At oxygen tensions of 100 mm Hg or more, hemoglobin is virtually 100% saturated, and approximately 1.34 ml of oxygen is then combined with each gram of hemoglobin.

The absorption spectra which are obtained when white light is passed through solutions of hemoglobin or closely related derivatives are of value in distinguishing these compounds from one another. Oxyhemoglobin or diluted arterial blood shows 3 absorption bands: a narrow band of light absorption at a wavelength of λ = 578 nm, a wider band at 542 nm, and a third with its center at 425 nm at the extreme violet end of the spectrum. Deoxygenated (ie, reduced) hemoglobin, on the other hand, shows only one broad band with its center at 559 nm.

When blood is treated with ozone, potassium permanganate, potassium ferricyanide, chlorates, nitrites, nitrobenzene, pyrogallic acid, acetanilid, or certain other oxidizing substances, **methemoglobin** is formed. In this compound, the iron which is in the ferrous (Fe^{2+}) state in hemoglobin is oxidized to the ferric (Fe^{3+}) state, in which form the hemoglobin cannot carry oxygen. In acid solution, methemoglobin has one absorption band with its center at λ = 634 nm.

Carbon monoxide combines with hemoglobin even more readily than does oxygen. Carbon monoxide hemoglobin shows 2 absorption bands, the middle of the first at 570 nm and the second at 542 nm. Combinations of hemoglobin with hydrogen sulfide or hydrocyanic acid also give characteristic absorption spectra. This provides a valuable means of detecting these com-

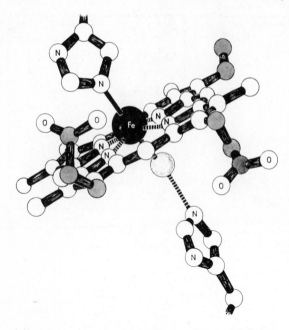

Figure 32–10. Addition of oxygen to heme iron in oxygenation. Shown also are the imidazole side chains of the 2 important histidine residues of globin which attach to the heme iron. (Reproduced, with permission, from Harper HA & others: *Physiologische Chemie.* Springer-Verlag, 1975.)

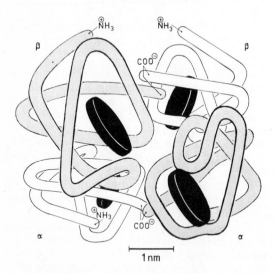

Figure 32–11. Conformation of the hemoglobin tetramer (two α and two β chains). The disks represent the heme porphyrin moieties. (Reproduced, with permission, from Harper HA & others: *Physiologische Chemie.* Springer-Verlag, 1975.)

pounds in the blood of individuals suspected of having been exposed to H_2S or HCN.

The average life of a red blood cell in the human body is about 120 days. When the red cells are destroyed, the porphyrin moiety of hemoglobin is broken down and thus forms the bile pigments bili-

verdin and bilirubin, which are carried to the liver for excretion into the intestine by way of the bile. The details of this process are described in Chapter 14.

Conformational Changes of Hemoglobin on Oxygenation

Reference has been made to the significant and unique characteristics of hemoglobin in the carriage of oxygen and the effect of CO_2 thereon. In addition, there is another compound, produced in the erythrocyte, that exerts an important effect on the carriage of oxygen by red cell hemoglobin. This compound is **2,3-diphosphoglyceric acid (DPG)**, also called bisphosphoglycerate (BPG). Its effect on oxygen carriage by hemoglobin is similar to that of CO_2. A more complete discussion of the origin of DPG in connection with the metabolic characteristics of the erythrocyte is given later in this chapter.

With the arrival of detailed information on the chemistry of hemoglobin and the conformational changes that occur in the molecule as it passes from the deoxygenated to the oxygenated state, it is now possible to attempt an explanation of the mechanisms for oxygen carriage and the effects of CO_2 and DPG thereon. The diagrams in Fig 32–12 represent the concepts of M.F. Perutz with respect to these events.

In the deoxygenated form, the 4 subunits, ie, α and β chains, of hemoglobin are assumed to be relatively tightly associated by means of several noncovalent bonds connecting the chains. These are as shown in Fig 32–12, namely the two α chains which form salt bridges with each other from the α-amino group of α_2-valine (the N-terminal amino acid of the α chain) to the C-terminal carboxyl group of α_1 arginine (amino acid at position 141), as well as from the guanidium group of α_1 arginine-141 to α_2 aspartic acid-126. The corresponding linkages from α_1 valine to α_2 arginine also exist. There are, in addition, bonds between the α COOH of histidine-146 (β_1) to the ϵ-amino of lysine-40 (α_2) and the imidazole of histidine-146 (β_1) to aspartic acid-94 (β_1). Also present are corresponding linkages from histidine-146 (β_2) to lysine-40 (α_1).

The next to last amino acids in all of the 4 chains of hemoglobin are tyrosine residues. These occur in hydrophobic pockets in the helical structure of the globin peptide chains. Finally, one molecule of 2,3-DPG may form 4 salt bridges with cationic groups in the β chains of hemoglobin, exerting a further constraint on the molecule. In normal adult deoxygenated human hemoglobin, 2,3-DPG is bound to hemoglobin in a mole-to-mole relationship. On the other hand, oxygenated hemoglobin has a low affinity for DPG. As indicated above, DPG brings about a tightening of the β chains close to one another. This interferes with carriage of oxygen; thus, deoxygenation (unloading of oxygen) is facilitated because the affinity of hemoglobin for oxygen is diminished by DPG.

The remaining diagrams of Fig 32–12 show the progress of events in the oxygenation of hemoglobin, starting with α_1, proceeding to α_2, and thence to the liberation of 2,3-DPG and oxygenation of β_1 and β_2.

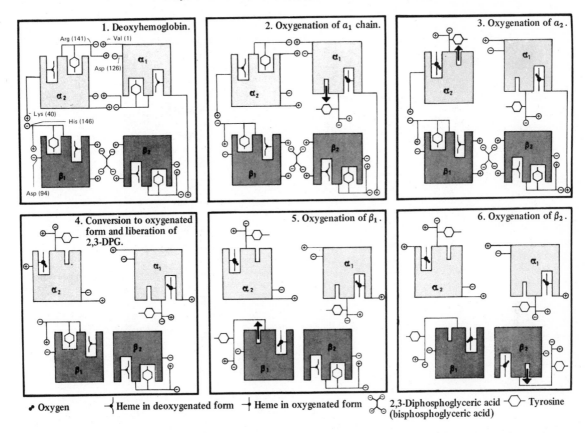

Figure 32–12. Diagrammatic representation of the molecular changes occurring during conversion of deoxyhemoglobin to oxyhemoglobin. (Reproduced, with permission, from Harper HA & others: *Physiologische Chemie.* Springer-Verlag, 1975.)

In deoxygenated hemoglobin, the salt bridges are intact and a mole of DPG is held between the two β chains. The 4 atoms of iron are out of the plane of the porphyrins within which they are contained, and the 4 tyrosine residues are present in hydrophobic pockets. In the oxygenated form, all of the salt bridges of hemoglobin have been broken and the DPG has been released; in addition, the 4 tyrosine residues have been released from the pockets.

The oxygenation of hemoglobin is depicted in Fig 32–12 as a gradual process, although the actual sequence of the changes is not certain. The stepwise oxygenation as shown would explain the sigmoidal character of the curve of oxygenation (Fig 33–1) by the increasing affinity of hemoglobin for oxygen as oxygenation occurs. The Bohr effect would be explained as representing changes in ionization constants of groups that form salt bridges in hemoglobin but are free in oxyhemoglobin.

Abnormal Hemoglobins

The first evidence that more than one type of hemoglobin exists may be traced back to the mid 19th century, when it was reported that newborn humans possessed a type of hemoglobin which was more resistant to denaturation by alkali than the hemoglobin present in the adult. When first reported, this hemoglobin, now referred to as fetal hemoglobin or hemoglobin F, was called hemochromogen. It was not until 1928 that Anson and Mirsky showed that this substance was actually a hemoglobin and, as now known, differs from normal adult hemoglobin only in the globin (protein) portion of the molecule. Although the production of fetal hemoglobin is normal during fetal life, in certain forms of anemia it has been observed that the anemic patient may still be producing fetal hemoglobin F at an age when it has entirely disappeared from the blood of normal adult individuals.

In 1949, Pauling, Itano, and others, using electrophoretic technics, separated 2 components of hemoglobin occurring in the blood of a patient afflicted with sickle cell anemia. One component was called hemoglobin (Hb) A and the other Hb B; the latter is now referred to as hemoglobin S, the abnormal hemoglobin of sickle cell disease.

The mechanism for the synthesis of hemoglobin protein is inherited from each parent in a manner similar to that of other genetically controlled protein synthesizing systems. Most individuals have inherited a normal mechanism from each parent, and their red blood cells contain only normal adult (A) hemoglobin, except for the first few months of postnatal life, when some fetal hemoglobin is still present.

The most useful technic for the detection of ab-

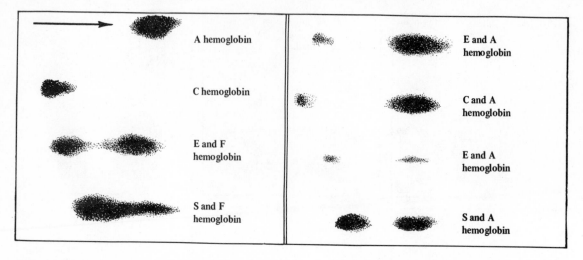

Figure 32–13. Paper electrophoresis of a number of hemoglobin specimens containing various types of hemoglobins. (Redrawn from Chernoff & Minnich: Hemoglobin E, a hereditary abnormality of human hemoglobin. Science 120:605, 1954.)

normal hemoglobins is that of electrophoresis. This is because differences in the amino acid composition of the globins may be such as to produce a variation in the mobilities of the hemoglobins on the supporting medium which is used. By means of paper electrophoresis, patterns of some abnormal hemoglobins as well as normal hemoglobin A are shown in Fig 32–13.

Various supporting media are now used for conducting electrophoretic determination in clinical laboratories not only for detection of abnormal hemoglobins but also for separation of immunoglobulins (see also Chapter 34). The different supporting media include paper, cellulose acetate, agar gel, starch gel, and starch block. In the USA, the most frequent mutant hemoglobins that occur are those of Hb S (sickle cell) and Hb C. Both of these are readily detectable by electrophoresis on cellulose acetate in alkaline buffers. There is, however, the problem of differentiating them from many other hemoglobins, which, while structurally different, nonetheless may not carry a sufficiently different electrical charge to permit significant differences in electrophoretic mobility. Electrophoresis on citrate agar, a method which depends on many factors other than charge, may confirm the identification of both Hb S and Hb C as well as several dozen rarer mutants. It can also reveal the presence of small amounts of Hb A and Hb F. The finding of both Hb A and Hb S is important as a means of differentiating the harmless "trait" (heterozygous) condition from the serious homozygous condition, particularly in sickle cell disease. In the trait, there is always more Hb A than Hb S (or Hb C).

The presence of abnormal hemoglobins in the blood is often associated with abnormalities in red cell morphology as well as definite clinical manifestations. Each abnormality appears to be transmitted as a mendelian-recessive characteristic. If the abnormality is heterozygous, ie, inherited from only one parent, and is associated with normal hemoglobin inherited from the other parent, the patient will have only a so-called "trait" (eg, sickle cell trait) and may be free of clinical findings, although the presence of the abnormality can still be detected electrophoretically.

The chemical differences between the hemoglobins are established by identification of the amino acid sequences (primary structures) of the globins. In the earliest studies of the composition of the globins, a purified preparation was split into a number of peptide fragments by treating the protein preparation with the proteolytic enzyme trypsin. This enzyme splits the polypeptide chain at sites occupied by lysine or arginine residues. The peptide fragments were then separated by chromatography on paper, using electrophoresis to induce amino acid migration in one direction, and conventional solvent chromatography further to separate the peptides in another direction. (See Fig 32–14.)

The pattern of the separated peptides as seen on the developed chromatogram is referred to as the "fingerprint" of the protein. By such a fingerprinting technic, Ingram was able to study the amino acid composition of the abnormal hemoglobin (S) which occurs in so-called sickle cell anemia, as had been indicated by Pauling (1949) in his illustration of what he termed a **"molecular disease."** As a result of these studies of the amino acid composition of sickle cell globin (hemoglobin S), it was discovered that while the alpha chains have the same amino acid sequence as those of normal hemoglobin, in both of the beta chains a valine residue occurs at position 6 (counting from the N-terminal amino acid), whereas in normal hemoglobin A, glutamic acid occurs at that position. This single amino acid substitution (valine for glutamic acid) is the only chemical difference between hemoglobins A and S among the 574 amino acids in the molecule. It is explained genetically as due to a mutation in the gene that controls synthesis of the beta chains. Such a mutation resulting in the replacement of one amino acid by

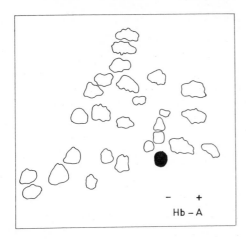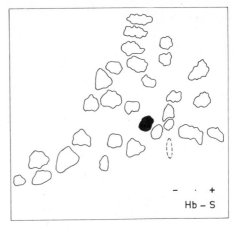

Figure 32–14. Two-dimensional chromatograms of peptide fragments produced by the action of trypsin on normal globin from hemoglobin A and on sickle cell hemoglobin S. The so-called "fingerprint" of the 2 proteins differs only within one peptide (shown as darker than the others). This peptide, when separated and its amino acid sequence determined, reveals that there is but a single amino acid difference in the composition of the 2 peptides. (Reproduced, with permission, from Harper HA & others: *Physiologische Chemie.* Springer-Verlag, 1975.)

another could result from only a single nucleotide base change in a coding triplet.

The solubility of hemoglobin S in the oxygenated state is not very different from that of hemoglobin A, but in the reduced (deoxygenated) state hemoglobin S is only about 2% as soluble as reduced hemoglobin A and about 1% as soluble as its own oxy- form. It is likely that the loss of the glutamate residue with its 2 carboxylic residues alters the distribution of positive and negative charges on the protein surface and thus changes its solubility. As a result of this insolubility of hemoglobin S, a significant increase in viscosity occurs when concentrated solutions of this protein become deoxygenated. Crystals of this form of the protein are crescent-shaped, resembling the so-called "sickled erythrocytes" of the patient with sickle cell disease. Thus it is the marked insolubility of the reduced hemoglobin S that is responsible for the clinical tests used to diagnose sickle cell disease as well as all of the signs and symptoms of the disease itself.

Sickle cell anemia is an inherited disorder that affects more than 50,000 Americans (10% of the black population in the USA is estimated to carry the gene for the disease) and others throughout the world although the incidence of this disease is concentrated in certain areas. In Africa, for example, up to 46% of the population has been estimated to carry the gene for sickle cell disease.

A promising agent for treating sickle cell anemia is sodium (or potassium) cyanate. In vitro, cyanate in concentrations as low as 0.01 M inhibits sickling of red blood cells. Cyanate is thought to act by carbamylating the terminal amino acid group of the beta chains of hemoglobin. Such carbamylation is believed to prevent the bonding of hemoglobin molecules to one another and thus to inhibit formation of the abnormal chains of hemoglobin characteristic of sickle cells.

The possible effectiveness of urea as a means of preventing sickling was studied. This compound is effective in vitro, possibly by breaking hydrophobic bonds or inhibiting the formation of such bonds between adjacent hemoglobin molecules, which would break or prevent the formation of the undesirable hemoglobin chains that occur in conjunction with the sickling phenomenon. Unfortunately, the results of a 2-year study of the effectiveness of urea as a treatment for sickle cell disease have been disappointing. It is now regarded as having no special value.

The blood of normal human adults contains a small amount (2.5% of the total) of a slowly migrating (in paper electrophoresis) type of hemoglobin A. This type is called hemoglobin A_2 to distinguish it from the much more abundant hemoglobin A_1. In hemoglobin A_2, replacing the beta chains of A_1 are chains having an arginine residue at position 16 instead of glycine as would be found at that position in a normal beta chain. These variant chains are designated **delta chains**.

In the fetal hemoglobin (F) referred to above, the alpha chains of A are present; however, instead of the beta chains, there are 2 **gamma chains**, which differ in composition from that of the beta chains of A_1 by having a lysine residue at position 6 rather than glutamic acid.

Hemoglobin H is an abnormal hemoglobin which has no alpha chains; instead, the molecule is composed of 4 beta chains, thus designated as β_4A. **Hemoglobin Barts** contains only gamma chains. These 2 types of hemoglobin may be found in the thalassemias, further discussed below.

Although most of the amino acid substitutions in the sequence of hemoglobins do not result in significant impairment of oxygen carrying power, there are conspicuous exceptions. Examples are the M types, wherein the histidine residues in position 58 of the *a*

Table 32—4. Composition of some abnormal hemoglobins.

Hemoglobin	Substitution	Designation
I. Amino Acid Substitutions in the Alpha Chains		
J (Toronto)	Ala → Asp at 5	$\alpha_2{}^5\text{Asp}\beta_2 A$
J (Paris)	Ala → Asp at 12	$\alpha_2{}^{12}\text{Asp}\beta_2 A$
J (Oxford)	Gly → Asp at 15	$\alpha_2{}^{15}\text{Asp}\beta_2 A$
I	Lys → Glu at 16	$\alpha_2{}^{16}\text{Glu}\beta_2 A$
J (Medellin)	Gly → Asp at 22	$\alpha_2{}^{22}\text{Asp}\beta_2 A$
(Memphis)	Glu → Gln at 23	$\alpha_2{}^{23}\text{Gln}\beta_2 A$
G (Honolulu; Singapore; Hong Kong)	Glu → Gln at 30	$\alpha_2{}^{30}\text{Gln}\beta_2 A$
(Torino)	Phe → Val at 43	$\alpha_2{}^{43}\text{Val}\beta_2 A$
L (Ferrara)	Asp → Gly at 47	$\alpha_2{}^{47}\text{Gly}\beta_2 A$
(Mexico)	Gln → Glu at 54	$\alpha_2{}^{54}\text{Glu}\beta_2 A$
(Shimonoseki)	Gln → Arg at 54	$\alpha_2{}^{54}\text{Arg}\beta_2 A$
(Norfolk)	Gly → Asp at 57	$\alpha_2{}^{57}\text{Asp}\beta_2 A$
M (Osaka; Boston)	His → Tyr at 58	$\alpha_2{}^{58}\text{Tyr}\beta_2 A$
G (Philadelphia)	Asn → Lys at 68	$\alpha_2{}^{68}\text{Lys}\beta_2 A$
M (Iwate; Kankakee)	His → Tyr at 87	$\alpha_2{}^{87}\text{Tyr}\beta_2 A$
(Chesapeake)	Arg → Leu at 92	$\alpha_2{}^{92}\text{Leu}\beta_2 A$
J (Capetown)	Arg → Gln at 92	$\alpha_2{}^{92}\text{Gln}\beta_2 A$
J (Tongariki)	Ala → Asp at 115	$\alpha_2{}^{115}\text{Asp}\beta_2 A$
O (Indonesia)	Glu → Lys at 116	$\alpha_2{}^{116}\text{Lys}\beta_2 A$
II. Amino Acid Substitutions in the Beta Chains		
C	Glu → Lys at 6	$\alpha_2 A\beta_2{}^6\text{Lys}$
S (Sickle cell)	Glu → Val at 6	$\alpha_2 A\beta_2{}^6\text{Val}$
C (Harlem)	Glu → Val at 6 Asp → Asn at 73	$\alpha_2 A\beta_2{}^6\text{Val} + {}^{73}\text{Asn}$
G (San Jose, Calif.)	Glu → Gly at 7	$\alpha_2 A\beta_2{}^7\text{Gly}$
J (Baltimore)	Gly → Asp at 16	$\alpha_2 A\beta_2{}^{16}\text{Asp}$
E (Saskatoon)	Glu → Lys at 22	$\alpha_2 A\beta_2{}^{22}\text{Lys}$
G (Saskatoon)	Glu → Ala at 22	$\alpha_2 A\beta_2{}^{22}\text{Ala}$
E	Glu → Lys at 26	$\alpha_2 A\beta_2{}^{26}\text{Lys}$
E (Genoa)	Leu → Pro at 28	$\alpha_2 A\beta_2{}^{28}\text{Pro}$
(Hammersmith)	Phe → Ser at 42	$\alpha_2 A\beta_2{}^{42}\text{Ser}$
G (Copenhagen)	Asp → Asn at 47	$\alpha_2 A\beta_2{}^{47}\text{Asn}$
(Hikari)	Lys → Asn at 61	$\alpha_2 A\beta_2{}^{61}\text{Asn}$
M (Hyde Park)	His → Tyr at 62	$\alpha_2 A\beta_2{}^{62}\text{Tyr}$
(Saskatoon)	His → Tyr at 63	$\alpha_2 A\beta_2{}^{63}\text{Tyr}$
(Zurich)	His → Arg at 63	$\alpha_2 A\beta_2{}^{63}\text{Arg}$
(Sydney)	Val → Ala at 67	$\alpha_2 A\beta_2{}^{67}\text{Ala}$
M (Milwaukee)	Val → Glu at 67	$\alpha_2 A\beta_2{}^{67}\text{Glu}$
J (Cambridge)	Gly → Asp at 69	$\alpha_2 A\beta_2{}^{69}\text{Asp}$
(Seattle)	Ala → Glu at 70	$\alpha_2 A\beta_2{}^{70}\text{Glu}$
G (Accra)	Asp → Asn at 79	$\alpha_2 A\beta_2{}^{79}\text{Asn}$
(Sabine)	Leu → Pro at 91	$\alpha_2 A\beta_2{}^{91}\text{Pro}$
N (Baltimore)	Lys → Glu at 95	$\alpha_2 A\beta_2{}^{95}\text{Glu}$
(Yakima)	Asp → His at 99	$\alpha_2 A\beta_2{}^{99}\text{His}$
(Kansas)	Asn → Thr at 102	$\alpha_2 A\beta_2{}^{102}\text{Thr}$
(New York)	Val → Glu at 113	$\alpha_2 A\beta_2{}^{113}\text{Glu}$
D (Punjab)	Glu → Gln at 121	$\alpha_2 A\beta_2{}^{121}\text{Gln}$
O (Arab)	Glu → Lys at 121	$\alpha_2 A\beta_2{}^{121}\text{Lys}$
K (Woolwich)	Lys → Glu at 132	$\alpha_2 A\beta_2{}^{132}\text{Glu}$
(Hope)	Gly → Asp at 136	$\alpha_2 A\beta_2{}^{136}\text{Asp}$
(Kenwood)	His → Asp at 143	$\alpha_2 A\beta_2{}^{143}\text{Asp}$
(Rainier)	Tyr → His at 145	$\alpha_2 A\beta_2{}^{145}\text{His}$

chains, or position 63 of the beta chains, are replaced by tyrosine residues. Because the histidine is involved in attachment of oxygen to heme iron, there does occur an impairment of oxygen transport. Furthermore, the heme iron in the variant chains is spontaneously oxidized to the ferric (Fe^{3+}) state, thus producing **methemoglobin** (hence the letter M used to designate these abnormal hemoglobins). It is evident that, in the hemoglobins M, two of the peptides (those in which the amino acid sequence is normal) will have ferrous iron heme molecules; the other two, the variant peptides, will have ferric iron hemin groups. The hemin ferric iron peptides cannot bind oxygen and therefore will not serve as oxygen carriers. The heme ferrous iron peptides function normally, but the fact that 2 of the 4 peptides of the hemoglobin molecule are not functioning in oxygen transport results in only half the normal capacity for oxygen binding. Despite this circumstance, individuals with heterozygous inheritance of hemoglobin M do not exhibit signs of an oxygen deficit, although the increased concentration of methemoglobin in their blood produces a dusky appearance of the skin.

Hemoglobin Gun Hill is another variant of adult hemoglobin. This abnormal hemoglobin has only half the expected number of heme groups. It appears that 5 amino acid residues are missing from the beta chains of the globin. The missing residues normally occur in a linear sequence in the beta chain in the region which is involved in binding of heme to globin. It would appear that the reason for the absence of half of the normal number of heme groups is related to the deletion of the 5 amino acids which normally would be involved in binding of heme to globin beta chains. The origin of the Gun Hill mutant may be genetically explained by unequal crossing over during meiosis.

Hemoglobin Sabine is an example of an abnormal hemoglobin which may predispose to mechanical injury to the erythrocyte. Patients afflicted with this disorder (substitution in the β chain of proline for leucine at position 91) exhibit methemoglobinemia and inclusion body anemia. In one such patient there was abnormally rapid turnover of erythrocytes (half-life 4 days in contrast to the normal 28 days). Since the amino acid substitution occurs in the vicinity of the point of attachment of heme, there may occur a diminished attraction of the a and β chains for heme so that free heme is liberated and metabolized to dipyrroles which are then excreted in the urine. The globin moiety not attached to heme precipitates in the erythrocyte and is visible as the so-called Heinz (inclusion) bodies not infrequently noted in various blood dyscrasias. Attachment of the inclusion bodies to the cell membrane alters the permeability of the cell. As a result, osmotic damage (hemolysis) occurs. This is the ultimate cause of the anemia, which may be quite serious even in heterozygotes.

"Unstable" hemoglobins are those which have a stability which is less than that of Hb A when placed in an organic solvent or when subjected to a temperature greater than 50° C. This instability may result from substitution of an amino acid which is in contact with a heme group or one which may interfere with the contacts between the helices. This interference often involves a proline residue. Also, the deletion of a residue may cause a decrease in the stability of the molecule. Unstable hemoglobins were first discovered in a patient with the abnormal hemoglobin M (Zurich) wherein histidine is replaced by arginine in position 63 of the beta chains. In this patient, a severe hemolytic anemia developed after the administration of sulfonamides. It was concluded that hemoglobin Zurich is an example of what may be termed a "silent" mutation, causing no abnormal clinical symptoms until a chemical "insult" occurs such as exposure to oxidative drugs or chemicals. There have now been identified approximately 50 unstable hemoglobin variants which may be a factor in varying degrees of hemolysis from little or none to severe.

Nomenclature of the Abnormal Hemoglobins

In the years intervening since the discovery of the abnormality of the composition of sickle cell hemoglobin, many additional hemoglobins have been described which may be considered abnormal in the sense that the amino acid composition of certain of the globin chains differs from that of hemoglobin A. The amino acid substitution may or may not change notably the properties of the hemoglobin molecule, but it often leads to diminished rate of production of messenger RNA, resulting in a reduced amount of the altered hemoglobin and an increased amount of hemoglobin F in the red blood cells of an individual heterozygous for the defect. If the defect is inherited from both parents, ie, the inheritance is homozygous, anemia will occur because of the decreased rate of hemoglobin synthesis.

In certain areas of the world (West Africa, the Mediterranean area, Southeast Asia), characteristic hemoglobin variants occur in a large proportion of the population, usually inherited as a heterozygous character and thus occurring as a "trait." Examples are hemoglobins S, C, D (Punjab), and E.

Originally, newly found hemoglobins were designated alphabetically in the order of their discovery. For example, the next abnormal hemoglobin to be reported after S was called C (B having at one time been used to designate sickle cell hemoglobin). This lettering system is no longer entirely suitable because, as the actual differences in composition of the hemoglobins are established, it becomes clear that in several instances different letters have been assigned by different investigators to the same protein. Furthermore, some hemoglobins have differences in amino acid composition which are not electrophoretically evident; as a result, the same letter may be used when in fact the hemoglobins so designated are not identical. This has necessitated the addition of the name of the original geographic origin of the variant. Examples are found among hemoglobins M, C, D, G, and J.

In the present system of nomenclature for the hemoglobins, the peptide chains of the major components of normal adult (A_1) and fetal (F) hemoglobin are designated as alpha, beta, or gamma. By this system, adult hemoglobin (A_1) is written as $a_2 A\beta_2 A$ and fetal hemoglobin as $a_2 A\gamma_2 F$. The superscripts refer to the fact that the particular chain is that found in human adult or fetal hemoglobin. Hemoglobin S would be written as $a_2 A\beta_2 S$, indicating that the chains corresponding to the beta chains of A are of a different type—namely, that of hemoglobin S. When the actual site and the nature of the amino acid substitution become known, the nomenclature will so designate. For example, the defect in hemoglobin S consists in the substitution of a valine residue for a glutamic acid residue at position 6 (counting from the N-terminal of the peptide chain) within the beta chains. Hemoglobin S is therefore designated $a_2 A\beta_2 \,6\,Glu \rightarrow Val$, or $a_2 A\beta_2 \,6\,Val$. The symbol $\beta_2 \,6\,Glu \rightarrow Val$ is read as, "in both of the beta chains, at position 6 a glutamic residue is replaced by a valine."

Table 32–4 summarizes the current information on the nature of the amino acid substitution in a number of abnormal hemoglobins exhibiting variations in composition of either alpha or beta chains.

Thalassemia

The abnormal hemoglobins discussed above result from mutations affecting coding for amino acid sequences in globin peptide chains. Other mutations may occur which affect the *rate* of synthesis of these chains, the amino acid sequences remaining unaffected. These latter mutations are the causes of the **thalassemias**. They appear to result from mutations affecting regulator genes rather than structural genes, as would be the case in the abnormal hemoglobins exhibiting amino acid substitutions. The thalassemia gene may affect the synthesis of either the alpha or the beta chain of normal hemoglobin. In so-called alpha chain thalassemia, wherein synthesis of a chains is repressed, there will be a compensatory increase in synthesis of other chains of which the cell is capable. An example is the pure β chain hemoglobin H mentioned above or the pure γ chain of hemoglobin Barts. Likewise, in β chain thalassemia, when the thalassemia gene represses β chain synthesis, an excess of a chains results which can combine with δ chains, producing an increase in A_2 hemoglobin, or with γ chains, producing an increase in fetal hemoglobin (F). Beta thalassemia is allelic with hemoglobins S or C, so that by interaction with the S or C gene there results a mixture of hemoglobins wherein S or C may comprise as much as 80–90% of the total hemoglobin. Alpha thalassemia is not allelic with S or C. Consequently, there is no interaction; hemoglobin S or C then constitutes but half of the total hemoglobin.

The abnormal hemoglobins consisting of only beta, gamma, or delta chains do not function as normal hemoglobin, having an abnormal oxygen dissociation curve including absence of a Bohr effect. **Thalassemia major** (Cooley's anemia; Mediterranean anemia) is the result of homozygous inheritance of thalassemia genes. **Thalassemia minor** is the heterozygous form.

Thalassemia may be difficult to diagnose; the electrophoretic pattern may exhibit no sign of an abnormal hemoglobin, although thalassemia may be found in combination with hemoglobin variants. The most common is Hb S-β-thalassemia, in which, if there is complete suppression (termed 0-thalassemia) of the β chain, the electrophoretic pattern will appear to be that of homozygous sickle cell anemia. Hb C-β-thalassemia is another hemoglobinopathy that may occasionally be found. If the inheritance is homozygous, the individual will appear to have Hb CC. Quantitation of the amount of hemoglobin A_2 is an important aid to the diagnosis of thalassemia. A patient with β thalassemia will generally have an **increased** amount of Hb A_2, usually 4–6%. In a thalassemia, Hb A_2 is usually slightly **decreased** to 1–2%.

A review of the subject of the abnormal hemoglobins and the diseases with which they are associated has been prepared by Lehmann & Huntsman (1972).

METABOLIC CHARACTERISTICS OF THE ERYTHROCYTE

The red blood cell is structurally and metabolically unique among the cells of the body. The mature erythrocyte does not possess a nucleus nor cytoplasmic subcellular structures. Metabolically, the red blood cell is able to function almost entirely by glycolysis; only vestiges of aerobic metabolism via the tricarboxylic acid cycle and of biosynthetic activities remain. However, glycolysis in red blood cells exhibits several special features. Noteworthy among these is the ability to maintain a high steady-state concentration of 2,3-bisphosphoglyceric acid (Fig 32–15). Glucose enters the red blood cell immediately, with little relation to the extracellular concentration of glucose. Within the red cell, glucose is converted to lactic acid via a series of enzymatically catalyzed reactions similar to those of the Embden-Meyerhof pathway of glycolysis well known in most cells. However, glucose is not oxidized to CO_2 except under special circumstances.

Although the mature human red blood cell does not possess the subcellular structures that are present in other cells, such as microsomes or mitochondria, the stromal component of the erythrocyte does exhibit a form of organization that may serve in the fashion of an ordered metabolic compartment as evidenced by the fact that this area of the cell contains firmly bound enzymes and metabolites. As a result of this stromal affinity on the part of several enzymes, there is a differential distribution of enzymes between the interior and the structural stroma that envelops the cell. A number of enzymes of the hydrolytic class are found only in the stromal portion of the red blood cell. These may be inactive in the intact cell because of their substantial affinity for the lipoprotein matrix of the stroma; however, when the stromal structure is damaged, dissociation of the enzymes from the matrix will occur with the result that enzymatic activity now becomes detectable. Examples of these stroma-bound enzymes are certain peptidases, acetylcholinesterase, ATPase, and NADase.

Certain enzymes of the glycolytic pathway within the red cell may be directly involved in the transport of metabolites across the red cell membrane when such enzymes are located at the cell surface. As an example, glyceraldehyde-3-phosphate dehydrogenase could play a role in the transport of inorganic phosphate (P_i) across the membrane of the erythrocyte since glyceraldehyde-3-phosphate dehydrogenase catalyzes the reaction whereby P_i enters the glycolytic pathway to form 1,3-bisphosphoglycerate from glyceraldehyde 3-phosphate. This idea finds support in the observation that P_i enters the interior of the red cell as organically bound phosphate; it is this phosphate moiety which is used to form ATP by phosphorylation at the substrate level in the subsequent step catalyzed by phosphoglycerate kinase (Fig 19–2). On the other hand, red cell intracellular P_i arises only from breakdown of ester phosphates rather than from extracellular P_i that has simply diffused into the cell.

Glycolysis in the Red Blood Cell

In primates, the red blood cells are directly permeable to glucose, and phosphorylation of the sugar then occurs within the cell. As is the case in the reactions of the classical Embden-Meyerhof pathway of glycolysis (Fig 19–2), the following enzymes catalyze the reactions of glycolysis in the erythrocyte. These are, in order of their participation: hexokinase, phosphohexose isomerase, phosphofructokinase, aldolase, phosphotriose isomerase, glyceraldehyde-3-phosphate dehydrogenase, phosphoglycerate kinase, phosphoglycerate mutase, enolase, pyruvate kinase, and lactic dehydrogenase.

The Rapoport-Luebering Cycle

The Rapoport-Luebering cycle describes a series of reactions in red blood cells of man and certain other mammals that may be considered as supplementary to glycolysis commencing at the triosephosphate level. The functional significance of this series of reactions is found in the fact that the red blood cell utilizes more glucose than it requires to maintain its cellular integrity; consequently, there must be developed some mechanism to dissipate the excess energy that is produced. Other factors in respect to the necessity for the red cell to "waste" energy are the circumstances that energy-demanding (endergonic) reactions that would utilize ATP are not present in the mature human erythrocyte, and ATPase activity, which controls ATP and ADP concentrations in the other cells of the organism, is functionally inactive. In the absence of a system to dispose of excess high-energy phosphate, ATP and 1,3-bisphosphoglycerate would accumulate, resulting in a decrease in ADP and P_i with consequent slowing or even complete cessation of glycolysis (see Chapter 17).

The Rapoport-Luebering cycle is a 2-step system

that serves as a mechanism to "waste" the energy not needed by the red cell. Commencing at the triosephosphate (glyceraldehyde 3-phosphate) level of glycolysis, the metabolic interrelationships of the various systems mentioned above are illustrated in Fig 32–15. Reactions IV and V constitute the Rapoport-Luebering cycle. They bring about a total energy loss of 14 kilocalories: 10 in reaction IV and 4 in reaction V. Reactions I, II, and III are essentially the same as those of the classical Embden-Meyerhof pathway of glycolysis as found in other tissues.

In Chapter 33 there is a discussion of the transport of oxygen by the blood. Organic phosphates bind to hemoglobin, resulting in a decrease in the affinity for oxygen of the hemoglobin molecule. The effective compounds in this respect are 2,3-bisphosphoglycerate—the most important—and, of somewhat lesser importance, ATP and inositol hexaphosphate. As noted above, bisphosphoglycerate and, to a lesser extent, ATP are present in significant amounts in red blood cells. Bisphosphoglycerate may be considered to exert an effect on hemoglobin dissociation (ie, release of oxygen) similar to that of CO_2 (the Bohr effect). It is customary to express these activities with respect to hemoglobin oxygen transport in terms of an effect on the P-50, ie, partial pressure (mm Hg) at which hemoglobin is 50% saturated. Thus, increasing tensions of CO_2 (P_{CO_2}) shift the P-50 "to the right" (Fig 33–1). A similar effect on P-50 occurs with increasing concentrations of bisphosphoglycerate. These effects on oxygen transport may be interpreted as favoring the delivery of oxygen to the tissues in circumstances of low oxygen tension, as is usually the case at the tissues when the arterial blood is being delivered; indeed, it is precisely at that site that the CO_2 tension is rising, thus favoring oxygen delivery.

Although bisphosphoglycerate markedly reduces the affinity of hemoglobin for oxygen, the extent of the effect as well as its nature are affected by several variables. For example, there is a diminished binding of bisphosphoglycerate to fetal hemoglobin (hemoglobin F) as compared to normal adult hemoglobin (hemoglobin A). Several hereditary defects in red cell glycolysis that affect red cell bisphosphoglycerate concentration, such as the rare hexokinase deficiency and the much more commonly occurring pyruvate kinase deficiency, also exhibit alterations in red cell bisphosphoglycerate concentration; in a patient with red cell hexokinase deficiency, there was a decrease in bisphosphoglycerate concentration to about two-thirds of normal, whereas in pyruvate kinase deficiency bisphosphoglycerate is more than twice normal. As a result, affinity for oxygen of hemoglobin is greater than normal in hexokinase deficiency and less than normal in pyruvate kinase deficiency.

Other Aspects of Red Cell Bisphosphoglycerate

Tissue hypoxia has an important effect on the level of red cell bisphosphoglycerate. For example, pulmonary hypoxic hypoxia, stagnant hypoxia either as a result of cardiovascular failure or shock, and anemic

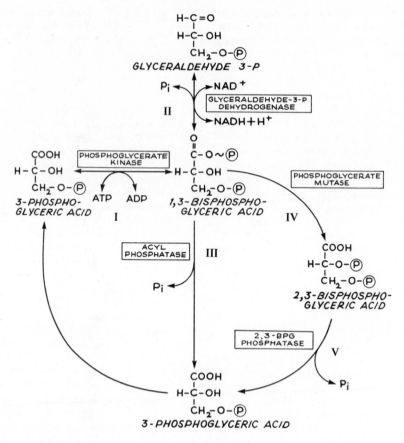

Figure 32–15. The Rapoport-Luebering cycle in red blood cells and its relationship to the Embden-Meyerhof pathway of glycolysis at the triosephosphate level. BPG = bisphosphoglycerate.

hypoxia, as in a deficit of red cell mass—all favor an increase in red cell organic phosphates, thus enhancing unloading of oxygen at the tissues. When normal individuals ascend to a height of 4500 meters, there is a rise in red cell bisphosphoglycerate level. The maximum rise occurs by 48 hours and returns to normal within a similar period after descent to sea level. It is believed that the mechanisms responsible for these changes in red cell bisphosphoglycerate during hypoxic states are associated with the red cell pH.

In preservation of red blood cells intended for transfusion, it is important to make certain that oxygen transport and release on the part of these cells are not altered. When blood is collected in acid-citrate-dextrose, there is an increased affinity for oxygen by hemoglobin in the stored cells and an associated decrease in bisphosphoglycerate concentration. The addition of pyruvate, inosine, and phosphate to the various media in which stored blood is collected replenishes the levels of red cell bisphosphoglycerate and ATP and restores the oxyhemoglobin dissociation curve toward normal.

A decline in red cell bisphosphoglycerate is a complication of the prolonged intravenous infusion of large concentrations of glucose, as may be necessary in patients who must be maintained by intravenous

hyperalimentation using solutions containing hypertonic (20–25%) glucose. Obviously, this is an undesirable occurrence in situations where it is particularly desirable that there be no impairment in oxygen delivery to the tissues.

Pyruvate Kinase Deficiency

Among the hereditary hemolytic anemias, there is a syndrome attributable to a deficiency of pyruvate kinase in red blood cells. This enzyme functions to catalyze transfer of a high-energy phosphate moiety from phosphoenolpyruvate to ADP to form ATP, thus liberating enolpyruvate, which itself promptly spontaneously reverts to ketopyruvate. Under anaerobic circumstances, the reduction of the pyruvate to lactate serves to reoxidize NADH to NAD, which is important earlier in the glycolytic pathway for the oxidation of glyceraldehyde (Fig 19–2).

Among the chemical abnormalities of red cell metabolism in pyruvate kinase-deficient patients there is an accumulation of glycolytic intermediates above the site of the enzymatic defect, such as phosphoenolpyruvate, 3-phosphoglycerate, and, especially, bisphosphoglycerate, whereas pyruvate and lactate levels tend to be decreased or possibly normal. It is very likely that the increase in 3-phosphoglycerate which occurs in glycolysis just before the site of enzyme deficiency in pyruvate kinase favors the synthesis of bisphosphoglycerate. As noted above with respect to the effect of bisphosphoglycerate on the P-50, this also explains the fact that the hemoglobin in the red cells of pyruvate kinase-deficient patients has an increased capacity to deliver oxygen to the tissues. On the other hand, there is a deficiency of ATP production by the pyruvate kinase-deficient red cells since the step at which pyruvate kinase operates is one of the few sources of ATP in glycolysis under the usual anaerobic circumstances. The impairment in pyruvate and in lactate production by these pyruvate kinase-deficient cells imposes a further handicap by contributing to a deficiency of NAD necessary to continuing glycolysis.

Although the mature red cell has a very limited need for ATP by virtue of its loss of the mechanisms to carry out endergonic reactions such as protein and enzyme synthesis, it is nonetheless necessary that it have sufficient ability to preserve its cellular integrity, including that of the cell membrane, and to maintain its capacity to defend against ionic imbalance—well illustrated by the need to concentrate potassium within the cell against an osmotic gradient, a process that requires ATP as a source of energy. A functioning glutathione reductase system is important to the red cell to protect against conversion of hemoglobin to methemoglobin. The production of NADPH by the pentose phosphate pathway of the red cell serves to supply a source of reducing equivalents for these reactions. The pyruvate kinase-deficient cell has no observed defect of these latter pathways, but the shortage of ATP and of oxidized niacin adenine dinucleotide (NAD) is critical. Even under normal circumstances, the red cell approaches destruction ultimately as a result of the slow but inevitable breakdown of metabolic machinery that it does not have the capacity to replace. When a genetic defect is present that further impairs already limited resources, it is not surprising that red cell survival is shortened and that a hemolytic anemia, as is characteristic of pyruvate kinase deficiency, will result.

Over 100 cases of pyruvate kinase deficiency hemolytic anemia have now been reported in the literature since the first description of this syndrome in 1961. Patients with this disorder have been found primarily in the USA and in Europe but also in Australia, New Zealand, Canada, and Japan. The disease is most common among peoples of northern European origin. A particularly high incidence of pyruvate kinase deficiency has been found among the Amish families in a certain region of Pennsylvania.

THE ANEMIAS

The concentration of hemoglobin in the blood may be measured by a number of methods, including iron analysis and oxygen combining power and, most commonly, by the color of the acid heme formed

Table 32–5. Characteristic values in 3 types of anemia.*

	MCV (fl)	MCH (pg)	MCHC (g/dl red cells)
Normal blood†	84–95	28–32	33–38
Macrocytic	95–160	30–52	31–38
Microcytic	72–79	22–26	31–38
Hypochromic	50–71	14–21	21–29

*Modified and reproduced, with permission, from Krupp & others: *Physician's Handbook,* 18th ed. Lange, 1976.
†Or normocytic anemia.

when a measured quantity of blood is treated with acid or alkali. Anemia exists when the hemoglobin content of the blood falls below normal.

Anemia may result from a decreased rate of production or from an increased loss or destruction of red blood cells. This may occur in acute or chronic hemorrhages, or may be produced by toxic factors (poisons or infections) which cause hemolysis and increased erythrocyte destruction. Decreased production of blood may be due to destruction or loss of function of the blood-forming tissue, as in the leukemias, Hodgkin's disease, multiple myeloma, and aplastic anemia. Certain drugs (benzene, gold salts, arsphenamine), chronic infections, and radiation may also lead to severe anemias because of their destructive or suppressive effect on erythrogenic tissue. Anemias related to inherited defects in production of hemoglobin have been discussed above.

Failure of erythrocyte production may also be caused by a lack of iron and protein in the diet. These nutritional or hypochromic anemias are common in infancy and childhood as well as pregnancy and in chronic blood loss where the iron or protein intake (or both) is inadequate.

Pernicious anemia is due to a failure in red cell production occasioned by a lack of a factor (or factors) necessary to erythrocyte maturation. In uncomplicated pernicious anemia this deficiency is completely corrected by vitamin B_{12}. According to Castle, 2 factors are necessary for the formation of red blood cells: (1) **extrinsic factor,** found in meat, yeast, liver, rice-polishings, eggs, and milk; and (2) the **intrinsic factor,** produced by the gastric mucosa and possibly also by the duodenal mucosa. Vitamin B_{12} is the extrinsic factor. It is now apparent that the function of the intrinsic factor is to assure absorption of vitamin B_{12} from the intestine. It has no direct effect on erythrocyte production, since parenterally administered vitamin B_{12} is itself sufficient to correct pernicious anemia.

Anemias are classified in one or both of 2 ways: (1) according to the predominating size of the erythrocytes, ie, macrocytic (large cell), microcytic (small cell), or normocytic (no significant alteration); and (2) according to the hemoglobin content of the red cell, ie, hyperchromic, hypochromic, or normochromic. There are 3 red cell indices which are useful in the differential diagnosis of the anemias:

Table 32—6. Blood, plasma, or serum values.

Determination	Material Analyzed	Amount Required* (F = fasting)	Normal Values (Values vary with procedure used)	SI Units†
Acetone bodies	Plasma	2 ml	0.3—2 mg/dl	3—20 mg/l
Aldosterone	Plasma		0.003—0.01 µg/dl	0.03—0.1 µg/l
Amino acid nitrogen	Plasma	2 ml F	3—5.5 mg/dl	2.1—3.9 mmol/l
Ammonia†	Blood	2 ml	40—70 µg/dl	22.16—38.78 µmol/l
Amylase	Serum	2 ml	80—180 Somogyi units/dl; 0.8—3.2 IU/liter	2.48—5.58 µkat/l
Ascorbic acid	Plasma	1 ml F	0.4—1.5 mg/dl (fasting)	23—85 µmol/l
	White cells (blood)	10 ml F	25—40 mg/dl	1420—2272 µmol/l
Bilirubin	Serum	2 ml	Direct: 0.1—0.4 mg/dl	1.71—6.84 µmol/l
			Indirect: 0.2—0.7 mg/dl	3.42—11.97 µmol/l
Calcium	Serum	2 ml F	9—10.6 mg/dl; 4.5—5.3 mEq/liter (varies with protein concentration)	2.25—2.65 mmol/l
Carbon dioxide: Content	Serum or plasma	1 ml	24—29 mEq/liter; 55—65 vol %	24—29 mmol/l
Combining power	Serum or plasma	1 ml	55—75 vol %	
Carotenoids	Serum	2 ml F	50—300 µg/dl	
Vitamin A	Serum	2 ml F	24—60 IU/dl; 24—60 µg/dl	0.84—2.10 µmol/l
Chloride	Serum	1 ml	100—106 mEq/liter; 350—375 mg/dl (as chloride)	100—106 mmol/l
Cholesterol	Serum	1 ml	150—280 mg/dl	3.9—7.3 mmol/l
Cholesterol esters	Serum	1 ml	50—65% of total cholesterol	
Copper	Serum	5 ml	100—200 µg/dl	16—31 µmol/l
Cortisol (free)	Plasma		4—18 µg/dl	110—497 nmol/l
Creatinine	Blood or serum	1 ml	0.7—1.5 mg/dl	60—130 µmol/l
Glucose (Folin)	Blood	0.1—1 ml F	80—120 mg/dl (fasting)	4.4—6.6 mmol/l
Glucose (true)	Blood	0.1—1 ml F	60—100 mg/dl	3.3—5.5 mmol/l
Hemoglobin	Blood	0.05 ml	Women: 12—16 g/dl	1.86—2.48 mmol/l
			Men: 14—18 g/dl	2.17—2.79 mmol/l
Iodine (BEI)	Serum	2 ml	3—6.5 µg/dl	0.24—0.51 µmol/l
Iodine, protein-bound	Serum	5 ml	4—8 µg/dl	0.32—0.63 µmol/l
Iron	Serum	5 ml	65—175 µg/dl	11.6—31.3 µmol/l
Iron-binding capacity	Serum	5 ml	250—410 µg/dl	44.8—73.3 µmol/l
Lactic acid	Blood (in iodoacetate)	2 ml	0.44—1.8 mM/liter; 4—16 mg/dl	0.44—1.28 µmol/l
Lactic dehydrogenase	Serum	2 ml	90—200 IU/liter	1.50—3.34 µkat/l
Lipase	Serum	2 ml	0.2—1.5 units (ml of 0.1 N NaOH)	0.93—6.96 µkat/l
Lipids, total	Serum	5 ml	500—600 mg/dl	5—6 g/l
Magnesium	Serum	2 ml	1.5—2.5 mEq/liter; 1—3 mg/dl	0.75—1.25 mmol/l
Nonprotein nitrogen‡	Serum or blood	1 ml	15—35 mg/dl	10.7—25 mmol/l
Oxygen: Capacity	Blood	5 ml	16—24 vol % (varies with Hb concentration)	0.16—0.24 of volume
Arterial content	Blood	5 ml	15—23 vol % (varies with Hb content)	0.15—0.23 of volume
Arterial % sat.			94—100% of capacity	0.94—1.00 of total
Venous content	Blood	5 ml	10—16 vol %	0.1—0.16 of total
Venous % sat.			60—85% of capacity	0.6—0.85 of total
Phosphatase, acid	Plasma	2 ml	1—5 units (King-Armstrong); 0.5—2 units (Bodansky); 0.5—2 units (Gutman); 0.1—1 unit (Shinowara); 0.1—0.63 unit (Bessey-Lowry) Women: 0.2—9.5 IU/liter Men: 0.5—11 IU/liter	4.48—17.94 µkat/l 0.90—8.97 µkat/l 27.5—175.14 µkat/l 3.34—158.65 nkat/l 8.35—183.7 nkat/l

*Minimum amount required for any procedure.

†SI (Système International d'Unités) units express clinical laboratory data according to internationally recommended names and symbols for quantities and units. This system attempts to establish a common language for reporting laboratory observations and measurements. A description of the system with conversion factors to translate the present normal values to SI units in whole blood, serum, and plasma as well as in urine may be obtained by reference to Lehmann HP: Metrication of clinical laboratory data in SI units. Am J Clin Pathol 65:2, 1976. ***Note:*** The **katal** is a suggested unit to define the catalytic amount of an enzyme. It is defined as the catalytic amount of any catalyst (including an enzyme) that catalyzes a reaction rate of 1 mole per second in an assay system. (The reaction conditions are not specified as a part of the definition.)

‡Do not use anticoagulant containing ammonium oxalate.

Table 32–6 (cont'd). Blood, plasma, or serum values.

Determination	Material Analyzed	Amount Required* (F = fasting)	Normal Values (Values vary with procedure used)	SI Units†
Phosphatase, alkaline	Plasma	2 ml	5–13 units (King-Armstrong);	59–153.4 µkat/l
			2–4.5 units (Bodansky);	17.94–40.37 µkat/l
			3–10 units (Gutman);	
			2.2–8.6 units (Shinowara);	19.73–77.14 µkat/l
			Children: 0.1–0.63 unit (Bessey-Lowry)	27.8–175.14 µkat/l
			Adults: 30–85 IU/liter;	501–1419 nkat/l
			0.8–2.3 units (Bessey-Lowry)	222.4–639.4 µkat/l
Phospholipid	Serum	2 ml	145–200 mg/dl	1.87–2.58 mmol/l
Phosphorus, inorganic	Serum	1 ml F	3–4.5 mg/dl (children, 4–7 mg)	1–1.5 mmol/l
Potassium	Serum	1 ml	2.5–5 mEq/liter; 14–20 mg/dl	2.5–5.0 mmol/l
Protein: Total	Serum	1 ml	5–8 g/dl	60–80 g/l
Albumin‡	Serum	1 ml	3.5–5.5 g/dl	0.54–0.847 mmol/l
Globulin‡	Serum		1.5–3 g/dl	15–30 g/l
Fibrinogen	Plasma	1 ml	0.2–0.6 g/dl	5.8–6.8 µmol/l
Pyruvic acid	Blood	2 ml	0.07–0.2 mM/liter; 0.7–2 mg/dl	79.8–228 µmol/l
Sodium	Serum	1 ml	136–145 mEq/liter; 310–340 mg/dl	136–145 mmol/l
Sulfate	Plasma or serum	2 ml	0.5–1.5 mEq/liter	50–150 µmol/l
Transaminases:				
Glutamic-oxaloacetic (SGOT)	Serum		5–40 units 6–25 IU/liter	40.1–320.8 nkat/l
Glutamic-pyruvic (SGPT)	Serum		5–35 units 3–26 IU/liter	40.1–280.7 nkat/l
Triglycerides	Serum	1 ml	< 165 mg/dl	< 18 mmol/l
Urea nitrogen§	Serum or blood	1 ml	8–20 mg/dl	2.86–7.14 mmol/l
Uric acid	Serum	1 ml	3–7.5 mg/dl	0.18–0.29 mmol/l

Blood volume (Evans blue dye method): Adults, 2990–6980 ml. (Women, 46.3–85.5 ml/kg; men, 66.2–99.7 ml/kg.)

*Minimum amount required for any procedure.

†See note (†) on previous page.

‡Albumin and globulin values obtained by use of 22% sodium sulfate; not in agreement with electrophoretic data. (See p 566.)

§Do not use anticoagulant containing ammonium oxalate.

A. Mean Corpuscular Volume (MCV): The range of normal MCV expressed in femtoliters is 80–94 fl; average, 87 fl. MCV is calculated from the volume of packed red cells (VPRC) and the red blood cell count. *Example:* VPRC = 0.45 1/1. RBC = 5.34 × 10¹²/1.

$$\frac{\text{VPRC (liters/liter)}}{\text{RBC (number} \times 10^{12}/\text{liter)}} = \frac{0.45}{5.34 \times 10^{12}} \times 1000 = 84.3 \text{ fl}$$

B. Mean Corpuscular Hemoglobin (MCH): This expresses the amount of hemoglobin per red blood cell. It is reported in picograms (pg). The normal range is 27–32 pg; average, 29.5 pg. For children, the range is 20–27 pg. MCH is calculated from the red blood cell count and the hemoglobin concentration. *Example:* Hemoglobin = 15.6 g/dl. RBC = 5.34 × 10¹²/1.

$$\frac{\text{Hb (g/dl blood)}}{\text{RBC (number} \times 10^{12}/\text{liter)}} = \frac{15.6}{5.34} \times 10 = 29.2 \text{ pg}$$

C. Mean Corpuscular Hemoglobin Concentration (MCHC): This is the amount of hemoglobin as percentage of the volume of a red blood cell. It is expressed in SI units as grams/deciliter of red blood cells. The normal range is 33–38 g/dl; average, 35 g/dl. It is calculated from the hemoglobin concentration and the volume of packed red blood cells. *Example:* Hemoglobin = 15.6 g/dl blood. VPRC = 0.45.

$$\frac{\text{Hb (g/dl blood)}}{\text{VPRC}} = \frac{15.6}{0.45} = 34.7 \text{ g/dl}$$

BLOOD CHEMISTRY

Determination of the content of various compounds in the blood is of increasing importance in the diagnosis and treatment of disease. The blood not only reflects the overall metabolism of the tissues but affords the most accessible method for the sampling of body fluids.

Many of the methods of blood chemistry require the preparation of a protein-free filtrate which is then analyzed for those constituents which remain. The most common technic for the preparation of a protein-free filtrate is the method of Folin and Wu, which utilizes sodium tungstate and sulfuric acid to make tungstic acid for the precipitation of the plasma proteins. Other protein precipitants include trichloroacetic acid or picric acid and a mixture of sodium hydroxide and zinc sulfate (the Somogyi precipitants). Urea, nonprotein nitrogen, uric acid, sugar, and creatinine are examples of blood constituents commonly determined in protein-free filtrates. Many other substances are determined directly, using oxalated whole blood, blood serum, or blood plasma without prior removal of protein.

The normal ranges in concentration of many of the important constituents of the blood are listed in Table 32–6.

LYMPH

The lymphatic fluid is a transudate formed from the plasma by filtration through the wall of the capillary. It resembles plasma in its content of substances which can permeate the capillary wall, although there are some differences in the electrolyte concentrations. The distribution of the nonelectrolytes such as glucose and urea is about equal in plasma and lymph, but the protein concentration of the lymph is definitely lower than that of plasma.

In its broadest aspects, the term "lymph" includes not only the fluid in the lymph vessels but also the fluid which bathes the cells, the "tissue" or "interstitial" fluid. The chemical composition of lymph would therefore be expected to vary with the source of the sample investigated. Thus, the fluid from the leg contains 2–3% protein, whereas that from the intestines contains 4–6% and that from the liver 6–8%.

The lymphatic vessels of the abdominal viscera, the "lacteals," absorb the majority of fat from the intestine. After a meal, this chylous fluid, milky-white in appearance because of its high content of neutral fat, can be readily demonstrated. Except for this high fat content, the chyle is similar in chemical composition to the lymph in other parts of the body.

CEREBROSPINAL FLUID

The cerebrospinal fluid is formed as an ultrafiltrate of the plasma by the choroid plexuses of the brain. The process is not one of simple filtration, since active secretory processes are involved. The normal fluid is water-clear, with a specific gravity of 1.003–1.008. Normally, the protein content is low, about 20–45 mg/dl, with an albumin-globulin ratio of 3:1, but in disease an increase in protein, particularly in globulin, is characteristic. In inflammatory meningitis, for example, the protein may rise as high as 125 mg to over 1 g/dl.

Various diseases of the brain (neurosyphilis, encephalitis, abscess, tumor) show protein elevations above normal of 20–300 mg/dl. The Pandy globulin test and the Lange colloidal gold test are diagnostic tests based on changes in the cerebrospinal fluid proteins.

The sugar in cerebrospinal fluid is somewhat less than in blood, 50–85 mg/dl in the fasting adult. It is raised in encephalitis, central nervous system syphilis, abscesses, and tumors. It is decreased in purulent meningitis.

The chloride concentration is normally 700–750 mg/dl (expressed as NaCl) or 120–130 mEq/liter. It is generally decreased in meningitis and unchanged in syphilis, encephalitis, poliomyelitis, and other diseases of the central nervous system. The chloride is especially low in tuberculous meningitis.

The concentration of calcium in normal human cerebrospinal fluid is 2.43 ± 0.05 mEq/liter; that of magnesium, 2.40 ± 0.14 mEq/liter. Thus, the calcium content of the cerebrospinal fluid is considerably less than that of the serum, whereas that of magnesium is slightly higher; the ratio of calcium to magnesium was found to be 1.01 ± 0.06.

• • •

References

Albritton EC (editor): *Standard Values in Blood.* Saunders, 1952.

Biggs R, Macfarlane RG: *Human Blood Coagulation and Its Disorders.* Davis, 1962.

Broheck JR (editor): *Best & Taylor's Physiological Basis of Medical Practice,* 9th ed. Williams & Wilkins, 1973.

Ingram VM, Stretton OW: Genetic basis of the thalassemia disease. Nature 184:1903, 1959.

Lehmann H, Huntsman RG: The hemoglobinopathies. Page 1398 in: *The Metabolic Basis of Inherited Disease,* 3rd ed. Stanbury JB, Wyngaarden JB, Fredrickson DS (editors). McGraw-Hill, 1972.

Milner PF, Gooden HM, General RT: Citrate-agar electrophoresis in routine screening for hemoglobinopathies using a simple hemolysate. Am J Clin Pathol 64:58, 1975.

Pauling L & others: Sickle cell anemia, a molecular disease. Science 110:543, 1949.

Putnam FW (editor): *The Plasma Proteins.* 2 vols. Academic Press, 1960.

Rosen FS, Merler E: Genetic defects in gamma-globulin synthesis. Page 1643 in: *The Metabolic Basis of Inherited Disease,* 3rd ed. Stanbury JB, Wyngaarden JB, Fredrickson DS (editors). McGraw-Hill, 1972.

Roughton FJW, Kendrew JC (editors): *Haemoglobin.* Interscience, 1949.

Schneider RG, Schmidt RM: Electrophoretic screening for abnormal hemoglobins. In: *Abnormal Hemoglobins and Thalassaemia.* Schmidt RM (editor). Academic Press, 1975.

Schultze HE, Heremans JF: *Molecular Biology of Human Proteins.* Elsevier, 1966.

33...
The Chemistry of Respiration

PHYSICAL EXCHANGE OF GASES

The term "respiration" is here applied to the interchange of the 2 gases, oxygen and CO_2, between the body and its environment.

Composition of Atmospheric Air

The atmospheric air which we inhale has the following composition: oxygen, 20.96%; CO_2, 0.04%; and nitrogen, 79%. Other gases are present in trace amounts but are not of physiologic importance.

Composition of Expired Air

The expired air contains the same amount of nitrogen as the inspired air, but the oxygen has been reduced to about 15% and the CO_2 increased to about 5%. About one-fourth of the oxygen of the inspired air has passed into the blood and has been replaced in the expired air by an equal amount of CO_2 which has left the blood.

Partial Pressure of Gases

In the mixture of gases in air, each gas exerts its own partial pressure. For example, the partial pressure of oxygen at sea level would be 20% of the total pressure of 760 mm Hg; ie, the partial pressure of oxygen (P_{O_2}) = 760 × 0.20 = 152 mm Hg. In the alveoli of the lung the oxygen content is 15%. The total pressure after correction for the vapor pressure of water in the alveolar air (47 mm Hg at 37° C) is 760 − 47 = 713 mm Hg. The partial pressure of oxygen in the lung is therefore about 107 mm Hg (713 × 0.15 = 107); that of CO_2, 36 mm Hg (713 × 0.05 = 36).

Diffusion of Gases in the Lungs

When the gases of the inspired air come in contact with the alveolar membrane of the lung, it is assumed that the exchange of gases takes place in accordance with the usual physical laws of diffusion. Thus, the gas passes through the membrane and into the blood, or in the reverse direction, in accordance with the difference in the pressure of that particular gas on either side of the membrane. The gas pressures in the blood are usually expressed as gas "tensions"; for example, the CO_2 "tension" (P_{CO_2}) is the pressure of the dry gas (mm Hg) with which the dissolved carbonic acid in the blood is in equilibrium; similarly P_{O_2} (oxygen tension) is the pressure of the dry gas with which the dissolved oxygen in the blood is in equilibrium.

The exchange of gases between the alveoli and the blood is illustrated by the following:

Oxygen tension in alveolar air:	107 mm Hg
Oxygen tension in venous blood:	40 mm Hg

A pressure difference of 67 mm Hg serves to drive oxygen from the alveoli of the lung into the blood.

CO_2 tension in alveolar air:	36 mm Hg
CO_2 tension in venous blood:	46 mm Hg

A relatively small difference of 10 mm Hg is sufficient to drive CO_2 from the blood into the lung. This small difference in pressure is adequate because of the rapidity of the diffusion of CO_2 through the alveolar membrane. In the resting state, a difference of as little as 0.12 mm Hg in CO_2 tension will still provide for the elimination of this gas.

The tension of nitrogen is essentially the same in both venous blood and lung alveoli (570 mm Hg). This gas is therefore physiologically inert.

After this exchange of gases has occurred, the blood becomes arterial (in a chemical sense). Arterial blood has an oxygen tension of about 100 mm Hg and a CO_2 tension of 40 mm Hg. The nitrogen tension is, of course, unchanged (570 mm Hg). These gases are dissolved in the blood in simple physical solution, and the quantity of each gas which might be carried in the blood in this manner can be calculated according to Henry's law from their absorption coefficients.

It is of interest to compare the quantities of each of these gases which could be dissolved (under physiologic conditions of temperature and pressure) with the actual quantities found in the blood.

Table 33–1. Comparison of the calculated content with the actual content of oxygen, CO_2, and nitrogen in the blood.

	ml/dl		
	O_2	CO_2	N_2
Calculated content in blood	0.393	2.96	1.04
Actually present:			
Arterial blood	20.0	50.0	1.70
Venous blood	14.0	56.0	1.70

It is apparent that considerable quantities of oxygen and CO_2 are carried in the blood in other than simple solution. The mechanisms by which these increased amounts of oxygen and CO_2 are transported will now be discussed.

THE TRANSPORT OF OXYGEN BY THE BLOOD

Function of Hemoglobin

The transport of oxygen by the blood from the lungs to the tissues is due mainly to the ability of hemoglobin to combine reversibly with oxygen. This may be represented by the equation:

$$Hb + O_2 \rightleftharpoons HbO_2$$

(Hb = reduced [ie, deoxygenated] hemoglobin; HbO_2 = oxyhemoglobin)

The combination of hemoglobin and oxygen is not that of a compound or a chemical combination such as an oxide. The nature of the oxygen-hemoglobin affinity was not understood until the discoveries of Perutz on the molecular events of the hemoglobin-oxyhemoglobin interchange were made. This is discussed in detail in Chapter 32.

The degree of combination of oxygen with hemoglobin or of its reversal, ie, dissociation of oxyhemoglobin to release oxygen, is determined by the tension of the oxygen in the medium surrounding the hemoglobin. At a tension of 100 mm Hg or more, hemoglobin is completely saturated. Under these conditions, approximately 1.34 ml of oxygen are combined with each gram of hemoglobin. Assuming a hemoglobin concentration of 14.5 g/dl of blood, the total oxygen which would be carried as oxyhemoglobin would be 14.5 × 1.34, or 19.43 ml/dl (19.43 vol%). To this may be added the 0.393 ml physically dissolved; the total, approximately 20 vol%, is the oxygen capacity of blood which contains 14.5 g/dl of hemoglobin. It is apparent that the oxygen carrying power of the blood (the oxygen content) is largely a function of the hemoglobin (red cell) concentration.

Dissociation of Oxyhemoglobin (See Fig 33–1.)

The important relationship between the saturation of hemoglobin and the oxygen tension may be perceived by an examination of the dissociation curve of oxyhemoglobin, in which the percent saturation is plotted against the oxygen tension. The shape of the dissociation curve varies with the tension of CO_2. The curve drawn with CO_2 at a tension of 40 mm Hg is to be considered as representative of the normal physiologic condition. It will be noted that at the oxygen tension which exists in arterial blood (100 mm Hg), the hemoglobin is 95–98% saturated; that is, almost complete formation of oxyhemoglobin has occurred. A further increase in oxygen tension has only a slight effect on the saturation of hemoglobin.

As the oxygen tension falls, the saturation of hemoglobin declines slowly until the oxygen tension drops to about 50 mm Hg, at which point a rapid evolution of oxygen occurs. This is the "unloading tension" of hemoglobin. This initial lag in dissociation of oxyhemoglobin provides a fairly wide margin of safety which permits the oxygen tension in the lung to fall as low as 80 mm Hg before any significant decrease in the oxygenation of hemoglobin occurs.

In the tissues, where the oxygen tension is about 40 mm Hg (approximately the unloading tension of

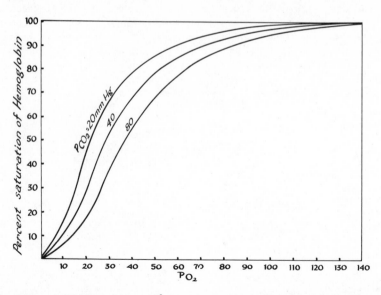

Figure 33–1. The dissociation curves of hemoglobin at 38° C and at partial pressures of CO_2 equal to 20, 40, and 80 mm Hg. (Redrawn from Davenport: *The ABC of Acid-Base Chemistry*, 4th ed. Univ of Chicago Press, 1958.)

hemoglobin), oxyhemoglobin dissociates and oxygen is readily made available to the cells. In the course of a single passage of the blood through the tissues, the oxygen content of the blood falls only from 20 to about 15 vol%. This provides a considerable reserve of oxygenated blood in the event of inadequate oxygenation at the lung.

Clinical Signs of Variation in Hemoglobin Saturation

The red color of deoxygenated hemoglobin is darker than the bright red of oxyhemoglobin. For this reason arterial blood is always brighter than venous blood. A decrease in normal oxygenation of the blood, with a consequent increase in deoxygenated hemoglobin, gives a characteristic bluish appearance to the skin. This is spoken of as cyanosis. It is characteristic of cyanide poisoning, where respiration is also impaired. A cyanotic appearance is dependent on the presence of at least 5 g of **deoxygenated hemoglobin** per deciliter of capillary blood (Lundsgaard). In severe anemia, the concentration of hemoglobin may be so low as to make cyanosis impossible even though the oxygen content of the blood is reduced. In CO poisoning, the formation of the cherry-red carbon monoxide-hemoglobin often produces a characteristic ruddy appearance, particularly noticeable in the lips, though dusky cyanosis may also be seen clinically.

Factors Which Affect the Dissociation of Oxyhemoglobin

A. Temperature: A rise in temperature decreases hemoglobin saturation. For example, at an oxygen tension of 100 mm Hg, hemoglobin is 93% saturated at 38° C but 98% saturated at 25° C. If the saturation of hemoglobin is measured at 10 mm Hg oxygen tension, these differences are even greater: at 25° C, hemoglobin is still 88% saturated, whereas at 37° C it is only 56% saturated. This last observation is of physiologic interest since it indicates that in warm-blooded animals hemoglobin gives up oxygen more readily when passing from high to low oxygen tensions (as from lungs to tissues) than it does in cold-blooded animals.

B. Electrolytes: At low oxygen tensions, oxyhemoglobin gives up oxygen more readily in the presence of electrolytes than it does in pure solution.

C. Effect of CO_2: The effect of CO_2 is illustrated in Fig 33–1, in which the curves for percentage saturation of hemoglobin at various tensions of oxygen are shown to vary with different tensions of CO_2. It is probable that the influence of CO_2 on the shape of the dissociation curve is actually the effect of carbonic acid formation, with consequent lowering of the pH of the environment. The increase in acidity, by altering the pH of the medium to the acid side of the isoelectric point of hemoglobin, facilitates the dissociation of oxyhemoglobin. The ability of CO_2 to shift the slope of the oxyhemoglobin dissociation curve to the right is known as the **Bohr effect**. The effect is often described as causing a shift of the P-50 to the right (Fig 33–1). The P-50 is the partial pressure (mm Hg) at which hemoglobin is 50% saturated. As is discussed in Chap-

ter 32, 2,3-bisphosphoglycerate, a compound readily produced during glycolysis in the red cell, also causes a significant shift of the P-50 to the right.

Under physiologic circumstances, these actions of electrolytes, CO_2, and 2,3-bisphosphoglycerate on delivery of oxygen to the tissues are of considerable importance.

Carboxyhemoglobin

As has been noted, hemoglobin combines with carbon monoxide even more readily than with oxygen (210 times as fast) to form cherry-red carboxyhemoglobin. This reduces the amount of hemoglobin available to carry oxygen. When the carbon monoxide in the inspired air is as low as 0.02%, headache and nausea occur. If the carbon monoxide concentration is only 1/210 that of oxygen in the air (approximately 0.1% carbon monoxide), unconsciousness will occur in 1 hour and death in 4 hours.

THE TRANSPORT OF CO_2 IN THE BLOOD

CO_2 is carried by the blood both in the cells and in the plasma. The CO_2 content of the arterial blood is 50–53 vol%, and in venous blood it is 54–60 vol% (ml CO_2 per 100 ml = vol%). In accordance with the data on the solubility of CO_2, 100 ml of blood at 37° C, exposed to a CO_2 tension of 40 mm Hg (as it is, for example, in alveolar air or arterial blood), would dissolve only about 2.9 ml. It is obvious that, as was shown for oxygen, the large majority of the blood CO_2 is not physically dissolved in the plasma but must exist in other forms. These comprise 3 main fractions: (1) a small amount of carbonic acid; (2) the "carbamino-bound" CO_2, which is transported in combination with proteins (mainly hemoglobin); and (3) that carried as bicarbonate in combination with the cations sodium or potassium.

The carbamino-bound CO_2, although it constitutes only about 20% of the total blood CO_2, is important in the exchange of this gas because of the relatively high rate of the reaction:

$$Hb \cdot NH_2 \underset{\longleftarrow}{\overset{CO_2}{\longrightarrow}} Hb \cdot NH \cdot COOH$$

where $Hb \cdot NH_2$ represents a free amino group of hemoglobin (or other blood protein) which is capable of combination with CO_2 to form the carbamino compound.

The amount of CO_2 physically dissolved in the blood is not large, but it is important because any change in its concentration will cause the following equilibrium to shift:

$$\uparrow CO_2 + H_2O \rightleftharpoons H_2CO_3 \rightleftharpoons H^+ + HCO_3^-$$

Carbonic Anhydrase

The rate at which equilibrium in the above reaction is attained is almost 100 times too slow to account for the amount of CO_2 which is eliminated from the blood in the 1 second allowed for passage through the pulmonary capillaries. Nevertheless, about 70% of the CO_2 is derived from that fraction which is carried as bicarbonates in the blood. This apparent inconsistency is explained by the action of an enzyme, **carbonic anhydrase,** which is associated with the hemoglobin in the red cells (never in the plasma). The enzyme has been isolated in highly purified form and shown to be a zinc-protein complex. It specifically catalyzes the removal of CO_2 from H_2CO_3. The reaction is, however, reversible. At the tissues, the formation of H_2CO_3 from CO_2 and H_2O is also accelerated by carbonic anhydrase. Small amounts of carbonic anhydrase are also found in muscle tissue, in the pancreas, and in spermatozoa. Much larger quantities occur in the parietal cells of the stomach, where the enzyme is involved in the secretion of hydrochloric acid. Carbonic anhydrase also occurs in the tubules of the kidney; here its function is also involved in hydrogen ion secretion.

Effect of CO_2 on Blood pH

Although it is true that the CO_2 evolved from the tissues will form carbonic acid, as shown in the above reaction, very little CO_2 can actually be carried in this form because of the effect of carbonic acid on the pH of the blood. It is estimated that in 24 hours the lungs remove the equivalent of 20–40 liters of 1 N acid as carbonic acid. This large acid load is successfully transported by the blood with hardly any variation in the blood pH, since most of the carbonic acid formed is promptly converted to bicarbonate, as shown in the equation below (B^+ represents cations in the blood, principally Na^+ or K^+).

$$H_2CO_3 \leftrightharpoons H^+ + HCO_3^- + B^+ \leftrightharpoons BHCO_3 + H^+$$

At the pH of blood (7.40), a ratio of 20:1 must exist between the bicarbonate and carbonic acid fractions. This ratio is calculated from the Henderson-Hasselbalch equation as follows:

$$7.4 = \text{pH of blood}$$
$$6.1 = \text{pKa, } H_2CO_3$$
$$\text{pH} = \text{pKa} + \log \frac{[\text{salt}]}{[\text{acid}]}$$
$$7.40 = 6.10 + \log \frac{S^*}{A}$$
$$1.30 = \log \frac{[BHCO_3]}{[H_2CO_3]}$$
$$\text{antilog } 1.3 = 20$$
$$\text{therefore} \quad \frac{20}{1} = \frac{[BHCO_3]}{[H_2CO_3]}$$

*S = salt (bicarbonate); A = acid (carbonic acid).

Any change in H ion activity will be met by an adjustment in the reaction. **As long as this ratio is**

maintained, the blood pH will be normal. Any alteration in the ratio will disturb the acid-base balance of the blood in the direction of acidemia or alkalemia.

THE BUFFER SYSTEMS OF THE BLOOD

Although venous blood carries considerably more CO_2 than does arterial blood, the buffers of the blood are so efficient that the pH of venous blood is more acid than that of arterial blood by only 0.01–0.03 units, ie, pH 7.40 vs pH 7.43. These blood buffers consist of the plasma proteins, hemoglobin, and oxyhemoglobin, and bicarbonates and inorganic phosphates. The small decrease in pH which occurs when CO_2 enters the venous blood at the tissues has the effect of shifting the ratio of acid to salt in all of these buffer pairs. In the sense that less cation is required to balance anions of the salt component of each of these buffers, when the ratio is shifted to form more of the acid, cation becomes available to form additional bicarbonate derived from the incoming CO_2. In this respect, the plasma phosphates and bicarbonates play a minor role. The buffering effect of the plasma proteins is of greater importance since they release sufficient cation to account for the carriage of about 10% of the total CO_2. The phosphates within the red cell are responsible for about 25% of the total CO_2 carried. Most important, however, is the unique buffering role of hemoglobin and oxyhemoglobin, which accounts for 60% of the CO_2 carrying capacity of whole blood. This role, described below, is, of course, in addition to the part hemoglobin plays in the carriage of carbamino-bound CO_2.

The Hemoglobin Buffers

The remarkable buffering capacity of hemoglobin is due to the fact that this protein in the oxy form is a stronger acid than in the reduced (deoxygenated) form. This is shown by the respective dissociation constants of the 2 forms of hemoglobin:

$$K, \text{oxyhemoglobin} = 2.4 \times 10^{-7}$$
$$K, \text{reduced oxyhemoglobin} = 6.6 \times 10^{-9}$$

At the lungs the formation of oxyhemoglobin from reduced hemoglobin must therefore release hydrogen ions, which will react with bicarbonate to form H_2CO_3. Because of the low CO_2 tension in the lung, the equilibrium then shifts toward the production of CO_2, which is continually eliminated in the expired air:

$$H^+ + HCO_3^- \leftrightarrow H_2CO_3 \leftrightarrow H_2O + CO_2$$

However, in the tissues, where oxygen tension is reduced, oxyhemoglobin dissociates (aided by CO_2, Bohr effect; see above), delivering oxygen to the cells, and reduced hemoglobin is formed. At the same time,

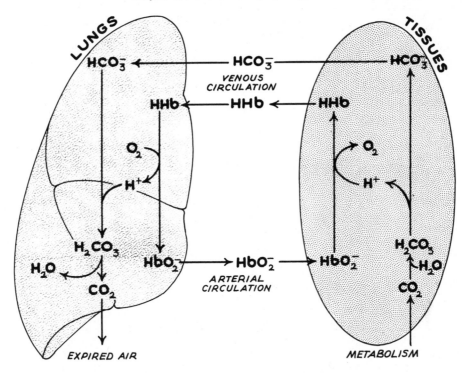

Figure 33–2. The buffering action of hemoglobin.

CO_2 produced in the course of metabolism enters the blood, where it is hydrated to form H_2CO_3, which ionizes to form H^+ and HCO_3^-. Reduced hemoglobin acting as an anion accepts the H^+ ions, forming so-called acid-reduced hemoglobin, HHb. Very little change in pH occurs because the newly arrived H^+ ions are buffered by formation of a very weak acid, ie, one in which ionization of hydrogen is suppressed. Then, as noted above, when the blood returns to the lungs these H^+ ions will be released as a result of the formation of a stronger acid, oxyhemoglobin, and the newly released H^+ will promptly be neutralized by HCO_3^-. Indeed, this reaction is essential to the liberation of CO_2 in the lungs.

These relationships of hemoglobin and oxyhemoglobin to the transport of CO_2 are illustrated in Fig 33–2.

At a pH of 7.25, 1 mol of oxyhemoglobin donates 1.88 mEq of H^+; 1 mol of reduced hemoglobin, on the other hand, because it is less ionized, donates only 1.28 mEq of H^+. It may therefore be calculated that at the tissues a change of 1 mol of oxyhemoglobin to reduced hemoglobin allows 0.6 mEq of H^+ to be bound (buffered) so that these newly formed H^+ ions do not bring about a change in pH. This circumstance as it relates to the role of the hemoglobin buffers is sometimes referred to as the **isohydric transport of CO_2**.

The Chloride Shift

It has been shown above that hemoglobin is responsible for about 60% of the buffering capacity of the blood. The red blood cell phosphates contribute another 25%. Thus some 85% of the CO_2 carrying power of the blood resides within the red cell. It is for this reason that the buffering power of whole blood greatly exceeds that of plasma or serum. However, it is also true that most of the buffered CO_2 is carried as bicarbonate in the plasma. These observations pose the question of how it is possible for the majority of the buffer capacity of the blood to reside in the red cells but to be exerted in the plasma.

CO_2 reacts with water to form carbonic acid, mainly inside the red cell since the catalyzing enzyme, carbonic anhydrase, is found only within the erythrocyte. The carbonic acid is then buffered by the intracellular buffers, phosphate and hemoglobin, combining in this case with potassium. Bicarbonate ion also returns to the plasma and exchanges with chloride, which shifts into the cell when the tension of CO_2 increases in the blood. The process is reversible, so that chloride leaves the cells and enters the plasma when the CO_2 tension is reduced. This fact is confirmed by the finding of a higher chloride content in arterial plasma than in venous plasma.

It is considered that under normal conditions the red cell is virtually impermeable to sodium or potassium. But since it is permeable to hydrogen, bicarbonate, and chloride ions, intracellular sources of cation (potassium) are indirectly made available to the plasma by chloride (anion) exchange. This permits the carriage of additional CO_2 (as sodium bicarbonate) by plasma.

The reactions of the chloride shift are summarized in Fig 33–3.

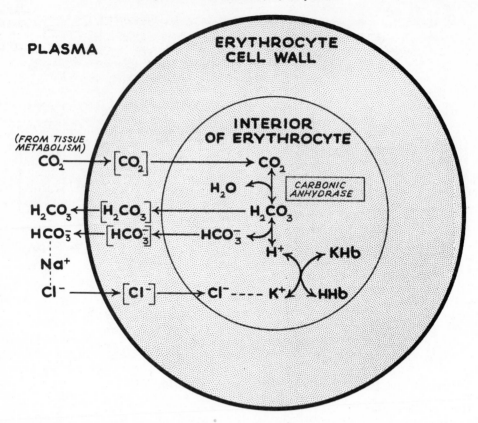

Figure 33—3. The chloride shift.

The CO_2 entering the blood from the tissues passes into the red cells, where it forms carbonic acid, a reaction catalyzed by carbonic anhydrase. Some of the carbonic acid returns to the plasma. The remainder reacts with the hemoglobin buffers to form bicarbonate, which then returns to the plasma where it exchanges with chloride. Sodium bicarbonate is formed in the plasma; and the chloride which the bicarbonate has replaced enters the red cells, where it is neutralized by potassium.

All of these reactions are reversible. At the lung, when the blood becomes arterial, chloride shifts back into the plasma, thus liberating intracellular potassium to buffer the newly formed oxyhemoglobin and, in the plasma, neutralizing the sodium liberated by the removal of CO_2 during respiration.

ACID-BASE BALANCE

It has been noted above that as long as the ratio of carbonic acid to bicarbonate in the blood is 1:20, the pH of the blood remains normal; and that any alteration in this ratio, which was calculated from the Henderson-Hasselbalch equation at the normal pH of the blood (see above), will disturb the acid-base balance of the blood and tissues in the direction of acidosis or alkalosis.

The content of H_2CO_3 in the blood is under the control of the respiratory system because of the dependence of carbonic acid on the PCO_2, which in turn is controlled by the organs of respiration. In consequence, disturbances in acid-base balance which are due to alterations in content of H_2CO_3 of the blood are said to be respiratory in origin. Thus **respiratory acidosis** will occur when circumstances are such as to cause an accumulation of H_2CO_3 in the blood; and **respiratory alkalosis** will occur when the rate of elimination of CO_2 is excessive, so that a reduction of H_2CO_3 occurs in the blood. In either instance, the normal 1:20 ratio of H_2CO_3 to bicarbonate is disturbed, and the pH of the blood will fall or rise in accordance with the retention or the excessive elimination of CO_2. If, however, the bicarbonate content of the blood can be adjusted to restore the 1:20 ratio between carbonic acid and bicarbonate, the pH will once more return to normal. Such an adjustment can be accomplished by the kidneys—in respiratory acidosis by reabsorption of more bicarbonate in the renal tubules, and in respiratory alkalosis by permitting more bicarbonate to escape reabsorption and thus to be excreted into the urine. The respiratory acidosis or alkalosis is then said to be **compensated**, which means that even though the amounts of H_2CO_3 and of bicarbonate in the blood are abnormal, the pH is normal because the ratio of the two has been restored to the normal 1:20. It follows from the above discussion that the CO_2 content (see below) of the plasma, which is a measure of both carbonic acid and bicarbonate, will be higher than normal in compensated respiratory acidosis and lower than normal in compensated respiratory alkalosis.

Disturbances in acid-base balance which are due to alterations in the content of bicarbonate in the blood are said to be metabolic in origin. A deficit of bicarbonate without any change in H_2CO_3 will produce a **metabolic acidosis**; an excess of bicarbonate, a **metabolic alkalosis**. Compensation will occur by adjustments of the carbonic acid concentrations, in the first instance by elimination of more CO_2 (hyperventilation) and in the latter instance by retention of CO_2 (depressed respirations). The CO_2 content of the plasma will obviously be lower than normal in meta-

bolic acidosis and higher than normal in metabolic alkalosis.

The biochemical changes which occur in the various types of acidosis and alkalosis, both uncompensated and compensated, are summarized in Fig 33–4.

Causes of Disturbances in Acid-Base Balance

A. Metabolic Acidosis: Caused by a decrease in the bicarbonate fraction, with either no change or a relatively smaller change in the carbonic acid fraction. This is the most common, classical type of acidosis. It occurs in uncontrolled diabetes with ketosis, in some cases of vomiting when the fluids lost are not acid, in renal disease, poisoning by an acid salt, excessive loss of intestinal fluids (particularly from the lower small intestine and colon, as in diarrhea or colitis), and whenever excessive losses of electrolyte have occurred. Increased respirations (hyperpnea) may be an important sign of an uncompensated acidosis.

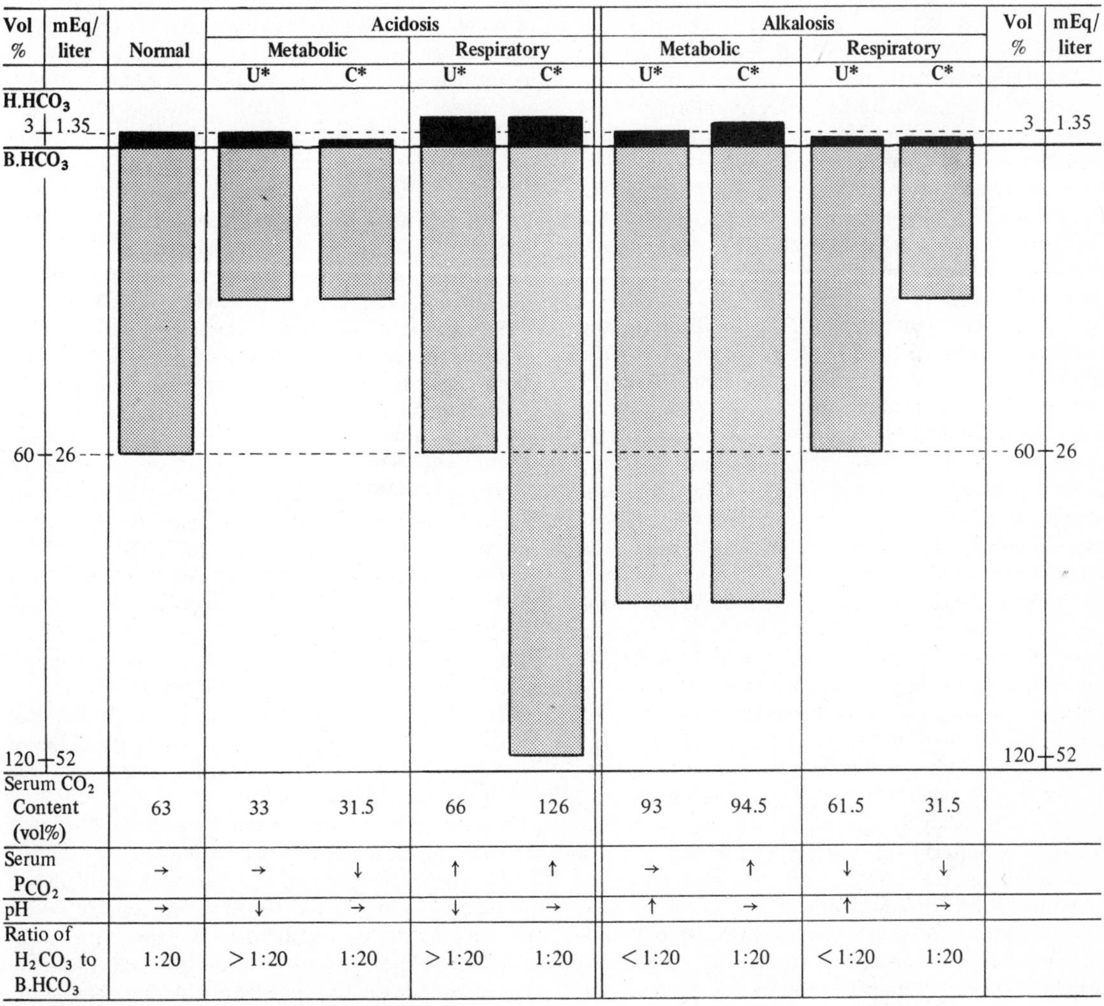

Vol % / mEq liter	Normal	Acidosis — Metabolic U*	Metabolic C*	Respiratory U*	Respiratory C*	Alkalosis — Metabolic U*	Metabolic C*	Respiratory U*	Respiratory C*	Vol % / mEq liter
H.HCO₃ (3 / 1.35) — B.HCO₃ (60 / 26 — 120 / 52) bar chart										3 / 1.35 · 60 / 26 · 120 / 52
Serum CO₂ Content (vol%)	63	33	31.5	66	126	93	94.5	61.5	31.5	
Serum P_{CO_2}	→	→	↓	↑	↑	→	↑	↓	↓	
pH	→	↓	→	↓	→	↑	→	↑	→	
Ratio of H₂CO₃ to B.HCO₃	1:20	>1:20	1:20	>1:20	1:20	<1:20	1:20	<1:20	1:20	

*U = Uncompensated. C = Compensated.

Figure 33—4. Biochemical changes in acidosis and alkalosis.

B. Respiratory Acidosis: Caused by an increase in carbonic acid relative to bicarbonate. This may occur in any disease which impairs respiration, such as pneumonia, emphysema, congestive failure, asthma, or in depression of the respiratory center (as by morphine poisoning). A poorly functioning respirator may also contribute to respiratory acidosis.

C. Metabolic Alkalosis: Occurs when there is an increase in the bicarbonate fraction, with either no change or a relatively smaller change in the carbonic acid fraction. A simple alkali excess leading to alkalosis is produced by the ingestion of large quantities of alkali, such as might occur in patients under treatment for peptic ulcer. But this type of alkalosis occurs much more commonly as a consequence of high intestinal obstruction (as in pyloric stenosis), after prolonged vomiting, or after the excessive removal of gastric secretions containing hydrochloric acid (as in gastric suction). The elevated blood pH of an uncompensated alkalosis often leads to tetany, possibly by inducing a decrease in ionized serum calcium. This is sometimes referred to as gastric tetany, although its relation to the stomach is, of course, incidental. The common denominator in this form of alkalosis is a chloride deficit caused by the removal of gastric secretions which are low in sodium but high in chloride (ie, as hydrochloric acid). The chloride ions which are lost are then replaced by bicarbonate. This type of metabolic alkalosis is aptly termed "hypochloremic" alkalosis. Potassium deficiency is frequently associated with the development of hypochloremic alkalosis. It also occurs in Cushing's disease and during corticotropin or cortisone administration.

In all types of uncompensated alkalosis, the respirations are slow and shallow; the urine may be alkaline, but usually, because of a concomitant deficit of sodium and potassium, will give an acid reaction even though the blood bicarbonate is elevated. This paradox is attributable in part to the fact that the excretion of the excess bicarbonate by the kidney will require an accompanying loss of sodium which under the conditions described (low sodium) cannot be spared. Thus the kidney defers to the necessity for maintaining sodium concentrations in the extracellular fluid at the expense of acid-base balance. However, an equal—if not, in the usual situations, a more important —cause of the excretion of an acid urine in the presence of an elevated plasma bicarbonate is the effect of a potassium deficit on the excretion of hydrogen ions by the kidney. Metabolic alkalosis as usually encountered clinically is almost always associated with a concomitant deficiency of potassium.

D. Respiratory Alkalosis: Occurs when there is a decrease in the carbonic acid fraction with no corresponding change in bicarbonate. This is brought about by hyperventilation, either voluntary or forced. Examples are hysterical hyperventilation, central nervous system disease affecting the respiratory system, the early stages of salicylate poisoning (see below), or injudicious use of respirators. Respiratory alkalosis may also occur in patients in hepatic coma.

Measurement of Acid-Base Balance; pH of Blood

The existence of uncompensated acidosis or alkalosis is most accurately determined by measurement of the pH of the blood. In respiratory acidosis or alkalosis, blood pH determination is essential to a satisfactory biochemical diagnosis. However, determination of the pH of the blood may not be feasible in some clinical circumstances. Furthermore, it is necessary to know to what extent the electrolyte pattern of the blood is disturbed in order to prescribe the proper corrective therapy. For these reasons, a determination of the CO_2 derived from a sample of blood plasma after treatment with acid (CO_2 capacity or CO_2 combining power) is also used. This measures essentially the total quantity of H_2CO_3 and of bicarbonate in the plasma but gives no information as to the ratio of distribution of the 2 components of the bicarbonate buffer system (and hence of the blood pH). It should also be noted that such a single determination also fails to take into account the concentration of other buffer systems such as hemoglobin (both oxygenated and reduced), serum protein, and phosphates. In disease, these may be notably altered and thus exert important effects on acid-base balance. However, the total blood CO_2 determination is reasonably satisfactory when taken in association with clinical observations and the history of the case. In addition, as noted above, it yields information on the degree of depletion or excess of bicarbonate so that the proper correction may be instituted.

In a clinical appraisal of the severity of a metabolic acidosis or alkalosis, the bicarbonate fraction of the blood is of primary interest. The plasma bicarbonate is sometimes designated the **alkali reserve** because it is this fraction of the plasma electrolyte which is used to neutralize all acidic compounds entering the blood and tissues. In this capacity, the plasma bicarbonate constitutes a sort of first line of defense. As a result, any threat to the acid-base equilibrium of the body will be reflected in a change in this component of the electrolyte structure. The concentration of the plasma bicarbonate, which is used to measure the alkali reserve, can be obtained from the CO_2 combining power. For this purpose, it is assumed that a 20:1 ratio exists between bicarbonate and carbonic acid; by dividing the CO_2 combining power (expressed in vol%) by 2.24, plasma bicarbonate concentration in mEq/liter is derived. A reduction in the plasma bicarbonate is usually sufficient to make a diagnosis of acidosis, although this may be erroneous since the ratio of carbonic acid to bicarbonate, which determines the blood pH, is not known.

The Role of the Kidney in Acid-Base Balance

In addition to carbonic acid, which is eliminated by the respiratory organs as CO_2, other acids, which are not volatile, are produced by metabolic processes. These include lactic and pyruvic acids and the more important inorganic acids, hydrochloric, phosphoric, and sulfuric. About 50–150 mEq of these inorganic acids are eliminated by the kidneys in a 24-hour period. It is of course necessary that these acids be partially buffered with cation, largely sodium; but in the distal tubules of the kidney some of this cation is reabsorbed (actually exchanged for hydrogen ion), and the pH of the urine is allowed to fall. This acidification of the urine in the distal tubule is a valuable function of the kidney in conserving the reserves of cation in the body.

Another device used by the kidney to buffer acids and thus to conserve fixed base (cation) is the production of ammonia from amino acids. The ammonia is substituted for alkali cations, and the amounts of ammonia mobilized for this purpose may be markedly increased when the production of acid within the body is excessive (eg, as in metabolic acidosis such as occurs as a result of the ketosis of uncontrolled diabetes).

When alkali is in excess, the kidney excretes an alkaline urine to correct this imbalance. The details of the renal regulation of acid-base equilibrium are discussed in Chapter 35.

In kidney disease, glomerular and tubular damage results in considerable impairment of these important renal mechanisms for the regulation of acid-base balance. Tubular reabsorption of sodium in exchange for hydrogen is poor, and excessive retention of acid catabolites, such as phosphates and sulfates, occurs because of decreased glomerular filtration. In addition, the mechanism for ammonia production by the tubules is inoperative. As a result, acidosis is a common finding in nephritis.

•   •   •

References

Anderson OS: The acid-base status of the blood. Scand J Clin Lab Invest 15 (Suppl 70):1, 1963.

Astrup P: A new approach to acid-base metabolism. Clin Chem 7:1, 1961.

Best CH, Taylor NB: *The Physiological Basis of Medical Practice,* 9th ed. Williams & Wilkins, 1973.

Christensen, HN: *Body Fluids and the Acid-Base Balance.* Saunders, 1964.

Davenport HW: *The ABC of Acid-Base Chemistry,* 6th ed. Univ of Chicago Press, 1974.

Filley GF: *Acid-Base and Gas Regulation.* Lea & Febiger, 1971.

Goldberger E: *A Primer of Water, Electrolyte, and Acid-Base Syndromes,* 5th ed. Lea & Febiger, 1975.

Hills AG: *Acid-Base Balance: Chemistry, Physiology, Pathophysiology.* Williams & Wilkins, 1973.

Robinson JR: *Fundamentals of Acid-Base Regulation,* 5th ed. Blackwell, 1975.

34 . . .

Immunochemistry

The immune system is comprised of 2 components, exhibited as cellular immunity or as humoral immunity. The lymphocyte is the primary cell involved in both components. The detection of various immunologic markers on the lymphocyte membrane as well as the functional characteristics of lymphocytes have permitted identification of 2 distinct populations of lymphocytes called T cells and B cells. The **T lymphocytes** (T cells) are thymus-derived or thymus-influenced during their development. T cells are responsible

for cellular immunity (ie, delayed skin reactivity, allograft rejection, antitumor immunity, and cellular defense against fungi, intracellular pathogens, and pox-viruses). The **B lymphocytes** (B cells) develop in the bursa of Fabricius in birds but are believed to be derived from bone marrow in mammals. The B cells are responsible for humoral immunity, which is expressed by the production of specific circulating plasma proteins termed antibodies or immunoglobulins.

This chapter is primarily concerned with the B

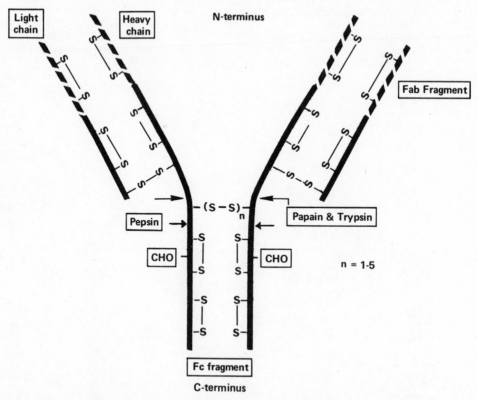

Figure 34–1. Structure of immunoglobulins. Electron microscopic studies have demonstrated that immunoglobulin molecules are Y-shaped. Solid lines indicate regions of constant amino acid sequences; broken lines indicate variable regions. Note symmetry in structure of molecule. One intrachain disulfide loop recurs for every 110–120 amino acid residues along heavy and light chains; about 60 residues are contained within each loop. From 1–5 inter-heavy chain disulfide bonds are present in each molecule depending on subclass of heavy chain. Points of cleavage of heavy chains by the proteolytic enzymes papain, trypsin, and pepsin, in relation to the inter-heavy chain disulfide bonds, are indicated. (Reproduced, with permission, from Freedman SO [editor] : *Clinical Immunology.* Harper, 1971.)

lymphocytes. The immunoglobulins produced by B lymphocytes will be discussed first, followed by a discussion of the biochemical characteristics of those substances which stimulate B lymphocytes to produce immunoglobulins.

STRUCTURE OF IMMUNOGLOBULINS

The basic unit of all immunoglobulin molecules consists of 4 polypeptide chains linked by disulfide bonds (Fig 34–1). There are 2 identical heavy (H) chains (MW 53,000–75,000) and 2 identical light (L) chains (MW 23,000). Immunoglobulins composed of more than one basic monomeric unit are termed **polymers**. The main examples are IgA dimers (2 units), IgA

trimers (3 units), and IgM pentamers (5 units) (Fig 34–2). Both heavy and light chains have C-terminal constant C regions (ie, constant amino acid sequences within a class or type) and N-terminal variable (V) regions, with considerable variation in amino acid sequence from molecule to molecule. The polypeptide chains are not straight sequences of amino acids but are folded 3-dimensionally with disulfide bonds to form areas called **domains**.

The part of the antibody molecule which combines with antigens is formed by a few amino acids in the V region of H and L chains. These amino acids are brought into close relationship by the folding of the V regions (domains) mentioned above.

Enzymes such as papain cleave IgG in the presence of cystine into 3 fragments: 2 Fab fragments (MW 52,000) and an Fc fragment (MW 48,000) (Fig 34–1). The isolated Fab fragments bear the entire antibody-

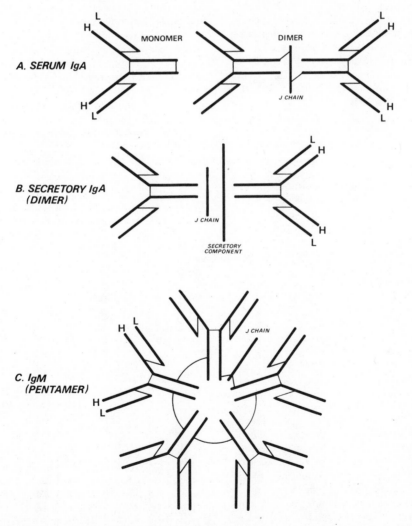

Figure 34–2. Highly schematic illustration of polymeric human immunoglobulins. Polypeptide chains are represented by thick lines; disulfide bonds linking different polypeptide chains are represented by thin lines. (Reproduced, with permission, from Fudenberg HH & others [editors] : *Basic & Clinical Immunology.* Lange, 1976.)

Table 34–1. Properties of human immunoglobulin chains.*

Designation	H Chains					L Chains		Secretory Component	J Chain
	γ	a	μ	δ	ϵ	κ	λ	SC	J
Classes in which chains occur	IgG	IgA	IgM	IgD	IgE	All classes	All classes	IgA	IgA,IgM
Subclasses or subtypes	1,2,3,4	1,2	1,2	...	...	...	1,2,3,4	...	...
Molecular weight (approximate)	50,000†	55,000	70,000	62,000	70,000	23,000	23,000	70,000	15,000
Carbohydrate (average percentage)	4	10	15	18	18	0	0	16	8
Number of oligosaccharides	1	2 or 3	5	?	5	0	0	?	1

*Reproduced, with permission, from Fudenberg HH & others (editors): *Basic & Clinical Immunology.* Lange, 1976.
†60,000 for γ3.

combining site for the antigen. The Fc fragment contains the lower halves of the H chains and is not involved in antibody specificity (Fig 34–1).

Several classes of L and H chains have been described. There are, however, only 2 major types of L chains in man, the kappa (κ) and lambda (λ) chains, distinguishable serologically as well as by their specific amino acid sequences. Either type of light chain can be associated with each of the heavy chain classes. Approximately 70% of the human immunoglobulin molecules carry κ light chains and 30% carry λ light chains. However, the H chain is unique to the class. In IgG, the H chain is termed a gamma (γ) chain; in IgA, an alpha (a) chain; in IgM, a mu (μ) chain; in IgD, a delta (δ) chain; and in IgE, an epsilon (ϵ) chain. The classification and properties of the H and L chains are listed in Table 34–1 and their amino acid composition in Table 34–2.

Carbohydrate residues are found within the immunoglobulin molecule attached to polypeptide chains (Table 34–1). There appear to be 2 carbohydrate units per molecule of IgG and 3 per molecule of IgM. Carbohydrate residues identified in the immunoglobulins include D-mannose, D-galactose, L-fructose, D-acetylneuraminic acid, and glucosamine.

The class of heavy chain is determined by the amino acid sequence in the constant region. The amino acid sequence is important in both the constant and the variable regions of the light chains.

These differences in amino acid sequence affect the conformation of the molecule (ie, secondary and higher orders of protein structure), which is important to assure antigen-antibody specificity.

Direct studies of amino acid sequence in a single species of IgG protein are possible with an immunoglobulin obtained from the serum of a patient with multiple myeloma. In this form of hypergammaglobulinemia, proliferation of a single type of an IgG-producing cell leads to the production of a large quantity of a single protein species. This is an example of so-called **monoclonal gammopathy,** in which one immunoglobulin with homologous composition predominates as a single peak in the electrophoretic pattern. L chains from a number of individual IgG molecules from myeloma patients have been partially or totally sequenced. None was found to be identical with an-

other. Data on H chains are not complete, but the evidence so far obtained indicates that the same degree of individuality in amino acid sequence prevails in H and L chains.

On the basis of electrophoretic, immunologic, and ultracentrifugal studies, the immunoglobulins have been divided into 5 groups.

(1) IgG globulin, the major antibody-containing fraction, comprises 80% of the gamma globulins. IgG is a single basic immunoglobulin unit with γ heavy chains. By ultracentrifugal analysis, it would be designated as a 7S gamma globulin in accordance with its sedimentation constant. Its molecular weight ranges from 150,000–160,000, and it contains 2–4% carbohydrates. It has the slowest electrophoretic mobility of all immunoglobulins. IgG is distributed in the extracellular fluid and is unique in its ability to cross the pla-

Table 34–2. Approximate amino acid compositions (in percent) of various immunoglobulin polypeptide chains. Values for γ, a, μ, κ, and λ chains were based on data from immunoglobulins isolated from normal human adults. The total of all amino acids measured was taken as unity. Tryptophan was excluded from the calculation.*

Amino Acid	Chain					Secretory Component	J Chain
	γ	a	μ	κ	λ		
Lys	7.0	4.7	4.8	6.4	5.4	5.6	4.3
His	2.0	2.2	2.0	1.1	1.7	0.9	0.8
Arg	3.0	3.8	4.0	3.5	2.5	4.9	7.3
Asn	7.9	7.4	8.0	8.2	7.0	10.7	17.0
Thr	7.4	10.0	10.8	8.1	9.3	6.0	9.7
Ser	12.1	10.8	10.5	14.0	14.5	8.6	5.8
Gln	9.6	9.7	10.3	11.2	10.5	10.8	11.2
Pro	8.8	9.1	8.0	5.5	6.3	5.2	6.0
Gly	7.3	7.7	5.7	6.6	7.6	9.9	1.6
Ala	4.8	6.7	6.2	6.4	8.2	5.9	4.4
Cys	2.4	2.8	2.6	2.3	2.4	3.1	5.6
Val	9.6	7.2	9.3	6.7	7.9	8.5	7.6
Met	1.4	0.6	1.3	0.5	0.3	0.0	0.7
Ile	1.8	1.4	3.3	3.2	2.6	3.5	6.5
Leu	6.9	9.9	6.8	8.0	7.0	9.2	6.0
Tyr	4.3	2.7	2.9	4.0	4.5	4.0	4.5
Phe	3.7	3.3	3.5	4.3	2.4	3.2	1.0

*Reproduced, with permission, from Fudenberg HH & others (editors): *Basic & Clinical Immunology.* Lange, 1976.

centa. Both IgG and IgM molecules bind complement by means of a receptor present in the constant regions of the γ or μ heavy chains.

(2) IgA has a molecular weight of approximately 180,000–400,000, and its S rate is 6.6–13. It differs from IgG in that it has a higher content of carbohydrate (5–10%). IgA is present in high concentrations in the blood, in seromucous secretions such as saliva, colostrum, and tears, and in secretions of the bronchi and the gastrointestinal tract. IgA found in serum is a single basic immunoglobulin unit with heavy a chains. Exocrine or secretory IgA is made up of 2 basic units connected by a J chain. A 60,000 MW molecule called **transport piece (t piece)** is attached to the Fc portion. This is necessary for the transport of IgA molecules into the lumens of exocrine glands. Secretory IgA appears to play an important part in host defense mechanisms against viral and bacterial infections. IgA does not cross the placenta.

(3) IgM is the largest protein yet to be sequenced. It contains 576 amino acids and has a mass of 950,000 daltons. IgM is the first antibody to be formed in a newborn animal or human. The cells that produce IgM later divide into daughter cells that produce IgG. IgM (with IgD) is the major immunoglobulin expressed on the surface of B cells. Its carbohydrate content is 10–12%. IgM globulins can be dissociated into subunits designated IgMs. Each monomer is comprised of two L chains and two H chains (μ) with 2 combining sites, so that the intact molecule has a total of 10 combining sites (Fig 34–2). The basic units are connected by disulfide bond bridges and a small polypeptide J chain. IgM does not cross the placenta.

(4) IgD:. No antibody activity has been associated with IgD. Although a significant number of patients with IgD myeloma have been reported, the physiologic significance of this class of globulins is not known.

(5) IgE is present in the serum in very low concentrations as a single basic immunoglobulin unit with heavy ϵ chains. The molecular weight of IgE is approximately 190,000 (8S). About half of patients with allergic diseases have increased serum IgE levels. IgE is a skin-sensitizing or reaginic antibody by virtue of a mast cell attachment site present on the constant region of the ϵ heavy chain. The specific interaction between antigen and IgE bound to the surface of mast cells results in the release of inflammatory mast cell products such as serotonin and histamine. A wheal and flare reaction or severe bronchospasms may be precipitated by such interaction in the tissues of the skin or lungs, respectively. The properties of human immunoglobulins are summarized in Table 34–3.

ELECTROPHORETIC DETERMINATION OF IMMUNOGLOBULINS

The immunoglobulins are composed of a heterogeneous group of serum proteins which account for approximately 20% of the plasma proteins. By the technic of electrophoresis, the various protein fractions can be separated.

Electrophoresis is the migration of charged particles in an electrolyte solution which occurs when an electric current is passed through the solution. Various protein components of the serum, at pH values above and below their isoelectric points, will migrate at varying rates because they possess different surface charges. The separation of proteins in electrical fields was per-

Table 34–3. Properties of human immunoglobulins.*

	IgG	IgA	IgM	IgD	IgE
H chain class	γ	a	μ	δ	ϵ
H chain subclass	$\gamma1,\gamma2,\gamma3,\gamma4$	$a1,a2$	$\mu1,\mu2$		
L chain type	κ and λ	κ and λ	κ and λ	κ and λ	κ and λ
Molecular formula	$\gamma_2 L_2$	$a_2 L_2$† or $(a_2 L_2)_2 SG\ddagger J\S$	$(a_2 L_2)_5 J\S$	$\delta_2 L_2$	$\epsilon_2 L_2$
Sedimentation coefficient (S)	6–7	7	19	7–8	8
Molecular weight (approximate)	150,000	160,000† 400,000**	900,000	180,000	190,000
Electrophoretic mobility (average)	γ	Fast γ to β	Fast γ to β	Fast γ	Fast γ
Complement fixation (classical)	+	0	++++	0	0
Serum concentration (approximate; mg/dl)	1000	200	120	3	0.05
Placental transfer	+	0	0	0	0
Reaginic activity	?	0	0	0	++++
Antibacterial lysis	+	+	+++	?	?
Antiviral activity	+	+++	+	?	?

*Reproduced, with permission, from Fudenberg HH & others (editors): *Basic & Clinical Immunology.* Lange, 1976.
†For monomeric serum IgA.
‡Secretory component.
§J chain.
**For secretory IgA.

fected in 1937 by Tiselius. However, owing to the relative complexity of this method, zone electrophoresis on a stabilizing medium has replaced electrophoresis in a free solution.

Zone Electrophoresis

Zone electrophoresis uses a supporting medium (ie, paper or cellulose acetate) which is inert and which does not impede or enhance the flow of molecules in an electrical field. The major advantage of cellulose acetate is the speed of completion of the electrophoretic migration (ie, 60–90 minutes compared to hours for paper). Serum or other biologic fluid samples are placed on the cellulose acetate and separated by electrophoresis for 90 minutes using alkaline buffer solutions (Fig 34–3). The strips are then stained and scanned. Densitometer scanning converts the bands into peaks which can be quantitated. Normal serum proteins are separated by this procedure into 5 major electrophoretic bands (albumin, α_1-globulin, α_2-globulin, β-globulin, and γ-globulin). Zone electrophoresis is very useful for the diagnosis of human paraprotein disorders such as multiple myeloma and hypogammaglobulinemia (Fig 34–4). In hypogammaglobulinemia, the decrease in serum γ-globulin is easily detected by this technic.

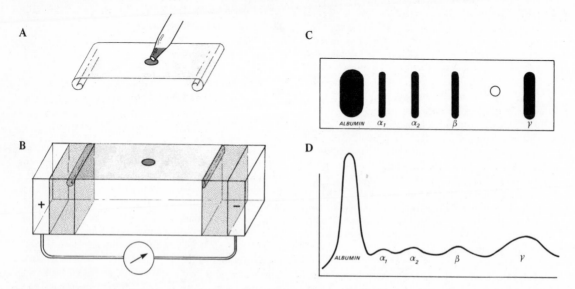

Figure 34–3. Technic of cellulose acetate zone electrophoresis. *A:* Small amount of serum or other fluid is applied to cellulose acetate strip. *B:* Electrophoresis of sample in electrolyte buffer is performed. *C:* Separated protein bands are visualized in characteristic position after being stained. *D:* Densitometer scanning from cellulose acetate strip converts bands to characteristic peaks of albumin, α_1-globulin, α_2-globulin, β-globulin, and γ-globulin. (Reproduced, with permission, from Fudenberg HH & others [editors] : *Basic & Clinical Immunology.* Lange, 1976.)

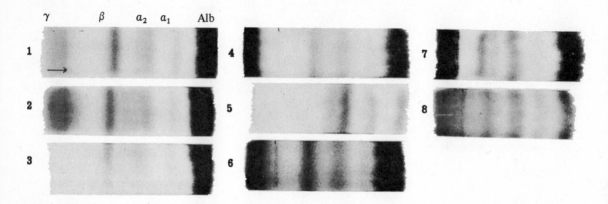

Figure 34–4. Examples of abnormalities in serum protein distribution which are evident on inspection of electrophoretic patterns obtained by electrophoresis on filter paper at pH 8.6. The direction of migration is indicated by the arrow. (1) Normal. (2) Infectious mononucleosis. (3) Hypogammaglobulinemia. (4) Leukemia (type undetermined). (5) Nephrotic syndrome. (6) Infectious hepatitis. (7) Multiple myeloma. (8) Sarcoidosis. (Reproduced, with permission, from Jencks & others: Am J Med 21:387, 1956.)

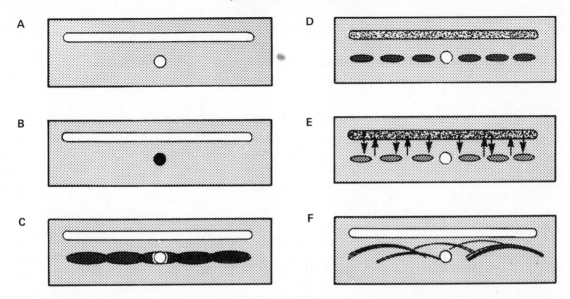

Figure 34–5. Technic of immunoelectrophoresis. *A:* Semi-solid agar poured onto glass slide and antigen well and antiserum trough cut out of agar. *B:* Antigen well filled with human serum. *C:* Serum separated by electrophoresis. *D:* Antiserum trough filled with antiserum to whole human serum. *E:* Serum and antiserum diffuse into agar. *F:* Precipitin lines form for individual serum proteins. (Reproduced, with permission, from Fudenberg HH & others [editors] : *Basic & Clinical Immunology.* Lange, 1976.)

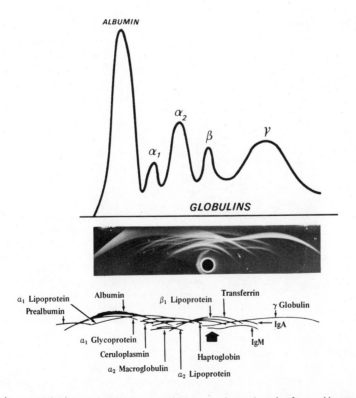

Figure 34–6. *Above:* Comparison of patterns of zone and immunoelectrophoresis of normal human serum. (Reproduced, with permission, from Fudenberg HH & others [editors] : *Basic & Clinical Immunology.* Lange, 1976.) *Below:* Immunoelectrophoresis of normal serum developed with a horse antiserum to whole normal serum. The broad vertical arrow indicates the starting point. (Reproduced, with permission, from White, Handler, & Smith: *Principles of Biochemistry,* 5th ed. Blakiston, 1973.)

Immunoelectrophoresis (IEP)

Immunoelectrophoresis combines both electrophoretic separation and immune precipitation of proteins. The test is performed on a glass slide covered with buffered molten agar (pH 8.2, ionic strength 0.025). After the agar has cooled, an antigen (serum) well and an antibody trough are cut in the agar (Fig 34–5). The serum sample is placed in the well, and the various proteins are then separated in an electrical field. Antiserum is next placed in the trough and allowed to diffuse for 18–24 hours in the direction of the separated proteins. When the various protein fractions meet the migrating antibody, precipitin lines are formed. These lines may be stained or photographed to make a permanent record. A comparison of the results of immunoelectrophoresis with those of zone electrophoresis is shown in Fig 34–6.

Immunoelectrophoresis is used as a screening device for semiquantitative estimates of immunoglobulin in serum and for identifying abnormal immunoglobulins (eg, myeloma protein). In addition, the absence of certain immunoglobulin classes or the presence of abnormal immunoglobulin molecules can be detected even in very low concentrations that are not apparent by zone electrophoresis.

QUANTITATIVE IMMUNOGLOBULIN DETERMINATIONS
(Radial Diffusion Technic)

Quantitative determinations of the serum IgG, IgA, and IgM levels can be accomplished by use of the radial diffusion technic (Fig 34–7). Wells are cut in an agar plate impregnated with a specific antiserum directed against a single human immunoglobulin class. A circular precipitin ring will form after the human serum proteins placed in the well diffuse through the agar. The diameter of the precipitin ring is proportionate to the concentration of serum immunoglobulin. The precise immunoglobulin level is determined by comparing the diameter of the unknown serum to that of a standard containing known levels of immunoglobulins.

This test does not differentiate between normal and abnormal immunoglobulin molecules, as does the immunoelectrophoresis procedure.

The normal serum concentrations of the 3 major immunoglobulin classes are as follows:

IgG, 710–1530 mg/dl (92–207 IU/ml)
IgA, 60–490 mg/dl (54–268 IU/ml)
IgM, 40–210 mg/dl (69–287 IU/ml)

Table 34–4 indicates the serum immunoglobulin concentration in diseases associated with polyclonal gammopathies.

The patient's age is important in interpreting immunoglobulin levels. The entire IgG portion of hu-

A
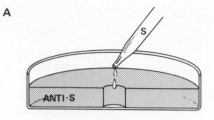

B
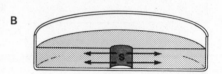

C
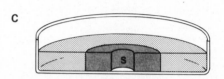

D
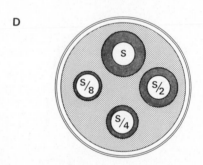

Figure 34–7. Single radial diffusion in agar (radial immunodiffusion). *A:* Petri dish is filled with semisolid agar solution containing antibody to antigen S. After agar hardens, the center well is filled with a precisely measured amount of material containing antigen S. *B:* Antigen S is allowed to diffuse radially from the center well for 24–48 hours. *C:* Where antigen S meets corresponding antibody to S in the agar, precipitation results. After reaction proceeds to completion, a sharp border or a ring is formed. *D:* By serial dilution of a known standard quantity of antigen S–S/1, S/2, S/4, S/8–rings of progressively decreasing size are formed. The amount of antigen S in unknown specimens can be calculated and compared with standard. (Reproduced, with permission, from Fudenberg HH & others [editors] : *Basic & Clinical Immunology.* Lange, 1976.)

man newborn cord blood has been transferred transplacentally from the mother (Fig 34–8). After birth, the maternal IgG decays, resulting in a falling serum IgG level. Autologous immunoglobulin synthesis begins early and increases progressively until late adolescence, when normal adult levels of IgG, IgA, and IgM are

Table 34—4. Serum immunoglobulin concentrations in diseases associated with polyclonal gammopathies.*

Diseases	Serum Immunoglobulin Concentration		
	IgG	IgA	IgM
Liver diseases			
Infectious hepatitis	↑ ↔ ↑↑	N ↔ ↑	N ↔ ↑↑
Laennec's cirrhosis	↑ ↔ ↑↑↑	↑ ↔ ↑↑↑	N ↔ ↑↑
Biliary cirrhosis	N	N	↑ ↔ ↑↑
Lupoid hepatitis	↑↑↑	↑	N ↔ ↑↑
Collagen disorders			
Lupus erythematosus	↑ ↔ ↑↑	N ↔ ↑	N ↔ ↑↑
Rheumatoid arthritis	N ↔ ↑	↑ ↔ ↑↑↑	N ↔ ↑
Sjögren's syndrome	N ↔ ↑	N ↔ ↑	↓ ↔ ↑↑
Scleroderma	N ↔ ↑	N	↑
Infections			
Tuberculosis	↑ ↔ ↑↑	N ↔ ↑↑↑	↓ ↔ N
Subacute bacterial endocarditis	↑ ↔ ↑↑	↓ ↔ N	↑ ↔ ↑↑
Leprosy	↑ ↔ ↑↑	N	↑
Trypanosomiasis	N ↔ ↑	N ↔ ↑	↑↑ ↔ ↑↑↑
Malaria	↓ ↔ ↑	N	↑ ↔ ↑↑
Kala-azar	↑↑	N	N
Infectious mono-nucleosis	↑ ↔ ↑↑	N ↔ ↑	↑ ↔ ↑↑
Fungus diseases	N	N ↔ ↑	N
Bartonellosis	↑	↓ ↔ N	↑↑ ↔ ↑↑↑
Lymphogranuloma venereum	↑↑	N	N
Actinomycosis	↑↑↑	↑↑	↑↑↑
Sarcoidosis	N ↔ ↑↑	N ↔ ↑↑	N ↔ ↑
Miscellaneous			
Hodgkin's disease	↓ ↔ ↑↑	↓ ↔ ↑	↓ ↔ ↑↑
Monocytic leukemia	↑	↑	↑↑
Cystic fibrosis	↑ ↔ ↑↑	↑ ↔ ↑↑	N ↔ ↑↑

N = Essentially normal serum immunoglobulin levels.
↓ = Decreased immunoglobulin concentrations.
↑, ↑↑, ↑↑↑ = Slight, moderate, or marked increases in serum immunoglobulin concentrations.
↔ = Range of immunoglobulin levels.

*Reproduced, with permission, from Ritzmann & Levin: Lab Synopsis 2:17, 1967.

attained. The half-life and rate of synthesis (in a 70-kg man) of the various immunoglobulins is as follows:

	Half-Life (days)	Rate of Synthesis (g/day)
IgG	25	2.3
IgA	6	1.7
IgM	5	0.3

• • •

The biochemical characteristics which enable a substance to stimulate an animal to produce immunoglobulins will now be considered. In addition, some of the physiologic and chemical events associated with antigen-antibody reactions will be discussed.

ANTIGENS

Substances which can induce an immune response (humoral, cellular, or mixed T and B cells) when introduced into an animal are called **immunogens** or **antigens**. Although most antigens are macromolecular proteins, polysaccharides, synthetic polypeptides, and other synthetic polymers may also be immunogenic. Furthermore, there are antibodies which react with nucleic acids. However, these must be produced by immunization with nucleoproteins. Such antibodies appear spontaneously in the sera of patients with systemic lupus erythematosus.

The immunogenicity of a molecule is not an inherent property but is dependent upon the experimental conditions of the system. Thus, the antigen, the mode of immunization, the species being immunized, and the sensitivity of the method of detection are all important. Although characteristics of antigens are complex and are not completely understood, certain conditions must be satisfied in order that a molecule be immunogenic, as follows:

(1) Only molecules that are foreign to the host are immunogenic.

(2) As a general rule, molecules smaller than MW 10,000 are only weakly immunogenic. Macromolecular proteins with molecular weights greater than 100,000 are the most potent immunogens.

(3) A molecule must possess a certain degree of complexity to be antigenic. Immunogenicity increases with structural complexity. In addition, aromatic amino acids contribute more to immunogenicity than do nonaromatic amino acid residues. Random polypeptides containing tyrosine are better antigens than the same polymers without tyrosine, and the immunogenicity of these polypeptides is proportionate to the tyrosine content of the molecule.

(4) Finally, the ability to respond to a particular antigen varies with the genetic constitution of the animal (eg, inbred strain No. 2 guinea pigs respond to poly-L-lysine but strain No. 13 guinea pigs do not). This ability to respond to antigens is inherited as an autosomal dominant trait.

ANTIGENIC DETERMINANTS

It is now widely accepted that the initiation of immunoglobulin production requires binding of the antigen to the lymphocyte surface. The combining sites on the surface of the lymphocyte are antibody-like molecules called **antigen receptors**.

Only restricted portions of antigenic molecules are involved in actual binding with antibody combining sites. These areas are termed **antigenic determinants**, and they determine the specificity of antigen-antibody reactions.

Most of the information about antigenic determi-

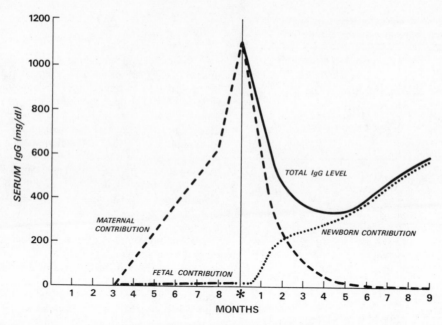

Figure 34–8. Development of IgG levels with age. Relationship of development of serum levels of IgG during fetal and newborn stages and maternal contribution. (Modified from Allansmith & others: J Pediatr 72:289, 1968.)

nants and the specificity of antigen-antibody reactions has been provided by studies involving haptens.

Haptens are small, chemically defined substances which, while not immunogenic, do react with antibodies. Karl Landsteiner prepared haptens by covalently coupling diazonium derivatives of aromatic amines to lysine, tyrosine, and histidine residues of immunogenic proteins (Fig 34–9). These proteins were called **carriers**. The protein-hapten conjugates induced the formation of antihapten antibody which was specific for the azo groups on the protein-hapten conjugate. The conjugated haptens thus behave as the complete antigenic determinant of the molecules. However, in certain instances the determinant may also include the

amino acids in the protein to which the hapten is linked (ie, azoprotein, dinitrophenylated and penicilloid proteins). The protein carrier has its own set of native antigenic determinants as well as the new determinants of the conjugated hapten (Fig 34–10).

The use of hapten-protein conjugates has demonstrated the diversity of the immune mechanisms and the very fine structural specificity of the antigen-antibody reactions. Landsteiner produced antibodies against *m*-aminobenzenesulfonate and tested its ability to bind other isomers of the hapten. The antibody was also tested with other related molecules in which the sulfonate group was replaced by arsonate or carboxylate groups (Table 34–5). The antisera could readily

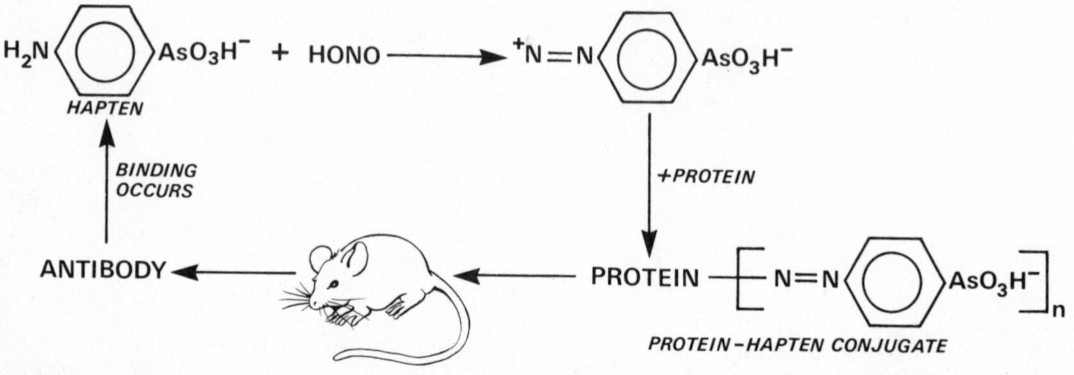

Figure 34–9. The preparation of hapten-protein conjugates and their capacity to induce the formation of antihapten antibody to the azophenylarsonate group in this example. (Reproduced, with permission, from Fudenberg HH & others [editors]: *Basic & Clinical Immunology.* Lange, 1976.)

Table 34—5. Effect of variation in hapten structure on strength of binding to *m*-aminobenzenesulfonate antibodies.

	ortho	*meta*	*para* isomers
R = sulfonate	++	+++	±
R = arsonate	−	+	−
R = carboxylate	−	±	−

Strength of binding is graded from negative (−) to very strong (+++). (From Landsteiner K, van der Scheer J: On cross reactions of immune sera to azoproteins. J Exp Med 63:325, 1936.)

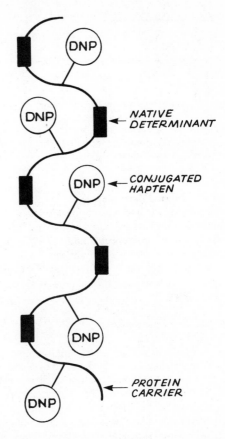

Figure 34—10. Diagrammatic illustration of a hapten-protein conjugate. The protein has several native or integral antigenic determinants denoted by thickened areas. The conjugated dinitrophenyl (DNP) hapten introduces new antigenic determinants. (Reproduced, with permission, from Fudenberg HH & others [editors]: *Basic & Clinical Immunology.* Lange, 1976.)

distinguish between the compounds with the sulfonate in the meta, ortho, or para position. The **meta isomer**, as expected, gave the strongest reaction since it was the **homologous hapten.** The substitution of arsonate or carboxylate for sulfonate gave only weak binding with the antibody.

The amazing specificity of the antigen determinants and the immune reaction was further demonstrated by Avery and Goebel. They immunized animals with simple sugar-protein conjugates (Table 34—6). The resulting antibodies could distinguish between glucose and galactose, which differ only by the orientation of hydrogen and hydroxyl groups on one carbon. Likewise, *p*-aminophenol *α*-glucoside and the *β*-glucosides—which are of identical configuration but differ stereochemically—could be distinguished in spite of some cross-reactivity.

This type of study indicates that, in general, antibodies recognize the overall 3-dimensional shape of the **antigenic determinant** rather than any specific chemical structure.

Table 34—6. Reactions of antisera with isomeric glucoside protein conjugates.[*]
(+ represents precipitation)

	p-Aminophenol *α*-glucoside	*p*-Aminophenol *β*-glucoside	*p*-Aminophenol *β*-galactoside
Antisera against:			
α-Glucoside	+++	++	0
β-Glucoside	++	+++	0
β-Galactoside	0	0	+++

[*]Reproduced, with permission, from Humphrey JH, White RG: *Immunology for Students of Medicine.* Davis, 1970.

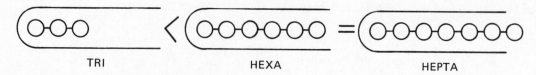

Figure 34—11. Illustration of how hapten binding with antibody permits assessment of the size of antigenic determinants. In the dextran-antidextran system, the hexasaccharide was a better ligand with antibody than smaller oligosaccharides and those equal to the heptasaccharide. It was concluded that the hexasaccharide just filled the antibody combining site, providing maximum binding energy. Additional sugar residues lay outside the site, making no contribution to binding. (Reproduced, with permission, from Fudenberg HH & others [editors] : *Basic & Clinical Immunology.* Lange, 1976.)

Number of Antigenic Determinants

The number of determinants on a single antigen molecule varies with its size and complexity. Valence estimates have been made on the number of antibody molecules bound per molecule of antigen. Using these estimates, ovalbumin (MW 42,000) has 5 antigenic determinants, whereas thyroglobulin (MW 700,000) has approximately 40.

Size of Antigenic Determinants

Antigenic determinants and antibody combining sites are believed to possess a structural complementarity that is similar to a "lock and key" arrangement. Therefore, the binding affinity between the antigen and antibody site is directly proportionate to the closeness of fit. The most precise analyses of antigenic determinant size were performed using single sugar (glucose) polysaccharides (dextran). These single-chain polysaccharides with few branch points were used to produce antibodies. The antigenic determinants were estimated using an ordered series of polysaccharides as inhibitors (ligands) of the dextran-antidextran precipitant reaction (Fig 34—11). The hexasaccharide was the best inhibitor of the antidextran

antibody. The heptasaccharide was not a better ligand since the hexasaccharide completely filled the antibody combining site. This is assumed to be the size of the antigenic determinant and also the size of the complementary region antibody. Numerous investigators using homopolymers of amino acids or multichain polymer-protein conjugates as antigens have yielded antigenic determinant sizes similar to the dextran model (Table 34—7). The most precise and convincing evaluation of the determinant size was obtained using (D-Ala)$_n$-Gly-RNAse as an antigen. The antigenic determinant was found to be a tetrapeptide; the lysine residue of the protein carrier participated as a determinant only if the inhibiting conjugated hapten was smaller than a tetrapeptide. These and other observations constitute compelling evidence that the antibody combining site will accommodate 4 amino acid residues.

IMMUNOPOTENCY

The capacity of the region of the **antigen** molecule to serve as an **antigenic determinant** and to induce the formation of specific antibodies is called **immunopotency.** Several factors influence immunopotency:

(1) Exposure to the aqueous environment is important in immunopotency. The most exposed and immunopotent regions of polysaccharides are the terminal side chains; therefore, the terminal side chains act as the antigenic determinant. Multichain synthetic polypeptides with sequences of tyrosine on the outside and alanine closer to the backbone, or the reverse, have been used to demonstrate that the most exposed sequence was the most immunopotent (Fig 34—12). When these 2 polysaccharides were used to immunize animals, the resulting antibodies were specific for the most exposed sequence (tyrosine or alanine). The most exposed sequence was in each instance the most immunopotent.

Internal sequences within proteins or polysaccharides may be determinants if the configuration of the macromolecule exposes these sequences to the environment (eg, as occurs with sperm whale myoglobin).

(2) As a general rule, charge residues will contrib-

Table 34—7. Estimation of the size of sequentially defined antigenic determinants.*

Antigen	Species	Determinant
Dextran	Man	Isomaltohexaose
Dextran	Rabbit	$\geqslant$ Isomaltohexaose
Poly-γ—glutamic acid (killed *B anthracis*)	Rabbit	Hexaglutamic acid
Polyalanyl-bovine serum albumin	Rabbit	Pentaalanine
Polylysyl-rabbit serum albumin	Rabbit	Penta- or hexalysine
Polylysyl-phosphoryl-bovine serum albumin	Rabbit	Pentalysine
α-Dinitrophenyl—(lysine)$_{11}$	Guinea pig	α-Dinitrophenyl—heptalysine
α-Dinitrophenyl—polylysine	Guinea pig	α-Dinitrophenyl—trilysine
(D—Ala)$_n$—Gly—RNase	Rabbit	Tetrapeptide
Denatured DNA	Man†	Pentanucleotide

*Reproduced, with permission, from Fudenberg HH & others (editors): *Basic & Clinical Immunology.* Lange, 1976.
†Sera from patients with systemic lupus erythematosus.

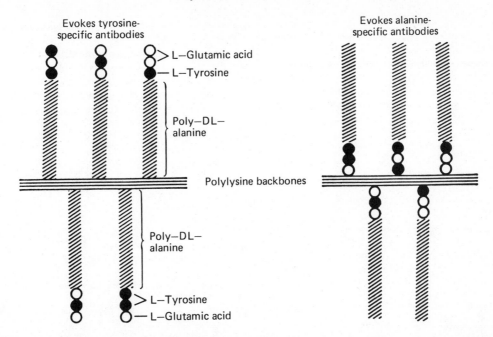

Figure 34–12. *Left:* A multichain copolymer in which L-tyrosine and L-glutamic acid residues are attached to multi-poly—DL—alanyl—poly—L—lysine(poly—[Tyr,Glu] —poly—DL—Ala—poly Lys). *Right:* Copolymer in which tyrosine and glutamic acid are attached directly to the polylysine backbone with alanine peptides on the ends of the side chains. Horizontal lines: poly—L—lysine; diagonal hatching: poly—DL—alanine; closed circles: L-tyrosine; open circles: L-glutamic acid. (From Sela M: Antigenicity: Some molecular aspects. Science 166:1365, 1969. Copyright © 1969 by The American Association for the Advancement of Science.)

ute significantly to the specificity of antigens. This may be because charged groups are hydrophilic and would therefore be in closer contact with the environment.

(3) As already mentioned, genetic factors play an important role in the ability of different animals to produce antibodies of different specificities against the same antigen.

Immunopotency concerns factors that determine why a particular region of an antigen molecule acts as an antigenic determinant.

The dominant component of the antigenic determinant, ie, that which contributes most to the reactivity with antibody, is termed **immunodominant**. The factors that determine immunopotency also influence immunodominance. Other factors (as indicated below) are also important in determining the immunodominant component of the antigenic determinant.

(1) The immunodominant feature of an antigenic determinant may be its **conformation** rather than a particular subunit of its structure. Polymers of the tripeptide L-tyrosyl-L-alanyl-L-glutamic acid form an α-helix under physiologic conditions. The α-helix conformation, and not the various subunits, is the immunodominant element of this polymer. Antibodies against the helical polymer will not cross-react with the tripeptide itself or with the tripeptide attached to a branched synthetic polypeptide. However, antibodies

against the branched polymer will bind to the simple tripeptide since the immunodominant component of the antigenic determinant rests in its subunits.

In human adult hemoglobin (ie, hemoglobin A_1) the immunodominant element is its quaternary structure.

(2) Antigenic determinants whose specificity is dictated by the sequence of the subunits (amino acids or sugars) within the determinant rather than by the conformation of the antigen molecule are termed **sequential determinants**. Sequential determinants may be either terminal or internal sequences of macromolecules. When the antigenic determinant is a terminal sequence, the terminal residue of the sequence is the **immunodominant subunit**. When specificity is directed toward an internal sequence of an antigen, there is still a **gradient of binding energy** for different subunits of the determinant.

(3) **Optical configuration:** Antibodies display a pronounced stereospecificity. In general, amino acid polymers of the D- optical configuration are poor immunogens. However, D-amino acids can be antigenic determinants when conjugated to immunogenic carriers.

In general, some antibodies are specific for the conformation of the antigenic molecule. For other antibodies, specificity is directed against sequential determinants.

Antibodies against sequential determinants will normally react with small fragments of the antigens, whereas antibodies specific for conformational features will not react because the antigen superstructure has been destroyed. Consequently, the antigenic determinants of simple linear or coiled molecules, peptidyl protein conjugates, and synthetic antigens (homopolymers of single amino acids, simple polypeptides) have all been easy to delineate in detail. However, antigenic determinants of the more complex globular proteins have been difficult to delineate because of the highly ordered structure of the antigen molecules. In fact, the simple antigens and particularly the synthetic antigens have provided the most information concerning the size and nature of the antigenic determinants.

●   ●   ●

References

Amos B (editor): *Progress in Immunology.* Vol 1. Academic Press, 1971.

Brent L, Holborrow J (editors): *Progress in Immunology.* Vol 2. North-Holland Publishing Co., 1975.

Butler VP Jr, Beiser SM: Antibodies to small molecules: Biological and clinical applications. Adv Immunol 17:255, 1973.

Goodman JW: Antigenic determinants and antibody combining sites. Page 127 in: *The Antigens.* Sela M (editor). Academic Press, 1975.

Eisen HN: *Immunology.* Harper & Row, 1974.

Gergely J, Medgyesi GA (editors): *Antibody Structure and Molecular Immunology.* North-Holland Publishing Co., 1975.

Kowchwa S, Kunkel HG (editors): Immunoglobulins. Ann NY Acad Sci 190:5, 1971.

Landsteiner K: *The Specificity of Serological Reactions.* Harvard Univ Press, 1945.

Nisonoff A, Hopper JE, Spring SB: *The Antibody Molecule.* Academic Press, 1975.

Pressman D, Grossberg AL: *The Structural Basis of Antibody Specificity.* Benjamin, 1968.

Reichlin M: Amino acid substitution and the antigenicity of globular proteins. Adv Immunol 20:71, 1975.

Sela M: Antigenicity: Some molecular aspects. Science 166:1365, 1969.

Tomasi TB, Grey HM: Structure and function of immunoglobulin A. Prog Allergy 16:81, 1972.

35...

The Kidney & the Urine

The extracellular fluid constitutes the internal environment of the cells of the body. It is in this medium that the cells carry out their vital activities. Since changes in extracellular fluid necessarily are reflected in changes in the fluid within the cells and thus also in cell functions, it is essential to the normal function of the cells that this fluid be maintained relatively constant in composition.

This internal environment (the *milieu intérieur* of Claude Bernard) is regulated mainly by 2 pairs of organs: the lungs, which control the concentrations of oxygen and CO_2; and the kidneys, which maintain optimal chemical composition of the body fluids. Thus, the kidney is an organ which does not merely remove metabolic wastes but actually performs highly important homeostatic functions. It also has a considerable metabolic capacity.

Role of the Kidney in Homeostasis

The regulation of the internal environment by the kidneys is a composite of 3 processes: (1) filtration of the blood plasma by the glomeruli; (2) selective reabsorption by the tubules of substances such as salts, water, simple sugars, and amino acids which are necessary to maintain the internal environment or to contribute to metabolic processes; and (3) secretion by the tubules of substances from the blood into the tubular lumen for excretion into the urine. This latter secretory process involves the handling of potassium, uric acid, organic anions, and hydrogen ion. It serves both as a means of regenerating components of the blood buffers and as a means of eliminating potentially harmful substances.

Structure of the Nephron

Urine is formed by a summation of the 3 processes mentioned above. The anatomic unit that carries out these functions is the nephron. Each kidney possesses about 1 million nephrons. Fig 35–1 illustrates this unit.

Blood is transmitted from the aorta via the renal artery and a series of renal arterial subdivisions to the afferent arterioles. Directly distal to this structure is the glomerulus, a tuftlike network of capillaries which comprises the filtering unit. These capillaries combine to form the efferent arteriole, a blood vessel with a muscular wall which is thus capable of changes in the diameter of its lumen. The efferent arteriole immediately divides again into a second capillary network which surrounds the remaining portions of the nephron.

The glomerular tuft lies within Bowman's capsule, a double-walled epithelial sac, which is the most proximal portion of the tubular system. Bowman's capsule leads directly into the proximal convoluted tubule and from there into the following components: (1) the straight proximal tubule and (2) the loop of Henle itself, consisting of the descending, thin ascending, and thick ascending limbs. The latter lies within both the renal medulla and the cortex. The thick ascending limb of the loop of Henle leads to the distal convoluted tubule, cortical collecting tubule, and medullary and papillary collecting tubule. Each of these portions of the tubular system has specific functions which will be discussed in subsequent sections.

FORMATION OF URINE

Filtration

The first step in urine formation is filtration of the blood plasma. A large volume of blood, approximately 1 liter/minute (or 25% of the entire cardiac output at rest), flows through the kidneys. Thus, in 4–5 minutes a volume of blood equal to the total blood volume passes through the renal circulation. This is made possible by a very extensive circulatory system in these organs. By the same token, the kidneys are particularly susceptible to damage by diffuse vascular disease.

The formation of glomerular filtrate is a process governed largely by the algebraic sum of the transcapillary hydrostatic and oncotic pressure differences. Stated in terms of the familiar Starling equation, the rate of formation of ultrafiltrate in Bowman's space of a single glomerulus is as follows:

$$SNGFR = K_f \times a \; [(P_g - P_t) - (\pi_g - \pi_t)]$$

where SNGFR is the filtration rate for a single nephron; K_f and a are the permeability coefficient and area, respectively, of the membrane; P_g and P_t are the

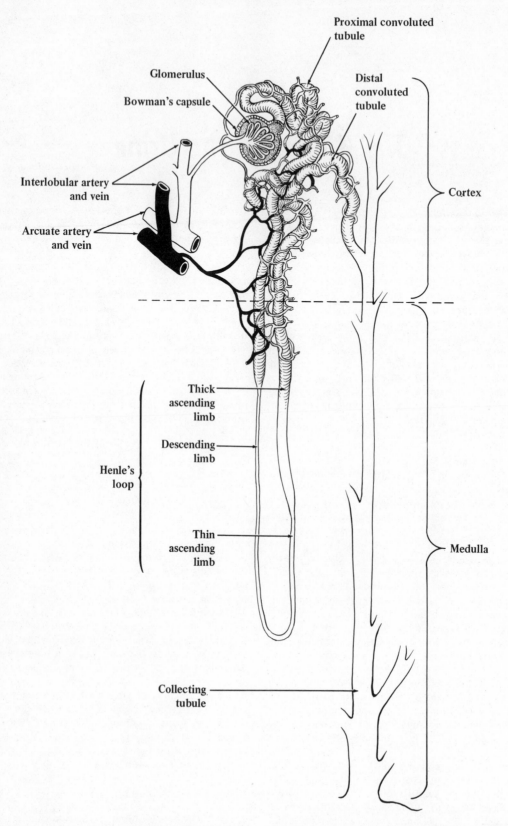

Figure 35–1. Vascular supply of the nephron in the outer zone of the cortex. (Reproduced, with permission, from Junqueira LC, Carneiro J, Contopoulos A: *Basic Histology,* 2nd ed. Lange, 1977.)

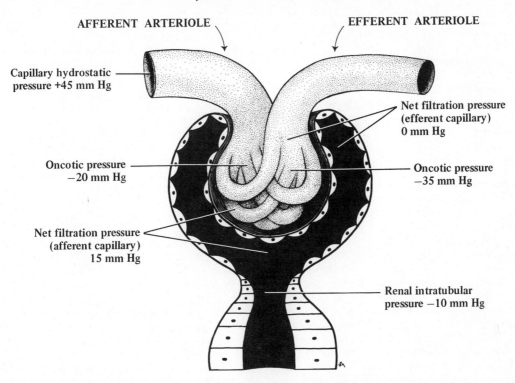

AFFERENT ARTERIOLE

EFFERENT ARTERIOLE

Capillary hydrostatic
pressure +45 mm Hg

Net filtration pressure
(efferent capillary)
0 mm Hg

Oncotic pressure
−20 mm Hg

Oncotic pressure
−35 mm Hg

Net filtration pressure
(afferent capillary)
15 mm Hg

Renal intratubular
pressure −10 mm Hg

Figure 35–2. Factors affecting the net filtration pressure. Beginning at the afferent side of the glomerular capillaries, the hydrostatic pressure averages 45 mm Hg. This is opposed by the intravascular oncotic pressure of 20 mm Hg and a renal intratubular pressure of 10 mm Hg. Thus, at this site the net filtration pressure is 15 mm Hg. As the efferent arteriole is approached, oncotic pressure gradually increases to 35 mm Hg, because of filtration of water, which has the effect of concentrating plasma. This oncotic increase (by 15 mm Hg) equals the original net filtration pressure, so that it is now virtually zero. (Modified and reproduced, with permission, from Merck Sharp & Dohme: *Seminar.* Vol 9, No 3, 1947.)

hydrostatic pressures within the glomerular capillary and Bowman's space; and π_g and π_t represent the oncotic forces within the glomerular capillary and Bowman's space.

Recent advances have permitted direct assessment of the hydrostatic forces in question. Under hydropenic control circumstances, glomerular capillary hydrostatic pressure averages 45 mm Hg (Fig 35–2), or approximately 40% of mean aortic pressure. Tubular hydrostatic pressure averages 10 mm Hg. Thus, a hydrostatic pressure gradient of 35 mm Hg is present which appears to be unchanged along the entire length of the capillary. Tubular oncotic pressure is zero; oncotic pressure within the capillary increases from about 20 mm Hg at the beginning to 35 mm Hg at the termination of the glomerulus. Thus, a net filtration pressure of ~15 mm Hg exists at the beginning of the capillary and diminishes as blood flow proceeds across the glomerulus.

Control of filtration is believed to be related to plasma flow because it affects the manner in which glomerular oncotic pressure increases. In addition, it is speculated that modification of surface area for filtration may occur by an increase or decrease in the number of capillaries through which blood is permitted to flow.

Under most physiologic circumstances, blood flow to the glomerulus and the filtration rate are maintained at a relatively constant level despite reasonably significant changes in blood pressure. This is accomplished by means of appropriate modulation of afferent arteriolar tone. Under conditions of shock, however, when aortic pressure falls below about 50–60 mm Hg, net filtration forces become negligible, filtration ceases, and anuria results until blood pressure is restored.

Other factors which affect filtration include obstruction of the arterial pathway to the glomerulus, increased interstitial pressure as may be caused by an inflammatory process, and increased resistance to flow within the tubular systems—such as by obstruction of the collecting tubules, ureters, or urethra.

The glomerular membrane may also be so injured by disease that it fails to function as a filter for the blood. Ultimately, the capillary may be completely occluded and thus removed from the active circulation. During the progress of such a disease, blood cells and plasma proteins will leak through the injured capillary and will be excreted in the urine. Such a pathologic process is illustrated by glomerulonephritis.

Glomerular Filtration Rate

In the normal adult, 1 liter of blood is filtered each minute by the combined action of the 2 million nephrons of both kidneys, and 120 ml/minute of glomerular filtrate are formed at Bowman's capsule. The **glomerular filtration rate** in adults is therefore about 120 ml/minute. Chemically, glomerular filtrate is an essentially protein-free extracellular fluid or a protein- and cell-free filtrate of whole blood.

The Action of the Tubule

The composition of the urine is quite different from that of glomerular filtrate. There is also a vast difference in the volume of fluid formed at the glomerulus each minute and the amount which arrives during the same period at the papilla. The glomeruli act only as a filter; the composition of the glomerular filtrate is thus determined solely by the permeability of the capillary membrane to the constituents of the blood. As a result, the glomerular filtrate contains many substances necessary for normal metabolism, such as water, glucose, amino acids, and electrolytes, as well as substances to be excreted and removed, such as urea, creatinine, and uric acid. Furthermore, under various conditions, greater or lesser amounts of essential substances are retained in accordance with the need to maintain constancy in the internal environment.

This highly selective function of the kidney is the task of the tubule. By reabsorption and secretion, it modifies the glomerular filtrate and thus produces the urine.

Reabsorption of Sodium, Chloride, & Water

Sixty to 80% of glomerular ultrafiltrate is normally reabsorbed by the proximal tubule. In this process, the tubular fluid remains isosmotic with respect to plasma. Although under most circumstances no transepithelial concentration gradient exists for sodium, under conditions of mannitol infusion the tubular concentration of sodium can be demonstrated to fall below that of plasma—a finding which suggests active transport of sodium. Further evidence for active sodium transport in this segment is the demonstration of a significant transepithelial electrical potential difference of about −2 to −6 mV within the lumen and the demonstration that this potential difference can be abolished by the removal of various metabolic substrates.

It is now proposed that salt and water reabsorption in the proximal tubule occur as shown schematically in Fig 35–3. Sodium, chloride, and water diffuse passively into the cell from the tubular lumen. Sodium is then actively transported into the intercellular space (stippled area), with chloride and water following pas-

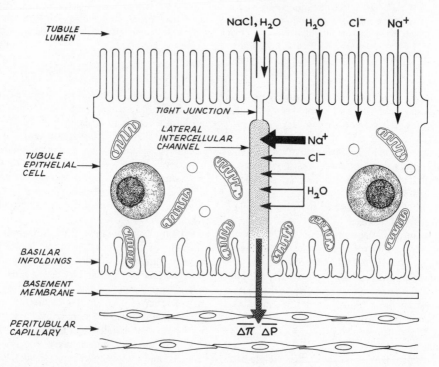

Figure 35–3. Idealized proximal tubule epithelial cells under normal hydropenic conditions. $\Delta\pi$, mean peritubular transcapillary colloid osmotic pressure difference; ΔP, mean peritubular transcapillary hydrostatic pressure difference. Heavy solid arrow denotes active Na^+ transport. Arrows coming from the right labeled Cl^- and H_2O denote passive transport. Heavy shaded arrow extending downward denotes the path of fluid movement as a function of the peritubular transcapillary Starling forces, $\Delta\pi$ and ΔP. (Modified, redrawn, and reproduced, with permission, from Mercer PF, Maddox DA, Brenner BM: Current concepts of sodium chloride and water transport by the mammalian nephron. West J Med 120:33, 1974.)

sively to maintain—respectively—electrical and osmotic equilibrium: This fluid is then reabsorbed into the peritubular space and capillary lumen.

Several hypotheses have been advanced to explain the alterations in proximal tubular reabsorption that occur in response to various pathophysiologic manipulations. Among these are the existence of a humoral agent, the so-called third factor, which increases or decreases sodium reabsorption; intrinsic capability of the tubular epithelium to alter reabsorption (this has been ruled out largely by direct experimental testing); alterations of reabsorption effected by oncotic and hydrostatic forces within tubule and capillary; and alteration in the volume of fluid which diffuses back into the tubule by variation in the "tightness" of the tight junctions (Fig 35–3) at the luminal border. This last hypothesis, proposed by Lewy and Windhager in 1968, appears to agree with current concepts of the mechanism of reabsorption of filtrate in the proximal tubule.

Loop of Henle

The loop of Henle is anatomically divisible into 3 distinct portions (Fig 35–1); each section possesses unique physiologic properties affecting salt and water transport.

The descending limb of the loop of Henle is a thin-walled structure whose cells are devoid of obvious intracellular structures which might be associated with energy-dependent functions. Isosmotic fluid delivered into this segment from the proximal tubule becomes increasingly hypertonic as it progresses from the renal cortex toward the papilla until it reaches a maximum concentration of approximately 1200 mosmol/liter at the hairpin turn of the loop. Although it is controversial whether solute (urea, NaCl) enters the descending

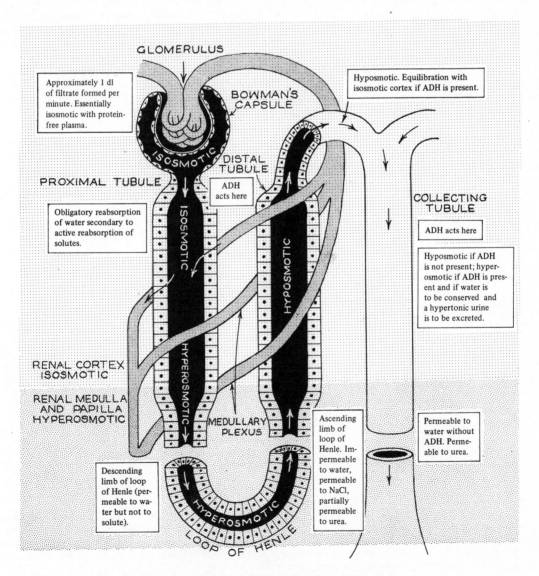

Figure 35–4. Summary of normal physiology of the nephron.

limb, it is clear that the major portion of the tubular fluid concentration process is accomplished by diffusion of water from the tubule in accordance with an established osmotic gradient. As illustrated in Fig 35–4, the interstitium of the medulla is hypertonic; the membrane of the descending limb is more permeable to water than solute, and, in order to effect equilibrium, water is removed. By this process, of the 30% of glomerular filtrate that leaves the proximal tubule, approximately 75% of the water is reabsorbed in the descending limb; solutes remain, so that the intratubular fluid becomes hypertonic.

At the hairpin turn (Fig 35–4), the tubular epithelium, although structurally unaltered, changes its functional character. It is now impermeable to water, freely permeable to NaCl, and partially permeable to urea. As the tubular fluid flows back toward the cortex in the thin-walled portion of the ascending limb of Henle, it becomes progressively less concentrated. In contrast to events which occurred in the descending limb, these changes occur as a consequence of loss of NaCl from the tubule by a process of passive diffusion. Although it has been suggested that this might be an active process, there is no experimental evidence to substantiate this idea. Since water does not enter the tubule, the volume of tubular fluid is not altered in this segment or in the thick-walled portion of the ascending limb of Henle which follows.

Either late in the thin or early in the thick segment of the ascending limb, the tubular fluid once again becomes isosmolar. This point is referred to as the end of the "functional" proximal tubule. Reabsorption of NaCl in the thick ascending limb distal to this isosmolar locus results in the formation of hypotonic intratubular fluid; this is the manner by which intertubular "free" water (water in excess of solute) is

formed. It is the mechanism by which ingested water is excreted. It has been demonstrated recently that NaCl is reabsorbed from both cortical and medullary thick ascending limbs by active chloride reabsorption but that reabsorption of sodium is by means of a passive reabsorptive process to maintain electrical neutrality. At the end of the cortical thick ascending limb, tubular fluid is notably hypotonic (30–70 mosmol/liter).

Fluid now enters the distal nephron, which comprises the distal convoluted tubule, the cortical collecting tubule, and the medullary collecting duct. Each of these segments is sensitive to stimulation by vasopressin (antidiuretic hormone; ADH), a hormone secreted by the posterior lobe of the pituitary which controls permeability to water of the epithelium of the distal nephron. Throughout the distal nephron, active reabsorption of sodium chloride continues, although to a lesser extent than previously; there is still controversy about the exact mechanism by which this occurs. In addition, in the distal convoluted tubule, specialized processes for sodium reabsorption occur through exchange with secreted hydrogen ion and potassium. These will be discussed in a later section.

The major function of the distal nephron is to reabsorb free water only to the extent required, as regulated by various stimuli such as plasma osmolarity and intravascular volume.

Under normal circumstances, the osmotic pressure of the plasma varies only slightly despite wide variations in the intake of fluid and solutes. The normal osmolarity of the plasma (285–295 mosmol/liter of water*) is largely attributable to its content of inorganic salts (electrolytes). It is maintained by the kidney by varying the volume flow as well as the osmolar concentration of the urine. For example, an excess of water, which would tend to dilute the plasma and thus

---

*The osmotic activity of solutions of substances which ionize is higher than that of substances which do not. Thus, a solution of sodium chloride which is 100% ionized would have an osmotic pressure twice that calculated from its concentration because it dissociates into 2 particles (ions) per mole. A solution of glucose, on the other hand, which does not ionize, would have an osmotic pressure equal only to that calculated from its molar concentration since it contains in solution only one particle per mole. These relationships between molar concentration and osmotic activity are conveniently expressed by the use of the term osmol. The osmolarity of a solution of a given compound is determined by multiplying the molar concentration by the number of particles per mole obtained by ionization.

$$\text{Osmolarity} = \text{Molarity} \times \begin{array}{c}\text{Number of particles}\\ \text{per mole resulting}\\ \text{from ionization}\end{array}$$

The concentrations of ionizable substance in physiologic fluids are so weak that complete ionization is assumed to occur. It is therefore possible to convert molar concentrations directly to osmolarity by reference to the number of ions per mole produced. It is also more convenient to express these dilute concentrations in terms of millimoles and milliosmoles, ie, 1/1000 mol or 1/1000 osmol.

Example:
  NaCl ($Na^+ + Cl^-$) at a concentration of 70 mmol/liter = 140 mmol/liter
  $Na_2 HPO_4$ ($2Na^+ + HPO_4^{2+}$) at a concentration of 1.3 mosmol/liter - 3.9 mosmol/liter.

The osmotic activity of physiologic fluids such as plasma and urine is due to the combined osmotic activity of a number of substances which are dissolved in them. The osmolarity of such fluids is therefore most easily determined by measurement of the freezing point depression rather than by attempting to calculate it from the concentration and degree of ionization of each constituent in the mixture. Electrically operated instruments for measurement of osmotic pressure by freezing point depression (osmometers) have been devised to measure very small changes in temperature. A depression in the freezing point of a solution of $0.00186° C$ below that of water (taken as $0° C$) is equivalent to 1 mosmol of osmotic activity/liter.

$$1 \text{ mosmol} = \Delta 0.00186° \text{ C}$$

Example: The freezing point of a sample of human blood plasma was found to be $-0.59° C$; the osmolarity would then be 317 mosmol/liter (0.59/0.00186).

reduce its osmotic pressure, produces a renal response which results in excretion of an increased volume of urine with an osmolarity less than that of plasma, ie, less than 285 μosmol/ml of urine water. By thus excreting water in excess of solute, the kidney defends the osmolarity of plasma. On the other hand, an increase in plasma osmolarity would be corrected by the excretion of a "concentrated" urine with an osmolarity higher than that of plasma, which indicates that, relative to the plasma, solute is being excreted in excess of water. The capacity of the kidney to control water loss from the body is illustrated by the fact that, although as much as 100 ml/minute of glomerular filtrate may normally be formed, as little as 1 ml of urine may remain by the time the fluid has passed down the collecting tubule. Under conditions of water deprivation, an even greater renal conservation of water may be effected.

Countercurrent Multiplication

As originally proposed by Wirz and Hargity, the loop of Henle acts as a countercurrent multiplier with energy provided by active chloride reabsorption in the thick portion of the ascending limb and with differential permeabilities ascribed to the various segments to assist in establishing the hypertonicity of the medulla and papilla. The key steps in establishing the concentration gradient in the medulla and papilla appear to be (1) the permeability to water and relative impermeability to solute of the descending limb; (2) the free permeability to NaCl and lesser degree of permeability to urea of the thin ascending limb; (3) active chloride transport in the thick ascending limb; (4) the permeability to water of the collecting duct and the permeability to urea of the papillary collecting duct; and (5) intact blood flow in the vasa recta.

Mechanism of Central Control of Antidiuretic Hormone Secretion

According to Verney, the mechanism for reabsorption of water which operates through pituitary antidiuretic hormone (ADH) is controlled by the activity of osmoreceptors located in the anterior hypothalamic region of the brain. When the blood is diluted, as by the ingestion of large amounts of water, the osmoreceptors detect the resultant decrease in the osmolarity of the blood brought to that region via the internal carotid artery. As a result, the osmoreceptors, over nervous connections to the posterior pituitary, transmit impulses that produce inhibition of pituitary secretion of ADH. The resultant suppression of ADH then permits excretion of more water in the distal and collecting tubules by impairing free water back-diffusion; thus, a large volume of dilute urine results. In contrast, after deprivation of water, the blood becomes more hypertonic and the osmoreceptors then act to stimulate ADH secretion, which returns more water to the blood in an effort to compensate for the hypertonicity. Under these circumstances, a concentrated urine of small volume results. The tubular reaction to ADH is one of the most sensitive of the homeostatic mechanisms of the kidney. For this reason, determination of maximal concentrating power of the tubule is one of the most useful clinical tests of renal function. In addition to the effects of plasma osmolarity on ADH release, regulation is also accomplished by an effective arterial volume and serum sodium concentration. The profound effect of volume explains the occurrence of hyposmolar states that are observed in volume-contracted states secondary to vomiting and the action of diuretic agents as well as in volume-depleted states such as those that occur in congestive heart failure.

A number of drugs, including ingested alcohol, act to suppress ADH secretion and thus to increase urine flow. On the other hand, certain stresses such as those of surgery or severe trauma, as well as those created by some of the drugs used in anesthesia, induce excessive production of ADH. In the immediate postoperative period these effects on ADH secretion contribute to excessive retention of water by the kidney and thus to oliguria. Failure to recognize this has led to serious overhydration of patients in an effort to correct the oliguria which, under the circumstances, is, in fact, a normal physiologic response.

Mechanism of Action of Vasopressin (Antidiuretic Hormone, ADH)

Vasopressin is the single most important regulator of the renal handling of water in mammals. The cellular mechanism of action of this hormone has been the subject of intensive investigation during the past several years.

The current theory of the biochemical mechanisms involved in the effect of vasopressin on water transport begins with binding of the hormone to a specific receptor located in the basal plasma membrane of the collecting tubular cell (Fig 35—5). The interaction of the hormone and its receptor initiates enzymatic formation of cyclic adenosine 3',5'-monophosphate (cyclic AMP, cAMP), the intracellular mediator of vasopressin. The AMP which is formed then activates a protein kinase which is probably responsible for phosphorylation of proteins located in the luminal plasma membranes. It is speculated that this latter event is responsible for the increase in permeability of the luminal membrane.

Since specific clinical syndromes have been associated with specific defects in this scheme of action, it is possible that the surge of basic research activity in this area will lead to improved methods of managing clinical disorders of water metabolism. For example, nephrogenic diabetes insipidus caused by hypothyroidism or hypercalcemia seems to be due to deficient formation of cAMP. The abnormality responds to treatment with stable analogs of cAMP such as dibutyryl cAMP. In hypokalemia, the defect appears to occur distal to the formation of cAMP so that a different therapeutic approach appears necessary. On the other hand, in diseases in which there is an excess of vasopressin, drugs known to interfere with vasopressin action (eg, demeclocycline, lithium) have proved useful.

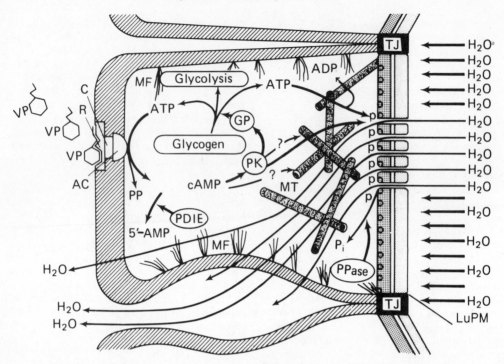

Figure 35–5. Scheme of the current view of the cellular action of vasopressin. AC, adenylate cyclase; ADP, adenosine 5′-diphosphate; 5′-AMP, adenosine 5′-monophosphate; ATP, adenosine 5′-triphosphate; C, coupling component of adenylate cyclase; GP, glycogen phosphorylase; MF, microfilaments; MT, microtubules; LuPM, luminal plasma membrane; p, phosphate attached to protein; cAMP, cyclic adenosine 3′,5′-monophosphate; PDIE, cAMP phosphodiesterase; PK, cAMP-dependent protein kinase; P_i, inorganic phosphorus; PP, pyrophosphate; PPase, protein phosphatase; R, receptor for vasopressin; TJ, tight junction; VP, vasopressin molecule. Loci showing water penetration through the LuPM do not necessarily mean structural pores but only areas in the membrane where water flux increases as a consequence of the action of cAMP. (Reproduced, with permission, from Dousa & Valtin: Kidney Internat 10:48, July 1976.)

Threshold Substances

Certain substances are reabsorbed almost completely by the tubule when their concentrations in the plasma are within the normal range but appear in the urine (ie, are not completely reabsorbed) when their normal plasma levels are exceeded. These are spoken of as threshold substances. A substance reabsorbed only slightly or not at all is a low-threshold substance (eg, creatinine, urea, and uric acid). Those materials necessary to the body which are reabsorbed very efficiently are high-threshold substances (eg, amino acids and glucose). The reabsorption of glucose is typical of this mechanism of the renal tubule. It is now recognized that factors which affect proximal tubular reabsorption of sodium chloride and water (eg, volume depletion or expansion) also alter the reabsorption of substances which were previously believed to behave entirely as Tm-limited substances (eg, glucose).

Reabsorption of Glucose

At an arterial plasma level of 100 mg/dl and a glomerular filtration rate of 120 ml/minute, 120 mg of glucose are delivered into the glomerular filtrate each minute. Normally, all of this glucose is reabsorbed into the blood in the proximal convoluted tubule.

The capacity of the glucose transporting system is limited. If the arterial plasma level of glucose rises—for example, to 200 mg/dl—and the glomerular filtration rate remains the same, twice as much glucose (240 mg/minute) is presented for reabsorption as before. All of this additional glucose is reabsorbed until the full capacity of the tubular transfer system is reached; the excess, which is filtered but cannot be reabsorbed, remains in the tubular fluid and passes on into the urine. This excess glucose also carries water with it, resulting in the characteristic diuresis of glycosuria.

The maximum rate at which glucose can be reabsorbed has been determined to be about 350 mg/minute. This is designated the Tm_G, or tubular maximum for glucose. If the glomerular filtration rate decreases, less glucose is presented per minute to the reabsorbing cells. This permits the concentration of glucose in the blood to rise above those levels at which glucose normally spills into the urine, and glycosuria is not actually observed. The reabsorptive capacity of the tubule for glucose probably does not change under normal conditions, although it may be above normal in hyperthyroidism, diabetes mellitus, and during the tubular hypertrophy that occurs during progressive renal failure.

Defects in Reabsorption by the Renal Tubules

The mechanisms for selective reabsorption in the kidney tubules may exhibit various defects, which are frequently inherited. Such tubular defects may be confined to a failure in the reabsorption of a single substance (eg, phosphates, glucose), or a combination of several reabsorptive defects may be found. The presence of glucose in the urine when the level of glucose in the blood is normal indicates a tubular defect in the reabsorption of glucose. Such a reduction in the "renal threshold" for glucose is called renal diabetes or renal glycosuria.

Those individuals who have a decreased capacity for the reabsorption of phosphates exhibit changes in the metabolism of bone as a result of excessive losses of phosphorus from the body. Evidence for such changes can be found in the blood, where the phosphorus is low and the alkaline phosphatase activity is high. Such cases may be designated as vitamin D-resistant rickets in children or idiopathic osteomalacia (Milkman's syndrome) in adults. These diseases are "resistant" to vitamin D only when it is given in ordinary doses. Large doses of the vitamin (50,000 units/ day) bring about a decrease in urinary excretion of phosphates and healing of the bones.

Renal tubular reabsorption of phosphate is normally accomplished by 2 different mechanisms. The first is by a system that is sensitive to parathyroid hormone; it is responsible for conservation of about two-thirds of the filtered phosphorus. The remainder of the filtered phosphorus is responsive to calcium but not to parathyroid hormone. It is the former system that is defective in patients with familial hypophosphatemic rickets. The existence of a component of phosphate reabsorption sensitive to calcium explains the fact that infusion of calcium will reverse temporarily the renal tubular phosphate leak in familial hypophosphatemic rickets.

The existence of hyperphosphaturia of renal tubular origin may be detected by measurement of the serum phosphate level and of the amounts of phosphate excreted in a 24-hour urine sample. These data are then used to calculate phosphate clearance. In normal individuals, phosphate clearance does not exceed 12% of the glomerular filtration rate. It should be emphasized that the metabolic effects of a renal tubular defect may be masked by a decline in glomerular filtration. Thus, a marked reduction in filtration would compensate for a decreased tubular reabsorptive capacity for phosphate, so that the serum levels would rise and healing of the bones could then occur. The urinary excretion of phosphate is therefore unreliable as a diagnostic tool in the presence of reduced glomerular filtration.

A third tubular defect which often occurs in combination with those mentioned above is characterized by excessive excretion of amino acids. In normal subjects, the content of amino acids in the urine is very low, but in individuals having this renal tubular deficiency, generalized aminoaciduria occurs, even though the levels of amino acids in the blood are normal.

The occurrence of all 3 tubular defects was first described in children by Fanconi, who called it **hypophosphatemic-glycosuric rickets**. It is now referred to as the **De Toni-Fanconi syndrome.** Similar cases have since been reported in adults. A peculiar feature of the disease in children is the accumulation of cystine crystals in the reticuloendothelial system and other tissues, including the cornea. Such cystine storage (cystinosis) without any of the other features of the De Toni-Fanconi syndrome has also been found in an otherwise normal individual. This suggests that the genetic defect responsible for cystine storage is not directly related to that involved in the causation of the renal tubular abnormalities of the De Toni-Fanconi syndrome, as might otherwise have been inferred from the almost inevitable coexistence of cystinosis and the De Toni-Fanconi syndrome in children.

In severe cases of the De Toni-Fanconi syndrome there is also a failure to reabsorb water and potassium properly as well as to acidify the urine. Such patients, if untreated, suffer from metabolic acidosis and dehydration as well as severe potassium deficiency, and this combination of tubular defects is usually fatal at an early age.

As was pointed out above in connection with tubular hyperphosphaturia, a decline in the glomerular filtration rate may obscure the aminoaciduria which would otherwise occur in the De Toni-Fanconi syndrome. For this reason, it is important to measure the glomerular filtration rate (eg, creatinine clearance) in order to interpret correctly the extent of aminoaciduria in cases where this tubular defect is suspected.

Another group of renal tubular defects, which, unlike those described above, is usually acquired rather than inherited, is characterized by increased urinary losses of calcium, phosphate, and potassium and a failure to acidify the urine. There may also be decreased ammonia formation by the kidneys (eg, nephrocalcinosis, hyperchloremic nephrocalcinosis, Butler-Albright syndrome). The primary defect in these cases is the inability to form an acid urine. Chronic acidosis results, leading to increased urinary excretion of alkali cations (sodium, potassium, and calcium), which are used to neutralize the excess acid. The losses of calcium and phosphorus in the urine produce changes in the bones (osteomalacia). Correction of the acidosis by administration of an alkaline salt (sodium bicarbonate) produces healing of the bones.

In contrast to the generalized aminoaciduria of the De Toni-Fanconi syndrome, a limited excretion of only a few amino acids without evidence of any other renal tubular defect may also occur. An example is the excessive excretion of cystine, lysine, arginine, and ornithine in "cystinuria."

Tubular Secretion

Creatinine is secreted by the tubules when the blood levels rise above normal. Uric acid, although completely filtered by the glomerulus, is almost completely reabsorbed in the proximal tubule. It is subse-

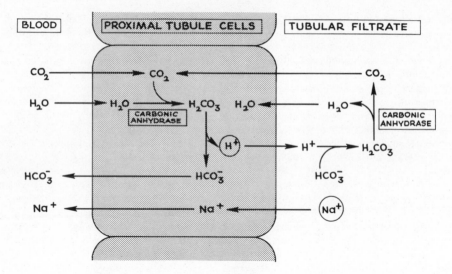

Figure 35—6. Mobilization of hydrogen ions in proximal tubule.

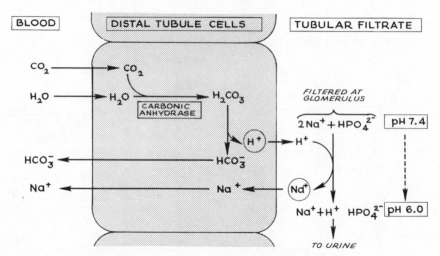

Figure 35—7. Secretion of hydrogen ions in distal tubule.

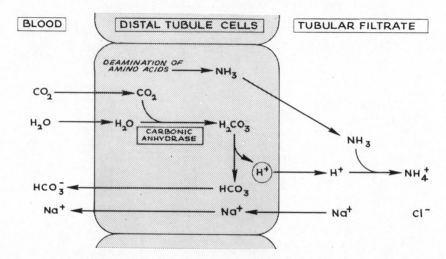

Figure 35—8. Production of ammonia in distal tubule.

quently secreted in a more distal portion of the proximal tubule, and a portion of this secreted uric acid may again be reabsorbed. In any event, most of the uric acid in the urine is present as a consequence of secretion. Potassium is secreted from the blood by the cells of the distal convoluted tubule. The exchange of hydrogen ions for sodium described below might also be considered a secretory function of the tubules.

In addition, a variety of organic anions which are protein-bound in plasma because of insolubility at physiologic pH are transported by tubular cells and excreted in urine either in their original or in biotransformed states. These substances are present in small quantities in plasma and urine of individuals with normal renal function but increase markedly in those with impairment of function.

Many foreign substances are readily secreted by the tubules. An example is the dye phenol red (phenolsulfonphthalein, PSP), which is secreted by the proximal tubule utilizing a carrier system similar to that for glucose but acting, of course, in reverse. The same carrier system is mainly responsible for the secretion of iodopyracetate (iodopyracet NF XIII; Diodrast, ie, 3,5-diiodo-4-pyridone-*N*-acetate which is loosely combined with diethanolamine), iodohippurate (Hippuran, ie, *o*-iodohippurate), penicillin, and *p*-aminohippurate.

Investigations into some of the energy sources for renal tubular transport indicate that energy from oxidation of succinate and other citric acid cycle oxidations is directly involved in tubular secretory processes. Various inhibitors of the succinic oxidase system are known to alter the secretion of aminohippurate and of the dye phenolsulfonphthalein. It is also possible that the glutathione *S*-transferase system is operative as an intracellular binding protein in the tubular cell.

The maximal rate at which the tubule can accomplish secretion is determined by the capacity of these carrier systems. This is measured and expressed as the **maximal tubular secretory capacity**, or **secretory Tm.** For aminohippurate this is about 80 mg/minute in normal persons. This value is useful in measuring the amount of functioning tubular tissue since it represents the total effect of all the tubules working together. Iodopyracetate, which is opaque to x-ray, is used for roentgenologic examinations of the urinary tract. It

may also be used like aminohippurate to measure tubular activity. The normal secretory Tm for iodopyracetate is about 50 mg/minute.

ACIDIFICATION OF THE URINE

The pH of blood is maintained within a normal range despite addition of acid and alkali into extracellular fluid both from the diet and as a result of metabolic reactions. Both extracellular and intracellular compartments contain numerous buffer systems; however, in extracellular fluid one particular buffer pair dominates. This is the carbon dioxide-bicarbonate system, the acid conjugate of which (H_2CO_3) is regulated by the respiratory center and lungs (CO_2) and the base (HCO_3^-) by the kidneys.

The kidneys regulate plasma bicarbonate concentration by 2 processes. In the first, filtered bicarbonate is completely reabsorbed by the tubules; in the second, bicarbonate is regenerated in the distal tubule to replace that which has been utilized by the presence of nonvolatile acids (HCl, H_3PO_4, H_2SO_4, and organic acids) within extracellular fluids as a consequence of metabolic processes.

Micropuncture studies have indicated that, by the time the urine has arrived at the end of the accessible portion of the proximal tubule, approximately 80–85% of filtered bicarbonate has been reabsorbed. Fig 35–6 shows diagrammatically the mechanism by which bicarbonate is reabsorbed. Inside the cell, CO_2 and H_2O react in the presence of the enzyme carbonic anhydrase to produce carbonic acid which dissociates into H^+ and HCO_3^-. The H^+, secreted into the tubular lumen in exchange for Na^+, reacts with filtered HCO_3^- to form H_2CO_3, which, again in the presence of carbonic anhydrase (located intraluminally in the brush border of the proximal tubule), dissociates into CO_2 and H_2O. CO_2 is freely diffusible back into the tubule cell. The originally filtered Na^+ and the HCO_3^- formed within the cell are then reabsorbed into blood. The net, albeit indirect, effect is reabsorption of filtered $NaHCO_3$.

At concentrations of plasma bicarbonate below about 25 mEq/liter, recovery of HCO_3^- by the proximal tubule is virtually complete; what small amounts of HCO_3^- remain to be delivered to the distal nephron are completely reabsorbed and the urine is now rendered free of bicarbonate. The relationships between bicarbonate reabsorption and plasma bicarbonate concentration are shown in Fig 35–9. The solid line depicts this relationship when effective arterial volume, P_{CO_2}, plasma K^+, and Cl^- are normal. At concentrations of HCO_3^- below 25 mEq/liter, reabsorption is complete and no bicarbonate appears in the urine. Above 25 mEq/liter, reabsorption remains constant at about 2.5 mEq/dl of filtrate. It is obvious that if the plasma HCO_3^- concentrations were to be elevated, as by ingestion of alkali, HCO_3^- would be excreted in

Iodopyracetate (Diodrast)

***p*-Aminohippurate**

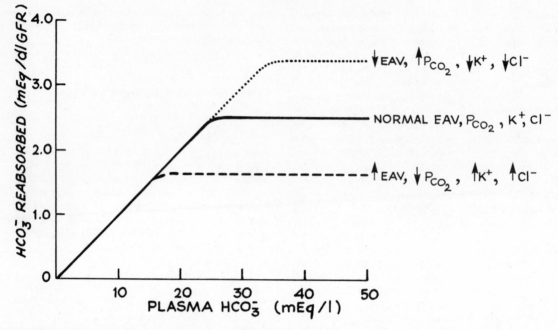

Figure 35—9. Relationships between reabsorption of bicarbonate and the concentration of bicarbonate in the plasma. (EAV = effective arterial volume; P_{CO_2} = partial pressure of carbon dioxide.)

urine until the plasma concentration of HCO_3^- had once again reached 25 mEq/liter. The dotted line reflects alterations in this relationship induced by volume depletion, hypokalemia, and hypochloremia, all of which increase the ability of the proximal tubule to reabsorb bicarbonate. The dashed line depicts alterations in bicarbonate reabsorption induced by volume expansion, hyperkalemia, and hyperchloremia, all of which inhibit the ability of the proximal tubule to reabsorb HCO_3^-. These relationships partially explain the alkalosis observed in volume contraction and the acidosis observed during saline infusion.

The response of the renal tubule to the CO_2 tension of the body fluids provides an explanation for the renal response to states of respiratory acidosis or alkalosis (Fig 35—9). In respiratory acidosis, compensation is achieved by an increase in the bicarbonate levels of the blood in an attempt to restore the normal 1:20 ratio of carbonic acid to bicarbonate that exists at physiologic pH. The increased bicarbonate may be obtained by the response of the kidney to the high CO_2 tension which prevails in respiratory acidosis. The situation is reversed in respiratory alkalosis. Here compensation is achieved by elimination of bicarbonate; the lowered CO_2 tension which prevails in this condition induces a renal response that reduces the rate of reabsorption of bicarbonate until the normal ratio of carbonic acid to bicarbonate is restored.

In the cells of the distal nephron (Fig 35—7), a process identical to that in proximal tubular cells occurs. Hydrogen ion is generated from CO_2 and H_2O and secreted into the lumen in exchange for sodium ion. This exchange process can continue in normal

individuals until the pH of the tubular fluid has dropped to about 4.5. Once this occurs, further net secretion ceases since the H^+ ion gradient between the cell and the tubular filtrate is too steep. Two mechanisms are present to prevent this low pH from being reached and to assure that sufficient bicarbonate may be generated by the cell to prevent the occurrence of metabolic acidosis. These mechanisms are (1) buffering by filtered HPO_4^{2-} ion and (2) ammonia secretion (Fig 35—8). After all of the bicarbonate has been reabsorbed, hydrogen ion secretion then proceeds against Na_2HPO_4. The exchange of a sodium ion for the secreted hydrogen ion changes Na_2HPO_4 to NaH_2PO_4, with a consequent increase in the acidity of the urine and a decrease in the urinary pH.

Ammonia is obtained principally by deamination of amino acids within the distal tubule. Deamination of glutamine catalyzed by renal glutaminase serves as the major source of the urinary ammonia. The ammonia formed within the renal tubule cell may react directly with hydrogen ions so that ammonium ions rather than hydrogen ions are secreted, or ammonia may diffuse into the tubular filtrate and there form ammonium ion. Such a mechanism operating against sodium chloride is illustrated in Fig 35—8.

The lower the pH of the urine (ie, the greater the concentration of hydrogen ions), the more rapidly will ammonia diffuse into the urine. Thus, ammonia production is greatly increased in metabolic acidosis and is negligible in alkalosis. It has also been proposed that the activity of renal glutaminase is enhanced by acidosis. The ammonia mechanism is a valuable device for the conservation of cation. Under normal conditions, 30–50 mEq of hydrogen ion are eliminated per day by combination with ammonia and about 10–30 mEq as titratable acid (ie, buffered with phosphate).

ABNORMALITIES OF ACID-BASE REGULATION BY THE KIDNEY

The Henderson-Hasselbalch equation as it applies to the ratio of the buffer pair HCO_3^-/CO_2 states that

$$pH = 6.10 + \log \frac{HCO_3^-}{0.0301\ P_{CO_2}}$$

The denominator of this ratio, ie, the CO_2 tension of blood, is regulated by the lungs; changes in this value are characteristic of so-called "respiratory" acidosis or alkalosis, depending on whether the P_{CO_2} increases or decreases. Changes in the numerator of the ratio are characteristic of "metabolic" acidosis or alkalosis. These are brought about either by addition of acid or base to the body fluids or by subtraction of acid or base from the body fluids. Table 35–1 lists the major causes of metabolic alkalosis and acidosis seen in clinical practice.

Metabolic alkalosis can be generated by loss of acid such as occurs in gastric vomiting or nasogastric secretion, or by ingestion of alkali by, for example, excessive use of sodium bicarbonate as an antacid. Alternatively, it can be generated by the kidney either as a proximal tubular event (Fig 35–9) secondary to volume depletion, hypercapnia (elevated P_{CO_2}), hypokalemia (decreased $[K^+]$), or hypochloremia, or as a distal tubular event secondary to adrenal mineralocorticoid excess (see p 490). Once the alkalosis is generated by one of these events, the kidney will rapidly correct the alkalosis by excreting the excess bicarbonate in the urine unless the reabsorptive ability of the proximal tubule is modified such that increased bicarbonate is instead reabsorbed, or unless there is mineralocorticoid excess or hypokalemia. Correction of metabolic alkalosis must therefore be directed to reversal of the underlying conditions which result in either the excessive reabsorption or regeneration of bicarbonate by the kidney.

Metabolic acidosis (a decrease in the numerator of the Henderson-Hasselbalch equation) can occur either when the chloride concentration of serum is normal or decreased or when the chloride concentration is increased relative to the decrease in bicarbonate. In the former variety, if one adds up the total **measured** cations and total **measured** anions in serum, there is a larger than normal difference (about 15 mEq/liter, due largely to plasma proteins) between the two. This is spoken of as an "anion gap" (Table 35–1). In general, anion gap metabolic acidosis is due to (1) diabetic acidosis, in which ketone bodies form the unmeasured anions; (2) lactic acidosis because of accumulated lac-

Table 35–1. Metabolic alkalosis and acidosis.

Causes of metabolic alkalosis:
1. Loss of acid (vomiting, gastric drainage)
2. Diuretic therapy
3. Posthypercapnic alkalosis
4. Mineralocorticoid excess syndromes: aldosteronism, Cushing's syndrome, Bartter's syndrome, ACTH-secreting tumors, licorice ingestion
5. Excessive alkali administration
6. Severe potassium depletion
7. Contraction alkalosis

Causes of metabolic acidosis divided according to the anion gap:
A. Increased Unmeasured Anions:
  1. Diabetic ketoacidosis
  2. Azotemic renal failure
  3. Lactic acidosis
  4. Ingestions
    a. Salicylate
    b. Methyl alcohol
    c. Paraldehyde
    d. Ethylene glycol
B. Normal Unmeasured Anions (Hyperchloremic Metabolic Acidosis):
  1. Diarrhea and draining fistulas
  2. Ammonium chloride administration
  3. Renal tubular acidosis (proximal and distal)
  4. Ureterosigmoidostomy
  5. Carbonic anhydrase inhibitors
  6. "Expansion" acidosis

tate anions; (3) poisoning with acid compounds; or (4) kidney failure, wherein there is an accumulation of a variety of anions that are normally excreted by the kidney.

These are to be contrasted with hyperchloremic metabolic acidosis, due either to ingestion of acid substances such as ammonium chloride or loss of bicarbonate occurring as a result of profuse diarrhea or enteric fistulas. A third form of hyperchloremic acidosis results from the inability of the kidney either to reabsorb (proximal tubule) or to regenerate bicarbonate appropriately—hence the term renal tubular acidosis (RTA) to describe this syndrome. The proximal tubular form of this disease is usually traceable to a hereditary defect, often associated with disorders of phosphate, glucose, and amino acid reabsorption as well. In this form of the disease, a lowered threshold for the appearance of bicarbonate in urine is observed, often associated with a decreased maximal ability of the tubule to reabsorb bicarbonate. Although severe bone disease and hypercalciuria are seen in proximal renal tubular acidosis, nephrocalcinosis and ureteral stones are not common.

The other form of renal tubular acidosis is that caused by inability of the distal nephron to acidify the urine adequately and thus to regenerate sufficient cation to maintain normal acid-base balance. The defect is probably due to increased back-diffusion of H^+ into the distal tubular cell. This form of the disease is associated with hypokalemia, bone disease, and, in contrast to proximal renal tubular acidosis, nephrocalcinosis and stones. The difference is attributable to decreased concentrations of citrate and other chelating substances in urine. Carbonic anhydrase inhibitors produce an acidosis which is actually a mixed form of renal tubular acidosis.

Treatment of distal renal tubular acidosis is simple, requiring only the addition of moderate amounts of bicarbonate to the diet. In proximal renal tubular acidosis, massive doses of HCO_3^- are required, and diuretics are also of value to produce some decrease of plasma volume.

Relation of Potassium Excretion to Acid-Base Equilibrium

The administration of potassium salts in excess produces a decrease in hydrogen ion concentration within the cells and an increase (acidosis) in the extracellular fluid accompanied by the excretion of an alkaline urine. Conversely, potassium depletion is associated with the development of alkalosis in the extracellular fluid and an increase in hydrogen ion concentration within the cell (intracellular acidosis) followed by the excretion of a highly acid urine despite the high bicarbonate content of the plasma (paradoxic aciduria). These latter circumstances may occur in patients treated with cortisone or corticotropin (ACTH) or in those with the hypercorticism of Cushing's syndrome. It is also a common occurrence in postoperative patients maintained largely on potassium-free fluids in whom depletion of potassium may result because of continued excretion of this cation in the urine and in the gastrointestinal fluids. Although the alkalosis in these surgical cases is usually accompanied by depletion of chloride (hypochloremic alkalosis), correction cannot be attained by the administration of sodium chloride alone but only by the administration of potassium salts as well. When adequate repletion of potassium has been accomplished, a fall in serum bicarbonate and a rise in serum chloride together with elevation of the urine pH to normal levels will occur.

As noted above, potassium is secreted by the distal tubule. Furthermore, parallel and coupled mechanisms which provide for the secretion of hydrogen ions in exchange for sodium are utilized for the secretion of potassium, also in exchange for sodium. The capacity of this parallel system is limited. Ordinarily it is represented by the sum of the secretion of hydrogen and potassium ions. When intracellular potassium levels are low and intracellular hydrogen ions are elevated, as occurs in potassium-deficient states, more hydrogen ions can be secreted by the distal tubule cells. Under these circumstances, bicarbonate reabsorption proceeds together with excess hydrogen ion secretion, and a highly acid urine is formed.

The effect of acid-base balance (in this instance, alkalosis) on the excretion of potassium in the urine can be further demonstrated by administration of a quantity of sodium bicarbonate sufficient to lower hydrogen ion concentration both intracellularly and extracellularly. Within the renal tubular cells, the decline in hydrogen ion concentration permits an increase in secretion of potassium because of the normal competition for secretion which exists between hydrogen and potassium ions in the distal tubule. Marked enhancement of potassium excretion will thus be produced in response to the alkalosis following bicarbonate administration. In fact, in man, the excretion of potassium is so closely related to alkalosis that simple hyperventilation (producing respiratory alkalosis) will raise the rate of excretion of potassium from 87–266 μEq/minute.

The ability of acetazolamide (Diamox) to increase excretion of potassium into the urine is attributable to its inhibiting effect on carbonic anhydrase activity, which thus brings about a reduction in hydrogen ion concentration within the renal tubule cell. Consequently, secretion of potassium can be increased.

Summary of the Mechanisms for Sodium Reabsorption

The relative importance of each of the mechanisms for the conservation of sodium by the kidney may be assessed by a consideration of the following data.

A. Sodium Reabsorbed With Fixed Anion (Mostly Chloride): 12,000 μEq/minute.

B. Na^+–H^+ Exchange:

1. $NaHCO_3$ –3200 μEq/minute.

2. NH_4 –20 μEq/minute.

3. Titratable acid (decrease in urine pH)–30 μEq/minute.

4. Free acid (1 ml urine at pH 5.0)–0.01 μEq/minute.

C. NA^+–K^+ Exchange (K^+ Excreted): 50 μEq/minute.

MECHANISM OF ACTION OF DIURETICS

Diuretics are drugs which promote losses of water and salt via the urine through interference with normal reabsorptive mechanisms. Table 35–2 lists the various classes of these drugs.

Osmotic diuretics are nonreabsorbable substances which increase tubular osmolarity progressively as salt and water are reabsorbed. When the fluid reaches the loop of Henle and collecting tubules where passive secretion of water occurs, the osmotic substances within the tubular fluid limit the amount of water which can diffuse out secondary to osmotic gradients. Urine flow is thus increased. These types of diuretics are not useful in the treatment of pathologic states like congestive heart failure because of their tendency to expand the vascular volume. Osmotic diuresis is responsible for the serious dehydration which accompanies diabetic ketoacidosis.

Acetazolamide (Diamox) is a potent carbonic anhydrase inhibitor. Thus, it blocks both HCO_3^- reabsorption in the proximal tubule and regeneration in the distal tubule. Although acutely it is an effective di-

Table 35–2. Diuretics.

Osmotic substances:
Mannitol
Glucose
Carbonic anhydrase inhibitors:
Acetazolamide
Thiazides ⎱ Not primary action
Furosemide ⎰
Thick ascending limb action:
Medullary thick-walled ascending limb:
Furosemide
Ethacrynic acid
Cortical thick-walled ascending limb:
Thiazides
Furosemide
Ethacrynic acid
Aldosterone antagonists:
Spironolactone
Triamterene
Tubular poisons: Organic mercurials

uretic, its effect depends on the presence of adequate bicarbonate concentrations in plasma. For this reason the drug's effectiveness diminishes rapidly as systemic acidosis develops. Thiazide diuretics and furosemide also have weak activity as carbonic anhydrase inhibitors; however, this is not the primary basis of their ability to induce diuresis.

As previously discussed, there are 2 portions of the thick-walled ascending lumb, cortical and medullary, which contribute to free water formation, but only the medullary portion contributes to urinary concentration. Thiazide diuretics, furosemide, ethacrynic acid, and mercurials all inhibit chloride reabsorption in the cortical thick-walled ascending limb, perhaps by different mechanisms, but only furosemide, ethacrynic acid, and probably mercurials have an effect in the medullary thick-walled ascending limb. Thus, thiazides have a much weaker diuretic effect than furosemide and ethacrynic acid.

The final class of diuretic drugs includes those which antagonize the action of aldosterone in the distal tubule. Since only a small portion ($< 1\%$) of sodium is reabsorbed by this mechanism, these are relatively poor diuretics. They have been used in combination with other diuretics because of their potassium-sparing action.

TESTS OF RENAL FUNCTION

Clearance

For the purpose of expressing quantitatively the rate of excretion of a given substance by the kidney, its "clearance" is frequently measured. This is a volume of blood or plasma which contains the amount of the substance which is excreted in the urine in 1 minute. Alternatively, the clearance of a substance may be defined as that volume of blood or plasma cleared of the amount of the substance found in 1 minute's excretion of urine. The calculation of clearance can be illustrated by measurement of the clearance of inulin.

A. Inulin Clearance: The polysaccharide inulin is filtered at the glomerulus but neither secreted nor reabsorbed by the tubule. The clearance of inulin is therefore a measure of glomerular filtration rate. **Mannitol** can also be used for the same purpose. These clearances, like many other physiologic phenomena, vary with body size. They are therefore expressed on the basis of a given size, eg, normal inulin clearance is 120 ml/1.73 sq m body surface area. To facilitate interpretation, the results of an actual clearance study are usually calculated ("corrected clearance") on the basis of ml/1.73 sq m.

In measuring inulin clearance it is desirable to maintain a constant plasma level of the test substance during the period of urine collections. Simultaneous measurement of the plasma inulin level and the quantity excreted in a given time supplies the data necessary to calculate the clearance according to the following formula:

$$C_{in} = \frac{U \times V}{P}$$

Where C_{in} = Clearance of inulin (ml/minute)
       U = Urinary inulin (mg/dl)
       P = Plasma inulin (mg/dl)
       V = Volume of urine (ml/minute)

B. Endogenous Creatinine Clearance: At normal levels of creatinine in the serum, this metabolite is filtered at the glomerulus but not secreted nor reabsorbed by the tubule. Consequently, its clearance may also be measured to obtain the GFR. This is a convenient clinical method for estimation of the GFR since it does not require the intravenous administration of a test substance, as is the case with an exogenous clearance study using inulin. Normal values for creatinine clearance are 95–105 ml/minute.

Measurement of Renal Plasma Flow

Aminohippurate is filtered at the glomeruli and secreted by the tubules. At low blood concentrations (2 mg or less/dl of plasma), aminohippurate is removed almost completely during a single circulation of the blood through the kidneys. Thus, the amount of aminohippurate in the urine becomes a measure of the volume of plasma cleared of aminohippurate in a unit of time. In other words, aminohippurate clearance at low blood levels estimates **renal plasma flow**. This is about 574 ml/minute for a surface area of 1.73 sq m.

Filtration Fraction

The filtration fraction, ie, the fraction of plasma passing through the kidney which is filtered at the glomerulus, is obtained by dividing the inulin clearance by the aminohippurate clearance (glomerular filtration rate/renal plasma flow = filtration fraction). For a glomerular filtration rate of 125 and a renal plasma flow of 574, the filtration fraction would then be 125/574 = 0.217 (21.7%). The filtration fraction tends to be normal in early essential hypertension, but as the disease progresses the decrease in renal plasma flow is greater than the decrease in glomerular filtration. This produces an increase in the filtration fraction. In the malignant phase of hypertension, these changes are much greater; consequently, the filtration fraction rises considerably. The reverse situation prevails in glomerulonephritis. In all stages of this disease, a decrease in the filtration fraction is characteristic because of the much greater decline in glomerular filtration than in renal plasma flow.

Measurement of Tubular Secretory Mass

This is accomplished by measuring the Tm (tubular maximum) for aminohippurate, ie, the maximal secretory capacity of the tubule for aminohippurate. In this case, aminohippurate must be raised to relatively high levels in the blood, eg, 50 mg/dl. At these levels, the tubular secretory carriers are working at maximal capacity. By correcting the urine aminohippurate for that filtered as calculated from the glomerular filtration rate, the quantity of aminohippurate secreted is obtained. The normal maximum is about 80 mg/minute/1.73 sq m. Iodopyracetate (Diodrast) clearance may be similarly used to measure tubular excretion. The Tm for aminohippurate can be used to gauge the extent of tubular damage in renal disease because, as tubular cells cease to function or are destroyed, excretion of aminohippurate is proportionately diminished.

Phenolsulfonphthalein Test

Dyes are widely used for excretion tests. An example is phenolsulfonphthalein (phenol red). The test is conducted by measuring the rate of excretion of the dye following intramuscular or intravenous administration. The intravenous test is the more valid since it eliminates the uncertainties of absorption which exist in the intramuscular test. Urine specimens may be collected at 15, 30, 60, and 120 minutes after the injection of the dye. If the 15-minute urine contains 25% or more of the injected phenolsulfonphthalein, the test is normal. Forty to 60% of the dye is normally excreted in the first hour and 20–25% in the second. The most useful information is obtained from the original 15-minute specimen since by the end of 2 hours the amount of dye excreted, although originally delayed, may now appear normal. The dye is readily excreted by the tubules, and therefore the result is not abnormal until impairment of renal function is extreme.

Concentration Tests

Impairment of the capacity of the tubule to perform osmotic work is an early feature of renal disease. The determination of the osmolarity of the urine after a period of water deprivation becomes, therefore, a valuable and sensitive indicator of renal function. If the kidneys do absolutely no work, a fluid is excreted with osmolarity the same as that of the glomerular filtrate, ie, 1.010 specific gravity. As has been pointed out, any deviation from this value (ie, dilution or concentration) requires osmotic work by the renal tubule.

The most reliable clinical method of measuring concentrating ability is through overnight water deprivation and determination of the urine osmolality on the morning specimen. If an osmometer is not available, a specific gravity in excess of 1.018 probably rules out any need for further tests of concentrating ability. If polyuria exists or if there is suspicion of a serious disturbance of concentrating ability, a more formal water deprivation test, under careful supervision, with vasopressin stimulation at the end, is indicated.

COMPOSITION OF URINE

Characteristics of Urine (Table 35–3.)

A. Volume: In the normal adult, 600–2500 ml of urine are formed daily. The quantity generally depends on the water intake, the external temperature, the diet, and the individual's mental and physical state. Urine volume is less in summer or in warm climates, for it is inversely related, roughly, to the extent of perspiration. Nitrogenous end products and coffee, tea, and alcoholic beverages have a diuretic effect. About half as much urine is formed during sleep as during activity.

B. Specific Gravity: This normally ranges from 1.003–1.030 and varies according to concentration of solutes in the urine. The figures in the second and third decimal places, multiplied by 2.66 (Long's coefficient), give roughly the total solids in the urine in g/liter; 50 g of solids in 1200 ml are an average normal for the day.

C. Reaction: The urine is normally acid, with a pH less than 6.0 (range: 4.7–8.0). Ordinarily, over 250 ml of 0.1 N acid, 25 mEq H ion (titratable acidity), are excreted daily. When the protein intake is high, the urine is acid because excess phosphate and sulfate are produced in the catabolism of protein. Acidity is also increased in acidosis and in fevers.

The urine becomes alkaline on standing because of conversion of urea to ammonia and loss of CO_2 to air. It may also be alkaline in alkalosis such as after excessive vomiting, at least at the early stages, and after meals due to H^+ secretion in the stomach (the "alkaline tide").

D. Color: Normal urine is pale yellow or amber. The color varies with the quantity and concentration of urine voided. The chief pigment is urochrome, but small quantities of urobilin and hematoporphyrin are also present.

In fever, because of concentration, the urine may be dark yellow or brownish. In liver disease, bile pigments may color the urine green, brown, or deep yellow. Blood or hemoglobin gives the urine a smoky to red color. Methemoglobin and homogentisic acid color it dark brown. Drugs may color the urine. For example, methylene blue gives the urine a green appear-

Table 35—3. Composition of normal urine.*

Specific Gravity: 1.003—1.030
Reaction (pH): 4.7—8.0 (avg 6.0)
Volume: Normal range: 600—2500 ml/24 hours (avg 1200 ml). Night/day ratio of volume: 1:2—1:4 if 8:00 a.m. and 8:00 p.m. are the divisions. Night urine usually does not exceed 500—700 ml and usually has a specific gravity of more than 1.018.
Titratable acidity of 100 ml (depending on pH): 250—700 ml of 0.1 N NaOH for acid urine.
Total solids: 30—70 g/liter (avg 50 g). Long's coefficient to estimate total solids per liter: multiply last 2 figures of specific gravity by 2.66.

Inorganic Constituents (per 24 hours):

Chlorides (as NaCl)	10 (9—16) g on usual diet	Sulfur (total) (as SO_3)	2 (0.7—3.5) g
Sodium	4 g on usual diet	Calcium	0.2 (0.1—0.2) g
(varies with intake)		Magnesium	0.15 (0.05—0.2) g
Phosphorus	2.2 (2—2.5) g	Iodine	50—250 μg
Potassium	2 g	Arsenic	50 μg or less
(varies with intake)		Lead	50 μg or less

Organic Constituents (per 24 hours):

		Nitrogen Equivalent
Nitrogenous (total)	25—35 g	10—14 g
Urea (half of total urine solids varies with diet)	25—30 g	10—12 g
Creatinine	1.4 (1—1.8) g	0.5 g
Ammonia	0.7 (0.3—1) g	0.4 g
Uric acid	0.7 (0.5—0.8) g	0.2 g
Undetermined N (amino acid, etc)		0.5 g
Protein, as such ("albumin")	0—0.2 g	
Creatine	60—150 mg (increased in liver or muscle diseases or thyrotoxicosis)	

Other Organic Constituents (per 24 hours):

Hippuric acid 0.1—1 g	Oxalic acid 15—20 mg	Indican 4—20 mg	Coproporphyrins 60—280 μg
Purine bases 10 mg	Ketone bodies 3—15 mg	Allantoin 30 mg	Phenols (total) 0.2—0.5 g

Sugar: 50% of people have 2—3 mg/100 ml after a heavy meal. A diabetic can lose up to 100 g/day.

Ascorbic Acid: Adults excrete 15—50 mg/24 hours; in scurvy, less than 15 mg/24 hours.

*Modified from Krupp MA & others: *Physician's Handbook,* 18th ed. Lange, 1976.

ance, and cascara and some other cathartics give it a brown color.

The urine is usually transparent, but in alkaline urine a turbidity may develop by precipitation of calcium phosphate. Strongly acid urine precipitates uric acid salts, which have a pink color.

E. Odor: Fresh urine is normally aromatic but the odor may be modified by substances in the diet such as asparagus (methyl mercaptan odor?). In ketosis, the odor of excreted acetone may be detected.

Normal Constituents of Urine (See Table 35—4.)

Urea constitutes about half (25 g) of the urine solids. Sodium chloride constitutes about one-fourth (9—16 g).

A. Urea: This is the principal end product of protein metabolism in mammals. Its excretion is directly related to the protein intake. Normally it comprises 80—90% of the total urinary nitrogen; but on a low-protein diet this is less because certain other nitrogenous constituents tend to remain relatively unaffected by diet.

Urea excretion is increased whenever protein catabolism is increased, as in fever, diabetes, or excess adrenocortical activity. In the last stages of fatal liver disease, decreased urea production may lead to decreased excretion. There is also a decrease in urine urea in acidosis since some of the nitrogen which would

have been converted to urea is diverted to ammonia formation. The urea does not, however, give rise to the ammonia directly.

B. Ammonia: Normally there is very little ammonia in freshly voided urine. Its formation by the kidney in acidosis has been described earlier. In acidosis of renal origin, this mechanism may fail. Therefore, such acidosis is accompanied by a low concentration of ammonia in the urine. On the other hand, the ketosis and resultant acidosis of uncontrolled diabetes mellitus, in which renal function is unimpaired, will cause a high ammonia output in the urine.

C. Creatinine and Creatine: Creatinine is the product of the breakdown of creatine. In a given subject it is excreted in relatively constant amounts regardless of diet. The creatinine coefficient is the ratio between the amount of creatinine excreted in 24 hours and the body weight in kg. It is usually 20—26 mg/kg/day in normal men and 14—22 mg/kg/day in normal women. Because this rate is so constant in a given individual, the creatinine coefficient may serve as a reliable index of the adequacy of the 24-hour urine collection. The excretion of creatinine is decreased in many pathologic states.

Creatine is present in the urine of children and, in much smaller amounts, in the urine of adults as well. In men the creatine excretion is about 6% of the total creatinine output (probably 60—150 mg/day). In wom-

Table 35–4. Variations in some urinary constituents with different protein levels in the diet.[*][†]

	Usual Protein Intake		Protein-Rich Diet		Protein-Poor Diet	
	g	%N	g	%N	g	%N
Total urinary nitrogen	13.20		23.28		4.20	
Protein represented by above N	82.50		145.50		26.25	
Urea nitrogen	11.36	86.1	20.45	87.9	2.90	69.0
Ammonia nitrogen	0.40	3.0	0.82	3.5	0.17	4.0
Creatinine nitrogen	0.61	4.6	0.64	2.7	0.60	14.3
Uric acid nitrogen	0.21	1.6	0.30	1.3	0.11	2.6
Undetermined nitrogen	0.62	4.7	1.07	4.6	0.52	12.4
Titratable acidity (ml 0.1 N)	284.0 ml		655.0 ml		160.0 ml	
Volume of urine	1260.0 ml		1550.0 ml		960.0 ml	
Total sulfur (as SO_3)	2.65 g		3.55 g		0.86 g	
Inorganic sulfate (as SO_3)	2.16		2.82		0.64	
Ethereal sulfate (as SO_3)	0.18		0.36		0.11	
Neutral sulfate (as SO_3)	0.31		0.37		0.11	
Total inorganic phosphate (as P_2O_5)	2.59		4.07		1.06	
Chloride (as NaCl)	12.10		15.10		9.80	

[*]Reprinted, with permission, from Bodansky: *Introduction to Physiological Chemistry,* 4th ed. Wiley, 1938.
[†]A balance between intake of protein nitrogen and the excretion of nitrogen (nitrogen balance) is presumed to exist in these experiments.

en creatinuria is much more variable (usually 2–2½ times that of normal men), although in about one-fifth of the normal women studied the creatinuria did not exceed that found in men. In pregnancy, creatine excretion is increased. Creatinuria is also found in pathologic states such as starvation, impaired carbohydrate metabolism, hyperthyroidism, and certain myopathies and infections. Excretion of creatine is decreased in hypothyroidism.

Creatinine is measured colorimetrically by adding alkaline picrate to the urine. In the presence of creatinine, the mixture develops an amber color (Jaffé reaction). The color is read against a creatinine standard similarly treated with alkaline picrate solution.

Creatine, when heated in acid solution, is converted to creatinine, which can be measured as described. The difference in the creatinine content of the urine before and after boiling with acid gives the creatine content.

D. Uric Acid: This is the most important end product of the oxidation of purines in the body. It is derived not only from dietary nucleoprotein but also from the breakdown of cellular nucleoprotein in the body.

Uric acid is very slightly soluble in water but forms soluble salts with alkali. For this reason it precipitates readily from acid urine on standing.

The output of uric acid is increased in leukemia, severe liver disease, and various stages of gout.

The blue color which uric acid gives in the presence of arsenophosphotungstic acid sodium cyanide is the basis of the Folin colorimetric test. This is not a specific reaction, however. Salicylates raise the color value due to the excretion of gentisic acid and other similar metabolites. This may raise the apparent excretion of uric acid as much as 25% in 24 hours after a large dose of aspirin.

The specificity of the analysis for uric acid may be increased by treatment of the sample with uricase, the enzyme (from hog kidney) which causes the conversion of uric acid to allantoin. The decline in apparent uric acid concentration after uricase treatment is taken as a measure of the true uric acid content of the sample.

E. Amino Acids: In adults, only about 150–200 mg of amino acid nitrogen are excreted in the urine in 24 hours. The full-term infant at birth excretes about 3 mg amino acid nitrogen per pound of body weight; this excretion declines gradually up to the age of 6 months, when it reaches a value of 1 mg/lb that is maintained throughout childhood. Premature infants may excrete as much as 10 times as much amino acid nitrogen as the full-term infant.

The reason such very small amounts of amino acids are lost into the urine is that the renal thresholds for these substances are quite high. However, all of the naturally occurring amino acids have been found in the urine, some in relatively large quantities when compared to the trace quantities characteristic of most. It is also of interest that a high percentage of some excreted amino acids is in combined forms and can be liberated by acid hydrolysis. Diet alters the pattern of amino acid excretion to some extent.

The amounts of free amino acids found in the urine of normal subjects are shown in Table 35–5.

In terminal liver disease and in certain types of poisoning (chloroform, carbon tetrachloride), the quantity of amino acids excreted is increased. This "overflow" type of aminoaciduria is to be distinguished from renal aminoaciduria due to an inherited tubular defect in reabsorption. In "cystinuria" a considerable increase in excretion of 4 amino acids occurs: arginine, cystine, lysine, and ornithine. The amounts of all other amino acids excreted remain normal.

Table 35–5. Amino acids in urine (maximum normal levels; expressed as μmol/24 hours).*

Amino Acid	Children	Adults
Alanine	438	225
α-Amino-*n*-butyric acid	44	14
β-Aminoisobutyric acid	165	1640
Arginine		26
Aspartic acid		145
Citrulline		6
Cystine	100	45
Ethanolamine		280
Glutamic acid		44
Glycine	1280	2600
Histidine	1110	1300
Hydroxyproline		8
Isoleucine	54	40
Leucine	76	75
Lysine	506	224
Methionine	94	38
1-Methylhistidine		570
3-Methylhistidine		360
Ornithine		27
Phenylalanine	103	90
Proline		22
Serine	543	770
Taurine	970	1230
Threonine	244	234
Tryptophan		125
Tyrosine	166	167
Valine	43	37

*From Dickinson JC & others: Pediatrics 36:2, 1965; Moore S, Stein W: J Biol Chem 211:908, 1956; King JS: Clin Chem Acta 9:441, 1964. (Courtesy of Bio-Science Laboratories.)

F. Allantoin: This is derived from partial oxidation of uric acid. There are very small quantities in human urine, but in other subprimate mammals allantoin is the principal end product of purine metabolism, replacing uric acid.

G. Chlorides: These are mainly excreted as sodium chloride. Because most of the chlorides are of dietary origin, output varies considerably with intake.

H. Sulfates: The urine sulfur is derived mainly from protein because of the presence of the sulfur-containing amino acids, methionine and cystine, in the protein molecule. Its output therefore varies with the protein intake. The total urine sulfur is usually partitioned into 3 forms. It is customary to express all sulfur concentrations in the urine as SO_3.

1. Inorganic (sulfate) sulfur—This is the completely oxidized sulfur precipitated from urine when barium chloride is added. It is roughly proportionate to the ingested protein with a ratio of 5:1 between urine nitrogen and inorganic sulfate (expressed as SO_3). Together with the total urinary nitrogen, this fraction of urine sulfur is an index of protein catabolism.

2. Ethereal sulfur (conjugated sulfates)—This fraction (about 10% of the total sulfur) includes the organic combinations of sulfur excreted in the urine. Examples are the phenol and cresol sulfuric acids, indoxyl and skatoxyl sulfuric acids, and other sulfur conjugates formed in detoxification.

The ethereal sulfate fraction is in part derived from protein metabolism; but in indican and some of the phenols, putrefactive activity in the intestine is also represented.

After hydrolysis with hot hydrochloric acid, the ethereal sulfates may be precipitated with barium chloride.

3. Neutral sulfur—This fraction is the sulfur which is incompletely oxidized, such as that which is contained in cystine, taurine, thiocyanate, or sulfides. It does not vary with the diet to the same extent that the other fractions do.

Neutral sulfur is determined as the difference between the total sulfur and the sum of the inorganic and ethereal sulfur.

I. Phosphates: The urine phosphates are combinations of sodium and potassium phosphate (the alkaline phosphates) as well as of calcium and magnesium (so-called earthy) phosphate. The latter forms are precipitated in alkaline urines.

The diet, particularly the protein content, influences phosphate excretion. Some is also derived from cellular breakdown.

In certain bone diseases, such as osteomalacia and so-called renal tubular rickets, the output of phosphorus in the urine is increased. In hyperparathyroidism the excretion of phosphorus is also markedly increased. A decrease is sometimes noted in renal and infectious diseases and in hypoparathyroidism.

J. Oxalates: Ordinarily the amount of oxalate in the urine is low, but in an inherited metabolic disease (primary hyperoxaluria) relatively large quantities of oxalate may be continuously excreted.

K. Minerals: Sodium, potassium, calcium, and magnesium—the 4 cations of the extracellular fluid—are present in the urine. The sodium content varies considerably with intake and physiologic requirements. Urine potassium rises when the intake is increased or in the presence of excessive tissue catabolism, in which case it is derived from intracellular materials. The excretion of potassium is also affected by acid-base equilibrium, most notably by alkalosis, which inevitably increases potassium excretion. Sodium and potassium excretions are also controlled by the activity of the adrenal cortex.

Most of the calcium and magnesium is lost to the body by the intestine, representing unabsorbed mineral; the content of these elements in the urine is, therefore, relatively low. However, this will vary in certain pathologic states, particularly those involving bone metabolism.

L. Vitamins, Hormones, and Enzymes: These can be detected in small quantities in normal urine. The urinary content of these substances is often of diagnostic importance.

Abnormal Constituents of the Urine

A. Proteins: Proteinuria (albuminuria) is the presence of albumin and globulin in the urine in abnormal concentrations. Normally not more than 30–200 mg of protein are excreted daily in the urine.

1. Physiologic proteinuria, in which less than 0.5% protein is present, may occur after severe exercise, after a high-protein meal, or as a result of some temporary impairment in renal circulation when a person stands erect (orthostatic or postural proteinuria).

In 30–35% of the cases, pregnancy is accompanied by proteinuria.

2. Pathologic proteinurias are sometimes classified as prerenal, when the primary causes are factors operating before the kidney is reached, although the kidney may also be involved; renal, when the lesion is intrinsic to the kidney; and postrenal, when the proteinuria is due to inflammation in the lower urinary tract. In glomerulonephritis proteinuria is marked during the degenerative phase; the lowest excretion of albumin is during the latent phase and may increase terminally. In nephrotic syndrome a marked proteinuria occurs, accompanied by edema and low concentrations of serum albumin. Nephrosclerosis, a vascular form of renal disease, is related to arterial hypertension. The proteinuria observed in this disease increases with the increasing severity of the renal lesion. The loss of protein in nephrosclerosis is generally less than that in glomerulonephritis. Proteinuria is also observed in poisoning of the renal tubules by heavy metals like mercury, arsenic, or bismuth unless the poisoning is severe enough to cause anuria.

3. Albumin may be detected by heating the urine, preferably after centrifuging to remove the sediment, then adding a little dilute acetic acid. A white cloud or precipitate which persists after addition of the acid indicates that protein is present. In quantitative measurement of urine protein, the protein is precipitated with trichloroacetic acid and then separated for analysis, either colorimetrically (biuret) or by Kjeldahl analysis.

4. Bence Jones proteins—These peculiar proteins are light chain fragments of globulins which occur in the urine, most commonly in multiple myeloma and rarely in leukemia, Hodgkin's disease, and lymphosarcoma. They may be identified in the urine by their ability to precipitate when the urine is warmed to 50–60° C and to redissolve almost completely at 100° C. The precipitate reforms on cooling.

B. Glucose: Normally not more than 1 g of sugar is excreted per day. Glycosuria is indicated when more than this quantity is found. The various causes of glycosuria have been discussed. Transient glycosuria may be noted after emotional stress, such as an exciting athletic contest. Fifteen percent of cases of glycosuria are not due to diabetes. Usually, however, glycosuria suggests diabetes; this must be confirmed by blood studies to eliminate the possibility of renal glycosuria.

A simple test for the presence of glucose in the urine is often performed by using paper test strips containing the peroxidase enzyme. It has been reported that peroxidase is inhibited by homogentisic acid (found in alkaptonuric urine), bilirubin glucuronide (as occurs in urine of jaundiced patients), ascorbic acid,

and epinephrine. In the presence of these inhibitory compounds, the enzyme paper strips may therefore give false-negative results when used to test for glucose in the urine.

C. Other Sugars:

1. Fructosuria is a rare anomaly in which the metabolism of fructose but not that of other carbohydrates is disturbed.

2. Galactosuria and lactosuria may occur occasionally in infants and in the mother during pregnancy, lactation, and the weaning period. In congenital galactosemia, the inherited disease which is characterized by impaired ability to convert galactose to glucose, the blood levels of galactose are much elevated and galactose spills over into the urine.

3. Pentosuria may occur transiently after ingestion of foods containing large quantities of pentoses, such as plums, cherries, grapes, and prunes. Congenital pentosuria is a benign genetic defect characterized by inability to metabolize L-xylulose, a constituent of the uronic acid pathway.

All of the above sugars reduce Benedict's solution. When it is suspected that sugars other than glucose are present, it has been customary to perform a fermentation test with baker's yeast. If all of the reducing action is removed by the yeast, this suggests that only glucose is present. However, more specific tests are preferred. The introduction of a specific analytic test for glucose by the use of the enzyme glucose oxidase is one such test. A comparison of the apparent glucose content of the urine (as determined by total reducing action) with the absolute glucose content (as determined by glucose oxidase) would indicate more definitely whether sugars other than glucose were present. If so, these other sugars can be identified readily by paper chromatography or in some cases by preparation of specific osazones.

D. Ketone Bodies: Normally, only 3–15 mg of ketones are excreted in a day. The quantity is increased in starvation, impaired carbohydrate metabolism (eg, diabetes), pregnancy, ether anesthesia, and some types of alkalosis. In many animals, excess fat metabolism will also induce a ketonuria. The acidosis accompanying ketosis will cause increased ammonia excretion as a result of the body's effort to conserve cations.

E. Bilirubin: The presence of bilirubin in the urine and its relationship to jaundice are discussed in Chapter 14.

F. Blood: In addition to its occurrence in nephritis, blood in the urine (hematuria) may be the result of a lesion in the kidney or urinary tract (eg, after trauma to the urinary tract). However, free hemoglobin (hemoglobinuria) may also be found in the urine after rapid hemolysis, eg, in blackwater fever (a complication of malaria) or after severe burns.

G. Porphyrins: (see Chapter 14). The excretion of coproporphyrins in the urine of the normal adult is 60–280 μg/day. Coproporphyrin I normally constitutes less than half of the total coproporphyrin; the III

isomer is usually the predominant form of coproporphyrin excreted by a healthy individual. However, this
ratio may be reversed in certain diseases of the liver.

The occurrence of uroporphyrins as well as increased amounts of coproporphyrins in the urine is a
distinctive chemical characteristic of the urine of patients suffering from porphyria.

HORMONES OF THE KIDNEY

In addition to excretory functions, the kidney
acts as an endocrine organ, elaborating a variety of
hormones which affect other organs and tissues and
several substances which may act only locally within
the kidney itself. The kidney also plays a major role in
the destruction of several hormones that are elaborated
in other endocrine organs.

Table 35–6 lists some of these hormones. The
hormones produced may be divided into 3 broad categories: those that have a direct or indirect effect on the
vascular system, those that stimulate red cell production, and a hormone that partially regulates calcium
metabolism.

The chemical mechanism of the action of renin is
as follows: In response to several stimuli (including
decreased arterial volume, decreased sodium presentation at the distal nephron, and hypokalemia), the juxtaglomerular cells of the renal cortex (specialized tissue
located adjacent to the afferent arteriole) manufacture
the proteolytic enzyme **renin** and secrete it into the
blood via the renal vein. In the blood, renin acts upon
its specific substrate, an α_2-globulin that is normally
present in blood plasma although it is produced in the
liver. This globulin is termed renin substrate or **angiotensinogen**. From angiotensinogen, the enzyme renin
splits off a polypeptide fragment called **angiotensin I**
which is a decapeptide containing 10 amino acids (Fig
35–10). Another enzyme in endothelial cells of the
capillaries of the lung acts on angiotensin I to split off
2 amino acids and thus to form the octapeptide **angiotensin II**. The decapeptide angiotensin I is only slightly
active. Antiotensin II is the active material, having a
pressor activity about 200 times that of norepinephrine. Angiotensin increases the force of the heartbeat
and constricts the arterioles, and this often results in
diminished renal blood flow even though peripheral
blood flow may remain unchanged. In addition to rais-

Table 35–6. A summary of some endocrine
functions of the kidney.

Hormones and substances affecting other organs and tissues:
  Renin
  Renomedullary prostaglandins
  Antihypertensive neutral renomedullary lipids
  Kininogen
  Erythropoietin
  Erythrogenin
  1,25-Dihydroxycholecalciferol
**Hormones and substances destroyed or physiologically altered
  by the kidney:**
  Insulin
  Glucagon
  25-Hydroxycholecalciferol (by conversion to 24,25-dihy-
    droxycholecalciferol)
  Aldosterone

ing blood pressure, angiotensin also brings about contraction of smooth muscle (myotropic effect).

Normal kidneys, plasma, and, to a lesser extent,
other tissues contain proteolytic enzymes called **angio-
tensinases** which are capable of destroying angiotensin.

The reactions of the renal pressor system may be
summarized as shown in Fig 35–10.

The amino acid sequence of the angiotensins is
shown in Fig 35–11. It will be noted that conversion
of angiotensin I to angiotensin II involves removal of
the 2 C-terminal amino acids leucine and histidine. It
is probable that the secondary form of angiotensin
involves a helical structure which may be maintained
by hydrogen bonds. This is indicated by the fact that
treatment of angiotensin with a 10% solution of urea,
which is known to rupture hydrogen bonds, brings
about a 50% decrease in myotropic activity of the pressor compound.

It has been shown that intravenous infusion of
angiotensin inevitably produces an increase in the rate
of secretion of aldosterone, the electrolyte-regulating
steroid of the adrenal cortex. Thus, aldosterone secretion is affected by a renal-adrenal endocrine system in
which angiotensin is acting as a tropic hormone in a
manner similar to the action of pituitary ACTH as it
relates to production of the adrenocorticosteroids
other than aldosterone. Aldosterone, by causing retention of sodium and water, tends to increase effective
volume and thus to effect suppression of renin production.

It is still uncertain whether the renin-angiotensin

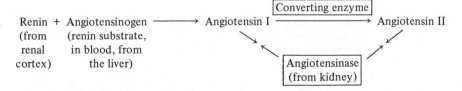

Figure 35–10. Reactions of the renal pressor system.

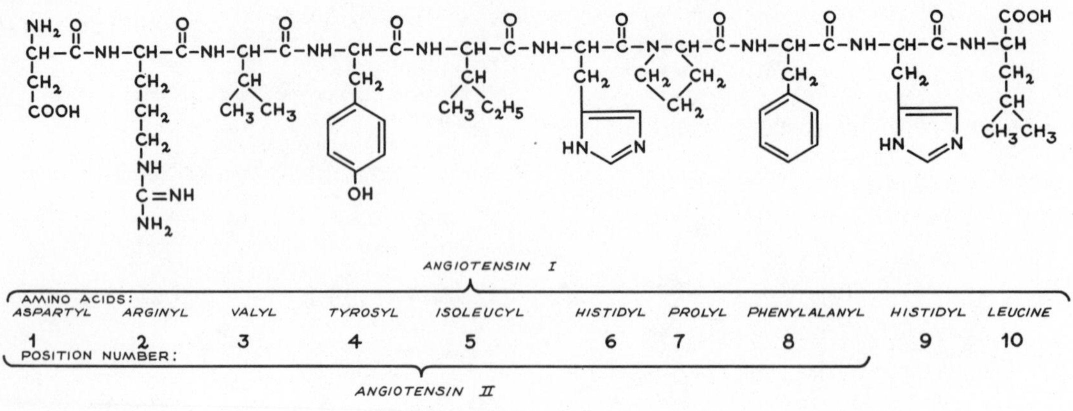

Figure 35–11. Amino acid sequence of angiotensins.

system plays any role in normal blood pressure regulation. When renal circulation is impaired, however, the pressor system is certainly more active than in the presence of normal renal circulation, and there is now increasing clinical evidence that some forms of hypertension may be greatly benefited (if not cured) by methods successful in restoring adequate circulation to the kidneys. In malignant hypertension, aldosterone hypersecretion is a much more consistent finding than in any other type. This suggests that malignant hypertension is a clinical counterpart to the Goldblatt experimental hypertension which was produced by compression of the renal artery in animals but which may occur clinically by the formation of many small occlusions to the circulation of both kidneys. The finding of increased aldosterone in the urine of the hypertensive patient should aid in the differential diagnosis of hypertension as a means of evaluating whether a renal pressor substance is involved in the etiology of the disease.

The discovery of the renal pressor system has clarified the long-recognized association between renal and cardiovascular disease, but increased amounts of renin have not been found consistently in many types of chronic hypertension. The true role of the renin-angiotensin system in clinical hypertension remains to be delineated.

The other vasoactive hormones of the kidney have a more direct effect on blood vessels. Prostaglandins are a group of naturally occurring and synthetic 20-carbon derivatives of a "parent" acid, prostanoic acid (Fig 35–12). These derivatives are produced in many tissues throughout the body, including the seminal vesicles, thymus, brain, and kidney. In the kidney, the primary prostaglandins that are produced—principally in the renal medulla—are PGA_2, PGE_2, and PGF_{2a} (Fig 35–12). Their effect is to produce short-lived but marked relaxation of smooth muscle. The actions of these hormones on the arteries cause vasodilatation and a decrease in blood pressure. In the kid-

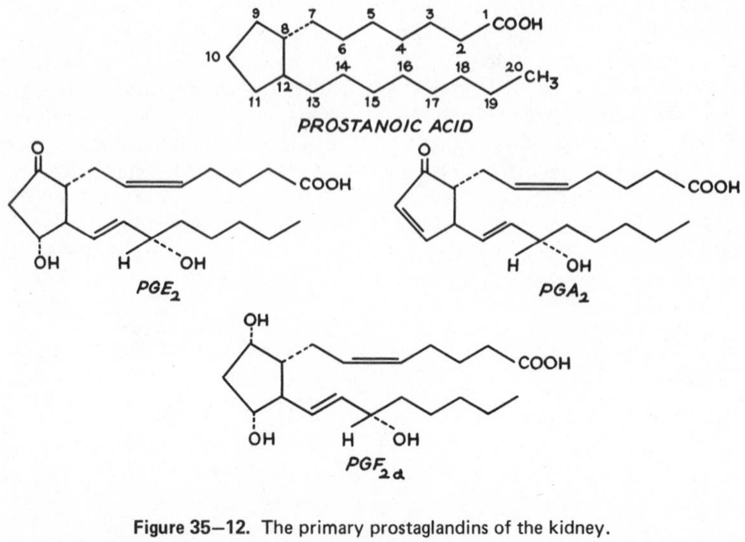

Figure 35–12. The primary prostaglandins of the kidney.

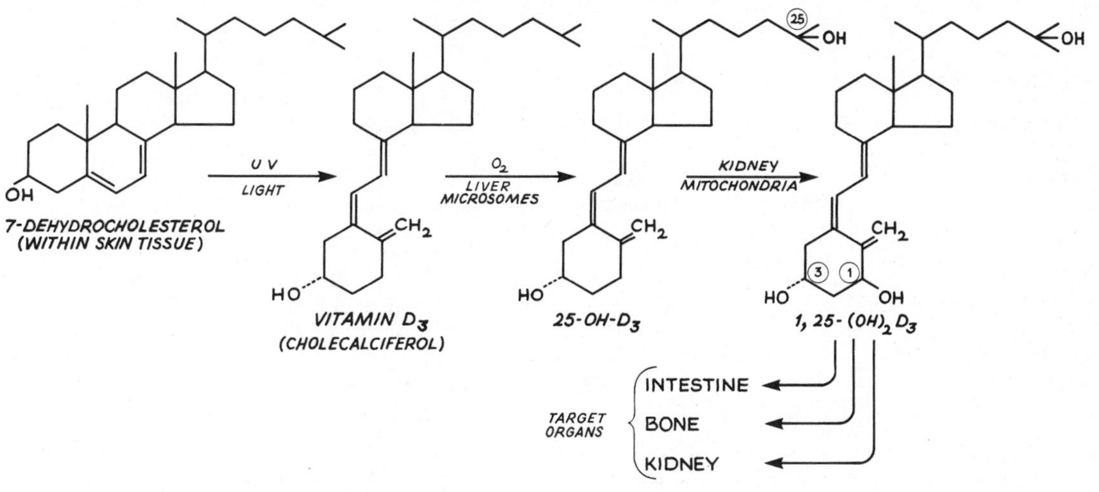

Figure 35—13. Metabolism of vitamin D required for its function.

ney, prostaglandins cause an increase in renal blood flow as well as vasodilatation. Natriuresis (sodium excretion) occurs in response to the vasodilatation. There is at present considerable speculation about the role of prostaglandins in the etiology of hypertension.

Antihypertensive, neutral, renomedullary lipids are a recently discovered group of nonprostaglandin, extractable, neutral lipids which have a long-acting effect on blood pressure, establishing a floor for the arterial pressure. **Kininogen** is another substance produced by the kidney which has an antihypertensive effect. Investigation into the biologic effect of these substances on regulating the blood pressure has just begun.

Erythropoietin and erythrogenin are 2 hormones which have an effect on bone marrow to stimulate production of red cells. One of the problems associated with chronic renal failure is a profound anemia which may be related in part to a deficiency of these substances as well as a variety of other abnormalities.

One of the most important and exciting recent advances has been the discovery that the kidney plays an important role in vitamin D metabolism (Fig 35–13). 7-Dehydrocholesterol, produced in the skin under the influence of ultraviolet light, undergoes a cleavage of a carbon-to-carbon bond, opening ring B of the steroid nucleus, to become cholecalciferol (vitamin D_3). This substance appears to possess biologic activity as an antirachitic vitamin, but in the liver it is hydroxylated at position 25, on the side chain, to become 25-OH-D_3, a form of vitamin D with a biologic potency approximately 25 times that of the parent compound, cholecalciferol. In the kidney, 25-OH-D_3 is further hydroxylated at position 1 to become 1,25-dihydroxy-D_3, the most active known form of vitamin D. This steroid hormone has its primary effect in the intestine, where it promotes calcium absorption, but it also acts on bone to effect deposition of calcium salts and thus to heal rachitic bone. In the kidney, 1,25-dihydroxy-D_3 acts on the tubule to decrease phosphate reabsorption.

Parathyroid hormone affects the 1-hydroxylation of 25-OH-D_3, and this seems to be an additional means by which this hormone acts to increase serum calcium. Under the influence of calcitonin, a hormone produced in the thyroid gland which lowers serum calcium, 25-OH-D_3 is hydroxylated within the kidney at position 24 to produce 24,25(OH)$_2$-D_3, a metabolite which has no biologic activity. A very potent feedback regulation system is thus present in the kidney to help regulate serum calcium concentration.

In addition to this renal inactivation of vitamin D_3, several other hormones are also destroyed within the kidney; among them are insulin and glucagon, 2 hormones secreted by the pancreas to regulate blood sugar, as well as aldosterone, the end product of the renin-aldosterone system.

It can thus be appreciated that the kidney plays a vital role as an endocrine organ, acting as a receptor organ for such hormones as parathyroid hormone, aldosterone, and vasopressin, and as a metabolic factory for the hormones shown in Table 35–6 as well as an inactivator of other hormones.

• • •

References

Anaemia in chronic renal failure. (Editorial). Lancet 1:959, 1975.

Bricker NS: Adaptations in chronic uremia: Pathophysiologic "trade-offs." Hosp Pract 9:119, 1974.

Burton BT: Current concepts of nutrition and diet in diseases of the kidney. 1. General principles of dietary management. 2. Dietary regimen in specific kidney disorders. J Am Diet Assoc 65:623, 1974.

Defronzo RA & others: Carbohydrate metabolism in uremia: A review. Medicine 52:469, 1973.

DeLuca HF: The kidney as an endocrine organ involved in the function of vitamin D. Am J Med 58:39, 1975.

Dousa TP: Cellular action of antidiuretic hormone in nephrogenic diabetes insipidus. Proc Mayo Clin 49:188, 1974.

Harrington JT, Cohen JJ: Clinical disorders of urine concentration and dilution. Arch Intern Med 131:810, 1973.

Klahr S, Slatopolsky E: Renal regulation of sodium excretion. Arch Intern Med 131:780, 1973.

Laragh & others: The renin axis and vasoconstriction volume analysis for understanding and treating renovascular and renal hypertension. Am J Med 58:4, 1975.

Makoff DL: Acid-base metabolism. Pages 297–346 in: *Clinical Disorders of Fluid and Electrolyte Metabolism,* 2nd ed. Maxwell MH, Kleeman CR (editors). McGraw-Hill, 1972.

Martinez-Maldonado M, Eknoyan G, Suki WN: Diuretics in non-edematous states. Arch Intern Med 131:797, 1973.

Massry SG, Friedler RM, Coburn JW: The physiology of the renal excretion of phosphate and calcium and its relation to clinical medicine. Arch Intern Med 131:828, 1973.

Schultze RG: Recent advances in the physiology and pathophysiology of potassium excretion. Arch Intern Med 131:885, 1973.

Walser M: Treatment of renal failure with ketoacids. Hosp Pract 9:59, 1975.

36 . . .
Muscle Tissue

There are 3 types of muscle tissue in the body: striated (voluntary) or skeletal muscle, nonstriated (involuntary) or smooth muscle, and cardiac muscle.

The chemical constitution of the skeletal muscle has been most completely studied: 75% is water, 20% is protein, and the remaining 5% is composed of inorganic material, certain organic "extractives," and carbohydrate (glycogen and its derivatives).

MUSCLE STRUCTURE

Striated muscle is comprised of fibrils surrounded by an electrically excitable membrane, the **sarcolemma**. When an individual muscle fiber is examined microscopically, it will be found to consist of a bundle of many myofibrils arranged in parallel; these are embedded in a type of intracellular fluid termed the **sarcoplasm**. Within this fluid is contained glycogen, the high-energy compounds ATP and phosphocreatine, and the enzymes of glycolysis.

The **sarcomere** is the functional unit of muscle. It is repeated along the axis of a fibril at distances of 2.5 μm (23,000 Å) (Fig 36–1). When the myofibril is examined by electron microscopy, alternating dark and light bands (A bands and I bands) can be observed. The central region of the A band (the H zone) appears less dense than the rest of the band. The I band is bisected by a very dense and narrow Z line. These structural details are illustrated diagrammatically in Fig 36–2.

When cross-sections of a myofibril are examined in an electron micrograph, it appears that each myo-

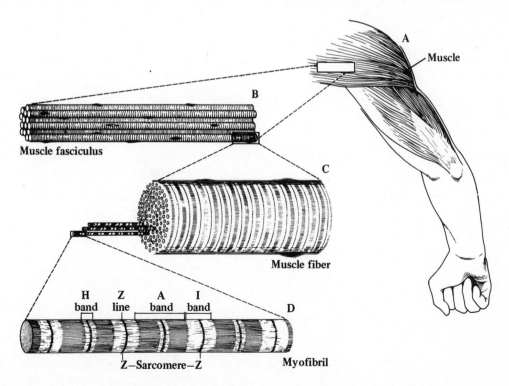

Figure 36–1. The structure of voluntary muscle. (Drawing by Sylvia Colard Keene. Reproduced, with permission, from Bloom W, Fawcett DW: *A Textbook of Histology,* 10th ed. Saunders, 1975.)

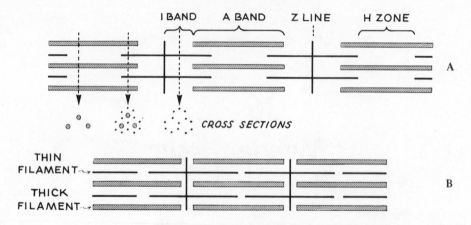

Figure 36—2. Arrangement of filaments in striated muscle. *A:* Extended. *B:* Contracted.

fibril is constructed of 2 types of longitudinal fila-ments. One type, confined to the A band (the thick filament), contains primarily the protein myosin. These filaments are about 16 nm in diameter, arranged in cross-section in a hexagonal array. The other fila-ment (the thin filament) lies in the I band but extends also into the A band. The thin filaments are smaller than those of myosin (about 6 nm in diameter). In the A band, they are arranged around the thick (myosin) filaments as a secondary hexagonal array. The thin fila-ments contain the proteins **actin, tropomyosin,** and **troponin.** As shown in Fig 36—2, each thin filament lies symmetrically between 3 thick filaments. The thick and thin filaments interact by cross-bridges emerging at intervals along the thick filaments; the contractile force of the muscle is generated at the sites of the cross-bridges.

When muscle contracts, the A bands remain the same length, but the I bands disappear, suggesting that a change in length of a muscle, ie, contraction, is accomplished by sliding the 2 arrays of filaments into or out of each other.

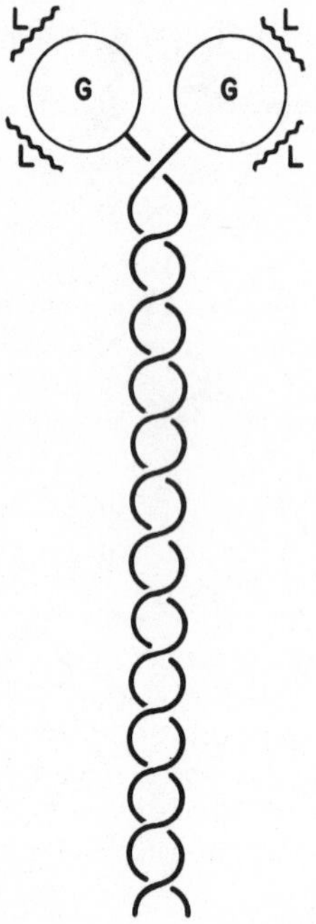

THE PROTEINS IN MUSCLE

The muscle fibrils are composed mainly of pro-teins; in fact, 20% of the chemical constituents of this tissue is protein, 75% is water, and the remaining 5% is comprised of inorganic material, certain organic "ex-tractives," and carbohydrates (glycogen and its deriva-tives). Muscle proteins are characterized by their elas-ticity, which confers contractile power on this tissue.

Myosin

The most abundant muscle protein is **myosin,** which is a globulin, soluble in dilute salt solutions (eg, alkaline 0.6 M KCl) and insoluble in water. Myosin is a very large molecule (MW 500,000) containing 2 identi-cal major chains (~ 200,000 MW each) and 4 light chains (~ 20,000 MW each). Structurally, myosin ap-pears to consist of 2 globular regions (each 9 nm in diameter), to each of which is joined a tail-like append-age (134 nm long). Each appendage is arranged as one strand of a double-stranded α-helix (Fig 36—3).

Myosin can be enzymatically cleaved by trypsin into 2 components—**meromyosins**—of unequal size; they are therefore termed **light** and **heavy** meromyo-sins (Fig 36—4). Intact myosin has the activity of the enzyme adenosine triphosphatase (ATPase). This is not, however, retained by light meromyosin, although it still forms filaments, as myosin will also, in solutions at physiologic pH and ionic strength. Myosin character-istically binds to the polymerized form of another

Figure 36—3. Diagram of a myosin molecule. G = globular re-gion; L = light chains.

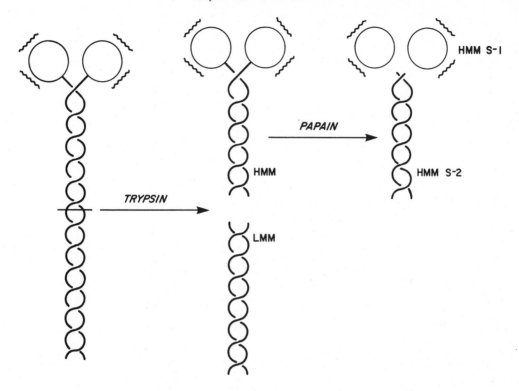

Figure 36—4. Enzymatic cleavage of myosin. HMM = heavy meromyosin; LMM = light meromyosin.

muscle protein, **actin** (see below), and the resultant product is termed **actomyosin.*** Light meromyosin, structurally arranged as a double-stranded α-helical rod, does not combine with actin.

Heavy meromyosin is very different in its activity from light meromyosin. It retains ATPase activity and binds to actin; however, it does not form filaments. As shown in Fig 36—4, heavy meromyosin is a rod-shaped protein fragment attached to the 2 globular components of the parent protein, myosin. The rod portion can be split off of the globular region by the action of papain; the resulting portions are designated HMM (heavy meromyosin) S-2 (the rod) or HMM S-1 (the globular portions). Each HMM S-1 fragment possesses an active site for ATPase activity as well as a binding site for actin.

The 4 light chains of the intact myosin molecule are bound to the HMM S-1 fragments; it is believed that these light chains may function as modulators of ATPase activity.

As has been noted above, myosin binds to the polymerized form of actin to form actomyosin, a protein complex of 3 myosin molecules with 1 actin molecule. This complex can be obtained by extraction of

muscle tissue with water followed by prolonged extraction of the residue with alkaline 0.6 M KCl. This latter extract is highly viscous and exhibits birefringence of flow as a result of the presence of actomyosin. The interaction of actin and myosin is essential to the generation of the force involved in the movements of the thick and thin filaments in muscle contraction (Fig 36—2).

Actin

Actin is a globulin of MW 60,000 which is the major constituent of the thin filaments in striated muscle (Fig 36—2). When actin is prepared by extraction with solutions of low ionic strength, it is obtained as an MW 42,000 monomer in a globular configuration called **G-actin** (Fig 36—5A). As the ionic strength increases, and in the presence of Mg^{2+}, G-actin polymerizes to the fibrous form, **F-actin** (Fig 36—5B), which in an electron micrograph appears as a double-stranded helix of actin monomers. During polymerization of G-actin to F-actin, ATP is hydrolyzed to ADP and P_i is released. Therefore, ATP must be added to accomplish depolymerization of F-actin to G-actin.

As has been noted, actomyosin is formed when a solution of actin is added to a solution of myosin. ATP dissociates actomyosin into actin and myosin:

---

*Actin and myosin are found not only in muscle but also in other cells and tissues. For example, actin and myosin are present in blood platelets, where they form a contractile complex very much resembling actomyosin. Recall that contraction of blood platelets is an essential element in clot retraction.

$$\text{ACTIN} + \text{MYOSIN} \xrightleftharpoons[\text{ATP}]{} \text{ACTOMYOSIN}$$

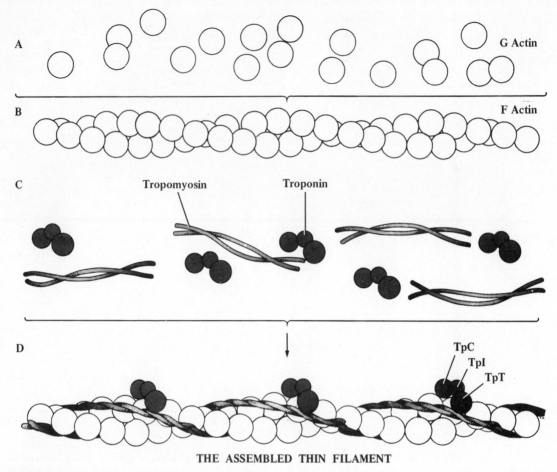

Figure 36–5. Schematic representation of the thin filament, showing the spatial configuration of the 3 major protein components—actin, tropomyosin, and troponin.

In a classical experiment, Szent-Györgyi prepared threads of actomyosin which contracted when immersed in a solution containing ATP, K^+ and Mg^{2+}. Threads of myosin alone did not contract. From this observation, Szent-Györgyi concluded that the force of muscular contraction emanates from an interaction of myosin, actin, and ATP.

Tropomyosin & Troponin

Tropomyosin and the troponin complex (Fig 36–5C) are proteins located in the thin filaments of muscle, comprising about one-third of its mass. Calcium ion, which is a physiologic regulator of muscle contraction, exerts its effect on the interaction of actin and myosin, which in turn is mediated by tropomyosin and troponin.

Tropomyosin is a double-stranded a-helical rod (MW 70,000) located between the 2 strands of F-actin. Troponin is a complex of 3 polypeptide chains designated TpC, TpI, and TpT (Fig 36–5D). The troponin complex is also located in the thin actin filaments at intervals of 38.5 nm. A troponin complex, bound to a

tropomyosin molecule, regulates the activity of about 7 actin monomers.

MOLECULAR EVENTS IN MUSCLE CONTRACTION

The fundamental reaction in muscle activity—the interaction of actin and myosin—is inhibited by troponin and tropomyosin when calcium ions are absent. Excitation of a motor nerve to the muscle brings about release of Ca^{2+} from the sarcolemma. The released calcium binds to the TpC portion of the troponin complex, producing conformational changes which are transmitted to tropomyosin and then to actin. This permits actin to interact with myosin with resultant muscular contraction, accompanied by hydrolysis of ATP acting as an energy source. These events persist until Ca^{2+} is removed. It may be concluded that calcium ions exert a control on the initiation of contraction by an allosteric mechanism proceeding as follows:

$$Ca^{2+} \longrightarrow TROPONIN \longrightarrow TROPOMYOSIN \longrightarrow ACTIN \longrightarrow MYOSIN$$

When a nerve impulse arrives at the junction between the nerve ending and the muscle (the end plate), the outer membrane of a muscle fiber is depolarized; subsequently, the depolarization of the outer membrane is transmitted to the interior of the muscle fiber by a system in close proximity to a plexus of channels, the **sarcoplasmic reticulum**. Calcium ions are maintained in this sarcoplasmic reticulum when a muscle is in the resting state. This is accomplished by an energy-requiring active transport system for calcium ions. The system, energized by ATP, lowers the concentration of calcium ions in the sarcoplasm (cytoplasm) of resting muscle cells while increasing Ca^{2+} within the sarcoplasmic reticulum, bound there by a calcium-binding protein called **calsequestrin**. When calcium is released from the sarcoplasmic reticulum, there is initiation of muscular contraction via the troponin-tropomyosin system described above.

MUSCLE PHOSPHAGENS

Although ATP is the immediate source of energy for muscular contraction, the amount of ATP in muscle is extremely small—only enough to sustain contraction for a fraction of a second. In vertebrate muscle, there is, however, a back-up source of high-energy phosphate in the form of **phosphocreatine**. Since this compound has a higher phosphate group-transfer potential than ATP, it can donate a high-energy phosphate group to ADP to reform ATP. Phosphocreatine is an example of a **phosphagen**. Some invertebrates utilize **phosphoarginine** in an analogous manner. Consequently, this compound may be regarded as the invertebrate phosphagen; phosphocreatine is the vertebrate phosphagen.

In the resting state, mammalian muscle contains 4–6 times as much phosphocreatine as ATP. The transfer of high-energy phosphate from creatine phosphate to ADP (the Lohmann reaction) is catalyzed by the enzyme **creatine kinase** (creatine phosphokinase, CPK). The reaction is reversible, so that resynthesis of creatine phosphate can take place when ATP later becomes available, as during the recovery period following a period of muscular contraction. Transfer of phosphate from ATP to creatine to form creatine phosphate is catalyzed by the enzyme **ATP-creatine transphosphorylase**. These relationships between ATP and creatine phosphate are represented in Fig 36–6.

A further source of ATP in muscle is attributable to the presence of another enzyme, **myokinase** (adenylate kinase), which catalyzes the transfer of a high-energy phosphate from one molecule of ADP to another to form ATP and adenosine monophosphate (AMP).

$$2ADP \xrightleftharpoons[\text{MYOKINASE}]{} AMP + ATP$$

Resynthesis of ATP and phosphocreatine may be blocked by poisoning an isolated muscle with iodoacetate, which prevents glycolysis. The muscle may contract for a while, but contraction ceases when all reserves of ATP and phosphocreatine have been used. This experiment demonstrates that the energy required for regeneration of ATP under such conditions is derived mainly from glycolysis. However, it is probable that, in vivo, other fuels such as free fatty acids and ketone bodies are used as well as glucose to supply contracting muscle with ATP. Fat must be the ultimate source of energy for long periods of muscular exertion, such as in migratory birds, whose total carbohydrate stores are quite inadequate to serve as the sole source of energy and whose fat stores become depleted during migration. The flight muscles of birds ("red meat") are particularly well developed for aerobic oxidation of fuels such as pyruvate, free fatty acids, and ketone bodies, having a well developed vasculature to increase oxygenation and a high content of enzymes of the respiratory chain as well as of cytochromes and myoglobin.

Thus, skeletal muscle is adapted to its function of providing for a very rapid output of energy by means of various mechanisms which allow it to produce ATP under anaerobic conditions, viz, the decomposition of phosphocreatine, the myokinase reaction, and provision of glycogen stores which can be glycolyzed to lactate. The liver aids oxidation in muscle by converting lactate back to glucose for reuse in muscle. It is

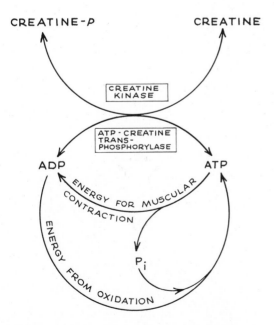

Figure 36–6. Formation and breakdown of creatine phosphate and the relationship of these events to ATP in muscular contraction.

probable that the energy required to convert lactate to glucose is furnished by the oxidation of free fatty acids in the liver. In this way, oxidation in the liver could be providing indirectly some of the energy for contraction in muscles.

Biochemically, heart muscle is similar to the flight muscles of birds in that it is capable of sustained activity and can utilize fuels such as free fatty acids, ketone bodies, and even lactate, which require aerobic conditions for their oxidation.

INORGANIC CONSTITUENTS OF MUSCLE

The cations of muscle (potassium, sodium, magnesium, and calcium) are the same as in extracellular fluids except that, in muscle, potassium predominates. The anions include phosphate, chloride, and small amounts of sulfate. The apparent high inorganic phosphate content may actually be an artifact produced by the breakdown of the organic phosphates of ATP and phosphocreatine in the course of the analysis.

Intracellular potassium plays an important role in muscle metabolism. When glycogen is deposited in muscle and when protein is being synthesized, a considerable amount of potassium is also incorporated into the tissue. Muscle weakness is a cardinal sign of potassium deficiency. The calcium and magnesium of muscle appear to function as activators or inhibitors of intramuscular enzyme systems.

●   ●   ●

References

Huxley HE: *The Mechanism of Muscular Contraction.* Cold Spring Harbor Symposia on Quantitative Biology. Vol 37. Cold Spring Harbor Laboratory, 1972.

Huxley HE: The structural basis of muscle contraction. Proc R Soc Lond (Biol) 179:131, 1971.

Murray JM, Weber A: The cooperative action of muscle proteins. Sci Am 230:59, Feb 1974.

Orten JM, Neuhaus OW: *Human Biochemistry,* 9th ed. Mosby, 1975.

Stryer L: *Biochemistry.* Freeman, 1975.

37 . . .

Epithelial, Connective, & Nerve Tissues

EPITHELIAL TISSUE

Epithelial tissue covers the surface of the body and lines hollow organs such as those of the respiratory, digestive, and urinary tracts.

Keratin

A major constituent of the epidermal portion of the skin and of other epidermal derivatives, such as hair, horn, hoof, feathers, and nails, is the protein keratin. This protein is notable for its great insolubility and resistance to attack by proteolytic enzymes of the stomach and intestine, and for its high content of the sulfur-containing amino acid cystine.

The composition of human hair differs in accordance with its color and with the race, sex, age, and genetic origin of the individual. The amino acid cystine accounts for about 20% of the amino acid content of the protein in human hair; this very high cystine content differentiates human hair from all other types of hair.

Melanin

The color of the skin is due to a variety of pigments, of which melanin, a tyrosine derivative, is the most important. It is said that racial differences in skin, hair, and eye color are due entirely to the amount of melanin present and that there is no qualitative difference in skin pigmentation of different races.

CONNECTIVE TISSUE

Connective tissue comprises all of that which supports or binds the other tissues of the body. In the widest sense it includes the bones and teeth as well as cartilage and fibrous tissue.

The connective tissue compartment is located between the blood circulation and the functioning parenchymal cells of a tissue. This tissue is comprised of 3 separate components: specialized cells, fibers, and the amorphous "ground substance." The cells are of 2 types: (1) the **fibroblasts**, which are responsible for the production of collagen fibers and the so-called acid

mucopolysaccharides (further discussed below as mucopolysaccharides); and (2) the **mast cells**, which probably both synthesize and store heparin.

There are 2 chemically and morphologically distinct types of fibers in connective tissue: **collagen** and **elastin**. Each will be further discussed below.

Ground substance is a complex mixture which contains substances that are in transit between cells and circulation, as well as certain components that are peculiar to the ground substance compartment. The most extensively studied of these ground substance components are the mucopolysaccharides.

Mucopolysaccharides (Glycosaminoglycans)
(Dorfman & Matalon, 1972.)

The mucopolysaccharides (sometimes referred to as "acid" mucopolysaccharides) constitute a group of closely related yet specific substances found singly in some tissues and in mixtures in others. A new nomenclature to describe these compounds is gradually being adopted (Table 37–1) (Jeanloz, 1960). It will be noted that the mucopolysaccharide group itself is now preferably termed "glycosaminoglycans."

A mucopolysaccharide characteristic of cartilage is **chondroitin-4-sulfate**. This polysaccharide consists of chains of varying length in which a fundamental disaccharide unit is repeated (Fig 37–1). A similar compound is **chondroitin-6-sulfate**. In both of these compounds, the fundamental disaccharide repeating unit consists of a β-glucuronic acid moiety linked through a

Table 37–1. Nomenclature of mucopolysaccharides (glycosaminoglycans).

Former Term	New Term
Chondroitin	Chondroitin
Chondroitin sulfate A	Chondroitin-4-sulfate
Chondroitin sulfate C	Chondroitin-6-sulfate
Chondroitin sulfate B (β-heparin)	Dermatan sulfate
Heparitin sulfate Heparin monosulfate	Heparan sulfate
Corneal keratosulfate	Keratan sulfate I
Skeletal keratosulfate	Keratan sulfate II
Chondromucoprotein (protein polysaccharide complex)	Proteoglycan

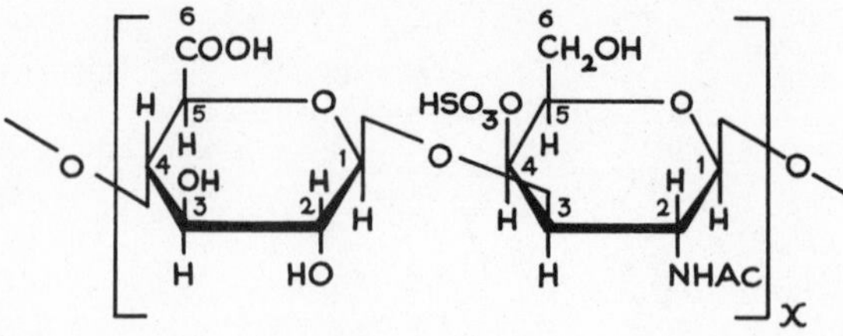

Figure 37–1. Disaccharide-repeating structure of chondroitin-4-sulfate.

glycosidic bond to N-acetylgalactosamine sulfate. The sulfate is attached at position 4 or 6, as indicated in the nomenclature.

The cartilage of elasmobranchs contains the 6-sulfate compound whereas that of the notochord contains the 4-sulfate. In the chick embryo, the cartilage contains a mixture of the 4- and 6-sulfates, the proportions of each varying with the age of the embryo. It should also be noted that chondroitin sulfates do not always contain only one sulfate per disaccharide unit. An example is a chondroitin sulfate isolated from the cartilage of the shark that resembles chondroitin-6-sulfate except that it has a second sulfate attached probably at carbon 2 or 3 of the uronic acid moiety. A similar disulfate has been isolated from a preparation of dermatan sulfate.

Chondroitin fractions have also been isolated that are lower in sulfate than is expected. One such fraction, termed simply chondroitin, has been found in corneal tissue. Low-sulfate chondroitin fractions may also be isolated from the cranial cartilage of tadpoles and from the epiphyseal cartilage of embryonic chicks. Furthermore, there is considerable heterogeneity among chondroitin sulfates with respect to both polysaccharide chain length and degree of sulfation. Some disaccharide units lack sulfation; others contain sulfate on both the 4 and 6 positions of the hexosamine or on the 2 and 3 positions of the glucuronic acid.

Among the many important functions of proteins is their ability to serve as structural elements of tissues. In higher animals, the fibrous protein **collagen** is synthesized by the fibroblasts. It is the major extracellular structural protein in connective tissue and bone. Collagen fibrils also aid in forming a structural continuum to bind a group of cells together in the formation of a tissue. **Elastin** is the other important structural protein of connective tissue. It is secreted by the cells of yellow elastic tissue and is a constituent of the *a*-keratin of skin, hair, nails, horn, and feathers. These 2 proteins will be discussed further below.

Many of the polysaccharide compounds discussed in this section occur in part bound to proteins in the tissue. The binding is by covalent linkages to specific amino acids in the protein, most likely with a hydroxy group as on serine and threonine residues. Hydrolysates of proteins containing chondroitin-4-sulfate have considerable quantities of serine. Compounds with chondroitin-4-sulfate or chondroitin-6-sulfate, dermatan sulfate, heparan sulfate, and heparin polysaccharide chains are linked through the trisaccharide sequence: — [galactose-galactose-xylose] — to the hydroxyl group of serine residues in the protein (Fig 37–2). Thus, serine functions are the point at which the polysaccharide prosthetic group branches from the protein. Threonine may also serve a similar fashion.

Dermatan sulfate, present in skin, tendon, and heart valves, differs from chondroitin-4- or 6-sulfate in that the prominent uronic acid is **L-iduronic acid,** a derivative of the hexose L-idose. D-Glucuronic acid is, however, present in variable amounts. The biosynthesis of L-iduronic acid is shown in Fig 37–3. This sugar derivative is produced in the tissues from glucuronic acid by the action of an epimerase which acts on the active form of glucuronic acid, uridine diphospho-D-glucuronic acid (UDP-D-glucuronic acid). The epimerizing enzyme uridine diphospho-D-glucuronic acid-5-epimerase has been detedted in extracts of rabbit skin. The reactions shown in Fig 37–3 seem to account for the origin of L-iduronic acid in the skin, where it is required for the synthesis of dermatan sulfate.

In dermatan sulfate, the glycosidic linkages are the same in position and configuration as in the chondroitin sulfates. In the dermatan sulfate of skin, the sulfate group is in the 4 position; in the dermatan of umbilical cord, it is in the 6 position.

The physiologic functions of dermatan sulfates are not well understood. Dermatan sulfate has been designated as β-heparin because it has weak anticoagulant properties. But, in contrast to heparin, its lipid-clearing activity is minimal.

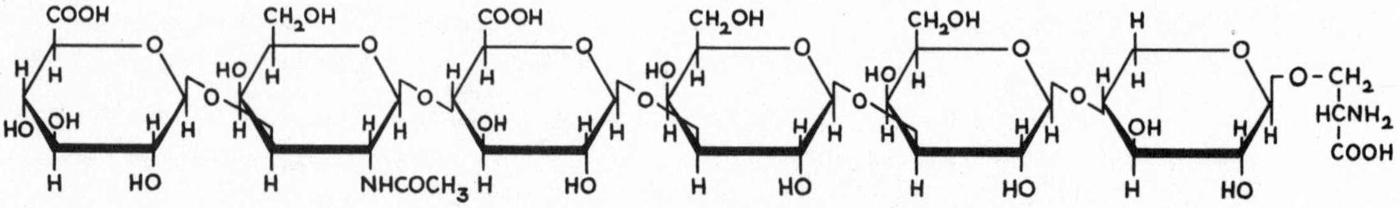

Figure 37–2. The linkage region of chondromucoprotein.

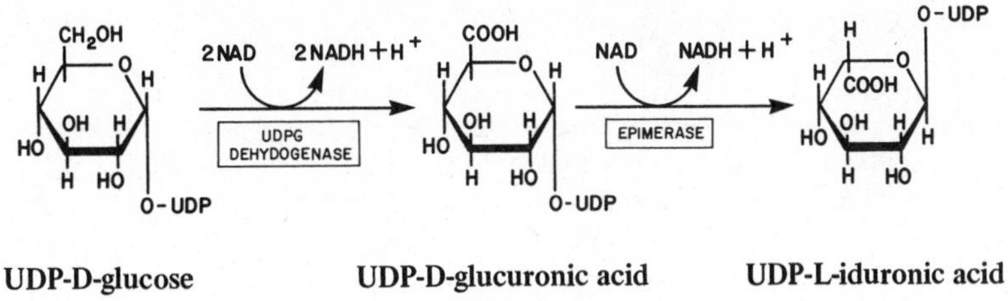

UDP-D-glucose   UDP-D-glucuronic acid   UDP-L-iduronic acid

Figure 37–3. Biosynthesis of L-iduronic acid.

Keratan sulfate is characterized by much more molecular heterogeneity than is the case with the chondroitins. The polysaccharide of the keratans is principally composed of a repeating disaccharide unit consisting of N-acetylglucosamine and galactose. There are no uronic acids in the molecule. Total sulfate content varies, but there is ester sulfate present at carbon 6 of both the N-acetylglucosamine and the galactose residues. At least 2 types of keratan sulfate have been described: keratan sulfate I, occurring in the cornea; and keratan sulfate II, occurring in skeletal tissues. In addition to the principal monosaccharides described above as constituting the repeating disaccharide unit of the keratans, mannose, fucose, sialic acid, and N-acetylgalactosamine have been found in the keratan sulfates, the latter hexosamine only in keratan sulfate II. Linkage to protein in corneal keratan sulfate I is between N-acetylglucosamine and an asparagine residue to form the N-glycoside bonding typical of glycoproteins. In skeletal keratan sulfate II, at least a portion of the linkage to protein is by way of hydroxyl groups on serine and threonine residues of the protein.

Heparin is not a homogeneous compound but rather a group of polymers within an extremely heterogeneous family of polysaccharides. This fact was made clear by the discovery of **heparan sulfate**, which was first thought to be a discrete polysaccharide species but is now believed to be only one end of a number of similar compounds commencing with heparin and terminating with heparan sulfate. Thus, there appears to be a number of heparin-like polysaccharides.

The structural features of heparin suggest that this polysaccharide is composed of alternating uronic acid and α-D-glucosamine units, joined by 1 → 4 glycosidic linkages. The uronic acid monosaccharide units may be either α-L-iduronic acid or β-D-glucuronic acid.

The glucosamine residues mainly possess sulfated amino groups, although in minor instances the amino groups of the glucosamine may be acetylated. Most of the glucosamine units have O-sulfate groups attached at carbon atom 6; in addition, most (not all) of the iduronic acid residues are sulfated at C_2. In contrast, the glucuronic acid component appears invariably to be nonsulfated (Fig 37–4).

Heparan sulfate generally contains less sulfate and iduronic acid than heparin; instead, there are more N-acetyl groups and glucuronic acid. Because of the poorly delineated differences in chemical structures of the heparin-like polymers, the anticoagulant activity is relied upon for purposes of classification, the heparins being more potent in anticoagulant activity and the heparans less so.

Heparin under normal physiologic conditions has been found only intracellularly, in mast cells or basophilic leucocytes, whereas heparan sulfate appears to be widely distributed on cell surfaces.

The presently recognized structural features of heparin are shown below in Fig 37–4.

Hyaluronic acid is another mucopolysaccharide. The repeating disaccharide units of hyaluronic acid consist of glucuronic acid linked to N-acetylglucosamine. Its composition is therefore similar to that of chondroitin, the essential difference between the 2 structures being the occurrence of galactosamine in chondroitin instead of glucosamine, as in hyaluronic acid. Hyaluronic acid is a component of the capsules of certain strains of pneumococci, streptococci, and certain other organisms as well as the vitreous humor, synovial fluid, and umbilical cord (Wharton's jelly). The hyaluronic acid of the tissues acts as a lubricant in the joints, as a jelly-like cementing substance, and as a means of holding water in the interstitial spaces.

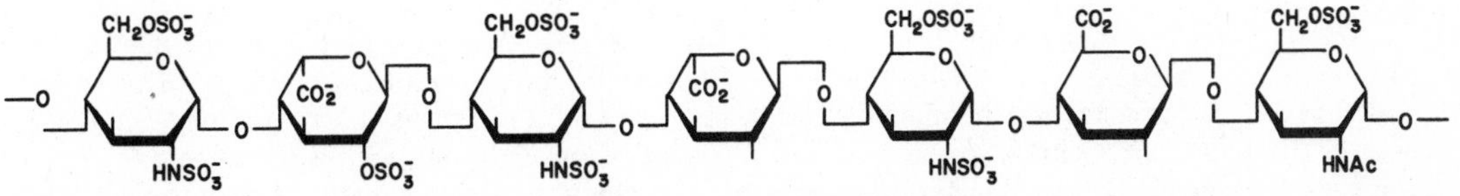

Figure 37–4. Structure of heparin. The polymer section illustrates structural features typical of heparin; however, the sequence of variously substituted repeating disaccharide units has been arbitrarily selected. In addition, non-O-sulfated or 3-O-sulfated glucosamine residues may also occur. (Redrawn and reproduced, with permission, from Lindahl U & others: Structure and biosynthesis of heparin-like polysaccharides. Fed Proc 36:19, 1977.)

Hyaluronidase is an enzyme present in certain tissues, notably testicular tissue and spleen, as well as in several types of pneumococci and the hemolytic streptococci. An enzyme similar to testicular hyaluronidase has been detected also in rat and guinea pig liver, lung, and kidney and in human kidney, urine, plasma, and synovial fluid and tissue.

Hyaluronidase, by destroying tissue hyaluronic acid, reduces viscosity and thus permits greater spreading of materials in tissue spaces. Hyaluronidase is therefore sometimes designated the "**spreading factor.**" Its activity may be measured by the extent of spread of injected India ink as indicator. The invasive power of some pathogenic organisms may be enhanced because they secrete hyaluronidase. In the testicular secretions, the enzyme may dissolve the viscid substances surrounding the ovum and thus permit penetration of the ovum by the sperm cell. Hyaluronidase is used clinically to increase the efficiency of absorption of solutions administered by clysis.

The Connective Tissue Proteins

Collagen is the principal solid substance in white fibrous connective tissue. This fibrous protein is synthesized by the fibroblasts. Collagen is difficult to dissolve and somewhat resistant to chemical attack although not to the same extent as keratin. Some animals possess collagenase, an enzyme capable of hydrolyzing collagen, in their digestive tracts.

The amino acid composition of collagen is quite different from that of keratin; glycine replaces cystine as the principal amino acid and in fact accounts for as much as one-third of all the amino acids present. Proline and hydroxyproline constitute another third. In addition to the most common form of hydroxyproline (2-hydroxyproline), small amounts (0.26% in cattle Achilles tendon) of 3-hydroxyproline have also been found in collagen. Collagen can be slowly digested by pepsin and hydrochloric acid; it can be digested by trypsin only after pepsin treatment or at temperatures over 40° C.

An important property of collagen is convertibility to **gelatin** by boiling with water or acid. This seems to involve only a physical change, since there is no chemical evidence that hydrolysis has occurred. Gelatin contains no tryptophan and only small amounts of tyrosine and cystine. It differs from collagen and keratin in being easily soluble and digestible. It may therefore be used as a source of protein in the diet, but only in a supplementary role because of its amino acid deficiencies.

The collagen of bone, skin, cartilage, and ligaments differs in chemical composition from that of white fibrous tissue.

Elastin is the characteristic protein of yellow elastic tissue. The nuchal ligaments exemplify yellow elastic tissue; the composition of nuchal ligament is 31.7% elastin, 7.2% collagen, and 0.5% mucoid. In contrast, in white fibrous tissue, elastin makes up only about 1.6% of the protein content whereas collagen makes up about 31.6%.

Elastin is insoluble in water but digestible by enzymes. It is not converted to gelatin by boiling. The sulfur content of elastin is low; 90% of the amino acid content of elastin is accounted for by only 5 amino acids: leucine, isoleucine, glycine, proline, and valine.

Chondroalbumoid is a protein found in the organic matrix of cartilage. This protein is similar to keratin and to elastin, but, in contrast to keratin, the sulfur content of chondroalbumoid is low and it is soluble in gastric juice.

Glycoproteins

Until recently, it was assumed that covalent binding of carbohydrate to protein occurred only in the slimy proteins such as may be found in saliva, the so-called mucin. As a result, the term **mucoprotein** was used to describe these substances. With the introduction of improved methods of isolation, purification, and identification, it is now apparent that protein-carbohydrate complexes are widely distributed in nature and that they participate in many metabolic processes. In fact, it is now evident that a majority of naturally occurring proteins are glycoproteins. Examples of proteins that are known to have side chains of carbohydrate are most of the proteins of the plasma, including the agglutinins that determine human blood types and many enzymes and hormones. Collagen, mentioned above in association with connective tissue proteins, is also a glycoprotein, as is **interferon**, an antiviral agent produced in the tissues.

Plants also contain glycoproteins, as was first revealed in studies of soybean agglutinins. Many other plant agglutinins, termed **lectins**, have been shown to contain carbohydrates. Glycoproteins are also found in some bacteria and viruses.

Much interest attaches to studies of the glycoproteins occurring on the surfaces of cells. The importance of these glycoproteins as constituents of cell membranes derives from the fact that they are believed to be responsible, at least in part, for determining the "individuality" of a cell. Thus, these surface glycoproteins may serve as antigenic determinants, as virus receptors, and as "markers" of cellular identity.

Of the 100 or more carbohydrates that are known to occur in natural materials, only 9 have been found in glycoproteins, and these are usually combined in chains of no more than 15 sugar units. Although glucose is a frequently occurring compound in natural substances, it is not found in the glycoproteins except for the collagens. Two other hexose sugars, galactose and mannose, are much more common in glycoproteins. **Fucose** (6-deoxy galactose), **acetylglucosamine,** and **acetylgalactosamine** are the most frequently found hexoses in the glycoproteins, and 2 pentoses, arabinose and xylose, also occur in glycoproteins. A common constituent of glycoproteins is neuraminic acid.

The glycoproteins that have been studied range in size from MW 15,000 to more than a million; in carbohydrate content, from 1% to more than 85%. Examples are ovalbumin, the major protein of egg white (MW 45,000), and the enzyme ribonuclease B (MW

14,700), each of which possesses only one carbohydrate side chain per molecule, whereas the salivary mucin secreted by the submaxillary gland of sheep contains about 800 sugar units per molecule, the units being arranged in disaccharide side chains, one for every 6 or 7 amino acids in the protein chain.

Although much remains to be learned about glycoprotein structure, certain details have emerged from recent studies. For example, fucose and sialic acid always occupy peripheral positions some distance from the polypeptide chain. In contrast, acetylglucosamine and galactose are usually found nearest the protein, often forming a part of the carbohydrate-to-protein linkage. It is of interest that only 5 of the 20 naturally occurring amino acids are known to form linkages with carbohydrates in the glycoproteins. These are asparagine, serine, threonine, hydroxylysine, and hydroxyproline. It will be remembered that the hydroxy group of these latter 2 amino acids is added to the lysine or proline moiety only after the amino acid has been incorporated into the peptide chain.

The first carbohydrate-to-protein linkage to be identified was that between acetylglucosamine and asparagine as it occurs in ovalbumin. This linkage is illustrated in Fig 37–5. The same linkage has been identified in a preparation of soybean agglutinin.

The glycosidic linkage between carbohydrate and protein occurs more frequently through an oxygen atom rather than nitrogen, as was illustrated above, where asparagine is linked to glucosamine. Examples

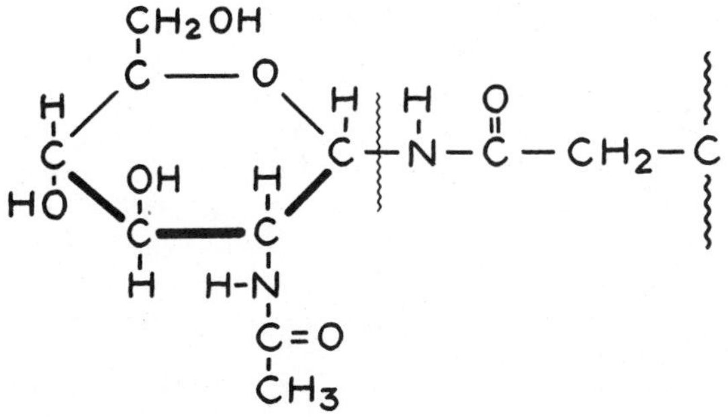

are linkages between the sugars and threonine, serine, hydroxylysine, or hydroxyproline within peptide chains. Such a linkage between N-acetylgalactosamine and threonine is illustrated in Fig 37–6. Galactose, xylose, and arabinose similarly may form glycosidic bonds with hydroxy amino acids within a peptide chain.

It has been noted that considerable heterogeneity exists in the carbohydrate portion of different molecules of a glycoprotein. This is so because the polysaccharide side chain may branch extensively, making possible a greater variety of polysaccharide chains than of amino acids in the connecting peptide. This can be understood when the mechanism of synthesis of the glycoproteins is considered.

Biosynthesis of glycoproteins begins in the same manner as with other proteins, by the formation of the polypeptide of the molecule in accordance with the information communicated to the ribosome from the DNA via the RNA messenger. On the other hand, the carbohydrate moiety of a glycoprotein is added to the already formed polypeptide at another site in the cell and by another mechanism.

The carbohydrate side chains on the glycoprotein molecule are synthesized at sites on membranes. The process is catalyzed by enzymes specific to each saccharide component. Thus, an enzyme can cause binding of a sugar to the glycoprotein molecule wherever the particular reaction catalyzed by the enzyme is possible. In the sense that the enzymes are themselves coded by the usual protein synthetic genetic mechanisms, the organism maintains indirect genetic control of the saccharide structure as well as the protein portion of the glycoproteins.

It appears that a very important step in the synthesis of the carbohydrate side chains of glycoproteins is attachment of the first sugar unit to the completed polypeptide chain. In many glycoproteins there is a particular tripeptide that acts as a linking region for attachment of the saccharide. This tripeptide is -Asn-Y-Ser- or -Asn-Y-Thr-, where Y can be any amino acid. Bonded to the asparagine of this tripeptide is acetylglucosamine.

An excellent example of genetic control of glycoprotein synthesis is found in the human blood group factors. The substances specific to both type A and type B blood are glycoproteins. It appears that the polypeptide component and most of each carbohydrate side chain are quite similar, differing only in the sugar that occupies a peripheral position. In type A blood, this sugar is acetylgalactosamine; in type B, it is galactose. The presence or absence of both peripheral sugars is determined by genetically specified enzymes—**glycosyltransferases**—that catalyze the attachment of the sugars to the protein moiety of the glycoprotein. Individuals with type A blood possess a transferase that attaches acetylgalactosamine to the protein; those with type B have an enzyme that transfers galactose. (In each instance, the sugars are actually derived from their activated nucleotide precursors, ie, UDP-acetylgalactosamine or UDP-galactose. Individuals lacking both of the specific transferases are type O, and those

Figure 37–5. Linkage of N-acetylglucosamine to asparagine as it occurs in ovalbumin.

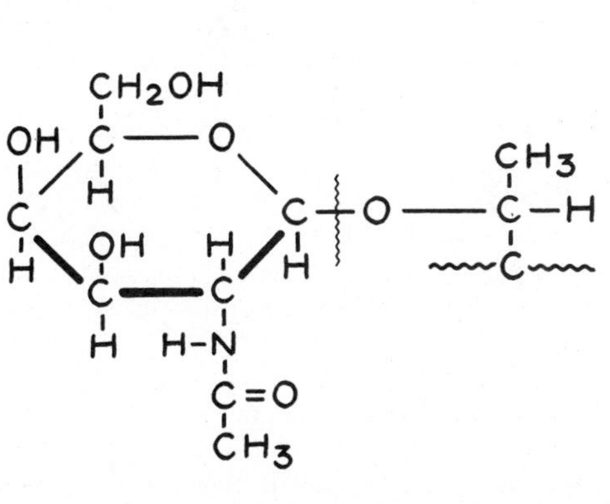

Figure 37–6. Linkage of N-acetylgalactosamine and threonine.

with both are type AB. As has long been known, the blood types are inherited in the classical autosomal manner; consequently, this must also be true of genetic control of the transferases.

Much speculation still attaches to the function of the carbohydrate moiety of glycoproteins. One interesting suggestion is that the sugars of glycoproteins may be essential components of the mechanism by which cells recognize other cells as if these sugars, located at the surface of the cell, were acting as methods of cellular communication in the sense of letters or words. It has often been noted, for example, that, whereas normal cells stop growing when they touch each other, cancer cells grow without restraint. It may be that this critical difference in the behavior of malignant cells is related to changes at the cell surface, possibly changes in the nature of the sugar side chains of the glycoproteins.

Bone

A. Chemistry: The water content of bone varies from 14–44%. From 30–35% of the fat-free dry material is organic. In some cases as much as 25% is fat. The organic material in bone, the bone matrix, is similar to that of cartilage in that it contains collagen, which can be converted to gelatin (ossein gelatin). There are also a glycoprotein named **osseomucoid** and an **osseo-albumoid**. The presence of citrate (about 1%) in bone has also been reported.

The inorganic material of bone consists mainly of phosphate and carbonate salts of calcium. There are also small amounts of magnesium, hydroxide, fluoride, and sulfate. A study of the x-ray pattern of the bone salts indicates a similarity to the naturally occurring mineral hydroxyapatite. The formula of hydroxyapatite is said to be

$$Ca(OH)_2 \cdot 3 Ca_3(PO_4)_2$$

or

$$Ca_{10}(OH)_2(PO_4)_6$$

It is believed that the crystal lattices of bone are similar to the lattices of these apatite minerals but that elements may be substituted in bone without disturbing the structure. For example, calcium and phosphorus atoms may be replaced by carbon; magnesium, sodium, and potassium may replace calcium; and fluorine may replace hydroxide. This probably accounts for the alterations in bone composition which occur with increasing age, in rickets, as a result of dietary factors, or subsequent to changes in acid-base equilibrium (eg, the acidosis of chronic renal disease).

B. Metabolism: Like all of the tissues of the body, the constituents of bone are constantly in exchange with those of the plasma. Demineralization of bone occurs when the intake of minerals necessary for bone formation is inadequate or when their loss is excessive.

The calcium and phosphorus content of the diet is obviously an important factor in ossification. Vitamin D raises the level of blood phosphate and calcium, and this may in turn raise the calcium-phosphorus

product to the point where calcium phosphate is precipitated in the bone. There is evidence that the vitamin not only acts to promote better absorption of the minerals but also acts locally in the bone. In rickets, osteitis deformans, and other bone disorders the blood alkaline phosphatase rises, possibly in an effort to supply more phosphate. Treatment with vitamin D is accompanied by a reduction in phosphatase.

The influence of hormones on calcification has been described in Chapter 29. The parathyroids, thyroid, anterior pituitary, adrenal, and sex glands are all important in this respect. They act either at the site of calcification or by altering absorption or excretion of calcium and phosphorus.

Ossification supposedly involves precipitation of bone salts in the matrix by means of a physicochemical equilibrium involving Ca^{2+}, HPO_4^{2-}, and PO_4^{3-}. The enzyme alkaline phosphatase, which liberates phosphate from organic phosphate esters, may produce the inorganic phosphate; this phosphate then reacts with the calcium to form insoluble calcium phosphate. Phosphatase is not found in the matrix but only in the osteoblasts of the growing bone.

The deposition of bone salt is not entirely explainable as due simply to physicochemical laws governing the solubility of the inorganic components of bone. The deposition of the bone salt in the presence of concentrations of inorganic phosphate and calcium similar to those of normal plasma may require the expenditure of energy from associated metabolic systems. In cartilage, calcification in vitro can be blocked with iodoacetate, fluoride, or cyanide, substances which are known to inhibit various enzymes involved in glycolysis. Furthermore, the deposition of bone salts in calcifying cartilage is preceded by swelling of the cartilage cells due to intracellular deposition of glycogen. Just prior to or simultaneously with the appearance of bone salt in the matrix of the cartilage, the stores of glycogen seem to disappear, which suggests that the breakdown of glycogen is necessary for the calcification of cartilage. All of the enzymes and intermediate compounds involved in glycolysis have been identified in calcifying cartilage, and, as noted above, enzyme inhibitors interfere with calcification in vitro.

It must be remembered that there are 2 important components in bone: the matrix, which is rich in proteins, and the mineral or inorganic component. Demineralization may result from effects on either. Steroids aid in the maintenance of osteoblasts and matrix; thus, in the absence of these hormones, osteoporosis may occur even though alkaline phosphatase is normal and, presumably, a favorable mineral environment exists. Changes in the concentration of alkaline phosphatase reflect activity of the osteoblasts, which are stimulated by stress on a weakened skeleton (as may be found in rickets).

Teeth

Enamel, dentin, and cementum of the teeth are all calcified tissues containing both organic and inorganic matter. In the center of the tooth is the **pulp**, a

Table 37—2. Average composition of human enamel and of dentin.*

	(% Dry Weight)	
	Enamel	Dentin
Calcium	35.8	26.5
Magnesium	0.27	0.79
Sodium	0.25	0.19
Potassium	0.05	0.07
Phosphorus	17.4	12.7
CO_2 (from carbonate)	2.97	3.06
Chlorine	0.3	0.0
Fluorine	0.0112	0.0204
Iron	0.0218	0.0072
Organic matter	1.0	25.0

*From Hawk, Oser, & Summerson: *Practical Physiological Chemistry*, 12th ed. Blakiston, 1947.

soft, uncalcified organic mass containing also the blood vessels and nerves.

A. Composition and Structure: The average composition of human enamel and of dentin is shown in Table 37—2.

According to x-ray studies, the inorganic matter in the enamel and dentin of the teeth is arranged similarly to that in bone; it consists mainly of hydroxyapatite salts.

Keratin is the principal organic constituent of the enamel. There are also small amounts of cholesterol and phospholipid. In the dentin, collagen and elastin occur together with a glycoprotein and the lipids of the enamel.

Collagen is a major organic constituent in the cementum. Both dentin and, to a lesser extent, enamel contain citrate.

B. Metabolism of Teeth: Studies with radioactive isotopes (radiophosphorus) indicate that the enamel and especially the dentin undergo constant turnover; this is slow in adult teeth. The diet must contain adequate calcium and phosphorus and also vitamins A, C, and D to ensure proper calcification. However, when the diet is low in calcium and phosphorus, the demineralization of bone exceeds that of the teeth, which may actually calcify during the restricted period but at a slower than normal rate. This and other data suggest that the mineral metabolism of teeth and that of bones are not necessarily parallel.

NERVE TISSUE

The tissues of the brain, spinal cord, the cranial and spinal nerves and their ganglia and plexuses, and those of the autonomic nervous system contain a considerable quantity of water. The gray matter, which represents a concentration of nerve cell bodies, always contains more water than the white matter, where the nerve fibers are found. In the adult brain, where gray and white matter are mixed, the water content aver-

Table 37—3. Lipid compounds in nerve tissue.

Compound Lipids in Nerve Tissue	Percent of Total Solids
Phospholipids (lecithins, cephalins, and sphingomyelins)	28%
Cholesterol	10%
Cerebrosides or galactolipids (glycolipids)	7%
Sulfur-containing lipids, aminolipids, etc	9%
	54%

ages 78%; in the cord the water content is slightly less, about 75%.

The solids of nerve tissue consist mainly of protein and lipids. There are also smaller amounts of organic extractives and of inorganic salts.

The Proteins of Nerve Tissue

These constitute 38—40% of the total solids. They include various globulins, nucleoprotein, and a characteristic albuminoid called **neurokeratin.**

The Lipids of Nerve Tissue

Over one-half (51—54%) of the solid content of nerve tissue is lipid material. In fact, this tissue is one of the highest in lipid content. It is noteworthy that very little if any simple lipid is present.

Representatives of all types of lipid compounds are found (Table 37—3).

The chemistry of these substances is discussed in Chapter 9.

The rate at which the lipids of the brain are exchanged is relatively slow in comparison to that in an active organ such as the liver. Tracer studies with deuterium indicate that while 50% of the liver fats may be exchanged in 24 hours, only 20% of the brain fat is replaced in 7 days.

Inorganic Salts

These substances in nervous tissue are components of the 1% ash produced as the result of combustion. The principal inorganic salts are potassium phosphate and chloride, with smaller amounts of sodium and other alkaline elements. The potassium of the nerve is thought to be important in the electrical nature of the nerve impulse, which depends on depolarization and repolarization at the membrane boundary of the nerve fiber.

Metabolism of Brain & Nerve

When a nerve is stimulated to conduct an impulse, a small but measurable amount of heat is produced. The heat is produced in 2 stages, as it is in working muscle. This suggests that the rapidly released initial heat represents the energy involved in transmission of the impulse, and that the delayed or recovery heat (which may continue for 30—45 minutes) is related to restoration of the energy mechanisms. Similarly, the nerve may conduct impulses and develop heat under anaerobic conditions as, for example, in an atmosphere of nitrogen; but recovery depends on the admission of oxygen, as indicated by the extra consumption of readmitted oxygen.

The respiratory quotient of metabolizing nerve is very close to 1, which suggests that the nerve is utilizing carbohydrate almost exclusively. Studies with rat brain mitochondria indicate that, contrary to earlier assumptions, brain mitochondria are not capable of oxidizing glucose. Glycolytic enzymes are apparently contained only in soluble cytoplasmic material of some cellular fragments present as contaminants of the original mitochondrial preparations, which thus appear to possess glycolytic activity. Mitochondria do, however, appear to possess significant quantities of the hexokinase activity identified in preparations from rat brain.

The metabolism of carbohydrate in nerve tissue seems to be similar to that of muscle, since lactic and pyruvic acids appear under anaerobic conditions. These end products disappear very slowly; oxygen does not accelerate the process.

The synthesis of glycogen by brain tissue has been shown to take place by way of uridine diphosphate glucose, as was described for liver and muscle. The glycogen stores of brain and nerve are very small; hence a minute-to-minute supply of blood glucose is particularly important to the nervous system. This may be the major reason for the prominence of nervous symptoms in hypoglycemia. In contrast to muscle extracts, brain extracts act more readily on glucose than on glycogen.

Glutamic acid seems to be the only amino acid metabolized by brain tissue. However, this amino acid is of considerable importance in brain metabolism. It serves as a precursor of γ-aminobutyric acid and is a major acceptor of ammonia produced either in the metabolism of the brain or delivered to the brain when the arterial blood ammonia is elevated. In this latter reaction, glutamic acid accepts 1 mol of ammonia and is thus converted to glutamine. Although it has been shown that the brain can form urea, the formation of urea does not play a significant role in removal of ammonia in the brain. This is accomplished almost entirely by reactions involving the formation of glutamic acid by amination of ketoglutaric acid as well as by the formation of glutamine.

When the levels of ammonia in the brain are elevated, usually as a result of increased ammonia in the blood, the supply of glutamic acid available from the blood may be insufficient to form the additional amounts of glutamine required to detoxify the ammonia in the brain. Under these circumstances glutamic acid is synthesized in the brain by amination of the ketoglutaric acid produced in the citric acid cycle within the brain itself. However, continuous utilization of ketoglutaric acid for this purpose would rapidly deplete the citric acid cycle of its intermediates unless a method of replenishing the cycle were available. Repletion is accomplished by CO_2 fixation, involving pyruvate, to form oxaloacetic acid, which enters the citric acid cycle and proceeds to the formation of keto-

glutarate. The reaction in brain is precisely analogous to that which occurs in the liver.

Fixation of CO_2 in isolated retinal tissue has been demonstrated and studies of CO_2 fixation in brain base also been described. CO_2 fixation into amino acids occurs to a significant degree in the cerebral cortex. The highest specific activity among metabolites in the brain was found in aspartate, which would be expected if the initial reaction involved formation of malate and then oxaloacetate, this latter compound forming aspartate by transamination. However, after infusion of ammonia, it was apparent that oxaloacetate was now being used for the synthesis of ketoglutarate, glutamate, and glutamine at a faster rate than it was being converted to aspartate. This suggests that ammonia causes channeling of oxaloacetate to the formation of glutamine.

The formation of γ-aminobutyrate in central nervous system tissue from glutamate has been discussed. The significance of γ-aminobutyrate as an important regulatory factor in neuronal activity has also been mentioned.

The synthesis of long-chain fatty acids by enzyme preparations from rat brain tissue has been demonstrated. The pathway of synthesis was that of the extramitochondrial system, in which malonyl coenzyme A is a required intermediate.

From the examples cited above and the results of other recent investigations of brain metabolism, it is becoming apparent that cerebral tissue possesses all of the enzymatic activities necessary to support the major metabolic pathways which are found in other organs of the body. This has been referred to as the "autonomy of cerebral metabolism."

The ability of the brain to fix CO_2 introduces interesting speculations with respect to the influence of CO_2 on the operations of the citric acid cycle in the brain. Because the metabolism of glucose provides virtually the sole source of energy for brain metabolism, if CO_2 tension did exert a controlling influence on the citric acid cycle an additional explanation for the effects of CO_2 on the brain might be forthcoming.

Chemical Mediators of Nerve Activity

The action of many nerve pathways is mediated by a chemical substance. A conspicuous example is that of transmission of a nerve impulse from a nerve to an effector skeletal muscle. This occurs at the **myoneural junction**, the area where a motor nerve terminates on a skeletal muscle fiber. Although the nature of the chemical mediators at many of the synapses is not known, it is clear that **acetylcholine** is the chemical mediator at all synapses between preganglionic and postganglionic fibers of the autonomic nervous system as well as at the myoneural junctions and at all postganglionic parasympathetic and some postganglionic sympathetic endings. The nerve impulse arriving at the end of the motor neuron evokes liberation of acetylcholine from the vesicles in the nerve synaptic terminals. Fibers utilizing acetylcholine as mediator are referred to as **cholinergic**.

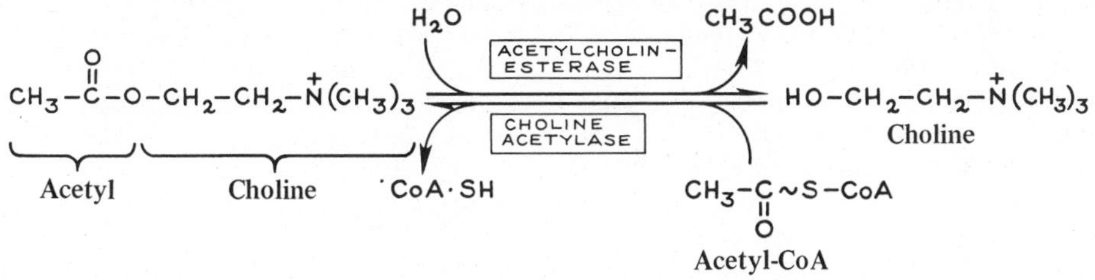

Figure 37–7. Formation and breakdown of acetylcholine.

The chemical mediator at most sympathetic post-ganglionic nerve endings is **norepinephrine**. It is stored in vesicles at the ends of presynaptic **adrenergic fibers** (synaptic knobs). Epinephrine, the N-methyl derivative of norepinephrine, while only of minor importance as a chemical mediator in the sympathetic nervous system, is, however, liberated by the adrenal medulla upon stimulation of the nerve supplying that endocrine organ. The circulating epinephrine derived from the adrenal medulla duplicates many of the metabolic effects that follow stimulation of the sympathetic nervous system (adrenergic effects).

Chemistry of the Mediators of Nerve Activity

Norepinephrine, epinephrine, and dopamine are the principal examples in the body of chemical compounds belonging to a group of tyrosine derivatives referred to as **catecholamines.**

The synthesis and hydrolytic breakdown of acetylcholine are illustrated in Fig 37–7. Acetylcholine is readily hydrolyzed to choline and acetic acid by the action of the enzyme **acetylcholinesterase,** found not only at the nerve endings but also within the nerve fiber.

The action of acetylcholine in the body is controlled by the inactivating effect of acetylcholinesterase.

The breakdown of acetylcholine is an exergonic reaction since energy is required for its resynthesis. Active acetate (CoA-acetate) serves as donor for the acetylation of choline. The enzyme **choline acetylase,** which is activated by potassium and magnesium ions, catalyzes the transfer of acetyl from CoA-acetate to choline.

Anticholinesterases. Inhibition of acetylcholine esterase with resultant prolongation of parasympathetic activity is effected by physostigmine (eserine). The action is reversible.

Neostigmine (Prostigmin) is an alkaloid which is thought to function also as an inhibitor of cholinesterase and thus to prolong acetylcholine or parasympathetic action. It has been used in the treatment of

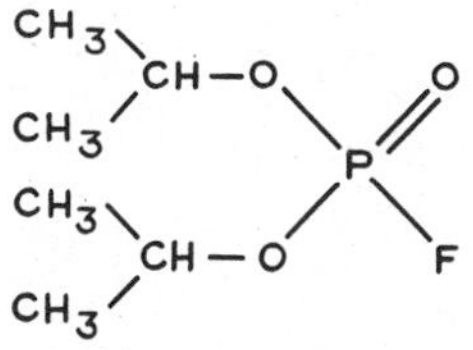

Figure 37–8. Diisopropylfluorophosphate.

myasthenia gravis, a chronic progressive muscular weakness with atrophy.

A synthetic compound, **diisopropylfluorophosphate** (Fig 37–8), also inhibits the esterase activity but in an irreversible manner.

This compound appears to be the most powerful and specific enzyme inhibitor yet discovered. It inhibits acetylcholinesterase when present in concentrations as low as 1×10^{-10} M. A mechanism for detoxifying diisopropylfluorophosphate exists in the body in the action of an enzyme capable of bringing about the hydrolysis of the compound to fluoride and diisopropylphosphate. This enzyme, diisopropylfluorophosphatase, has been identified in the kidney. The enzyme is activated by Mn^{2+} or Co^{2+} and specific cofactors such as imidazole and pyridine derivatives (eg, proline or hydroxyproline).

Diisopropylfluorophosphate has also been used in the treatment of myasthenia gravis, although not with clinical results equal to those obtainable with neostigmine. It is a dangerous drug to use, since the toxic dose is too close to the effective dose.

A number of **anticholinesterases** similar in their action to diisopropylfluorophosphate have been investigated. They serve as the active principle of insecticides. The so-called "nerve gases" proposed for gas warfare, as well as many insecticides (eg, parathion), are also anticholinesterases. These insecticides may produce toxic effects in individuals exposed to high concentrations when they are used as plant sprays.

Atropine is used as an antidote to the toxic effects of diisopropylfluorophosphate and other anticholinesterases.

• • •

References

Brimacombe JS, Webber JM: *Mucopolysaccharides.* Elsevier, 1964.

Dorfman A, Matalon R: The mucopolysaccharidoses. Page 1218 in: *The Metabolic Basis of Inherited Disease,* 3rd ed. Stanbury, JB, Wyngaarden JB, Fredrickson DS (editors). McGraw-Hill, 1972.

Elliott KAC, Page IH, Quastel JH (editors): *Neurochemistry: The Chemistry of Brain and Nerve,* 2nd ed. Thomas, 1962.

Ganong WF: *Review of Medical Physiology,* 8th ed. Lange, 1977.

Jeanloz BW: The nomenclature of acid mucopolysaccharides. Arthritis Rheum 3:323, 1960.

Jeanloz BW, Balasz EA (editors): *Amino Sugars.* Vols I and II. Academic Press, 1965.

Lindahl U & others: Structure and biosynthesis of heparin-like polysaccharides. Fed Proc 36:19, 1977.

McLean FC, Urist MR: *Bone: An Introduction to the Physiology of Skeletal Tissue,* 2nd ed. Univ of Chicago Press, 1961.

Oser BL: *Hawk's Physiological Chemistry,* 14th ed. Blakiston, 1965.

Sourkes TL: *Biochemistry of Mental Disease.* Hoeber, 1962.

Waelsch H (editor): *Biochemistry of the Developing Nervous System.* Academic Press, 1955.

West ES & others: *Textbook of Biochemistry,* 4th ed. Macmillan, 1966.

White A, Handler P, Smith EL: *Principles of Biochemistry,* 5th ed. McGraw-Hill, 1973.

A (Å)	Angstrom unit(s) (10^{-10} m, 0.1 nm)
AA	Amino acid
a-AA	*a*-Amino acid
ACTH	Adrenocorticotropic hormone, adrenocorticotropin, corticotropin
Acyl-CoA	An acyl derivative of CoA (eg, butyryl-CoA)
ADH	Alcohol dehydrogenase
ADH	Antidiuretic hormone
AHG	Antihemophilic globulin
Ala	Alanine
ALA	Aminolevulinic acid
AmLev	Aminolevulinic acid
AMP	Adenosine monophosphate
Arg	Arginine
Asn	Asparagine
Asp	Aspartic acid
ATP	Adenosine triphosphate
BAL	Dimercaprol (British anti-lewisite)
Cal	Calorie (ie, kilocalorie, kcal)
CBG	Corticosteroid-binding globulin
CBZ	Carbobenzoxy
CCCP	m-Chlorocarbonyl cyanide phenylhydrazone
CCK-PZ	Cholecystokinin-pancreozymin
CDP	Cytidine diphosphocholine
Cer	Ceramide
CI	Chain-initiating
CK	Creatine phosphokinase (see also CPK)
CMP	Cytidine monophosphate; 5′-phosphoribosyl cytosine
CoA.SH	Free (uncombined) coenzyme A. A pantothenic acid-containing nucleotide which functions in the metabolism of fatty acids, ketone bodies, acetate, and amino acids

$$\text{CoA.S.C.CH}_3 \quad \overset{\overset{\text{O}}{\|}}{}$$

CoA.S.C.CH₃ Acetyl-CoA, "activated acetate." The form in which acetate is "activated" by combination with coenzyme A for participation in various reactions

CPK	Creatine phosphokinase (see also CK)
CRF	Corticotropin-releasing factor
CRH	Corticotropin-releasing hormone
CRP	C-reactive protein
CTP	Cytidine triphosphate
Cys	Cysteine
D-	Dextrorotatory
D_2 (vitamin)	Ergocalciferol
D_3 (vitamin)	Cholecalciferol
1,25-$(OH)_2$-D_3	1,25-Dihydroxycholecalciferol
dA	Deoxyadenosine
dC	Deoxycytosine
dG	Deoxyguanosine
DNA	Deoxyribonucleic acid
DNP	Dinitrophenol
dopa	3,4-Dihydroxyphenylalanine
DPN	Diphosphopyridine nucleotide (now replaced by NAD)
dT	Deoxythymidine

dUMP	Deoxyribose uridine-5′-phosphate
E	Enzyme (also Enz)
E.C.	Enzyme code number (IUB system)
EDTA	Ethylenediaminetetraacetic acid. A reagent used to chelate divalent metals
Enz	Enzyme (also E)
Eq	Equivalent
eu	Enzyme unit
FAD	Flavin adenine dinucleotide (oxidized form)
$FADH_2$	Flavin adenine dinucleotide (reduced form)
FDA	Food & Drug Administration
FFA	Free fatty acids
figlu	Formiminoglutamic acid
FMN	Flavin mononucleotide
FP	Flavoprotein
FSF	Fibrin stabilizing factor
FSH	Follicle-stimulating hormone
FSHRF	Follicle-stimulating hormone-releasing factor
FSHRH	Follicle-stimulating hormone-releasing hormone
g	Gram(s)
g	Gravity
Gal	Galactose
GalNAc	N-Acetylgalactose
GDP	Guanosine diphosphate
GFR	Glomerular filtration rate
GH	Growth hormone
GHRF	Growth hormone-releasing factor
GHRH	Growth hormone-releasing hormone
GH-RIF	Growth hormone release-inhibiting factor
GHRIH	Growth hormone release-inhibiting hormone
GIH	Growth hormone release-inhibiting hormone
GLC	Gas-liquid chromatography
Glc	Glucose
GlcUA	Glucuronic acid
Gln	Glutamine
Glu	Glutamic acid
Gly	Glycine
GMP	Guanosine monophosphate
GRH	Growth hormone-releasing hormone
Hb	Hemoglobin
HCG	Human chorionic gonadotropin
HDL	High density lipoproteins
H_2folate	Dihydrofolate
H_4folate	Tetrahydrofolate
His	Histidine
HMG-CoA	β-Hydroxy-β-methylglutaryl coenzyme A
Hyl	Hydroxylysine
Hyp	4-Hydroxyproline
ICD	Isocitric dehydrogenase
IDP	Inosine diphosphate
IF	Initiation factor (for protein synthesis)
Ile	Isoleucine
IMP	Inosine monophosphate; hypoxanthine ribonucleotide

INH	Isonicotinic acid hydrazide (isoniazid)
I_3 Thn	Triiodothyronine
I_4 Thn	Tetraiodothyronine (thyroxine)
ITP	Inosine triphosphate
ITyr	Monoiodotyrosine
I_2 Tyr	Diiodotyrosine
IU	International unit(s)
IUB	International Union of Biochemistry
a-KA	*a*-Keto acid
kcal	Kilocalorie
a-KG	*a*-Ketoglutarate
kJ	Kilojoule
K_m	Substrate concentration producing half-maximal velocity (Michaelis constant)
L-	Levo-
LCAT	Lecithin:cholesterol acyltransferase
LD	Lactate dehydrogenase (see also LDH)
LDH	Lactic dehydrogenase
LDL	Low density lipoproteins
Leu	Leucine
LH	Luteinizing hormone
LHRF	Luteinizing hormone-releasing factor
LHRH	Luteinizing hormone-releasing hormone
LLF	Laki-Lorand factor
LTH	Luteotropic hormone
Lys	Lysine
M	Molar
MAO	Monoamine oxidase
MCH	Mean corpuscular hemoglobin
MCHC	Mean corpuscular hemoglobin concentration
MCV	Mean corpuscular volume
Met	Methionine
MIF	Melanocyte inhibiting factor
mol	Mole
MRF	Melanocyte releasing factor
MRH	Melanocyte releasing hormone
MRIH	Melanocyte release-inhibiting hormone
mRNA	Messenger RNA
MSH	Melanocyte-stimulating hormone
MW	Molecular weight
NAD	Nicotinamide adenine dinucleotide (oxidized)
NADH	Nicotinamide adenine dinucleotide (reduced)
NADP	Nicotinamide adenine dinucleotide phosphate (oxidized)
NADPH	Nicotinamide adenine dinucleotide phosphate (reduced)
NANA	N-Acetylneuraminic acid
NDP	Any nucleoside diphosphate
NTP	Any nucleoside triphosphate
OA	Oxaloacetic acid
OD	Optical density
P	Phosphate (radical)
PCV	Packed cell volume
PGH	Plasma growth hormone
Phe	Phenylalanine
P_i	Inorganic phosphate (orthophosphate)
PIF	Prolactin release-inhibiting factor
PL	Prolactin
PL	Pyridoxal

PLP	Pyridoxal phosphate
PP_i	Pyrophosphate
PRF	Prolactin-release-inhibiting factor
PRH	Prolactin-release-inhibiting hormone
PRIH	Prolactin release-inhibiting hormone
Pro	Proline
PRPP	5-Phosphoribosyl 1-pyrophosphate
PTA	Plasma thromboplastin antecedent
PTC	Plasma thromboplastin component
RBC	Red blood cell
RDA	Recommended daily allowance
RE	Retinol equivalents
RNA	Ribonucleic acid
RQ	Respiratory quotient
S (Sf) units	Svedberg units of flotation
SDA	Specific dynamic action
SDS	Sodium dodecyl sulfate
Ser	Serine
SGOT	Serum glutamic oxalacetic transaminase
SGPT	Serum glutamic pyruvic transaminase
SH	Sulfhydryl
SLR	*Streptococcus lactis* R
SPCA	Serum prothrombin conversion accelerator
sRNA	Soluble RNA (same as tRNA, which term is preferred)
STP	Standard temperature and pressure (273° absolute, 760 mm Hg)
T_3	Triiodothyronine
T_4	Tetraiodothyronine
TBG	Testosterone-binding globulin
TG	Triacylglycerols (formerly called triglycerides)
Thr	Threonine
TLC	Thin layer chromotography
Tm_{Ca}	Tubular maximum for calcium
Tm_G	Tubular maximum for glucose
dTMP	Thymidine monophosphate (5'-phosphoribosyl-thymine)
TPN	Triphosphopyridine nucleotide (now replaced by NADP)
TRF	Thyrotropin-releasing factor
TRH	Thyrotropin-releasing hormone
Tris	Tris(hydroxymethyl)aminomethane, a buffer (tromethamine)
tRNA	Transfer RNA
Trp	Tryptophan
TSH	Thyroid-stimulating hormone; thyrotropin
Tyr	Tyrosine
UDP	Uridine diphosphate
UDPG	Uridine diphosphoglucose
UDPGal	Uridine diphosphogalactose
UDPGlcUA	Uridine diphosphoglucuronic acid
UDPGluc	Uridine diphosphoglucuronic acid
UMP	Uridine monophosphate; uridine-5'-phosphate; uridylic acid
UTP	Uridine triphosphate
Val	Valine
VLDL	Very low density lipoproteins
VMA	Vanilmandelic acid
V_{max}	Maximal velocity
vol%	Volumes percent

Index

VLDL (cont'd)
  remnant, 306
  secretion, 319
β-VLDL, 303
VMA, 483, 485
Von Gierke's disease, 265, 407
VPRC, 559

Waldenström's macroglobulinemia, 517
Warburg's respiratory enzyme, 226
Water, 11–17
  body, total, 516
  dissociation of, 12
  hydrogen bonds in, 12
  intake and loss of, 516
  loss or restriction causing dehydration, 520
  macromolecular structure of, 12
  metabolic, 280
  metabolism, 516
  molecular structure of, 11
  in nutrition, 555
  properties of, 516
  reabsorption of, 612
Water-soluble vitamins, 553
  recommended daily allowance, 551
Watson and Crick, 416
  model of double helical structure of DNA, 134
Waxes, 108

Wear and tear quota, 549
Weight reduction, 302
Westergren technic, 559
Whale muscle myoglobin molecule, 39
Wilson's disease, 535
Wintrobe technic, 559
Wobble, 436

Xanthine, 123, 391, 392, 401
  dehydrogenase, 227
  lithiasis, 408
  oxidase, 392, 399, 401, 538
    deficiency, 408
    in purine or pyrimidine metabolism, 83
  riboside, 391
  ribotide, 391
Xanthinuria, 407, 408, 538
Xanthinylic acid, 391
Xanthomas, 319, 320
Xanthoproteic reaction, 25, 45
Xanthosine, 391
  monophosphate, 395
Xanthurenic acid, 353, 354
Xeroderma pigmentosum, 421
Xerophthalmia, 145
XMP, 395
X-ray
  crystallography in determination of protein structure, 41

X-ray (cont'd)
  diffraction in determination of protein structure, 40
Xylitol, 275
Xylose, 253, 474, 642
D-Xylose, 96, 97, 273, 275
L-Xylulose, 273, 275
Xylulose 5-phosphate, 266, 268, 269, 270

Yanofsky, Charles, 433
Yeast, fermentation in, 253

Z
  gene, 450
  line, 633
Zeta
  potential, 559
  sedimentation ratio, 560
Zimmermann reaction, 495
Zinc, 228, 536, 556
  atom, 44
  deficiency, 537
  recommended daily allowance, 551
Zollinger-Ellison syndrome, 512
Zone electrophoresis, 600
Zwitterion, 19
Zymogens, 205
Zymosterol, 316